ARTS, IDEAS AND CIVILIZATION

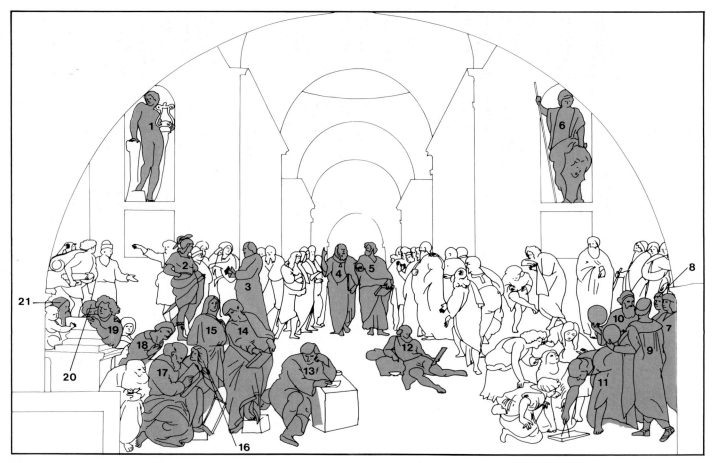

The front cover shows a detail from *The School of Athens* by Raphael.

1 Apollo, **2** Alcibiades or Alexander, **3** Socrates, **4** Plato (Leonardo), **5** Aristotle, **6** Minerva, **7** Sodoma, **8** Raphael, **9** Ptolemy, **10** Zoroaster (Pietro Bembo?), **11** Euclid (Bramante), **12** Diogenes, **13** Heraclitus (Michelangelo), **14** Parmenides, Xenocrates or Aristossenus, **15** Francesco Maria della Rovere, **16** Telauges, **17** Pythagoras, **18** Averrhoës, **19** Epicurus, **20** Federico Gonzaga, **21** Zeno.

ARTS, IDEAS AND CIVILIZATION

Jack A. Hobbs & Robert L. Duncan

Illinois State University

Prentice-Hall, Inc., Englewood Cliffs, New Jersey

To Marge and Betty

ISBN 0–13–048711–2

This book was designed and produced by
JOHN CALMANN AND KING LTD, LONDON
Designer: Karen Osborne

Phototypeset by Keyspools Ltd, England
Printed in Hong Kong

Contents

Preface *10*

CHAPTER ONE

BEGINNINGS *14*
Introduction *16*
 Prehistoric Cultures *14* Mesopotamia *15*
 Egypt *19*
Literature *20*
 Psalm 8 *20* Genesis *1–11 21* The Prophets *21*
 Amos *21* Hosea *22* The Book of Job *22*
 Isaiah 53: The Suffering Servant *24*
The Beginnings of Art *25*
 Ice-Age Art *25* Peasant Village Art *28* The
 Cities of Mesopotamia *29* Egyptian Art *34*
Music *41*
Conclusion *43*

CHAPTER TWO

CLASSICISM I: GREECE AND ROME *44*
The Classical World *46*
 The Greeks *46* The Romans *47*
The Homeric Epic *49*
 The Iliad *49* The Odyssey *49*
Archaic Art 650–450 B.C. *50*
 Archaic Sculpture *50*
 Archaic Architecture *52*
Early Greek Music *54*
Literature of the Golden Age *55*
 Greek Tragedy *55* Aeschylus *56* Sophocles *57*
 Euripides *59* Other Athenian Writers *60*
Classical Art *62*
 Sculpture: free-standing *62* Sculpture:
 architectural *65* The Parthenon *66* Hellenistic
 Art 323–27 B.C. *70*
Music of the Golden Age *73*
The Roman Epic *75*
 Virgil's *Aeneid 75*
Roman Art *79*
 Sculpture *80* Architecture *82*
Roman Music *91*

CHAPTER THREE

CLASSICISM II: THE RENAISSANCE *92*
Introduction *94*
Italian Humanism *97*
 Petrarch *97* Boccaccio *98*
 Pico della Mirandola *99*
Fifteenth-Century Italian Art *99*
 Brunelleschi *102* Donatello *105*
 Masaccio *107* Florentine Art in the later
 1400s *110* Art outside Florence *113*
Music in the Renaissance *116*
 Early Renaissance *116* Dufay *118*
 Ockeghem *118* Secular Music in Italy *118*

Sixteenth-Century Literature *119*
    Machiavelli *119*   Castiglione *120*
    Montaigne *121*   Shakespeare's *Hamlet* *122*
Sixteenth-Century Italian Art *124*
    High Renaissance Art *124*   Leonardo *125*
    Michelangelo *130*   Raphael *136*
    Architecture *138*   Late Renaissance and
    Mannerism *141*   Titian *141*   Mannerism *145*
Sixteenth-Century Music *146*
    Josquin *146*   Instrumental Music *147*
    The Madrigal *147*

CHAPTER FOUR   **CLASSICISM III: 17th AND 18th CENTURIES** *148*
Introduction *150*
    The Enlightenment *151*
Seventeenth-Century Literature *153*
    Molière *153*   Racine *155*
Eighteenth-Century Literature *156*
    Swift *156*   Voltaire *158*   Counterpoint to
    Rationalism *160*
Seventeenth-Century Art *161*
    Classicism in Seventeenth-Century Art *166*
    Poussin *166*   Claude *167*   The Palace of
    Versailles *169*   St. Paul's Cathedral *170*
Eighteenth-Century Art *172*
    The Neoclassical Movement *177*   David *177*
    Ingres *178*   Neoclassical Sculpture *179*
    Neoclassical Architecture *180*
Baroque Music *181*
    Opera *182*   Instrumental Forms *184*
    Handel *184*   Bach *184*   The Rococo Spirit *187*
Classical Music *187*
    Characteristics of Classical Music *187*
    The Classical Symphony *188*   The Sonata
    Form *188*   Haydn *189*   Mozart *191*
Conclusion *193*

CHAPTER FIVE   **THE CELEBRATION OF FEELING** *194*
Romanticism *196*
Literature *200*
    Rousseau *200*   Goethe *201*   Wordsworth *203*
Romantic Art *206*
    Watteau *207*   Goya *207*   Characteristics of
    Romantic Art *208*   Géricault *211*
    Delacroix *212*   Nature in Romantic Art *213*
    Friedrich *214*   Turner *215*   Constable *217*
    Sculpture—Rodin *218*
Architecture *220*
Romantic Music *222*
    Precursors of Romantic Music *223*
    Beethoven *223*   Berlioz *226*   Schumann *227*
    Wagner *229*   Late Romantic Music *231*

CHAPTER SIX   **CHRISTIANITY I** *232*
Introduction *234*
Literature *237*
     The New Testament *237*   St. Augustine *239*
Early Christian Art *243*
     From 42 to 200 A.D. *243*   From 200 to 313 A.D. *244*
     From 313 to 527 A.D.: Architecture *247*   Mosaic *251*
     Sculpture *252*
Byzantine Art *254*
Early Christian Music *261*
     Liturgy and Music up to 313 *261*   Liturgy and
     Music from 313 to 604 *263*   The Services of the
     Divine Office *264*   The Service of the Mass *265*

CHAPTER SEVEN   **CHRISTIANITY II: THE MIDDLE AGES** *266*
Introduction *268*
Literature *271*
     The *Song of Roland* *271*   The Thirteenth-Century
     Synthesis *272*   Dante *275*
Art of the Middle Ages *278*
     The Carolingian Renaissance *279*   Interim: The
     Ninth and Tenth Centuries *281*   Romanesque
     Architecture *281*   Romanesque Architectural
     Sculpture *289*   The Gothic Age *291*   Gothic
     Architecture *293*   Gothic Sculpture *300*   Late
     Medieval Tuscan Painting *304*   Late Gothic:
     Flemish Painting *308*
Music *313*
     Post-Gregorian Music *313*   Polyphony *314*   The
     School of Notre Dame *315*   Secular Music *316*
     Ars Nova *317*   Machaut *317*

CHAPTER EIGHT   **CHRISTIANITY III: THE ERA OF THE
REFORMATION** *320*
Introduction *322*
Literature *325*
     Erasmus *325*   Luther *327*   Calvin *329*
     The Counter Reformation: Loyola *331*
Reformation and Counter-Reformation Art *332*
     Reformation Art *332*   Dürer *332*
     Grünewald *337*   *The Last Judgment* *341*
     Counter-Reformation Art *341*   El Greco *342*
     Baroque Religious Art *344*   Art in the
     Netherlands *347*   Rembrandt *347*
Music *351*
     Reformation Music *351*   Counter-Reformation
     Music *352*   Protestant Baroque Music *353*
Conclusion *355*

CHAPTER NINE   **REALISM AND MATERIALISM** *356*
Introduction to Realism *358*
Literature *360*
     Flaubert *360*   Dostoyevsky *362*   Tolstoy *364*

Realism in Art *367*
    Realism in Seventeenth-Century Painting *368*
    Nineteenth-Century Realism *370*   Courbet *370*
    Winslow Homer *371*   Manet *373*
    Impressionism: Monet *374*   Degas *379*
Architecture *379*
    Frame Construction *379*   The Crystal
    Palace *380*   Sullivan and the Chicago School *381*

CHAPTER TEN   **MODERNISM I** *382*
The Conditions of Modernism *384*
Literature *387*
    Conrad *387*   Kafka *389*   Mann *391*
    Joyce *394*   Eliot *395*
Painting *397*
    The Avant-Garde *397*   Post-Impressionism *397*
    Cézanne *398*   Van Gogh *400*   Fin de Siècle
    Art *403*   Early Twentieth Century *407*
    Fauvism: Matisse *407*   German
    Expressionism *409*   Cubism: Picasso *412*
    Variations of Cubism *416*   Duchamp, Dada, and
    Surrealism *420*
Sculpture *425*
Architecture *429*
    Wright *431*   The Bauhaus and the International
    Style *431*
Music *434*
    The Late Nineteenth Century *434*
    Debussy *434*   From 1900 to 1950 *435*
    Stravinsky *436*   Schoenberg *438*

CHAPTER ELEVEN   **MODERNISM II** *442*
Modernism and the Transcendent *444*
Literature *445*
    Camus *445*   Beckett and the Theater of the
    Absurd *449*   Wiesel *451*   Solzhenitsyn *453*
Visual Arts *455*
    From the Armory Show to World War II *455*
    The Crisis of Transition *458*   Abstract
    Expressionism *462*   Alternatives to Abstract
    Expressionism *464*   Pop Art *465*   Hard-Edge
    Abstraction *467*   Op Art *469*   Photo-
    Realism *469*   Three-Dimensional Postwar
    Art *469*   Temporary Art *475*   Summary of
    Postwar Art *476*
Architecture *477*
The New Music *482*
    Developments in Postwar Europe *482*
    Developments in Pre-war America *485*
    Developments in Postwar America *485*
    Cage *488*

CHAPTER TWELVE POST-MODERNISM *490*
Introduction *492*
Literature *493*
Visual Arts *495*
Architecture *501*
The New Music *502*
    Minimalism *502*
Conclusion *504*

Glossary *505*
Notes *516*
Further Reading *519*
Index *526*

Preface

Arts, Ideas and Civilization is a survey of the major developments of Western civilization as expressed through literature, art, and music. As much as possible, these arts have been integrated in order to provide a coherent introduction to the humanities and to the ways in which human beings conceive and express their understanding of life and the world.

In structuring the content of a humanities text, an author usually chooses one of two options: thematic—dividing the subject into major themes—or historical—chronicling the great periods of history. In this text, however, we have chosen a third option: a combination of thematic and chronological approaches. Although each chapter addresses a theme (or one part of a thematic trilogy), it also presents developments and examples which are confined primarily, though not exclusively, to a particular historical period.

Following the first chapter, "Beginnings," which treats of prehistoric societies and ancient civilizations, the theme of Classicism is traced in three sequential chapters, focusing especially on fifth-century Greece (Chapter 2), the Italian Renaissance (Chapter 3), and French Neo-classicism and the Enlightenment (Chapter 4). To point up the contrast between Classicism and Romanticism, Chapter 5, "The Celebration of Feeling," examines the "romantic temper" in some examples predating the Romantic movement, as well as the unfolding of the movement itself in the eighteenth and nineteenth centuries. Christianity—

like Classicism, a major cultural influence in Western civilization—is also traced in three sequential chapters, in this case, from Roman times through the Middle Ages to the agonizing period of the Reformation and Counter Reformation. Realism is treated in Chapter 9 by referring to its manifestations in earlier periods, but with major emphasis, of course, on developments in the nineteenth century. The proliferation of radical questioning of traditional values and of experimenting with varied styles and modes in nineteenth- and twentieth-century Modernism is treated in Chapters 10 and 11, followed by Chapter 12, "Post-Modernism," which examines what many believe to be a new cultural era.

As stated above, the chapters are grouped thematically and chronologically within each theme. The three main themes—Classicism, Christianity, and the Modern World—are presented in sequential chapters. Instructors who wish to follow a strictly chronological approach with this book may easily do so by rearranging the order of the chapters and by supplementing a few of the chapters with reading assignments from other chapters. Mainly, the chronological order would be: 1, 2, 6, 7, 3, 4, 5, 9, 10, 11, and 12, with Chapter 8 being "dismembered" and subsumed into the second halves of 3 and 4. This is clarified in the table opposite, which shows the order of chapters in the left-hand column and any specific topics to be integrated from other chapters in the right-hand column.

Historical Chronology of Chapters

Chapters	Supplements from other chapters
1: BEGINNINGS	(None)
2: CLASSICISM I: GREECE AND ROME	(None)
6: CHRISTIANITY I	(None)
7: CHRISTIANITY II: THE MIDDLE AGES	(None)
3: CLASSICISM II: THE RENAISSANCE	
Sixteenth-Century Literature (p. 119)	Chapter 8 (p. 325): Erasmus, Luther, Calvin, Loyola
Sixteenth-Century Art (p. 124)	Chapter 8 (p. 332): Dürer, Grünewald, Michelangelo, El Greco
Sixteenth-Century Music (p. 145)	Chapter 8 (p. 351): Reformation Music / Counter-Reformation Music
4: CLASSICISM III: 17th & 18th CENTURIES	
Seventeenth-Century Art (p. 161)	Chapter 8 (p. 344): Baroque Religious Art, Rembrandt / Chapter 9 (p. 368): Velasquez, Vermeer / Chapter 5 (p. 213) Van Ruisdael / Chapter 5 (p. 207) Watteau
Eighteenth-Century Art (p. 172)	
Baroque Music (p. 181)	Chapter 8 (p. 353): Protestant Baroque Music
(8: CHRISTIANITY III—see Chapters 3 and 4)	
5: CELEBRATION OF FEELING	(None)
9: REALISM AND MATERIALISM	(None)
10: MODERNISM I	(None)
11: MODERNISM II	(None)
12: POST-MODERNISM	(None)

Acknowledgements

We wish to thank the many individuals whose expertise and counsel we sought while compiling this book. We are especially grateful to Gary R. Sudano, Chair of the Department of Creative Arts at Purdue University, and Don L. Peterson, Professor of Music at Illinois State University, who generously gave of their time in examining the music sections of the manuscript; also to Charles B. Harris, Chair of the English Department at Illinois State University, and Stanley W. Renner, Professor of English at Illinois State University, who provided helpful suggestions for certain of the literature sections. In addition, we wish to recognize our many colleagues at Illinois State University—Susan Amster, Barry Blinderman, and Harold Gregor of the Art Department; Paul Borg, and Timothy Hurtz of the Music Department; and Eric Hradecky of WGLT Radio—for their advice and help with various aspects of the project.

We thank Betty Duncan and Brian Arnold for the many hours they spent transcribing the chapter introductions and literature discussions on the word processor. Finally, we wish to thank the following: Norwell F. Therien of Prentice Hall, Inc.; Laurence King, editors Rosemary Bradley and Carolyn Yates of Calmann and King Ltd; Eleanor van Zandt and designer Karen Osborne.

Picture Credits

The authors, the publishers, and John Calmann and King Ltd wish to thank the artists, museums, galleries, collectors, and other owners who have kindly allowed works to be reproduced in this book. In general, museums have supplied their own photographs; other sources, photographs, and copyright holders are listed here.

Chapter 1: 1, 7: Scala, Florence; 5: Colorphoto Hans Hinz, Allschwil, Switzerland; 6, 8, 13: Musées Nationaux, Paris; 9, 17, 22, 23, 24, 25: Hirmer Fotarchiv, Munich; 11, 14, 27: Mansell Collection.

Chapter 2: 1: Sonia Halliday Photographs, Weston Turville, UK; 4, 12, 21, 23, 25, 26, 31, 35: Hirmer Fotoarchiv, Munich; 7, 13, 14, 15, 16, 17, 18, 19: Mansell Collection; 11, 27, 43, 53: Ralph Lieberman; 22, 41: Alinari, Florence; 30: Bildarchiv Foto Marburg; 38: Ancient Art and Architecture Collection; 42: Scala; 44: A. F. Kersting, FRPS; 50, 52, 55: Fototeca Unione, Rome; 56: Leonard von Matt, Buochs, Switzerland.

Chapter 3: 1, 7, 13, 14, 15, 16, 18, 19, 20, 21, 28, 33, 34, 37, 38, 41, 42, 47, 48, 49, 50, 51: Scala; 5, 10, 12, 22: Alinari; 4, 11, 17, 29, 30: Mansell Collection; 6: Caisse Nationale des Monuments Historiques/SPADEM/Jean Feuillie; 8: Michael Holford/Clyde; 32: Bulloz, Paris; 35, 43: Musées Nationaux, Paris; 40: Anderson-Alinari; 44: Ralph Lieberman; 46: Leonard von Matt.

Chapter 4: 1: Musées Nationaux, Paris; 5, 26: Giraudon, Paris; 6, 7, 8, 38: Mansell Collection; 9: Sonia Halliday Photographs/Jane Taylor; 10, 12, 13, 14, 16: Scala; 11: Alinari; 19: A. F. Kersting, FRPS; 25: Bridgeman Art Library; 28: Studio O'Sughrue, Montpellier; 29: Trustees of the Victoria & Albert Museum; 31: BBC Hulton Picture Library.

Chapter 5: 2, 5, 6, 19: Mansell Collection; 3, 7, 14: Bridgeman Art Library; 10: Giraudon; 12: Scala; 15: Ralph Kleinhempel, Hamburg; 21, 22: A. F. Kersting, FRPS.

Chapter 6: 1, 25, 27, 28, 29: Scala; 3, 26: Sonia Halliday Photographs; 6: Ancient Art and Architecture Collection; 7, 10: Fototeca Unione, Rome; 8: Pontifica Commissione della Arte Sacra, Rome: 11, 13, 16, 17: Alinari; 14: A. F. Kersting, FRPS; 18, 21, 22: Hirmer Fotarchiv; 19, 30: Anderson-Alinari; 20: Ralph Lieberman.

Chapter 7: 1, 43, 44, 45, 46, 48, 50: Scala; 4, 47: Giraudon/Musée Condé, Chantilly; 5: Alinari; 6, 36: Mansell Collection; 9, 49: Institut du Patrimoine Royale des Beaux-Arts, Brussels; 11: Giraudon/Epernay, Bibliothèque Municipale; 14, 17: Photo Yan, Toulouse; 18: Anderson-Giraudon; 19, 20, 32, 35: A. F. Kersting, FRPS; 22: Caisse Nationale des Monuments Historiques; 23, 33, 39, 40, 41, 42: Giraudon; 24, 30, 38: CNMH/SPADEM; 27: Aerofilms; 28: Ralph Lieberman; 37: Arxiu M.A.S., Barcelona.

Chapter 8: 1, 5, 11, 14, 15, 18: Scala; 4: Musées Nationaux, Paris; 6, 7: Mansell Collection; 8, 21, 22: Artothek, Munich; 12: Prestel Verlag, Munich; 13: Giraudon; 16: Oronoz, Madrid; 17: Institut Royale du Patrimoine des Beaux Arts, Brussels; 19: Anderson-Alinari; 25: Novosti.

Chapter 9: 1, 8, 10, 14, 16: Musées Nationaux, Paris; 2, 4, 5: Mansell Collection, London; 6: Trustees of the Victoria & Albert Museum; 12: Fotomas Index; 18: Cervin Robinson, New York.

Chapter 10: 1, 22, 25, 26, 28, 35, 38, 40 © ADAGP, Paris and DACS, London 1988; 3: Mansell Collection; 4: BBC Hulton Picture Library/Bettmann Archive; 5, 6, 7: BBC Hulton; 17, 18, 23, 24, 27, 33, 39, 53: © DACS 1988; 21: Prestel Verlag, © COSMOPRESS, Geneva/DACS, London 1988; 30: Christie's Colour Library, London, © DACS 1988; 34: © DEMART PRO ARTE BV 1988; 42: Martin Charles; 43: Wayne Andrews; 44: Library of Congress, Washington; 45: RIBA/British Architectural Library; 47: Harcourt Brace Jovanovitch; 48: Lucien Herve/© SPADEM.

Chapter 11: 4, 6: BBC Hulton/UPI/Bettmann Newsphotos; 5: Camera Press; 11: Hans Namuth; 13: Steven Sloman, New York; 16: © DACS 1988, courtesy of the artist; 17: © DACS 1988; 18: © DACS 1988; 21: © DACS 1988, courtesy of the artist; 22: O. K. Harris Works of Art, New York; 23: © DACS 1988; 26: Leo Castelli Gallery, New York; 29: Fred McDarrah, New York; 30: Gianfranco Gorgoni, New York; 32: Esto Photographics © 1958 Ezra Stoller; 33: Lucien Herve © SPADEM; 34: Camera Press © John Fairfax; 35: Architectural Press; 37: Fondation Le Corbusier, Paris © SPADEM.

Chapter 12: 3: Timothy Hursley; 4: Esto Photographics © Ezra Stoller; 5: Courtesy of the Artist; 6: Mary Boone Gallery, New York; 7: Charles Saatchi Collection, London; 8: Harcourt Brace Jovanovich/Metro Pictures, New York; 9: Esto/Wayne Andrews; 10: Venturi, Rauch/Tom Crane; 11: Esto/Wolfgang Hoyt; 12: Camera Press.

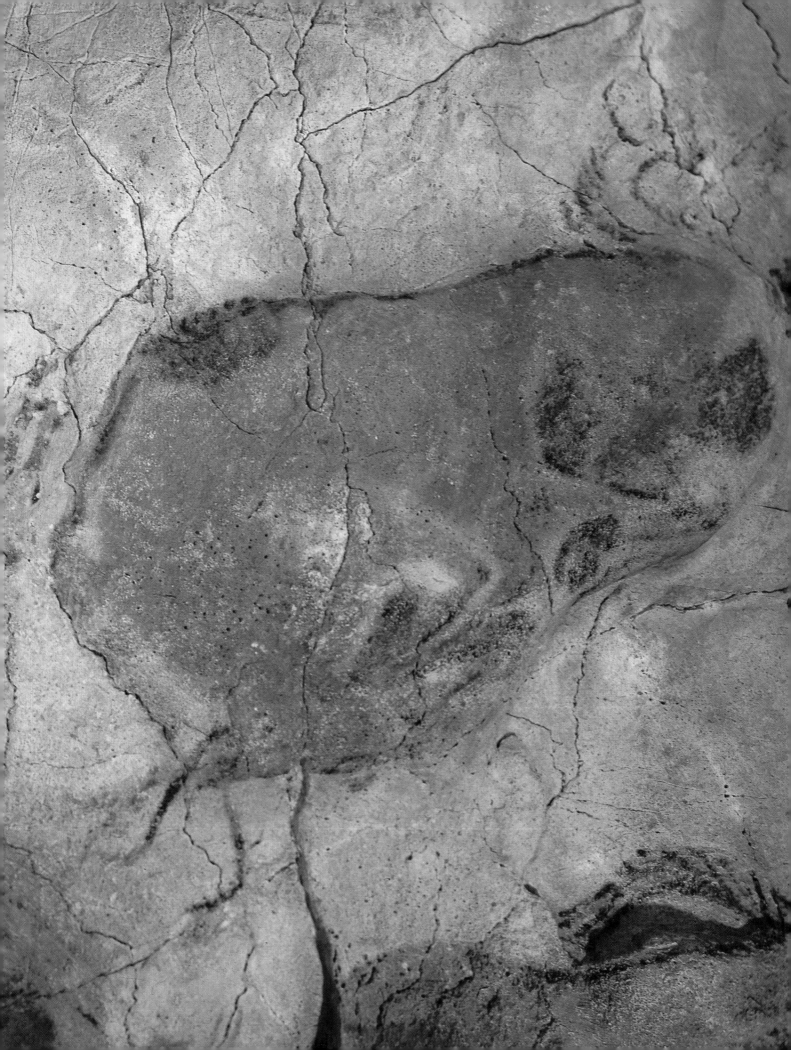

CHAPTER ONE

Beginnings

What is man that thou art mindful of him, and the son of man that thou dost care for him?

PSALM 8, v.4

1.1 *Wounded Bison*, Altamira, Spain, c. 15,000–10,000 BC

Introduction

Prehistoric Cultures

Human beings roamed the world many thousands of years ago. For the purposes of this text, however, we shall begin with a hunter-gatherer culture of approximately 10,000 BC (Fig. 1.3). It falls within the period called the Paleolithic (Old Stone Age) because of the crude stone tools humans employed. The Mesolithic (Middle Stone Age) lasted from 7000 BC until about 6000 BC, and was followed by the Neolithic (New Stone Age), so-called because of the development of sharper and more effective stone tools. This era also marked a shift from the hunter-gatherer mode of living to the peasant-village mode.

Some 10,000 years before the birth of Christ the last glacial period was coming to an end. In this period, Britain and Scandinavia were, like Greenland today, permanently covered with ice. Southern France, like northeastern Canada, was cold and relatively treeless. But these areas teemed with cold-adapted animals such as reindeer, antelope, bison, horses, bears, and mammoths, to name a few. Thus, despite the inhospitable climate, Europe was able to support human life, in the form of a hunter-gatherer culture who had to eke out an existence by hunting and killing animals.

Sometimes called the "Ice-Age" people, they were tall with large craniums and, physically, were the same as modern humans. They wore animal skins, used fire, and fashioned tools mainly from stones but also from bones, ivory, and wood. They were also, as we shall see, the creators of sophisticated art depicting animals. They did not live in caves, but sought shelter in overhanging cliffs along river banks (in Western Europe) or in trenches covered with hides (in Eastern Europe). But because they had to follow herds in search of game, they did not linger anywhere for long periods. This nomadic existence typified the hunter-gatherer culture.

However, at the end of the Ice Age, temperatures warmed, forests covered the land, and these large cold-adapted animals moved to other locations or became extinct. Ice-Age people were forced to seek other game, mostly easier-to-kill. As their hunting habits changed, so did their social structure and skills. An agricultural revolution which began around 7000 BC and gradually spread from the Middle East to Europe, was to have a profound effect upon their way of life. Instead of following herds and wandering in search of edible plants, men and women began to settle down and grow their own food—a style of culture called peasant-village.

The implications of this change were enormous. Growing food was associated not only with the arts of cattle rearing, sheep herding, and land cultivation, but also with the development of such skills as pottery and tool making, weaving, and the building of sun-baked brick huts and granaries—skills required to maintain a simple agricultural economy. In addition, warriors were needed to protect against enemy tribes; and shamans, to protect against evil forces. All this required some division of responsibilities, which in turn led to the development of social organization and the necessity of leaders such as chieftains and priests. Furthermore, land cultivation required knowledge of the seasons, and hence at least a rudimentary knowledge of astronomy and mathematics. Peasant-village life being less precarious than that of the hunter-gatherer, people had more time to ponder the supernatural: the creation of the world, good and evil, the meaning of human existence, life after death. Thus innate religious longings were shaped into more sophisticated beliefs expressed through chant and other kinds of music.

The rudimentary yet impressive beginnings of civilization, therefore, are traceable in both the hunter-gatherer and the peasant-village cultures. Especially notable for the study of humanities are the strikingly realistic and skillfully-executed animal paintings made by the Ice-Age people on the cave walls of southern France and northern Spain: the first evidence of symbolizing ideas, of embodying form and meaning in visible signs, and thus a momentous step in human development. More speculatively, one may assume that the beginnings of music and literature in Western civilization are to be found in the chants used in the religious ritual of the peasant-village people and perhaps also in those providing cadence for performing large tasks requiring united efforts.

But civilization, as defined by historians, requires cities; and cities require more than the subsistence level of food produced by the peasant-villagers. Cities require extra food—enough to allow substantial numbers of people to pursue occupations other than farming. Like the agricultural revolution, the transition to city life involved profound changes: the introduction of trade, an intense division of labor with people devoting all of their time to individual skills and professions, and a heightened need for a social organization and direction.

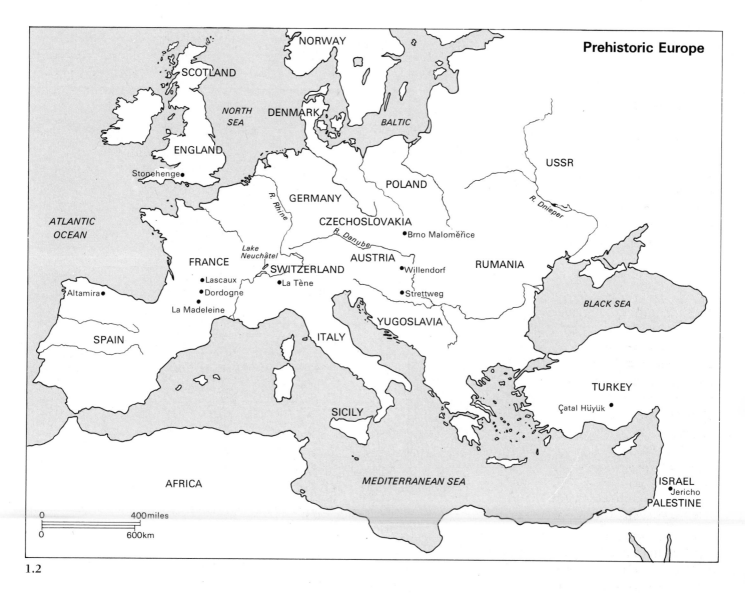

Prehistoric Europe

1.2

Mesopotamia

Although the evidence of excavations suggests that at
least two cities—prehistoric Jericho (in modern Israel) and
Catal Huyuk (in modern Turkey)—may go back as far as
the peasant-village culture itself, the first cities to leave a
significant legacy were those emerging a little after
4000 BC along the banks of the Tigris and Euphrates rivers
in Mesopotamia ("land between the rivers"), modern Iraq.
This was one of the two river valleys of the ancient Near
East—the other being the Nile Valley—that produced
sophisticated civilizations. A fertile plain, ideal for farming
and spawning a civilization, Mesopotamia was also
subject to violent storms and unpredictable floods. The
geopolitics of this area—the magnet for invaders and a
place where many races, languages, and cultures com-
peted for some 3000 years—was as volatile as the climate.
It was also a land of city-states, which became a single,
unified civilization only through brutal conquest, and

then only for brief periods. Thus it was a land where kings
were required to be military leaders. The religions of
Mesopotamia were as pluralistic as the cultures, and the
gods within each religion were also pluralistic.

For more than a thousand years (3500–2400 BC) the
southern part of Mesopotamia was controlled by people
called Sumerians. They were the founders of Ur, among
other cities. Among the major contributions these people
made to Near Eastern civilization—literary, scientific, and
artistic—was the invention of writing. History begins with
writing; thus we know much more about the Sumerians
than about the peoples who preceded them. Their writing
is called "cuneiform" (from Latin *cuneus*, "wedge")
because it was made with a wedge-shaped stylus, which
produced correspondingly wedge-shaped marks in the soft
clay used as a writing surface. The clay tablets were then
baked hard. In literature, the Sumerians are best known
for the creation of epics concerning a legendary king
named Gilgamesh—poems that influenced biblical litera-

DATES	SOCIAL AND POLITICAL DEVELOPMENTS	LITERATURE AND PHILOSOPHY	VISUAL ARTS	ARCHITECTURE	MUSIC
15,000–7,000 BC	Old Stone Age Hunter-gatherer culture New Stone Age Peasant-village culture		Lascaux paintings (**1.5**) Altamira paintings (**1.1, 1.7**) Bison carved in reindeer horn (**1.6**)		Religious dances Incantations
6,000			Painted beaker from Susa (**1.8**)		
4,000	First Mesopotamian cities Beginning of Old Kingdom, Egypt	Cuneiform writing *Epic of Gilgamesh* Hieroglyphic writing	Mycerinus and his Queen (**1.20**) Painted relief of Ti, Saqqara (**1.22**) Tomb paintings (**1.27**)	Mastabas (**1.21**) Pyramids at Giza (**1.17**) Ziggurat at Ur (**1.9**)	Sumerian harp from Ur (**1.12**)
2,000	Beginning of Middle Kingdom, Egypt Old Babylonian Empire Hammurabi Hyksos Beginning of New Kingdom, Egypt Akhenaton Rameses II Israelite Exodus	Code of Hammurabi Development of alphabet (Phoenician)	Stele of Hammurabi (**1.13**)	Funerary temple of Hatshepsut (**1.24**) Portrait statue of Akhenaton (**1.25**) Painted relief of Smenkhkare (**1.26**)	Musicians and musical instruments depicted in Tomb of Nakht (**1.27**)
1,000	Assyrian Empire Neo-Babylonian Empire Babylonian Exile (Jews) Persian Empire	Amos Hosea Isaiah Book of Job(?)		Citadel of Sargon (**1.15**) Tower of Babel	Musical instruments: trumpets, kissor, harps, lyres Psalteries Solomon's temple

1.3 Prehistory to the Persian Empire

ture. In architecture, they are famous for the building of tower-temples called ziggurats (cf. Genesis 11:1–9).

The Sumerians were conquered after 2400 BC by the Akkadians, whose control of Mesopotamia was relatively short-lived. The Amorite rulers of Babylon, a Semitic people, brought order out of the chaos resulting from the fall of the Akkadian Empire. Thus was born what historians term the Old Babylonian Empire. Hammurabi, the most powerful of the Amorite rulers, brought all of Mesopotamia under his control in the eighteenth century. He is remembered for having formulated a code of laws which has some parallels with those imparted to the Israelites at Mount Sinai. Hammurabi's code, however, has been shown by recent historians to be derived from Sumerian laws—an indication of the powerful influence of Sumerian civilization on subsequent cultures.

In northern Mesopotamia, the Assyrians, who had long endured the domination of the southern kingdoms, finally took advantage of the political turmoil that occurred at the end of the second millennium and assumed control—a supremacy that lasted from about 1300 to 612 BC.

Ambitious and aggressive, they acquired an empire that reached from Egypt to the Persian Gulf, and, in the process, gained a considerable reputation for barbarism. In the eighth century BC, the Israelites (also known as Hebrews or Jews), as predicted by their prophets, became victims of the Assyrians' notorious savagery. II Kings (chapters 17–19) describes how the Assyrian king Shalmaneser devastated Samaria and how Sennacherib, another Assyrian king, threatened Jerusalem, humiliated King Hezekiah, and even blasphemed against the Lord. The short Book of Nahum in the Old Testament is devoted entirely to denouncing the Assyrians and rejoicing in their final destruction.

An empire that thrived on terror was bound to meet with increasing opposition. In the seventh century the Assyrians were overpowered by a combined force of Medes, Babylonians, and Scythians, who captured Nineveh (capital of Assyria), the event celebrated in such vivid language by the prophet Nahum. Following this came the re-emergence of Babylonia, called Neo-Babylon by historians, an empire that survived less than a century. In biblical history this period is even more infamous than the Assyrian era because of the exploits of Babylon's most legendary king, Nebuchadnezzar, who, in 587 BC, destroyed Jerusalem, razed the Temple of Solomon, and carried the leading Jews into exile in Babylon. In the Book of Daniel he is presented both as a villain and, later, as a convert to the worship of the God of the Jews. The Neo-Babylonian Empire was brought to an end by Cyrus, king of the Medes and Persians, who, in 538 BC, decreed that the Jewish exiles could return to their homeland.

Egypt

Unlike the sprawling "land between the rivers" that produced the Mesopotamian civilizations, the Nile Valley is a relatively narrow stretch of fertile land. This has two distinct sections: Upper Egypt, consisting of narrow strips of cultivation on either side of the Nile; and Lower Egypt, consisting of the river's delta, a triangle of sediment and distributaries emptying into the Mediterranean. On the map the Valley resembles a long, thin stem topped by a lotus, Egypt's national flower. To the north is sea; to the south, crocodile-infested wilderness; on either side of the stem, desert. The river and its banks were sources of many things needed in daily life—fish and game, papyrus, clay

for pottery—but it was the annual flooding of the river, which irrigated and enriched the valley and delta with silt, that made possible the miracle of agriculture. In ancient times the river's overflow was so regular that it could be predicted almost to the day—between July 19 and 21 at Heliopolis (now Cairo). Even the climate, much milder than that of Mesopotamia, was predictable.

The Egyptian civilization, reflecting the regularity of its river and serenity of its climate, was one of the most stable and abiding of any in history. Because of the Nile's dependability, Egypt was spared the upheavals that come with periodic famines (although, according to Genesis [chapter 41], famine might have occurred on one occasion, had it not been for Joseph's wise advice to the pharaoh). Because of its isolation, Egypt was free to develop without interference. Unlike Mesopotamia it was neither an arena for feuding city-states, nor a magnet for invading armies. Its leaders were sacred kings, not military commanders. Egypt's religion stressed the eternal, not the here and now; its gods were cosmic rather than human. To an Egyptian, heaven itself was conceived as an extension of life in Egypt.

Ancient Egyptian history is divided into three periods: the Old Kingdom (about c. 2686–c. 2160 BC), the era in

1.4

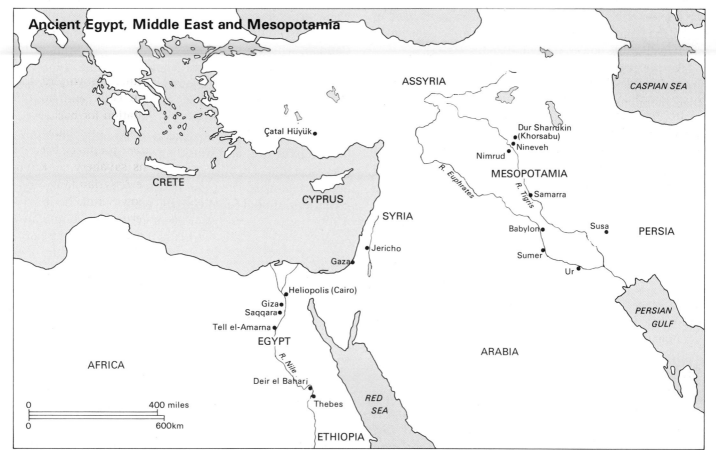

Ancient Egypt, Middle East and Mesopotamia

which the great pyramids were built; the Middle Kingdom (c. 2040–1786 BC); and the New Kingdom (1570–1085 BC), also called the Empire because of the aggressive imperialism that characterized Egyptian rule in this period. The gap between the Old and the Middle kingdoms was a period of instability resulting from a succession of weak pharaohs. The gap between the Middle Kingdom and the Empire resulted from the invasion of a people called the Hyksos, who ruled Egypt for more than a century. It may have been during the rule of these "shepherd kings" that Joseph and his family moved into Egypt (Genesis, chapters 37–50). It has been speculated that this may account for the favorable treatment accorded Joseph's family, also shepherds, who were settled by the pharaoh in the eastern region of the Delta. Thus the new king "who did not know Joseph" (Exodus 1:8) and who enslaved the Israelites would have been a member of the Egyptian dynasty restored after the expulsion of the Hyksos. If the exodus of the Israelites from Egypt occurred in the thirteenth century BC, as many scholars believe, it took place in the nineteenth dynasty (1320–1200 BC), perhaps in the reign of Rameses II (1304–1237 BC).

Although the Egyptians, like the people of Mesopotamia, worshipped several gods, the most basic fact of their religion was the belief that the pharaoh himself was a god. Thus when Moses came before the pharoah demanding the release of his people in the name of Yahweh, God of Israel, the pharaoh would have seen this as a challenge to his own absolute power in Egypt (Exodus 5:1–2).

Like the people of Mesopotamia, the Egyptians made significant contributions to Near Eastern civilization. Their monumental architecture, their serene sculptures, their colorful wall paintings—all are timelessly impressive. But the Egyptians were also a literary people. Their system of writing is called hieroglyphic (Greek, "sacred carving") and was composed of pictograms: pictures of physical objects. Some of the signs, however, became conventions for abstract ideas. Hieroglyphic symbols were also used for artistic decoration. Unlike the Sumerians, who wrote on clay tablets, the Egyptians used scrolls made of papyrus, a fiber from the papyrus plant (and the source of the word "paper"). The Egyptians were not as competent in mathematics as the Mesopotamians, but their knowledge of medicine was remarkable. And although they did not create a work analogous to the epic of Gilgamesh, they produced literature of many kinds, much of it religious in nature. Their philosophical writings focused on ethical and political issues. Perhaps their most significant contribution to civilization was the invention of the principle of the alphabet (the use of syllables for voice sounds). The Phoenicians later combined this principle with their own form of writing and carried the system to other peoples.

Thus the two great river valleys of the ancient Near East served as the cradles for the cultures that marked the beginnings of Western civilization. The peoples of Mesopotamia and Egypt created sophisticated civilizations which produced, among other things, monumental architecture, skillfully wrought sculptures, and, in the case of Egypt, tomb paintings which provide insights into the daily life of that society. One may also speculate that both Egypt and Mesopotamia created some form of music comparable to their other cultural achievements. The first chapter of this book, therefore, will focus partly on the visual art and (speculatively) the music of these cultures. In contrast to these two mighty civilizations, the Land of Canaan, which lies between them, produced little in the way of art or architecture (though possibly some fine music—now lost, like all ancient music). But its people, the Hebrews, were supreme in literature; and through their creation of the Bible were to have a lasting impact on Western civilization. Our religion, philosophy, literature, art, architecture, and music all bear the profound and pervasive marks of biblical stories and thought. Thus it is appropriate that a study of the Humanities in this civilization should begin with the Bible.

Literature

Psalm 8

The Bible is profoundly concerned with the question implied by the word "humanities" itself: What does it mean to be human? The psalmist explicitly asks this question: "What is man that thou art mindful of him? and the son of man that thou dost care for him?" (8:4).[1] The question is not asked in despair and frustration, as in the Book of Job (7:17–18), but in wonderment at the privileges and prerogatives granted to humans. Though seemingly so insignificant, as compared with the "heavens" (v.3), man is the object of God's special "care" (v.4), and indeed is "little less than God" (v.5); for God has "given him dominion" over creation (vs.6–8).

Psalm 8 epitomizes the biblical view of the relationship of human beings to God. They are unique, created in the image of God (Genesis 1:27), special creatures in God's world. But this uniqueness is a gift of God. Thus the privileges of being human can be worthily enjoyed and fulfilled only within the will of God. Moreover, humanness cannot be eradicated, remaining intact however depraved or tortured the human condition may become. This biblical view of humanness, though often challenged by artists and writers, runs deep in the Western tradition.

Genesis 1–11

The first 11 chapters of Genesis may be regarded as a prologue not only to the stories of the patriarchs of Israel (Abraham, Isaac, Jacob, and Jacob's sons, especially Joseph), but also to the entire Bible. Here the basic biblical premises of the human condition are set forth: creation by God, the problem of sin, and God's judgment tempered by his grace. The Bible illustrates and works out the implications of this view. God's provisions for this human situation are the choice of a nation, Israel, in the Old Testament, and the sending of his son, Jesus Christ, in the New Testament—the latter provision, according to the New Testament, fulfilling the redemptive promises of the former.

Biblical scholars often refer to the stories of Genesis 1–11 as "myth." Because of the devaluation of this term in common usage—it is often used to refer to what is not true—it is important to understand what is meant when it is used in reference to these stories. Broadly speaking, myth, in this sense, refers to stories that convey profound religious truths, that attempt to answer such perennial human questions as 'Who are we?' 'What is our origin?' 'What is our destiny?' and 'What were we meant to be?' Genesis 1–11 addresses all these questions. But this is truth of a particular kind. It is not the factual truth of science, or even the truth of historicity. Rather, it is the kind of truth found in the parables of Jesus, the truth of being and meaning—religious truth. It is also permanently relevant truth; that is, myth is intended to explain not simply how things *were* but how they always *are*. Thus, for example, the story of Adam and Eve is not merely the story of a man and woman of the past but of every-man and every-woman, each of us, in all times and places. The flood story likewise is about a continuing reality, the reality of evil in the world, and God's judgment upon it.

Genesis 1–11 has also been described as a radical analysis of the human situation, an analysis, that is, which goes to the root of the human problem. This is evident in the stories of creation and the fall and those that follow. Human beings, created by God for a special relation to him and finding fulfillment in that relationship, become dissatisfied and rebel, seeking godhood instead. The result is alienation from God and from each other. Though God judges and punishes them for this, he also maintains his concern for them, making provision for their welfare. Thus these ancient stories do not merely focus on a moment of the past but seek to penetrate for all time the enigma of human sin and the divine response.

The Prophets

Although Moses is regarded as the paradigm of the true prophet (Deut. 18:15–18), most of the prophets did not appear until later, especially in conjunction with the rise of kingship. This is significant, for the prophet often served as both advisor to and critic of the king and his policies. His authority for performing this important function was simply that the Lord had called him to be his spokesman. Unlike that of king and priest, his office was not hereditary. His authority resided in the authenticity of his divine summons. The prophet, therefore, often stresses the circumstances of his call as a guarantee of the validity of his message.

Amos

Amos, who prophesied around the middle of the eighth century BC, is often referred to as the first of the "writing prophets." This merely means that he is the earliest prophet whose oracles, or messages, have been recorded, probably by Amos himself. Prophetic writings often reflect messages proclaimed to live audiences. Amos, for example, did much of his preaching at Bethel, a religious sanctuary in the northern kingdom of Israel. Because much of what the prophet proclaimed pertained to contemporary spiritual and political conditions, he often encountered strident, even violent, opposition.

Jeroboam II (784–744 BC), king of Israel during the ministry of Amos, presided over a time of political security and economic growth. A middle class, composed of merchants and landowners, was becoming increasingly prosperous. Their prosperity, however, was often at the expense of the poor and powerless. Compounding this problem, ironically, was the superficial piety of the wealthy, who believed that their prosperity was the seal of God's approval. Because of this social injustice and Israel's general unfaithfulness to the moral and spiritual demands of their covenant relationship with the Lord, Amos foresaw the Lord's destruction of Israel some 30 years before it was effected, in 722 BC, by the Assyrians.

Amos attacks the sins of his time with vivid language, drawing upon his considerable poetic gifts to drive home his moral and spiritual judgments. He does not confine himself to the denunciation of Israel. In fact, the book begins with his attack on surrounding pagan nations for their violation of the moral law, a clear sign of Amos's conviction that God is no mere national deity, but the sovereign Lord of the nations. The series of denunciations, however, reaches its climax with Judah and Israel (2:4–8). From this point on the focus is on Israel's prosperous middle class, "because they sell the righteous for silver, / and the needy for a pair of shoes...." The perpetrators of such injustices are warned: "Because you trample upon the poor / and take from him exactions of wheat, / you have built houses of hewn stone, / but you shall not dwell in them; / you have planted pleasant vinyards, / but you shall not drink their wine" (5:11).

To their callous treatment of the poor, wealthy Israelites added the sin of hypocrisy, in the form of showy but superficial religiosity. The futility and offensiveness of their shallow devotions are devastatingly presented by Amos in the words of the Lord himself: "I hate, I despise your feasts, and I take no delight in your solemn assemblies" (5:21). To find favor in the eyes of God, they must, writes the prophet, in one of his most memorable passages, "let justice roll down like waters, / and righteousness like an ever-flowing stream" (5:25). It is not surprising that Amos has traditionally been regarded as the champion of the poor and the oppressed.

Amos has also been called the prophet of judgment. Yet, for all his relentless denunciation of the sins of Israel, his book ends on a note of high promise (9:9–15). Indeed, it was typical of the prophets to see divine salvation beyond divine judgment in their sure belief that the Lord's redemptive purposes would not fail. This hope of ultimate redemption becomes even more pronounced—certainly more dramatic and personal—in the prophecy of Hosea, a somewhat later contemporary of Amos.

Hosea

Soon after Hosea began to prophesy, the prosperous reign of Jeroboam came to an end. It was followed by a period of economic and political decline which was ultimately to be fatal. The Jehu dynasty, to which Jeroboam had belonged, and which lasted for nearly a century, was brought to an end within six months of Jeroboam's death by the assassination of his son Zechariah. Shallum, Zechariah's assassin, was himself murdered by Menahem, who ruled until 738 BC. At this point he began to pay tribute to Assyria, which under the leadership of Tiglath-Pileser III had moved westward, using its powerful and brutal army

to subdue the smaller kingdoms. For Israel, this was the beginning of the end. It was against the background of this turbulent political situation that Hosea carried out his preaching mission to the people of Israel.

The dominant image used by Hosea to convey Israel's spiritual waywardness is that of a harlot: "For a spirit of harlotry has led them astray, and they have left their God to play the harlot" (4:12). The personal significance of this imagery becomes clear in the account of Hosea's call to become a prophet: "When the Lord first spoke to Hosea, the Lord said to Hosea, 'Go take to yourself a wife of harlotry, and have children of harlotry, for the land commits great harlotry by forsaking the Lord.' So he went and took Gomer" (1:3). Thus Hosea's own marital tragedy became for him the symbol of the spiritual adultery of Israel, their idolatrous turning to other gods. But as Hosea continued to love the adulterous Gomer, and sought to reclaim her as his wife—as God later commanded him—so also the Lord's tenacious love for his people compelled him to pursue their redemption, despite their idolatrous and disobedient ways (3:1–5; 11.8). Thus, Hosea's profound insight into the relationship of the Lord to his people is that his justice does not preclude his love—indeed, is tempered by it. But as Hosea's understanding of the steadfast love of God for his people grew out of his personal experience with an adulterous wife, so also did his recognition that such love does not come cheap. A price must be paid by the lover who refuses to give up on his beloved. Thus the suffering love of Hosea for Gomer dramatizes on a human scale the suffering love of the Lord for his straying people.

The Book of Job

The author of the Book of Job, one of the great books in world literature, is unknown. So also is the date of its composition; in its present form it is usually placed somewhere between 600 and 400 BC. The prose prologue and epilogue perhaps came from a traditional tale about Job which the author of the poetic dialogues that form the heart of the story used for his own purposes. Fortunately, the significance of Job is not limited by matters of authorship and dating; for its subject—the meaning of suffering for the person of deep religious faith—is timeless and its impact independent of authorship.

The Book of Job is based on the conviction that God *is* and that he *cares*—he is involved in human affairs and works for the good of his people. This belief is the source of much of Job's anguish. Not only is his body devastated by disease and his emotions shattered by the loss of his possessions and children; his conception of God has also been smashed on the jagged rock of his personal experience. Yet he must pursue the answers to his anguished questions within the parameters of his faith in God. Thus his search is for a more adequate, more realistic theology which will meet the test of concrete human experience.

The author of Job has presented this search in the form of a series of poetic dialogues set within the framework of a prose prologue and epilogue. The prologue tells how Job's devastating losses are the result of encounters in heaven between the Lord and Satan. The dialogues consist of three rounds of debate on the reason for Job's suffering, with each of Job's friends (Eliphaz, Bildad, and Zophar) making one speech in each round, with the exception of the third round, in which Zophar does not speak. Job responds to each of the speeches, then, after a poem in praise of wisdom (chapter 28), he presents his final defense. Elihu, who is not referred to elsewhere in the poem, then makes a lengthy speech, which Job does not answer. (Some scholars believe that the Elihu section is a later interpolation.) At this point the Lord himself enters the picture and responds to Job. The book concludes with Job's penitent submission to the Lord (42:6) and an epilogue in which the Lord rebukes Job's friends, thus vindicating Job, and restores his possessions and his family.

The poet introduces Job as a righteous and God-fearing man who was very wealthy and had many children. The scene then shifts from the earth to the court of the Lord (compare the discussion of Goethe's *Faust*, Chapter 5). There Satan appears among the "sons of God" and challenges the Lord, asserting that his cherished servant Job serves him only because his righteousness guarantees divinely-provided prosperity and security. In this and a subsequent appearance Satan contends that if he is permitted to strip Job of his wealth, children, and health, he will be reduced to cursing God. Although the Lord accepts the challenge, and Job consequently suffers these devastating losses, Job maintains his integrity and his faith in God. The prologue thus provides part of the poet's response to the problem of undeserved suffering: God may have worthy purposes that can be fulfilled only through suffering. In Job's case this purpose is to demonstrate that a human being can be righteous purely for the sake of righteousness, not because it always pays off in divine blessings.

The three friends of Job now appear, having "made an appointment together to condole with him and comfort him" (2:11). They are overwhelmed by his devastated appearance, weep, and then sit in silence with him for seven days, "for they saw that his suffering was very great" (2:13). Thus concludes the prose prologue.

The dialogues open with a soliloquy by Job in which he curses the day of his birth. Job's friends contend through-

out the dialogues that there is always a causal connection between sin/righteousness and suffering/prosperity; that is, sin always produces suffering and righteousness always produces prosperity. This is how divine justice operates.

The friends do not believe in the hereafter. Thus they argue from the premise that God's justice must be accomplished in this life. Although Job gropes after an ultimate justice beyond death, he cannot sustain such a hope (14:7–17; 19:25–26). It is the absence of such a faith on the part of Job and his friends that makes Job's suffering so crucial in this drama. If God's justice is to be confirmed, it must be in this world. As the friends see things, God has already demonstrated his justice: Job has sinned and God is now punishing him.

Although Job himself has previously held the same belief, he knows that it cannot explain his own loss and pain. While not regarding himself as perfect, he knows that he has done nothing to deserve his terrible plight. Indeed, the reader knows this, too; for both the narrator (1:1) and the Lord (1:8; 2:3) have witnessed to his righteousness and integrity. Thus the poet-theologian, through his drama on the experience of Job, seeks a more realistic faith—one that will take account of suffering that cannot be explained as resulting from sin.

Job is caught in the painful position of a religious person whose present faith is inadequate to the experience of real life, but who has not found a more mature faith to replace it. Thus Job's anguish over his suffering is primarily theological *angst*; that is, his suffering is essentially the pain resulting from his inability to understand how a just and loving God could visit physical and emotional pain such as he now endures on a good man. Nonetheless, though he argues with God, though he even comes close to blaspheming God, Job never denies, or even questions, God's existence. Here we see the caliber of the poet's faith: he does not shut his eyes to the reality of undeserved human suffering; he does not offer platitudes to explain it away. But neither does he deny the existence of a loving and omnipotent God, whose reality is as much a part of his own experience as is the reality of undeserved suffering.

Eventually Job's friends fall silent; Job, it would appear, has won the argument. But now (passing over Elihu's speeches) the Lord himself enters the debate—not to be questioned but to ask questions (chapters 38–41). Job himself is now put on the witness stand to be interrogated by the Lord, speaking "out of the whirlwind" (38:1). The central thrust of the divine questioning is this: what do you know, Job, of my creative power and wise providence in the universe? "Where were you," asks the Lord, "when I laid the foundations of the earth?" (38:4). The Lord's questioning demonstrates repeatedly his powerful and concerned involvement in his creation. With but one brief and weak exception (40:3–5), Job is unable to respond to these speeches. Finally, however, after the Lord has finished, Job cries out, "I had heard of thee by the hearing of the ear, but now my eye sees thee; therefore I despise myself, and repent in dust and ashes" (42:5–6). Job's faith, previously derived from tradition, is now founded upon a personal encounter with the Lord. Because of this, he repents of his presumptuousness. No longer is he compelled to cry out "Why?" He has found peace for his anguished spirit—he rests in God.

The question, however, remains: how can this be? Implicitly, the poet offers three answers[2]: (1) *Job has had a personal encounter with God which is altogether convincing.* The victory over suffering, the poet implies, comes not through clever verbal solutions to the problem of evil, but through the actual experience of God's presence and love in the seething cauldron of pain and loss. Job has had such an experience. (2) *Job is persuaded that the Lord's wisdom is at work in his own case through the panoramic view of his power and providence in creation.* Job's meager knowledge of the Lord's role in the creation and preservation of his universe teaches him humility with respect to the divine purpose in his own case. Moreover, if the Lord so cares for the rest of his creation, he must also care for Job. (3) *Job's penitent submission is the only means by which he can cope with his grief and suffering.* The sufferer does not need rational solutions but the means of transcending his pain. Because Job's encounter with the Lord changes his relationship with him, he undergoes a change in his very being. Thus his soul is healed, and he is able to find rest in God.

The restoration of Job's material fortunes occurs in the epilogue. Here, the special regard of the Lord for Job is illustrated by his instructions to Eliphaz and his two friends to offer sacrifice and ask Job to intercede for them. The importance of this intercessory role is underscored by the fact that it is only after Job has prayed for his friends that his family and material possessions are restored (in fact, his possessions are doubled). Though much less profound than the dialogue of Job's encounter with the Lord, this ending is the tangible proof to Job's friends of the Lord's approval of him. Since no clear hope of justification in the hereafter is provided by the poet, Job's vindication must be shown to his friends in the context of this life.

Isaiah 53: The Suffering Servant

The problem of suffering is presented in yet another key in Isaiah 53, one of the most significant and controversial passages in the Old Testament. It is the fourth and longest of four "servant songs" in Isaiah (42:1–4; 49:1–6; 50:4–11; 52:13–53:12), poems that speak of a mysterious figure whose suffering—rather than being punishment for sin or a divine mystery—will be vicarious, the means of reconciling mankind to God.

Of the numerous interpretations of the Servant, the two that are most representative are (1) that the Servant is Israel; (2) that the Servant foreshadows the redemptive role of Jesus. In the first interpretation Israel's suffering, rather than resulting simply from her own sins, is for the sins of the nations and will be the means by which God will redeem the Gentiles. Thus Isaiah 53, in this view, represents a profound enlargement of Israel's role among the nations at whose hands she has so often suffered. The poem, however, is given yet another dimension in the New Testament interpretation of Jesus as its historical embodiment—an interpretation which, there is good reason to believe, originated with Jesus himself. Through Jesus and the New Testament, then, the Suffering Servant concept became specifically historical and individualized. It is in this Christianized form that the concept of the Suffering Servant has had its greatest impact on the Western tradition.

Whether one approaches the poem as an explanatory vision of the meaning of Israel's suffering or as the foreshadowing of the suffering of Jesus as the Messiah, it is unique in that it presents suffering as the means by which the Servant *fulfills* the divine mission of reconciliation. There is nothing like this elsewhere in the Old Testament. Because of its unique interpretation of the suffering of the Servant, this passage serves as an appropriate bridge to the New Testament presentation of Jesus as the Messiah whose suffering is the means by which God forgives sin and reconciles mankind to himself (see Chapter 6).

The Beginnings of Art

When did art begin? To answer that we have to determine what we mean by art. If, for example, we think of it only in terms of pictures and sculptures made for their *aesthetic* appeal—that is, to be viewed for their own sake in galleries, museums, office lobbies, and private homes, then we exclude not only architecture but a great many interesting and important examples of our visual heritage. Throughout much of history, buildings, paintings, and sculptures were made to fulfill important social needs—usually related to religious beliefs—rather than aesthetic needs, though at times they performed this function as well. In fact, only a minority of the world's images and virtually none of the world's buildings have been made for aesthetic purposes only. Obviously, we would not wish to define our subject so narrowly as to omit the majority of our visual culture. On the other hand, our visual heritage is so vast that we must accept some limits.

Henceforth architecture will be limited to those buildings that are considered significant "monuments" of architecture—that is, large, surviving edifices that are highly representative of their period's construction technologies and noblest values. And of these, we will be able to consider only a small sample. The definition of the other visual arts—paintings, murals, sculptures, relief carvings, and so forth—will be broad enough to include works intended not only for aesthetic purposes but also for ritualistic, religious, and even magical purposes. As with architecture, however, these will be limited to works that are highly representative of their respective periods.

Given these parameters, we might say that architecture began around 3000 BC, since monumental construction probably did not exist earlier than that time (later in this section we will review examples of Mesopotamian and Egyptian architecture). But painting and sculpture began much earlier—around 15,000 BC.

Ice-Age Art

The discovery of the earliest-known art is a history in itself. A little more than 100 years ago people were just beginning to be aware that the human race, not to mention human culture, pre-dated the peoples of Ancient Egypt and the Old Testament. Archeology was in its infancy; the idea of saving old bones, tools, and artifacts found at random—perhaps even deliberately searching for such things—was just catching on. But already enough of these objects had been found in various parts of Europe to suggest that unknown tribes of people roamed that continent long before such ancient people as the Goths and Huns. The fact that these unknown people painted images—indeed very impressive ones—was discovered by chance in 1879, when a five-year-old girl accompanying her father in one of the Altamira Caves in Spain noticed paintings on the ceiling. The father, who was an amateur archeologist, deduced that they were prehistoric; but when he announced this amazing find to the scientific community, he was met with disbelief. It was not until 1896, when some other cave paintings, partially covered with calcareous deposits, were discovered in southern France, that authorities became convinced. Because the deposits required thousands of years to accumulate, scientists knew that the paintings had to be very old, and therefore that skilled artists must have lived in the area of southern France and northern Spain some 10–12,000 years before the time of Christ. That would have been at the end of the last glacial period. Europe at that time, as we have seen, was thinly populated by a hunter-gatherer culture we now call Ice-Age people.

We have also noted that these people were primarily nomadic and did not live in caves. If this is true, why are some caves in western Europe, like the one near Lascaux, France (Fig. 1.5), full of paintings of animals? One theory is that they served as "way stations" on chase routes, to which hunters returned again and again. And what about the paintings? Why were they made? Why were they painted in caves? How were they made? What do they mean? Answers to these questions can be deduced partly from carefully studying the paintings. Like all art, they can be analyzed in terms of four basic components: subject matter, medium, style, and content.

The "subject matter" (or subject) is what is represented in a picture. In the paintings of these Ice-Age people the subject matter is overwhelmingly that of animals. Other subjects—people, tools, trees, terrain features, and so forth—are found only rarely, if at all. Those that do exist are rudimentary.

The "medium" (pl. "media") includes the methods and materials employed. Knowing the medium can help answer the question of how the pictures were made. Basically, the medium is *mural*: picture or pictures applied directly to a wall. Specifically the method was painting; the pigments, or coloring matter, were probably obtained from the earth or even from a campsite: gypsum for white; charcoal for black; and metal oxides for different shades of red, brown, and yellow-brown. These were probably mixed with animal fat or blood and applied with brushes

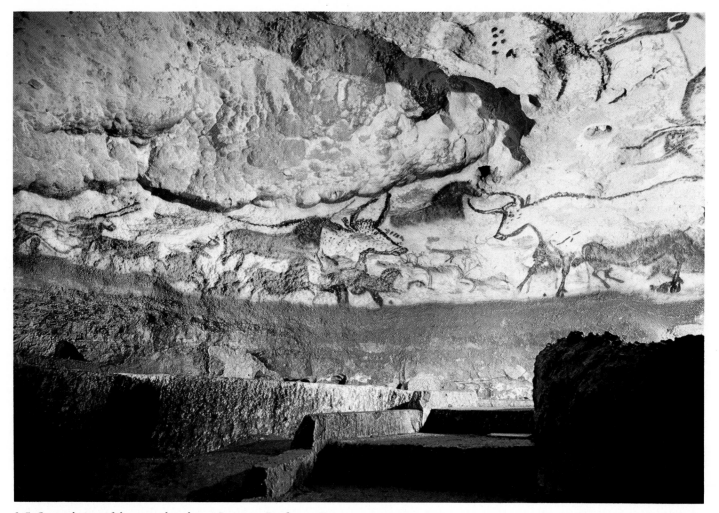

1.5 General view of the cave chamber at Lascaux, Dordogne, France

made of animal tails and/or frayed sticks. In some cases—as we shall see in one example—the mixture may have been blown onto the wall through hollow tubes of horn or wood. Although Ice-Age artists also created images in clay, bone, and ivory (Fig. 1.6), the focus here will be on the murals.

Analyzing the "style" is a bit more complicated and requires a close examination of the pictures' *forms*: the shapes and colors of the images, and how they are arranged or composed. The individual shapes reveal a high level of observation and drawing skill, their contours conforming rather accurately to those of real animals. Most are shown running or in other active positions. The colors, though limited to yellows, browns, reds, black, and white, not only suggest the patterns of their subjects' hides, but in places have been applied with varying degrees of light and dark to suggest roundness. This effect was employed with particular skill at Altamira to evoke the massive form of a bison (Figs. 1.1, 1.7).

Experts believe that this artist may have applied the

paint with a blow gun, much as artists today use airbrushes for similar effects. In addition to the shading, the drawing of this crouching, wounded animal (Fig. 1.1) is evidence not only of skill but a level of intelligence and sensitivity to equal that of any animal drawing in the history of art. Such an achievement obviously demonstrates the hunter-artist's intimate knowledge of the appearance and movements of animals. The fact that he or she also possessed the sophisticated concepts and skills needed to transform this knowledge into a realistic picture, for example, the use of shading to suggest depth, is nothing less than remarkable.

Still, even the bison displays a limitation common to all Ice-Age painting: it shows only a side view. Not one of these animals is represented in a truly *foreshortened position* that is, either all or part of it being seen from the front, rear, or an angle. But this limitation scarcely detracts from the vividness of individual images. A more fundamental limitation is the relative lack of *composition*, that is, organizing several images into a unified, single picture. Rarely are two or more animals intentionally related to one another, either spatially or sequentially, to tell a story. When they are, they are arranged in tandem, never by using one of the simple ways of suggesting depth, such as overlapping or making distant things smaller and higher on the picture plane—let alone such sophisticated techniques as linear or aerial perspective (see Chapter 3). There is no evidence that hunter-artists were concerned about design—even to the extent of controlling the sizes and placement of the figures so that they and the intervals between them are somewhat harmonized. Instead, the positioning of the images, like that of graffiti, seems to have been determined by chance—as though each artist left his or her mark on the cave wall irrespective of what had been placed there earlier. Although the space separating two animals may be small, the time separating them might be as little as a day or as long as a century, for the hunter-artists returned again and again to these caves over long periods.

The "content" of a work of art is its meaning. In this case, we need to ask what these paintings meant to the

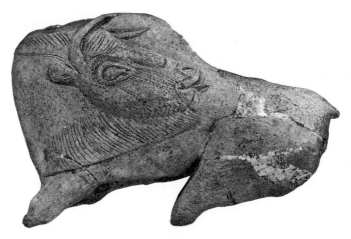

1.6 *Bison*, from La Madeleine, Dordogne, c. 15,000–10,000 BC
Reindeer horn, 4 ins (10 cm) long
Museum of National Antiquities, St-Germain-en-Laye, France

1.7 *Bison*, c. 14,000–10,000 BC
8 ft 3 ins (2.5 m) long
Altamira, Spain

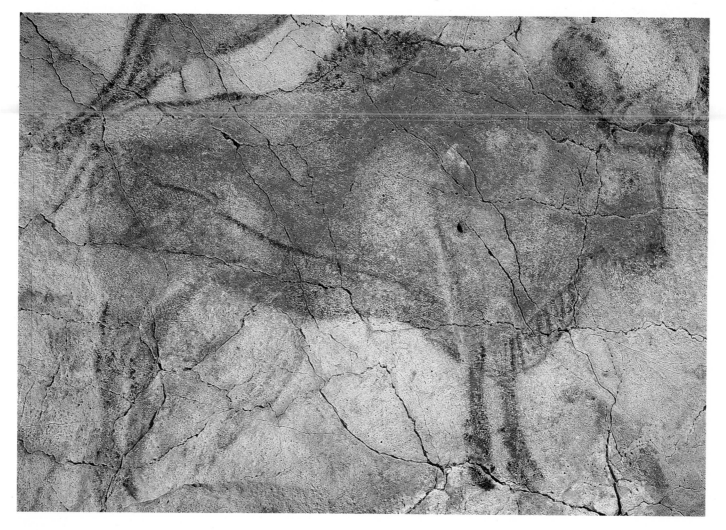

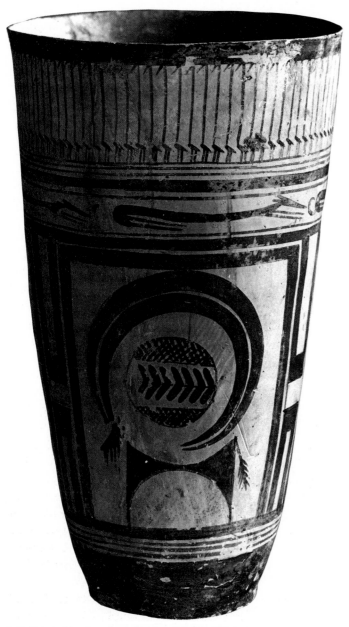

1.8 Painted beaker, from Susa, c. 5000–4000 BC
11¼ ins (28.5 cm) high
Louvre, Paris

arrows, spears, traps, and other devices related to the chase. Some even bear the marks of real spears, arrows, and rocks. Putting these facts together with those of the aesthetic analysis—the vivid rendering of individual animals, the haphazard placement of each, and even the lack of foreshortening—suggests (though it may never be proved completely) that Ice-Age art was a form of magic; that the making of an image conferred power over an animal (or its kind) on the artist and his or her tribe. The more realistic the representation, the more effective the magic. Yet, despite this impulse towards realism, foreshortening was probably avoided deliberately; its use might have been regarded as a distortion of an animal's shape which thus would make it magically less desirable. But if distortion was unacceptable, mutilation of the image with spears or rocks was apparently accepted as a form of ritual killing, a rehearsal for the real kill. The purpose of this magical art, then, was to ensure success in the hunt.

It may be hard to believe that such realistic and vivid animal images could be produced by a hunter-gatherer society. As we shall see in a later chapter, it was not easy for artists in the relatively advanced civilization of fifteenth-century Europe to develop the skills needed to paint convincing images of people. But it is possible that Ice-Age painters, like Renaissance painters, had nurtured their own art "tradition" in which each generation learned from and improved upon the methods of the preceding generation. Thus the preceptual habits and skills needed to produce such sophisticated works as the wounded bison might have been developed and refined over hundreds, or even thousands of years. At any rate, we now know that image-making, the symbolizing of experience in intelligible visual forms, is a very ancient practice, that it was followed even in the earliest type of culture: that of the hunter-gatherers.

Eventually, warmer temperatures led to changes in the ecology of Europe, affecting the animal population and methods of hunting. The need for painting animals, since it was related to these methods, disappeared. Thus the amazing image-making ability of hunter-artists languished and died; the images themselves lay hidden in the caves of Europe until the nineteenth and twentieth centuries. Ice-Age art was neither handed down nor revived by following generations. Thus it cannot be considered a part of our Western heritage, though it is certainly a testimony to the antiquity of our human urge to make images.

Peasant-Village Art

Given the higher degree of sophistication associated with peasant-village cultures, it may come as a surprise to learn

people who made them. We said earlier that the answer could be deduced partly from an analysis of the pictures. To complete the puzzle, however, we must consider some other pieces of evidence. One of the most telling facts is that many of the paintings are hidden away in cramped, damp, or otherwise inaccessible locations. Since such spaces are not conducive to strolling or congregating, the possibility of the caves serving as "art galleries" or as temples of animal worship can probably be ruled out. Some of the animals are accompanied by symbols of

that animals in peasant-village art, unlike those in the older Ice-Age paintings, are not realistic but schematic and decorative. Although it may be risky to generalize about the art of the thousands of individual peasant-village societies that have existed, all over the world, from 7000 BC to modern times, we have chosen just one item, a beaker from Susa in western Iran (Fig. **1.8**), to exemplify the ornamental tendencies of this cultural style. Note the extent to which the animal figures have been simplified and distorted for the purpose of fitting them to the surface of the beaker. Around the rim, long-necked cranes become vertical repeats; below them, racing hounds are reduced to horizontal bands; in the large space, the horns of a goat become huge crescents surrounding a round symbol. But the loss in realism of the individual figures is offset by the gain in organization and design, a reflection, no doubt, of the organization and rhythm of peasant-village life. In other words, the impulse to maintain order and continuity in their communities had apparently carried over into their handicrafts. As people must conform to the rules of the group, so must the images on a utensil conform to the principles of design.

The tendency to abstract may also stem from the need to embody ideas unknown to their hunter-gatherer forebears. Given the narrowly focused life of Ice-Age people, it is little wonder that they painted animals almost exclusively and became very proficient at representing them. Although the life of peasant-villagers was only slightly less marginal, it did allow for imagining a supernatural and other unseen forces—intangible things that are better represented in abstract forms than in realistic ones. Thus the life of these rural, self-sufficient societies, steeped as they were in their religious beliefs and customs, is perfectly expressed in the static, abstract forms of their art.

The Cities of Mesopotamia

Cities, as we noted in the introduction, are a prerequisite for a civilization. Besides the division of labor, which makes art possible, cities also contain institutions and individuals of power and wealth, who create a demand for art. Since the beginning of civilization, the artistic life of all civilizations has been concentrated in their cities.

Despite the cultural variety of Mesopotamia, and the changes that occurred there over three millennia, some generalizations can be made about its art. Compared with Ice-Age and peasant-village societies, the cities of Mesopotamia had a greater variety of materials, including precious metals and stones, as well as much better tools, with which to produce art. But compared to Egypt (which will be discussed next), this area did not have substantial quantities of stone, a condition that adversely affected their production of architecture and monumental sculpture. Regarding pictorial art, Mesopotamian subject matter is considerably more varied than that of tribal societies. Although animals are quite common, humans, gods, hybrid creatures, weapons, tools, musical instruments, and even indications of surroundings (trees, buildings, walls, and so forth) are also common. Significantly, these things are combined by Mesopotamian artists to create allegories or tell stories. Though this culture comprised several kingdoms—Sumer, Akkad, Babylonia, and Assyria—over a length of time, only a few examples will be considered in this chapter.

Mesopotamia's most significant form of architecture was the *ziggurat*, a terraced, or stepped, pyramid with each story smaller than the one below. The earliest ones made their appearance long before the pyramids of Egypt and were probably built by the Sumerians, the first agricultural people to control floods, build strong-walled towns, develop a complex religion, and, most importantly, invent writing. The ziggurat that stands at Ur (Fig. **1.9**), though not the earliest, is the best preserved. Essentially a mound of bricks (sun-dried on the inside, baked on the outside), this one was originally three stories—topped by a little shrine (Fig. **1.10**). Only the partly restored, 50-foot (15-meter) bottom story remains to offer some idea of its original appearance. The layouts of Ur and other Sumerian cities reveal that ziggurats stood at the physical center, and thus, probably, at the spiritual center of the community. The exact origin and purpose of the ziggurat form are unknown, but a reasonable assumption is that its height was related to the pride and respect that the gods held in the minds of the Sumerians, who were compelled to "look up" to them literally and symbolically.

The best-known ziggurat was the "Tower of Babel," referred to in Genesis 11. A lofty mound of 650 feet (200 meters), it was built in Babylon during the reign of Nebuchadnezzar, the king who also oversaw the construction of the famous hanging gardens. Because of these projects and others, including a system of avenues and canals, Babylon was perhaps the most magnificent city of the ancient world. Unfortunately, because of the lack of stone in southern Mesopotamia, these structures were realized in baked or glazed brick, a comparatively fragile material. Thus, except for a few meager remains, Babylon's architectural splendor is left to our imagination (Fig. **1.11**).

We have a little more evidence of Mesopotamian skill in image making. The inlaid panel shown in Fig. **1.12**, from a soundbox of a harp, illustrates the pictorial abilities of the Sumerians, as well as giving evidence that they played music. Made of pieces of shell, the figures on the panel are

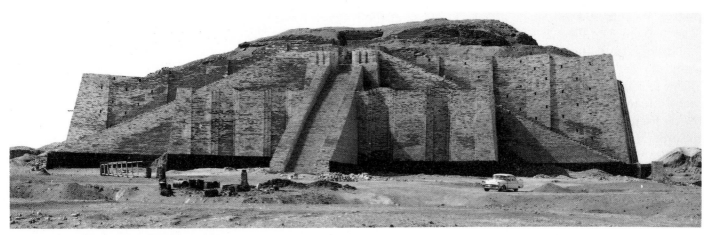

1.9 Ziggurat of King Urnammu, Ur, c. 2500 BC

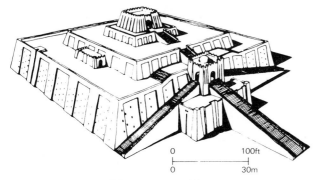

1.10 Reconstruction of the ziggurat at Ur

1.11 Reconstructed view of Babylon

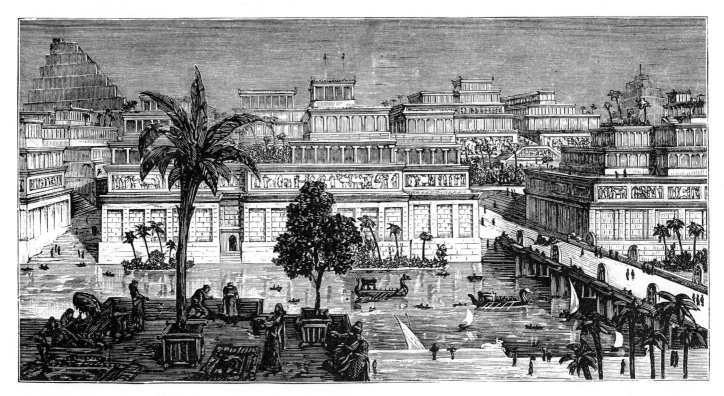

divided into registers like those of a modern-day comic strip and include (reading from top to bottom) a hero struggling with two bulls; a dog and a lion preparing a feast; a donkey, bear, and miniature jackal playing music for the occasion; and a goat offering wine to a hybrid man. Of all the figures, the men are the most *conventionalized*— that is, they conform more to the rules of Sumerian image making than to the appearance of real men. Although the animals are engaged in fantastic activities—walking on hind feet, performing human tasks, and so forth—their forms are more natural and varied than those of the men. They also remind us of the whimsical creatures that frolic in children's stories, from Br'er Rabbit to Mickey Mouse. But the Sumerians may have seen them quite differently, perhaps as personifications of their gods.

How does the soundbox compare artistically to the prehistoric examples? The animal figures are stiffer and less natural than those painted 7000 years earlier in the caves but are much more realistic than those on the peasant-village beaker. On the other hand, the arrangement of the figures, especially the way in which they are displayed in bands and fitted into a small space, resembles that of the beaker and is much more organized than the chaotic collection of animals found in the caves. But unlike both prehistoric examples—in fact, unlike most known prehistoric art—the Sumerian piece tells a story. The figures not only are involved in purposeful actions but relate to one another both spatially and psychologically.

The method of illustrating the human figure with head and legs in profile and shoulders frontally was to become a pervasive convention in the pictorial art of the various Mesopotamian cultures. This can be seen in the relief figures on the upper part of a stone slab, or *stele* (Fig. 1.13), commemorating Hammurabi, the king who established the city-state of Babylon. According to legend, and as revealed in the stele, Hammurabi was also responsible for the world's first successful legal system. Just as Moses received the Ten Commandments from God, Hammurabi receives the Babylonian code of laws from the throned figure of Shamash, god of the sun, who holds the symbols of divine authority while he dictates the laws (the laws themselves are inscribed on the stele below the figures). The convention of combining frontal shoulders with profile head and legs persists even when legs are hidden by gowns or bent in a seated position. The rigidness of this formula is softened only by the position of Hammurabi's arms: the right elbow resting on his left forearm and the right hand raised to his face. Although probably a gesture of reverence, this pose, ironically, appears nonchalant to us, as though Hammurabi and Shamash were casually chatting.

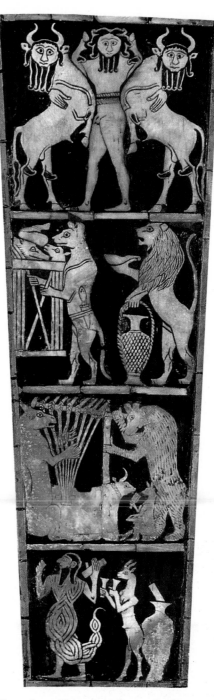

1.12 Soundbox of royal harp from the tomb of Queen Puabi at Ur, c. 2600 BC
Shell inlay set in bitumen, 13 ins (33 cm) high.
University Museum, Philadelphia.

The Assyrians, after wresting control from the cities of southern Mesopotamia, built grand palaces like the enormous citadel of Sargon II—a complex of apartments, courtyards, ramps, temples, and ziggurat surrounded by a fortress wall (Figs. 1.15, 1.16). But their greatest artistic legacy consists of the relief carvings of hunting scenes remaining from some of the walls of the palaces. To the Assyrians, especially their kings, hunting was a sport, not a means of survival as it was to the Ice-Age people. Rather than pursuing lions in the field, a king and his party typically killed captive lions released from cages under rather controlled conditions. Such a royal hunt, carved on the Palace of Ashurnasirpal II at Nimrud (Fig. 1.14) shows the king taking aim at a lion from the back of his chariot. The convention of displaying broad shoulders, like that used for the bodies of Hammurabi and Shamash, not only emphasizes Ashurnasirpal's physique but effectively describes the action of drawing a bow. This relief, more than in the previous examples, relates objects through overlapping, thereby suggesting a degree of depth. Overlapping was used for the soldiers in the rear, as well as for the troika of horses in the front (contrast their stiff stride with the fluid movements of Ice-Age painted animals). It was also used, but in a more subtle way, to suggest the relationship between the king and his charioteer. The Assyrian sculptors, however, invested their greatest talents in depicting the two lions—by far the most expressive images in the relief. Only artists who, like the cave painters, knew animals first hand (and probably at close range) could define so well the outer contours and movements of those animals and also articulate so incisively the muscles and tendons bulging under their hides. And only those who were in the presence of real lions could capture their ferocity so vividly.

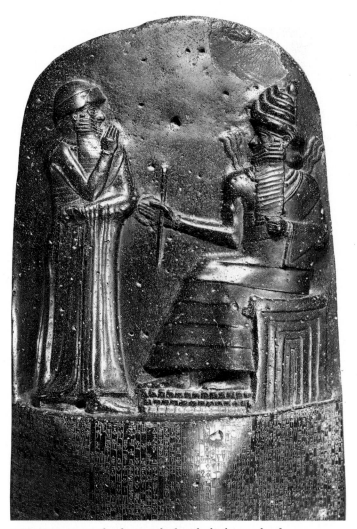

1.13 Upper part of stele inscribed with the law code of Hammurabi, c. 1760 BC Basalt, 88 ins (223.5 cm) high Louvre, Paris

1.14 *Ashurnasirpal II Killing Lions*, from Nimrud (Calah), c. 850 BC Limestone, 3 ft 3 ins × 8 ft 4 ins (97 cm × 250 cm) British Museum, London

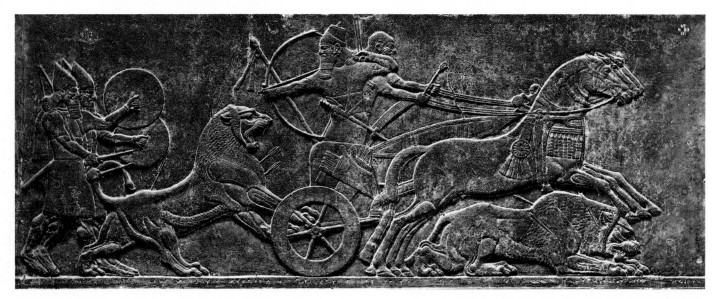

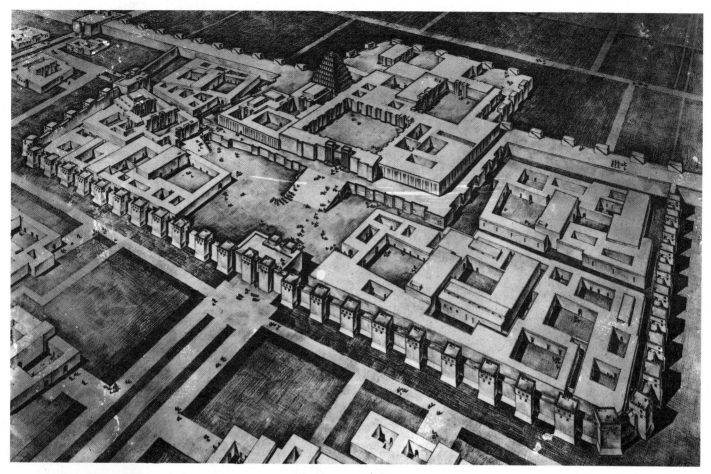

1.15 Citadel of King Sargon II at Dur Sharrukin, (Khorsabad), c. 742–706 BC (reconstruction).

1.16 Plan of Sargon II's citadel at Dur Sharrukin

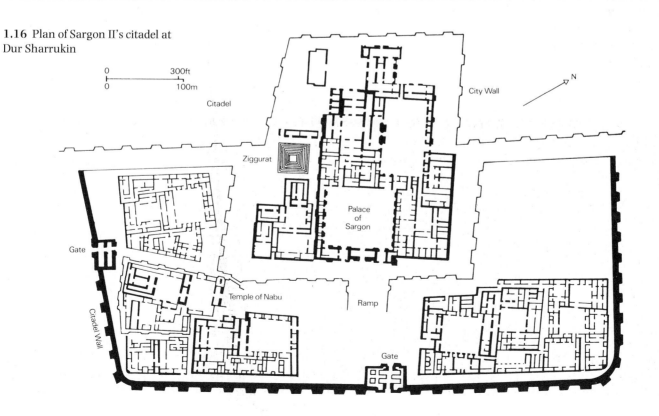

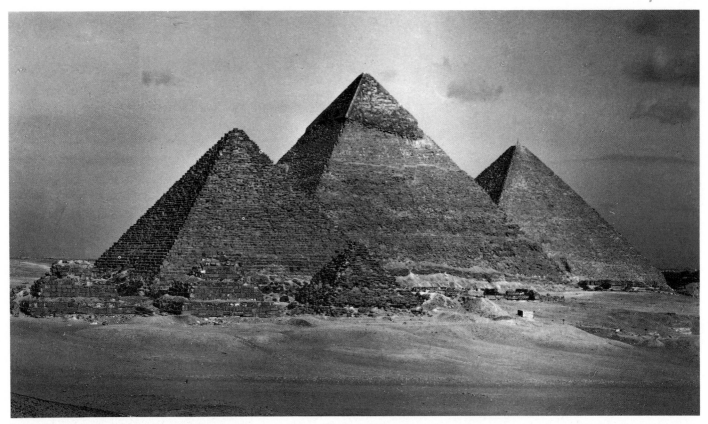

1.17 The pyramids of Mycerinus, Chefren & Cheops, at Giza, c. 2530–2470 BC

1.18 Plan of the pyramids at Giza

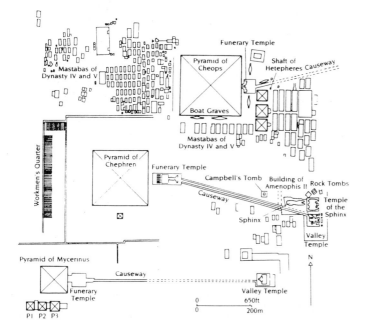

Egyptian Art

Egyptian art, like all Egyptian culture, is characterized by serenity and a sense of permanence. The figures of people are static, though very legible, as opposed to the lively, sometimes uneven, figures found in Mesopotamian art; Egyptian animals are loving or detached, rather than wild or fantastic. Because of an artistic "bureaucracy" and an almost uninterrupted use of the same conventions for thousands of years, Egyptian art often seems more stereotyped than its Asian counterparts, but it also seems more self-assured and professional. Finally, because of the abundance of stone in Egypt, Egyptian artisans were able to produce enduring monuments of architecture and sculpture in greater quantity and quality than their Mesopotamian contemporaries.

"Enduring" is an appropriate word for Egyptian art, as most of it was intended to last for eternity. The Egyptian religion, though polytheistic like that of Mesopotamia, was distinguished by a very important feature: belief in life after death, or *immortality*. Immortality was not a privilege of everyone in Egypt; only a person of high station—pharaoh (king), priest, nobleman, bureaucrat, and, sometimes, a scribe (secretary)—was assured that his/her soul would live in the hereafter. They also believed that the best home for a soul was the dead body itself—or, if the body should decay, that a soul could take up residence in an image. Hence, in addition to embalming and mummification, the production of funerary images was an important industry in ancient Egypt. The society took great pains not only to preserve the body of a dignitary but to surround it with images—paintings and sculptures of the deceased, along with the images of people and things needed to serve that person in the hereafter: servants, slaves, crops, animals, and so forth. To preserve the whole *ménage*, Egyptians built strong, supposedly impenetrable tombs. Thus, the vast majority of the surviving paintings and sculptures of Egypt are from tombs; the surviving architecture consists of the tombs themselves or temples. That this art has held up so well for so long is due not only to the dry, desert climate, but to the fact that Egyptians went to such great lengths to comply with their concept of immortality.

The most impressive tombs—not only in Egypt, but anywhere—were built during the Old Kingdom (c. 2686–c. 2160 BC), the earliest sub-period of Egyptian history. The largest and most legendary, of course, are the enormous pyramids at Giza (Figs. 1.17, 1.18). Built for three pharaohs of the fourth dynasty, they are smooth-sided—a form that had evolved from a ziggurat-like stepped pyramid used in the preceding dynasty. The tomb of Cheops (Khufu), the largest and oldest of the three, is 450 feet (137 meters) tall, as high as a skyscraper, and covers an area of 13 acres (5 hectares). Except for a small burial chamber and a few narrow passageways contained within (Fig. 1.19), it is a solid mass of limestone. Yet despite its prodigious mass, this pyramid, like almost all of Egypt's tombs, was penetrated and looted by grave robbers. Because of such roguery, posterity, as well as the Egyptian dead, was deprived of innumerable pieces of statuary, furniture, utensils, pottery, jewelry, and other handicrafts. Fortunately, the robbers could not carry off the heavier statues or peel the paintings off the walls.

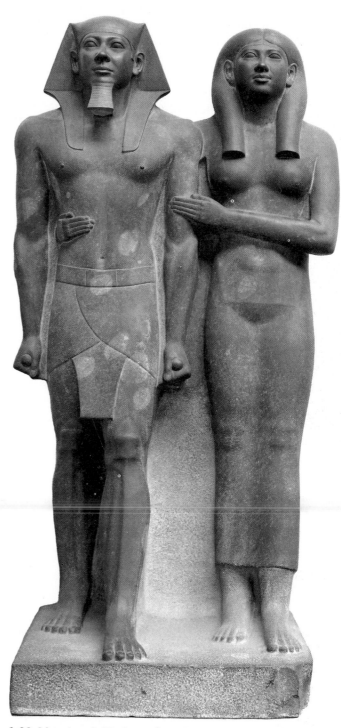

1.20 *Mycerinus & His Queen*, from Giza, c. 2470 BC
Slate, 56 ins (142 cm) high
Museum of Fine Arts, Boston

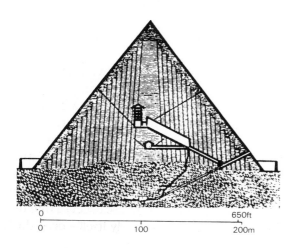

1.19 North-south section of the pyramid of Cheops (after L. Borchardt)

In their own way, the portrait statues of the Old Kingdom are as imposing as the pyramids. Among these, the sculpture of Mycerinus, builder of the third pyramid, accompanied by his queen (Fig. 1.20), is a prime example. The pair's regalia, contrary to what we usually expect of royalty, is quite simple: nothing more than a linen headdress, false beard, and royal kilt for him, and a thin sheath robe for her. But their aristocratic bearing matches that of any other royal couple embodied in stone. In addition the sculptor endowed them with the serenity needed for eternal existence. These qualities are the result not only of great skill and hard work but also of the constraints of the medium and the rules of Egyptian art. Cubic in character, Egyptian sculptures always suggest the blocks of stone from which they were carved—a tedious, almost heroic process of subtraction using bronze chisels. The stiffness, the severity of the forms, and the limited movement of this pair is due to the difficulty of this process, as well as to the artist's adherence to a set of conventions—the idealization of the body, the frontal posture, the placement of the feet, even the articulation of the kneecaps—for representing human figures, especially those of important people. The end result is truly majestic; the image of Mycerinus exemplifies Egyptian royal portraiture at its best. But what makes this sculpture, as a pair, particularly fascinating is the contrast of masculine and

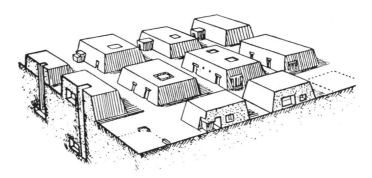

1.21 Group of mastabas (after A. Badawy), 4th Dynasty

feminine: his angular body versus her delicate curves, his military bearing versus her tender embrace.

Egyptian paintings, if anything, are more rule-bound than Egyptian sculptures. The greatest legacy of this art is found not in royal tombs but in *mastabas* (Fig. 1.21): modest-sized, flat-topped tombs for people below the rank of pharaoh. A painted relief in the mastaba of Ti, an overseer of the pyramids, shows the deceased enjoying one of his earthly pursuits: hunting in the marshes of the Nile (Fig. 1.23). His erect, idealized body, which is larger than those of the busy servants doing the actual hunting, symbolizes his noble detachment as well as his importance. It also follows a strict formula: head, legs, and feet shown in profile while one eye and the trunk of the body

1.22 *Cattle fording a river*
Painted limestone relief
Tomb of Ti, Saqqara

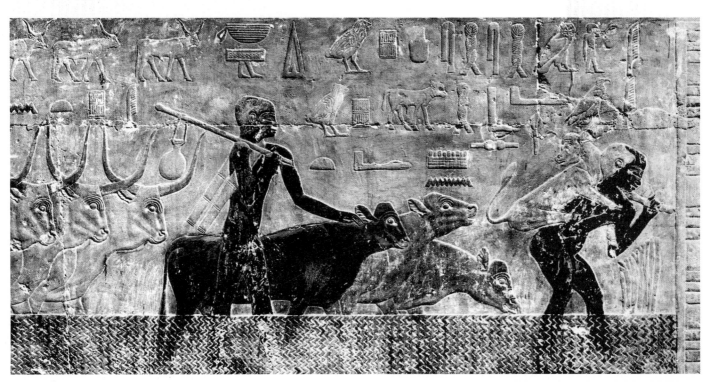

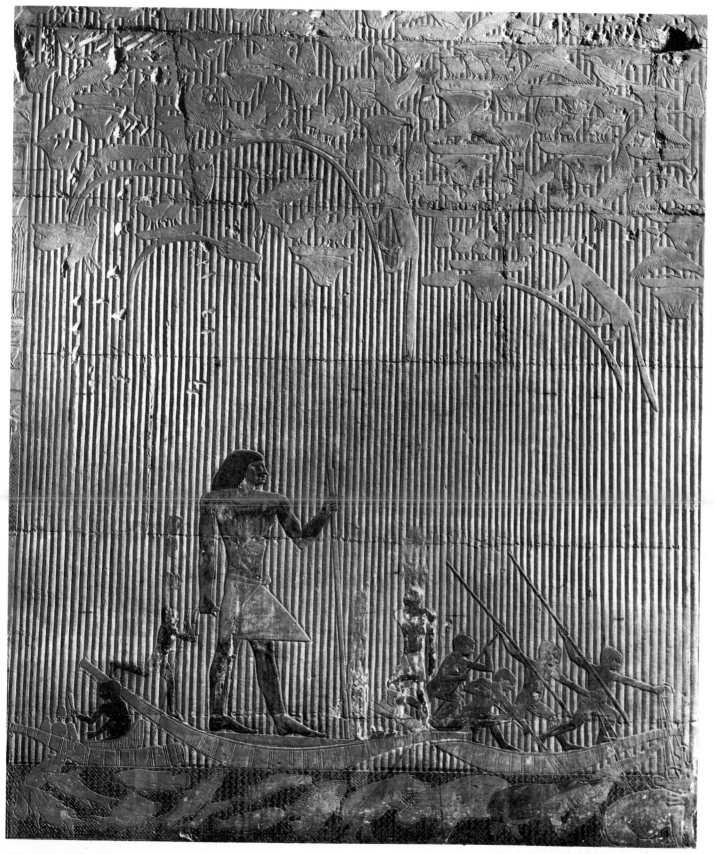

1.23 *Ti Watching a Hippopotamus Hunt*, c. 2400 BC
Painted limestone relief, approx. 48 ins (122 cm) high
Tomb of Ti. Saqqara

are shown frontally. Even the servants' bodies, despite their activity and variety, follow the same formula. Similar in some respects to the conventions of Mesopotamian art, this style was applied strictly and with little change over thousands of years. Its staying power was due in part to the conservatism of Egyptian society, but also to the magical role images played in the context of Egyptian religion. For example, had Ti's head been shown from the back, or one of his legs hidden behind the other, or his feet hidden inside the boat, then his anatomy would have been considered incomplete and therefore an inadequate home for his soul. It was therefore necessary to provide a complete view of the main parts not only of Ti's body but also of those of the people and creatures that were to serve him forever. A similar solution was applied to the background, for it, too, was conceived as a sum of clearly depicted individual parts: the thicket of papyrus stalks behind the men, the papyrus tops teeming with animals, the birds overhead, and the river, with its upper edge forming a simple baseline for the boats, teeming with aquatic life below. Apart from a modicum of overlapping, this scene, like those of the Babylonian and Assyrian reliefs, lacks any of the devices needed to create a sense of spatial depth. Moreover, the figures of the men are as flat as cutouts, lacking even a trace of the kind of shading that makes Ice-Age paintings of animals so vividly three-dimensional. An Egyptian painting, like a map, is to be read as a two-dimensional surface.

Other walls in the mastaba illustrate workers in the daily tasks of maintaining Ti's rich estate: peasants harvesting grain and caring for his cattle (Fig. **1.22**), cooks and bakers preparing his food, servants dusting his statues, and so forth. Typical of Old Kingdom tomb paintings, those in Ti's mastaba are, in effect, a record, almost a calendar, of the recurring activities of his life on earth.

Perhaps the huge sums lavished on the pyramids at Giza were responsible for the gradual weakening and decline of the Old Kingdom. Thereafter, at any rate, royal tombs were scaled down considerably, never again to equal those of the fourth dynasty. The tombs of the Middle Kingdom (c. 2040–1786 BC) were not even visible, being hollowed out of cliffs along the Nile with sealed and concealed entrances. By the New Kingdom (c.1570–

1.24 Funerary temple of Queen Hatshepsut, Deir el-Bahari, c. 1480 BC

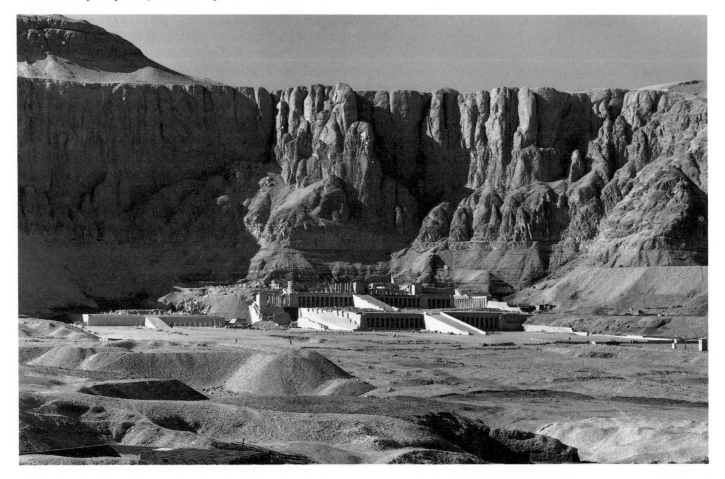

1085 BC) the custom of building mortuary temples had been established; these were endowed with the grandeur, if not the scale, of Old Kingdom pyramids. Built into the banks of the Nile, at some distance from the pharaoh's hidden tomb, a mortuary temple served as a memorial chapel and a home for the deceased ruler's patron god. Among the grandest of them is the temple complex at Deir el-Bahari, built for Queen Hatshepsut during the time of the Israelite captivity and dedicated to Amon (Fig. **1.24**). Leading to the temple, the chamber of which is carved into the cliff, are three grand terraces, each marked by broad colonnades on progressively ascending levels and linked by ramps. Although much of the complex is cut into rock, the colonnades themselves are built of vertical columns and horizontal beams, an example of the *post and lintel* method of construction used throughout the ancient world.

Of the same dynasty as Hatshepsut but following her by a century was a most unusual pharaoh: Amenhotep IV. Unlike his predecessors—who either approved of the religious establishment or were too preoccupied with governing the country to care—Amenhotep challenged the practices and ideas of the priesthood, the most powerful force in Egypt society next to the pharaoh. He protested their keeping of concubines in the Temple of Amon and their trafficking in magic and charms. More seriously, he opposed the mysticism of the Amon cult and its many deities and proclaimed the worship of one god, Aton, whom he identified with the sun. He changed his own name to Akhnaton ("glory to Aton"), replaced Amon with Aton on all monuments, and moved the capital from Thebes to a new site, near modern Tell-el-Amarna. (For this reason Akhnaton's reign is called the Amarna period.) He even wrote hymns and poems to Aton. Theologically, the changes meant not only a sudden switch from polytheism to monotheism, but also less preoccupation with death and the hereafter.

The art of Akhnaton's court was equally heretical: old conventions were transgressed as angular form gave way to curvilinear, stereotype yielded to naturalism, and subject matter became more personalized. The extent of these departures can be seen in the rounded forms of Akhnaton's monumental portrait (Fig. **1.25**). Although it is frontal, symmetrical, and stiff, and though it wears the obligatory royal costume, this version of kingship differs dramatically from the masculine ideal embodied in portraits like Mycerinus's. The body, with its swelling abdomen and hips, is epicene; the head, with its long face and full lips, is languid; and the whole sculpture lacks the sturdy, cubic character typical of Egyptian statuary. Whether the artist was responding to Akhnaton's actual appearance, or experimenting with style, or both, is

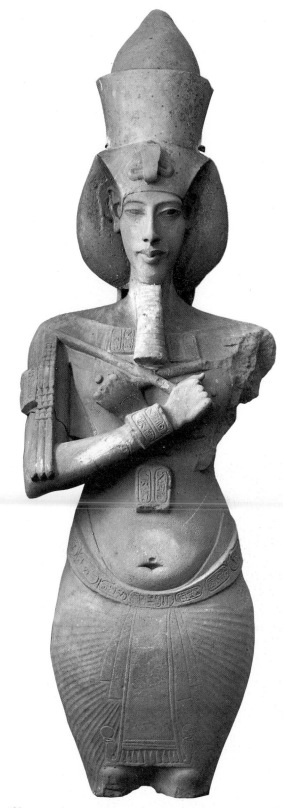

1.25 *Akhenaton*, from a pillar statue in the Temple of Aton, Tell el-Amarna, c. 1375 BC
Sandstone, approx. 13 ins (32.5 cm) high
Egyptian Museum, Cairo

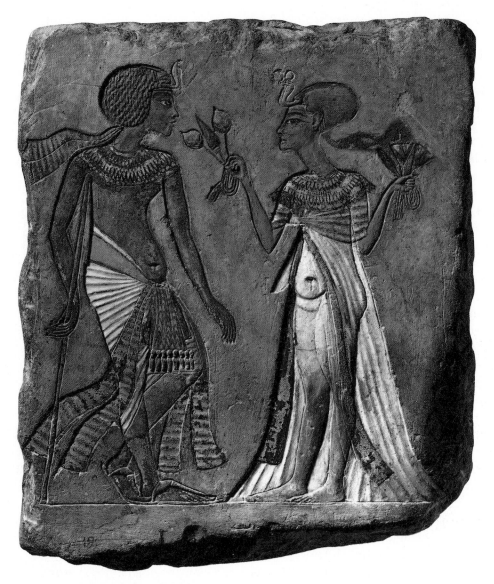

1.26 *King Smenkhkare and Meritaten*, Tell el-Amarna, c. 1360 BC
Painted limestone relief, approx. 60 ins (152.5 cm) high
Staatliche Museen, Berlin

uncertain. Any of these motives would have constituted a defiance of established practice. The same experimental spirit also affected portraits of family members, such as the painted relief of Smenkhakare and Meritaten, Akhnaton's half-brother and his wife, which immortalizes the pair in a seemingly offhand moment (Fig. **1.26**). Their bodies, unlike those of Ti and his retinue, are uncharacteristically relaxed: Smenkhakare lazily supports his sagging frame on a cane and one leg; Meritaten waves handfuls of flowers in her husband's face; both display a heretofore unknown degree of naturalism. Meanwhile, the informality of the subject is enhanced by a free and fluid style which contrasts noticeably with the stasis of traditional pictorial art.

During Akhnaton's reign, Egypt lost its colonies in the Near East, and its treasury was drained. The young pharaoh died at the age of 30, supposedly a failure. His city was abandoned, the ancient gods were restored, Amon was re-engraved on the monuments and Aton erased. Art reverted to what it had been, but not immediately and not completely. The Akhnaton style is clearly visible in the art and craft associated with King Tutankhamen, his son-in-law and successor. After that, it soon faded, though the vestiges of it can be detected in later examples. Apart from the brief reign of Akhnaton, Egyptian art was a relatively smooth continuum which lasted 3000 years, changing little, even in the final days when Egypt was exposed to the influences of Greece and Rome.

Music

Because it is not tangible, at least not in the way art and architecture are, music has left relatively few material remains for later generations to study, let alone experience directly. In recent times, of course, much of the world's music *has* been given a permanent physical form by being recorded. Assuming that future generations will always possess the necessary hardware and technology to avail themselves of it, this legacy of recordings will endow those generations with an extensive and highly accurate reproduction of our music.

But there is at least one other type of musical record that enables people to recover and experience music of the past; this consists of paper, papyrus, or clay inscribed with symbols representing a series of musical tones—in other words, musical *notation*. Such a record assumes the existence of performers or scholars who can read the symbols, and further, possess the right instruments, if needed, to perform the music. An account of the development of Western musical notation can be found in Chapter 7. For our purposes here, it should be observed that before the ninth century, most music was not written down at all, while that which was (a few fragments of Greek music) is virtually indecipherable. Indeed, much of the music written in Western Europe between the ninth and thirteenth centuries is also difficult to decipher. But that written since 1200 or so can be read, or translated, well enough to be performed and listened to with some degree of confidence in its fidelity. The notation of music of the Classical and Romantic eras (see Chapters 4 and 5) is so thorough, and our knowledge of those works so complete, that this music can be performed to sound almost as it did in its original settings. Needless to say, however, our system of notation is no help at all in understanding, let alone directly experiencing, the music of prehistoric and ancient cultures. For this kind of music we are forced to rely on indirect records: pictures, surviving instruments, ancient writings, and the music of present-day tribal societies and tradition-centered ethnic groups. From such evidence a few inferences about early music have been made.

Some ancient murals, like the one found in the tomb of Nakht (Fig. 1.27) contain depictions of musical instruments, with or without people playing them. (There is even a cave painting from the Ice Age showing what may be a primitive stringed instrument in the hands of a hunter.) In addition, musical instruments themselves, or parts thereof, have survived over the centuries—for example, the panel of a soundbox of a Sumerian harp which we examined earlier in this chapter (Fig. 1.11). But beyond establishing the existence of music in a given era, these examples tell us little about the music itself. Ancient writings containing references to music are not much more helpful. Like art, they cannot tell us how the music sounded, but they can and do describe how it was used, performed, and/or perceived in their respective societies. Among the best and and most available of these sources is the Old Testament. According to the chronicler, on the occasion of moving the ark of the covenant to a new location, David ordered Levites to sing and play harps, *psalteries* (stringed instruments), and cymbals (I Chronicles 15:16–22); years later, to consecrate Solomon's temple and open the ark, Levites again performed, but this time accompanied by 120 priests playing trumpets: "It came even to pass, as the trumpeters and singers were as one, to make one sound to be heard in praising and thanking the Lord . . ." (II Chronicles 5:13). Such passages tell us a number of things: that music was valued, especially for ritual celebrations; that certain kinds of instruments were used, as well as the fact that they accompanied singing; and that musicians were organized in large ensembles to perform simultaneously.

In the case of prehistoric cultures that left little art and no writing, musical researchers often turn to present-day tribal cultures to find clues. They reason that early societies passed through stages of development similar to those found in various preliterate societies existing today and that, therefore, their music is also similar. If this is true, then not only the possible sounds of early music can be determined, but also the evolution of early music as it progressed from simple to complex. The conclusions of this kind of research are manifold. Music began with singing—probably as *incantation*, casting magical spells through chants. In this respect, singing and metered speech, or *poetry*, were virtually synonymous. The earliest melodies had just two tones—later three. Prehistoric music was probably characterized by three styles: word-related, emotion-related, and melodic. The first, a vehicle for words, maintained moderate levels of pitch and loudness; the second, related to the release of emotions, varied dramatically in loudness and pitch; the third, related to both words and emotions, fell somewhere between the extremes. Musical design was additive; that is, performers improvised by spontaneously extending their melodies, as opposed to planning musical compositions as unities. The earliest form of rhythm consisted of slapping hands, chest, or legs to accent melodies. In time,

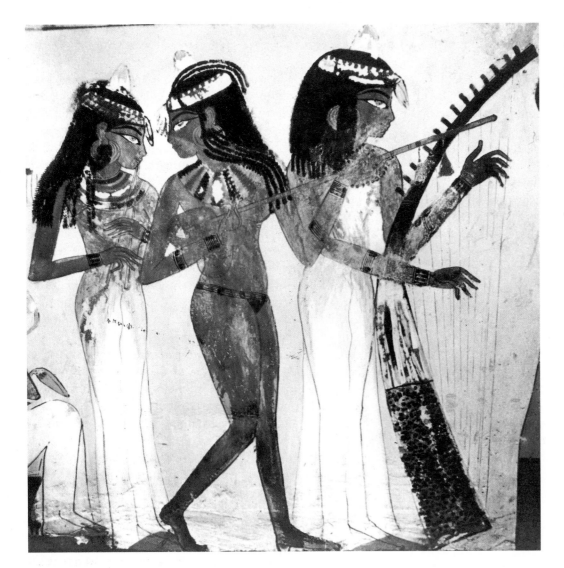

1.27 *Players with double oboe, lute and harp*, 15th century BC Mural from the tomb of Nakht, near Thebes, approx. 15 ins (40 cm) high

this was extended by rattles, clappers, paddles, and drums. Some early societies probably even engaged in part singing, two or more people singing at different pitches simultaneously. Such a practice may have grown out of the natural differences of voices, as in men and women, or men and boys. Finally, some societies practiced responsive singing—that is, the alternate repeating of musical phrases—an outgrowth of either competitive singing or work crews singing to the rhythms of their labor.

To add to what is already known about the music of ancient civilizations, researchers study certain subcultures that cling to antiquated forms of music—the assumption being that such music may have ancient bloodlines. Thus, insights about the music of ancient Egypt can perhaps be gained from observing the music of the Copts, a subculture of Egyptians christianized during the Roman era, or that of the Nubians, a peasant subculture living in Upper Egypt. Clues to the music of ancient Mesopotamia, meanwhile, might be observed in

the singing of isolated Jewish congregations living in such places as Yemen and Iran. Inferences based on this research have led to the belief that the ancient cultures of Mesopotamia and Egypt used a four-tone scale not unlike that of Greece (see Chapter 2); that their melodies were chiefly word-related, or *syllabic*; and that ancient musicians did not think of melodies consisting of series of notes, as we do, but as patterns of sounds. Responsive singing, so popular with Yemenite Jews today, has led to the theory that it was also prevalent in ancient Jewish congregations, and perhaps in Babylonian choruses as well.

How did the music of ancient civilizations differ from that of the more advanced primitive societies of the same time? Mainly, it was conceived of as a medium subject to logic and measure and was identified with education, skill and knowledge, as opposed to being primarily instinctual. It also had more sub-categories: amateur and professional, secular and religious, lower class (folk music) and upper class (educated music). In addition, it could be as intimate as one singer accompanied by a harp or as grand as a large chorus and orchestra. Ancient music progressed from a condition in which everyone sang and played instruments to one in which highly skilled, possibly professional musicians had an important role—an evolution reflected in the history of the Jews (if we take the chronicler's account as true), particularly in the life of David. As a shepherd, he was an amateur musician who played for Saul. As a king, he organized the first group of official musicians when he commanded the Levites "to be the singers with instruments of musick, psalteries and harps and cymbals, sounding, by lifting up the voice with joy" (I Chronicles 15:16). By the time of Solomon, the body of musicians had increased dramatically when, as we saw in II Chronicles, the psalteries, harps, cymbals, and voices, were augmented by 120 trumpets. There is every reason to believe that the court orchestras and temple choruses of Egypt and Babylon were just as—perhaps even more—splendid. Unfortunately, we shall never hear this music; it remains one of the most tantalizing mysteries of ancient civilization.

Conclusion

Judging by the evidence of Ice-Age cave paintings, the art of painting is at least 15,000 years old. This means that the ability to seize an aspect of experience and convert it into a two-dimensional sign—in this case, a vivid image of an animal—has an ancient heritage. There is also reason to believe that the purpose of such an image was magical, the hunter's attempt to control his environment through making the sign. The evidence for the genesis of early music, on the other hand, is very sparse, though we are fairly certain that music also had tribal beginnings and probably had a magical purpose.

The heritage of literature is less ancient. It is believed that the city-dwelling Sumerians were the first to employ the art of writing; if so, literature did not develop until people started to live in cities. Its beginnings probably consisted of written transcriptions of beliefs and myths handed down orally from tribal forebears. Like literature, the arts of architecture and monumental sculpture, which depend on higher levels of technology and administration, had to wait until the evolution of an urban culture.

The examples of literature, painting, sculpture, architecture, and music reviewed in this chapter—whether tribal or civilized—are evidence of the depth and richness of our cultural heritage. But not all of these examples are exclusively a part of our *Western* cultural heritage, that is, the stream of developments that characterize the histories of ancient Greece and Rome, and, later, Europe and America. Cave paintings and prehistoric music (which is still unknown) obviously predate that heritage. Although the mythical tower of Babel and the exploits of the Assyrians and Babylonians are part of the literature of the Hebrews, our current knowledge of ancient Near Eastern cultures is largely dependent on recent excavations and modern research. Even the pyramids, which, along with Egypt herself, have been in existence since the days of the Old Kingdom, were an enigma to Europeans until Napoleon's armies conquered Cairo, and later, European scholars discovered the Rosetta Stone, which enabled them to decipher the Egyptian language.

A major reason why the ancient civilizations of Mesopotamia and Egypt lay virtually forgotten for so many centuries is the supremacy of Greece, that other ancient culture that flourished on the edge of the Mediterranean before the days of Christ. It was not only that those civilizations were superseded by the power of the Greeks, but that the legacy of literature, philosophy, and arts left by the Greeks was so overwhelming.

Thus, the legacies of the Sumerians, Babylonians, Assyrians, and Egyptians, for all their splendor, had to wait until recent times, and the painstaking work of archeologists and historians, for their riches to be fully appreciated. Up to then their heritage was transmitted, at best indirectly, through the Greeks—but for one exception in which a part of that heritage was transmitted directly. A small subculture, a mere outpost of the greater Mesopotamian culture is responsible for a most important collection of writings. The subculture was the Jews; the collection, of course, is the Old Testament, the most fundamental text in Western civilization.

Later in this book we will survey some of the many ways in which the Old Testament played such a profound role in the development of Western civilization. However, the next chapter is the first of a series on that other major source of Western culture: *classicism*. Both an outlook on the world and a set of guiding principles for the arts, classicism originated in the city-states of Greece.

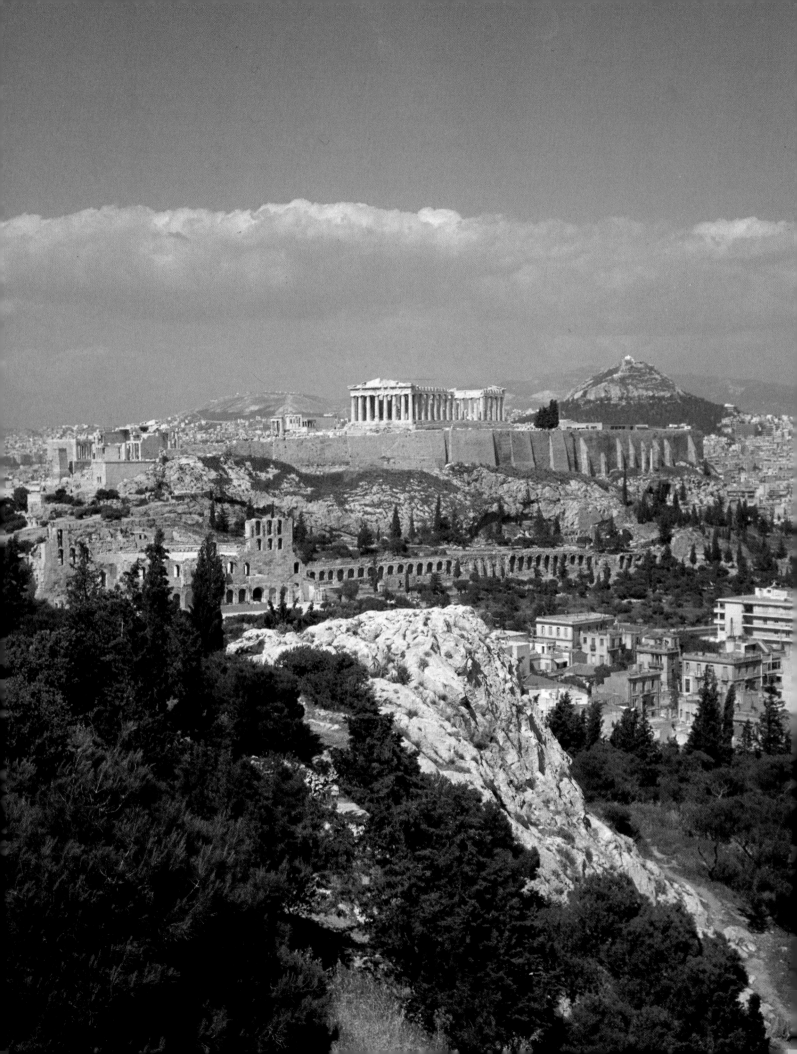

CHAPTER TWO

Classicism I: Greece and Rome

*Wonders are many, and
none is more wonderful
than man.*

SOPHOCLES, *ANTIGONE*

2.1 Acropolis, Athens

The Classical World

The Greeks

The history of Classical antiquity is the history of the Greeks and Romans. However, because much of Roman culture was borrowed from and imitative of Greek culture, the classical component of European civilization is primarily derived from the Greeks. More precisely, it is rooted in the period which includes most of the fifth and fourth centuries BC; during these approximately 150 years Greek art, music, literature and architecture were at their highest level of refinement. However Greek civilization began to flourish long before this. Our summary will begin with the Homeric Age (c.1200–900 BC); that is, the period reflected in the two great epics, the *Iliad* and the *Odyssey*, traditionally attributed to an Ionian poet named Homer, who is believed to have lived during the ninth century BC. The influx of tribes from the north, whose integration with the Mycenean culture of the Greek mainland produced early Greek civilization, preceded but also continued into the Homeric age. About 1000 BC, however, these migrations had ended, and city-states had begun to develop.

Much of what is known about the period comes from the Homeric poems. It was a period of turmoil and warfare, exemplified by the Trojan War, the context for both the *Iliad* and the *Odyssey*. It was also a time of remarkable social and economic equality. This equality was not to endure, however, for with the rise of the monarchy power was concentrated in the hands of a few.

Little is known about the Greek age of monarchs (c.900 –700 BC. It is a murky period because there is no creative literature analogous to the Homeric epics to reveal its culture and customs. It is also a dark age because the despotism of the monarchs suppressed the freedom characteristic of the Greek spirit at its best. This concentration of authority in the monarch, however, was gradually weakened by the rise of powerful nobles, who eventually either radically reduced the power of the king or in some cases eliminated the office. By about 700 BC, kingship had disappeared, and rivalries among the nobles had led to the rise of tyrants (*tyrannoi*). The Greek word did not carry as pejorative a sense as its English equivalent but designated a strong leader who came to power by unconstitutional means and imposed order on a politically unstable society.

Athens was fortunate in having four tyrants who made major contributions to its civilization. Draco and Solon were largely responsible for bringing order out of the chaos of Athenian law. Peisistratus, though something of a demagogue, made Greek drama an institution by providing it with state support. He was also responsible for reawakening interest in the Homeric epics and encouraging the editing of their texts. Cleisthenes divided the Athenian people into districts (*demes*) and instituted the council (*Boule*), composed of representatives from these districts. Moreover, he discouraged the intrusion of tyrants into Athenian polity by inaugurating the system of ostracism, by which demagogues could be sent into exile. Thus Cleisthenes prepared the way for the rise of Athenian democracy, a profoundly significant contribution to Western civilization.

The rise of Athens in the fifth century BC to leadership of the Greeks was the result of the role it played in the defeat of the Persians. First at Marathon (490 BC) under Darius, and later at Salamis and Plataea (479 BC) under Xerxes, the Persians, seeking to extend their power into the Hellenic world, were decisively defeated by the Greeks, led by the Athenians.

Athens' hegemony, as well as her folly in foreign policy, is illustrated by the history of the Delian League. This was formed at the close of the Persian wars to enable the Greeks to cooperate in defending themselves against further Persian incursions, as well as to support the Ionian Greeks of Asia Minor in their revolt against Persian domination. The treasury of the League was located on the tiny Aegean island of Delos, for which the league was named. The Athenians, however, in an arbitrary power play, transferred the treasury from Delos to Athens (454 BC), thus transforming the Delian League into an Athenian empire, an action that would eventually lead to war with Sparta and the downfall of Athens.

The man who presided over and directed the rising fortunes of Athens, and who personified the Golden Age of Athenian civilization was Pericles (c.495–429 BC). This Athenian general and statesman sponsored a cultural flowering hardly to be equaled in European history. In the drama, architecture, and sculpture of this period, Athens provided models for Western culture that dominated the Renaissance, the Neoclassicism of the seventeenth and eighteenth centuries, and the Enlightenment, and that have perhaps influenced most, if not all, of the great artists, architects, and writers of the European tradition. But at the time of Pericles' death from plague in 429 BC, Athens was already two years deep into the disastrous Peloponnesian War (431–404 BC) with Sparta, which ended in Sparta's invasion of Athens and the destruction of the Long Wall built by Pericles for the defense of the city.

Athens was never again to retrieve its vanished great-

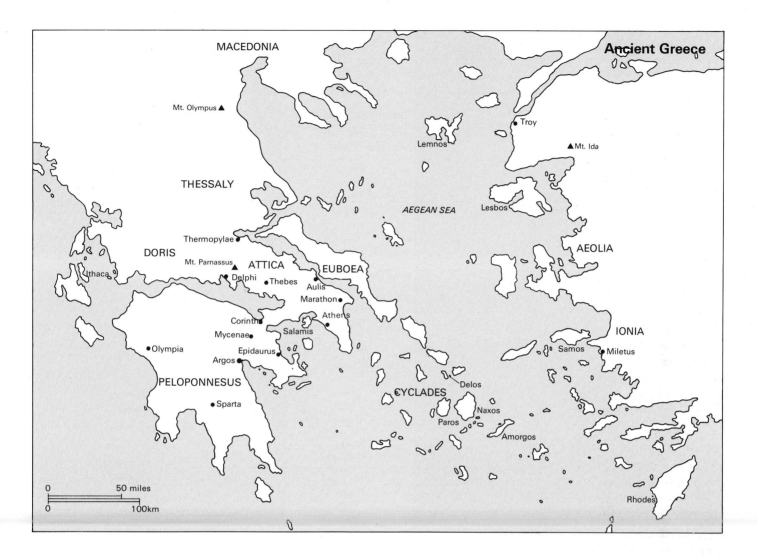

ness. The great work of Plato and Aristotle in philosophy was yet to come, but the philosopher-kings of Plato's *Republic* were fictional. There was never to be another Pericles for Athens.

Eventually (338 BC) Athens was defeated by Philip of Macedon, who also brought the rest of Greece within his dominion. After his assassination, Philip was succeeded by his ambitious son Alexander, who, because of his brilliant generalship and rapid conquest of the eastern Mediterranean and Asian worlds, was to be known in history as "the Great". Upon his death in 323 BC, Alexander's empire was divided among his generals and quickly disintegrated. The next empire to dominate the Mediterranean arena, in the West as well as the East, was that of Rome.

The Romans

Although the legendary date of the founding of Rome is 753 BC, the site was settled much earlier. Throughout much of the seventh and sixth centuries the Romans were governed by Etruscan kings, but with the help of Latin allies, they were able to throw off this yoke in 509 BC. Subsequently, a republic with two elected consuls was established. Over a period of centuries the Romans increasingly extended their power in the Italian peninsula, so that by 265 BC, with the incorporation of the Greek colonies in southern Italy, they had succeeded in bringing the entire peninsula under their control.

At about this same time (264 BC), the first of three vicious and devastating conflicts (the Punic wars) began with the wealthy city of Carthage, which had been established by Phoenicia as a trading post on the coast of North Africa. The first of these wars ended in 241 BC, with Carthage ceding Sicily to the Romans; the second, in 201 BC, with Roman annexation of Spain; the third, in 146 BC, with Rome adding Africa to its possessions and wiping Carthage from the face of the earth.

In the meantime, Roman troops were campaigning in the Eastern Mediterranean, and in the same year that Carthage was destroyed, these troops sacked Corinth. Thus the Romans extended their political and military

DATES	SOCIAL AND POLITICAL DEVELOPMENTS	LITERATURE AND PHILOSOPHY	VISUAL ARTS	ARCHITECTURE	MUSIC
1,500 BC 1,200 800	Mycenaean civilization Trojan War (legendary) Age of Monarchs (Greece)	Homer (2.4)	*Helmet-maker* (2.5)		Epic poetry accompanied by lyres
700	Rise of Tyrants		*Youth from Tenea* (2.6)		
600		Pythagoras	*Peplos Maiden* (2.7)	Basilica at Paestum (2.11)	Pythagorus's theory of music Choric dance festivals Instruments: aulos, lyres, salpinx, panpipe, tympanon
500	Persian Wars Delian League Pericles Golden Age of Athens Peloponnesian War	Aeschylus (2.13) Herodotus Sophocles (2.14) Aristophanes Euripides (2.15) Thucydides Socrates (2.16)	*Kritios Boy* (2.21) *Spear Carrier* (2.22) Parthenon sculptures: *Horsemen* (2.25) *Three Goddesses* (2.24)	Acropolis (2.1, 2.19) Parthenon (2.27)	Classical unity between music and poetry
400	Philip of Macedon Alexander the Great	Xenophon Plato (2.17) Aristotle (2.18) Menander	*Hermes and Dionysus* (2.23)	Tholos at Epidaurus (2.30) Theater at Epidaurus (2.12) Temple of Apollo, Didyma (2.35)	Aristotle's theory of music Mass concerts, huge choirs
300		Epicurus Zeno	*Aphrodite* (2.31) *Demosthenes* (2.33)		
200 100 0					
100 AD			*Laocoon and his Two Sons* (2.32)		

2.3 Ancient Greece

power over the Greeks; but their cultural submission to the Greeks was signified by the fact that they levied only a light tribute on the Greek city-states and granted them a large measure of self-rule.

The plundering and enslavement of conquered peoples made the wealthy Romans even wealthier but also made it impossible for the common people to compete with the cheap labor and imports. Social unrest ensued, with open revolt breaking out in 90 BC. The Roman general Sulla succeeded in quelling this revolt, but he then gave himself dictatorial powers, denouncing and executing his enemies. Much bitterness resulted from Sulla's heavy-handed actions, and a period of feuding began which led, a few decades later, to the death of the Republic. The remarkable man who emerged from the violence and counter-violence of this tragic era to bring peace to Rome and become the first Roman emperor was Octavian, given the reverential title of Augustus by a grateful Senate.

The Homeric Epic

The history of European literature begins with the Homeric poems, the *Iliad* and the *Odyssey*. The sophisticated use of epic techniques in these poems, however, shows that poetry was already highly developed at the time Homer lived. Western literature begins with the Homeric epics because they, unlike earlier works, have survived. An epic poem is a long narrative poem featuring larger-than-life heroes performing heroic deeds. The Greek tribal leaders of the nineth and eighth centuries BC sought to establish traditions by looking back to an heroic age celebrated in poetry by bards who transmitted these epic traditions through oral recitation. Homer and other epic poets drew upon these orally transmitted poems in developing their own epics.

Little is known about Homer's life. Indeed, it was once thought that no such person ever lived and that the poems ascribed to him were of composite authorship. One modern view is that there was, in fact, a historical Homer and that he, using sources and re-working his material, was the author of both poems.

The Iliad

The *Iliad* is the story of a brief episode in the Trojan War, a conflict that lasted ten years. The historical basis for this poem and the myth behind it is that there was an ancient city called Ilios (Troy) located in Asia Minor near the Hellespont (modern Dardanelles). According to Greek tradition, the city fell in 1184 BC. The mythological cause of the war between the Greeks and the Trojans was the abduction by Paris, son of the Trojan king, Priam, of Helen, wife of Menelaus, King of Sparta. Paris had been awarded Helen by Aphrodite, the goddess of love, because he chose Aphrodite as the fairest in a beauty contest with the goddesses Athena and Hera. Agamemnon, King of Mycenae and brother of Menelaus, then assembled a Greek fleet which sailed against Troy to recover Helen and punish the Trojans.

The central conflict of the *Iliad* is the quarrel of Achilles, the greatest of the Greek heroes, with Agamemnon, and the consequences of that quarrel. Agamemnon had taken as his concubine Chryseis, the daughter of Chryses, priest of Apollo. Because Agamemnon refused to return Chryseis to her father, Apollo sent a plague upon the Greeks, which forced Agamemnon to relent. In compensation, however, he demanded Briseis, the concubine of Achilles. This is the point at which the poem begins. In a rage, Achilles withdraws from the conflict to sulk in isolation from his Greek comrades. The battle sways back and forth inconclusively until Patrocles, Achilles' beloved friend, borrows Achilles' armor and is killed by Hector, another son of King Priam. Enraged and grief-stricken, Achilles re-enters the struggle and kills Hector in personal combat; in his anger, he abuses the body of the slain Trojan prince. He is able to curb his emotions to the extent of admitting Priam to his tent and, after much pleading on the part of Priam, releasing the body of Hector for ransom. Achilles is a prototype of the tragic hero of Greek drama, a noble man of great gifts who, through excessive pride in his greatness, is the cause of much suffering, to himself and others. The funeral of Hector brings the *Iliad* to an end.

The Odyssey

There is no historical basis for the *Odyssey*. The mythological background is this: Achilles is killed by Paris, and the Greeks pretend to give up the struggle, boarding their ships and apparently sailing away. Before leaving, however, they build a huge hollow horse and fill it with Greek soldiers. Sinon, a Greek soldier posing as a deserter, persuades the Trojans to draw the horse into the city. That very night he releases the Greek soldiers confined within the horse, who then open the gates of the city to those Greeks who pretended to sail homeward. Thus Troy is

2.4 Homer

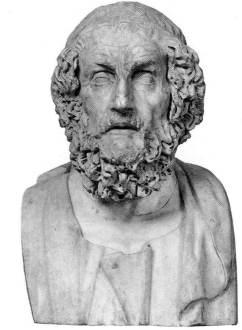

destroyed, Helen recovered, and the Greeks then truly set out for their homes.

The *Odyssey* tells the story of how one of the Greek warriors, Odysseus, finally makes his way home, experiencing many adventures before he is able to settle down once more in Ithaca with his beloved and faithful wife Penelope. En route, he does battle with the fierce Cycones; meets the lotus-eaters, whose food induces a listlessness in his men; arrives in the land of the Cyclops and through his cleverness is able to blind the one-eyed Polyphemus; experiences near-shipwreck; stays for a time with the enchantress Circe, who changes his men into pigs (they are restored through the herb *moly* provided by Hermes, the messenger god); consults the spirit of the dead prophet Tiresias; escapes the beautiful but deadly Sirens; eludes the sea monsters Scylla and Charybdis; is shipwrecked because his men have eaten the sacred cattle of Hyperion, the sun god; is washed ashore at Ogygia, the island of Calypso; is shipwrecked again and saved by Alcinous, king of the Phaeacians; and finally arrives home in Ithaca. Even there, however, he must overcome the opposition posed by the suitors of Penelope and therefore remains in the disguise of a beggar until the crucial moment when he reveals his identity and kills the suitors. Finally, then, Odysseus and Penelope are happily reunited.

Although Odysseus is a heroic type, he is of a more human dimension than is the handsome and youthful Achilles. He is middle-aged, short, overweight, and appears awkward as he prepares to speak to an audience. But he possesses in full measure the gifts of wit and eloquence. Thus Odysseus, the consummate survivor, is described in the opening lines of the poem as "the man who was never at a loss." Apparently defeated repeatedly, opposed by overwhelming odds, delayed for years on end, Odysseus continues to cherish wife and home in his heart and finally—through his wit, tenacity, and courage—is able to reach his home.

Although Homeric epic, because we know more about it, dominates early Greek literature in our thinking, other types of poetry were also developed by the Greeks in the period preceding the Greek defeat of the Persians in 480 BC. The didactic poet Hesiod and the lyric poet Sappho are the best known among these early writers. Tragedy and comedy also began to be developed, tragedy being incorporated into the festival of Dionysus at Athens in the late sixth century BC and comedy in the early fifth. From 323 BC, the date of Alexander's death, Athens was the dominant influence in literature. Early in this period Greek tragedy reached its highest point of development in the plays of Aeschylus, Sophocles, and Euripides (see *Literature of the Golden Age* below).

Archaic Art 650–450 BC

The art of the eighth century is certainly not the equal of the epic poetry of the time. Most of it, like the little bronze statuette of a helmet-maker (Fig. 2.5), reveals little understanding of anatomy and is anything but heroic. But by the middle of the seventh century, the beginning of the *Archaic* period, an art befitting the spirit of Homer began to appear in Greece.

Archaic sculpture

Many of the categories of sculpture that continued through later periods of Greek art were established during this period. Greek sculptors extended their techniques to include large-scale stone carving, hollow bronze casting, and *chryselephantine*—constructions of wood covered with layers of ivory and gold. (However, because many of the bronze works were melted down to make weapons and the chryselephantine works robbed of their precious materials, most of the surviving statues are of stone.) The

purpose of most Archaic art was religious—cult statues for temple interiors, images of gods and heroes to decorate temple exteriors, and votive statues used as offerings—but some of it was only partly religious. Among the latter are life-size statues dedicated to noblemen, who, as young men, had been obliged to compete in the Olympic (Panhellenic) games in the nude. Like their subjects these statues display ideal physiques; they were once thought to be images of Apollo, the god of youthful manly beauty.

As trade contacts between Greece and Egypt increased during the Archaic period the impressive monumental art of that older civilization became more accessible. It is probably for this reason that Archaic statues, especially those of naked youths, show a marked Egyptian influence. This can be seen in the *Youth from Tenea* (Fig. 2.6). Like the Egyptian statue of Mycerinus (Fig. 1.20), it is rigidly frontal; the two also share the positions of their arms, fists, and feet and the delineations of some of their anatomy, including even the kneecaps. But unlike the Egyptian king, the Greek youth is nude and animated by a subtle vigor, evident in its trim body and the typical Archaic smile. For the Greeks, statues like this one personified not only physical beauty but also the virtues of physical fitness and self-discipline and the correct balance between bodily and spiritual concerns—in short, the ethics of Greece's male-dominated aristocracy.

Statues of young women, such as the *Peplos Maiden* (so named because she wears a woolen garment called a *peplos*—Fig. **2.7**), were the counterparts of male statues. Like the *Youth from Tenea*, it smiles and expresses a sense of youthful vitality, despite its stiffly frontal posture. But like all Archaic statues of women, this one is fully clothed. Because of this and the fact that one arm (now broken) bends, it has more variety than the male statue. And originally it was much more colorful. Although all stone sculptures were painted, statues of women in particular were liberally decorated, with color being applied to, among other things, borders of garments, earrings, diadems, bracelets, and facial details. With statues of men, only the facial details were decorated, the rest of their bodies remaining the color of the stone. Moreover the *Peplos Maiden* was not intended to represent an ordinary woman, but a goddess: Athena, patron goddess of Athens.

2.5 Helmet-maker, c. 700 BC
Bronze, 2 ins (5.1 cm) high
Metropolitan Museum of Art, New York, Fletcher Fund, 1942

2.6 *Youth from Tenea*, c. 600 BC
Marble, 73½ ins (1.84 m) high
Metropolitan Museum of Art, New York

2.7 *Peplos Maiden* c. 530 BC
Marble, approx. 48 ins (122 cm) high
Acropolis Museum, Athens

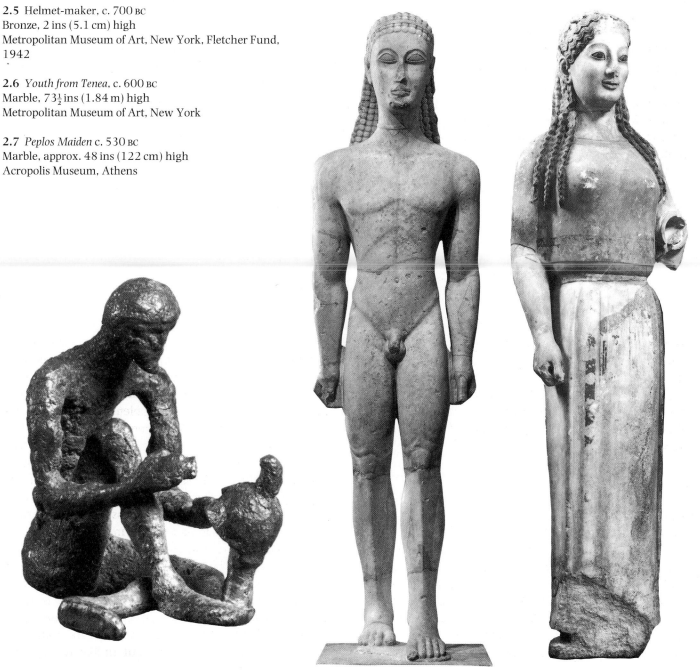

Archaic Architecture

Masonry-constructed public architecture included market buildings, theatres, concert halls, gymnasiums, and various ritualistic structures: treasury buildings, altars, elaborate gateways, and temples. Chief among all the buildings, both religious and non-religious, was the temple, which set the style for the rest.

The basic temple plan (Fig. **2.8**)—a simple rectangle, open at one or both ends of its long axis—was established even before the Archaic era. By the Archaic period, some temples were very large. Typically, a large temple (Fig. **2.9**) was circumscribed by a row of columns, or *colonnade*, inside of which was a walled enclosure called a *cella*. The interior of a cella was intended to house a cult statue of a god or goddess, rather than a large congregation of worshippers. The latter gathered outside the temple on various occasions for festivals, processions, and sacrifices. Only priests and a small number of pilgrims could be accommodated in the chamber containing the statue.

As Greek sculptors had established basic categories in their medium during the Archaic period, so Greek architects had articulated two basic styles, called *orders*: the Doric and the Ionic. The similarities and differences between the orders is manifested not so much in their plans as in their elevations (Fig. **2.10**). Common to both orders (starting at the top of the temple) are: the *pediment*, a gable-like triangle space at either end of the building; the

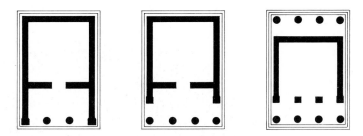

2.8 Representative Greek temple plans

2.9 Plans of Temple of Hera at Olympia (left) and Temple of Aphaia at Aegina (right)

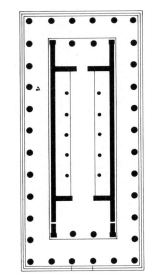

2.10 Doric and Ionic Orders (after Grinnell)

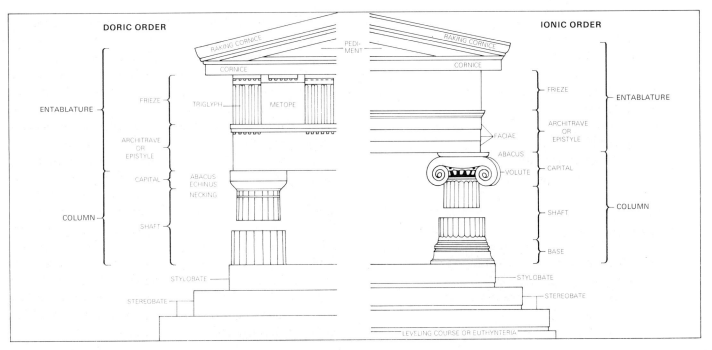

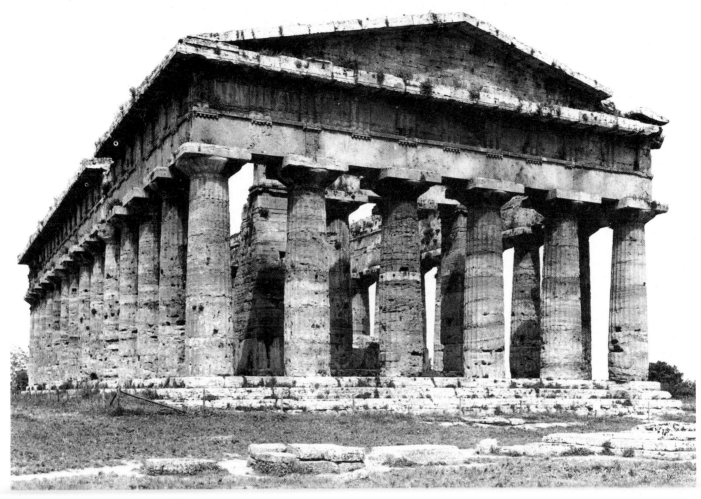

2.11 The Basilica, Paestum, c. 550 BC

entablature, the part between the pediment and column, consisting mainly of a *frieze* and *architrave*; the *column*, consisting of a *capital, shaft*, and, in the Ionic order only, a base; and the *stylobate*, or platform. The most conspicuous difference has to do with the form of the capital, the Doric being a simple rectangular block (*abacus*) above a circular support (*echinus*) and the Ionic having an ornate *echinus* with double scrolls called *volutes*. The other important difference – especially for sculptural decoration – is that the Doric frieze consists of a series of large rectangles called *metopes*, separated by small, ornate rectangles called *triglyphs*, whereas the Ionic frieze is a continuous, uninterrupted surface.

Few temples have survived above the foundation level and none are intact. Among Archaic examples, one of the best preserved is a Doric temple built in the mid-sixth century at the Greek colony of Paestum, in Italy (Fig. 2.11). Note especially the bulging columns, broad capitals, and high entablature. (More will be said about

the evolution of Doric proportions under *Classical Art 480–323 BC*, below.)

The Doric order—identified with the Dorian people—was popular on the Greek mainland and the western colonies, whereas the Ionic order—identified with the Ionians and other ethnic groups that fled the Peloponnesus—was popular on the various islands of the Aegean and the coast of Asia Minor. In addition to differences related to ethnicity and geography there are obvious aesthetic differences—Doric emphasizing the qualities of simplicity, directness, and "masculinity," and Ionic the qualities of grace, refinement, and "femininity." Such distinctions also apply to Archaic sculpture: male subjects—the starkly simple nude youths—were very prevalent in the Peloponnesus; female subjects—the brightly decorated maidens—were more popular in Asia Minor; both subjects were common in ethnically-mixed Athens. Later in this chapter, we will find similar dichotomies in Greek music.

Early Greek Music

Unlike examples of Greek literature, art, and architecture, of which there is an abundance, examples of Greek music survive only in a few fragments transcribed on stone and papyrus; and most of these are from later periods. Furthermore, there is little agreement among music historians on how they were meant to sound. Therefore, the knowledge we have about Greek music comes mainly from writings about it, not from the music itself.

Music was highly honored in Greek society. To understand the status of anything in ancient Greece, one looks to its myths. To begin with, the word "music" derives from *Muse*; music was considered the art of the *Muses*, mythical nymphs and daughters of Zeus whose collective purpose was that of presiding over the various arts and sciences. These lovely creatures held a special place in Greek imagination as embodiments of intellectual and artistic inspiration and, especially, of poetic-musical creation. A musician was a person possessed by the Muses, that is, an instrument of divine power. The leader of the Muses was Apollo, god of beauty and reason, whose attributes were music, prophecy, medicine, and archery, and whose musical gift was playing the lyre. Among the heroes of music were Linos, son of Apollo and the Muse Urania, and Orpheus, Linos' pupil.

Historically, our knowledge of Greek music does not go back earlier than the Dorians. During the age of epic poetry (the early part of the Archaic period), poets, as musical servants in the houses of aristocratic families, sang their verses about the deeds of heroes to the accompaniment of lyres. Indeed, the word "lyric", designating a type of graceful, expressive poetry, is derived from the musical lyre, which indicates the close association between music and poetry during this time and throughout antiquity. Music also played a role in the larger community, for choruses sang for various social occasions—weddings, funerals, and athletic victories—and religious rites. These were accompanied either by a lyre—associated with the worship of Apollo—or by a reed pipe, called an *aulos* associated with the worship of Dionysus. The music of the lyre, the instrument of the epic poet as well as Apollo, was considered to exemplify both beauty and rationality. The aulos, like Dionysus, was associated with drinking wine and carousing. These two instruments, together with the cults they represented, came to symbolize a division not only in music but in Greek culture itself: on the one hand, Apollonian restraint and sublimity and, on the other, Dionysian excitement and sensuality.

Other stringed instruments were known to the Greeks, but most of them were variations of the lyre. Although almost all the instruments referred to in Homer are stringed, an ancient trumpet called a *salpinx*, believed to have been invented by the Etruscans, is mentioned in the *Iliad*.[1] Both the aulos and salpinx were used in military campaigns and ceremonies. The *panpipes* (attributed to Pan, god of the shepherds), a wind instrument comprising several reed tubes of varying lengths tied together in a row and played by blowing across the open upper ends, was used by shepherds and, perhaps, to accompany folk dances. Some percussion instruments, particularly the *tympanon*, a hand drum used to accompany dances, were known to the Greeks. But the lyre and aulos, and variants thereof, were the main instruments used.

As to its form, Greek music was primarily *monophonic*; that is, consisting of a single melody without the support of harmony; every member of even large choruses sang the same tune. (Accompanying instruments are thought to have struck single tones, the main notes of a tune, or played passages of it responsively with the chorus.) As mentioned earlier, music was linked to poetry. The rise and fall of the melody was related to the inflection of spoken words; the rhythm to the rhythms of syllables. Although by the end of the sixth century the Greeks were aware of octave intervals (for example, from middle C to treble C), their basic unit consisted of four tones, called a *tetrachord*. Unlike our system, in which the smallest standard intervals are half-steps or semitones (e.g. C to C♯, theirs could apparently accommodate very small micro-intervals. A Greek chorus, in which all sang in unison a narrow, sliding melodic line, would sound strange indeed to our ears. We can only imagine a concert of *paeans* in praise of Apollo, *dithyrambs* in praise of Dionysus, or other kinds of *hymnoi*. Choruses of dithyrambs, incidentally, were the forerunners of Greek drama.

Unfortunately, no early Greek musical pieces exist, and we are unable to trace the development of music during the pre-Classical period. But we know that music was very popular in early Greece and played a central role in the life of its citizens at all levels. While most musical participation was amateur, professionalism increased during this time, in particular with regard to the playing of instruments. By the sixth century, major competitions featuring the lyre or aulos were taking place. By the beginning of the Classical period (c. 500 BC), music, like architecture, sculpture, and literature, was a developed form of artistic expression.

Literature of the Golden Age

Greek Tragedy

The origins of Greek tragedy are unclear and thus controversial. The explanation most widely accepted— originally proposed by Aristotle in his *Poetics* (fourth century BC)—is that tragedy began with the choral dithyrambs or hymns sung and danced in honor of Dionysus, god of plant and animal life. This theory is supported by the fact that the chorus remained a part of Athenian tragedy throughout the fifth century BC, even when its role had become largely perfunctory, as in the plays of Euripides; also by the fact that the City Dionysia, a festival in honor of Dionysus instituted by Athens in the seventh century BC, was the occasion for the presentation of tragedies. In fact, the altar of Dionysus stood in full view of the spectators in the middle of the orchestra, the area between the stage and the audience where the chorus sang and danced.

The chorus itself related the story in the earliest Greek tragedies. The first individual actor, or "answerer" (*hypocrites*, from which "hypocrite" is derived), was reputedly introduced by the poet Thespis in the sixth century BC. "Answerer" signified his role as respondent to the chorus. Aeschylus later added a second actor, and Sophocles, still later, a third. The early Greek playwrights drew their stories and metric forms from the epic and lyric traditions of an even more distant past. Many of these stories were found in the *Iliad* and the *Odyssey* of Homer, as well as in the so-called Epic Cycle, poems intended to supplement and complete the story of the Trojan War as told by Homer. The Athenian tragic poets best known to us— Aeschylus, Sophocles, and Euripides—also drew copi-

2.12 Theater at Epidaurus, Greece, c. 350 BC
Diameter 375 ft (114 m), orchestra 66 ft (20 m) across

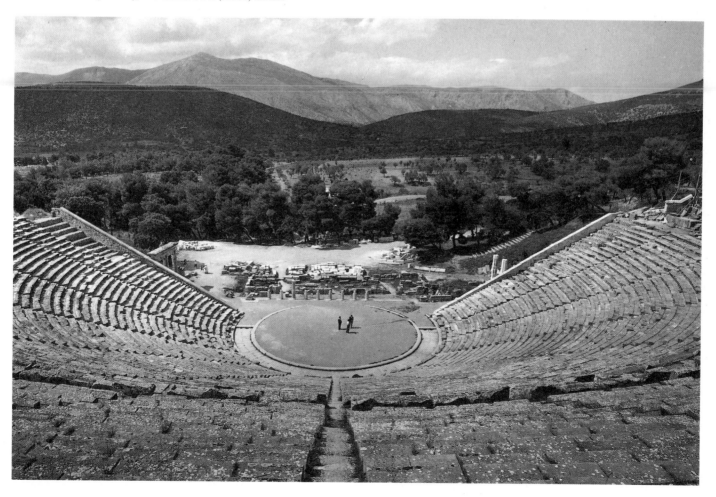

ously upon this legendary material. Thus they reworked material already familiar to their audiences. A dramatist's originality and the source of special interest to the spectators lay in his choice of a particular version of a story and in his interpretation and presentation of that version.

The actors (always male) wore elaborate costumes and masks representing the various roles they played. Greek plays were presented outdoors at the base of a hillside which formed a natural amphitheater, the spectators sitting on benches which covered the hillside (Fig. 2.12). The orchestra, in which the chorus danced and chanted its lines, was a semi-circular area at the focal point of the amphitheater. Although scholars disagree on the question of whether there was an actual stage, it is thought by some that behind the orchestra was a stage on which the actors delivered their lines. The building that provided the backdrop for this stage also served as a dressing room. Central doors in the stage building made it possible for a scene within to be displayed, and a moveable platform (the *ekkuklema*) could be used to bring spectacles within into the full view of the audience. (The *ekkuklema* may have come into use later than the fifth century BC.) On the roof of the stage building was a crane, used for lowering onto the stage deities who provided resolutions to otherwise impossible conflicts. This device is the source of the phrase *deus ex machina*, "god from the machine," used in drama for an arbitrary ending imposed upon a play by the playwright.

Perhaps the most puzzling element in Greek drama for the modern reader or playgoer is the chorus. The choral beginnings of drama provide a partial explanation of the continuing importance of this element; but the chorus, at least as used by Aeschylus and Sophocles, is much more than a vestigial remnant of an early age. Most obviously it provided poetic beauty as well as spectacle through dance and song. It may also be regarded as a very perceptive group of spectators with profound insights into the implications of the dialogue and actions of the drama. Thus it often calls attention to the universal meanings implied by the experience of particular characters. Oedipus' plight, for example, represents, according to the chorus, the uncertainty that haunts all human beings until the day they die. Yet the chorus is not omniscient. For example, it does not at first, in Aeschylus' *Oresteia*, understand the prophetess Cassandra's predictions that both she and King Agamemnon will be murdered by Queen Clytemnestra.

The practice of offering prizes for outstanding plays began in the fifth century BC. Each of three playwrights prepared four plays: a tragic trilogy and a satyr play. At first the trilogy treated only one theme, an example being Aeschylus' *Oresteia*. Satyr plays were bawdy and satirical comedies. The plays were presented competitively to the Athenian audience at the City Dionysia.

Aeschylus

Because the writers of the earliest tragedies are such shadowy figures, tragedy, for us, must begin with Aeschylus (c. 525–456 BC). Little is known for certain about his life. It is curious, in the light of his monumental significance as a dramatist, that his epitaph speaks of where he died (Gela, Sicily) and his prowess in battle against the Persians at Marathon, but says nothing of his skill and prodigious output as a playwright. Although he wrote more than 70 plays, only seven have survived. Among these are *Agamemnon*, *The Libation Bearers*, and *The Eumenides*, which make up the *Oresteia*, the only extant tragic trilogy. During his lifetime he is reported to have won first prize in the dramatic competition on thirteen occasions; and his plays continued to win prizes even after his death.

In writing the *Oresteia*—so named because of the importance of Orestes, son of Agamemnon and Clytemnestra, in two of the three plays—Aeschylus drew upon the myth of the curse upon the House of Atreus. According to this story, Thyestes, disputing the throne of

2.13 Aeschylus

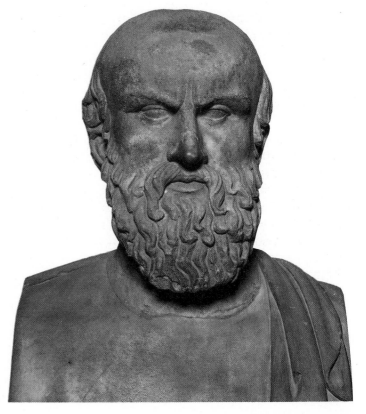

Argos with his brother Atreus, seduced Atreus' wife. In revenge, Atreus, pretending reconciliation, invited Thyestes to a banquet at which he served all but one of his brother's sons as a meat dish. Upon learning what he had eaten, Thyestes placed a curse upon the family of Atreus and fled from Argos with Aegisthus, his surviving son.

This myth is linked with the Trojan War through Agamemnon and Menelaus, sons of Atreus. These brothers led the Greek expedition against Troy to recover Menelaus' wife Helen, who had been abducted by Paris (see the *Iliad* above). Agamemnon's wife was Clytemnestra, sister of Helen. During the absence of her husband, Clytemnestra took Aegisthus as her lover. Justifying her actions by Agamemnon's sacrifice of their daughter Iphigenia at Aulis in order to gain favorable winds for the becalmed Greek fleet, Clytemnestra, in collusion with Aegisthus, planned the assassination of Agamemnon. Thus the curse upon the House of Atreus began to work its way through the family of Agamemnon. But the theme of retribution in the play is carried not only by this curse but also by the suffering of the Trojan War perpetrated by the Greeks for the sake of an unworthy woman.

Agamemnon, the first play of the trilogy, opens with the news of a Greek victory at Troy. Much of this play is taken up with the theological reflections by the chorus on the various aspects of the Trojan War, especially Agamemnon's sacrifice of Iphigenia and the suffering caused by the war. Through their poetic meditations and reminiscences, they reach several theological certainties—in particular, that Zeus, the ruler of the Greek gods, teaches mankind through suffering:

> *Zeus, who guided men to think,*
> *who has laid it down that wisdom*
> *comes alone through suffering.*[2]

It also becomes evident that Zeus is working through the Trojan War to bring retribution upon the Trojans and the Greeks, in general, as well as the descendants of Atreus. Indeed, this play and the two plays that follow affirm that the law of retribution reigns supreme, as Troy is destroyed by the Greeks (in punishment for the sin of Paris), the Greeks are scattered by storms (because of their lack of restraint in the sacking of Troy), Agamemnon is murdered by Clytemnestra (because of his sacrifice of Iphigenia), Clytemnestra and Aegisthus are killed by Orestes (in revenge for his father's death), and he, in turn, is pursued by the Furies because he has killed his mother. Thus retribution runs rampant as crime punishes crime—and all under the controlling hand of Zeus as he teaches mankind that "the doer must suffer."

This Zeus-driven cycle of sin and retribution is under-

scored by the chorus as they chant in response to the revelation of Clytemnestra's murder of Agamemnon:

> *. . . all through Zeus, Zeus,*
> *first cause, prime mover.*
> *For what thing without Zeus is done among mortals?*
> *What here is without God's blessing?*[3]

Thus the curse upon the House of Atreus threads its way, under divine guidance, through the events of the trilogy. But where is it to end? There is no logical stopping place for such justice. Each act of retributive violence breeds another. To this dilemma Aeschylus provides a solution in *The Eumenides*, the final play of the trilogy. Orestes, who in the second play, *The Libation Bearers*, has murdered his mother and Aegisthus, is pursued in the final play by the Furies for the crime of matricide. Defenders of the rights of kindred, in this case of the mother, they demand the punishment of Orestes. But Apollo, defender of male authority, had commanded Orestes to kill Clytemnestra and thus defends him against the accusations of the Furies. The result is an impasse. Aeschylus' solution is to cause Orestes to be tried by a jury at the newly established court of the Areopagus in Athens. When the jury becomes deadlocked in a six–six tie, Athena casts the decisive vote in favor of Orestes and thus brings the curse and the cycle of retribution to an end. The primitive rights represented by the Furies are vindicated when these frightful creatures are made the protectors of Athens as the Eumenides ("Kindly Ones").

The *Oresteia* is a powerful moral and social myth about the evolution of justice from the primitive form of the passionate vendetta to the Athenian court system based upon the rational decision of a dispassionate jury. But it is also a powerful religious myth about the evolution of the god Zeus, who grows from a god whose justice is violently retributive to a god who can temper justice with wisdom and compassion. This striking change is made evident by the role of his daughter Athena at the jury trial. For those steeped in Judaeo-Christian thought, a god that evolves and changes is a contradiction in terms. But it is clear from this trilogy, as well as from his *Prometheus*—in which Zeus is superior in power to Prometheus but lacking in his compassion, wisdom, and foreknowledge— that Aeschylus conceived of Zeus in this way.

Sophocles

Born at Colonus about 30 years later than Aeschylus, Sophocles (c. 496–406 BC) was too young to fight the Persians. And when the Peloponnesian War began in 431 BC, he was too old to fight the Spartans; he died before they finally defeated the Athenians. He was an active participant, however, in the politics of his time and saw the development of Athens into a democracy under the leadership of Pericles.

Although Sophocles learned from Aeschylus, he did not merely imitate him. For example, he created a unified whole in the single play, rather than developing his themes through a tragic trilogy. Other changes introduced by Sophocles were the addition of a third actor, the reduction of the role of the chorus and the fixing of its number at fifteen, and the use of painted scenery.

Like Aeschylus, Sophocles wrote many more plays than have been preserved. Of more than 120 plays written by him, only seven of his tragedies are extant. Among these is the Theban Trilogy—consisting of three related but self-contained plays: *Oedipus the King*, *Oedipus at Colonus*, and *Antigone*—so named because Thebes is the location for two of the three plays and has a significant role in the third. The order in which the three plays were written differs from their dramatic chronology. Thus, although *Antigone* was written first (c. 441 BC), its events take place last. The events of *Oedipus the King* occur first, and those of *Oedipus at Colonus* follow.

Perhaps the best-known Greek myth inherited by Western culture is that of King Oedipus, and Sophocles' tragedy based upon this story is certainly the best-known Greek play. Not only has this story permeated Western literature, it also is the source of a significant aspect of Freudian psychoanalytic theory, the "Oedipus complex," signifying a male child's erotic attachment to his mother.

The story of Oedipus is as follows. The oracle of Apollo at Delphi revealed that King Laius and Queen Jocasta of Thebes would have a son who would kill his father and marry his mother. Seeking to evade the fulfillment of this prediction, Laius and Jocasta, upon the birth of a son, gave him to a herdsman with the instruction that he was to be abandoned. The child's feet were fastened together with an iron pin, giving rise to the name Oedipus (":Swollenfoot"). The herdsman, however, pitying the child, gave him to another herdsman from Corinth, who, in turn, gave him to Polybus and Merope, the childless king and queen of Corinth. The royal couple brought up Oedipus as their own son, not revealing his origins to him. During a drunken party, however, he was called a bastard and was thus prompted to set out for Delphi to learn the truth of his origins. Here he received no answer to his inquiry except that he would murder his father and marry his mother. Thinking to avert this calamity, Oedipus determined not to return to Corinth and instead set out for Thebes. En route he met Laius and his royal party at a crossroads. A quarrel ensued, and Oedipus, unaware of Laius' identity, killed his father and all of his servants, except one who

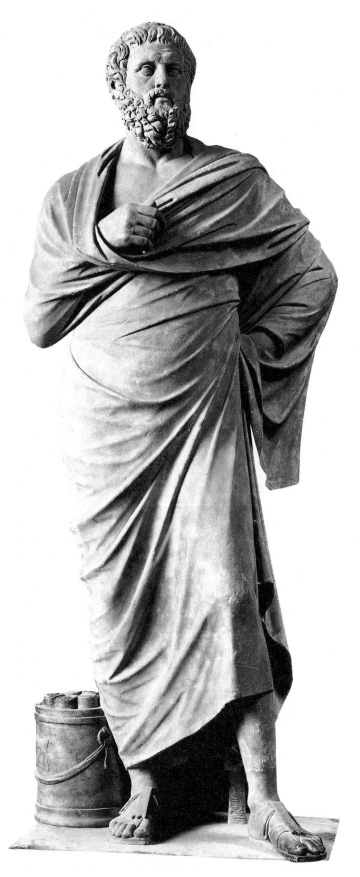

2.14 Sophocles

escaped, and would later be forced to identify Oedipus. Oedipus then continued his journey to Thebes; before arriving, however, he solved the riddle of the Sphinx who was ravaging the countryside. His reward from a grateful Thebes was the kingship and the widowed queen Jocasta for his wife. She bore him four children: Eteocles, Polyneices, Antigone, and Ismene. This is the background for Sophocles' play, which tells of the revelation of Oedipus' true identity—a discovery that results in the suicide of Jocasta and the self-blinding and exile of Oedipus.

Oedipus is permeated with dramatic irony, for the audience knows the identity of Oedipus while he does not. Thus viewers are fully aware that his relentless efforts to discover, first, who is the cause of a plague ravaging Thebes because the killer of Laius has not been punished and, later, his own identity, simply tighten the noose around his own neck. Indeed, the play contains numerous ironies: for example, Oedipus could solve the riddle of the Sphinx but is ignorant of his own identity; he is at first blind though he sees, and cannot see until he is blind; he is both the pursuer and the pursued; he is at the outset the healer of Thebes' woes and yet the cause of the plague that later afflicts the city.

Typically, readers of *Oedipus* conclude that the protagonist is the plaything of fate, or a puppet manipulated by Apollo. But these interpretations fail to do justice to the care with which Sophocles has drawn his human characters, especially Oedipus. The critic H. D. F. Kitto has commented: "Oedipus, as we see him time after time, is intelligent, determined, self-reliant, but hot-tempered and too sure of himself; and an apparently malignant chain of circumstances combine now with the strong, now with the weak side of his character to produce the catastrophe."[4] For example, a weak man would have simply accepted the insult at Corinth, but Oedipus was determined to discover the truth about himself, and having heard the oracle he resolutely turned his back upon Corinth to avoid bringing ruin upon himself and his supposed parents. By coincidence, as he was en route to Thebes, he encountered his real father; and since both were hot-tempered, violence and murder ensued. He could have arrived in Thebes unknown and safe, but since he was intelligent, he interpreted the riddle of the Sphinx and became the savior of the city. What happens to him, therefore, is the result of the interaction of his virtues and vices and those of others in combination with a series of circumstances.

At the same time, however, we are made aware of another plane of action besides that of autonomous human characters. Although the gods do not appear personally in *Oedipus*, as they do in the *Oresteia*, their presence is apparent. The dramatic irony of the play continually points to the oracle and its fulfillment by Oedipus. And the plague is explicit evidence of a hidden divine power. Thus there are two levels of action: one human, the other divine. But the human level is so realistic that it is not plausible to interpret the play as an example of divine determinism.

How, then, if not deterministically, are we to interpret the oracles in this play? The gods do not foreordain the future through their oracles; rather, they merely foresee it. Their predictions, therefore, do not negate human will and choice. Moreover, in Sophoclean philosophy the universe in all of its aspects is controlled by law, or reason (Greek *Logos*), and any action in violation of this law, in nature or human affairs, triggers a reaction. Thus it is as inevitable that Oedipus' murder of his father and marriage to his mother will result in suffering as it is that a man who stumbles in the dark and falls from a building must plunge to the ground. In both cases ignorance is not a saving factor and the consequences are certain and devastating. What Sophocles affirms in the play, therefore, is that although life may be cruel, it is not chaotic. There is a pattern to life; there is a world order, though it cannot be manipulated by the good intentions of human beings.

In the second play, *Oedipus at Colonus*, the aged king, accompanied in his exile by his daughter Antigone, finally achieves peace and is honored by the king of Athens and by the gods. In *Antigone*, Oedipus' daughter defies her uncle, Creon, now king of Thebes, who has refused to allow her to bury her brother, Polyneices, a victim of the recent civil war. The timelessness of the play's central conflict, between the individual, represented by Antigone, and the state, represented by Creon, has made it one of the most enduringly thought-provoking of Greek tragedies.

Euripides

Although he did not enjoy great success with the judges of the City Dionysia in his lifetime, Euripides (c. 480–407) had more influence than Aeschylus and Sophocles in later periods, especially on Latin drama and French Neoclassical playwrights. His strong individualism and his questioning of the religious certainties affirmed by Aeschylus and Sophocles may have contributed to his lack of success with his contemporaries. Being somewhat alienated from society and individualistic, Euripides saw tragedy in terms of conflicts within the soul of the ordinary person rather than between the heroic figure and external forces. This perception of tragedy lends a realistic and modern aspect to Euripides' plays that sometimes approaches naturalism.

Of the some 90 plays that he wrote, 19 have survived, as compared with seven each for Aeschylus and Sophocles. Among his extant plays are *Medea*, which treats

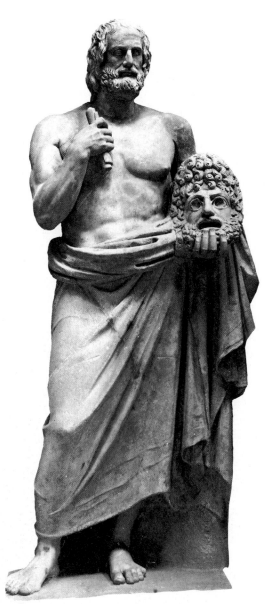

2.15 Euripides

Other Athenian Writers

In addition to tragedy, we should note other Athenian literary and intellectual achievements of the period ending with the death of Alexander (323 BC). Among these are the comedy of Aristophanes (c. 450–c. 385 BC), one of the great comic geniuses in Western literature. Like tragedy and comedy, the discipline of writing history also has its origins with the Greeks of fifth-century Athens (with the possible exception of certain Old Testament narratives), in the *Histories* of Herodotus, *The History of the Peloponnesian War* by Thucydides, and the works of Xenophon. In philosophy the great names are Socrates, his disciple Plato, and Plato's pupil Aristotle, whose philosophy profoundly influenced Western thought, especially through the Scholasticism of Thomas Aquinas (see Chapter 7). Plato made a major contribution to Western thought with his Theory of Ideas: the concept that ultimate reality is an unseen world of ideas existing objectively outside space and time and providing the perfect models for all that we observe and experience. These ideas can be known by reason, through dialectic, which is possible because the soul, prior to its embodiment, has known these ideas in the unseen world. Thus Plato believed in the immortality and transmigration of

2.16 Socrates

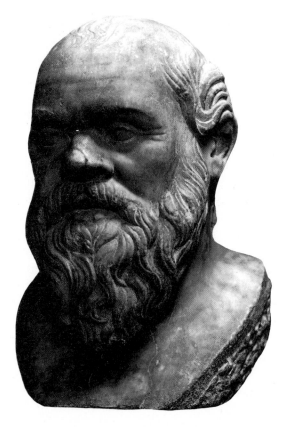

the theme of the destructive force of unrestrained passion; *Hippolytus*, also on the theme of passion, in this case in conflict with chastity; *The Trojan Women*, dealing with the brutality of war through the suffering of the women of Troy who survived the Greek destruction of their city; *Electra*, a play that presents the daughter of Agamemnon more realistically than Aeschylus' *The Libation Bearers* or Sophocles' *Electra; Orestes*, another play on the myth used by Aeschylus; and *The Bacchae*, a play which, like *Hippolytus*, treats the theme of irresistible passion, but passion as revealed in the religious ecstasy that characterized the worship of Dionysus, the god of Greek theater.

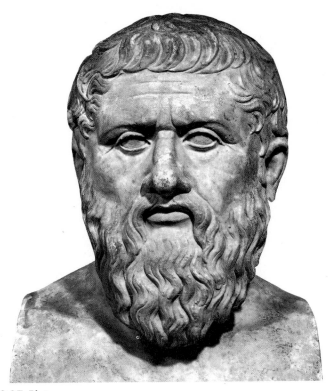

2.17 Plato

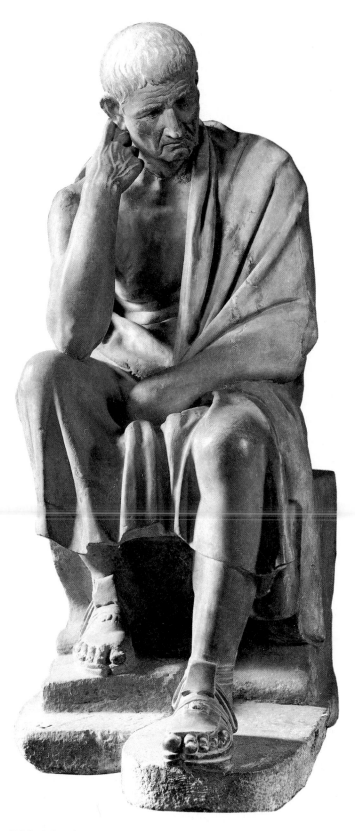

the soul, and explained learning as a process of recollecting what the soul has previously known. The Neoplatonists, such as Plotinus and Porphyry in the early Christian era and Pico della Mirandola and Marsilio Ficino in the Renaissance, are evidence of the far-reaching influence of Plato's thinking. Indeed, St. Augustine, who provided the theological underpinnings of both Catholicism and, later, Protestantism, was greatly indebted to the Neoplatonism of Plotinus and Porphyry. Medieval emphasis on the dualism of body and soul and of this world and the eternal world, resulting in contempt for both the body and the physical world, is no doubt traceable in part to Platonic influence.

Although Athens' political dominance declined during and after the Peloponnesian War with Sparta (431–404 BC), she was able to retain her intellectual dominance. However, in the period extending from the death of Alexander the Great to the Roman sack of Corinth (146 BC), Greek cultural leadership shifted from Athens to Alexandria, Egypt. Early in this period Athens was still able to produce such important figures as the philosophers Zeno (stoicism) and Epicurus (epicureanism) and the comic dramatist Menander, but the writings of these men were not equal in quality to those of the Periclean age. The contribution of the Alexandrians was largely scholarly rather than creative—literary and textual criticism, historical study, and biography. In sum, the literary output of the Alexandrian age simply did not measure up to that of the Periclean.

2.18 Aristotle

Classical Art

At the start of the Classical period, Athens was in its prime and the leader of the Greek world. Athenians, therefore, felt compelled to make their city the artistic marvel of that world. They rebuilt the *Acropolis* ("high city"; Figs. **2.19, 2.20**), a dramatic mound of rock and architecture overlooking the city. Earlier, it had been a fortress; now it was to be an imposing religious-ceremonial precinct. Work began on the new Acropolis soon after the victory at Marathon (490 BC), only for it to be razed to the ground by the Persians during the battle of Salamis (480 BC). The final rebuilding began under the leadership of Pericles in 448 BC, following a treaty with the Persians.

Although Periclean Athens is often cited as a watershed in the progress of democracy and civil liberties, the forces of conservatism were still strong. Nearly half of the Athenian population were slaves; of the free, only males were allowed political participation; of these, only a small percentage served in the general assembly (*ecclesia*). Most of the great figures of the period, including Aeschylus, Herodotus, Thucydides, and Pericles, came from noble families; Sophocles and Plato, who came from middle-class families, identified themselves with the aristocracy.

The contest between freedom and tradition existing in Greek political life was reflected in the tension between humanism and idealism found in Classical art. We know, for example, that in painting a desire for truth to nature was tempered by a commitment to representing ideal figures in an ideal world. However, our knowledge of this

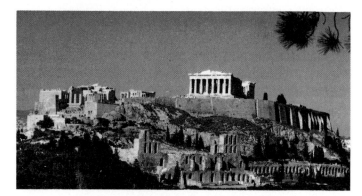

2.19 View of the Acropolis, Athens

art is almost entirely based on written accounts since, apart from vases, very few examples of Greek painting—whether easel or mural—have survived. Thus, we must turn to sculpture to see the developments in Greek art as well as the Greek values it embodies.

Sculpture: free-standing

The extraordinary series of changes that took place in representing the male nude in the early part of the fifth century paralleled the greater naturalism introduced in dramatic tragedy and in philosophy during this period. In their striving for visual truth, Greek artists liberated sculpture from the fixed framework of the Archaic style.

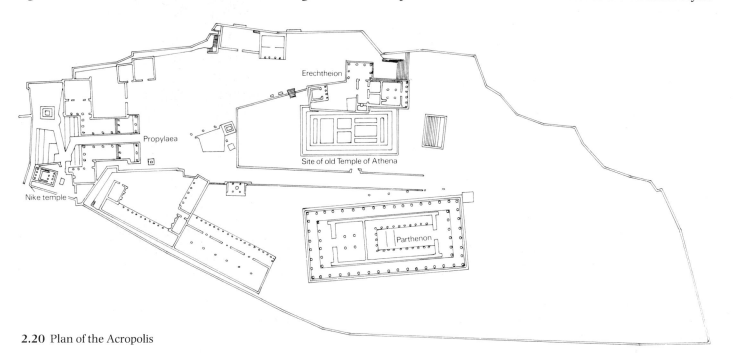

2.20 Plan of the Acropolis

The anatomy of *Kritios Boy* (Fig. **2.21**), sculpted in 480 BC, is obviously more naturalistic than that of *Youth from Tenea*. But, more significantly, by the slight turning of its upper body and head and the shifting of its weight from two feet to one (now missing), *Kritios Boy* breaks the bonds of thousands of years of sculptural frontality and opens the way for new formal and expressive possibilities.

A realization of those possibilities appears as early as 450 BC in a work by the renowned Polykleitos (born c. 480 BC). His *Spear Carrier* (Fig. **2.22**)—which, unfortunately, survives only in Roman copies—is often used as a prime example of the Classical moment in Greek sculpture. In contrast to earlier nudes, this one is an organic unit with the shape and structure of a real adult male. Unlike *Kritios Boy*, whose movements are timid, this one firmly places the weight of its body over the right foot. By so doing, the right hip is raised higher than the left. Then, to counter the slant of the hips and prevent the figure from tipping to its left, the trunk is bent so that the left shoulder is higher than the right and the head directly above the right ankle. Although this kind of posture, natural for standing or strolling, is commonplace in everyday life, it was a breakthrough in the art of figure sculpture.

Despite its realism, *Spear Carrier* is obviously not a representation of an ordinary young man. Not only does it have an athletic physique; several of its parts—the planes of the chest and abdomen, the pelvic girdle, and the bony but definitive kneecaps—have been simplified to reinforce the sense of its being an ideal. Most of all, the passive, expressionless face—characteristic of all Classical sculptures, male or female—helps both to idealize and to depersonalize the whole figure.

Thus, on the one hand, *Spear Carrier* reflects a humanizing trend in Greek thought, epitomized in the statement of Protagoras (480–411 BC): "Man is the measure of all things." Its realism is clearly a symptom of this new attitude. On the other hand, Polykleitos' work reflects a conservative, idealizing tendency, a tendency best represented in the writings of Plato. In addition to the eternal verities—truth, beauty, and goodness—Plato's world of ideas provides for the perfect forms for all things, including men and women. *Spear Carrier* is, above all, an image of such an ideal. Indeed, it is based on a numerical system—a *canon*—of correct proportions devised by the artist, which was supposedly referred to by other artists throughout the Classical world.

Spear Carrier's round head, broad shoulders, thick torso, and overall simplicity of conception are sculptural counterparts of the simple, sturdy columns of the Doric order. And like a Doric temple, it is an ideal of strength, not grace.

If Polykleitos is the Aeschylus of Classical sculpture then the fourth-century Praxiteles (born c. 390 BC) is its

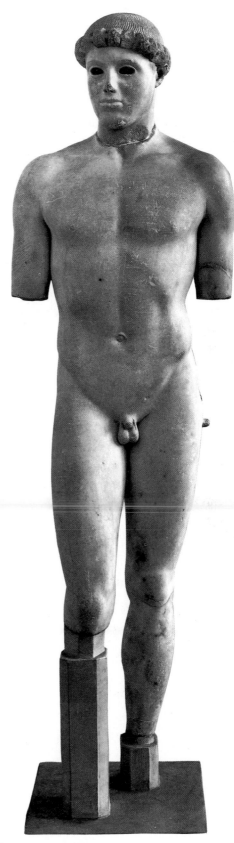

2.21 *Kritios Boy*, c. 480 BC
Marble, c. 34 ins (86 cm) high.
Acropolis Museum, Athens

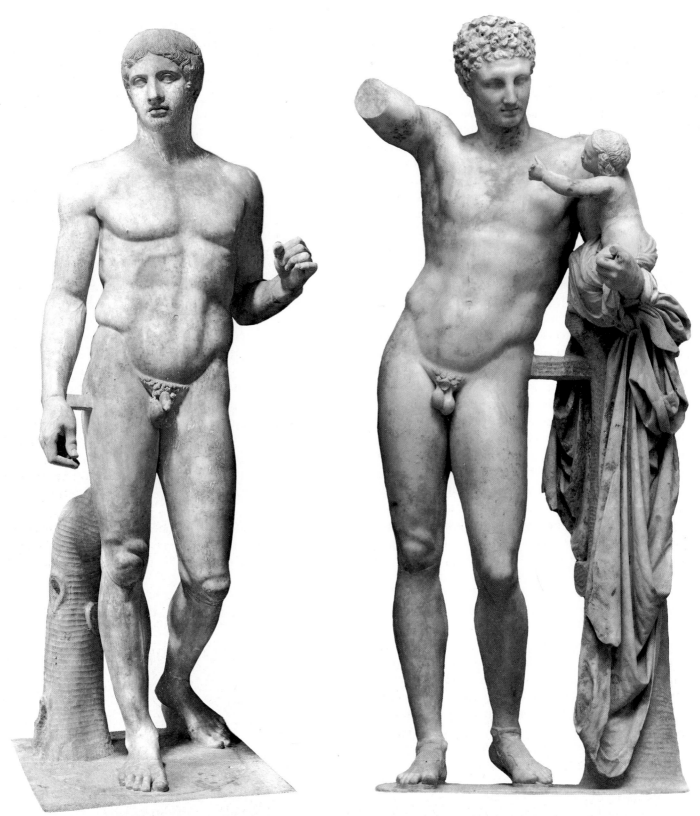

2.22 *Spear-Carrier*, c. 450–440 BC
Roman copy after original by Polykleitos
National Museum, Naples

2.23 *Hermes and Dionysus*, Praxiteles, c. 330–320 BC
Marble, 7 ft 1 in (2.16 m) high
Museum, Olympia

Euripides—the poet who injected not only a greater degree of realism into Greek drama but also the complexities of human emotions and interrelationships. In Praxiteles' *Hermes and Dionysus* (Fig. **2.23**), sculpted about 100 years later than *Spear Carrier*, the figure of the messenger-god supports Dionysus with its left arm (and dangled a bunch of grapes before the infant with its now absent right arm). The Hermes shares with the earlier figure the ideal physique, classical posture, and serene countenance. But there the similarity ends. Lacking the lucid anatomical definitions of the *Spear Carrier*'s body, Hermes' body is softer, more realistic, and much more sensuous—qualities echoed in its graceful, supple movement. Its weight is partially supported by its left arm—thus displacing the center of gravity to the left—while the right arm reaches out into space. More importantly, through a combination of pose, gesture, and facial expression, *Hermes* expresses a sense of tenderness, the consequence of a relationship between the two subjects—the infant and the messenger-god. Such human qualities in art increased as the Classical period progressed.

Sculpture: architectural

Polykleitos' main rival was Phidias (c. 490–432 BC), the artist appointed by Pericles to supervise the artistic aspects of rebuilding the Acropolis. The Parthenon (Fig. **2.27**), a new temple to Athena, was the major project. Phidias' greatest challenge was producing sculptures for the temple's 92 metopes for the 542-foot (165-meter)-long frieze (an Ionic element) which was to go around the cella

for the two pediments, and for the sanctuary interior—which was to be filled with a colossal cult statue of Athena (made of chryselephantine). Although the sculptures were probably carved by platoons of assistants, the designs were drawn by Phidias, who presumably supervised their implementation.

Of the huge figures made for the pediments, only a few fragments survive. Among those from the east pediment (which illustrated the legend of Athena's birth) are the *Three Goddesses* (Fig. **2.24**), now in the British Museum. Robust in body, but languid in posture, the three goddesses, despite their monumental appearance, were made to fit into a corner of the pediment. Very important to the overall character of the group are the folds of drapery. Since real Greek clothing was loose and untailored, Greek sculptors were free to invent the ways in which it covered the body. Phidias was a master at this. Prior to his time, drapery was conceived of as plain (as with the *Peplos Maiden*, Fig. **2.7**) or as a simple pattern of repeated folds. On the Parthenon figures, it assumes a variety of forms that swell, collapse, gather, or cling to the body. In all cases, the presence of the underlying body is never lost. Not only is Phidias' drapery more natural than earlier drapery, it is more expressive and boldly rhythmic. The patterns of folds help both to dramatize the individual figures and to integrate the group.

The frieze (also now in the British Museum) is a rhythmical series of low-relief sculptures illustrating a procession in honor of Athena. (Starting at the west end, it culminates at the east end with the ceremony of presenting a ritual *peplos* for Athena's statue.) The elements of the procession include horsemen (Fig. **2.25**), chariots and a

2.24 *Three Goddesses*, from the east pediment of the Parthenon, Athens, c. 438–432 BC
Marble, over life-size
British Museum, London

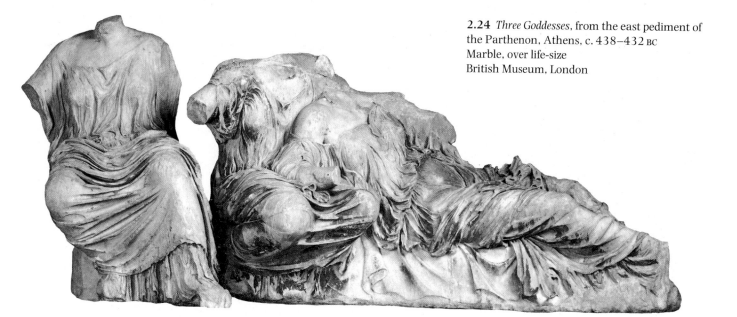

variety of people on foot: among others, parade marshals, musicians, and young men carrying ritual vessels. There is also a variety of action, especially among the men and horses: a man lacing a boot, an unmounted horse restlessly tossing its head, a man restraining a lively horse, and mounted horses in various stages of movement. Since the frieze, as a unit, could not be experienced in a single glance, but only by walking around the building, it existed in time as well as space—like a real parade. The meter of a real parade, a mixture of rapid and halting movements, is captured in the abstract lines and rhythms of the carving as well as in the variety of actions of the characters.

The fact that the subject consists primarily of ordinary people, the citizens of Athens, rather than noblemen or gods (although some seated gods are placed at the end of the parade) was an innovation in the ancient world. (Pericles may have intended the frieze to provide a democratic contrast to a frieze on a Persian temple showing a procession of subject peoples bearing tribute to the King.) Nevertheless, the people in the frieze resemble gods. Like all Classical sculptures, the bodies are idealized and the faces have that characteristic passive gaze.

The carvings on both the frieze and the metopes (Fig. 2.26) vary in quality and even style. Many stonecar-

vers were involved in the project, and their efforts had to be coordinated with the agenda of the temple construction. The 92 metopes, for example, had to be completed before the ceiling beams could be attached. Phidias, the supervisor, was apparently preoccupied with the huge statue of Athena, an overwhelming project in its own right. Nevertheless the Parthenon sculptures, as a whole, are recognized as the greatest achievement of fifth-century art and Phidias as perhaps the greatest artist of antiquity. His fully developed, mobile figures enriched the Classical style, endowing it with a heightened sense of rhythm and energy. He raised the depiction of drapery to the level of art. His work, which is less severe than Polykleitos', combines Doric and Ionic tendencies and anticipates late Classical art, such as Praxiteles', and Hellenistic art.

The Parthenon

It is likely that Phidias played a decisive role in the planning of the Parthenon (Fig. 2.27), even though two other men—Ictinus and Callicrates—were the actual architects. Built of Pentelic marble over the foundations of the earlier temple, the present Parthenon is more grandi-

2.25 *Horsemen*, from the west frieze of the Parthenon, c. 440 BC
Marble, 43 ins (107 cm) high
British Museum, London

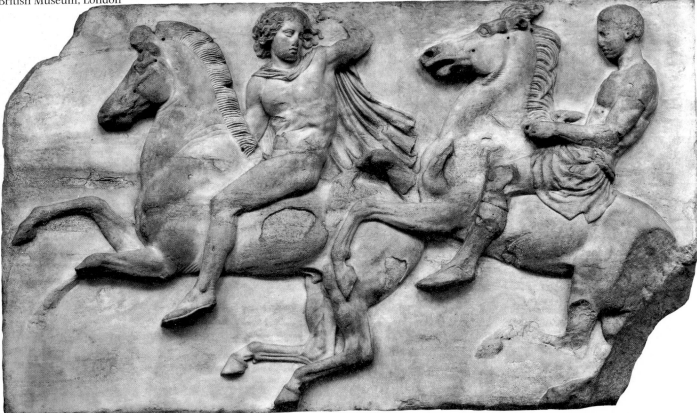

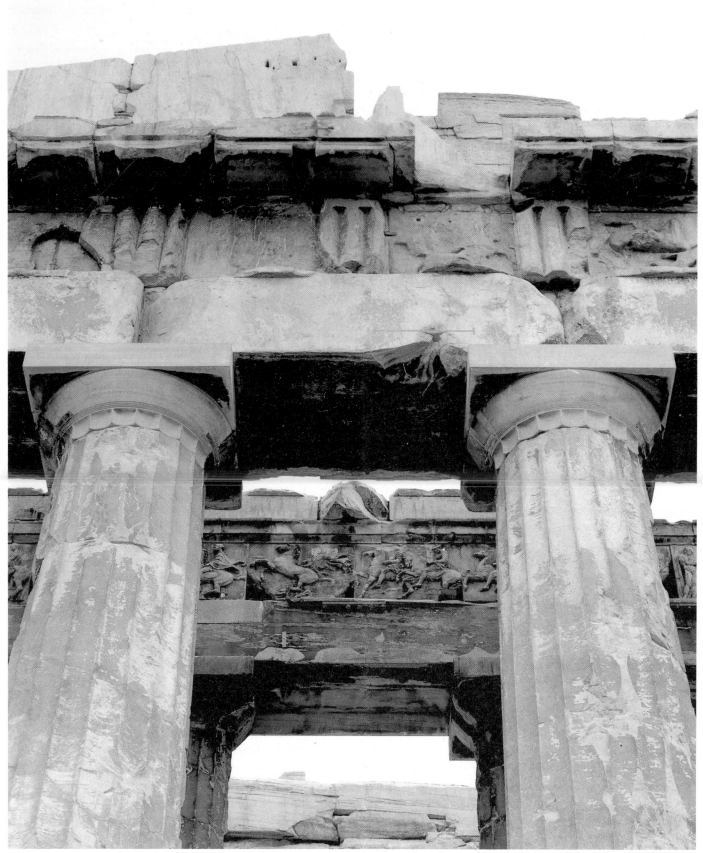

2.26 West entrance of the cella of the Parthenon, showing a portion of the Panathenaic procession, c. 440 BC
Marble frieze

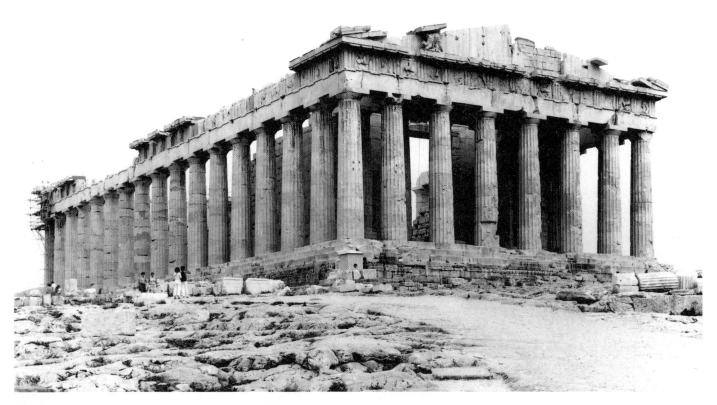

2.27 Parthenon, view from the north-west, 448–432 BC

ose in plan (Fig. **2.28**) than its predecessor. Mainly, it is wider, with eight columns across, rather than the traditional six. Also, unlike most Doric plans, this one has two cella chambers: the large one for Phidias' statue of Athena and the small one for the treasury of the Delian League. The interior of the small one contains four majestic Ionic columns, another innovation for a mainly Doric temple.

Still another innovation is the Ionic frieze discussed above (Fig. **2.26**). No previous Doric temple had been endowed with such a frieze. By so doing, Phidias and the architects not only provided a secondary sculptural rhythm inside the colonnade to complement the metopes on the entablature; they also united the Ionic and Doric orders, symbolically resolving that ancient cultural dualism.

But the fame of the Parthenon, the highest achievement of the Doric order, rests not on its innovations, but on its unique refinements. The most visible of these refinements are the proportions of its columns, which, compared to those of the Archaic temple (Fig. 2.11) appear slender (Fig. **2.29**). This is because they are narrower in relation to their height; their capitals, too, are considerably smaller and narrower than the earlier ones. Also, relative to the entablature they are taller; or, to put it differently, the Parthenon entablature, relative to its columns, is shorter than the Archaic entablature. In many places, the ratio of

9:4 (or nearly) is employed: the length of the temple to its width, the width to the height, the column intervals to the column diameters, and so forth. This particular ratio demonstrates the preoccupation of the Greeks with number. The lessons of Pythagoras, the famous philosopher-mathematician, were not lost on fifth-century architects. Like Polykleitos, they also felt that a rule based on numerical relationships was good for their craft.

Other refinements, though less visible, are called, paradoxically, "optical" refinements. These consist of subtle deviations from what the eye expects to see or thinks it sees. The most apparent of these has to do with adjusting the position of the end columns relative to the metopes and triglyphs. Notice that all the columns, except the end ones, are centered beneath a triglyph. To prevent the capitals of the end columns from extending beyond the edge of the entablature, the interval between each end column and its neighbor has been reduced (corresponding adjustments have been made to the dimensions of the end triglyphs and metopes). The least apparent of the optical refinements are the many deviations from lines that are expected to be straight, vertical, and horizontal. Rather than taper straight, the columns gently swell in the middle—called *entasis*. Also, rather than being perfectly plumb, the columns lean slightly inward. The plane of the stylobate, rather than being perfectly level, is slightly convex—being higher in the center by $4\frac{5}{16}$ inches (11 cm).

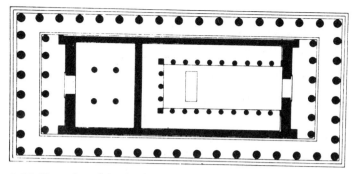

2.28 Floor plan of the Parthenon

Because the columns do not vary in height, the curvature of the stylobate is thus repeated on the entablature. According to students of Greek architecture, the purpose of such optical refinements was to make the temple appear more stable than it would otherwise. Without the effect of entasis, the columns would seem weak, without their inward tilt, they would appear to be falling outward; without its curvature, the stylobate would seem to be sagging in the middle; and so forth. In other words, deviations from *geometrical* perfection were used in order to achieve *optical* perfection. (It should be pointed out that, originally, parts of the Parthenon were painted—the details of sculptures, the backgrounds of metopes and

frieze, the triglyphs, and the finials (carved ornaments) on the roof. The rest remained the natural color of Pentelic marble.)

Like fifth-century sculpture, the Parthenon exemplifies a balance between humanistic and idealistic tendencies. Although majestic, the Greek temple is not nearly so large as Egyptian temples, to say nothing of Egyptian pyramids. It is built to a human scale. Further, it could be said that the optical refinements were made to satisfy the human eye rather than the dictates of geometry. But the Parthenon also reflects the striving of Greek architects to achieve perfection, to approximate as closely as humanly possible that which can exist only in the ideal world. Even the 9:4 ratio may have been perceived as some sort of divine proportion. The Parthenon continues to impress the Western mind; it is probably the most renowned architectual monument in the Western world. More significantly, Greek temple architecture supplied the Roman Empire and, later, Western Europe and America, with an endless supply of architectural motifs—columns, capitals, entablatures, pediments, and so forth—for centuries.

Finally, before leaving the Classical period, we should note the invention of a third order, *Corinthian*, which differs from the Ionic order mainly in the design of its capital (Fig. **2.30**). Even the capital is akin to the Ionic in

2.29 Evolution of Doric-order proportions, Archaic to Classical

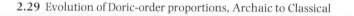

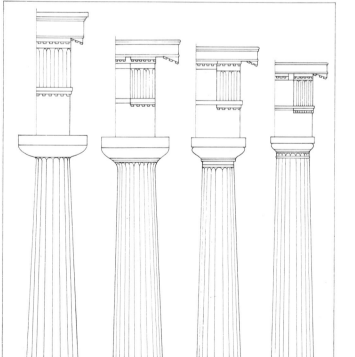

2.30 Corinthian capital, from the tholos at Epidaurus, c. 350 BC

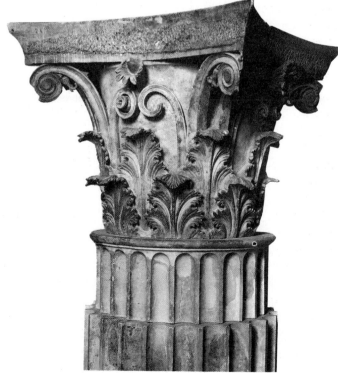

that it consists of four volutes; but these have been reduced in size and combined with a number of stylized acanthus leaves. The design is a successful solution to the challenge of providing a gradual transition between the circular form of a column and the rectangular form of an entablature. Although invented in the fifth century, it was not used on the outside of a building until the fourth century, and then, sparingly.

Hellenistic Art 323–27 BC

The traumatic changes undergone by the Greek world following its conquest by Alexander profoundly affected Greek art—not just in style and subject matter but also in

2.31 *Aphrodite*, Doidalsas

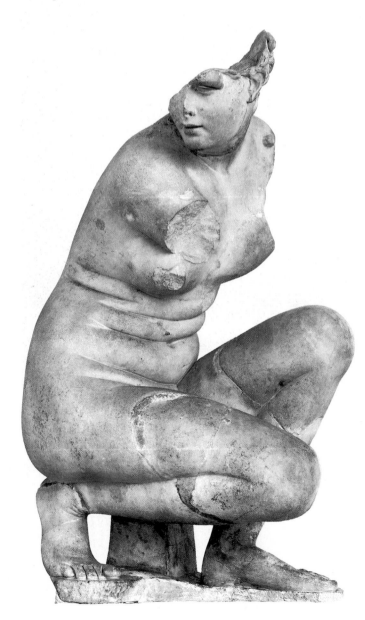

its relationship to the public. As city-states gave way to larger political units and culture became international-ized, artists and artistic styles became less identified with particular cities or ethnic groups. Athens—no longer the major political/economic power—was also no longer the principal center of cultural developments. That role was dispersed and divided among the large cosmopolitan cities of the East, principally Alexandria. The status of the aristocracy, as arbiter of spiritual and artistic standards, declined sharply. Their influence was increasingly usur-ped by the middle classes—the segment of population whose wealth and status depended on commerce rather than land ownership and birthright. The new hero, in a world of money economy and international trade, was the merchant prince.

Although religious subjects were still popular, their lessons were no longer taken seriously. Neither the gods nor the old culture had much authority anymore. Previ-ously unknown categories of subject matter, such as portraits and scenes of everyday life, or *genre*, came into existence. The new public—more pragmatic and less idealistic—tended to prefer art that showed life as it is, not as it should be. Female nudes, which first appeared in the late fourth century, superseded male nudes in popularity. In the guise of goddesses, usually Aphrodite, goddess of love, these sculptures were primarily erotic—that is, intended to inspire sexual fantasies (Fig. **2.31**).

The increased secularism of themes was matched by an increased realism of style. The Hellenistic artist was less limited than his Classical predecessor in the ability to impart movement. Thus, he freely animated his figures by turning their axes in a variety of directions. And because of the new interest in human psychology, he became skilled at providing his figures with intense expressions. However, vivid treatment of movement and facial ex-pression often led to mere virtuosity and melodramatic effects rather than more realism (Fig. **2.32**).

It would appear that Hellenistic culture was a victory of humanism over idealism; that the lessons of the Sophists and the aesthetics of Euripides had come into their own. To a large extent this was true. But artists persisted in giving their figures idealized shapes (though the canons of proportion differed from Polykleitos') and, as mentioned before, religious subjects continued. The new toleration, after all, meant that any theme or style was acceptable, including an old-fashioned one. Indeed, because Hellen-istic Greeks were interested in history (and sometimes sentimental about the past), Hellenistic artists were motivated at times to revive older themes and styles. Hellenistic art, therefore, was not only pluralistic, it was eclectic—selecting from various sources, including the past. Eclecticism led to copying old masterworks, a

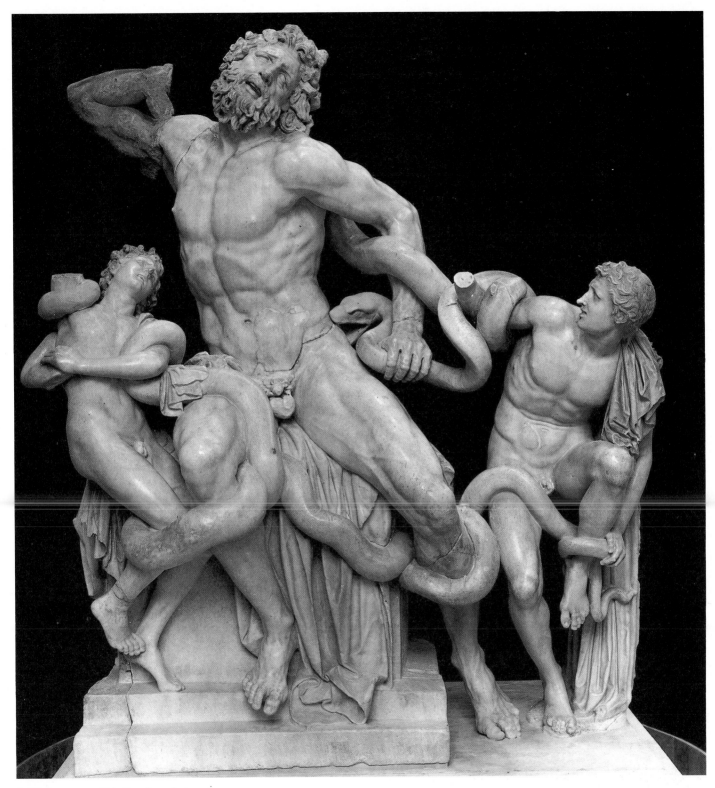

2.32 *Laocoon and his Two Sons*, 1st century AD
Marble, 8 ft (2.24 m) high
Vatican Museums, Rome

practice that became a major industry in the Hellenistic period. Systematic collection of art for its own sake also occurred. Hellenistic art collections anticipated the art museums that we have today. The concept of "art" as we now know it—a body of objects having no utility other than providing private pleasure—was first realized in this period.

The statue of *Demosthenes*, the greatest orator of ancient Athens (Fig. **2.33**), exemplifies several characteristics of Hellenistic art, especially realism. Sculpted in 280 BC, some 42 years after the subject's death, its actual similarity to the man who bravely spoke out against Philip, king of Macedonia, is doubtful. Nevertheless, it is a convincing image of a serious, reflective man whose body shows the stress of physical aging and a troubled spirit. The lines of the face, the scrubby hair and beard, the sagging shoulders, even the customary, though hastily draped, gown are thoroughly lifelike. Furthermore, by means of a somber pose and withdrawn expression, and without traditional idealizing, the statue effectively symbolizes the life of a man who fought a courageous battle with words, lost, and was eventually forced to commit suicide. Demosthenes at this moment could be pondering the fate of his city, himself, or both.

Although impressive buildings were erected during the Hellenistic period, nothing new was added to the traditional Classical orders, at least not on the outsides of temples. In general, buildings were larger (both in plan and elevation), interior spaces were emphasized more than before, and the Ionic order superseded the Doric in popularity. The Temple of Apollo at Didyma (Fig. **2.34**), Ionic on the outside, features a large open court rather than an enclosed cella on the inside (Fig. **2.35**). Entry from the columned porch to the court consists of two concealed barrel-vaulted ramps—another slight innovation as well as a foreshadowing of Roman architecture.

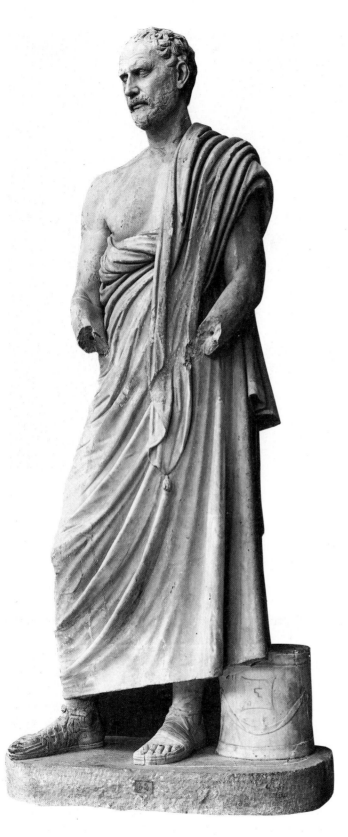

2.33 *Demosthenes*, attrib. Polyeuktos, c. 280 BC
Roman marble copy of bronze original, 80 ins (2 m) high
Vatican Museums, Rome.

2.34 Plan of the Temple of Apollo, Didyma

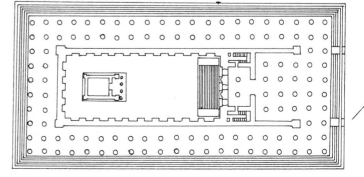

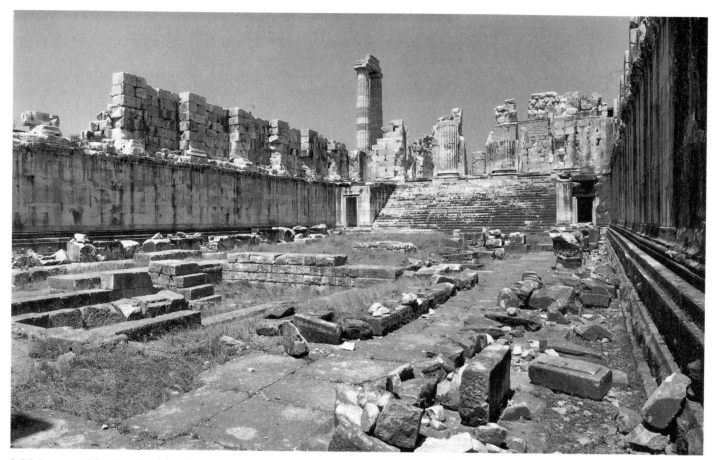

2.35 Interior of the Temple of Apollo, Didyma, near Miletus, Turkey, c. 313 BC

Music of the Golden Age

In the fifth century, important developments in music, like those in drama, sculpture, and architecture, were centered in Athens. In fact, it was in Athens that Greek music—which was, if anything, more highly respected than the visual arts—reached its fullest expression.

Unlike us, Greeks did not think of music and drama being separate, for plays were outgrowths and extensions of dithyrambs, choric hymns to Dionysus. Even in the hands of Aeschylus, Sophocles, and Euripides they were combinations of music, poetry, and dance. The two or three actors sang their lines; so did the chorus, who also often performed a dance, or *orchesis*, in front of the stage, a special place that is still known as the "orchestra" in modern theaters. The Athenian dramatists, unlike playwrights today, who just write words, composed with words and music simultaneously. Indeed all three dramatists were praised by Greeks as musicians as well as poets. We have already studied their works as literary master-

pieces. Unfortunately, we have no real knowledge of them as musical masterpieces, nor any bases for a real understanding of the ways in which these works contributed to the development of music in the fifth century. But we do have, through the parodies of Aristophanes (448–380 BC), an Athenian writer of satirical dramas, an idea of how the music of Aeschylus compared to that of Euripides. In a play called *The Frogs*, a contest is staged between the two, in which Dionysus commands the musico-dramatists to weigh their musical lines on balance scales. It turns out that one mighty line of Aeschylus' is equal to twelve of Euripides'. The latter's music, like his writing, was apparently perceived as insubstantial in comparison to that of the earlier dramatist.

Although we may never know the sound of their music, we do know something of Greek musical theory. According to tradition, it was based on the speculations of Pythagoras, whose own insights were supposedly gathered from Oriental sciences and cults of Egyptian priests. He formulated a cosmology—an explanation of the universe—grounded in numbers. All elements of the system, whether musical notes or planetary bodies, were subject to the same numerical proportions. He discovered that if one string is twice as long as another, though of equal thickness and tension, it will sound exactly one octave lower (middle C to treble C). A 3:2 ratio produces a difference equal to the interval of a fifth (C to G); 4:3, a fourth (C to F—a tetrachord), and so forth. Thus every musical interval could be calculated. Pythagoras' discoveries are still basic to modern acoustical theory. However, some of his other speculations—though influential at the time and, later, during the Middle Ages—have no credibility today. He reasoned that the planets—supposedly moving in orbits around the earth—also produce sounds, "the music of the spheres," the pitch of each depending on its size and speed. The universe, a perfect system numerically and symbolically, was conceived of as a model for a musical system, and vice versa.

The principal elements of Greek music were rhythm, genus, and mode. The rhythm, as we have seen, was related to the rhythm of the poetic text. *Genus* refers to one of three basic types, or *genera*, of tetrachords. Since the outer tones of each of the genera were of the same interval (that is, a fourth), the inner tones and their intervals formed the basis for the differences between the genera. (Since some of these intervals were less than a half step, or semi tone, Greek ears must have been quite sensitive to subtle distinctions of pitch.) *Mode* refers to characteristic patterns of tones—usually based on one of the three genera—associated with different kinds of music (often corresponding to differing ethnic origins). The words "mode" and "mood" have a common Greek root; accordingly, each of the musical modes had a specific emotional quality, evoking a particular mood. According to Aristotle, the Mixolydian mode made men "sad and grave," the Dorian produced "a moderate and settled temper," the Phrygian inspired "enthusiasm," and so forth.[5] The belief that music could affect people thus—not just their moods but their personalities—was known as the doctrine of *ethos*.

Largely because of the doctrine of ethos, music was made a staple of Greek education in the Classical period. Available only to freeborn males, this education included, in addition to music, writing and gymnastics. Of the three subjects, however, music was probably the most important. For one thing, it was civic duty of every free man to participate in community dances and choirs; being unmusical in fifth-century Greece was synonymous with being uneducated. But above all, music, according to the doctrine of ethos, played a leading role in the formation of character; therefore, the kind of music used in teaching was a matter of great concern. Plato, as a critic of fourth-century education and music, had very definite ideas about both. Much of his writing on the subject was motivated by what he perceived to be a contemporary corruption of fifth-century standards. He proposed three years of instruction at a time when it was reduced to two. In his education of "guardians"—the ruling elite of his proposed ideal society—he recommends a proper balance between gymnastics and music. Too much of the former tended to make a man brutish; too much of the latter, soft. As to music, in an analogy between rich food and certain kinds of music that "engender licentiousness," he allows that simplicity in music "begets sobriety in the soul." He preferred stringed instruments ("the instruments of Apollo") to wind instruments and the Dorian mode to the Ionian. The latter was too "soft and convivial" and inappropriate for warriors, whereas the former befitted the character and behavior of both "brave and temperate" men[6]. Essentially, Plato was attempting to save the Classical tradition in education.

Both Plato and Aristotle felt that music had declined in their time. The debilitating effects of the Peloponnesian War may have been a cause. Because of financial restrictions the choruses were reduced in size. Musical education, as we have seen, was cut back; the best school of music in Athens was closed. More seriously, musical structure of the fifth century, along with the standards of taste that supported that structure, seemed to be unraveling. Aristophanes chides Euripidean music for its wavering, formless melodic line, implying that Classical tonality was breaking down. Plato berates poets who were "ignorant of the laws of music," judging it by the pleasure it gave rather than by more objective standards.[7] He accused the composers of dithyrambs of pandering to popular taste by consciously rejecting educated standards and engaging in sensationalism. Under these conditions, the art of the virtuoso performer comes to the fore and begins to compete with that of the poet-musician and the amateur singer-dancer—the people who were so vital to the Classical tradition. Unfortunately for posterity, the Classical styles of music that Plato, Aristotle, and Aristophanes admired existed in their memories, not in notes inscribed on papyrus or stone. Therefore, when these styles evolved into newer and different forms, whether for good or ill, they ceased to be played. And when eventually they ceased to be remembered, they disappeared. Unlike Classical art, Classical music could not be revived.

The decline continued into the Hellenistic period to such an extent that the musical culture of Greece perhaps reached its nadir. The emphasis on entertainment and virtuosity, begun in the late Classical period, became the rule rather than the exception. Variety shows featuring comedy, bad jokes, pantomime, and acrobatics replaced tragedy. Mass concerts featuring huge choirs, instrumental solos, or instrumental duets replaced performances of epic poets. By this time, virtuoso performers were more famous than poet-composers; patrons no longer demanded original music. Therefore the production of new music was devalued and the role of amateur performers was trivialized. The Classical unity of music and poetry was broken: poets could no longer make music; professional musicians could not write verse. Popular musical performers in Hellenistic Greece, like some today, were highly paid, but of low social standing. Although some music was written down, little was stored because none was valued. Music was, at best, an enjoyable diversion; at worst, a vulgarizing influence. The middle classes did not take it seriously; the upper classes no longer pursued it. Needless to say, music in education languished.

Thus, a once-lively, creative art form had declined to the level of mere entertainment. However, Greek music did not die; it survived, not in sound, but as a body of theories. Although Plato and Aristotle, the greatest philosophers of the ancient world, truly understood the music of their time (including the practice of it), their credentials in philosophy were so overwhelming that later writers misconstrued and transformed their musical insights into a branch of philosophy. Texts by these writers were filled with speculations on the music of the spheres, the science of number, and non-existent scales. Indeed, this false legacy of Greek music held philosophers, musical scholars, and even architects in thrall for centuries. On the positive side, it contributed to the formulations of, among other things, medieval music and Renaissance architecture. But it had nothing to do with the practice of Greek music, only with the metaphysics of it.

The Roman Epic

Roman literature, like Roman art, was primarily imitative of the Greeks. But this is not to disparage the Roman contribution to the literature of Western civilization. The so-called Golden Age of Latin literature (70 BC–AD 14) produced, at its outset, such major writers as the philosopher Lucretius and the orator Cicero. In the literary period following the accession of Augustus in 27 BC (named, appropriately, the Augustan age), Roman civilization reached its peak, as Athenian civilization had under Pericles. Virgil, Horace, Ovid, and Livy were the outstanding literary figures of this era, but their influence was not confined to the Golden Age—they were destined to play a major role in the development of the Western literary tradition. This is pre-eminently true of Virgil and of his best-known work, the *Aeneid*.

Virgil's Aeneid

Publius Vergilius Maro (70–19 BC) was born near Mantua in northern Italy, where his parents, who were moderately well-to-do, owned a farm. He obtained a good education, completing his studies in Rome. There he perhaps first met the young Octavian, later to become Augustus Caesar, the first Roman emperor. Virgil, shy and in poor health, was not of the disposition to enter public life, so he retired to his father's farm to write poetry. This phase of his career, however, could not last. His ancestral property was confiscated in the political chaos attending the civil war that brought the Republic to an end and prepared the way for the rise of Augustus, who later restored Virgil's property.

Between 42 and 37 BC Virgil composed a series of ten pastoral poems entitled the *Eclogues*, or *Bucolics*. These poems are characterized by an ideal beauty manifested in nature and the songs sung by shepherds. The most famous of the Eclogues, the Fourth, predicts the birth of a child who will usher in a golden age of peace and joy. Because of the messianic overtones of this poem, Virgil was regarded during the Middle Ages as a pagan prophet of the birth of Christ—one of the reasons for his great significance in this period. The identity of Virgil's messianic child remains unknown.

The *Eclogues* perhaps offer some evidence of the restoration of Virgil's property. What can be said with certainty, however, is that by the time they were published, he had become a member of the literary circle of Maecenas, the chief minister of Augustus. As a result of this patronage, he was granted an estate and provided with the financial backing and encouragement to continue his writing career.

It was in this period that Virgil, urged by Maecenas, who sought support for Augustus' policy of agricultural revival, composed his *Georgics*, a poem on the duties of those who work the soil. Idealizing the role of the Roman farmer, this poem traces the activities of farm life throughout the year. There is much practical advice in this work,

DATES	SOCIAL AND POLITICAL DEVELOPMENTS	LITERATURE AND PHILOSOPHY	VISUAL ARTS	ARCHITECTURE	MUSIC
753 BC	Legendary founding of Rome				
300	First Punic War Second Punic War				
200	Third Punic War Destruction of Carthage			First stone theaters in Rome Temple of Fortuna, Rome (**2.43**)	Instruments: harp, kithara, tibia, cornu, lithus, drum, cymbols, tambourine, utricularius, organ
100 0	Julius Caesar Augustus – founding of Roman Empire	Golden Age of Latin Literature Lucretius and Cicero Virgil (**2.38**) Horace Ovid Livy	*Augustus of Primaporta* (**2.42**)	Pont du Gard (aqueduct) (**2.44**) Temple of Mars Ultor (**2.46**)	
100 AD	Nero		Portrait bust (**2.41**)	Forum of Augustus (**2.45**) The Colosseum (**2.50**)	Nero's concerts in Greece
200				Pantheon, Rome (**2.52**, **2.53**)	

2.36 Ancient Rome

but its true significance lies in its presentation of the beauty of nature and of all living things, patriotic duty, and the mystery at the heart of life, a profound concern of Virgil's.

Perhaps sometime during the seven years that he worked on the *Georgics*, Virgil began to lay plans for the writing of an epic in praise of Rome and Augustus. He devoted the last ten years of his life (29–19 BC) to this task. At the time of his death, which occurred shortly after his return to Italy from a trip to Greece, he had completed this major work but intended to spend three years revising it. The poem, in his view, fell so far short of his conception that he wished to have it destroyed. Augustus, however, would not allow this, and it was published two years later.

Begun in 29 BC, two years after the battle of Actium brought an end to the half century of civil wars that had ravaged Italy and the provinces, Virgil's *Aeneid* was written during the transition period from the Republic to the Empire. In the transition Augustus assumed dictatorial powers, but under the forms of the Republic. Virgil saw in Augustus the hope of the establishment of peace and order and the restoration of Roman greatness. Thus he set out to celebrate Augustus and Rome in his national epic. In doing so he turned his gaze to the past; not, however, the historical but the legendary past. The heart of the legend, accepted as fact by the Romans, was that the

Roman nation was founded by Trojan survivors of the Greek overthrow of Troy and that Aeneas, a Trojan prince and their leader, was the ancestor of Augustus. In fuller form, the story told was that Aeneas (son of Anchises and the goddess Venus) fought through and survived the final battle of Troy because he was destined to rule his people. In his escape from the doomed city, he lost his wife Creusa, but was able to save his father and his son Ascanius (also called Iulus). Gathering a band of survivors, Aeneas built a ship and set out to establish a home for his people in Italy. After seven years of wandering, they finally arrived in Sicily, where Anchises died. Setting out once again for the Italian mainland, they encountered a raging storm sent by the goddess Juno and were driven on to the coast of Africa, near the spot where Dido, an exile from Tyre, was building the city of Carthage. Although it involved compromising her reputation and neglecting the building of Carthage, Dido, prompted by Aeneas' divine mother Venus, fell passionately in love with him. Aeneas seemed to reciprocate this love, but was brought back to an awareness of his divine destiny to found a kingdom in Italy by a message from Jupiter (Greek Zeus). Obediently he slipped away from Dido and set sail for Italy. Dido, overwhelmed by grief and frustrated love, committed suicide.

The first landing of the Trojans in Italy was near

Cumae. There Aeneas, under the guidance of the prophetic Sibyl, descended into Hades, the realm of the dead; Anchises (now among the blessed) then became his guide and pointed out the souls of great Romans yet unborn. Thus Aeneas was given a glimpse of his destiny.

Sailing northward along the west coast of Italy, the Trojans landed at Latium, near the mouth of the Tiber River. King Latinus of Latium had a daughter, Lavinia, who, according to an oracle, was to marry a foreign prince. The king identified Aeneas as the predicted prince and offered him Lavinia. Juno, however, always opposed to the Trojans, stirred up Turnus, king of the Rutulians and a suitor of Lavinia, to attack the Trojans. Each side found allies, and a bitter protracted struggle ensued, ending only after Aeneas succeeded in killing Turnus. Aeneas then was able to build the city of Lavinium, named

for his wife. After ruling three years, he was taken up into heaven. His son Ascanius succeeded him and moved his people to Alba Longa. There Romulus and Remus, the legendary founders of Rome, were born. Virgil concludes his poem, however, with the death of Turnus, who had been the final obstacle to the fulfillment of Aeneas' destiny as the ancestor of the Romans.

Instead of telling this story in chronological order, Virgil follows the epic convention of beginning *in medias res* ("in the midst of things"). In this Homeric convention (well illustrated by the *Iliad*) the story begins at a high point of the action, and background information is supplied by flashbacks. Thus Virgil commences his poem with the storm that drives Aeneas to Carthage. Then, during the feast that Dido holds in Aeneas' honor (Book II), Virgil has his hero tell the story of the escape from Troy and the

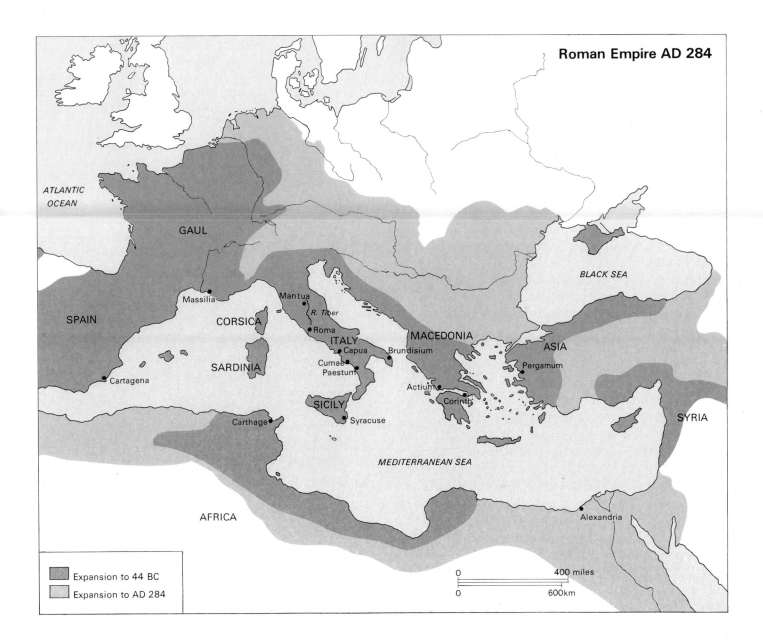

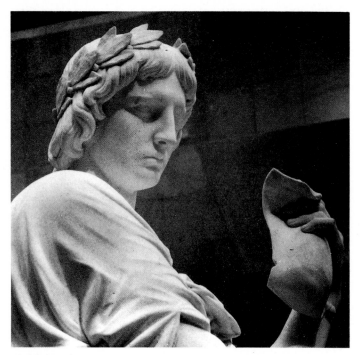

2.38 Virgil

wanderings that brought the Trojans to Carthage.

Virgil borrowed often and extensively from Homer, but did so creatively. The wanderings of Aeneas (Books I – VI) are patterned after those of Odysseus in the *Odyssey*—for example the storm and shipwreck, the hero's narration of his adventures at a banquet held in his honor, and the descent into Hades, where the hero's future is predicted. Books VII – XII, which tell the story of the war in Italy, are indebted to the *Iliad*—for example, in the battle scenes, the attack on the ships, the armor of the hero being fashioned by a god, the funeral games, and the duel at the end between the protagonists of the opposing armies.

But Virgil's hero is very different from Homeric heroes. The chief responsibility of the Homeric hero is to his sense of his own excellence as a warrior, vividly illustrated by Achilles, who withdraws his support from the Greeks because he has been insulted by King Agamemnon. Aeneas, however, bears the burden of destiny, which takes precedence over all personal considerations. Thus, when the message comes from Jupiter recalling Aeneas to the fulfillment of that destiny, he is swiftly brought back to his sense of duty, as a consequence forsaking Dido. It is for this devotion to the duty imposed by destiny that Virgil gives him the epithet, "Aeneas the True" (*pius*). On occasion, Aeneas can become sidetracked from his destiny, as in his romantic involvement with Dido, but never does he become permanently deterred by egocentric considerations. He is true to his family, his friends, the gods and, above all, his destiny to become the founder of

Roman civilization. It is this commitment that causes some readers to conclude that he is cold and inhuman, especially in his relationship with Dido.

Indeed, Dido has fared much better than Aeneas with romantic readers of Virgil's poem. They admire her warm and passionate nature and applaud her spurning of Aeneas when he encounters her in Hades. In his pre-conversion days, St. Augustine (see Chapter 6), so he tells us in his *Confessions*, lamented her suicide for love. But to the Romans of Virgil's day, Dido, as the founder of Carthage, represented the violent and prolonged Punic wars which ravaged Italy and Carthage in the third and second centuries BC. She also would have reminded them of the disastrous involvement of Mark Antony with Cleopatra.

The philosophic underpinnings of Virgil's poem, reflected especially in Book VI, are eclectic. The Stoic element is illustrated by Anchises' speech on the "World Soul" that permeates all things. It is also shown in the poem's dramatization of the dangers of excessive emotion, as when Aeneas becomes involved with Dido. Pythagorean philosophy is evident in the doctrine of reincarnation explicated by Anchises as he points out to Aeneas the line of previously embodied Roman souls awaiting re-embodiment. There is also evidence of Platonic mysticism in the view that affirms the pre-existence of the soul and its

2.39 *Dido sacrificing*, illustration to Virgil's *Aeneid*, early 5th century AD, Biblioteca Apostolica, Vatican. Ms. lat. 3225 f.33v.

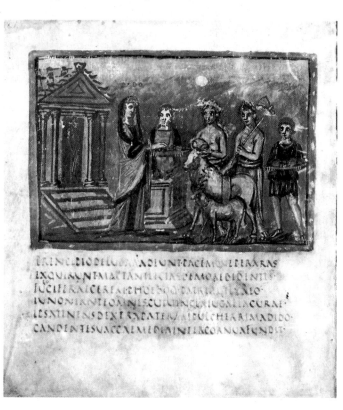

involvement with an unseen eternal world before entrance into this world.

Regarded by modern critics as the best of the Roman poets, Virgil was also held in high regard by the critics of his own time, not to mention Augustus and the imperial court, who accorded him honors and patronage that enabled him to become a wealthy man. The Roman people also greatly respected him, and his influence on later Roman writers was profound. He continued to be read and to exert a strong influence on the Christians of the Middle Ages, a veneration especially evident in the fact that Dante called him his "sweet master" and used him as his guide through the inferno and the purgatory of his *Divine Comedy*. In fact, Virgil was worshipped as a god not long after his death and was regarded by Christians as "the prophet of the Gentiles." He was also believed to be a white magician, and in the Middle Ages books were written extolling his miracles.

Roman Art

Rome's rise to power occurred within the context of Hellenistic culture. Therefore most of its own early culture was inherited rather than indigenous; this was especially true in the visual arts. Roman artists, like Roman writers, freely borrowed from the Greeks. However, many artists did more than borrow; they copied Greek works outright.

2.40 *Ulysses in the Land of the Lestrygonians*, part of the *Odyssey Landscapes*, wall painting from a house in Rome, late first century BC. Approx 60 ins (152 cm) high. Vatican Library, Rome

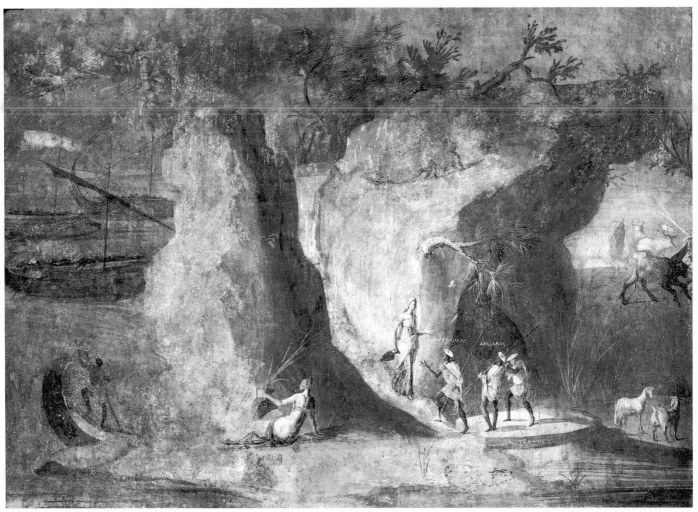

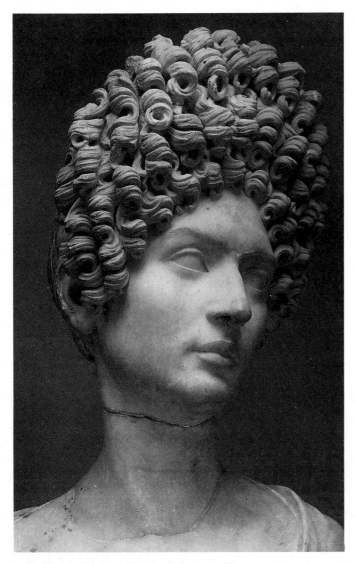

2.41 Portrait bust of a Roman lady, c. AD 90
Marble, life-size
Museo Capitalino, Rome

And many supposedly "Roman" artists were actually Greeks. Thus, the thread of continuity between Hellenistic art and Roman art—particularly during the Republic and early Empire—was virtually unbroken. Nevertheless, by the time of Augustus, important developments within this tradition began to take place in Rome, not the eastern Mediterranean.

Most Roman art was secular. Some of it, serving as objects to be admired and collected, performed the same function in Roman society that fine art does in our own time. Other examples, intended to entertain and provide escape from everyday life, or even to decorate a home (Fig. **2.40**), satisfied the same needs as today's popular art. Still other works of art were intended to glorify the emperor or the state.

Oppositions in Greek art, such as Ionic versus Doric, have already been discussed. In Roman art there is one overriding opposition: Greek versus Roman. In other words, to what extent is a work of art Hellenistic? To what extent is it native Roman? The answer depends not only on the period of time, but also on which of the visual arts is under consideration. With the passage of time Greek influence decreased; by the third century—when the copying of Greek art stopped—the evolution of Roman art became more independent. In the early Empire—the period we will be examining—Greek qualities predominate in the arts of sculpture and painting, whereas Roman ideas and methods play a major role in the art of architecture.

Sculpture

Apparently the extensive plundering of Hellenistic cities had not satisfied the insatiable demand of wealthy Romans for Greek art. Therefore, a large copy industry developed, exceeding even the thriving one run by the Hellenistic Greeks. Around 100 BC the Romans invented a method of copying using points mapped out on the copy that correspond exactly to points on the original. Capable of producing virtually exact copies, the method tended to obscure the difference between original and copy. Our modern notion of "fake" art had either not occurred to Romans or not been a cause of concern. Nevertheless, because of Roman ingenuity, many Greek works that exist only in copies, can be appreciated and studied with some degree of confidence.

Copies aside, even Roman originals produced during the reign of Augustus are very Greek in style. Compare the emperor's portrait, *Augustus of Primaporta* (Fig. **2.42**), with *Spear Carrier*. Both share the same stocky proportions, calm bearing, position of the feet, round head, triangular face, and even the same hair style. The resemblance is no accident, for Augustus himself was an admirer of Greek culture and deliberately promoted the Classical period as a model for the new imperial art. However, some things on the statue are unmistakably Roman: the breastplate (bearing a relief of a Roman theme) and the particular details of the face, which probably resemble more the features of Augustus' face than those of a Greek god. Commitment to realism at the time was very strong in Roman art, particularly in portrait busts (Fig. **2.41**). Some of this has made its way into Augustus' portrait despite its classicism.

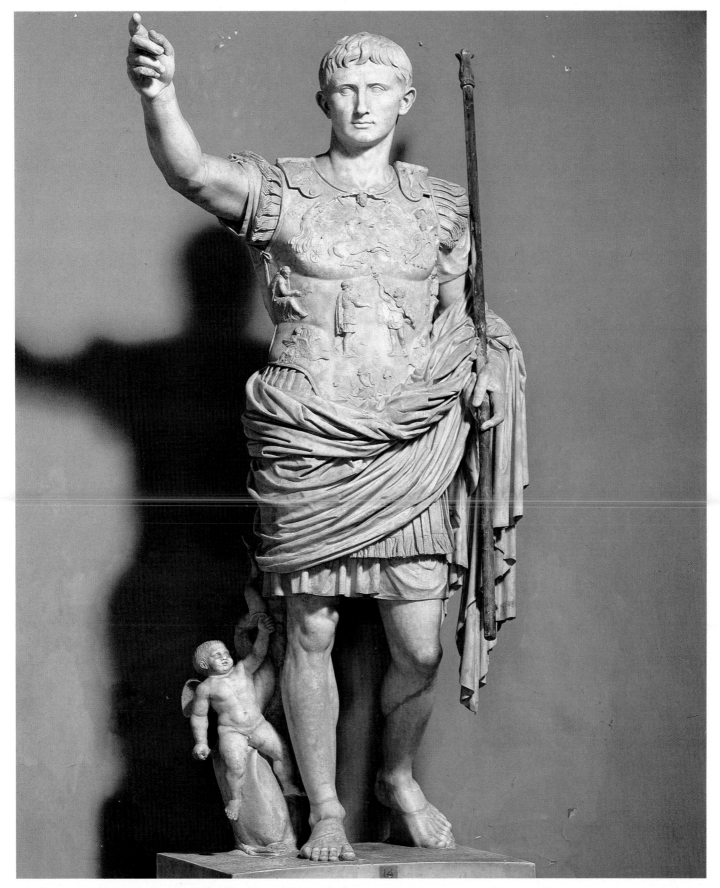

2.42 *Augustus of Primaporta*, c. 20 BC. Marble, 80 ins (203 cm) high. Vatican Museums, Rome

Architecture

Like Roman religion, Roman temples—particularly those that are column-supported rectangular buildings (Fig. 2.43)—are indebted to the Greeks (and also the Etruscans). Also, many of the law courts, money exchanges, treasuries, record offices, assemblies, and so forth, found in Roman civic centers or *fora*, remind one of Greek temples and stoas. But the various structures designed for recreation and entertainment—gymnasiums, public baths, theatres, race tracks, and stadiums (Fig. 2.50)—are larger and far more innovative than any found even in Hellenistic Greece. Further, as engineer-architects, Romans were bolder than their Greek counter-

parts, building impressive utilitarian projects—harbors, bridges, sewers, and water conduits called *aqueducts* (Fig. 2.44)—not only in Rome but all over Italy and the provinces.

As we saw earlier, Greek influence peaked during the reign of Augustus. And this was as true for architecture as it was for sculpture. Importing foreign craftsmen and architects, the emperor set out to make Rome in the image of Classical Greece. He rebuilt temples and created the Forum of Augustus (Fig. 2.45) just north of the old Roman forum; his son-in-law Agrippa laid out a new building complex in the northwest section of the city and repaired its sewers. But Augustus' most important project was transforming the old forum—at the time a crowded

2.43 Temple of Fortuna, Rome, late 2nd century BC

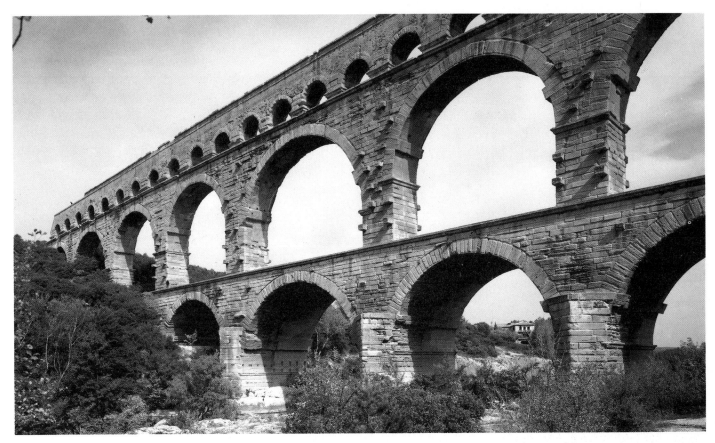

2.44 Aqueduct, Pont du Gard, near Nîmes, France, 1st century BC

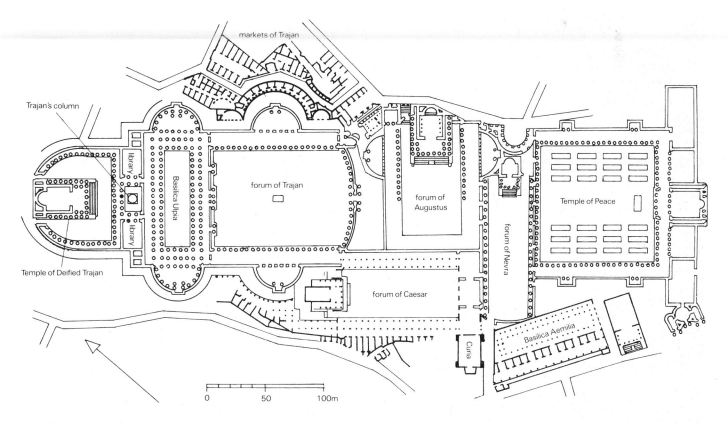

2.45 Plan of the Forums at Rome

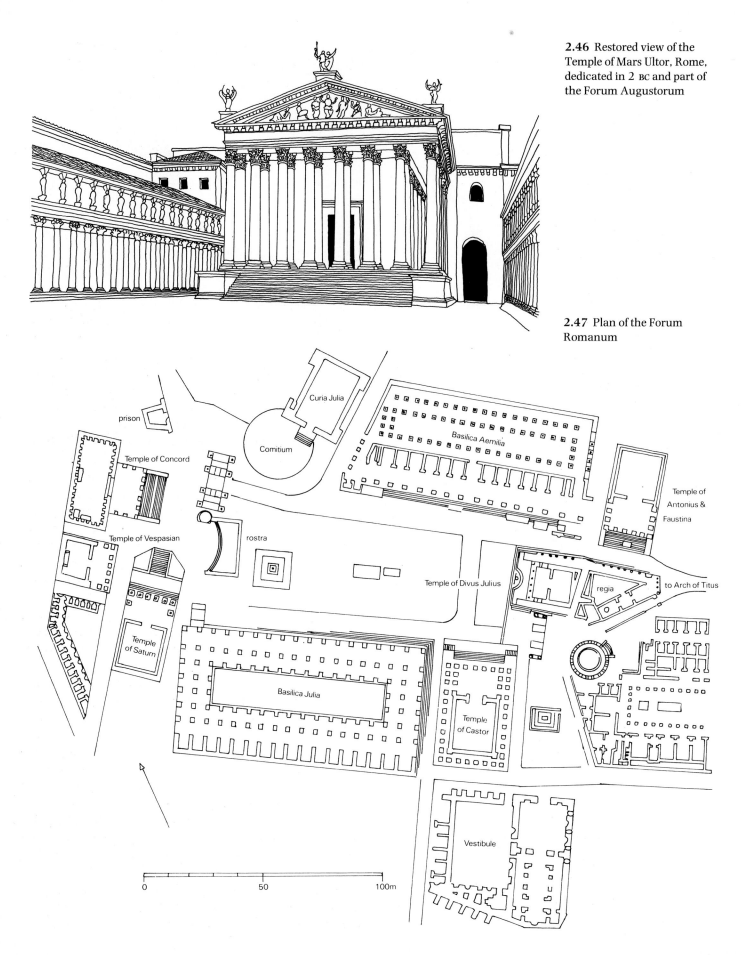

2.46 Restored view of the Temple of Mars Ultor, Rome, dedicated in 2 BC and part of the Forum Augustorum

2.47 Plan of the Forum Romanum

prison

Curia Julia

Comitium

Temple of Concord

Basilica Aemilia

Temple of Antonius & Faustina

Temple of Vespasian

rostra

Temple of Divus Julius

regia

to Arch of Titus

Temple of Saturn

Basilica Julia

Temple of Castor

Vestibule

0   50   100m

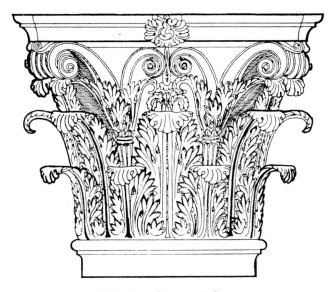

2.48 Corinthian capital

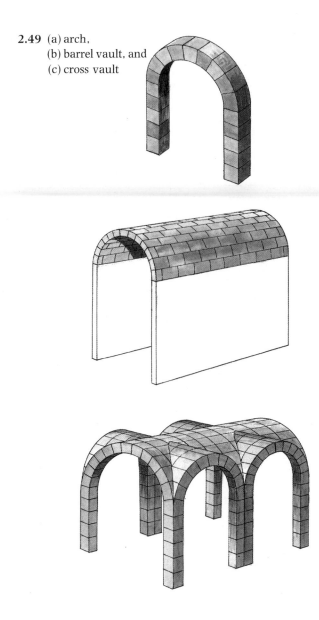

2.49 (a) arch,
(b) barrel vault, and
(c) cross vault

marketplace. There, he oversaw the completion of two large basilicas (legal centers), a meeting place for the senate and three temples, including that of Mars Ultor (Fig. **2.46**). The Arch of Titus and the Arch of Septimius Severus were added at a later date. According to Suetonius, Augustus boasted that he "found Rome a city of brick and left it a city of marble". The style of the new forum (Fig. **2.47**) was essentially Hellenistic—large buildings with pediments, double colonnades, and Corinthian capitals. But the effort was not entirely a matter of borrowing Greek forms; the emperor's architects also improved on some of them. For one thing, they developed the Roman Corinthian order, a refined version of the Greek original and the style used throughout the Empire for the next three centuries (Fig. **2.48**).

Under Augustus, Rome became a center of Hellenistic art and architecture. It served not only to train its own artisans in Greek styles and methods but to set high standards for coming generations. Nevertheless, the most impressive examples of Roman building are those based on Roman inventiveness, not Greek principles. Before reviewing those examples it will be necessary first to understand the *arch system* of construction.

The post and lintel method, as we saw earlier, is limited because of stone's inherent lack of tensile strength. A masonry lintel or beam cannot span much more than 20 feet (6 meters). Because of this the interior of an Egyptian temple is a dark and crowded forest of columns. Because of this Greeks used wooden ceiling beams (which are both lighter and stronger in tensile strength) on the insides of their temples; but, of course, wood is not permanent. An arch (Fig. **2.49**), which uses a number of small stones in a curve rather than a single horizontal stone to span a space, overcomes stone's disadvantage. The wedge-shaped blocks press against one another rather than falling. During construction, the stones of an arch are supported by a temporary wooden framework—or *centering*—until the last stone is in place. The vertical pull of gravity, which is thwarted by the arch, is converted to horizontal thrust, which exerts outward pressure on the supporting posts. A *barrel vault* (Fig. **2.49**)—an arch extended in depth—can be used to cover a rectangular area. However, because of the problem of horizontal thrust, it requires heavy walls for support along its entire length. A *cross vault* (Fig. **2.49**), formed by two intersecting barrel vaults, is an improvement on the barrel vault because it permits the support to be focused at just four points. Finally, another variation is the *dome* which is simply a radial form of the arch to cover a circular area.

The Romans did not invent the arch, but they alone among the ancients developed it. Another technology—also developed, though not invented, by the Romans—

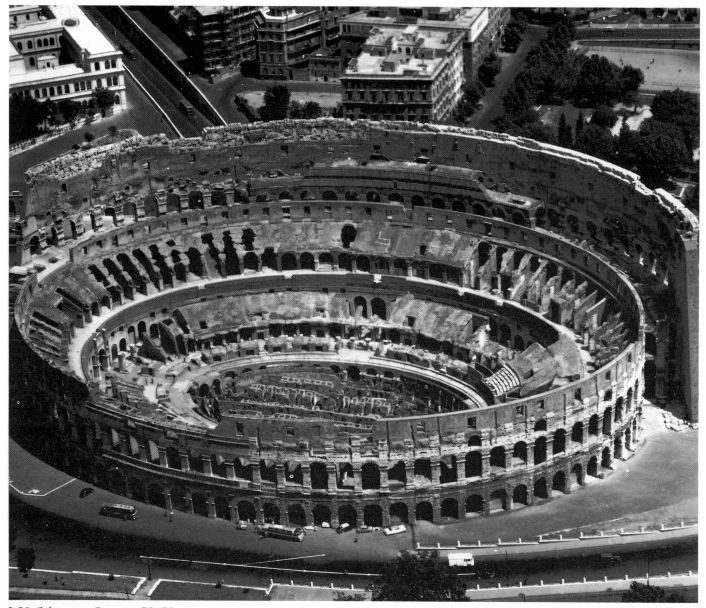

2.50 Colosseum, Rome, c. 70–82 AD

2.51 Sectional diagram of the Colosseum

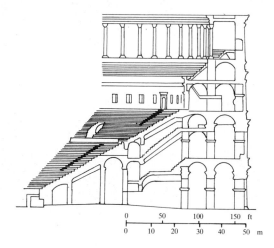

was equally important to their architectural achievements; this was the making of concrete. By the third century BC, the Romans had evolved a strong mortar which, in combination with an aggregate of small stones and facing bricks, produced strong walls. By the time of Augustus, they were making the mixture even stronger with the addition of a reddish volcanic dust. When using concrete, Roman architects resorted to the same forms described above: arches, barrel vaults, cross vaults, and domes. Concrete, like stone, is a type of masonry. Without the reinforcement of steel rods (as in modern ferroconcrete construction), it also lacks tensile strength. Therefore, to span a space and not crack, concrete must be cast in curved configurations like those of the arch system. Both technologies—arch and concrete—answered Roman needs for durable, practical structures featuring interior space. By using both—separately or in combination—they created striking new architectural forms.

Apart from being an extraordinary piece of architecture, the legendary Colosseum—started under Vespasian and dedicated by Titus—is a textbook of Roman construction methods (Figs. **2.50, 2.51**). Using a combination of stone and concrete, its builders exploited the arch system (excepting the dome) to its fullest: three levels of *arcades*—repeated arches—ring the outside (Fig. **2.52**), one system of barrel-vaulted corridors radiates from the arena, ano-

ther system runs concentrically around the stadium at all levels, cross vaults occur at intersections, and all the vaults combined provide a superstructure to support the stadium seats (which at one time held 50,000). The materials are travertine—a hard limestone—on the outside, with tufa—a porous volcanic stone—and concrete on the inside. Oval shaped, the Colosseum is 620 feet (189 meters) long, 513 feet (156 meters) wide, and 157 feet (47 meters) high—as tall as a 13-story building. In area alone it is ten times the size of the Parthenon. Beneath its arena is an infrastructure of vaults and compartments which at

2.52 Colosseum exterior, showing the three orders

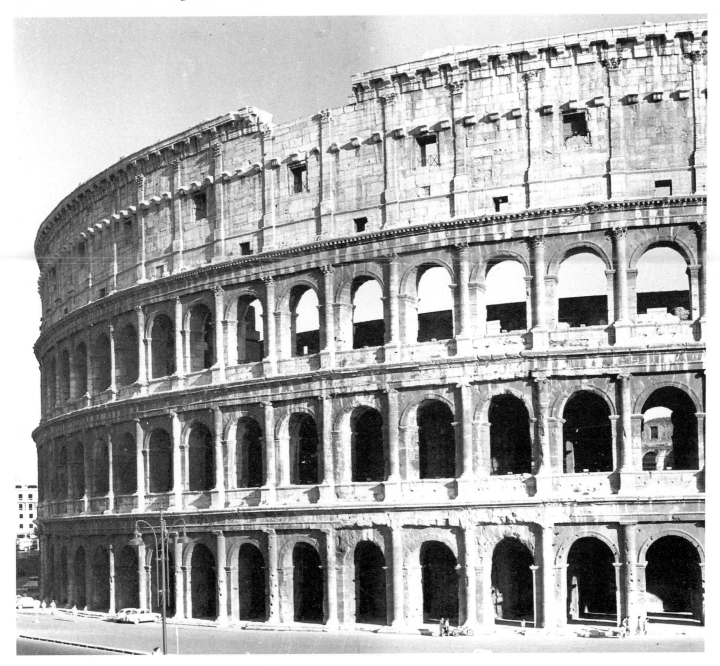

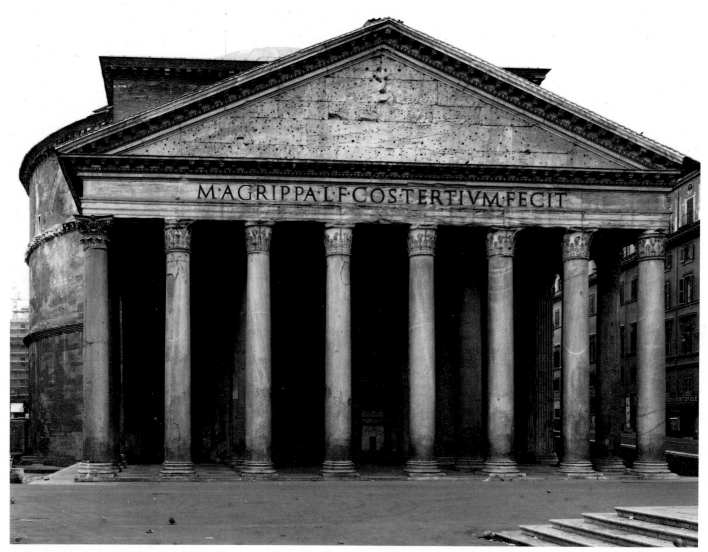

2.53 The Pantheon, Rome, c. 118–125 AD

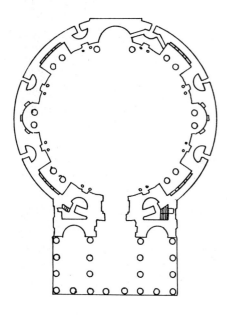

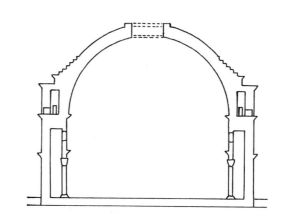

2.54 Plan and section of the Pantheon

one time included 32 cells for wild animals. At its dedication more than 5000 animals were killed. For the opening performance the arena was flooded for a mock naval battle involving 3000 actors. It was built in just five years—perhaps the most impressive statistic of all.

Is there anything Greek at all about a marvel of Roman engineering used for such profane purposes? Yes, there is. On the exterior, the arches are framed with attached, non-functional columns consisting of, starting at the bottom, Tuscan (a Roman order similar to the Doric), Ionic, and Corinthian orders. Corinthian pilasters (flat columns) and entablature adorn the fourth story. Thus, the dualism:

Roman technology overlaid with Greek decoration.

With the Pantheon (Figs. **2.53**, **2.54**)—constructed during the reign of Hadrian—Roman technology is almost completely concealed, from the front, by a Greek porch. Approaching the building at street level, a visitor can barely see its dome above the massive pediment. (Originally, when the street level was several steps lower, the dome was even less visible.) Its vast dimensions—144 feet (44 meters) in diameter and 144 feet (44 meters) off the floor—become apparent only when one is inside (Fig. **2.55**). Resting on a thick masonry drum, the dome itself is a solid concrete shell with an *oculus*, or round

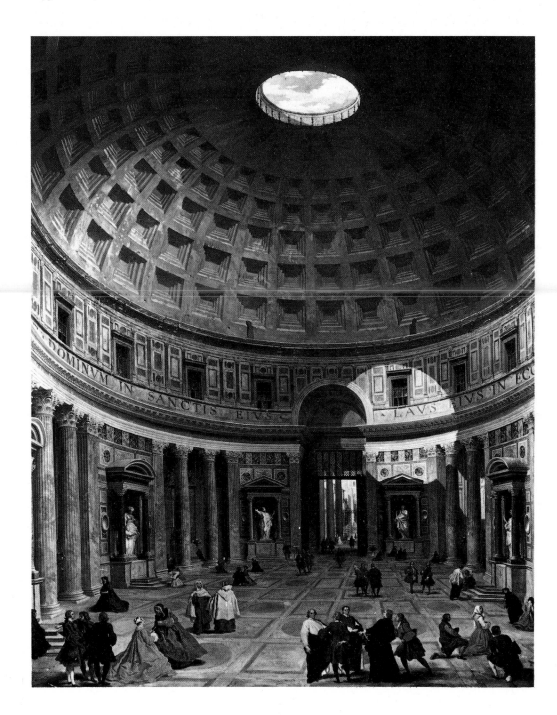

2.55 *The Interior of the Pantheon*, Giovanni Paolo Panini, c. 1740
National Gallery of Art, Washington DC
(Samuel H. Kress Collection)

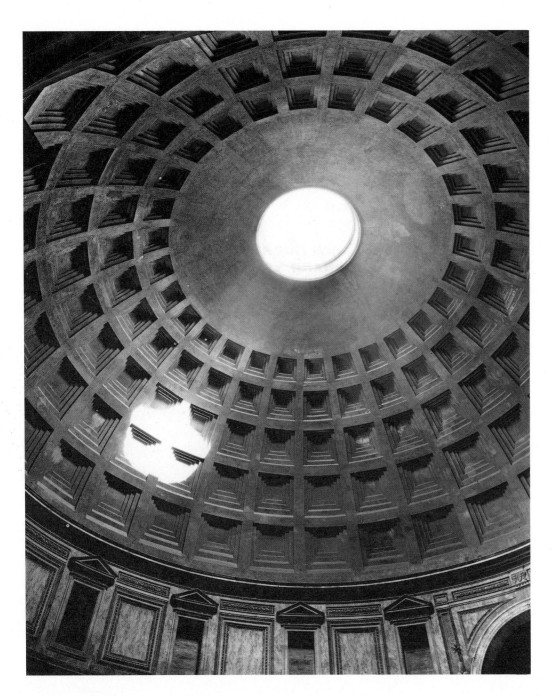

opening, at the top. Dedicated to the seven planetary gods it is a simulacrum of the dome of the sky—not unlike a planetarium. On sunlit days the sun, streaming through the oculus, forms a disk which moves across the surface of the walls and floor with the speed of the sun itself (Fig. **2.56**). In antiquity, the 140 *coffers*, or sunken panels, lining the dome were decorated with bronze rosettes—perhaps to suggest stars. Immediately below the dome the upper part of the drum consists of a series of rectangles alternating with blind windows sporting pediments. The walls of the lower part contain seven recesses (for each of the seven gods) flanked by Corinthian pilasters, alternat-

ing with four pairs of massive Corinthian columns—an echo of the portico, on which Hadrian had inscribed the name of Agrippa, the builder of the original Pantheon.

One of the best-preserved examples of all pre-Christian Roman architecture, the Pantheon was converted to a church in the seventh century and thus escaped the dismantling that befell almost all other Roman buildings. It inspired architects of both the Byzantine and Renaissance eras. The dome, in particular, served as a model for Renaissance architects, who went on to develop elongated versions that crown many religious and civic buildings throughout Europe and America.

Roman Music

Scholars are divided over the significance of Roman music. Some say that, at best, it was Greek music transplanted to Roman soil, at worst, a further degeneration of a tradition which had started to decay in the fourth century BC. Even Romans denounced it; poets, especially, satirized it for its pretentiousness and, at times, vulgarity. Other scholars, while conceding some of these faults, argue that Roman music at least played an important role in its own society.

Like Roman art, Roman music was not entirely indigenous, owing much of its character to both Etruscan and Greek influences. After the conquest of Greece in 146 BC, Roman music, like much of Roman culture, became virtually Hellenistic. Nevertheless, Roman musicians adapted from their sources and modified musical traditions to suit native requirements. Like Roman architecture, Roman music was practical, an "applied" art form intended to serve the needs of Roman daily and public life. Roman music was marked by the same dualism as Roman art: it was both Greek and Roman, though the dividing line between the two is uncertain, especially in the case of music.

Roman musicians, unlike Roman artists, had no access to the works of Classical Greece in their discipline. As we have seen, fifth-century Greek music was little more than a memory even in the time of Plato; after that it disappeared. Accordingly, there is little reason to believe that during the reign of Augustus the musical arts experienced a Classical revival, as did the visual arts and literature. In fact, there is no evidence to suggest that Augustus himself was even interested in music.

The lyre almost disappeared, while its cousin, the *kithara*, acquired more strings and a larger sounding-board. The harp, rarely used by Greeks, was popular with Romans. To the panpipes, aulos (Roman *tibia*), and salpinx (Roman *tuba*), Romans added the *cornu*, a bronze horn bent into a half circle, and the *lituus*, a J-shaped bronze horn. Other wind instruments included the *utricularius*, a type of bagpipe, and an organ driven by water pressure. Percussion instruments included several kinds of drum, cymbals, tambourines, and bells.

Music was played during and after banquets, sometimes, apparently, to the detriment of conversation. The rich could afford concerts in their homes and sometimes commanded slaves to play music continually for their pleasure (and often, no doubt, the displeasure of their neighbors). Commoners could enjoy the antics of street musicians, who not only played music but juggled and performed acrobatics. No funeral was complete without the accompaniment of horns.

In public performances a division between serious and popular music seems to have existed, not unlike our own distinction between "classical" and "popular". Pantomimes—dances performed without words by single actors—appealed only to those with "educated" tastes, people who knew the stories and could recognize the dance movements. Most Romans tended to prefer the music played in amphitheaters such as the Colosseum; there, the various shows, including gladiatorial contests, were introduced by performances of tubas and organs. In one series of games one hundred horns played together. Like Hellenistic Greeks, the Romans were attracted to virtuoso performances; exceptionally talented soloists were in great demand and received enormous fees.

But amateur music-making also thrived. Many members of the aristocracy and royalty, including several emperors, took pride in their musical ability. Among the musically talented Roman emperors were Caligula, Titus, Hadrian, Commodus, and, of course, Nero. Notorious for having, according to legend, played his harp while Rome burned (and for many acts of cruelty), he was, in fact, an accomplished musician. In AD 66–68 he toured Greece, playing in concerts and festivals, (accompanied by a claque of several thousand paid applauders).

The fact that he toured Greece suggests that Nero, for all his power, shared the awe that many other Romans still felt for Greek culture. Though now merely a Roman possession, Greece was still acknowledged as the wellspring of classical civilization. The next chapter, "Classicism II: The Renaissance," calls attention to generations of Europeans living 1300 to 1500 years later for whom the arts of both Greece and Rome were touchstones of culture.

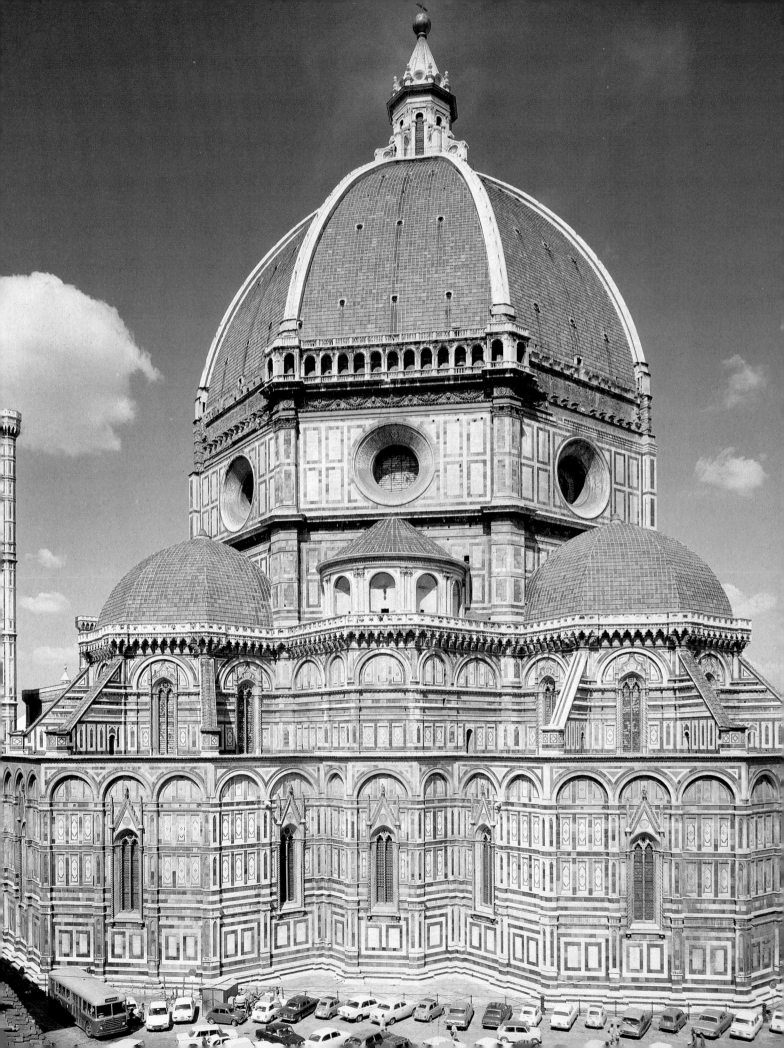

CHAPTER THREE

Classicism II: The Renaissance

When the darkness breaks, the generations to come may contrive to find their way back to the clear splendor of the ancient past.

PETRARCH

3.1 The Cathedral of Florence, 1296–1436

Introduction

"Renaissance" is the term used for the historical period following the Middle Ages, but the chronological boundary between the two periods has been much debated. Reacting to the sharply defined distinction between the Renaissance and Middle Ages propounded by certain nineteenth-century historians, especially Jacob Burckhardt, twentieth-century scholars have tended to push the origins of the Renaissance farther and farther back into the medieval period, some finding its beginning in the twelfth century, others even as early as the time of Charlemagne (AD 742–814). For our purposes, and in keeping with widely-held scholarly opinion, we will use the fourteenth and early seventeenth centuries as the chronological boundaries of the period. However it is important to keep in mind that the Renaissance did not represent a sharp and sudden break with the Middle Ages, but, in many respects, grew out of roots embedded in that period. There is, of course, a chronological overlap between the Renaissance and the Reformation, which began in the early sixteenth century and was in many ways a religious expression of Renaissance ideas. However, since the Reformation is essentially, though not exclusively, a religious movement, whereas the Renaissance movement is largely secular, we shall treat it in a separate chapter.

"Renaissance" means "rebirth" and expresses the conviction of the Renaissance humanists that they were restoring the culture and spirit of Classical antiquity. But the revival of classical literature, so fundamental to humanism, was not merely the result of new opportunities to study this literature. It was also the result of the rise of a secular spirit in the Renaissance that gave new appeal to this material. Thus the passion for classical literature was derived in large part from the recovery of the secular spirit and outlook during this period. Indeed, secularism—compelling interest in this world, its pleasures and possibilities—is central to the meaning of the Renaissance in Italy. Northern Europe is another matter. There, humanistic scholars such as John Colet, Desiderius, Erasmus, and Thomas More used their classical learning in efforts to reform the Church and to establish accurate texts and interpretations of the Bible and the Church fathers. But we will treat this aspect of the Renaissance in the chapter on the Reformation. Here we shall focus on the largely secular Italian Renaissance, which, though it seemed to serve the cause of religion through its art and scholarship, was imbued with a secular spirit which contrasted with the other-worldly values of medieval society: values that played down or even rejected the pleasures of physical life in a physical world. Italian humanists rejoiced in secular pleasures and earthly beauty, though not always, as we shall see in the case of Petrarch, without some painful stabbings of the lingering medieval conscience.

Akin to humanistic secularism was humanistic individualism—the concern for full development of human potential, a concern also at odds with the medieval emphasis on self-abnegation. In the medieval view the individual was expected to suppress his own desires and aspirations for the good of the community—an ideal that was fostered and encouraged both by feudalism and by the Church. Thus the humanists turned to Classical antiquity, not out of mere antiquarian interest, but because it was there that they found inspiration and models for their secular and individualistic pursuits. The Renaissance ideal, therefore, exemplified by Castiglione's "universal man" and the achievements of Leonardo da Vinci, celebrated the multi-talented individual who sought to give highly-developed expression to all of his possibilities.

Humanistic secularism and individualism were also fostered and expressed in the Renaissance Church. The fourteenth century was the period in which the papacy was transferred from Rome to Avignon through the appointment of a French pope by Philip IV of France. The Babylonian Captivity, as it was called (an allusion to the exile of the Jews in the sixth century BC) lasted until 1377. In fact, in 1378, there were two claimants to the papacy, Urban VI in Rome and Clement VII in Avignon, a political controversy hardly calculated to create respect for the office believed to represent Christ on earth. Many Renaissance popes were scarcely distinguishable from the secular princes, in their love of luxury and greed for wealth and power. Moreover, the Dominicans and the Franciscans, religious orders created in the Middle Ages out of high spiritual idealism, were also subverted by the greed and love of power that so often typified the Church in the Renaissance. Thus the Church as a whole dismally failed to provide the spiritual leadership expected of it by devout and thoughtful people. These factors led to the deterioration of religious authority and ultimately contributed to the success of the sixteenth-century reformers.

But the Renaissance involved a reaction not only against medieval religion but also against medieval authority and standards generally: literature, philosophy, architecture, sculpture, science, political theory—all of these areas of human thought and creativity underwent profound changes under the impulse of the humanist rejection of the Middle Ages and its achievements. In literature, this meant a return to the spirit and forms of classical writings and also the creation of writings in the vernacular languages; in philosophy, a rejection of the authority of Aristotle in favor of Plato (Neoplatonism); in architecture, a rejection of the Gothic style and a return to classical orders and building types; in sculpture, an admiration for, and imitation of, Roman antiquities; in science, the questioning of authoritarian pronouncements based on Aristotelian deductive reason and the beginnings of experimental approaches based on observation and induction; and in political theory, the rejection of theological and philosophical ideals in favor of what was put forth as objective analysis of human psychology and behavior. Such luminaries as Leonardo da Vinci, Raphael, Donatello, and Michelangelo (art), Machiavelli (political theory), Ficino and Pico della Mirandola (philosophy), Petrarch, Boccaccio, Ariosto, and Tasso (literature) made Italy the center of cultural and intellectual ferment.

In drama, however, Renaissance humanism, especially in Italy and France, was characterized by an unsuccessful attempt to model plays after Classical examples, particularly the tragedies of Seneca (4 BC–AD 65). But in England, where a strong dramatic tradition was already established, classical influence was minimal. The English were to experience a golden age in drama in the late sixteenth and early seventeenth centuries with the work of such playwrights as Christopher Marlowe and William Shakespeare.

In music, also, the major figures of the early Renaissance were non-Italians; not Englishmen but Netherlanders—from Flanders (now part of Belgium). However, Italy was the place where many of these Netherlandish composers spent considerable time, met Italian humanists and artists, were inspired by the "new age," and, because of Italian patronage, did most of their writing. Like Italian artists, they were caught up in the new creative spirit, taking pride in the fact that their work broke free of the stilted forms of earlier music. In this respect, they differed somewhat from their Netherlandish

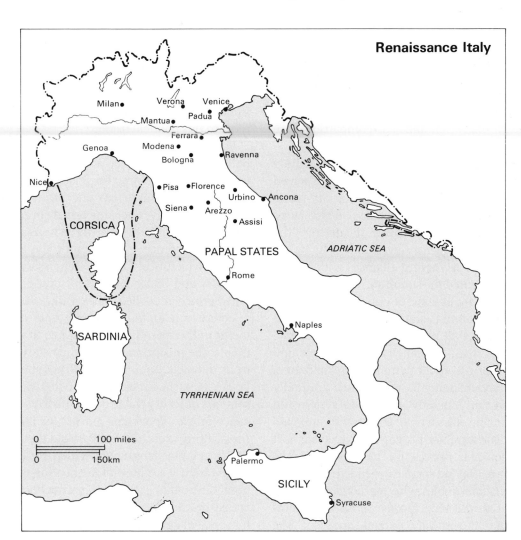

Renaissance Italy

DATES	SOCIAL AND POLITICAL DEVELOPMENTS	LITERATURE AND PHILOSOPHY	VISUAL ARTS	ARCHITECTURE	MUSIC
1250 1300	Black Death "Babylonian Captivity" Renaissance beginnings	Dante Petrarch (3.4) Boccaccio (3.5)		Sainte-Chapelle (3.6)	
1400	Invention of printing press Lorenzo de Medici (the Magnificent) Rise of national states	Neo-Platonism Ficino Pico della Mirandola	Donatello (3.11, 3.12) Masaccio (3.15, 3.16) Gentile da Fabriano (3.14) Ghiberti (3.17) Verrochio (3.19) Botticelli (3.20) Piero della Francesca(3.21) Mantegna (3.22)	Brunelleschi: Pazzi Chapel (3.7); Dome – Cathedral of Florence (3.8); Ospedale degli Innocenti (3.10)	Dunstable (3.23) Dufay (3.27) Ockegham Homophony Josquin des Prez (3.52)
1500		Machiavelli (3.28) Castiglione	Leonardo da Vinci (3.34) Michelangelo (3.36, 3.38) Raphael (3.42) Parmigianino (3.50) Titian (3.48)	Bramante: Tempietto (3.44)	Madrigal Rise of instrumental music (3.26)
1550		Montaigne (3.29) Shakespeare (3.30)		Michelangelo: St Peter's (3.46)	Yonge's portfolio of Italian madrigals
1600				Maderno: St Peter's façade (3.47)	

3.3 The Renaissance

counterparts in art, the so-called *Flemish painters*. These artists, including Campin, Van Eyck, Van der Weyden, and Bouts, were among the most skilled of the Renaissance; however, their themes and styles are so Gothic in spirit that they, unlike their musical compatriots, are surveyed in Chapter 7.

Although culturally and intellectually advanced, Italy remained politically chaotic. Political power was dispersed among quarrelsome and violent kingdoms and city-states (including those controlled by the papacy), which were often at one another's throats. Moreover, the rulers of the Holy Roman Empire and France loved to fish in Italy's troubled waters, and their varying alliances with Italian princes further complicated the situation.

Outside Italy, the major political development in Europe was the growth of national states. This phenomenon resulted from the rise of strong rulers whose centralized political control was made possible by the economic and social changes resulting from the dynamic development of commerce. A money economy based on trade gradually supplanted the agrarian economy of the feudal system and produced a new middle class who lived in towns and paid taxes to the king; the king, for his part, provided support and protection for the tax-paying merchants. Royal authority, therefore, was no longer dependent upon the support of quarrelsome nobles who, ensconced in their fortresses, could defy the king himself. Thus a combination of economic and social changes produced the political phenomenon of the centralized nation state ruled by a powerful king. England, France, and Spain all developed centralized monarchies during the Renaissance. Germany and Italy, however, were notable exceptions to this political trend.

Economic changes in the Renaissance affected not only politics but also culture. Wealthy middle-class merchants and bankers, looking for instant prestige and status, became patrons of artists and humanist scholars. Some patrons themselves became noted connoisseurs of art and scholars in their own right, as demonstrated by the Medici family of Florence. Castiglione's *The Book of the Courtier* gives us a picture of the ideal Renaissance court, including scholars and philosophers and presided over by a cultivated prince, modelled on the Duke of Urbino.

Before concluding we must note another important factor in the spread of Renaissance thought and achievements: the invention (some time before 1450) of printing from movable type, making it possible to mass-produce books. Thus the Greek and Latin literature rediscovered by scholars quickly achieved wide distribution, as did Renaissance music. The wider market for literature created by the printing press also encouraged the writing of works in the vernacular languages, which could be read by more people than were literate in the Classical languages. The great importance of these vernacular writings is illustrated by the stature of Petrarch and Boccaccio, whose fame rested largely on their writings in Italian.

Italian Humanism

Petrarch

Petrarch (Francesco Petrarca; 1304–1374) was the first great Italian humanist. He was deeply interested in the classical writers—especially Cicero, Virgil, and Seneca—and sought to emulate the spirit as well as the style of such men. He searched ardently for ancient manuscripts and encouraged the study of both Greek and Latin literature as the means of communing with the great minds of classical antiquity. Thus his passionate interest in the Greek and Roman classics was not merely pedantic but a manifestation of the revival of the classical spirit as well as of classical learning. This is important to an understanding of the Renaissance. Medieval scholars, too, had known classical writings but lacked the secular and human-centered outlook of the Renaissance that gave these ancient sources renewed life. Thus the Renaissance was the result of the revival not only of classical studies but also of the classical spirit, and it was the combination of these two that made Petrarch the first Italian humanist.

But Petrarch was not a thoroughgoing secular man. He lived in the tension created by the opposing Christian and classical views of human existence. Thus he took clerical orders (although for the purpose of receiving Church benefices) and began a work about 1342 titled *Secretum*, a series of imaginary dialogues with St. Augustine (see Chapter 6) in which he confessed his inner conflicts. When he climbed Mount Ventoux, in Provence, he took with him a copy of Augustine's *Confessions*, so he relates, thus combining natural enjoyment of the experience with a theological perspective.

Petrarch's father, a Florentine notary, was exiled from Florence for political reasons in 1302, and Petrarch was born two years later in Arezzo. Petrarch's youth, however, was spent in Avignon, where the papal court was then located. In his later life Petrarch often returned to this cultured city which played a significant role in his career.

In fact it was in Avignon that Petrarch claimed to have had his first encounter, in 1327, with the mysterious Laura (who, according to some scholars, was his own creation). As Beatrice was for Dante (though in a more sensual key), she became the inspiration for Petrarch's writing—in particular his *Canzoniere*, lyric poems in the Italian language written and continually revised throughout the remainder of his life. These poems provided Petrarch with his first literary renown. They continue to be the basis for his fame as a poet, though he believed that his Latin works alone deserved to be considered serious literature. Though written in a variety of forms, the majority of the poems were sonnets, lyric poems of 14 lines with a rhyme scheme of abba, abba, cde, cde. The octave (first eight lines) states the theme or sets the problem while the sestet (last six lines) provides the resolution. Both the form and the content of the Petrarchan sonnet were to provide the poet with a permanent reputation in European literature. The rhyme scheme of the Petrarchan sonnet became one of the two basic sonnet patterns, the other being the English, or Shakespearean.

3.4 Petrarch

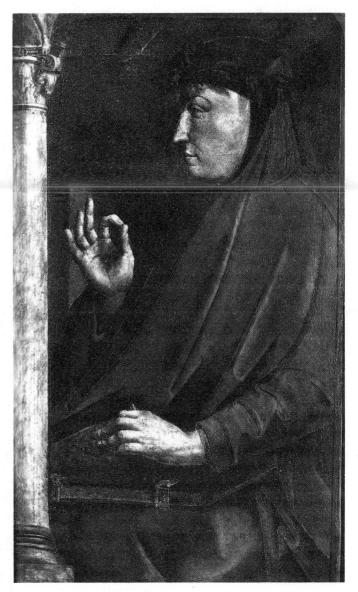

Moreover, the dominant theme of these poems, Petrarch's love for Laura, a married woman, became the paradigm of hopeless passion tempered by spirituality. In the poems, Petrarch minutely analyzes his feelings as he struggles over the conflict between the flesh and the spirit. Thus his physical passion for Laura is given a mystical dimension through its conflict with religious convictions.

Although he wrote some works in Latin, Petrarch's significance as a classicist did not lie principally in these writings but in the role he played in the revival of classical literature and scholarship. He encouraged the reading of Greek and Latin writings, (he persuaded his friend Boccaccio to study Greek), collected and copied ancient manuscripts, amassed an extensive personal library, and promoted the study of Cicero by other humanists. Admirer of all things classical, Petrarch was stirred by the monuments to Rome's ancient glory and hoped for a day when it would once more become the center of a reborn and reunited classical civilization. Thus Petrarch's significance for the beginnings of the Renaissance lay in the fact that he was the first humanist, as demonstrated by his recovery of both the literature and the spirit of classical antiquity. Yet the transitional nature of the fourteenth century between the waning of the Middle Ages and the dawning of the Renaissance is strikingly illustrated in Petrarch through the conflict engendered by his simultaneous commitment to the Christian and the classical traditions.

Boccaccio

Giovanni Boccaccio (1313–1375), one of the three foremost literary figures in fourteenth-century Italy, had significant connections with the other two. A deep admirer of Dante and his writings, his *Life of Dante* (1353) was the first biography of the great author. His public lectures on Dante's *Divine Comedy*, given at the invitation of the city of Florence in 1373, were also a "first." His admiration for Dante and devotion to Petrarch are illustrated by the fact that he commissioned the copying of Dante's *Divine Comedy* for Petrarch's use. Boccaccio was too young to have known Dante personally, but his admiration for Petrarch was based on a personal relationship. The two poets met for the first time in Florence in the autumn of 1350. Boccaccio had held Petrarch and his classical scholarship in the highest regard for many years, and from the time of their first meeting until Boccaccio's death, he saw himself as the disciple and Petrarch as his master (for a brief period in 1363 the two shared a house in Venice). Petrarch was the major influence on Boccaccio during the latter half of his life, and encouraged him to give up writing in the vernacular to compose serious works in Latin.

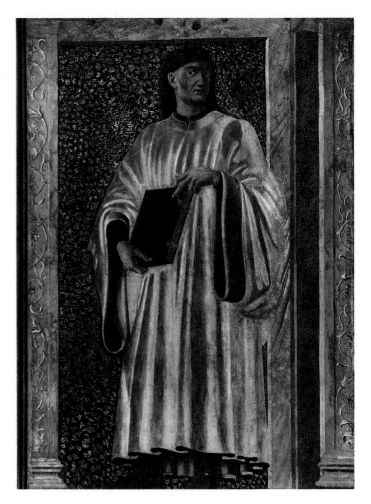

3.5 Giovanni Boccaccio, by Andrea del Castagno

But the dominant influence on Boccaccio in the first half of his career as a poet was a person of a very different sort. Like both Petrarch and Dante, Boccaccio was inspired—at least in his early writings—by a woman. His relationship with Maria d'Aquino, or Fiammetta ("Little Flame"), as he called her, was, however, a physical one. He took her as his mistress for a brief period, but she soon jilted him, apparently out of boredom. As brief as this experience was, it made Boccaccio a poet. Six of his early works reflect Maria's influence; these include the *Amorosa Visione*, an allegory glorifying both Maria and love.

Important as these early works are, Boccaccio is known chiefly for his *Decameron*, a collection of prose tales written between 1348 and 1353. The *novella* (short novel), a staple in Italian literature from Boccaccio to the present, became especially popular in the sixteenth century, and the stories told in *The Decameron* were the model for the genre. Thus Boccaccio's fame, though depending in the early Renaissance on his Latin treatises, later came to rest on his stories in the vernacular. Like Petrarch, he deprecated his vernacular writings; but also like his master, his literary reputation would eventually rest on what he had written in Italian.

The Decameron, meaning "ten days," was a "frame" story set in plague-ravaged Florence (an historical situation). The frame for the 100 stories of *The Decameron* is this: ten young people, seven women and three men, seek refuge from the plague by moving to the countryside outside Florence. The ten take turns presiding over ten days of story-telling, each one appointing his or her successor and selecting the theme for the next day's stories. Each person tells one story on the theme of the day, resulting in a total of 100 stories.

These stories are generally short and often bawdy. The style is direct and the story line uncomplicated. The fourteenth-century temporal world provides the subject matter for *The Decameron*—not the eternal world that preoccupied most medieval writers. Moreover, Boccaccio obviously takes pleasure in this temporal world. He does not seek to impose a thesis or theology but tolerantly depicts the human comedy (and tragedy), with all its foibles and follies. Thus *The Decameron* has a decidedly modern flavor, which is especially evident in Boccaccio's unembarrassed and frank treatment of love and sex. Indeed, *The Decameron* provides a panoramic view of fourteenth-century Italy.

Thus, although Boccaccio lived at the end of the Middle Ages and, like Petrarch, was still influenced by medieval attitudes, he was nevertheless a man of the Renaissance. His Latin treatises on classical mythology, lives of famous men and women of classical antiquity, and ancient geography became authoritative works for later Renaissance scholars. Moreover, the individualism and focus on this world that became the hallmarks of the Renaissance were evident in Boccaccio's vernacular writings. Some scholars regard him as the first modern man.

Pico della Mirandola

The growing emphasis on a human-centered world characteristic of fifteenth-century Italy is evident in the *Oration on the Dignity of Man* by Pico della Mirandola (1463–1494). In this impressive and influential presentation of the humanistic view, published in 1486, Pico celebrated the human capacity for unlimited improvement through reason—a confidence not always to be maintained, as we shall see, in the later stages of humanism. Pico sought to construct a system of thought that would reconcile the major sources of knowledge: Greek (especially Plato and Aristotle), Christian, and even Hebrew. It was possible, he believed, to harmonize all philosophies and religions—a belief that testifies to Renaissance optimism about human reason. Indeed, Pico viewed human beings as the epitome of God's creative genius, for they alone were granted the divine gift of reason.

Pico and Marsilio Ficino were mentioned previously in connection with our discussion of the influence of Plato's Theory of Ideas as it was extended through Neoplatonism (see Chapter 2), for both were members of the Platonic Academy in Florence. This academy is evidence of the strong interest in Neoplatonism on the part of the Italian humanists, who were fascinated by Plato's attempt, through his Theory of Ideas, to bring all things together in a unity culminating in God. The ideas generated and disseminated by the Platonic Academy influenced such important Renaissance figures as Castiglione, Erasmus, More, Botticelli, and Michelangelo.

Fifteenth-Century Italian Art

The classical spirit that guided Florentine literature in the mid-fourteenth century did not affect developments in Florentine art for another 50 years. Thus our survey of Renaissance art begins with the fifteenth century.

As noted earlier, the chronological boundary between the Middle Ages and the Renaissance is debatable. But so far as the visual arts are concerned, the changes that occurred in the early 1400s, particularly in Florence, are dramatic enough to quell all debate.

A comparison of two works of architecture, one Gothic and the other Renaissance, demonstrates the thorough-ness of the fifteenth-century break with the past: the Sainte-Chapelle (Fig. 3.6) was built in the 1200s for the private use of the French monarchy; the Pazzi Chapel (Fig. 3.7), in the 1400s for a wealthy Florentine banking family. Both are small structures; originally, both were intended as chapels for privileged clients. But here their similarities end. The walls of the Sainte-Chapelle—if they can be called that—are screens of stained glass windows framed by thin columns of colored stone which stress the chapel's vertical proportions. Like most Gothic architecture, the chapel is ornate and complex—qualities that

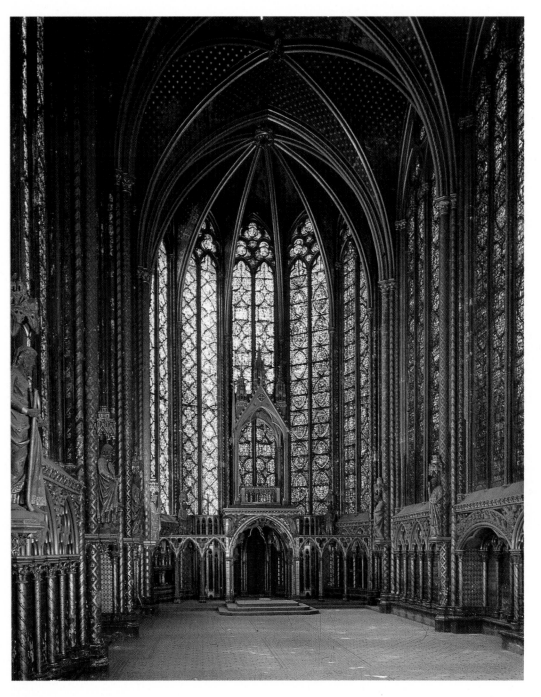

3.6 Sainte-Chapelle, Paris, interior view, 1243–48

came to be associated with late medieval culture. By contrast, the flat surfaces of the Pazzi Chapel are an affirmation of the walls. The ornamentation and color accents are designed to clarify, not confuse; the proportions stress balance between vertical and horizontal. The whole design is comprehensible and rational; in other words, it is classical.

The city of Florence provided ideal conditions for the classicizing of the visual arts. The largest city of Europe in the fifteenth century, it was well endowed with wealthy traders and bankers, eager to buy art and subsidize major projects. It also had a spirit of individualism, which encouraged private initiative; a climate of humanism (the creation of scholars and writers such as Petrarch and Boccaccio), with its independent thought and love of classical culture; and the good luck of being blessed with several talented artists born in or near the city itself. Finally, it should be pointed out that Gothic styles of architecture and sculpture did not strike such deep roots in Italy as in other parts of Europe. Therefore, Italian artists, including those in Florence, had less to react against.

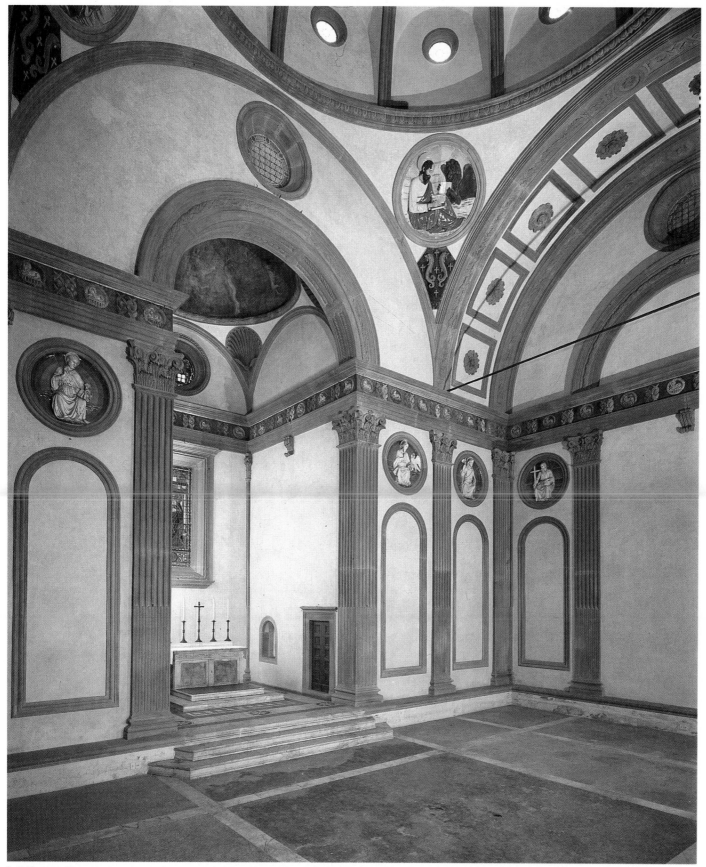

3.7 FILIPPO BRUNELLESCHI
Pazzi Chapel, Santa Croce, Florence, interior view, begun 1430–33

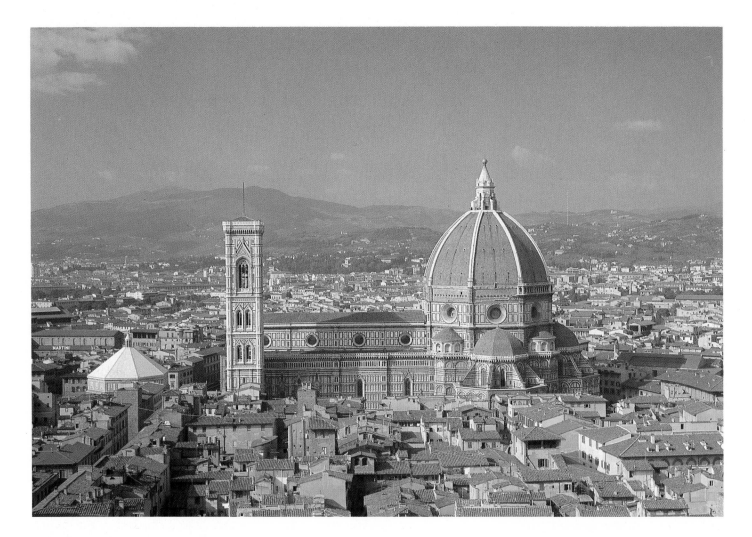

3.8 Filippo Brunelleschi
Cathedral of Florence,
1296–1436 (Dome, 1420–36)

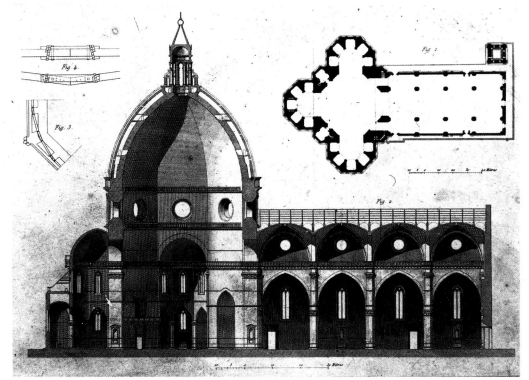

3.9 Plan and Section of
Florence Cathedral

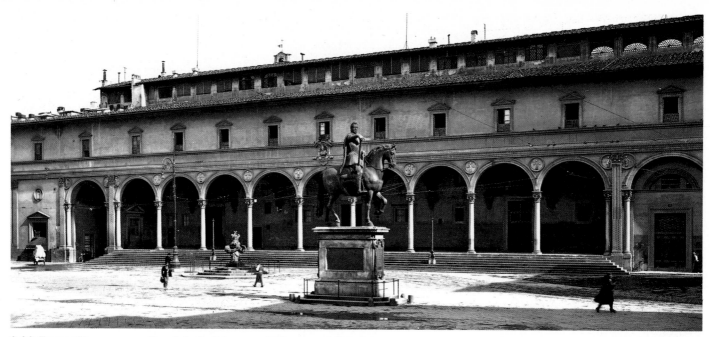

3.10 FILIPPO BRUNELLESCHI Ospedale degli Innocenti, Florence, 1419–24

Brunelleschi

The Pazzi Chapel was designed by Filippo Brunelleschi (1377–1446), though it was completed after his death. Like many men of his generation, Brunelleschi was widely talented—at least in the visual arts. Trained as a goldsmith, he was a noted sculptor before turning to architecture. He was supposedly the inventor of *linear perspective*, a method of representing spatial depth in a picture, which was later refined by his fellow architect and humanist, Leon Battista Alberti. Linear perspective played a role in the development of fifteenth-century drawing, painting, and relief sculpture.

Brunelleschi was also something of an archeologist. Like Petrarch, he admired Roman ruins and buildings, particularly the Pantheon, which inspired his greatest, and still most famous, project: the dome of the Cathedral of Florence (Fig. **3.8**). One of the major landmarks of Europe and a symbol of the Renaissance, the cathedral is dominated by its dome; the rest of it—built in the thirteenth and fourteenth centuries—is mostly Italian-style Gothic (Fig. **3.9**). The dome spans a diameter of 140 feet (43 meters). No dome this wide had been built since the Pantheon. No dome this tall had ever been built. Unlike any of its predecessors, Brunelleschi's dome is pointed, reinforced with 24 "ribs" (eight of which are visible on the outside), and crowned by an elaborate "lantern" for stability. In addition to designing the dome Brunelleschi had to invent new methods for building it. Because the centering of such a large dome would have required a veritable forest of timber, Brunelleschi built it in self-supporting stages, using temporary, movable scaffolding at each stage. He even invented a hoisting machine for lifting stones and bricks to the scaffold.

The shape of the dome and the use of rib reinforcements are related to the pointed arches and ribbed vaults of Gothic architecture (see page 293). But the boldness of the concept, in both its scale and its departure from traditional architecture, is clearly of the Renaissance. The top of the dome is 300 feet (93 meters) from the floor, more than twice the heights of the Pantheon dome and the tallest Gothic vaults; the top of the lantern is 351 feet (107 meters) from the floor. Giorgio Vasari, the sixteenth-century biographer and art historian, said of the dome, "The mountains about Florence look like its fellows."[1] It is the prototype of all the famous domes in the Western world, including St. Peter's in Rome, St. Paul's in London, and the United States Capitol.

Although not as dramatic as the dome, Brunelleschi's other projects were nevertheless original for their time in terms of style. His series of column-supported arches for the front of Florence's Ospedale degli Innocenti ("children's hospital," Fig. **3.10**) was, like the dome, inspired by classical architecture. The capitals are Corinthian, and the long entablature above the arches is an example of the use of classical motifs. But Brunelleschi's combining of columns and arches to create a colonnade is characteristic neither of the Greeks, who rarely used arches, or of the Romans, who rarely put columns under their arches. Equally uncharacteristic of classical building are the delicate proportions: the thin columns and the sharply-pointed convergences of the arches above the capitals. Although this building bears the influence of the classical language of architecture, it is original—in effect, the beginning of a new language of architecture.

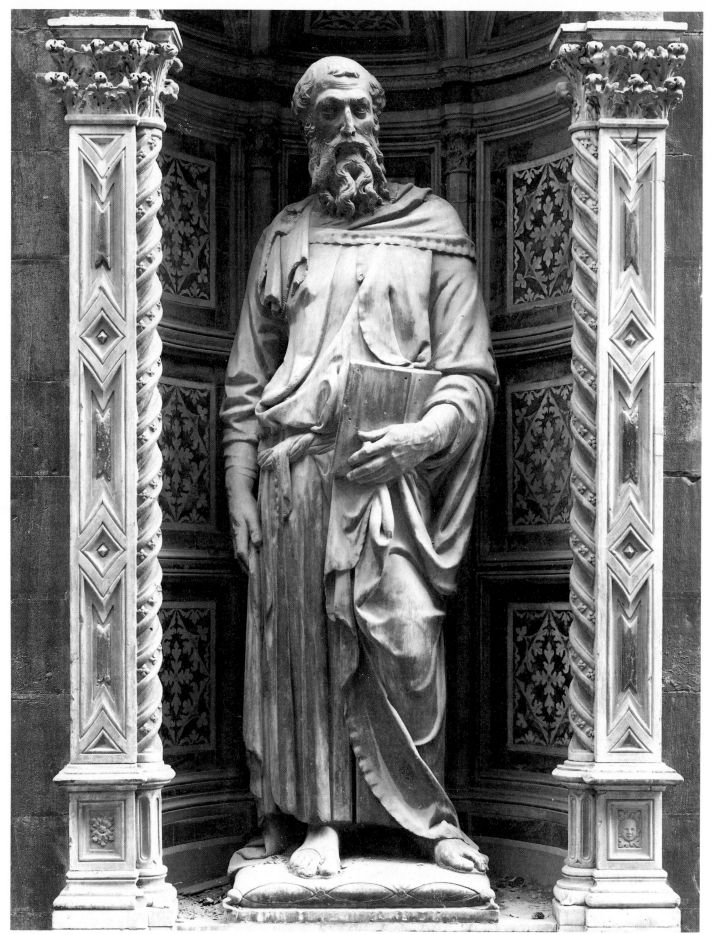

3.11 DONATELLO *St Mark* 1411–13, Marble, approx. 7 ft 9 ins (2.36 m) high, Or San Michelle, Florence

Donatello

The sculptor Donatello (Donato di Niccolo Bardi; 1386–1466) accompanied Brunelleschi on his trips to Rome, where they measured and drew the ruins. Like Brunelleschi, he not only studied classicism but reflected its principles in his work. And also like Brunelleschi, Donatello was responsible for several innovations in his medium. He broke new ground stylistically, endowing his works with a degree of realism not seen before, freeing his statuary from its medieval dependence on architecture and investing it with great intensity of expression. Although most of his subjects are Old Testament heroes, apostles, and saints, he helped to establish new categories such as portraits and classical subjects. Often he combined religious and secular qualities in a single work: using a Christian saint to symbolize non-religious ideas, such as the virtues of classical antiquity or the struggles between Florence and her enemies; or using a statue of a secular hero to express religious fervor.

St. Mark (Fig. **3.11**), an early work, demonstrates Donatello's originality and powers of expression. Like many late medieval statues, it was designed for an architectural niche (in this case, in Or San Michele, church of the Florentine guilds). But because of its realism and commanding authority, *St. Mark* could very well stand alone, free of its restrictive environment. Although late medieval works show movement, even weight-shift postures at times, this is the first statue since antiquity to build on the legacy of Polykleitos. In addition, it successfully relates anatomy and clothing, conveying the presence of a real human being beneath its garment. Most importantly, *St. Mark* is not beautiful, at least not in any traditional sense. The gown, though quite realistic, does not fall, like medieval drapery, in regular, rhythmical folds; it bunches, pouches, and sags, looking as if the Evangelist has slept in it. The face, though noble, is stern and serious, the look of the most plain-spoken of the four Evangelists. It could also be the look of a Florentine humanist exhorting his fellow citizens to show courage during their times of crisis. *St. Mark* is an engaging statue, especially when compared to the bland sculpture that preceded it. Imagine how it must have affected Florentines as it glared at them from its niche.

Another of Donatello's religious statues has multiple, even contrasting meanings. *David* (Fig. **3.12**), symbol of Jewish glory (and perhaps also of Florence), stands triumphantly with one foot on the head of Goliath, symbol of evil (and perhaps of Florence's enemies, the city-states of Milan and Naples). But significantly, he is naked—except for helmet and boots—and young. Being the first classical nude since classical times the statue is as much

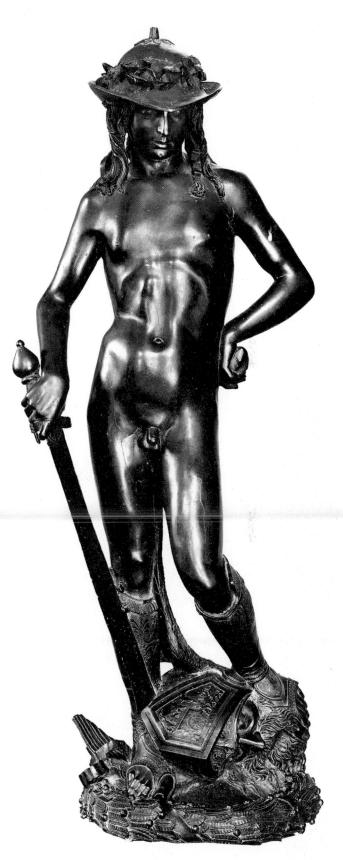

3.12 DONATELLO
David, 1425–30
Bronze, approx. 62 ins (157.5 cm) high
National Museum, Florence

Greek god as Old Testament hero. And this, too, is consistent with its representing Florence, the new Athens. As *St. Mark*, with its dour expression and dowdy clothes, symbolizes abstinence and moral rectitude, *David* represents pleasure. It is a puzzling work, particularly in light of Donatello's other sculptures. Since the history of its commission and where it was originally placed are unknown, there is little evidence other than its subject from which to deduce Donatello's intentions. But it demonstrates again his remarkable originality. *David* anticipates the traits of nudity, classicism, beauty, and pleasure that were to become so prevalent in future art.

Donatello was called to Padua to produce a large bronze equestrian statue—to commemorate the memory of a Venetian military hero, Erasmo da Narni, known as *Gattamelata* ("honey cat"—Fig. **3.13**). Like *St. Mark* and *David*, it was an innovation for its time: the only free-standing equestrian statue of a non-religious personage since the fall of Rome, apart from the so-called Statuette of Charlemagne, c. 860–70. Indeed, Donatello may have had a Roman work in mind; but the virility of the *Gattamelata* is unmatched by that of any classical statue. To express immutable power, Donatello limited the design to a few large, uncomplicated massses while emphasizing the weight and density of both horse and rider. The fiercely determined expression of the commander's face, the focal point of the composition, is itself a landmark in the history of sculpture. *Gattamelata* personifies the ambitious and willful Renaissance leader, a sculptural embodiment of Machiavelli's ruler in *The Prince*.

3.13 DONATELLO
Equestrian Statue of Gattamelata, 1445–50,
Bronze, c.11 × 13 ft (3.4 × 4 m)
Piazza del Santo, Padua

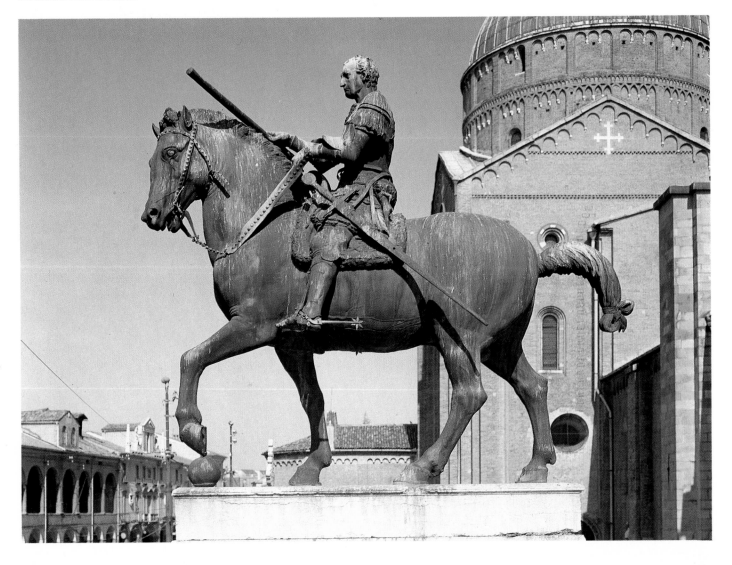

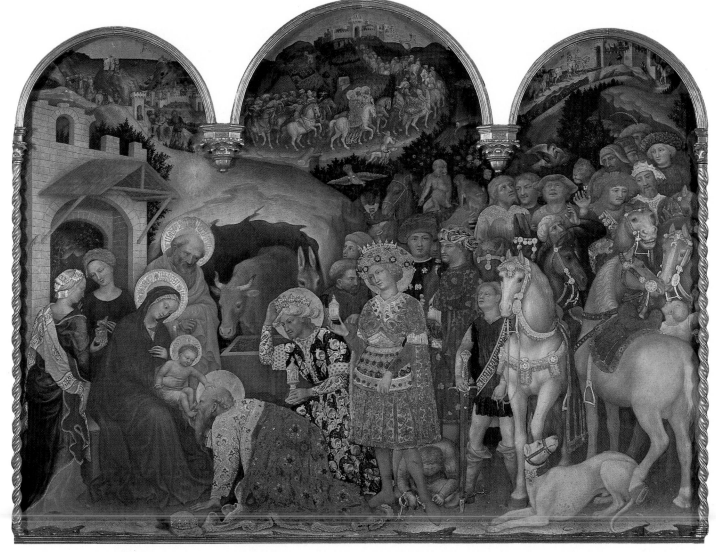

3.14 GENTILE DA FABRIANO
The Adoration of the Magi, 1423
Tempera on wood panel, 119 × 111 ins (302 × 282 cm)
Uffizi Gallery, Florence

Masaccio

Unlike Donatello, the painter Masaccio (Tommaso Guidi; 1401–1428) did not introduce new categories of subject matter. Because he died young he produced few works, all of them religious, but they were a turning point in the history of painting.

To understand Masaccio's revolutionary importance it will be helpful to study briefly the *Adoration of the Magi* (Fig. 3.14), by Gentile da Fabriano, a late-Gothic painter who was active in Florence at this time. Gentile had a brilliant reputation for, among other things, vivid realism. A battle scene he created in Venice reputedly filled observers with terror. Some of this realism can be seen in the altarpiece: the variety of shape, texture, and activity (seen in both people and animals), and the loving

attention given to the finest of details. Moreover, through skillful use of shading the artist endowed everything with a degree of roundness; he also employed foreshortening daringly in the stable animals, the servant on the ground behind the young king in the middle, and the horses on the right. In other respects, however, the painting is very unrealistic. The composition is unnaturally crowded. The procession scene in the background does not fit spatially with the Nativity scene in the foreground. Although perspective is used in the stable on the left, it has not been applied consistently. The detail, if anything, detracts from the realism, making the figures resemble cutouts rather than real people. Although the people show emotions, their personalities seem as bland as their bodies are flat. The *Adoration* is a beautiful work, full of late-Gothic splendor, but it lacks the kind of realism—optical, emo-

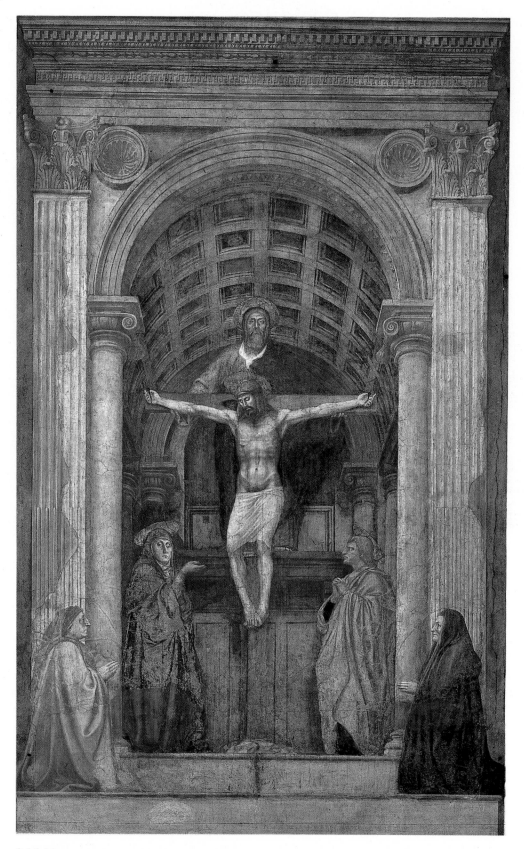

3.15 MASACCIO
The Holy Trinity with the Virgin and St John, 1425
Fresco, 21 ft 9 ins × 9 ft 4 ins (6.67 × 3.17 m)
Santa Maria Novella, Florence

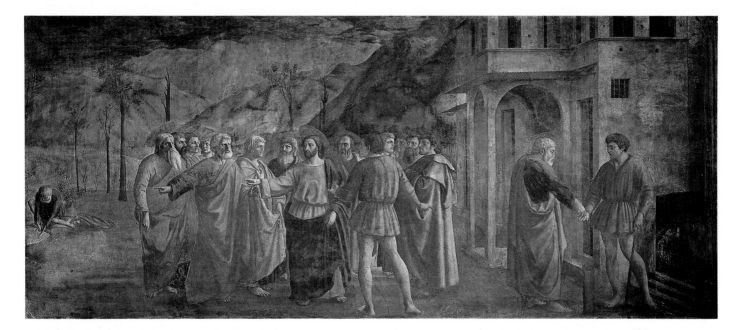

3.16 Masaccio
The Tribute Money, c. 1427
Fresco, 8 ft 4 ins × 19 ft 8 ins (2.54 × 5.9 m)
Brancacci Chapel, Santa Maria del Carmine, Florence

tional, and philosophical—of the work of Donatello.

Like the *Adoration*, the *Holy Trinity with the Virgin and St. John* (Fig. **3.15**), a mural by Masaccio in a Florence church, is a religious picture. In fact, no subject in Christianity is more profoundly theological than the Trinity. But unlike the Gentile picture, the *Trinity* contains monumental figures in a simple, spatially coherent composition, full of the kind of earthy realism expected of a Donatello. God the Father stands behind the crucified Jesus (the dove of the Holy Spirit hovering between their heads) with Mary and John at the foot of the cross. Kneeling before the scene, which is enacted in a narrow, vaulted room, are two Florentines, perhaps the donors. Each figure has physical substance and weight; each face expresses an individual, though somber, personality. The organic relationship between clothes and body suggests that Masaccio used live models as well as Donatello's sculptures as his sources. The partially nude, athletic body of Christ suggests the use of classical sculptures. But the most advanced aspect of the *Trinity* is its use of "true" linear perspective—a technique used here possibly for the first time. The barrel vault above the figures' heads is so accurately drawn that its measurement can be deduced. The vanishing point is directly beneath the cross on the ledge above the crypt—a radically low eye level which conveys the impression that the viewer is below the cross. (Around 5 feet [1.5 meters] above the floor, the eye level

corresponds to the height of an actual viewer in the church.) Finally, unlike the *Adoration*, which is set in a Gothic frame, the *Trinity* is set in the new surroundings of Renaissance architecture.

The Tribute Money (Fig. **3.16**), one of a series of murals on the subject of St. Peter, is located in the Brancacci Chapel in Florence. Based on the story in St. Matthew (17:24–7), it is about a tax collector who approaches Peter and the disciples in Capernaum. The tax collector, clad in a short tunic, is shown both in the middle and on the right. St. Peter is shown in three places: in the middle, where he is told by Jesus to obtain a coin from the mouth of a fish; on the left, where he is gathering the coin; and on the right, where he appears to be thrusting the coin in the collector's hand. The figures of the men, painted in bold strokes of chiaroscuro, are consistently illuminated from the right. They are as weighty and solid as the horse and rider in *Gattamelata*, and their intense expressions recall the face of Donatello's *St. Mark*. In this painting Masaccio created men capable of risking their lives to start a religious revolution. They could also be members of the Florentine *Signoria* (government) assembled for an emergency meeting. At any rate, the artist provided for them a spatially real world in which to carry out their vocations. The house on the right, for example, conforms to the rules of one-point perspective. But depth is effected mainly through the contrast between the men in the foreground and the Tuscan hills in the background. Unlike hills represented in other pictures, these resemble real terrain and harmonize with the rest of the picture in terms of scale and eye level. Moreover, Masaccio created the impression of air and space through the heretofore unknown method of *aerial perspective*—softening color contrasts and blurring the edges of things in the distance. For its time, *The Tribute Money* was a textbook of pictorial innovations. According to Giorgio Vasari, the Brancacci Chapel became a "school of art" for the most celebrated sculptors and painters of the time, including Botticelli, Leonardo da Vinci, and Michelangelo—artists we shall discuss later in this chapter.

Florentine Art in the later *1400s*

The artistic trends set by Donatello and Masaccio were not invariably pursued by following generations of Florentine artists; the emphasis on realism and intensity of expression often yielded to a preference for beauty and refinement.

This preference can already be seen in the *Jacob and Esau* panel (Fig. 3.17) on the *Gates of Paradise* by Lorenzo Ghiberti (1378–1455). Although Ghiberti was older than

3.17 Lorenzo Ghiberti
The Story of Jacob and Esau, panel from the 'Gates of Paradise', c. 1435
Gilt bronze, $31\frac{1}{4}$ ins (79 cm) square
Baptistery, Florence

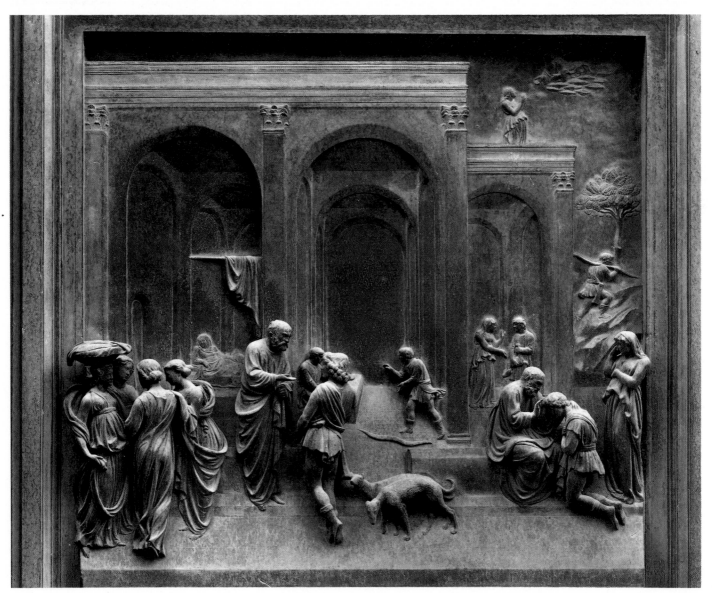

3.18 LORENZO GHIBERTI
Gates of Paradise, entire, approx. 17 ft (5.2 m) high

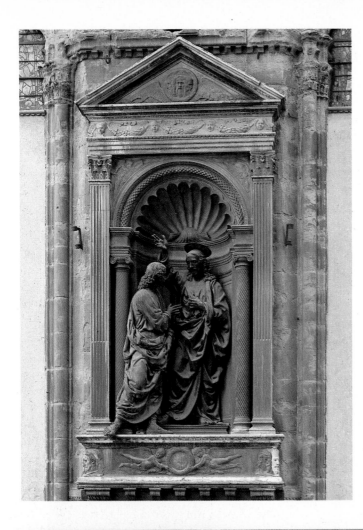

3.19 ANDREA DEL VERROCHIO
Doubting of Thomas, 1465–83
Bronze, life-size
Or San Michelle, Florence

3.20 SANDRO BOTTICELLI
The Birth of Venus, c. 1480
Tempera on canvas, 68 × 109 ins (175 × 228 cm)
Uffizi Gallery, Florence

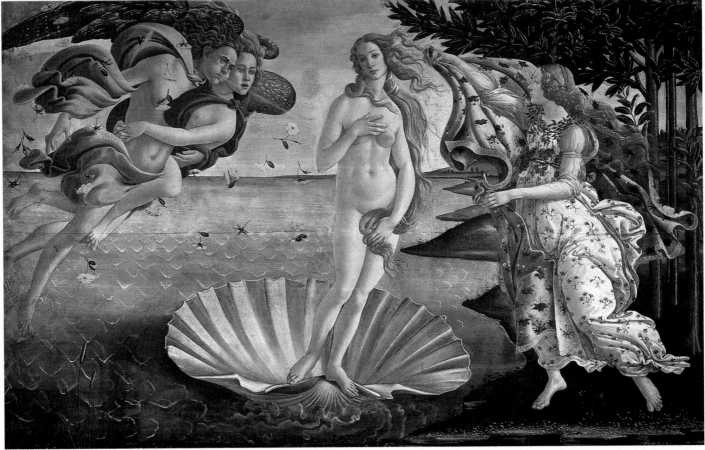

Donatello (and even his teacher for a brief time) his famous east doors of the Florence Baptistery (Fig. 3.18) were not completed until the mid-fifteenth century. Unlike earlier relief sculptures, including those made in the classical world, *Jacob and Esau* presents an illusion of depth by means of the same methods used in painting: linear perspective (found in the foreground paving stones as well as in the open-vaulted temple in the background) and aerial perspective (seen in the way that people and objects in the distance tend to dissolve into the background). The result is an environment that is both harmonious and full of space—echoed in the graceful lines and movement of the figures of the foreground. It is not surprising that Ghiberti's doors were, and still are, much loved. They offer realism without the harshness of early Florentine art; they also lack some of the substance of that art.

The taste for graceful lines and movement is also satisfied in *The Doubting of Thomas* (Fig. 3.19) by one of Ghiberti's apprentices, Andrea del Verrocchio (1432–88). Occupying another niche of the same church that contains Donatello's *St. Mark*, this pair of figures illustrates the dramatic moment when the disciple is shown the wound in the side of his risen Lord. Verrocchio, however, did not explore the psychological possibilities of such an encounter, as Donatello might have done. Instead he has idealized it, perhaps to emphasize the eternal life promised by the Resurrection. Reminiscent of Gothic angels, the figures of Thomas and Christ are almost overwhelmed by the beauty of the deeply-cut drapery of their robes.

In the late fifteenth century, when Sandro Botticelli (1444–1510) was active, a great deal of Florentine art was made for the private pleasure of well-to-do patrons, many of whom were educated or advised by humanist scholars. This perhaps explains why so much of it leans toward the sensuous and the esoteric. Botticelli was certainly well qualified to gratify this taste, for his work is unparalleled in its command of lyrical proportion, felicity of line, and nuance of feeling. *The Birth of Venus* (Fig. 3.20), painted in 1482, presents Venus in the center, blown by *zephyrs* (west winds) on the left, and an *hour* (one of the seasons) on the right. This work was a birth in more ways than one: the first large-scale painting to display a naked woman and the first to celebrate a pagan deity since pagan times. In fact, it started the "Venus tradition" which was to become so familiar in European art. Yet in 1482 medieval attitudes about nudity and sexual morality were still rather strong; such a painting must have been controversial. Although naked, however, Botticelli's Venus was not intended to be erotic, and thus, perhaps, not as shocking as one might think. It was painted for Lorenzo di Pierfrancesco de' Medici, second cousin to the famous Lorenzo the Magnificent and intimate friend of

Marsilio Ficino, Neoplatonist and a member of the Platonic Academy in Florence. In Ficino's philosophy, Venus was a goddess not of erotic love but of Beauty; and beauty with a capital "B" was divine, transcending earthly life and physical desire. Thus *The Birth of Venus* was, so to speak, an altarpiece for the cult of Neoplatonic philosophy. And just as that philosophy is not really Greek, neither is Botticelli's figure of Venus, even though based on a classical statue. Instead of a physical goddess of love, his is a pale, lovely spirit, one that floats rather than stands. The rest of the picture is equally dream-like: the angelic zephyrs, the lovely *hour*, with her billowing gown and cape, and the placid sea touched with V-shaped ripples. Except for its nudity, *The Birth of Venus* could almost be a late-Gothic altarpiece.

Art Outside Florence

The tradition of Donatello and Masaccio was, ironically, stronger elsewhere in Italy than in Florence.

Piero della Francesca (c. 1420–92) began his career as a painter in Florence as an apprentice of Domenico Veneziano. At that time he was exposed to the works of Ghiberti, Donatello, and Masaccio. But rather than remaining in the exhilarating atmosphere of Florence, Piero chose to work in the much quieter town of Arezzo, Petrarch's birthplace. Thus he was out of touch with the fast-moving developments of Florentine art. Perhaps for this reason he continued to retain a taste for the monumental, volumetric figures of early Renaissance painting. We can see evidence of this taste in his *Resurrection* (Fig. 3.21). Christ, staring resolutely at the viewer, is as stiffly frontal as an Archaic statue. With one foot on the edge of the sepulcher, he towers triumphantly over the sleeping guards, whose bodies, in contrast to his own, show more variety of posture. Although they seem to bend and turn at all the joints, these bodies are nevertheless as substantial as Masaccio's.

The legacy of Masaccio seems to live even more in the works of Andrea Mantegna (c. 1431–83). But it was Donatello, not Masaccio, who influenced Mantegna directly. The two had probably met in Padua, Mantegna's home town, where the sculptor worked for a period of time. From the latter's statues Mantegna may have discovered classical proportion; from his relief sculptures, perspective. Indeed, Mantegna's own works have the solid, dense look of sculpture. In black-and-white reproduction, *St. James Led to Execution* (Fig. 3.22) looks more like a relief carving than a painting. Both figures and architecture suggest the crisp clarity of incised lines. But perhaps the most striking aspect of this work is its radical perspective. Like Masaccio's *Trinity*, it presents a dramatic

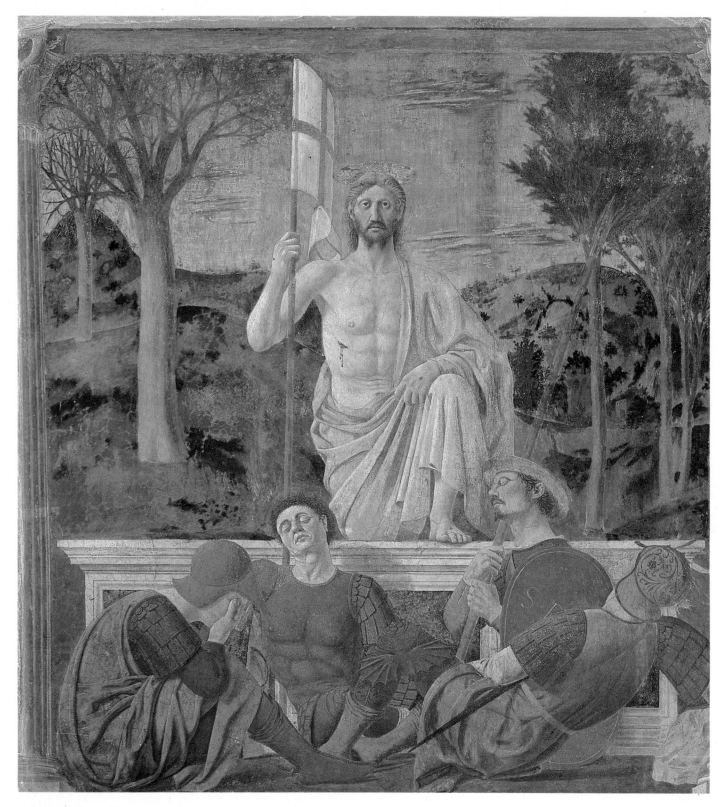

3.21 Piero Della Francesca
Resurrection, c. 1463
Fresco, 9 ft 6 ins × 8 ft 4 ins (2.9 × 2.54 m)
Piazza Communale, Borgo San Sepolcro

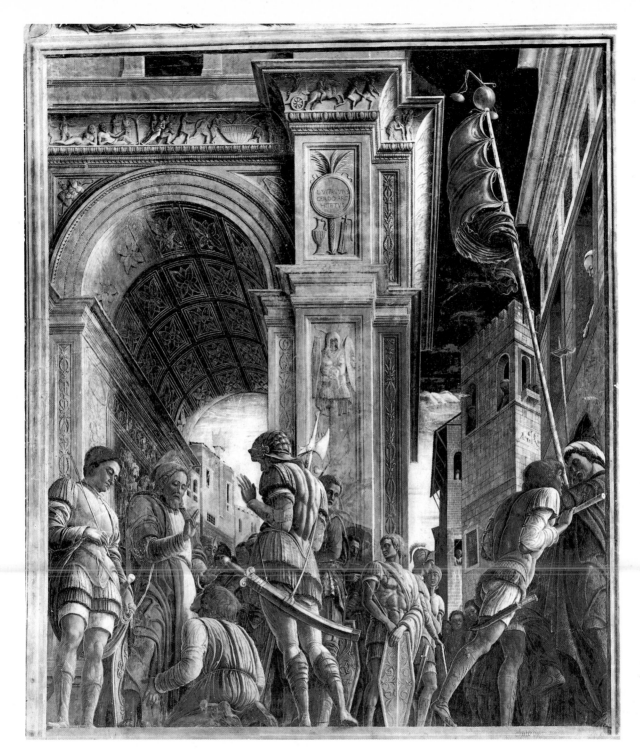

3.22 Andrea Mantegna
St James Led to his Execution, c. 1455
Fresco (destroyed in 1944)
Ovetari Chapel, Padua

"worm's-eye-view" of the scene, in this case, the saint surrounded by Roman soldiers beneath an imposing triumphal arch. The eye level is below the picture so that the feet of the more distant figures are obscured.

Thus, near the end of the fifteenth century, we see two trends in Italian art: one stressing the physical nature of the world; the other stressing its lyrical and allegorical side. Both trends reflect the classical revival and the pictorial advances set in motion at the beginning of the century—even though Botticelli's lightweight figures seem, in some respects, to be atavisms of late Gothic art. A merging of these trends began to be achieved in the work of Leonardo da Vinci at the turn of the century (see *Sixteenth-Century Italian Art* below).

Music in the Renaissance

The relationship of music to the classical spirit of the Renaissance is somewhat more oblique than that of art and literature. Unlike their counterparts in the other arts, composers did not have any Greek or Roman models to study and emulate. As we have noted, of the few manuscripts of Greek music that survived, none have been deciphered so as to reveal how the music sounded. Thus, developments in Renaissance music, though informed by the spirit of the time, built upon forms established in medieval music. These developments were less revolutionary than corresponding developments in painting, for example; and although music of this period has an ever-growing number of admirers in our own time, its composers are not exactly household names. Everyone knows of Leonardo, Michelangelo and Shakespeare. But how many people have heard of Dufay, Ockeghem, or Josquin—let alone heard any of their music?

As their names suggest, most of the leading composers of the early Renaissance were not Italian. They were of Netherlandish or French origin; however many of them lived in Italy and knew first hand such people as Alberti, Leonardo, and Ficino; worked for such patrons as the Medici, the dukes of Milan, Urbino, and Mantua, and the popes; and presented their works in Italian courts and cathedrals. Like their artist friends, they were excited by the rebirth of classical art and learning. And though they had little to study in terms of authentic music from the Greco-Roman era, they shared with artists and writers an admiration for antiquity, equating it, ironically, with the "new age." Like artists, they looked upon their own work as new and innovative, a break with what they perceived to be the stilted forms of the "Gothic" past. Both composers and performers, who were allowed much more freedom than before, basked in this new creative environment.

Music of the Renaissance, like art and literature, witnessed a dramatic increase in activity; more of it was written and performed than ever before. There were other parallels: as artists began to judge their work in terms of the visible world and writers like Boccaccio depicted the panorama of real life, so musicians began to judge music on how it sounded to the ears rather than on a set of abstract rules. Compositions were conceived of as units or wholes, rather than as collections of separate pieces of musical material. Greater emphasis was placed on sonority—beautiful, agreeable sound. A closer relationship was fostered between music and words—sometimes called "text painting"; composers strove not only to adhere a better match between tones and words, but also to express the meanings of texts. Such pursuits, which were closely related to the humanistic movement, laid the foundations for musical thinking for generations to come.

Early Renaissance

Despite all the characteristics that identify a certain body of music as "Renaissance" rather than "medieval" or "Gothic," it is important to remember that music of the fourteenth century was a highly developed art form and that many of its characteristics survived in fifteenth-century music. In other words, the break between the two was anything but total; indeed, the basic elements and forms of the former were carried over into the latter. At this point it will be helpful to compare these elements and forms with those of Greek music.

In contrast to Greek music, which, as we have noted, was monophonic, European music by this time was largely *polyphonic*—having two or more independent melodic lines sung or played at the same time. A small section of liturgical music by John Dunstable is a good illustration (Fig. **3.23**). Note that the three parts have different melodic lines and different words. But increasingly Renaissance music employed chordal writing or *homophony*—two or more voices singing together at the same rhythm and tempo, but at different pitches. However, choruses, who alternated with soloists in performances of liturgical music, continued the ancient practice of singing monophonically (from a body of music called Gregorian chant; see page 263).

Whereas the basic unit of Greek music was the tetrachord, the basic unit of European music was an eight-note scale. But, rather than being limited to just two modes (major and minor), a fifteenth-century scale could

3.23 Liturgical music by Dunstable

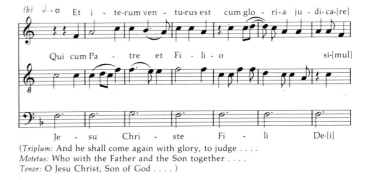

(*Triplum:* And he shall come again with glory, to judge . . . .
Motetus: Who with the Father and the Son together . . . .
Tenor: O Jesu Christ, Son of God . . . .)

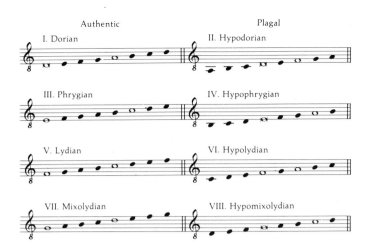

Authentic   Plagal
I. Dorian   II. Hypodorian

III. Phrygian   IV. Hypophrygian

V. Lydian   VI. Hypolydian

VII. Mixolydian   VIII. Hypomixolydian

3.24 Medieval Church modes

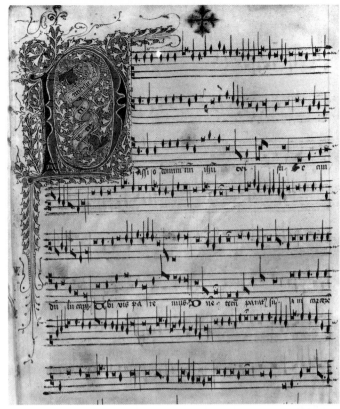

3.25 Opening of a three-part passion according to St Luke
British Museum MS. Egerton 3307, fo. 20

3.26 Plate from Michael Praetorius' *Syntagma musicum*

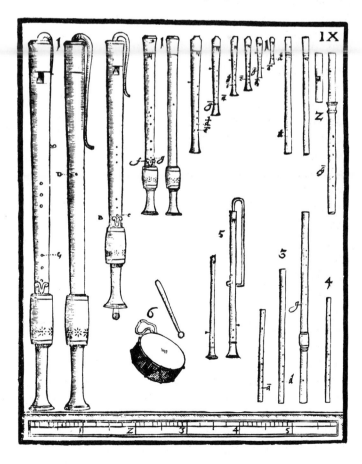

be played in one of eight modes. Although related to Greek modes in their terminologies (Dorian, Phrygian, and so forth), Renaissance modes did not sound like them. Some, along with their classical labels, are displayed in modern notation in Fig. **3.24**.

Performers now had the benefit of a fairly logical system of notation. Symbols for designating time values and rhythmic patterns of notes and *staffs*, frameworks of horizontal lines to locate the pitch of each note, were in use by the fifteenth century (Fig. **3.25**). (*Bars*, vertical lines to divide staffs into *measures*, were added in the sixteenth century.) Improved notation, besides being helpful to performers, was an important factor in the dissemination and circulation of new music.

Fifteenth-century music included both religious and secular works: songs, hymns, choral music, and dance music. The major form was the *Mass*, music written to accompany the Eucharist. The various sections of the Mass fall into two categories: the "Proper," which varies according to the Church calendar, and the "Ordinary," which includes the Kyrie, Gloria, Creed, Sanctus, Benedictus, and Agnus Dei, and remains the same throughout the year. The *motet*, a polyphonic composition in Latin text, is usually religious, though never serves as part of a Mass Ordinary. The *chanson* (French for "song") of this period was a secular song, often accompanied by a *lute*. Although little music was written for instruments alone, instrumental music adapted from vocal compositions was performed for dances, fanfares, processions, festivals, and other special occasions.

For such occasions, Renaissance musicians could avail themselves of a variety of wind instruments: *sackbuts* (forerunners of trombones) and trumpets in all sizes and shapes (*cornetts* of wood or ivory, *recorders* (Fig. **3.26**) like modern flutes but played vertically), and double-reed winds called *shawms*. Stringed instruments included *viols*, which were bowed, and lutes, which were plucked. Keyboard instruments included *clavichords*, *virginals* and organs.

Dufay

Guillaume Dufay (c. 1400–1470), one of the Netherlandish composers who transformed the music of the period, was born in the Burgundian province of Hainaut (now on the French-Belgian border). Ruling this area were the dukes of Burgundy, who, in the fourteenth and fifteenth centuries, were wealthy, powerful, and great patrons of the arts.

Despite the brilliance of the Burgundian court, Dufay chose to spend at least 20 of his productive years (1420–40) in Italy (the same years in which Brunelleschi, Donatello, and Masaccio were active). There he composed motets for all kinds of occasions: state weddings, signing of political treaties, and consecrations of churches and cathedrals. Once he was even called upon to write a motet lamenting the fall of Constantinople. One of his better known motets, *Nuper rosarum flores—Terribilis est locus iste* (Fig. 3.27), was written for the dedication of Brunelleschi's dome (Fig. 3.8). To make it more ceremonious, Dufay included brass, strings, and woodwinds.

Music was not his only forte. A student of law, Dufay was ordained as a priest in 1420 and appointed to influential offices in the Church. Like Leonardo da Vinci,

3.27 *Nuper rosarum flores—Terribilis est locus iste*, Dufay

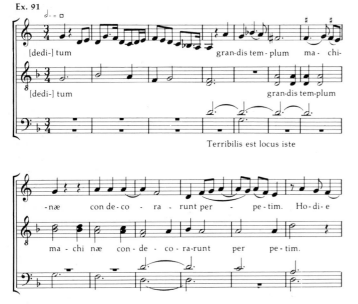

(. . . the splendid shrine dedicated [to thee, flowers] have continually adorned.)

he traveled between North and South and was honored in courts, chapels, and capitals all over the Continent. His travels and his many contacts probably accounted for the richness and diversity of his music. He was one of the first to combine the intricate polyphony of northern music with the simpler rhythms and harmonic textures of Italian music. He experimented with the addition of a (heretofore absent) bass voice. His Masses, in which the lead melodies were uncommonly supple, anticipated later developments in that form. Impressed with the rhythmic qualities of the Italian language, especially as embodied in the works of Petrarch, he contributed significantly to the custom of fitting music to words in his motets.

Ockeghem

Johannes Ockeghem (c. 1420–1496), a member of the next generation of Renaissance composers, worked continuously in the North, mostly at the French court. His active period of time corresponds roughly to that of Verrocchio and Mantegna, and his work, like theirs, occupies an intermediate position in the history of Renaissance developments.

In some respects, Ockeghem simplified musical language. He contributed to the development of musical *imitation*—that is, the repetition of themes by different voices (as in a musical "round"). Thus a theme introduced by the tenor voice, for example, would provide the substance for a whole polyphonic composition. This concept was also used in the form of providing thematic links between the various movements of the Mass Ordinary.

Ockeghem not only emphasized the ideas of the text—even more than Dufay—he sought ways of dramatizing the text of the Mass through changes in its structure. Up to the fifteenth century, only soloists sang polyphonic sections of the Mass, while choruses sang monophonic passages, called *plainchants*. Under the influence of Ockeghem and his students, it became customary for the chorus, also, to sing polyphonically. Masses now featured alternations between choruses and duets, trios, or quartets of soloists, all singing similar themes.

Secular Music in Italy

While Netherlandish composers dominated the serious music of the Early Renaissance, the Italians exerted a strong influence on popular music. Mainly because of its simplicity and homophonic texture, this music provided a foil to the more difficult polyphonic structure of official music.

The *lauda*, an Italian devotional hymn, was developed

in the late fifteenth century during the time Savonarola was in power. Sung in Italian or Latin, laudas are rhythmic, mostly homophonic, and noted for their clarity of expression.

Although some music was composed expecially for laudas, most of it was adapted from carnival songs with the original words changed to sacred ones. This music owes its viability, surprisingly, to Lorenzo the Magnificent. Under his leadership the Florentine carnival reached a high level of brilliance, and he himself wrote songs for these events. The words of carnival songs—always in Italian—are amorous, suggestive, and often obscene, while the music is marked by simple harmonies, pronounced rhythm, and clear phrases.

Various kinds of secular song—collectively called *frottolas*—were also converted to laudas. Although considered a type of popular music, the frottola was not sung by commoners in the streets but by noblemen, chiefly in the northern Italian courts of Mantua, Venice, Urbino, and Florence. The form was especially favored by Isabella d'Este, wife of the Duke of Mantua, and famous patron of poets and artists. As did Lorenzo in Florence, she promoted the establishment of the Italian language as a worthy companion to music. Although there are different kinds of frottolas, in general they are more melodic than carnival songs. However, they share with the latter their simplicity and declamatory style. Their harmonies come very close to our own major and minor keys.

Sixteenth-Century Literature

Machiavelli

Secularism in the Italian Renaissance reaches its summit in the political thought of Niccolò Machiavelli (1469–1527). Although Machiavelli regarded himself as a man of integrity, his name, since the sixteenth century, has become synonymous with ruthless political scheming. This reputation derives from his best-known work, *The Prince*, in which he describes politics and human behavior, not as they ought to be, but as they actually were in his time. For this reason he has often been described as the first political realist. In order to evaluate his views accurately, however, one must be aware of the conditions in Italy and of his personal experience of those conditions, which prompted him to write *The Prince*.

Machiavelli grew up during the golden age of humanism in a Florence that was dominated by the personality of the great Medici ruler, Lorenzo the Magnificent. After the Medici rule ended, Machiavelli served the Florentine Republic for 14 years in a diplomatic role which required much travel and contact with princes and popes. He thus became acutely aware of the unscrupulous power politics practiced by the city-states of Italy and by those nations, such as France and Spain, which intervened in Italian politics. With the return to power of the Medici in 1512, the Republic was brought to an abrupt end, and Machiavelli, who was mistrusted by the Medici, was excluded from the government. He wrote *The Prince* (1513) partly at least, to gain the favor of the Medici; thus when the Republic was restored a few years later, he was also

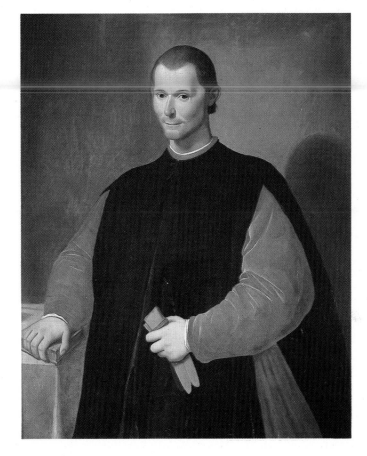

3.28 Niccolo Machiavelli

rejected from participation in that government.

The Prince is a striking example of the secularity of the Italian Renaissance, for it broke radically with the medieval concept of a Christian social order ruled, under God, by a prince whose responsibility was the distribution of justice in accordance with moral and theological principles. In this view, politics and the duties of the prince were treated as a branch of Christian ethics, with the prince held accountable to God for his political stewardship.

Machiavelli began with a very different premise: the belief that the most pressing need was the unification of Italy. This premise was a natural one for Machiavelli to assume, given his own sense of patriotism and the political chaos that dominated Italy in this period. In Machiavelli's view, the only escape from this political turmoil was through the rule of a strong prince, the type of powerful leader represented by Donatello's *Gattamelata* (Fig. 3.13). Thus he dedicated his book to Lorenzo de' Medici (grandson of Lorenzo the Magnificent), an ironic choice since Lorenzo was an unlikely candidate for the role Machiavelli mapped out for his prince and may not have even read the book.

To understand *The Prince*, then, one must be aware of the political context in which it was written. Because Machiavelli saw Italian reunification as the greatest good, he subjects all other considerations, moral and theological, to this overriding concern. Thus he exhorts his prince to use whatever methods are necessary to gain and retain power. He may choose to act in keeping with moral/theological principles, but only if such behavior is conducive to obtaining and maintaining political power. Thus the good of the state takes precedence over all other values. All means to this end are therefore justified. In the light of this approach to politics, one can understand why *The Prince* has becomes a textbook for tyrants; in fact, it may serve as a handbook to any political view that assumes that the welfare of the state takes precedence over all other considerations.

The Prince, then, is thoroughly of its time. But Machiavelli also (as he points out in his dedication addressed to Lorenzo) drew upon classical authors in developing his theories. Thus, in true Renaissance fashion, he, like Petrarch and Boccaccio, found that his own spirit and understanding were inspired and enlightened by the classical sources, especially the ancient historians.

Machiavelli was a true representative of the mature Italian Renaissance. Unlike Petrarch, he was apparently untroubled by a faith-driven conscience. Like him, however, he found the classics a source of inspiration, full of relevance for the kind of Italy he hoped to see realized. Wholly secular in his approach to life, he was concerned with the political and material well-being of Italy and, unlike the medieval ascetics, sought his pleasures in this world. Moreover, his political theories were based upon his study of classical history and personal observation of how the "political animal," as Aristotle defined man, behaves. The measure of his achievement is illustrated by the fact that *The Prince* is one of the most profoundly influential books in the history of Western thought.

Castiglione

Baldassare Castiglione (1478–1529), like Machiavelli, is also a product of the Italian Renaissance, but in a different sense. Diplomat, soldier, and humanist scholar, he embodied the Renaissance ideal of the well-rounded courtier which he described in *The Book of the Courtier*. His friend Raphael has provided us with a visual impression of his considerable gifts through a portrait which now hangs in the Louvre (Fig. 3.43).

Although his famous book is associated with the court of Urbino, Castiglione was born near Mantua and obtained his humanist education at Milan. Here he studied Greek and Latin, the Italian poets, music, and painting. He also learned horsemanship and developed the skills of the soldier. Upon the death of his father he was recalled to Mantua, where his talents were put to use by Francesco Gonzaga, Marquis of Mantua, for a few years prior to his invitation to enter the service of Guidobaldo di Montefeltro, Duke of Urbino.

Guidobaldo attracted to his court a remarkable company of poets, philosophers, scholars, musicans, and artists, and Urbino became an important center of Renaissance art and learning. Though imaginatively conceived, the dialogues in *The Book of the Courtier* are spoken by characters bearing the names of members of the Duke's court and are no doubt modeled on the urbane conversation that took place there. Begun in 1508, the book was in circulation by 1516, but Castiglione did not allow it to be printed until 1528. It became one of the most widely-read books of the time.

The ideal of the Courtier is that of the universal man (*uomo universale*), skilled in all the arts and sciences valued by the Renaissance. He must be handsome and of noble birth, a soldier and athlete, a poet and student of literature, a skilled conversationalist and dancer—and every manifestation of his skills must be characterized by *sprezzatura*, the nonchalance that makes the difficult look easy. This model of the ideal courtier gradually emerges from the first two books of *The Courtier*. The ideal lady at court is not neglected; her characteristics of femininity, chastity, and knowledge of arts and letters are treated in the third book. Book Four deals with the relationship of the courtier to his prince and stresses the necessity of the courtier's making a careful choice because he will be likely to imitate his master.

The most famous passage of *The Courtier* is found in the fourth book. Here the humanist and poet Pietro Bembo, later to become a cardinal, holds forth eloquently on the Neoplatonic ladder of love, a synthesis of Christian and pagan thought developed in the fifteenth century by Ficino, whose philosophy of divine love has been noted in our discussion of Botticelli. Love, according to Bembo, is the longing to enjoy beauty, and beauty is integrally connected to goodness. The lover seeks ultimate beauty and goodness, which is God himself; but as he moves up the hierarchy of love he will also love beautiful creatures, for beauty is a sign of goodness and is of God. Eventually, however, he will leave created beauty behind and focus his love on the uncreated beauty of God himself.

Castiglione's book was the principal means of popularizing this conception among Renaissance humanists. Moreover, *The Courtier*, through its many translations, became one instrument by which the achievements of Renaissance Italy were communicated to northern Europe, including England, where educated people— including Shakespeare, presumably—read it in the translation (1566) by Sir Thomas Hoby.

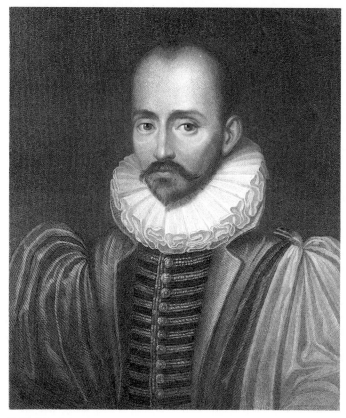

3.29 Montaigne

Montaigne

Michel de Montaigne (1533–1592), essayist and philosopher, was born at the Chateau of Montaigne in southwestern France. His father was a French Catholic; his mother, a Protestant, came from a family of Spanish Jews living in France who had converted to Christianity. Thus Montaigne, notable for his tolerance in a bigoted age, learned toleration from the cradle. His father, who deeply admired Italian humanistic learning, placed him, when he first began to speak, under the tutelage of a German physician who spoke no French and, therefore, conversed with his young pupil in Latin. Even his mother and the servants of the family were required to speak to Montaigne in Latin. Very early, therefore, Montaigne came under the classical influence and so was reading on his own, at the age of seven or eight, writers such as Ovid and Virgil. The young boy, so we are informed, was awakened in the morning by music. By thus providing a highly civilized environment for his son, Montaigne's father sought to instill in the boy a natural love of learning. His efforts were rewarded: the adult Montaigne both exemplified and advocated the benefits of this approach to knowledge.

Having completed his basic education at the College de Guyenne in Bordeaux, Montaigne studied law, after which he began service as a counselor with the Parlia-

ment (provincial high court) of Bordeaux. He resigned from this position in 1570 and retired to his chateau at the age of 38. It was here, in the famous round tower which he used as a study, that he began work on his essays (a literary genre that he created), two books of which appeared in 1580.

Not long after the publication of these essays, Montaigne set out on a tour of Europe, returning to France in 1581 to serve two terms as mayor of Bordeaux. In 1586 he retired once more to his chateau, and in 1588 he published a new edition of his essays containing the extensively revised and enlarged first two books plus a third book. In 1595, three years after his death, Marie le Jars de Gournay, a young intellectual and admirer of Montaigne, published yet another edition of the essays.

In revising his essays, Montaigne did not strike out what he had written but simply inserted his new ideas into the existing text. This method reflects the kind of mind Montaigne possessed, a mind always hospitable to new ideas and ways of seeing things. His essays, both new and revised, mirror the growth of his thought as he moved from one philosophical stance to another, including stoicism, skepticism, and epicureanism. The French word *assai*, first used by Montaigne for the essay, suggests a testing or trying. Montaigne saw his essays as a means of exploring and testing himself: "Thus, reader, I am myself the matter of my book."[2]

Montaigne is, of course, a man of the Renaissance. This is evident in his individualism and interest in human beings (especially himself), his classical education, and his devotion to and interaction with ancient writers (Plutarch and Seneca were his favorites). But his essays also reveal a skeptical point of view uncharacteristic of the earlier Renaissance, a skepticism so comprehensive that it undermines vaunted human reason and the very possibility of human knowledge. Allied to this skepticism is his opposition to discipline, his belief that abandoning oneself to nature and to one's own nature is the best way of life. Here we find a point of view quite unlike that of Castiglione's *Courtier*, with its glorification of the universal man, who, in order to master the arts and sciences, has vigorously disciplined his body and mind.

It is especially in this skeptical attitude toward reason and the possibility of human knowledge that Montaigne, the Renaissance man, undermines the attitudes of the Renaissance. Among the 54 quotations inscribed on the beams of his study's ceiling was the corrosive line, "There is no reason which is not opposed by an equal reason." Indeed, his skepticism is so radical as to deny the final word to reason in all human experience and endeavor. How very unlike Pico della Mirandola's humanistic confidence in the perfectability of human nature through reason! One is also reminded of the contrast we shall later find (page 145) between the ideal figures painted by Raphael and the questioning of this classical clarity in the distortions of Parmigianino's manneristic style. In both Montaigne and Parmigianino, Renaissance humanism is confronted by the possibility that there is always an alternate view, however clearly truth may seem to have been captured in the currently reigning perspective on reality. For Montaigne, human knowledge can never be a certain thing, for reason is fallible. There is always the possibility that some new discovery or experience will modify or even contradict what one has previously believed. Montaigne's personal motto, "Que scais-je?" ("What do I know?") captures the essence of his skeptical attitude toward the possibility of possessing absolute truth.

The ultimate danger in such radical skepticism is that a person can become so overwhelmed by the relativity of all seeming truth and experience as to become paralyzed. This is the fate of Shakespeare's Hamlet, who moves beyond Montaigne's bland skepticism to a radical denial of all meaning.

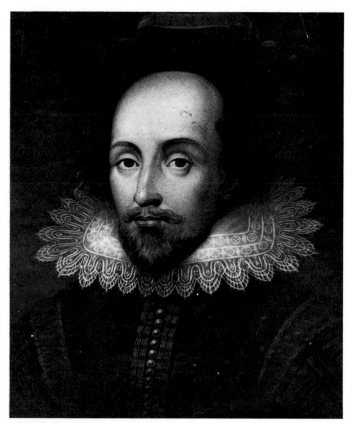

3.30 Shakespeare

Shakespeare's Hamlet

William Shakespeare (1564–1616) (Fig. **3.30**) was born in Stratford-on-Avon, a town, at that time, of some 2,000 inhabitants. Although little is known of Shakespeare's early life, this is not unusual; actors and playwrights did not have a high status in Elizabethan society, and their lives, therefore, were not of great interest. Shakespeare's father was a respected and prosperous citizen of Stratford, and it is believed that Shakespeare attended the town's fine grammar school. He married Anne Hathaway, who was seven or eight years older than he, at the age of 18. Baptismal records mark the births of their children, Susanna (1583), born five months after the marriage, and the twins Hamnet and Judith (1585).

We next hear of Shakespeare seven years later, when he was living in London and had already achieved success as a playwright. He was also a successful composer of poems, both narrative (*Venus and Adonis*, 1593; *The Rape of Lucrece*, 1594) and lyric (*Sonnets*, written, perhaps, in the 1590s and published in 1609). By 1596 he had written several of his best-known plays, including *The Taming of the Shrew*, *Romeo and Juliet*, and *Henry IV*, parts 1 and 2.

Shakespeare also shared—as actor, playwright, and business partner—in a well-known theatrical company of which the Lord Chamberlain was the patron. In 1599 this company built the famous Globe Theatre. When James I came to the throne in 1603, the Chamberlain's Men came under royal patronage and were henceforth known as the King's Men. Shakespeare's growing prosperity also brought social recognition, so that, in 1596, he was granted a coat of arms and the title of "Gentleman." In this same period he bought New Place, a large house in Stratford; later he purchased other properties in Stratford and London. Most of Shakespeare's major tragedies, including *Hamlet*, *Othello*, *King Lear* and *Macbeth*, were written in the first ten years or so of the seventeenth century. Sometime near the end of this period he retired to Stratford, where he lived most of the time until his death there on April 23, 1616.

As Shakespeare's plays constitute the most significant corpus of dramatic literature in the world, so *Hamlet* (1606) is the world's most famous play and its protagonist the most discussed dramatic character. Indeed, there is hardly a European country in which the play, in translation, has not been published. One reason for critics' fascination with *Hamlet* is the many-sided character of its protagonist. He has provoked a plethora of interpretations unequalled in literary criticism. How are we to explain the character of Hamlet? Is he the "sweet prince" who is the victim of circumstances he cannot control, or the cruel and ambitious aspirant to the Danish throne who can commit murder and then heap ignominy upon the corpse of his victim? Is he the poetic dreamer, so obsessed with the life of the mind that he cannot act, or is he simply blocked by circumstances from complying with the admonition of his murdered father's ghost? Is he paralyzed by melancholy? Or does he delay action because, in the Freudian view, he suffers from an unresolved Oedipus complex and identifies with Claudius' killing of his father and marriage to his mother? Or does he, by erroneously assuming that the Ghost is truly that of his father, fall victim to an evil spirit and thus, in violation of Christian teachings, cause the destruction of two entire families?

This chapter has previously dealt with two images of the Renaissance court, the Machiavellian and the Castiglionian: the one provides a context for the amoral seizure and maintenance of power by the prince; the other, a context for urbane rational dialogue among intellectual equals concerning the training and education of the ideal courtier. As dissimilar as these two images may appear, both are based on the assumption that this world provides a context for meaningful action. Machiavelli's ideal prince is supremely rational in his assessment of the possibilities and liabilities of power; and having embraced power as his supreme value, he is thoroughly capable of the decisions and actions necessary to achieving that goal. Although Castiglione's courtier is trained to serve a prince, his book

does not support the Machiavellian view that political power is the ultimate good; rather, it is based upon the assumption that the Renaissance ideal of the universal man, competent in all areas of endeavor, is worthy of the rigorous mental and physical discipline necessary to attaining it. Thus both Machiavelli and Castiglione base their presentations of the court upon positive assumptions about human reason and its possibilities.

Not so the court of Shakespeare's *Hamlet*. Hamlet possesses the qualifications of the ideal courtier, as Ophelia observes when she speaks of him as a courtier, soldier, and scholar—and so he is. But having mastered these accomplishments, Hamlet places no value on his achievement. It fails to provide him with a basis for being and acting. His most famous utterance, "To be, or not to be, that is the question," calls the value of life itself into question; and when he acts, he does so spasmodically and compulsively. Hamlet finds no basis, in heaven or earth, for meaningful action; this is his tragedy. What is the cause of this void in Hamlet's world?

Writing in the late nineteenth century, the English poet and critic Matthew Arnold stated that *Hamlet* is a "puzzle" because "Shakespere [sic] conceived this play with his mind running on Montaigne, and placed its action and its hero in Montaigne's atmosphere and world." He goes on to describe that world as one "of man viewed as a being *ondoyant et divers* [undulating and diverse], balancing and indeterminate, the plaything of cross-motives and shifting impulses, swayed by a thousand subtle influences...."[3] Arnold's statement reflects the relativism of Montaigne, his position that no point of view, however rationally convincing, is exempt from modification or even refutation because of new reasons and/or new experiences. Montaigne did not apply his rational methods to his Catholic beliefs, but the tool of radical relativism which he made accessible to other thinkers could not, in the hands of a less complacent person, be confined to secular issues. It is an intriguing question why Montaigne, though arguing for the *relativity* of all things, does not, like Hamlet, follow through with the next step, the *futility* of all things. Is it a matter of temperament, a cheerful disposition that by its very nature cannot entertain a sense of the tragic? One wonders.

Whatever may be the answer to this question, the typical Renaissance mind usually asks at some point what is the ultimate meaning of the intellectual activity it so highly prizes. Thus that mind, in a suicidal gesture, turns its sharply honed rational weapons against itself, raising the fundamental question as to whether there is any meaning in human activity. The result of this questioning, for some, is a failure of nerve, the paralysis of self-doubt. Having lost their confidence in the concept of a divinely revealed and executed cosmic plan, such persons find themselves confronted by a void where they can find no footing, human or divine, from which to launch meaningful human action.

Such is the case with Hamlet, who, unlike Montaigne, moves beyond relativity to futility. Hence, his speeches are permeated with irony—so often the refuge of the disillusioned and cynical. Hence also his inconsistent plans and purposes, giving rise to the multiplicity of interpretations of his character; for there is no course of action or thought that can claim his wholehearted commitment. Such is the nature of the world inhabited by Hamlet, a fictional incarnation of Montaigne's "undulating and diverse" creature, the late-Renaissance intellectual.

Shakespeare makes it clear that Hamlet has not always been so disillusioned. Ophelia describes him as having been "the expectancy and rose of the fair state,/The glass of fashion, and the mould of form," possessed of a "noble and most sovereign reason...." It is his mother's incestuous and sudden marriage after his father's death and the unworthiness of Claudius, his father's successor to the throne—later compounded in evil by the revelation of his father's murder by Claudius—that snap the moorings of Hamlet's intellectual and moral confidence. Indeed, in his first soliloquy, even before his encounter with his father's ghost, Hamlet expresses a total cynicism, toward the world, the state, and human nature. Later, after the Ghost's revelation, in his speech to Rosencrantz and Guildenstern, he reveals his disillusionment, first with the macrocosm (the universe)—the earth is a "sterile promontory," the air "a foul and pestilent congregation of vapours"—and then with the microcosm (humanity)—"this quintessence of dust." Significantly, these are the very areas of medieval certainty challenged by Renaissance thought. In the hierarchial medieval view, divine ordering was apparent in both the macrocosm and the microcosm—the God-given gift of reason being the means by which the human being, the apex of God's creation, perceived this order. The state likewise was a manifestation of divine hierarchy, with the king, under God but over his subjects, ruling justly and wisely in accordance with God's will. The theories of Copernicus put in question the central significance of the world and its inhabitants by replacing the earth with the sun as the center of the cosmos. Machiavelli's purely secular view of the state challenged the idea of politics as a branch of Christian ethics. Finally, as we have seen, Montaigne denied the reliability of reason, the faculty that, in Christian teaching, elevated the human being above the rest of creation and by means of which the reality of God's orderly hierarchy was perceived.

This is the background for Shakespeare's presentation of Hamlet, whose personal tragedy opens the door to the void of cosmic meaninglessness which, potentially, was already the habitation of Renaissance man. The character of Hamlet, therefore, is the fictional representation of Renaissance disillusionment with Renaissance humanism. Hamlet, the ideal courtier, embodiment of Castiglione's universal man, disillusioned by the hypocrisy and corruption within his family and the state, is forced to confront the question of whether there is meaning in his own life and in human experience in general. But in a world where all truth is merely relative and there is no grand design, he cannot find a place to stand. He launches projects that point to decisive action but they fail to produce it. He acts impulsively (his murder of Polonius) or under compulsion (the final duel); but he never methodically undertakes the fulfillment of the task with which the Ghost has entrusted him, and so indirectly causes the carnage of the last scene. Aeschylus' *Oresteia* shows a chain of retributive justice that is, potentially, unending. Shakespeare's *Hamlet* suggests that the neglect of retributive justice can also produce victims. Neither course offers a satisfactory prospect. However, Aeschylus believed, like medieval humans, in ultimate certainties. Thus he offered a resolution of the problem of retributive justice in the Athenian jury system. Shakespeare's play offers no such resolution. The indeterminate and uncertain Renaissance world of *Hamlet* is more like that of Euripides—and therefore more modern.

Sixteenth-Century Italian Art

High Renaissance Art

In the early fifteenth century the seat of the papacy was removed from Avignon and returned to Rome, the former capital of the ancient world. At that time, while Florence was thriving, Rome was a collection of old ruins, dirt roads, and cow pastures. Smaller than Florence, Milan, or Venice, it was one of the least civilized cities of Italy, teeming with disease (caused partly by its impure water). Thanks to the efforts of some of the popes, however, old aqueducts and walls were restored, old churches were renovated, and new construction was started in mid-century. Through "jubilees" and other money-raising schemes, the revenues of the Church were increased, and large sums of money began to flow into the city. In addition, Greek and Roman manuscripts were assiduously collected, humanist scholars were courted, and Florentine artists were brought in to decorate the papal apartments, including the Sistine Chapel, and to work on other projects. By the end of the century, the wealth of the papacy was greater than that of many princes, and Rome began to rival Florence as a cultural capital. In the early sixteenth century it overtook Florence and became the new focus of major developments—though Florence continued to be a major breeding ground for artists.

The flowering of art in sixteenth-century Rome is comparable to the flowering of Greek Classical art nearly 2,000 years earlier. Referred to as the *High Renaissance*, this period represents the fruition of prior developments (in this case, in Florence) and is marked by the emergence of Olympian figures such as Leonardo and Michelangelo. High Renaissance artists, more than those of earlier civilizations, including even Classical Greece, were showered with praise and monetary rewards. Had he chosen to, Michelangelo could have lived like a prince; Titian actually did. These artists and others fulfilled the potential of fifteenth-century artists—bringing to perfection both the realistic and the idealistic trends found in Florentine art. But High Renaissance art is more than just a continuation of that earlier art; it projects a new world, containing, as art historian Heinrich Wölfflin puts it, "a new race of men." It is peopled by athletic, fully-developed, larger-than-life men and women who move through their surroundings with the stately, unhurried assurance of Castiglione's aristocrats. Nowhere in the High Renaissance world does one see the awkwardness of a Masaccio or Piero, the brittleness of a Donatello or Mantegna, or the tentativeness of a Ghiberti or Botticelli. In painting, the fictional settings of this world—subject to the controls of linear perspective—are both rational and spacious, befitting the dignity of the people within them; the grandeur of the fictional architecture of painting has its counterpart in the real architecture designed by Michelangelo, the major architect of the early sixteenth century.

Leonardo

The considerable popular fame of Leonardo da Vinci (1452–1519) rests almost entirely on two very well-known works of art, *The Last Supper* and the *Mona Lisa*. The public reputation of these works belies the true greatness of a man who was a genius in several fields: engineering, astronomy, hydrology, sound, optics, and physiology. More than just knowledgeable in these fields, he was ahead of his time, inventing hundreds of machines that were centuries ahead of their time. He filled the pages of his notebooks with drawings and written descriptions of such things as band brakes, machine guns, mortars, armored cars, flying machines, and a differential transmission. (In recent times working models based on his drawings have actually been built.) His considerable curiosity about nature led him to observe and diagram the movements of water, growths of plants, moods of the atmosphere, and shapes of mountains. His main fascination, however, was with the human body (Fig. **3.31**); and he is said to have dissected as many as 50 cadavers. Scholars today consider him the greatest physicist of the sixteenth century and one of the most important names in anatomy before the time of modern medicine.

Born in 1452, Leonardo was only eight years younger than Botticelli, yet his art was so advanced that he could well have lived a generation later. Apprenticed to Verrocchio in his twenties, he demonstrated such precocity as a painter that, according to legend, the master discarded his own brushes and concentrated henceforward on sculpture. Leonardo was indifferent to Neoplatonic musings, the intellectual vogue of the time. Perhaps because of this,

3.31 LEONARDO DA VINCI
Embryo in the Womb, c. 1510
Pen drawing
Royal Library, Windsor Castle

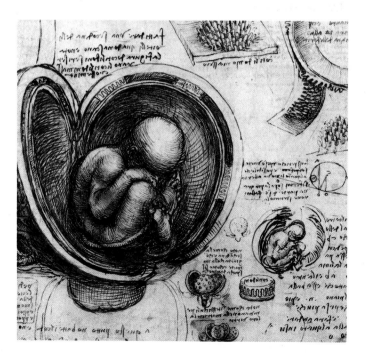

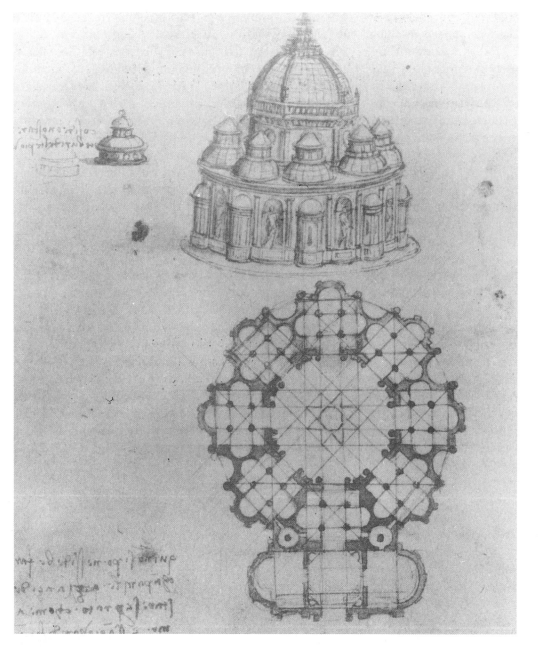

3.32 LEONARDO DA VINCI
Project for a Church, c. 1490,
Pen drawing
Bibliothèque de l'Arsenal, Paris

or because the Medici family was indifferent to his talents, he went to Milan to work for Lodovico Sforza, Regent of Milan. There his talents did not go unnoticed; he was idolized by both patrons and artists as he painted portraits, completed important commissions, including *The Last Supper*, and worked on pageants. After 17 years in Milan he visited many places: Mantua, Venice, Florence, the Romagna (with Cesare Borgia), and Rome. His last destination was France, where he served as the designated painter, architect, and engineer to Francis I. There he died at the age of 67.

Although his notebooks show that Leonardo was the first to design churches in the High Renaissance style (Fig. 3.32), his architecture never got beyond the proposal stage. His only major sculpture, an enormous equestrian statue of Francesco Sforza, the Regent's father, fell victim to French soldiers, who used it for target practice, before it could be cast. Thus Leonardo's output consists of drawings and paintings.

Although it remained unfinished, *The Adoration of the Magi* (Fig. 3.33) is considered the most important work of Leonardo's first Florentine period. Unlike Gentile's painting of the Adoration, this one has no procession in the background; instead it has fantastic, open architecture—an indication of the artist's imagination as well as his mastery of perspective. More importantly, the people in

3.33 LEONARDO DA VINCI
Adoration of the Magi, begun
1481
Underpainting on panel,
96 × 97 ins (244 × 246 cm)
Uffizi Gallery, Florence

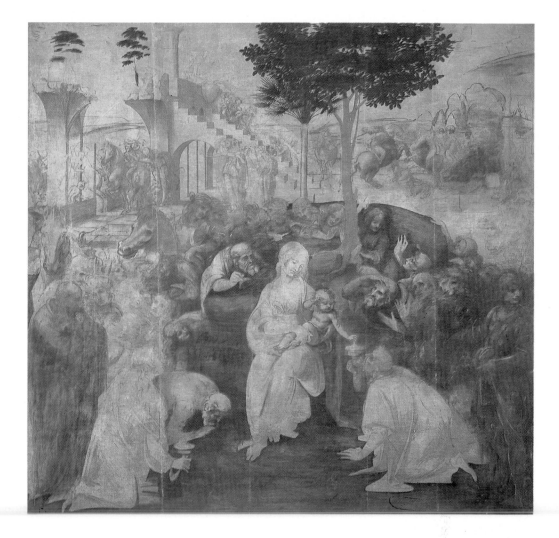

3.34 Leonardo Da Vinci
The Last Supper
Mural painting,
15 ft 1 in × 28 ft 10½ ins
(4.6 × 8.56 m)
Santa Maria delle Grazie, Milan

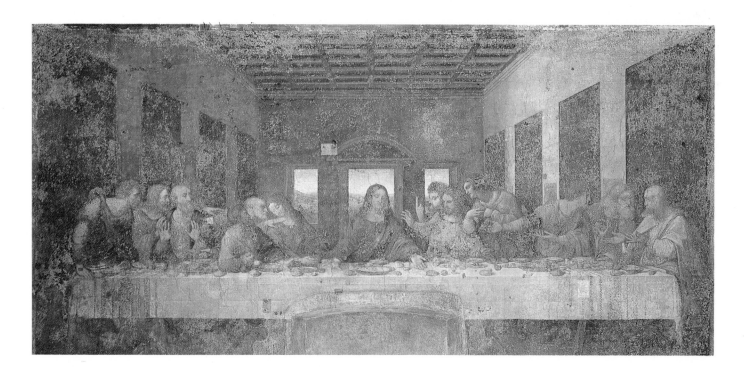

this Adoration, as seen in the crowd of agitated characters pressing around the Virgin, are clearly focused on the central event. Less visible, though equally important, is the evidence of Leonardo's struggle to solve compositional problems. Although Renaissance painting had progressed significantly in depicting both human bodies and a plausible, spatial world for them to inhabit, it had not succeeded very well in putting the two together. The problem of relating figures, especially active ones, to their spatial surroundings seemed to boil down to two unsatisfactory alternatives: Either movement was sacrificed in favor of compositional stability (as in Masaccio's *Tribute Money*, Fig. 3.16) or stability was sacrificed in favor of movement (as in Mantegna's *St. James*, Fig. 3.22). Clearly, in its present state, Leonardo's *Adoration* has plenty of movement but suffers from being chaotic. (Indeed, if it had been finished in colors and details, it would have been even more chaotic.) But a closer look reveals a latent triangular shape in the foreground, with its apex at the top of Mary's head and with sides extending along the backs of the two foreground Magi terminating at the bottom corners of the picture. Had Leonardo finished the *Adoration*, he might have developed this compositional device further and thus imposed some order on the chaos.

The Last Supper (Fig. 3.34), in which Leonardo did solve the problem of reconciling movement and stability, is also, unfortunately, difficult to see. Painted on the wall of a Milan monastery with a special, still unknown, preparation invented by the artist, it began to peel off the wall less than 20 years after it was finished. After that it suffered still more abuses: a door being cut through it (at the bottom of the picture), Napoleon's soldiers using the room for a mess hall, a number of ill-advised restorations, and World War II bombings. It is a wonder that the painting looks as good as it does.

One of the reasons *The Last Supper* is so well known has to do with its deceptive simplicity. The setting is simply a square room with several large openings and a long rectangular table in the foreground. The table, along with the disciples arrayed behind it, stresses the horizontal shape of the picture itself. The shape of the environment is determined by one-point perspective, the lines terminating at a point in the exact center, the position of Christ's head. In addition to his central location, Christ is further set off by the window behind him (the only one with a curved pediment) and his separation from the disciples, who are arranged in groups of three. Along with being the pictorial focus, Christ is also the psychological focus. *The Last Supper* illustrates the moment when he says, "one of you will betray me," setting off an explosion of reactions among the men. The most animated are those to the immediate left (Judas, Peter, and John) and the right

(Thomas, James, and Philip). Philip, his hands pressed to his breast, seems to be protesting his Lord that it is not he. In a masterful piece of understatement, Leonardo has marked off Judas symbolically and formally by making him the only one in shadow. Leaning back with one arm on the table, he seems to be recoiling from Christ and from the knowledge that he is the betrayer.

The first truly High Renaissance painting, *The Last Supper* is a successful integration of active figures in a real spatial world. By means of using a symmetrical and horizontal format as a stage for physical and psychological action, Leonardo resolved the Renaissance dichotomy of movement versus stability. Though all the men are idealized, each has a different personality. Though all are psychologically focused and clearly part of the same dramatic circumstance, each has a different reaction to it. But their expressions, unlike those in the *Adoration*, are dignified, not exaggerated. Finally, their gestures, though individual and purposeful, are nevertheless graceful. *The Last Supper* is a marvelous integration of subject matter and form, which accounts for its reputation as one of the greatest works of all time.

The *Mona Lisa* (Fig. 3.35), is the other of Leonardo's two most famous paintings. When he finished it in 1503, during his second Florentine period, it was original in several ways.

The triangle, which was latent in the *Adoration*, can be seen in the pyramidal shape of the sitter, whose form dominates the picture plane and whose body is visible from head to lap. (Previous portraits confined the view to just the head and shoulders.) Though in repose, the subject's body exhibits a subtle movement with the shoulders facing three-quarters to the left, the head turned more toward the viewer, and the eyes looking directly at the viewer. The vivid landscape in the background is remarkable in its own right, especially when compared to the limited, stage-set conceptions of earlier art. To integrate the landscape with the sitter, Leonardo raised the horizon to the level of her eyes. To do this and still maintain correct perspective, he placed her on a high plane (perhaps, a balcony of a villa on a mountaintop), a solution that imparts a sense of loftiness. Sitter and background are further united by Leonardo's own version of aerial perspective called *sfumato*—blurring the edges of objects and people to create the effect of smoky atmosphere.

The subject, the 24-year-old wife of Francesco del Giocondo, a Florentine banker, must have been very patient, for the artist took three years to complete the portrait. Perhaps this accounts for the passive, though personal, expression of the face. In *The Last Supper* a psychological relationship exists among the subjects; in

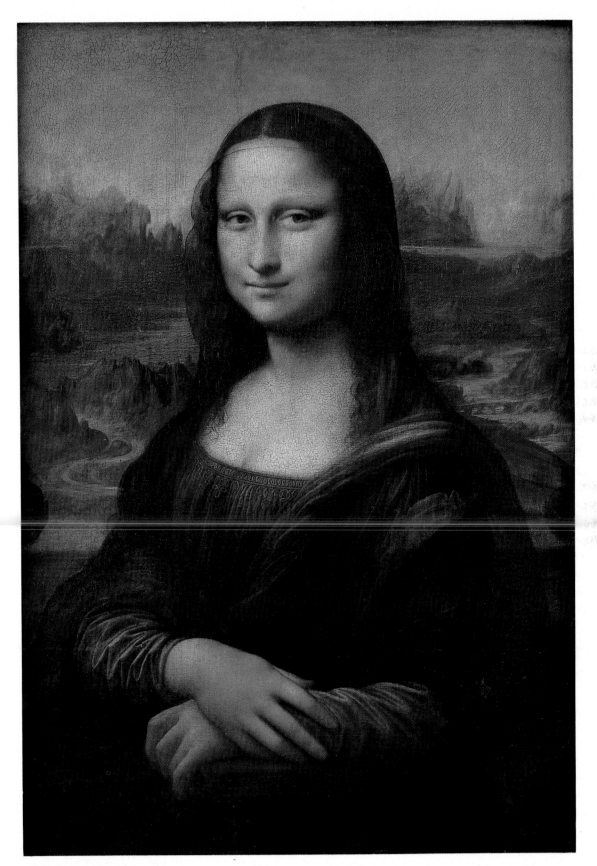

3.35 LEONARDO DA VINCI
Mona Lisa, c. 1503–5
Oil on panel, 30¼ ins × 21 ins (76.8 × 53.3 cm)
Louvre, Paris

the *Mona Lisa* the relationship is between the subject and the viewer. But the nature of this relationship is unclear. Its subtlety and elusiveness, conveyed by the sitter's "enigmatic smile," has been the source of an endless supply of commentary, romantic writing, even songs. The cold, craggy, uninhabited background enhances the aura of mystery and isolation. The *Mona Lisa* was the first portrait to exhibit the essential characteristics of a High Renaissance painting. It has the monumental figure and balanced composition to provide stability and repose; it has a breathtaking view to give it grandeur; finally, the naturalness of the sitter and the enigmatic psychology give it the necessary life and human interest.

Michelangelo

In 1504 Michelangelo Buonarroti (1474–1564) was commissioned to paint a mural in Florence's Palazzo Vecchio, the town hall, just opposite one that Leonardo had started working on. Each was to portray a Florentine military triumph. Leonardo was then 52; Michelangelo, 30—young enough to be the elder artist's son, but already a famous sculptor. At first the enterprise was viewed by Florentines as a contest between giants. They were disappointed. Because of technical errors, the colors of Leonardo's mural began to run before it was half finished; because of a summons from the pope to do a sculpture, Michelangelo abandoned the mural project after making only a few sketches.

Unlike Leonardo, Michelangelo was not active in fields outside art; but within that world his gargantuan talents and energies ranged from sculpture to painting to architecture. Although his preferred medium was sculpture, he produced what many believe to be the greatest single painting in the world—the ceiling of the Sistine Chapel. And his architectural projects in Florence and Rome, including part of the design of St. Peter's, established him as the leading architect of the era.

Born in 1474 in the little village of Caprese, he was apprenticed at the age of 13 to the painter Domenico Ghirlandaio, and two years later joined the Medici household, then led by Lorenzo the Magnificent. During the next few, crucially formative years, Michelangelo was able to study and produce sculpture in their gardens and to sit at the same table with Lorenzo, Politian (Poliziano), Pico, and Ficino. There, at the very center of Florentine culture, the young artist was indoctrinated with a love of the high world of classicism, in both art and philosophy. Among other things, he became a passionate admirer of the naked body—particularly the male body—which, in keeping with Renaissance Neoplatonism, he saw as both a manifestation of divine beauty and a prison of the soul.

But during those same formative years he also heard the sermons of Savonarola, the Dominican monk who, preaching the ideals of the early Church, denounced the culture of the humanists as pagan and immoral and predicted that the sins of the Italian people would be avenged in a holocaust. His denunciations spared no one, not even Lorenzo and the pope himself. Thus, a contrasting side of the young Michelangelo was cultivated: a deep sense of sin and the fear of divine retribution. These two sides found an uneasy, at times very disturbed, synthesis in both his personality and his art.

Many elements of that synthesis are reflected in a monumental work completed in 1504, the same year as the ill-fated mural commission. Given a 14-foot- (4-meter)-tall block of marble, Michelangelo signed a contract in 1501 to produce a gigantic male statue for the Cathedral of Florence. The result was the *David* (Fig. 3.36), conceived by the artist as an embodiment of both Christian and civic virtues. The city fathers were so pleased with the result that they placed it at the entrance of the Palazzo Vecchio instead of the Cathedral. Michelangelo's choice of David, a symbol of the triumph of good over evil, signifies his admiration for Old Testament heroes as well as his commitment to Christianity. However, because this David, like Donatello's (Fig. 3.12), is nude, it is also a sign of the artist's admiration for pagan art and commitment to Neoplatonism. Still, because its proportions are more those of a sturdy farm lad than those of a lithe adolescent, it is very different from Donatello's nude and, for that matter, Greek nudes. With head, arms, and hands too large for its hips and legs, it was likened by Wölfflin to "a gigantic hobbledehoy." But what especially distinguishes Michelangelo's nude from one by Polykleitos or Praxiteles, for example, is its complete lack of classical passivity. Clearly it expresses defiance, even latent violence, rather than ideal calm or sensuousness. And this is because of the many subtle evidences of tension that can be seen in the moody face, the tendons of the neck, the muscles of the thorax, and the veins of the statue's right hand. Such tension was to become more overt in much of the artist's later work. Despite its lack of perfect proportions, according to Greek canons, the *David* does possess beauty, but a beauty charged with pent-up emotion. Though a masterpiece of the High Renaissance, the *David's* representation of human nature is, appropriately, closer to the Old Testament than to classicism, with idealism and emotion being held in precarious balance. Vasari wrote that "it surpasses all others, both ancient and modern."

In 1505 Michelangelo was summoned to Rome by Pope Julius II to create his tomb. Probably the most powerful and ambitious pope ever to occupy the chair, Julius

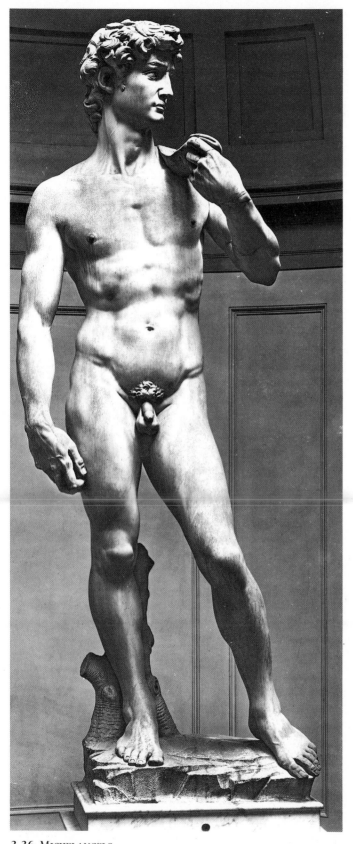

3.36 MICHELANGELO
David, 1501–4
Marble, 13 ft 5 ins (4.08 m) high
Academy, Florence

wanted a grandiose monument to proclaim his greatness. Savonarola, were he still alive in the sixteenth century, would have reviled him in his sermons; Erasmus, Dutch theologian and scholar, did revile him in a vicious satire, *Iulius exclusus* (*Julius Excluded from Heaven*). For the tomb Michelangelo proposed a three-story mausoleum with niches and pedestals for 40 statues. But not long after the marble was secured, the project was called off—perhaps because funds were needed for another of Julius' projects, the new St. Peter's. Michelangelo was outraged, but the pope asked him instead to paint the ceiling of the Sistine Chapel (Fig. **3.37**).

Protesting that he was a sculptor, not a painter, Michelangelo nonetheless yielded to the pope and began in 1508 to paint a mural on the subject of God's Creation. Michelangelo's creation itself was almost superhuman. Seventy feet (21 meters) above the floor and 5800 square feet (537 square meters) in area, the enormous vault had been given only a coat of blue dotted with gold stars under Pope Sixtus in the fifteenth century. (The walls below the windows had been covered with murals by several fifteenth-century artists, including Botticelli and Ghirlandaio.) Four years after beginning work, Michelangelo had transformed that surface into a complex pictorial drama (Fig. **3.38**).

Episodes from the Book of Genesis—the Creation, the Fall, and the Flood—are chronicled in a series of nine panels in the center, running the full length of the ceiling (Fig. **3.39**). The whole mural, however, intermingles themes from both testaments and from pagan mythology. Although Christ is not pictured anywhere, he is represented symbolically.

There is no single vantage point for viewing the ceiling that would enable one to see all the scenes right side up. Furthermore, there is no preferred sequence for viewing parts of it. However, its overall structure can be divided into three main sections: the lowest section—physically and symbolically—consists of the eight *lunettes* (triangular shapes just above the windows) containing the Jewish kings and queens, ordinary mortals who were the ancestors of Christ. The larger lunettes at the corners contain events from the Old Testament which are believed to have portended the Crucifixion. The middle section consists of the 12 niches between the lunettes which contain the Old Testament prophets and Greek sibyls (prophetesses)—clairvoyant mortals who predicted the coming of Christ. Above them is the third section, the scenes of Genesis, containing, in addition to God, the most significant people of the Old Testament. Finally, there is a supporting cast of characters: *putti* (cupids) appear as relief carvings on the pedestals that flank the prophets' and sibyls' niches; *genii* (guardian spirits) are dimly visible

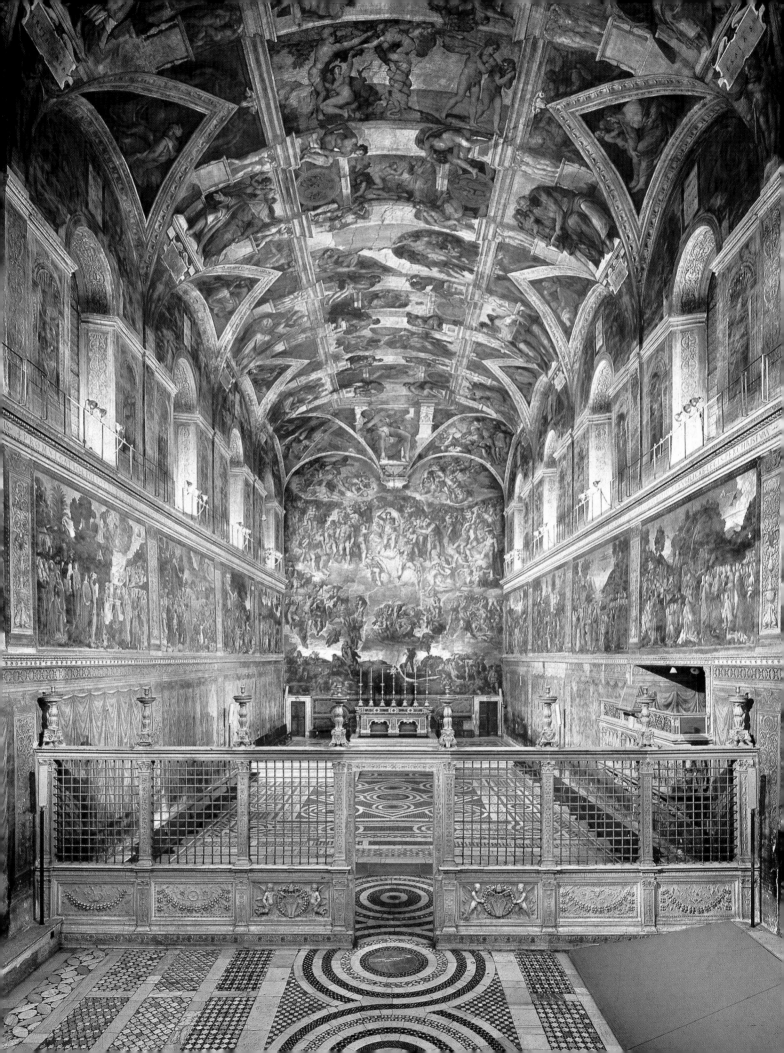

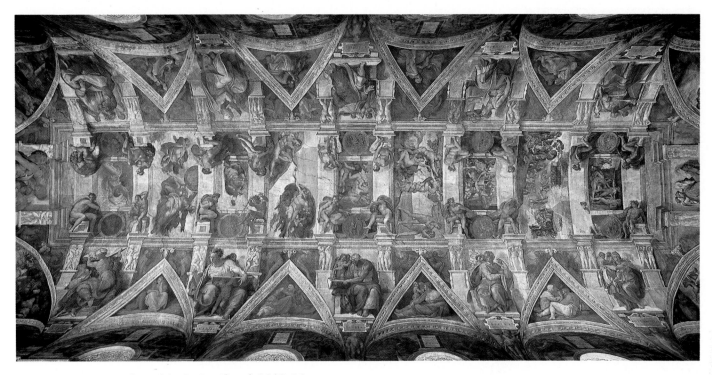

3.38 MICHELANGELO Ceiling of the Sistine Chapel, 1508–12.

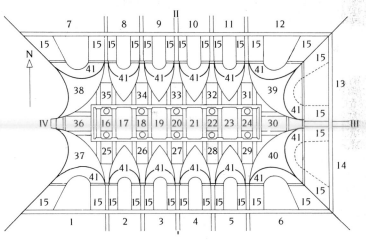

3.39 Diagram of the Sistine Chapel ceiling frescoes

I South Wall with scenes from the life of Moses (1–6)
II North wall with scenes from the life of Christ (7–12)
III East wall with entrance (13–14)
IV West wall with Last Judgment

15 Window niches with 24 portraits of the first Popes
41 Lunettes above the windows with portraits of the ancestors of Christ and scenes from the Old Testament

The Frescoes on the Ceiling

16 God Separates Light and Darkness
17 God Creates the Sun and the Moon and the Plants on Earth
18 God Separates the Water and Earth and Blesses his Work
19 Creation of Adam
20 Creation of Eve
21 Fall of Man and Expulsion from Paradise
22 Sacrifice of Noah
23 The Flood
24 The Intoxication of Noah
25 Jeremiah
26 Persian Sibyl
27 Ezekiel
28 Eritrean Sibyl
29 Joel
30 Zechariah
31 Delphic Sibyl
32 Isaiah
33 Cumaean Sibyl
34 Daniel
35 Libyan Sibyl
36 Jonah
37 The Punishment of Haman
38 The Brazen Serpent
39 Judith with the Head of Holofernes
40 David Slaying Goliath

3.37 (left) MICHELANGELO
Interior of the Sistine Chapel, showing ceiling frescoes, 1508–12
The Vatican, Rome

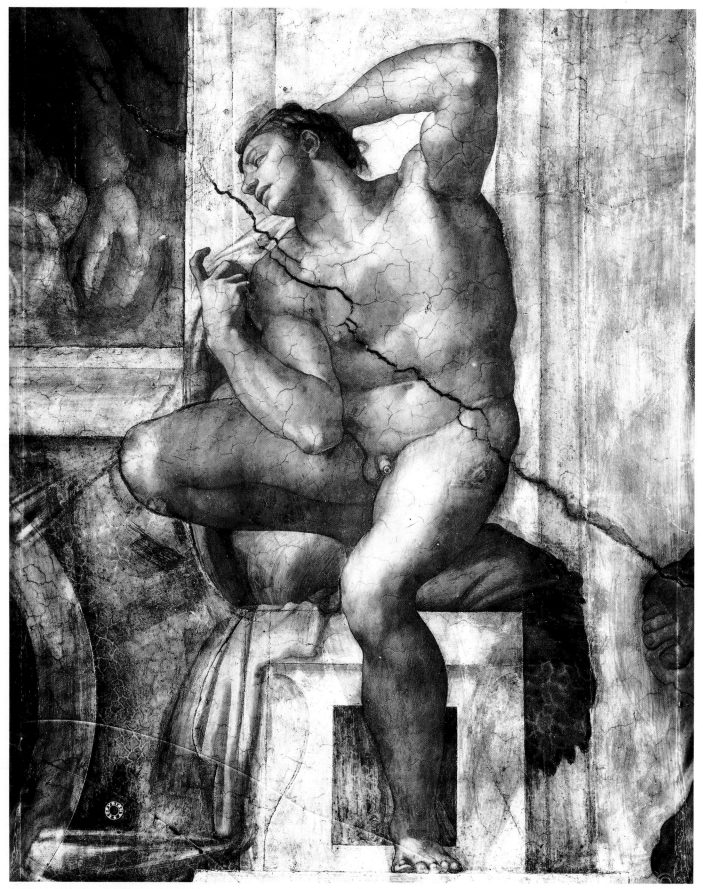

3.40 MICHELANGELO *Naked Youth*, detail of fresco from the Sistine Chapel ceiling

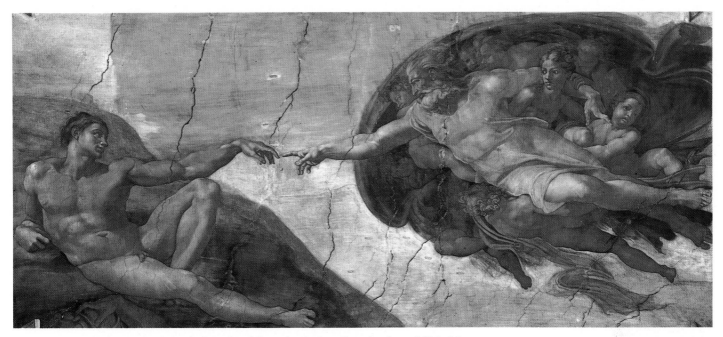

3.41 MICHELANGELO *The Creation of Adam*, detail from the Sistine Chapel ceiling, 1508–12

behind each of the prophets and sibyls; and naked youths, or "slaves" (Fig. **3.40**), can be seen sitting uneasily on the pedestals just above the putti. Although the slaves' nudity suggest Greek art, their role in this work is similar to that of Christian angels—intermediaries between God and people.

The Creation of Adam (Fig. **3.41**), the fourth of the Genesis scenes, is divided between two dominant shapes: a triangle of barren earth supporting Adam on the left, opposite an oval-shaped, billowing mantle supporting God and the angels on the right (the young woman under God's arm is either Eve or Mary). Between them is empty space—except for the extended hands of Adam and God whose fingers do not quite touch. Thus, the two masses are united by the tiny, charged field of energy between their fingertips, as Adam is about to be given life. Adam's body, though heroic in its proportions, is anything but heroic in its languid pose—as if waiting to be awakened from a long sleep. Lying as it does on bare ground, it could also symbolize Prometheus, the Greek god who was bound to a rock because he defied Zeus—just as Adam was to suffer the Fall because he defied God. Unlike Adam's passive body, God's is dynamic, full of divine energy. Although it has the titanic proportions of, say, Zeus, chief of all the Greek gods, it also has the fear-inspiring expression of Jehovah, God of the Old Testament. (Julius may have been the model.) *The Creation of Adam*, like Leonardo's *Last Supper*, is deceptively simple, a perfect fusion of form and content—in this case, expressing the drama of the most profound moment of the story of the Creation. Unlike *The Last Supper*, however, it is asymmetrical. The two masses of *The Creation of Adam* are unequal in both visual and symbolic weight. Yet they complement each other perfectly. And in this episode, as in the rest of the mural, Michelangelo has also brought Judaeo-Christian theology into dialectical relationship with pagan myth. According to the art historian Frederick Hartt:

> *A century of Early Renaissance research into the nature and possibilities of human anatomy seems in retrospect to lead to this single, unrecapturable moment, in which all the pride of pagan antiquity in the glory of the body, all the yearning of Christianity for the spirit, have reached a mysterious and perfect harmony.*[4]

In the Sistine Ceiling Michelangelo gave new meaning to the word "heroic" and demonstrated the expressive power of energetic figures. His mastery of anatomy, along with the exploitation of its motile possibilities, influenced centuries of painting, particularly seventeenth-century Baroque painting (see page 344). Each of the restless slaves, for example, illustrates a different posture and movement. All of this may be artistically effective; on the other hand, energy and restlessness also tend to violate the High Renaissance principle of serenity. Indeed, this vaunted principle is violated in the Ceiling by many things: there are more than 300 figures, all of which are in motion; many of the figures are drawn to different scales; scenes take place on different planes and in different directions; and too many events—worlds being created, prophecy, sin, worlds being destroyed—coexist in the same picture. Yet, almost miraculously, Michelangelo imposed an order on this potential chaos and brought everything into complex harmony through dividing the composition into a framework of rectangular and triangular spaces. The harmony of the composition is paralleled in the balance of the themes: the Christian emphasis on the life of the spirit is balanced by the pagan love of beauty, while the fear of divine retribution is balanced by the hope of Christ's redemption.

Raphael

Raffaello Sanzio (1483–1520), known as Raphael (the name of the fairest of the archangels), is the third of the three monumental figures of the High Renaissance. His work, more than that of the other two, represents a summation, a "textbook," of High Renaissance traits and ideals. Much younger than Leonardo, Raphael did not lead the way into the style; nor did he take risks and expand its limits as did Michelangelo. His work, having neither the mysteries of a Leonardo nor the storms of a Michelangelo, is full of charm and optimism, like the man himself.

Born not far from Urbino, Raphael had the good luck of having for a father a well-educated artist, who was attached to the court of Urbino. Thus he gained an early taste of the High Renaissance graces that he would later display in his art. Having access to the ducal palace, he was exposed to works by such people as Botticelli and Piero. Later he absorbed the style of Perugino, the artist to whom he was apprenticed during adolescence. Consisting

3.42 RAPHAEL
The School of Athens, 1508
Fresco, 26 × 18 ft (7.92 × 5.49 m)
Stanza della Segnatura, Vatican, Rome

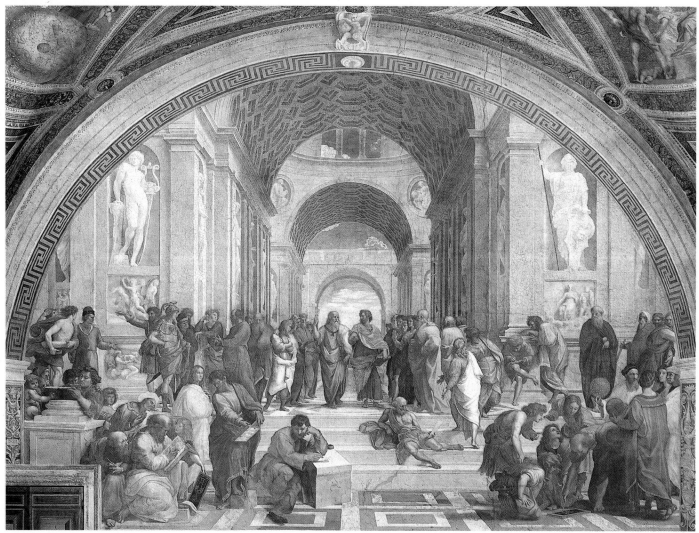

of scenes of gentle people in quiet settings, painted in clear, simple colors, the work of Perugino (who had served in Verrocchio's shop) had a lasting effect on that of Raphael.

In his early twenties Raphael decided to settle in Florence, where his master had spent so many years. He arrived in 1505, in time to learn of the rivalry between Leonardo and Michelangelo, which was being enacted in the Palazzo Vecchio. Combining influences of Leonardo and Perugino, Raphael's early works were on a more modest scale than those of Leonardo and Michelangelo who, by this time, were inaccessible to anyone other than princes or popes. He made a series of Madonna paintings which, though beautiful, lacked the anatomical realism of his two great contemporaries.

But apparently this work was good enough to attract the attention of the right people—advisors to Julius II— who recommended him to the pope. Arriving at the Vatican in 1508, Raphael was assigned to decorate the Stanza della Segnatura (room for signing papers) just a short distance from the chapel where Michelangelo was beginning to work.

The School of Athens (Fig. **3.42**), a painting of the great figures of ancient Greek philosophy, was designed to complement an earlier mural in that room by Raphael of the fathers of the Church. Called to a miraculous convention, the greatest sages of the ancient world are gathered in a noble hall beneath statues of Apollo and Minerva (goddess of wisdom). The lords of philosophy, Plato and Aristotle, are in the center, framed by an open arch. Plato (a portrait of Leonardo) points to the sky, the realm of divine ideas; Aristotle gestures toward the ground, a symbol of the earthly world. Socrates can be seen on the left arguing with students, accenting each point with a separate finger. On the lower level is a kneeling Pythagoras, writing harmonic scales in a book. A short distance away is Herakleitos (probably Michelangelo) resting, appropriately, on a block of marble. To the right of him students observe Euclid as he bends down to draw on a slate with a compass. (He is probably the architect Bramante, designer of the new St. Peter's.) To the right of Euclid, next to the arch, stand Raphael and an artist friend, Sodoma, observing the august throng.

In theme, form, and spirit, *The School of Athens* is, as much as any monument in ancient Greece itself, a summation of classicism. The subject is a celebration of pagan thought and ideals. The composition, based on one-point perspective (the point lies between Plato and Aristotle, about where Plato's left hand is), is balanced and harmonious. All the conditions for figurative representation—ideal bodies, noble bearing, grand gestures, stately movements, and aristocratic reserve—are fully satisfied, enough so to elicit the admiration of a Plato

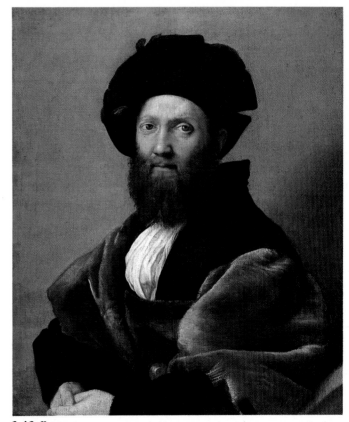

3.43 RAPHAEL
Baldassare Castiglione, c. 1514
Oil on canvas, approx. $30\frac{1}{4} \times 26\frac{1}{2}$ ins (77×67 cm)
Louvre, Paris

or Castiglione. While staying within these limits, Raphael, fortunately, did not neglect variety: no two individuals are doing the same thing; each action, though stylized, is natural; some actions are very inventive—one man straining to see over the shoulder of another, an old man sprawled on steps like a derelict, a standing boy propping up a knee to use as a base for writing notes—while not disrupting the harmony of the whole. The setting, an imposing, open-vaulted hall, is equally imaginative. Perhaps Raphael had seen the open vaults of Ghiberti's *Jacob and Esau* relief on the doors of the Florence Baptistery. The style of the hall, however, is based on Bramante's designs for the new St. Peter's. Thus this work could be seen as the representation of an essence, like a Platonic idea, which preceded the actual existence of St. Peter's. By opening the roof to the sky, Raphael filled the scene with light, a symbol of knowledge, and open air, a symbol of freedom. *The School of Athens* is a sort of Neoplatonic paradise or, perhaps, a glimpse of Plato's ideal world.

Baldassare Castiglione (Fig. **3.43**), a portrait of the well-known author of *The Book of the Courtier*, is more down to earth. Following the style of portraiture established in the

Mona Lisa, this painting has a pyramidal composition and three-quarter-view figure—with the same subtle turning of body, head, and eyes—filling the canvas. Even the proportions are similar, though the Castiglione portrait does not include the sitter's lap. Both works are subdued in color, expressive of the emotional sobriety and restraint which are, in the case of Castiglione, appropriate for the members of his class. But there are some differences between the two, besides their gender: the predominately brown, gray, and black colors of the Raphael are a degree or two warmer than the shadowy greens of the Leonardo; the plain, but slightly modulated, background contrasts with the detail and mystery of the landscape in *Mona Lisa*; and, significantly, the *Castiglione*, owing to the special quality of the eyes, displays a different sense of humanity. It is more like a real person caught in a given moment of life; whereas the *Mona Lisa*, despite its famous gaze, is more like a legend, an archetype, than a flesh-and-blood woman. Castiglione, the paradigm of the gentleman, appears dignified, yet sufficiently humble, a model of propriety, yet sincere enough to be human, a man of means who does not flaunt wealth, and a man of decency in a world of intrigue and corruption. Because Raphael and Castiglione were friends, the humanity embodied in this portrait may say as much about the artist as about its subject. This is one of the few portraits before Rembrandt's truly to penetrate the character of an individual person.

Architecture

The sculptural quality of High Renaissance painting is reflected in the heavy forms and solemn proportions of sixteenth-century architecture. These qualities were already present in the Tempietto (Fig. **3.44**), a chapel completed in 1508 by Donato Bramante (1444–1514). Though unpretentious in scale, this building is nonetheless High Renaissance in spirit and the first building in the sixteenth century to employ a central-plan—one that is round, square, or polygonal as opposed to rectangular. The Tempietto is a model of compact unity and sculptural density. The columns, balustrade posts, windows, and dome ribs provide vertical continuity, while the repetitions of these same elements, together with the round design, provide an emphatic horizontal unity.

When commissioned by Julius in 1505 to replace the original St. Peter's, a centuries-old early Christian structure, Bramante may have had the Tempietto in mind when he devised an ambitious central-plan structure (Fig. **3.45**). Resembling an eight-pointed star (or two overlapping squares), the basilica consisted of four aisles of equal length extending out from the center, or crossing. The crossing was to be topped by a large central dome, flanked

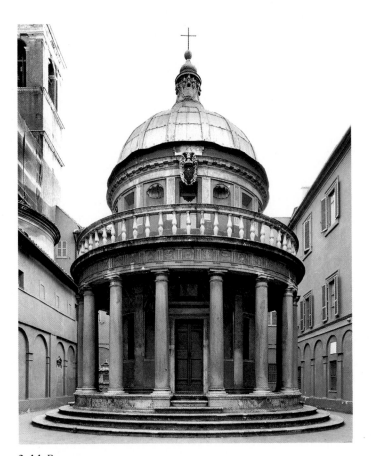

3.44 BRAMANTE
The Tempietto, S Pietro in Montorio, Rome, 1502

by four smaller ones. Bramante lived long enough to see only the completion of the four arches that were to support the central dome.

After several architects and delays the project was eventually taken over by Michelangelo (under Pope Paul III), who simplified Bramante's plan by eliminating some of the spaces and making the bearings thicker (Fig. **3.46**). The exterior of the west end of the basilica, the part that supports the dome, is the result of Michelangelo's design using the revised plan of Bramante's. (The dome itself, though based on Michelangelo's design, was modified by Giacomo della Porta after Michelangelo's death.) The Corinthian order, the main architectural motif, takes the form of gigantic pilasters on the lower stories and paired columns on the drum of the dome. On all the levels, bracketed by either pilasters or paired columns, are windows with heavy pediments. The ribs of the dome, corresponding to the paired columns, continue the motif up to the lantern, which is also of the Corinthian order. Comparing the west end of St. Peter's with a building of the Early Renaissance, such as the Ospedale degli Innocenti (children's hospital; Fig. 3.10), illustrates both the similarities and differences between fifteenth-century

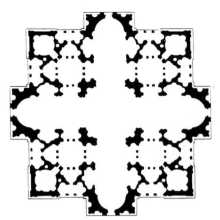

3.45 Original plan for St. Peter's, Rome, 1506 Bramante (after Geymuller)

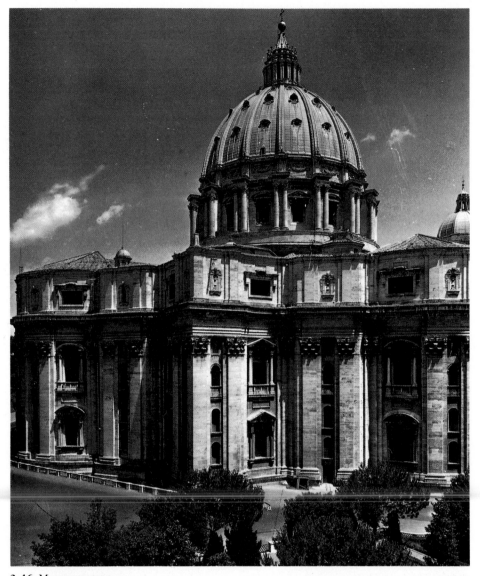

3.46 MICHELANGELO
St. Peter's, Rome, seen from the west, with plan for the Cathedral, 1546–64

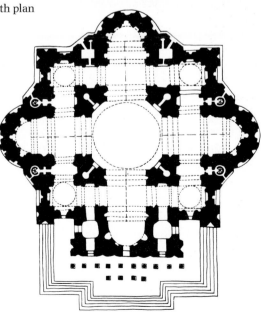

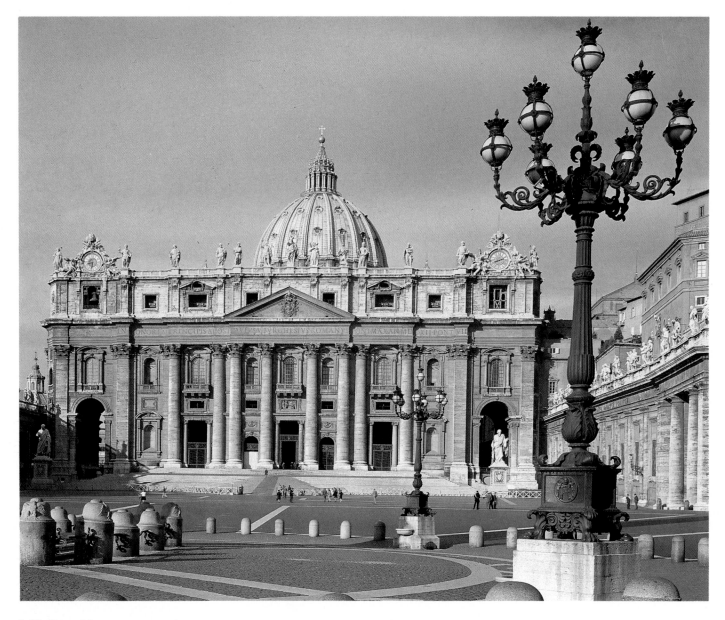

3.47 CARLO MADERNO
Façade of St. Peter's, designed 1607

architecture and High Renaissance architecture. Whereas the overall effect of the Ospedale is grace and lightness, that of the Basilica is density and weight, a fitting symbol of power for the headquarters of the Church. The east extension and façade (Fig. **3.47**), completed in the early seventeenth century by Carlo Maderno (1556–1629), are often criticized because these additions not only eliminated the central-plan concept, but also detract from the dome. Still, by employing the Corinthian order, along with clustering the attached columns and pilasters in the façade itself, Maderno complied with the spirit of Michelangelo's design.

A review of sixteenth-century architecture would not

be complete without mention of Andrea Palladio (1508–1580) whose designs, in many ways, are a synthesis of the graceful proportions of Brunelleschi's and the compactness of Michelangelo's. The villas, palaces, and churches he built in and around Venice demonstrate this synthesis as well as his skill in adapting the architectural language of antiquity. In addition to designing buildings, Palladio wrote his own treatise on architecture, *I quattro libri dell' architettura (Four Books on Architecture)*, which was to have perhaps more influence on succeeding generations of architects than his buildings. His impact on the Neoclassical architecture of England and America, as we shall see in Chapter 4, was particularly important.

Late Renaissance and Mannerism

A vigorous painting tradition had existed in Venice and its surroundings ever since Giovanni Bellini (c. 1430–1516), the brother-in-law of Mantegna. By the sixteenth century the Venetian school began to rival the Roman, and after Raphael's death (1520), it came to dominate European art—mostly in the person of Tiziano Vecillio, known as Titian. By eliminating the need for "underpainting," Venetian painters made the medium of oil on canvas the most popular of all visual arts media, a position that it holds even to this day. Previously, figures and objects were drawn and shaded in brownish tones of *tempera*, a water-based paint, before oil colors were applied. Venetian artists boldly began to use the oil medium from the very start of a painting. Thus they were the first to exploit the many sensuous possibilities not only of the colors and textures of their subjects but also the inherent qualities of the oil medium itself. Florentine and Roman artists, on the other hand, were so preoccupied with the structure of the human figure and pictorial space, that they often tended to overlook these possibilities.

Titian

The career of Titian (1488/90–1576) like that of Michelangelo, was long and productive; though, in other ways, it was more like Raphael's, who perfected the art of his time without transcending it. By 1538, when he painted the *Venus of Urbino* (Fig. **3.48**), Titian was already famous and rich enough to buy an expensive villa. This may explain why this painting expresses, among other things, such a high degree of relaxed luxury. In what appears to be a palatial residence, a lovely nude with a dog at her feet lies on a couch in the foreground separated by a heavy curtain from a tapestried room in the background where servants

3.48 TITIAN
Venus of Urbino, c. 1533
Oil on canvas, 47¼ ins × 65 ins (120 × 165 cm)
Uffizi Gallery, Florence

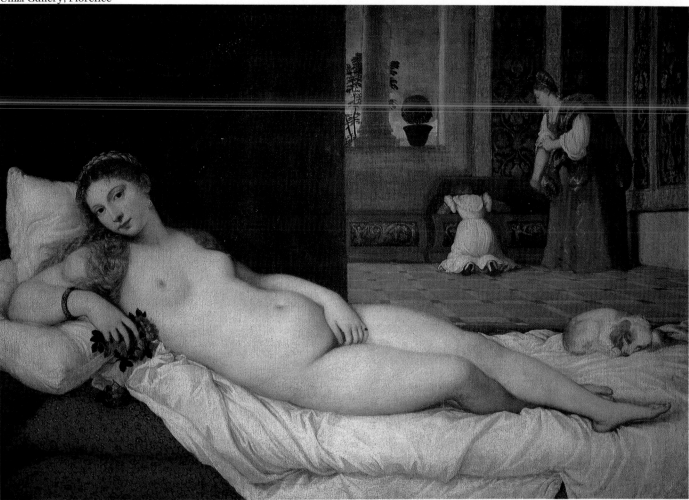

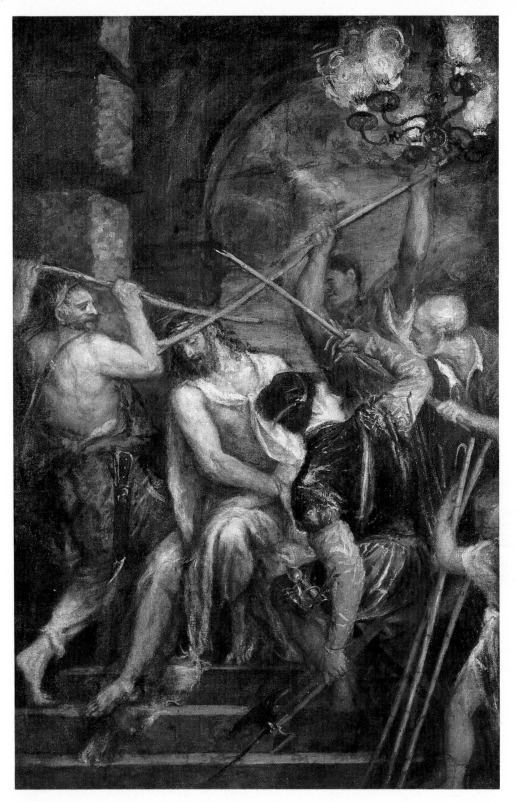

3.49 TITIAN
Christ Crowned with Thorns,
c. 1570
Oil on canvas, 110 × 72 ins
(280 × 183 cm)
Alte Pinokothek, Munich

search for something in a chest. The deep colors and variety of textures—silk, velvet, brocade, carved wood, and marble—are signs of Titian's newly acquired tastes as a gentleman as well as his skills as an artist. That the woman is naked, beautiful, and available for pleasure is probably a sign of the taste of his patron, the duke of Urbino. Unlike Botticelli's Venus, this one is, quite obviously, a goddess of love. Her passive posture and seductive expression were to reappear again and again in the erotic art of Europe.

Christ Crowned with Thorns (Fig. **3.49**), a religious picture made in the late years of the artist's life, illustrates not only another side of the artist's expressive abilities but also the freedom and boldness with which he was able to employ the oil medium. The bodies of Christ and his tormentors are titanic and mobile, like those of Michelangelo's. The composition employs diagonals—a device found in works by Mantegna and Leonardo. But the

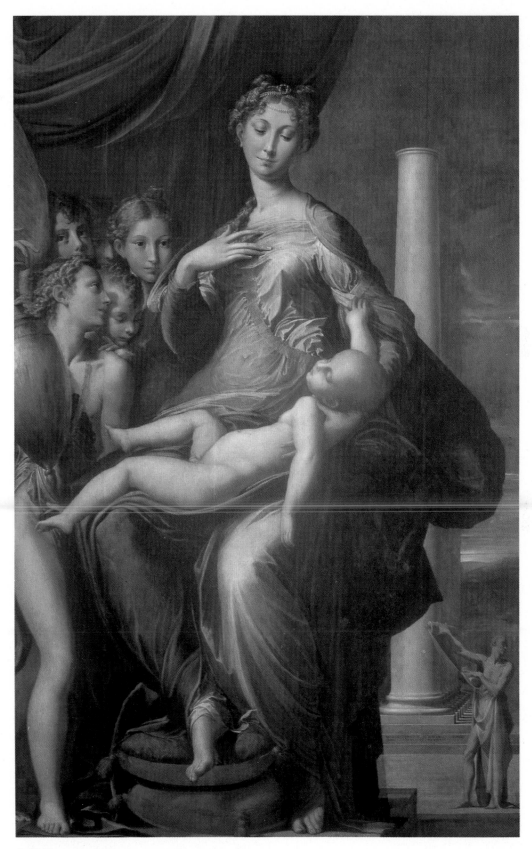

3.50 Parmigianino
Madonna with the Long Neck, c. 1535
Oil on panel, approx 85 × 52 ins (216 × 132 cm)
Uffizi Gallery, Florence

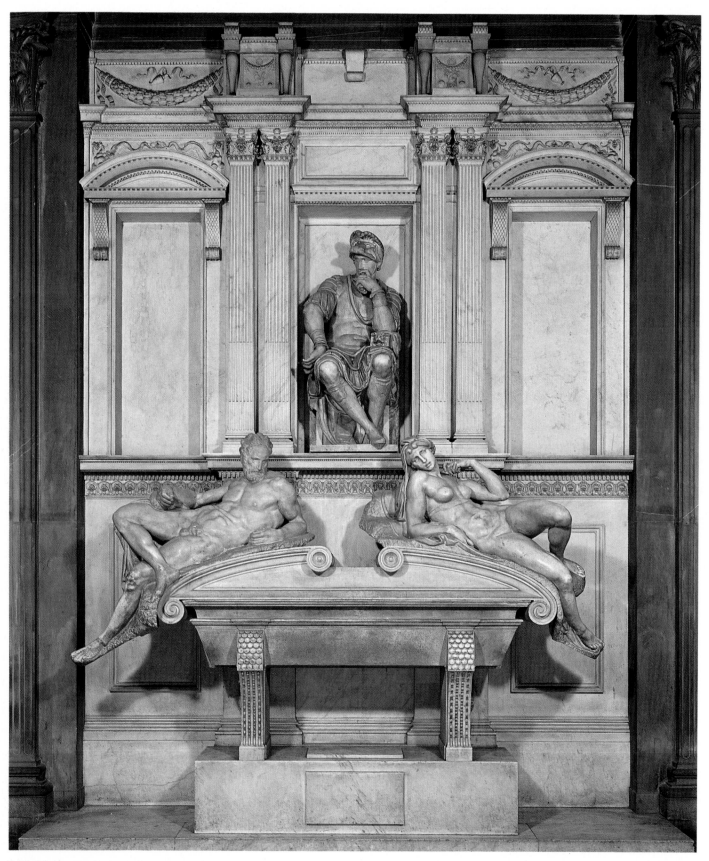

3.51 Michelangelo
Tomb of Lorenzo, Duke of Urbino, 1534
Medici chapels, Rome

drama is communicated mainly by thick paint, vivid colors, and vibrant brushwork—traits that anticipated the Baroque paintings of the next century.

Mannerism

Used to describe a particular period of art or style of art, the term "mannerism" has caused more controversy than perhaps any other in art history. Some of the controversy stems from the word itself. *Maniera*, the original term, was intended by seventeenth-century artists and writers, critical of post High Renaissance art, to mean over-emphasis on manual dexterity, whereas the English word, mannerism, means "excessive use of some distinctive, often affected, manner or style in art." Some of it has to do with the lack of consensus over the merits of this art. It is obviously both a decline of the High Renaissance and an important stage of development between that period and the Baroque. The *Madonna with the Long Neck* (Fig. **3.50**) by Parmigianino, a virtual summation of Mannerist traits, will do as a good example of the focus of this controversy. The most obvious trait is the abnormal elongation of the figures of Mary and Jesus. The ratio of Mary's head to her body is about 1:10 (a normal body is about 1:7). Jesus' body is spread across his mother's lap as if in a coma—almost the antithesis of conventional illustrations of the Madonna and Child theme, although in the Venetian tradition of a "sleeping" infant Christ, prefiguring his death. The composition, which is overcrowded on the left and relatively empty on the right, is just as disturbing as the freakish proportions of the figures. There is little apparent reason for the crowd of semi-nude figures on the left, nor is there any explanation for the free-standing column, lone figure of a man (believed to be St. Jerome), and ambiguous scale of the right. If, as his size suggests, the man is in the distance, then the Madonna and throng are crowded precariously on a high platform overlooking him and the strange column which supports nothing. Although it has some of the stylistic tendencies of a Leonardo or Raphael, the *Madonna with a Long Neck* is, in effect, a denial of everything the High Renaissance stands for: ideal proportions; graceful, relaxed movements; comprehensible space and environment; balanced composition.

Many of these same traits can be found in the sculpture group (Fig. **3.51**) for Lorenzo de' Medici (descendent of Lorenzo the Magnificent, and the one to whom Machiavelli dedicated *The Prince*) which Michelangelo completed in 1534, the same year as Parmigianino's painting. Beneath the figure of Lorenzo are two allegorical figures: on the left, a man symbolizing Twilight, on the right, a woman symbolizing Dawn. All three, especially Lorenzo, have the attenuated proportions and languid postures of the *Madonna with a Long Neck*. The two nudes, because they recline so restlessly on pedestals too short for their bodies, are particularly unsettling. It has been said that they represent Michelangelo's weariness with life. (Even during the production of these sculptures, the artist lived through the overthrow of two Florentine governments, being pressed into designing fortifications, and being sent into hiding because of an order for his assassination.) The figure of Lorenzo, nicknamed *il Penseroso*, the thinker, is perhaps the most poignant. Dressed in Roman armor, a symbol of his status as leader, he listlessly rests his head on his left hand. With his face in permanent shadow under his helmet, he personifies the impotence of a leader who, struggling with his conscience, is a captive of indecision—a cardinal sin according to Machiavelli. At the same time this image of melancholia also anticipates the tormented diffidence of Shakespeare's Hamlet.

Sixteenth-Century Music

While homophony increased (see page 116), polyphony still ruled in sixteenth-century music. A new form of secular vocal music called the *madrigal* (which has little in common with a fourteenth-century musical form of the same name) made its appearance at this time. Madrigals were usually sung *a cappella*—without instrumental accompaniment—a style that was very popular in the sixteenth century. At the same time, instrumental music was also gaining in popularity. Before this time, instruments were used mainly to accompany vocal music or to play music written for voice. Now, some compositions were being written for instruments alone, a sign that this medium was slowly acquiring independence and status. The sixteenth century also saw the beginning of music printing. Following the invention of printing with movable type by Johann Gutenberg in the mid-1400s, printed music began to appear early in the sixteenth century. The first major collection of printed polyphonic music came out in 1501 by a Venetian publisher, Ottaviano de' Petrucci.

Josquin

The most renowned composer at the turn of the century was Josquin des Prez (c. 1440–1521). Praised by personages as widely separated (geographically and philosophically) as Castiglione and Luther, he was bestowed with almost as many honors as Michelangelo. In fact, he was even compared to Michelangelo—the claim being made that he was without peer in music, just as the artist was in sculpture and architecture. The first of Petrucci's series of printed Masses was a volume by Josquin. Like Dufay, Josquin came from the province of Hainaut and spent a great deal of time in Italy. He held several posts there, being attached to the ducal chapel in Milan, the papal chapel in Rome, and the court at Ferrara. He also spent a number of years in the service of the French king Louis XII. About the same age as Botticelli, Josquin lived long enough to have had his productive career overlap those of Leonardo, Raphael, and Michelangelo.

Just as he was renowned during his time, Josquin is recognized today as the leading figure of musical culture at the turn of the century and as having had a fundamental influence on sixteenth-century music. He combined the tendencies of North and South into a beautiful synthesis. In his work the high art of polyphony was enlivened by the four-part harmonies and "toe-tapping" rhythms of the frottola; the austerity of the northern Mass was humanized by elements of the Italian lauda.

Josquin raised text-painting to the status of a high art. He took great care to ensure not only that his notes matched syllables and his rhythms the patterns of human speech, but also that performers could read his scores in order to produce the correct effects. In addition to matching notes to words, he used every musical means at his disposal to express the ideas of a text. Moods were described by variations in tempo, cadence, harmonic textures, and the rise or fall of melodic lines. More than any previous composer, Josquin chose musical motifs to serve the interpretation of the word. Nothing illustrates this better than the first lines of his motet *Absalon fili mi* (Fig. 3.52). The words are David's "O My Son Absalom," mourning the death of his son (II Samuel 18:33). With a slow, stately tempo, each syllable of the lament is proclaimed by a whole or half note. The first line, *Absalon fili mi*, is introduced by the top voice, then repeated in staggered, imitative fashion by the other voices. Each voice enters four or five notes lower than the one preceding it. By the sixth measure all four voices have made their entries; by the ninth all four end on the word *mi* (my) as the doleful music finishes its first cycle.

Josquin created the form of the *parody Mass*, that is, one using musical material of secular motets, such as amorous

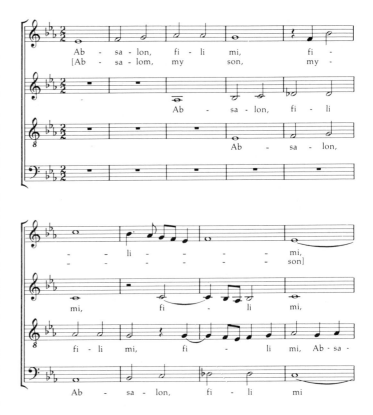

3.52 *Absalon fili mi*, Josquin des Prez

chansons, disguising them with sacred words and embedding them in the composition. If the borrowed material was familiar, and particularly if it was bawdy, the irony of its presence in a sacred context could amuse alert listeners. In addition to its occasional entertainment value, the inclusion of parody in the Mass helped to bring greater musical diversity to the Mass itself. Josquin's most popular medium, though, was the motet, because it allowed him more freedom to experiment than even the parody Mass. Motets, whose cadences are often concealed by the overlapping of voices, tended toward formlessness and monotony. To overcome this, Josquin attended to the "architecture" of his compositions, in this case, through variation and repetition of musical elements. At times certain notes or rhythms are given stress, at other times a theme is repeated by means of imitation. One of his loveliest motets, *Ave Maria*, demonstrates Josquin's ability to attain a "High Renaissance" balance between flowing melody and a firm musical structure (Fig. 3.53). The imitative principle at work among the four voices, as each repeats the "Ave Maria" phrase identically but at different octaves, is obvious. Yet this repetition is tempered by the flow of the melody and, as the piece progresses, variations in melodic line.

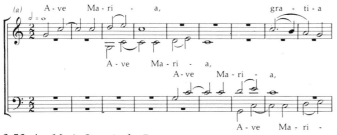

3.53 *Ave Maria*, Josquin des Prez

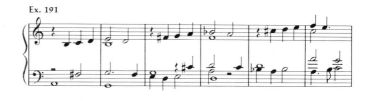

Ex. 191

3.54 Ricercar for organ, Marco Antonio

Instrumental Music

As the Renaissance progressed, instrumental music became increasingly popular. Like vocal music, it benefitted from the invention of the printing press, which even provided different symbols for various kinds of instruments. The *ricercar*, the instrumental counterpart of the motet, achieved its distinctive form by the middle of the sixteenth century. Although most were intended for instrumental ensembles, some ricercars, such as this one for organ by Marco Antonio, (Fig. 3.54) were written for solo keyboard instruments. Like the music of Josquin, this piece has clear, simple phrasing, though less reliance on imitation.

As social dancing became even more refined and varied, music featuring regular rhythm patterns and clearly defined tempos was needed. Therefore, unlike the ricercar, music for dancing could not be modeled after the motet. Instead it had to be based on folk idioms and developed according to its own internal logic. The needs of the dance thus provided a laboratory in which instrumental music could grow as an independent art form—leading eventually to its dominant status in the classical and romantic eras.

The Madrigal

In addition to dancing, the court life of Renaissance Italy required a type of refined vocal music that could express its ideals. The *madrigal*, a short poem set to music, fulfilled that need. Since it was secular, the art of the madrigal was not subject to the limitations of text or style imposed by religion (although a few sacred madrigals were written). Usually erotic, often humorous, madrigal poetry ranges from pathos to hilarity, and from sentimentality to obscenity. Early madrigals had words by minor poets, but composers increasingly used the poems by such writers as Petrarch and Boccaccio. Musically, these composers were free to experiment, but at the same time they were required to express the drama and variety of moods called for in the literature. Using several voices, typically alternating between polyphony and homophony, madrigals are models of text painting. They even include the calculated use of *dissonance* (inharmonious sound), which not only acts as a foil to *consonance* (harmonious sound) but creates musical tensions appropriate for expressing the full range of human emotions.

One might suppose that sixteenth-century England, because of the quality of its poetry, would be fertile ground for the madrigal; and in fact it was. Under Queen Elizabeth, this art form reached a new peak of refinement. Initially, Englishmen looked to the Italians for their models; Nicholas Yonge printed the first portfolio of Italian madrigals in 1588, the year of the Spanish Armada. However, by the end of the century Englishmen were writing their own madrigals. Remarkably, in the age of Marlowe and Shakespeare, English madrigals are distinguished more by their music than by their poetry, which consists mostly of pastoral poems. According to music historian Donald J. Grout:

> *The expressive and pictorial traits in the music of the madrigals are combined with accurate, nimble declamation of the English texts. The accents of the words are maintained independently in each voice, so that the ensembles produce sparkling counterpoints of endless rhythmic vitality.*[4]

The sixteenth-century madrigal, with its variegated vocal harmonies and text painting, foreshadowed the seventeenth-century opera. The next chapter, "Classicism III: 17th and 18th Centuries," will review the beginnings of the opera, along with other musical developments during a period that had the same importance for music that the fifteenth and sixteenth centuries had for art.

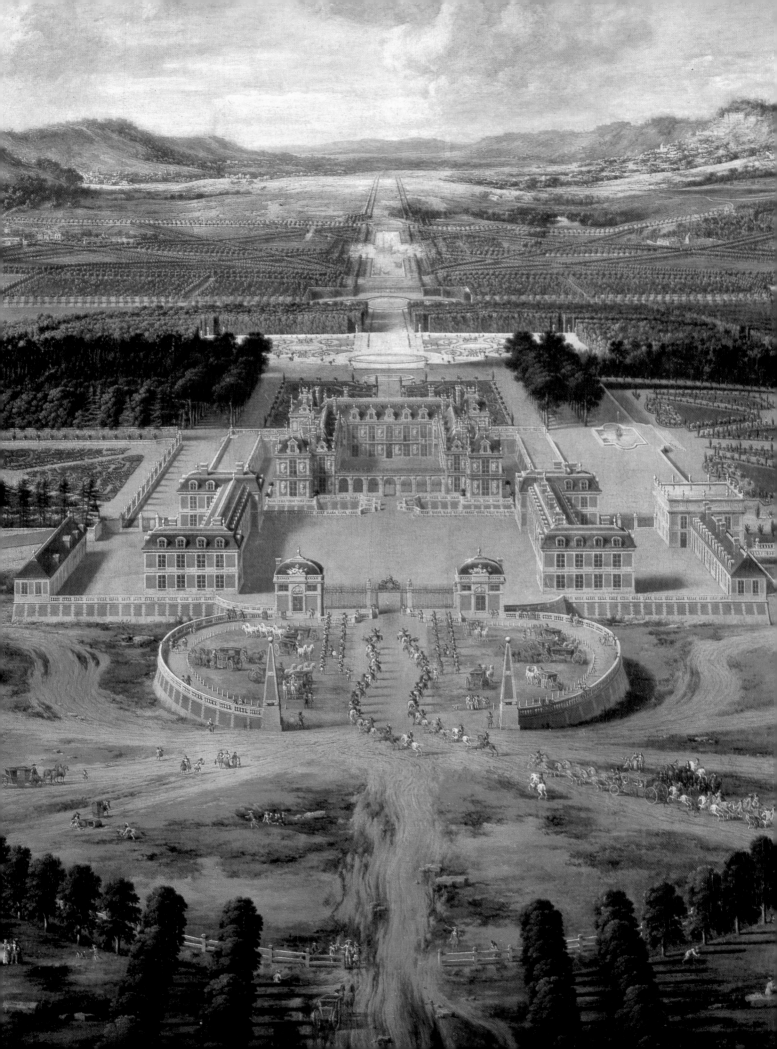

CHAPTER FOUR

Classicism III: 17th and 18th Centuries

These rules of old discovered, not devised
Are Nature still, but Nature methodised;
Nature, like Liberty, is but restrained,
By the same laws which first herself ordained.

POPE, *ESSAY ON CRITICISM*

4.1 Versailles, from a painting by Pierre Patel, 1688

Introduction

Classicism, as we have seen, is an attempt to recover the classical ideals of form, balance, and reason in both literature and the arts, as manifested in ancient Greece and Rome. Reverence for classical models, an important aspect of humanism in the Renaissance, continued into the seventeenth century on the part of writers and some artists. But whereas in the Renaissance the classical spirit was mixed with individualism—the Renaissance writers and artists asserting themselves against the Gothic past— in the seventeenth century it was often a matter of conforming to rules. This was especially true in literature.

Some distinctions must be made between art, music, and literature with regard to both their manifestations of classicism and their individual developments. Of the three, only literature enjoyed a significant period of classicism (called *Neoclassicism*) in both the seventeenth and the eighteenth centuries. Art and music of the seventeenth century were less governed by classical ideals of restraint; both were characterized by a style called *Baroque*—a style that, in its extreme versions, was almost anti-classical. But there were exceptions, such as in France, where painting, architecture, and music observed classical precepts, and in England, where toward the end of the seventeenth century the influence of classical architecture took root. Whereas France was the home of significant literary developments throughout the seventeenth century, Italy—at least in the early 1600s—continued to be the cradle of developments in art and music. Later, Baroque

art spread from Italy to other countries—most notably Spain, France and the Low Countries (Flanders and the Dutch Republic)—where individual variations of the style matured independently. Baroque music also took root in other countries but continued to be dependent on and nurtured by Italian music throughout most of the century.

By the middle of the seventeenth century, France, under the rule of the "Sun King," Louis XIV, entered a golden age. Considering himself the earthly representative of God (as did most monarchs of the time), Louis, who ruled from 1643 to 1715, is reported to have said, "L'État, c'est moi" ("*I* am the state"). The classic example of an absolute monarch, Louis expected his subjects to conform to his will, whether in paying heavy taxes to support his lavish court or in following his tastes in literature and the arts. He transformed his country estate at Versailles into the most magnificent palace in Europe, the supreme example of grandeur and sophistication. Indeed, the court of Versailles became the model for rulers, both powerful and provincial, throughout Europe. France, probably the richest and strongest country in Europe during Louis' reign, was also beginning to appropriate the cultural leadership held so long by the Italians.

Classicism and absolutism combined under Louis to produce an attitude that discouraged nonconformity in the arts as well as in language and behavior. Writers were expected to observe the rules of elegance and good taste, in

4.2 The seventeenth century

DATES	SOCIAL AND POLITICAL DEVELOPMENTS	LITERATURE AND PHILOSOPHY	VISUAL ARTS	ARCHITECTURE	MUSIC
1600	Defeat of Spanish Armada	Descartes	Baroque style Rubens (4.12) De Hooch (4.13)	Bernini: Colonnade, St Peter's (4.9); Baldacchino (4.10)	Birth of opera Oratoria; cantata Monteverdi
	Louis XIV	Blaise Pascal	Poussin (4.14) Claude (4.15)	Borromini (4.11)	
1650	Beheading of Charles I Oliver Cromwell – Commonwealth	Moliere (4.5) Racine (4.6)			
	Restoration of Stuart monarchy				Corelli Lully (4.36) Purcell
		Newton's *Principia*		Palace of Versailles (4.16) Wren: St Paul's (4.19)	
1700	Glorious Revolution				Scarlotti

both form and content, rather than be original. Artists were to emulate the classical standards of Italian art (ironically, Italian artists of the seventeenth century had gotten away from these standards). Composers were to show restraint in their medium. Such rules and restraints were regarded as universal, as unquestionably "right" as were the commandments of Louis himself, God's representative. Such an atmosphere would seem to stifle rather than nurture the growth of the arts. Louis, however, who was an even greater patron of the arts than Pope Julius II or Lorenzo de' Medici, bought so much painting and sculpture from Italy that further export was forbidden by the pope. More importantly, he encouraged the growth of French arts and letters through lavish commissions and by establishing royal academies to train professionals and maintain standards.

With the defeat of the formidable Spanish Armada (1588), the naval arm of the most powerful nation in Europe at the time, England's long dominance of the sea had its inception. Thus, this island nation came to rival France in power in the seventeenth century—although France maintained its cultural pre-eminence. Following the English Civil War, which led to the beheading of the Stuart king Charles I (1649), the victorious Parliament established the Commonwealth under Oliver Cromwell. The Stuart monarchy was restored under Charles II in 1660; but its cherished concept of the divine right of kings continued to be rejected by a Parliament that had achieved the ascendancy during the Civil War. Charles was circumspect about asserting his royal power, but his brother, James II, who succeeded him, was not. A Catholic convert, James also had his son and heir, born in 1688, baptized a Catholic, thus generating fear that the Catholic Church would gain control in England. As a result, the leading members of Parliament invited William III of Holland and his wife Mary, the Protestant daughter of James, to land an army in England. James fled to France, and the Glorious Revolution (so called because it was nonviolent) was achieved in 1688. Thus, in the same period when Louis XIV was promoting royal absolutism, the English Parliament was rejecting it and asserting its own prerogatives—a difference in the political systems of the two nations that Voltaire was later to emphasize to the embarrassment of France. Monarchical absolutism was to become a major cause of the outbreak of the French Revolution in 1789.

Partly because of its Protestantism and its rejection of absolute monarchy, Britain did not provide a fertile soil for Baroque art, although a relatively restrained version of Baroque architecture flourished there, in the works of Christopher Wren, John Vanbrugh, and others. In the eighteenth century, British architects found inspiration in the works of Italian Renaissance architects such as Palladio and, later, in the original classical buildings of ancient Greece and Rome. Baroque music was more readily embraced by the British than its visual counterparts. Wren's near-contemporary Henry Purcell was the finest English-born composer in this style; and a few years later another Baroque composer, the German-born George Frideric Handel, enjoyed enormous popularity in England. William Hogarth, England's first artist of note, satirized his operas. Literary Neoclassicism also came late to England, arriving during the Restoration, with Neoclassical drama being its earliest manifestation. But it found a home there and became an effective influence. In the eighteenth century, satire was the dominant manifestation of English Neoclassical literature. Skillful satirists such as Pope and Swift maintained complete rational control of their medium, whether the heroic couplet or prose, however caustic their criticism.

In France, following the death of Louis XIV, the Rococo style, a frivolous offshoot of Baroque art, began to emerge. Rococo thrived until the end of the eighteenth century, when it gave way to a classical revival in the visual arts called Neoclassicism (the same term used for the dominant literary style of the seventeenth and eighteenth centuries). Although Neoclassical art and architecture developed under Louis XVI, it later became associated with the ideals of the French Revolution and Louis' tragic downfall. At about the same time that Paris was hosting the Neoclassical movement in art, Vienna, the capital of the Holy Roman Empire (see page 269), was the center for a new style of music, called Classical because of its clarity, restraint, and elegant sense of proportion.

The Enlightenment

The emphasis on reason and order in the classicism of the seventeenth and eighteenth centuries had its counterpart in the scientific and philosophical rationalism of the same period. In his *Principia* (1687), Isaac Newton demonstrated mathematically that the universe is governed by universal laws. Certain eighteenth-century French intellectuals—mostly literary people rather than scientists—were deeply impressed by such discoveries and sought to develop a rational philosophy that would correspond to this scientific rationalism. Although Newton himself held conservative religious views, this combination of philosophical rationalism and scientific discovery led to *deism*, which conceived the universe as a giant machine operating according to orderly laws discoverable by reason, a view that radically altered the traditional status of God in relation to his creation. In place of the personal God of the Judaeo-Christian tradition, who

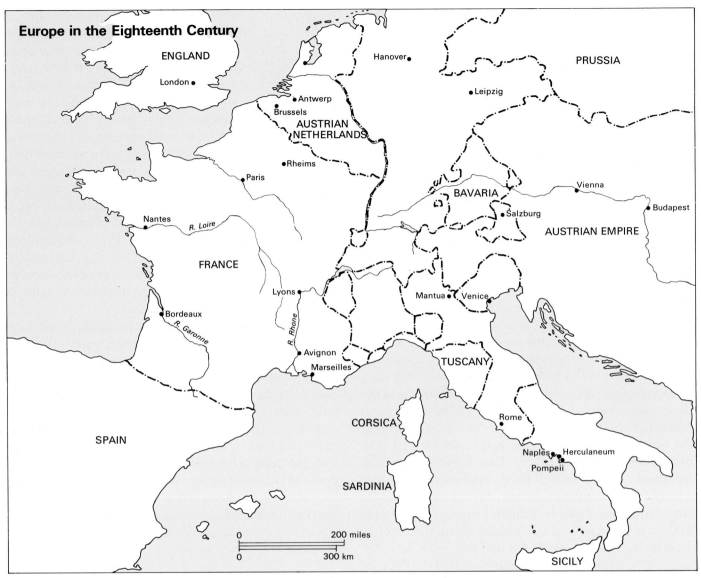

Europe in the Eighteenth Century

4.3

4.4 The eighteenth century

DATES	SOCIAL AND POLITICAL DEVELOPMENTS	LITERATURE AND PHILOSOPHY	VISUAL ARTS	ARCHITECTURE	MUSIC
1700	Death of Louis XIV	Swift (**4.7**) Pope Leibnitz Voltaire (**4.8**)			Couperin Bach (**4.38**) Handel (**4.39**)
	Herculaneum and Pompeii ruins discovered		Hogarth (**4.23**) Chardin (**4.24**)	Bouffrand: Salon de la Princesse (**4.21**)	
1750	Lisbon earthquake	Diderot: *Encyclopedia of the Sciences, Arts, & Trades* Winckelmann	Fragonard (**4.22**) Piranesi (**4.25**) David (**4.26**) Houdon (**4.28**)	Jefferson: State Capitol, Virginia (**4.30**)	Haydn (**4.45**) Classical sonatas Mozart (**4.50**)
	French Revolution				
1800			Canova (**4.29**) Ingres (**4.27**)		

intervened in nature and history to perform miracles, the deists posited the existence of a "Watchmaker God," who had created the universe and set it in motion, causing it to operate according to natural laws with which even he dare not tinker. The rejection of the biblical role of God by the deists was pushed by others in this skeptical era to the point of rejection of the very idea of God, or atheism.

Rationalism dominated most of the eighteenth century, not only in philosophy, science, and religion, but also in social and political criticism. This is evident in the writings of Voltaire and other *philosophes*, the term for those who saw themselves, somewhat immodestly, as the "enlightened" proclaimers of the new rational view of the universe. Hence the term "Enlightenment" for this period.

These thinkers were contributors to what was perhaps the most significant publication of the Enlightenment, the *Encyclopedia, or Practical Dictionary of the Sciences, of the Arts, and of the Trades* (1751–1776), in 35 volumes. Edited by Denis Diderot, this work attempted to collect current knowledge of the sciences, arts, and trades and to present it systematically. Contributors also used the *Encyclopedia* as a forum for damning tyranny and extolling reason and liberty. Thus it became an important influence in shaping the ideas that led to the French Revolution, the event which, ironically, in its ultimate pathological violence became the tragic negation of the Enlightenment ideals of reason and liberty.

Seventeenth-Century Literature

Neoclassicism in literature, as the term suggests, was an attempt to attain the classical ideals of order, balance, and restraint in writing, especially in the composition of drama. This is illustrated by the so-called "three unities" of time, place, and action. In his *Poetics*, Aristotle emphasized unity of action (the exclusion of irrelevant episodes or sub-plots) and noted that the action in Greek drama usually took place within a single day. Neoclassical critics made rules of both unity of action and unity of time and derived unity of place from the latter.

Although classicism implies order and restraint, this does not preclude the expression of emotion. Racine's adherence to the formal structure of the three unities, as we shall see, did not prevent him from exploring the full range of Phaedra's sexual passion. But classicism, unlike Romanticism, confines this potentially dangerous emotional power within rules and structures, rather than allowing it precedence. Racine shows the danger of the emotions in that Phaedra's passion is presented as a disorder that threatens both herself and others. Indeed, Seneca, the first-century Stoic philosopher, in his play on the Phaedra myth, used Phaedra as a negative example to teach the Stoic value of rational control of the passions.

All of the Neoclassical writers to be discussed in this chapter reveal a serious moral point of view, but three of them do so, paradoxically, through comedy. Molière, Swift, and Voltaire employ satire to attack the foibles and follies of mankind. Typically they focus on excess in human behaviour, a favorite target of Neoclassical writers because of their adherence to classical restraint and their determination to initiate and to preserve order and

balance in human affairs. The ethical seriousness of satire is based on the assumption that human beings are rational enough to discern the criticism in the comedy of satire and moral enough to effect the changes called for in themselves and in society. Thus some critics contend that the satirist is by definition an optimist about human nature—an attitude not easily discerned in the biting rhetoric of Swift and Voltaire, or, as we shall see, in the damning caricatures of the artist Hogarth.

Molière

Jean Baptiste Poquelin, known by his stage name, Molière (1622–1673), is widely recognized as the master of dramatic comedy. His comic genius is demonstrated through a technique that emphasizes some aspect of human behavior which, through exaggeration, is held up to ridicule. His standard of measurement for such behavior is reason and moderation, the norms of classicism. Thus, for example, Molière takes a trait such as hypocrisy (*Tartuffe*); or its opposite, absolute honesty (*The Misanthrope*); avarice (*The Miser*); or hypochondria (*The Imaginary Invalid*), and develops a character who embodies that trait in exaggerated form. He then provides a slight plot, just substantial enough to support his character, placing his protagonist in a set of circumstances that reveals the folly of his or her behavior when contrasted with a balanced view and common sense. Through this contrast, Molière generates his humor and the laughter of the audience. Molière's plays focus on character types well known in seventeenth-century France, but also univers-

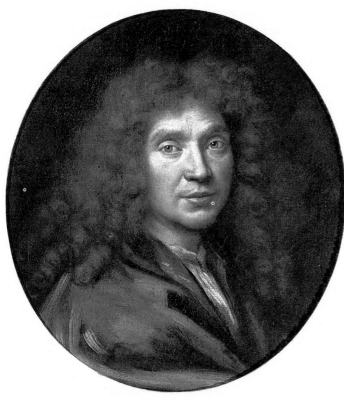

4.5 Moliere

ally familiar. Thus his plays are not dated, as anyone can verify who has had the pleasure of seeing them.

Molière was born in Paris, the son of a prosperous upholsterer, and received a good education in a Jesuit school. He could have inherited his father's position as upholsterer to Louis XIV but chose instead to become, in 1643, one of the founders of the Illustrious Theater, a business venture that soon failed. He then took to the provinces, where he built up a solid body of experience in all aspects of the theater, including playwriting, over the next 12 years. He returned to Paris in 1658, having written two plays. But it was his next play, *The High-Brow Ladies* (1659), a play satirizing the affectation and the cultural pretensions of the salons, which attracted the interest of the Parisians and of Louis XIV himself.

Over the next 14 years, Molière wrote many successful plays, including, in addition to those mentioned above, *The School for Wives* (1662); *Don Juan, or The Stone Guest* (1665), a tragicomedy which the librettist Lorenzo Da Ponte adapted for Mozart's opera *Don Giovanni*; *The Physician in Spite of Himself* (1666), one of four of his plays satirizing the medical profession; *The Would-Be Gentleman* (1670), a comedy-ballet on which Molière and Jean-Baptiste Lully collaborated; and *The Learned Women* (1672), another play satirizing the women who held forth

in the salons. His last play, *The Imaginary Invalid* (1673), written and produced during his final illness, also satirized the medical profession and, like his other plays on that theme, probably reflected his own experience with doctors. Appropriately, the crowning irony of the career of this master of comedy occurred at the end of his life; for he died shortly after his fourth performance in the leading role in this play—a fatally ill man playing the role of a perfectly healthy hypochondriac. Through the king's intervention Molière was allowed a quiet funeral service despite the fact that actors were normally denied Christian burial because of the ill-repute of the theater in the eyes of the clergy and society.

Tartuffe, a satire on religious hypocrisy, is probably the most controversial of Molière's plays. It was rewritten twice and was not performed publicly in Paris until five years after it first appeared in 1664. Louis XIV saw the original version of the play without finding fault, but the opposition to it was formidable, including the archbishop of Paris. The version of *Tartuffe* now extant is the final rewritten version, and there is no doubt that Molière made changes that emphasize the hypocrisy of Tartuffe far more than was the case in the original. The critics complained that Molière was attacking true religion; thus he sought to clarify beyond doubt that he was satirizing the abuse of religion, not faith itself. Even so, critics still wonder whether *Tartuffe* may, after all, be fundamentally an anti-religious play.

The Misanthrope, first presented in 1666, is probably the most thought-provoking of Molière's comedies because of the ambiguity of the role of the protagonist, Alceste. Typically, Molière's plays show how the eccentric individual is punished by the society whose norms he violates. In this play, however, Molière shows that the punishable eccentricity can be a virtue.

Alceste, a completely honest man, lives in a hypocritical society in which the rules of etiquette dictate that its members be deceitful and affected in their relationships. Thus they fawn upon and flatter one another, when in reality they hold each other in contempt. Alceste's revelation of the brutal truth in these circumstances is both shocking and amusing. For example, he ridicules the mediocre verses of a foppish and affected would-be poet, and even berates Célimène, the woman he loves, for her hypocritical praise of the courtiers who surround her.

The ambiguity results from this clash of Alceste's honesty with society's falsity. Alceste may be seen as an honorable and honest man whose refusal to compromise his high ideals is the cause of his suffering. But he may also be viewed as a foolish and unreasonable man who creates himself in the image of his own coldly intellectual ideal and then dramatizes himself in order to validate this act of self-creation. The play, therefore, hovers on the borderline between comedy and tragedy, as both genres involve extravagant behavior. Alceste's excesses can be viewed as comic; but the results of that behavior, for example Alceste's increasing isolation from others for whom he cares—above all Célimène—can be perceived as tragic. At the end of the play, Alceste, true misanthrope that he is, rejects Célimène and stalks off the stage determined to live entirely alone. But his friends, Philinte and Eliante, more flexible in their views and behavior, decide to marry. The contrast is both provocative and instructive.

Racine

Jean Racine (1639–1699), a younger contemporary of Molière, whose chosen genre was tragedy rather than comedy, was the most effective exponent of French Neoclassicism. Unlike Corneille, his predecessor, whose *The Cid* was attacked by the Neoclassical critics, Racine had no difficulty restricting his dramas to the three unities of time, place, and action. Choosing a dramatic moment of psychological tension, Racine focuses on an emotion, frequently love, in his protagonist, often a woman. This focus emphasizes characterization and little action occurs. The tragedy arises from the inability of the protagonist to control this passion.

Although Racine's sources for his plays were ancient and exotic (Greek and Roman mythology, the Bible, Oriental history), he was able to portray characters and situations convincingly because of his remarkably accurate insight into human, especially feminine, psychology. Racine's dramatic conception of human nature has been ascribed to two powerful influences: Jansenism and Greek drama. Both of these influences were brought to bear upon Racine through his education at Port-Royal, the center of Jansenism in France. Jansenism was a reform movement in French Catholicism that stressed salvation by God's grace and predestination—thus, in the minds of some people, diminishing or eliminating human choice and effort in salvation. This theology, combined with the element of fate in the Greek literature that was the foundation of his education at Port-Royal, imbued Racine with a deep sense of human weakness and vulnerability to the passions of the heart. The young Racine remained at Port-Royal until 1658, when he went to Paris to study law. Later he reacted against his early religious training, even denouncing his Jansenist teachers, who had censured him for his involvement with theater people and other worldly friends in Paris—an involvement that launched his career as a playwright.

His first two extant dramas are not significant, except that he was associated with Molière and his theater company in their production. His first successful drama, *Andromache* (1667), treats the themes of sexual passion and hatred through Greek mythology. Over the next ten years there followed such works as *Britannicus*, set in Nero's court; *Bérénice*, a tragedy on the emperor Titus's painful relinquishment of Bérénice because of Roman law; *Mithradates*; and *Iphigénie*, based on Euripides' *Iphigenia at Aulis*.

Racine's last secular play was *Phaedra* (1677), a drama that apparently precipitated his return to Jansenism. Though now regarded as the best of Racine's plays, *Phaedra* was a source of humiliation to the playwright because a group of his enemies bought a block of tickets for the play and then did not show up for the performance. Racine interpreted this as a judgment of God for his treatment of his Jansenist friends, and he later returned to Port-Royal to be reconciled to them. As evidence of his about-face, he subsequently gave up playwriting—except for two biblical plays (*Esther* and *Athalie*)—accepted the post of historiographer to Louis XIV, married a pious woman, and raised a large family.

Phaedra struck an appropriate note to herald Racine's return to Jansenism. This is illustrated by his preface, which strongly emphasizes the play's moral purpose. If we take this preface at face value, we must conclude that he

4.6 Jean Racine

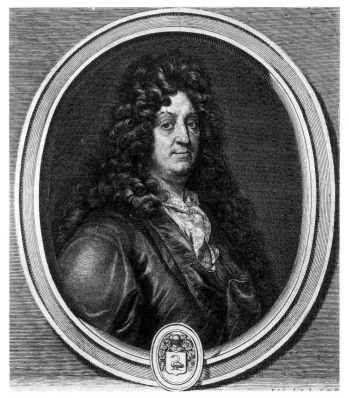

intended, through *Phaedra*, to reveal the evil of unchecked passion and its tragic consequences. He does this in such a manner, however, that one might conclude that such restraint is possible only through divine grace. For Phaedra, though a pagan protagonist, struggles against her illicit passion with a conscience worthy of a Jansenist—but to no avail.

The chief source of Racine's play, as he acknowledged, was Euripides' *Hippolytus*. The source of both plays was a Greek myth which told the story of Hippolytus, the son of Theseus of Athens by Hippolyte, queen of the Amazons. Theseus' wife, Phaedra, fell in love with the chaste and handsome Hippolytus, who spurned her. To avenge herself, Phaedra falsely accused Hippolytus of attempting to seduce her and committed suicide. Theseus then called down a curse from Poseidon upon his son. As a result, Hippolytus suffered a violent and mutilating death when his horses were frightened by a sea monster.

Racine's change of title is significant, for his play concentrates on the passionate Phaedra rather than on the chaste Hippolytus. (In Racine's view, women are more likely than men to be the victims of their emotions.) In Euripides' play, Hippolytus is a worshiper of Artemis (the Roman Diana), the virgin goddess of the hunt, and will therefore have nothing to do with Phaedra or any other woman. He thus rejects the goddess of love, Aphrodite (the Roman Venus), an act of hubris that leads to his destruction at the instigation of the goddess. Thus Eurip-

ides' protagonist is Hippolytus, not Phaedra (who in fact dies halfway through the play).

Racine, on the other hand, concentrates on the struggle of Phaedra to overcome her passion for her stepson and her deep sense of guilt resulting from her illicit love, a guilt that is Jansenist rather than Greek. She sincerely seeks to control her fatal passion, causing Hippolytus to be exiled from Athens to Troezen, away from her sight, and confessing her love to him only when she is assured that Theseus is dead. But Theseus returns alive, and Phaedra, to protect herself, consents to her nurse's deception of the king, who is led to believe that Hippolytus has tried to seduce Phaedra. Significantly, however, she does this only after her jealousy has been whipped to a fury by the news that Hippolytus loves Aricia, a claimant to the throne of Athens. Here is one of the more significant changes Racine made in Euripides' play, for Euripides' Hippolytus rejects all women. This change allows Racine to add the motive of jealousy to the emotional maelstrom of Phaedra's passion-obsessed mind. Theseus, infuriated at Hippolytus, invokes the curse of Neptune (Greek Poseidon) upon him, causing his death. Both Oenone, the nurse, and Phaedra commit suicide, but Phaedra, in her dying words, confesses her guilt. To appease the shade of Hippolytus, Theseus then takes Aricia as his daughter. Thus there is a tragic resolution of the conflict caused by Phaedra's passion, illustrating the classical principle of creating tensions and then resolving them.

Eighteenth-Century Literature

Swift

Jonathan Swift (1667–1745), like Racine, was profoundly concerned with the danger of human excess, especially pride, but like Molière, he attacked this excess by means of satiric comedy rather than tragedy.

Swift was born in Ireland of English parents. Although he lived in England for extended periods and was ambitious for a bishopric there, he often returned to Ireland, where he eventually became Dean of St. Patrick's Cathedral in Dublin (1714) and where he spent the last 30 years of his life. He endeared himself to the Irish (then under British rule) as the champion of their rights. It was during this 30-year period that Swift wrote some of his most significant works, including *A Modest Proposal* (1729) and *Gulliver's Travels* (1726). Swift is famous for

his satire, and these two works brilliantly illustrate his use of this genre. The first is an essay ironically proposing that the Irish cope with English oppression by raising children to be sold in the English markets for food; the second, a narrative satirizing human folly more generally.

One of the many ironies of *Gulliver's Travels* is that it has come to be widely regarded as a children's book. The book can provide an exciting fantasy experience for children, but just beneath the surface lies the adult satire, which is far removed from children's fare—indeed, so far removed that Swift has been tagged a misanthrope by some who, mistakenly, regard his view of human nature as cynical and bitter. Swift wrote his own epitaph, which read, "He has gone where fierce indignation can lacerate his heart no more." Such "indignation," as the literary critic Samuel Monk has pointed out, did not result from

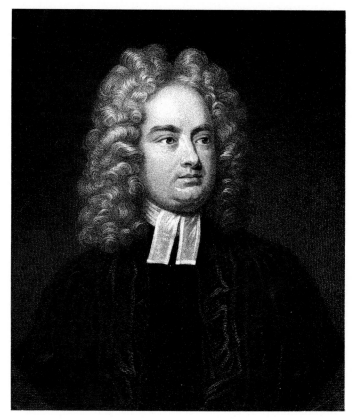

4.7 Jonathan Swift

cynicism; rather, it came from Swift's recognition of the failure of human beings to live up to their moral and spiritual potential.

Swift wrote *Gulliver's Travels* during the Enlightenment, regarded by some scholars as the beginning of modern times. However, he opposed some of the characteristics of this period, attacking, for example, rationalism (the tendency to see truth merely as intellectual concepts and to reject the wisdom of the past generated by experience), experimental and theoretical science (which he regarded as lacking in moral concern), the concept that human nature is essentially good (a view that failed to take account of the fallen nature of human beings (see page 153) and the growth of centralized government (because of its isolation from real human need). All of these developments so characteristic of the Enlightenment are attacked and satirized by Swift in *Gulliver's Travels*.

Although broadly a satire on the physical, political, intellectual, and moral aspects of human nature, *Gulliver's Travels* is specifically an attack on pride, the besetting sin of fallen human beings in Swift's Christian view. Monk has pointed out that Swift uses the "great chain of being" concept, widely accepted in his time, in developing his attack on human pride. This was a hierarchial view of reality relating all being in an ascend-

ing chain, from inanimate objects, through animals, human beings, and angels, ultimately reaching God. Significantly, human beings are uncomfortably poised on the chain between animals and angels; that is, they are both sensual and rational. This concept is vividly illustrated by a passage from Alexander Pope's *Essay on Man*, published seven years after *Gulliver's Travels*:

> *Placed on this isthmus of a middle state,*
> *A being darkly wise, and rudely great:*
> *With too much knowledge for the sceptic side,*
> *With too much weakness for the stoic's pride,*
> *He hangs between: in doubt to act, or rest;*
> *In doubt to deem himself a god, or beast;*
> *In doubt his mind or body to prefer;*
> *Born but to die, and reasoning but to err;*
> *Alike in ignorance, his reason such,*
> *Whether he thinks too little, or too much:*
> *Chaos of Thought and Passion, all confused;*
> *Still by himself abused, or disabused;*
> *Created half to rise, and half to fall;*
> *Great lord of all things, yet a prey to all;*
> *Sole judge of truth, in endless error hurl'd:*
> *The glory, jest, and riddle of the world![1]*

Proud humans, in Swift's view, are strongly inclined to rebel against this painful duality, claiming powers of reason that belong to angels, not human beings.

Gulliver's Travels is divided into four books, or "voyages." The concept of the "chain of being" is reflected in three of them. In the first two voyages, Gulliver is made aware of his middle state, both physically and morally. Among the Lilliputians he looks down the chain. Though much larger than they, he is not brutish but kind and gentle, while the Lilliputians, though superficially appealing and clever, are in fact vicious and violent—yet proud. Thus they appear to Gulliver as humans must appear to superior beings. Among the giant Brobdingnagians in Voyage 2, Gulliver looks up the chain, for now *he* is the "little odious vermin" (as the king calls Europeans), whose pretentious and corrupted moral views are disproportionate to his insignificant size. The contrast is especially evident in his confrontation with the king, who is appalled at Gulliver's account of European warfare and his attempt to persuade the king of the value of making and using gunpowder. For Gulliver, this is the result of "narrow principles and short views." But the reader knows that it is the king, not Gulliver, who sees European warfare for what it really is: a gross violation of the common-sense morality of the Brobdingnagians.

Voyage 3 departs from the chain of being theme and satirizes politics and the abuse of reason through the metaphor of science. Swift was familiar with contemporary scientific ideas and experiments, but he distrusted these popular Enlightenment pursuits because, in his view, they were divorced from practical human needs and morality. Thus, for example, he portrays the scientists of the Flying Island as so lost in abstractions that they neglect their wives and are even incapable of measuring Gulliver for a suit of clothes.

The Flying Island is also a symbol of centralized government controlled by a faction far removed from the needs of their subjects. They govern according to rationalized scientific theory rather than practical morality. Their subjects are poor, oppressed, and frightened, controlled by the ruling clique through spies and informers. Swift thus takes dead aim at the Enlightenment's hubristic confidence in the classical ideal of reason.

In Voyage 4, the most criticized and the least understood of the four parts of *Gulliver's Travels*, Swift continues his attack on arrogant human reason as well as human sensuality, using the powerful symbolism of the Houyhnhnms (highly intelligent horses) and the Yahoos (degenerate humanoid beings). Adapting the idea of the great chain of being, he portrays humans through Gulliver, poised as he is between purely rational creatures (the Houyhnhnms) and purely sensual creatures (the Yahoos). Gulliver makes the fatal mistake of concluding that human beings are merely violent and lustful Yahoos, and as a result he goes mad. His madness is revealed in his rejection of all humans including his own family, and in his attempt to become a Houyhnhnm. But the human being (Gulliver) is no more purely rational than he is purely sensual—he is a mixture of the two. This is his tragic duality on the chain of being. It is only through pride that Gulliver, like the *philosophes*, can assume that he *is* a rational creature (the Enlightenment definition of the human being) rather than merely *capable* of reason (Swift's own definition). The Houyhnhnms, therefore, are not Swift's ideal for human beings. They incarnate the pure reason of Cartesianism, a philosophical system named for René Descartes (1596–1650) which, in Swift's view, placed too much confidence in human reason. They also lack love, the highest Christian virtue, and manifest the characteristics of Stoicism, a philosophy concerning rational indifference to pleasure or pain, of which Swift once remarked, "The Stoical scheme of supplying our wants by lopping off our desires, is like cutting off our feet when we want shoes."

It is Gulliver, therefore, not Swift, who, like Enlightenment man, falls into the grave error of deifying reason. In his mistaken pride, he rejects the true human condition and, as is illustrated by his encounter with Don Pedro de Mendez (Voyage 4), blinds himself to the possibility of transcending his tragic "middle state" through compassion and kindness. Finally, he closes his account of his

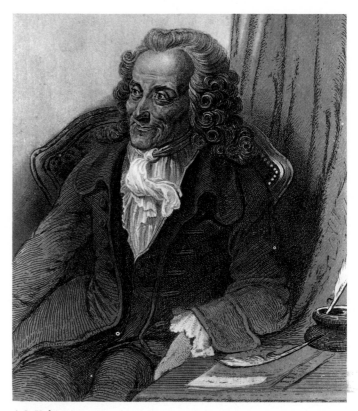

4.8 Voltaire

travels with an attack on human pride which, ironically, reveals his own pride in dissociating himself from humankind.

Voltaire

Born François-Marie Arouet, Voltaire (1694–1778), like Swift and Molière, was critical of human folly. Although he also wrote plays, histories, essays and poetry, he is best known for his philosophical novel *Candide*. Like Swift, he employs in his own novel the literary device of the travel story as the means of exposing human wickedness; unlike Gulliver's, this journey, despite its numerous improbable coincidences, takes place in a real world rather than a fantastic one, and the evil comes from natural as well as human causes. Both Swift and Voltaire, however, attack those who stretch the powers of reason too far. Instead, they offer more limited, and yet more demanding, possibilities for human achievement. For both, to act with rational restraint in a world overgrown with immoderate and proud human behavior is a full-time task and requires a large measure of modesty. Whereas Swift's comic rhetoric sometimes has a tragic power and intensity, Voltaire's rhetorical touch is light and playful. Both writers, however, are deadly serious about the evils they attack.

Voltaire is the best-known representative of the Enlightenment. He personifies the period in many respects—in his rational approach to political, social, and religious issues and institutions, and in his devastating attacks on hypocrisy, prejudice, bigotry, and superstition—although he did not share the optimism of most Enlightenment thinkers. Although he is frequently associated with the skepticism that typified the age, he called himself a theist and professed his belief in a God whose existence is revealed through design in the natural world. This God, however, was impersonal and removed from human affairs. Thus Voltaire rejected the Judaeo-Christian doctrine of providence and even sometimes questioned the goodness of God.

Throughout his life, Voltaire—whose intelligence and skeptical outlook are captured by Houdon's bust (Fig. 4.28)—was involved in controversy because of his caustic wit and satirical attacks on the beliefs, institutions, and customs of his time. He was imprisoned in the Bastille and was forced to flee France on more than one occasion, including a three-year exile in England (1726–1729). While there, he met such famous Englishmen as Pope, Swift, and the philosopher John Locke and became an admirer of English literature, science, government, and religion. Later, in his famous *Philosophic Letters on the English* (1734), he expressed this admiration in such a manner that the French authorities recognized his attack on their own institutions in the contrasts he drew with those of the English. When the executioner burned the work, Voltaire again had to flee, this time to Cirey, in Champagne, where he took refuge with Madame du Châtelet. He remained there until her death in 1749.

Shortly afterward, he moved to Prussia at the invitation of Frederick the Great. He and Frederick were not compatible, however, and he left Prussia in 1753 for Switzerland. He moved to an estate just across the French border in 1758, and remained there until his death 20 years later. During these last years he wrote, under various pen names, numerous pamphlets, including those that eventually grew into his six-volume *Philosophical Dictionary* (1764).

Voltaire was a prolific writer who published in almost every genre of the day, an output that ran to 97 volumes. His most significant works, however, were in the genre of the philosophical tale, especially *Zadig* (1748), a Job-like story of the loss and recovery of prosperity in a Babylonian setting, and *Candide* (1759). The philosophic tale is an episodic narrative that employs satire and comedy to defend or attack an idea. This genre allowed Voltaire to express his criticism under the guise of a story and to communicate his ideas to those who would read them because they were entertaining.

The theme of *Candide* is the problem of evil. This problem arises out of the presence of evil and suffering in a world created, according to traditional Christian belief, by a good God who is all-powerful. If God is omnipotent and beneficent, the question goes, how is one to account for evil? The Christian doctrine of the Fall is intended to explain this paradox. In this interpretation evil is the result of human rebellion against the God who originally created humans in his own image and provided a perfect setting for their development. In *Candide* Voltaire launched a devastating attack upon all rationalizations of the problem of evil, but especially upon Baron Gottfried Wilhelm von Leibnitz's *Theodicy* (1710).

According to Leibnitz, God had a choice from among the possible worlds he might create that would not violate the laws of reason. From these he chose the best possible world—one, however, that necessarily contained evil, because a world without evil would not be as good as one with evil, in that some "goods" are dependent upon evil. Free will, for example, depends upon the possibility of making the wrong choice as well as the right one. In Leibnitz's view, however, the good outweighs the bad in the universe, and the presence of evil in God's creation therefore does not disprove his benevolence. Thus Leibnitz, while maintaining that God is good, also sought to develop a theology that would account for evil without contravening the laws of reason. Although Leibnitz himself is a respected figure, some of his disciples, such as Christian von Wolff and Alexander Pope, developed his ideas in such a manner as to make them vulnerable to Voltaire's biting satire. The last lines of the first epistle of Pope's *Essay on Man* strikingly illustrate this:

> *All Nature is but art, unknown to thee*
> *All chance, direction, which thou canst not see;*
> *All discord, harmony not understood;*
> *All partial evil, universal good:*
> *And, spite of pride, in erring reason's spite,*
> *One truth is clear, WHATEVER IS, IS RIGHT.*[2]

Although some critics regard Pope's *Essay on Man* as an impressive synthesis of Christian apologetics, the last line quoted above made his system an easy target for a caricaturist and satirist like Voltaire. Pope seems to affirm that evil itself has a part to play in the divine perfection of the universe. Prideful humans may not understand why God permits evil to exist, but since he does, it must have a purpose in the grand design of things.

In *Candide* Voltaire attacks the idea that "whatever is, is right" and makes it appear absurd. His protagonist, Candide, brought up under the tutelage of a Leibnitzian philosopher named Pangloss (a Greek compound meaning "All-Tongue"), experiences and observes the most horrifying instances of human suffering and evil and yet continues to parrot Pangloss's axiom, "All is for the best in the best of all possible worlds." Candide's experiences often reflect actual incidents, including the devastating Lisbon earthquake of 1755. Yet the suffering is presented by Voltaire in such a detached, satirical manner that readers do not become involved with it. Thus Voltaire is able to divert attention to the ideas that permeate the narrative. The necessity of this detached approach is suggested from the outset by the title, *Candide, or Optimism*. The protagonist is thus equated with an idea, and readers are alerted to the fact that they must be on the lookout for the ideas conveyed by the narrative rather than becoming involved with the characters themselves. This detachment is also encouraged by the episodic nature of the narrative. Candide moves rapidly from place to place, in the Old World and the New, undergoing so many incredible experiences so rapidly that readers cannot be misled into thinking that Voltaire is striving for realism. Thus attention is directed, not to the reality of the characters and their world, but rather to the ideas that Voltaire is attacking.

The impact of Voltaire's satire is strengthened by the character of his protagonist. Candide is naive and innocent, always willing to invoke the optimistic Leibnitzian philosophy of Pangloss in the face of the most grotesque and horrendous evil. Thus Voltaire ridicules the philosophy of optimism. But even Candide finally grows weary of the hopeless task of declaring that "all is for the best in the best of all possible worlds." At the end of the novel, having settled on a farm with his friends and his childhood sweetheart Cunegonde, he gently brushes aside Pangloss's optimistic bromides and advises, "That is well said, but we must tend our gardens," the only positive view offered in the novel. Although the inveterate optimism of the innocent Candide is finally worn away by the evils of the world, he does not become cynical but offers a positive alternative. Thus, Voltaire seems to say, there is hope in the acceptance of the world as it is, without optimistic rationalizations of its evils, if human beings will devote themselves to the practical task at hand. He does not, however, consider the result if the task should be unworthy or cruel.

Counterpoint to Rationalism

The age of the Enlightenment and the *philosophes* ended not long after the death of Voltaire. Although the *philosophes* might seem to be the antithesis of Candide, they too were (except for Voltaire) inveterate optimists. They believed in the power of education to dispel ignor-

ance, eliminate superstition, and transform human nature. They had faith in the ability of reason to undermine evil, in the ability of science to enlarge knowledge and solve society's problems, and in the ultimate triumph of rationality for the betterment of the human race. In the last decades of the eighteenth century their views gained considerable credibility, even among the institutions and leaders who would have had the most to lose by the implementation of these views. But in the light of the cataclysmic events of the French Revolution at the end of the century these views turned out to be as much of an illusion as Pangloss's "All is for the best in the best of all possible worlds."

Meanwhile, Enlightenment intellectuals were either unable to understand or unwilling to respect the persistently non-rational side of human nature. Jean-Jacques Rousseau (1712–1778) is an exception, but he was in many ways a Romantic living in the Enlightenment and will be treated as such in Chapter 5. Others, however, were impatient with the demands of imagination and sentiment, played down the powers of love and hatred, were arrogant about mysticism and the persistence of religious belief, and denigrated the roles of tradition and custom. But the emotional, sexual, instinctive, religious, mystical, and superstitious aspects of human nature are real in all ages and cannot indefinitely be ignored. They are reflected not only in the writings of Rousseau, but also, as we shall see, in the classical and Neoclassical arts.

It should also be remembered that even while the rationalist ideals of the Enlightenment were gaining currency in the late 1600s, one of the leading scientists of the time, the Frenchman Blaise Pascal (1623–1662) was espousing more intuitive beliefs. Pascal was a mathematical and scientific genius who, as the result of a powerful conversion experience (to Jansenism), undertook to prepare an apologetic for biblical Christianity in which he rejected the rationalistic "God of the philosophers" for the "God of Jesus Christ." He died before he was able to complete this work, but his notes were published under the title *Pensées* ("Thoughts"). In these notes he argues that "the heart has its reasons of which reason knows nothing," thus recognizing the religious longing expressed by St. Augustine in the well-known opening of his *Confessions*: "You made us for yourself and our hearts find no peace until they rest in you"[3] (see Chapter 6) Here, then, is a profound thinker, who, in the beginnings of modern science, recognized the intuitive longing of human beings for knowledge that transcends reason and scientific facts. It is no surprise, therefore, that Enlightenment rationalism, even before the outbreak of the French Revolution in 1789, began to give way to the romanticism that made room for such mystical yearnings.

Seventeenth-Century Art

Sixteenth-century art, as we saw in Chapter 3, began with the High Renaissance style and ended with Mannerism. Having inherited the grandeur of the first and the restlessness of the second, Baroque art can be seen as the offspring of both styles. Born in Italy in the late sixteenth and early seventeenth centuries, Baroque soon spread from there to the rest of Europe.

Although its derivation is uncertain, the term Baroque first came into use as a negative label by nineteenth-

century critics to denounce most seventeenth-century art. Among other things, the art of that time was considered a betrayal of the classical ideals of the High Renaissance: order, balance, objectivity, and restraint. Even today, the word as a general term, refers to anything perceived as excessive. But the negative attitude toward seventeenth-century art itself, even those works that particularly exemplify the Baroque style, has moderated. Modern writers are quick to point out the dangers of generalizing

4.9 BERNINI
Colonnade, St. Peter's, Rome

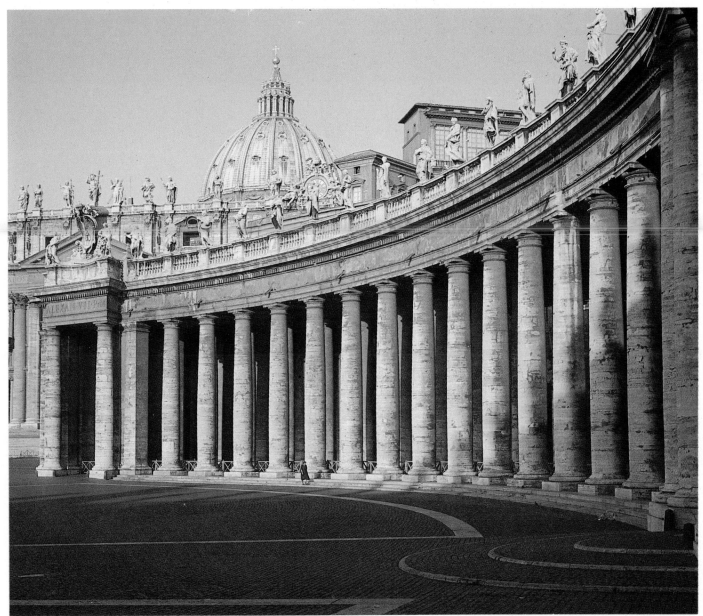

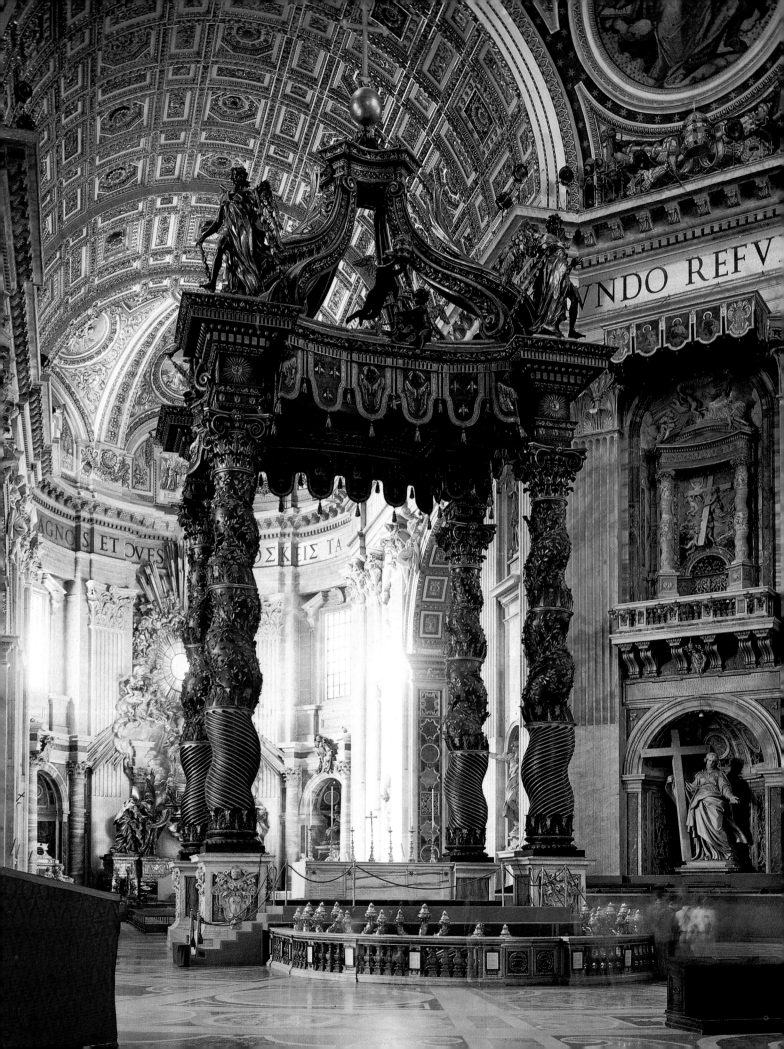

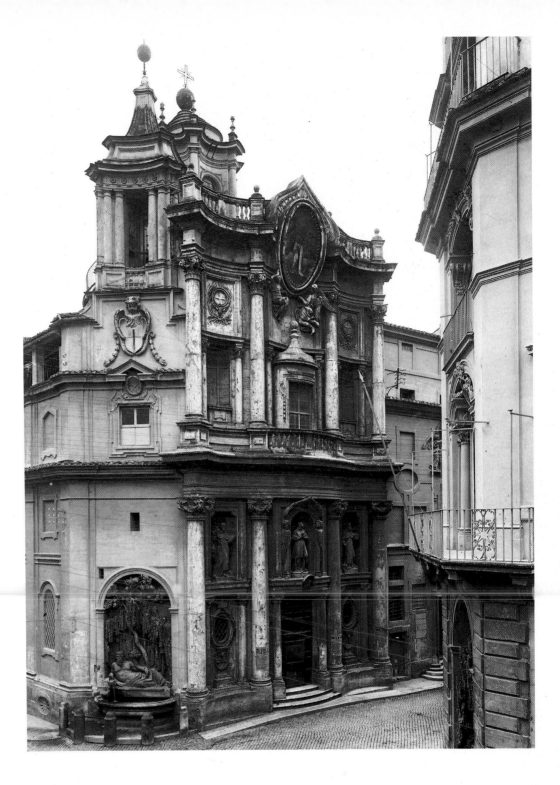

4.10 (left) BERNINI
Baldacchino, St. Peter's,
Rome, 1624–33
Gilded bronze,
c. 100 ft (30.5 m) high

4.11 BORROMINI
San Carlo Alle Quatro
Fontana, Rome, begun 1635

about this art, for it contains a great deal of diversity. A wide variety of styles can be found in the works of some individual Baroque artists, such as Gianlorenzo Bernini (1598–1680). For example, his famous *colonnade* in front of St. Peter's (Fig. **4.9**), consisting of a majestic arrangement of Tuscan columns, the plainest column used in ancient Rome, is very classical. On the other hand, his *baldacchino* inside St. Peter's (Fig. **4.10**), whose ornate columns curve and twist like the legs of some fantastic beast, is very unclassical. The following section will review examples of art in the seventeenth century with

special emphasis given to those that reflect in one way or another the qualities of classicism.

The range of diversity in seventeenth-century art is even broader when one makes comparisons across national boundaries. To some extent this diversity is a reflection of the regional, religious, and economic tapestry of seventeenth-century Europe. Italian architecture, compared with that of northern countries, is known for its complexity and ornamentation. The front of a small Roman church (Fig. **4.11**) designed by Bernini's rival, Francesco Borromini (1599–1667), is a mixture of con-

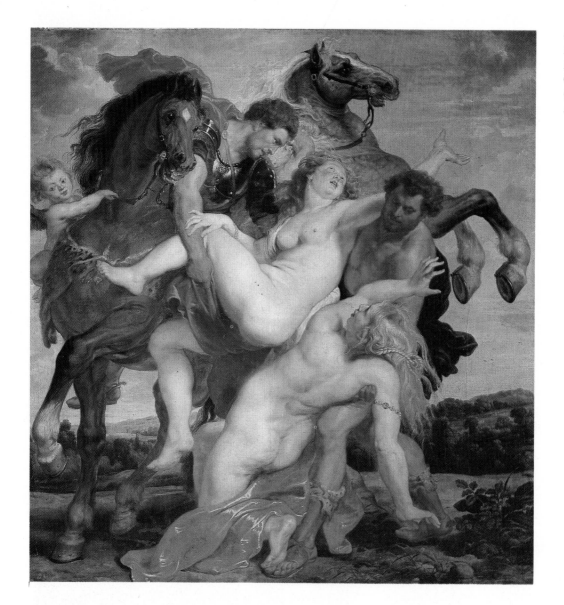

4.12 PETER PAUL RUBENS
*Rape of the Daughters of
Leucippus,* 1617
Oil on canvas, $87\frac{1}{2} \times 82\frac{1}{4}$ ins
$(222 \times 209$ cm)
Alte Pinakothek, Munich

cave and convex surfaces, deeply recessed niches, balustrades, medallions, and Corinthian columns. Seventeenth-century architecture in France and England, as we shall see later, is much more restrained. Because Italian ideas in painting had become completely assimilated by non-Italian artists, the differences in this art form had more to do with religion and politics than with region. Catholic Flanders was the home of Peter Paul Rubens (1577–1640), whose lively painting *The Rape of the Daughters of Leucippus* (Fig. **4.12**), brimming with heroic figures engaged in athletic struggle, can be contrasted with the staid domestic scene (Fig. **4.13**) of one of his Protestant contemporaries in the neighboring Dutch Republic. Whereas Rubens' patrons were members of the aristocracy and monarchy all over Europe, as well as the Catholic Church, the Dutch artists' patrons were the practical, prosperous traders and bankers of Amsterdam and Leiden. Some art critics divide seventeenth-century

art into "Catholic Baroque" and "Protestant Baroque" or "aristocratic style" and "bourgeois style."

Nevertheless, all Baroque works tend to share, to greater or lesser degrees, a set of family traits: complexity, unity, and drama (in both painting and architecture), and pictorial realism and heroic figures (in painting).

Complexity can be seen in each of the examples given, especially in Bernini's baldacchino, Borromini's church, and Rubens' abduction scene. Sometimes complexity is compounded by the Baroque tendency to mix two or more media in the same work, such as the mixture of sculpture and architecture in the baldacchino. But complexity, no matter how great, is always tempered by the Baroque passion for unity. Unity in these examples is illustrated by the repetitions and rhythms of Bernini's architecture, the concentration of heavy features in the center of the Borromini façade, and the directional forces that swirl around the central nude of the Rubens. Unity is closely

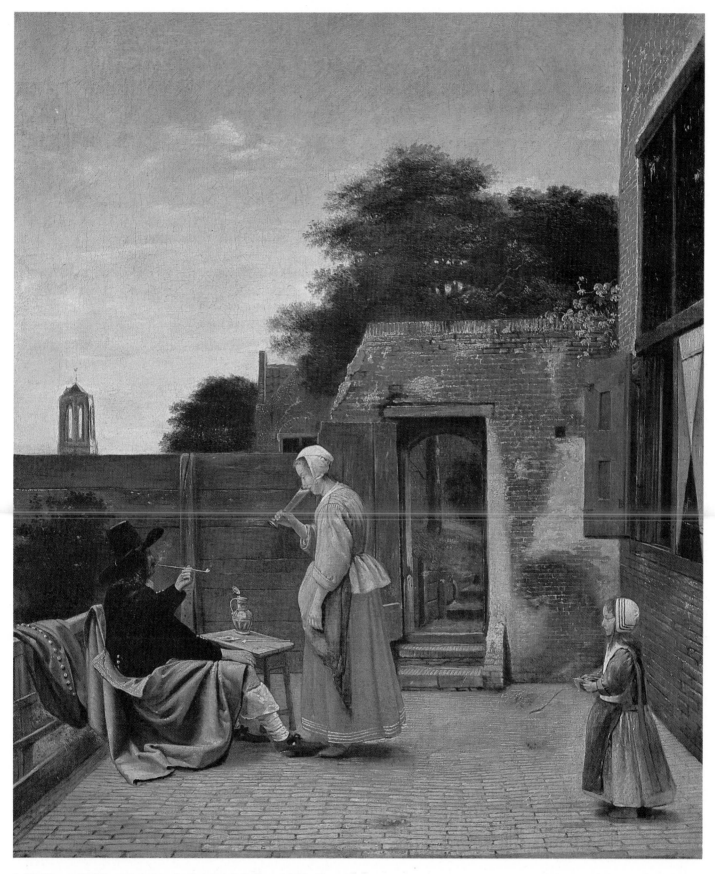

4.13 PIETER DE HOOCH *Interior of a Courtyard, Delft*, c. 1658–60
Oil on canvas, 26¾ × 23 ins (68 × 59 cm), Mauritshuis, The Hague

related to drama, because the dramatic impact is greater when given focus by compositional unity. Drama can be seen in the subject matter and energy of the Rubens painting and in the scale and pomp of the architecture. Common to all Baroque painting is pictorial realism. Seventeenth-century painters had the skills to create convincing illusions of even the most fantastic subjects. And because much Baroque art was designed to appeal to the senses, many painters took special delight in exploiting their skill in representing textures: human flesh, horse flesh, satin brocade, wispy clouds, anything. Finally, like Rubens, most painters seemed to be fascinated with the beauty of the human body, which, in Baroque pictures, is usually endowed with heroic proportions and restless movement.

Classicism in Seventeenth-Century Art

Are there any classical traits in a style of art that extols complexity, drama, sensuousness, and exaggerated movement? Though different from Renaissance art in import-ant respects, Baroque art inherited a legacy from that style that can be seen in the idealized figures and mythological themes of its painting and in the columns and other classical motifs of its architecture. But the reverence for order, balance, and harmony, as well as the breathing room necessary to nurture these qualities, has clearly been sacrificed in much Baroque art. There are, however, exceptions—notably in the art of France.

Poussin

Of all the countries of Europe, France seems to have had the strongest instinct for classicism. The works of her architects and painters, as well as her Neoclassical dramatists, exhibit a classical restraint which is unique in seventeenth-century culture. In the paintings of Nicolas Poussin (1594–1665) the tradition of classicism, particularly as exemplified in High Renaissance art, was not only preserved but given a new expression.

Except for brief service as court painter to Louis XIII of France, Poussin spent most of his productive life in Rome.

4.14 NICOLAS POUSSIN *Landscape with the Burial of Phocion*, 1648
Oil on canvas, 70 × 47 ins (178 × 120 cm), Louvre, Paris

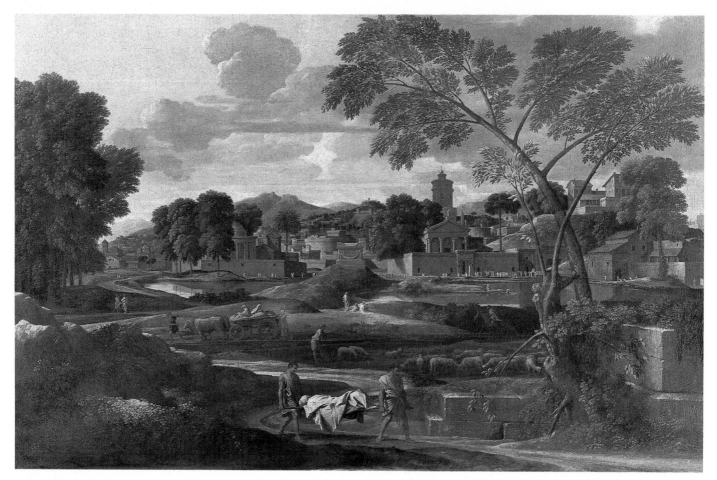

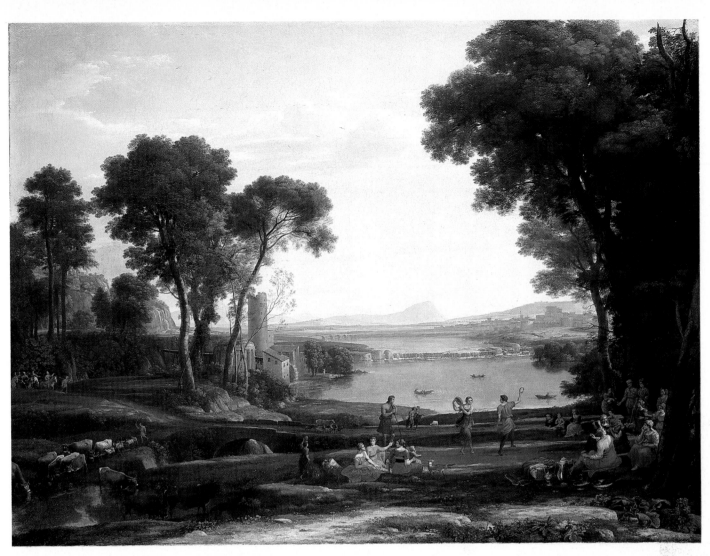

4.15 CLAUDE *The Marriage of Isaac and Rebekah*, 1642
Oil on canvas, 59 × 77 ins (150 × 195 cm), National Gallery, London

In that city, the expatriate Frenchman preferred the works of Titian and Raphael to the contemporary works of Rome's Baroque artists. However, it was Rome itself that made the biggest impression on him. Poussin's love of that city's squares, trees, hills, and especially of its ancient ruins, anticipated the sentiments of nineteenth-century Romantics (see Chapter 5).

The results of these obsessions can be seen in *The Burial of Phocion* (Fig. **4.14**). Like Racine, an ardent student of classical literature, Poussin derived the story from Plutarch's accounts of Greek and Roman heroes. True to classical requirements, the forms are clearly defined, the people—especially those in the foreground bearing Phocion's corpse—have the bodily proportions of Greek statues or of Raphael's men in *The School of Athens* (Fig. 3.42), and the buildings in the background are vaguely based on Greek and Roman models. But Poussin has introduced something new: the use of landscape as the principal subject matter and focus of attention—an unusual practice in Western art up to that time. Yet because each object—building, wall, or tree—is so lucidly

revealed by the late afternoon light, the land so carefully terraced and cultivated, and the mood so quiet and stately, we seem to be transported into antiquity itself.

Claude

Poussin and his contemporary, Claude Gellee (known as Claude or Claude Lorraine) (1600–82), were kindred spirits in many ways. Like Poussin, Claude was an expatriate Frenchman who worked in Rome and loved ancient ruins; he also painted idealised landscapes as imaginative reconstructions of another era. His subjects, however, were often derived from the biblical past, as in *The Marriage of Isaac and Rebekah* (Fig. **4.15**), rather than the classical past. And, as opposed to Poussin's architectonic, "heroic" style, Claude's is softer, more carefree, and atmospheric. Romantic artists (Chapter 5), who often conceived of landscapes as metaphors of longing and nostalgia, were inspired by Claude. But in the final analysis, the Frenchman's paintings, despite their alleged romantic tendencies, affirm the characteristics of harmony, balance, and repose typical of classical art.

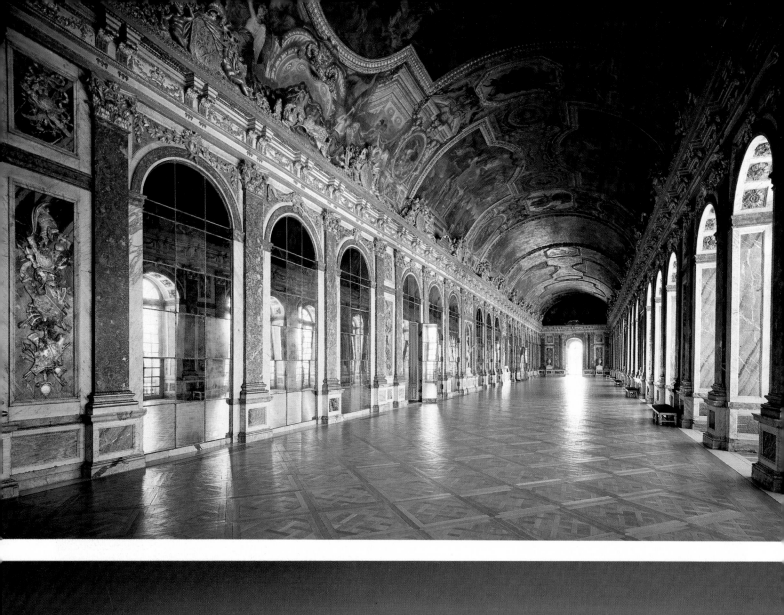

4.16 (top left) MANSART
and LEBRUN
Hall of Mirrors, Versailles
begun 1676
Length 240 ft (73.15 m)
Width 34 ft (10.36 m)
Height 43 ft (13.11 m)

4.17 (bottom left)
Versailles, Garden façade

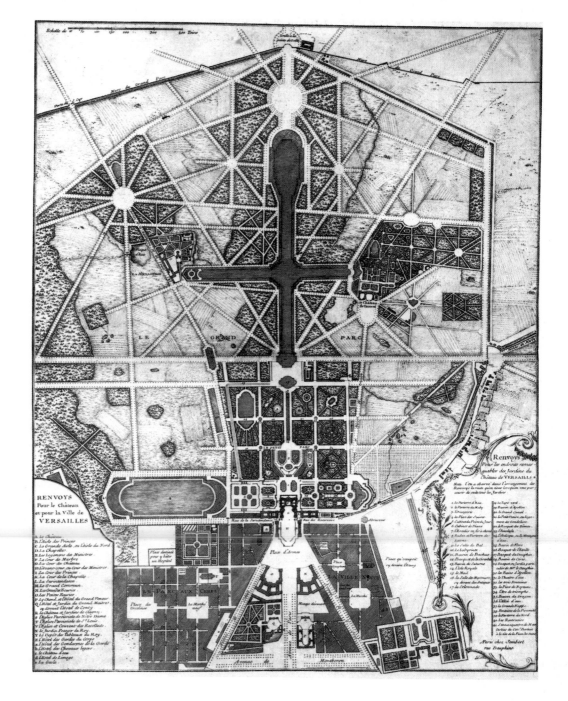

4.18 Contemporary plan of
the Palace of Versailles

The Palace of Versailles

In many ways Louis XIV's Palace of Versailles, represented here by its sumptuous Galerie des Glaces, or Hall of Mirrors (Fig. **4.16**), is the ultimate example of Baroque excess. Built by an army of architects, landscape designers, painters, sculptors, stonemasons, and decorators (which, during the peak of the construction in 1685, totaled 36,000 men, plus 6000 horses), the palace and grounds are perhaps the most enormous architectural project ever undertaken for a single purpose (Fig. **4.18**). However, the exteriors of the individual buildings, such as the garden façade of the palace (Fig. **4.17**), are comparatively restrained, resembling High Renaissance architecture more than Baroque. Unlike the walls of Borromini's church, these are uncomplicated and relatively flat; the use of ornament—sculptures, medallions, carving—is moderate. Finally, the symmetry, balance, and overall proportions, especially the use of three stories, recall the designs of Michelangelo and Maderno for St. Peter's Basilica (p. 139–40). One reason for the persistence of classicism in an otherwise Baroque enterprise could be that Charles le Brun (1619–1690), manager of the project, was a student of Poussin's.

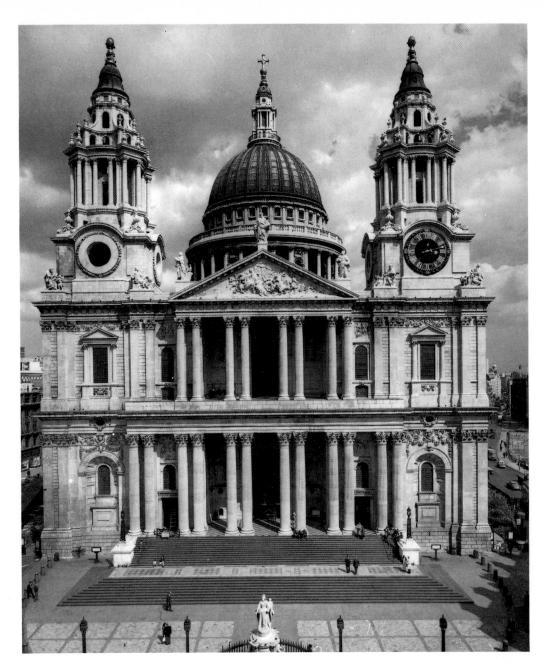

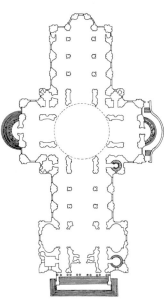

4.19 CHRISTOPHER WREN
St. Paul's Cathedral, facade
and plan, 1675–1710

St. Paul's Cathedral

Across the Channel, developments in art were far behind those on the Continent. England had no painters to compare with Rubens or Poussin, and her architects were only just beginning to assimilate Italian ideas. But during the Restoration period English architecture began to flourish.

Christopher Wren (1632–1723) was already a skilled scientist, engineer, and astronomy professor before turning to architecture in his thirties. On a visit to France in 1665–66 he experienced French Baroque architecture at first hand and, through the study of prints, and perhaps also of Palladio's treatise (see Chapter 3), he acquired knowledge of the Renaissance and Baroque architecture of Italy.

St. Paul's Cathedral (Figs. **4.19**, **4.20**)—which Wren designed in 1666 after the original St. Paul's, a Gothic structure, burned down in the Great Fire of that year—is a synthesis of High Renaissance, Baroque, and even Gothic concepts. The basically rectilinear façade, the use of paired columns, and the big dome are High Renaissance—reminiscent of both Versailles and St. Peter's. The dome itself is closely based on Bramante's Tempietto, at the church of S. Pietro in Montorio, Rome. The two flanking towers, like the kind Borromini used on his church (Fig. 4.11), are Baroque. The rest of the cathedral, consisting of a long nave supported by flying buttresses (though the latter are hidden by the second story of the outer wall), is a continuation of Gothic principles. Despite the mixture of sources, the overall appearance of Wren's church is basically classical.

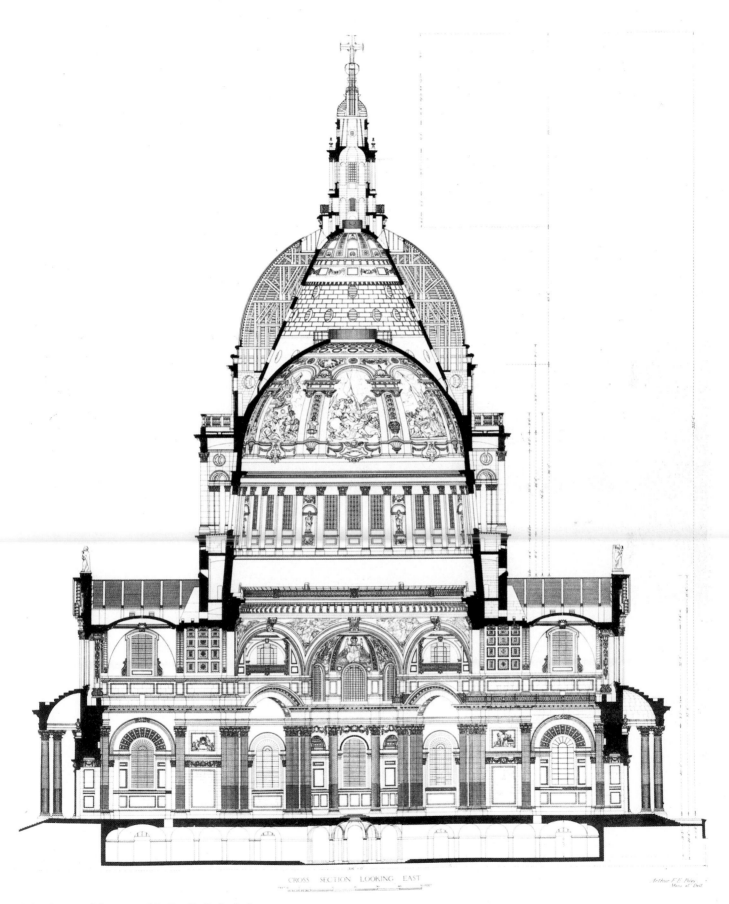

CROSS SECTION LOOKING EAST

4.20 Sectional drawing of St. Paul's Cathedral

Eighteenth-Century Art

Largely because of the splendor of Louis XIV's court, France had become the cultural arbiter of Europe. Louis' death in 1715 signaled a change of taste in the art of France, and ultimately other European countries as well. The Regent, who governed France until the young Louis XV came of age in 1723, was more interested in amusement and pleasure than power.

When the Regent moved the government from Versailles back to Paris, the French nobility—so long in thrall to tedious court etiquette—reasserted itself. At the same time, they rejected the heavy Baroque style associated with Versailles and turned to a lighter, more delicate style known as Rococo, a style perfectly suited to the relatively smaller salons of Parisian townhouses, such as the Salon de la Princesse (Fig. **4.21**) in the Palais Soubise. In such rooms as this, aristocratic French society met for intimate concerts, dances and evenings of refined and witty conversation. The outlook of this society is admirably depicted in *The Swing* by Jean-Honoré Fragonard (1732–1806), a scene of aristocrats at play in a make-

4.21 GERMAIN BOFFRAND
Salon de la Princesse, Palais Soubise, Paris, c. 1740

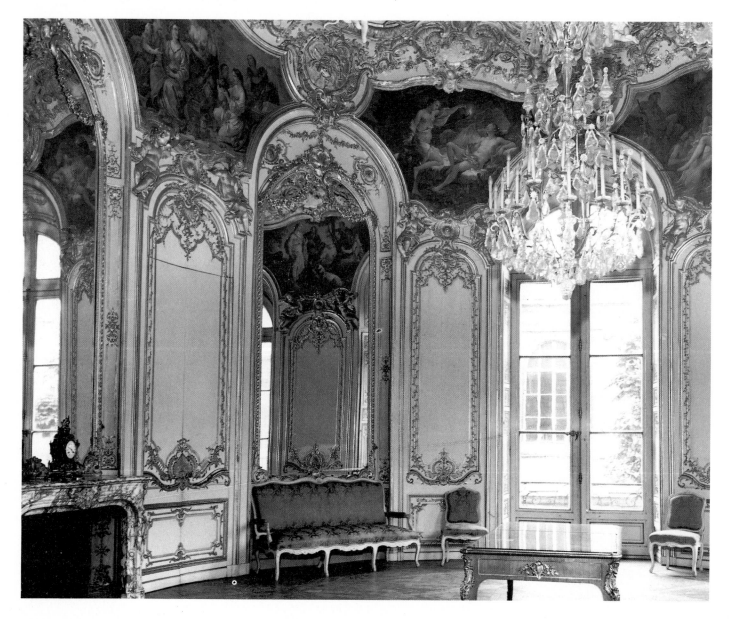

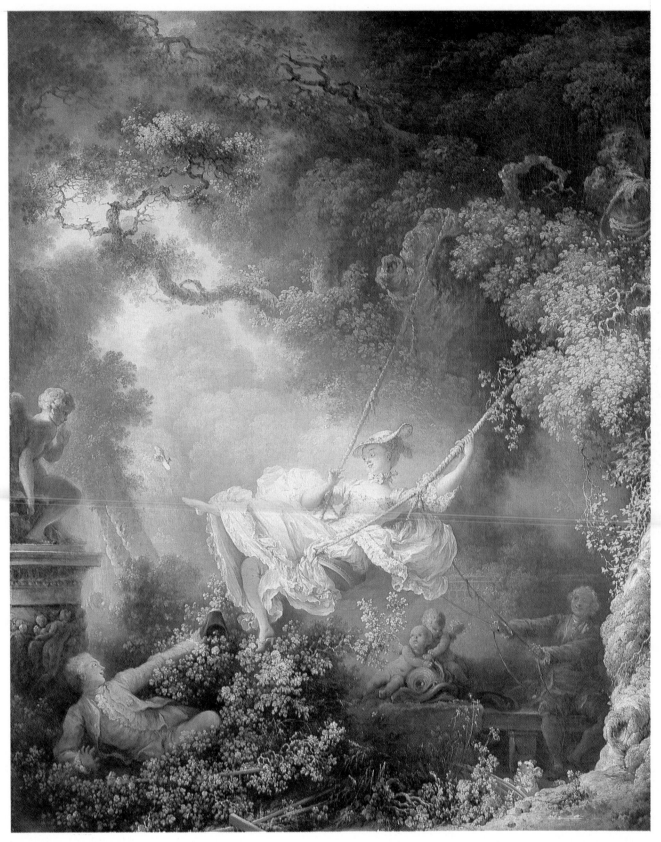

4.22 Jean-Honore Fragonard
The Swing, c. 1768–69
Oil on canvas, 32 × 25 ins (83 × 62.5 cm)
Wallace Collection, London

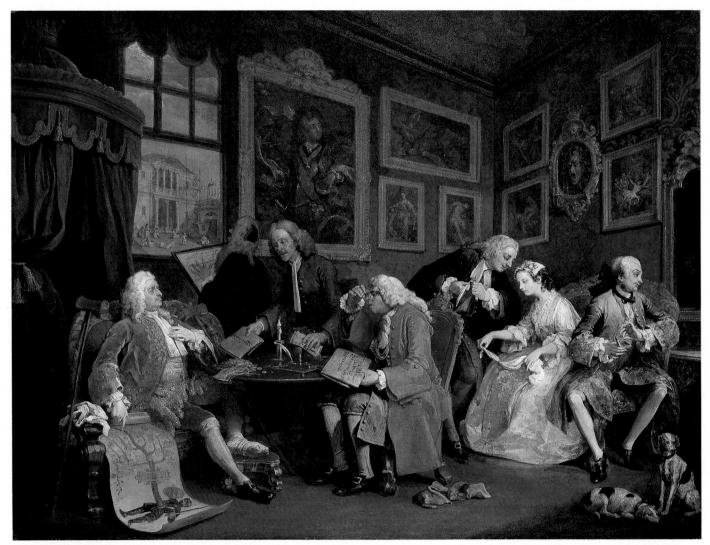

4.23 WILLIAM HOGARTH
The Marriage Contract from *Marriage à la Mode*, c. 1745
Oil on canvas, approx 28 × 36 ins (71 × 91.5 cm)
National Gallery, London

believe world (Fig. **4.22**). A young lady coquettishly kicks off a slipper while her lover admires the view from below. The lovely textures of her swirling, expensive clothes are echoed in the feathery foliage of the fantasy landscape. Rococo painting acquired a more thoughtful, poetic dimension in the work of Antoine Watteau (1684–1721). But because the dreamlike quality of so many of his paintings clearly foreshadows the Romantic period, he will be discussed more fully in Chapter 5.

Primarily associated with the decorative arts, Rococo features pastel colors, irregular, curvilinear shapes (often based on plant forms or *rocaille*—little shells), delicate lines, and soft textures—traits that can be seen in both the salon and Fragonard's painting. Rococo evolved from Baroque, but the kind of Baroque exemplified by the Hall

of Mirrors and Rubens' *Rape of the Daughters of Leucippus*; for Rococo has little in common with the classicism of Poussin. Although it shares with Baroque a love of sensuous colors, fluid forms, and lively movement, Rococo treats all of these things, including the depictions of human figures, with a much lighter touch. It is also more light-hearted in content, and, some would say, light-headed. It perfectly expressed the values and pastimes of a pleasure-loving aristocracy.

Rococo did not express the values and concerns of the middle classes, a segment of society that grew dramatically in size and power during the eighteenth century. The style's many critics perceived it as both frivolous and immoral and tried to promote a different art to take its place. One such critic was William Hogarth

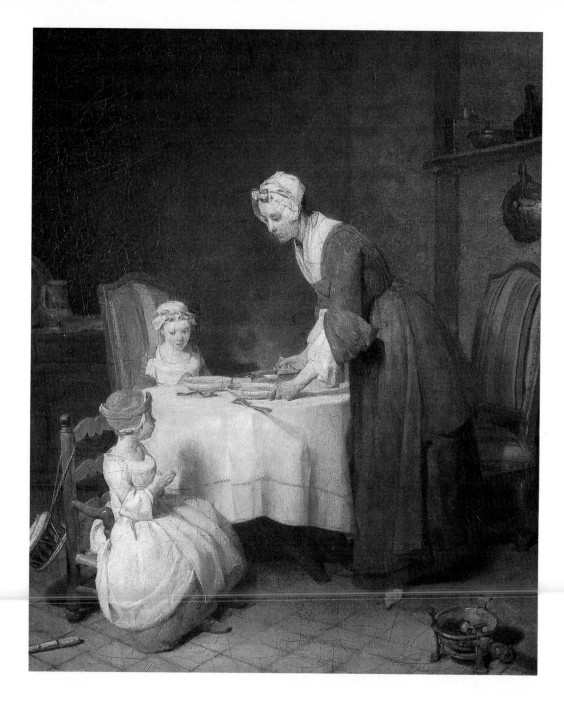

4.24 JEAN-BAPTISTE CHARDIN
Grace at Table, 1740
Oil on canvas, 19 × 15 ins
(48 × 38 cm)
Louvre, Paris

(1697–1764), the first important English painter since the Middle Ages. Like Swift, Hogarth combined serious moral purpose and wit in his art and is best known for several series of paintings (and etchings derived from them) exposing human follies and vices, especially those of the upper classes. For example, *Marriage à la Mode*, a six-part story, lampoons the cynical custom of using marriage as a means to gain title or wealth. In the first scene, *The Marriage Contract* (Fig. **4.23**), the groom's father, an impoverished nobleman, proudly displays his family tree, while the bride's father, a wealthy merchant, squints at the contract. The son and daughter, the bargaining chips of the deal, sit with their backs to each other—the groom-to-be completely indifferent to his future wife, who is flirting with another man. Their short, farcical marriage,

chronicled in five additional scenes, ends with the wife, a suicide, in the hands of her father, who is interested only in salvaging the ring on her finger. Hogarth also satirized art, especially the pretensions of Baroque opera, which was popular in his day. He illustrated several scenes for John Gay's *Beggar's Opera* (1728), which poked fun at the operas of Handel, among others.

Meanwhile, one French artist, Jean-Baptiste-Siméon Chardin (1699–1779), countered the Rococo style more gently than did Hogarth. At first glance one might think that the quiet domestic scene of *Grace at Table* (Fig. **4.24**) was painted by a seventeenth-century Dutch master, such as Vermeer (see Chapter 9). The subject—middle class people in their modest but comfortable home—and the appropriately subdued colors are reminiscent of Dutch

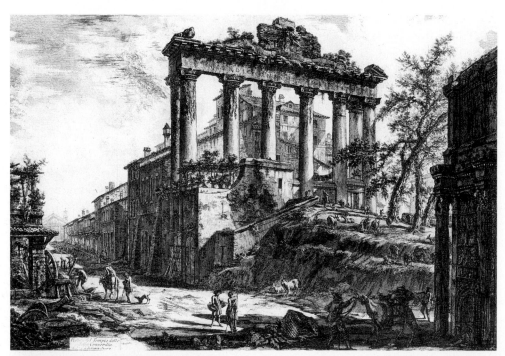

4.25 GIOVANNI BATTISTA PIRANESI
The Temple of Saturn,
Etching from *The Views of Rome*
c. 1774
Metropolitan Museum of Art,
New York

4.26 JACQUES-LOUIS DAVID
Oath of the Horatii, 1784
Oil on canvas, approx 14 × 11 ft
(4.26 × 3.35 m)
Louvre, Paris

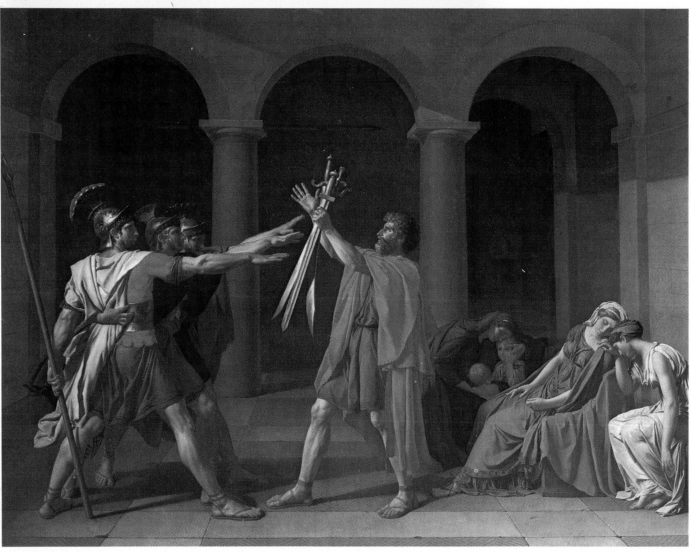

genre painting. Nearly all of Chardin's paintings are of such ordinary people, depicted with a subtlety and quiet restraint that make the frivolous Rococo style—and its equally frivolous subjects, the aristocracy—look shallow indeed.

Thus at mid-century, when the Age of Enlightenment was reaching its peak, Europe had a dominant style, Rococo, which represented the aristocracy, and the art of such "anti-Rococo" painters as Hogarth and Chardin, which represented the middle class, or bourgeoisie. None of this art was genuinely classical. Rococo artists' use of classical themes was motivated more by a desire to display the charms of female goddesses than by a reverence for classicism. The opposing styles were simply not concerned with classical themes (although the work of Chardin certainly exhibits a classical sense of decorum).

The Neoclassical Movement

A number of intellectual, artistic, and social currents of the time were influential in dramatically changing the art of Europe before the end of the eighteenth century.

Because of the Enlightenment, and the concomitant decline of the influence of the Church, education for the general public became more important and more widespread. The breakthrough of the printed word produced the unexpected phenomenon of a large reading public, a public that expected more of art than fluff.

The *philosophes*, who attacked the social and political order of France, also disapproved of Rococo art. Diderot—who, among other things, was an art critic—ridiculed some artists and championed others, in an attempt to influence the direction of art through his writing. He was especially concerned about the need for morality and seriousness in art.

Changes in patronage occurred as the middle classes, who could not afford to collect large, expensive works, bought prints (such as Hogarth's) and commissioned portraits from minor artists. Meanwhile large works of the past, which had previously been seen only by noblemen or kings, became available to the general public as former palaces became art museums. Both the Vatican (the former palace of the popes) and the Louvre (the former palace of the French royalty) were opened to the public.

New interest in the classical civilizations surfaced in the wake of the discoveries of Herculaneum (1738) and Pompeii (1748), Roman towns preserved in volcanic ash since the eruption of Mount Vesuvius in AD 79. The almost-intact remains provided glimpses of everyday Roman life which stimulated scholars and public alike. Giovanni Battista Piranesi (1720–1778) further stirred imaginations by causing people to see Roman ruins in a

new way through his famous *Views of Rome* (Fig. **4.25**). A German art historian, Johann Joachim Winckelmann (1717–1768), gave articulate shape to the classical past through his "cycles-of-growth" theory of artistic developments. Because of his writing, people began to distinguish between Greek and Roman sculpture and to honor early "Archaic" forms more than they had before.

Winckelmann was the leading spokesman for a new kind of art which came to be called *Neoclassical*. While studying Greek art he became impressed with its "noble simplicity and calm grandeur." Obviously Rococo is completely lacking in these qualities. The art of Chardin, although simple and calm, is not noble and grand. True art, according to Winckelmann, should embody three things: the "universal," the "ideal," and "moral force."

All the necessary conditions for Winckelmann's art were present in the late eighteenth century: an educated public, middle-class patrons, a new knowledge of classical culture, and the desire for something new. But, except for a few examples of architecture, no art clearly embodied true Neoclassical qualities until the French artist David began to give visual expression to Winckelmann's three touchstones in the 1780s.

David

The Oath of the Horatii (Fig. **4.26**) by Jacques Louis David (1748–1825) was not only the first painting to fulfill Winckelmann's criteria, it has remained a prime symbol of Neoclassicism ever since. Inspired by the legendary history of ancient Rome by Livy (59 BC–AD 17) and *Horace*, a play by the French dramatist Pierre Corneille (1606–1684), the painting depicts three Roman brothers' commitment to a death-duel with three Alban brothers to decide a war between Rome and Alba. It personifies patriotism and stoicism, the highest virtues of the Roman Republic. David chose the moment of the oath to express and crystallize these values, infusing the subject with visual and psychological tension. The triangular rigidity of the male figures contrasts with the curvilinear softness of the women—two sisters (one betrothed to one of the Albans) and an older woman—who are slumped in despair. This contrast between left and right and, symbolically, between male and female, is echoed in other contrasts. The starkly defined figures, assembled across the front like sculptures in a classical frieze, are set against a plain background, a simple arcade supported by Tuscan columns. The relative complexity of the lower half of the painting is opposed by the simplicity of the upper. The darks and lights are strong; the colors, besides brown, black, and white, are mostly primary. *The Oath of the Horatii* is an intense, concentrated image. According to the art historian Hugh Honour, David achieved in this painting "a perfect fusion of form and content in an image of extraordinary lucidity and visual punch." The differences in theme, composition and mood between it and *The Swing*, made by David's compatriot Fragonard just 18 years earlier, could not be more dramatic.

The success of David's painting was both artistic and political. When shown in the Paris Salon of 1785, it signaled the victory of Neoclassicism over Rococo and was applauded as a vivid allegory of patriotism. Eventually it came to symbolize the French Revolution, inspiring the bourgeoisie in their struggle for liberty. Ironically, it was Louis XVI, the Revolution's main victim, who had commissioned David to make the painting in the first place.

The Jacobin society, the most radical of the revolutionary factions, adopted Neoclassicism as its official artistic style. David was elected to the National Convention (the governing body of France during the Revolution) and eventually became Napoleon's court painter. Thus David's reputation, both ideological and artistic, assured his place in history as the foremost Neoclassicist in the field of painting. But for many years in the nineteenth century, one of his students held this distinction.

Ingres

In the early stages of his career Jean-Auguste Dominique Ingres (1780–1867) was accused of deviating from Neoclassicial principles; but later, as the Romantic movement began to gain ascendancy, he became known as the archetypal Neoclassical painter and the main spokesman of a by-then conservative tradition. The contrast between his work and that of Eugène Delacroix, the famous Romantic painter, was played up at the time by both critics and the press (see Chapter 5).

Although Ingres' art seemed very Neoclassical to his contemporaries, in retrospect it departs from David's brand of Neoclassicism in many ways. The figures are sinuous and sensual rather than monumental. The content often leans to pomp, fantasy, and, sometimes cool eroticism, as in the *Grande Odalisque* (Fig. **4.27**). In the final analysis, the Neoclassicism of Ingres' painting lies mainly in its carefully-rendered and clearly-defined shapes and its studied composition.

The artist admired certain kinds of art in the classical tradition—Greek reliefs, Raphael, Poussin—which exemplified a keen sensitivity for contour. The splendid

4.27 JEAN-AUGUSTE-DOMINIQUE INGRES
La Grande Odalisque, 1874
Oil on canvas, approx $36\frac{1}{4} \times 63\frac{3}{4}$ ins (92×110 cm)
Louvre, Paris

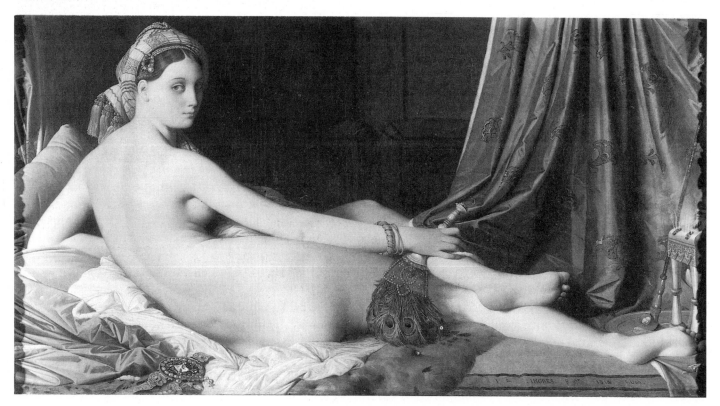

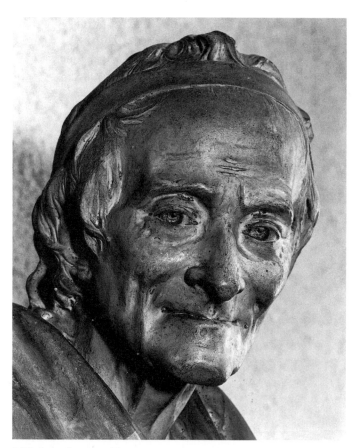

4.28 JEAN ANTOINE HOUDON
Voltaire, 1781
Terracotta and plaster, after a marble statue
now in the Comedie Française, Paris
Fabre Museum, Montpellier, France

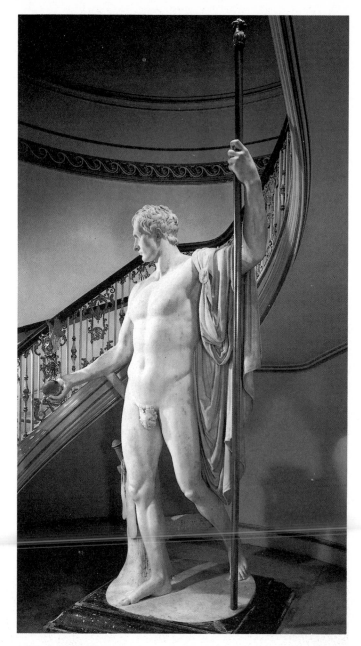

4.29 ANTONIO CANOVA
Napoleon, 1802–10
Marble, 11 ft 8 ins (3.56 m) high
Wellington Museum, London

lines of the *Grande Odalisque* reflect this obsession. Other aspects of the painting, however, reflect additional influences, two of which are from the sixteenth century. The subject—a passive reclining nude—shows the legacy of Titian's *Venus of Urbino* (Fig. 3.48). The abnormal elongation of her torso (critics in Ingres' day accused her of having three vertebrae too many) is reminiscent of the languid figures in Parmigianino's *Madonna with the Long Neck* (Fig. 3.50). Finally, the fact that she is an odalisque—a female slave in a Turkish harem—shows that Ingres, like the Romantics with whom he disagreed, had a taste for the exotic.

Neoclassical Sculpture

Like painting, sculpture underwent a transition in the late eighteenth century from frivolity to seriousness. Nevertheless a modicum of Rococo whimsy can be detected in the portrait of Voltaire (Fig. **4.28**) by the Neoclassical sculptor Jean Antoine Houdon (1744–1828). Of course, to overlook the satirist's brilliant sense of humor would

have been a serious omission. Although Houdon sculpted full figures he is best known for portraits of leading Enlightenment heroes, including the Americans Franklin, Jefferson, and Washington.

David's counterpart in sculpture was an Italian, Antonio Canova (1757–1822). Like David, Canova changed his style while working in Rome, around the time that David painted *The Oath of the Horatii*. Later David became first painter to Napoleon, while Canova was the Emperor's favorite sculptor. The head of his portrait of Napoleon (Fig. **4.29**) may resemble that of the famous ruler, but the nude body resembles that of Polykleitos's *Spear Carrier* (Fig. 2.21).

Neoclassical Architecture

The term Neoclassical is applied to architecture of the late eighteenth and early nineteenth centuries that sought to emulate antique styles—especially the Greek—more faithfully than had the classically inspired styles of preceding periods. Some fine Neoclassical architecture was produced in France, Britain, and other European countries; but the style was especially popular in the young republic of the United States, where its most illustrious exponent was Thomas Jefferson (1743–1826), an amateur architect and follower of the principles of Palladio (see Chapter 3).

While ambassador to France (1785–1789) during the height of the Neoclassical style, Jefferson admired a Roman temple in Nîmes, the Maison Carrée, which he used as a model for the Virginia State Capitol (Fig. **4.30**). Thus he was the first architect since the Romans to use a temple form for a public building. By doing so he imported Neoclassicism to the shores of America, where it became popular. Architecturally, Washington DC is the most Neoclassical city in the world.

The prevalence of Neoclassical architecture persisted well into the nineteenth century, while Neoclassical painting was supplanted by Romanticism. Despite its obvious Neoclassicism, David's painting contains the seeds of Romanticism, especially with regard to its latent emotion and violence. In some respects it parallels the music of David's contemporary Beethoven, which contained both classical and Romantic elements and which will be examined in Chapter 5.

4.30 THOMAS JEFFERSON
State Capitol, Richmond, Virginia, designed 1785–89

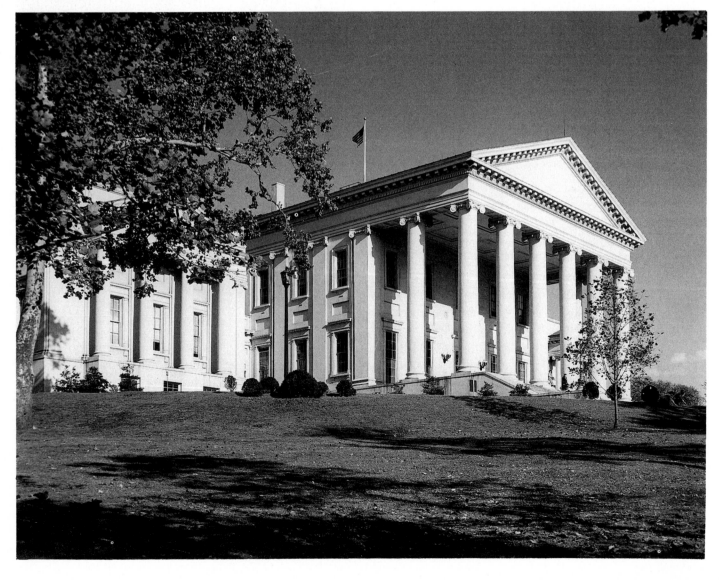

Baroque Music

The Baroque period of music (1600–1750) roughly parallels the Baroque and Rococo periods of art. Like the paintings and buildings of that era, Baroque operas, oratorios, and concertos are replete with detail and brimming with energy and movement. These similarities can be attributed partly to the fact that Baroque music was written for the same institutions that commissioned and collected Baroque art: the Church, royalty, and nobility.

But the Baroque period has a special meaning for music that it does not have for art. This was the period when European music came of age, just as the Renaissance was

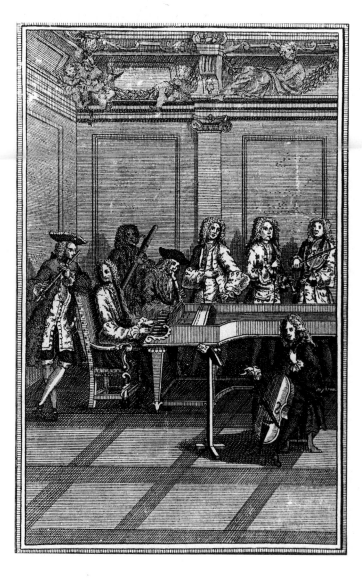

4.31 *A Baroque Orchestra*, eighteenth-century German engraving
The Bettmann Archive

the great period for art. Baroque composers, like Renaissance artists, conceived a wealth of original forms in their quest for new musical ideas and expressive possibilities. Bach and Handel, like Leonardo and Michelangelo, reached the summit of their art, and their names have become familiar even to the general public.

As we have noted in connection with Renaissance music (see page 116), Classical antiquity had little influence on developments in music—there being no ancient music remaining to serve as inspiration—although the legends of antiquity were to provide a rich vein of subject matter for opera. Toward the end of the eighteenth century the ideals of classicism came increasingly to dominate musical language, so that we describe music of this period as being in the Classical style. But there were foreshadowings of classicism in Baroque music too. In this section we will be looking at, among other things, some of those foreshadowings.

During the Baroque age, instrumental music became much more important, while the size of the orchestra grew to between ten and 40 members. The nucleus of the Baroque orchestra consisted of strings and a *basso continuo*: a combination of a low-sounding melodic instrument (cello or bassoon) and a keyboard instrument (harpsichord or organ) which played the bass-line melody (Fig. **4.31**). The basso continuo provided not only rhythm but a firm foundation for the harmonic structure. It also provided greater distinction between base and treble in the polyphonic texture. Compared to Renaissance music, Baroque music has a stronger rhythm, a steady driving force. A Baroque melody, like a Borromini façade, is frequently embellished with ornament, such as trills and tremolos. Baroque composition is also characterized by *terraced dynamics*: abrupt changes in loudness or softness, after which the dynamic (loudness) level stays constant for a long segment, if not for a whole movement.

The old church modes were replaced by the eight-tone major and minor scales, used to this day. Either type of scale is characterized by having a *tonic*, or basic note. The tonic of the major scale shown in Fig. **4.32** is C (the note at the bottom and top of the scale); whenever sounded in the context of this scale, C conveys a sense of rest or finality. This scale, as well as any music based on it, is said to be in

4.32 Major scale, key of C

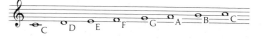

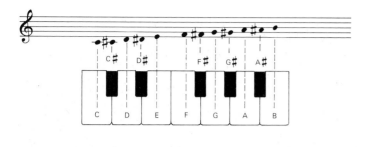

4.33 Twelve tones

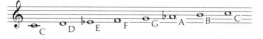

4.35 Minor scale, key of C

the *key* of C. Any of the 12 available tones (both white and black keys on a keyboard instrument; Fig. **4.33**) can serve as a tonic. For example, a major scale with G as its tonic (or key note) is shown in Figure **4.34**. In a major scale, all the intervals are whole steps, except those between the third and fourth notes, and between the seventh and eighth notes, which are half steps. In a minor scale (Fig. **4.35**) the arrangement of intervals is different, as the half steps typically (but not always) occur between the second and third notes and between the fifth and sixth notes. Of the two types of scale the major is the more popular—perhaps because music written in that scale tends to sound more optimistic and reassuring; music in a minor scale tends to sound more serious, somber, or even ominous.

The types of scale used in music are fundamental to the nature of that music, regardless of whether it employs monophony, polyphony, or homophony. During the Baroque period the polyphonic style inherited from the Renaissance was refined into perhaps its greatest form of expression in the fugue (see below). In this period we also find increased use of homophony, the style of musical texture that was to become conventional in Classical music.

Opera

Of all the arts, opera illustrates best the Baroque tendency to combine different media. Essentially a musical play on a grand scale, opera combines music, prose, poetry, acting, dance, scenery, and costumes (Fig. **4.36**). It requires the services not only of a composer, but also of a *librettist* to write the text, as well as an army of singers, dancers, and instrumentalists.

Opera began in the early seventeenth century with a small group of musicians and intellectuals in Florence

who were interested in reviving what was believed to be the music drama of the Greeks. Taking exception to traditional Renaissance polyphony, they proposed a style of music that would better accommodate spoken dialogue. It would consist of *arias*, songs for solo voice, and *recitatives*, declamatory singing used to provide the dialogue and advance the action of the story between arias. The new music was basically homophonic with single melodic lines to reflect the pitch and rhythms of real speech.

Claudio Monteverdi (1567–1643) was the first composer to breathe life into the new form, when he composed *Orfeo* (1607) for the ducal court of Mantua. Initially limited to performances in courts, opera soon became available to anyone with the price of admission when the first public opera house opened in Venice in 1637. The

4.36 Scene from Lully's opera *Phaëton*, First performed at Versailles in 1683

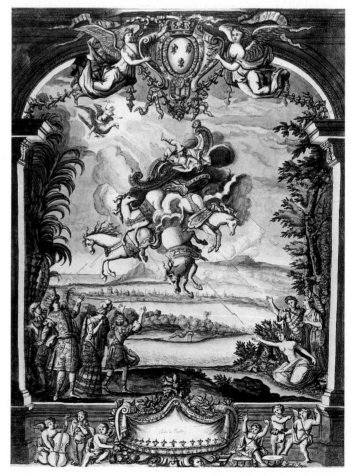

4.34 Major scale, key of G

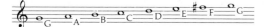

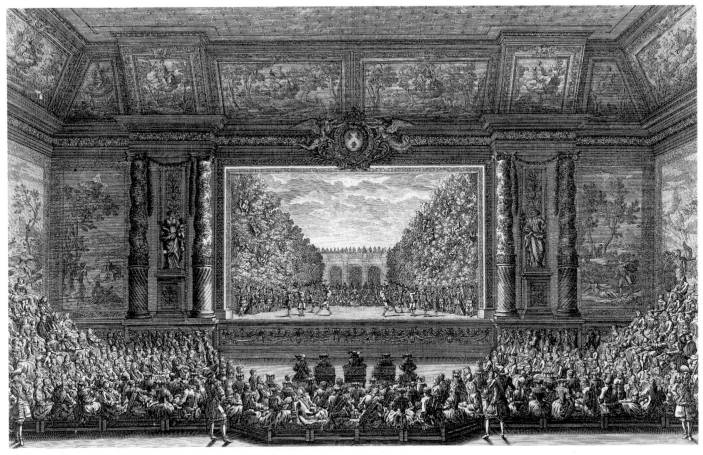

4.37 Scene from Lully's opera *Les Fêtes de l'amour et de Bacchus*
Bibliothèque Nationale, Paris

idea of public opera caught on in Italy, where several cities opened their own houses. In other European cities public opera waited until the eighteenth century; but in the meantime court opera (mostly Italian in style) spread rapidly.

In France, Jean-Baptiste Lully (1623–1687), an Italian who came to Paris at a young age, presented his operas at Versailles (Figs. 4.36, 4.37). In the spirit of the Louis XIV court, with its stress on classicism and stately pomp, Lully's compositions, like Poussin's paintings and the plays of Racine, emphasize symmetry and clarity while avoiding the tendency to over-embellish. Before composing operas, Lully had collaborated with the dramatist Molière on a number of comedy-ballets. No doubt his work with Molière, along with his observations of the declamative styles used in the French theater, helped him to write recitatives in that tongue, the rhythmic patterns of which are quite different from Italian. He also invented the French *overture*, a short, two-part composition used to introduce a vocal or instrumental work. The first part is homophonic, slow and majestic; the second, which is faster and more polyphonic, eventually returns to the slower tempo of the beginning.

In England, Henry Purcell (1659–1695) used the French overture to introduce his *Dido and Aeneas* (1689), an hour-long opera based on the *Aeneid* (see page 75). Although the plot is set in such exotic places as Troy and Carthage and involves love, witches, and suicide, it does not overwhelm the beauty of Purcell's music. He and his librettist Nahum Tate were sensitive to the inflections of English speech, for which relatively few operas, until this century, have been written. Purcell, who died at the age of 36, was Britain's last native-born composer of international stature before the late nineteenth century.

Besides opera, there were two other popular forms of vocal music: the *oratorio* and the *cantata*. Though resembling an opera in some ways, an oratorio differs from it in others: it is rarely performed with actors and costumes, and often has no fixed character part for each voice. Usually the chorus, like that in a Greek drama, is used for narrative purposes. A cantata is a vocal composition for chorus, solo voices, and orchestra. Instead of having acts and scenes, it is divided into *movements*—major parts with their own beginnings and endings. Both forms can use either secular or religious texts. Sacred versions of both forms will be analyzed in Chapter 8.

Instrumental Forms

Like opera, much of Baroque instrumental music is indebted to the innovations of seventeenth-century Italian musicians and composers. They perfected the violin—a descendant of the Renaissance viol—whose flexibility and tonal range liberated composers and performers. From Renaissance madrigals, motets, and ricercars, they developed such forms as the *sonata* and the *concerto grosso*, both of these having several movements.

The career of Arcangelo Corelli (1653–1713), is a good example of exploiting the mutual advantages of being both composer and performer. A virtuoso violinist, he composed *trio sonatas* (two melody instruments over, usually, a keyboard instrument serving as a basso continuo) featuring the violin. His skill as a performer helped to popularize his works. Domenico Scarlatti (1685–1757), who played the harpsichord, wrote more than 550 sonatas for his favorite instrument. Corelli also pioneered the *concerto grosso*. A multi-movement form, a concerto grosso pits a small group of solo instruments against a small orchestra, each returning to play modified versions of the opening theme or melody throughout a movement. In the eighteenth century Antonio Vivaldi (1678–1741) pioneered the *solo concerto*, in which only one instrument is contrasted with a large ensemble. Both the sonata and concerto forms were to be significantly transformed in the Classical era.

The *suite* and *fugue* were primarily German contributions. The suite is a composition of several movements, usually dances having a constant key but different rhythms from dance to dance. This form obviously owes its heritage to the ricercar as well as to the court dances of the Renaissance and Baroque periods. Probably no form of music symbolizes the Baroque era more than the fugue, a polyphonic composition based on a single melody, and a descendant of Ockeghem's imitation (see Chapter 3). Called a "subject," the melody is played in turn by each "voice" (one or more instruments), not unlike the singing of a round. In a fugue, however, the subject can vary from voice to voice and from one repetition to the next by changing keys and adding different melodic and rhythmic ideas as it goes along. The expressive range of fugues is wide. One written in a minor key can be dark and despondent, while one in a major key can be joyous. Some compositions were written entirely as fugues; others as fugues, but mixed with homophonic harmonies. As a developed form of polyphony, the fugue greatly enriched the musical repertoire of Baroque composers.

Handel

Two Germans, born a month apart in towns separated by only 100 miles (160 km) brought Baroque music to a glorious climax. Both George Frideric Handel and Johann Sebastian Bach wrote major choral works (which will be examined in Chapter 8) and some of the most cherished instrumental works in all of Western music. But beyond these general similarities their lives and works differ significantly.

Although not born to a musical family, Handel (1685–1759) came under the spell of music early in life. By the age of 20 he had produced his first opera (*Almira*) and by 25, had conquered Italy, the capital of Baroque music. His reputation earned him the post of *Kapellmeister* (conductor of a choir or orchestra) in the court of the Elector of Hanover in northern Germany. But his stay there was brief, as he was impatient to see London. In that city, and at the court of Queen Anne, who were passionately fond of music, Handel was an instant success. When Queen Anne died in 1714, who should take her place but the Elector of Hanover, Handel's former German patron, who became King George I. According to legend, the composer reinstated himself in the favor of His Majesty by writing the *Water Music* (see below).

Handel spent the remaining 47 years of his life in England where he was the toast of that country's music, and became virtually the most famous composer in Europe. His operas were extremely popular, but in the 1730s the opera company of which he was director ran into financial difficulties, and he turned to writing religious oratorios, a form that had an immense following among the middle classes. Buried in Westminster Abbey, Handel still ranks as one of Britain's favorite composers. He never married. Although he was not particularly devout, he wrote the *Messiah*, perhaps the best-loved of all religious works.

Bach

During his lifetime (1688–1750), Johann Sebastian Bach was much less celebrated than Handel. Born into a dynasty of professional musicians, he raised four more (out of 20 children from two marriages, nine survived him) (Fig. 4.38). While Handel was winning over the Italians, Bach played the organ for a minor German court. While Handel was recruiting Europe's best singers for his London opera company, Bach directed a choir in Leipzig. But Bach was just as busy as his contemporary. A devout Lutheran, he composed and rehearsed the music for four Leipzig churches every Sunday and regularly gave organ recitals, not to mention teaching music and sponsoring

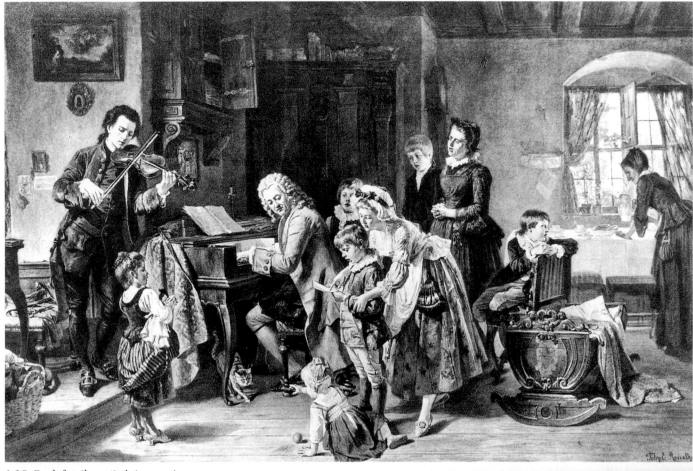

4.38 Bach family, artist's impression
New York Public Library

the music club at St. Thomas' school. With so many responsibilities, it is a wonder that he was able to write so many great and lasting works of music. Unlike the cosmopolitan Handel, Bach rarely traveled. His reputation and circle of acquaintances were confined to Germany, where he was recognized as a superb organist and a master of the fugue.

The music of the two composers was as different as their lives. Handel sought to communicate dramatic ideas; Bach was preoccupied with musical ideas. Handel's music was considered progressive; Bach's, especially its persistent use of polyphony, was considered old-fashioned. Even his third son, Carl Philipp Emanuel Bach (1714–1788), also a composer, criticized him for this. Bach's natural medium was the organ; he probably thought of that instrument even when he wrote for the voice. Handel's music is nearly always clear and intelligible; Bach's is more complex and often difficult to follow. Handel wrote for the glory of the world; Bach wrote for the glory of God.

Handel's *Water Music* is a collection of some 20 movements, mainly dances, written in 1715 and 1717. It was performed as a single suite by an orchestra of 50 players on a barge floating up the Thames on a July night in 1717. The occasion was a water party for King George I and his friends, who had the pleasure of listening to the music from accompanying barges. Today's orchestras perform a shorter version with movements that vary from an expansive French overture to a playful hornpipe (sailors' dance) and from an elegant minuet to a plaintive andante in D minor. But the overall mood is triumphant and festive, befitting the pomp of the occasion of the original royal performance. The hymn-like "air" (Fig. **4.39**), played by strings in a stately 4/4 meter, strikes a proper balance between seriousness and showiness and therefore exemplifies the entire suite.

Bach's *Goldberg Variations*, a set of 30 variations on a theme for harpsichord, were written in 1742 for a German count who suffered from insomnia. He commissioned the music to be played on long sleepless nights by his private musician, Johann Goldberg. The theme itself is a *saraband* (a slow, graceful Spanish dance) (Fig. **4.40**). Decorated with occasional trills, the stately melody,

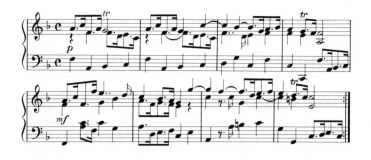

4.39 Handel's *Water Music*

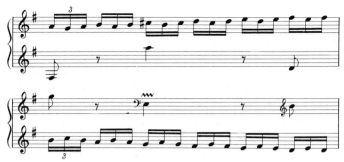

4.41 Bach's *Goldberg Variations, Variation No. 20*

played by the right hand, is firmly supported by a sturdy bass melody, played by the left. The variations which follow demonstrate Bach's enormous powers of invention with their astonishing variety. Syncopated rhythms, subtle changes of texture, bold changes of tempo, and other musical ingenuities follow each other in rich profusion. Yet all the variations comply with the basic harmonic and rhythmic structure established in the original theme. In variation No. 20, the triplets, rapidly played by one hand and then by the other, both in a high register, sound like laughter (Fig. 4.41). The fluttering sixteenth notes of variation No. 28, played simultaneously by both hands, are even more jubilant (Fig. 4.42). By contrast, the relatively slow tempo, wandering melodic line, and dissonant harmonies of variation No. 25 could not be sadder (Fig. 4.43). Wanda Landowska, the noted harpsichordist, called this variation "the Crown of Thorns."

While Bach's musical craftsmanship and ability to invent were unequaled, his work is admired today for its expressive depth. Yet in his day, his style became unfashionable, as polyphony lost out to homophony and people began to prefer lighter, less complicated music. After he died public performances of his music virtually ceased, finally to be resurrected in 1829 by Felix Mendelssohn, who discovered and had performed his *St. Matthew Passion*. Since then, Bach has been acknowledged as one of the greatest geniuses in the history of music.

In Chapter 8 the religious works of Handel and Bach

4.42 Bach's *Goldberg Variations, Variation No. 28*

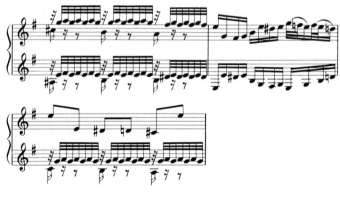

4.40 Bach's *Goldberg Variations, Saraband*

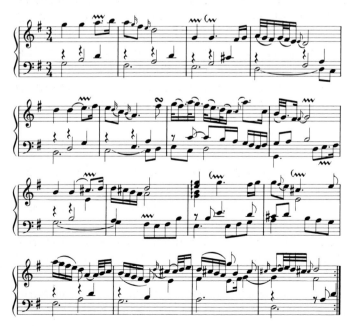

4.43 Bach's *Goldberg Variations, Variation No. 25*

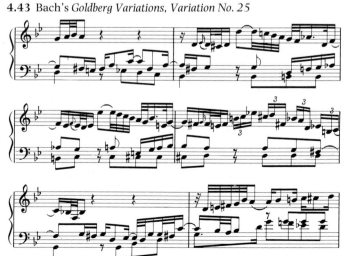

will be examined. Here we have looked at secular works of theirs that exemplified classical principles, but in different ways: the *Water Music*, because of its stately rhythms, measured tempo, and broad homophonic harmonies, which foreshadowed the Classical style; the *Goldberg Variations*, because of their symmetry, subtle proportions, and lapidary craftsmanship, as well as their composer's ability to discover infinite creative possibilities within narrow, self-imposed rules.

The Rococo spirit

In the second half of the eighteenth century, music experienced a shift from seriousness to lightness similar to the shift in art from the Baroque style to Rococo. Rising in popularity to rival the traditional Baroque opera was *opera buffa* (comic opera), which featured simpler music, often sung in local dialects, and comic situations about every-day life, rather than serious allegories involving gods and emperors. The Rococo spirit was also reflected in the instrumental music of French composers, particularly that of François Couperin (1668–1733). Characterized by subtle tones and delicate expression, Couperin's compositions for keyboard instruments were perfectly suited to the elegant, sophisticated milieu of the salons. In Germany a musical idiom known as *empfindsamer Stil* ("sensitive style"), also featuring subtlety of tone and mood, was developed by, among others, Carl Philipp Emanuel Bach, who was much better known in mid-century than his father. This music and the music that evolved from it, including the early work of Haydn (see below), overlapped the late years of Handel and Bach. Unlike Rococo art, the music of this period, was not considered decadent, or a corruption of the Baroque style. Rather, it was seen as a progressive development in its own right and, later, as a bridge between Baroque and Classical music.

Classical Music

The same intellectual and social currents that had affected art in the second half of the eighteenth century also affected the music world. Spreading through Europe were the revolutionary ideas of Voltaire's and other *philosophes*. Middle-class listeners were asserting their right to the spiritual rewards of music by organizing public concerts and thereby making their own tastes known. An increase in amateur music making created a demand for music of clarity as well as elegance. Moreover, composers were responding to the spirit of classicism which was infecting all the arts.

Vienna now became the musical center of Europe. The capital of the Holy Roman Empire, it was much more conservative than Paris, the home of the *philosophes*, and not so permeated with classical antiquity as Rome. However, its loosely-governed empire (which comprised, among other territories, Austria, Hungary, and parts of present-day Germany) was a hive of musical activity. Every court that could afford to do so had its own composer and private orchestra. The Bachs were only one of several dynasties of professional musicians, while amateur musicians flourished among the aristocracy as princes, dukes, and counts prided themselves on being able to play an instrument or sing. Even Empress Maria Theresa sang, and her son, Emperor Joseph II, played the violoncello, viola, and clavier.

The main developments in the Classical period came in instrumental music. These affected not only the major instrumental forms of the period—the symphony, concerto, and chamber music—but also opera, the most popular vocal form. By the late eighteenth century orchestras had grown to include as many as 50 members, acquiring very much the shape that they have today. The basso continuo went out of style as instruments were no longer strictly designated bass-accompaniment or melody. The piano (Fig. 4.44), originally called the *pianoforte* ("soft-loud") began to supplant the harpsichord. Unlike earlier keyboard instruments, the piano allows a performer to vary dynamics by varying the pressure of the fingers. This permits crescendos (gradual increases in loudness) and decrescendos (gradual decreases)—a change from the terraced dynamics of the Baroque era.

Characteristics of Classical Music

Music of this period is called Classical because it embodies the ideals of classicism—order, restraint, and balance. And it does so more than the music of any other period of Western music. In the next chapter Classical music will be contrasted with Romantic music; here we shall compare it to Baroque music.

In some ways Classical music is less complicated than Baroque. Classical harmonies, which are homophonic rather than polyphonic, are usually simple and easy to

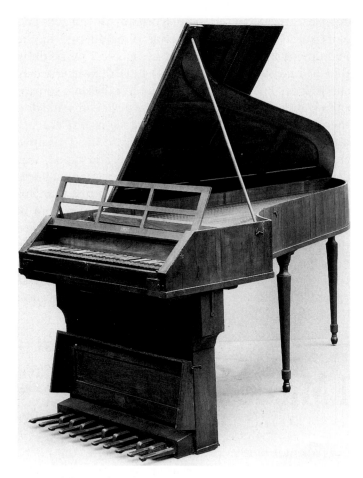

4.44 Pedal piano by Johann Andreas Stein, 1778
Metropolitan Museum, New York, Crosby Brown Collection

grasp; some can even be strummed on a guitar. Classical melodies are also usually simple, sometimes disarmingly so; many can be hummed by anyone who is not tone-deaf. Classical music in general abstains from trills, tremolos, and other musical flourishes which typify the Baroque style. Indeed, Classical music satisfies Winckelmann's precept of "noble simplicity" as much as Neoclassical art does. A Classical composition, like a David painting in which the images are lucid and unmistakable, contains clear and simply stated themes.

Still, in other ways Classical music is more complicated than Baroque music. It is much freer than Baroque music to vary such things as dynamics, tempo, rhythm, and key in a single movement or even in a single theme. The variety of Bach's *Goldberg Variations*, as we noted, exists *between* the pieces, rather than within each piece. Once it is set in motion, a Baroque piece or a Baroque movement, like a clock, continues the same pattern to the end. In such music, modulations (shifting from one key to another) as well as crescendos and decrescendos would be out of the question. In Classical music, however, gradual changes or abrupt changes, such as a sudden pause, can occur in the middle of a bar. Contrasts like these contribute to contrasts in expression, as moods can change from turbulence to serenity or from gaiety to tragedy. Such contrasts are reminiscent of the bold oppositions between the Horatii men and Horatii women in David's painting (Fig. 4.26), or the barely restrained passion of Racine's *Phaedra*. Yet such oppositions, if resolved, help, rather than harm, clarity and unity. The use of contrasts to create tensions and the resolution of these tensions is fundamental to Classical music.

The Classical Symphony

The symphony, perhaps the greatest contribution of the Classical period, is to this day the main framework—apart from opera—within which serious composers essay major musical ideas. A composition of grand proportions, the symphony is to a composer what a novel is to a writer or a mural cycle to a painter. The Classical symphony consists of four movements, each having a traditional form of its own as well as a particular role in the overall scheme of the composition. Typically they are:

First movement
Sonata Form (to be discussed in detail below): a relatively fast and dramatic movement which sometimes includes a special introduction and ending.

Second movement
Theme and Variations. Slow and lyrical and in a different key, this movement repeats a melody several times in different ways .

Third movement
Minuet and Trio. This movement consists of a stylized minuet, including a softer middle section, called a trio because it was originally written in three-part harmony.

Fourth movement
Sonata Form or Rondo Form. A rondo consists of a main theme that alternates with one or two other themes. If the main theme is A and the other two are B and C, a rondo pattern could be A B A C A or A B A C A B A, and so forth.

The Sonata Form

Besides forming part of symphonies, the sonata form is also used in movements of Classical concertos and chamber music. More than the other forms, it embodies the classical principle of creating tensions and then resolving them. A typical sonata movement consists of three main sections: *exposition, development,* and *recapitulation.* The first movement of the *Symphony No. 94 in G Major* ("Surprise Symphony") by Franz Joseph Haydn (1732–1809) will serve as our illustration.

Haydn's symphony opens with a slow introduction before launching into the main tempo (marked *vivace*

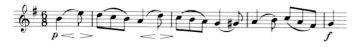

4.45 Haydn's *Symphony No. 94 in G Major*, first movement, first theme

assai—very lively, or fast) and the exposition section itself. The purpose of the exposition is to introduce two themes. The orchestra, led by violins, takes less than 30 seconds to play the first theme, a sprightly melody in the home key of G major (Fig. **4.45**). Coming to a complete stop, the orchestra then begins to play it a second time, but a little differently, as it mixes the melody with a *bridge* passage—a transition section in which the orchestra modulates to the key of D major, the key of the second theme (Fig. **4.46**). Though equally fast, the second theme is softer and more lyrical than the first (and consequently can be easily missed by the novice listener). Because of the differences, in both key and mood, between the two themes, a musical opposition or tension is established. The exposition section is repeated, lasting approximately one more minute.

The purpose of the development section is to increase the musical tension. Opening with a variation of the first theme (Fig. **4.47**), it manipulates fragments of the two themes through a series of changes in key, rhythm, and dynamics. At one moment a fragment may be playful, at another aggressive, while being subjected to a variety of permutations. This section lasts approximately one minute.

In the recapitulation section, which lasts about two minutes, we see a return of the original two themes, but this time both are in the original key. Thus the conflict has been resolved and the tension is reduced. The movement ends with a triumphant *coda* ("tail" in Italian) or ending.

4.46 Haydn's *Symphony No. 94 in G Major*, first movement, second theme

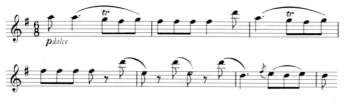

4.47 Haydn's *Symphony No. 94 in G Major*, first movement, variation of first theme

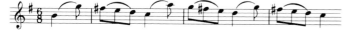

Haydn

The Symphony No. 94, one of 12 "London" symphonies by Haydn, was enthusiastically received at its first performance in 1792. Especially exciting to the London audience was the "surprise," an unexpectedly loud chord at the end of a simple, folk-like melody appearing early in the second movement.

The use of novelty or humor was typical of this composer. Born of relatively humble origins Haydn learned folk music from his wheelwright father before becoming a professional choirboy, a job that lasted until his voice changed. After many trying years as a music teacher and performer he obtained a position with the Esterházys, the richest family of the Hungarian aristocracy. In addition to composing on demand, Haydn was responsible for all music functions—conducting, directing singers, even tending the music library—in the splendid, but isolated, Esterházy palace (Fig. **4.48**). Still, with good pay and the loving support of his employers, Haydn was able to develop steadily, though slowly, as a composer. Even the isolation was an advantage because, as Haydn explained, it forced him to be original. Other parts of Europe came to appreciate his originality as Haydn's compositions were copied and circulated by the Esterházys.

When the head of the family, Prince Nicholas I, died in 1790, Haydn felt free to accept the offer of a London impresario to compose and conduct symphonies in England. There he wrote some of his best works, the "London" symphonies, and was such a success that he was given an honorary doctorate by Oxford University. Now a celebrity, Haydn returned to the continent, remaining in contact with the Esterházys while living in Vienna. He continued to write music, including two important Masses, and to receive honors until his death at the age of 77.

A prolific composer, Haydn is credited with 104 symphonies, 68 string quartets, numerous piano sonatas and trios and several operas and Masses. But compared to most artists he was a late starter, not achieving mastery of his art until his thirties and peaking in his sixties! Haydn's remarkable success was due not only to his genius but also to persistence, sweat, and good health. Like the man, his music was robust and down-to-earth.' He united the charm of folk-like melodies with superb craftsmanship when composing string quartets for Prince Nicholas. In his mature work he infused this combination with a sense of urgency and greater depth. He acknowledged his debts to others, including Carl Philipp Emanuel Bach and Mozart (see below), but the music world of the late eighteenth century owed a great deal to Haydn, who

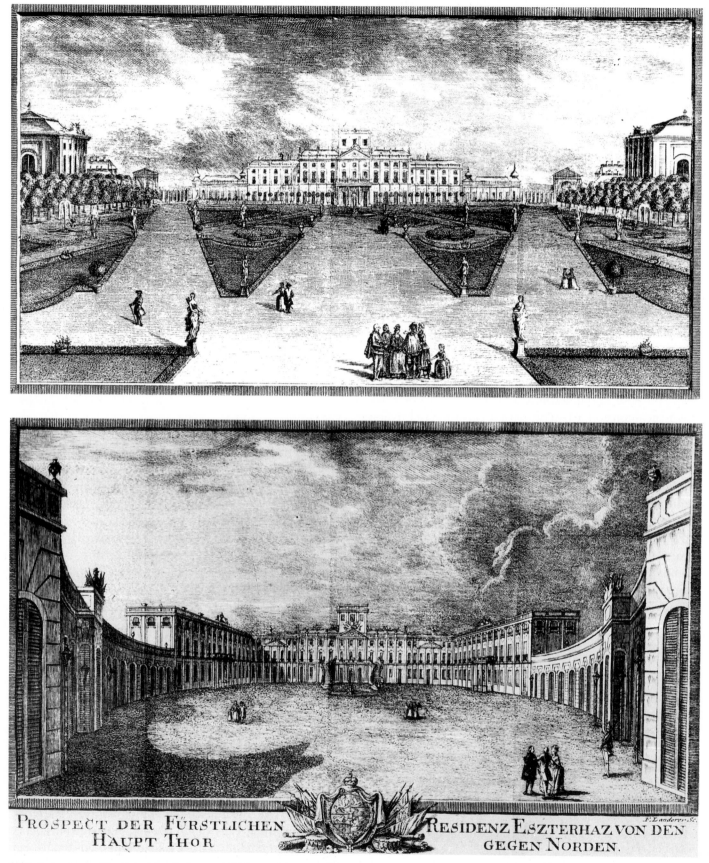

PROSPECT DER FÜRSTLICHEN
HAUPT THOR

RESIDENZ ESZTERHAZ VON DEN
GEGEN NORDEN.

F. Landerer. Sc.

4.48 Two views of the Esterházy Palace, c. 1784
Austrian National Library

blazed trails in the Classical idiom and the development of the symphony.

Mozart

Although the music of Wolfgang Amadeus Mozart (1756–1791) bears some similarity to that of Haydn, his life could hardly have been more different. At the age of six Mozart possessed perfect pitch and could sight-read scores and play several instruments. Eager to further his son's talent—and perhaps also to exploit it—Leopold Mozart booked Wolfgang for performances at noble and royal palaces all over Europe. Besides playing and improvising on the harpsichord, Mozart would also amuse his hosts by naming the correct note of anything they would strike, such as a bell or glass. Despite the pressures of traveling and performing, Mozart found time to compose. By the age of 12, he had written a symphony, an oratorio, and an opera, as well as numerous smaller works. At age 14 in Milan he received his first public success as a composer of an opera, *Mitridate* (with a libretto taken from Racine).

When his career as a prodigy came to an end, Mozart tried working for the Prince-Archbishop of Salzburg, his father's employer. But the former child wonder could not tolerate being treated like a servant (as musicians generally were in those days). When the arrangement ended in failure, Mozart moved to Vienna (Fig. **4.49**), where he married a young soprano named Constanze Weber. Forsaking the security of working for a court, he tried to establish a career as a freelance musician in Vienna. For a while he tasted celebrity again. Two operas—*The Abduction from the Seraglio* (1782) and *The Marriage of Figaro* (1786)—were successes. He enjoyed the friendship and respect of Haydn (24 years his senior), who told Leopold, "Your son is the greatest composer that I know either in person or by name." But after his next opera, *Don Giovanni* (1787), received a lukewarm reception in Vienna, Mozart began to experience a series of seemingly irreversible setbacks. Without the protection of a patron, he had to depend on the fickle tastes of the Viennese concert-going public. His popularity as a performer and composer plunged. Had the Mozarts been better at managing

4.49 St Peter's church and square, Vienna
Austrian National Library

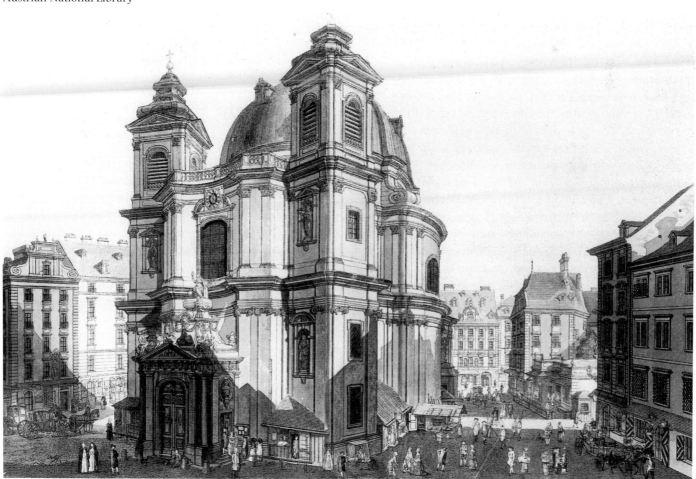

money, or Constanze not continually ill or pregnant, the couple might have weathered the storm. Still, Mozart continued to write. Some of his best work—including the opera *Così Fan Tutte* and symphonies 39, 40, and 41—was written during these trying times. In 1791, in deteriorating health, he wrote two operas and part of a Requiem Mass. He died before his 36th birthday and was buried in a paupers' vault at St. Mark's cemetery in Vienna in 1791.

Don Giovanni is often cited as Mozart's greatest achievement. Considered too heavy by the Viennese public, it was, however, written in the *opera buffa* idiom and contains a great deal of humor. The story is based on the tale of *Don Juan*, a Spanish count, whose legendary sexual exploits provided the grist for a number of plays and comedies, including one by Molière. There are really two plots. One is a situation comedy of Giovanni's many attempts at seduction enlivened by the capers of his servant, Leporello. In his famous "catalogue aria" Leporello presents Donna Elvira (one of Giovanni's earlier conquests) with his master's scorecard of seductions—"640 in Italy, 231 in Germany, 100 in France, 91 in Turkey—but in Spain already 1003!" The other plot involves Giovanni's consistent refusal to repent of his sins, which leads to his destruction. Early in the opera he kills a nobleman, the father of one of his conquests, in a duel. In the end, the dead nobleman, in the form of a statue, orders the Don to beg for forgiveness. He refuses and is dragged down into the flames of Hell. Of course, both plots are absurd. The first has been exaggerated to comic proportions; the second is really a satire on supernatural retribution. But the absurdity is a foil to the seriousness of Mozart's portrait of the human condition—in this case, passion, betrayal, and revenge—through the medium of opera.

In most previous operas, character and plot development depended mostly on recitatives, while the arias were little more than a static series of beautiful songs. In Mozart's later operas, including *Don Giovanni*, character development is in the music itself. Aristocratic women sing in ornate styles, peasant women sing in simpler styles, while the clever Don sings in the style of the woman he is trying to seduce. Changing character is revealed through subtle combinations of music and words. The duet between Giovanni and Zerlina, a pretty peasant girl, is marked *legato* (smooth) as he tries to tempt her with a promise of marriage. She replies, "I'd like to, but yet I would not." Later, she sings the same line but in unison with him. Lastly, when Zerlina surrenders, both sing together, "Let us go, let us go, my beloved," to joyful, faster music. The conflicting emotions of Elvira, who was deserted by the Don and yet remains devoted to him, are echoed in a sighing orchestral passage which varies from

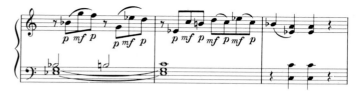

4.50 Theme from Mozart's *Don Giovanni*, expressing Elvira's sighs

soft (*p*) to moderately loud (*mf*) between eighth notes (Fig. **4.50**).

Mozart's knowledge of human character and his ability to describe it musically may have been informed by his own tragic life. His instrumental works, no less than his operas, also speak to the human heart, showing the same richness and variety of mood. Some nineteenth-century musicians and critics tried to envisage Mozart as a Romantic, or perhaps a "pre-Romantic," composer. But this view overlooks the fact that in his music he always maintained a sense of proportion and balance. For example, in the overture to *Don Giovanni*, a sinister foretaste of the Don's impending doom is set against brisk tunes evoking the comic elements of the opera; in his concertos, the orchestra and solo instrument are in perfect balance, responding to and echoing each other. Musical ideas are developed fully, but never belabored. In other words, Mozart's music is persistently Classical. As the music scholar Edward Dent explains:

> *Whether Mozart is inwardly romantic or not every listener will decide for himself; it is a matter of personal temperament rather than of hard fact; but it is difficult to find in Mozart any traces of a consciously romantic technique. He knows all depths of human emotion, but he is always Italian and strictly realistic; his music is often complex in the extreme but invariably clear.*[4]

Because of correspondences of time, culture, style, and musical philosophy, the works of Mozart and Haydn, the giants of the Classical period, are similar in many respects. But there are differences. Although perhaps subtle to inexperienced ears, these differences are significant and reflective not only of the personality differences between the two men but also of the traditional dualism of classicism going back to the fifth century BC. Haydn's music leans toward optimism and predictability; Mozart's tends more toward fragile beauty and melancholy. Haydn's might be compared to the sturdy proportions of the Doric order; Mozart's, to the more graceful Ionic. Yet both are associated with the rationality symbolized by Apollo, rather than with the qualities of Prometheus or Dionysus, gods of Romantic music. Prometheus, symbol of eternal struggle, whose presence is already latent in the paintings of David, thrives in the music of Beethoven. Dionysus, god of wine and the release of emotions, is the sovereign lord of the Romantic movement.

Conclusion

Ever since the flowering of Greek philosophy, drama, and art in the fifth century BC, a system of ideals that we call classicism has been a major legacy of Western history—interrupted only by the period of the Dark Ages (see page 268). In the last three chapters we have seen how this legacy was nurtured by different people in different ways: from Virgil modeling his epic poem on the epic poems of Homer, to Michelangelo and Raphael emulating the qualities of Greek art in their own works, and to Haydn and Mozart bringing classical ideals of proportion, clarity and balance into Western music. Leaders in other fields—philosophy, education, and politics—also nurtured and were nurtured by the legacy.

Does the end of this series of chapters mean that the legacy itself came to an end? Well, partly, yes. Romanticism, as we shall see in the next chapter, captured the imaginations of writers, artists, and composers to such an extent that it overwhelmed Neoclassicism as a significant force in the arts. More importantly, there have been no broad movements since Neoclassicism that could be attributed to anything that resembles the classical legacy. As either a generator of new ideas or an inspiration for artistic creativity, classicism seems to have indeed come to an end. Few philosophers any longer are personally committed to the theories of Plato or Neoplatonism, or the perfectability of humanity. Writers rarely take to heart the principles outlined in Aristotle's *Poetics*. Artists have long since abandoned the ideal nude as a touchstone of excellence. And few musicians are committed to the sonata form. The reign of Apollo and the Muses seems to be over.

But as a heritage—rich in content and emotional resonance—classicism survives in Greek tragedies, which continue to be frequently performed; in the music of Mozart, which is more loved and revered than ever; in the works of Leonardo and Michelangelo, which continue to be among the most cherished in the visual arts; and in the works of hundreds of other authors, composers, and artists who, in the past 25 centuries, have been guided by its principles. In addition, it survives in every major city in Europe and America, where public buildings are graced with columns, arches, and domes; and even in the political institutions of the great democracies, whose governments have been influenced by, or—in the case of the United States—founded on, the democratic principles outlined by the philosophers of the Enlightenment. And finally, the heritage survives in those contemporary forms of art, music, and architecture (Chapters 10 and 11) that reflect in abstract ways the principles of order and restraint.

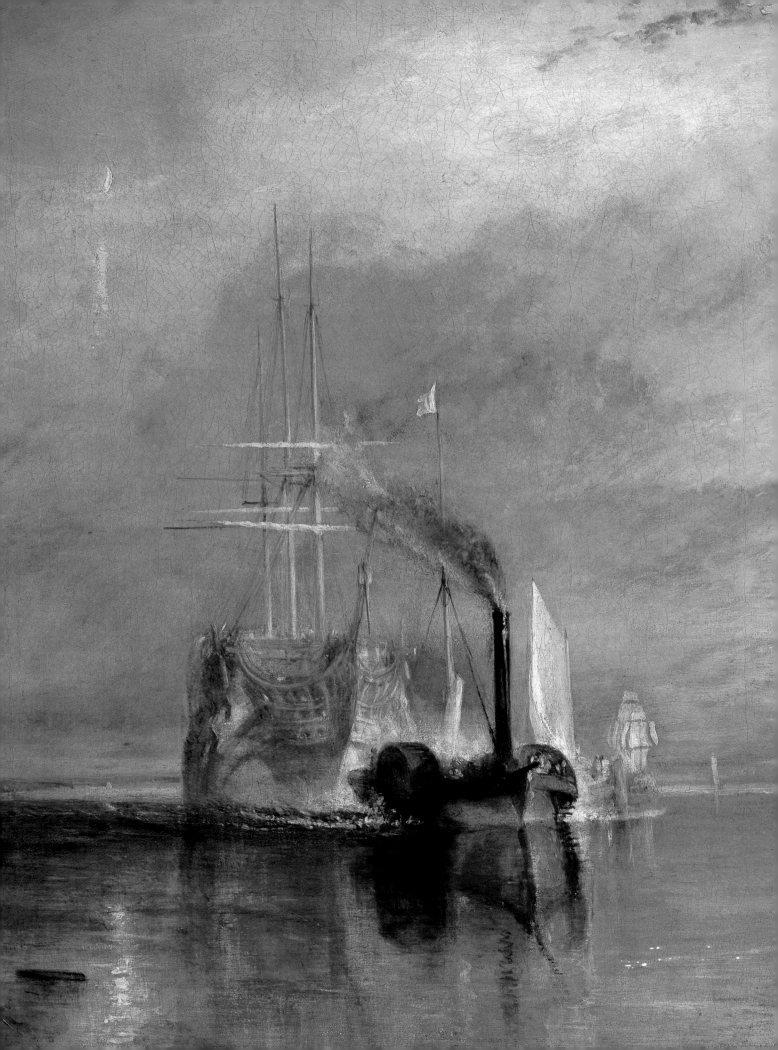

CHAPTER FIVE

The Celebration of Feeling

I am made unlike anyone I have ever met; I will even venture to say that I am like no one in the whole world. I may be no better, but at least I am different.

ROUSSEAU, *CONFESSIONS*

Romanticism

The term *Romanticism* is ordinarily used for a movement in literature and art of the late eighteenth and the first half of the nineteenth centuries, and for a development in music that began somewhat later and continued much longer—in fact into the early twentieth century (Fig. 5.3). But certain of the characteristics of Romanticism, such as individualism, subjectivism, and love of nature, reflect attitudes that may be seen in certain persons at various stages in history. Thus, for example, Euripides, the Greek tragedian, was an alienated individualist who wrote tragedies exploring the inner conflicts of the individual (see Chapter 2), and Michelangelo, another alienated individualist, created sculptures expressing frustration and anxiety. Even St. Francis (see Chapter 6) had a religious relationship with nature which, in some respects, foreshadows the mystical experience of nature that characterized many Romantics (although he, unlike the pantheistic Romantics, distinguished between nature and its Creator). Romanticism, then, is a slippery term because it includes aspects of human thought and behavior that surface periodically in individuals and cultures. For this reason, some scholars prefer to think of Romanticism not as a single movement but as a group of allied characteristics.

It should also be noted that Romanticism was not of equal strength in all the countries that experienced a Romantic movement. In general, whereas French culture was the most strongly influenced by classicism, German culture was the most strongly influenced by Romanticism. The characteristics of the movement also varied from country to country. The interest in folklore, for example, was very slight in France, whereas in Germany it was a prime characteristic of the Romantic movement. But despite the recurrence of Romantic personality types and the variable uses of the term, critics are generally agreed that there is a sufficient clustering of the attributes of Romanticism in the art, literature, and music of the late eighteenth and nineteenth centuries to speak of a movement.

What is distinctive about the Romantics can perhaps be understood most clearly by contrasting their beliefs with those of the Neoclassicists. Classical purists believed that truth, for both the individual and society, is embedded in and transmitted by a tradition derived from the philosophy, art, and literature of the Greeks and Romans. Thus the Neoclassicists did not seek to surpass the achievements of the past but to recover and imitate them by reason and skill. The fundamental assumptions here are

that human beings are basically the same in all ages, and that since the ideal has already been achieved by the Greeks and the Romans in all areas of human achievement, human beings in every age can do no better than to recover and imitate that ideal.

The Romantics, however, rejected both of these assumptions. The intensity of their emphasis on the uniqueness of the individual is epitomized by the assertion of Rousseau in the opening lines of his *Confessions*: "I am made unlike any one I have ever met; I will even venture to say that I am like no one in the whole world. I may be no better, but at least I am different."[1] The Romantics thus rejected the idea that all human beings are made of the same stuff. They regarded themselves as geniuses whose perception of the real and the true came not from the Greeks or Romans but from within themselves. The ideal, therefore, was not to be grasped by objective rational analysis of classical models supposedly embodying the ideal, but from subjective emotional (even mystical) response to present experience. To be sure, the Romantics were often intensely interested in the past, but they generally turned to the medieval period and its styles, especially the Gothic. In Germany they were also deeply concerned with the recovery of national folklore and traditions. Although imitation of the past can be found in Romanticism—for example in the fad of reproducing Gothic architecture—the historicism of the Romantics, unlike that of the classicists, was not an attempt to imitate meticulously the models of the past but to find inspiration and affirmation of their own ideals.

This contrast between classicism and Romanticism, however, should not be exaggerated. The same individual could be both a classicist and a Romantic. Goethe, for example, was profoundly involved with the early (1770s) Romantic *Sturm und Drang* ("storm and stress") movement in Germany. But he turned toward classicism about the time of his sojourn in Italy in the 1780s and sought to join the two traditions in his drama *Faust*, symbolized by the marriage of Faust and Helen of Troy. Beethoven, in his music, also combined Romanticism and classicism. But the contrasts between the two traditions are striking enough to justify the distinctions drawn in the discussion above. The bottom line, of course, is that one must not insist on defining Romanticism too precisely. Having said this, however, we shall now attempt to define Romanticism more precisely than we have above! The reader must, however, maintain a degree of skepticism toward this attempt "to nail down" the characteristics of an extremely complex period in cultural history.

In addition to the *individualism* and *subjectivism* which, as we have noted, were prime indices to Romanticism, one must also include a *sense of alienation*, which fits into the same cluster of characteristics. An extremely individualistic and subjective personality is likely to feel misunderstood and hence alienated. A kind of *melancholy*—called by the French *mal du siècle* ("sickness of the age"), by the Germans *Weltschmerz* ("world-pain")—is another phenomenon of the Romantic era, and is also connected with this cluster.

Love of nature is also closely related to these ideas. For the Romantics—Rousseau is a specific case in point—often, though not always (see the discussion of Nature in *Romantic Art* below), found solace for their loneliness and feeling of alienation in the bosom of nature. Indeed, this sense of comfort and communication could be so profound as to produce a nature mysticism, a belief that one had encountered the Infinite, a kind of "World Soul" in the experience of nature.

Romantics also manifested an *exoticism* through their interest in the long ago and far away. Rousseau thus glorified the "noble savage"; the writer Chateaubriand and the artist Girodet did the same for the American Indian, while Delacroix was fascinated by the ancient Assyrians and idealized the Arabs of Morocco. This interest often reflects the Romantics' disillusionment with civilization in their belief that primitive peoples, being closer to nature, are also more truly human.

Nationalism is linked with exoticism in that nostalgia for the remote past sometimes expressed itself in an intense interest in the history and folklore of the peoples who constituted, as in the case of Germany, an emerging nation state (though German national unity was not to be achieved until 1870). Romantic composers of symphonies and operas enthusiastically used folk music and dances to express their nationalistic sentiments. Some Romantics, such as Lord Byron, even fought on behalf of peoples seeking independence (in Byron's case, for the Greeks).

Romanticism contributed not only to nationalism but also to the revolutions that were endemic during the Romantic era. The American Revolution (1776), the French Revolution (1789), the revolutions of 1830 and 1848—all took place within the age of Romanticism. The explosive and inflammatory first sentence of Rousseau's *Social Contract* (1762) is a manifesto of revolution: "Man is born free, and is everywhere in chains." In this powerful document, Rousseau argued that sovereignty rests in the people and called for a representative government serving the people rather than itself. Authentic government exists, he contended, because the people enter into a contract in which they surrender a measure of their natural freedom—never their sovereignty—to the governors, who in turn maintain order and operate the machinery of government. Thus government should be based on a mutual contract between the governed and the state, the state being held accountable to the people for its actions. Indeed, Rousseau called for the overthrow of governments that violate the natural rights of the people through arbitrary rule. It is not surprising that *The Social Contract* became a powerful impetus to the French Revolution.

Ironically, however, the French Revolution, like most of those that followed it in the early nineteenth century, ended in a return to conservative forms of government. Having begun with a justifiable attack on monarchical and aristocratic privileges and arbitrary power, it degenerated into a blood bath in which the revolutionaries not only executed royalty and nobility, but eventually massacred a good many of their own sympathizers. Then, in one of the great ironies of history, this revolution which grew out of belief in the sovereignty of the people ended, in 1804, with Napoleon's crowning himself Emperor of the French. Napoleon's coup was made possible by the fact that he was able to bring order out of the chaos into which the Revolution had descended. The price of this order, however—as so often in history—was the creation of a

5.2 Jean-Jacques Rousseau

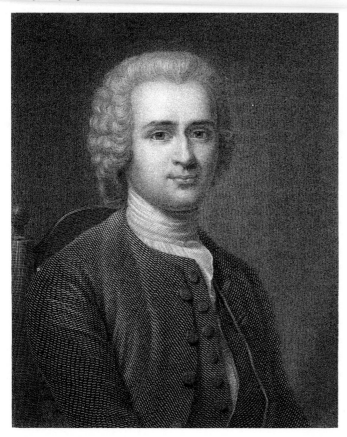

DATES	SOCIAL AND POLITICAL DEVELOPMENTS	LITERATURE AND PHILOSOPHY	VISUAL ARTS	ARCHITECTURE	MUSIC
1700			Watteau (5.7)		
1750		Kant Diderot Rousseau (5.4) Herder Storm and Stress movement			Haydn (4.45)
1775	American Revolution French Revolution	Goethe (5.5) Schiller Hegel Schelling Wordsworth (5.6)			
1800	Napoleon crowned Emperor	Coleridge Shelley Keats Byron Chateaubriand	Goya (5.4, 5.8, 5.9) Géricault (5.10, 5.11) Friedrich (5.14) Turner (5.16) Constable (5.18)	Nash: Royal Pavilion (5.22)	Beethoven (5.23–28) Schubert Mendelssohn Berlioz (5.29) Chopin
1825			Ingres (4.26) Delacroix (5.12)	Houses of Parliament (5.21)	Schumann (5.33) Liszt Wagner (5.33)
1850	Revolution in Europe		 Rodin (5.19)		Brahms Verdi Gounod Saint-Saens Bruckner Tchaikovsky Greig Mahler Elgar

5.3 Romanticism

dictatorial government. The visual image that perhaps best captures the essence of this tragic reversal is Francisco Goya's *The Third of May 1808* (Fig. 5.4), in which a firing squad of Napoleon's soldiers is depicted in the act of executing a pathetic band of Madrid civilians.

The Romantic era also saw significant contributions in philosophy, especially in Germany. The German philosopher Immanuel Kant (1724–1804) was a transition figure from the Enlightenment confidence in reason and science to the Romantic disillusionment that followed. Himself a scientist, Kant nonetheless contended that our perceptions of external objects are affected by preconceived categories held in the mind and imposed upon these objects. What the scientist perceives, therefore, is not the real world but a mental construct of it. This theory puts in question the reliability of reason and empiricism, the chief tools of the scientist. Thus scientific knowledge, though useful, is limited. Moreover, it cannot speak at all on such matters as the knowledge of God and moral duties, which

are known by intuition. (One is reminded of Pascal's dictum: "The heart has its reasons of which reason knows nothing." See page 160.) The evidence of this reality is the fact that human beings instinctively seek a law of morality that transcends what they can know with their senses. Kant called this absolute moral law the categorical imperative.

Friedrich W. J. Schelling (1775–1854) believed, like Kant, in a universal principle, but his *Weltseele* ("World Soul") included nature as well as human beings. The individual and nature are one in the sense that they share and manifest in common the World Soul. This universal presence is experienced especially through the phenomena of nature. This pantheistic concept is typical of the Romantic view of nature; indeed, Schelling's philosophy influenced such Romantic poets as Coleridge and Shelley.

Georg Wilhelm Friedrich Hegel (1770–1831), like St. Augustine, believed that history is the theater in which the divine purpose is unfolded. For Hegel, however, this

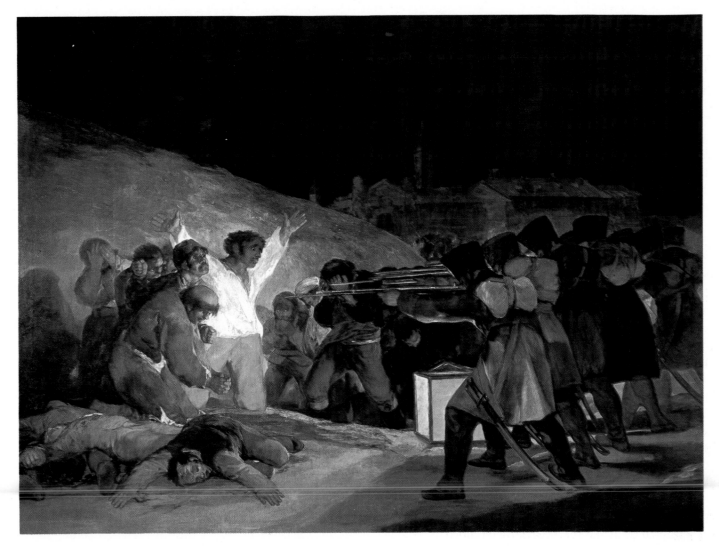

5.4 FRANCISCO GOYA
The Third of May, 1808, 1814,
Oil on canvas, approx. 8 ft 8 ins × 11 ft 4 ins (2.6 × 3.45 m)
Prado, Madrid

purpose is revealed in the dialectic of ideas in history. The prevailing idea at any point in history he called the *thesis*. The opposing idea called forth by the imperfections in the thesis is the *antithesis*. The amalgamation of the two is the *synthesis*, which, in turn, becomes another thesis. Thus social progress is the product of struggle—a view that was later to go hand in glove with the Darwinian concept of the survival of the fittest. But in Hegel's optimistic philosophy, that which survives is not simply the strongest but also the best.

To summarize, then, it may be seen that Romanticism was a movement that influenced all aspects of culture. Although extremely complex and varied, it had one essential ingredient: the elevation of feeling above reason; the belief that truth and beauty are best discerned, not through objective rational analysis, but through passionate involvement in all aspects of human experience. Since both feeling and reason are basic features of human nature which demand recognition, it is not surprising that following the Enlightenment's exaltation of reason, there should be a reaction in favor of feeling as the prime human characteristic.

Literature

Rousseau

Although Jean-Jacques Rousseau (1712–1788) lived during the Enlightenment and died before the Romantic period had fully developed, he has been called the father of Romanticism. Indeed, he embodies most of the characteristics of Romanticism discussed above. Unlike the *philosophes*, Rousseau did not trust reason as a means of solving human problems. Rather, he believed that many things are known through intuition and emotion.

It has been said of Rousseau that "he invented nothing and inflamed everything." His genius lay not in original thought but in the ability to give voice to the deep yearnings of the people of his time—and of other times as well. He was not only the forerunner of the Romantic movement but also the harbinger of the French Revolution and of democratic ideals in general, along with the English philosopher John Locke (1632–1704). But it was his rhetoric, not the man himself, that inspired; for Rousseau was not an easy man to like. Petulant, oversensitive to the point of paranoia, egocentric, he wandered into and out of relationships with people much as he wandered into and out of different communities and countries throughout his life.

Much of what we know of Rousseau's childhood comes from his *Confessions* (1782), a work whose reliability is undermined by its self-serving character. Born in Geneva, Rousseau was the son of a Swiss Protestant watchmaker. The father's relationship with his son was marked from the outset by the fact that his wife died in giving birth to him. According to Rousseau, his father's feelings toward him were a mixture of affection and regret, because he saw in the boy both the features of his wife and the cause of her death. During his first ten years he lived with his father, the two of them often sharing the pleasure of reading to one another the romances enjoyed by his mother. But Jean-Jacques' reading fare also included more substantial French and classical authors whose works he found in his grandfather's library.

When Rousseau's father became involved in a dispute in Geneva, he left the city, taking his son with him. Subsequently, he sent Jean-Jacques to school under Pastor Lambercier of Boissy. After two years, Rousseau dropped out and became an apprentice, first to the city registrar and later to an engraver. Failing in both of these ventures, he ran away in 1728 and eventually ended up, while yet in his teens, in the home of Madame Louise de Warens at Annecy; five years later, she became his mistress. Some 12 years older than Rousseau, she is the woman called "*Maman*" in the *Confessions*. During this period Rousseau converted to Catholicism, the religion of Madame de Warens (he later returned to Protestantism). It was also during this period that he became a student of music, an interest that he pursued as composer and teacher.

Rousseau went to Paris in 1741, thinking to impress others with the superiority of a system of musical notation that he had invented. Although his invention was not successful, he did gain admission to Parisian society, where he was recognized as a philosopher and poet. For the next 15 years he was in and out of Paris. During this period he became the friend of Diderot, the *philosophe* and encyclopedist. Indeed, he contributed several articles to Diderot's prestigous *Encyclopedia* (see page 153). It was during this time also that he became involved with a servant girl, Thérèse Levasseur, who bore him five children. Later to be the author of a highly influential work on the education of children, Rousseau sent all of his own children to a foundling home.

Fame first came to Rousseau when he was granted first prize by the Academy of Dijon for his essay titled, *Discourse on the Sciences and the Arts* (1750). The Academy had invited responses to the question: "Has the progress of sciences and arts contributed to corrupt or purify morrals?" Rousseau's prize-winning response asserted that morals *had* been corrupted; thus he fired his opening salvo at civilization. Five years later he continued the attack with his *Discourse on the Origin of Inequality* (1755), which argued that the "noble savage" is the natural man and is superior to civilized man. Inequality and corruption were introduced into society through the desire for property and power.

Rousseau's *Julie: or The New Eloise* (1761), an epistolary novel, was patterned after the famous medieval love story of Abelard and Héloïse. It tells the story of the frustrated love affair of Julie and her tutor Saint-Preux, who seduces her, as Abelard did Héloïse. Rousseau idealizes this relationship through the purity of their feelings for one another. In passages where Saint-Preux describes the natural beauty of the countryside, Rousseau shows that nature itself responds to such emotions, a truly Romantic concept.

Rousseau's famous political work *The Social Contract* was published in 1762. Here Rousseau sets for himself the problem of whether it is possible to establish a contract between the individual and the government that will not infringe upon the rights of the individual yet will also promote the common good. His solution is offered through the concept of the general will, which is the collective expression of the will of the individuals who make up society. The question raised by the "solution," of course, is how the general will is to be determined—that is, who is to specify what is the will of the people? The multitude of voices claiming to speak for "the people" in our own time illustrates the problem.

Rousseau's highly influential treatise on education, *Émile* (1762), takes the form of a didactic novel. In this work Rousseau further develops his thesis that human beings are naturally good, but, once civilized, have defaced everything that God has given them, including their own natures. Through the experience of Émile, Rousseau seeks to show how it is possible to educate children so that they will develop in accordance with their true natures rather than under compulsion—hence without loss of their freedom as human beings. Rousseau's dual standards for males and females is demonstrated, however, in the fact that Sophie, whom Émile marries, is trained so as to please him. Nevertheless, *Émile* is now regarded as a basic work in the history of education and a forerunner of modern educational theory.

One of Rousseau's most famous passages occurs in this novel. Although the section is titled "The Profession of Faith of the Savoyard Vicar," in reality it is the author's own profession. The Vicar, who is called in to give religious instruction to Émile, is essentially a deist. His God, however, is known not by reason but by feeling. Thus Rousseau confronts the deism of the *philosophes*. Rousseau's God, essentially, is a God who manifests himself in nature and is known through feeling—not, as in Christianity, through revelation. Wordsworth and other Romantics were greatly influenced by the Vicar's profession of faith.

Because *The Social Contract* and *Émile* were condemned by the French authorities, Rousseau found it convenient to accept an invitation from the philosopher David Hume to seek asylum in England. But the relationship with Hume was broken off, as so frequently with Rousseau's friendships, because of his belief that he was being persecuted by his friend. The following year, 1767, he returned to France. While still in England, however, he was able to complete most of his *Confessions*, his autobiographical masterpiece, which provides us with a fascinating portrait of a complex personality.

Rousseau has been branded as a neurotic posing as a genius, but his achievements will not permit us to brush him aside so lightly. He undoubtedly articulated the longings of many of his contemporaries—as was later evident in the rhetoric of the French revolutionaries. But he also continued to speak, through his writings, to

succeeding generations, in his educational theories, for example, as well as his political ideas. Moreover, in his emphasis on the uniqueness of his personality, his unabashed releasing of his emotions—in sharp contrast with the Enlightenment emphasis on the necessary restraint of reason—and his love of nature and reliance upon it as a refuge, he was a transition figure from the Enlightenment to Romanticism.

Goethe

Johann Wolfgang von Goethe (1749–1832) is one of the four or five greatest names in world literature. A brilliant scientist and successful administrator, he was an accomplished writer in all the literary genres, including the epic, the novel, the lyric poem, and the drama. He also wrote scientific articles, literary criticism, and autobiography. For good reason, therefore, he has been called a "universal genius." His complete writings fill 120 volumes.

Goethe was born in Frankfurt-am-Main to middle-class parents whose cultural and intellectual interests assured their son of a good education. After his early schooling in Frankfurt, Goethe, at the age of 16, began to study law and other subjects at the University of Leipzig. Because of illness, however, he found it necessary to interrupt his

5.5 Johann Wolfgang von Goethe

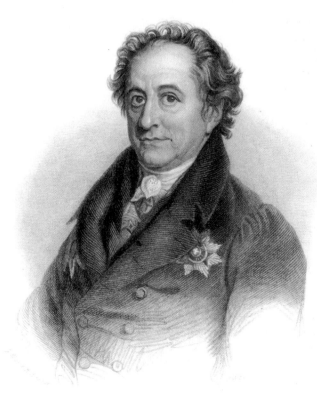

education. After a year and a half at home, he returned to his studies, completing his legal education at the University of Strassburg in 1771.

Goethe's most significant experience at Strassburg, however, was not his legal training but his exposure to the ideas of Johann Gottfried Herder, a Lutheran pastor who was deeply interested in literature and was leading an effort to throw off the restraints of French Neoclassicism in favor of folk literature. Influenced by Rousseau, Herder advocated a return to the primitive and to nature, insisting that nature is to be known, not through reason, but through feeling. Herder's Romantic ideas had a profound effect upon Goethe and other young German writers, whose literary interest and activities in the 1770s are called the *Sturm und Drang* ("Storm and Stress") movement, an early instance of Romanticism. Thus, although Romanticism, like Neoclassicism, had its origins in France, it was Germany that took the lead in the spread of Rousseau's ideas. Goethe played a significant role in this early Romantic movement in his homeland.

During this period Goethe began work on what was to be his masterpiece, *Faust*, whose completion, however, lay many years in the future. In 1773, he published *Götz von Berlichingen*, the story of a German noble of the sixteenth century who joined the peasants in their revolt against oppression, a powerful expression of the *Sturm und Drang* movement. Shortly afterward Goethe published *The Sorrows of Young Werther* (1774), an epistolary novel in the frustrated-love tradition of Rousseau's *New Eloise*. In Goethe's story, however, unlike Rousseau's, the protagonist ends the frustration of his hopeless love for a married woman by committing suicide. This work had a sensational effect upon Europeans, who wept with young Werther and in some cases even followed his example. In its emphasis on sentiment and subjectivism, *Werther* is an outstanding example of the *Sturm und Drang* trend.

In 1775, the Duke of Weimar, impressed by Goethe's writings, invited him to visit his court, and Weimar became Goethe's home for the remainder of his life. He was one of several literary notables, including Herder and Schiller, that the young Duke gathered around him. After a period of ten years, in which Goethe held several administrative positions in Weimar, and thus had little time for writing, he set out on a journey to Italy. This was to mark a significant change in his literary orientation, from the Romanticism of Herder to the classicism represented by Italy. During this sojourn Goethe completed several plays, including *Iphigenia in Taurus* and *Torquato Tasso*, which demonstrated his shift toward classicism. At about this same time (1790) he also published *Faust, a Fragment*, the first version of this work. He published Part I in 1808 and completed Part II a few months before he died

(1832), sealing it with the instructions that it was to be published posthumously.

The Faust story was based on a sixteenth-century German legend of a historical figure named Doctor Johann Faust. A practitioner of black magic, he sold his soul to the Devil to gain knowledge and power. The first of numerous dramas to be written on the Faust theme was by the Elizabethan playwright Christopher Marlowe, who wrote *The Tragical History of Doctor Faustus* (?1588). In this version, Faust makes a pact with Mephistopheles, a minion of Lucifer. Mephistopheles is to serve him for 24 years, after which Faust will, for eternity, become the servant of Mephistopheles in Hell. Although Goethe, like Marlowe, treats the ancient themes of the meaning of human existence and the human struggle against limitations on knowledge, he presents these in a new key. Marlowe explores these issues in terms of a conflict between the medieval view of the human being as a pilgrim of eternity and the Renaissance view, which emphasized the ever-expanding possibilities for humans. It is the medieval view that emerges triumphant; for Faust, abusing power and knowledge, becomes hardened to the redemptive possibilities of divine grace. Thus he loses his soul. In Goethe's version, however, Faust is ultimately saved because he has remained true to the conception of the human being as an endlessly searching and striving creature, a romantic view of human nature proclaimed by God himself in the Prologue of Goethe's drama.

Indeed, Goethe's Prologue in Heaven is a key to understanding the nature of the conflict between Faust and Mephistopheles. This section is patterned after the prologue to the Book of Job in the Old Testament (see page 23). In both, there is an assembly of celestial beings presided over by the Lord, before whom the tempter (Satan in Job; Mephistopheles in *Faust*) appears. Although the terms differ, the central issue in both stories is a conflict between God and the tempter over the human condition, as represented by one man; and the quarrel results in a wager between the Lord and the tempter in which the Lord affirms his confidence in his chosen one.

Mephistopheles appears before the Lord and the heavenly host rather like—it has been suggested—a jester before a feudal lord; for there is ironic humor in Mephistopheles' argument. As Satan in Job is the opposer of both God and man, so the cynical Mephistopheles seeks to defeat the Lord by destroying Faust. First, however, he contends that the Lord has made a grievous error in granting man (Faust) the gift of reason, which he "merely uses to be more beastly than any beast."[2] Ironically, it is in this opening speech that, for the first time, we see reflected the Lord's conception of the human being as a constantly striving creature—Mephistopheles compares the "little

God of this world" to a grasshopper that is constantly leaping up, only to fall to the ground. When the Lord identifies Faust as his servant, Mephistopheles taunts him, so he thinks, by saying that Faust is a peculiar servant since "nothing, whether near or far, satisfies his deeply turbulent breast." But the Lord affirms that Faust is serving him, though confusedly, and that he himself "shall soon lead him into light." He then states the premise that "man errs as long as he strives." Thus Faust can avoid error only if he does nothing. Here Goethe sets forth the fundamental concept of his drama: so long as Faust continues to strive he will never be lost. This dynamic view of the human being as an endlessly striving, though erring, creature is quintessentially Romantic.

Mephistopheles, like Satan in the Book of Job, then wagers that if he is given a free hand with Faust, the Lord will lose his servant. And, also as in Job, the Lord agrees to the terms of this bet. In the earlier versions, including Marlowe's, it is Faust only who makes a compact with the devil. In Goethe's version, however, the wager between Mephistopheles and Faust, which occurs later in the drama, is the earthly fulfillment of the Lord's purpose demonstrated in the Prologue, though Faust himself is unaware of this. In the barbed dialogue between the Lord and Mephistopheles that follows the wager, the Lord further states his confidence in Faust: "A good man, for all the obscurity of his impulses, is well aware of the one right way." He then defines the negative role of Mephistopheles in the ultimate salvation of Faust: "Of all the spirits that deny, the roguish knave burdens me least. Man's activity can flag only too easily, and soon he gets to liking absolute passivity; hence I like to give him an associate who prods and pushes and must act like a devil." Thus the Lord will employ Mephistopheles, a negative force, as a creative stimulus to the positive dynamic activity that defines human nature.

The negative role of Mephistopheles is also apparent in his wager with Faust. Faust, like the Lord, affirms that human life has meaning only if it is lived dynamically, in persistent aspiration after ever-fleeting fulfillment and satisfaction. Mephistopheles, however, contends that he will bring Faust to a time when he will "want to feast on something in tranquility." Faust responds, "If ever I lay myself tranquilly upon a bed of ease, then let that be my immediate end!" As he and Mephistopheles seal their pact, he further states, "If ever I shall say to any moment: 'Do stay with me, you are so good!' Then you may put fetters upon me, then you are free of your service." The clock, he says, may then stop.[3]

An understanding of the wager scenes is crucial to understanding Goethe's drama. When we are first introduced to Faust in his study, we see him as a frustrated seeker after ultimate truth and experience, the essence of the Romantic quest. The consummate scholar, he has exhausted all the possibilities of traditional knowledge yet remains dissatisfied. Thus he has resorted to magic so that he "may discern what holds the universe together in its deepest center."[4] Unlike Rousseau and other Romantics, however, he longs to experience such truth through a union with nature that would be magical rather than mystical.

His romantic involvement with Margaret (or Gretchen) is a further demonstration of his aspiring nature. Mephistopheles thinks to satisfy Faust by giving him the mere physical conquest of the young girl, but he fails to take account of the spiritual possibilities in love. Love, in the Romantic view, is not merely a game, with conquest as the only objective. Rather, it is a spiritual quest with profound philosophical implications. Thus Faust's sexual conquest of Margaret does not give him the ultimate satisfaction which Mephistopheles seeks to provide. Instead, it creates a tragic situation which causes the death of Margaret's mother and baby, and, finally, of Margaret herself. As a result, Faust experiences a sense of guilt, seeing in Margaret a depth of love that, just prior to her death, transforms his feeling for her from mere sexual passion into a spiritual ideal and thus an endless yearning. Again, Mephistopheles is foiled.

This yearning after the ideal continues to the end of Faust's life. Near the close of Part II of the drama, Faust, now an old man, contemplates the draining of a marsh and the opening up of arable land, by means of which he will create a happy and prosperous community. Anticipating the joy of such a humanitarian achievement, he pronounces the fateful words, "to that moment I'd have a right to say, 'Do stay with me, you are so good,'" and dies. Mephistopheles, thinking that he has finally won the wager, quotes Faust's own provisional promise, "the clock may stop," as fulfilled. But once more, he appears to be thwarted. For the angels of the Lord bear away the spirit of Faust chanting, "We can redeem anyone who keeps on striving and struggling."[5] Eckermann, Goethe's secretary, reported that Goethe told him that the passage in which these lines are found "contain[s] the key to Faust's salvation." So did Mephistopheles actually win the wager? Goethe's apparent answer is no. For even at his death, as an aged man, Faust, in his plans at least, is still "striving and struggling."

Wordsworth

Although English Romanticism boasts such brilliant luminaries as Shelley, Keats, Byron, and Coleridge, it is William Wordsworth (1770–1850) whose splendid

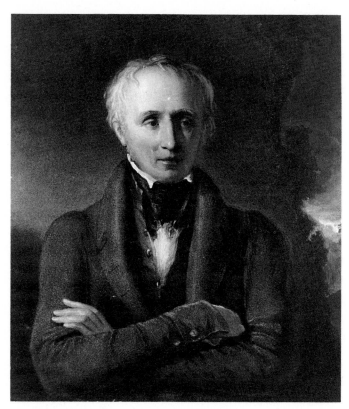

5.6 William Wordsworth

nature poetry is best known and who stated the poetic principles that marked the beginning of Romanticism in England.

Born on the northern edge of the Lake District in northwestern England, Wordsworth was orphaned at 13. He received his early education at Hawkshead, in the very area whose natural beauty he would celebrate in his poetry. Even as a child he loved to roam the hills and woods of the Lake Country, "drinking in," as he liked to term it, the loveliness of his natural surroundings. Although Wordsworth received a Bachelor of Arts degree from Cambridge in 1791, his academic record was quite ordinary.

Before graduation he had made a walking tour of France; and he returned to that country in 1791 to study the language. He spent more than a year in France on this second visit. This was the period of the French Revolution, and Wordsworth was caught up in the democratic excitement that attended the early years of this conflict— an enthusiasm that would fade as he grew older. He also became passionately involved with a French girl, Annette Vallon, who bore him a daughter, Caroline. Shortly afterward, Wordsworth was compelled, for financial reasons, to return to England; thus he and Annette, as it turned out, never married. Feeling guilty over this affair, disillusioned by the tide of the Revolution, and torn by the

war between England and France, Wordsworth passed through a period of suffering and despair, eventually regaining his equilibrium under the healing effect of writing poetry.

At about this time he received a legacy which allowed him to devote himself completely to his poetry; he also entered into close relationships with two persons who were to exert a profound influence upon him: Dorothy, his sister and secretary, and Samuel Taylor Coleridge, his collaborator in the writing of poetry and the development of his poetic theories. Wordsworth and Dorothy took up residence together at Racedown in Dorset, later moving to Alfoxden in Somerset, near which Coleridge lived. The collaboration of Wordsworth and Coleridge led, in 1798, to their joint publication of a collection of their poems entitled *Lyrical Ballads*, the event that marks the beginning of the English Romantic movement. Wordsworth also wrote a famous preface to the second edition of the book (1800), which set forth his views of how poetry should be written (see below).

Wordsworth and Dorothy returned to the Lake District in 1799, settling in Dove Cottage (as it later was to be called) at Grasmere. Here they were to remain, except for occasional travel, for the remainder of their lives. Coleridge also moved to this area to be near Wordsworth. Unfortunately, Wordsworth's relationship with Coleridge deteriorated, although a reconciliation occurred many years later. Wordsworth, who had married a Lake District girl, Mary Hutchinson, also suffered the loss of two of his children and the death by drowning of his brother, John. Moreover, his beloved Dorothy began to deteriorate mentally in the 1830s, although she was to outlive him by five years. Despite such grief and suffering, however, Wordsworth's poetic reputation grew, and he was duly recognized by his countrymen. In 1813, he received the sinecure of Distributor of Stamps. Evidence of his departure from the political liberalism of his youth is seen in his appointment, in 1843, as Poet Laureate. Even before his death his homes became tourist attractions, as Dove Cottage remains today.

Although much of his best poetry was written before 1807, it was not published until many years afterward. Indeed, *The Prelude*, his poetic autobiography, partly completed by 1805, was not published until after his death in 1850. Even then, though often revised, it had not been completed.

Although Wordsworth's famous preface to the *Lyrical Ballads* is the source of much critical controversy, there is no doubt that his intention was to set forth a theory of poetry that would dislodge Neoclassical views. He argued that ordinary experience and people were appropriate to poetry and that the language of poetry should not be elevated and artificial but "the language really used by men." Thus he took issue with the Neoclassical notion that only persons of elevated status, such as nobles and kings, were appropriate protagonists in epic and tragedy, and that elevated language should be used to match the status of such persons and their deeds.

Unlike the Neoclassical view that poetry must follow prescribed rules based on the literary practices of classical antiquity, Wordsworth defined poetry as "the spontaneous overflow of powerful feelings," a definition especially suitable to lyric poetry. He did not mean, however, that the poet, at the moment of the upsurge of his feelings in response to his experience, sets those feelings to language. No such chaos of emotional language is evident in Wordsworth's poetry. His expansion of his definition at a later point in his preface is vital: "I have said that poetry is the spontaneous overflow of powerful feelings: it takes its origin from emotion recollected in tranquility." Thus it is not the immediate emotional experience that is the proper subject of poetry, according to Wordsworth, but that experience as it is perceived when the poet is in a tranquil mood: "The emotion is contemplated till, by a species of reaction, the tranquility gradually disappears, and an emotion kindred to that which was before the subject of contemplation, is gradually produced, and does itself actually exist in the mind. In this mood successful composition generally begins. . . ." The poem is the "overflow" of the poet's feelings, therefore, but the raw feelings as originally experienced must be recovered in a time of tranquility before they are appropriate subject matter for poetry.

Understanding of this necessary combination of emotion and thoughtful tranquility is important to the reader who would appreciate and understand Wordsworth's philosophical observations on the significance of his emotional experiences of nature. Such reflections result from moments of tranquility as he looks back upon an earlier experience. One of his best-known lyrical poems, "I Wandered Lonely as a Cloud," may be used to illustrate his theory:

> I wandered lonely as a cloud
> That floats on high o'er vales and hills,
> When all at once I saw a crowd,
> A host, of golden daffodils;
> Beside the lake, beneath the trees,
> Fluttering and dancing in the breeze.
>
> Continuous as the stars that shine,
> And twinkle on the milky way,
> They stretched in never-ending line
> Along the margin of a bay:
> Ten thousand saw I at a glance,
> Tossing their heads in sprightly dance.

> The waves beside them danced; but they
> Out-did the sparkling waves in glee:
> A poet could not but be gay,
> In such a jocund company:
> I gazed—and gazed—but little thought
> What wealth the show to me had brought:
>
> For oft, when on my couch I lie
> In vacant or in pensive mood,
> They flash upon that inward eye
> Which is the bliss of solitude;
> And then my heart with pleasure fills,
> And dances with the daffodils.

Although the first three stanzas of this poem, for the most part, might have been written at the time of, or shortly after, Wordsworth's wander among the daffodils, the last stanza reveals that he is composing the poem in retrospect. Indeed, "oft" suggests that a considerable period of time has elapsed. Even within the third stanza there is a hint of the poet's retrospective view when he confesses that at the time of the experience he "little thought/What wealth the show to me had brought." The last stanza reveals the nature of the "wealth" Wordsworth continues to derive from the original experience. Here he depicts himself as absorbed in thought, again "wandering lonely as a cloud," when once more he suddenly, as in the original experience, sees—this time with his "inward eye"—the daffodils. And now, as then, they communicate their joy to him so effectively that he shares in it. Thus Wordsworth, "recollecting in tranquility" an earlier "spontaneous overflow of powerful feelings," composes a poem about the continuing significance of that experience in his life. Obviously, such a poem could not have been written at the time he saw the daffodils or even shortly after, for the poetic reflection is dependent upon the passage of time and the accumulation of repeated experiences of the meaning of the event. The result of this process is a poem about the capacity of nature to share its joy with the poet both in the immediate experience and in retrospect.

"Lines composed a few miles above Tintern Abbey," the concluding poem of *Lyrical Ballads*, though not a lyric, also illustrates Wordsworth's poetic theory. Here he gives the reader a triple perspective. For he not only reflects upon the past from the perspective of the present but also projects the significance of the experience into the future.

The poem was written as a result of a walking tour he and Dorothy took in 1798 which led them to a spot on the Wye River, not far above Tintern Abbey. Wordsworth, traveling by himself, had experienced the same scene five years earlier. Hence the duality of perspective that is evident in the opening line, "Five years have passed," which contrasts with the "and now" at the beginning of the fourth stanza, in which he not only reflects on "present pleasure" (l. 63) as he contemplates the "wild secluded scene" (l. 6) but also experiences "pleasing thoughts/That in this moment there is life and food/For future years."

In this poem Wordsworth meditates upon the difference between his earlier and his present experience of the scene. In his youthful response, nature was external and his enjoyment of it sensuous and spontaneous, "... a feeling and love,/That had no need of a remoter charm,/By thought supplied, nor any interest/Unborrowed from the eye." "That time," he affirms, "is past." But he has been more than repaid for this loss, for "other gifts/Have followed." Now he has learned "To look on nature, not as in the hour/Of thoughtless youth; but hearing oftentimes/The still, sad music of humanity" which has "ample power/To chasten and subdue." In his mature perspective he also has felt "A presence that disturbs me with the joy/Of elevated thoughts," a divine presence which he also describes as "A motion and a spirit, that impels/All thinking things, all objects of all thought,/And rolls through all things." Such transcendent experiences, however, are yet rooted in external nature, which is the "anchor of my purest thoughts, the nurse,/The guide, the guardian of my heart, and soul/Of all my moral being."

In the final stanza Wordsworth addresses Dorothy, hearing in her voice "the language of my former heart" and reading in her "wild eyes" his "former pleasures." Thus he sees Dorothy as being at the same level of perception that he was on his first visit to the Wye. But he looks forward to the time "when those wild ecstasies shall be matured/Into a sober pleasure; when thy mind/Shall be a mansion for all lovely forms,/Thy memory be as a dwelling place/For all sweet sounds and harmonies." Then, should she experience pain or loneliness, she will remember him and his "exhortations" with "healing thoughts/Of tender joy." Even though he be dead and thus no longer capable of hearing her voice or seeing his "past experience" in her eyes, she will not forget "that on the banks of this delightful stream/We stood together" and how he "a worshiper of Nature" came to the Wye "unwearied in that service." Nor will she forget,

That after many wanderings, many years
Of absence, these steep woods and lofty cliffs,
And this green pastoral landscape, were to me
More dear, both for themselves and for thy sake.

Thus Wordsworth returns at the end of his poem to the scene that gave rise to his lengthy meditation on the healing and comforting power of nature already experienced by himself and to be experienced by Dorothy. Indeed, nature not only communicates her consolation to William and Dorothy, but is the common denominator by which they communicate with one another—and with the divine. But this entire meditation is triggered by Wordsworth's double exposure to the scene on the Wye and his puzzlement over the difference between the two experiences. It is therefore his "recollection in tranquility" of his earlier emotions and of the ongoing and maturing meaning of the original experience that enables him to compose this poem about the second experience and to see in both a pattern that Dorothy will share with him.

For Wordsworth, therefore, Romanticism was not simply a self-indulgent spilling-over of immature emotions. His own poetic principles, as stated in the preface to *Lyrical Ballads*, combined feeling with deep reflection. These principles not only gave a philosophical dimension to his own poetry, but also—in thus being articulated—provided that same potential dimension for all Romantic poetry. Romanticism sometimes produced writing so emotionally laden as to be adolescent—Rousseau's *The New Eloise* and Goethe's *The Sorrows of Young Werther* may be cases in point. But it is clear from Wordsworth's poetry and Goethe's *Faust* that Romanticism was also capable of producing literature imbued with provocative ideas that speak convincingly to the deepest experience of the mature human heart.

Romantic Art

As we noted in the introduction to this chapter, many of the characteristics associated with the Romantic movement of the late eighteenth and early nineteenth centuries have been found in individuals and works of art of other periods. This is as true of art as it is for literature. In this section we shall concentrate on works of art that are associated with the Romantic movement itself. But first we shall consider two artists whose works display Romantic tendencies though they are not of the Romantic period: Watteau and Goya.

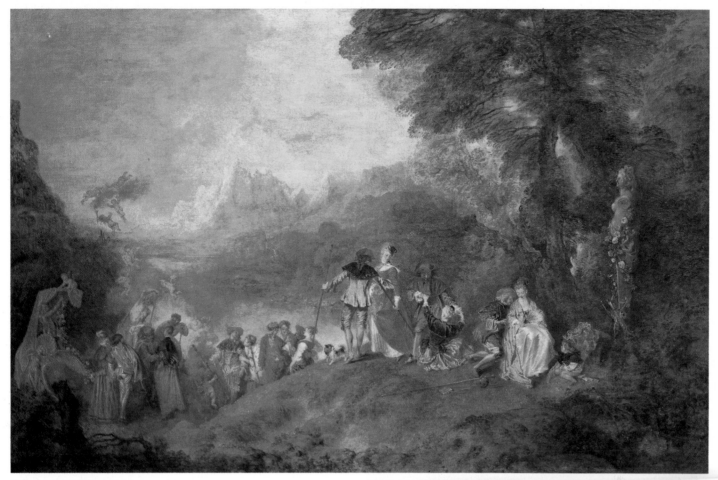

5.7 ANTOINE WATTEAU
A Pilgrimage to Cythera, 1717
Oil on canvas, 51 × 76½ ins (129.5 × 194.5 cm)
Louvre, Paris

Watteau

Although Jean-Antoine Watteau (1684–1721) was a highly celebrated painter, he was too weak (because of tuberculosis) to enjoy the society of the fashionable ladies and gallant gentlemen whom he depicted. Perhaps this is why he portrayed this society in shades of pessimism. Watteau's best-known work, *A Pilgrimage to Cythera* (Fig. **5.7**) shows a group of such people preparing to board a golden boat on a lake. According to legend, Cythera was the island home of Venus; thus, couples went there for one reason, to make love. In Watteau's picture, couples are seen about to go to the island, or perhaps about to leave it. To the right of them, in the shadow of trees, stands a garlanded statue of Venus herself; to the left, at the bottom of the hill under hovering cupids, lies the boat, presided over by a pair of gods; in the distance, through the evening haze, is a faint view of snow-capped mountains. Painted in pastel hues and delicate shades of brown and green,

Cythera, like its subject, is muted and dream-like. Though obviously an allegory of sexual love, it is far from being a picture of pure bliss. With its dusky setting and the wistfulness of the people, it is tinged with sadness and yearning. The idea of departure itself has poignant overtones; and travel by boat (as on the River Styx in classical myth or Dante) is an ancient symbol of death. The art historian Michael Levey compares this work to a Mozart opera: "In every way, the picture is imbued with a poignant sense of the losing battle love fights against the reality of time."[6] Watteau was the greatest of the Rococo painters (see page 172). In his art, one can find all the characteristics of the Rococo style, which he helped to establish. But it also transcends that style to say something profound about life.

Goya

In his early works the Spanish artist Francisco Goya

(1746–1828) displayed a mastery of the Rococo style; his portraits of the Spanish nobility are elegant and charming. Later, however, he revealed a fascination with more disturbing subjects. In *The Third of May, 1808,* (Fig. 5.4) he anticipates the Romantic preoccupations with nationalism and tragedy. He was also a prophet of the irrational and one of the first painters deliberately to use morbid subject matter. After a serious illness that left him totally deaf at the age of 47, Goya made a series of etchings entitled *Caprichos* (1823–1824). Though supposedly a commentary on Spanish customs and superstitions, the series raises several questions about the artist's real intentions. Is it supposed to be serious, or is it a satire? Is it about society or Goya's own capricious imagination? Does it probe the depths of hell or the artist's subconscious? Truth and dream, reason and absurdity mingle so freely in the *Caprichos* that it frustrates a quest for answers. As Goya declared: "The world is a masquerade, all would seem to be what they are not, all deceive and nobody

knows himself."

Like an *opera buffa* the series opens with scenes of urchins, flirting maidens, gossips, and lechers on the streets of Madrid; but soon it turns ominous. A sinister glance, a grotesque face, and the gray tones of Goya's etchings foreshadow such scenes as a kidnapping, a lover in the throes of death, and a hanged man being robbed of his teeth. Goya's titles and comments provide some insight into what all this means. Plate 3 (Fig. **5.8**), showing a mother and her frightened children confronted by a hooded figure, is entitled *The Bogeyman Is Coming*. Goya's notes suggest that he was condemning superstitions that warp human nature, and the use of fear in raising children. But we cannot be sure if this is all he meant by the picture itself.

The *Caprichos* are a virtual textbook of Spanish demonology: screech owls, goats, cats, corpses of the newborn, skulls, and broomsticks. These are often found in the company of dwarfs, giants, witches, and hybrid creatures of Goya's own invention. They cavort about, often with hapless victims. Some of these, together with owls and bats, fill the twilight void in Plate 43 (Fig. **5.9**). Goya's title, *The Sleep of Reason Produces Monsters*, could be either a comment on the backwardness of Spanish society or a premonition of the Romantic era.

Characteristics of Romantic Art

In order to understand some of the defining characteristics of nineteenth-century Romantic art it will be helpful to compare it with Neoclassical art. Both are marked by strong emotion and *high seriousness*. David's *Oath of the Horatii* (Fig. 4.25), for example, embodies personal sacrifice. But whereas Neoclassical works tend to stress "noble" emotions, such as courage and patriotism, Romantic works stress darker, more private emotions: nostalgia, despair, yearning, eroticism, narcissism, and morbidity. Correspondingly, Romantic subject matter tends toward the exotic and the dramatic: the long ago and far away, romantic love, sex and violence, death, and, most importantly, nature. (The only taboo subjects are satires, genre scenes, and romping aristocrats.) The range of styles in Romantic art is wider. Despite the occasional heroic character, most works feature lively figures, vigorous brushstrokes, and crowded composition. Whereas color, the most evocative of the visual elements, is not too important in Neoclassical art, it certainly figures prominently in Romantic art. One story about Delacroix relates how he removed one of his pictures at an exhibition and spent four days retouching it before putting it back—all because he was impressed by the vibrant colors of Constable's *The Hay Wain*, which also hung there.

5.8 FRANCISCO GOYA
The Bogeyman is Coming from *Los Caprichos*, 1797–98,
Etching and aquatint, 8½ × 6 ins (21.6 × 15 cm)
Metropolitan Museum, New York

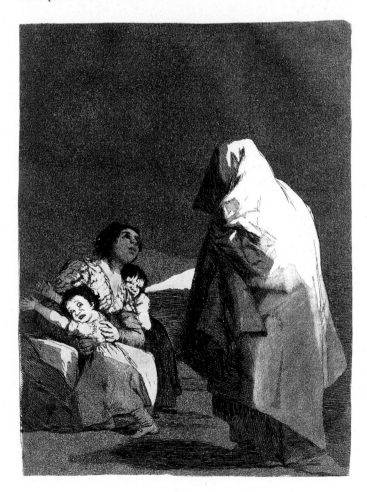

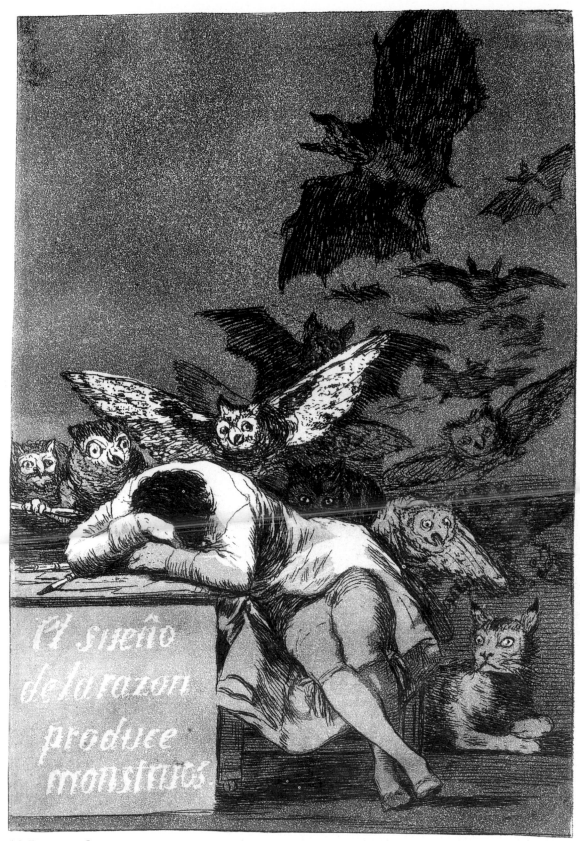

5.9 FRANCISCO GOYA
The Sleep of Reason Produces Monsters from *Los Caprichos*, 1799
Etching and aquatint, $8\frac{1}{2} \times 6$ ins (21.6 ins $\times$ 15 cm)
Metropolitan Museum, New York

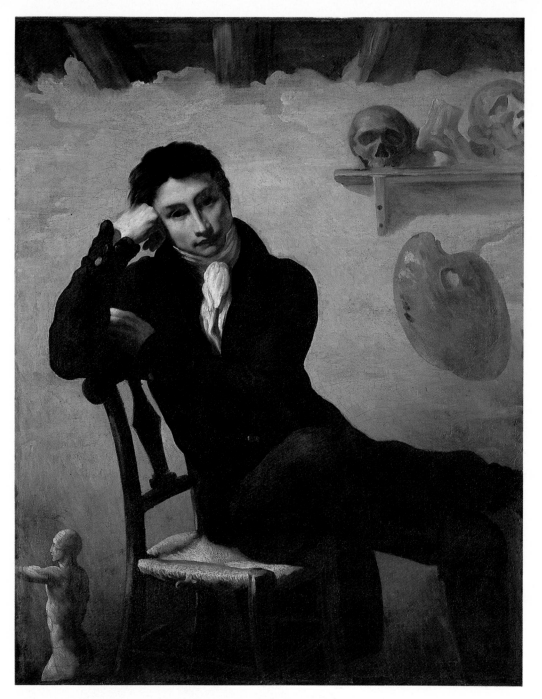

5.10 THÉODORE GERICAULT
*Portrait of a Young Man in an
Artist's Studio*, c. 1818–19
Oil on canvas, 58 × 40 ins
(146.7 × 101.4 cm)
Louvre, Paris

One of the reasons for the triumph of Neoclassicism, as we saw in Chapter 4, was due to the cultural pressures of the rising middle class. But it was the French Revolution that brought these pressures to their full realization. In 1793 the Louvre (former royal palace) and some of its collection were opened to the public. There, for the first time, ordinary people could view works of art that had been available only to kings and their guests. The term *salon* acquired an additional meaning: it was now applied to annual exhibitions of current art, again, open to the public. All of this, of course, affected the working conditions of artists. As middle-class patronage became more important than that of the aristocracy and the Church, artists were more independent but also less secure—

though the successful, like Delacroix and Turner, were always in demand.

But all artists, whether financially successful or not, shared a special status: like the introspective young man in Theodore Géricault's portrait (Fig. **5.10**), they were perceived as being a special breed, engaged in lonely struggles with their doubts and sense of alienation (a notion about artists that persists today). Art, then, was a special calling, not unlike that of a saint in earlier times. Some artists took this notion—and themselves—so seriously that they became opponents of middle-class culture, the original source of their emancipation. Thus we see in the Romantic era the beginnings of a growing alienation between artist and public.

Géricault

The earliest works of Théodore Géricault (1791–1824), a gifted young painter who had matured during the French Revolution and the Napoleonic wars, reflect the artist's fascination with themes of violence. These were usually taken from the point of view of the victor, but Géricault's most significant work, *The Raft of the Medusa* (Fig. 5.11)—a painting that became a landmark in the history of Romantic art—is taken from the point of view of the victim. Based on an actual event—passengers of a French ship that had foundered off the coast of Africa being set adrift on a raft—Géricault's picture dramatizes a moment of that event: the sighting of a ship in the distance. If read from left to right, the crowded scene of survivors could be interpreted as despair changing to hope, symbolized by the youth in the upper right who is vigorously signaling the rescuers. But if read the opposite way, it could suggest the vain attempt to attract a ship, and the fleeting hope of

rescue turning into even deeper despondency.

More harrowing than heroic, the actual event involved pointless mutinies, drownings, and even cannibalism before the few remaining survivors were finally rescued. In planning the picture, Géricault, like a news reporter, interviewed the survivors, studied corpses and dying men in a hospital, and even had the ship's carpenter make a model of the raft. The artist's preparations notwithstanding, the final product is more theater (in a Romantic vein) than objective reporting. Stylistically it is not very original, for it contains elements of Michelangelo (the figures) as well as elements of Rubens (both figures and composition). The originality of *The Raft of the Medusa* consists in its use of a grand style and heroic scale (16 by 23 feet [4.8 by 7 meters]) to depict the suffering of ordinary humanity. In earlier art, ordinary humanity—as in Dutch genre paintings (see page 347)—did not suffer. Conversely, suffering humanity—as in *Laocoon and his Two Sons* (Fig. 2.32) or Titian's *Christ Crowned with Thorns*

5.11 THÉODORE GERICAULT
The Raft of the Medusa, 1818–19
Oil on canvas, approx. 16 × 23 ft (4.8 × 7 m)
Louvre, Paris

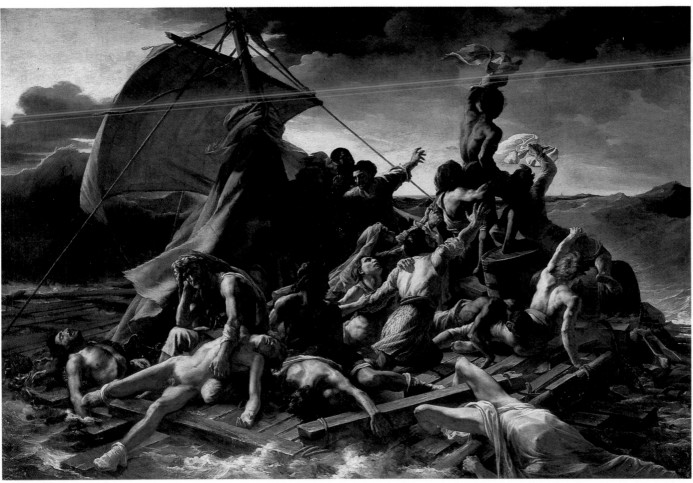

(Fig. 3.49)—was not ordinary.

The *Medusa* incident was a major scandal, perceived as a case of bureaucratic bungling. Therefore the unveiling of *The Raft of the Medusa* was timely, and its effect on the public was powerful. Its effect on the art world was equally powerful—that is, if we may judge by the reaction of a young painter at the time: Eugène Delacroix. Many years later Delacroix recalled that the impression it gave him "was so strong that as I left the studio I broke into a run, and kept running like a fool all the way back to the rue de la Planche where I lived."[7]

Delacroix

The name of Delacroix (1798–1863) is synonymous with Romanticism—as much for his vivid, paradoxical personality as for his art. Since he was the principal antagonist of Ingres, the conservator of Neoclassicism (see page 178), Delacroix was the idol of Romantic painters. Literate, charming, and a man of the world, he had many influential friends in the arts (including the composer Chopin and the writer Baudelaire). Despite these credentials, Delacroix condemned the society in which he flourished. Like Rousseau, he believed that urban culture was corrupt and that true virtue could be found only in nature. Fascinated by wild animals, especially tigers, which he described in numerous sketches and paintings, he revered them as symbols of nature. He also revered the people of Morocco—which he often visited—as the cultural opposite of his own people. In his eyes, they were more dignified, indeed, much closer in spirit and appearance to the ancient Greeks, than were Europeans. Finally, like legendary Romantic geniuses, he suffered from fits of depression and was thoroughly contemptuous of the public. Ironically, his personal charisma was due as much to this dark side of his personality as to the bright, sociable side.

The Death of Sardanapalus (Fig. **5.12**) a paradigm of Romantic painting, reflects some of these aspects of Delacroix's personality. Based on a poem by the Romantic poet Byron (which in turn was inspired by the story of Ashurbanipal, an ancient Assyrian king), it illustrates the final minutes of an Oriental despot, who, encircled by enemies, sacrifices all of his possessions before setting fire to himself. Here, the death wish, a popular theme in Romantic art, is mingled with sadism—as, for example, in the almost ecstatic sacrifice of the concubine in the foreground. Meanwhile, the passive king, who observes this orgy with ironic detachment, provides a striking contrast. The sexuality and violence of the subject are echoed in the sumptuous colors, the impetuous strokes of paint, and the turbulent, crowded composition.

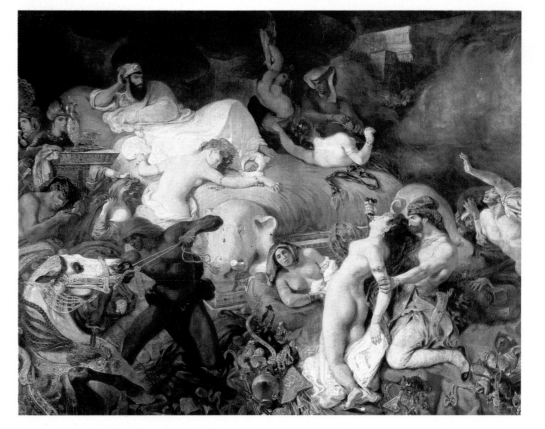

5.12 EUGENE DELACROIX
The Death of Sardanapalus, 1826
Oil on canvas,
12 ft 10 ins × 16 ft 3 ins
(3.92 × 4.96 m)
Louvre, Paris

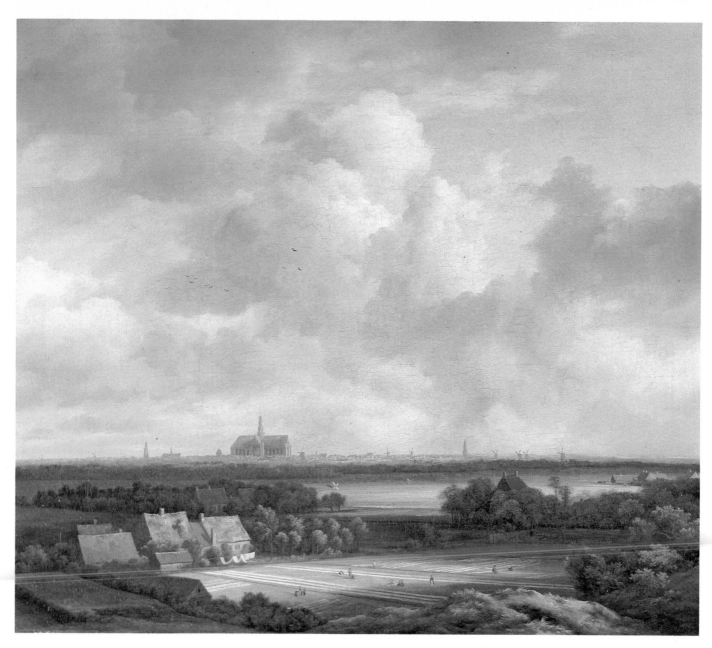

5.13 JACOB VAN RUISDAEL
View of Haarlem from the Dunes at Overveen, c. 1670
Oil on canvas, approx. 22 ins × 25 ins (55.8 × 63.5 cm)
Mauritshuis, The Hague

Nature in Romantic Art

Delacroix saw beauty in the violence of nature: scenes of beasts fighting beasts or beasts fighting men, as in tigers attacking Arabs. They express his obsession with blood and primordial forces. But the worship of nature, a central theme of Romanticism, so evident in Rousseau and Wordsworth, could be expressed in more subdued ways. Thus the nineteenth century was a peak period for the production of landscapes and seascapes.

The art of the landscape goes back at least to the seventeenth century (that is, if we exclude the backgrounds of some earlier pictures such as Leonardo's *Mona Lisa*). At that time there were essentially two kinds of landscape: ideal and realistic. An example of the first is Poussin's *Burial of Phocion* (Fig. 4.14) which is about an imaginary place and includes references to the classical past. An example of the second is Jacob van Ruisdael's *View of Haarlem from the Dunes at Overveen* (Fig. **5.13**) which is about an actual place and has no reference to either the classical or the biblical past. It was made in Holland during a time when religious art was actively discouraged by the Dutch Reformed (Calvinist) Church. Thus it could be said that Ruisdael's landscape is Protestant in a negative sense, that is, because it represents a turning away from traditional Catholic subject matter.

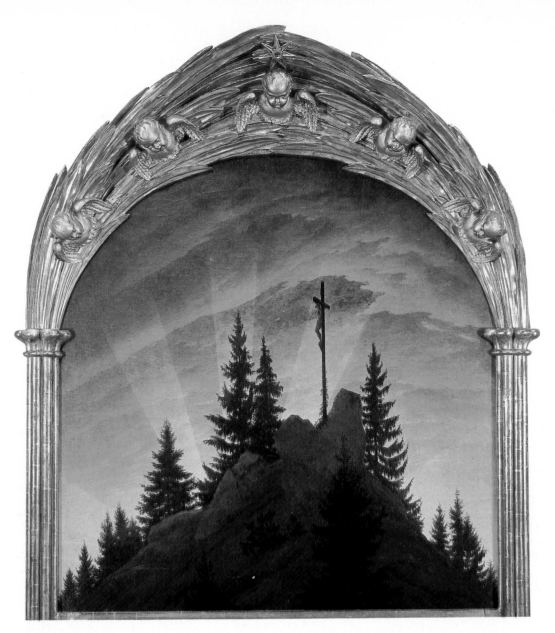

5.14 Caspar David Friedrich
Cross in the Mountains, 1807–8,
Oil on canvas, $45\frac{1}{2} \times 43\frac{1}{2}$ ins
(115×110.5 cm)
Gemäldegalerie, Dresden

Friedrich

A landscape by Caspar David Friedrich (1774–1840) is Protestant in a positive sense. Rather than avoiding religion, his paintings proclaim it. But this kind of religion must be seen in the context of the worship of God as revealed in nature. The physical landscape is seen as a revelation of God's power and love, while the painted landscape is its sacred icon. Friedrich's work is Protestant, in a sense, because the revelation is cast in a personal, idiosyncratic form of expression. As in the doctrine of the "priesthood of all believers," in which the pursuit of salvation is independent of religious authority, Friedrich's art asserts its independence of artistic authority. The artist himself was a devout Lutheran who insisted on the "private judgment" of the individual as the only valid guide to interpreting the Bible or art. His artistic interpretation of nature is indeed private and unorthodox.

Cross in the Mountains (Fig. **5.14**), an early work, illustrates this unorthodoxy, especially relative to the time when it was made. The subject itself is odd: a mountain peak as a setting for the Crucifixion. (This intriguing juxtaposition of the Christian symbol of the Atonement with a scene from nature marks a departure from the typical religious experiences of the Romantics—for example, those of Rousseau and Wordsworth—in which they encountered the Infinite through mystical communion with nature.) The composition is also quite unconventional: the landscape, in which the mountain is almost a silhouette, has no foreground or background. Unlike a Poussin or Ruisdael, it lacks transitional features such as fields, hills, or trees to guide the eye into the picture. The position of the viewer—either suspended in air or on a nearby mountain—is also unusual. The religious symbolism is both original and ambiguous. The extra-thin cross is visually and symbolically unstable.

There is uncertainty as to whether the sun is rising or setting and whether Christ is facing or turning his back on the viewer. *Cross in the Mountains* is a troubling picture because of these visual and symbolic ambiguities. As the art historian Hugh Honour explains, "It is an image of that 'honest doubt' in which, paradoxically, nineteenth-century faith lived most fully and painfully."[8] The peculiar spatial relationships give the picture an air of mystery, suggestive of the supernatural; its disturbing qualities evoke a sense of yearning, a condition of sin or of being separated from God. Thus the painting, paradoxically, combines an image of the certainty of salvation through divine grace with a manner of composition that introduces uneasiness and perhaps doubt.

Though *The Polar Sea* (Fig. **5.15**) is less obviously religious, it nevertheless proclaims the awesome power of God—as manifested in nature—in contrast to the helplessness of Man. It also demonstrates the compelling power of Friedrich's imagination. Inspired by an actual event—an Arctic exploration in 1819—Friedrich chose to show the quiet aftermath of disaster. The result, as haunting as the *Cross in the Mountains*, evokes a sense of uncompromising stillness and desolation.

Turner

Compare *The Polar Sea* with *The Shipwreck* (Fig. **5.16**), an early work by J. M. W. Turner (1775–1851). The two paintings, of course, share some features: the theme of maritime disaster, in which nature is no longer the symbol of consolation that it was for Rousseau and Wordsworth, and a composition of interlocking diagonals. In other

5.15 Caspar David Friedrich *The Polar Sea*, 1824
Oil on canvas, $38\frac{1}{2}$ ins × $50\frac{1}{2}$ ins (97.8 × 128 cm)
Kunsthalle, Hamburg

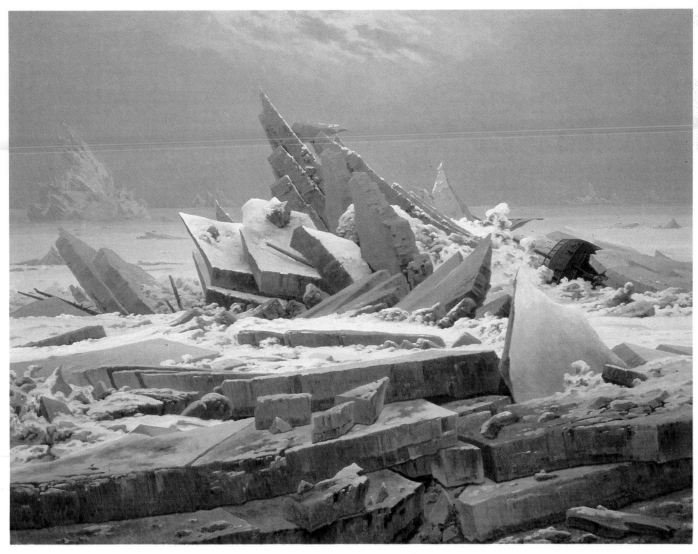

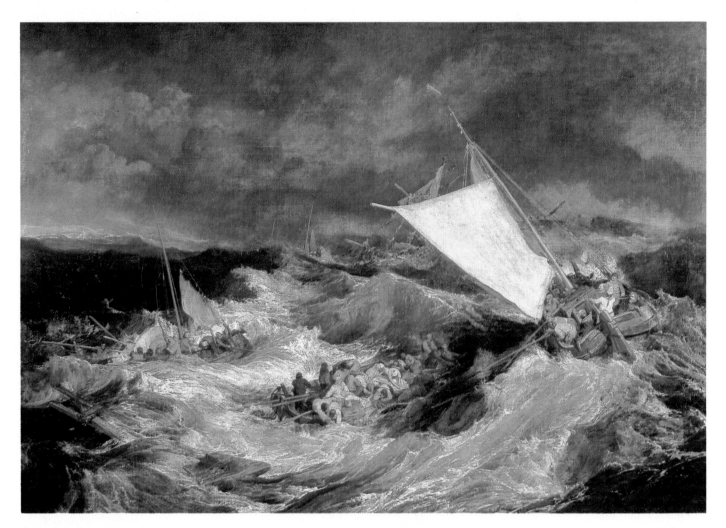

5.16 J. M. W. TURNER
The Shipwreck, 1805
Oil on canvas, 67½ × 95 ins (171.5 × 241 cm)
Tate Gallery, London

respects, however, they are as different as day (the Friedrich) and night (the Turner). *The Polar Sea* is as still as death—the aftermath of violence. *The Shipwreck* roars with the sounds of active violence—furious waves and desperate screams. Friedrich's careful drawing, meticulous detail, and smooth, "laconic" paint surface tend to make the forms every bit as frozen as the subject itself. By contrast, Turner's savage brushwork is fitting for a subject of turbulent sea and chaos. *The Shipwreck*, despite its maritime subject, has more in common with Delacroix's *The Death of Sardanapalus* than it does with *The Polar Sea*.

Turner continued to paint disasters—shipwrecks, storms, fires, avalanches. As time went on, they became more apocalyptic and more radical in style: full of slashing diagonals, sweeping whorls, and paint so loose that the forms almost disappeared. Remarkably, these works anticipated abstract art of the Modern movement by almost a century. But Turner also painted calm scenes: Venetian canals in the evening, English castles in the morning, and harbor scenes at sunset, such as *The Fighting Temeraire* (Fig. **5.17**), his most famous picture. It shows a veteran battleship—a heroic, old sailing vessel—being drawn by a tug—a steam vessel—to its destruction. In the context of the Industrial Revolution, the contrast between the two symbolizes the passing of an age. As such, the painting could prompt one to think of the past or the future, of nostalgia or progress; all are typical Romantic themes. At any rate, Turner saw to it that the air and water of the harbor were suffused with the golden colors of a sunset sky (in itself an original subject). Light and its ultimate source, the sun, were to him metaphors of divine creation. This explains why so many of his late, more tranquil paintings are also scenes full of mist drenched in light and color.

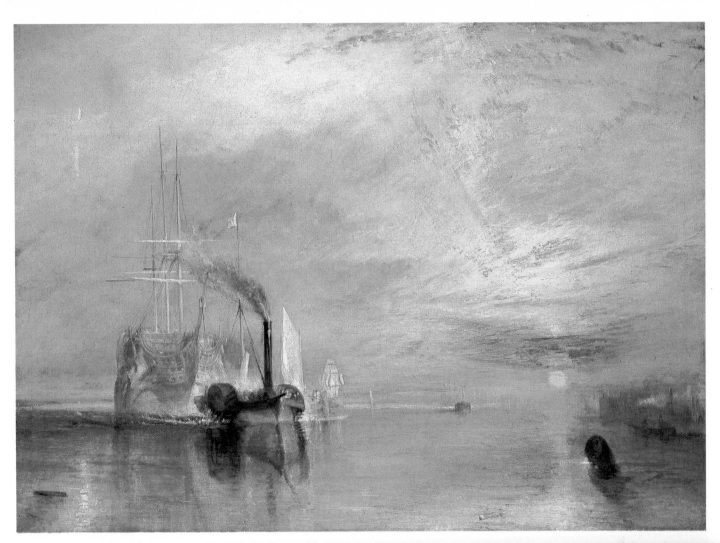

5.17 J. M. W. Turner
The Fighting Temeraire,
Oil on canvas, $35\frac{1}{2} \times 48$ ins (90×121 cm)
National Gallery, London

Constable

John Constable (1776–1837) and Turner were compatriots and almost exact contemporaries. But their art is very different. Constable's interpretation of nature is placid and untroubled, never tempestuous or epic. Form is always intact, never dissolved. His scenes of the English countryside are the result of keen observation and faithful rendering of what the eye sees. His work is also very different from Friedrich's; it never employs spatial ambiguities or unusual eye levels. The paint surface is vibrant, not smooth and matte. The content is always cheerful and open, never moody or mysterious. Moreover, unlike that of either Turner or Friedrich, Constable's work is not particularly visionary. So, if his art is neither visionary, wild, nor strange, what makes it Romantic? The answer is that although Constable's paintings, like those of the other two, are epiphanies of God's creation, his are *optimistic*. Also, unlike the paintings of the other

two, they are not given to the rhetoric of grandeur. They celebrate the humblest features of the countryside—mill dams, stagnant ponds, old rotten planks, even dung heaps—as well as its picturesque aspects.

Constable and Wordsworth were contemporaries and friends. Both valued childhood visions and their influence on adult character. Almost all of Constable's paintings depict the East Anglian countryside where he grew up; as such they express the same sentiment as Wordsworth's lines:

> *My heart leaps up when I behold*
> *A Rainbow in the sky;*
> *So was it when my life began;*
> *So is it when I shall grow old,*
>   *Or let me die!*
> *The Child is father of the Man....*[9]

Compared to Turner's or Friedrich's compositions, Constable's are relatively traditional, with no big, looping

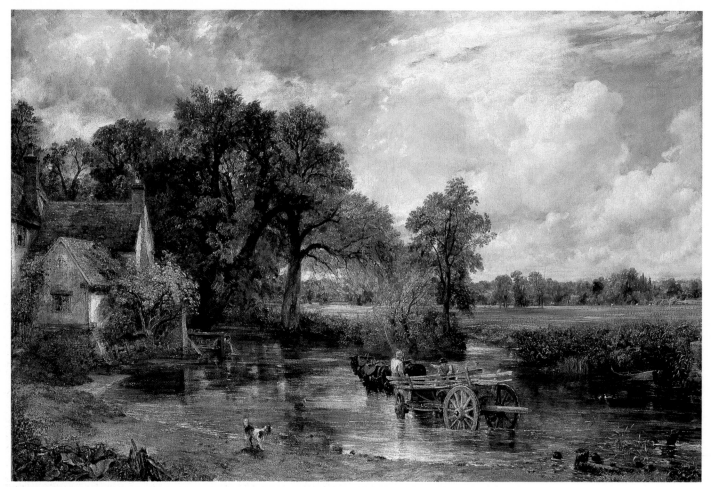

5.18 JOHN CONSTABLE
The Hay Wain, 1821
Oil on canvas, $51\frac{1}{4} \times 73$ ins (130×185 cm)
National Gallery, London

swirls of apocalyptic storms or unconventional points of view. What is more, they are realistic, like Ruisdael's. Indeed, the works of both Ruisdael and Poussin influenced Constable. But his paintings differ from earlier and contemporary art in at least one important respect: the use of *broken color*. None of the objects or natural features in *The Hay Wain* (Fig. **5.18**) are smoothly finished and carefully shaded; rather they are enlivened by small flecks of pure color or white applied with a brush or palette knife. This was the painting in the Paris Salon of 1824 that caused Delacroix to rework the colors in one of his own paintings (see above). The use of broken color was eventually transmitted, through Delacroix, to the Impressionists (see Chapter 9).

Sculpture—Rodin

According to official chronologies, the Romantic movement was followed by Realism, which began around 1850

in both art and literature. But in fact Romantic art and literature overlapped later styles, coexisting with them for years. In music, as we shall see, Romanticism continued into the twentieth century. In sculpture, the Romantic movement found its greatest exponent in Auguste Rodin, who was of the same generation as the Impressionists. Rodin was a rebel too, a member of the *avant garde*, and in continual trouble with critics and patrons. Also, some aspects of his work, especially the vibrant modeling of his bronze surfaces, recall the broken colors of the Impressionists. But, in the main, his artistic goals differed from theirs. The seriousness and heavy drama of his subjects are completely alien to the emotional detachment of Impressionism. In other words, Rodin, despite some affinities with the Impressionists, was persistently Romantic.

The Kiss (Fig. **5.19**), a sculpture of a nude couple in a passionate embrace, is another outstanding example of Romantic art—not only because of its obvious eroticism

5.19 AUGUSTE RODIN
The Kiss, 1886–98,
Marble, over life-size
Rodin Museum, Paris

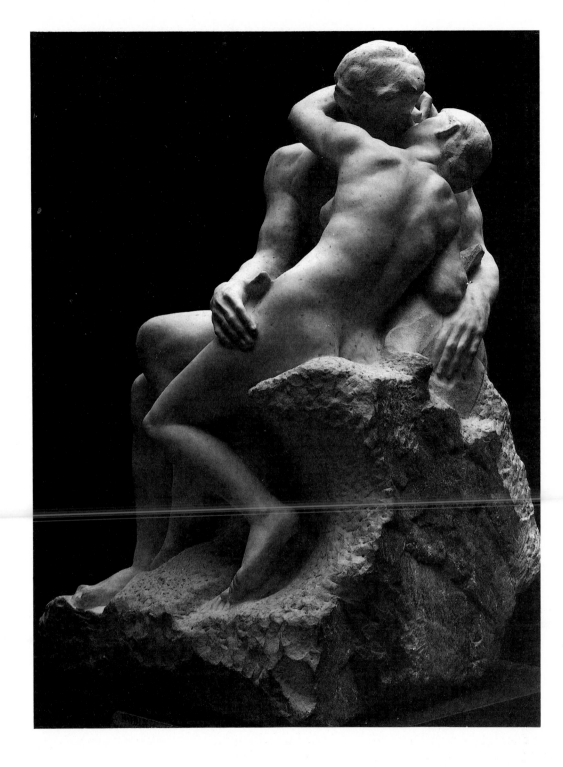

but because of the stylistic strategies used by the artist to stress that eroticism. To Rodin, who was an admirer of Michelangelo, the nude was both a vehicle of expression and a metaphor of abstract ideas. *The Kiss*, one of the most provocative sculptures in the history of art, demonstrates the obvious point that nudity is a powerful means of expressing sexual desire. Rodin endowed the bodies of the pair with the same restless energy found in Michelangelo's nude ''Slaves'' on the Sistine Ceiling—a quality that has

overtones of guilt as well as of passion. He also left some of the stone unfinished, as Michelangelo often did with his sculptures (usually for lack of time). Thus, by opposing the smooth texture of flesh with the rough texture of unfinished stone, he heightened the sculpture's sensuality.

As both a sculptor and a man, Rodin belonged to two generations: the Romantic and the early modern. We shall look at his Modern role in Chapter 10.

Architecture

Architecture responded to the Romantic impulse mainly through reviving styles of the past—in particular, Gothic (which, as we noted earlier, fell out of favor during the Renaissance). Buildings inspired by the Gothic style first appeared (or reappeared) in England as early as the mid-eighteenth century. In the nineteenth century, when Romanticism became a broad movement, the taste for Gothic and for "medievalism" in general acquired the status of a cult. This was expressed in many ways, not just in architecture: Delacroix painted dramatic pictures of Crusaders and thirteenth-century battle scenes based on the novels of Sir Walter Scott. Friedrich, characteristically, painted moody pictures, such as the one of a desolate, snow-covered landscape presided over by a towering Gothic ruin (Fig. **5.20**). In the applied arts, "Neo-Gothic" appeared in the designs of houses and furniture. As a literary example of medievalism, *Faust* is presented in a Gothic setting; in music, Richard Wagner was enthralled by the Middle Ages. Interest in medievalism led to intensified efforts to recover a European past which had been allowed to atrophy since the Renaissance.

This fascination with the Middle Ages acquired nationalistic overtones as each European country began to emphasize its medieval origins. The seat of the English legislature is a case in point. The Houses of Parliament which had burned down in 1834 were replaced with new ones designed by Charles Barry (1795–1860) and A. W. N. Pugin (1812–52) in 1835.

The concept of the building (Fig. **5.21**), with its rectangularity and (on the river front) symmetry, reflects the classical principles of its main architect, Barry. But its details, the contribution of Pugin, are thoroughly Gothic, right down to the thinnest molding and spikiest pinnacle; and the spirit of this imposing building—a symbol not only of the British government but of the continuity and venerability of Britain itself—evokes the Middle Ages.

Although Gothic was the most popular, it was just one of many revivalist styles in the nineteenth century: Islamic, Egyptian, Italian Renaissance, and Baroque. Neoclassicism, also known as Greek revival, especially in the United States, continued to have its adherents. The prevailing spirit of nineteenth-century architecture was eclectic: architects freely adapted and combined styles to suit their purpose, or the requirements of the client.

A striking example of this, as well as of the Romantic taste for the exotic in general, is the Royal Pavilion (Fig. **5.22**) at Brighton by the predominantly Neoclassical architect John Nash (1752–1835). A remodeling of an earlier royal residence, this extraordinary building, with its onion-shaped domes, minarets, and horseshoe arches, is a fantastic miscellany of styles sometimes called "Indian Gothic."

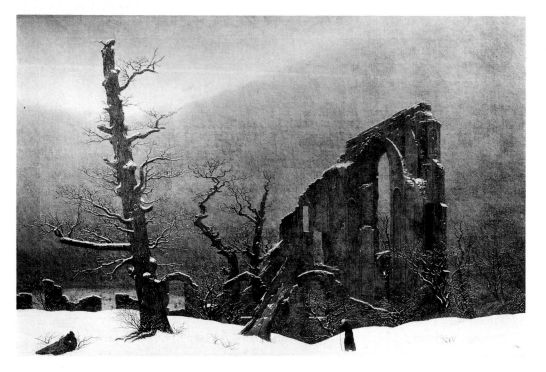

5.20 Caspar David Friedrich
Winter, 1808
Oil on canvas, painting
destroyed during World War II

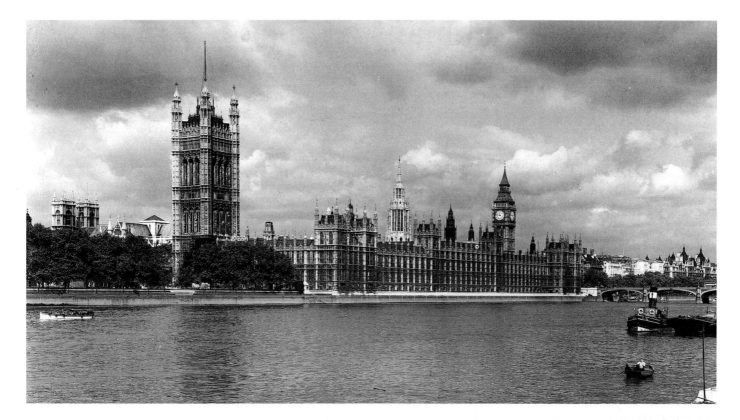

5.21 CHARLES BARRY and A. W. PUGIN
The Houses of Parliament, London, begun 1836

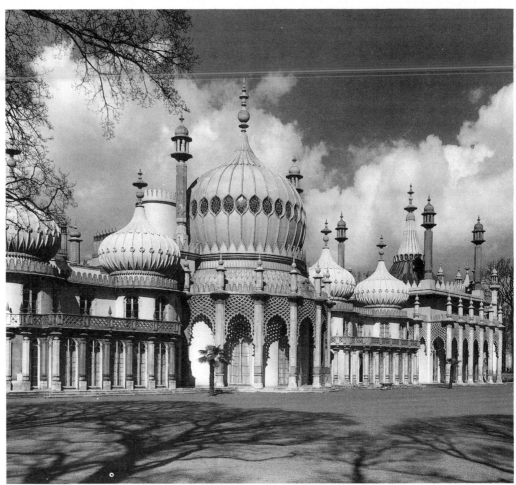

5.22 JOHN NASH
The Royal Pavilion, Brighton, 1815–18

Romantic Music

The spell of Romanticism was deeper and more enduring in music than it was in poetry, painting and sculpture. Music was seen by many Romantics, not just composers, as the purest form of art. As the art critic Walter Pater (1839–1894) said: "All art constantly aspires towards the condition of music."

This is an indication of the status of music in the nineteenth century. No longer merely a servant of the Church or an ornament of the rich, music was now seen as fundamental to civilization itself. Whereas a painting could try to picture Plato's ideal world (as in, perhaps, Raphael's *School of Athens*; Fig. 3.42), music could strive to create its actual conditions.

In contrast to their earlier servile status, composers now began to be respected, even venerated. Previously, they had served aristocrats; now, some aristocrats actually served composers, at least the successful ones. No longer were composers obliged to perform or to hold petty bureaucratic positions—as *Kapellmeisters*, organists, music librarians, and so forth—to earn their keep; now, many were "pure" composers, devoting all their time to writing music. Rather than being commissioned to produce scores, they wrote the music first, in hopes that their efforts would be repaid by proceeds from mass concerts or by royalties from publishers. Earlier, the vocation of music was typically passed down from father to son (as in farming or carpentry); now it was a career freely chosen by people from the educated middle class. Music was a calling—maybe even a "divine" one—which was often resisted by conservative fathers.

Romantic music is full of contrasts, if not contradictions. Compositions tended to get both larger and smaller: some late Romantics, such as Mahler, wrote symphonies lasting over an hour; Chopin wrote a waltz lasting less than a minute. While some composers explored personal areas of the soul through sensitive, intimate music, others dazzled audiences with loudness and brilliance, as orchestras got larger and larger. At the same time when individualism was so much in vogue, musical "nationalism" became a serious issue. Both *absolute* music (music completely free of extra-musical associations) and *program* music (music written to tell a story or describe nonmusical ideas) were championed. Some composers and performers were idolized by mass audiences yet, paradoxically, many felt alienated, as did their counterparts in art and literature. In the nineteenth century, when the musical public—previously consisting mainly of the aristocracy—was broadened, it included many who were

musically unsophisticated. For the first time serious differences arose between music and the public, as some composers deliberately distanced themselves from the tastes of middle-class audiences. This period also saw the first popular music—music intended for mass audiences.

Although music of the Romantic era is full of such contradictions, it is guided by one basic belief: that a work of art is a medium for transmitting feelings, an invitation for shared experience. To this end, nineteenth-century music is characterized by a common constellation of traits. Like poetry and art, it is partial to Romantic themes: exotic places, romantic love, the beauty and violence of nature, and so forth. But, obviously, such themes are embodied differently in music—whether absolute or programmatic. Unlike painting, music cannot represent the visual world. Unlike poetry or prose, it cannot describe events. But it can evoke moods and feelings more directly and, often, more vividly than either art or poetry. Indeed, it can set loose a flood of emotions that are experienced by listeners in a most immediate way. Because of its detachment from the tangible world and its ability to affect the listener, music was seen by some as spiritually superior to the other arts and, therefore, ultimately more capable of conveying Romantic ideas.

Romantic composers, like Romantic painters, loosened the rules of classical design, bending them where necessary and even breaking them. Content now dictated form, instead of the other way around. *Chromatic* harmony (using semitones and tones not in the main key) became more frequent, adding to the richness and variety of Romantic sound. Melodies were less restricted in phrasing and length; meter and rhythmic patterns are not only more varied, but more subject to change within movements or sections of a work. Still, although Romantic composers tampered with the musical legacy of Mozart and Haydn, they did not destroy it. They retained all of its basic elements: the major and minor keys, primarily homophonic textures, the sonata form, and essentially the same instruments and orchestration. That legacy, a highly developed musical language, was (and still is) capable of infinite possibilities. Just as Turner in his most radical works never really abandoned basic pictorial devices, Romantic composers operated within musical parameters established by Baroque and Classical composers more than they might have been willing to admit.

Instrumental music assumed a growing importance in the nineteenth century. Music without words, whether in solo instruments or huge orchestras, came to equal, if not surpass, vocal music as a vehicle of expression (although opera continued to develop and flourish, as we shall see). Instruments could "sing" as well as the human voice. When composed to accompany voices, instrumental parts were sometimes the main carriers of ideas—voice parts serving simply as added commentary. Romantic composers made careers out of exploiting the capacities of instruments and refining the art of orchestration. To these ends, new instruments or newly-improved instruments, notably trumpets and French horns with modern valve systems, were added to the orchestral palette. Melodic ranges were expanded and musical textures made denser than ever. Just as Romantic artists were addicted to rich, evocative color, so Romantic musicians reveled in *sonority*—deep, rich, resonant sound.

In keeping with the new relationship to the past, Romantic composers rediscovered medieval, Renaissance, and Baroque music. Whereas in earlier times, composers tended to ignore, if not completely forget, their predecessors, Romantic composers began to venerate them. But this veneration was cast in Romantic terms. For example, Bach was rediscovered in 1829 when his *Passion According to St. Matthew* was presented by Mendelssohn. This was the first public performance of one of Bach's major choral works since his death. Yet the music of that performance was a travesty of the original. According to the musical scholar Alfred Einstein: "It was no longer the Bach of the Bible, of the Lutheran faith, of the magnificent simplicity, but a Romanticized Bach, reduced to Mendelssohnian formulae."[10] Nevertheless, such efforts to recover the past led to the establishment of *musicology*, the scholarly study of music, including its history and scientific principles.

Perhaps even more than the other arts, music responded to the stirrings of nationalism. In earlier centuries little concern was shown over a composer's nationality: Netherlanders worked in Italy, Germans worked in England, and so forth; there was no "English," "German," "French," or "Italian" music in any restrictive sense. In the nineteenth century, people became more conscious of national origins, even believing that different musical traits were indigenous to different countries. Some composers emphasized this: Wagner was chauvinistic about his Germanic origins and "Teutonic" music. Others also capitalized on nationalism—writing music in the "costume" of a particular country, not necessarily their own: Liszt (Hungarian) wrote *Hungarian Rhapsodies*; but Berlioz (French) wrote *Harold in Italy*; Mendelssohn (German) wrote the *Italian Symphony and Scottish Symphony*; and Bizet (French) wrote *Carmen* (an opera set in Spain). These composers were simply reflecting a well-known Romantic theme—that of the lonely wanderer.

Precursors of Romantic Music

Just as Rousseau's veneration of nature foreshadows Romanticism in literature, and as the poignancy of Watteau and the fantasies of Goya foreshadow similar tendencies in Romantic painting, so the tenderness of feeling in C. P. E. Bach (one of Johann Sebastian Bach's sons; see page 185) anticipates similar effects in Romantic songs. Even the great Classicists, Haydn and Mozart (see Chapter 4), who observed formal rules in their music, had their moments of Romanticism. The loud chord in the second movement of Haydn's "Surprise" Symphony is a forerunner of all the harmonic jolts and sudden changes of mood in nineteenth-century music. The opening bars of his Symphony No. 103 (the "Drum Roll") are as dark and foreboding as any found in the most brooding Romantic piece. The opening bars of Mozart's overture to *Don Giovanni* are equally foreboding.

Beethoven

Was Ludwig van Beethoven (1770–1827) the last of the great Classical composers or the first of the Romantics? Some say he was neither; he was purely Beethoven. Some say he was both. Less than a generation younger than Mozart, whom he met briefly as a youth, Beethoven studied with Haydn for two years. His early works, particularly his First Symphony, strongly resemble the music of these two composers. His later works, in which he coaxed out the Romantic possibilities of this heritage, go well beyond the limitations of strict classicism, while at the same time preserving its structural principles. Formal coherence is not sacrificed to emotional content. Indeed, his multi-movement compositions can be said to have an emotional "program," like a novel that has a consistent point of view throughout. Still, it was the subjective and revolutionary aspects of Beethoven's work, rather than its sense of order, that impressed and influenced the Romantic generation. In 1792, at the age of 22, Beethoven left Bonn to study, compose, and perform in Vienna, where he met Haydn and other teachers and people of influence. By 24 he had gained a reputation as the most exciting pianist in Vienna, and by 27 had published a number of works, amongst them his First Symphony and several piano sonatas including the famous "Moonlight" Sonata.

He was not handsome: according to friends he was short, stocky, untidy in dress, with a pockmarked face, small eyes, and broad nose. Nevertheless, he was imposing: his broad shoulders, bristling hair, and bushy eyebrows gave him an image befitting his powerful music (Fig. 5.23). His personality was equally overwhelming. He

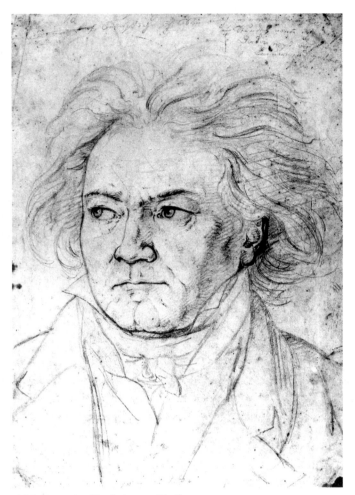

5.23 Portrait of Ludwig van Beethoven
Pencil drawing by Carl Friedrich Auguste von Kloeber, c. 1818
Beethovenhaus, Bonn

could be brusque with servants, impatient with his peers, ruthless to rivals, and even rude at times to nobles, who, paradoxically, treated him with the utmost respect. But some, if not all, of this behavior can be attributed to a growing handicap: deafness. This condition struck him at the early age of 27. In a letter of 1801 he revealed to a friend that he had been suffering from it for three years:

> *I must confess that I lead a wretched life. For almost two years I have ceased to attend any social functions, just because I find it impossible to say to people: I am deaf. If I had any other profession I might be able to cope with my infirmity; but in my profession it is a terrible calamity.*[11]

Despite, or perhaps because of, this "terrible calamity," he continued to write ever more majestic music: the Third Symphony, "Eroica" (1803–4), the opera *Fidelio* (1805), his Fourth, Fifth, and Sixth symphonies (1806–8), and the "Emperor" Concerto (1809); in addition to these, string quartets and piano sonatas. During this period Napoleon's armies twice marched on Vienna. Born in the same year as Wordsworth, Beethoven, too, was at first an ardent sympathizer with the causes of the French Revolution; but their enthusiasm waned: Wordsworth's gradually; Beethoven's suddenly, when Napoleon proclaimed himself Emperor. By 1813 Beethoven was the most acclaimed composer in Europe, but his deafness was so severe that he ceased performing on the piano. His last symphony, the Ninth, was received with jubilation at its first performance in 1824. But because its composer and conductor was not facing the audience, he was unaware of the applause until someone turned him around.

The similarities between Beethoven and Michelangelo are striking: both had stocky builds, saturnine personalities, and a generous measure of egotism. Neither married. They lived through changing, dangerous times: Michelangelo, a child of the Renaissance, was caught between rival political factions in Florence; Beethoven, a child of the Enlightenment and the Revolution, was caught between his own political sympathies and loyalty to his titled friends in Vienna. But their times were also favorable: just as art approached a climax of unprecedented growth and heroic stature at the turn of the sixteenth century, so did music at the turn of the nineteenth. Both men not only built on the achievements of their predecessors, but also dominated their respective arts. And their larger-than-life artistic statements involve Promethean struggles between the forces of despair and triumph. Michelangelo's themes of the Creation, Fall, and Redemption were inspired by Christianity and Neoplatonism; Beethoven's themes of freedom and universal brotherhood were inspired by the ideals of the French Revolution. Both of these geniuses gave new meaning to the word "heroic."

In addition to a number of piano sonatas and chamber works, Beethoven wrote nine symphonies, five piano concertos, two Masses, one oratorio, and one opera. Compare this output with Mozart's 600 works, including over 59 symphonies (of these a dozen or so were written as a youth) and 22 operas, or Haydn's 100-odd symphonies. These statistics illustrate the contrast between their working styles. His own sternest critic, he reworked every composition extensively. *Fidelio*, his only opera, came out in three versions with four overtures; parts of Act Two were revised 18 times. The urge to perfectionism was in his nature, but its realization was made possible by his relationship with his patrons. Unlike Haydn for example, who had to write on demand for employers, Beethoven took all the time he needed to write for an imaginary, ideal audience. He lived on proceeds from performances of his music or advances from patrons.

Beethoven changed the form of the symphony by expanding the first movement, making the second movement sadder and more hymn-like, replacing the minuet of the third movement with the antic, rapid music (though still in triple time) of a *scherzo* (Italian, "a joke"), and lengthening the fourth movement. Aside from these structural changes, his music is marked by abrupt contrasts—sudden changes in pitch, loudness, rhythm, even style. Planted in the middle of the glorious finale of his Ninth Symphony, for example, is an incongruous tune called a "Turkish march." Such contrasts provide light relief but can also evoke sweeping changes of mood. Beethoven's music is often stormy: fate, conflict, despair, triumph, and joy are recurring themes.

These ideas were given musical life in an 1808 concert in which both the Fifth and Sixth symphonies were premiered. It was appropriate that these two works should share the same program—not only because they were written at about the same time but also because the two are complementary: the Fifth is intense and brooding; the Sixth, relaxed and optimistic.

The opening C-minor motif (Fig. 5.24) of the Fifth, like Hamlet's "To be or not to be" or the Mona Lisa's smile, is one of those deceptively simple artistic creations that have captured the attention of a wide public. Unfortunately, because of this, it has also become a musical cliché, a situation that tends to obscure its real significance. Though simple, it is full of foreboding, like "Fate knocking at the door." Stated with strings, it forms the basis of the first theme. Essentially the rhythm, rather than the melody, is the motive; it is restated in a variety of permutations as the texture thickens and the tension builds. The second theme (Fig. 5.25), though lyrical and in a major key, provides only temporary relief from the essentially troubled quality of the first theme. After a

5.24 Opening motive of Beethoven's *Fifth Symphony*

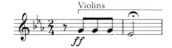

5.25 Second theme of Beethoven's *Fifth Symphony*

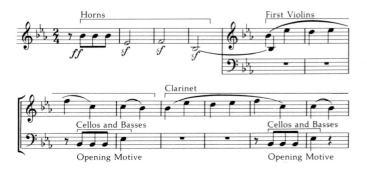

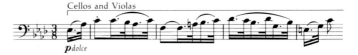

5.26 First theme of second movement of Beethoven's *Fifth Symphony*

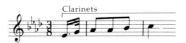

5.27 Second theme of second movement of Beethoven's *Fifth Symphony*

tempestuous development and recapitulation, the movement ends on very loud C-minor chords. The second movement, unlike that of a Haydn symphony, is in *double* theme and variation form. The first theme (Fig. 5.26) is solemn and stately. The second (Fig. 5.27), also solemn, starts quietly but soon becomes loud as its simple melody is doubled with brass instruments. After undergoing numerous variations of both its themes, the second movement ends with an expansive, though brief, coda. The third movement, or scherzo, is in A B A form and consists of a first theme in C minor interrupted by a playful second theme in C major before returning to the original theme. The quiet playing of *pizzicato* (plucked) strings at the ending of the third movement in the minor key imperceptibly blends into the bowed strings at the onset of the C-major fourth movement. Starting very quietly, this transitional section soon explodes into a *fortissimo* burst from the full orchestra. One of the most dramatic moments in music, the opening theme (Fig. 5.28) of the final movement must have raised the people out of their seats in that original 1808 performance. The change from minor to major, from *pianissimo* to *fortissimo*, and from *pizzicato* strings to full orchestra (including the first symphonic use of trombones) is a musical incarnation of triumph. Consisting of four themes, alternating between fast and very fast tempos, the last movement is a brilliant exercise in contrasts, modulations, variations, and recombinations of musical material. It ends on a repeated C-major chord.

Although it ends triumphantly, the Fifth Symphony is, on balance, a somber artistic statement—especially when compared to the unqualified joy of the Sixth Symphony, also known as the "Pastoral," because of its rural themes. Beethoven labeled the five movements: "Awakening of happy feelings on arriving in the country," "By the brook," "Joyous gathering of country folk," "Storm," and "Shepherd's song; happy and thankful feelings after the

5.28 First theme of the final movement of Beethoven's *Fifth Symphony*

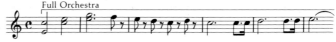

storm." Some people consider the Sixth Symphony to be program music—that is, music that attempts to describe scenes or tell stories. Such music usually follows no particular organization, since the form depends on a story, and relies heavily on "tone painting," the imitation of natural sounds. The Sixth Symphony, however, follows the usual Classical pattern. The first, second, and final movements are in sonata form, while the third movement is not unlike a traditional Beethoven scherzo. (If the ultra-short "Storm" movement is regarded as a transition between the third and final movements, the Sixth could be seen as conforming to the traditional four-movement pattern.) Further, the tone painting is limited to the storm and some "bird calls" inserted at the end of the second movement. Beethoven intended to relate this music to its pastoral theme in ways other than imitations of nature, as he explained: "More an expression of feeling, than painting." Some of the "rural" effects of the Sixth Symphony are based on musical sounds and themes associated with peasants that were familiar to nineteenth-century ears: yodeling tunes, sounds of bagpipes (a peasant instrument) in the bass parts, and village dances in the scherzo. This is analogous to using guitar sounds and country-western songs in, say, a twentieth-century American pastorale. In the final analysis, the main carrier of bucolic sentiment is Beethoven's relating the character of the music to feelings associated with nature. The use, primarily, of the major mode and the slow harmonic changes throughout create a prevailing mood of serenity. The tonal richness and expansive melodies of the first movement suggest the refreshing experience of open countryside. The quieter, lyrical melodies of the second movement ("By the brook") continue the serenity but also suggest a more intimate contact with the finer aspects of nature. The scherzo, which features abrupt modulations and a parody of village music-making, provides comic relief and another side of rural life. The storm interlude, in addition to sounding somewhat like a real storm, injects the only anxious note; it is more turbulent even than the first movement of the Fifth Symphony. The opening of the final movement not only signals the end of the ordeal but also introduces the beginning of some of the most joyful music ever written. Starting quietly, it transposes to a yodel melody (played by oboes and French horns) and then to the main melody, which slowly grows in loudness and harmonic richness to a climax. This final movement is expansive, like the first, but more uplifting. The Sixth Symphony is the musical cousin of Wordsworth's poetry and Constable's peaceful landscapes. Beethoven, like other Romantics, found spiritual refreshment and solace in nature: "O God, what majesty in woods like these. In the heights there is peace—peace to serve Him."[12]

Despite the pictorial associations of its movements, the Sixth Symphony is just that: a symphony, not a piece of program music. But it is also an essay on a sequence of emotional experiences with nature. Therefore, Beethoven was compelled to ensure that the work was unified around this sequence as well as following the abstract sequence of the symphonic form. And to do this it was necessary in places to stretch that form.

Berlioz

Critics accused Hector Berlioz (1803–1869) of stretching the form to the breaking point in his *Symphonie Fantastique*. Its melodies are exceptionally long and asymmetrical; its dissonant harmonies and clashing rhythms were appropriately revolutionary for 1830, the year in which the Bourbon monarchy was overthrown for the second time and also the year of its first performance. It was (and perhaps still is) as eccentric as its name suggests. Moreover, Berlioz had added a *program*—a story to go with each movement—that was as bizarre as the music.

Born during the First French Republic and the height of Neoclassical style, Berlioz was given the classical name of Hector (Trojan hero of the *Iliad*). At the age of 18 he was sent to Paris to study medicine, but discovered that he preferred analyzing harmony to examining cadavers. At 21 he decided, over the objections of his family, to pursue music and became a full-time student at the Paris Conservatoire. In 1827, at a stirring performance of *Hamlet*, he fell passionately in love with the beautiful Irish actress Harriet Smithson (who played Ophelia). But try as he would, he was unable to see her offstage. To attract her attention he went to the unprecedented lengths of producing his own concert in 1828. Musically, it was a success, but it failed to make an impression on Miss Smithson. That year Berlioz had another electrifying experience: attending a series of Beethoven concerts. The young composer realized what was missing from his education at the conservatory. Meanwhile, he also discovered Goethe's *Faust* (through a French translation by Gérard de Nerval).

All of these impressions, including his sexual longings, were brought to bear in the writing of the *Symphonie Fantastique*. According to one of Berlioz's biographers, Jacques Barzun, the composer, inspired by the example of Beethoven, intended merely to create a dramatic symphony. If so, he confused the public not only about his intentions but about the work itself by attaching a written program describing an "Episode in the Life of an Artist" (the symphony's original title). Following the outline of the five movements ("Reveries, Passions"; "A Ball"; "In the Country"; "March to the Scaffold"; and "Dream of a Witches' Sabbath") it introduces the artist and his obsession about a young woman that takes the form of an *idée fixe* (fixed idea), in this case a musical thought as beautiful as the woman herself. The *idée fixe* follows him to a ball, and then to the country, and even appears in an opium-induced dream in which he imagines he kills his beloved and is condemned to death and executed. The last scene finds him, like Faust, in the middle of a wild witches' sabbath in which his former beloved, now a prostitute, mocks him and joins in the revelry. As Berlioz had made no attempt to keep his feelings about Harriet a secret, the hopeless love affair was common knowledge. Meanwhile, however, Berlioz had fallen in love with another young woman and virtually forgotten Harriet. But when the newspaper *Le Figaro* published the program (in anticipation of a forthcoming performance) the public quite naturally identified the *idée fixe* with Harriet.

The *idée fixe* motive, a long, sweetly lyrical and languid melody (Fig. **5.29**), enters after six minutes of playing time, and then only briefly. However, the whole first movement consists of variants of the melody as its characteristics are echoed in countless musical fragments. Though marked by tremendous contrasts of loud and soft, the music is not epic like Beethoven's; rather, it seems to swell and shrink as crescendos and decrescendos come in waves. The quiet opening of the second movement soon becomes a flourish that introduces a beautiful waltz. The *idée fixe* appears as a waltz, but, unlike the main themes, it is distant, almost spectral. It returns briefly as a ghostly solo sandwiched between loud passages toward the end of the movement. The third movement is announced by the bucolic sounds of a shepherd's call, a beautiful *adagio* sounded first by flutes and oboes and later by strings. The serenity gives way to louder and more frenzied music just before the return of the motif which, this time, is forced to struggle with cellos and full orchestra. The movement ends with the quiet strains of the shepherd's call alternating with the sounds of thunder. The fourth movement, which starts ominously with drum-rolls and a theme based on a descending G-minor scale (Fig. **5.30**) soon erupts into a loud march. At length the *idée fixe* returns, only to be cut off by a crashing loud chord, followed by two plunks on the cellos. After the macabre introduction of the final movement, the *idée fixe* returns stronger than ever, but now with dissonant harmony and jolting rhythm, a mockery of its earlier incarnations. It is joined by the sounding of bells and a parody of the *Dies Irae* ("Day of Wrath"), plainchant theme of the Requiem Mass. The last

5.29 *Idée fixe* from Berlioz' *Symphonie fantastique*

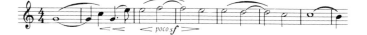

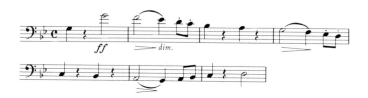

5.30 First theme of fourth movement from Berlioz' *Symphonie fantastique*

movement is as fantastic as Goya's *Caprichos*.

Performed with the largest orchestra up to that time, the *Symphonie Fantastique* was as revolutionary, in its way, as the political events surrounding its premiere. And—unusually for revolutionary music—it was a great success. The audience was enthusiastic. *Le Figaro* described it as "bizarre" and "monstrous"—compliments in Romantic terminology. The last two movements, the most original of the work, both shocked and pleased. Still modern by today's standards, these movements' traits can be heard in many later works: *The Sorcerer's Apprentice* (Dukas), *Pictures at an Exhibition* (Mussorgsky-Ravel), *The Rite of Spring* (Stravinsky), and, perhaps, every scare-movie soundtrack. The expansive beginning of the waltz in the second movement anticipates similar treatments in the music of Johann Strauss; the protracted melodies and *adagios* of the third movement foreshadow Wagner's *Tristan and Isolde*. The symphony was a turning point in Berlioz's career. The Hungarian composer Franz Liszt was in the audience, marking the beginning not only of a long friendship between the two, but of the music of Berlioz becoming known by everyone involved in the Romantic movement. For a period of time, he was one of the most seminal musical minds in Europe. As Delacroix was to painting and Byron to English poetry, Berlioz was to music: the first complete Romantic.

Schumann

In 1835, Robert Schumann (1810–1856) published an article on Berlioz. Without hearing the *Symphonie Fantastique* (and having seen only a piano version of its score), the young Leipzig composer and writer was able to appreciate the originality of Berlioz's musical ideas. At the time, Schumann was the sole editor of *Neue Zeitschrift für Musik* ("New Journal for Music") and better known as a journalist than as a composer for the piano. He himself did not distinguish between the two; his purpose was to attack musical "philistinism" and raise musical taste, whether through articles or piano compositions. According to Schumann, German music since Beethoven had declined seriously. To enliven his crusade in the journal, he often posed some of his arguments as debates between Florestan and Eusebius, pseudonyms for two sides of his character. At times he was Florestan (hero of Beethoven's *Fidelio*): passionate and impetuous; at other times he was Eusebius (a fourth-century saint): reserved, cautious, and vulnerable.

Like Berlioz, Schumann was obsessed by a young woman: Clara Wieck, a concert pianist. However, Clara, unlike Harriet, was not just a fantasy; furthermore, she returned Schumann's love. The daughter of Schumann's piano teacher, Clara was a famous performer at 16 when she and Schumann (nine years older) fell in love. Unfortunately, her father, Friedrich Wieck, prevented them from seeing each other and even from exchanging letters. Schumann got so desperate that, when Clara was 19, he started legal proceedings against Wieck. (Many in the Leipzig music world, including Felix Mendelssohn, came to his support.) Amid the tension of the hearings, accusations, Wieck's stalling tactics, and, most poignantly, Clara and Robert's frustrated love, Schumann turned to writing *Lieder* (German songs). In fact he wrote more than 120 songs during the course of the crisis.

A German Lied (pl. Lieder) is a poem set to music. A Romantic Lied is almost always presented by a combination of voice and piano. Rather than simply accompanying the voice, the piano part shares equally in the task of illuminating the emotional content of the poem. Although solo songs go back to antiquity and were highly refined in the Renaissance, their full flowering as an art form was accomplished by Franz Schubert (1797–1828) who wrote more than 600. His songs, among the most beautiful ever written, vary from simple folk-like tunes to creations of sophisticated artistry. His piano accompaniments are especially inventive in their contribution to the mood or action of the text.

Among the many contrasts within Romantic music is that between super-large forms, like the *Symphonie Fantastique*, and very small forms, like the Lied. Both are simply two sides of the same coin. One, like Goethe's *Faust*, is powerful and overwhelming; the other, like a short poem by Wordsworth, demands a great deal from the reader/listener. To grasp the full meaning of an art song depends on refined taste and the ability to respond to the slightest nuance of form or feeling. Yet both large and small forms of Romantic music are committed to the exploration of emotion, especially the yearnings and conflicts of the human heart. Of the whole spectrum of Romantic themes, the art song leans to those that are acutely intimate, such as the melancholic heart, tender passion, and the confessional.

Schumann, inheriting the Lieder tradition from Schubert, made of it a completely Romantic idiom. Whereas Schubert's songs retain an element of classical balance, Schumann's are freer and less predictable. In content they are more psychological and autobiographical. They also reflect Schumann's more acute literary instincts. Having grown up in a bookish family and written poetry as a youngster, he had more feeling for prosody than any previous song-writer. Unlike Schubert, who occasionally set to music the lines of mediocre poets, Schumann used none but the finest of contemporary poets, such as Goethe and Heinrich Heine. Even so, the music, not the text, is the primary vehicle of meaning. For Schumann, setting a poem was not a matter of musically imitating words but of discovering its essence, its interior meaning, and refracting it through his own personality before expressing it musically. Sometimes music and text move together; sometimes they are in contrast; but always the music dominates. Theoretically, listening to a Schumann Lied and not knowing the German language would not prevent one from grasping its essence. This is true up to a point. Nevertheless, the ability to understand nineteenth-century German poetry (not just the German language) certainly enhances one's appreciation of both the text and the subtle interactions between text and music.

The fluctuating moods of Heine's poetry—between hope and pessimism and between tenderness and irony—perfectly suited Schumann's own changeable temperament. The *Liederkreis* (Opus 24), written in 1840, is a setting of nine of Heine's poems. The story of the third song, *Ich wandelte unter den Bäumen* ("I wandered amid the green trees"), is about a lonely man preoccupied with his grief who experiences old dreams and pain because some birds try to "steal his grief." When the birds, who have learned of a "golden word" from a young maiden, offer to tell the man the secret of his love, he refuses to hear it. Although the piano introduction contains a few unusual modulations, it employs traditional harmony and a slow, broad 4/4 meter, like a thoughtful hymn. This simplicity continues after the entry of the voice until the fourth line, "Und schlich mir ins Herz hinein" ("and stole into my heart"), when the rhythm vacillates and the music ceases to follow the words precisely (Fig. **5.31**). The change, however, is as subtle as a sigh. The same pattern is repeated in the eighth line ("I'll feel all my pain anew")

5.31 Extract from Schumann's setting of *Ich wandelte unter den Baumen*

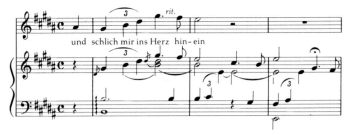

just prior to the birds' reply, which is sung quietly in a different key. After that, the song returns to its original 4/4 meter and harmonic simplicity as the man returns to the comfort of his loneliness and grief. As the musical scholar Martin Cooper explains:

> *The eeriness of the whole poem arises from the suggestion of the "secret" which the poet refuses to be told, although it would lighten his grief. It is this which gives the neurotic, "psycho-analytical" atmosphere to so many of Heine's poems, the suggestion of a split personality and a self-torturing, masochistic rapture beneath the conventional roses and nightingales.*[13]

If Cooper is right about Heine, then Schumann's musical embodiment is a subtle understatement of the poem's and Heine's intentions. The psychological atmosphere of Adelbert von Chamisso's poems in the song cycle, *Frauenliebe und Leben* ("A Woman's Love and Life"), is more conventionally Romantic. Of course the point of view, that of a woman, is also different. Here, one can imagine Clara's happiness and yearning as she thinks of Schumann. The second song, *Er, der Herrlichste von allen* ("He, the noblest of all") in words and music (Fig. **5.32**) is eulogistic, like a hymn of praise. Modern listeners, however, will question Chamisso's (and Schumann's) interpretation of the female mind and what it implies about the relationship between men and women. For example, the young woman is made to say of her lover, "... dedicated only to your fortune; a lowly maid you may not know, high star of splendor!" One is reminded of the relationship of Sophie to Émile in Rousseau's novel *Émile*.

Wagner

The music of Richard Wagner (1813–1883), unlike that of Schumann, is vocal music writ large. Indeed, a persistent stereotype of opera—huge choruses and overweight soloists dressed in medieval costume—is actually a caricature of a Wagnerian music-drama.

Wagner was, and still is, one of the most controversial figures in the history of the arts. During his lifetime the music world was split between his followers, who treated him like a god, and his detractors, who criticized both his music and his theories. Today, although the particular musical issues are no longer hotly debated, the assessment of Wagner—his music, the values he professed, and his place in history—still is. To some people, he represents the efflorescence of the whole Romantic movement; to others he is a symbol of decadence, both musical and cultural.

Probably more than any other, Wagner's music is intoxicating. Its effect on the senses is almost visceral, its effect on the mind hypnotic. It glories in dense textures of sound played by huge ensembles and in flowing musical lines marked by rich chromaticism (Fig. **5.33**). Although the dynamic contrasts are as extreme as those in Beethoven, they are less abrupt, more gradual, even than those in Berlioz. In addition, Wagner de-emphasized rhythm and virtually dispensed with conventional melodic phrasing, making it impossible to tell where one melody ends and another begins. His music is like a seamless continuity of sound, in which, as the conductor Pierre Boulez put it, "everything is melody, unending melody."[14] This dissolution of form is the musical counterpart of the swirling, formless storms of Turner's later paintings.

Dissatisfied with traditional opera, particularly its alternation of recitative and aria, Wagner created the *music-drama*. One distinguishing feature of this new form was

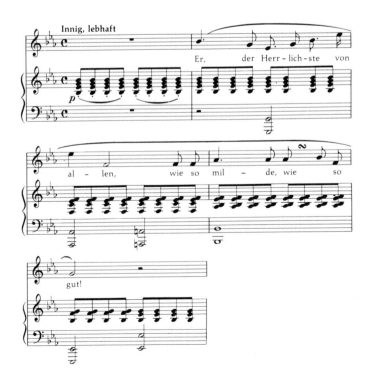

5.32 Extract from Schumann's setting of *Er, der Herrlichste von allen*

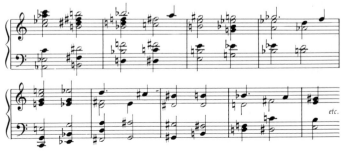

5.33 Theme from Wagner

the concept of the *leitmotif*—a melodic fragment standing for an object, character, situation, or idea. Though somewhat like Berlioz's *idée fixe*, leitmotifs are not confined to single themes. In *Tristan und Isolde*, for example, there is a different one for each character, the love potion, death, day, fate, and so forth. Relying on a continuous mosaic of melody fragments to structure his dramas, Wagner virtually eliminated the usual series of self-contained arias found in conventional operas. The other salient feature of the music-drama was the concept of *Gesamtkunstwerk*—the complete uniting of poetry, music, and theater. The idea of mixing media, of course, is as old as the idea of opera itself (see page 73). But the concept of *Gesamtkunstwerk* entails uniting the media so closely that the boundaries between them disappear and that all merge into one single, unified work of art. Wagner's purpose was to fuse plot, action, music, and meaning into an all-embracing, overwhelming experience. Because of the totality of his conceptions, it was necessary for him to write texts as well as scores and to provide complete instructions for executing productions. Indeed, to stage his music-dramas Wagner even designed a special theater, located in Bayreuth, Germany.

To the extent that the composer succeeded in his ambitions, his music was, and still is to some degree, criticized by those who see it as overstated and lacking in structure. Even more controversial is his obsessive nationalism. Ardent about not only the superiority of German music but also the quality of the German *Volk*, the mythical soul of the German people, Wagner peopled his stage with Teutonic knights and Norse gods, and blond and blue-eyed heroines and goddesses.

But everyone—friend or foe—agrees that Wagner's music, at times, is awesome in its beauty and power. Two of his greatest music-dramas, composed in mid-career, are *Tristan und Isolde* and *Die Meistersinger von Nurnberg* (The Mastersingers of Nuremberg). As a pair, they are complementary: *Tristan* is dark and serious; *Die Meistersinger* is light and cheerful, especially for Wagner.

The plot of *Tristan*, briefly, is as follows: Tristan, a knight, falls in love with Princess Isolde, the bride-to-be of his uncle, King Mark of Cornwall. When the two are discovered making love, Tristan, refusing to defend himself, is mortally wounded by one of the king's men. He lives long enough for his squire to take him back to his own castle. There he is joined by Isolde, and both die. Although the drama also includes Isolde's maid, other knights, courtiers, and sailors, it is entirely focused on the two lovers and their tragic passion. Wagner wrote *Tristan* while he himself was in love with Mathilde Wesendonk, wife of a close friend and patron. The themes of betrayal, adulterous love, and guilt illuminated in his opera thus

had parallels in his own life. Perhaps this is why, of the hundreds of operas about love, none expresses all-consuming sexual passion as vividly as *Tristan*. Wagner was a master at exploring human emotions—perhaps even subconscious impulses as well. Some of these are evoked through his skillful use of leitmotifs. But the most visceral ones are evoked through other aspects of the music: ceaseless chromaticism (in which the sense of a "home" key is lacking) expresses yearning. Languid melodic lines and dense tone colors embody sexual desire. And in the love duet of the Second Act, the gradual increase of the power and intensity of the music until it breaks out in soaring melody is a vivid portrayal of sexual union.

Die Meistersinger is a different world entirely. Set in sixteenth-century Nuremberg (unlike *Tristan*'s timeless, legendary setting), it is about a song-writing contest among members of the Mastersingers' Guild. The hero, Walther von Stolzing, with the help of a leading Mastersinger, the wise cobbler Hans Sachs, wins the contest and the hand in marriage of his sweetheart Eva, daughter of the Guild Master.

The contrast between *Die Meistersinger* and *Tristan* is striking: its characters—burghers, craftsmen, and apprentices—are drawn from real life rather than the abstract world of myth; its music is diatonic (confined to the five whole-steps and two half-steps of the major and minor scales) rather than chromatic; and its mood is comic and full of zest for life rather than tragic and serious. The opening bars of the two operas (Fig. **5.34**) illustrate their contrasting musical personalities.

The musical counterpart of genre painting, *Die Meistersinger* is Wagner's affectionate tribute to ordinary people. Yet it is anything but simple-minded. Through its celebration of the German *Volk* it allegorizes the nineteenth-century dream of German nationhood. It also allegorizes the issues of nineteenth-century music: Walther, whose

5.34 Opening bars of *Tristan und Isolde* and *Die Meistersinger*

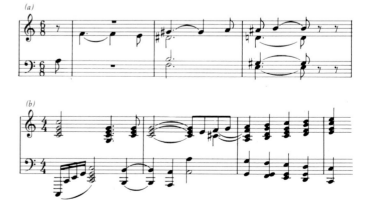

music is at first rejected by the Mastersingers, represents the innovative side of Wagner, frequently in conflict with the musical establishment; Sachs, rooted in ancient musical tradition (though still able to accept the new) represents his more conservative side; while the ridiculous Beckmesser, Walther's rival, who tallies Walther's many mistakes in his trial song, is a caricature of one of Wagner's harshest critics. The music itself is a happy resolution of the dramatic conflict: a transmutation of earlier, simpler musical styles into the new language of music-drama.

Late Romantic Music

Every important musician in Europe knew Wagner, or at least his music. Liszt was the father of his second wife, Cosima. Berlioz met him in Paris and Dresden. Mendelssohn and Schumann entertained him in Leipzig. Charles Gounod (1818–1893) and Camille Saint-Saens (1835–1921) attended his salon in Paris. Anton Bruckner (1824–1896), Peter Ilyich Tchaikovsky (1840–1893), Edvard Grieg (1843–1907), Gustav Mahler (1860–1911), and Saint-Saens attended his festivals at Bayreuth. His greatest rival, the opera composer Giuseppe Verdi (1813–1901), never met him, but attended the first performance of *Lohengrin.*

Despite his considerable reputation as an opera composer, Wagner's influence on opera was not as great as one might have expected. Verdi's later operas compare in orchestral richness and dramatic intensity with Wagner's, but they are still clearly in the Italian operatic tradition. They contain recognizable arias, although the musical texture is more integrated than in earlier operas. The lush orchestration in the works of Giacomo Puccini (1858–1924), Verdi's successor in Italian opera, could be attributed to the influence of Verdi as well as Wagner.

Wagner's legacy was strongest in the field of orchestral music, which, in the late nineteenth century, was divided between followers of Johannes Brahms (1833–1897) and followers of Wagner. Although Brahms's music was Romantic in its scale and expansiveness, its masterly structure, notably in the use of the sonata form, made it a link with Beethoven and the Classical period. The influence of both Wagner and Brahms can be heard in the music of Bruckner, Mahler, Saint-Saens, and Edward Elgar (1857–1934), while that of Wagner can be heard especially in the music of Richard Strauss (1864–1949). Well known for his *symphonic poems* (programmatic orchestral compositions in one movement), Strauss used orchestral music to develop character, describe action, and tell stories. Such concert favorites as *Don Quixote* and *Till Eulenspiegel* contain abrupt key changes, lyrical melodies, and rich orchestration which bear the stamp of Wagner.

The major point is that all of these composers wrote music in the Romantic style well into the 1880s and '90s. By contrast, both literature and painting had experienced at least two major new movements by this time: Realism and Naturalism (in literature), and Realism and Impressionism (in art). (Indeed, the 1890s saw the beginning of *Post-Impressionism.*) Some of the composers we have discussed were writing Romantic music in the early twentieth century, when the visual arts had been swept up into the Modern movement. Arnold Schoenberg, (1874–1951), another of Wagner's musical heirs, can be contrasted with Strauss. Whereas Strauss generally followed *Die Meistersinger*'s path of diatonic harmony, Schoenberg followed *Tristan*'s chromaticism. Before long he transformed this heritage into a style that was highly intellectual and the very opposite of Romantic. Schoenberg became one of the most important and influential of modern composers. But that is a story for another chapter.

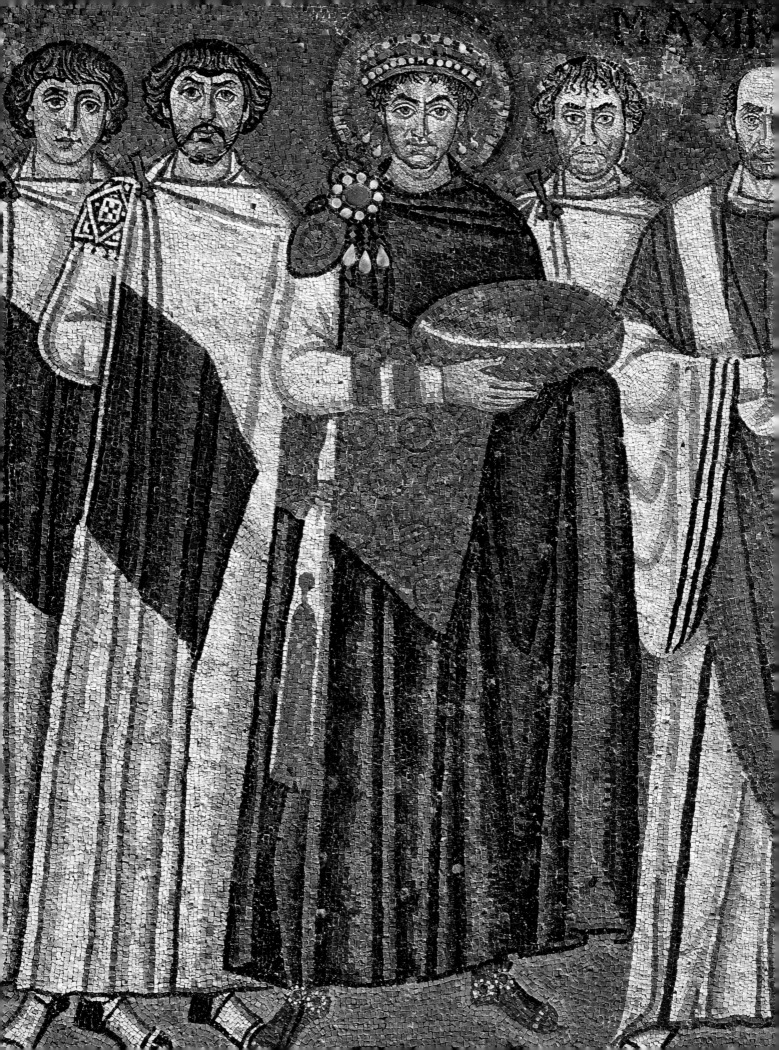

CHAPTER SIX

Christianity I

*In the beginning was the Word,
and the Word was with God and
the Word was God.*

JOHN 1:1

Introduction

"But when the time had fully come, God sent forth his Son" (Galatians 4:4). Thus the apostle Paul saw the coming of Christ as the consummation of God's purpose to bless all of mankind through a descendant of Abraham (Galatians 3:16; cf. Genesis 22:18). There were also political and cultural circumstances that support the view that the coming of Christ and the subsequent rise of Christianity occurred at the appropriate historical moment.

After the Babylonian conquest of Judah in 587 BC, the leading Jews were taken as exiles to Babylon. Many never returned to Judah, and others migrated to the various cities of the Mediterranean world, especially Alexandria in Egypt. Thus began the Diaspora, or dispersion of the Jews. This, plus the fact that there were Jewish synagogues in most of the places where Jews were living, assured Paul and other Christian missionaries of audiences that would understand the Scriptures in the cities they sought to evangelize.

Because of Alexander the Great's conquests during the late fourth century BC the use of the Greek language had become nearly universal in the Mediterranean world. Thus the spread of the Christian faith was immensely facilitated because the Christian evangelists were able to preach their message in a common tongue throughout much of the Roman Empire. Indeed, the New Testament, though most of its authors were Christianized Jews, was written in the Greek language. Moreover, the Hebrew Scriptures had been translated into Greek (the Septuagint), a translation used by the early Christians in their proclamations of the Gospel (there was no New Testament until much later). Numerous New Testament quotations from the Old Testament are taken from the Septuagint.

Various conditions within the Roman Empire also facilitated the spread of Christianity. The birth of Jesus occurred in the reign of Augustus Caesar, who had assumed power as the first Roman emperor but under the outward forms of the defunct Republic. In his reign the *Pax Romana* ("peace of Rome") was imposed upon the Mediterranean world, providing the stability and protection that facilitated relatively safe travel within the Empire. Excellent roads made land travel more feasible, and travel by sea was made safer by the fact that piracy had been almost completely suppressed. Moreover, human energies were not being drained away by constant warfare. All of these factors contributed to the rapid spread of Christianity under Roman rule, as is evident from the story of Paul's missionary journeys in the Book of Acts.

Other less tangible factors also prepared the way for the rise of the Christian faith. The classical religion of the Greeks and the Romans had run its course; indeed, belief

6.2 Early Christianity

DATES	SOCIAL AND POLITICAL DEVELOPMENTS	LITERATURE AND PHILOSOPHY	VISUAL ARTS	ARCHITECTURE	MUSIC

0	Birth of Apostle Paul
	Nero
	
	Beginnings of ascetic
	  monasticism
		Books of New Testament
		
		Manichaeism
			Catacomb paintings (6.8)		Responsorial chanting
					
					Oral church music/
					  chants
					Psalms
					Holy Eucharist

300
 	
400
 	
500
	Constantine declares
	  Christianity a legal
	  religion
	Constantine moves capital
	  to Constantinople
	Sack of Rome by Visigoths
	
	Council of Chalcedon
		St Augustine: *Confessions*
		  and *City of God* (6.6)
		
		Boethius' *Philosophy of
		  Music*
			Sarcophagus of
			  Julius Bassius (6.18)
			
			Mosaic: Parting of Lot
			and Abraham (6.17)
				Arch of Constantine
				  (6.10)
				Santa Costanza c. 350
				  (6.15)
				
				Santa Maria Maggiore
				  (6.12)
					Ambrosian lyre
					
					Divine Office
					Boethius' development
					  of church modes

600	Pope Gregory		Apse mosaics, S. Vitale (6.27)	Hagia Sophia (6.20) S Vitale, Ravenna (6.26)	Gregorian Chant Reorganization of Schola Cantorum

in the traditional gods and goddesses was derided by intellectuals. Some of the ancient cults remained in place, but largely for their social and political value. Emperor worship was supported by the state because of the political stability it provided, but it did not supply any sense of personal salvation. Many people turned to the mystery religions for gratification of this longing. These religions—developed around such figures as Orpheus, Magna Mater (the Great Mother), Osiris, and Mithra—centered on myths about the death and resurrection of savior gods. Worshipers could share in the immortality of these gods by participating in sacramental rites, such as baptism and communion, which guaranteed new birth. Although similarities to the Christian faith are obvious, a distinction must be drawn: mystery religions were founded upon myths about gods who died and arose annually, not, as was Christianity, upon a remarkable historical person. The popularity of these cults, however, bespoke a universal longing for redemption and immortality, such as were offered in the Christian Gospel.

At the heart of the faith of the early Church was the story of the redemptive death and resurrection of Christ, termed the *kerygma* ("the thing preached"). An early example of *kerygma* is found in the apostle Paul's first letter to the church of Corinth (I Cor. 15:1–4). (Paul's letters provide the earliest documentary evidence of the faith and life of the first-century Church.) Here Paul reveals that his preaching focused on the death and resurrection of Christ. Paul's teaching on the Lord's Supper, or Eucharist, was also based on the death and resurrection (I Cor. 11:23–26). Moreover, the ceremony of baptism practiced by the early Church was a re-enactment of the death, burial, and resurrection of Jesus (Romans 6:3–4).

In his first letter to the Corinthians, Paul identifies the fundamental credo of the early Christians: "Jesus is Lord" (I Cor. 12:3). Consisting of only two words in Greek, this simple statement has been identified as the earliest Christian confession of faith. Despite its brevity, it was a creed with profound implications for the early Christians as they sought to work out in their lives the meaning of the Lordship of Jesus. In their relationship to the Roman government, for example, their commitment to Jesus as their only Lord prevented them from acknowledging Caesar as Lord; they were thus regarded as political dissidents—as was their Lord—dangerous to the stability of the Empire.

Indeed, persecution was an important factor in the growth of the early Church. The Carthaginian theologian Tertullian wrote, "The blood of the martyrs is the seed" (of the Church). At first, persecution was spasmodic and local. Later, however, Nero blamed the Christians for the burning of Rome and used them as scapegoats (AD 64),

mounting a savage attack on them in the city and its environs. More general persecutions in the Empire occurred later in the third and early fourth centuries.

Opposition to the Christian movement, according to the Gospels, had begun even during the ministry of Jesus. Although popular with the masses, at least for a time, he was strongly opposed by the religious leaders of his people, largely on the grounds that his teachings were heretical and his claims for himself blasphemous. The apostle Paul encountered opposition to his mission to the Gentiles both from within and without the Church. In the second and third centuries, the young Church was greatly strengthened in its struggle with its critics by the addition to its membership of able intellectuals such as Justin Martyr, Irenaeus, Tertullian, and Origen. Such leaders, called "Church Fathers," wrote sophisticated works defending the Christian faith which both answered the critics and sharpened the definitions of that faith.

Eventually, however, despite opposition, Christianity gained such a foothold in the Empire that the Roman Emperor Constantine himself was converted; in 313, he declared it a legal religion. In 395, it became the official religion of the state. This state recognition of the Church was, according to some historians, a devastating development, because it marked the beginnings of the Church's involvement in politics and consequent deterioration of its spiritual vitality. The emperors gained effective control over the Church in the Eastern Empire after Constantine moved the capital to Constantinople (Byzantium) in AD 330. The Emperor Justinian, for example, defined true doctrine and, in large measure, controlled Church administration. In the Western Empire, however, the papacy exercised greater authority because of imperial weakness in Italy. Indeed, when the Roman Empire went into decline under the onslaught of the Gothic invasions, the Roman Church picked up the reins of authority.

Doctrinally and institutionally the Roman Church gained strength in the fourth and fifth centuries. More precise and authoritarian definitions of Church doctrine, development of the liturgy, and growth of the hierarchy—all characterized the Roman Church's history during this period. Basic Christian theology was summed up in the Nicene Creed (Council of Nicea, 325), and the Creed of Chalcedon (Council of Chalcedon, 451). St. Ambrose's contributions to hymnology and the liturgy and the brilliant writings of St. Augustine, which became the foundation for Catholic theology, also appeared in this era. In 445, Leo I, one of the ablest of the Roman popes, declared that the Bishop of Rome was the successor to the authority of St. Peter. The authority of the Roman hierarchy was an important unifying factor in the cultural and political chaos that followed the barbarian invasions.

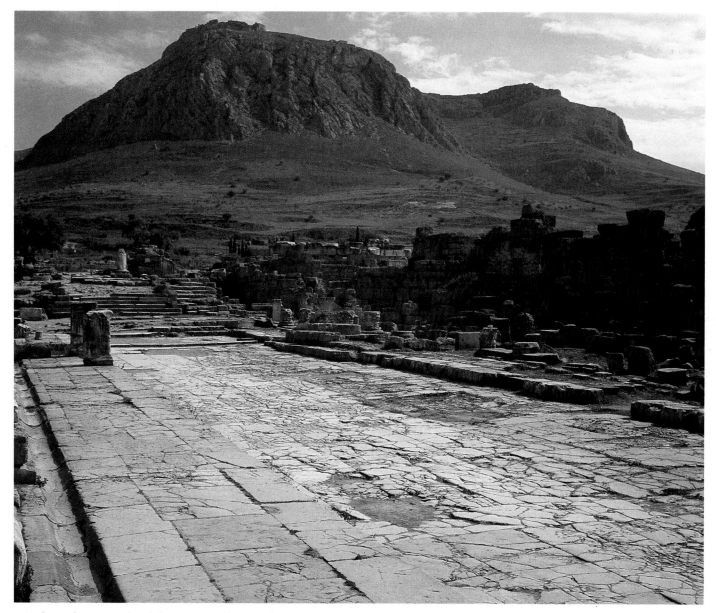

6.3 The Lechaion Road and the Acrocorinth, Corinth, Greece

Moreover, the scholars and manuscript copyists of the Western Church sustained the Christian tradition and were responsible for the preservation of the classical writings, which otherwise might have sunk into oblivion in Western Europe.

The Christian story is anchored in the real and the tangible. It is linked with such historical figures as Caesar Augustus, Herod the Great, and Pontius Pilate—not with a legendary past. Unlike Gnosticism, its main rival, and other such dualistic systems of thought, which taught that matter was sinful, Christianity sanctified matter through the belief that God created the world and that he revealed himself in human flesh (John 1:1–3, 14). Thus the Christian faith consecrated life in this world. It is no

surprise, then, that this faith has been a prime source of artistic inspiration, for the artist celebrates the tangible, the concrete. The story of Christianity in Europe, cannot be told without at the same time telling the story of European art. And the Christian story itself has often been told most effectively through art, especially for those in the early and medieval Church who were incapable of reading the Gospels or without access to them. Indeed, art and Christianity are, for much of the history of Western civilization, inextricably connected—Christian faith supplying the subject matter and inspiration; Christian artists providing the talents which, they believed, were gifts of the God who had redeemed them in Christ.

Literature

The New Testament

No other book can compare with the New Testament in its impact on Western civilization. The word "testament" (or "covenant"), modified by the adjective "new," implies both a contrast and a comparison with the Old Testament, which tells the story of the Exodus (God's deliverance of his people Israel from Egyptian slavery), the subsequent covenant he made with them through Moses at Mt. Sinai (Exodus 19–20:19), and of the development in Israel's history of that special relationship (see Chapter 1). More than six centuries after the Exodus, the prophet Jeremiah (31:31–34) spoke of a "new covenant" that God would one day make with his people; the early Christians believed that this prediction was fulfilled in Jesus of Nazareth. The new covenant thus emerged from the old.

The documents of the New Testament are the outgrowth of this covenant and are the main sources for our knowledge of early Christianity. These documents, how-ever, were not written in the infancy of that faith. The earliest of the New Testament books was written about 20 years, and the latest about 70 years, after Jesus' crucifixion. Thus the New Testament is the product of various Christian communities which were proclaiming the Gospel ("good news") of salvation in Christ and preserving the Christian tradition through oral communication long before the books of the New Testament were even completed—let alone gathered into a single authoritative collection. The New Testament sources, therefore, reflect both the beginnings of the Christian faith in the ministry of Jesus and the developing beliefs and practices of the Church as it sought to establish itself in an alien world. These are the documents upon which we are largely dependent for our knowledge of Christianity in the first century of our era.

The first four books of the New Testament, the Gospels, contain accounts of the life and teachings of Jesus. Three of these (Matthew, Mark, and Luke) are designated the

6.4

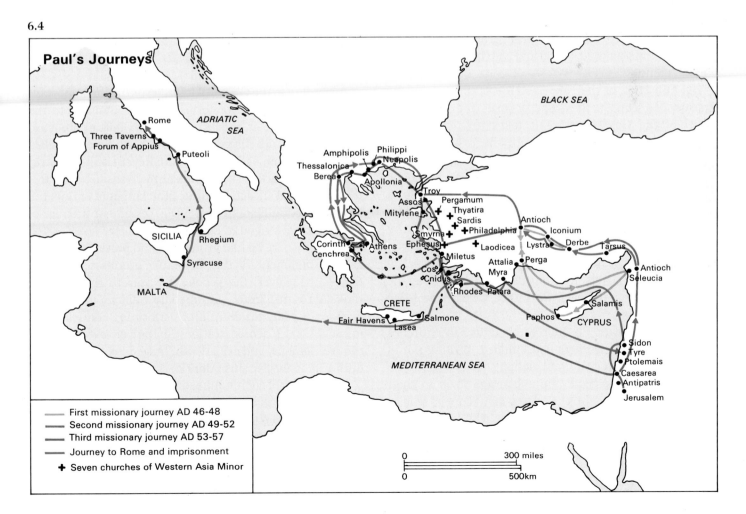

Paul's Journeys

BLACK SEA

ADRIATIC SEA

Rome
Three Taverns
Forum of Appius
Puteoli

Amphipolis · Philippi
Neapolis
Thessalonica
Berea
Apollonia

Troy
Assos · Pergamum
Mitylene · Thyatira
Sardis
Smyrna · Philadelphia
Ephesus · Laodicea
Miletus

Antioch
Iconium
Lystra · Derbe
Tarsus
Attalia · Perga
Myra

Antioch
Seleucia

SICILIA
Rhegium
Syracuse

Corinth
Cenchrea · Athens

Cos
Cnidus
Rhodes · Patara

Salamis
Paphos · CYPRUS

MALTA

CRETE
Fair Havens · Salmone
Lasea

Sidon
Tyre
Ptolemais
Caesarea
Antipatris
Jerusalem

MEDITERRANEAN SEA

— First missionary journey AD 46-48
— Second missionary journey AD 49-52
— Third missionary journey AD 53-57
— Journey to Rome and imprisonment
✚ Seven churches of Western Asia Minor

0   300 miles
0   500km

Synoptic Gospels (Greek *synopsis*, a "viewing together"), because they include many of the same events presented in much the same order. The Gospel of John is quite different from the Synoptics. It includes many discourses of Jesus and events in his life not contained in the other Gospels. It also attempts to plumb the theological depths of the personality of Jesus in a manner not typical of the Synoptics. Thus it begins, not with narratives of the virgin birth, as do Matthew and Luke, but with Jesus as the pre-existent Word (Greek *Logos*) sharing in the deity of God and his creation of the universe.

Strictly speaking, the Gospels are not biographies. Indeed, they do not contain adequate material for a biography of Jesus. Rather, they are selective and interpretive accounts of his life and teachings which emphasize who he was and what he came to do, those factors essential for the preaching and teaching of the early Christians. Apart from the Nativity stories in Matthew and Luke, they focus on a few events in the last three years of his life, including detailed accounts of the few days preceding his crucifixion—an indication of the significance for the early Christians of his death and resurrection. The profound influence of the Gospels on Western religion and culture suggests that the peculiar focus of the authors has been effective. Although they have not provided us with a photographic likeness of Jesus, they have painted a vivid and convincing composite portrait of him.

The fifth book of the New Testament, the Acts of the Apostles, is a sequel to the Gospel of Luke—for that matter, to all of the Gospels, since it takes up the story of Christianity where they end, with the resurrection of Jesus, and then goes on to tell the story of the spread of the Christian faith along the roads that led to Rome. The Book of Acts is strategically located in the New Testament, for it is not only a sequel to the Gospels but also background for several of the books that follow, especially those written by St. Paul, whose conversion from a zealous persecutor of Christians to a passionate proclaimer of the Gospel of Christ is related in Acts. As many as 13 of the books of the New Testament have been attributed to Paul by some modern scholars.

For the most part, Paul wrote his letters to churches that he and his co-workers had founded. Writing out of deep pastoral concern, Paul sought to answer their questions and to instruct and encourage them in their newly received faith. Thus his letters should not be read as highly organized theological treatises. His letter to the Romans comes closest to being a systematic presentation of the Gospel he preached.

The non-Pauline "catholic" (general) epistles (for example, James and I John) are those not written to specific churches or individuals. The anonymous "letter" to the Hebrews (actually, more a treatise than a letter) was written to show the superiority of the Christian faith to the law of Moses. Finally, the Book of Revelation is an example of Christian apocalyptic writing, a highly symbolic representation of the conflict between Christ and Satan which proclaims that Christ and his kingdom will ultimately be victorious (Rev. 17:14).

The dynamic force that generated the documents of the New Testament and the cause of their profound influence on the world was Jesus of Nazareth. Who was he? The New Testament declares that he was both human and divine, the son of the Virgin Mary and the Son of God. His birth must have occurred sometime prior to 4 BC, since Herod the Great, who sought his life, according to Matthew, died in that year. He apparently learned the trade of carpenter from his father Joseph (Mark 6:3; cf. Matthew 13:55). At the age of 30 he presented himself for baptism to John the Baptist, whose role as the forerunner of Christ is revealed in all of the Gospels. This marked the beginning of Jesus' public ministry—the significance is marked by the Holy Spirit's descent upon him in the form of a dove and the declaration of the voice from heaven, "This is my beloved Son, with whom I am well pleased" (Matt. 3:16–17). After his baptism, the Synoptics tell us, Jesus was led by the Spirit into the wilderness. There he rejected Satan's efforts to divert him from his divine destiny as a suffering Messiah (Matt. 4:1–11)..

According to the Gospel of John, Jesus had an important ministry in Judaea prior to his Galilean ministry. In the Synoptics, however, the focus is on his Galilean ministry, which began with his proclamation, "The time is fulfilled and the kingdom of God is at hand: Repent and believe in the gospel" (Mark 1:15). Significantly, Jesus here declares that his appearance inaugurates the kingdom of God, the long-delayed fulfillment of the Old Testament promise of the Messianic kingdom. Early in his ministry Jesus visited Nazareth, where he had grown up, and presented himself as the fulfillment of the Messianic promises in Isaiah 61:1–2. However, the people of Nazareth rejected him (Luke 4:16–30). Jesus continued his Galilean ministry for perhaps a year, teaching and performing miracles. His miracles were demonstrations of power over disease, nature, demons, and even death. Indeed, he even claimed authority to forgive sins (Mark 2:1–12).

In the light of such a ministry, it is not surprising that Jesus, for a time at least, was enormously popular with the people. But this popularity faded, according to the Gospel of John, when it became apparent that Jesus would not allow himself to be crowned a Messianic king (John 6:14—15). His reason for refusing becomes apparent in an episode, recorded in the Synoptics, that occurred at

Caesarea Philippi. Here Peter, speaking for all the Apostles of Jesus, declared him to be the Messiah, Israel's promised redeemer. Though accepting this confession, Jesus warned his disciples not to publicize his identity as the Messiah, for he must suffer at the hands of the religious leaders, be put to death, and finally be raised from the dead (Mark 8:27–33). Indeed, all of the Gospels focus on the rejection, suffering, and death of Jesus as essential to his redemptive role and as the prelude to his resurrection. But a suffering Messiah was impossible for the Jewish mind to accept—the Messiah was to be a conquering king! What, then, was the source of this concept of a suffering Messiah? The answer is, the Suffering Servant poems of Isaiah, especially Isaiah 53 (see Chapter 1). Apparently it was Jesus himself who, for the first time in Jewish tradition, linked the Suffering Servant theme of Isaiah with the Messianic role. This conception of redemptive suffering has had a profound influence on the formulation of the message of the Gospel and on Christian tradition, as illustrated by the countless works of art dramatizing Jesus' death upon the cross. It is expressed in the conviction that on the cross, as Paul puts it, Christ "died for all" and that there God "through Christ reconciled us to himself" (II Cor. 5:15, 18).

According to the Gospels, Jesus, throughout his ministry, encountered opposition from the religious leaders and teachers of his own people, who resented his popularity and considered his teaching heretical and blasphemous. This opposition rose to a crescendo in the last week of his life and climaxed in his crucifixion. He had returned to Jerusalem to observe the Passover with his Apostles; but shortly after he had done so, he was arrested in the Garden of Gethsemane by temple soldiers led to him by Judas Iscariot, one of his twelve Apostles, who had made a deal with the chief priest to betray him (Matt. 26:14–16). During his trial Jesus did not deny that he was the Messiah and the Son of God. Consequently, the Sanhedrin (the Jewish high court) "condemned him as deserving death" (Mark 14:64). Since Rome alone could administer the death penalty (John 18:31), Jesus was taken before Pontius Pilate, the Roman governor of Judaea. But Pilate, realizing that Jesus had no political aspirations, sought to release him. Certain religious leaders, however, stirred up the crowds to shout for his crucifixion, and Pilate had to order Jesus to be put to death by Roman soldiers.

It must be noted that some New Testament scholars, both Jewish and Christian, are convinced that it was the Romans who were actually responsible for the execution of Jesus and not—as the Gospels claim—Jesus' Jewish opponents. Another view is that the responsibility rests with a relatively small number of Jewish religious leaders who, seeing Jesus as a threat to their authority and influence, manipulated the crowd so as to bring about his execution.

Because of his death, the disciples of Jesus seemed to lose faith in his Messiahship (Luke 24:11). Thus the Gospels do not support the view that the disciples were wistfully hoping that Jesus would somehow overcome death. Yet they are unanimous in reporting that he did so. All of the Gospels attest that Jesus appeared to his disciples after his resurrection—appearances that continued over a period of 40 days, according to Acts 1:3. Then, having instructed the Apostles to make disciples of all nations, he ascended to his Father, assuring his followers that he would be with them to "the close of the age" (Matt. 28:18–20). The Book of Acts traces the beginning of the fulfillment of this mission.

This discussion of the beginnings of Christianity has focused on the death and resurrection of Jesus, for it is the proclamation of these events and of their significance that is the heart of the New Testament and that best explains the rapid spread of the Christian faith in the Roman world. As charismatic as was Jesus himself, as persuasive as were his teachings, they do not adequately account for the remarkable success of the Gospel in the early centuries of the Christian era. The religious malaise that permeated the Roman world, the longing for spiritual and moral rebirth, could not be satisfied by the old gods. Many people hoped for an intervention in human affairs that would give assurance of divine concern and forgiveness, the opportunity to begin anew and a hope reaching beyond death. The Christian proclamation that God had revealed himself in the compassionate Jesus, who, because of his great love, had died on the cross to make forgiveness and new life available to all, and whose right to die for others and power over death had been demonstrated in his resurrection—this was the message that satisfied the longings of many people of the first century—and beyond.

St. Augustine

Aurelius Augustinus (354–430), second only to St. Paul (excluding Jesus, of course) in his influence on the formulation of Christian thought, was born at Tagaste in North Africa of a Christian mother, Monica, and a pagan father, Patricius. His devout mother naturally wished her son to be a Christian, but her hopes were not to be realized for many years to come. Augustine received his early education in Tagaste and a neighboring town, but shortly after reaching the age of 16 he traveled to Carthage to complete his studies.

There he studied rhetoric, developing a special interest in Virgil and Cicero. There also he took a mistress, whom he never names; she bore him a son, Adeodatus. While

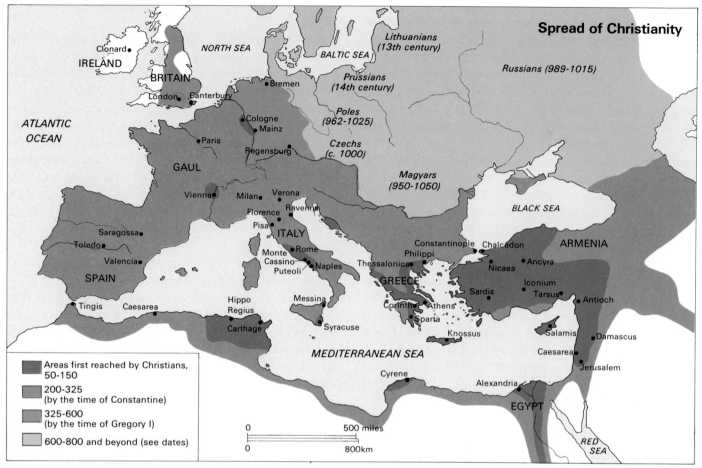

Spread of Christianity

Clonard •
IRELAND
NORTH SEA
BALTIC SEA
Lithuanians (13th century)
Russians (989-1015)
BRITAIN
• Bremen
London •
Canterbury
Prussians (14th century)
ATLANTIC OCEAN
Cologne •
Mainz
Poles (962-1025)
Paris •
Regensburg
Czechs (c. 1000)
GAUL
Magyars (950-1050)
Vienna •
Milan •
Verona •
BLACK SEA
Florence •
Ravenna
Pisa •
ITALY
Saragossa •
Rome •
Constantinople
Chalcedon
ARMENIA
Toledo •
Monte Cassino
Philippi
Ancyra •
Nicaea •
Valencia •
Puteoli
Naples •
Thessalonica •
Iconium •
SPAIN
GREECE
Sardis •
Tarsus •
Antioch
Tingis •
Caesarea
Hippo Regius
Messina
Corinth •
Athens •
Salamis •
Damascus
Sparta •
Knossus •
Caesarea •
Carthage •
Syracuse •
Jerusalem
MEDITERRANEAN SEA
Cyrene •
Alexandria •
Caesarea •
EGYPT
RED SEA

Areas first reached by Christians, 50-150
200-325 (by the time of Constantine)
325-600 (by the time of Gregory I)
600-800 and beyond (see dates)

0   500 miles
0   800km

6.5

studying in Carthage, Augustine was converted to Manichaeism, a religion that he was to profess for almost ten years. Its teachings seemed to solve a problem that had baffled him: how there could be evil in a world created by a good God. According to the Manichees (named for Mani, a religious teacher martyred in Persia in AD 277), there were in the beginning two principles, Good and Evil, or Light and Darkness. Because evil invaded the realm of good, the two became intermingled. Thus matter is made up of a mixture of both good and evil, in conflict with one another. For Augustine, this view offered an explanation of the problem of evil in that it posited an independent realm of evil. (After his conversion he sought to solve this problem by arguing that evil does not have an independent existence but is the absence of being.) As the result of an encounter with Faustus, a Manichaean bishop of inflated reputation who was unable to resolve the serious doubts that were plaguing him, Augustine finally became disillusioned with Manichaeism.

After he had completed his studies, Augustine taught rhetoric for a few years at Carthage and Tagaste. Because of the undisciplined behavior of his African students, however, he determined to go to Rome. There he came under the influence of the Skeptics, who argued that sure knowledge of the physical world was impossible because of the unreliability of our sensory experiences. Augustine was a seeker after knowledge, especially religious knowledge, but how could one hope to attain sure knowledge of God if even mundane knowledge was only a matter of opinion?

Augustine was delivered from this agnosticism by Neoplatonism, the philosophy that also influenced such Renaissance figures as Pico della Mirandola and Michelangelo (see Chapter 3). Indeed, this philosophy was to become a bridge to his conversion and a permanent component of his fully developed theology. For Augustine, the One, the pure being at the apex of the ascending order of being in Neoplatonism, was the God revealed in Scripture and the teaching of the Church. In this God, posited in Neoplatonism and revealed in Scripture, Augustine discovered the true goal of his philosophical quest. Thus, intellectually, Augustine was ready for conversion. His passions, however, especially his sexual passion, dictated otherwise.

In the meantime he once more became discouraged with his students' lack of discipline (this time in Rome) and moved on to Milan. There he was joined by his devoted mother and came under the influence of St. Ambrose, whose learning and eloquence made a deep impression upon him. He learned from Ambrose that Scripture need not be interpreted literally, that depths of meaning previously unknown to him lay in the allegorical exegesis of the Bible. This experience also removed a stumbling block for Augustine, for he had once thought that the Bible was unworthy of the attention of the true philosopher.

The crisis that broke through the impasse in which Augustine found himself—poised between the old life of his passions and the new of Christian conversion—is the subject of one of the best-known scenes in his famous autobiographical work, the *Confessions*. He relates how he was once weeping over his bondage to sin, when he heard from a neighboring garden the voice of a child chanting, "Take up and read." He was puzzled because he knew of no child's game that involved such a chant. Concluding that the words were a divine admonition to look into the Scriptures, he seized a copy of Paul's epistles and began reading. The passage upon which his eyes first fell was Romans 13:13–14: "Not in reveling and drunkenness, not in debauchery and licentiousness, not in quarrelling and jealousy. But put on the Lord Jesus Christ, and make no provision for the flesh to gratify its desires." At this point, he tells us, he "had no wish to read more and no need to do so. For in an instant, as I came to the end of the sentence, it was as though the light of confidence flooded into my heart and all the darkness of doubt was dispelled."[1] Thus Augustine broke with his past and was converted in July, AD 386. He was baptized by Ambrose at Milan on April 25 (Easter week) of the next year. Shortly afterward, he returned to Tagaste (without his mother, who had died on the journey).

Having forsaken his teaching profession, Augustine devoted himself to meditation and theological studies. Later he moved to Hippo, a city on the coast north of Tagaste. There he was ordained a priest in AD 391; five years later he was consecrated Bishop of Hippo. His administrative responsibilities in this office compelled him to study closely the nature of the Church and to defend its teachings. The result was a voluminous body of theological writings whose concepts were to shape the thinking of Christian scholars and Church leaders for many centuries to come. Indeed, his writings continue to be a rich source for theologians. Augustine lived in Hippo until his death, which occurred in the midst of a siege by the Vandals.

Of Augustine's many writings the most widely known today are the *Confessions* and *The City of God*. The former was completed in AD 400; the latter in 426. *The City of God*, on which Augustine worked for some 13 years, was his

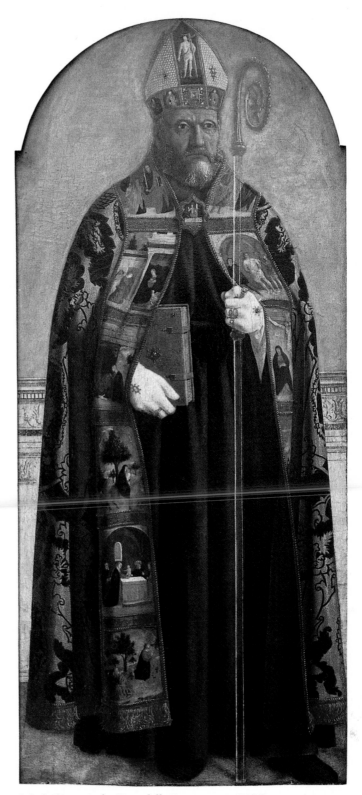

6.6 *St Augustine* by Piero della Francesca, c. 1465

response to the criticism of Christianity rising out of the Visigoths' sacking of Rome in 410. This event shocked the world, for Rome had been for centuries the center of a great civilization. Those pagans who resented Christianity's status as the official religion of the Empire argued that the cause of this catastrophe was the abandonment of the old gods who had protected Rome, in favor of the impotent God of the Christians. Thus the question of the meaning of history was raised; and Augustine responded with his monumental *The City of God*.

Augustine's philosophy of history is based on the idea that there are two cities in the world, the City of God and the City of Satan. The latter originated with the rebellion of certain angels against God and manifested itself in this world with the disobedience of Adam. The City of God consists of angels and humans who are loyal to God—specifically, since the coming of Christ, those who are believers in him and members of his Church. Rome, like Babylon and all worldly powers, was a manifestation of the City of Satan. Its downfall therefore, was not the calamity the pagans imagined it to be. Ultimately, all such powers will be destroyed, for the Church alone is the earthly representation of the City of God. Although the City of Satan and the City of God are mingled together in this world, at the final judgment they will be decisively and eternally separated.

The *Confessions*, Augustine's spiritual autobiography, is undoubtedly his most widely read book today. It has been described as "one of the greatest books ever composed in Latin, famous not only for its deep religious fervor and its tumultuous emotions, but for its psychological insight and its vast descriptive powers."[2] It was written a few years after Augustine's conversion, in the form of a confession/prayer to God. Unlike Rousseau in his *Confessions*, (see Chapter 5), Augustine was not confessing to other human beings, seeking their sympathy. From the very outset he is addressing God, praising him for his grace in redeeming him, despite his waywardness, and lamenting the things that separate him from God. However, the book is also addressed indirectly to other humans as well as to God. That is, Augustine wrote the book to edify and instruct his fellow Christians, who are allowed to "eavesdrop" on his confessions. But his primary concern is his confession to the God who discerns his innermost thoughts and motives.

In the first nine books he tells how he came to experience the redemption that he now enjoys; and thus they constitute a kind of autobiography. (Book 10 deals with his present life, while books 11–13 are a commentary on Genesis 1:1–2:2.) It is important to note that he selects those memories that suit his purpose, which is to reveal a pattern of providence in his life. He evaluates and interprets these memories from the perspective of his present state as a mature Christian thinker. For example, he relates an incident from his youth in which he and some friends stole some pears, then uses this to illustrate a moral point. He had not really wanted the pears (they were thrown to some pigs) but the pleasure of stealing; it was the sin itself that he "relished and enjoyed."

The *Confessions* are shaped by Augustine in keeping with his profound conviction that his earlier life—his lust for worldly achievement, his sexual adventures, his attraction to Manichaeism—was a demonstration of divine providence at work preparing him for conversion to Christ. Providence was also revealed in the fact that, despite his waywardness, he never gave up his search for Truth. Ultimately, therefore, he was confronted by Reality, Christ himself, and was compelled to decide. This is the moment toward which the *Confessions* are directed, and it is this climax that dictates Augustine's choice and interpretation of episodes from his earlier life.

Augustine is a highly significant transition figure between Classical antiquity and the Middle Ages. Steeped in classical literature and philosophy, he is a Roman writer who lived through the fall of classical civilization and summed up its destiny in a comprehensive philosophy of history. But he is also a medieval writer, employing faith and reason to combat the heresies that threatened to split the Church, thus assuring its survival and laying the foundations that shaped Christian theology down to the thirteenth century. The sixteenth-century Protestant reformers also studied Augustine's theology, particularly his teaching on grace, in their attempt to recover a biblical faith. Indeed, "without St. Augustine's massive intellect and deep spiritual perception, Western theology would never have taken the shape in which it is familiar to us."[3]

Augustine's *Confessions* are important as the earliest example of an authentic autobiography and as the first contemporary account of the childhood of a major historical figure. The work is also highly regarded because of its psychological penetration of the religious mind and emotions. It is no surprise, therefore, that Augustine is an endlessly fascinating figure to theologians and historians—and, indeed, to all who, for whatever reason, are deeply curious about human thought and personality.

Early Christian Art

Just as the early Church developed in the context of the declining Roman Empire, so Early Christian art developed in the context of Roman art. Most of it was made in Italy, primarily in Rome. Although its subject matter and content differ from Roman art, its style does not. Christian artists, after all, were simply baptized Romans. However, as we shall see, that style changed over the course of five centuries. Early Christian art may be usefully divided into three rough periods:

42–200: from the time the Apostles left Jerusalem to the end of the second century
200–313: from the beginning of the third century to the Edict of Toleration
313–527: from the Edict of Toleration to the beginning of the reign of Justinian I

Among all of the persecuted minority faiths that existed in the Hellenistic world. Christianity was the only one to prevail. One advantage it had was the fact that the organization of the Church was modeled on that of Rome. A ruling cadre of bishops, presbyters (priests or elders), and deacons, together with a system of regional *dioceses*, provided an authority structure to fill the vacuum created by the collapse of the old Empire. But its main advantages lay in the special ways in which its message appealed to the "Gentiles"—non-Jewish people of Rome and other parts of the Hellenistic world. The books of the Old Testament countered Greek and Roman myths with the history of God and the human race. The resurrection of Christ resolved the riddle of death. Unlike a pagan figure, Jesus was neither a god nor a hero; he was God who became man. Facts were known about his human family; during his life he was surrounded by ordinary men, not heroes and aristocrats. These themes and the meanings behind them are reflected in Early Christian architecture and art.

From 42 to 200 AD

The letters of Paul refer to churches in Rome, Greece, and Asia Minor. The Book of Revelation makes specific reference to seven churches in Asia. Today, "church" evokes a mental image of a special building designated for Christian worship. But in this period Christians were not permitted to build public houses of worship, and so they met in private homes or rented buildings.

Although Christian architecture per se did not exist, the beginnings of Christian art appeared in the second century, despite the fact that early Christian leaders were opposed to art because of the Jewish concept of idolatry and a perceived association between imagery and pagan culture. This first Christian art appeared on the walls of underground cemeteries called *catacombs*: a vast network of galleries and burial chambers. There were several reasons for this method of interring the dead. Burial was preferred over cremation (which was used by pagan Romans); Christians did not want to be buried with unbelievers, thus they needed their own cemeteries; and catacombs were much cheaper than regular cemeteries, which required valuable surface land. Contrary to popular belief, catacombs were permitted by Roman authorities, and were not primarily used as refuges or secret meeting places. Originally, the galleries were simply narrow corridors (around 3 feet [1 meter] wide) leading to small rooms for burial chambers. But eventually, the walls of the galleries were excavated to hold shelf-like graves (Fig. **6.7**) for the less distinguished—thus adding immensely to

6.7 View of catacombs with shelf-like graves

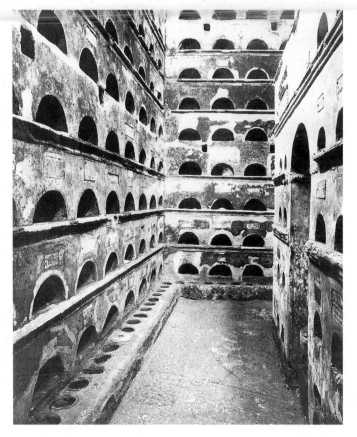

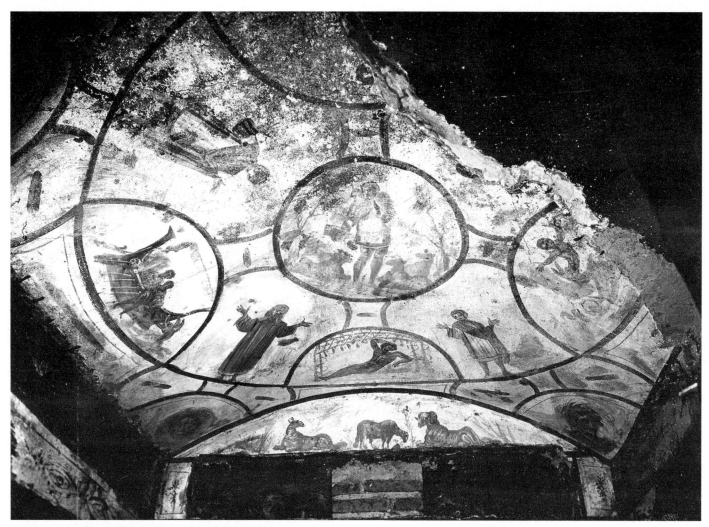

6.8 Painted ceiling, 4th century AD
Catacomb of SS. Pietro e Marcellino, Rome

the capacity of catacombs. Probably because of the need to relieve the gloom, the chambers were decorated—at first with abstract ornament, then later with images of Christ and scenes from the Old Testament. More will be said about the nature of these images—their subject matter, style, and purpose—in the discussion of the next period.

From 200 to 313 AD

Although Christianity was still an illegal religion, it grew substantially during this period. In 304 the Emperor Diocletian ordered all property used for Christian worship to be destroyed; therefore it is uncertain whether actual churches were built prior to this time. During this period the form of Christian worship was being developed; and this form, along with the very nature of the religion itself, would eventually produce a distinctively Christian form of architecture.

Meanwhile, the painting of frescoes in the catacombs flourished. Although subjects were taken from both testaments, those of the Old Testament were more popular at first—perhaps because the canon of New Testament books was not completely set. The theme uniting most of these subjects, regardless of which testament they came from, is that of deliverance: the Old Testament stories of Daniel among the lions, Jonah and the whale, Isaac saved from sacrifice, and Shadrach, Meshach, and Abednego rescued from the fiery furnace; and the miracles of Christ's healing ministry from the New Testament. It is not surprising, of course, that such subjects were used in a Christian burial ground. The deliverance of one's soul, eternal salvation, was (and is) the hope of all Christians. A non-biblical image, called an *orant* (figure on lower left side of Fig. **6.8**) was intended to symbolize the soul itself. Always shown with outstretched arms, the ancient attitude of prayer, an orant represented the deceased either as a portrait or as an abstract spirit (usually female). Popular during the second and third centuries was the figure of Christ as the Good Shepherd (central figure of Fig. 6.8), an image rooted in both biblical and pagan sources. The New Testament contains allegorical references to faithful Christians as sheep and to Jesus as shepherd. The Old Testament contains the 23rd Psalm, in which the shepherd leads his sheep "through the valley of the shadow of death." Statues of herdsmen, as votive offerings for various gods, had been produced by Greeks as early as the Archaic period (Fig. **6.9**). Thus there was pagan precedent as well as biblical authority to inspire the use of the Good Shepherd image.

The style of these catacomb frescoes is Hellenistic. The figure of Christ, for example, reveals the by-now familiar posture of weight shift. These images differ from standard Roman art of the time only insofar as the Christian artists were probably amateurs, and their working conditions were, to say the least, not ideal in terms of lighting, space, and ventilation. Such factors undoubtedly account for the imperfections in proportion and spatial depth, which would not be found, for example, in pagan frescoes in luxurious private homes. This art is best understood as an easy-to-read, popular form of art, indicative of a persecuted, mostly lower-class people and of the personal, humanistic religion which ministered to these people.

By the late third century an *anti-classical* tendency—an impulse toward abstraction—began to appear in Roman art, as the realism and idealized figures typical of the Hellenistic style were being modified or subverted. This change did not occur as a consistent, linear development; nor was it present everywhere at the same time. But the fact that it existed at all is significant. It was probably one of the inevitable side effects of a weary civilization disillusioned with old spiritual values and in search of new ones. The old art forms, like the old values, were also losing their power. Although this tendency was not necessarily caused by the presence of Christianity in Roman culture, it affected Christian art, and lent itself to the expression of spiritual content.

The contrast between the classical and anti-classical is demonstrated in the relief sculptures contained on the Arch of Constantine (Fig. **6.10**). Intended to commemorate the emperor's victory over Maxentius, a political rival, this monument has nothing to do with Christianity (though Constantine had by this time professed the Christian faith). Most of the sculptures were appropriated from second-century monuments. However, a set of narrow friezes, one of which is shown just below a pair of second-century medallion reliefs, was made by Constantine's artists (Fig. **6.11**). Everything about the frieze is a rejection of classical principles: dwarfish figures

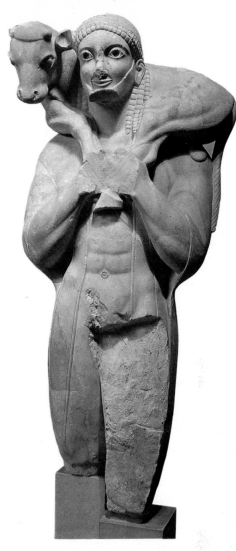

6.9 *Calf-bearer*, c. 570 BC
Marble, 77 ins (195 cm) high
Acropolis Museum, Athens

with oversize heads; lack of movement, particularly, graceful movement; shallow depth; static, repetitive composition. It could almost be a throwback to the frontality of Greek Archaic sculpture and the geometrical simplicity of Egyptian reliefs. The reason for this cannot be lack of skill on the part of an artist attempting to emulate the traditional style. Surely, with so many models to observe and copy, a skilled artist would have no difficulty following the older style; and, just as surely, Constantine would have availed himself of the best artists. No, everything seems to suggest that the change in style was intentional, that the frieze was not meant to be judged by the old standards, that the artist was working with new and different artistic criteria.

Although the anti-classical trend was accelerated by Christianity in the fourth and fifth centuries, it was interrupted by "revivals" of classicism. Indeed, the alternation between classicism and anti-classicism was to become a theme in the art of the Middle Ages.

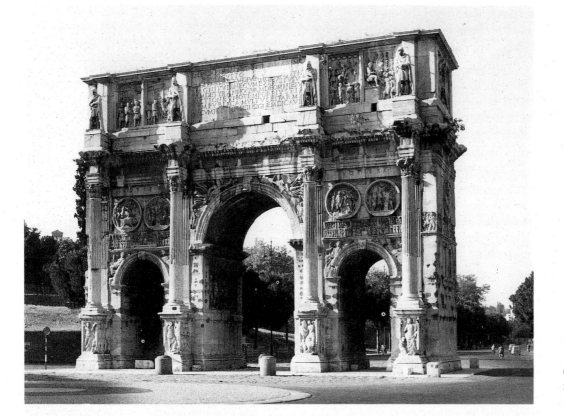

6.10 The Arch of Constantine, Rome, 312–315 AD

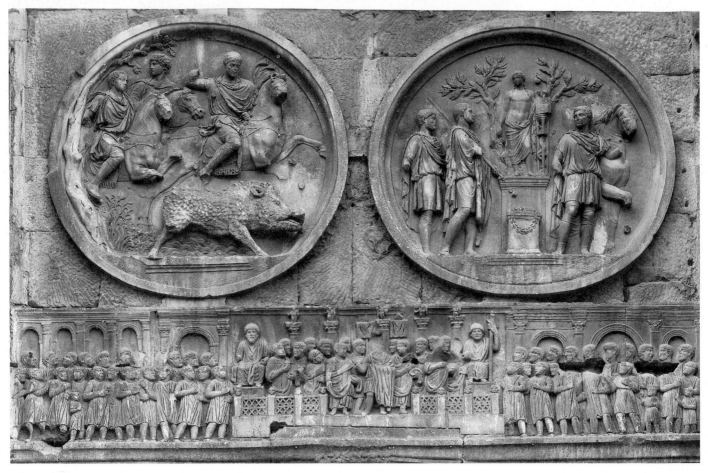

6.11 The Arch of Constantine, medallions (117–138 AD) and frieze (early 4th century)

From 313 to 527 AD: Architecture

When Christianity was emancipated under Constantine in 313, a great church-building program, encouraged by the emperor himself, was undertaken. Not only was public worship legal, but the buildings destroyed a decade earlier by Diocletian had to be replaced. In seeking models for their churches, Christians turned not to Roman temples, with their pagan associations, but to secular buildings whose forms could be adapted to Christian worship. Chief among these was the basilica, a large rectangular building used for courts (Fig. **2.47**) and other types of meeting. With slight modifications this became the Christian basilica, used for large congregations. Another building type, the centrally planned, domed mausoleum, served as the inspiration for Christian tombs and baptisteries.

The plan of Santa Maria Maggiore (Fig. **6.12**), a church erected in Rome shortly after the death of St. Augustine, illustrates some of the basic components of the basilica. Mainly it consists of a *nave*, a large central aisle flanked by *side aisles* (in some basilicas the entrance to the nave and

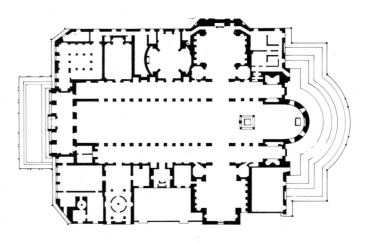

6.12 Plan of Santa Maria Maggiore, Rome (Structure surrounding nave added later.)

6.13 Central nave of Santa Maria Maggiore, Rome

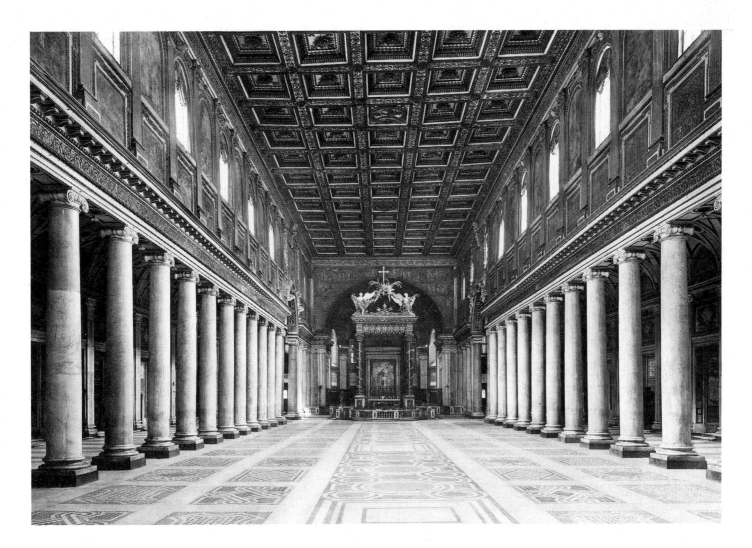

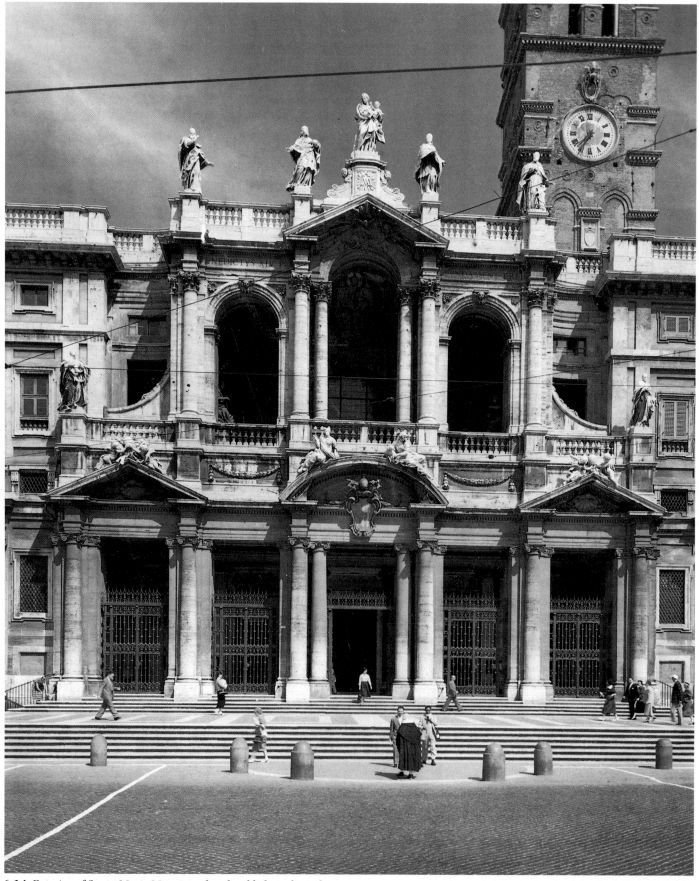

6.14 Exterior of Santa Maria Maggiore, façade added at a later date.

6.15 Plan and cross-section
of Santa Costanza, Rome

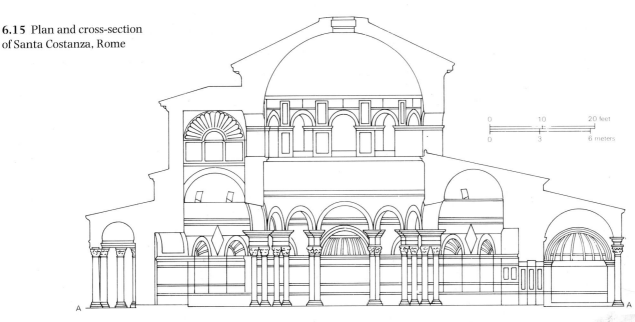

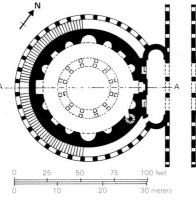

side aisles is articulated by a *narthex*, a sort of vestibule).
The nave leads to the *transept*, a rectangular area whose
long axis is perpendicular to that of the nave (in some
basilicas the ends of the transept extend beyond the sides
of the church itself); the intersection of the nave and
transept is called the *crossing*. Beyond the transept is a
semicircular niche called an *apse*. These same components, as we shall see in Chapter 7, became basic to almost
all churches of Western Europe. A view of the interior (Fig.
6.13) helps to explain how Santa Maria Maggiore is
constructed as well as how it was used for worship. The
most basic features, visually and structurally, are the rows
of columns (colonnades) which not only support the walls
of the nave but separate it from the aisles. Above the
colonnades is the *clerestory*, pierced by windows; the
ceiling beams are wood, not stone. Long and narrow, the
nave of a basilica tends to aim one's attention in one
direction. Everything—colonnades, clerestory, even the
coffered ceiling—leads to the *chancel*, the part at the end of
the building wherein the Holy Eucharist is celebrated.
There, in the crossing, separated from the nave by a
railing, are the altar (under a canopy) and pulpits (one for

reading the Epistle; the other, the Gospel). There were no
pews; except for bishop (if present) and priests, everyone
stood: congregation, altar boys, even the deacons.

Unlike other early public buildings, the basilica is
comparatively spacious. Because the ceiling is not stone or
vaulted, the walls and bearings are thin, and the nave is
roomy and uncluttered. The emphasis in an early Christian church, unlike that in a pagan temple, is on *interior*
space. It is not a beautiful monument containing a god,
outside which the faithful perform their rituals; it is a place
in which to congregate and celebrate with God. Thus, it is
like a temple turned outside-in. This is the reason why
Early Christian churches are so plain on the outside.

Domed buildings used for baptisteries and tombs were
probably modeled after rotunda-type buildings like the
Pantheon, and, as we shall see below, influenced the
church architecture of eastern (*Byzantine*) Christendom.
A baptistery, a small building used, as the name suggests,
for baptism, was adjacent to a basilica. Baptisteries are
rare in northern Europe, but continued to be built well
into the Middle Ages in Italy. A splendid example of tomb
architecture is Santa Costanza in Rome, built by Constantine as the mausoleum for his daughters. Its plan (Fig.
6.15) is circular and contains a central space—analogous
to the nave of a basilica—ringed by two aisles (one on the
exterior). In its section (Fig. 6.15) we see that this space,
which is taller than the aisles, is enclosed by a ring of
paired columns supporting a drum-shaped clerestory
pierced by windows and topped by a vaulted dome. Note
that the drum enclosing the inner aisle, though containing several niches, is very thick. This is necessary to
provide support for the inner drum which in turn supports
the vaulted ceiling.

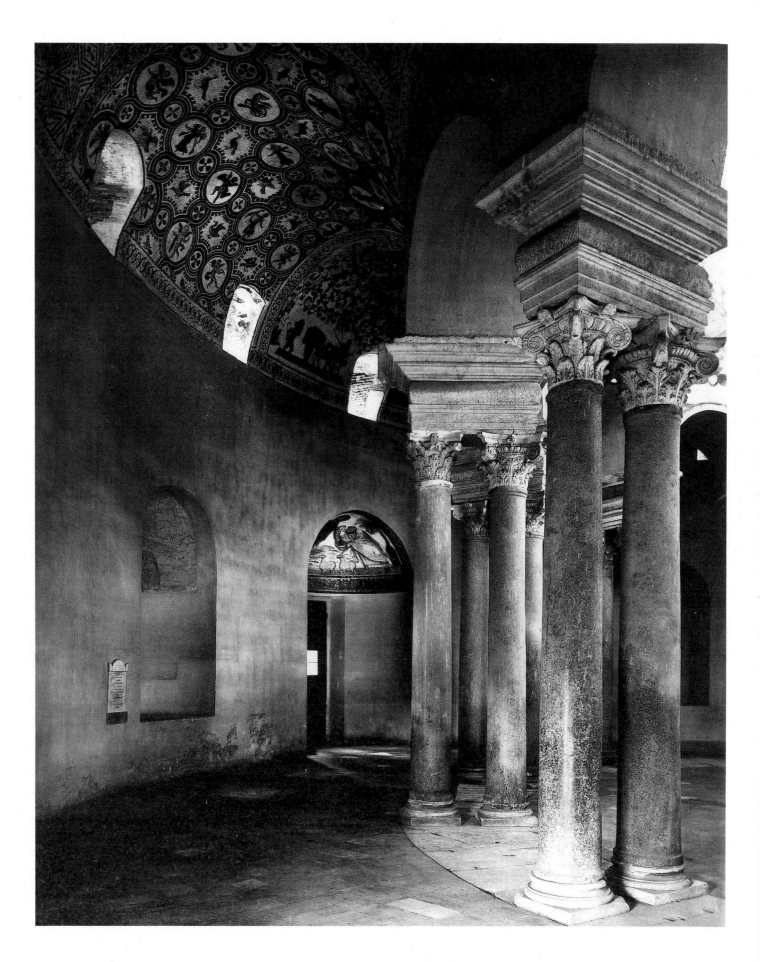

Mosaic

The vault over the inner aisle of Santa Costanza is decorated with *mosaic*—small bits of inlaid material (Fig. 6.16). Although this particular one is largely abstract, most Christian mosaics are pictorial. Indeed, mosaic, rather than fresco, was the preferred medium for illustrating biblical stories on the walls of basilicas. Compared to fresco, or any other painting method, the medium of mosaic is less tractable for making smooth transitions of color or light and dark. But compensating for this is its ability to produce sparkling surfaces. Most Roman mosaics were used for floors and made of marble; but Christian mosaics, designed for walls, were made with bits of glass sometimes faced with gold—each inlay, or *tessera* (pl. tesserae), being a small reflector. Their radiance enhanced the sense of mystery during the Eucharist. Santa Maria Maggiore's *The Parting of Lot and Abraham* (Fig. 6.17), part of a large cycle of stories from Genesis, Exodus, and Joshua, illustrates the use of the medium in the early fifth century. The scene of separation between the two patriarchs is stated with dramatic simplicity: Abraham on the left, Lot on the right, both gesturing in the directions they are headed while glancing backward at each other. Their figures divide the composition into symmetrical halves: Abraham's family went to the blessed land of Canaan, symbolized by a tree and a basilica on the left; Lot chose the Jordan valley and the wicked city of Sodom, the walled city on the right. Other than these symbols, there is no particular indication of the contrast between good and evil, or, even, between the personalities of the two main characters, Abraham and Lot. But there is no doubt—given their proportions, their dress, their gestures, and the determined expressions of their faces—that they are the leading actors in a drama of parting. Although some of this simplicity and directness of approach may be due to the natural limitations of the medium, most was due to the needs of narrative clarity. Like a book illustration, *The Parting of Lot and Abraham* was required to make its point unequivocally. To this end, the anti-classical tendencies of late Roman art were expedient. These can be seen in the shallow space and the shorthand means used to represent groups of people or cityscapes. Nevertheless, traces of the old tradition can be seen in the figures of Lot and Abraham: their proportions, the variety of their postures and their actions, even the relative naturalness in the folds of their gowns. In later Christian art, these classical traces decreased.

6.16 (left) Interior, Santa Constanza

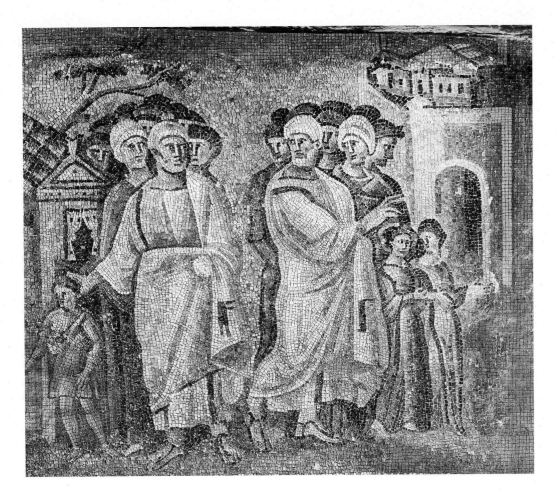

6.17 *The Parting of Lot and Abraham*, c. 430 AD
Santa Maria Maggiore, Rome

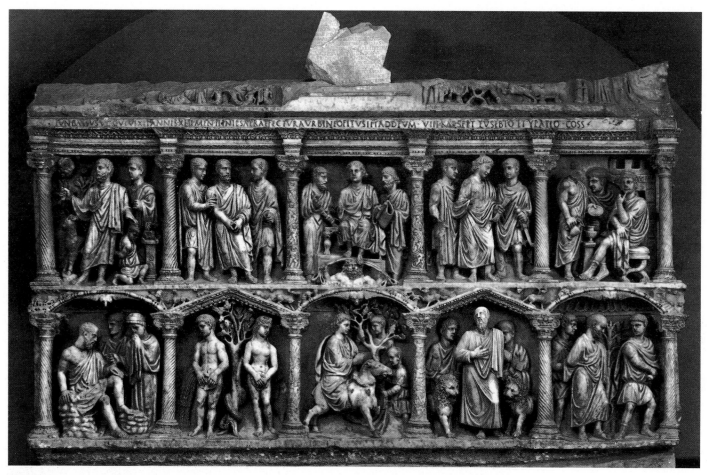

6.18 Sarcophagus of Junius Bassus, c. 359 AD
Marble, 3 ft 10½ ins × 8 ft (118 × 244 cm)
Vatican Grottoes, Rome

Sculpture

A similar mixture of classicism and anti-classicism exists in the scenes on the stone coffin of Junius Bassus (Fig. **6.18**). As with the earliest examples of Christian painting, Early Christian sculpture was strongly influenced by burial needs: specifically, the making of coffins. Because of their high cost, these coffins were available only to the wealthy (Bassus was the mayor of Rome), and because of the length of time needed to produce one, they could not be made on order in cases of unexpected death. Though some were carved with decorations acceptable to both Christians and non-Christians, many were clearly intended to be for one or the other. Obviously, Bassus' coffin was intended for a Christian, as all of its ten niches contain biblical scenes and symbols: in the upper row, the sacrifice of Isaac, the arrest of Peter, Christ enthroned, Christ before Pilate (repeated); in the lower, Job, Adam and Eve, Christ's entry into Jerusalem, Daniel among the lions, and Paul being led to execution. In the lower-left, Job is seen sitting

on a pile of potsherds as two people, including his wife, on the right, attend him in his misery. (His wife keeps her distance as she gives him food on the end of a stick and covers her nose with her garment.) In the upper middle is Christ—not as the Good Shepherd, but as a ruler seated on a throne above a symbol of the sky and flanked by Peter and Paul (Fig. **6.19**). As the fortunes of Christianity improved dramatically in the wake of Constantine's conversion, so did the image of Jesus change from a peasant to a prince. Compared to the forms on the Arch of Constantine frieze (Fig. 6.11), those on the sarcophagus are relatively classical. The figures are in high relief; their bodies—including that of the suffering Job—are athletic and involved in a variety of actions; their heads, relatively handsome; and their faces, passive. Yet this classicism is tempered by the fact that the proportions of the puppet-like figures—particularly those of Adam and Eve—are clearly not ideal. The ratio between their bodies and heads is 5:1 or less (the ideal ratio is around 7:1).

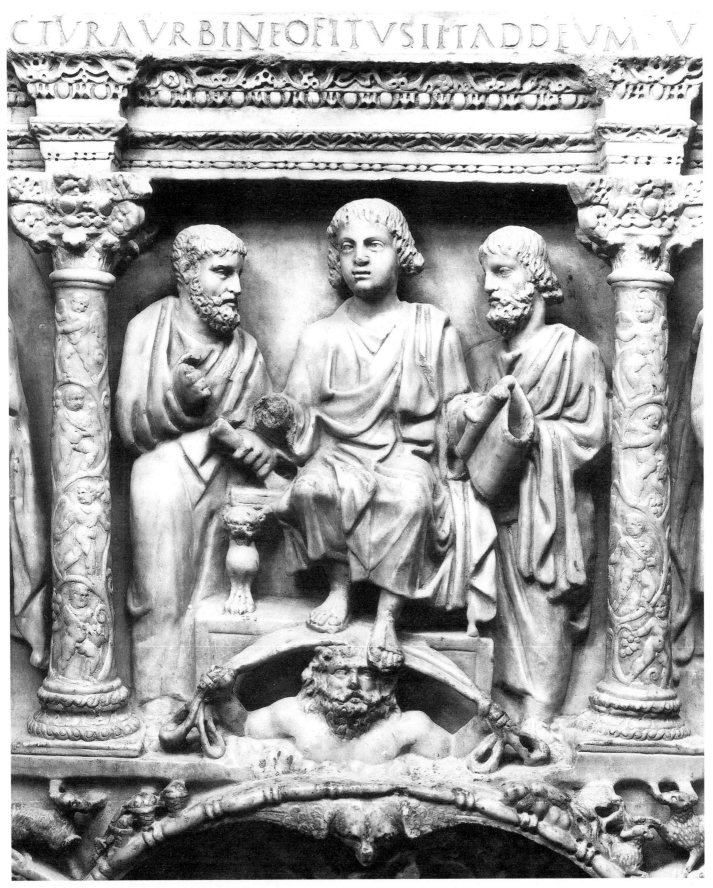

6.19 *Christ Enthroned*, detail of sarcophagus of Junius Bassus

Byzantine Art

The division of the Roman Empire begun by Diocletian was completed by Theodosius making Milan the western capital and Constantinople the eastern. The eastern half, embracing Greece and Asia Minor (and for a while parts of Italy, the Middle East, and North Africa), became the real heir to the power and splendor of the old Empire and came to be known as the *Byzantine* Empire (after *Byzantium*, the Greek name for Constantinople). While the West lost population, regressed from an urban to a rural society, and slipped ever deeper into an age of darkness, the new Empire flourished. Located on the Bosporus and surrounded on three sides by water, Constantinople became a center of industry and trade, and achieved a population of over one million by the fifth century. The city was remarkably cosmopolitan, full of glittering palaces, treasure, and endless festivities, as magnificent as Babylon, Alexandria, Rome, or any metropolis to this time. But unlike its predecessors, Constantinople was founded as a Christian city. And the Byzantine Empire, unlike the Roman, was a theocracy, ruled by an absolute monarch—considered the vicar of Christ—whose court was shrouded in secrecy and whose power was reinforced by layers of officialdom. In the West power was increasingly ceded to certain leading clergy, particularly the

6.20 Hagia Sophia, Istanbul, 532–537 AD
Anthemius & Isidorus

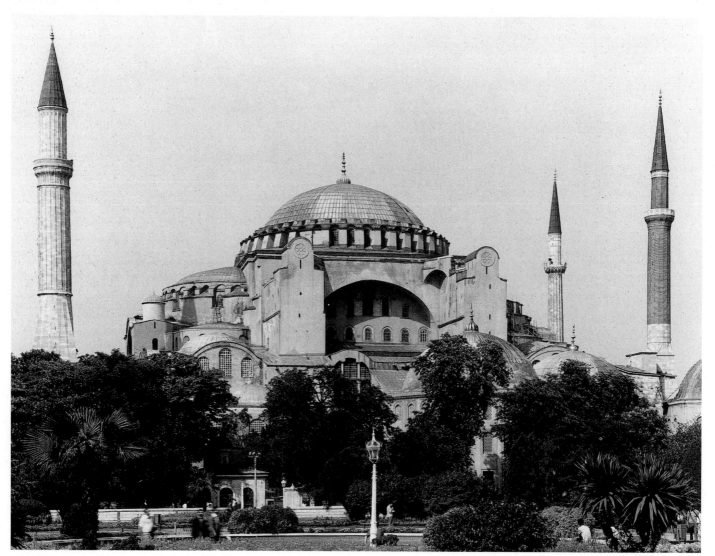

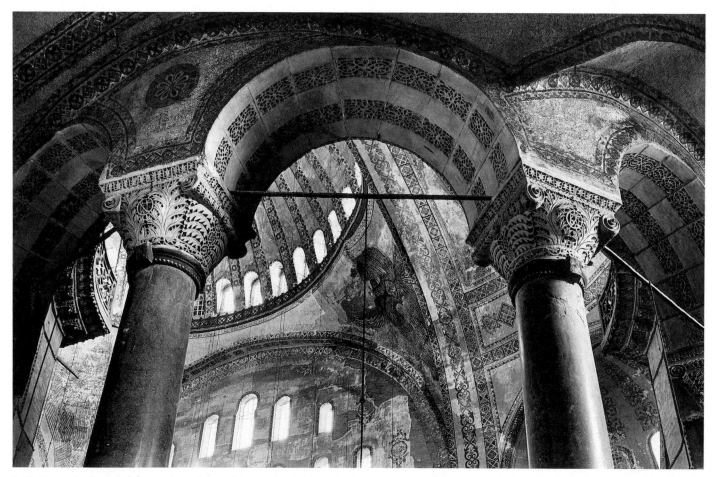

6.21 Hagia Sophia, view from the galleries showing capitals

bishop of Rome (the *pope*), while in the East secular and religious powers were retained by the emperor, who was a sort of caesar and pope in one.

The combination of central authority, strong economy, and strategically located capital helped the Empire to survive a thousand years. But it also fostered conservatism. In contrast to the West, whose checkered politics and history were dynamic, the East emphasized stability and control. Little cultural innovation occurred over all those years. Here we will study only a short part of that history, the sixth century. However, it should be noted that the existence of the East was crucial to the West—not only for the latter's cultural development but also possibly for its very existence as a historical entity. Though different in so many ways, both societies were Christian, one acting as a sort of rich, educated cousin to the other. Constantinople—retainer and codifier of Greco-Roman traditions, collector and preserver of the writings of classical poets and philosophers—tutored the West and served as cultural model. But also, through holding off a succession of eastern invaders (Persians, Arabs, and Turks), it gave the West that most precious of commodities

needed for growth: time.

Our study will focus on art under Justinian, the emperor who tried to reunite East and West. Indeed, he succeeded in recapturing parts of Italy and other former Roman holdings; but, when he died, most of the new territory slipped away. Italy, exhausted by Justinian's project, joined Western Europe and the Dark Ages. If he did not finally succeed in his military objectives, Justinian's artistic record was superb; like Augustus and Hadrian before him, he was a great patron of the arts. The architecture and mosaics produced under his direct or indirect patronage can be seen as part of a golden age and the beginning of a Byzantine style. But this art can also be seen as the climax of Early Christian art.

In 532 a series of riots in Constantinople threatened Justinian's court. Only the intervention of the Empress Theodora, his remarkable wife, prevented flight. The revolt was quelled, but half the city was left in ruins. Justinian began immediately to rebuild everything, including the church of *Hagia Sophia* ("Holy Wisdom;" Fig. **6.20**). Built in five years, this combination of cathedral and palace church was proclaimed at the time to be a

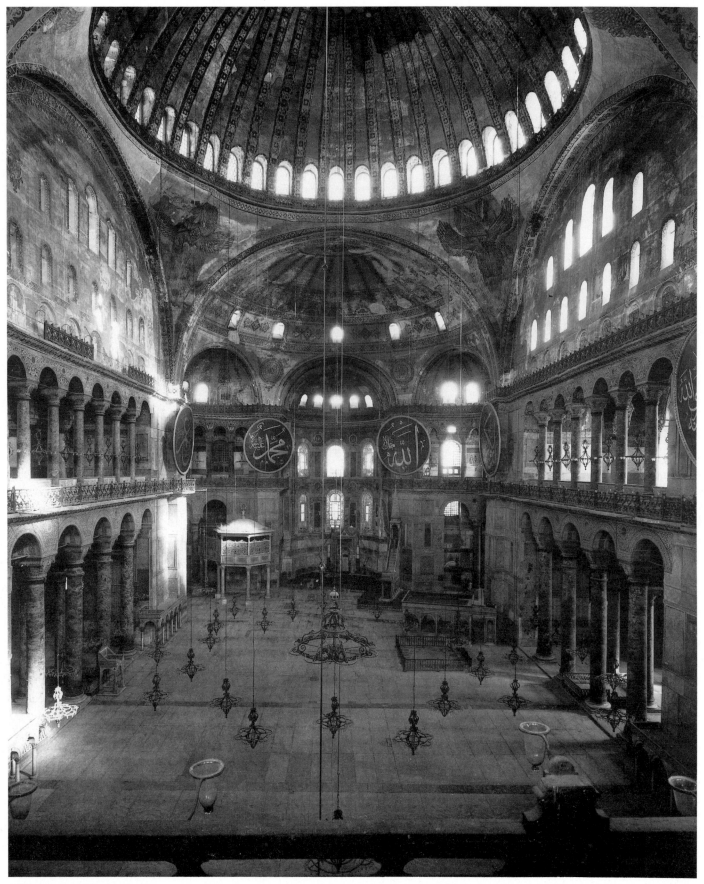

6.22 Interior of Hagia Sophia

marvel, a judgment that still holds. The later additions of buttresses and Turkish minarets, if anything, enhance the appearance of the exterior—a fascinating orchestration of cubes, cylinders, half-cylinders, cones and hemispheres. But the transcendental effects are reserved for the interior (Figs. **6.21**, **6.22**), in which the volumes of this geometry come into play. The dome, a soaring canopy over the central area, is 108 feet (33 meters) in diameter and 180 feet (55 meters) off the floor. Ringing its base are 40 windows which suggest that the dome is floating on beads of light. In reality it is supported by four lofty arches (unlike the domes of the Pantheon and Santa Costanza, which rest on heavy cylindrical drums) that form massive piers at the corners. On the east and west these arches are open, exposing large adjoining half-domed areas which, in turn, open out into smaller half-domed apses. The view in Fig. 6.22 shows three apses, including the central one which contained the altar. The north and south arches are filled with masonry screens, each containing two rows of arcades supporting a semicircular wall pierced with windows. The upper arcades form galleries for members of the congregation. The plan and diagram (Figs **6.23**, **6.24**) help to clarify the complexity of the interrelated volumes,

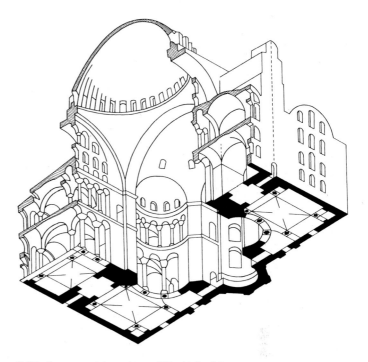

6.24 Axonometric section of Hagia Sophia

6.23 Section and plan of Hagia Sophia

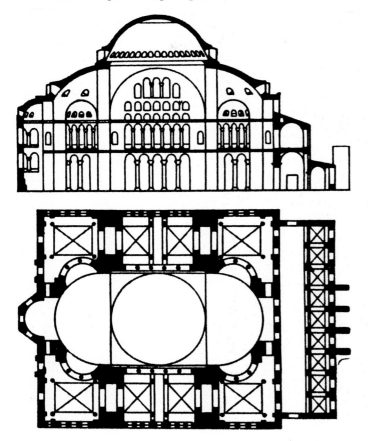

as well as revealing that the concept of space is a compromise between the two styles of architecture originating under Constantine. Despite its central dome, Hagia Sophia is oblong, not radial, in plan, though not nearly so narrow as a basilica. The church has an outer and an inner narthex, a central nave, side aisles, and apse—all the elements of a basilica, except the crossing and transept. Justinian, the *patriarchs* (bishops), and their respective attendants were the only people privileged to occupy the nave; Theodora and her attendants sat in one of the galleries; commoners, if any, were confined to the side aisles and remaining galleries.

Hagia Sophia is a blend of architectural principles from Rome and Oriental splendor from places such as Antioch (Syria) and Alexandria. Its immense scale was made possible by an arch technology that had been practiced for centuries on everything from temples to public baths. But its many-faceted spaces, along with rays of light streaming in from all directions from hundreds of small openings reflecting off vast areas of (now-effaced) glass and gold mosaic surpassed even the most magnificent of Roman projects. "In short," writes the art historian John Beckwith, "Hagia Sophia was the largest and most expensive religious theatre imaginable, built and furnished for the semi-private performances of the sacred and imperial liturgy."[4]

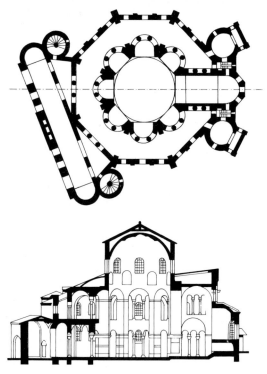

6.25 Plan and transverse section of San Vitale, Ravenna, Italy, 526–47 AD

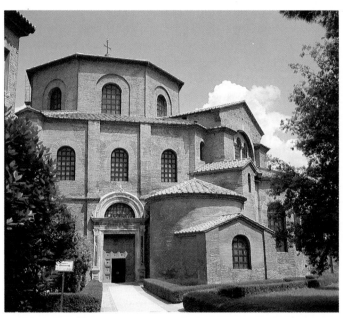

6.26 Facade of San Vitale, Ravenna

6.27 Interior view from apse, San Vitale, Ravenna

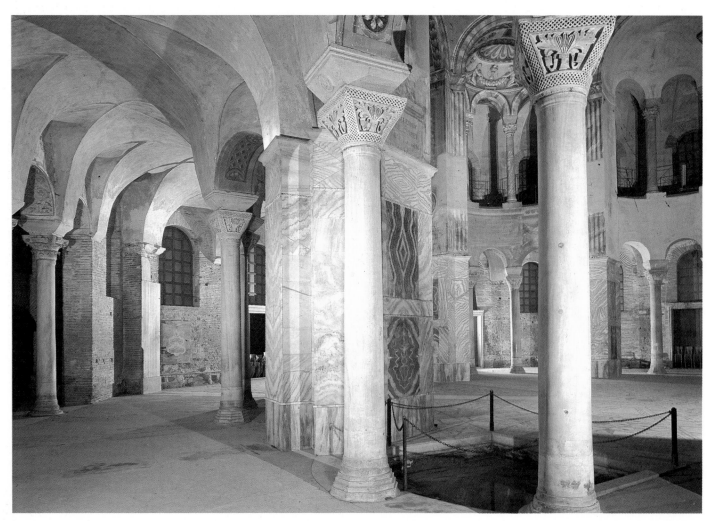

The sacred and imperial were also celebrated at San Vitale, a much smaller church in Ravenna, Italy, Justinian's western outpost. Although its plan is radial, like Santa Costanza, its outer shape is octagonal, while the central drum is supported by a ring of seven semicircular niches which also divide nave and aisle (Fig. **6.25**). At the east end, the eighth side of the octagon, is the apse. Like that of Hagia Sophia, its plain-brick exterior is an essay in prismatic geometry (Fig. **6.26**)—though less impressive in terms of scale and complexity. But San Vitale compensates for whatever it lacks in scale by the sheer elegance of its interior (Fig. **6.27**). Below the clerestory are the vaults covering the seven towering niches, each with two levels of arcades: the lower leading to the aisle; the upper, to the gallery. Framed by a tall archway, each niche is concave, penetrating the space of the aisle and contrasting with the plane of the outside wall. The round columns are topped by capitals that resemble double inverted baskets carved with stylized acanthus leaves. Also framed by a tall archway, but rectilinear rather than concave, is the approach to the apse, the part of the chancel where the altar is located. The apse itself, which extends beyond the plane of the octagon, is one-storied. The profusion of levels, contrasting perspectives, openings, and interlocking volumes, though complex and mystifying, are subtly and delicately proportioned. Added to this are surfaces skillfully decorated with different colors of mar-

ble, porphyry, and some of the best-preserved and most brilliant mosaics in Christendom.

On one wall of the apse, on the "Gospel" side of the chancel, Justinian is pictured holding a gold dish, standing in the center of a line of men, all staring at the viewer (Fig. **6.28**). To his right are attendants and soldiers (one holding a shield bearing a *chi-rho* monogram, the first two Greek letters in the word "Christ"); to his left, and behind him, a secretary; to his left, and slightly in front of him, are Maximian, the archbishop of Ravenna who supervised the completion of San Vitale, and two clergymen, one of whom holds a gem-encrusted book. Rank is indicated by size, position, costume, and halo. On some counts, Justinian and Maximian rival each other. The archbishop is larger and, according to the forward position of his feet, in front of the emperor. Yet, according to the occlusion of their bodies, the emperor is in front. And by virtue of his regal costume, central location, and halo (symbolizing his godlike status), Justinian clearly outranks Maximian.

There is no question that Theodora, though not in the center, is the ranking figure in the mosaic on the opposite wall, the "Epistle" side (Fig. **6.29**). Tall and proud, dressed in full regalia (including a hem embroidered with images of the Three Kings) and embellished with jewels, tiara, and halo, she stands before a niche holding a gold chalice. This mosaic contains more variety than Justinian's: it includes both men and women, more movement (not all of the

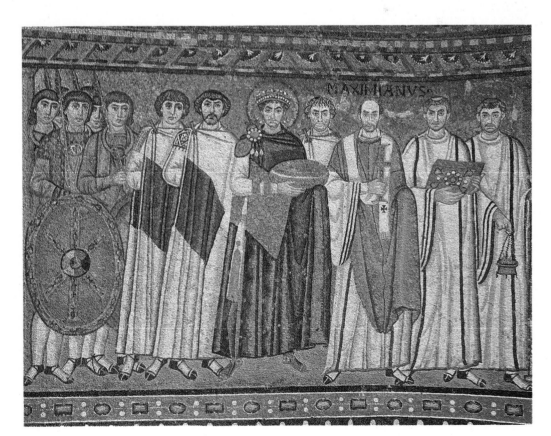

6.28 *Justinian and Attendants,* 547 AD Apse mosaic from San Vitale

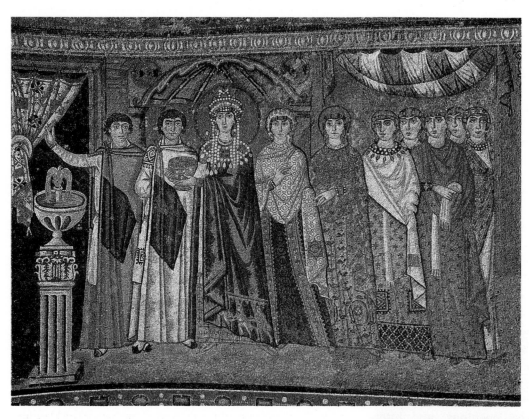

6.29 *Theodora and Attendants,* 547 AD Apse mosaic from San Vitale

6.30 Detail of attendant's head in *Justinian and Attendants* Mosaic, San Vitale

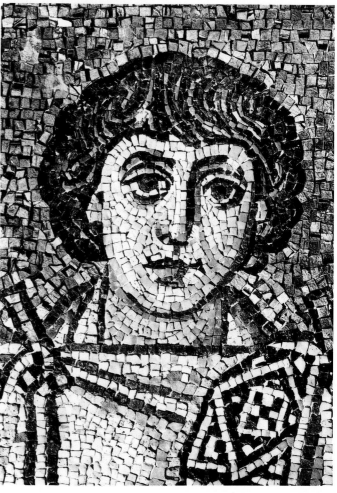

figures are staring straight ahead), and several architectural features—the niche, a doorway with a hanging curtain, a fountain, and a furled canopy. Some experts believe that the mosaics were meant to represent royal processionals celebrating the Eucharist. Others maintain that they were intended to show Justinian and Theodora bearing gifts, a symbol of their support for Maximian, and to remind the faithful of the two spheres of authority: the religious and the imperial. The images of the royal couple (who probably never visited Ravenna) served as magical epiphanies of their spiritual presence.

In addition to the triumphs of Justinian and Christianity we can see in these mosaics the victory of a stylized, symbolic form of art: flattened figures, frontality, shallow depth, and "cookie-cutter" repetition. The use of foreshortening is minimal; nearly everything—heads, bodies, shields, vessels, and so forth—is shown in its most characteristic, readable view. This approach at times produces what we perceive as spatial contradictions, as, for example, in the conflicting eye-levels of the fountain. But to the Byzantine artist and the faithful, such unrealistic elements were not contradictions; or at least they were not important. Even the relatively natural folds of the gowns show signs of becoming frozen into permanent, stylized patterns. The most telling aspect of Byzantine art is the fact that the people's faces are both generalized and individualized. All of them are frontal (most are bilaterally symmetrical) with large, staring eyes. Those of lower rank, like the soldiers and attendants, have the same features and hair styles (Fig. **6.30**). But those of higher rank, particularly the officials in the Justinian mosaic as well as Justinian himself, are clearly individualized: the attendant to the emperor's right is young with neatly groomed hair and beard, the one to his left is older with stringier hair, and so on for each of the officials. These are personalized portraits in an otherwise impersonal procession.

The San Vitale mosaics are partially the product of the anti-classical process that we saw on Constantine's arch—though, significantly, the figures are tall and angular rather than short and plump. They are also the product of influences from folk-art traditions of Syria and Palestine which tended to be more abstract and to stress the mystical rather than the objective. In addition, they are a product of two fundamental conditions of the Byzantine world: religion and state. On the one hand, the impulse to abstract corresponds to the need to subordinate physical reality to spiritual reality. By reducing people and physical objects to formulas, by schematizing detail, and by hardening these into stereotypes, the Byzantine artist was literally "denaturing" reality. In such art it is not the seen, but the *unseen* that matters. Images are signs of the inner, spiritual life. Their function is to symbolize, to direct one's attention to the mystery that lies hidden behind appearances. The staring eyes, the highly charged gaze, is a token of the inner life, the new person, illuminated by faith and born again in the Spirit. On the other hand, this is the art of a theocracy, a society in which the ruler and God are one. The symmetrical, carefully regulated composition is a simulacrum of the political order itself. The formality of the style is in tune with the formality of the state, its rituals and etiquette, and, above all, the demand that all be subservient to its rules. The figures of the officials were designed to inspire awe in the beholder-citizen. The portraits of Justinian and the ranking officials, the only hint of realism in a rigidly formal work, are not inconsistent with any of these themes. They are like epiphanies of remote personages of divine status, in other words, magical stand-ins for an archbishop, the supreme authority in Ravenna, and for an emperor-god residing in distant Constantinople. Finally, it should be pointed out that just as religion and state were one, so were religion and art. The latter was completely in the service of belief. All forms of art—architecture, mosaics, relief carvings, the crafts—had been, so to speak, "baptized."

We have seen a remarkable evolution in Christian art: from amateurish paintings on cemetery walls to dazzling mosaics on the walls of splendid churches, from humanistic realism to hieratic formalism, and from the patronage of a persecuted minority to that of a powerful state led by a supposedly divine ruler.

Early Christian Music

As we have learned, classicism—the heritage of Greece and Rome—played a major role in the development of European art and literature. The classical legacy was particularly important to the fields of painting, sculpture, and architecture. The history of European music, however, is different. It did not originate in the dithyrambs and paeans of the Greeks, or in the fanfares of the Romans, but in the psalms, hymns, and chants sung by early Christians.

Of course folk music of various kinds continued to develop, and later on secular songs and dances were performed in the courts of nobility and royalty. All of these musical forms would eventually find their way into the mainstream of European serious music. But at the beginning of the Christian era and throughout the Dark Ages, when virtually the only literate people in Europe were the clergy, it was inevitably the Church that served as the guardian of the remaining fragments of ancient musical theory and the cradle of a system of notation which was to make possible the subsequent flowering of Western music in all its rich profusion. Thus, in a sense, the music of the early Church is the direct ancestor of modern Western music. In this chapter we shall look at Christian music in its infancy.

Liturgy and Music

The music of the Early Christian period, like that of the early Greeks and Romans, was transmitted orally, through memory and repetition. Without any manuscripts, we therefore do not know what it sounded like. But we can infer some things about it from other kinds of evidence, including the Bible.

The development of music in the early Church was both similar to and different from that of art. Most early Christians viewed the use of music for non-religious purposes, such as drama, entertainment, and social occasions, as immoral. So opposed were they to secular, "pagan" music that they even resisted the use of instruments, including simple ones like the kithara (see Chapter 2)—just as Christian artists rejected nudity and sculpture in the round. But whereas Christian art and architecture inevitably drew some of their inspiration from classical models, Christian music had a more suitable source of inspiration: the music of the Jews. (Western art might have developed quite differently had there been a Jewish tradition in the visual arts to emulate.) Music played a central role in Jewish worship; and it is now believed that the main source of Early Christian music was Jewish, specifically, the psalms and hymns sung in the synagogues.

There is abundant evidence in written documents, including the New Testament itself, to support this belief. According to Matthew (26:30) and Mark (14:26), Jesus and the disciples sang a hymn after the Last Supper. In Ephesians (5:18–20) and Colossians (3:16), St. Paul exhorts the faithful to sing "psalms and hymns and spiritual songs." Musical scholars think that this music was based on the psalms of the Old Testament, music basic to the Jewish liturgy. There are also psalms in the New Testament—the *Magnificat*, Mary's song of praise (Luke 1:46–55), and the *Nunc Dimittis*, Simeon's song of thanksgiving (Luke 2:29–32). It is believed that the words of these psalms were set to traditional Jewish tunes. In addition to musical references in the New Testament there are writings by early Church Fathers that indicate a close connection between Christian and Jewish music: Eusebius (265–340) of Caesarea (the church scholar whose name was used by Schumann in his musical journal; see page 228) says of Christians: "We are in this fashion 'Jews inwardly' when we sing God's praise in spiritual songs...."[5] St. Augustine speaks of the Jewish influence in church singing, pointing out that the Alleluia was chanted according to Jewish tradition.[6]

The early Church of this period seems to have been closely linked musically (and, to some extent liturgically) to the Jewish synagogue. The Jewish Christians, especially, were essentially the same people that they had been as members of the synagogue. And the converted Gentiles, no doubt, imitated their traditions. Instead of Rome, places like Caesarea and Jerusalem in Palestine and Antioch in Syria were centers of musical influence. If Early Christian artists were "baptized Romans," Early Christian musicians were "baptized Jews."

There were two types of service: the Holy Eucharist, celebrated on Sunday morning, and psalm singing, performed at different times on Saturday and early Sunday morning in small gatherings or "vigils." The Holy Eucha-rist service later came to be known as the Mass; psalm singing in vigils was the forerunner of the Divine Office—daily devotional observances in the monasteries. The music in either of these services was basically *chant*: uninterrupted, monophonic vocal music lacking strict meter. Chant is halfway between speech and singing, the meter being dependent on speech rhythms. Like Greek paeans and dithyrambs, Jewish and early Christian chants were based on a system of modes. Scriptural verses set to chants were recited in, mainly, two ways: *responsorial*, in which a soloist (such as the priest) and the congregation sang lines of verses alternately, and *antiphonal*, in which two choruses alternated verses with extra lines set to a different melody.

The development of liturgy and music in the early Church was related to the development of the Church itself. As it grew in numbers it spread from towns and cities to surrounding territories. It spread even to parts of "barbaric" Europe, including distant Spain (Romans 15:28). By the fourth century, Gentiles came to outnumber Jewish Christians; heretical sects had come and gone; and, in the West, Latin had replaced Greek as the language of the liturgy. Given the variety of local traditions, the admixture of cultures, the dominance of Gentiles, the change of language, and the introduction of heretical ideas, it is easy to see how Christian liturgy would have begun to assume a character of its own, becoming increasingly different from that of the synagogue. It also became pluralistic—a situation that led to a demand for standardizing the literature in the West in later centuries.

The evidence for the use of instruments is mixed. They were certainly not unknown to the Jews. In addition to David's legendary harp (I Samuel 18:10), harps, tambourines, flutes, and lyres are mentioned in I Samuel 10:5, and trumpets and pipes are mentioned in I Kings 1:39–40. Services in Jewish temples may have included instruments, but music in the synagogues was probably unaccompanied. Statements of Church Fathers were both pro and con: some approved of instrumental music, others condemned it. Like nudity in art, it tended to be associated in the minds of Christians with revelry and moral depravity. The musical scholar Russel N. Squire thinks instruments were cautiously used for a while but were banned in the fourth century. Ironically, early Christians must have felt the same way about the singing of women. Although the female voice was accepted as a part of congregational singing in the first two centuries, it later fell into disfavor. Like the harp and the lyre, it came to be linked with the dangers of heresy and immorality. By the sixth century it was generally prohibited.

Thus, through piecing together bits of evidence we can begin to formulate a general notion of the practice of early Church music—although it is unlikely that anyone will ever be able to reconstruct either its sound or the ways in which it was experienced by the people who used it.

We know more about the theories underlying early Church music. Numerous writings reveal that Christian thinkers were more indebted to classical notions than to Jewish notions. These notions, as we saw in Chapter 2, are based partly on the theories of Pythagoras, Plato, and Aristotle, and partly on interpretations of their theories in the writings of later classical scholars. Greek theories, as we noted, had little to do with the actual practice of Greek music. So there is little reason to believe that Christian theories, based as they were on Greek theories, had much to do with the actual practice of early church music. For example, St. Augustine, in *De Musica*, describes Pythagoras' theories of number and Plato's notions of morality, rather than the ways in which the music of his own time was played and sounded.

Thus, in the early Church, we find a curious situation in which the heritage of musical theory is Greek, while that of the music itself is basically Jewish.

Liturgy and Music from 313 to 604 AD

By the fourth century there were several liturgies in the West—all using the Latin language. Of these, the most influential was the "Ambrosian," named for St. Ambrose (c.340–397).

Next to Rome, the most important religious center in the West was Milan, a city with some cultural ties to Eastern centers such as Constantinople. Its most famous bishop was the popular and capable Ambrose, the man who converted St. Augustine. Just how much Ambrose was personally involved with creating the liturgy that bears his name is difficult to say. Ambrosian liturgy, it is believed, imported Jewish and Syrian practices—particularly, responsorial and antiphonal singing—into the West. Ambrose himself is given credit for introducing the singing of hymns, which, essentially, are non-biblical sacred poems. According to legend, the custom arose when the saint led his followers in hymns during a demonstration to prevent Empress Justina from taking over a Milan church. Significantly, the texts of hymns need not be scriptural so long as they celebrate Christian principles or events. Therefore the practice of hymn singing created a new poetry for Christian music.

Still another factor in the development of the liturgy was monasticism (from the Greek *monazein*, "to dwell alone"). Although the idea of the religious community originated with St. Anthony of Egypt (c.251–c.356), it

became institutionalized in Europe under the auspices of St. Benedict (c.480–c.543). In essence, Benedict established a commune, where all activities—eating, sleeping, labor, and religious observances—were regulated by the commune, called the Order. In addition to attending Mass, a Benedictine monk was enjoined to celebrate the Divine Office, a series of eight services (see below) held at intervals from dawn to midnight daily. The Divine Office (sometimes referred to as the canonical hours) became a staple of monastic liturgy, and like most Christian liturgy it was sung. Thus St. Benedict, through the founding of the first European monastic order, contributed to the development of a major category of medieval music.

Boethius (c.480–524), a Roman philosopher and statesman, influenced the theoretical foundation of that music. Echoing Pythagoras and St. Augustine, he idealized it as a system of divine numbers; echoing Plato, he stressed its effects on human character (the doctrine of ethos; see Chapter 2). Most important for medieval musical practice, however, were Boethius' translations of the Greek modes (see page 74). Though far from accurate, they nevertheless formed the basis for what came to be known as the church modes. The many copies of his writings preserved in medieval libraries attest to their influence, as well as to their intermediate position between classical antiquity and the Middle Ages.

But the greatest milestone in the evolution of European music was the establishment of *Gregorian chant* (also called plainchant or plainsong). This involved not so much the creation of new forms as the codification of old forms. Although its origin is a matter of debate, Gregorian chant is named after one of the most respected popes of all time, Gregory I (c.540–604). Born into a rich and noble family, Gregory lived like a monk, spending his fortune on charity rather than on himself. After he became pope, he continued his ascetic way of life and service to others. Under him the papacy became, for the first time, an important power—the only one in the West during that time to rival the emperor in Constantinople. Among his papal duties, Gregory placed a high priority on music. He reorganized the *Schola Cantorum*, a school for training men and boys to sing in choirs, and supplied the impulse to reform and standardize the various forms of worship that the Roman Church had inherited.

Since musical notation did not exist, the melodies for the Gregorian liturgy were not compiled during Gregory's time. However, it is believed that they were preserved and passed on orally by the Schola Cantorum until the ninth century, when it became possible to preserve them in written form. (The texts of the Divine Office are collected in a liturgical book called the *Antiphonal*; those of the Mass, in a book called the *Graduale*.) Just how true these

stereotyped and impersonal. The problem of appreciating it involves not so much what is there but what is *not* there. As the music scholar, Donald Grout explains:

> *We feel the lack of supporting harmony or accompaniment; or we miss clearly defined time values and regular accents; or we notice that the melodic line sometimes turns strangely and often does not cadence on the expected note; or we are perhaps resentfully conscious that the music makes no attempt to thrill our senses or entangle our emotions.*[7]

Yet if we approach plainchant on its own terms and with an open mind, we can discover a world of music that is not only worthy of our attention but also, in its way, very beautiful. To do so we must understand its liturgical setting, that is, the Divine Office and the Mass. The names of the various offices along with their times are listed below:

1	Matins—after midnight	5	Sext—Noon
2	Lauds—at daybreak	6	None—3 p.m.
3	Prime—6 a.m.	7	Vespers—early evening
4	Terce—9 a.m.	8	Compline—before bedtime

Of the eight offices, Matins, Lauds, and Vespers are the lengthiest and most important musically. But although they differ from one another in some respects, each office is introduced with the singing of the first verse of Psalm 70, *Deus in adjutorium*, ("Make haste, O God"), and each includes its own collection of antiphonal music, Bible readings, and prayers. The selection of texts varies within each office according to whether or not performances occur on Sundays or religious feast days—Christmas, Easter, All Saints' Day, and so forth. As we saw in Chapter 3, texts that do not vary from day to day are referred to as the Ordinary; those that vary according to the liturgical calendar are known as the Proper.

For the most part, texts are taken from the Old Testament's Book of Psalms (indeed the Office was designed so that all 150 psalms would be sung each week). Additionally, every office includes at least one hymn and a song of praise (*canticle*) from the New Testament, such as the *Magnificat* (at Vespers) and the *Nunc Dimittis* (at Compline). The method of singing is antiphonal—though whether this involved solo voice and choir or two half choirs in Gregory's time is uncertain. Individual verses of a psalm or canticle are sung according to a recitation formula rooted in one of the eight church modes; in places several syllables are recited on one note, or *psalm tone* (notice the syllables "te-bor ti-bi Do-mi-ne in to-to" in Fig. **6.32**). The verses are alternated with an *antiphon*, an additional verse set to a free melody in the same mode (Fig. **6.33**). The method of alternation can vary: A V1 A V2 etc.; or A V1–2 A V3–4 A etc. (A = antiphon; V = verse).

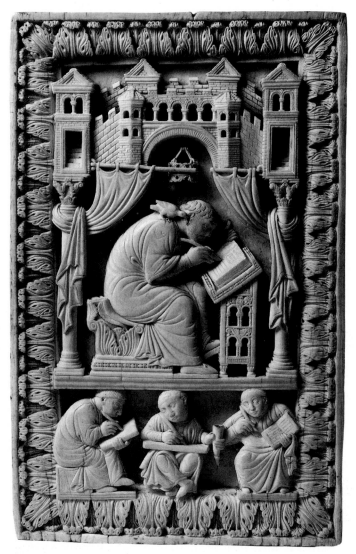

6.31 St Gregory with three scribes, 10th century
Ivory book case

manuscripts are to the original chants ascribed to Gregory's papacy is open to speculation. But we do know some of the characteristics common to all Gregorian chant, whether in original or evolved forms. Musically, it is monophonic and exclusively vocal; its range is limited to the normal range of the male voice (monks sang in monasteries; monks, clergy, and/or male choirs sang in churches); its melodic structure is mostly *conjunct* (stepwise), having relatively few intervals of even as great as a third or a fourth; its rhythmic structure lacks recognizable meter; finally, it is based on what later came to be known as the eight church modes (Fig. 3.24).

The Services of the Divine Office

Gregorian chant sounds foreign to modern ears, at least on a first hearing. It may strike one as overly stylized,

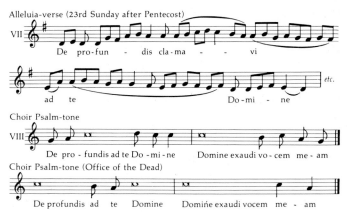

Intonation Tenor   Mediant of 2 accents

1. Con-fi - te-bor ti - bi Do-mi - ne   in to-to   cor - de me - o:
2.   Ma-gna   o-pe - ra Do-mi - ni
3.   Con-fes-si - o   et ma-gni - fi - cen-ti - a   o - pus e - jus:

6.32 Extract from Psalm 110, Office of Second Vespers

The Service of the Mass

Organized around the re-enactment of the Last Supper, the Mass consists of a series of processionals, offertory rites, prayers, biblical readings (Epistle and Gospel), and psalms and canticles sung both antiphonally and responsorially. Although its forms have varied throughout the centuries, most of its basic elements were in place by the late seventeenth century. At that time, the sung parts consisted of the following:

1 *Introit*: an antiphon; originally sung as a processional for the entrance of a bishop.

2 *Kyrie*: a responsorial chant involving alternations of the Greek words *Kyrie eleison* ("Lord have mercy") and *Christe eleison* ("Christ have mercy").

3 *Gloria*: ("Glory to God in the highest") a responsorial chant in which the opening phrase was sung by the bishop or celebrating priest and the rest by the choir and, possibly, the congregation.

4 *Gradual*: a responsorial chant sung between the reading of the Epistles and the reading of the Gospel.

5 *Alleluia* or *Tract*: a responsorial chant of praise (Hebrew: *Hallelu Ja*; English: "Praise ye Jehovah") following the Gradual. During the season of Lent, when solemnity is called for, the Alleluia is replaced by the Tract, a series of verses from the Bible.

6 *Credo*: the statement of Christian belief. The Nicene Creed (beginning "I believe in one God") was established at the Council of Nicea in 325.

7 *Offertory*: an antiphon for the offertory processional. It stands at the beginning of the sacrificial part of the Mass and was originally sung by clergy and congregation at the presentation of bread and wine.

8 *Sanctus*: ("Holy, Holy, Holy, Lord God of Hosts") a responsorial chant, following the reading of prayers and the preparation of the bread and wine, which the congregation was allowed to sing. This was followed by the *Benedictus* ("Blessed is he that cometh in the name of the Lord").

9 *Agnus Dei*: ("Lamb of God") a responsorial chant sung by the choir following the Sanctus and a recitation of the *Pater noster* (Lord's Prayer).

10 *Communion*: an antiphonal chant sung by the choir after the bread and wine have been consumed.

11 *Ite, Missa Est*: ("Go, it is the dismissal") a responsorial chant that ends the service. In time, the word *missa* came to stand for the service itself and was adapted in the European vernaculars (hence the English "Mass").

Like the Divine Office, the Mass has its own Proper components that change depending on the church calendar, and Ordinary components that remain the same:

Proper		Ordinary	
1	Introit		
		2	Kyrie
		3	Gloria
4	Gradual		
5	Alleluia or Tract		
		6	Credo
7	Offertory		
		8	Sanctus
		9	Agnus Dei
10	Communion		
11	Ite, Missa Est		

Gregorian chant is not so expressionless that it is indifferent to the occasion or musical setting. For example, the lines, *De profundis clamavi ad te, Domine: Domine exaudi vocem meam* ("From the depths I have cried to thee, O Lord; Lord, hear my voice") from Psalm 130 were set to different melodies to fit different times and purposes as, for example, in a chant for the Alleluia and a choir psalm tone (Fig. **6.34**). Though unfamiliar with the subtleties of the church modes and the Gregorian style, we can nonetheless sense the dramatic difference between the joy of the ornate Alleluia and seriousness of the psalm tone.

Like the simple plan of the Early Christian basilica, Gregorian chant served as the foundation on which the elaborate edifices of the medieval period would be constructed.

6.34 Vespers antiphon, in modern notation

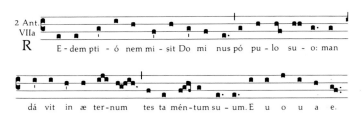

Alleluia-verse (23rd Sunday after Pentecost)

VII De pro-fun - dis cla-ma - - vi

ad te   Do - mi - ne   *etc.*

Choir Psalm-tone

VIII De pro - fundis ad te Do-mi-ne   Domine exaudi vo-cem me - am

Choir Psalm-tone (Office of the Dead)

De profundis ad te Domine   Domine exaudi vocem me - am

6.33 An antiphon

2 Ant.
VIIa
R   E - dem pti - ó nem mi - sit Do mi nus pó pu - lo su - o: man

dá vit in æ ter-num   tes ta mén-tum su - um. E u o u a e.

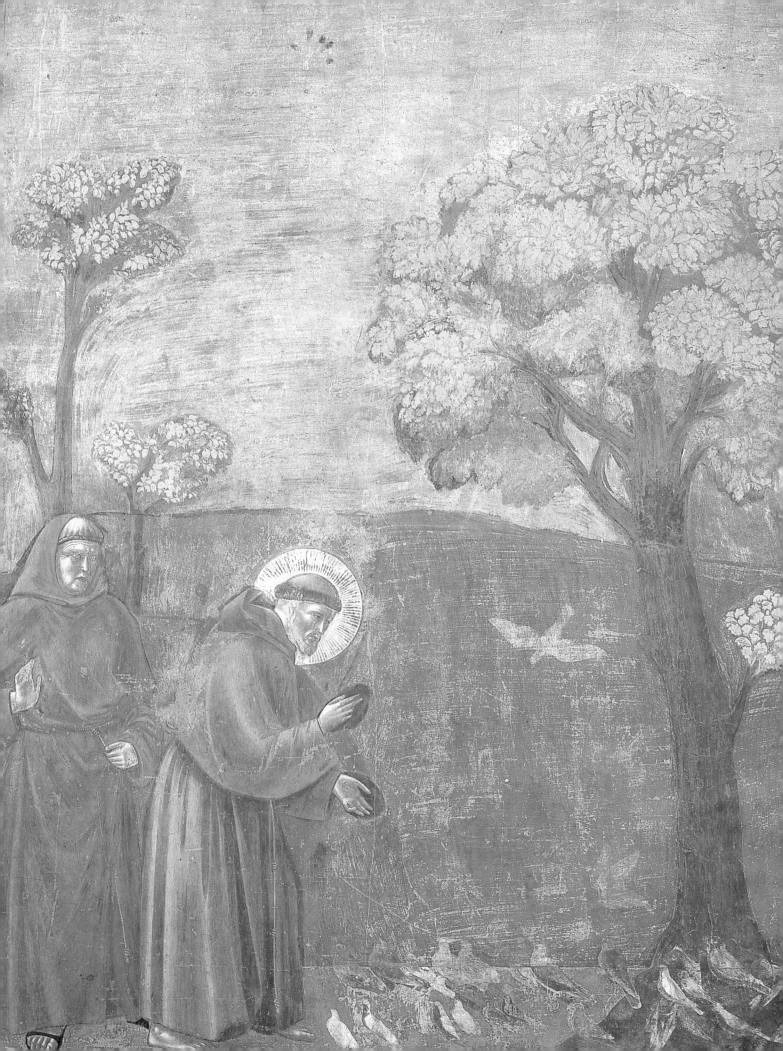

CHAPTER SEVEN

Christianity II: The Middle Ages

Be thou praised, my Lord,
with all thy creatures.

ST FRANCIS OF ASSISI

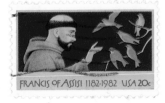

7.1 GIOTTO(?) *St. Francis' Sermon to the Birds,* Assisi

Introduction

The Middle Ages, also called the medieval period, is that span of European history between the ancient and modern worlds, often dated from the fall of Rome in the fifth century to the fall of Constantinople in the fifteenth (Fig. 7.2). The early part of this period, between 500 and 800, is called the Dark Ages because of the economic, social, and cultural chaos that descended upon Western Europe in the aftermath of the Germanic invasions that brought about the final destruction of the Roman Empire. Rome itself was devastated by warfare and disease, reduced to a fraction of its former population. Across the Alps, the Gauls, the most Romanized people of Western Europe, were also prey to barbaric invasions. These invasions, however, as destructive as they were, added a new dimension to the Roman culture, which, as the result of Constantine's decree legitimizing the Christian faith, embraced both classical and Judaeo-Christian elements. Thus the cultural ancestry of Western civilization was eventually to be made up of a mixture of the classical, Christian, and Germanic cultures. The Germanic peoples quite readily received the Christian faith and adapted themselves to its teachings and practices, at the same time infusing it with their own traits, such as their love of action and independence. Classicism, however, was barely preserved, largely through the monasteries, in the cultural darkness of the period extending from the sixth to the eighth centuries.

The classical culture of Rome, as well as the Orthodox tradition in Christianity, was preserved and extended in this period primarily through Constantinople (Byzantium), the capital of the Eastern Empire (see Chapter 6). Even here, however, though classical philosophy and literature were preserved, significant original contributions occurred in art alone. The high point of Byzantine civilization is associated with the name of Justinian, who controlled both Church and Empire.

7.2 The Middle Ages

DATES	SOCIAL AND POLITICAL DEVELOPMENTS	LITERATURE AND PHILOSOPHY	VISUAL ARTS	ARCHITECTURE	MUSIC
500		Code of Justinian	Purse cover from Sutton Hoo (7.7)		
	Spread of Islam				
700	Islamic culture (8th–11th centuries) Charlemagne crowned			Palace Chapel of Charlemagne (7.9)	
800	Cluniac order founded Growth of monasticism		Gospel Book of Charlemagne (7.10) Gospel Book of Rheims (7.11)		Musical notation Polyphony
1000		Growth of vernacular literature *Song of Roland* (7.4)	Moissac carvings (7.22)	Cluny III (7.13) St Sernin (7.14) Pisa Cathedral (7.18)	Guido d'Arezzo Solmization
	Crusades (1096–1204)				
1100	Growth of town life First universities	Impact of Islamic Scholars Anselm and Abelard *De contemptu mundi*	Jamb statues at Chartres (7.39)	Durham Cathedral (7.21) St-Denis, Paris (7.24) Chartres Cathedral (7.27)	
1200		*The Song of Brother Sun* Thomas Aquinas	Cimabue (7.44)	Amiens Cathedral (7.31) Salisbury Cathedral (7.35) Cologne Cathedral (7.36)	Minnesingers School of Notre Dame Organ
1300	Popes in Avignon Hundred Years War Black Death	Dante (7.6) Petrarch Boccaccio	Virgin of Paris (7.41) Sluter (7.42) Giotto (7.1, 7.43) Limbourg Brothers (7.47)	Palma Cathedral (7.37)	De Vitry: *Roman de Fauvel* (7.55) *Ars Nova* Machaut (7.56)
1400	First printed book Columbus discovers America		Van Eyck (7.48)		
1500					

Through his powerful influence, the Byzantine Empire prospered and expanded, Roman law was organized into the great Justinian Code, and art flourished, evidenced especially by the creation of the magnificent church *Hagia Sophia*. Later, in the ninth century, the Byzantine Church was also responsible for the evangelizing of the Slavic peoples of the Balkans and Russia.

But the preservation of the classical traditions was accomplished not only through Christianity—the Byzantine Empire in the East and the monasteries, minimally, in the West—but also through the rise of another great world religion: Islam. Beginning with Mohammed's flight from Mecca in 622, this religion spread like wildfire throughout the Middle East, Central Asia, and North Africa, finally to be checked by Charles Martel at Tours (732), in central France. In the period between the eighth and eleventh centuries, Islam created a magnificent civilization composed of elements from the East (India and Persia) and the West (the Greeks). The Muslims recovered Greek philosophical and scientific works and, through their translations into Arabic, made these works, along with their own distinctive art and music, available to Western Europe as it gradually emerged from the Dark Ages.

In the West this recovery first began to occur under the Frankish rulers, most notably Charlemagne (Charles the Great, 768–814), who was crowned the first Holy Roman Emperor by Pope Leo III on Christmas Day, 800. In this act (which apparently came as a surprise to Charlemagne), the pope formally sanctioned what Charlemagne had already set out to accomplish: the unification of Europe under the banner of the Church.

Eventually Charlemagne's empire reached from the North Sea to Rome, from Denmark to Spain, and from the Atlantic to the Danube valley. He presided over this new political entity from his capital Aachen (West Germany). Along with his program of christianizing Europe, Charlemagne launched a revival of the arts and learning known as the Carolingian Renaissance (from the Latin *Carolus*, Charles). He brought to Aachen Europe's best scholars—including the English theologian Alcuin (735–804), whom he charged with recovering the true text of the Bible—and artists from as far away as Constantinople. Although the Carolingian Renaissance was not innovative, it encouraged the copying of the ancient Latin authors and thus contributed significantly to their survival. It also revived early church architecture and the sculpture and painting of the Mediterranean world.

The fortunes of the Church were varied in the early medieval period. Constantinople, under the patriarchs, and Rome, under the popes, became the two centers of authority for the Christian faith. The patriarchs, though initially in the more powerful position because of the backing of the wealthy Eastern Empire, eventually found themselves under the thumb of the emperors, who controlled both state and Church. The popes, on the other hand, were often in conflict with the secular rulers, a struggle from which they eventually emerged triumphant—the reverse of the situation in Constantinople. This was also a period of missionary activity in the West, with monks such as the Irishman Columbanus and the Englishman Boniface evangelizing the Continent and founding monasteries. A scholar as well as a missionary, Boniface was a significant figure in the Carolingian Renaissance, improving existing monastic schools as well as founding new ones. Despite the occasional appearance of such religious luminaries, however, the early medieval period was in many ways an age of spiritual as well as cultural darkness.

In the ninth century the peace achieved by the Carolingian dynasty was disrupted by another wave of barbarian raids and by Muslim attacks. Since there was no central government strong enough to protect the inhabitants of the Frankish kingdom, they sought security in the protection of powerful local leaders. Thus developed a feudal society, with its hierarchical organization consisting of political leaders, including the king, who granted land to their vassals in exchange for personal service, chiefly military. This is the political and social structure that is assumed in the *Song of Roland*, as we shall see.

The tenth and eleventh centuries marked the beginning of a spiritual and secular revival in Western Europe. The growth of monasticism was a major factor in this change. The Benedictine abbey of Cluny, founded in 910 in Burgundy, sought to achieve spiritual renewal through a more faithful adherence to the rule formulated by Benedict of Nursia in the sixth century. Indeed, the Cluniac monks sought to reform the Church in general, including the papacy. Their effort to free the papacy from the control of Italian politics resulted eventually in the creation of the College of Cardinals, to whom was given the task of electing the pope. One of the supporters of their reform movement was Pope Gregory VII (1077–1088), who excommunicated the Holy Roman Emperor himself, Henry IV, when Henry sought to depose him because Gregory had prohibited lay appointment of church officials.

Among the numerous other monastic orders founded in this period and dedicated to reform and renewal were the Cistercians in the twelfth century, founded by St. Bernard of Clairvaux; the Franciscans in the thirteenth century, founded by St. Francis of Assisi; and, also in the thirteenth century, the Dominicans, founded by St. Dominic.

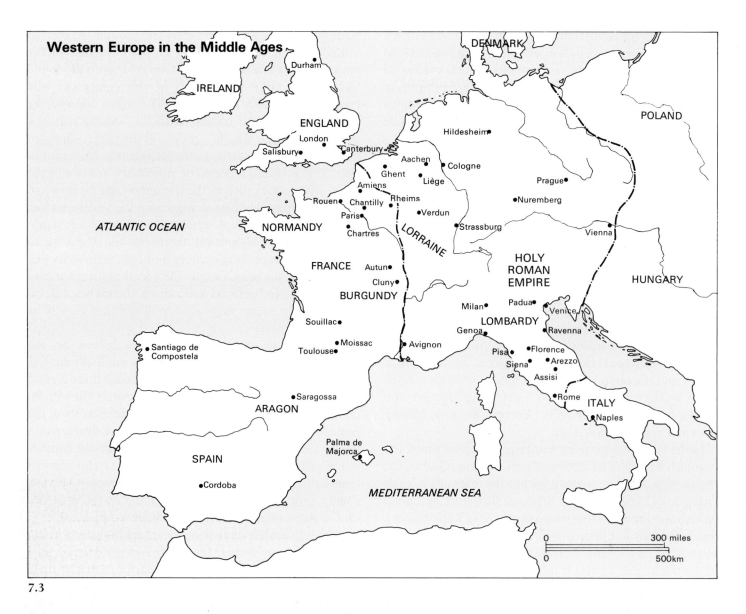

Western Europe in the Middle Ages

DENMARK

IRELAND

POLAND

ENGLAND

Durham

Hildesheim

London

Salisbury

Canterbury

Aachen

Cologne

Prague

Ghent

Liège

ATLANTIC OCEAN

Amiens

Rheims

Nuremberg

Rouen

Chantilly

Paris

Verdun

NORMANDY

Chartres

LORRAINE

Strassburg

Vienna

HOLY
ROMAN
EMPIRE

FRANCE

Autun

HUNGARY

Cluny

BURGUNDY

Milan

Padua

Venice

LOMBARDY

Souillac

Genoa

Ravenna

Santiago de
Compostela

Moissac

Avignon

Pisa

Florence

Toulouse

Siena

Arezzo

Assisi

Saragossa

Rome

ITALY

ARAGON

Naples

Palma de
Majorca

SPAIN

Cordoba

MEDITERRANEAN SEA

0   300 miles

0   500km

7.3

Although the high ideals of monasticism were often subverted and corrupted by human weakness, the monastic orders were a stimulus for spiritual reform both in the Church and in society at large. Moreover, they made significant contributions in the missionary outreach of the Church.

The eleventh century saw both secular states and the Church gaining power, developments that made conflict inevitable. The kings sought to enhance their power at the expense of the nobles, and the papacy sought to consolidate its control over all of society. Both efforts were largely successful. Politically, economically, intellectually, the Church, from Gregory VI in the eleventh century, to the Protestant Reformation of the sixteenth, dominated Western Europe. Since the eternal salvation of the individual was dependent upon the sacraments administered by the Church, the papal hierarchy's control extended to the private life of every person, including the king. During the

Crusades, the Latin Church also extended its power to the East.

The eleventh century was also the period of the upsurge of the middle class and the growth of town life, beginning in Italy and spreading to the west and the north. This development was, among other things, a significant factor in the generation and transmission of ideas. This was also the century of the elaboration of the Romanesque style in church architecture, the development of the philosophy of St. Anselm, and the writing of a large body of Latin literature, as well as poetry in the vernacular (native) languages, including the *Song of Roland*.

Medieval culture reached its apogee in the twelfth and thirteenth centuries. Prior to the twelfth century, the monasteries had been the centers of learning and had thus attracted the best scholars. The growth of town prosperity, however, provided new support and prestige for the secular clergy—priests and bishops (monks belonged to the "religious" clergy). Thus the cathedral schools, run by the secular clergy, also grew in importance, and certain ones of them, such as the cathedral school of Notre Dame in Paris, became the great medieval universities. These universities were very cosmopolitan, attracting students and teachers from all over Europe, and thus fostered a unity in medieval thought. Their faculties included some scholars and poets; Dante and St. Thomas Aquinas, for example, were among those who studied at the University of Paris. This period also saw the development of Gothic architecture out of the Romanesque style, as well as the creation of chivalric romance. Significant developments also occurred in the performance and theory of music.

Among the cultural contributions of the thirteenth century, three in particular stand out: the Gothic cathedral, the *Summa Theologica* of Thomas Aquinas, and the *Divine Comedy* of Dante. One could find no greater monuments to the prestige of the medieval Church and the cultural achievement of the high medieval period than these. Gothic architecture and Aquinas's *Summa*, in which he attempts to link reason and revelation in a comprehensive system of thought, were, of course, produced in the service of the Church. Dante's *Commedia*, though not written for the Church, is an expression of Thomist theology, as will be shown, and, in its own way, also sums up medieval theology. All three are achievements of enormous significance, not only for thirteenth-century religion and culture but for all time. This chapter, therefore, will give special attention to these works; and the literary section will culminate with a discussion of Dante. The art section, however, because of the continuation of medieval symbolism and subject matter into the fifteenth century, will end with Flemish art of that later period. Like literature, the music section will end in the fourteenth century, but with *ars nova*, exemplified by Machaut's *Notre Dame Mass*, his most significant work.

Literature

The Song of Roland

The *chanson de geste* ("song of [heroic] deeds") was a medieval French narrative poem celebrating acts of bravery, especially those of Charlemagne and his knights. The *Chanson de Roland* is of this genre; it recounts the heroism of one Roland, the nephew of Charlemagne. The *Song of Roland* was written in Old French (the ancestor of the modern French language and one of the ancestors of English).The event it commemorates occurred in the late eighth century, but the poem itself was probably written in the eleventh century. The historical event was quite minor. Charlemagne had attempted to extend his power into Spain through an alliance with a Saracen faction. After a six-week siege of Saragossa, a city that was supposed to welcome him, Charlemagne withdrew and headed back to France. As the army moved through a pass in the Pyrenees, the rear guard was attacked and annihilated by Christian Basques (AD 778). Einhard, Charlemagne's biographer, who, some 50 years later, tells the story, names three nobles who fell. One of the three was Roland, prefect of Brittany. This is the slight historical kernel that evolved into the *Song of Roland*.

Although the stages by which the changes occurred are unknown, the idealistic transformation of this story in the *Song of Roland* is apparent. For example, Christian Basques are changed into pagan Saracens, Muslims who worship false gods (a fantastic notion in view of the passionate

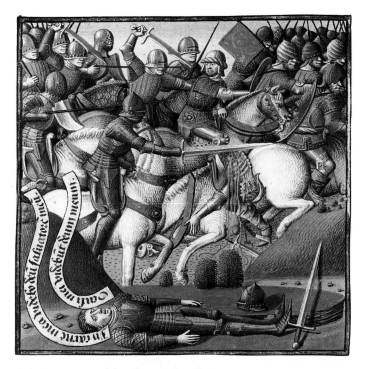

7.4 Manuscript of the *Chanson de Roland*
Illumination, fifteenth century
Musée Condé, Chantilly, France

monotheism of Islam). This metamorphosis made it possible for the poet to turn a minor skirmish involving Christians only into a great Christian crusade against paganism. Thus Charlemagne is transformed from an ambitious king in his thirties, out to expand his political horizon, into an august gray-bearded ancient of 200 years, guided by the angel Gabriel and weighed down by the heavy burden of the divine purpose in history.

Roland, as the title suggests, is the key figure in the story. He is bound in a close friendship with Oliver, another of the king's faithful retainers, and possesses a remarkable horn which he can cause to be heard at a distance of 30 leagues. The villain of the piece is Ganelon, Roland's stepfather, whose spite toward Roland leads to his treacherous collusion with the Saracens and the annihilation of Roland and his rear guard when Roland, out of fear that he might be called a coward, refuses, until it is too late, to sound the horn call that would have brought Charlemagne and his army to the rescue. He dies, not at the hands of the Saracens, but because his temples burst under the pressure of his blowing the Oliphant, his mighty horn. Although Charlemagne arrives too late to save Roland and his men, he defeats the Saracen army. Eventually, the king brings Ganelon to trial and, despite Ganelon's claim that his aggression against Roland should not be regarded as treason against his king, executes him.

Like the Homeric epics, the *Song of Roland* developed out of an oral tradition. This is evident from the numerous examples of repetition in the poem, especially in the description of single combat involving notable heroes from both sides. The same words and phrases are employed repeatedly. This is typical of epic poetry originating in an oral tradition, since it was made to be recited and heard, not read. Both the performer and the audience would be aided by this repetition, the performer in his recitation of the poem from memory and the audience through the reassuring sound of familiar diction.

The *Song of Roland's* dramatization of the interlocked ideals of God, king, and country, combined with its literary power, achieved through poetry and interesting heroic characters, explains its immense popularity in the French tradition. God, king, and country form a unity so ideal as to suggest the realization of the kingdom of God on earth.[1] Vassal, king, and God are bound in ascending order in the perfect hierarchy that was the feudal ideal. Roland, the ideal vassal, is loyal to the religion about whose truth he never entertains the slightest doubt; to the king, whose wisdom and goodness are near-divine; and to "sweet France," which he can never dishonor by cowardice. Indeed, the poem reveals a kingdom that is ideal, a near

fulfillment of the biblical predictions of the establishment of God's kingdom on earth and certainly a model for kingdoms yet to come. It is no surprise, therefore, that some critics see the poem as a glorification of royal authority and thus intended to provide support for the Capetian kings of France, who, in the eleventh century, sought to establish their authority over their barons.

In any case, the poem provides us with a portrait, not of the kingdom of Charlemagne, but of the way the past was viewed by eleventh-century France. The ahistorical nature of the presentation notwithstanding, the *Song of Roland* wields a power in the French tradition that puts it in the category of other great idealistic poeticized renditions of the past such as Homer's *Iliad* for the Greeks and Virgil's *Aeneid* for the Romans (see Chapter 2).

The Thirteenth-Century Synthesis

The title of Pope Innocent III's famous work, *De contemptu mundi* ("On Contempt of the World"), written in 1195, epitomizes the medieval view of the world as evil, a vale of sorrows and temptations through which Christians must painfully make their way in order, finally, to enter Paradise. Shortly before the dawning of the Renaissance, however, there was a shift in attitude which has been called the "thirteenth-century synthesis."[2] In this development, nature and God, rather than being viewed as antithetical, came to be regarded as interpenetrating aspects of a divine Reality which formed a coherent synthesis.

The life and thought of St. Francis of Assisi (1182–1226) beautifully illustrate this synthesis. After a dramatic conversion in which he turned his back on a life of wealth and luxury, Francis embraced poverty and dedicated himself to helping the poor and weak—principles on which he later founded the Franciscan Order. A gentle and compassionate man, Francis saw nature and all its creatures as gifts of God; thus, rather than rejecting this physical world, he related to it in a very personal and devout manner. He is, for example, reputed to have preached to the birds—an incident immortalized in his "Sermon to the Birds" and in Giotto's (?) fresco of the scene (Fig. 7.1). The same devotional linking of nature with God is evident in his poem "The Song of Brother Sun":

> MOST HIGH, Omnipotent, Good Lord.
> Thine be the praise, the glory, the honour, and all benediction.
> To Thee alone, Most High, they are due, and no man is worthy to mention Thee.
>
> Be Thou praised, my Lord, with all Thy creatures, above all
> Brother Sun, who gives the day and lightens us therewith.

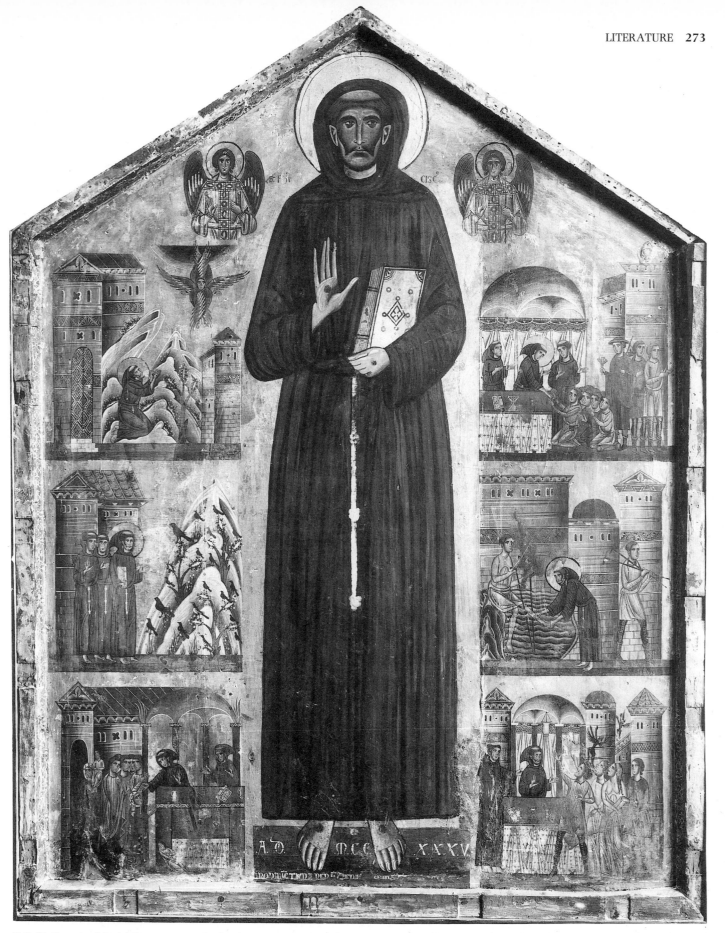

7.5 *St. Francis of Assisi*, Bonaventura Berlinghieri, 1235
Oil on panel, about 60 × 42 ins (152 × 107 cm)
San Francesco, Pescia

*And he is beautiful and radiant with great splendour, of Thee,
Most High, he bears similitude.*

*Be Thou praised, my Lord, of Sister Moon and the stars, in the
heaven hast Thou formed them, clear and precious and comely.*

*Be Thou praised, my Lord, of Brother Wind, and of the air, and
the cloud, and of fair and of all weather, by which Thou givest to
Thy creatures sustenance.*

*Be Thou praised, my Lord, of Sister Water, which is much useful
and humble and precious and pure.*

*Be Thou praised, my Lord, of Brother Fire, by which Thou hast
lightened the night, and he is beautiful and joyful and robust and
strong.*

*Be Thou praised, my Lord, of our Sister Mother Earth, which
sustains and hath us in rule, and produces divers fruits with
coloured flowers and herbs.*

*Be Thou praised, my Lord, of those who pardon for Thy love and
endure sickness and tribulations.*

*Blessed are they who will endure it in peace, for by Thee, Most
High, they shall be crowned.*

*Be Thou praised, my Lord, of our Sister Bodily Death, from
whom no man living may escape: woe to those who die in mortal
sin:*

*Blessed are they who are found in Thy most holy will, for the
second death shall not work them ill.*

*Praise ye and bless my Lord, and give Him thanks, and serve Him
with great humility.*[3]

Thus Francis praises God for his natural and his
spiritual gifts. It is clearly both a religious and a nature
poem, emphasizing the loveliness of nature so subjectively
as to foreshadow the Romantic movement of the
nineteenth century. For Francis, nature is an expression of
the love and mercy of God, who is the source of all good
things. Death itself, the ultimate destructive force in
nature, is Francis' "sister" and an item in his litany of
praise. Even the "second death" is not to be feared by those
who do not die in "mortal sin" and have served with
"great humility" the God who has lavished his gifts upon
them.

For Francis, therefore, the natural world is not a barrier
to eternal life, but the manifestation of divine goodness. He
sanctified the ordinary and the secular and proclaimed
that the commonplace not only provides an opportunity
for praise but is in itself a form of praise. Thus he affirmed
the goodness of life in this world. This sanctification of the

secular and the ordinary is a theme that dominates the
popular literature of the thirteenth century, especially
stories based on the cult of Mary, the mother of Jesus.

The cult of the Virgin was a great source of comfort to
the ordinary worshiper in the twelfth and thirteenth
centuries. Its popularity is attested by the many churches
dedicated to "Our Lady" in Europe ("Notre Dame" in
France) and the numerous paintings, sculptures, stories,
poems, and hymns glorifying Mary. Patient and kind, she
interceded for sinners with God and Christ, both having
become remote in popular medieval belief. It is this
humanizing element provided by Mary that serves as
background for stories such as "Our Lady's Tumbler,"
which also illustrates the sanctification of the ordinary.

The tumbler of this story, grown weary of his life in the
world, enters a monastery. Since he cannot read or write,
however, he is incapable of participating in the daily
round of prayer and praise that occupies the lives of the
other monks. Frustrated, he prays for Mary's help. As he
wanders about the monastery he comes upon an altar
presided over by a statue of the Virgin. Hearing the bell
sounding for Mass, he decides that he will offer to his
beloved Mary the one thing that he does well. Thus he
begins to perform acrobatics in the presence of the statue.
Although he knows that he is an accomplished acrobat,
he offers his gift with the greatest humility. Tumbling with
all his might, he begins to sweat profusely. At this point,
Mary herself begins to fan him. But it is the abbot of the
monastery who sees her, not the tumbler, absorbed as he
is so unselfconsciously in his strenuous efforts to offer his
best to the Virgin.

This story and St. Francis' song illustrate the belief that
the natural and the commonplace belong to God and
provide a means of praising and serving him. Salvation is
therefore not a matter of rejecting life in this world, but of
recognizing the value of that life as a divine gift.

This thirteenth-century synthesis reached its pinnacle
with the immensely detailed philosophical system of
Scholasticism, introduced in the twelfth century by the
insistence of St. Anselm and Abelard on the use of reason
in defense of Christian belief, and fully developed by St.
Thomas Aquinas (1225–1274), who grounded his theology in the philosophy of Aristotle. Aquinas rejected the
antithetical isolation of nature and God, reason and
revelation, arguing that "grace does not deny nature but
perfects it." As reason is the means of discovering truth in
nature, so revelation (the Bible) is the means of discovering truth in the spiritual world. Some truths can be known
through reason; others can be known only through
revelation. Both kinds of truth, however, belong to God's
total Reality and are thus not discontinuous but connected. In his vast *Summa Theologica* (c. 1265–1274) Aquinas

sought to demonstrate this connection. Thus, for Aquinas, the revelation of God's nature and purpose as presented in the Bible, rather than conflicting with reason, was the culmination of what could already be known by human beings through reason. The influence of Aquinas's thought is far-reaching. Indeed, Scholasticism became the official philosophy of the Catholic Church. It also pervades Dante's immensely significant *Divine Comedy*.

Dante

The monumental importance of Dante Alighieri (1265–1321) in the Western literary tradition is captured by the remark of the poet T. S. Eliot: "Dante and Shakespeare divide the modern world between them; there is no third." Although not all critics would agree with this exclusive evaluation of the Italian poet (Fig. 7.6), it is unlikely that any would exclude him from the category of the greatest poets of the Western world. He stood at the zenith of the medieval era, and, in his *Divine Comedy*, achieved what the Gothic churches of his time did in architecture: summed up and consummated the great theological and philosophical traditions of the period. He was also a harbinger of the Renaissance in his close study of classical rhetoric and philosophy and his defense of the vernacular, which he employed in writing his great poem.

Dante was a man of many parts—poet, philosopher, soldier, politician—and it was his involvement in the tumultuous politics of Florence, where he was born and grew up, that led to the exile of his last years (1302–1321). Dante had sided with the Guelphs (supporters of the pope) against the Ghibellines (supporters of the Holy Roman Emperor); in his exile he would become a Ghibelline. But after the Guelphs gained control of Florence, they split into two factions. As a result of this inter-party struggle, Dante, while on a diplomatic mission to the papacy, was exiled and threatened with death should he return to the city. He spent the remainder of his life in sad wandering from patron to patron. But it was during this exile that he wrote *The Divine Comedy*. After his death in Ravenna, the last cantos of the *Paradiso* were discovered in his study; apparently he had only recently completed the poem.

In his exile, Dante developed political theories intended to bring the feuding and factionalism of the Italian city-states to an end. These he set forth in *The Banquet*, *Concerning Monarchy*, and, finally, *The Divine Comedy*. Although he held the Aristotelian view that human beings can reach their potential only in a social context, he also recognized that greed and envy often set them at one another's throats. Hence the warring of the Italian city-states. What was needed, therefore, was some centra-lized authority that would implement universal law. The Roman Empire had once played this civilizing and pacifying role; and like Virgil, Dante believed that this function was divinely imposed. Thus he places Brutus and Cassius, assassins of Julius Caesar, Dante's personification of the Empire, in the mouths of Satan at the bottom of Hell, along with Judas Iscariot. As Judas had betrayed God's Redeemer, so they had betrayed God's government. Indeed, Dante argued that the Roman Empire (which, in his view, was represented in his time by the Holy Roman Empire) received its authority, as did the Church, directly from God. Thus the Empire was not dependent upon the Church for the exercise of its authority. However, to prevent tyranny, the Church must use its moral and spiritual authority to provide society with proper guidance and to prepare fit rulers. But it must not use political means to achieve its aims, lest it become corrupt. For Dante, the Empire, the secular arm of God's redemptive purpose, is based upon reason; the Church, the spirtual arm of that purpose, upon revelation. Here we see the influence of Aquinas's Scholasticism—reason and revelation complementing one another in the service of God. Dante's system was, of course, gravely flawed, because the

7.6 GIOTTO (?)
Portrait of Dante, c. 1325
Detail of fresco, Chapel of Palazzo del Podesta, Bargello, Florence

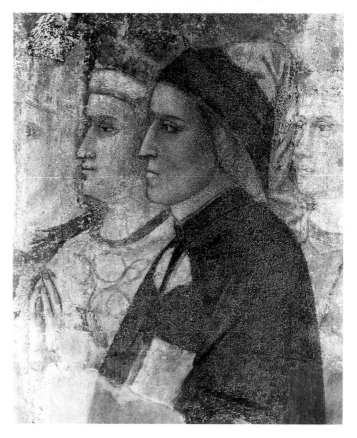

Empire lacked the power to impose peace on the Italian city-states, and the Church was not at all likely to withdraw from its deep involvement in politics. It is nonetheless important to bear in mind, as one reads *The Divine Comedy*, that Dante is concerned with the salvation of the state as well as of the individual.

The most significant incident in Dante's life with regard to *The Divine Comedy*, however, was not his exile from Florence and his subsequent frustration and political theorizing, but his encounter, at the age of nine, with Beatrice Portinare. Telling the story some 20 years later, he describes the impact of Beatrice upon him as though she were a divine being who was to rule his life. Although on the surface their relationship was a distant one—Beatrice died at 24, Dante having seen her only a few times—she became for him his inspiration and spiritual ideal. In the *Commedia* she is the symbol of divine grace and the instrument of the poet's redemption.

The entire *Divine Comedy* is symbolic, an allegory of Everyman's journey into self-knowledge (*Inferno*), through purgation from sin (*Purgatorio*), and into a state of grace (*Paradiso*). As with all allegories, the real significance of *The Divine Comedy* is not found in its literal meaning but in what the literal objects symbolize. Thus, for example, though Dante believed in a literal hell, purgatory, and paradise, the true significance of his poem is not found in such literalism but in the symbolic use that he makes of these realms and their inhabitants. His descent into Hell symbolizes the descent into the deepening possibilities for evil within themselves that all human beings must make if they are to be redeemed from sin. Once Everyman (Dante the Pilgrim) has become aware of the depths of sin, both potential and actual, within himself, he is ready for the discipline of repentance symbolized by the persons undergoing purgation on the seven encircling cornices of Mount Purgatory. Finally, he enters the state of grace symbolized by the vision of God himself in Paradise.

Dante's dependence upon Aquinas's Scholastic theology and its synthesis of reason and revelation is especially evident in the roles of Virgil and Beatrice. It is Virgil, Dante's "Sweet Master," representing classical reason and the best of paganism, who is sent by Beatrice, symbol of Christian revelation, to lead Dante out of the Dark Wood of error in which he has become lost. Virgil steers Dante through Hell and Purgatory and then relinquishes him to the guidance of Beatrice as he enters Paradise. Thus reason, under the direction of revelation, aids Everyman in the discovery of his sin and the repentance that follows; revelation alone is capable of conducting him into a state of grace. Following Aquinas, therefore, Dante saw reason and revelation as comple-

menting one another in human salvation.

As he uses historical figures to symbolize reason and revelation, so also Dante typically employs real persons, often from his own era, for other aspects of his allegorical purpose. It is at first puzzling that those who are in Hell say so little about the sins causing their damnation. They converse with Dante, but there is little moralizing over their sins and their punishment. This problem is solved, however, once one recognizes that the portrayed sinner suffering his/her particular punishment is indeed the personification of that sin. That is, Dante reveals the true nature of the sin by the image he creates of the sinner and his or her punishment. Thus, for example, Paolo and Francesca, swept by their overwhelming passion for each other into the adultery that destroyed them (they were murdered by Francesca's husband, who was also Paolo's brother), are portrayed in the second circle of the Inferno (reserved for the lustful) as locked in an eternal embrace and endlessly tumbled about by a powerful wind. This, Dante is saying, is the real state of the person who allows passion to overcome reason: out of control, rudderless, the prey of destructive desires. Thus he portrays and dramatizes the nature of this sin rather than moralizing over it.

The Divine Comedy opens with Dante lost in the Dark Wood, which symbolizes the sin-hardened state of mind that prevents a faithful response to God's offer of redemption. Although he sees the way out, a mountain-top bathed in sunlight, his attempts to climb the mountain, symbolizing repentance, are thwarted, in turn, by three animals: a leopard, a lion, and a wolf. These symbolize the sins that prevent Dante—and Everyman—from escaping the Dark Wood of error: respectively, incontinence (that is, uncontrolled appetites), violence, and fraud. These sins constitute the three major divisions of Hell through which Dante must pass as he penetrates ever more deeply into the wickedness of the human soul. As the frightened Dante turns his back, he encounters the shadowy figure of Virgil, who reveals that Dante must travel by another way if he is to ascend the mountain. That way, of course, will take him into the depths of the Inferno. There he must come to an awareness of the destructive power of sin before he will be ready to ascend the mountain of repentance and purgation.

Significantly, Dante, led by Virgil, enters Hell on Good Friday, the day of Christ's crucifixion, and emerges on Easter Sunday, the day of his resurrection. Like Christ, Dante must die (spiritually speaking) before he can rise to new life. But as Dante begins to follow Virgil, descending toward the Gate of Hell, he despairs because of his unworthiness. Virgil, however, reassures him by relating how Beatrice descended to the Inferno in order to send him to guide Dante. Thus divine grace, as well as reason, is necessary for Dante's redemption.

As the poets pass the gates of Hell, they enter the Vestibule, where hordes of people scream in pain while, stung by insects, they run after an elusive banner. These are the opportunists, the neutrals, those persons who have chosen neither good nor evil but have selfishly pursued their own interests only.

Dante and Virgil move on to Acheron, the first river of Hell, where they are met by Charon, who ferries the damned across to the other side. At first he refuses Dante because he is a living man and protected by divine grace; but then, advised by Virgil that it is God's will, he complies. Dante swoons and does not recover until they reach the other side.

The poets now enter the First Circle of Hell. Dante envisions Hell as a great funnel penetrating the earth in the northern hemisphere with its lowest point at the earth's center. Its Circles are concentric rings of ledges, each the place of punishment for a category of evil. Dante and Virgil move ever downward, crossing these ledges as they go; the deeper they penetrate, the more serious the sin. Thus Upper Hell (Circles I–V) includes the Vestibule, Limbo, and Circles for the *Incontinent*, such as the lustful, gluttons, and the greedy. Lower Hell is for the *Violent* (Circles VI–VII) and the *Fraudulent* (Circles VIII–IX). The category of the Violent includes heretics (VI), as well as murderers, suicides, and deicides (VII), because it is the obdurate rejection of God and his truth that leads to sins of violence. Circle VIII is reserved for persons who have defrauded those who have no special trust, while Circle IX is for those who have defrauded kindred, country, guests, and lords. At the very pit of Hell is Lucifer, submerged in ice, with Judas in his center mouth and Brutus and Cassius in the mouths on either side.

The First Circle, or Limbo, is inhabited by virtuous pagans and the unbaptized, those whose sins do not deserve Hell but who did not have the opportunity to choose Christ. Their only punishment is that they are without hope. Virgil, proclaimed by a voice "Prince of Poets," is welcomed back (as a virtuous pagan he occupies this part of Hell) by the other great poets: Homer (the greatest of the four), Horace, Ovid, and Lucan. With Virgil's smiling approval, they invite Dante into their elite group as a sixth member.

The sharp distinction between Limbo and Hell proper is symbolized by the passage of Dante and Virgil from light to darkness as they move from the First Circle to the Second. The distinction is also made evident by the figure of Minos, the Judge of Hell, who sits at its threshold assigning appropriate places of punishment to the arriving souls upon their confession of their sins. Though temporarily halted by a threat from Minos, the two poets move on into the Second Circle, the circle of the Lustful, where Dante encounters Paolo and Francesca.

In such a manner Dante, led by Virgil, descends ever more deeply into the bowels of Hell, and thus, symbolically, ever more deeply into the evil of the human heart. In each of Hell's Circles Dante encounters persons—some historical, some fictional—whose grotesque punishments symbolize the nature of the sin for which they are being punished. Thus Dante the Pilgrim's journey into self-knowledge is the means by which he comes to recognize both the possibilities and the realities of sin, the evil that every human being is capable of and the true nature of that evil.

Emerging from the pit of Hell on Easter Sunday, Dante and Virgil ascend Mount Purgatory—in Dante's poetic vision, a mountain in the southern hemisphere. Allegorically, however it is the image of repentance, the means by which Everyman, having discovered his sins, is cleansed. Suddenly, Beatrice appears to Dante and, overjoyed, he turns to Virgil to share the moment. But Virgil is gone, for he (Reason) can no longer lead. It is Beatrice (Revelation) who must conduct him into Paradise. Thus the two of them are set free of the encumbering earth and are swept upward toward Heaven.

Throughout the reading of Dante's great poem, it is imperative that one distinguish between its literal and its allegorical significance. Dante uses what to him were real places in the next world to symbolize the soul's journey to salvation *in this world*: through Hell (the soul's discovery of sin), up Mount Purgatory (the soul's repentance of sin), into Paradise (the soul's foretaste of eternal bliss). Dante's grand design, therefore, aimed at the redemption of life on earth, for the individual and the community, as well as in the world to come.

Thus we have encountered a connective theme in the literature discussed in this chapter. In the *Song of Roland* we are presented with a poetic rendering of the reign of Charlemagne—the first Holy Roman Emperor—that is so idealized as to suggest the realization of a divine kingdom on earth. "Our Lady's Tumbler" and the life and thought of St. Francis also suggest the possibility of living out the values of the heavenly kingdom in an earthly context. Thomas Aquinas, though setting forth the limitations of reason without revelation, also emphasizes its possibilities as a gift from God to be used in knowing and serving him. Finally, Dante, using Aquinas's Scholasticism as his philosophical substructure, erects the vast poetic "cathedral" of his *Divine Comedy* in which he argues the possibility of the redemption of the individual and the community—the latter through submission to the Holy Roman Emperor, Charlemagne's successor—in this world as well as the next, through the right use of the divine gifts of reason and revelation. Thus the vision of the Kingdom of God in this world, the redemption of earthly life, comes into focus in these works, contrasting with the darker medieval view of the world as a vale of sorrows, mere preparation ground for eternity. In the Renaissance, as we saw in Chapter 3, emphasis on the possibilities of this world becomes even stronger; in fact, in some cases, eclipses the possibilities of the next.

Art of the Middle Ages

During the Middle Ages, Europe experienced enormous growth in its material culture. It developed from a continent of rural, isolated villages to that of a civilization replete with monumental architecture and art. Because of the various stages of development within that period, together with regional differences, it is difficult to make meaningful generalizations regarding medieval art as a whole.

This development of a distinctively Western European civilization was strongly influenced by neighboring cultures; above all, by the Byzantine and Islamic. But the dominant influence was undoubtedly the Christian Church. Most artistic activity during the Middle Ages (with the significant exception of the building of castles) was dedicated to its service. The most visible evidence of this is the thousands of medieval churches, monasteries, convents, and cathedrals that still adorn the European landscape. Small-scale craftsmen, too, such as metal-

workers, jewelers, and embroiderers, worked mainly for the Church, producing candlesticks, chalices, vestments, and other precious liturgical objects. The subject matter of manuscript illustration, architectural sculpture, stained glass, and fresco and easel painting was primarily biblical.

A certain amount of myth has attached itself to the medieval artist. This takes the form of a notion that all of them were pious craftsmen wearing goatskins and working solely for the glory of God—an image perpetrated by writers of the Romantic era who believed that Gothic cathedrals were the product of anonymous creativity. But this view is not only sentimental, it is belied by the fact that a great number of stonemasons, metalworkers, and manuscript painters were highly respected and known by their personal styles; indeed numerous examples of Romanesque and Gothic painting and sculpture were signed. Moreover, the folklore of those periods tended to exaggerate the powers of artists, portraying them as sorcerers.

7.7 Purse cover from Sutton Hoo Ship Burial, 625–33 AD
Gold and enamel, 7½ ins (19 cm) long
British Museum, London

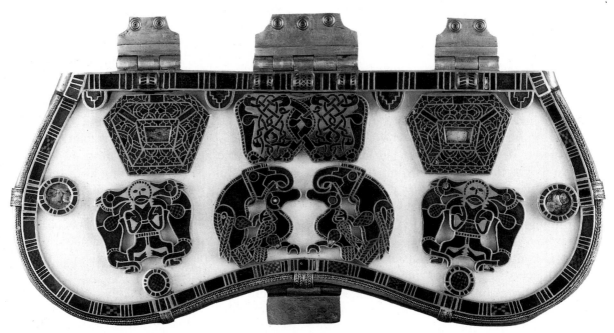

Nevertheless, it is true that most medieval artists, compared to their counterparts in the Renaissance, not to mention those of the Romantic era, were rather humble. Recruited from the ranks of serfs, the lowest rung of the feudal ladder (many used their services as barter for a higher rung on the ladder), they worked in relative obscurity.

The Carolingian Renaissance

During the Dark Ages (500–800), as we have seen, artistic activity in Western Europe languished. The production of monumental architecture and even sculpture virtually ceased, and the small amount of representational art that was produced—mostly that of illustrating biblical manuscripts—lacked the realistic portrayal of the human figure characteristic of classical art. The skill of Germanic and Celtic artists lay, rather, in interweaving stylized images of humans or beasts with geometric patterns—a tradition that grew out of decorating portable objects for a nomadic society (Fig. 7.7).

With the coronation of Charlemagne as Holy Roman Emperor in 800 this situation began to change. Charlemagne desired, in particular, to emulate and perpetuate the artistic achievements of the original Roman Empire (although, of course, in a Christian form). Among its main achievements was monumental architecture. Like successful emperors in the past, Charlemagne undertook an ambitious building program. But he had little to work with. Although Roman building practices had not been completely lost during the Dark Ages, masonry vaulting on a grand scale had disappeared. Several monasteries and churches were built under him, but few survive; all those that employed the basilica style (see page 247) have

7.8 Restored plan of Palace Chapel of Charlemagne, Aachen, 792–805 AD

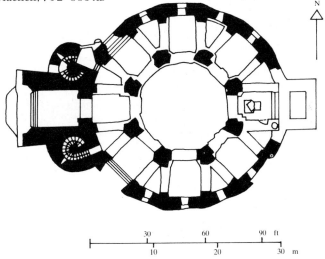

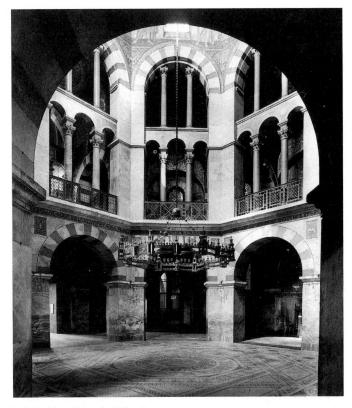

7.9 Palace Chapel of Charlemagne, interior

disappeared. The best-known surviving building is his Palatine (palace) Chapel at Aachen, which supposedly was inspired by San Vitale in Ravenna (though, according to recent theory, it was modeled after a now-destroyed building in the palace complex at Constantinople). However, about the only similarity between the San Vitale and the Palatine Chapel is the fact that both are domed, radially planned structures. The exterior wall of the Palatine is 16-sided, but its interior, like San Vitale's, is octagonal (Fig. 7.8). Thus, the cross-vaulting that links the 16-sided exterior to the eight-sided interior creates a curious network of alternating squares and triangles. It is the Palatine's interior (Fig. 7.9), however, that is so different in spirit from that of San Vitale.

The main supports are divided into two levels: a squat ground-level arcade which supports a taller, but equally massive, second-level arcade. The latter is further divided by a two-tiered screen of Corinthian columns. Despite the complexity of these arch systems, and Charlemagne's desire to emulate Eastern culture, the blunt geometry of this chapel differs markedly from the airy proportions of San Vitale. In the final analysis, it is neither Byzantine nor Roman, but Germanic—the first monument of an incipient Western architecture.

Charlemagne's stimulation of the arts was equally significant in small-scale works, particularly devotional

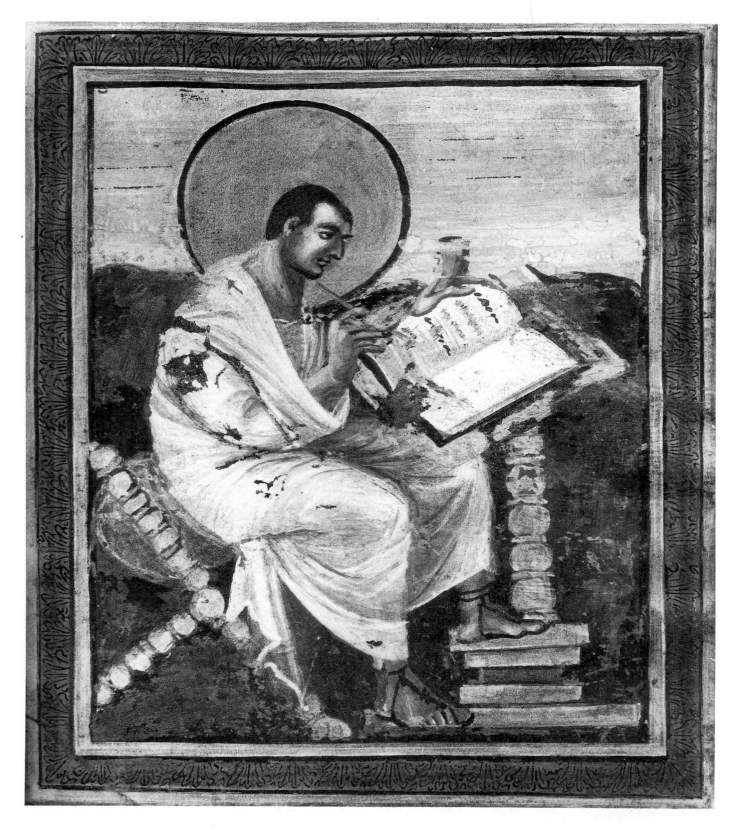

7.10 *St. Matthew* from the *Gospel Book of Charlemagne*, c. 800–810 AD
Approx. $6\frac{3}{4} \times 9$ ins (17×23 cm)
Kunsthistorisches Museum, Vienna

books. New churches, of course, required new copies of Gospels, Psalters (collections of psalms), sermons, and revised forms of Gregorian chant. While Alcuin and other resident scholars were busy authenticating the texts of the manuscripts, and calligraphers were busy transcribing them, Charlemagne's artists were busy decorating them. Carolingian representational art, like its architecture, was modeled on Early Christian and Byzantine examples—in this case, frescoes, mosaics, ivory reliefs, and manuscript illustrations. Some of Charlemagne's manuscripts were not only modeled on such sources but also probably executed by artists imported from Constantinople, Ravenna, or Rome. Only a person trained in the tradition of late Hellenism, it is believed, could have adequately understood and represented the ways in which a toga covers the human form, as in the illustration of St. Matthew (Fig. **7.10**). Another illustration of the saint, made a few years later, is probably by a northern artist attempting to appropriate this tradition (Fig. **7.11**). Although the painter misinterpreted the body-clothing relationship, he more than compensated for this defici-

7.11 *St. Matthew*, from the *Gospel Book of Archbishop Ebbo of Reims*, c. 816–35
Approx. 10 × 8 ins (25 × 20 cm)
Bibliotheque Nationale, Paris

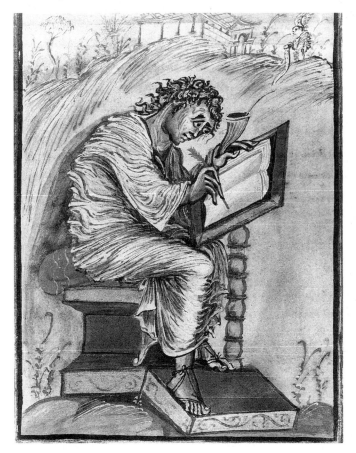

ency in other ways. His version, which shares with the earlier one the same composition and pose, is much livelier. The scene of the Evangelist, thoroughly absorbed in writing his Gospel, is enlivened by the expressive face, the agitated folds of the toga, the sketchy, animated landscape, and, especially, by the energy transmitted through the artist's restless, pulsating lines. Of course, we have no knowledge of the artist's real intentions. Perhaps he was simply doing his best to imitate the mannerisms of late Roman art rather than to transcend them.

The Carolingian revival was possible because of the politics, personality, and patronage of Charlemagne. His efforts resulted in what could be called "a culture in search of a style." Its source was the classical past—or, to be more precise, what Carolingian artists thought was the classical past, that is, Byzantine, Early Christian, and late Roman art. Furthermore, these artists did not comprehend what they copied. But this does not mean they failed. Like their musical counterparts, who tried to appropriate Greek modes, they misconstrued the classical past, but they succeeded, nevertheless, in planting the seeds of a new European art. Carolingian culture stands as an island in history, an anachronism in both directions: behind its time because it delved into obsolete art, ahead of its time because it anticipated the art of the future.

Interim: the Ninth and Tenth Centuries

Charlemagne's empire, which lasted only 30 years after his death, was followed by another period of confusion. But this period was not entirely a dark age. Two recognizable political entities evolved out of the breakup of the Carolingian empire: the Holy Roman Empire in central Europe (which in fact was a cluster of German kingdoms) and a Frankish kingdom on the Atlantic that prefigured the modern state of France. Meanwhile, the institutions of feudalism and monasticism became stronger and began increasingly to shape medieval economic and cultural life.

Although culture did not flourish in this period, it did not die. In the monasteries and convents, literacy was kept alive by preserving manuscripts and teaching Latin, music by chanting the liturgy, and the visual arts not only by manuscripts but by carving ivory, working metal, and embroidering vestments. Largely because of these religious orders, an original European culture began to emerge in the eleventh century.

Romanesque Architecture

Symbolizing this culture is the *Romanesque* church. Characterized by round arches, heavy supports, and, usually, a feeling of austere solidity, these churches are reminiscent

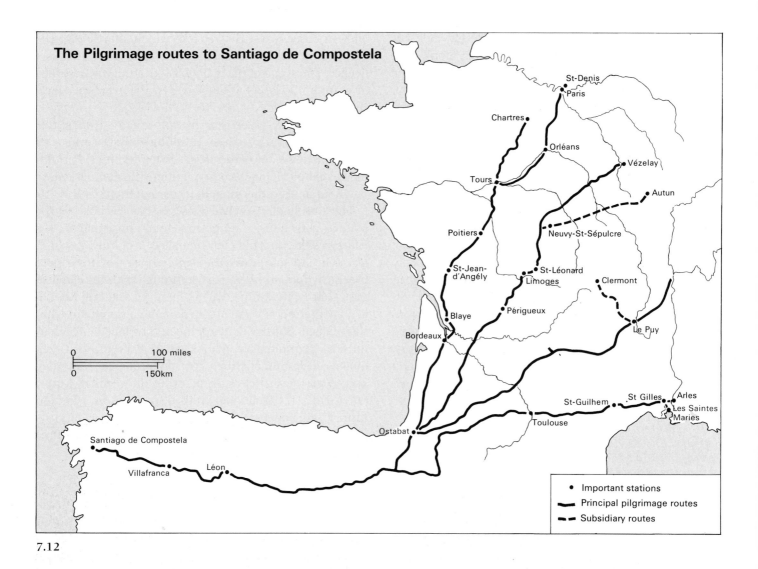

The Pilgrimage routes to Santiago de Compostela

St-Denis
Paris
Chartres
Orléans
Vézelay
Tours
Autun
Poitiers
Neuvy-St-Sépulcre
St-Jean-d'Angély
St-Léonard
Limoges
Clermont
Blaye
Périgueux
Bordeaux
Le Puy
St-Guilhem
St Gilles
Arles
St-Léonard
Toulouse
Les Saintes Maries
Ostabat
Santiago de Compostela
Villafranca
Léon

0   100 miles
0   150km

• Important stations
━ Principal pilgrimage routes
╍ Subsidiary routes

7.12

of Roman buildings—hence the name "Romanesque." The boldness of this architecture, together with the fact that so many churches were built in the eleventh and twelfth centuries, reflects the confidence of a new age. No longer subject entirely to forces outside of their control, Europeans began to master their own affairs and destinies. Former barbarians became converts to Christianity, thus helping to stabilize the political system and consolidate the borders of Europe. With increased stability at home, Europeans ventured beyond their borders in religious/military campaigns to the Holy Land: the Crusades. Although ultimately unsuccessful, the Crusades did have the side effects of stimulating building efforts in towns and port cities along Crusade routes and of bringing Europeans into contact with foreign peoples, particularly the Muslims and Byzantines.

More peacefully, Europeans were also on the move for another purpose, the pilgrimage. This was a trip to a shrine containing relics—venerated objects, usually the remains of a saint: his or her bones, hair, pieces of clothing, and so forth, which were believed to be divinely endowed. Pilgrims endured many dangers and hardships to see and be in the presence of these relics. They poured into the shrines to fulfill vows, atone for sins, seek miraculous cures, and also, in some cases, to see a bit of the world. Some traveled as far as Jerusalem, to visit the shrines associated with Holy Week. Within Europe, the leading pilgrimage centers were Rome (the shrine of St. Peter), Santiago de Compostela in Spain (St. James), and, later, Canterbury, shrine of the martyred St. Thomas Becket.

Like the Crusades, pilgrimages stimulated a need for buildings, and resulted not only in the enlargement and elaboration of the shrines themselves but also in the building of many other churches along the pilgrimage routes (Fig. 7.12). Revenues from the pilgrims' donations helped to finance the costs of construction. The impulse for both the pilgrimages and the building program came largely from Cluniac monks. Although Cluny itself was not on a route, the now-destroyed Cluniac monastery was the model for most of the shrines, as well as being an important example of the Romanesque style (Fig. **7.13**).

A distinguishing feature of many Romanesque churches is the barrel vault ceiling. By now, Europeans had learned from experience—through accidents and barbarian raids—that timber ceilings burn; thus they began to build them of stone. Stone ceilings could not, of course, be flat, because of the great weight; so, instead, they were constructed according to the principle of the arch. The resulting tunnel-like barrel vault had a further advantage: it provided the best acoustics for the singing of chants. But such a ceiling, as noted earlier (see page 85), exerts a great deal of downward and outward pressure along its entire length. Therefore, another distinguishing feature of a Romanesque church is the heaviness of its walls and supporting piers. More will be said about the vaulted ceiling and its effect on the rest of the structure as we study the specifics of St. Sernin in Toulouse, France— an important example of Romanesque architecture and

perhaps the most representative of the pilgrimage churches (Fig. **7.14**).

Even the plan of St. Sernin (1080–1096) reveals its walls and internal bearing members to be considerably thicker than those of an Early Christian basilica (Fig. **7.15**). In that it has a narthex, long nave, side aisles, transept, crossing and apse, St. Sernin's plan follows the basilican tradition. But a few new features have been added. Because of the lengthened transept and large apse, it resembles a cross (a configuration known as *cruciform*). Furthermore, the side aisles (which are double along the nave) extend around the perimeters of both transept and apse. Called an *ambulatory*, this extension was intended for the passage of pilgrims, who often paused for devotions in front of relics contained in one or more of the nine *radiating chapels* that project from the ambulatory. The east end of the building, sometimes including part of the nave, was often reserved for the intoning of chants by choirs of monks.

7.13 Elevation and plan of third abbey church, Cluny, c. 1095–1100
From an eighteenth-century engraving

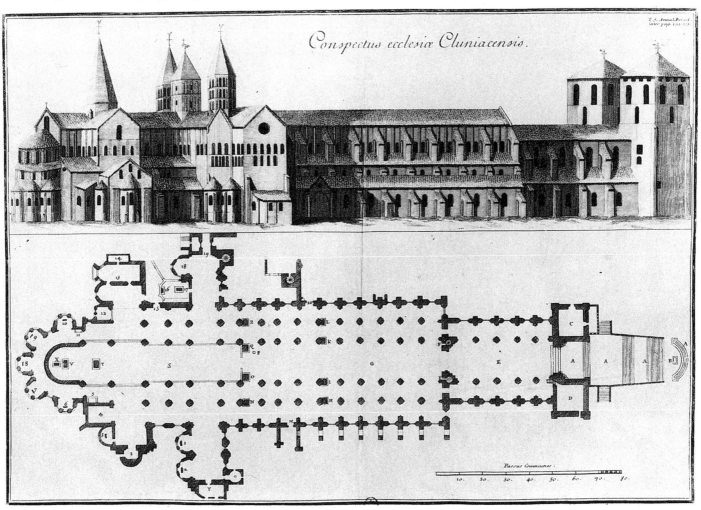

Conspectus ecclesiæ Cluniacensis.

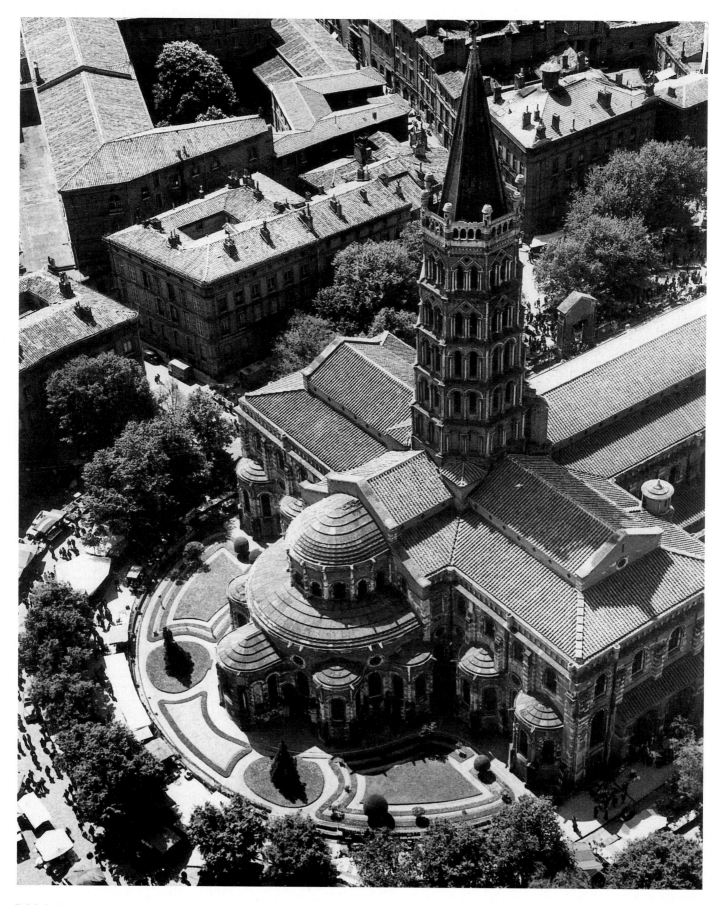

7.14 St. Sernin, Toulouse, c. 1080–1120

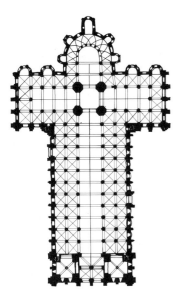

7.15 Plan of St. Sernin, Toulouse

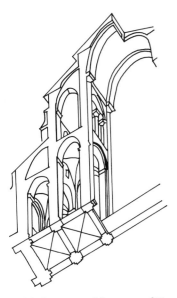

7.16 Segment of the nave of St. Sernin, Toulouse

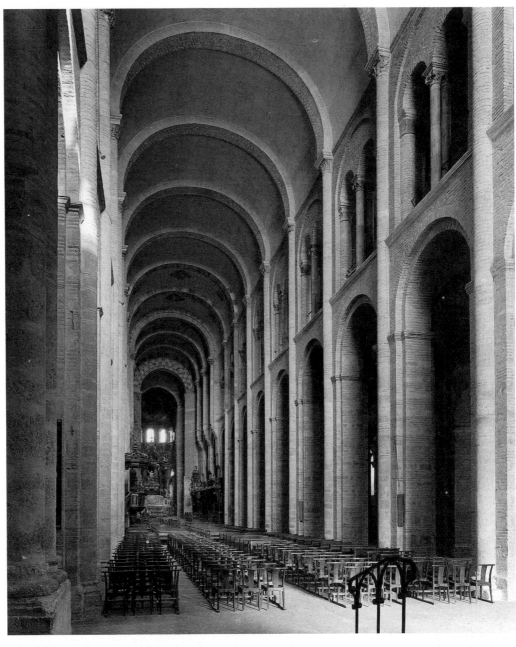

7.17 St. Sernin, nave and choir

The diagram in Fig. **7.16** shows a segment of the nave, along with its adjoining side aisles and gallery. In addition to accommodating pilgrims, the architecture of side aisles and gallery was needed to abut the lateral pressure of the barrel vault over the nave. From inside the nave this segment presents a unit called a *bay*. In a Romanesque or Gothic church, a bay comprises the area between two piers that frame one set of arch openings. In this case, since there is no clerestory in the nave, the unit consists of just two levels: the ground level arcade and the gallery. The piers are accented by *colonnettes*, attached half

columns which extend vertically to the ceiling and then continue as *transverse arches* across it. These vertical accents serve to accentuate the height of the bay, which climaxes in the curve of the ceiling. A series of bays, articulated by colonnettes and transverse arches, creates a solemn rhythm as it moves procession-like through the nave (Fig. **7.17**). Because St. Sernin lacks clerestory windows (except in the apse), outdoor light must come from window openings in the outer side aisle and the gallery. But this light has to pass through one or two arcades before it reaches the nave. Needless to say,

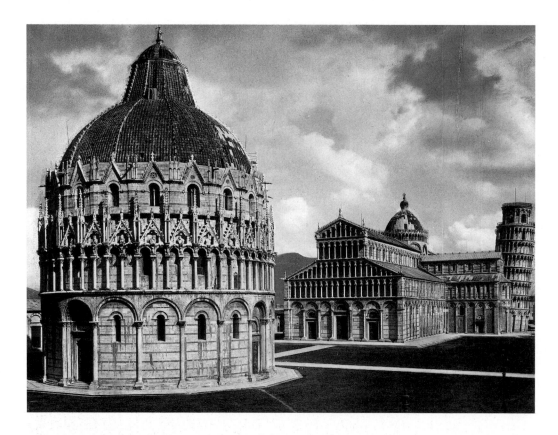

without the aid of artificial light, the inside of St. Sernin would be very dark.

The volumes of St. Sernin's interior are clearly echoed in the solid geometry of its exterior, where the forms of the nave, transept, apse, and radiating chapels are easily recognizable (Fig. **7.14**). Each bay is represented by a window. The different levels of ceiling vaults—as over the nave, galleries, outer aisles, radiating chapels, and so forth—are reflected in the different levels of roofs covering the vaults. Finally, the location of the crossing is marked by a tall octagonal bell tower. (Double towers, planned for the narthex at the west end, were never carried out.)

The differences between St. Sernin, a Romanesque church, and Santa Maria Maggiore, an Early Christian basilica (see Chapter 6), are dramatic. The former has a high ceiling reinforced by strong vertical accents; the latter, a flat, relatively low ceiling and horizontal accents. The wall plane in the pilgrimage church, segmented as it is by bays, is virtually eliminated, whereas the wall plane in Santa Maria, particularly in the clerestory above the columns, is intact.

Local variations—building traditions, availability of materials, proximity to trade or pilgrimage routes, and so forth—contributed to pronounced regional differences among Romanesque churches. Although space does not permit us to survey examples from each region, we can look at two widely separated churches that demonstrate

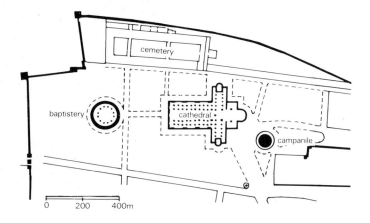

the extent of these differences.

The Pisa cathedral complex (Fig. **7.18**), one of the most beautiful architectural groupings in the world, was begun in 1063 after the victory of the Pisan navy over the Saracens near Palermo. Because it was a port for both Crusaders and traders, Pisa was the benefactor of Byzantine, Near Eastern, and Islamic influences. And being in Italy, where the memory of Early Christian architecture was never completely lost, it had stronger links to the past than northern centers. Pisa's separation of baptistery, church, and bell tower—a common practice in medieval Italy—dates back to the fourth century. Also typically Italian is the focus on surface decoration rather

7.19 Pisa Cathedral, interior

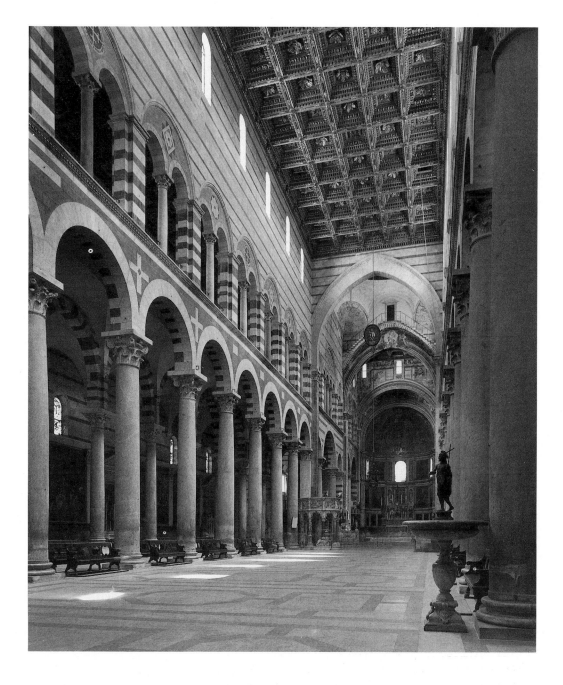

than on geometrical forms. Although the shape of the cathedral is cruciform, it lacks the three-dimensional complexity of St. Sernin. On the other hand, the flatness of its outer walls is relieved by rows of free-standing marble columns, a motif that is repeated in the famous cylindrical bell tower (which, because of insufficient foundations and uneven subsoil, began to lean even before it was completed). The low dome over the crossing, built in similar fashion to Islamic domes, adds an Oriental aspect that is echoed in the baptistery. True to Early Christian tradition, the latter is a radial, domed building. But the dome itself, a curious combination of hemisphere and cone shape, may have been modeled after a similar one existing in the Holy

Land (however, much of the decoration is Gothic). The interior, like the exterior, is an admixture of traditions: the use of supporting columns in the nave is Early Christian; the columns themselves were appropriated from a Roman temple (Fig. **7.19**). The gallery over the side aisle, together with the arcade that divides it from the nave, is Romanesque (the "zebra" striping of the piers could be Romanesque, Carolingian, or even Islamic), but the flat clerestory and timber ceiling above it is Early Christian. (Perhaps Pisa was less threatened by torch-carrying invaders.) The pointed archway leading to the crossing, another Islamic touch, foreshadows the Gothic style.

If the jewel-box look of Pisa represents the "feminine"

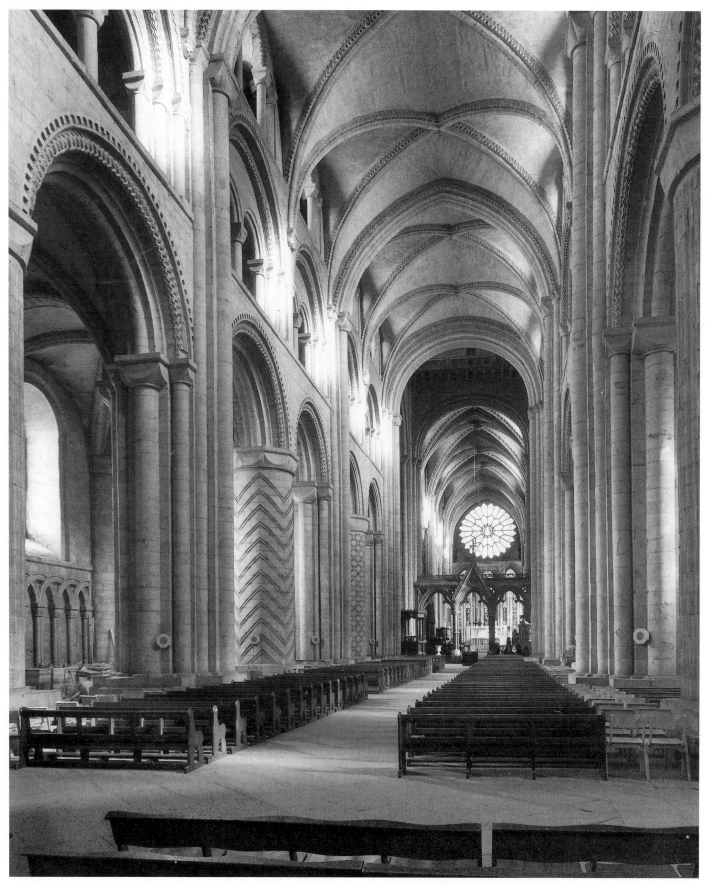

7.20 Durham Cathedral, view of nave, looking east

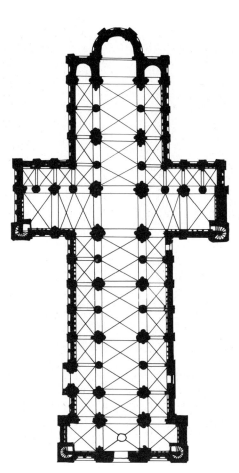

7.21 Durham Cathedral, 1093–1130

baric" chevron designs alternate with massive piers embellished with colonnettes which extend to the ceiling. The second story consists of an arcaded gallery, but without windows on the wall side. The clerestory windows pierce the vaulted ceiling; but, in this case, cross vaulting is used rather than barrel vaulting. Over each bay is a double cross vault; the diagonal lines ("groins") of the cross vaults are reinforced with ribs. In addition to these ribs are the huge, slightly-pointed transverse arches which lie above each pier and frame the double cross vaults. Durham is the first building to employ such *ribbed vaulting* in the nave and choir (although it had been used before in domes by Islamic architects and in small domes, narthexes, and porches by Christian architects).

Ribbed vaulting is both stronger and more efficient than regular cross vaulting—providing a stable "skeleton" for the whole unit (the "webs" between the ribs are filled in with thinner masonry) and allowing for greater speed of construction. Also, the cross vault itself has the advantages of concentrating greater weight at certain points (such as piers) and allowing for openings (such as clerestory windows). The Normans, as audacious in architecture as they were in military conquest, pushed Romanesque architecture to its greatest limits. Because of Durham's enlarged east end, windowless galleries, ribbed vaulting, and pointed arches, it anticipates the Gothic. On the other hand, because of its ponderous supports and relatively dark interior, it is still firmly a part of the Romanesque world.

Romanesque Architectural Sculpture

Since the fall of Rome, large-scale sculpture had been virtually nonexistent in the West. For a long time sculptural craftsmanship was dedicated to making small objects—crucifixes, book covers, ivory plaques, and reliquaries (containers for relics)—or cutting masonry stones; nothing in between. In the eleventh century, however, these two crafts began to merge to create architectural sculpture. First appearing in window moldings, doorway lintels, and column capitals, this sculpture had, by the twelfth century, extended to involve the carving of semicircular areas over doorways, called *tympanums* (Fig. **7.22**) and the posts that frame the doorways—the *jambs*, or *embrasures* (Fig. **7.23**).

Romanesque sculpture reflects many strains. Its predilection for beasts and monsters can be traced to barbaric roots, while the use of filigree pattern is both barbaric and Islamic in origin. Palmettes, rosettes, medallions, foliage scrolls (corruptions of acanthus leaves), volutes (corruptions of Ionic capitals), and combinations thereof are among the classically derived motifs in its rich decorative

side of Romanesque, then the fortress-like masonry of Norman architecture is the "masculine." Normans ("Northmen"), the last of the Scandinavian invaders to be converted and assimilated, settled in northern France in the tenth century and established the duchy of Normandy. Ever audacious, in the following century (1066) they invaded and conquered England, where they overwhelmed the existing Anglo-Saxon culture. Almost overnight, everything—government, Church, the official language, and architecture—became Norman. An outstanding example of this architecture is Durham Cathedral (Fig. **7.20**), which was begun in 1093. Its plan (Fig. **7.21**), like those of other Romanesque churches, is cruciform, but its east end is proportionately long compared to that of either St. Sernin or Pisa. This part of Durham is large enough to be considered (architecturally speaking) a *choir*, distinct from the nave. Except in the narthex and crossing, the internal supports consist of alternations between heavy piers and slightly smaller, but still heavy, columns. This creates "double" bays—two in the choir, three in the nave. These can be seen in a view of the nave where enormous columns adorned with "bar-

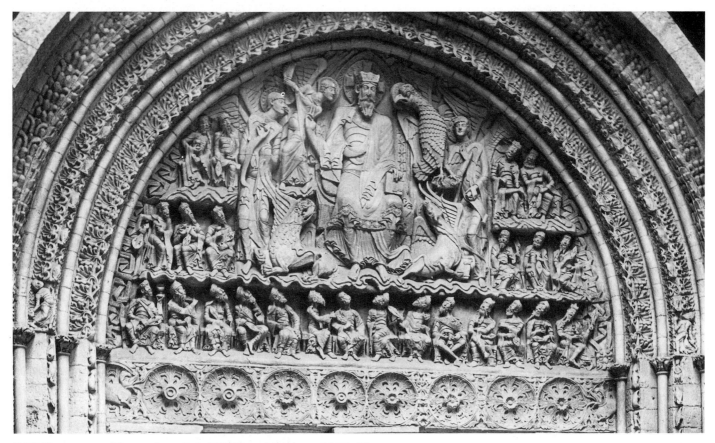

7.22 Tympanum of the south portral of St. Pierre, Moissac, c. 1115–35

lexicon. Highly stylized human figures show Byzantine effects or, sometimes, classical tendencies that started in the Carolingian era. The plethora of images and symbolism could have been inspired by influences from Assyria, Armenia, and the Holy Land, or even by the words of the Bible itself. *Revelation*, the most exotic book of the New Testament, was very popular at the time.

The tympanum of the Cluniac abbey church at Moissac in Gascony (c.1120), whose forms bear the influence of Islamic art and whose subject matter was inspired by the fourth chapter of Revelation, is a case in point (Fig. 7.22). To represent the miraculous vision of St. John the Divine, the sculptor filled the limited space with a dense composition enlivened by a profusion of figures. Surrounding the central figure of Christ are four "beasts"—described in Revelation and Ezekiel—used here to symbolize the four Evangelists: on Christ's right, the angel (Matthew) and winged lion (Mark); on his left, the eagle (John) and winged ox (Luke). Flanking the Evangelists are elongated angels holding scrolls. Filling the rest of the composition are the small figures of the 24 elders seated on clouds and with heads turned toward the central group. Above the tympanum are rows of ornamented *archivolts* (decorative

moldings), and below it is the lintel, decorated with medallions. Dominating the whole ensemble is the stiffly frontal Christ, who is portrayed not as the compassionate savior of the world but as a terrible apparition, a divine king, bent on judging the world and punishing sinners. Theologically and artistically, the human Jesus of the early Church has been forgotten.

Below this tympanum a flowing-locked Jeremiah shares the embrasure with stylized lions, all carved with extreme virtuosity and a keen sense of ornamental design (Fig. 7.23). The prophet strains restlessly within the confines of his stone environment, his body possessed by a miraculous dance, his face showing the effects of one under a spell. Among the best-known of Romanesque sculptures, the Moissac Jeremiah is often characterized as representing the intense spirituality of the period or, at least, of the Cluniac monks who commissioned it. In this respect it shares with Polykleitos' *Spear Carrier* (Fig. 2.22) the quality of representing an ideal: the latter, an archetype of physical beauty, proclaims the humanistic values of fifth-century BC Greek aristocrats; Jeremiah, a denial of the corporeal body, proclaims the spiritualistic values of a twelfth-century clerical elite. The comparison demonstrates, if nothing else, the enormous gulf between medieval civilization and its classical predecessor.

The Gothic Age

No sooner had the mortar dried on Romanesque churches than there emerged, in the twelfth century, a new style of architecture called *Gothic*. First appearing in the Île de France, the region surrounding Paris, and the heart of the then-small French kingdom, Gothic had, by the fifteenth century, spread to most of the Western world. Ironically, that was when the label first came into use, as a rough equivalent to "barbaric." Renaissance critics invented a pejorative term to condemn Gothic as the antithesis of classical architecture. When Renaissance ideals spread from Italy to northern Europe, Gothic went into eclipse and stayed there for centuries. However, since the nineteenth century, when appreciation of it returned dramatically, Gothic architecture has come to be regarded as the most visible evidence of medieval genius and one of the highest achievements of Western culture.

The emergence of a style inevitably relates to certain social and economic conditions. The improvements in European life that contributed to construction of Romanesque churches continued into the late twelfth, thirteenth, and fourteenth centuries. The victories of the Normans in Sicily and the Crusaders in the Near East cleared the way for trade and the input of new ideas. Elements of Islamic technology were utilized in Gothic settings, just as they had been in Romanesque. The effect of increased trade, especially its impact on the growth of towns and cities, was probably more important to the existence of Gothic than was anything else. Cathedrals were the sites of festivals, colorful processions, and even dramatic performances. Because peasants fled to towns to escape feudal servitude, and pilgrims flocked to their cathedrals for religious reasons, towns grew in size and wealth. They thus became capable of supporting artistic activities, including ambitious building programs. The French monarchy was more favorably disposed toward the development of towns than were feudal rulers elsewhere. This, together with the fact that the Île de France did not have a strong tradition of Romanesque architecture, explains why it was such fertile soil for a new style to take root.

By (inadvertently) increasing Europeans' awareness of other cultures, the Crusades may have, paradoxically, contributed to a climate of toleration. A gentler attitude can also be seen in the influence of such mystics as St. Francis of Assisi, who stressed the themes of love and brotherhood rather than sin and punishment. This can also be seen in the fact that romantic love and the idealizing of women, rather than the adventures of men,

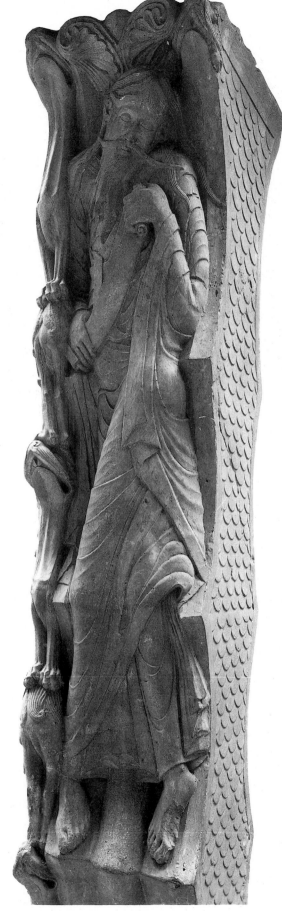

7.23 Door jamb of St. Pierre, Moissac

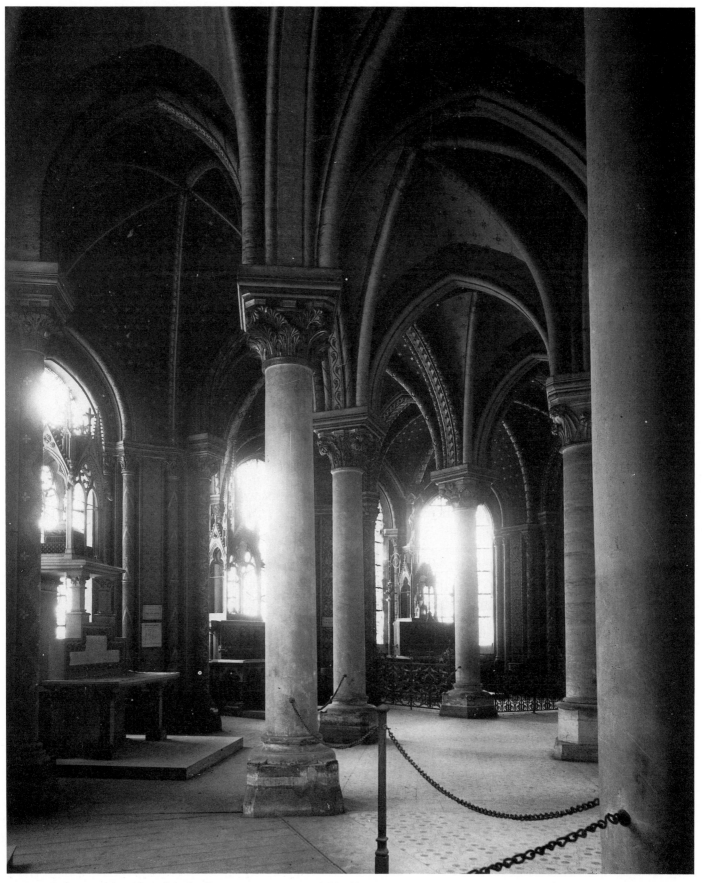

7.24 Ambulatory of the abbey church of St-Denis, near Paris, 1140–44

had become subjects of poetry and secular songs. This was the age of chivalry in social customs, and the beginnings of the cult of the Virgin Mary in religion. The new sensibility found its visual expression in Gothic architecture, which, as opposed to its more severe predecessor, emphasized light; and in Gothic sculpture which, as opposed to its spiritualistic predecessor, emphasized a degree of humanism.

Because its manifest divisions and subdivisions resemble the themes and sub-themes of reasoned argument, Gothic is also seen as akin to Scholasticism. As the latter strove to synthesize opposites in monuments of systematic thought, Gothic strove to reconcile the oppositions of opaque masonry and the need for space, air, and light in monuments of stone. Indeed, some see the parallels between Scholasticism and Gothic as more than just coincidence. The art historian Erwin Panofsky, who has analyzed the relationship between the two, sees both achievements as products of people who shared the same habits of mind.

Gothic Architecture

Many of the elements of Gothic architecture were already present in late Romanesque architecture: a basilican plan with ambulatories and radiating chapels, the vertically accentuated, three-storied bay, vaulted (sometimes ribbed) stone ceiling, a lengthened choir, and even limited use of the pointed arch. But the interiors of most Romanesque churches seemed oppressive to a new generation of builders, who took up the challenge of providing maximum space with minimum material. To meet this challenge they added two crucial elements: the *pointed arch* and the *flying buttress.*

A new choir built in 1140 for the abbey church of St. Denis near Paris, was the first to have its ambulatory and interconnecting chapels covered with vaults of uniform height (Fig. 7.24). This was possible because it used the pointed arch. A round arch is a semicircle; its height is strictly governed by its width. Therefore, when two round vaults of different widths intersect, their arches will not be

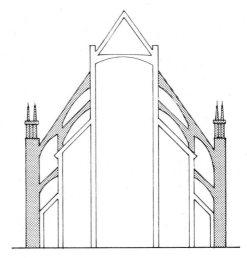

7.26 Flying buttress, in cross-section

the same height. A pointed arch, on the other hand, is more like a triangle; it allows the ratio of width to height to vary simply by changing the angle of the arch (Fig. 7.25). This, in turn, allows intersecting vaults of different widths to have the same height—an important advantage which made possible the rectangular cross vaults and complicated juxtapositions of ambulatories and chapels characteristic of Gothic plans. Moreover, the pointed arch is more stable than the round. Its sharper angle focuses the thrust of gravity downward more than outward. Finally, it has certain aesthetic and symbolic advantages. The glory of Gothic is based on the graceful configurations of pointed arches which literally and figuratively uplift the eyes, mind, and spirit.

The flying buttress, first used experimentally on the Cathedral of Notre Dame in Paris, is a method of reinforcing the ceiling vault and walls by a system of external half arches that absorbs much of the outward thrust (Fig. 7.26). Buttresses, positioned along the wall where the groins of the vault and the transverse arches meet, correspond to the piers in the nave; the space between two buttresses corresponds to a bay. Forming an exoskeleton around the outside of a church—a reflection of its interior—these vane-like buttresses have become a hallmark of the Gothic style, as seen here on Chartres Cathedral (Fig. 7.27). Although their effect on the outside is dramatic, flying buttresses, by absorbing the outward thrust of the vault and thus virtually eliminating the pressure on the walls, had an even more dramatic effect on the interior. Their invention constitutes the final step in medieval builders' goals of voiding walls and reducing the massiveness of internal supports.

Chartres Cathedral (completed in 1260), a prime example of Gothic architecture, was the first to have its

7.25 Pointed arch cross vault

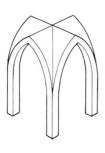

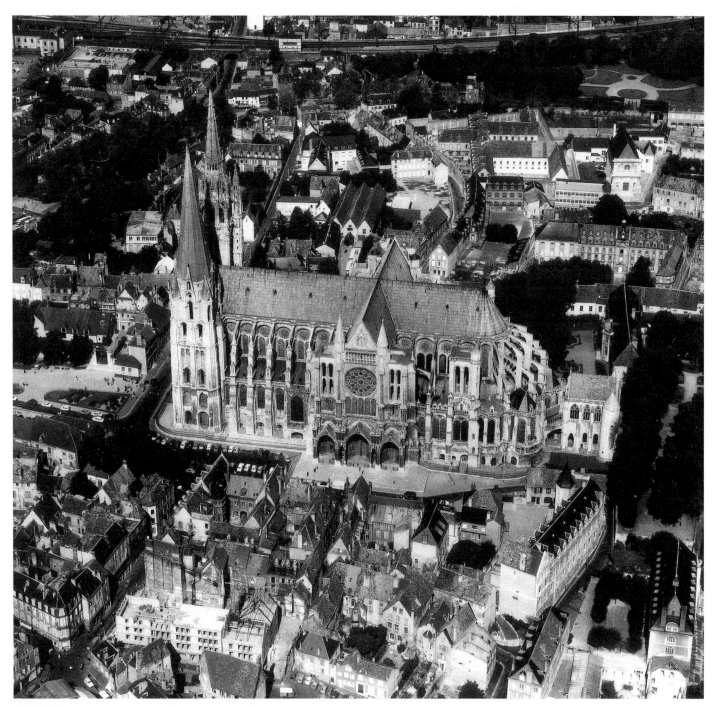

7.27 Chartres Cathedral, begun 1194

nave, transept, and choir constructed in the *High Gothic* style. Work began in 1194, following a fire which had destroyed all of the former, Early Gothic structure except the west façade—most of which was retained and incorporated into the new building (Fig. **7.28**). The circular window and north tower, added later, are not part of the original façade. Chartres is one of the best-known of all medieval buildings and possibly the best-loved. Like the Parthenon or the Cathedral of Florence, it symbolizes an

era—in this case, the "Age of Faith." A study of the plan of Chartres (Fig. **7.29**) shows that although it conforms to the cruciform pattern, it differs from Romanesque models in having porches at the ends of its transepts; it also differs from Durham in that the subdivisions of its nave vaults are in single rather than double units. Most significantly, it differs in its proportions; note the enlarged choir, shorter transept, and, especially, the small diameters of its internal supports.

7.28 Chartres Cathedral, view of west front

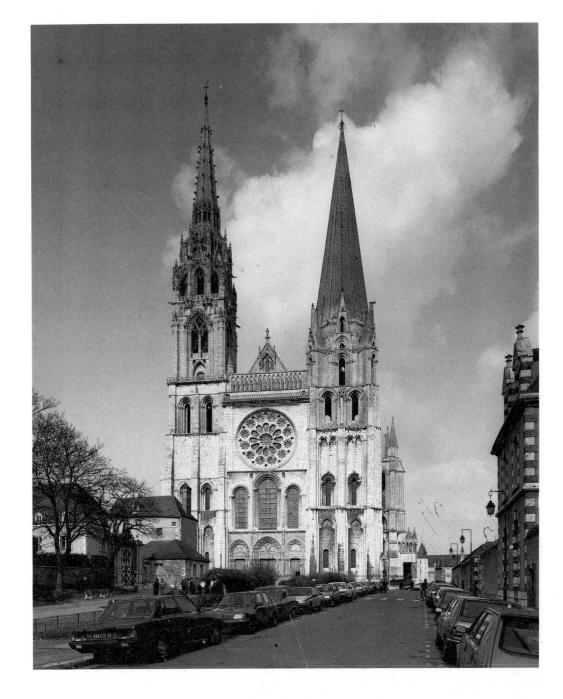

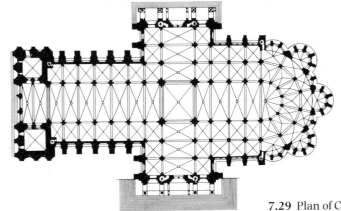

7.29 Plan of Chartres Cathedral

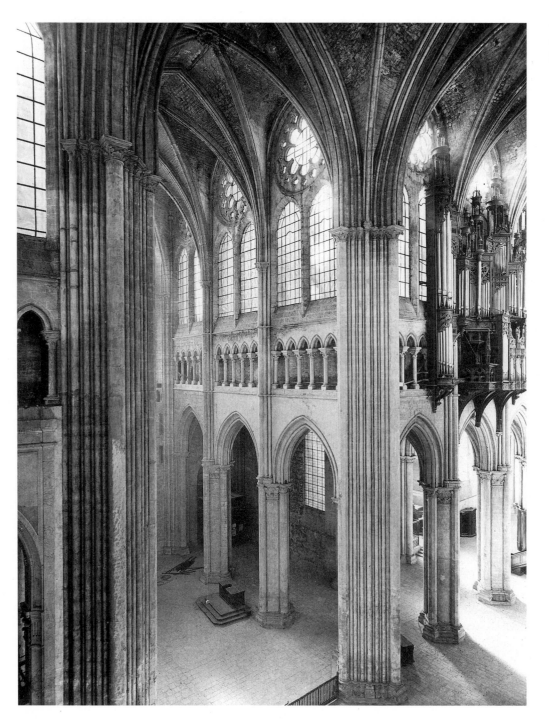

7.30 Chartres Cathedral, view of nave and crossing, begun 1194

The slenderness of the cathedral's piers is readily apparent in a view of the crossing (showing the nave, right, and north wing of the transept, left; Fig. 7.30). This, together with the voiding of walls made possible by flying buttresses, has allowed for very large arcade and window openings. The amount of light pouring into this interior is modified only by the coloration of the stained glass windows. Chartres' bays are three-storied, and more than half again as high as Durham's. Early Gothic designs were usually four-storied, consisting of arcade, gallery, *trifo-rium* (a small gallery whose exterior wall corresponds to the narrow space between the roof and vaults of the side aisle), and clerestory. In Chartres the gallery has been eliminated, leaving only a narrow triforium between a tall arcade and an equally tall clerestory. The basic schema and proportions of this kind of bay became the hallmark of the High Gothic interior. Its complexity, like that of Dante's *Divine Comedy* or a fully developed Scholastic argument, is tempered by the revealed consistency of its structural logic, a consistency that can be seen in the

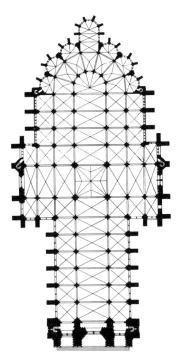

7.31 Plan of Amiens Cathedral

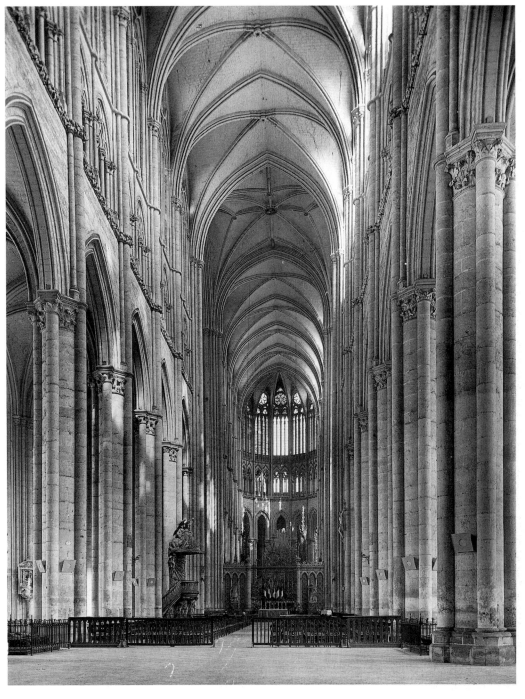

7.32 Nave of Amiens Cathedral, c. 1220–36

systemic connections between colonnettes, shafts, arches, and ribs where each of the four pier colonnettes is logically restated in the structural elements above it. The side of the pier facing the nave, for example, supports a cluster of shafts which extends to the ceiling, at which point each shaft becomes a transverse arch or rib. The many shafts lining a crossing pier have similar destinies. Indeed, much of the ''information'' about a Gothic structure is contained in a cross section of a pier.

As a successful solution to the problems addressed by

medieval builders, Chartres was widely emulated, particularly by the builders of Amiens Cathedral (Fig. **7.31**, **7.32**). Begun in 1220, Amiens reflects Chartres' plan, its bay schema, and many of its details, but it also refines them. The arcades are proportionately taller; the clusterings of colonnettes, shafts, ribs and arches are generally slenderer; and the design of the windows is more intricate. The soaring choir vaults, 144 feet (44 meters) above the floor, are a fitting climax to Amiens' sanctuary and to High Gothic brilliance (Fig. **7.33**). Here, as in Hagia

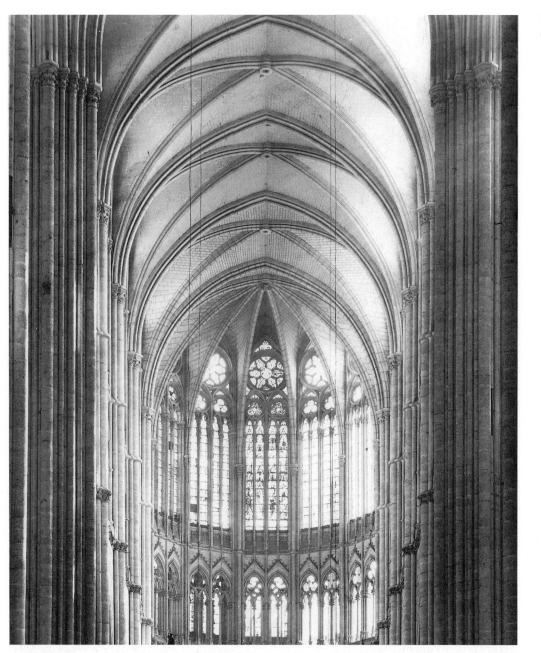

7.33 Amiens Cathedral, choir vault

Sophia (Fig. 6.22), the ceiling seems to float, giving full expression to the sense of loftiness. But this has been accomplished without sacrificing a sense of architectural mass. The two oppositions, mass and airy space, were maintained in delicate tension by High Gothic builders.

Later, this tension was violated in favor of airiness. At times, builders were too daring; they made vaults so high or insubstantial that they collapsed. At other times, they were too obsessed with refinement and elegant effects. They made bays ever narrower, colonnettes thinner, *tracery* (ornamental carving) more lavish, and walls that increasingly became screens of glass. These tendencies led to a pervasive *linear* quality of Late Gothic construction.

The Sainte-Chapelle, discussed in Chapter 3, is an early example of Late Gothic effects and linearity (Fig. 3.6). Like a marvelous crystal enclosure, this chapel conceals rather than reveals its masonry substance: the supports, resembling metal rods rather than stone piers, seem less substantial than the windows themselves. The painting of the piers and vaults, and the profusion of tracery further contribute to the illusion of immateriality. Late Gothic, unlike High Gothic which always reveals its structural substance, seems bent on concealing it. No wonder Renaissance writers, who tended to judge all of Gothic by late examples, were critical.

Once established in France, Gothic was soon exported to

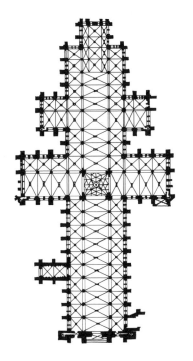

7.34 Plan of Salisbury Cathedral, 1220–70

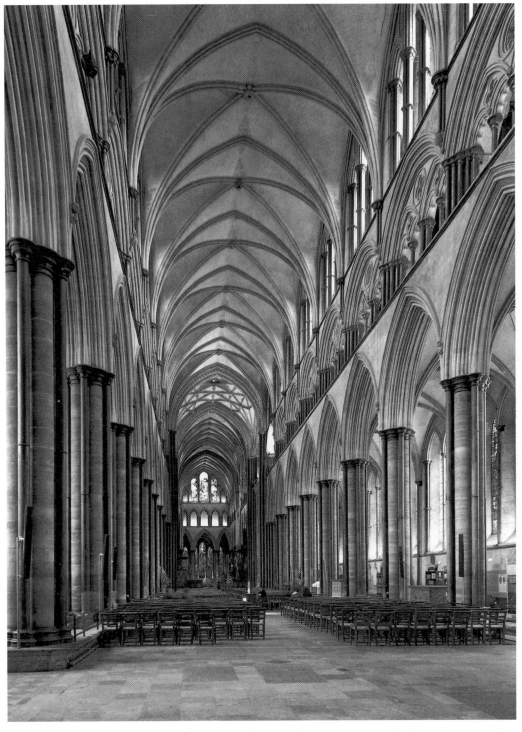

7.35 Salisbury Cathedral, nave and choir

other parts of Europe. Next to French Gothic, English Gothic is the most original and distinctive. Traces of its Norman tradition can be seen in Salisbury Cathedral (completed c. 1260). Its squarish plan (Fig. 7.34) and long proportions are more like Durham's than Chartres'. So also is the horizontal emphasis of its nave (Fig. 7.35). The slender piers, three-storied bays, ribbed vaulting, and single-unit vaults are High Gothic. But Salisbury's piers,

unlike those of its French counterparts, lack colonnettes and shafts traveling from floor to ceiling. Here, the emphasis is not so much on vertical divisions, but on horizontal ones, each of which continues with little interruption down the nave. This horizontality is typical of English Gothic—as is the emphasis on the pattern of the vaulting, which in Salisbury is accentuated by the use of a darker stone for details such as colonnettes and ribs.

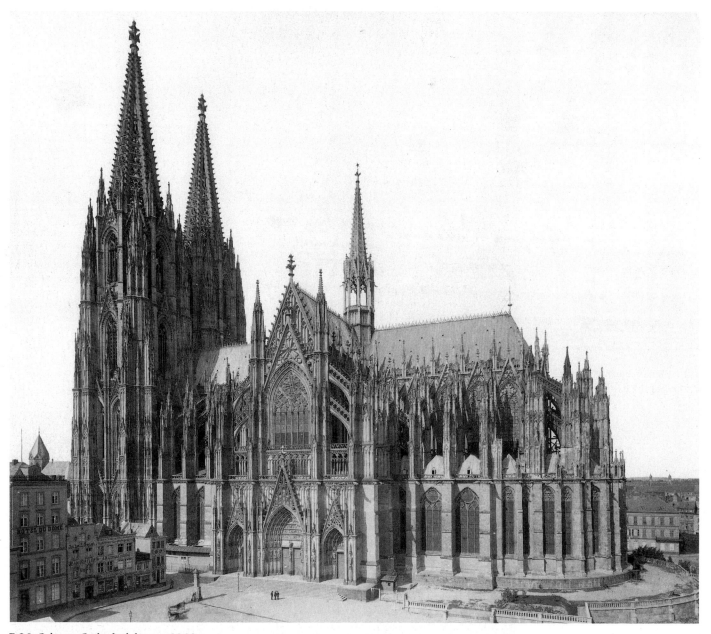

7.36 Cologne Cathedral, begun 1248

The Cathedral of Cologne, the most impressive Gothic structure in Germany, is a duplication of French ideas (Fig. **7.36**); its radiating chapels are copies of Amiens', its nave is similar to Amiens', but higher, rising to almost 160 feet (49 meters)! Although begun in 1248, the building was only completed in the nineteenth century. Some of the most unusual interpretations of the Gothic system are found in Spain. Several Spanish cathedrals, like the one at Palma, are lined with chapels—one for every bay (Fig. **7.37**). Palma's proportions, featuring a 100-foot-(30-meter)-high arcade, formed of simple octagonal columns, along with an extremely tall aisle, are also quite different from the French ideal. The country least

affected by Gothic, was Italy—where the wall plane was considered inviolable even in churches that were built in nominally Gothic styles (see Chapter 3).

Gothic Sculpture

The Gothic spirit effected changes in sculpture no less than in architecture. Once again, the Early Gothic façade of Chartres can be invoked to illustrate these changes; here we shall examine the sculpture around the door openings, known as the "royal portals." The differences between these sculptures and those of Moissac, which were made only a generation earlier, amount to a turning point in

7.37 Cathedral, Palma de
Majorca, interior view, late
13th century

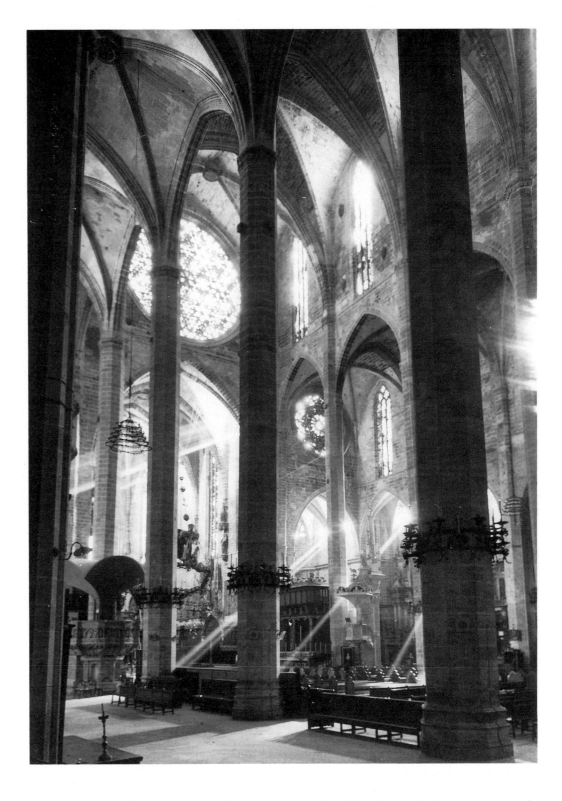

Christian art. The tympanum over the central door at
Chartres (Fig. **7.38**) is similar to Moissac's tympanum
(Fig. **7.22**) in subject and composition, but that is all.
Here, only the main actors—Christ (as the likeness of God
the Father) and the four Evangelists—appear in the
tympanum shape itself, making it less crowded. Each
figure, fitting comfortably in its own space, is sculpted
with more amplitude. The figure of Christ is not only
rounder but far more natural. The symbols of the
Evangelists, though still hybrid, are less fantastic and less
agitated. The minor characters are confined to the
perimeters: the twenty-four elders in the archivolts, the
twelve Apostles in the lintel beneath the tympanum.
Despite the spatial limitations of these places, particularly

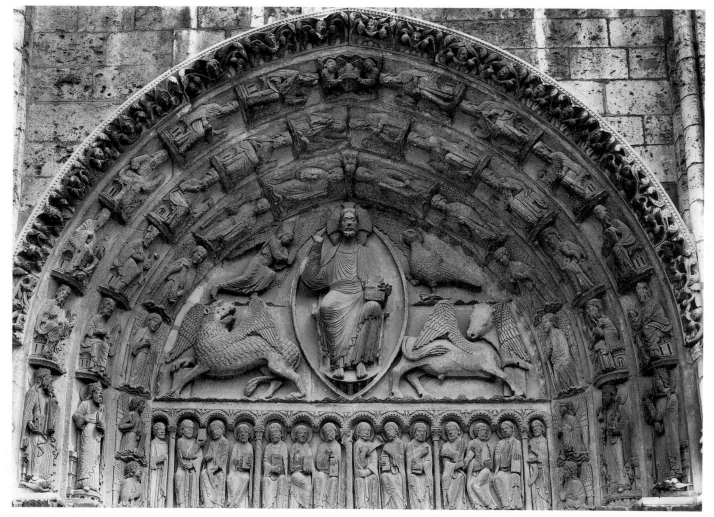

7.38 Tympanum over central door, Chartres Cathedral

in the archivolts, the figures in them are nevertheless more recognizably human than those at Moissac.

This turning point in art (which, incidentally, predates Francis of Assisi, Thomas Aquinas, and the "thirteenth-century synthesis") indicates the beginning of a liberal trend in medieval thought. A new, more balanced relationship between the Almighty and his creation, and between the divine world and the world of sensory experience, was emerging. This meant more acceptance of nature and of humanity's place in nature, and therefore more room for compassion, hope, and love. To be sure, neither the supernatural nor the Apocalypse had lost their hold on people's minds, but these were no longer the sole preoccupations. Like Gothic architecture, Gothic sculpture expresses the reconciliation of medieval dualisms.

Symbolizing the kings and queens of the Old Testament and perhaps also members of the French court (hence the name "royal" portals), the figures in the jambs are contained within narrow columnar forms (Fig. 7.39). But despite the seeming severity of their limiting shapes, they are rounder, more human-looking, and more independent of their architectural environment than the Jeremiah at Moissac. A further development in this evolution is represented by the High Gothic sculptures on the doors of the south transept of Chartres (Fig. 7.40). The figures of a knight and three saints, sculpted some 75 years later, are, by comparison, so independent and natural-looking that one can almost imagine them stepping down from their pedestals. In addition, their faces contain a spark of individualism, suggesting that they may have been based on living models, probably burghers or clerics in the city of Chartres. Although only a century separates these sculptures from those at Moissac, the distance traveled in terms of both religious interpretation and realism is remarkable. Yet, when we compare these to Donatello's sculptures (see Chapter 3), we can readily perceive that they are still far from being completely secular, far from classical, and, to some extent, lacking in realism.

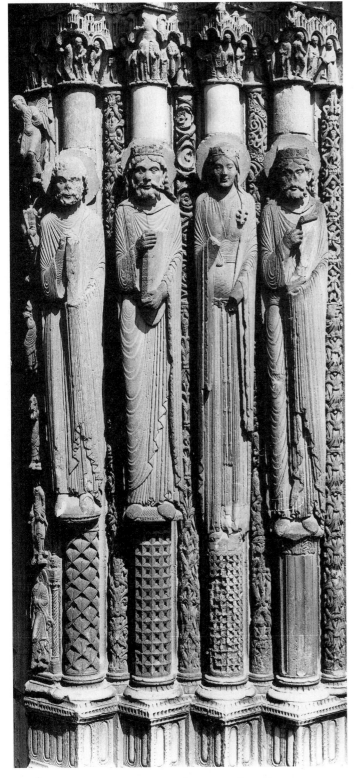

7.39 Jamb statues, west portals, Chartres Cathedral

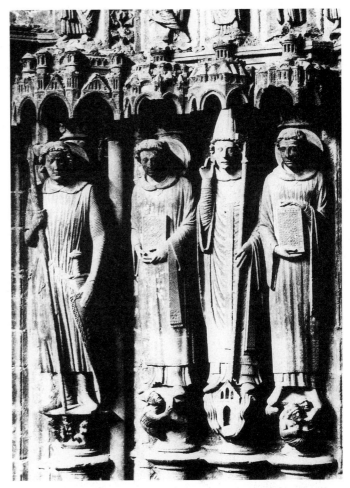

7.40 Jamb statues, south transept portals, Chartres Cathedral c. 1215–20

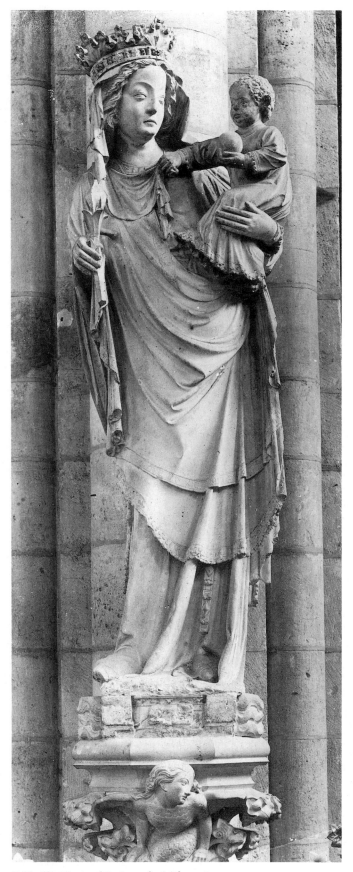

7.41 *The Virgin of Paris*, early 14th century
Notre Dame, Paris

As Late Gothic architecture tended toward courtly elegance, so did Late Gothic sculpture—as can be seen in the early fourteenth-century *The Virgin of Paris* (Fig. **7.41**). The pronounced curve in the posture, especially the projection of the hip, shows a kind of observation of real life—in this case the natural posture of a woman carrying a baby—which had not been seen since classical times. In other respects, however, the image of the Virgin differs markedly from classical statues of women. There is little emphasis on the female body underneath the drooping folds of the robe. Rather, the form is slender and linear, like a Late Gothic interior. Just as the ceiling of the Sainte-Chapelle seems to be miraculously supported by screens of glass and tracery, so the infant Christ is supported by his mother at shoulder height in a way that defies gravity.

The works of Claus Sluter (c.1350–1406), an artist from the province of Holland who worked for Philip, Duke of Burgundy, stand as a major achievement of medieval sculpture. For the Duke's mausoleum near Dijon, Sluter sculpted the "Well of Moses," an elaborate pedestal bearing images of Moses and five other prophets, all of whom boldly protrude into the space surrounding them (Fig. **7.42**). Far from being airy and linear like *The Virgin of Paris*, Sluter's representation of Moses is a paragon of weight and monumentality. With its suggestion of a powerful body under the flowing robes and the dramatically bearded head, it constitutes perhaps the most virile figure to be produced since the fall of Rome. The realism of the details, particularly in the wizened face, enhances rather than detracts from the expression of majesty and pathos. "We must recognize," as the art historian Henri Focillon explains, "not the reflection of a moment of history, but the continuity of a dynasty of the spirit, which ... descends to our own day through Michelangelo and Rodin."[4]

Late Medieval Tuscan Painting

Although his career falls within the Late Gothic period, and his life was almost exactly contemporary with Dante's, Giotto di Bondone (c.1276–c.1337) has been linked more with the Renaissance than with the Middle Ages. Indeed, important figures throughout the Renaissance praised him and proclaimed him as the progenitor of Western painting. In the late fourteenth century Boccaccio compared him favorably to the legendary Apelles of ancient Greece; in the fifteenth, Ghiberti said that the art of painting started with him; Leonardo claimed that art declined after him, only to be revived again by Masaccio, who, like Giotto, took his standard from nature; Vasari, in the sixteenth century, said that "Giotto alone ... set art upon the path that may be called the true one."[5]

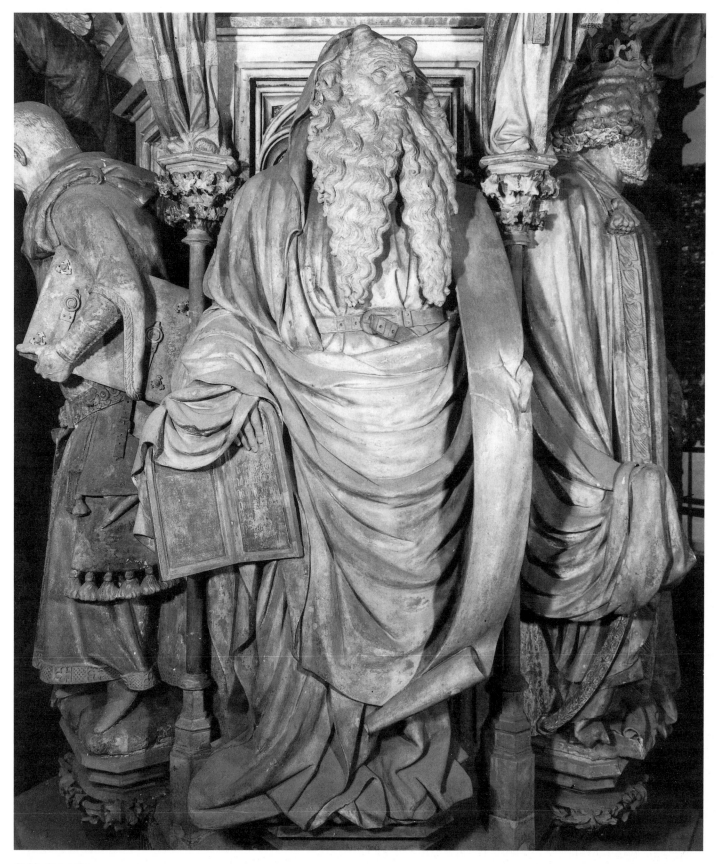

7.42 CLAUS SLUTER
Well of Moses, Mausoleum of Philip, Duke of Burgundy, nr. Dijon, 1395–1406.
Height of figures, c. 6 ft (1.82 m)

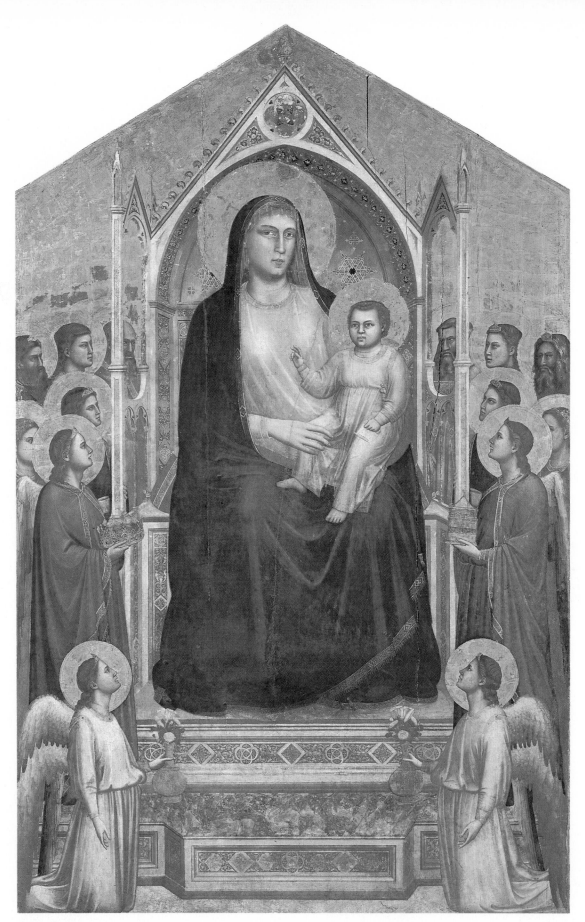

7.43 GIOTTO
Madonna Enthroned, c. 1310
Tempera on panel, 10 ft 8 ins × 6 ft 8 ins (3.25 × 2 m)
Uffizi Gallery, Florence

Giotto was held in high esteem during his life as well. The few records available suggest that he, among all the artists working in and around Florence, was singled out for major commissions; he achieved a level of fame and social standing typical more of a Renaissance artist than of a medieval one. Commenting in the *Purgatorio* on the transience of fame, Dante alludes to the artist's rising reputation:

> *O empty glory of human powers! How short the time its green endures at its peak, if it be not overtaken by crude ages! Cimabue thought to hold the field in painting, and now Giotto has the cry, so that the fame of the former is obscured.*[6]

Giotto's reputation as a forerunner of the Renaissance notwithstanding, his art remains part of the medieval world. Its subject matter, unlike that chosen by Renaissance artists, is exclusively religious; its content is characteristic of the humane Christianity of Gothic art. Even though the style, because of its simplicity and monumentality, is correctly associated with Masaccio's painting, it can also be associated with sculptures on the portals of Chartres and with Sluter's *Well of Moses*. Moreover, Gothic motifs can be found here and there in some of its minor details.

In addition to its subject matter, Giotto's *Madonna Enthroned*—an altarpiece painted in 1310 for a church in Florence—has obvious medieval traits: gold background, angels, solid haloes, and the characteristically Gothic canopy over the throne (Fig. 7.43). But, when it is compared to a similar altarpiece (Fig. 7.44) by Cimabue (c.1280), the other artist mentioned in the Dante extract, its "modern" qualities can also be appreciated. The people and objects in Giotto's altarpiece, unlike Cimabue's, have weight and physical substance. Because we see indications of Mary's anatomy under her gown, as in the forward projection of her knees, we sense that she has a real lap to support Jesus. Because of the throne's projecting canopy and sides, we sense that it occupies real space, providing a seat for Mary. Even minor details, such as a halo blocking the view of an angel or a saint peering through an opening in the side of the throne, help to reinforce the illusion of depth. Although all of the angels' faces are turned toward the Madonna, they possess at least a hint of individuality.

By contrast, in Cimabue's altarpiece, the angels on one side are almost a mirror image of those opposite; all of their faces, like that of the Virgin, are in three-quarter position. The body of the Virgin seems to be floating, rather than sitting, on the throne. The minor parts of Cimabue's altarpiece, unlike those of Giotto's, tend to be more fantastic than realistic—for example, the throne which

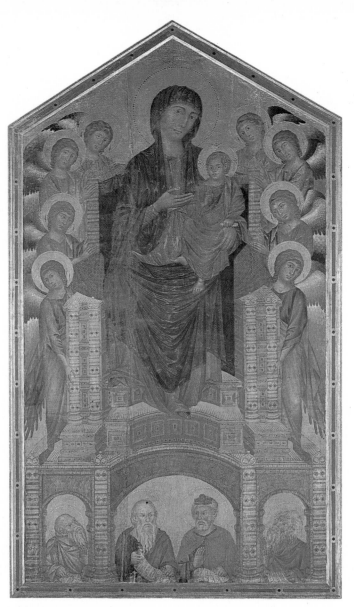

7.44 CIMABUE
Madonna Enthroned, c. 1280–90
Tempera on wood, c. 12 ft 7½ ins × 7 ft 4 ins (3.84 × 2.24 m)
Uffizi Gallery, Florence

miraculously becomes a piece of architecture beneath the Virgin's feet, and the gnomic prophets in the openings in the bottom of the throne/building.

Cimabue was a generation older than Giotto, and probably his teacher. In fairness, it should be pointed out that when his art is compared to typical fourteenth-century Tuscan art, it looks quite progressive. The Byzantine style (see Chapter 6), which may have been imported during the Crusades and which pervaded Tuscany and central Italy in the twelfth through fourteenth centuries, is the tradition out of which Cimabue developed. The style of the mosaics and altarpieces that he saw and emulated were rather stiff and somewhat abstract. Cimabue added significantly to this Italo-Byzantine tradition.

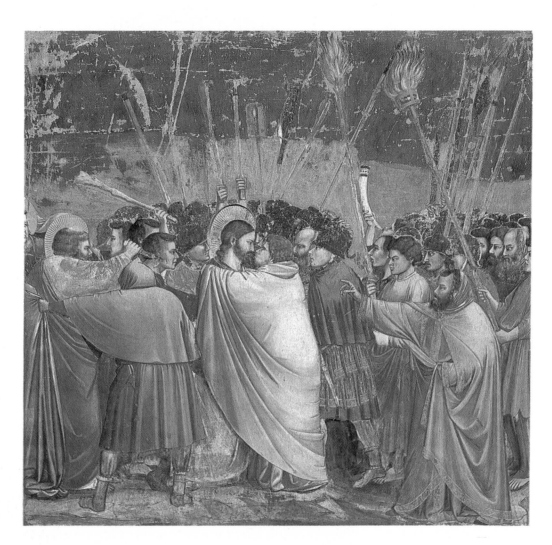

7.45 GIOTTO
The Kiss of Judas, c. 1305–6
Fresco, detail, Padua, Arena Chapel

Giotto's work, in addition to conveying a stronger sense of physical reality (when compared to Cimabue's painting, to say nothing of traditional Italo-Byzantine work), also conveys emotional reality. This is particularly true of *The Kiss of Judas* (Fig. **7.45**), one of the many vivid frescoes about Christ's life painted for Padua's Arena Chapel (Fig. **7.46**). In addition to Jesus and Judas, it shows the confrontation in the Garden of Gethsemane between the twelve Apostles and the priests and soldiers who arrived to arrest Jesus. Anxiety, seen in the crowding of the mob, the aggressive movements, and the angry faces, is reinforced by diagonals: a priest pointing, the hem of Judas's gown, and, especially, the torches and clubs held aloft by the soldiers. This anxiety is further intensified by our awareness of the loneliness of Christ. The only Apostles present (identified by their haloes) are Peter, seen cutting off the ear of a soldier, and another, apparently leaving the scene on the left. The psychological climax of the picture is the moment of betrayal, Judas's kiss. The dismal irony of a gesture of love being the sign of betrayal is tellingly conveyed by the squat figure of Judas pursing his lips as he embraces Jesus. The restraint of Giotto's treatment of this moment, one of the most dramatic of the New Testament, serves to intensify its credibility.

Giotto may have used live models. His desire to observe life, together with his ability to select from it and describe it in a painting, was no less than a breakthrough in art. The breakthrough, however, was not exploited to any great extent by other Florentine artists. After Giotto's death, Florence fell victim to a series of financial crises and insurrections, and to the Black Death, which struck harder there than in most cities. Artistic leadership passed to neighboring Siena until the early fifteenth century, when the Florence of Brunelleschi, Donatello, and Masaccio reclaimed it.

Late Gothic Flemish Painting

As Gothic architecture spread throughout Western Europe in the thirteenth century, so, too, did a style of

7.46 Arena Chapel, Padua, entire

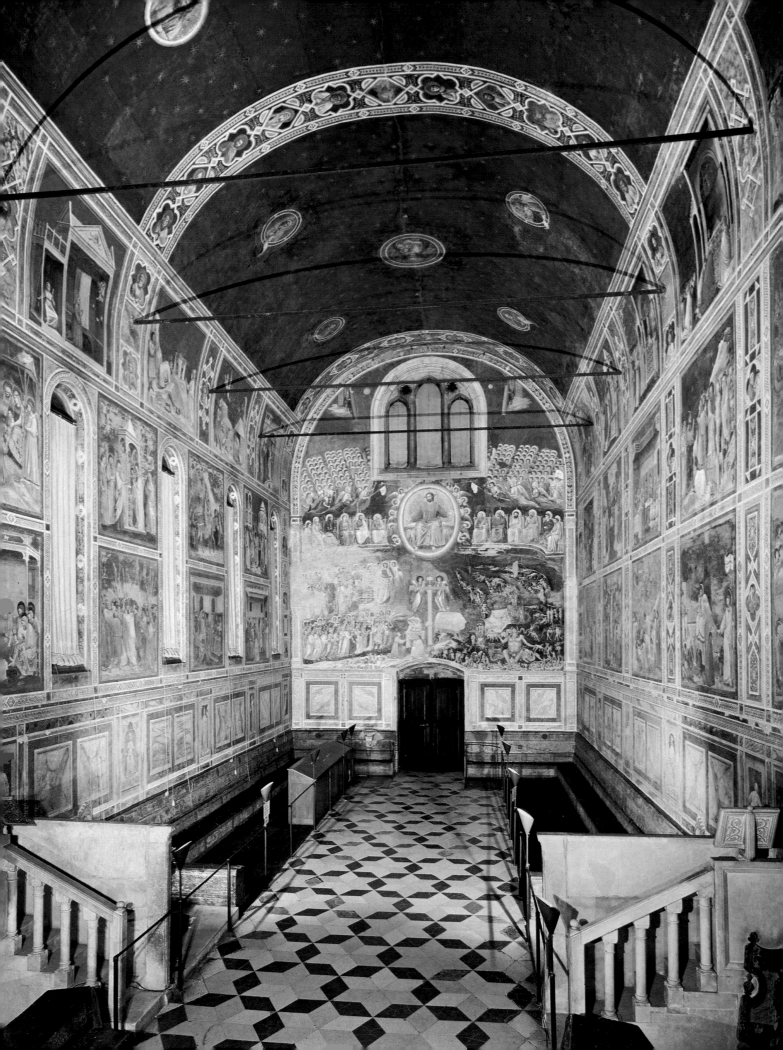

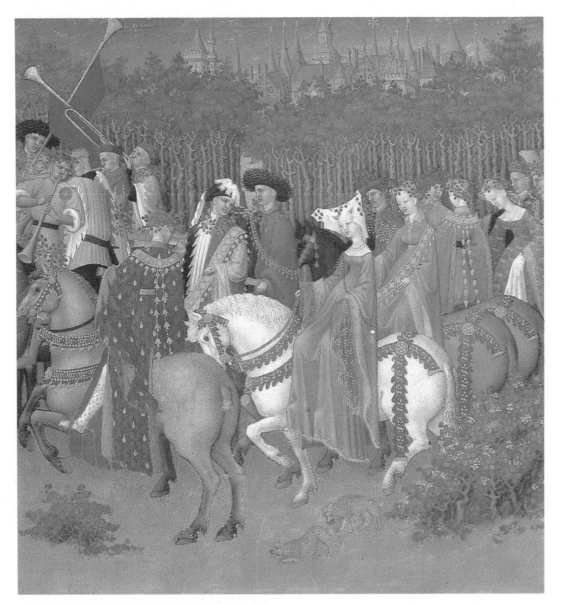

7.47 THE LIMBOURG BROTHERS
May, from *Les Trés Riches Heures du Duc de Berry*, 1413–1
Illumination, $8\frac{1}{2} \times 5\frac{1}{2}$ ins (21.6×14 cm)
Musée Condé, Chantilly, France

painting in the fourteenth and fifteenth centuries. Called appropriately the International Style, it developed out of Late Gothic architecture and sculpture, fourteenth-century Italian painting, and manuscript illustration. Like Late Gothic architecture, it leans to the delicate and charming. We have already seen an example by a famous exponent of the style, Gentile da Fabriano, a contemporary of Masaccio, in Florence (Fig. 3.14). Leading representatives in the North were to be found in Flanders, a group of provinces along the North Sea (today, northeastern

France, Belgium, and southern Holland). These exponents of the International Style were especially renowned for their skill in the production of *miniatures*, small paintings, particularly illustrations for liturgical books. One of the most famous of these is a book of "hours" made by three Flemish brothers: Pol, Hennequin, and Herman Limbourg and called the *Très Riches Heures* ("Very Rich Hours"). In addition to devotional readings for the eight services of the Divine Office (see page 264), the *Très Riches Heures* contains colorful illustrations for each of the feast days of

the calendar. The illustration for May (Fig. **7.47**) shows a
festive assembly of aristocrats which recalls the crowd of
kings and attendants in Gentile's *Adoration of the Magi*
(Fig. 3.14). Like Gentile, the Limbourg brothers gave
loving attention to details of ornament and finery. Even
the treatment of the landscape (at that time landscapes
were rare in painting) illustrates the pervasive emphasis
on elegance.

Growing out of the International Style, but transcending it, was a tradition of painting often referred to as
"Flemish" or "Northern" Renaissance. Its practitioners
were the counterparts of Netherlandish composers, as
well as being the contemporaries of Donatello and Masaccio (see Chapter 3). Indeed, the existence of this tradition
raises anew the question of the definition of Renaissance.
Flemings explored the details of optical experience so
intensely and with such craftsmanship that their work
breaks significantly with the medieval past. Indeed, the
technical skill involved in representing God's attire in *God
the Father*, by Hubert and Jan van Eyck, is a tour de force
even by later standards (Fig. **7.48**). Not even such
minutiae as a glint on a shining pearl or the needlework in
a section of brocade escaped the artists' attention. Yet,
with respect to subject matter and content, the paintings
of these and other Flemish artists use traditional medieval
symbols; the focus is on the divine world, a realm that
excludes the classical references found in the symbolism
and style of Italian art.

Flemish and Italian painters had in common a
heightened interest in representing the visible world more
faithfully, but their approaches to this pursuit differed
considerably. The Flemings were literalists, interested in
the particulars of optical experience; the Italians were
generalists, interested in the universals underlying the
physical world, rather than just its outward appearance.
Flemings were unsurpassed in their ability to render
surface textures; Italians concentrated on such things as
anatomical structure and how it is revealed by shading.
Flemings approached perspective "empirically," that is,
by observing how things appear in the spatial world and
recording this in their work; Italians developed the rules of
linear perspective and applied those rules in their work.
Flemings, whose tradition grew out of painting miniatures
and other small-scale works, emphasized clarity of detail;
Italians, whose tradition grew out of Giotto and painting
murals, stressed broadness of treatment.

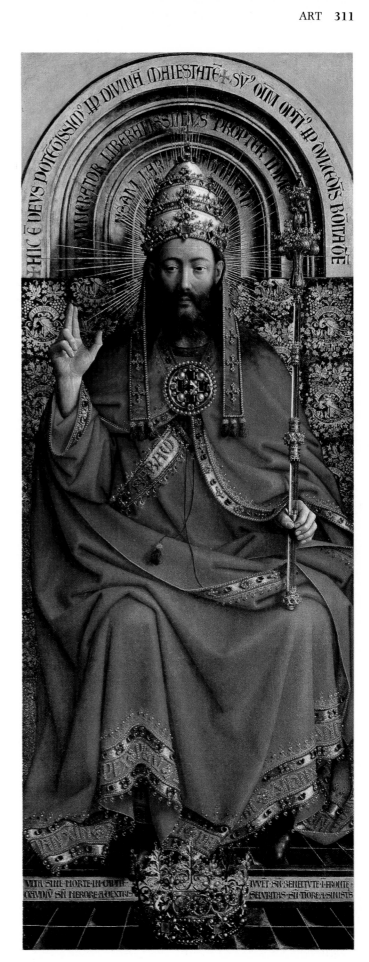

7.48 HUBERT and JAN VAN EYCK
God the Father, from *The Ghent Altarpiece*, 1432
St. Bavo, Ghent

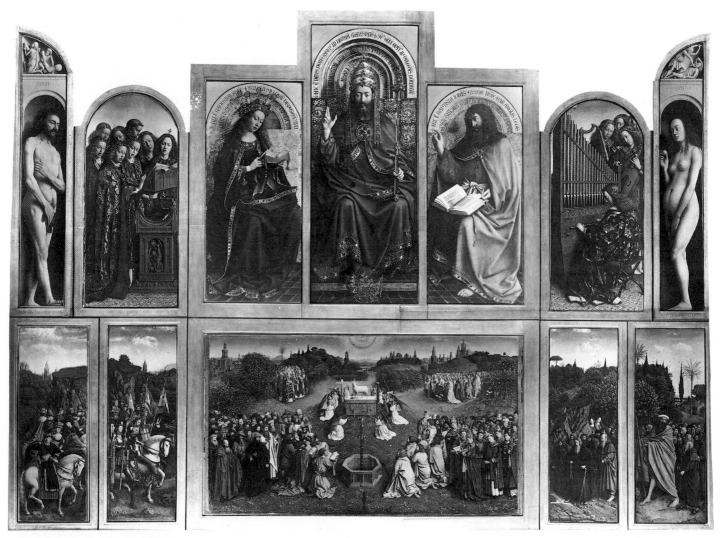

7.49 HUBERT and JAN VAN EYCK
The Ghent Altarpiece (open), 1432
Tempera and oil on panel, approx. 11 ft × 15 ft (3.3 × 4.6 m)
St. Bavo, Ghent

God the Father is one panel of the *Ghent Altarpiece* (1432), attributed to Hubert and Jan van Eyck (Fig. **7.49**). For reasons that we need not go into here, scholars dispute which parts of the work were painted by which brother, or even if Hubert, the older of the two, painted any of it. There is no question, however, that Jan was not only the principal author of this work, but the more important of the two brothers. Indeed, Jan van Eyck (c.1370–c.1440), who spent most of his working life in the city of Bruges, is generally considered the most important of all the fifteenth-century Flemish masters.

The *Ghent Altarpiece* is an ambitious work, a summation of Christian dogma, in this case, the Redemption. Because its outer wings, like shutters, open and close, not all of the panels are visible at one time. When open, the altarpiece reveals two registers: large figures of a celestial nature in the upper one; smaller, earthly figures in the lower one. On the outermost panels of the upper register are the images of Adam and Eve. Remarkably unclassical in their nakedness, they symbolize sin and the medieval view of the human body as indecent. Next to them are two groups of musical angels who flank the seated figures of the Virgin Mary and John the Baptist, intercessors for mankind and the forerunners of Christ. Climaxing the upper register is the resplendent figure of God Triumphant, the merciful Father of mankind.

The panels of the lower register are connected by a single, marvelous landscape filled with groups of pilgrims all converging on the center. On the left are defenders of the faith—judges and knights on horseback; on the right, hermits and pilgrims approaching on foot. At the center is *The Adoration of the Lamb* (Fig. **7.50**), a mystical scene that

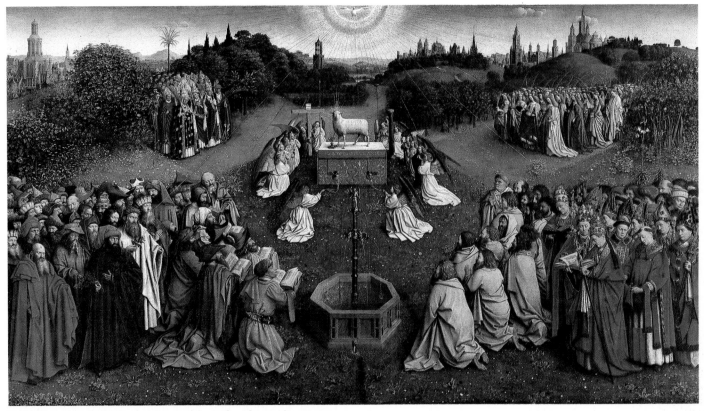

7.50 *The Adoration of the Lamb*, panel from the Ghent Altarpiece

brings the Redemption narrative to its logical and compositional climax. In the central axis, just below the figure of God, are the symbols of Christ the Redeemer: the dove of the Holy Spirit, the altar of the Lamb, and the fountain of life and truth. Approaching from four directions are groups of adoring humanity: confessors and holy virgins in the distance, Evangelists and Apostles surrounded by prophets and martyrs in the foreground. The procession, a glorious pageant of saints, painted with brilliant, enamel-like colors, is enacted in a garden filled with exotic plants and shrubs. All Flemish painters had a talent for rendering

details, and Van Eyck was first among equals. Because to him everything was God's creation, every object in his pictures had to be treated with the same reverent concern, including even objects in the distance. Atmospheric perspective—the blurring of detail in the background—was not part of Van Eyck's pictorial stock in trade. In truth, such fastidious attention to particulars detracts from the sense of realism rather than enhancing it. It does, however, enhance the sense of mysticism, and *The Adoration of the Lamb* is a very mystical picture.

Music

Post-Gregorian Music

Chapter 6 ended with the growth of European music up to the establishment of the Gregorian chant, or plainsong, in the sixth century. It must be stressed again that, without notated manuscripts to study, the full nature of this body of music as it existed in Gregory's time is a matter of

speculation. Because a system of musical notation was yet to be developed, the teaching and preservation of music was entirely oral. Performance of an antiphon from one time to the next was dependent on the memories, if not the whims, of individual singers. And, according to Guido d'Arezzo, an eleventh-century monk and music teacher, "... of all men, singers are the most foolish."[7] The point is not so much that singers are foolish, or even that they should be blamed for the lack of a notational system, but that to leave the preservation of a musical heritage solely to them would be folly.

The impetus for creating a viable system of preserving music may have begun with Charlemagne, who, because the pope had neglected to give him a complete set of books on the Gregorian liturgy, called on Alcuin to supplement it. To do so, Alcuin had to draw on materials from local traditions. Although his task involved organizing verbal rather than musical texts, his efforts may have set a precedent for systematic translation of available sources, including, eventually, the notation of music. At any rate, from this time until the Renaissance, growth in the liturgy was led more by French and German scholars and musicians than by Italians. During the latter half of the Middle Ages, the history of music, like the history of art, was enacted mostly in the North.

Musical notation, which began in the ninth century, was apparently a northern invention, as none of the earliest manuscripts were written in Italy. At first the system simply involved writing a sign, called a *neume*, above each syllable in a text to indicate whether the note for that syllable should be high or low in relation to the one preceding it. If several notes were sung to one syllable, single signs could be combined into two- or three-note neumes. Up to this point, the system was mute about sizes of intervals between notes or even the note on which the melody began; it served mainly as a memory aid for singers who already knew the melody. Later, sizes of intervals were shown by neumes at different heights on the page; this led to careful spacing and the use of lines to clarify which neumes were of the same pitch. When the lines themselves came to have fixed meanings in terms of their respective pitches, the method of staffing (see Chapter 4) was born. Still missing, however, was a method of indicating rhythm.

Meanwhile the church modes (see page 263) had become, in effect, the standard scales of medieval music. As we have seen, late Roman scholars had tried to relate these modes to what they thought were Greek modes. Tenth-century monks tried to perpetuate this tradition. But in the final analysis there was nothing Greek about the church modes except their names (Fig. 3.24). Regardless of their not being truly Greek, to modern ears they might as well be—not so much because of the scales themselves but because of the way they were used. In each mode two notes are important: the *dominant* (marked D in the figure) and the *final* (marked F). The final is usually the note on which a chant ends. It corresponds to the tonic in a modern major or minor scale. What sounds strange to a modern listener is that the finals of most of these modes do

not have semitones immediately below them as modern tonics have (that is, *ti* below *do*). Therefore the endings of plainchants tend to sound odd, as if they stopped in "mid-air." Nevertheless, the modes themselves, inasmuch as each consists of eight notes, with two semitone steps, are the ancestors of the major and minor scales to which our ears are accustomed.

Another advance in the progress of European harmony was the idea of *solmization*, the use of generic syllables for singing the tones of a scale (as in *do, re, mi*, etc.). Invented by Guido d'Arezzo in the eleventh century, the first system of solmization was limited to the tonal range of only six steps—*ut, re, me, fa, sol, la*—and was used as an aid in the teaching of plainchant melodies. Later, the system was completed with the addition of *ti* and the concluding *ut*, or *do*. In this form it continues to be used in vocal lessons to this day.

As musical systems were being developed, chant repertoires were being expanded and loosened. Old melodies were extended; new words were added to old melodies. Although the added words were not scriptural, they enlarged the meaning of a psalm or made more explicit the connection between a biblical verse and the feast day for which it was appointed. For example, added to the Kyrie ("Lord have mercy upon us") were such lines as "Auctor caelorum Deus eterne" (Author of the heavens, eternal God) and "Spiritus cordium illustrator" (Holy Spirit, illuminator of hearts). This practice not only provided greater latitude for poets and musicians; it led to one of the most important innovations in musical history: polyphony.

Polyphony

Polyphony—two or more voices singing (or, in the case of instruments, playing) independently began as an embellishment of the monophonic plainsong, probably in the form of new words sung simultaneously with old chants. (Another theory is that it began accidentally with a monk who could not stay in tune.) Polyphony flourished especially in southern France and northern Spain in the Cluniac monasteries; and it was to become the predominant style of music in the Renaissance (see Chapter 3). More significantly, polyphony was the basis on which the vertical, or harmonic, dimension of Western music was built.

Before describing early polyphonic forms, however, we must explain three monophonic forms: the *syllabic*, the *neumatic*, and the *melismatic*. In syllabic melodies, each syllable of a text has a single note; in neumatic passages, a single syllable is sung to several notes; a melismatic passage extends this principle, with a syllable being sung

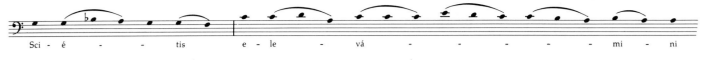

7.51 A melisma with positive accents

to a longer series of notes called a *melisma* (Fig. **7.51**). Many chants contain a mixture of the three, with syllabic and neumatic sections alternating with melismas. As to their respective effects on the listener, the three differ in degrees of ornateness, with the syllabic being the simplest and the melismatic, the most florid.

The earliest type of polyphony is called *organum* (pl. *organa*). It was limited to small groups of soloists; monophony was still the rule for choruses. (As we saw in Chapter 3, it was the fifteenth-century composer Ockegham who first gave polyphonic music to choirs.) The earliest organa were probably *parallel*, that is, voices following the same musical paths but separated in pitch by a few steps. Later the musical paths diverged slightly, leading to what is referred to as *free* organum—part singing by two or more relatively independent voices. The lowest part, known as the "cantus firmus" or "tenor" (from Latin *tenere*, "to hold") sang the melody; the other parts, from lowest to highest, were called respectively "duplum," "triplum," and "quadruplum."

Two styles of free organum flourished in the Middle Ages. The first, called *melismatic organum*, consists of a melody sung in long, sustained notes paired with a melisma in the duplum voice (Fig. **7.52**); the other, called *discant* style, consists of two or more melodies sung syllabically or neumatically (Fig. **7.53**). Unlike the florid melismatic organum, discant organum entails mostly "note-against-note" polyphony.

7.52 Example of melismatic organum

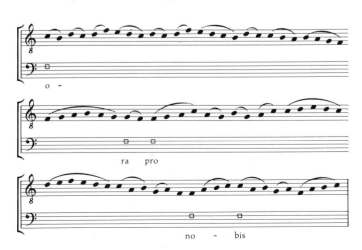

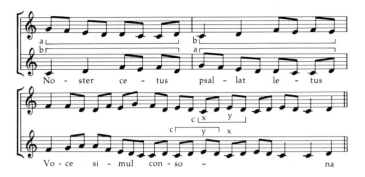

7.53 Example of discant style

The School of Notre Dame

The early development of Gothic architecture, as we have seen, occurred in the Île de France. Musical innovation in the thirteenth century also moved north to that province, particularly to Paris, site of one of the oldest medieval universities and of a famous Gothic cathedral, Notre Dame. Even as the cathedral itself was being built, a large body of polyphonic music, now credited to the "School of Notre Dame," was being composed.

Because the medieval system of notation did not provide time values for different neumes, it was difficult for two or more singers to coordinate their rhythms in polyphonic works. To address this problem, the composer-teachers at Notre Dame devised a system for notating rhythm. Unlike our own, in which notes have strictly determined time values (within a context of time signatures and bars), the early medieval system established a set of note patterns, or "rhythmic modes;" the relative value of a note was determined by the context of the note pattern in which it appeared. Although the system itself may have been awkward, the concept of rhythmic notation was a vital step in the development of Western music.

The composers associated with Notre Dame also pioneered the development of the *motet*, a musical form that would be used to great advantage by Dufay and Ockeghem (see pages 118–19) in the fifteenth century. Motets grew out of Latin sacred songs that were not officially part of the liturgy. Unlike organa, which were built on the styles and texts of plainchants, these songs were liturgically independent pieces—the first polyphonic compositions with original texts. Some of the Latin songs are simple, some rather embellished. The simpler ones re-

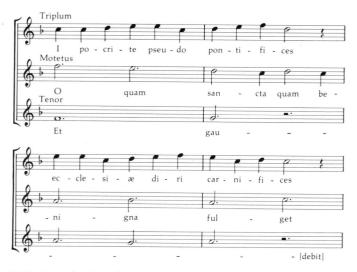

7.54 Example of conducti/motet

semble modern hymns and secular songs, in that their melodies are sung syllabically, their texts are organized in stanzas, and the music is repeated for each stanza. But, unlike a song (and also the organum) which uses the same text for all voices, a motet may employ different texts in the voices (Fig. 7.54).

Northern France in the thirteenth century was thus the center of developments in music, just as it was for architecture and sculpture. The development of rhythmic notation, the creation of beautiful organa, and the invention of the motet brought music to the next episode in its European development—*ars nova*. But before reviewing that style, we should say some things about non-religious music.

Secular Music

Alongside the development of religious polyphony was the development of another kind of music: the love song. Music dedicated to institutions outside the Church and inspired by forces outside religion is, of course, known as secular music. Such music may have anticipated the stories of Boccaccio and other manifestations of the secular spirit that arose in the fourteenth century. At the very least, twelfth-century secular music affected contemporary musical developments, both secular and religious. Nevertheless, it is mostly monophonic. Stylistically, the differences between it and sacred monophony are difficult to determine.

Even before the twelfth century, Frenchmen composed *chansons de geste* (songs of deeds), the most famous example being the *Song of Roland* (see above). In essence these are medieval epics of legendary French heroes, possibly sung to the accompaniment of stringed instru-

ments (harps or viols). As such, they played a role in medieval society similar to that of epic poetry in Archaic Greece (see Chapter 2).

At about the same time that organum was reaching its fullest development, *troubadours*, poet-musicians of Provence in southern France, were writing *cansos* (love songs) and *baladas* (dance songs) for the courts. Many early troubadours, like William IX, Duke of Aquitaine, were themselves of the nobility; later they were often professionals in the service of a royal or noble household. Troubadour songs, like modern songs, employ stanzas sung to the same melodies, and were usually sung syllabically. However, the style of troubadour melodies scarcely differs from that of Gregorian chant, even to the extent of adhering to the eight-mode system.

Although some troubadours also performed songs they generally composed them for *jongleurs*, wandering entertainers, to sing. Jongleurs' performances were well received, but they themselves were social outcasts. Despite their lowly status jongleurs spread the influence and example of troubadour music throughout southern France and beyond.

This influence eventually spawned the music of the *trouvère* in northern France and the *Minnesinger* in Germany, both of whom flourished in the thirteenth century. These were essentially the same as the troubadour and, like the troubadours, usually aristocrats. Later, in Germany, the Minnesingers were followed by Meistersingers (see page 230), who were members of the rising middle class. All of this music drew on multiple sources: the *chansons de geste*, plainchant, the songs of itinerant minstrels, and vernacular poetry, such as that of Celtic bards. In general, trouvère music has simpler melodies and more pronounced rhythms than its Provençal counterpart. In this respect it is more akin to folk music.

Love songs and other forms of secular music typically involved the use of instruments. Indeed, most of the instruments mentioned in Chapter 3 with regard to Renaissance music (lute, sackbut, trumpet, shawm, viol, organ, and so forth) had been invented by this time. But evidence of this comes mostly from pictures and written sources, rather than from musical manuscripts; none of the latter indicated instrumental parts. This is because vocal music was still the dominant medium and the basis of all music; instrumental performance was the province of jongleurs and other vagabond entertainers. Nevertheless, instruments were making important inroads, even in liturgical music. There is reason to believe that the performance of the tenor part in polyphonic compositions was taken over by the organ. By the second half of the thirteenth century this instrument had become common in many churches.

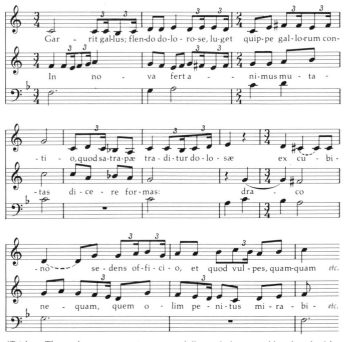

(*Triplum:* The cock crows, weeping sorrowfully, and the assembly of cocks [the French nation] mourns, for it is handed over to the cunning satrap.
Motetus: One is minded to tell of forms changed into something new.)

7.55 The *Fauvel* motet, de Vitry

Ars Nova

Ars nova (Latin, "new art"), the title of a musical treatise by Philippe de Vitry (1291–1361), was applied to a musical style that thrived in the fourteenth century. De Vitry, who came from the province of Champagne, attempted to clarify musical practices that were already taking place. He standardized time values, devised new codes for these values, and introduced the first "color coding," by using red ink for rhythmic changes in a score. These innovations enabled composers of his time to exploit the rhythmic possibilities of their medium more effectively.

Just how new was *ars nova*? Judging by its contemporary critics, it was radically new. Jacob of Liège, a writer on music, complained about its making use of "varied imperfections in notes, modes, measures. ..."[8] Pope John XXII issued a papal bull condemning composers for using too many short notes, rests, and endless melismas. But modern musicologists dispute the idea of *ars nova* being so new, tending to regard it more as an elaboration of thirteenth-century music, just as Late Gothic is an elaboration of thirteenth-century Gothic. They also see, in its increased complexity and use of novelty, a reflection of

the turmoil of late medieval Europe: the peasant uprising, the Hundred Years War, the Great Schism of the papacy, and a pervasive mood of disrespect for traditional institutions. This new aesthetic is exemplified by the poem, *Roman de Fauvel* (1316). The text, a satire on social corruption symbolized by a horse named Fauvel, is set to various pieces of music, including songs and motets—some written by de Vitry—which display early manifestations of the *ars nova* style.

Ars nova music, like Late Gothic architecture or International School miniatures, is characterized by refinement, subtlety, and complexity of detail. Specifically, it departs from earlier music by its incorporation of such things as shorter notes, rhythmic complexity, syncopation (adding an accent where one is not expected or removing an accent where one is expected), and duple meter (2/4 time signature). The *Fauvel* motet "Garrit gallus/In nova fert animus," by de Vitry, has many of these characteristics: eighth notes interspersed with sixteenth notes in the upper voices; rhythmic complexity, as seen in the alternations between 3/4 and 2/4 time; and syncopation resulting from this alternation as well as from the unexpected accents caused by the intermittent sixteenth notes (Fig. **7.55**). It is also a good example of repeating a long rhythmic pattern throughout a composition, a practice that was to become commonplace in fourteenth-century motets. Although de Vitry—a friend of Petrarch's—was highly celebrated in his time, few of his works have been preserved.

Machaut

Fortunately, many of the works of Guillaume de Machaut (c.1300–1377) have survived. Like de Vitry, he was born in Champagne and was a leader in the *ars nova* movement. Considered by many to be the greatest poet and composer of the fourteenth century, he was also a part-time trouvère, civil servant, ambassador, and cleric. On his travels he met, among others, the Duke of Berry, owner of the *Très Riches Heures*. In his later years the composer was appointed as canon of Rheims Cathedral, where he was buried.

Machaut, like many other *ars nova* composers, wrote more secular music than religious. Except for one important liturgical piece, he is best known for his love songs, dances, and secular motets. Some of the best examples of *ars nova* inventiveness are found in these works. "Se je chant," a hunting song, vividly illustrates the composer's joining of text and music for expressive effect (Fig. **7.56**). The rhythms of a hunt in full swing are skillfully brought to life by the syncopating pulse of syllables, sixteenth notes, and abrupt rests: "Ho, quiet there; ho, I see them;

Ex. 7

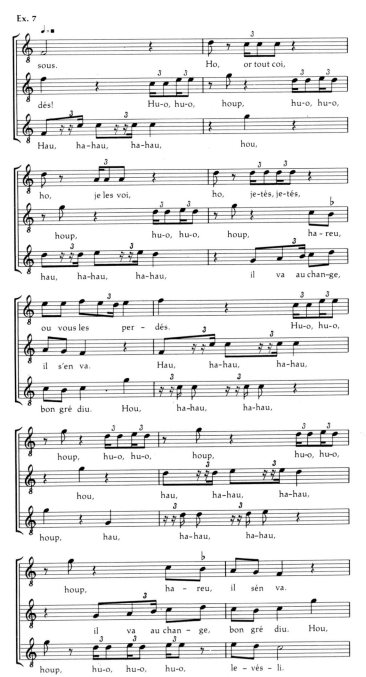

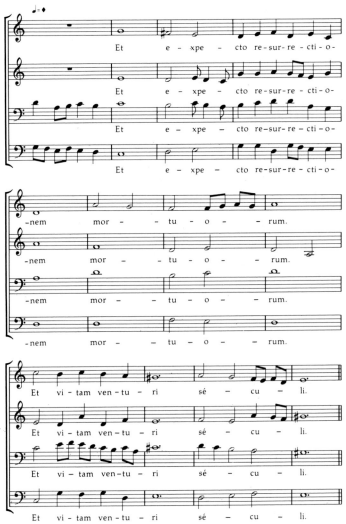

And I look for the resurrection of the dead, and the life of the world to come.

7.57 The credo

(Ho, quiet there: ho, I see them; ho, throw, throw, or you lose them. Huo, huo, houp; huo, huo, houp; hareu, he's got away. Hau, hahau, & c.; he's on the wrong scent, thank God. Hou, & c., pick him up. Hau, hahau, hahau; ha-ha, he's dead, let's go and feed our hawks.)

7.56 Hunting chant—"Se je chant..."

ho, throw, throw, or you lose them. . . ." In addition, the element of pursuit is suggested by the partial use of a round, in which voices seem to "chase" one another with similar lines sung at different times.

The brilliance of his secular poetry and music notwithstanding, Machaut's most enduring musical monument is a religious piece: the Notre Dame Mass (c. 1364). Up to this time, composers had written music for the Mass not as a unit, but as individual parts, particularly those of the Proper which are sung on feast days and special occasions. Now composers began treating the Mass as a unit, but only, of course, including the Ordinary: the Kyrie, Gloria, Credo, Sanctus, Agnus Dei and Ite missus est. These parts, then, became the separate movements of a total composition—the musical Mass we know today (although later Masses omit the last section). Machaut's Mass is a prototype, the first completely polyphonic Mass

Ordinary written by one person. Consisting of 730 measures, it is an ambitious piece, perhaps the composer's memorial to his many years of service at Rheims Cathedral. The movements, written mainly in motet style, use four voices, two of which may have been performed by or doubled with instruments; unlike motets, they use the same text in all voices. Machaut employed several devices to unify the composition: the repetition of a plainsong melody and isorhythm in four of the movements, the use of melismatic amens at the end of all movements, and the predominant use of 2/4 time signature throughout.

Despite the unifying devices, each of the movements is a unique expressive entity in which music and theme are closely related. For example, the Kyrie is solemn and elaborate, befitting a prayer for mercy. The Credo, illustrated here, is measured and stately, appropriate for an unwavering affirmation of faith (Fig. 7.57). More like a Latin song than a motet, this work is marked by a distinctly syllabic, note-against-note polyphony, with the same text used in all four voices. The contrast between the sobriety of the Credo and the vivacity of "Se je chant," the hunt song, demonstrates the range of Machaut's musical expression, a range that exemplifies the distance European music had traveled since the time of Pope Gregory.

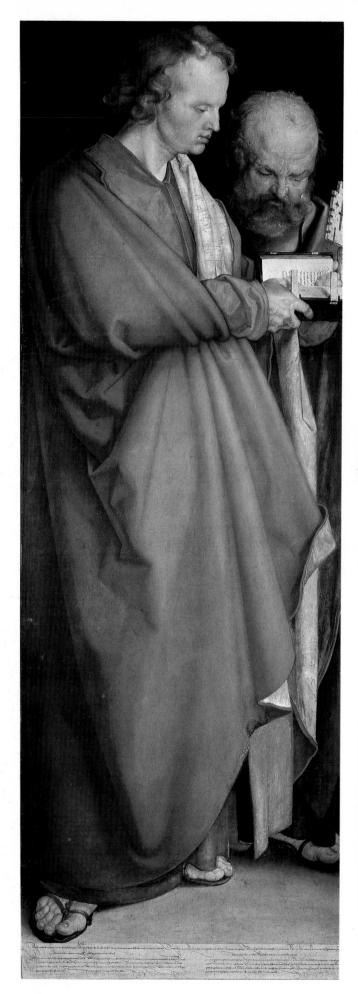
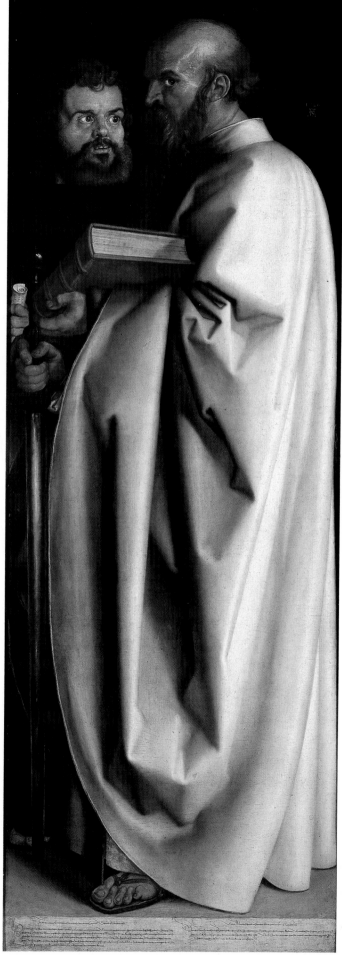

CHAPTER EIGHT

Christianity III: The Era of the Reformation

The just shall live by faith.

ROMANS 1:17

Introduction

The Reformation is the term used for the revolt which occurred within the Catholic Church in the sixteenth century and which led to the creation of the Protestant churches. "Revolt" is perhaps too negative a term; for the theology developed by Martin Luther and other reformers was not merely a critical response to the obvious abuses in the late medieval and Renaissance Church; it was, in essence, an attempt to answer, in biblical terms, the question, "What must I do to be saved?" As the Reformation progressed, many deep-seated concerns—political, economic, and social—were expressed through the demands for religious reform; but one must always be mindful that the precipitating factor in Luther's challenge to the Catholic Church was his discovery, in the writings of St. Paul, of what he believed to be the one right answer to the question of personal salvation. This was the seed of the German Reformation: the search of one sin-ridden man for the assurance that God had forgiven and accepted him.

Chronologically, the Reformation parallels, roughly, the period of the Renaissance, discussed in Chapter 3. Indeed, the two movements are, in significant ways, inextricably connected. By means of their linguistic skills, especially the knowledge of Greek, developed through their study of the classical writings, humanists prepared the way for the biblical interpretations of the Protestant reformers. The best-known German artist of the Reformation, Albrecht Dürer, studied painting in Italy and thus lent his classically influenced talent to the service of expressing its ideals. Much the same point may be made with respect to Reformation music: Luther's contribution to musical liturgy, as well as his appreciation of the polyphony of Josquin (see page 146), are examples.

As demonstrated by the monastic reform movements dealt with previously (see Chapter 7), concern for religious reform did not begin with Martin Luther. The abuses and superstitions perpetrated by the institutional Church, especially in the fourteenth and fifteenth centuries, had been attacked by men such as the Oxford philosopher John Wycliffe (1320?–1384) and Jan Hus (1369–1415), a Czech priest strongly influenced by Wycliffe. Wycliffe denied the universal power of the pope, condemned corrupt priests, and rejected the doctrine of transubstantiation (that the bread and wine literally become the body and blood of Christ in the Mass). He also taught that people could approach God directly, without priestly intercession. He is especially significant for his translation of the Latin Bible (the Vulgate) into English, thus enabling

the English to contrast the simplicity of the early Church with the power and wealth of the medieval Church. Eventually, he was forced by the religious authorities to leave Oxford. Like Wycliffe, Hus condemned clerical corruption and advocated the universal priesthood of all believers. He also condemned pilgrimages and the worship of images. He was finally excommunicated by the pope when he attacked the sale of indulgences, which had been initiated by the pope to finance a crusade against a Christian king. Though given a letter of safe conduct to attend the Council of Constance, where he hoped to explain his views, Hus was condemned by the council and burned as an heretic.

Further evidence of the desire for religious reform is found in the Conciliar Movement of the fifteenth century, which was the result of the Great Schism, the division among the cardinals over which of the two popes—one at Avignon, the other at Rome (see page 94)—was authentic. Certain scholars believed that only a general council could carry out a "reformation in head and members" of the Church. Thus the Council of Pisa was called in 1409—the result: a third pope elected by the council! The Council of Constance (1414–1418), however, was able to resolve the problem of the Schism. It was not so successful with reforms, largely because the new pope did not find it politically convenient to implement them. The Council of Basel (1431–1449) also failed to institute reforms.

By the end of the fifteenth century there was a general recognition among devout and thoughtful people of the need for religious reform. In its effort to adjust to the rise of the middle class, the increase of wealth, and the growing power of temporal rulers, the Church itself had become increasingly secularized and corrupt. Moreover, the corruption was so widespread, and so many political and religious leaders were profiting from it, that it seemed impossible to eradicate.

Luther, too, originally intended to reform the Church from within. In this he obviously failed. But he did not become simply one more unsuccessful reformer, like Wycliffe or Hus, rejected by the Church; instead, he received, from like-minded people, the protection and support he needed to mount a successful revolt against the Catholic Church and to found a new branch of Christianity.

What made the difference in the case of Luther? A modern authority on the Reformation, Harold J. Grimm, offers three answers to this question. Firstly, Germany had been heavily burdened by the financial demands of the papacy. Thus the German people were especially resentful of papal greed. Secondly, the German people were stronger in their determination to find an answer to the religious question: "What must I do to be saved?" Finally, there were in Germany larger numbers of educated bourgeoisie who were sensitive to the restraints imposed upon them by the Church. Therefore, as Grimm states, "the resentments, and the hopes, of the Germans were epitomized in the life and work of Martin Luther."[1] Thus, Luther was the right man in the right place at the right time. This chapter will briefly survey the road that led to his discovery, in the writings of St. Paul, of the doctrine of justification by faith and his subsequent break with the Catholic Church.

The protest that began with Luther eventually spread to other nations, giving rise to three basic forms of Protestantism (a term only coined in 1529). *Lutheranism* was, of course, the form that it took, under the influence of Luther, in most of Germany, but also in the Scandinavian countries. The doctrines of Lutheranism are classically expressed in the Augsburg Confession (1530). The *Reformed* Church (sometimes known as Calvinist, or Presbyterian) developed essentially out of the theology of John Calvin. It began in Switzerland, and spread to the Netherlands and Scotland. Reformed theology also had adherents in France and England, as well as in parts of Germany and Eastern Europe. The Reformed churches expressed their beliefs in a number of separate national confessions. The *Anglican* Church developed out of Henry VIII's defiance of papal authority in divorcing his wife Catherine of Aragon in order to marry Anne Boleyn, hoping thereby to obtain a male heir to the English throne. Although proclaiming himself head of the English Church, displacing the pope, Henry remained a Catholic in doctrine. The Anglican Church swerved sharply toward Protestantism under Henry's son Edward VI (1547–1553). Following the reign of Henry's elder daughter Mary I (1553–1558), during which Roman Catholicism was reinstated, Anglicanism was finally established under Elizabeth I (1558–1603), also Henry's daughter, and was given its final form in the Thirty-nine Articles, which reflected both Lutheran and Calvinist doctrines.

Indeed, all three manifestations of Protestantism, though developing under different social and political circumstances, shared certain theological convictions that originated with Luther. They believed that the Word of God (the Bible) is the source of religious authority, that salvation is by faith alone, and that all believers have the right of direct access to God (the priesthood of all believers).

The sixteenth century has been termed the Age of Reformations, emphasizing that the well-known Protestant Reformation was not the only one. The Counter Reformation, or Catholic Reformation, discussed later in this chapter, is the most obvious example of this fact. Humanists such as Erasmus (see below) were also clearly concerned for reform, and contributed to the Reformation.

The "Radical Reformation" was yet another manifestation of the deep-running concern for reform in the sixteenth century. The reformers belonging to this movement differed in the particulars of their theological views and programs—some were much more radical than others—but were in agreement that the principal reformers had not been radical enough, because they had failed to abolish the integral connection between state and Church; thus they rejected the idea of a state or national church.

Not surprisingly, much of the literature of this period was essentially religious: Bible commentaries, theological treatises, and textual and philological studies of Scripture. This chapter focuses on some examples of the Reformation writings of Luther and Calvin but also includes an analysis of Erasmus' book *The Praise of Folly*. This work well illustrates how Christian humanists helped prepare the soil for the seed sown by the reformers. Examples of sixteenth-century literature not directly related to the Reformation have been discussed in Chapter 3.

Apart from Albrecht Dürer and Matthias Grünewald, Lutheranism produced few great artists whose works are known chiefly for their religious content. In the seventeenth century, however, Reformed Protestantism did find artistic expression in The Netherlands, especially in the works of Rembrandt. His paintings are dramatic and provocative reinterpretations of biblical subjects which, like the reinterpretations of the reformers, made the Bible vibrant and relevant.

Counter-Reformation theology, unlike Lutheran, is linked with particular artistic traditions: Mannerism and, especially, the Baroque. The works of El Greco illustrate the former; those of Rubens, the latter. In sculpture the prime example of the Baroque style is the work of Bernini. Also expressive of Counter-Reformation theology are the imposing Baroque churches of the seventeenth and eighteenth centuries, which proclaim, in their splendid virtuosity, the renewed spiritual vigor (as well as the wealth and power) of the Catholic Church.

Music fared much better than art in German Protestantism. Beginning with Luther himself, a strong tradition of congregational and choir singing grew up in the Lutheran churches. Organ and choral music in the Lutheran tradition reached its apogee with Johann Sebastian Bach. The great German hymn tunes (which Bach used as a basis for many of his compositions) are still sung today in Lutheran and other Protestant churches. The Calvinist churches also employed congregational singing in their worship, but their song books included only psalms set to music. The *Genevan Psalter* was such a book, widely used by the Reformed churches on the Continent. Although the liturgical use of music in the Catholic Church was threatened by the Council of Trent's criticisms that its elaborate structure obscured its devotional content, it survived in the lucid, more restrained compositions of Palestrina.

Historians disagree on the question of whether the Reformation was essentially a modern or a medieval event. Although it began with a typically medieval question—"How can I be saved?"—it also introduced a principle of individualism—often associated with Modernism—in its emphasis on the priesthood of all believers. Moreover, it also contributed to a political-religious uprising, the Peasants' Revolt (or War), which broke out in Germany in 1524. Using Luther's defiance of the Catholic Church as a precedent, peasants demanded various rights and freedoms from their princes. In this instance Luther sided with the established authorities and condemned the uprising.

However much Luther and other reformers censured unbridled individualism, they were responsible for introducing this potentially explosive concept. Apart from the arguments of historians, the question of the continuing relevance of the Reformation will usually be answered on a subjective basis: that is, on the basis of whether its essentially theological concerns and principles, as contrasted with the particular historical circumstances in which it occurred, continue to speak to them.

8.2

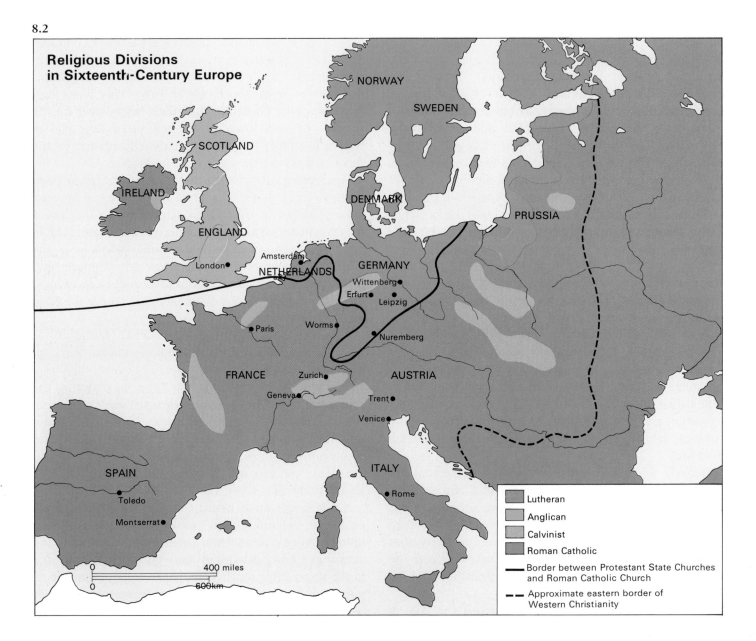

Religious Divisions in Sixteenth-Century Europe

	Lutheran
	Anglican
	Calvinist
	Roman Catholic
———	Border between Protestant State Churches and Roman Catholic Church
– – –	Approximate eastern border of Western Christianity

DATES	SOCIAL AND POLITICAL DEVELOPMENTS	LITERATURE AND PHILOSOPHY	VISUAL ARTS	ARCHITECTURE	MUSIC
1400		Wycliffe's translation of the Bible			
1500	Pope Julius II Luther: 95 Theses Diet of Worms	Erasmus (8.4) John Colet Thomas More Luther (8.5) St Ignatius Loyola (8.7)	Dürer (8.9) Grünewald (8.12) Holbein the Younger (8.4)		German chorale
1525	Henry VIII rejects papal authority Jesuits – Loyola Council of Trent	Calvin (8.6)	Michelangelo (8.14)		Palestrina
1550	Counter-Reformation Elizabeth I		Tintoretto (8.15) El Greco (8.16) Caravaggio (8.18)		
1600	Thirty Years War		Baroque style Rubens (8.17) Bernini (8.19) Rembrandt (8.21–25)		Organ in churches
1650	Oliver Cromwell – Commonwealth				Telemann
1700					Bach (8.27) Handel (8.28)

8.3 The Enlightenment

Literature

Erasmus

Desiderius Erasmus (1466?–1536), a Dutch scholar, has been called the "Prince of the Humanists." Born in Rotterdam, the illegitimate son of a priest, Erasmus spent nine years at Deventer in the School of the Brethren of the Common Life, an order that emphasized the example of Jesus as a guide to ethical conduct and the importance of Christian service and love. Ordained a priest in 1492, he later studied theology at the University of Paris, where he became disgusted with the hair-splitting disputations of the scholastic theologians.

Erasmus is the outstanding example of the Christian humanists of northern Europe, as contrasted with the more secular humanists of Italy. These northern scholars were especially concerned with the elimination of textual errors from the Bible and the establishment of correct methods of Scriptural interpretation. Although, like their Italian counterparts, the Christian humanists studied the classical texts, they did so not for the purpose of identifying with the attitudes and concerns of antiquity, but to develop and hone their philological tools so as to interpret correctly the Scriptural texts. Erasmus' most significant linguistic achievement, for example—though he was also a translator of both Latin and Greek classical texts—was the publication of a new edition of the Greek New Testament (1516), later used by Martin Luther in doing his profoundly influential German translation. Erasmus also published a new Latin translation of the New Testament which audaciously corrected errors in the Vulgate, St. Jerome's Latin translation, which had served as the authoritative Bible for a thousand years. Erasmus also used his philological skills to produce more accurate texts of the writings of the Church Fathers, the scholars who, in the early centuries of the Church's history, sought to define Christian doctrine (see page 235). Through such scholarly activity, Erasmus, like many other Christian humanists, believed that it would be possible to recover the authentic primitive Christian faith and thereby to reform the Church in his own day. Believing that the unity of Christendom must be preserved, he and other Christian humanists, unlike Luther, did not deny the basic doctrines of the Catholic Church but attacked its abuses and institutional corruption in the confidence that correct

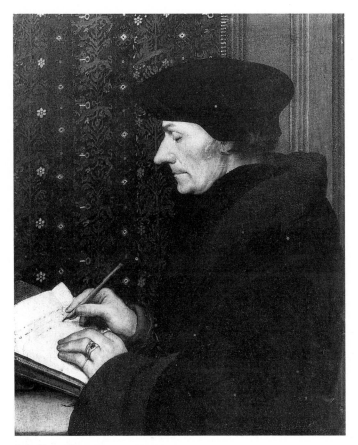

8.4 HANS HOLBEIN THE YOUNGER
Erasmus of Rotterdam, c. 1523
Oil on panel, $16\frac{1}{2} \times 12\frac{1}{2}$ ins (42×32 cm)
Louvre, Paris

reason and true learning would lead to reformation and piety.

In fact, Erasmus and Luther were widely separated in their attitudes toward human nature and its possibilities for salvation, as became evident in their debate (in the form of essays) on freedom of the will. Erasmus, though recognizing that human reason has its limits, placed considerable confidence in its possibilities and in the capacity of human beings to exercise freedom in achieving salvation. Not so Luther. In his view, reason, like every other aspect of human nature, is corrupted by sin and thus can be a barrier to faith or even become a servant of evil. So enthralled by sin are humans, in Luther's view, that God's grace alone is sufficient to redeem them. Thus no reconciliation between Erasmus and Luther was possible. This debate reveals the great gulf between the program of the Christian humanists and the theology of the reformers.

Even before the publication of his Greek New Testament, Erasmus published *Adages* (1500), a book that made him famous. Consisting of quotations from the Latin classics, it also included Erasmus' satirical comments on various groups, both religious and secular. Among his numerous religious works, Erasmus wrote the *Handbook of the Christian Knight* (1503), a book that sets forth his "philosophy of Christ," and *The Education of a Christian Prince* (1516), written for Charles I of Spain, later to become Charles V, the Holy Roman Emperor. Although this book was published only three years after Machiavelli wrote *The Prince*, it is poles apart from that amoral work, emphasizing as it does the moral responsibilities of a Christian ruler. Erasmus approached the subject in the traditional manner of such philosophers and theologians as Plato, Aristotle, and Aquinas, whereas Machiavelli (see Chapter 3) was a radical innovator. In 1517, four years after the death of the warlike pope and patron of the arts Julius II (see page 130), Erasmus wrote an anonymous dialogue entitled *Julius Exclusus* (*Julius Excluded from Heaven*), a satirical work that allowed him to express his pacifism. This dialogue was so successful that he wrote a series of dialogues (*Familiar Conversations*; 1518) which are rich in information about the times and contain much criticism of religious abuses.

Erasmus made six trips to England (the first occurring in 1499) which afforded him the opportunity to get to know such illustrious humanists as Sir Thomas More and John Colet. In fact, it was Colet who encouraged him to translate the New Testament, which he accomplished while lecturing at Cambridge (1510–1513). During his third visit to England, while recovering from lumbago in More's home, Erasmus wrote the book for which he is best known in modern times, his witty and satirical *The Praise of Folly* (1509).

In this book Erasmus speaks through a literary persona (fictitious character)—Folly—who makes a speech in praise of herself and her followers. Thus the question of whose views are being stated is raised. Are they Folly's or the views of Erasmus? In fact the book is highly ambiguous, for sometimes Erasmus is sincerely expressing his own views and in fact attacking a particular kind of folly, while at other times he is, in the guise of folly, ironically praising it. Contributing to the ambiguity of the book is the fact that Erasmus uses the concept of the "fool" in more than one sense, mostly negatively but sometimes positively, drawing on the medieval tradition of the "wisdom" of folly. Thus the tone of the book shifts from time to time, depending upon the type of folly under consideration.

Erasmus considers three main kinds of folly: natural, unnatural, and supernatural (divine), and the tone reflects this organization.[2] Thus, when Folly praises natural folly early in the book, the tone is wittily playful and ironic. But in the middle section, where Folly describes unnatural folly, it is as though Erasmus is speaking in his own person, and the tone becomes severely critical. He continues to speak his own mind directly in the final section, as he describes divine folly, and the tone now becomes quite devoutly serious.

In Part I, Folly argues that she is the source of all human pleasure. Indeed, she contends, to be human is to be foolish, and to expect more of humans is like expecting a horse to know grammar or a bull to dance—such is contrary to their natures. So with human beings: "A foolish man is no more unhappy than an illiterate horse: both are true to themselves."[3] Folly thus presents us with a view of human nature that is a compromise between Rousseau's idea that human beings are essentially good (see Chapter 7), and the medieval concept that they are evil. They are neither evil nor good but foolish.

In Part II, the irony of Part I gives way to open attack, because Erasmus wishes to leave no doubt as to his attitude toward the evils presented. Significantly, two-thirds of the criticism in this section is directed at the Church. The tone becomes increasingly serious, matching the nature of the evils treated.

His attack on the Church hierarchy is separated from his treatment of other churchmen by the section on political leaders, thus emphasizing that these religious officials are essentially political figures. Here he turns his big guns on bishops, cardinals, and popes, ending with an attack on priests. He is particularly savage in his treatment of popes, asserting that the Church has no "more deadly enemies than impious popes who by their silence cause Christ to be forsaken, who use His laws to make money, who adulterate His word with forced interpretations, and who crucify Him with their corrupt life!"[4] Indeed, he says that popes "can show how a man may draw a sword and run it through his brother's guts and at the same time live in that perfect charity which Christ tells us a Christian owes to his neighbor."

In the beginning of Part III, where he treats divine folly, Erasmus briefly reverts to irony, but the tone becomes more seriously religious as the discussion develops. In this section's key passage he states: "Christ himself, although He possessed the wisdom of the Father, became something like a fool in order to cure the folly of mankind, when he assumed the nature and being of a mortal.... He was made 'to be sin' in order to redeem sinners. He did not wish to redeem them by any way except the foolishness of the cross, and by weak and simple apostles."[5] Here Erasmus draws heavily on St. Paul (cf. I Corinthians 1:18–31) to demonstrate that the wisdom of God and the Christian Gospel that it produced are, from the worldly point of view, folly. But what seems absurd—God's Son becoming a human being and dying a criminal's death on a Roman cross—is, in fact, the divine means of curing human folly.

Both the tone and the content of these passages clearly reveal that Erasmus is not satirizing Christ and the Christian Gospel but, like St. Paul, is straightforwardly presenting their challenge. In Part III, therefore, as in Part II, Erasmus, though continuing to use the persona of Folly, speaks directly, not ironically. In Part II, he attacks the evils of the Church; in Part III, he sets forth the divine alternative to a corrupted Church. But one must remember that Erasmus, despite his severe satirical attacks on the Church and his presentation of the striking contrast between its practices and the nature of the Gospel, never broke with the Catholic faith itself.

Luther

Since, as we have noted, the Reformation was sparked by the personal religious crisis of Martin Luther (1483–1546), this discussion will focus on that crisis and its cataclysmic resolution.

Although Luther was born in Eisleben, in Thuringian Saxony, he and his parents soon moved to Mansfeld, where his father became a successful mining entrepreneur. He was able to provide his first-born son with an excellent education, first in the Latin school of Mansfeld, then in the cathedral school at Magdeburg, where (like Erasmus at Deventer) he studied under the tutelage of the Brethren of the Common Life. His basic education was completed at Eisenach. Subsequently, he matriculated at the University of Erfurt, from which he received a Bachelor's degree in 1502 and a Master's in 1505. His father expected him to take up legal studies so that he could become a prosperous lawyer; Luther intended to fulfill his father's wishes, but an incident in the summer of 1505 led to a profound change of direction which was to have enormous consequences.

Travelling toward Erfurt one day in July, he was caught in a thunderstorm and struck down by lightning. Fearing that he was about to die, he made a vow that he would enter a monastery if he should be spared—a vow he carried out two weeks later, despite the protestations of his father, when he entered the Augustinian monastery in Erfurt. There he studied for the priesthood and, the following year, took his monastic vows. Traditionally, such a step would have brought the reassurance of forgiveness of sin. But such was not the case with Luther. He sought assurance through the traditional monastic practices but found it impossible to believe that he could be accepted by a righteous God. His internal struggle became even more intense after his ordination and celebration of his first Mass. The key to Luther's struggle lay in his conception of the righteousness of God. In his view, God's perfect righteousness was the impossibly demanding standard by which human beings were judged. Thus, though diligently using the sacrament of penance, he could find no peace of conscience because of his deep awareness that he was incapable of the spiritual perfection God required.

Transferred to the University of Wittenberg in 1508 to continue his theological education, Luther studied and lectured, obtaining his Bachelor of the Bible degree in 1509, and his Doctor of Theology degree in 1512. He then began an extended course of lectures on various books of the Bible, including Psalms, Galatians, and Romans. It was his preparation of these lectures that led to the resolution of his internal struggle over divine righteousness and his sin. The key verse was Romans 1:17: "For in it [the Gospel] the righteousness of God is revealed through faith for faith: as it is written, 'He who through faith is righteous shall live.'" For Luther, these words became "the true gate of paradise."

Luther's discovery focuses on the meaning of "the righteousness of God." That righteousness, Paul declares, is revealed in the Gospel, the good news that God in Christ offers salvation to those who have faith. Such righteousness, Luther concluded, rather than being the standard by which people are judged and condemned, is a gift of God to those who believe; not an imperfect righteousness based on human achievement but the *perfect* righteousness bestowed by God's grace. Moreover, it is not dependent upon the intercessory role of a priest. This interpretation of Scripture was to have far-reaching implications, not only for Luther personally but also for all of Christendom. Because it had succeeded in resolving his own personal struggle, the doctrine of justification by faith alone came to have an increasing influence upon his interpretation of Scripture generally. Indeed, he was so convinced that he had come to a correct understanding of the truth of the Gospel, as revealed by Paul, that he was eventually compelled to oppose everything in the Catholic Church that, in his view, contradicted that understanding.

Although Luther's final break with the Church did not occur until 1521, when he was excommunicated by the pope and outlawed by the Emperor Charles V, the event that ultimately led to this took place in 1517, when he posted his 95 theses on the door of the castle church in Wittenberg. These theses were not of an incendiary nature but were proposals for scholarly debate (they were written in Latin, the language of scholarship, rather than German). However, they did reflect Luther's deep concern over the sale of indulgences by a Dominican friar named Johannes Tetzel, who was preaching near Wittenberg at the time.

Although interpretations of indulgences varied greatly,

the most extreme view, proclaimed by Tetzel, held that the pope could remit not only the *penalties* for sin on earth and in purgatory, but even sin itself. The theory behind indulgences was that Christ and the saints provided an excess of merits for salvation, a sort of "treasury" upon which the pope could draw on behalf of those who were deficient in such merit. In Luther's belief, of course, no such treasury existed. The indulgence Tetzel was offering, first inaugurated by Julius II (1503–1513) and revived by Leo X (1513–1521), was intended to provide funds for the rebuilding of Saint Peter's Basilica. Luther argued that if the pope really had the power of granting indulgences, he should freely use it, rather than milking the poor Germans for the support of this project.

Although the language of Luther's theses was generally moderate and academic, the controversy they engendered was neither. Luther, a man of strong passions as well as convictions, responded in kind. Thus he was pushed to define his theological views in opposition to Catholic belief and practice ever more sharply and to defend them with increasing vigor. Three pamphlets, published in 1520— shortly before the Diet (assembly) of Worms confirmed his excommunication and outlawed him—summarized the issues which were to separate him once and for all from the Roman Church.

The first of these pamphlets, *Address to the Christian Nobility of the German Nation*, was written in German and appealed to secular rulers to reform the Church. They must assume this responsibility, he maintained, because the Romanists (as Luther called the papacy and its supporters) not only had failed to lead in such reforms, but had surrounded themselves with three walls to protect themselves from reform. The first wall was the argument that the spiritual power has authority over the secular. When Scripture was used to reprove the Romanists, they erected the second wall, the contention that only the pope had the right to interpret Scripture. The third wall, the contention that only the pope could summon a Church council, provided protection for the Romanists against conciliar reform.

Luther sought to demolish the first wall by arguing from Scripture that all Christians, clergy and laity alike, are priests and belong to the spiritual class. He attacked the second wall on the ground that all believers are taught of God, citing John 6:45. The third wall, Luther contended, falls along with the first two; for if the pope fails to obey Scripture, it is the duty of the Church at large (he quotes Matthew 18:15–17) to come together and lay charges against him.

Written in Latin, the pamphlet entitled *The Babylonian Captivity of the Church* was intended mainly for scholars. Here Luther developed the implications for the sacraments

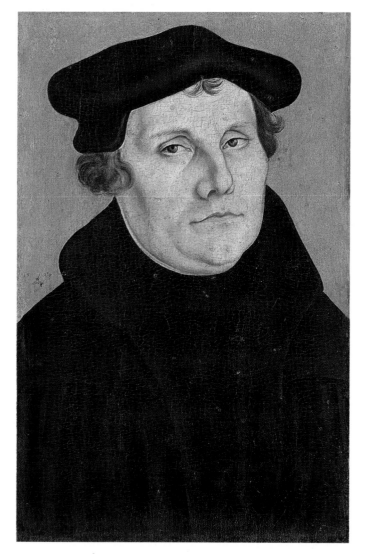

8.5 Martin Luther

by the priest. In his view, the believer experiences the presence of Christ in the Lord's Supper, not through the intercession of an ordained priest, but through faith. With this pamphlet, the crack that had opened between Luther and the Church because of his theses became a yawning chasm, not to be bridged.

Yet within a matter of weeks, Luther produced *The Freedom of the Christian Man*, a pamphlet written in Latin for the pope which struck a conciliatory note.[6] In this treatise Luther answered those critics who asked why one should do good works if it is faith alone that justifies one before God. Good works, he argued, are the *products* of faith, the fruit of the new life in Christ. "Good works do not make a man good, but a good man [one who is justified by God's grace through faith] does good works." He splendidly epitomized the relation of his ethical views to faith when he wrote, "I will give myself as a sort of Christ to my neighbor as Christ gave himself for me."

A few months after the publication of this pamphlet Luther was summoned by the Emperor Charles V to the Diet of Worms, which, in May 1521, declared him both a heretic and a rebel against imperial authority. Excommunicated by the Church and outlawed by the Empire, Luther had now broken completely with the powers of his world.

Of his voluminous literary output, one more work must be mentioned, his translation into German of the New Testament from the second edition of Erasmus' Greek New Testament. Luther accomplished this task during his stay at Wartburg Castle, where he lived in disguise as Junker Georg ("Knight George") for almost a year following his flight from Worms. Later he was to translate the Old Testament. As the Reformation scholar Roland Bainton has stated, "The German Bible is Luther's noblest achievement."[7] Creator of a standard German language, its enduring excellence is demonstrated by its continued use by many German Protestants.

Calvin

The most significant figure of the Protestant Reformation, next to Luther, the Frenchman John (Jean) Calvin (1509–1564), has been called the Thomas Aquinas of Protestantism; for just as Aquinas synthesized and systematized Christian thought for Catholicism in the thirteenth century (notably in the *Summa Theologica*), so did Calvin for Protestantism (in the *Institutes of the Christian Religion*) in the sixteenth. Calvin greatly admired Luther, and their theological differences were not extensive. Although Calvin, in his fully developed theology, emphasized predestination (see below) much more than did Luther, both agreed that human sinfulness was so

posed by his doctrine of justification by faith alone. Thus he argued that since all Christians are priests, all have the right of direct access to God through faith. With this one stroke, Luther undercut the entire sacerdotal system. For the claims of the Roman Church rested largely upon its teaching that the sacraments were the sole means of obtaining divine grace and that they could be administered only by ordained priests. Luther also reduced the number of sacraments from seven—baptism, confirmation, the Eucharist, marriage, ordination, penance, and extreme unction—to two—baptism and the Eucharist—on the grounds that a true sacrament must have been instituted by Christ himself. He rejected the doctrine of transubstantiation and also the dogma that through the Mass the incarnation and crucifixion of Christ were repeated, a miracle that could be accomplished only

profound that redemption was possible only through divine initiative, thus eliminating human achievement as a factor in salvation. Yet both also taught that the redeemed, out of gratitude for God's forgiveness, must commit themselves to acts of Christ-like love toward the human community.

In his youth Calvin studied liberal arts and theology in Paris, intending to enter the priesthood; but, influenced by his father, he later took up the study of law at Orléans and Bourges. Upon his father's death, Calvin turned his attentions to humanistic studies, including Greek and Hebrew (he had learned Latin at Paris), and published his *Commentary on Seneca's Treatise on Clemency* (1532). At this point he seems to have been embarked upon a humanistic career after the manner of Erasmus. Within two years, however, Calvin's writing, and his life, had taken a new turn. Henceforth he was to be intensely committed to the reformation of Christianity and to the scriptural explication that was to inform his efforts. It is not known for certain what led to his decisive break with Catholicism and this redirection of his life. He attributed

8.6 John Calvin

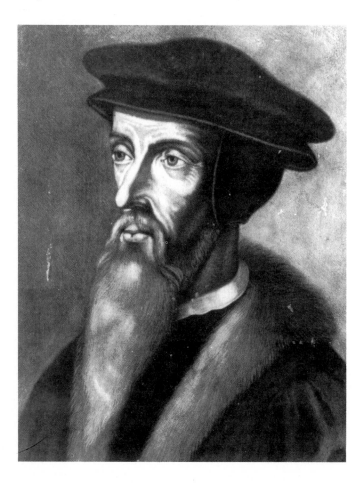

the changes to divine intervention: "God by a sudden conversion subdued my heart to teachableness." In any case, his dedicated and scholarly study of the Bible soon turned him into a theologian, despite his limited theological training. Ironically, "thousands of theologians," as John T. McNeill has pointed out, were to become "the readers and disciples of this man who never had a formal theological training."[8]

In 1536 Calvin published his first edition of the *Institutes of the Christian Religion*. Though containing much material basic to his theology, this book was a relatively modest beginning for what was to become in subsequent editions "the one comprehensive and systematic organization of Christian doctrine on a Scriptural basis that has become a classic."[9] The second edition (1539), containing 17 chapters and more than twice as large as the first, for the first time included a discussion of predestination, the doctrine most often identified with historic Calvinism. This doctrine was the logical outgrowth of the tremendous emphasis in Calvin's theology on the sovereignty of God, the absolute divine control of all things. Yet, even the theme of predestination, emphasized as it is by Calvin, "is treated," as McNeill has pointed out, "within the framework of the doctrine of salvation, the overarching concern in his theology."[10] His translation into French (1541) of the Latin text of the second edition of his *Institutes* played a significant role in the development of French as a literary language. Calvin continued to expand the *Institutes* until, in the final edition (1559), it contained 80 chapters and was five times the length of the original edition. This version had a fourfold structure: Book I dealt with the knowledge of God the Creator; Book II, with the knowledge of God the Redeemer in Christ; Book III, with the role of the Holy Spirit in communicating the benefits of Christ to believers; Book IV, with the Church, including its ministries and government. Thus the Christian doctrine of the Trinity and the biblical concept of the people of God provided Calvin with the basic structure of the definitive edition of his *Institutes*.

Although Calvin was much inclined toward a life of scholarly seclusion, his publication of the first edition of the *Institutes* in 1536 forced him into a position of leadership in the Reformation. Thus, when he stopped over briefly in Geneva, Switzerland, in July, 1536, Guillaume Farel, who was leading the Reformation forces in that strife-torn city, persuaded him to remain and assist him. There Calvin was to remain, apart from a brief exile, until his death in 1564. But, although diverted from a life devoted wholly to scholarly pursuits, and bearing the burden of organizing the Genevan Church and preaching as often as eight times a week, Calvin nonetheless continued to produce not only new editions of the

Institutes but also voluminous commentaries on Scripture which are cited by scholars today as models of felicitously written, insightful biblical exposition.

The Counter Reformation: Loyola

In the aftermath of the reformers' break with the Catholic Church, various reforming movements developed within that Church. This is especially evident in various reforming religious orders that sprang up. Nonetheless, as the Catholic Church neared the midpoint of the sixteenth century, it was still reeling under the blow struck by the reformers and demonstrated little spiritual vitality. What was required for the success of internal reform was strong leadership from a papacy that had itself been reformed. This was provided by Pope Paul III (1534–1549), who called the council that finally met in Trent (Trento, Italy), in 1545, and continued to meet intermittently until 1563. Trent marked the beginning of the Counter Reformation, sometimes called the Catholic Reformation. The significance of this council for the Catholic Church can hardly be overestimated. Its definition of Catholic belief and practice not only shored up the Church's defenses against the Protestant Reformation, even making possible the regaining of some of the ground lost to the reformers, but also became the definitive statement on Catholicism until the twentieth century. In general, Trent set forth tighter interpretations of the Catholic faith, doctrinal positions that were, at least in part, reactions to the teachings of the reformers. Thus the Council focused on those items— justification by faith alone, for example—that distinguished the Reformed faith from traditional Catholicism, and sought to define such doctrines in a distinctly Catholic manner. In opposition to the Protestant principle of *sola Scriptura*, Trent declared that Church teaching was to be equal with Scripture in authority. It also increased the power of bishops, giving them the authority to reform their dioceses.

Spain, long a zealous champion of Catholic orthodoxy, was the foremost advocate and supporter of the Counter Reformation. Thus it is appropriate that this country produced the Jesuits (Society of Jesus), who were a major means by which the doctrinal values of the Catholic Reformation became effective.

The story of the Jesuits begins with St. Ignatius Loyola (c. 1491–1556), the founder of this order. Born in northern Spain, Loyola was a soldier until severely wounded in 1521. During his recovery, he read lives of the saints and of Christ; challenged by these examples of spiritual heroism, he determined to become, like the knights of legend, a soldier of Christ. While on pilgrimage at the shrine of the Virgin Mary at Montserrat, he, like Luther,

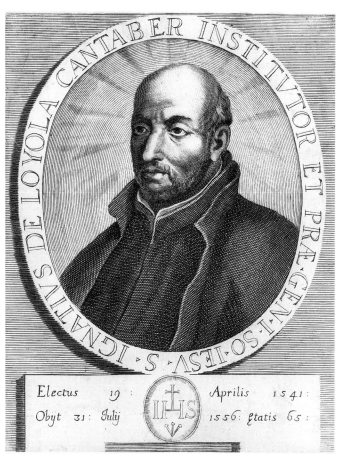

8.7 St. Ignatius Loyola, engraving

underwent a spiritual struggle. Unlike Luther, however, Loyola emerged from his crisis not with a new doctrine but with a new spiritual discipline, which enabled him, through force of will, to achieve the peace of soul that Luther also had sought.[11] Loyola set forth his method in *The Spiritual Exercises*, a book that was to become the foundation of the Jesuit order. The "exercises" dramatize the Christian story of redemption so as to make an imaginative appeal to the one who followed his instructions, thus enabling him to experience that story personally. The ultimate goal of this method was the disciplining of the human will into complete commitment to the service of Christ. Realizing the need of additional theological education to fulfill his commitment, Loyola spent several years studying at various universities. During this time he gathered around him a small band of like-minded followers. A few years later, in 1540, they were given recognition as an order, under the name of the Society of Jesus, by Pope Paul III.

Perhaps the most characteristic and basic feature of the Jesuits was unquestioning obedience to the pope. In implementing this obedience they became especially noted for their work in three areas: education, recovery of those persons and lands lost to the Protestant Reformation, and missionary expansion into non-Christian lands. Highly successful in achieving their goals, the Jesuits exerted extraordinary influence in all of these areas. Through their influence and sacrificial zeal—zeal that laid them open to the charge of justifying means by the ends sought—they became "the chief instrument" (Grimm) of the Counter Reformation.

Reformation and Counter-Reformation Art

In the previous chapter we concluded our discussion of medieval art by looking at fifteenth-century Flemish painting. In this, the last chapter to deal with Christianity in Western culture, we begin with German painting of the sixteenth century. As we have seen, that century marked the great split in Christianity. The split affected art, but not enough to divide it clearly into Catholic and Protestant styles, or even to account for all of the differences between the art produced in one part of Europe and that produced in another. The differences that did exist were due to a number of variables, in particular to local traditions which were in place before the Reformation began.

This chapter focuses on religious art of the sixteenth and seventeenth centuries, comparing that produced in Protestant areas with that produced in Catholic areas with respect to the ways in which the split in Christianity is expressed or implied.

Reformation Art

The early phase of the Reformation coincided with the High Renaissance in Italy and also with one of the finest periods of German painting. Albrecht Dürer and Matthias Grünewald, the greatest exponents of German Reformation painting were approximately the age of Michelangelo.

In the early 1500s German art was, in varying degrees, affected by three factors: religious fervor, reformers, and the Italian Renaissance. In reaction to the formality of the established Church, many German faithful sought religious experience in mysticism or extreme pietism. Some of this fervor is reflected in Dürer's woodcut of the *Apocalypse* (Fig. 8.9), in which the terror of the subject is heightened by the harshness of the style. German artists themselves were, in different ways, personally involved in the Protestant movement: Dürer (1471–1528) had close ties with reformers in Nuremberg; Lucas Cranach (1472–1553) was a friend of Luther and painted his portrait. Grünewald was directly involved in the Peasants' Revolt. Meanwhile, the effects of the religious revolution on art were amplified by the artistic revolution in Italy, as Renaissance styles began to spread from there to the rest of Europe.

Dürer

There are striking similarities between the Van Eycks' *God the Father* (Fig. 7.48) and Albrecht Dürer's painting of himself as Christ—*Self-Portrait in a Fur Coat* (Fig. 8.8). The bodies of both are symmetrical and frontal; the faces of both are solemn and idealized. The slender proportions and attention to detail in both are characteristic of Late Gothic painting. Dürer's work at the turn of the century, like other German work, relates to Flemish art. If there is a difference it would be that German art is more severe: its color is usually brighter and harsher; its line, like that in Dürer's woodcut, more angular; and its content, like that of Dürer's self-portrait, more intense. *Self-Portrait in a Fur Coat* could be considered an icon of the pre-Reformation: reflected in the face of young Dürer is the kind of fervor and self-determination that would defy the Church of Rome.

By 1500, Dürer had already made one of his trips to Italy; but other than the use of one-point perspective, few signs of this experience are visible in his art, at least not at this time. If we compare his self-portrait to Leonardo's *Mona Lisa* (Fig. 3.35), made only three years later, we see that the two belong to different worlds. Still we must not assume from this example that Dürer himself was unaffected by Italian art, or by the humanist spirit. Indeed, there are many parallels between him and that quintessential humanist: Leonardo. Like Leonardo, Dürer traveled often: twice across the Alps to Italy and at least once to Flanders. He was patronized by important rulers: first by Frederick the Wise, Prince of Saxony, who protected Luther, and later by Maximilian I, Holy Roman Emperor (1493–1519). Dürer was also a learned man. Like Leonardo, he compiled his theories—studies of linear perspective and proportions of the body—in written and illustrated forms. (Dürer's, however, were published in

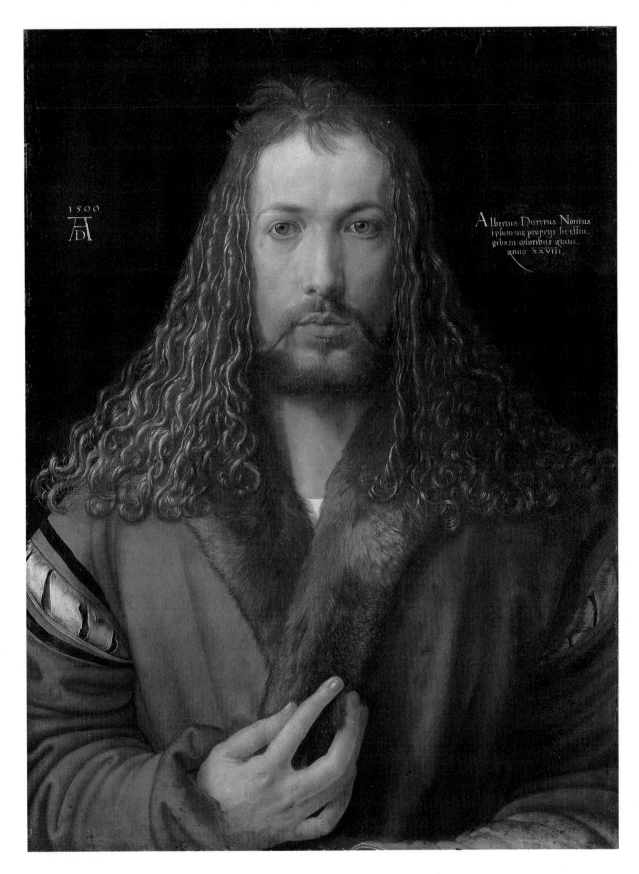

8.8 ALBRECHT DÜRER
Self-Portrait in a Fur Coat, 1500
Oil on panel, $26\frac{2}{5} \times 19\frac{3}{10}$ ins (67 × 49 cm)
Alte Pinakothek, Munich

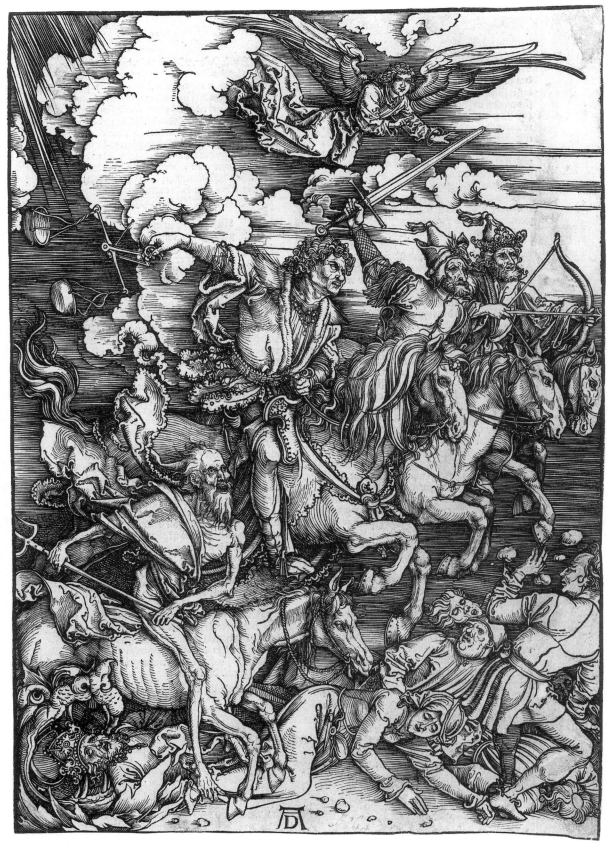

8.9 ALBRECHT DÜRER
The Four Horsemen of the Apocalypse, c. 1497–98
Woodcut, approx. $15\frac{1}{4} \times 11$ ins (38.7×28 cm)
Museum of Fine Arts, Boston

8.10 ALBRECHT DÜRER
Adam and Eve, 1504
Engraving
Museum of Fine Arts, Boston

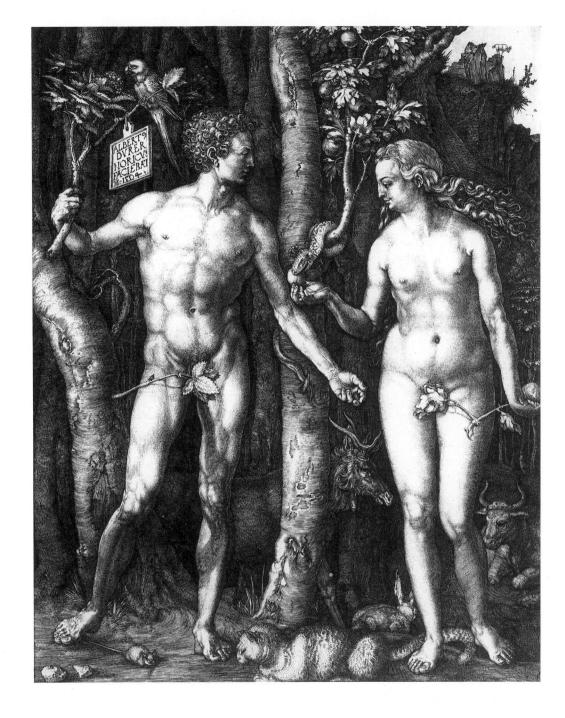

three volumes.)

As time passed, Dürer assimilated Renaissance influences into his own style, attempting to acquire in a few years what the Italians had developed over a century. Some of these influences are in evidence by 1504. In an engraving of Adam and Eve, the artist's intent was that of illustrating ideal beauty, as much as the Fall (Fig. **8.10**). The bodies of Adam and Eve in this 1504 work are quite classical. Yet the head of Eve is more that of a German *Hausfrau* than of the typically seductive classical Eve. The background—which could be a scene in the Black Forest—is also Germanic. Though not as angular and restless as the Apocalypse print, it is crowded with detail. Typical of Late Gothic art, much of this detail does double duty: representing natural objects while symbolizing ideas. The cat, elk, rabbit, and ox stand for the four cardinal humors: choler, black bile, blood, and phlegm. The serpent, of course, stands for evil. Compositionally, the pieces do not quite fit; the foreground is incompatible with the background, for example. *Adam and Eve* is inconsistent in yet more ways, being part Renaissance and part medieval, part Italian and part German.

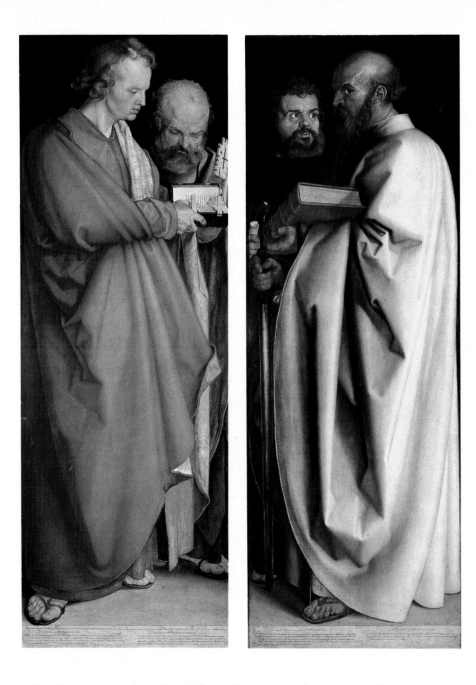

8.11 ALBRECHT DÜRER
Four Apostles, 1523–26
Oil on panel, each 85 × 30 ins
(216 × 76 cm)
Alte Pinakothek, Munich

By the 1520s, when the Reformation was under way, Dürer had successfully come to terms with the disparate elements of his art. He united not only the styles of North and South, but the content of Protestantism and of humanism. This kind of synthesis, as well as the artist's personal philosophy, is summed up in a painting that he presented to the city of Nuremberg in 1526, two years before he died. Called the *Four Apostles*, it is in two panels: John and Peter (both looking at the Gospel of John) in the left panel, Paul and Mark in the right (Fig. **8.11**). Its simple composition, balance, monumental figures, and calm movement recall Leonardo's *Last Supper* and Michelangelo's *David*. In other words, it is High Renaissance. But the realism and individual character of the faces are Northern. Unlike the *Last Supper* Apostles, with their aristocratic mien, these men resemble shopkeepers, burgomasters, German knights—the earthy heroes of the Protestant movement; the image of John is a portrait of Philipp Melanchthon, Luther's main disciple. Engraved on the frames are quotations from Luther's translation of the New Testament warning against the worship of false prophets, an implied disapproval of extremism, whether Catholic or Protestant (Luther condemned the actions of Protestant mobs). Dürer thus tempered religious fervor with reason. In the final stage of his life he arrived at a philosophical position close to that of Erasmus and the rational side of the Reformation: a blend of German passion and Italian humanism.

Dürer's art developed from Late Gothic to High Renaissance and, in the process, brought Italian ideas of art to the North. Still, he was very much a loyal German and a supporter of the Reformation. When Dürer died, northern Europe mourned just as Italy did for Michelangelo.

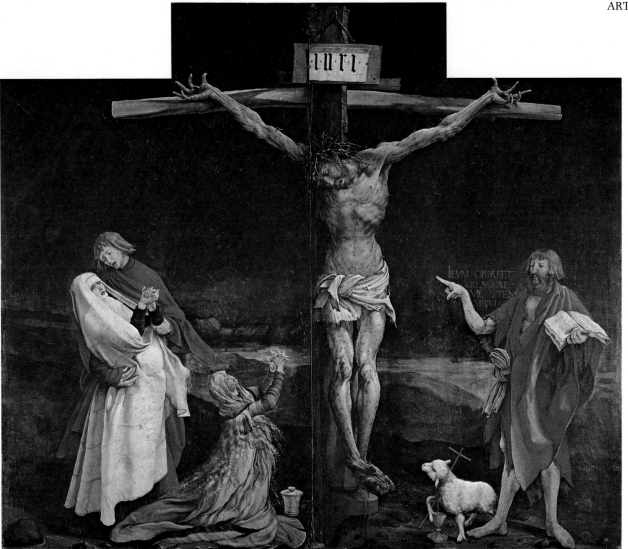

8.12 MATTHIAS GRÜNEWALD
The Crucifixion from *The Isenheim Altarpiece* (closed), c. 1510–15,
Oil on panel, 96 × 121 ins (2.4 × 3 m)
Musée Unterlinden, Colmar

Grünewald

Matthias Grünewald (1475?–1528) died the same year as Dürer, but in almost total obscurity. Although, like Dürer, a supporter of the Reformation, Grünewald was not on personal terms with its leaders or the intelligentsia of Germany. He made a living by serving as court painter to the archbishops of Mainz, and occasionally as a hydraulic engineer. In 1525 he participated in the Peasants' Revolt; later, when the revolt collapsed, he fled to northern Germany. He died in the Protestant town of Halle. Among his personal possessions were a "Riot List" (a sort of safe-passage for people suspected of sympathy for insurgent peasants and/or religious extremists) and a drawer full of books and pamphlets related to the Protestant movement.

All that remains of Grünewald's production are a few oil-on-wood altarpieces and some drawings. His style remained rooted in the Gothic tradition, with few traces of Renaissance tendencies. *The Crucifixion* is a powerful symbol of the more emotional side of the Protestant movement (Fig. **8.12**). Unlike most portrayals of this subject, in which an idealized Christ hangs gracefully from a smooth cross, Grünewald's shows a peasant whose heavy body twists awkwardly on a rough-hewn timber cross. The sallow, pock-marked skin suggests suffering and death; the sagging head, the fulcrum of the composition, is a portrait of agony. The other people respond to his suffering in different ways: those on the left—Mary, St. John, and Mary Magdalen—seem both repulsed by and drawn to it, as they bend away from Christ while reaching toward him with clasped hands and twisted fingers. John the Baptist, on the right, points to him with the words (written on the canvas), "He increases while I decrease." The loneliness of the group is stressed by the bleakness of

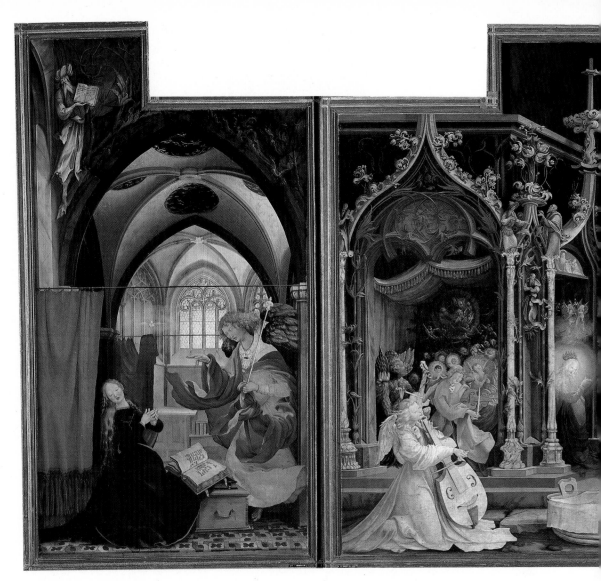

8.13 Matthias Grünewald
The Annunciation; Virgin and Child with Angels; The Resurrection
Second view of *The Isenheim Altarpiece*

their environment: a ghostly-green horizon beneath a heavy, blue-black sky, an image suggesting the end of the world. The absence of background detail, unusual in a Late Gothic work, allows us to focus on the drama of the Crucifixion itself. Grünewald does not evade the physical reality of a crucifixion: torture, humiliation, and horror. Nor does he compromise the religious meaning of the cross: sin and separation from God.

The Crucifixion is part of a larger work, the *Isenheim Altarpiece*, made for the hospital order of St. Anthony, in the Alsatian village of Isenheim. Essentially, it is a system of hinged panels which can be folded, partially folded, or opened to show different scenes for different occasions. On most days it was closed to reveal *The Crucifixion*. It has been said that the patients who could see that scene on a daily basis took comfort from the fact that Christ also suffered.

On Sundays, *The Crucifixion* disappeared, when the altarpiece was opened to reveal *The Annunciation; Virgin and Child with Angels; and The Resurrection* (Fig. **8.13**). The central panel, showing an angelic orchestra serenading the Virgin, is one of the most ecstatic pictures ever made. Radiating beautiful sound as well as golden light, the angels sing and play viols beneath a fantastic pavilion. In front of them, kneeling in the entrance, is the Virgin in transfigured state, glowing as though on fire. Delicate carvings of saints and prophets, in addition to vines, leaves, tendrils, and flowers, decorate the slender columns and arches of the pavilion itself. Outside the pavilion, in the bright light of day, is the Virgin adoring the Christ Child. Behind them, a city and a mountain are set aglow by a light that streams through clouds and flying seraphim. The source of the light is God the Father, at the top of the panel. The pavilion, the angels, and the overall naiveté of the conception are Late Gothic. But other aspects—the triangular form of the Virgin, the robust,

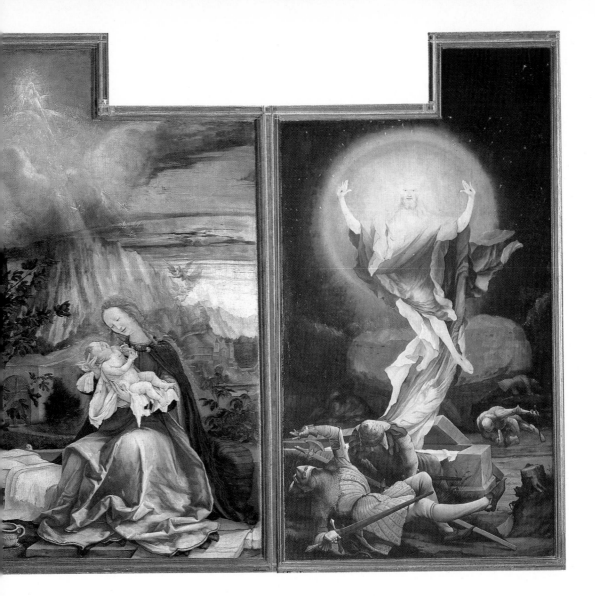

fleshy infant, and the fluid, vibrant colors—are High Renaissance, suggesting that Grünewald was aware of Italian painting of his time, particularly Venetian painting.

The *Annunciation*, the most conservative of the panels, is enacted within a Gothic interior. Mary is seen recoiling from the shock of seeing an angel, his billowing garments described with a flamboyance typical of Late Gothic. Grünewald's is one of very few versions of the Annunciation reflecting the passage in Luke 1:29: "And when she saw him she was troubled...."

In the *Resurrection*, as in the *Virgin and Child with Angels*, bold color is used to represent supernatural phenomena. Christ, bursting from the sepulcher, rises in a brilliant fireball halo. White in the center, the locus of Christ's head, the halo cools to bright orange at the edge, where it is encircled by a bluish aureole. Reflecting its incandescence are the objects beneath Christ: the trailing

shrouds, the stones of the sepulcher, and the uniforms of the guards who, caught by surprise and blinded by the light, are in disarray (their radical foreshortening, seen especially in the distant soldier, is another sign of Renaissance influence). The darkness of the sky serves to concentrate the brilliance of the scene, especially that of the risen Christ, who before our eyes is being transformed from flesh to spirit. Compare this Resurrection with Piero della Francesca's (Fig. 3.21). In the latter's, the setting is a peaceful, sunlit morning, the soldiers are asleep, and the figure of Christ is as calm and substantial as a stone statue.

The loosening of religious thought on the eve of the Great Schism made it possible for a visionary like Grünewald to produce works of art within the framework of the Church. It also allowed a learned German like Dürer to introduce Italian-style art to the courts of the North. Neither Dürer's nor Grünewald's work should be thought of as "official" Reformation art; it was never authorized as

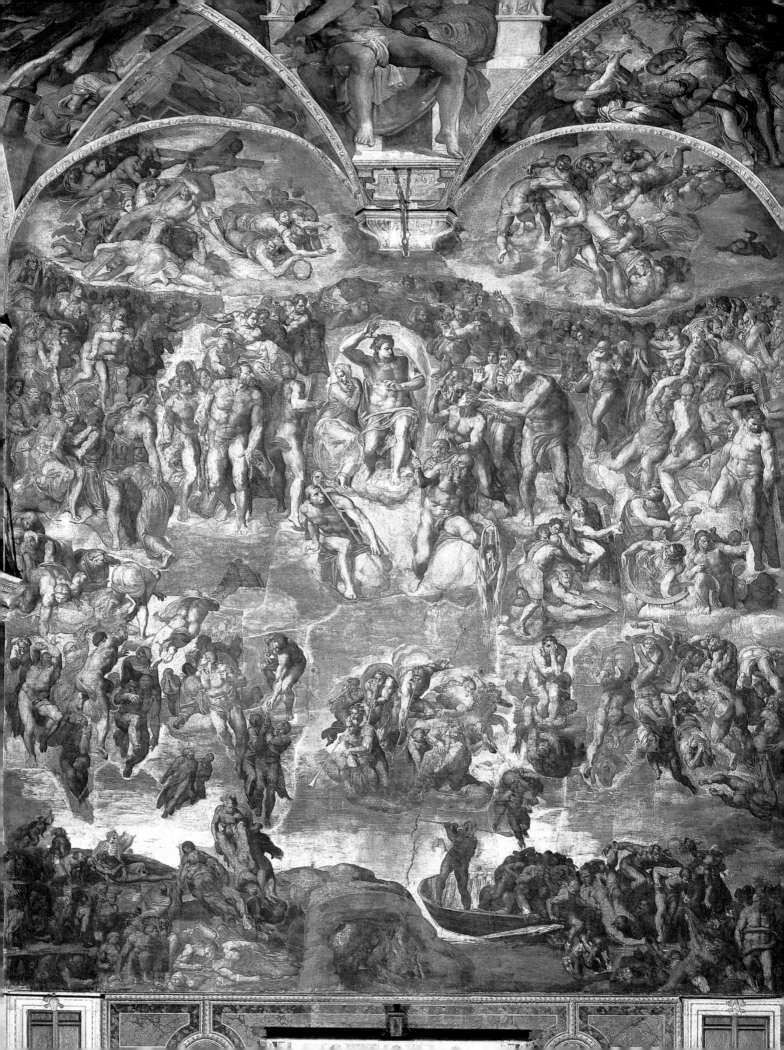

such by Protestant leaders. Nevertheless, it expresses in different, but equally valid, ways the spirit of the Reformation during the time that it was created.

Unfortunately, when Protestantism triumphed, religious art in Protestant countries languished. In the heat of the religious conflict, Protestant extremists wantonly destroyed church art. Erasmus, observing this kind of destruction in Basel, wrote: "Nothing has survived, neither in the cloisters nor on the portals, nor in the convents. The pictures were covered with whitewash; what could burn was thrown on the bonfire, the rest was smashed."[12] Although Luther and Calvin condemned these excesses, both disparaged religious art. Many of the reformers resented the lavishing of money on artistic projects such as the decoration of the Sistine Chapel and the rebuilding of St. Peter's, which ordinary Christians had to support. Both Lutherans and Calvinists also were strongly influenced by the Old Testament, which warns against the sin of idolatry. Thus religious patronage— which had been so important to the growth of art from Early Christian times through the Renaissance—became nonexistent in Protestant denominations, and a truly Protestant art, that is, a tradition of art directly related to the principles of the Protestant faith, never came into being.

The "Last Judgment"

Michelangelo, whose work is so closely identified with papal Rome, produced a second fresco for the Sistine Chapel which reflects the religious conflicts of the time. In 1534, 22 years after the completion of the ceiling fresco, the Medici pope, Clement VII, asked him to paint the wall behind the altar. The ceiling fresco, as we have seen (see pages 131–33), implied the coming of Christ as Redeemer. It would have been quite natural for the nearly 60-year-old Michelangelo to fulfill that promise artistically, creating perhaps a Neoplatonic interpretation of the Gospel. But when he began the project under Paul III (the pope who called the Council of Trent), he chose instead to paint *The Last Judgment*, and gave us Christ as Avenger (Fig. **8.14**). The visual narrative, based on Revelation, I Corinthians, and Dante's *Inferno*, starts in the upper center, where a titanic Jesus is seen denouncing the world. Below him, angels blow trumpets to start the process: the dead are wrested from their graves (lower left) to be lifted before Christ, who decides which are to remain with him

and which are to be dragged struggling into Hell (lower right). *The Last Judgment* is an image of fear and despair. The people, with their small heads and bulging muscles, are almost a mockery of the kind of heroic nudity one would expect to see. Even the saved have a grim aspect. The composition, like the theme, is equally depressing: uneven clusters of nude humanity swirling around the severe figure of Christ.

There are many theories to explain why Michelangelo produced such a negatively charged work. Involved in too many projects, he was harassed from all sides by those who had commissioned work from him—including Julius's lawyers, who were still trying to get him to finish the tomb. The world around him seemed to be a helpless victim of hostile forces: the Reformation that was threatening the Church; foreign soldiers who had sacked Rome (1527); and political factions that were destabilizing Florence, his home city. There were also religious/moral reasons: in addition to recalling Savonarola's prophecies of doom and denunciations of wickedness (see page 130), Michelangelo in later years belonged to a circle of Catholic reformers whose leader was influenced by the writings of Erasmus. His religious views, thus, may have been closer to those of Luther and Calvin than he realized. When *The Last Judgment* was unveiled in 1541, it was greeted with approval by Roman Catholics who themselves had begun to react against the failings and corruption of the Church. It was also greeted with approval by young Mannerist artists who were inspired by its unconventional figures and design. The style of Mannerism was to become a vehicle for expressing the spiritualism of the Counter Reformation.

Counter-Reformation Art

As we have seen, the Catholic Church eventually responded to the Protestant Reformation by launching a major reform of its own: the Counter Reformation. This aimed to purify Christian life within the framework of the existing order, and it placed great emphasis on the relationship between salvation and the institutional Church. The ideals of the movement are apparent in Counter-Reformation art, the religious art produced in Catholic countries following the Council of Trent.

Whereas Protestants had rejected the relationship between art and religion, Catholics turned to it more than ever as an important agent in the life and teachings of the Church. Stylistically, Counter-Reformation art conforms to the trends called Mannerism (see Chapter 3) and Baroque (see Chapter 4). Highly dramatic and emotional, it focuses on the lives of the saints, in ways clearly intended to inspire piety.

8.14 MICHELANGELO
The Last Judgment, altar wall of the Sistine Chapel, 1534–41

El Greco

Born Kyriakos Theotokopoulos on the Greek island of Crete, El Greco (c. 1548–c. 1614) emigrated to Italy as a youth. In Venice, he saw works by Titian (Figs. 3.48, 3.49) and the Venetian Mannerist Tintoretto (1518–1594), whose spirited version of *The Last Supper* (Fig. **8.15**) can be contrasted with Leonardo's. After spending some time in Rome, where he saw more Mannerist art (Fig. 3.50), he emigrated to Spain, and took up residence in Toledo. There he absorbed the religious thinking of Toledo church scholars and acquired the name *El Greco* ("The Greek").

These multiple influences are brought to bear in paintings such as *The Burial of Count Orgaz* (Fig. **8.16**)—a memorial to the benefactor of the church of Santo Tomé, who had died three centuries earlier. Through the magic of his brush, El Greco brought together present and past, earth and Heaven in one picture: legendary saints miraculously mingle with Toledo dignitaries as heavenly digni-

taries oversee the whole event. El Greco organized the picture around two axes: a vertical one, with Christ at the top and the dead count's armor-clad body at the bottom dividing the canvas into left and right; and a horizontal one, formed by the row of Spanish noblemen's heads, dividing it into lower and upper, or earth and Heaven. In the earthly sphere, the count is being lowered into his tomb by saints Stephen and Augustine, who, wearing gold-embroidered vestments, have descended from Heaven for the occasion. Directly above them, in the lower part of the heavenly sphere, an angel escorts the count's soul—looking like a ghostly fetus—upward along the vertical axis between the figures of Mary and John the Baptist, who intercede on its behalf before Christ. Looking on are St. Peter, behind Mary, and other heavenly figures, behind St. John.

The rich, flowing color in *The Burial of Count Orgaz* is a legacy of El Greco's knowledge of Venetian art; the elastic, elongated figures, ghostly light, and crowded composition are indebted to the Mannerist style; but the overall

8.15 Jacopo Tintoretto
The Last Supper, 1592–94
Oil on canvas, 12 ft × 18 ft 8 ins (3.65 × 5.7 m)
S Giorgio Maggiore, Venice

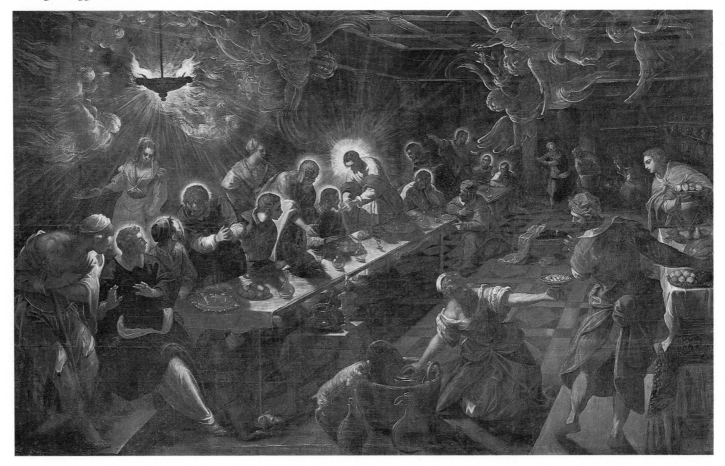

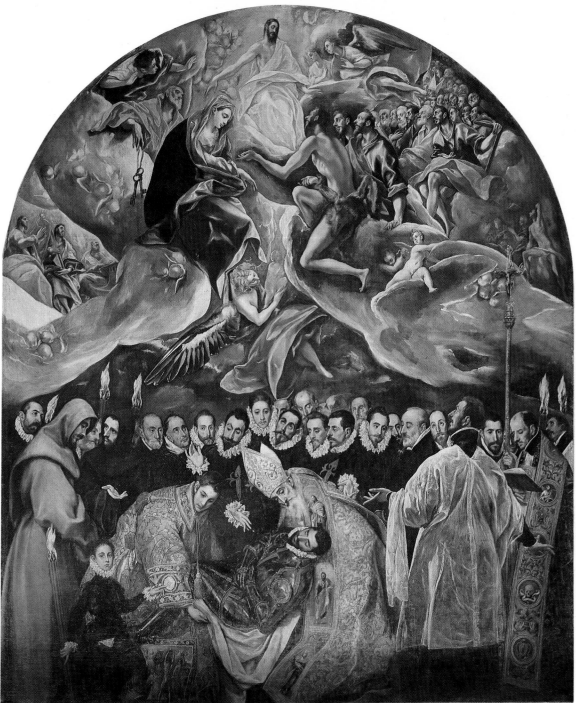

8.16 EL GRECO
The Burial of Count Orgaz, 1586
Oil on canvas, 16 ft × 11 ft 10 ins (4.87 × 3.6 m)
Santo Tomé, Toledo

splendor of line, color, and texture is due to memories of Byzantine art in his native Greece. These tendencies are effectively marshaled to express a Spanish variety of Counter-Reformation spiritualism.

The supernatural aspects of *The Burial of Count Orgaz* obviously relate to similar tendencies in Grünewald's *Virgin and Child with Angels* (Fig. 8.13); each work employs coloristic means to create the effects of an ecstatic experience. El Greco's, however, is based on Mannerism, a descendant of High Renaissance art. Although the Mannerist style is more complicated and restless than the High Renaissance style, it retains the earlier style's instinct for beautiful people and graceful gestures, an instinct completely lacking in Grünewald's Late Gothic style. El Greco's art, like the Counter-Reformation Church, continues a grand tradition, but in renewed form.

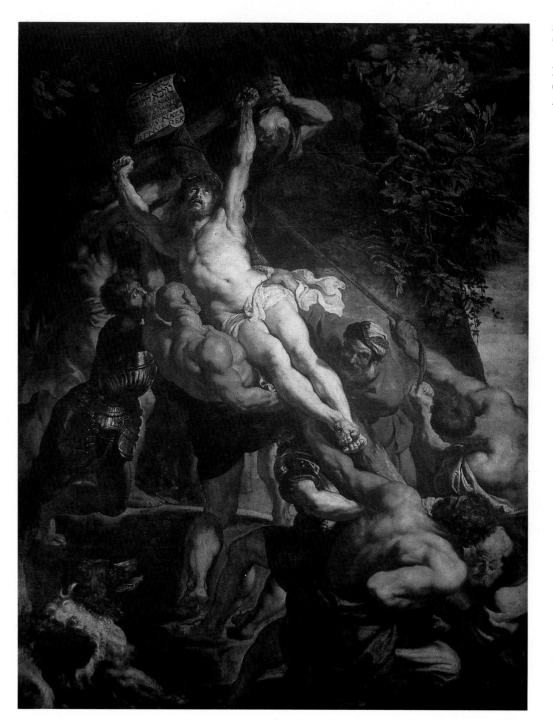

8.17 Peter Paul Rubens
The Raising of the Cross,
1609–10
Panel, 15 ft 2 ins × 11 ft 2 ins
(4.62 × 3.4 m)
Antwerp Cathedral

Baroque Religious Art

By the beginning of the seventeenth century, the classical tradition of art had evolved into the Baroque style. The chief exponent of Baroque painting was not an Italian, but a Fleming, Peter Paul Rubens, whose life and work were briefly discussed in Chapter 4.

Rubens's *The Raising of the Cross* (Fig. **8.17**) is typical of much Baroque religious art. It shows a crew of powerful men struggling mightily to accomplish a task that seems almost as difficult as raising the Washington Monument. To animate the composition, as well as add further drama, Rubens tilted the cross at a precarious 45-degree angle. The dynamic, crowded composition and energetic, muscular bodies are legacies of Michelangelo and Mannerism. The sharp contrast of light and dark, or *chiaroscuro*, is characteristic of Baroque painting. It is found especially in the work of Caravaggio (c. 1565–1609), an Italian

8.18 CARAVAGGIO
The Conversion of St. Paul,
c. 1601
Oil on canvas, approx.
90 × 69 ins (2.28 × 1.75 m)
Santa Maria del Popolo, Rome

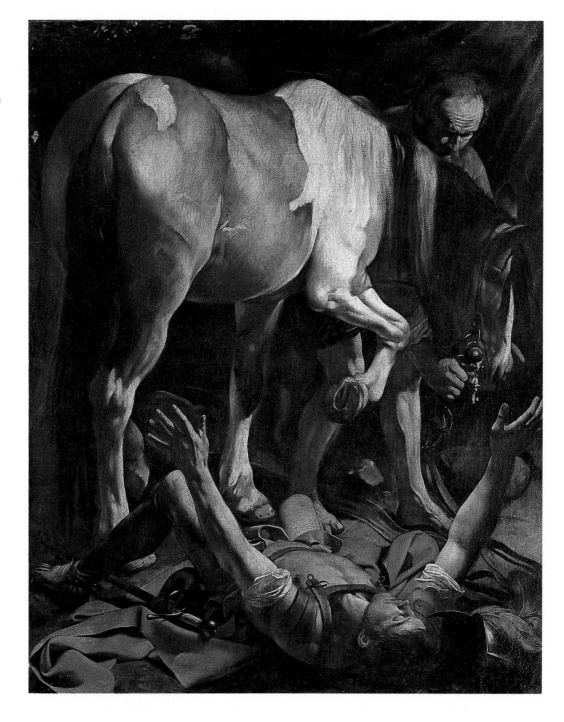

Baroque painter who pioneered the practice of revealing objects and figures with a powerful single source of light, as in *The Conversion of St. Paul* (Fig. **8.18**). Finally, the realism of details—leaves, anatomy, clothing, dog fur, and so forth—reflects Rubens's Flemish background.

Rubens took pains to unify *The Raising of the Cross* through subordinating everything to the figure of Christ, which dominates the composition not only by its symbolic weight but also by its visual weight. Although all the figures are large and idealized, Christ's is the only one in full view. The adjectives that come to mind in describing this Good Friday subject are "heroic," "grand," and, perhaps, "theatrical." Compare it in this respect to Grünewald's *The Crucifixion* or Michelangelo's *The Last Judgment.*

Rubens's counterpart in sculpture was Gianlorenzo Bernini (1598–1680), some of whose impressive works adorn the exterior and interior of St. Peter's Basilica (Figs. 4.9, and 4.10). But his *The Ecstasy of St. Theresa*, a project combining architecture, sculpture, and painting in a small chapel, is the ultimate Baroque work of art (Fig. **8.19**). It portrays a vision of Spain's most famous

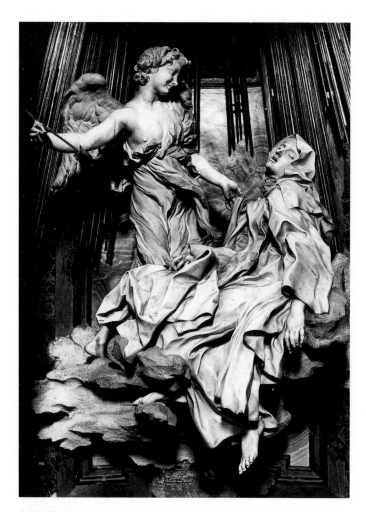

8.19 BERNINI
The Ecstasy of St. Theresa, 1645–52
Marble, life-size
Santa Maria della Vittoria, Rome

mystic, in which an angel repeatedly stabs her in the bosom with a fire-tipped dart. In her words:

> *So real was the pain that I was forced to moan aloud, yet it was so surpassingly sweet that I would not wish to be delivered from it. No delight of life can give more content. As the angel withdrew the dart, he left me all burning with a great love of God.*[13]

In Bernini's conception, the vision takes place on a layer of clouds beneath rays of the sun (bronze rods). As Rubens was supremely skilled in making illusions of textures in paint, so Bernini was in stone and bronze: in addition to clouds and rays, the artist has articulated the differences between flesh, drapery, and feathers. But even more impressive is his description of contrasting emotions as personified by the two characters: the roguish angel versus the swooning Theresa, whose heightened experience is both physical and spiritual. The angel's emotion is echoed in the swirling energy of his gown; by contrast, the

saint's is heavy and slack.

In the context of the whole chapel, the angel and saint are the focus of a much larger ensemble (Fig. **8.20**). Occupying an elaborate marble-columned niche in the center of the chapel, the two participants are "viewed" by spectators, the Cornaro family, whose sculpted images sit in recesses resembling theater boxes. Overhead, filling the vaulted ceiling, is a scene of angels and clouds, both painted and sculpted. This and the sculptural group in the niche are animated by real light that pours down from a hidden window, illuminates the bronze rods, and thereby, enhances the illusion of heavenly light.

The subject of Bernini's *The Ecstasy of St. Theresa*, like that of El Greco's *The Burial of Count Orgaz*, juxtaposes Heaven and earth. But Bernini's project goes beyond El Greco's. It is religious theater in the extreme, blurring the boundary between art and reality, between art and spectator, between reality and illusion, and between the flesh and the spirit. Bernini attempted literally to embody the mysteries of the divine world, to bring Heaven down to earth for all to see.

8.20 View of the Cornaro Chapel, Santa Maria della Vittoria, showing *The Ecstasy of St. Theresa* in its setting

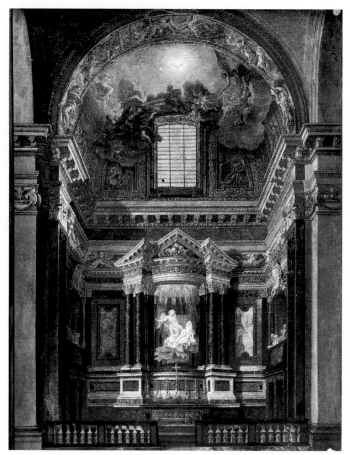

Art in the Netherlands

Following the deaths of Dürer and Grünewald, no important sacred art was produced on the Protestant side of the religious split for the rest of the century. Because of the Thirty Years' War, together with Protestant vandalism, the tradition of German art was broken. In other areas, either the Protestants were too weak or art was too weak, as in England, Scotland, and Scandinavia.

By the seventeenth century, there was just one country with both a strong Protestant Church and a strong artistic tradition: the Netherlands. A union of Protestant provinces along the North Sea, this small republic had recently broken away from the Spanish Netherlands (or Flanders), which was predominately Catholic. This part of Europe, as we learned in Chapter 7, had a strong art tradition dating back to the fourteenth century. The venerable Rubens, who resided in the part of the Netherlands that remained Catholic, continued to uphold the tradition in the seventeenth century.

For the Dutch, self-determination meant not only freedom to practice their Calvinist faith but economic opportunity as well. Taking advantage of the Netherlands' ports and seafaring history, hard-working Dutch traders proceeded to dominate the oceans and establish commercial relations all over the world. Amsterdam, the nation's richest and most powerful city, had become the banking center of Europe and an important commercial metropolis. The combination of Calvinism and capitalism served the nation well; in contrast to much of Europe, the Dutch Republic was mostly middle-class and prosperous.

Because of Calvinism's aversion to religious art, no art was commissioned by and for the Church. Yet despite the loss of this traditional form of patronage, art thrived in the Dutch Republic. Patronage shifted to the middle class, well-to-do burghers, who commissioned portraits or bought pictures from dealers, a new phenomenon in the art world. Like most things in a commercial society, art was transformed into a marketable commodity. In this new market, paintings with religious themes did fairly well; secular paintings did much better. Apparently Dutchmen enjoyed, or found comfort in, reflections of their own world: genre paintings, such as home interiors, street scenes, taverns and markets; landscapes; still lifes; and portraits of themselves.

Rembrandt

There were, basically, two artistic alternatives for a painter in the Dutch Republic when Rembrandt van Rijn (1606–1669) came of age: the "Italian" school (so called because the artists studied in Italy, or were influenced by those who did) and the emergent "Dutch" school. The first dealt with historical and religious subjects rendered in the

8.21 Rembrandt van Rijn
The Blinding of Samson, 1636
Oil on canvas, 93 × 119 ins
(236 × 302 cm)
Staedelisches Kunstinstitut,
Frankfurt

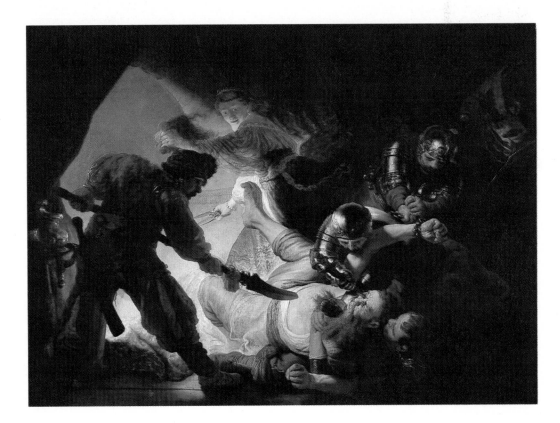

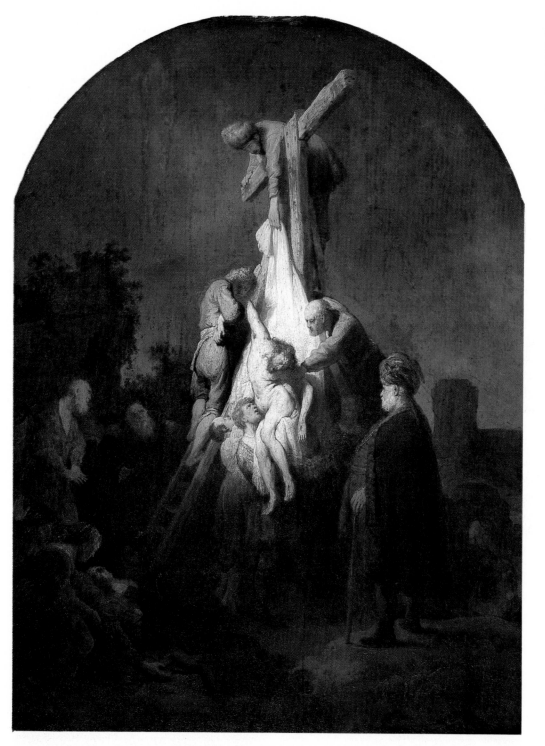

8.22 REMBRANDT VAN RIJN
The Descent from the Cross,
1633
Oil on canvas, $36\frac{1}{4} \times 27\frac{1}{4}$ ins
(92×69.2 cm)
Alte Pinakothek, Munich

grand manner; the second favored scenes of ordinary life. Rembrandt was influenced by both schools; his teacher, Pieter Lastman, was a member of the Italian. But Rembrandt's art does not belong to either school. Unlike the Italian, it involves non-heroic figures in humble settings. Unlike the Dutch, it includes a large proportion of religious themes (in all, around 800 drawings, prints, and paintings). In effect, Rembrandt used elements from both schools to achieve a unique synthesis: Old and New

Testament stories conceived of in terms of ordinary life. His interest in the Bible may have been the result of his mother's influence; if so, it was given artistic direction by Lastman. At any rate, Rembrandt's religious output is a rare, certainly the most profound, legacy of Protestant interpretation of the Scriptures by an artist. His work also includes non-religious subjects, notably portraits, including a series of remarkable self-portraits. These, too, are devoid of the pomposity of typical Baroque art and the triviality of much seventeenth-century Dutch painting.

Rembrandt's greatest period of personal happiness and professional success was the decade of the 1630s. At the age of 25 he moved his studio from Leiden, his home town, to Amsterdam, the art capital of the nation. There he obtained several important commissions, enjoyed the esteem of Amsterdam society, and married Saskia van Ulenburgh, the daughter of a burgomaster. By the end of the decade he was the most sought-after painter in Amsterdam, and was prosperous enough to make a down payment on a large house.

The work he produced during this period is relatively Baroque. *The Blinding of Samson* (Fig. **8.21**) is a case in point. Allegedly made to please a patron who had a taste for violence and horror, it uses typical Baroque methods —diagonals, strong contrasts, chiaroscuro—to create drama. But most of the drama is achieved by stark realism. The atrocity occurs in the tent of Delilah, who flees with the victim's hair as he is wrestled to the ground and stabbed in the eye. Pain is registered not only in Samson's face, but in his whole body: clenched fists, arched back, kicking legs, and even clenched toes. Unlike the men in Rubens's *The Raising of the Cross*, none of the figures is particularly muscular. Samson, though large, is fat and unprepossessing; the soldiers, if anything, are rather puny. By depicting ordinary humans, rather than extraordinary ones, Rembrandt made the scene more plausible, and therefore, more vivid. His bloodthirsty patron must not have been disappointed.

Chiaroscuro is used again to create contrast and dramatic focus in *The Descent from the Cross* (Fig. **8.22**). And again, characters with ordinary physiques fill the scene. Christ's body is poignantly ordinary, now broken from death and the ordeal of the cross, as it sinks into the arms of those who have the forlorn task of lowering it. In the darkness beyond the central group, onlookers recede into the shadows, while above them, the bloodstained cross rises nakedly into the barren sky. There is not a shred of beauty or heroism in *The Descent from the Cross*. It is obviously more in the spirit of Grünewald's Good Friday painting than of Rubens's *Raising of the Cross*.

In the 1640s Rembrandt's fortunes changed. Saskia died in 1642, the year often cited as the beginning of a series of setbacks. In addition to losing his wife, he apparently suffered a decline in reputation precipitated by the poor reception accorded a large group portrait finished that year. Although historians disagree over the reasons for Rembrandt's misfortunes, they agree that his life, both personal and professional, turned for the worse. The decline in reputation, for whatever reasons, affected the market for his work, which in turn, was aggravated by the public disapproval of his living with Hendrickje Stoffels, a

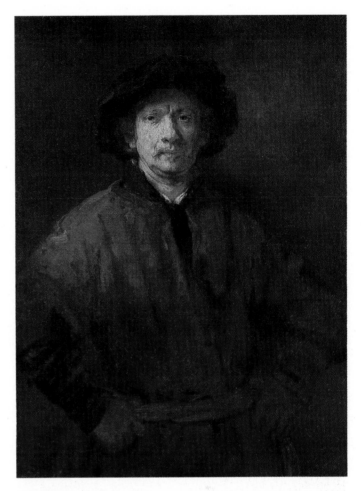

8.23 REMBRANDT VAN RIJN
Self-Portrait, 1652
Oil on canvas, 45 × 32 ins (114 × 81 cm)
Kunsthistorisches Museum, Vienna

servant girl with whom he fell in love after Saskia's death (and whom he could not marry because he would have lost his deceased wife's estate). Added to these difficulties was the fact that Rembrandt, an avid collector of curios as well as art, was poor at managing money.

The stress of these mounting problems seems to be reflected in a 1652 self-portrait in which the artist appears both defiant and insecure (Fig. **8.23**). Also reflected are changes that had taken place in his art. The composition is simpler, the details and textures are less pronounced, the brushwork is broader and softer. Light is still a major means of articulating form and of focusing attention, but Rembrandt has used it differently. Instead of a strong light to create drama, it is a soft light which probes the inner life and emotions of the subject, especially as these are revealed in the aging face. In spite of deaths, lawsuits, and bankruptcy proceedings, Rembrandt continued to paint as much as ever. Indeed, his later work includes many of the paintings which are now considered his best work.

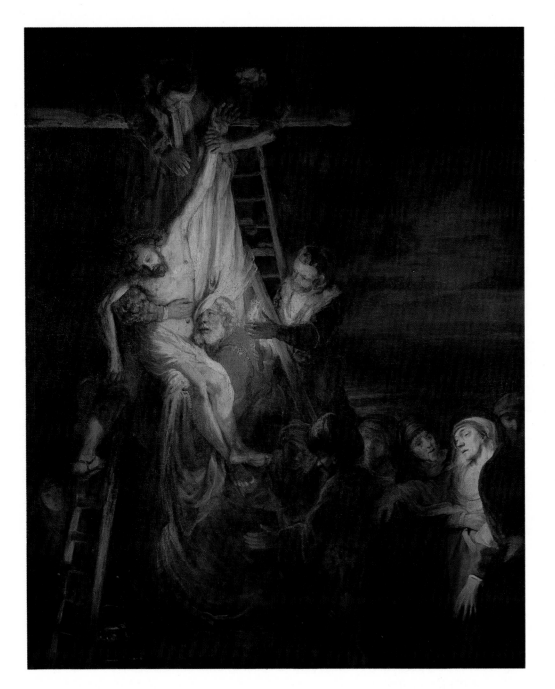

8.24 REMBRANDT VAN RIJN
Descent from the Cross, 1651
Oil on canvas, $56\frac{1}{4} \times 43\frac{3}{4}$ ins
$(1.43 \times 1.11\,\text{m})$
National Gallery of Art,
Washington DC

These changes are readily apparent when comparing his 1651 *Descent from the Cross* (Fig. **8.24**) with his 1633 version of the same subject. Both are basically pyramidal in composition, with the combined images of Christ, shrouds, workers, ladders, and so forth, spreading down and outward to join the people on the ground who form the base. But the later painting is simpler, more monumental, and yet more intimate. Fewer people and objects are visible to divert attention from the theme of death and mourning. The activity of the descent itself occupies a greater proportion of the total canvas, its off-center position effectively balanced by the grief-stricken Mary in the lower right. As viewers, we seem to be more involved, as if we were a part of the small circle of workers and mourners—in contrast to the earlier work in which we are merely spectators. The lighting in the later *Descent* is softer and warmer, though also used to structure the composition and to focus attention on areas of symbolic and/or emotional priority. Christ's body, equally broken and limp, seems to be handled with more affection and tenderness. An embracing arm, an extended hand, and especially the bearded face of Joseph of Arimethea, who grasps the lowered body from beneath, convey care and compassion—feelings deepened by the presence of Mary, the most vivid and compelling image of a mother in shock in the history of art.

Hendrickje died in 1662. Rembrandt lived seven more years, during which time his fortunes, along with the prices of his works, fell even further. *The Return of the Prodigal Son*, based on the parable (Luke 15:11–32) in which the younger of two sons returns home after a period of reckless living, is one of his last paintings (Fig. **8.25**). The simplicity of the scene, without any distracting movement, has the quality of a sacrament. The image of the younger son surrendering himself to his father expresses contrition. The image of the father tenderly embracing him expresses forgiveness—the healing message of Christian pardon. Unlike many artists depicting this parable, Rembrandt did not neglect to include the older son, the one who obeyed, stayed on the farm, and worked for the father. Seen standing off to the right, he expresses, though subtly, envy and suppressed anger.

In this and other late works Rembrandt stressed the psychological aspects of his subjects in simpler, more restrained compositions. Perhaps because of the problems he faced in his own life, his later art was extremely penetrating in its portrayal of human feelings. His religious subjects were not intended to portray the mysteries of Heaven, chronicle the miracles of saints, or even to teach Church doctrines. Instead they were intended to do something both more difficult and more valuable: provide credible accounts of God's ways with people.

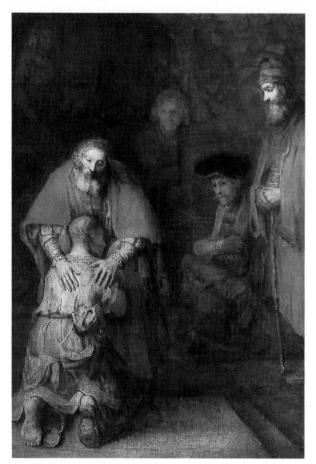

8.25 Rembrandt van Rijn
The Return of the Prodigal Son, c. 1665 (detail)
Oil on canvas, 8 ft 8 ins × 6 ft 8¾ ins (2.64 × 2.05 m)
Hermitage Museum, Leningrad

Music

Under the Protestants religious music fared much better than religious art. Although it had to be modified to conform to the demands of a different set of principles and a different approach to worship, music's existence in the Protestant community was never seriously threatened; in fact, most Protestant sects considered it vital to the life of the Church. Ultimately, sacred music was strengthened by the Reformation. Congregational singing began to play a greater role than it ever had under the Catholics. Many Protestant composers, including extremely gifted ones like Bach and Handel, were motivated to do their best work for the Church. Our discussion of religious music will begin with the Reformation and end in the Baroque period, well into the eighteenth century.

Reformation Music

The relationship between music and the Reformation, from the outset, was direct and positive. Much of this was due to Luther himself, who was very musical. He sang, played the lute, composed, and appreciated Netherlandish polyphony, particularly the works of Josquin (see page 146). Most importantly, he believed in the efficacy of religious music: "After theology I give music the highest place and highest honor."[14]

To Luther music was a basic way of praising God, an offering by the congregation, and an educational tool for the spreading of the Gospel. With such positive views about the role of sacred music on the part of the founder of

Lutheranism, there was no doubt that it would be used in the new Church, perhaps even more than in the old. But there was doubt about the form it would take. On this point Luther was somewhat ambivalent. Although he wanted to retain the Latin Mass, he also wanted the people, not just the clergy, to participate fully. He wrote a German Mass (which, apart from its language, differed from the Roman Mass only in certain details), but did not insist on its being used uniformly. Some congregations adopted it, some did not—resulting in liturgical pluralism and confusion in Lutheran churches. Although Luther was an admirer of complex polyphony, he knew that its performance was limited to trained monks and professional musicians, and this would not do. His concern for involving ordinary people in worship led to his greatest single contribution to the body of sacred music: the German chorale, a broad, unison song that could be sung by a congregation. His aim was to teach people to sing.

Some of the chorales were taken from Gregorian hymns; some were "parodies" of secular songs (sacred words set to secular tunes); and some were newly-written poems and melodies. They are all *strophic* in form—each stanza of a poem being sung to the same music—which helped to make them easy enough for a congregation to master and sing. A number of these chorales, like *Ein feste Burg*, "A Mighty Fortress is Our God" (whose words and, possibly, melody were written by Luther), are found in many of today's hymnals. Although we are familiar with them as four-part, harmonized hymns, in the mid-sixteenth century they were sung monophonically without accompaniment. (It was not until the seventeenth century that congregational singing began to be accompanied by organ.) The performance of chorales, of course, is not limited to monophony and simple four-part harmony; they can be adapted to more complicated musical forms. Lutheran composers did just that, setting them to the kinds of polyphonic styles available in the sixteenth century: old German Lieds with slow tenor parts, Netherlandish motets (as in the works of Ockeghem and Josquin), and the "modern" chordal style with the melody in the soprano. But, of course, these settings were intended only for the trained voices of a choir. Thus, we see emerging already in the late sixteenth century the kind of dual musical service that exists today in most Protestant denominations: on the one hand, simple congregational hymns and, on the other, elaborate music sung by a choir. Both aspects are outgrowths of this dual application of the German chorale.

Not only new tunes but also traditional ones were tapped for their possibilities in new polyphonic settings, as chorale themes came to be used with greater and greater artistic freedom. The German chorale, in addition to

modifying Christian worship, also established a tradition of German musical creativity that would lead to the emergence of such geniuses as Bach, Mozart, and Beethoven.

Outside Germany the role of music in the liturgy fared less well. Of all the reformers, only Ulrich Zwingli (1484–1531) strove to dispense with it altogether, substituting, in his Zurich church, the recitation of psalms and canticles (by the end of the century, the church had introduced congregational singing). Calvin, though less enthusiastic than Luther about music, did have a doctrine of sacred music: it should be simple, modest, and unaccompanied. More concerned about the inroads of secularism than their counterparts in Germany, Calvinists restricted their musical worship to the singing of the Psalms, which were set to new tunes or to popular ones adapted from plainchant. A number of French and Netherlandish composers devoted their talents to this end, composing or adapting melodies which became popular in several of the Protestant countries, including Germany, where some were transformed into chorales. The Church of England (Anglican), as we have noted, separated from the Roman Church for political, rather than doctrinal, reasons. Thus, except for the change in language, the English liturgy continued to resemble, as it does to this day, the Catholic. However, the change from Latin to English gave rise to a significant body of English church music. In the final analysis, the status of liturgical music in all areas of Protestant Europe seems to have benefited more than suffered because of the Reformation. Sacred music, unlike religious art, not only survived; it eventually thrived.

Counter-Reformation Music

In Catholic Europe, the situation was almost a complete reversal of that in Protestant areas. While religious art flourished, liturgical music—at least an important aspect of it—came under serious attack. In addition to its other deliberations, the Council of Trent also debated the function of the arts, especially music. Some of the concerns heard about music were relatively minor: the carelessness and irreverence of performers and the excessive use of instruments. Others were more serious, including, for example, composers' lack of regard for texts. Not unlike their Calvinist opponents, some Catholic prelates were upset over the incursions of secular music, such as the practice of parodying popular songs in the Mass. More seriously, they linked the issue of secularism to that of polyphony—which was also criticized for obscuring the text—and even recommended that polyphony itself be abolished. According to legend, it was saved only because a work by Giovanni Pierluigi da Palestrina (1524–1594), performed at the Council, convinced representatives that the polyphonic style could be conducive to reverence. Whether or not this actually happened, polyphony was allowed to remain, and the best exemplification of Counter-Reformation music, the kind that appeased the ears of reformist Catholics, can be found in the compositions of Palestrina. Not unlike Josquin's music, Palestrina's is essentially imitative polyphony in the tradition of Renaissance motets, but it is also, in a way, more "classical." The melodies are smooth and gently curved, the phrasing well-proportioned, and the relationship among voices carefully balanced.

The leading composer of Catholic church music in the second half of the century, Palestrina wrote over 100 Masses and over 400 sacred motets. On the whole, his work is conservative compared to most sixteenth-century music. While others were composing for five or more voices, Palestrina often wrote for four voices; almost all of his Masses are based on themes from Gregorian chant. The melodies of the four-part "Kyrie" in his *Missa brevis* (Short Mass) of 1570, a good example of his style (Fig. 8.26), are carefully rounded, with no intervals greater than a fourth. The polyphonic texture of the lines as they overlap is relatively "thin" until the beginning of the seventh measure, when the entry of the fourth voice is marked by a chord spanning an octave and a perfect fifth, the most dramatic moment in the example. Though mostly contrapuntal (independent or imitative) in their relationship, the lines at times parallel one another to

form chords, as in the two-part harmony of the upper voices in the seventh and eighth measures. Where harmony does occur, it is always consonant and essentially diatonic. Cool, elegant, reserved, and almost austere in its purity, Palestrina's music embodies the serious, conservative side of the Counter Reformation. In this respect it is quite unlike the theatrical sculptures of Bernini and exuberant paintings of Rubens, for example.

Protestant Baroque Music

In the Baroque era Protestant music went from strength to strength. A virtual "industry" of singers, organists, cantors, Kapellmeisters, and composers was needed to fulfill the musical requirements of churches, particularly Lutheran churches—even those in small provincial cities. A member of that industry was Johann Sebastian Bach, who, as we noted in Chapter 4, was employed in his later years as music director of St. Thomas's School and Church in Leipzig. Because of his position, together with the fact that he was recognized as a virtuoso organist and composer of contrapuntal works, he was well known in Lutheran musical circles. Still, he was not as famous as a half dozen or so other German composers (such as Georg Philipp Telemann, a very prolific composer who also worked in Leipzig for a time). It certainly was not for lack of production that Bach was less famous. In addition to hundreds of secular fugues and concerti grossi, he wrote an enormous body of religious pieces, including 170 organ settings of German chorales and more than 200 cantatas (a vocal composition for chorus, soloists, and orchestra). The demand for cantata performances in Leipzig churches—58 per year—was considerable. Not all of these had to be newly-written ones; but Bach, probably because he was responsible for directing the principal performances, felt compelled to write new cantatas on a regular basis. For these performances he used the "first" choir from his school, and an orchestra recruited from the school, the town, and a musical society at Leipzig University.

Cantata No. 80, written for the Reformation Festival (October 31), is based on Luther's chorale *Ein feste Burg* (above) whose stanzas declare God to be humans' fortress and Christ their savior, and proclaim the struggle against evil and the promise of reward after death. Consisting of eight movements, the cantata includes all four stanzas of the chorale, along with additional texts inserted in between. As in the *Goldberg Variations* (see page 185), the original melody serves as a point of departure for exploring related musical ideas and undergoes numerous transformations along the way. Unlike the *Variations*, however, Cantata No. 80 not only relates musical ideas to specific

8.26 Opening theme of the "Kyrie" in *Missa brevis*, Palestrina

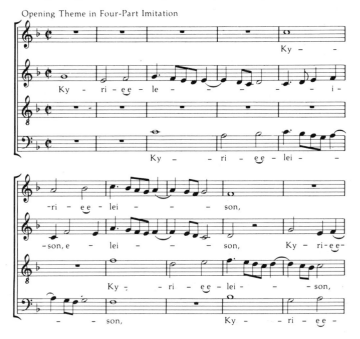

Opening Theme in Four-Part Imitation

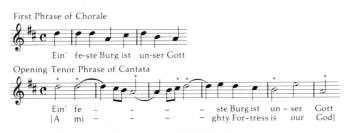

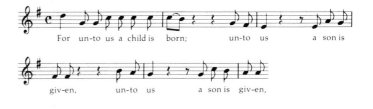

8.27 *Ein feste Burg*, Cantata No. 80, J S Bach

8.28 *For unto us a Child is Born*, first theme from Handel's *Messiah*

content, but returns the listener to a straightforward, triumphant exposition of the original music in the final movement.

The first movement involves a four-part polyphony with instruments doubling the voices of the choir while ornamented versions of each phrase of the first stanza are introduced imitatively. The difference between the simple, majestic line of the chorale melody's first phrase and its adaptation in the opening line of the cantata is illustrated in Fig. **8.27**. Woven into these adaptations are the original melodies of the phrases, stated triumphantly by soprano voices and trumpets. (Especially noticeable throughout is the octave-long descending scale of the second, fourth, and final phrases.) Although Bach's music is Baroque in its splendid, often florid effects, its structure—notably its manipulation of thematic material—is as thoroughly worked out as a medieval Scholastic argument or Gothic rib vault. The exposition of the first stanza is complex yet monumental. The second stanza, sung in ornate style by soprano voice, is pitted contrapuntally against an independent text and melody sung in the bass. The third and fourth movements consist of recitatives sung respectively by soprano and bass. In the fifth movement, the choir sings the third stanza of the original melody in unison, but the orchestral melody, driven by a faster, more energetic tempo, continues its contrary ways as it weaves in, out, and around the choir. After a recitative and duet by tenor and alto voices, the last movement (in which the congregation may have joined in) proclaims the fourth stanza of the chorale with full orchestra and choir. The long-note original tune is amplified by a simple homophony, embellished only by trumpet accents at the endings of some of the phrases. If the polyphony of the first movement recalls Gothic elegance, the sturdy chords of the final movement recall the monumentality of Romanesque.

The music of the hymn *Ein feste Burg* is familiar to most Americans, but the music of the cantata—which is heard mainly in concert-hall performances—is not. Ironically, Handel's *Messiah*, which was originally intended only for concert halls, is familiar to most churchgoers. Undoubtedly the most popular sacred work ever written, *Messiah*—in part or in whole—is frequently heard in both

churches and concert halls all over America, especially during the Christmas season.

An oratorio, as we saw in Chapter 4, is like an opera without the actors and stage sets. Handel's oratorios differ from his operas in another way: the use of English rather than Italian for the text. And his *Messiah* differs from his other oratorios in at least one way: its text is not a narrative but a series of contemplations on the major themes of Christianity—the birth of Jesus, his death and resurrection, and the redemption. In essence, the *Messiah* is a musical altarpiece. It is also a masterpiece of the Baroque: richly ornate, lively, full of beautiful melodies, pomp, and dramatic climaxes.

Although the "Hallelujah Chorus" is the most famous part of the *Messiah*, the chorus "For Unto Us a Child Is Born" (based on the text of Isaiah 9:6), with its characteristically Baroque runs of sixteenth notes, is more typical of the oratorio as a whole. The opening theme (Fig. **8.28**) is introduced in the key of G major by the orchestra, followed by the sopranos and tenors, respectively, who sing the theme imitatively, followed by the altos and basses. The next line of the Isaiah verse, "and the government shall be upon his shoulder," also presented contrapuntally, is sung to a new theme (Fig. **8.29**). The melodies of both themes are light, the tempo sprightly, the overlapping of voices superbly integrated, and the harmony without dissonance. This delightful polyphony continues for some 30 measures before an increase in intensity is sensed in the second repetition of the second theme. Still, the dramatic, pounding chords of "Wonderful! Counsellor!," the climax of the chorus, come as a surprise. Following this is the resolution of the climax, the declamatory singing of "The mighty God, The everlasting Father, The Prince of Peace," and then the resumption of the first theme. The full cycle is repeated twice, though with some variations.

8.29 Second theme from Handel's *Messiah*

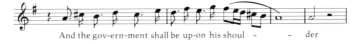

Although Handel's oratorios were written for a mainly middle-class audience in predominately Protestant England, the qualities of his music seem to relate less to the sober spirit of Protestantism than to the florid exuberance of Catholic Baroque. Its melodic richness, breadth, drama, and unabashed pomp recall similar tendencies found in the architecture of Bernini and Borromini (see Chapter 4) as well as the examples of Counter-Reformation art discussed in this chapter. In addition to being a great composer of oratorios, Handel was the greatest composer in his time of Italian opera. Like Rubens, he borrowed a foreign style and brought it to its pinnacle of excellence. At the very least, then, it can be said that the *Messiah*, the most famous of all oratorios, belongs not just to Protestantism but to all of Christianity.

Conclusion

The end of this chapter brings to a close a three-chapter series on Christianity in Western culture. An earlier three-chapter series (Chapters 2, 3, and 4) surveyed the tradition of classicism. The fact that both traditions are given "equal time" in this book implies a degree of symmetry between the two. Such an implication can be misleading.

The differences in content between classicism and Christianity—a legacy of learnings and manners shared by intellectuals and ruling elites versus a living faith shared by rich and poor—probably needs no further elaboration. The two also differ with regard to the fact that classicism is (or was) not only a set of guiding principles for the arts, but also, in many ways, a style that could be recognized in works as widely separated in time as Polykleitos' *Spear Carrier* (Fig. 2.22) and David's *Oath of the Horatii* (Fig. 4.26). Christianity, although it is responsible for some of the most enduring examples of literature, art, and music in the West, is neither of these. The Bible contains no guidelines for artists and musicians; the styles produced in the name of Christianity vary from that of the Justinian mosaic in San Vitale (Fig. 6.28) to that of Rembrandt's *Descent from the Cross* (Fig. 8.22), and from Machaut's *Notre Dame Mass* to Handel's *Messiah*. Finally, although they overlapped in time, classicism has exerted relatively little influence on the arts since the time of Napoleon; Christianity is still very much alive, though not as culturally influential as it once was.

Although in conflict at certain points in the early centuries of the Christian era, in the final analysis the two traditions were neither similar nor radically opposed. It would be more accurate to portray them as complementary, often working hand-in-hand. Examples of their synthesis include: the influence of Virgil's *Aeneid* (Chapter 2) on the medieval world, particularly in the writings of Dante (Chapter 7), the influence of Plato's writings (Chapter 2) on the theology of many early Christians (Chapter 6) and on Michelangelo's Sistine Ceiling (Chapter 3), the influence of Neoplatonism on St. Augustine's theology (Chapter 6), the merging of Christian faith and classical reason in the theology of Aquinas (Chapter 7), the combination of Reformation fervor and Renaissance style in the art of Dürer (Chapter 8), the dualism of Renaissance scholar and Reformation prophet in the character of Erasmus (Chapter 8), and the persistence of classical elements in the arts of the Counter Reformation (Chapter 8).

In the introduction to his book *What is Christianity?*, the renowned scholar Adolf von Harnack says: "The great English philosopher, John Stuart Mill, once commented that 'mankind can hardly be too often reminded that there was once a man named Socrates.' That is correct; but it is even more important to remind mankind that a man named Jesus Christ once stood in their midst."[15]

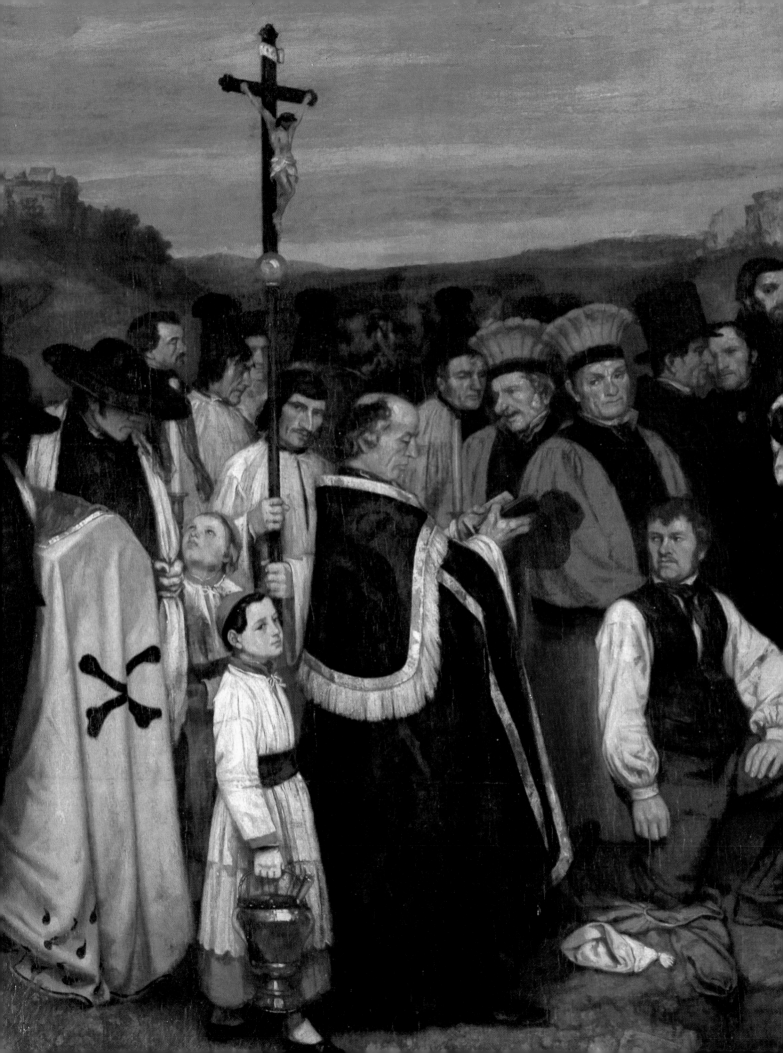

CHAPTER NINE

Realism and Materialism

I am...above all, a realist, that is, the sincere friend of real truth.

COURBET

Introduction to Realism

Realism, variously defined in terms of a truthful representation of reality, is associated in its beginnings with mid-nineteenth century France, especially in fiction and painting. For it was in these two forms of artistic expression that its possibilities were most fully explored. (Since there is no musical equivalent for Realism in literature and art, this chapter will not discuss music.) Neither in art, however, nor in literature does the nineteenth century mark the beginning of critical concern for truthful representation of the real world. Aristotle, writing in the fourth century BC, states at the beginning of his *Poetics* that all arts are types of imitation (Greek *mimesis*) and that tragedy is an imitation of an action. Erich Auerbach entitled his classic work of literary criticism *Mimesis: The Representation of Reality in Western Literature* and traced this theme throughout literary history. Going back to the origins of Western literature, to Homer himself, one finds "truthful representations" of reality in the *Odyssey*. The similes of Virgil's *Aeneid* provide glimpses of everyday Roman life. Certainly there is real life reflected in Chaucer's *Canterbury Tales* and Boccaccio's *Decameron*, as also in Elizabethan drama and Cervantes' *Don Quixote*. One could continue, but the point is clear: realism has a long history.

In both art and literature the unique quality of nineteenth-century Realism is its determined and systematic attempt to portray, honestly and faithfully, those segments of society that had been neglected by Romantic artists and writers: the middle and lower classes. Indeed, Realism was a reaction to Romanticism. One can reverse certain of the typical characteristics of Romanticism and have a description of Realism. The Romantic was obsessed with the *mystical past*; the Realist focused on *contemporary life*. The Romantic believed that truth was served best by a *subjective* approach to experience; the Realist sought *objectivity*. The Romantic indulged his *imagination*; the Realist aspired to a presentation of reality that would appeal to *reason* and *common sense*. The Romantic featured the *heroic*, the universal; the Realist portrayed the *ordinary*, the commonplace.

The contrast between the romantic and realistic approaches to subject matter is strikingly illustrated by a comparison of Goethe's *Faust* (see Chapter 5) with Tolstoy's *Ivan Ilych* (see below). Faust is no ordinary mortal. He is the consummate scholar, master of all knowledge, whose superhuman passions become the subject of a controversy between God and an evil spirit. Thus, when he dies, he is an aged wise man, still seeking,

like Alexander the Great, new worlds to conquer. And his death itself is no ordinary one: he is borne to heaven by angels. Ivan Ilych, on the other hand, is explicitly described by Tolstoy as "most ordinary," and he is portrayed throughout as a typical middle-class man whose submission to the moral compromises and materialism of the bourgeois routine constitutes his tragedy. Thus Tolstoy uses commonplaces to convey moral truth. Ilych dies in mid-life of a horrible wasting disease (perhaps cancer), experiencing in his long, drawn-out dying the agonizing, relentless pain and the consequent disintegration of personality effected by such a disease. Hardly the subject matter for a Romantic (or classical, for that matter) painting or novel!

Tolstoy's near-clinical description of the death of Ivan Ilych comes very close to the extreme form of Realism called *Naturalism*. Flaubert also does this in his description of the death by arsenic poisoning of Emma Bovary. Although some Realist artists portrayed sordid subjects in order to reveal social injustices, Naturalism was mainly the concern of writers. How, then, are Realism and Naturalism to be distinguished? In one sense, Naturalism can be regarded as an extension of the Realist principle of portraying all aspects of life objectively. The Naturalist writer, much more than the Realist writer, explored such matters as physical drives (hunger and sex, for example), poverty, oppression, and crime and sought to present them objectively, even scientifically. Émile Zola, for instance, saw himself in relation to his subject matter as a scientist conducting an experiment on society intended to reveal the objective truth about its various levels.

Both Realist and Naturalist writers liked to think of themselves as cutting into society to reveal a "slice of life." Such an exaggerated metaphor for objectivity cannot be taken at face value. Whether in literary or plastic art, total objectivity is not possible, or desirable. The artist is a maker, a creator, not a piece of unexposed film. The French novelist Stendhal said that a novel is a mirror walking along the road, but such a metaphor will not work for the writer or the artist. They are not merely reflectors. They choose their subject matter; they decide what aspects they will feature and how these will be interpreted. And they are not objective. They have attitudes, hold to certain views, espouse and promote programs and causes—all imbued with their own personalities. Flaubert, for example, made objectivity a primary value in his *Madame Bovary*; yet, it is apparent that he was more sympathetic toward some of his characters than

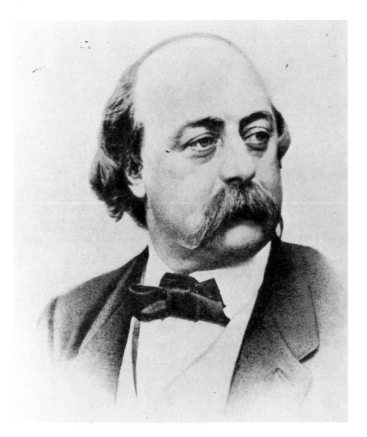

9.2 Gustave Flaubert

toward others. Courbet clearly espoused liberal causes in his work. The subject matter and the way it is presented inevitably provide an index to the views of the writer or the artist. What one can safely conclude about the Realists' concern for objectivity is that, first, they claimed the right to include all kinds of subjects in their work, seeking especially to portray contemporary life and matters accurately; and, second, that Realist writers shunned intervention in their narratives for the purpose of indulging in direct authorial comment, reflection, or philosophizing.

Several factors provided the context of the transition from Romanticism to Realism in the nineteenth century (Fig. 9.3)—indeed, often contributed to it: the failed revolutions of 1848, industrialism, materialism, the growing strength of the middle class, and scientism (the theory that scientific methods should be applied in all fields). The passion for liberty so typical of the nineteenth century is demonstrated by the cluster of revolutions occurring in 1848 in France, Italy, Germany, and Austria. The Romantic idealism driving these uprisings induced a number of writers and artists to become directly involved. The measure of their idealism was also the measure of their disillusionment when these revolutions failed and conservative reactions set in. Thus they became alienated

from a culture which they believed to be "Philistine"— Matthew Arnold's word for the smug and boorish middle class incapable of appreciating art or artists because of their inveterate ignorance. Liberalism experienced a crushing blow in France when Louis-Napoleon, nephew of Napoleon Bonaparte, declared himself, in 1852, Emperor Napoleon III, proclaiming the Second Empire.

The beginning of the Second Empire coincided roughly with the Great Exhibition of 1851, a celebration of science and technology held in the Crystal Palace in London (see *Frame Construction* below). Dostoyevsky used the Crystal Palace in his *Notes from Underground* to symbolize the vain attempt to solve all human problems through reason and technology. Other intellectuals were critical of the Great Exhibition on the grounds that although it celebrated England's industrial and technological achievements, it failed to speak to the needs of the poor and oppressed.

However, the growth of industry and technology and the wealth thereby created produced benefits that, in small degree at least, did improve the lot of the working class. But the middle class was the primary beneficiary, which is reflected, for example, in the Impressionist paintings that immortalized the hedonistic life-styles of the Parisian members of this class. The smug materialistic and commercial values of the middle class provided an easy target for the volleys of criticism fired off by alienated artists and writers. Yet the growth of technology and wealth, in the minds of many people, was good reason for optimism about the future—an optimism fed also by nineteenth-century science and philosophy.

The discoveries of Charles Darwin (1809–1882), which led to his publication of *On the Origin of Species* in 1859, seemed to provide in the theory of the survival of the fittest, a scientific rationale for the idea of progress. (Perhaps it should be noted that it also led some people to assume that if weak species eventually die out by a process of "natural selection," it was therefore perfectly right for strong (that is, rich and powerful) people to exploit weak (that is, poor and powerless) ones. Such ruthless behavior, according to this spin-off of Darwinian theory, was simply a natural part of "the survival of the fittest.") Auguste Comte's (1798–1857) philosophy of Positivism also was evolutionary in nature. In his view, human thinking had passed through three stages—theological, metaphysical, and positivistic. In the first stage, humans depended upon authority; in the second, on independent speculation; in the third, however, they are no longer dependent on speculation, for speculation has given way to exact, scientific demonstration. Utilitarianism, the philosophy proclaimed by John Stuart Mill (1806–1873), also declared that knowledge must be empirical. His attempt to treat morality empirically (using as the criterion of an

DATES	SOCIAL AND POLITICAL DEVELOPMENTS	LITERATURE AND PHILOSOPHY	VISUAL ARTS	ARCHITECTURE	MUSIC
1600			Velázquez (9.6) Vermeer (9.7)		
1800 1825 1850	Revolutions in Europe	Balzac			
1850	Growth of nationalism Great Exhibition	Comte: *Positivism* Mill: *Utilitarianism* Flaubert (9.2) Dostoyevsky (9.4) Tolstoy (9.5) Darwin: *Origin of Species* Marx: *Das Kapital*	Courbet (9.8) Manet (9.10) Winslow Homer (9.9) Monet (9.13, 9.15)	Paxton: Crystal Palace (9.17)	
1875 1900	Urbanization: growth of big business and rise of Labor Unions	Zola Nietzsche	Renoir (9.14) Degas (9.16)	Chicago School Louis Sullivan Wainwright Building First skyscraper) (9.18)	

9.3 Realism

act's morality the achievement of "the greatest good for the greatest number") was devastatingly satirized by Dostoyevsky in the character of Luzhin in *Crime and Punishment*. Karl Marx, in his book *Das Kapital* (1867), also set forth an empirical view in his theory of "dialectical materialism." He argued that social evolution is governed by certain discoverable laws which are moving society toward a consummation in which there will be no classes, no private property, and no government. Marx's book was but one example of variously motivated socialist theories attacking capitalism on behalf of labor, evidence of the growing significance of the proletariat.

Although some people found encouragement about the future of mankind in these political, social, economic, and intellectual developments, others found them deeply disturbing. For such people the hope of a perfected future offered by the theories of Comte and Marx had little relevance for the existing depressing realities. And the findings of Darwin, which seemed to imply that the struggle for existence was the only governing factor in human behavior, did not inspire optimism. Realist and Naturalist writers, ambivalently, sought to employ scientific methods in the formulation of their attacks on middle class materialism which was itself a by-product of scientific advances. Writers and painters, attacking the banality and egocentrism of society, lent form and significance to those conditions through their insights and perspectives.

In this chapter, therefore, we shall study examples of the stories, paintings, and architecture of the Realist tradition in order to understand better, not merely its external history, but also the artistic reflection and critique of the period. For it is often the artist who, by giving form to his ideas through his creations, provides us with the deepest insight into the inner structure of our past and thereby enlightens us as to our destiny as human beings.

Literature

Flaubert

Although Gustave Flaubert (1821–1880) was preceded by Honoré de Balzac, called "the father of modern realism," he is the most significant figure in the rise of French Realism. By temperament a romantic, Flaubert nonetheless realistically exposed the dangers of Romanticism in his greatest novel, *Madame Bovary*.

Flaubert's own life was quite unromantic. Born in Rouen, the city featured in *Madame Bovary*, he was the son of a doctor, a fact that influenced his literary works, especially *Madame Bovary*. His father wanted him to become a lawyer, but Flaubert, though he studied law in Paris for a few years, rejected this profession. After a period of traveling for his health, he returned to his family home at Croisset, near Rouen, to devote himself to writing. There he lived until his death of apoplexy in 1880.

Flaubert's Realistic approach to literature is evident in his meticulous methods of writing, for which he has become a father figure to other writers in the Realist tradition. He eschewed Romantic subjectivism and sought to present his characters and their milieu with careful objectivity. Through meticulous observation he strove for accuracy in the details by which he created his verbal pictures. He believed that there was only one correct word (*le mot juste*) in every case for what the writer wishes to express. Given such demanding standards, it is no surprise that he wrote few books. He was able to produce, in some instances, only one or two pages in a week, spending several years on each of his novels—five years, for example, on *Madame Bovary*.

Flaubert's Romantic fascination with the exotic past is revealed in *Salammbô* (1862), a novel about Carthage in the third century BC. His Realist side, however, is demonstrated by the fact that he traveled to North Africa in 1858 to document his story. Thus the novel had an exotic setting but was written in an objective style. His penchant for careful documentation is also evident in his novel *Sentimental Education* (1870), which is set in the revolutionary period of 1848. His most Romantic novel is *The Temptation of St. Anthony* (1874), an exotic story about the Devil's temptation of this third-century saint. His reputation as a writer of short stories rests upon *Three Tales* (1877), including *A Simple Heart*, which, in the character of the humble French maid Félicité, is an excellent example of Flaubert's ability to combine objectivity of method with sympathetic presentation. Flaubert's last novel, *Bouvard and Pécuchet*, though never completed, was published posthumously (1881).

Madame Bovary is the story of an attractive French girl, the daughter of a prosperous farmer, who marries a plodding doctor (actually, more like a health officer) named Charles Bovary. Educated in a convent but steeped in the syrupy romantic novels and poetry of the second quarter of the nineteenth century, Emma marries Charles in the hope that she will find in their relationship the fulfillment of her unrealistic romantic ideals. The unambitious Charles, easily pleased with the ordinary comforts of domestic life, cannot comprehend, let alone fulfill, such aspirations. Thus Emma soon becomes extremely bored.

Her boredom is temporarily suspended by an invitation to a ball given by a local aristocrat. Her attendance at the ball, however, simply makes her more aware of what she perceives as the realization of the romantic ideal in the lives of the wealthy, a world she aspires to but cannot attain. Thus her frustration increases and eventually manifests itself as illness. Hoping to improve her health, Charles moves from Tostes, their first home, to Yonville-l'Abbaye, near Rouen. To his delight, Emma is now pregnant. When the child she bears turns out to be a girl, however, rather than the son which she has romantically idealized in her imagination, she loses interest.

In Yonville Emma finds one person, the handsome young Léon Depuis, who identifies with her boredom and romanticism. They are strongly attracted to each other and carry on a flirtation, but their passion is not at this point consummated. Thus, disappointed, Léon leaves for Paris, to the frustration of Emma, who again lapses into illness.

Once more, however, Emma discovers, or is discovered by, a man on whom she can pin her romantic dreams, one Rodolphe Boulanger, a sexually experienced bachelor who wants Emma simply because she is physically attractive. Emma, of course, idealizes this relationship, and after he seduces her, she is ecstatic, repeating to herself, "I have a lover."

Not surprisingly, the philandering Rodolphe becomes bored with their relationship. In a weak moment, however, he agrees to run away with Emma, but does not show up for the journey and sends a deceitful note saying that he has gone away to avoid ruining Emma's life. Emma is devastated, and once more falls ill. She turns to religion for solace, but this merely transfers her romantic notions from her lover to God.

In the pursuit of her love affair, Emma has spent large sums of money on herself and Rodolphe. She was encouraged in this by the local draper, Lheureux, to whom she went heavily into debt without the knowledge of Charles.

Hoping to cure Emma's melancholy, Charles takes her to the opera in Rouen. There they meet—Léon! Much more sophisticated now, he eventually seduces Emma, and thus Emma begins another affair. In order to facilitate this relationship Emma pretends to be making regular trips to Rouen for music lessons. Now she must borrow more money from Lheureux to finance her trips.

This adulterous relationship, too, eventually runs its course, and Léon wants out because it threatens his possibilities for advancement. After a quarrel with Léon, Emma returns to Yonville to find that Lheureux has brought a court judgment against her and is demanding payment within 24 hours. Beside herself, Emma turns for help to first one and then another, including Lheureux and Rodolphe, but is rejected at every turn. Desperate, she rushes to the pharmacy, gains entrance to the drug closet, and gobbles a handful of arsenic. Flaubert's experience as a child at the hospital where his father worked and his study of arsenic poisoning now come into play as he describes in detail the slow and torturous death of Emma.

Not until after Emma's death does Charles learn of her extravagances and adulterous affairs. He dies of grief, and their daughter is sent first to her grandmother, then, upon her grandmother's death, to her aunt, who puts her to work as a factory hand.

The novel closes with an ironic note: the pompous, pseudo-intellectual pharmacist, Homais, after much self-centered posturing, is awarded the medal of the Legion of Honor.

Madame Bovary has been compared to Cervantes' *Don Quixote* (1605, 1615): as *Don Quixote* satirizes the chivalric code, dramatizing the absurd and disastrous consequences of taking it seriously, so does *Madame Bovary* for the romantic ideal. In attacking romanticism, however, Flaubert was exorcising part of himself, the romanticism endemic to his own personality. When asked who had been the model for his character (in fact, there had been at least two), Flaubert claimed, "My poor Bovary, without a doubt, is suffering and weeping in twenty villages in France," an indication of how widespread such frustrated dreams were among young women. Pressed further, he declared, "*I* am Madame Bovary," indicating his personal identification with the dangerous romantic passions of his protagonist. The decisive difference between Flaubert and his literary creation, of course, lay in the fact that whereas Emma Bovary tries to enact her romantic ideals, with fatal consequences, Flaubert was able to sublimate his romantic tendencies in creating a work of art.

Madame Bovary was controversial from its publication. In fact it became the subject of a celebrated court case instigated by the government on the grounds that, because of its treatment of adultery, it was an offense to public morals and religion. The trial ended in acquittal—and ensured instant fame for both Flaubert and *Madame Bovary.* Anyone who reads this novel can see that it does not condone adultery.

Although Flaubert, in his characterization of Emma Bovary, reveals the devastating consequences of sentimental and unthinking attachment to the romantic ideal, his implied criticism is basically sympathetic. His depiction of the middle class, which he despised, is a different matter. Homais, the pharmacist of Yonville, is the outstanding example. Although Flaubert sought to treat his characters objectively, there can be no question about his attitude toward this arrogant, self-seeking, pretentious pseudo-intellectual, who imagines himself an Enlightenment skeptic in the tradition of Voltaire.

Martin Turnell, an authority on French literature, states that "Flaubert was the greatest virtuoso who ever practiced prose fiction" and that "he was the creator of the contemporary novel, and the source of nearly every important technical advance made since the middle of the last century."[1] He supports this comment, in part, by an analysis of Flaubert's use of "an immensely elaborate network of interrelated images" (symbols) to create the meaning of *Madame Bovary.* For example, in Part I Emma comes across her wedding bouquet and casts it into the fireplace—one of several images symbolizing the destruction of her marriage. Later, she tears up a note she has written to Léon breaking off their relationship and scatters the pieces out of a cab window; the pieces of the note float like "butterflies" into a field, a reference to the pieces of Emma's wedding bouquet which floated up the chimney like "black butterflies."

But Flaubert's masterful use of interconnected images is but one measure of his achievement in creating this seminal novel of the Realist tradition in literature. His ironic and penetrating analysis of bourgeois character and culture in early nineteenth-century France, his meticulously crafted style, his skillful use of realistic detail—these are some of the other aspects of *Madame Bovary* that have caused it to be recognized as the Realist novel *par excellence* and perhaps the best-known of all French novels.

Dostoyevsky

Born in the same year, Flaubert and Fyodor Dostoyevsky (1821–1881) were almost exact contemporaries. Both were also the sons of doctors, but their attitudes toward their fathers differed markedly: whereas Flaubert's father is perhaps the model for the distinguished Doctor Larivière in *Madame Bovary,* Dostoyevsky's father, it has been suggested, is reflected in the dissolute Fyodor Pavlovich Karamazov, the father in *The Brothers Karamazov,* who is murdered by his illegitimate son. In fact, Dostoyevsky's harsh father *was* murdered—not by his son, but by his peasants.

The murder occurred while Dostoyevsky was a student at the College of Military Engineering at St. Petersburg, from which he graduated in 1843. His real interest, however, was literature, and he resigned his commission at the age of 23 in order to devote himself to writing. He became involved in this period with a group of radical socialists who were regarded by the Russian government as revolutionaries. Members of the group, including Dostoyevsky, were arrested in 1849 and sentenced to death. The czar allowed the process of execution to go as far as the blindfolding of the prisoners in preparation for

and Punishment (1866) were all written to pay off his devastating gambling debts. His debts were not covered by the money he received for these novels, however, and he remained in Western Europe for four more years (1867–1871) to escape his creditors. During this period, despite his poverty and illness, he was able to write two long novels, *The Idiot* (1869) and *The Possessed* (1871). He left Polina Suslova in 1867 and married his stenographer, Anna Snitkina (25 years younger than himself), a practical and competent woman who loved him and bore his children. After his return to Russia in 1871, Dostoyevsky entered upon a period of relative happiness, enjoying literary success and modest prosperity amidst the joys of family life. In this period he wrote *A Raw Youth* (1875) and what is regarded as the greatest of all his novels, *The Brothers Karamazov* (1879–1880).

The hallmark of Dostoyevsky's writings is his probing of the depths of the human psyche by which he reveals the dark, irrational underside of human nature. This is apparent in his *Notes from Underground*, in which the narrator, the Underground Man—who has become a classic literary persona for modern literature—reveals the irrational impulses of the human soul through his confession and his account of his attempts to relate to other human beings. This work has the perspective so often associated with the modern era: uncertainty, alienation, subjectivity, questioning of the relevance of rational thought, even nihilism (the denial of all values, including the value of life itself). It is paradoxical, therefore, that Dostoyevsky had a religious purpose in writing this work, a paradox that occurs often in Dostoyevsky because his profound analyses of the negative aspects of the human condition tend to overshadow his presentation of a positive religious response to that condition. In *Notes from Underground*, however, this misunderstanding, he contended in a letter to his brother, was the work of the censors. This letter supports the view that Dostoyevsky meant to show that the only way of escape for the Underground Man from the prison of his self-will is through surrender of his will to Christ. This is an example of Dostoyevsky's idea of the man-God versus the God-man (Christ). For Dostoyevsky, the sovereign deployment of the human will, by which the individual recognizes no will superior to his own, leads to the point where he deifies himself, thus becoming a man-God; or he discovers that he has become enslaved to his own will and surrenders that will to the God-man (Christ), who alone can make him truly free and enable him to become what he was meant to be. This religious understanding of freedom is integral to Dostoyevsky's meaning in his later novels.

A much more fully developed presentation of Dostoyevsky's Christian view is found in *Crime and*

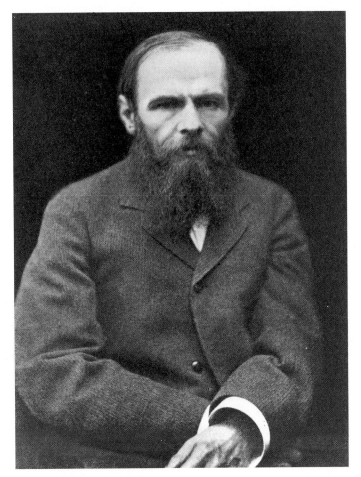

9.4 Fyodor M. Dostoyevsky

the firing squad before sending a message that their sentences had been commuted to imprisonment. Dostoyevsky was sentenced to eight years exile in Siberia, including five years at hard labor, the rest of the sentence to be served in the army. He was profoundly marked by his last-minute reprieve and by his subsequent exile. Not only did he gain insight into the criminal personality, both its capacity for violence and its capacity for nobility; but he also learned to accept suffering as necessary for the expiation of sin, an understanding of the redemptive value of suffering that permeates his novels. He wrote about his prison life in *The House of the Dead* (1862). Pardoned in 1859, Dostoyevsky returned to St. Petersburg to resume his literary career.

At the time of his first wife's death (1864), Dostoyevsky was already involved in a short, passionate affair with Polina Suslova, with whom he traveled in Western Europe, at the same time indulging another overmastering passion—gambling. Both passions are reflected in his works: the character of his mistress in several of his stories, and his gambling in *The Gambler* (1867). This short novel, *Notes from Underground* (1866), and *Crime*

Punishment. The Russian word translated as "crime" has the broader meaning of "stepping across" and thus can include the violation of moral and religious as well as civil restrictions. Indeed, it becomes evident that Raskolnikov, the protagonist, despite his attempts to convince himself otherwise, has violated moral, religious, and civil sanctions in committing a double murder and must therefore accept the consequences of his deed. Dostoyevsky's man-God versus the God-man theory is evident in *Crime and Punishment*, for Raskolnikov seeks to deploy his will without restriction, moral or otherwise, in the name of his Extraordinary Man theory, Dostoyevsky's version of Friedrich Nietzsche's concept of the Superman, a person who has transcended traditional moral and religious values. The Christian alternative is clearly evident here in the character of Sonya, who finally redeems Raskolnikov, and the Lazarus motif, which foreshadows Raskolnikov's "resurrection," under Sonya's influence, at the end of the novel.

Raskolnikov's crime consists in his murder of an old pawnbroker and her retarded sister, but the motives for this dual murder (he planned to kill only the pawnbroker, but her sister arrived on the scene unexpectedly and he also murdered her) are confused. In a previously published article Raskolnikov had developed his theory of the Extraordinary Man, the person (he especially likes to use Napoleon as his example) who is not restricted by traditional values and who can therefore, in the name of a "new word" (identified vaguely by Raskolnikov as a proclamation of a better future), "step across" these boundaries. Raskolnikov tries to convince himself that he is such a person, thus, in the view of Dostoyevsky, aspiring to become a man-God. But he also rationalizes that by killing the old woman he will be able to use her money to perform "thousands of good deeds" that will eradicate "one little crime."[2] Here Dostoyevsky is attacking the philosophy of Utilitarianism (see page 359), which he also attacks in *Notes from Underground*. Raskolnikov shows no interest in the few trifles that he steals at the time of the murder, revealing the weakness of his theorizing. He also realizes that were he truly an Extraordinary Man he would not be subject to the second thoughts and uncertainties that he experiences. Moreover, an Extraordinary Man, as defined by Raskolnikov, would not be neurotically obsessed, as he is, with confessing his crime.

Although this obsession draws Raskolnikov to the detective Porfiry, he does not immediately confess. Porfiry realizes early on that Raskolnikov is the murderer, but he intuits that Raskolnikov will not flee and will eventually confess of his own volition. Raskolnikov makes his first confession to Sonya, and it is through her influence that he ultimately confesses to Porfiry and accepts his punish-ment. Even so, it is much later, after he has been in penal servitude for a year, that he truly begins to undergo—again because of the presence of Sonya—the spiritual resurrection that will redeem him. Even this, Dostoyevsky emphasizes, is only a beginning. Thus Dostoyevsky offers no facile set of beliefs as a panacea for all of Raskolnikov's problems.

The spiritual resurrection of Raskolnikov that begins at the end of *Crime and Punishment* is foreshadowed by the Lazarus motif (see John 11:1–44). Shortly after the murders, he returns to his room and lapses into a state of semi-consciousness that lasts for almost four days, the period of time that Lazarus had been in the tomb when Christ restored him to life. Later, in Raskolnikov's first interview with Porfiry, the detective asks him if he believes in the raising of Lazarus, emphasizing his point by adding "literally?" Raskolnikov answers that he does. Then, not long before he confesses to Sonya, Raskolnikov demands that she read him the story of Lazarus. She reads almost the entire story. Finally, at the end of the novel, as Raskolnikov meditates on the renewal of life which has begun within him, he picks up the very New Testament from which Sonya had read and recalls the raising of Lazarus: "... one thought flashed through his mind: 'Is it possible that her convictions can be mine, too, now? Her feelings, her yearnings, at least....'" Dostoyevsky then closes his novel with the promise of a "gradual rebirth" for Raskolnikov.[3]

Thus Dostoyevsky presents the God-man (Christ) as the alternative to the man-God (Raskolnikov's Extraordinary Man). Raskolnikov has sought to will himself into the exclusive category of the Extraordinary Man. The result of his effort is that he "murders" his better self: "Was it the old hag that I killed? No, I killed myself, and not the old hag." But the Lazarus motif points to the power of Christ to give new life, even to the dead; and Sonya, through her example and her love, makes this an existential reality for Raskolnikov. Thus he finally submits to Sonya's urging that he "accept suffering and be redeemed by it," confesses his guilt, and begins, at the end of the novel, to experience the reality of Sonya's promise: "God will send you life again."[4]

Tolstoy

Although Dostoyevsky and Leo Tolstoy (1828–1910) were contemporaries, they never met. Moreover, Dostoyevsky, who was of the middle class, wrote about that class, and also about the poor; whereas Count Tolstoy wrote largely about his own class, the aristocracy, and their serfs. Both were passionate seekers after religious truth, but Dostoyevsky's intense awareness of the dark

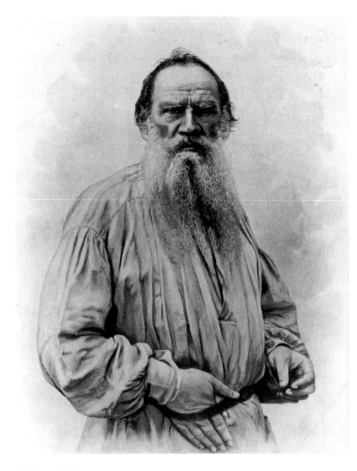

9.5 Leo Tolstoy

and irrational underside of human nature produced a theology that stressed the necessity of divine redemption; Tolstoy, on the other hand, felt that the kingdom of God lay within the reach of human reason, although, for him "reason" included the heart. Thus he rejected the supernatural elements in the Gospels—for example, the incarnation and atonement for sin—but dedicated himself to the personal and social realization of his conception of the ideals of the Sermon on the Mount (Matthew 5–7). Tolstoy's brother once told him that he had buried, in the woods near their house, a green stick containing the secret of universal love. Tolstoy spent most of his life in search of that mythical stick but never found it. His very death reveals this frustrated search, for he died (at 82) in the house of the stationmaster at Astopovo, having slipped away from his home and wife in the hope of discovering in solitude the peace that had always eluded him. Ironically, because of his fame, Tolstoy's dying attracted hordes of his disciples and news people, even including a movie camera. Appropriately, his last audible words were, "To seek, always to seek."

Tolstoy's early education was provided by tutors. He attended the University of Kazan, but never completed his

degree. Somewhat later, he enlisted in the army and served in the Caucasus, an experience reflected in *The Cossacks*, completed in 1854 but not published until 1862. He also served in the Crimean War. Thus his knowledge of army life and military tactics, so apparent in *War and Peace*, is not merely that of an armchair soldier. His *Sevastopol* (1855) also provides a realistic portrayal of war, in this case the defense of Sevastopol in the Crimean War. Earlier (1852), he had written the semi-autobiographical *Childhood*. These two works established Tolstoy's literary reputation.

After his military service, Tolstoy traveled intermittently in Western Europe, studying pedagogical methods. In the process he learned to distrust Western materialism even more than previously, and, like Dostoyevsky, he rejected the idea that Russia's salvation lay in imitating the West. Upon his return to his family estate, he set up a school for his peasants based on Rousseau's idea that the natural man—in this case the Russian serf—leads a life that is morally and intellectually superior to that of the sophisticated and educated. Tolstoy's idealistic view of peasant life was to remain a profound influence in his own life and work.

In 1862 Tolstoy married the much-younger Sophie Behrs (he was 34 and she was 18), who proved to be immensely helpful to him in his writing—for example, in copying and recopying his lengthy manuscripts—as well as bearing his 13 children. (Later, ironically, Tolstoy came to the conclusion that the chaste life is the ideal state.) The marriage was often rocky, largely because Sophie could not identify with the rigorous ideals which her husband pursued, especially in his later years—a pursuit that made him seem to be more concerned with personal peace of mind than with the needs and interests of his family. In the 15 years following his marriage Tolstoy wrote two of his three major novels, *War and Peace* (1862–1869) and *Anna Karenina* (1878).

War and Peace is an epic of Russian family life, especially that of the aristocracy, in the early nineteenth century, set against the background of the Napoleonic wars—hence, his mingled themes of war and peace. Although this gigantic novel may at first seem episodic, a coherent panoramic view of Russian life in that era eventually emerges from the multitudinous details and episodes with which Tolstoy builds his story. He also develops a philosophy of history, treated at length in the latter part, in which he rejects Nietzsche's idea that history is made by great men. On the contrary, he argues, history is made by forces, natural and supernatural, that lie beyond human control. Thus the Russian general Kutuzov was a greater man than Napoleon because, in retreating, he allowed himself to be an instrument of those forces, rather than attempting to manipulate them, as Napoleon did when he pushed ever more deeply into Russia, to be ultimately defeated by the land itself.

Anna Karenina, which is much more limited in scale than *War and Peace*, is the story of a woman who seeks to defy the conventional mores of her society and her own moral standards, and is, as a result, destroyed. Bound by a loveless marriage to Karenin, a government official, Anna falls in love with the dashing Alexei Vronsky. At first she resists her passion, but finally succumbs. She is unable to obtain a divorce from her husband, so she chooses to live with Vronsky out of wedlock. Anna's society tolerates, in some cases even encourages, discreet adultery, but not such open practice of it. Thus it rejects her. The relationship of Vronsky and Anna cannot sustain itself against the pressures of society, and eventually it sours. Anna becomes increasingly distraught and querulous, resorts to morphine, and finally commits suicide by throwing herself under the wheels of a train.

Tolstoy experienced a spiritual crisis not long after he completed *Anna Karenina*. *My Confession* (1879), often compared with St. Augustine's *Confessions* (see page 241), tells the story of his transformation. He suddenly found himself overwhelmed by the realization that he must ultimately die. So depressed was he by this awareness that he contemplated suicide to escape his anguish. Out of this suffering he began his search for meaning, a search that focused on the Russian peasants and the New Testament—especially the Sermon on the Mount—stripped of its supernatural elements. In the peasants he saw a natural acceptance of the rhythms of human existence, including death itself, which resulted from implicit faith in God. In the Sermon on the Mount he discovered the ethical principles that should govern human conduct.

The remainder of his life was given over to a lonely and often frustrating pursuit of these ideals. He dressed like the peasants and worked with them in the fields, rejected the state and its institutions as based on force—indeed, he rejected all forms of violence—and preached universal love. His rejection of wealth and of any art that lacked moral purpose led to his attempts to rid himself of property and royalties. Sophie balked at this, however; so he gave her the copyright of his earlier writings and made the numerous religious writings that followed his conversion available to all who wished to publish them. The royalties for his last major novel, *Resurrection* (1899), he donated to the Dukhobors, a Russian sect that objected to military service, to enable them to emigrate to Canada. Appropriately titled, this novel tells the story of the spiritual rebirth of Prince Nekhludov. He seduces a young girl, then later realizes that he is responsible for the life of prostitution into

which she has drifted. Like Tolstoy, he discovers the key to his salvation in the teachings of the Sermon on the Mount.

Of the numerous short stories and novellas written by Tolstoy, the best known is *The Death of Ivan Ilych* (1886), written after his conversion experience. This is the story of a man who, like the author himself, is compelled to seek the meaning of life because he becomes fully aware that he is sentenced to death.

It is clear that Tolstoy intends to indict the shallow concerns of the middle class from the opening statement of the flashback to Ilych's life: "Ivan Ilych's life had been most simple and most ordinary and therefore most terrible."[5] "Simple" and "ordinary" here refer to Ilych's almost unquestioning conformity to the expectations of his class. In the narrative that follows it becomes evident that, with the exception of his childhood and youth, Ilych, a successful member of the Court of Justice, has lived a life of opportunism, governed by the superficial values of a superficial society. The terrible irony of Ilych's life is captured in the detail that after his graduation from law school he hung a medallion from his watch chain enscribed with the words *respice finem* ("Provide for the end"). Ilych's failure to make such provision becomes apparent after the illness that strikes him down at the high point of his life, when he has achieved professional success and is happily decorating a new house.

In the midst of the suffering that encroaches ever more upon his existence, Ilych is driven to ask the question, "What is it all for?" But he cannot answer because he insists on justifying his life. Not long before his death, he briefly entertains the possibility that he has not lived as he should. But then he asks, "How could that be, when I did everything properly?" Tolstoy comments that he then "immediately dismissed from his mind this, the sole solution of all the riddles of life and death, as something quite impossible" (p. 295). Thus Tolstoy points up the profound significance of Ilych's self-questioning about the meaning of life.

Finally, as Ilych continues to question his life, a major breakthrough occurs, and he begins to consider seriously the possibility that his life has been wrong; thus he is forced to confront the alternative, "What then?" Now he reviews his life in a very different manner. As he contemplates the deceptive and superficial behavior of his family, his footman, and the doctor, he sees himself—"all that for which he had lived—and saw clearly that it was not real at all, but a terrible and huge deception which had hidden both life and death. This consciousness intensified his physical suffering tenfold" (p. 299).

But in these last days of his life a profound transformation takes place in Ivan Ilych—a transformation carefully delineated by the author. Up to this point Tolstoy has indicted Ilych for his selfish opportunism and shallow living. He now shows how Ilych is compelled to question his life radically because of the onrush of death—a questioning that ultimately leads him to reject the values by which he has lived. Stripped of his defenses, he now stands in naked confrontation with the event that will mark the end of all possibilities for change.

At this point Tolstoy produces the image of the "black sack" into which Ilych imagines he is being forced. This "sack" is quite clearly a symbol for the womb. Ilych is thus struggling to be born—or reborn. But he "was hindered from getting into the black sack by his conviction that his life had been a good one" (p. 301). He could not move forward through the sack, Tolstoy tells us, because he was held fast by self-justification.

But Tolstoy develops the "sack" image further. As Ilych struggles against being thrust into the sack, he once more comes to the conclusion that his life was not right. Then he asks, "But what *is* the right thing?" We are told that Ilych's question comes "at the end of the third day, two hours before his death." At that moment his young son Vasya approaches Ilych's bedside, and the father's hand falls on the boy's head. Vasya takes hold of his father's hand and begins to cry. "At that very moment Ivan Ilych fell through and caught sight of the light, and it was revealed to him that though his life had not been what it should have been, this could still be rectified." Significantly, Vasya is the only person who, according to Ilych, "understood and pitied him," with the exception of Gerasim, the peasant youth whose genuine compassion, expressed in practical acts of kindness and understanding, has comforted Ilych in his darkest hours. Thus the compassion of Vasya and Gerasim is Tolstoy's answer to Ilych's question. The "right thing" is compassion and love for the sufferer, especially when the sufferer is not lovable.

For the first time, now, Ilych becomes sensitive to the feelings of others and places their well-being before his own. He reflects on the suffering he is causing his wife and son and wants to tell them that it will be better for them when he dies, but he lacks the strength. His repentance for his failures is expressed in his attempt to say, "forgive me"—words that he cannot articulate, so that he actually says "forego." But he waves his hand, as if to say that this failure is unimportant, for "He whose understanding mattered would understand."

At this point the pace quickens: "... suddenly it grew clear to him that what had been oppressing him and would not leave him was all dropping away at once from two sides, from ten sides, and from all sides. He was sorry for them, he must act so as not to hurt them: release them and free himself from these sufferings. 'How good and simple,' he thought." Thus death is no longer an ominous darkness that poses a grim and inescapable threat to all human hopes but a release from suffering. "He sought his former accustomed fear of death and did not find it." Finally it appears that he is gone, and someone says, "It is finished!" But Ivan Ilych hears these words and repeats them, adding, "Death is finished.... It is no more!" (p. 362).

The Death of Ivan Ilych is the story of an ordinary man (one might say Everyman) who, in confronting death for the first time, is also forced for the first time to confront himself. Thus he is driven to ask, "Who am I? What has been the meaning of my life?" Tolstoy's own confrontation in mid-life with the inevitability of death compelled him to ask the same questions. However, he seems never to have arrived at that sense of absolute peace and certainty experienced by his fictional character in the last moments of his earthly existence.

Realism in Art

The term "Realism" refers to a particular movement in the visual arts that flourished in the mid-nineteenth century; by contrast, "realism" refers to a tendency in art to depict things as they appear in life, a tendency that goes back to the Stone Age and has been practiced to a greater or lesser extent up to the present time.

The impulse on the part of artists to fashion images resembling things in the visible world has a long history. Recall the lifelike animals recorded on cave walls tens of thousands of years ago by Ice-Age artists (see Chapter 1), the natural-looking, though idealized, men and women carved by Polykleitos and Phidias more than 2400 years ago (see Chapter 2), the development of linear perspective by Alberti and Brunelleschi some 500 years ago (see Chapter 3), and the painstakingly detailed representations of objects painted by Jan van Eyck at about the same time (see Chapter 7). Up until the end of the nineteenth century, philosophers of art in the West generally accepted the *mimesis*, or imitation, theory of art. Plato, the original author of that theory, explains in *The Republic* that the art of painting is the imitation of things as they *appear*, not as they are. The average person today still expects pictures and sculptures to resemble the physical world, at least to a degree—despite the fact that nineteenth- and twentieth-century philosophies of art dispute that notion.

Imitation has not always been the main impulse in art. In many cultures the purpose of sculpture and painting was not to duplicate appearances but to symbolize the known or unknown—as in ancient Egypt, where images were strictly regulated by religious-artistic convention, and Early Christian, Byzantine, and medieval cultures, in which artists depicted the world of God, not man. In the twentieth century, we see the prevalence of abstract art, which is not intended to imitate anything.

It should also be pointed out that realism in art is a relative concept; the degree to which an art style is perceived as realistic depends on who is looking at it. For example, Giotto's contemporaries in fourteenth-century Europe considered his paintings extremely lifelike, the very latest thing in representing appearances (Fig. 7.46). But to the eyes of, say, seventeenth-century Europeans, his paintings did not seem at all realistic. Thus the ways in which images are perceived, as well as the desire to pursue realism in art (or not to pursue it), have varied over time.

In its strictest sense Realism demands more of a work of art than that of just imitating appearances. It also means, at least theoretically, a complete absence of interpretation on the part of the artist. Therefore it is almost easier to explain what a picture should *not* have, that is: *no* distortion of what the eye naturally sees; *no* obvious use of design principles or other devices to give a picture harmony, unity, or drama; *no* use of imaginary subject matter; and *no* glorifying or sentimentalizing of whatever subject matter is used. Romanticism, or any kind of celebration of feeling, is taboo. These conditions were most closely adhered to in the nineteenth century, but it would be remiss not to point out examples of realism that occurred earlier.

Realism in Seventeenth-Century Painting

As we have seen, the theories and techniques of spatial depth—shading, foreshortening, linear perspective—were introduced by Italian artists in the fifteenth century (see Chapter 3), at the same time that Flemish painters were establishing the virtues of disciplined observation and meticulous detail (see Chapter 7). By the seventeenth century, the lessons of realism had been so thoroughly learned that Europe's painters—men like Caravaggio, Rubens, and Rembrandt—could represent even the spiritual world. Although they often used their astonishing

gifts to depict imaginary subjects—gods, angels, saints, and so forth—they also used them to depict mundane subjects. It seems, therefore, that an analysis of realism, even in the nineteenth-century sense, should start with painting of this period.

Two painters, the Spaniard Diego Velázquez (1599–1664) and the Dutchman Jan Vermeer (1632–1675), were particularly skilled in the treatment of commonplace subjects. Velázquez is best known as a royal painter, but before being appointed to that post he often painted Spanish peasants—sometimes incorporated into allegories with Greek gods, sometimes as independent subjects, as in *The Water Carrier of Seville* (Fig. 9.6). A simple scene, *The Water Carrier* shows a street vendor and two boys, one reaching for a glass and the other, in the shadows, drinking from a glass. As a quiet moment, captured for eternity, it is reminiscent of Rembrandt's *The Return of the Prodigal Son* (Fig. 8.25). The sense of permanence is owing to the triangular design—not only in the vendor's body but in the larger triangle formed by him, the boys, and the objects. Within that triangle, the

9.6 DIEGO VELAZQUEZ
The Water Carrier of Seville, c. 1619
Oil on canvas, $41\frac{1}{2} \times 31\frac{1}{2}$ ins (105.5×80 cm)
Wellington Museum, London (Crown copyright reserved)

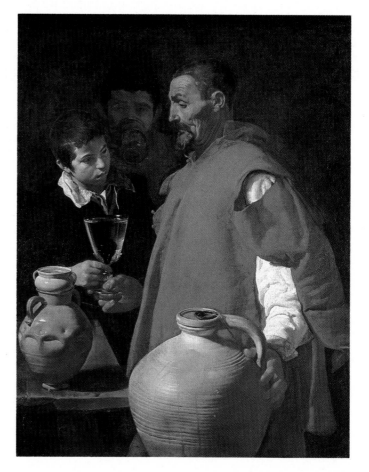

9.7 Jan Vermeer
Young Woman with a Water Jug,
c. 1665
Oil on canvas, 18 × 16 ins
(45.7 × 40.6 cm)
Metropolitan Museum, New
York

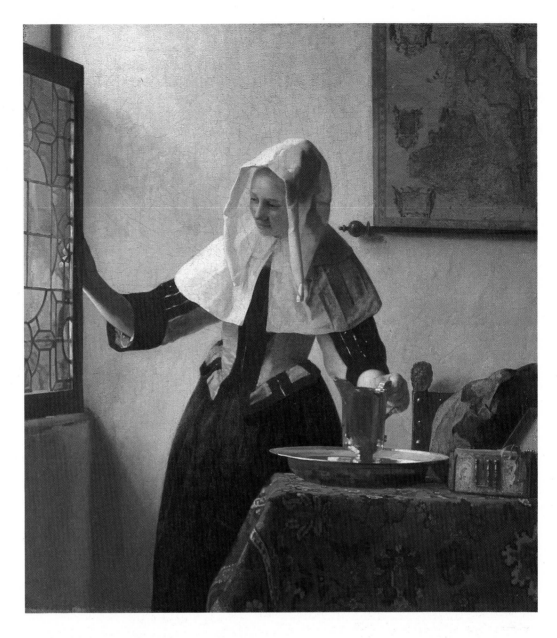

forms of the vendor and boys are echoed in the solid forms of the earthenware jugs. The use of chiaroscuro not only clarifies the forms but invests them with weight and tangibility. Thus, although the setting is humble, and though it is rendered with optical objectivity, it is also endowed with the dignity that might be accorded a sacred rite.

Young Woman with a Water Jug (Fig. **9.7**), by Vermeer is also about water, and also has a reverent quality, though in this case the artist has portrayed a middle-class woman in an affluent Delft home. A generation younger than Rembrandt, Vermeer is sometimes listed among the "little Dutch masters," mid-seventeenth-century painters who specialized in intensely realistic still lifes and interior scenes. They shared with their Flemish predecessor, Van Eyck, a fascination for detail, but unlike him they

generally did not paint religious subjects. Vermeer, the most highly regarded of this group, could observe and reproduce the subtleties of optical experience as well as the best of them, but he also imbued his scenes with a quiet mystery which transcends mere optical realism.

The key, again, is light. Like other artists of his time, Vermeer was a master of light, but instead of using chiaroscuro, like Rembrandt or Caravaggio, for example, he bathed his interiors in a soft, diffused light, often coming from an open window. Close examination of his canvases reveals an unusual awareness of the effects of back-lighting—surfaces of objects both illuminating and reflecting other objects. At times Vermeer used a forerunner of photography: the *camera obscura*—a darkened room with a pinhole through which light passed to project an image onto the opposite wall. The image, like that on a photographic film, is a perfect replica (though upside-down) of the actual scene on the other side of the pinhole. There is little reason to believe that Vermeer based entire pictures on camera-obscura images, but his own essays in realism and the effects of light were informed by them. Scientific objectivity, faithful observation, careful translation of optical experience, and, no doubt, patience were his guiding principles.

Nineteenth-Century Realism

In the mid-nineteenth century art consisted mostly of pompous historical subjects, allegories, idealized landscapes, and genre scenes—all painted with greater or lesser degrees of optical realism and all having romantic overtones, to a greater or lesser extent. Much of this art has been dubbed "academic," a word that, in an artistic context, means conservative, overly committed to rules, and derivative. Not all mid-nineteenth-century paintings were academic, however; and one that definitely was not appeared in the Paris Salon of 1850.

Courbet

To many of those who saw it, *Burial at Ornans* (Fig. **9.8**) by Gustave Courbet (1819–1877) was too coarse to be considered art. The subject—townspeople gathered around a grave—was lacking in drama and moral uplift. Courbet had neither cast it as an allegory nor shown the people as noble toilers of the soil; he had portrayed it matter-of-factly, without flattery or condescension. By the standards of 1850 the style, too, was coarse. Because Courbet often applied paint with a palette knife instead of brushes, the surface of *Burial* is thick and rough. Finally, the composition was deemed coarse. Besides being a picture of a graveside rite, *Burial* is a group portrait of Courbet's friends, the townspeople of Ornans. Rather than plan the composition, the artist added their portraits as each man or woman sat for him, on a first-come, first-served basis—a strategy that accounts not only for the randomness of the composition, but for the confusion of the group's costumes, positions, and gestures.

Burial is no more realistic in the optical sense than Vermeer's *Young Woman with a Water Jug*—perhaps even less so. What sets it apart from that work and all previous work is its uncompromising objectivity. Not only was the subject taken from ordinary life; the artist defied traditional conventions of style and composition and, supposedly, made no attempt to sentimentalize, ennoble, or even interpret the subject. Theoretically, the painting is a straightforward portrayal of real life. And how did the 1850 public react? They were divided: most despised it, calling it grotesque and sacreligious, but some praised it as courageous and "a harbinger of a new era." In either case

9.8 GUSTAVE COURBET
Burial at Ornans, 1849
Oil on canvas, 10 ft 3 ins × 21 ft 9 ins (3.14 × 6.63 m)
Louvre, Paris

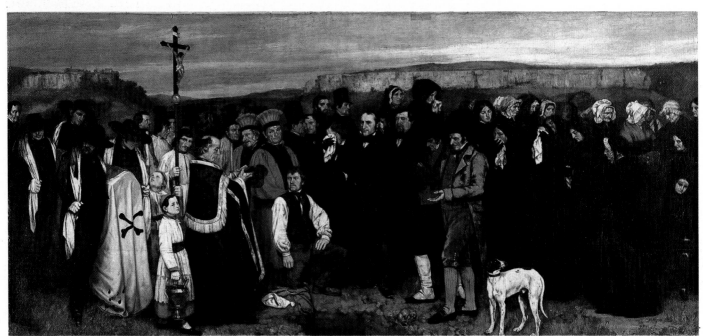

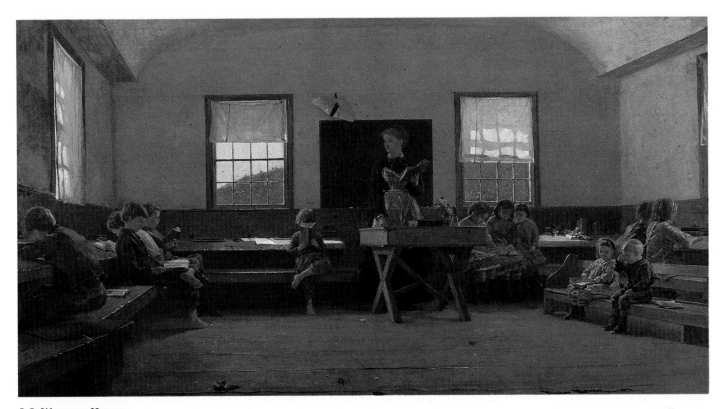

9.9 WINSLOW HOMER
The Country School, 1871
Oil on canvas, $21\frac{3}{8} \times 38\frac{3}{8}$ ins (214×279 cm)
St. Louis Art Museum

the reaction was extreme.

Burial at Ornans was completed in 1849, not long after the workers' revolution of 1848, an ugly class war fought mainly in the streets of Paris. Most of Courbet's critics identified the painting with these radical stirrings and accused the artist of bringing politics into art. Meanwhile a minority, mostly liberals and radicals, approved of it for the same reason. Pierre Proudhon, a French socialist and political writer, who read political meanings in all of Courbet's work, supported his art and sought to influence his politics. So for a time, Realism, despite its commitment to objectivity, had a political agenda. In 1851 Courbet wrote, "I am not only a socialist, but also a democrat and a republican, in a word, a partisan of revolution and, above all, a realist, that is, the sincere friend of the real truth."[6]

But as the fear of class uprising subsided, and the aversion to doctrinaire Realism softened, Courbet began to receive support from conservative middle-class patrons as well as from radicals. He reciprocated by making some paintings to please, rather than offend, these patrons. Furthermore, his politics often turned out to be more words than deeds. And just as Courbet may not have been the radical that he (and Proudhon) pretended that he was,

he was also not an absolute Realist. Many of his figure studies and still lifes are as conservative as those of the most staid academician. Sentimental about people and nature, Courbet even allowed Romantic attitudes to creep into his portraits and landscapes. Still, his place in art history, as the initiator not only of the Realist movement but also of the tradition of the artist as rebel, is assured.

Winslow Homer

The Realistic movement, minus the ideological overtones, soon spread to the United States. *The Country School*, by Winslow Homer (1836–1910), was not intended to incite revolution, or even to make a political point (Fig. **9.9**). Far from being a revolutionary, Homer was proud of his membership in the middle class. An illustrator for *Harpers Weekly* before becoming a serious painter, he wore conservative clothes and enjoyed city life. Yet the majority of his paintings are about country life. And like Courbet, Homer depicted that life without embellishment or condescension.

The setting of *The Country School* is as prosaic as a school lunch. Spartan simplicity is evident in its empty walls—

relieved only by the presence of a slate board and plain windows—and in the broad expanse of wooden floor. Children, some barefoot, are seated randomly around the room—one here, three there, and so forth—on furniture pushed against the walls, quietly reading. Like the moments captured in *The Water Carrier of Seville* and *Young Woman with a Water Jug*, this scene is devoid of story-telling implications. No particular actions on the part of the children or the teacher are anticipated. Framed by the slate board, the young teacher is the central figure—both visually and symbolically—and the psychological key to the work. An ambiguous image, she is neither stern nor friendly, defying the stereotypes of "schoolmarm" and nineteenth-century education. More than anything else her image seems, paradoxically, to express loneliness.

Because it lacks sentimentality, Homer's work is an excellent source for those interested in how America and Americans actually looked in the nineteenth century. The presence of nostalgia, if any, is due not to Homer, but to our own conceptions (or misconceptions) of that time. His work exemplifies all the tendencies of Realism, particularly the qualities of frankness and emotional detachment. Yet, because American art and artists were not highly respected in Europe, Homer was not recognized as a member of the Realist movement. Like Courbet, he had detractors among his own countrymen, but Homer's were in the minority. The author Henry James (1843–1916), who was familiar with European art and the grand manner, accused Homer's art of having too many "barren plank fences," "freckled, straight-haired Yankee urchins," and "flat-breasted maidens," yet confessed that "there is nevertheless something one likes about him." To most Americans it was precisely these homely subjects

9.10 EDOUARD MANET *Le Déjeuner sur l'Herbe*, 1863
Oil on canvas, 84 × 106 ins (214 × 279 cm), Louvre, Paris

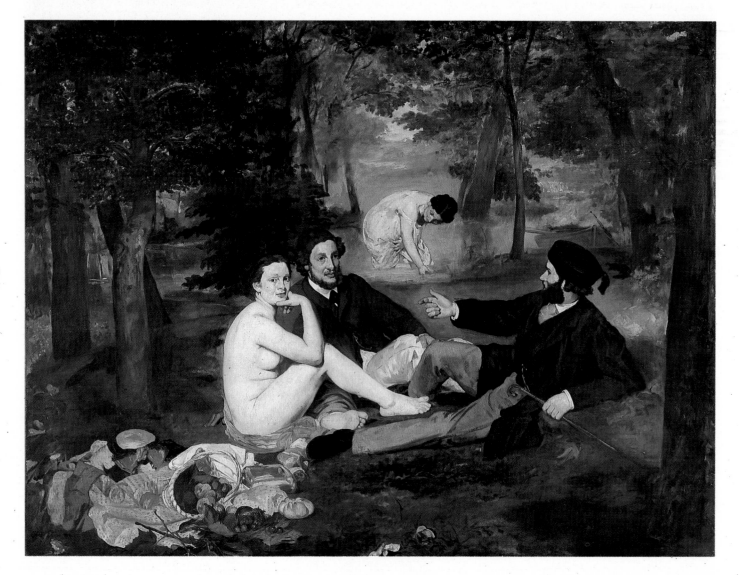

that made Homer's pictures appealing.

To summarize: nineteenth-century Realism was not a new phenomenon in all respects; realism, with a small "r," had been an important pursuit in Western art since the Renaissance. But some nineteenth-century artists carried the pursuit further. A reaction against Romanticism, Realism was intellectually related to the scientism and materialism of its time. In addition, it was a serious attempt to honor the injunction of French critic Charles Baudelaire: to express the "heroism of modern life."

By and large, the art of both Courbet and Homer satisfies the strict conditions demanded of Realist painting: optical realism, random composition, and truth to life. In addition to the examples shown here, Courbet produced some rather traditional portraits, nudes, still lifes, and landscapes. In addition to rural America, Homer specialized in hunting scenes and sea adventures. Curiously, neither artist touched on a very important aspect of their time: the city and its people.

Manet

It was left to Édouard Manet (1832–1883), Courbet's heir in the Realism movement, to crystallize an image of modern urban life. To some degree all art reflects its time; but some works manage to evoke the spirit of an age more than others. For example, a whole world of prosperous tranquility is captured in a Vermeer painting, though our awareness of this world is not describable in words—as if it exists at a deeper, more meaningful, level of consciousness. This sort of awareness is often conveyed by a painting of Manet's; however, in this case, it expresses the spirit of the upper middle classes of Paris, probably the liveliest city of the nineteenth century.

Manet submitted *Le Déjeuner sur l'Herbe* (Luncheon on the Grass) (Fig. 9.10) to the Paris Salon of 1863. Held annually, these exhibitions were the principal vehicle of exposure for professional artists in France. Reputations depended on the success of getting works into the annual Salon. Manet's painting was turned down. But so many works were rejected that year that an alternate show was opened for rejected works—called, appropriately, the "*Salon des Refusés.*" There, Manet's work was in a position to be seen by the public. Indeed, it received more attention than Manet bargained for. *Le Déjeuner sur l'Herbe* caused a scandal.

Female nudity, as we know, had been acceptable in European art since the time of Botticelli (Fig. 3.20). In the mid-nineteenth century it continued to be acceptable, even popular—despite the fact that this was during the Victorian age, when even words like "leg" were taboo in polite British and American society. Yet, as long as it was

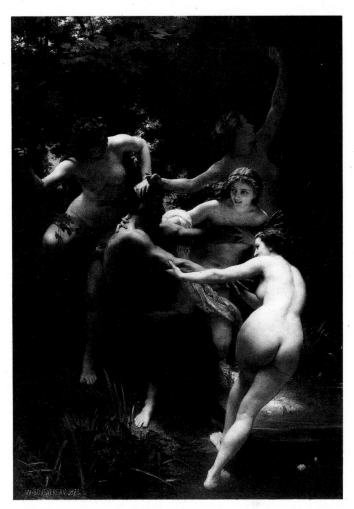

9.11 GUILLAUME ADOLPHE BOUGEREAU
Nymphs and Satyr, 1873
Oil on canvas, $102\frac{3}{8} \times 70\frac{7}{8}$ ins (260 × 180 cm)
Sterling and Francine Clark Institute, Williamstown, MA.

cast in terms of myth or allegory, even the most voyeuristic kind of nudity was approved in art (Fig. 9.11). *Déjeuner*, however, is neither a classical fable nor a sermon on life. The female figures are not Greek goddesses in a fairytale setting, but two young women—one loosely clothed and the other completely naked—in a contemporary setting, accompanied by two smartly dressed young men. Such behavior was considered indecent; and therefore, according to mid-nineteenth-century standards, the picture was also indecent.

Ironically, the motif of the central group was appropriated by Manet from a sixteenth-century print based on a classical myth; the figures of the two compositions share almost identical postures and gestures (Fig. 9.12). The lighting of Manet's group is indebted to Velázquez, whose works Manet admired and studied. The high contrasts of light and dark—a clustering of light tones in a single area, such as the naked woman's body, set against a clustering

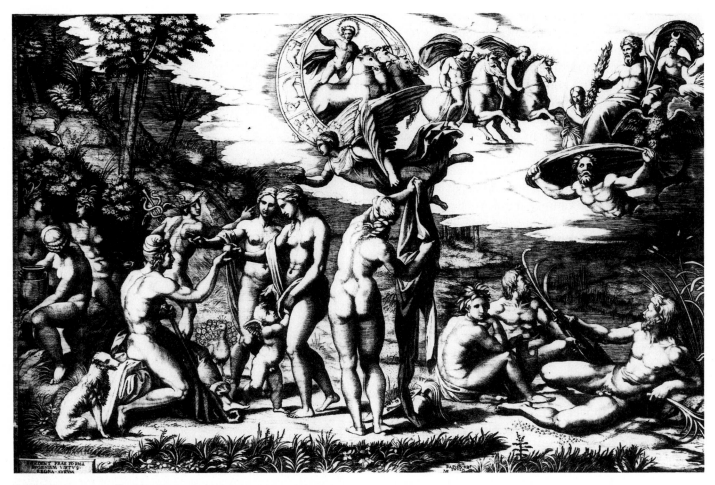

9.12 MARCANTONIO RAIMONDI
The Judgement of Paris, c. 1520, after Raphael
Engraving.

of dark tones in another area, such as the men's coats and the forest—resemble those of the seventeenth-century master. Notwithstanding this homage to tradition—of which the 1863 critics were probably unaware—*Le Déjeuner sur l'Herbe* was regarded as revolutionary. It was condemned for its style as well as its supposed moral indecency. The composition was perceived as loosely organized. (Indeed, to the extent that discontinuity exists between the foreground and background, the critics were probably correct.) What drew the most criticism, in the aesthetic area, was the flattening of forms—particularly in the nude—which was due to Manet's method of shading (or lack thereof). In traditional painting, both bodies and objects were carefully modeled with gradations of light and dark to make them appear soft and sculptural. Manet's, on the other hand, appear to reside in the glare of a noonday sun or a flashbulb. Even Courbet complained of this effect, saying that it made Manet's paintings look like playing cards.

The general public, however, was probably most offended by the casual attitudes of the people: the gentlemen visiting nonchalantly beside a naked demimondaine (a woman of easy morals) who looks casually and shamelessly at the viewer. In the final analysis, *Le Déjeuner sur l'Herbe* was too novel. The artist had taken too many liberties with subject matter, composition, and technique. He had offended contemporary sensibilities by violating the traditional relationship between art and good taste, confronting the public for the first time with a painting that portrayed an aspect of life that they preferred to ignore.

Impressionism: Monet

Manet's troubles with critics did not end with the Salon des Refusés but continued through most of his career. On the other hand, he enjoyed the support of writers such as Émile Zola, and the following of a small coterie of progressive artists. Among the latter was Claude Monet (1840–1926), who was influenced by Manet and was, for a time, his close associate. Like Manet, Monet favored contemporary subject matter, rendered in relatively flat forms and bright colors. But Monet went beyond Manet to pioneer an original style called *Impressionism*.

La Grenouillère ("Frog Pond"), the name of a popular restaurant that literally floated on the Seine, is also the name of Monet's painting of that restaurant, a good example of Impressionism (Fig. **9.13**). The restaurant itself is on the right, connected by a walkway to a dock in the middle of the rippling water, while boats for rent are in the foreground. Nothing in the scene is outlined in the conventional sense, for the entire canvas was painted with small strokes of bright color. In this regard nothing is given priority, not even people. At close range, everything consists of daubs of color. Viewed at a greater distance the daubs coalesce to form discrete images: men in frock coats, women in gowns, women in bathing costume—some standing, some sitting—as well as trees, dock, boats, and water (although there is some lack of precision in these things). In terms of optical realism, this loss of precision is more than offset by the gain in brilliance, the experience of being a part of a sunlit environment. The flickering reflection of the ripples is especially effective.

Monet's style is the result of a combination of three factors: painting out-of-doors, broken color, and science. Landscapes, a popular category of art for centuries, were traditionally painted in studios, not on the site. Among the reasons for this practice was the difficulty of carrying jars of paint to and from a location. The nineteenth-century innovation of packaging oil paint in tubes came just in

9.13 Claude Monet
La Grenouillère, 1869
Oil on canvas, 29½ × 39¼ ins (74.9 × 99.7 cm)
Metropolitan Museum, New York, H.O. Havermeyer Collection

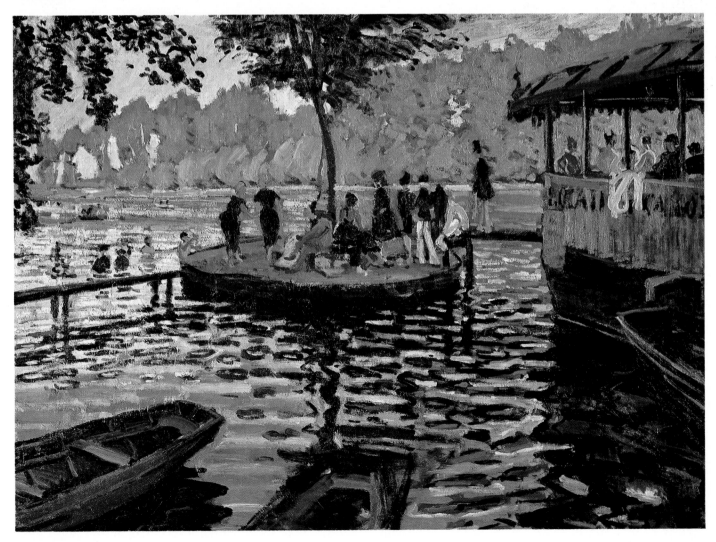

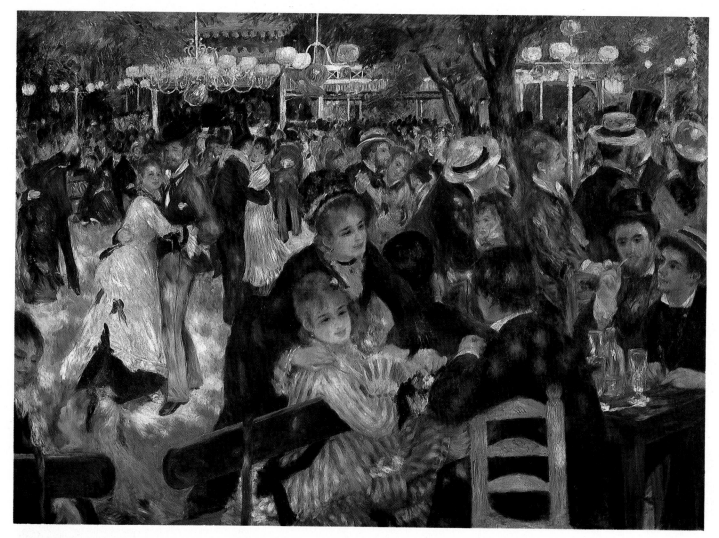

9.14 AUGUSTE RENOIR
Le Moulin de la Galette, 1876
Oil on canvas, $51\frac{1}{2} \times 69$ ins (131×175 cm)
Louvre, Paris

time for Monet. The advantage of tubes notwithstanding, painting outdoors requires the artist to work quickly; nature does not sit still for long. The technique of broken color was learned from Constable through Delacroix (see Chapter 5). When combined with working outdoors, it was carried to limits far beyond those envisioned by either of these Romantic artists. In Monet's hands broken color was further informed by scientific theories: the fact that colors leave after-images and that, therefore, an optically mixed green (perceived in adjacent strokes of blue and yellow) is, for example, more visually active than a physically mixed green. In addition Monet was aware that the local color of an object is modified by the quality and quantity of light in which it is seen; and that shadows are modified by the objects they overlay, by reflection, and

other conditions. At times Monet applied this knowledge in rather systematic ways by painting a single subject (such as Rouen Cathedral—see below) many times under varying conditions of light and atmosphere.

In the 1870s and '80s, the Impressionist movement, a small group of artists led by Monet, was at its peak. To a greater or lesser extent, the other artists reflected his approach. In *Le Moulin de la Galette*, Auguste Renoir, who made the most genial paintings of all, depicts an open-air dance in scintillating, luminous colors (Fig. **9.14**). Despite the obvious charm today of such pictures, Impressionism was vilified by critics for a number of years; indeed, the name was invented by a journalist as a term of derision. Because their works were barred from the official salons, Impressionists sponsored their own shows until the

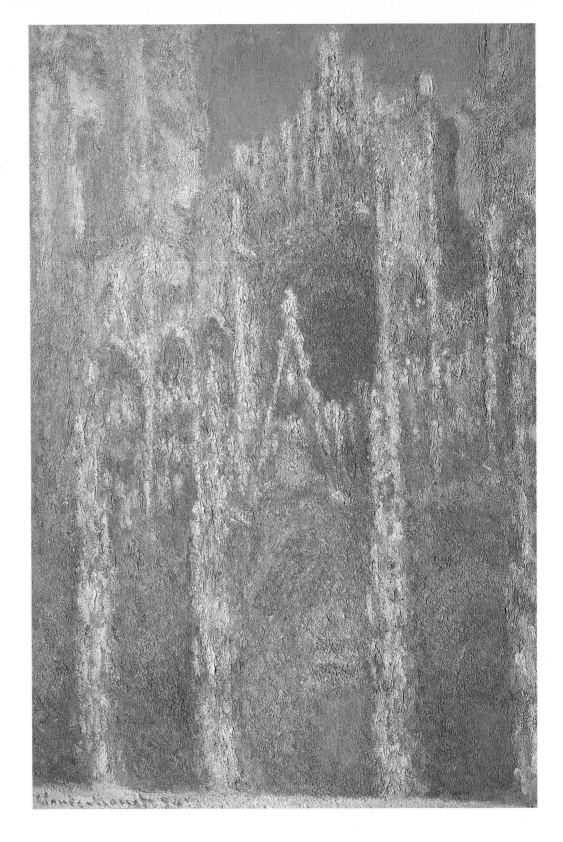

9.15 CLAUDE MONET
Rouen Cathedral, in Full Sunlight, 1894
Oil on canvas, $89\frac{1}{2} \times 25$ ins
$(100.5 \times 66.2$ cm$)$
Juliana Cheney Edwards
Collection, Courtesy Museum of
Fine Arts, Boston

1880s. However in the 1890s the movement had gained the acceptance of the official art world, and shortly thereafter of the general public.

The most exemplary works of the style, those that embody most thoroughly the principles associated with Impressionism, were painted by Monet himself. Above all, the style is noted for its freshness, a quality owing mainly to the spontaneous effects of making a painting on a site in just minutes. This freshness has not deteriorated over the years. Today Impressionism is the most popular of all schools of art. The brilliant, sunlit colors have not lost their physical appeal, nor the subjects their vicarious appeal; in these paintings we relive what seems a blithe past, a world of leisure—dancing, country strolls,

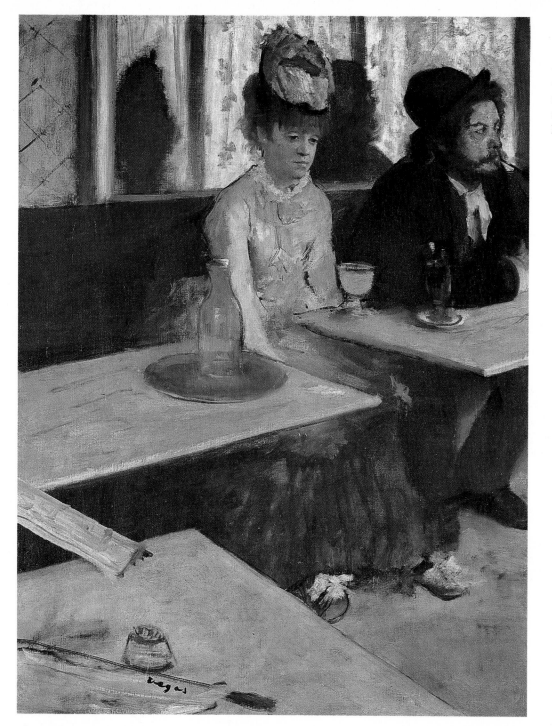

9.16 EDGAR DEGAS
The Glass of Absinthe, 1876
Oil on canvas, 36 × 27 ins
(91.5 × 68 cm)
Louvre, Paris

weekend outings—enjoyed by the French middle class. It is also a world without idealism, romanticism, religious connotations, or even social consciousness. In Monet's hands, this world is also impersonal. Whereas Manet was a student of human nature (though most of his humans display very little overt emotion), Monet was a student of the world of vision—the raw materials of light and color. His people, as in *La Grenouillère*, are part of the landscape—"humanscapes" as they are sometimes called. His paintings represent the same renunciation of melodrama, extremes, and moralizing that we find in Flaubert's *Madame Bovary*.

In fact, Rouen Cathedral, the scene of Léon's decision to seduce Emma, served as the subject of a series of paintings executed by Monet in the 1890s. He was interested in showing how the cathedral's appearance changed according to the time of day, "to reveal no more of reality than the shifting flux of appearances." In *Rouen Cathedral in Full Sunlight* (Fig. **9.15**), for example, the stone edifice seems to be little more than a tissue of reflected colors. Thus, Monet displays not only emotional detachment but also "color detachment." Color, the raw material of appearances, has become an independent entity. Such is the final destination of optical realism. It is also the beginning of an anti-realism in which forms—colors, lines, shapes, and textures—begin to have a life of their own, independent of the subject. But that is a story for the next chapter.

Degas

Edgar Degas (1834–1917) often captured in his own pictures the transient effects of candid photography. But just as often, these effects were based on a design strategy having nothing to do with photography. Like many other progressive artists of the 1880s, Degas was an admirer of Japanese woodcuts, and he assimilated their characteristics into his own work. The off-center composition, empty spaces, diagonals, and high eye level—all Japanese devices—can be seen in *The Glass of Absinthe* (Fig. **9.16**). These devices create not only a deceptive sense of informality but also interesting visual tensions. The man on the right, almost out of the picture himself, leads our attention even further in that direction by his gaze; meanwhile his female companion returns our attention to the scene by staring rather blankly in our direction. Visually, the two are balanced by the starkly geometric planes of two tables on the left.

Degas' works are also interesting because of their insights into human character. Like Manet, he was a student of urban Parisian society, though he depicted it even more dispassionately. His focus was usually on the well-to-do: people who attended ballets, concerts, regattas, and horse races, as opposed to those who, like the forlorn couple sharing a glass of absinthe, frequent cheap cafés. Still, the two occupy the same urban society as the wealthier citizens of Paris, being simply the other side of the same socio-economic coin. They also experienced anomie, a condition of purposelessness and rootlessness shared by many—rich and poor—in modern industrial society.

Our review of nineteenth-century paintings started with Courbet and ended with Degas, and has touched on two movements involving mainly French artists: Realism and Impressionism. One thing uniting all these examples is the secularism of their content. Eager to distance themselves from Romanticism, both Realists and Impressionists avoided even indirect references to either myth or religion. And unlike the Realists, Impressionist artists had no message to convey; they were concerned only to paint the world they knew and enjoyed.

Architecture

The new industrialized society that was emerging in Europe and America in the nineteenth century would inevitably change the landscape—especially the urban landscape. New building types were required: factories, warehouses, railroad stations, department stores, and office buildings. In previous ages architects had concerned themselves mainly with grand public buildings—such as temples, churches, palaces, and theaters—which, apart from their practical functions, had one or more symbolic dimensions, expressing, for example, the power and glory of the state, or the spiritual world, or classical antiquity. Within this large category of buildings, architectural language was adapted freely from one building type to another. We have seen, in Chapter 6, how Early Christian architects adapted the Roman basilica to their first churches. Later, the spires and pointed arches of Gothic churches were used for medieval town halls, which were thus endowed with an aura of quasi-divine authority. Still later, churches would be built in the style of Greek temples, thus implicitly linking the Christian faith with the rational principles of the Enlightenment.

This free adaptation of traditional building styles reached a peak in the nineteenth century. Architects borrowed and mixed styles freely (see Chapter 5), often with success. But when it came to designing the new "temples" of the industrial age, the traditional styles were clearly inappropriate. There might be a rationale for putting a Greek portico on an aristocrat's country house, for example, but it was hard to find one for putting it on a department store. There was, thus, a need for a new architectural language, suitable for new kinds of building.

Frame Construction

At the same time, new technologies were being developed which would, in turn, be instrumental in the development of the new architectural language. Among the most important of these was iron- (and later steel-) frame construction. Up until the nineteenth century, virtually all public buildings, and many houses, too (apart from those in areas where timber was the most plentiful building material), were of the *load-carrying* type; based on construction systems in which walls, columns, buttresses, and so forth, are used to support floors and ceilings. Frame

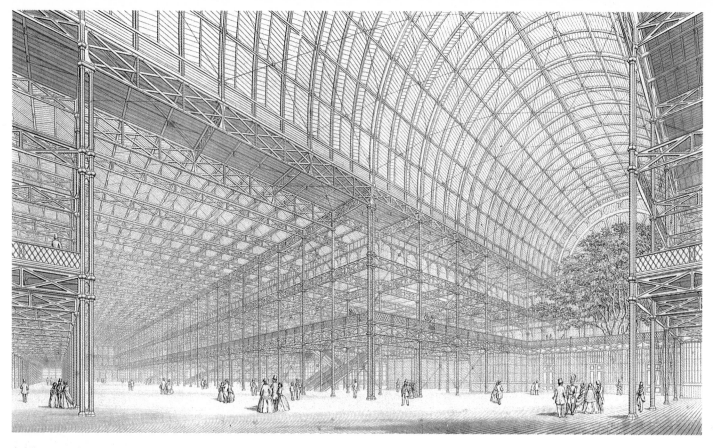

9.17 JOSEPH PAXTON
Interior view of the Crystal Palace, Hyde Park, 1851. From a print by R. Cuff after W. G. Brounger.

construction, on the other hand, is non-load-carrying, since it consists of joining thin, relatively lightweight beams to form a rigid framework like a cage. Walls are added to the framework as needed; since they are non-load-bearing, these walls may be of any material, even glass.

Prior to the nineteenth century, wood houses, such as those in the American colonies, were typically constructed of heavy rough-hewn beams supported by large posts and fireplaces (located either at the center or at the ends of the buildings). The posts and beams were joined by a cumbersome process of fitting tenons into mortices. In the 1830s, balloon-frame houses began to appear on the American frontier. Capitalising on mass-produced nails and pre-cut lumber (two-by-fours, two-by-sixes, etc.), the balloon frame was an early example of non-load-carrying construction. The ancestor of today's wood frame, it was not only quicker to build but stronger than the typical post-and-lintel house made up to that time.

The Crystal Palace

Built to house the Great Exhibition of 1851—the first world's fair—the Crystal Palace was daring even by the standards of subsequent fairs. It was designed by Joseph Paxton (1801–1865), a London engineer, and consisted essentially of a vast framework of iron rods and panes of glass (Fig. 9.17). Despite its enormous size—covering 800,000 square feet (74,000 square meters) of floor—it was erected in less than six months. Individual structural units, planned around the largest standard sheet of glass (at that time only 4 feet [1.22 meters] square), were prefabricated in Birmingham and fitted together on the site in London's Hyde Park. The edifice was the star attraction of the Exhibition, outshining all the new machines and marvelous artifacts displayed beneath its transparent roofs. It acquired the name Crystal Palace from the fairgoers themselves, who were impressed not only by its size but by the radiance of its spaces. Visitors from all parts of Europe came to this cathedral of progress to stroll among the venerated objects of technology, just as, centuries earlier, their ancestors had filed through the pilgrimage churches to view the relics of saints.

Despite the Crystal Palace's success—technologically and visually—it was deemed unworthy of the term architecture by most architects and critics, who believed real architecture was made of stone, not iron pipes and panes of glass. Still, the obvious advantages of frame construction could not be ignored. Others had experimented with it before Paxton, for example, in the construction of train sheds. But Paxton's stunning building dramatized the aesthetic and practical possibilities of frame construction. Apart from pavilions, greenhouses, and train sheds, iron and glass construction had limited applicability; but the principle of the frame itself was here to stay. As the century progressed, it would be used increasingly, for many kinds of structures, from prosaic factories to fanciful ones like the Eiffel Tower (1889). Eventually, it was to become the basis of twentieth-century architecture.

Sullivan and the Chicago School

The next stage in the development of frame construction took place, not in London or Paris, but in Chicago. During the 1890s, when Impressionists were pioneering new methods of painting to describe the pleasures of their city, Chicago builders were pioneering new methods of construction to rebuild their city in the wake of the great fire of 1873. Several factors combined to encourage innovation: opportunities caused by the building boom itself, the high prices of downtown real estate forcing the search for new solutions, the possibilities provided by the new technologies of metal-frame construction and the passenger elevator, and finally, the lack of strong architectural conventions (as existed in Europe) to inhibit the use of bold solutions. Chicago architects pioneered a new concept of building which took advantage of the inexpensive space of the sky instead of the costly space on the ground: the *skyscraper*. These turn-of-the-century innovators are now known as the "Chicago School," though they did projects for other cities as well. Some of them were engineer-architects, men who built bridges before trying their hand at commercial buildings.

Of the men associated with the Chicago School, the most outstanding was Louis Sullivan (1856–1924). In addition to designing buildings, Sullivan was a great advocate for new architecture and new thinking about it. He was just as revolutionary in his field as Courbet and Manet were in painting. Concerned about relating his designs to people, he asked, what is the proper form for democratic architecture, and how can a building enhance the actions of the people using it? Architecture during the 1880s and 1890s was, if anything, in a sorrier state than painting had been in the 1850s and 1860s. This was when eclecticism was fashionable; when Romanesque, Baroque, Neoclassical, and even hybrid styles were championed. Oftentimes metal-frame methods were used, but were hidden behind façades resembling Roman temples or Gothic cathedrals. The peak of this architectural deception occurred in Chicago itself—the Columbian Exposition of 1893: a world's fair nicknamed the "White City." Almost all of the fair buildings, though made with frame methods,

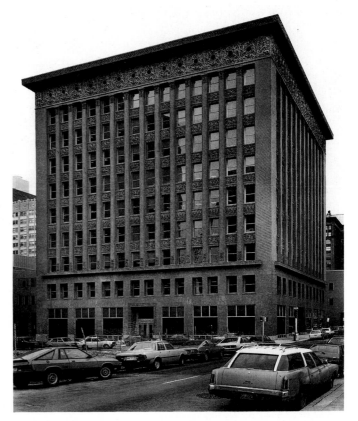

9.18 LOUIS SULLIVAN
Wainwright Building, St. Louis, Missouri, 1890–91

were furnished with Neoclassical exteriors and painted white. Sullivan, always outspoken, called the whole project a "sham."

Sullivan's first skyscraper, the Wainwright Building in St. Louis, is a simple, unpretentious block which expresses the world of business as well as its frame construction (Fig. **9.18**). The planes of the block are relieved by a three-level composition: a base, a middle section, and an ornate cornice. Although the grid pattern of the middle section reflects the internal steel frame, the continuous ribbons of brick which rise from base to cornice stress the vertical dimension. The Wainwright embodies Sullivan's motto: "form follows function," a phrase that would become the slogan of twentieth-century design. Sullivan himself, however, never intended the motto to mean the elimination of ornament. All of his buildings feature decorative accents, like those between the windows and on the cornice of the Wainwright, which were personally designed by the architect.

The Chicago School, Sullivan, and the idea that form must follow function are part of the history of Modernism, a subject that will be surveyed in the last three chapters.

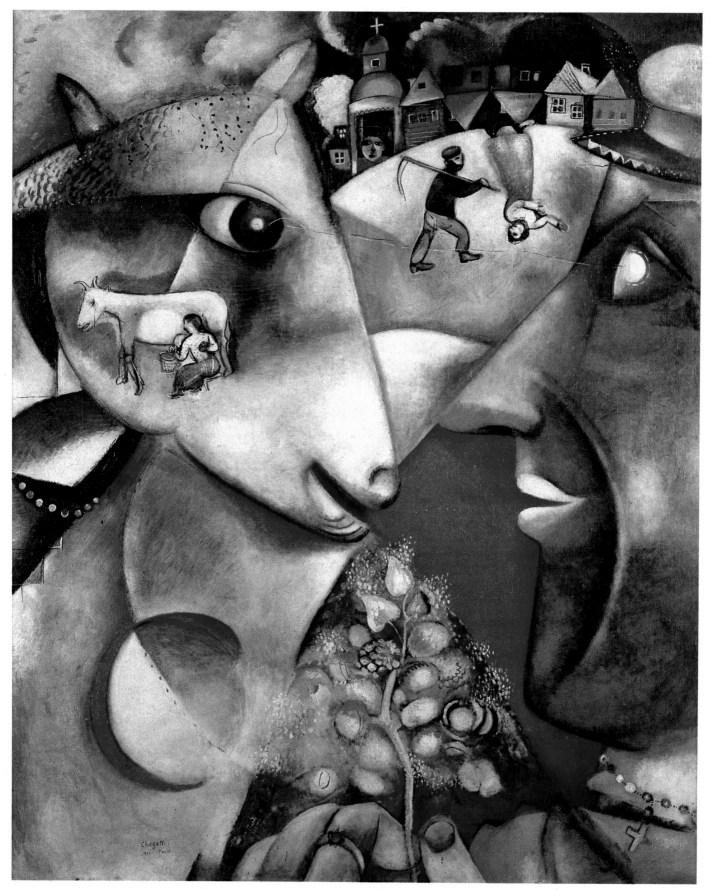

10.1 MARC CHAGALL *I and the Village*, 1911. Oil on canvas, 6 ft 3 ins × 59⅝ ins (192 × 151.5 cm)
Museum of Modern Art, New York, Mrs Simon Guggenheim Fund

CHAPTER TEN

Modernism I

Art comes to you proposing frankly to give nothing but the highest quality to your moments as they pass, and simply for those moments.

WALTER PATER

The Conditions of Modernism

"Modernism" is a term used to describe certain developments in literature, art, and music that peaked in the first half of the twentieth century (Fig. **10.2**). In one sense, the term is relative; what is modern to people of one period is outdated to those of the next. But the terms "Modernism," "Modernist," and "Modern movement" have been applied, for decades now, to certain tendencies in the arts, and thus have acquired a certain degree of descriptive validity. Moreover, the outlook and attitudes that produced these artistic developments continue to influence society, especially intellectuals, down to the present. It will perhaps be helpful to list and briefly discuss some of the characteristics of the Modernist outlook.

1 *History*, in the Modernist view of the early 1900s, had become a dead end. Traditional values and morals, along with any basis for hope in the future, which had already been eroded by nineteenth-century skepticism, were shattered by the apocalyptic struggle of World War I. It could no longer be taken for granted that Western civilization would survive; and if it did, one could no longer assume that it would do so in its traditional form with its traditional beliefs.

2 In the Modernist perspective, one of the most basic assumptions of Western culture concerning *human nature* was no longer credible; this was the assumption that human beings are rational and can thus solve their problems and discover and control their world through reason. This concept is of course basic to the Western achievement in science and technology. Freud's discovery of the unconscious and his conclusion that it, rather than reason, has the ultimate mastery in human behavior had a profound influence in the Modernist rejection of the primacy of reason. One expression of this view is the attempt of Modernist poets and artists to bypass the rational processes and get in touch with the unconscious through automatic writing and drawing.

3 *Primitivism* was another manifestation of the Modernist rejection of the sovereignty of reason. Paul Gauguin, for example, sought meaning for his life and matter for his art among the primitive peoples of Tahiti.

10.2 1875–1940

DATES	SOCIAL AND POLITICAL DEVELOPMENTS	LITERATURE AND PHILOSOPHY	VISUAL ARTS	ARCHITECTURE	MUSIC
1875	Invention of telegraph and telephone	French Symbolism Nietzsche Conrad (**10.3**)	Cézanne (**10.8**) Van Gogh (**10.10**) Gauguin (**10.12**) Seurat (**10.13**) Toulouse-Lautrec (**10.14**) Munch (**10.15**) Beardsley (**10.16**) Rodin (**10.36**)	Horta (**10.42**)	Mussorgsky Franck Rimsky-Korsakov Dvorak Grieg Mahler Saint-Sæns Fauré Debussy (**10.51**)
1900	Women's suffrage First World War Russian Revolution	Freud Jung Kafka (**10.4**) Mann (**10.5**) Joyce (**10.6**)	Modersohn-Becker (**10.19**) Matisse (**10.17, 10.18**) Picasso (**10.23, 10.24**) Braque (**10.25, 10.26**) De Chirico (**10.33**) Nolde (**10.20**) Duchamp (**10.28, 10.32**) Kokoschka (**10.21**) Kandinsky (**10.22**) Stella (**10.29**) Boccioni (**10.37**) Brancusi (**10.38**)	Louis Sullivan: Department store (**10.43**) Frank Lloyd Wright: Robie house (**10.44**) Behrens	Satie Stravinsky (**10.53, 10.54**) Schoenberg (**10.57**) Elgar Sibelius De Falla
1920 1940	Mussolini Hitler Second World War	T.S. Eliot (**10.7**)	Barlach Chagall (**10.1**) Mondrian (**10.30**) Miro (**10.35**) Gonzalez (**10.39**) Henry Moore (**10.41**) Calder (**10.40**)	Gropius (**10.46**) Bauhaus Le Corbusier: Villa Savoye (**10.48**) Mies van der Rohe: German Pavilion (**10.47**)	Berg Ravel Bartok Ives Webern

Dostoyevsky (see Chapter 9), a nineteenth-century prophet of Modernism, rejected what he regarded as decadent Western culture, with its overbearing and unwarranted confidence in reason and technology, and returned to the traditional Russian Orthodox faith. Dostoyevsky is, for Modernism, an ambivalent case. He foreshadowed the Modernist view of the problematic nature of human existence: the sense of alienation, extreme subjectivism, skepticism, irrationalism, even doubt as to the value of human existence. Yet he proposed religious faith as the only possible means of resolving the human dilemma, an answer typically spurned by Modernism.

Darwin's theory of evolution presented a more scientific aspect of the theme of primitivism. This theory—according to some interpretations—postulated forces at work in human behavior far more powerful than reason. These primitive forces, in the view of some Modernists—far from suggesting Rousseau's comforting talisman of the noble savage—are, under the suppression of civilization, like a temporarily subdued wild animal which, at unguarded moments, can spring forth and destroy all the humanistic assumptions of restraint and reason. Joseph Conrad explores this theme in his story *Heart of Darkness.* For Modernists like Conrad, what is especially revelatory of primitivism in human nature is that "civilized" human beings find themselves simultaneously repelled and drawn by it, as do Marlow, Conrad's narrator, and Kurtz, the altruistic ivory trader whose humanistic ideals are devastatingly subverted by the jungle. Further evidence of the Modernist fascination with the power of the primitive is found in Stravinsky's music for the ballet *The Rite of Spring* (*Le Sacré du printemps*) a musical exposition of the celebration in ancient cultures of the upsurge of vegetative and sexual vitality in springtime. The powerful influence of native African art on twentieth-century artists is further evidence of the attraction of primitivism.

Thomas Mann, in his story *Mario and the Magician*, also seeks to measure the depths of the irrational in human behavior, in order to show how easily these traits can be exploited by a political demagogue. (Mann's writings demonstrate the fact that a Modernist perspective does not necessitate an experimental method but can be couched in traditional literary form and style.)

The conclusion drawn by many Modernists from these discoveries of the unconscious, the primitive, and the irrational in human nature was that it is foolish, even absurd, to retain faith in human reason.

4 Contributing to this pessimistic view of the human lot held by Modernists was their equally pessimistic *view of the universe.* Deprived, as they felt, of the classical and Christian view of the cosmos as orderly and purposeful,

they came to see it as fragmented, chaotic, without transcendent meaning, and, if not aggressive, at least indifferent toward human values and aspirations. Indeed, this cosmic fragmentation and meaninglessness was of a piece with all reality.

5 This pessimistic Modernist conception of the world and human nature was reflected in their *art.* If the cosmos is fractured and fragmented, if life is chaotic and meaningless, if the self is a congeries of irrational and uncontrollable impulses, art must reflect this broken and disharmonious reality. The traditional role of the artist had been to assemble the broken pieces of reality into a unified and intelligible form that would please and inspire. The Modernists sought to create an art that would embody and communicate their disturbing perception of reality as fractured and chaotic, or at best paradoxical. Reflections of this perception can be discerned in the Cubism of Picasso and Braque, the complex rhythms of Stravinsky and the atonality of Schoenberg, and the enigmatic and threatening world of Kafka's stories. In part at least, the restless experimentation so characteristic of Modernist artists is the reflection of their ceaseless efforts to make their art an accurate image of their world view.

6 Since the human longing for knowledge and understanding could only be frustrated by external reality, the Modernists turned within, to their own *psyches as a source of truth.* Because of its primitive origins the psyche offered depths of meaning not accessible through reason or science. French Symbolism, a literary movement of the late nineteenth century led by Stéphane Mallarmé (1842–1898), anticipated this turning within. The aim of Symbolism was to disconnect the poem from everyday experience and make it an independent world of its own. Although it did not enshrine the unconscious, Symbolism rejected external reality as the subject matter of poetry. It saw the poem as a symbolic revelation of the poet's evanescent emotions, rather than a means of revealing some truth about the tangible world. In the early twentieth century, when the unconscious was "discovered" by Freud, the depths of the psyche began to be plumbed by Freudian and, later, Jungian psychology—the latter exploring Carl Jung's theory that myth reflects the unconscious of the race. The critic Irving Howe points out that Modernism's obsession with the inner life follows upon the breakdown of Romantic faith in the transcendent.[1] Rejecting traditional biblical faith in a transcendent personal God, the Romantics nonetheless continued to cling to the reassuring concept of a creative and beneficent power with which they could communicate through nature. But once belief in a spiritual source of truth in nature broke down, the only direction that one could turn was within. Thus, for the Modernist writer or artist, the mysterious psyche became the source of "revelation."

7 The intense focus of the Modernist on the inner life led to a self-consciousness at odds with society, a sense of *alienation* or *estrangement* from what Modernists regarded as the materialistic, banal, and hypocritical behavior of the middle class. This outlook, in turn, led to a kind of art that was so highly personal as to be, in some cases, incomprehensible. Indeed, some Modernist writers and artists apparently derived a perverse pleasure from producing art that shocked the public by its absurdity. Thus Modernist art tended to be a highly private affair, with an appeal limited to the initiated. What really mattered was not what the public could see with the physical eye but what the artist felt, and how he or she perceived this emotional inner world. The artistic attempt to give form to this inner world is especially evident in Expressionist painting and the stream-of-consciousness novel, which, as the term suggests, was an attempt to trace the uneven flow of consciousness in a fictional character.

8 Finally, Modernism was characterized by a pervasive and sometimes corrosive *skepticism*, a radical questioning of the value of society, of morality, of reason, of religion— indeed, of life itself. Some Modernists were driven by their skepticism to the ultimate act of despair, suicide. Others engaged in radical experimentation in an attempt to create more authentic values and art to replace what had been rejected. But the danger of nihilism was implicit in their radical skepticism, and it became, as Howe has pointed out, "the central preoccupation, the inner demon, at the heart of modern literature."[2] Significantly, Albert Camus (see Chapter 11) begins his philosophical treatise *The Myth of Sisyphus* with the statement that the fundamental philosophical issue is whether life is worth living. Dostoyevsky, again in the role of the prophet, had warned that the only alternative to religious faith is nihilism: "If God does not exist, all things are permitted"; that is, without God there is no foundation on which one can base values or beliefs—thus, anything goes and nothing matters. The Dadaists acted out Dostoyevsky's dictum: quite literally, in art as well as life, anything was permissible. One sees this same confrontation with the void of meaninglessness in the final outcry of Conrad's Kurtz, "The horror! The horror!"; and in the fruitless search of Joseph K., Kafka's protagonist in *The Trial*, for an affirmation of his right to exist.

What were the specifically artistic sources of Modernism? We have traced certain intellectual sources in the introduction to the preceding chapter and in this one: Darwinian evolution, Marx's attacks on the values of middle-class commercialism, Dostoyevsky's ambivalent dramatization of the human condition, and Freud's discovery of the unconscious. We must add Friedrich

Nietzsche's (1844–1900) exaltation of passion over reason, his affirmation of the Superman unhampered by Christian morality; indeed, his attempt to revise all values. Artistically, the sources of Modernism include *art-for-art's sake*, a slogan coined by Walter Pater in 1868, and a philosophy that divorces art from any didactic responsibility and evaluates the whole of life in terms of the aesthetic experience. The theoretical foundations for this attitude can be traced to the writings of Arthur Schopenhauer (1788–1860), the German philosopher who promoted the contemplation of art as a respite from the strivings and frustrations of life itself. Charles Baudelaire (1821–1867), a defender of Manet and forerunner of Symbolism, despised nature, extolled the charms of city life, and in general lived in accordance with this philosophy. As a way of life, art-for-art's sake probably reached its peak among the Symbolist poets: Mallarmé, cut off from ordinary life, lived only for literature. Jean Rimbaud (1854–1891) and Paul Gauguin, a painter associated with the Symbolists (see below), escaped ordinary life by fleeing to distant exotic lands. Although not all modern poets and artists have carried the philosophy to such extremes in their personal lives, the pervasive condition of Modernism in the arts is that of philosophical inbreeding and isolation from the concerns of everyday culture.

But the single event that was both the highly appropriate metaphor and in part the cause of Modernism's nihilistic tendencies was World War I. Following the Serbian assassination of the heir to the Austrian throne, Archduke Francis Ferdinand, on June 28, 1914, hostilities accelerated until all the major European powers were involved and also, eventually, the United States. Thus began a type of conflict that was to typify the twentieth century: the total war, that is, warfare involving whole populations and thus resulting in widespread devastation and human suffering. World War I was an especially savage war. Millions of soldiers died, and many who survived appeared to be walking cadavers because of their ghastly wounds, inflicted by such innovations as the machine gun, poison gas, liquid fire, and explosive bullets. The war seemed to develop a momentum of its own, becoming a kind of demonic monster which no individual or nation could restrain. It is not surprising, therefore, that writers and artists of the period—notably the Dadaists—were profoundly pessimistic about reason, society, and history.

Russia, one of the early belligerents, withdrew from the war in 1917, and in the ensuing Bolshevik Revolution gave birth to the first Communist state, a development of monumental significance for the twentieth century. The conditions giving rise to Fascism also grew out of World War I. The humiliation and economic devastation of

Germany resulting from the war prepared the way for Hitler's rise to power. Italy, although it emerged from the war on the winning side, suffered extensive casualties and felt humiliated by the paucity of its territorial gains. Thus it was receptive to the appeals of Mussolini, who became leader of a Fascist state (1922) more than ten years prior to the rise of Hitler in 1933. These political developments led, in turn, to World War II.

As we bring this introduction to a close, a word of warning is in order. Considerable space has been devoted to a discussion of the characteristics of Modernism. The reader should be aware, however, that this discussion is intended to characterize the movement as a whole; not all Modernist writers and artists reveal all of these characteristics. Moreover, we must emphasize that Modernism is not a chronological designation but refers to a number of tendencies in the arts, especially evident in the first half of the twentieth century but not confined to that period. Thus the perceptive reader of the last two chapters will see that certain Modernist assumptions and tendencies—far from being rejected—continue to influence the arts. Much of what has been said in this introduction—especially with regard to the Modernist conception of the problematical state of mankind in an alien universe—is therefore typical of the views held by many artists and writers of the twentieth century down to the present.

Literature

Conrad

It is appropriate that a discussion of Joseph Conrad (1857–1924) and his story *Heart of Darkness* (1902) should stand at the head of our treatment of twentieth-century literature. In many ways Conrad's work straddles the two centuries. He combines romanticism, in his use of exotic locales, with realistic detail, and thus includes attributes of two of the major movements in art and literature of the nineteenth century. But he also stands astride the two centuries in his use of impressionistic techniques in *Heart of Darkness*, for the story is told by a narrator, Marlow, whose subjective perceptions of his singular experience, especially in his jungle journey up the Congo River, evoke a mood of apprehensiveness in the reader that matches his own. This subjectivism in Conrad's stories, combined with a sense of loneliness and alienation—the inability of human beings to make genuine connections with one another—also provides a link between Dostoyevsky's *Notes from Underground* and the existential writers of the twentieth century who explore these themes. The judgment of Kurtz, the European ivory trader, upon his life and the human condition in general as he confronts death is reminiscent of Ivan Ilych's sense of the absurd in the face of death and points forward to the absurd in the thought of Albert Camus, which also stemmed largely from the inevitability of death. Moreover, Conrad's devastating revelation in *Heart of Darkness* of the potential of "civilized" European man for primitive cruelty and violence confirms, in its own way, Dostoyevsky's analysis of the underside of human nature, and fore-shadows the horrors of World War I, which was to

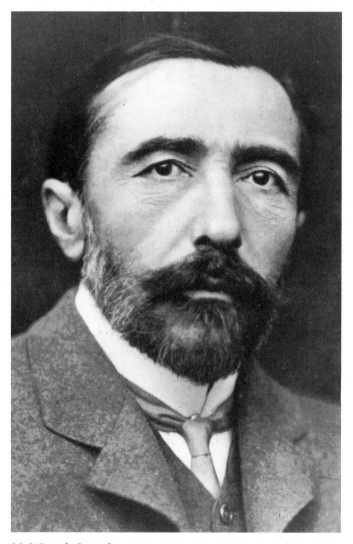

10.3 Joseph Conrad

explode across Europe just 12 years later.

Teodor Jósef Konrad Korzeniowski was born in southern Poland at a time when that country was (not for the last time) under Russian control. His father's revolutionary activities led to his arrest and exile in Russia. He took his family with him, and Conrad's mother died in Russia a few years later. His father also died, after he had been pardoned and had returned to Poland. Conrad's uncle thus became his guardian. Some three years later, at the age of 15, Conrad expressed his intention to become a sailor—a longing that he had conceived and fueled through reading stories of the sea since his early boyhood. At the age of 17, he became an apprentice aboard a French vessel. Twelve years later he had become master of his own ship. In this period, he also learned the English language, in which he was to write, and became a British citizen. He retired from the sea in 1894, and one year later published his first novel, *Almayer's Folly*. A succession of novels followed, including *Outcasts of the Islands* (1896), *The Nigger of the "Narcissus"* (1898), *Lord Jim* (1900), *Youth* (1902), *The Secret Agent* (1907), *Victory* (1915), and *The Rover* (1923), as well as numerous short stories and an autobiography.

Typically, Conrad places his characters in circumstances—usually at sea or in the jungle—where their values are put to the ultimate test because there are no external constraints upon them. Their choices thus become authentic pointers to what lies beneath the surface of lives ordinarily governed by the laws and expectations of civilization. "The sea [and the jungle, one may add] is a catalyst," Conrad once wrote. "It demands action. It is not taken in by pretense." Thus Conrad—unlike Naturalist writers, who depicted men and women as victims of hereditary and environment—believed that human beings are shapers of their own destinies. Life is always treacherous, in Conrad's view, but internal discipline and work can enable one (Marlow is a case in point) somehow to maintain the integrity of his soul, although it will be tainted by his encounter with the "heart of darkness."

Conrad's stories often reflect his experience in exotic places as a sailor. *Heart of Darkness* is such a story. Even as a boy, Conrad tells us, he expressed his intention to go to the then unknown and mysterious heart of Africa. In 1890 he had his opportunity, when he became an employee of the Belgian colonial enterprise that figures in his story. This organization purported to be set on civilizing and developing the Congo, but in fact, according to Conrad, it was a major participant in "the vilist scramble for loot that ever disfigured the history of human conscience and geographical exploration." Conrad, like Marlow, hired on to take a steamboat up the Congo for the trading company, but—refused command of his ship after it had been repaired—he was unable to complete his journey. He was there long enough, however, to become seriously ill and also to gather a wealth of experience and observation of colonialism which he channeled into *Heart of Darkness*. Thus his ironic presentation of the true motives of the "emissaries of progress" in *Heart of Darkness* was based upon first-hand knowledge.

Marlow tells his story to a small group of friends who sit with him aboard the *Nellie*, a cruising yawl which is anchored in the Thames River in London. Speaking of his voyage to the upper reaches of the Congo where he found Kurtz, he says, "It was the farthest point of navigation and the culminating point of my experience. It seems somehow to throw a kind of light on everything about me—and into my thoughts."[3] Thus he begins the tale of his journey into the heart of darkness.

Conrad's title has three levels of significance. Most obviously it refers to the heart of Africa penetrated by the Congo River. But it also signifies the heart of Kurtz, the megalomaniac ivory trader whom Marlow finally encounters in his voyage up the river. Finally, however, the heart of darkness is every human heart, with its potential for primitive violence. There are also three levels of meaning in the story itself. Superficially it may be read as an adventure story, though its rich and densely-textured style would discourage the reader looking for a fast-paced read. It is also quite clearly a devastating attack upon imperialism and colonial exploitation of primitive peoples. But at its greatest depth, *Heart of Darkness* is an exploration of the dark recesses of the human heart. Thus Marlow's voyage into the heart of Africa is also a voyage of self discovery by Marlow which reveals to him his own potential, and that of all humans, for brutish behavior.

The motif of the perilous journey into self-knowledge occurs often in literature. Dante, for example, must descend into Hell to discover the ever-deepening possibilities for evil in the individual and the community. So also Marlow makes his journey up the Congo River, ostensibly to find a man, Kurtz, but symbolically to penetrate the depths of the human heart of darkness. This evil is progressively revealed through the colonial exploiters but ultimately through Kurtz, the former humanitarian idealist whose potential for savagery has been actualized by the absence of the restraints of civilization. Thus Marlow, like Dante, must undergo an initiation into the knowledge of evil in order to understand himself and mankind at large.

But what is the source of this evil, this capacity for violence and primitive behavior in human beings? This question brings us to the controlling perspective of *Heart of Darkness*: Darwinism. For what the human beings in this story reveal—the "civilized" and uncivilized alike—is the animality resulting from their evolutionary origins. This is apparent enough in the African natives, who are not at all the noble savages of Rousseau and the Romantics. But it is also present, in more sinister form, in European men, lying just beneath the veneer of civilization that quickly peels away in the wilderness where there are no restraints on their egocentric passions. Kurtz is the prime example of this process. "All Europe contributed to [his] making," Marlow tells us. That is, Kurtz is the incarnation of vaunted nineteenth-century European humanism, the very best cultural missionary that Europe could send out to civilize the Africans. Yet he is utterly corrupted by the jungle, for it unleashes passions of which he has been completely naive because of his civilized upbringing. Quite literally, he makes himself a god to the natives he enslaves, accepting their worship and exercising the power of life and death as he uses them to accumulate vast holdings of ivory.

Marlow's voyage into the interior of Africa, and to Kurtz, therefore, is a voyage into primitive human nature. "Going up that river," Marlow reflects, "was like traveling back to the earliest beginnings of the world, when vegetation rioted on the earth and the big trees were kings."[4] The story therefore stands as a rebuke and a warning to Europeans, a censure of their colonial exploitation and also a warning of the potential for violence and cruelty lying just beneath the polished surface of humanism, a warning that would be amply justified by the subsequent history of the twentieth century.

Kafka

Franz Kafka (1883–1924) has, since World War II, become one of the most influential figures in twentieth-century literature. Few people, however, recognized his literary achievement during his lifetime. Although his works were all written in the first quarter of the century, he succeeded in capturing the spirit of the entire twentieth century—its fears, insecurity, and general malaise.

The typical Kafkaesque protagonist undergoes some disorienting change in his life which threatens his well-being and identity and, in some cases, his very existence. This change sometimes results from aggressive actions perpetrated by persons who claim to represent a faceless bureaucracy which holds sovereign sway over the lives of all who serve it and all whom it chooses to summon. The protagonist, thus summoned, finds himself increasingly absorbed in a frustrating effort to contact this amorphous, though pervasive, bureaucracy in order to vindicate himself. Though teased along by repeated assurances and promises given by the intermediaries, who themselves are

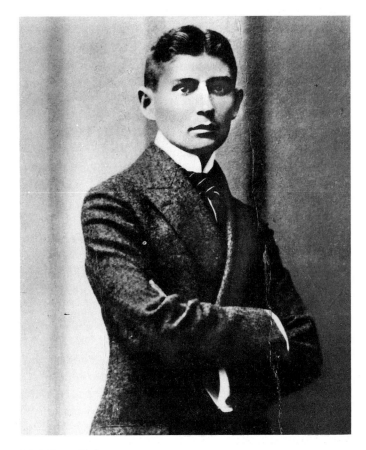

10.4 Franz Kafka

ignorant victims of the bureaucracy, he never succeeds.

Because Kafka's symbols are open to so many interpretations and because he offers no key to their interpretation, there is much disagreement among critics as to his meaning. Typically, there are three critical approaches, though they are not necessarily mutually exclusive. The *psychological approach* focuses particularly on Kafka's difficult relationship with an overbearing father who was disappointed with his son's commitment to art and whom Kafka therefore could not please. Thus he felt rejected by his father, who represented authority, and was frustrated in his attempt to justify his life to him. The *theological interpretation* identifies the bureaucracy with God and those who claim to represent him to mankind. Thus a remote God draws mankind toward himself, but because of the ignorance of his representatives in the world and his own unapproachableness, those summoned by him are frustrated in their attempt to respond to his call. The *institutional approach* sees the bureaucratic images in Kafka's stories as representing any faceless authoritarian institution that exercises control over the lives of people in a dehumanizing and irrational manner. It is best for the reader of Kafka to remain open to all these approaches, since there is strong evidence, both in the stories and in

Kafka's life, in support of each of them.

Born in Prague, Czechoslovakia, the son of Jewish parents, Kafka was the eldest of six children. His father was a strong-willed, self-made businessman who had prospered despite prejudice against the Jews. After attending a Prague gymnasium (secondary school), Kafka studied law at the University of Prague, from which he received his doctorate in 1906. Not long afterwards he took a position in the accident claims department of an insurance company, where he undoubtedly learned a great deal about the plight of the lonely individual who attempts to establish his or her claim upon a ponderous and obstinate bureaucracy. Because his job ended at two in the afternoon, Kafka was free to devote the rest of his day to writing, his true vocation.

Kafka never married. He became engaged to Felice Bauer (whom he refers to as "F. B.") in 1914, but their on-and-off relationship was finally ended in 1917, after he learned that he had tuberculosis. Kafka could not conceive of combining marriage and ordinary life with his passionate dedication to his writing, a conflict that plagued him incessantly. Thus the disease was, for him, a Godsend because it saved him from marriage. His later relationship with Milena Jesenska was also broken off because of his writing vocation. Dora Dyment, the one woman he apparently would have married and with whom he lived in Berlin, was denied him because her father refused to give his consent. Nonetheless, she remained with him during what were to be his last days as he sought treatment for his tuberculosis. Placed in a sanitorium near Vienna, he lapsed into a coma and died on June 3, 1924. His body was returned to Prague for burial. (The names of his sisters, who lived on into the Nazi era, are inscribed on a memorial to victims of the Holocaust in the synagogue behind which he is buried.)

Kafka left three unfinished novels—*The Trial*, *The Castle*, and *Amerika*—all published posthumously by Max Brod, his literary executor. He also wrote short stories, parables, letters, journals, and aphorisms.

The Trial (1925) opens with the arrest one morning of Joseph K. He is unaware of any crime that he may have committed, and the representatives of the court who notify him do not specify any violation of the law—nor do they confine him. Yet, beginning from this point and extending throughout the entire novel—even to the moment when he is finally "executed" (his death seems more like a murder)—his life is given over to repeatedly frustrated efforts to determine what the charges are and to vindicate himself before the mysterious court that has arrested him. A sober and responsible bank official at the time of his arrest, he becomes so obsessed with his efforts at self-justification that he cannot concentrate on his work. Compulsively, he seeks out various persons who seem to have connections with the court. Typically, these intermediaries give the appearance of knowing the Law but in fact are unable to offer K. any help.

The climactic encounter between K. and a spokesman for the court occurs in the Cathedral, where K. is confronted by a priest who relates a parable, ostensibly to enlighten K. In the parable, a man appears before the door of the Law seeking admission. The doorkeeper, however, tells him that at the moment he cannot be admitted. Year after year he waits, even bribing the doorkeeper, who accepts the bribes but does not relent. Finally, as the man is dying, the doorkeeper informs him that the door was for him alone, and thus he will now close it. The priest then proceeds to interpret the parable, hiding behind the authority of the Law so as to vindicate the doorkeeper; the casuistry of his argument, however, becomes evident to K., and he rejects it, contending that it is the man who has come to the doorkeeper who has been wronged. It is he, of course, who represents the plight of K. In the final chapter K. is apprehended by two fat comical characters wearing top hats, led out to a stone quarry, and knifed to death, still ignorant of his crime and of the court that has condemned him.

Kafka's best-known story, The *Metamorphosis*, clearly reflects his anguished relationship with his father. The story opens with Gregor Samsa waking up one morning to find that he has been transformed into a giant insect. Here Kafka employs a literary motif, that of physical transformation, that goes back at least as far as Homer's *Odyssey*, in which Circe changes Odysseus' men into pigs. The *Metamorphoses* of Ovid (a Roman poet of the first century AD) is a poetic collection of stories about such transformations. Although writers as widely separated chronologically as Aesop, Swift, and Orwell have used animals to represent human beings, the logic of their usage is more evident than is Kafka's: their animals clearly represent human traits that the authors are attacking or satirizing. Kafka's purpose is more subtle, as we shall see.

Gregor has previously been the breadwinner and mainstay of his father, mother, and sister. Ostensibly an invalid, the father remains at home while Gregor, a traveling salesman, must go forth every day to a job that depresses and dehumanizes him. Five years previously his father's business had failed. Gregor, assuming his father was financially ruined, shouldered the responsibility for supporting the family and also for paying off his employer for a debt incurred by his father. After his metamorphosis, however, he learns that his father has money from the sale of property and that he has also put aside some of the money that Gregor has turned over to him for the family, money that could have been used to pay off Gregor's employer, "which would have brought near the date of Gregor's release."[5] Nonetheless, Gregor bears no ill will toward his father; on the contrary, he is pleased that his father has exercised financial foresight. But because of Gregor's metamorphosis his father must now go to work to supplement the savings.

Thus it becomes evident—to the reader—that Gregor has been used by his father as well as by his employer. To his family he is a breadwinner; to his employer, a flunkey. His entire existence has been absorbed by these roles. Yet he has a capacity for values other than material ones. He loves music and had hoped to send his sister to the conservatory. He also has framed and hung on his wall a cut-out picture of a woman in furs—pathetic testimony to his capacity for aesthetic appreciation. The rigor of his work schedule, however, has allowed him no time for the cultivation of such values.

All of this points to the hidden conflict between Gregor and his father, the conflict of materialistic values with spiritual ones, the same conflict that ravaged the relationship of Kafka and his own father. No wonder that Gregor's father becomes so angry and frustrated at his son's metamorphosis. He is consistently belligerent toward him throughout the story, though prior to the metamorphosis he had seemed to be docile and grateful. Thus Gregor's metamorphosis may be understood, first, as an incarnation of what he was within the family: an insect alienated from people who used him as an object. This transformation is also an incarnation of his subconscious rebellion against the role imposed upon him. Moreover, it frees him from the materialistic bourgeois ambitions of his family which have previously controlled his life. Some critics have seen in Gregor's metamorphosis a reflection of Kafka's tuberculosis, which set him free from his job and from the prospect of marriage to pursue his art uninterruptedly.

Whereas the attitude of Gregor's father toward Gregor's changed state is typically bitter and resentful, his sister at first seems to care for him but eventually lapses into a negative attitude much like the father's. His mother, though afraid of Gregor, shows some sensitivity to his plight, even expressing the hope that he will one day be restored to them. But she lacks the strength to take effective action on his behalf. Here we see the literary theme of the testing of love by an object of disgust— illustrated, for example, by the well-known children's story of the frog transformed into a prince by the kiss of the princess, and by Chaucer's story of the ugly woman transformed by the devotion of her knight. Gregor, however, experiences no such transforming love. Thus he perishes.

Just before his death, however, his capacity for values that lie outside the boundaries of the bourgeois routine surface one last time as he, a loathsome creature from the darkness, creeps into the well-lighted room where his sister is playing the violin, so that he might hear and see her better. His sister, revolted by this intrusion, refuses to see "this monster" as her brother—"we must find some means of getting rid of it," she asserts. Shortly afterward, Gregor dies, and his carcass is thrown out by the cleaning woman. Father, mother, and daughter, immensely relieved, now plan an outing in the country. Smugly, Herr Samsa says, "Come, come, it's all past history now," and adds significantly, "You can start paying a little attention to me."[6] Once more, he is at the center of the family's attention and concern. The story ends with the three boarding a train for the country; and, freed of the spiritual challenge to their bourgeois materialism posed by Gregor's metamorphosis, they optimistically plan for a future based on good jobs, good neighborhood, and a good marriage for the daughter.

Mann

Thomas Mann (1875–1955), like Kafka, experienced a sense of guilt because of his art. His father, like Kafka's, was a successful middle-class merchant. But Mann's

10.5 Thomas Mann

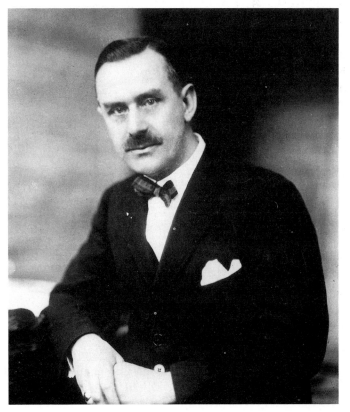

father was a highly respected scion of a well-established family, unlike Kafka's father who, as a Jew, had succeeded by his own efforts against the odds. In both writers, however, one sees a conflict resulting from family background: Kafka's resulting from his father's displeasure with his literary passion to the neglect of practical duties; Mann's, from his belief that the life of the artist is a departure from Germanic bourgeois discipline and is thus spiritually unhealthy, fraught with disease and death. Kafka also believed that there was something unwholesome about art and that it isolated the artist from family happiness. Both authors reflect this tension frequently in their writings.

Born in Lübeck, a city of northern Germany with a merchant aristocracy, Mann was the second of five children of a wealthy grain merchant and senator and a woman of mixed German and Creole stock who was of an artistic temperament. Hence Mann's ambivalence toward the relative merits of bourgeois discipline and the artistic life. Even as a boy he determined to become a writer. Indeed, his propensity for writing verses caused him to run afoul the Prussian schoolmasters at the Realgymnasium he attended, an experience that turned him against the German educational system. When his father died and his mother moved to Munich, Mann remained behind to complete his education before following her later. He attended the University of Munich, but never obtained a degree.

While visiting his brother Heinrich (also a novelist) in Italy, he began the long novel *Buddenbrooks*, which he completed (1900) upon his return to Munich. Significantly, this is the story of the gradual deterioration of a nineteenth-century merchant dynasty because of the encroachment of artistic values upon their disciplined lives. The success of this work was confirmed by the publication of the autobiographical novella *Tonio Kröger* (1903), another story about the clash of middle-class and artistic values, this time within the protagonist. Shortly after the publication of this story, Mann married Katja Pringsheim, the daughter of a Munich professor, who was to bear him six children.

In 1913 Mann published the major novella *Death in Venice*, the story of a writer, Gustav von Aschenbach, whose self-discipline is broken down by his homosexual obsession with a beautiful Polish boy whom he encounters in Venice. Although he never so much as speaks to the boy, Aschenbach stays on in Venice to be near him, despite a cholera epidemic. As a result, he dies of the disease. The deterioration of the character and values of Von Aschenbach seemed to some European leaders, on the eve of World War I, a prophetic insight into the breakdown of Western culture.

This story grew out of a vacation Mann spent with his family in Venice; similarly, his best-known novel, *The Magic Mountain*, resulted from Katja's hospitalization for tuberculosis at a sanitorium in Davos, Switzerland. Although this occurred in 1912, the novel was not completed until 1924. It is a *bildungsroman* ("novel of education," in the broad sense), a story about the maturation of Hans Castorp, who spends seven years in a tuberculosis sanitorium and thereby comes under the influence of persons representing various aspects of European culture. As it ends, he is facing possible death as a soldier in World War I.

Although Mann sought to avoid the maelstrom of European politics (as is evident in his treatise *Reflections of an Unpolitical Man* [1918]), he found it impossible to remain silent in the presence of the rising threat of fascism in Germany and Italy in the 1920s. Thus he spoke out against this movement in the story *Mario and the Magician* in 1929, the same year in which he won the Nobel Prize for literature. This story is set in Mussolini's Italy. Shortly afterward (1930), Mann launched another attack in a speech to the German people entitled *An Appeal to Reason*. At the time Hitler seized power (1933), Mann and his wife were in Switzerland. Warned of the danger by his family, they did not return. Indeed, Mann was never again to take up permanent residence in his homeland, although he visited Germany 16 years later. During his absence, the Nazis deprived him of his citizenship (1936) and his honorary doctorate, and burned his books. Mann settled in the United States in 1938, and in 1944, near the end of World War II, he became a citizen. Two especially significant works that he wrote during his exile were *Joseph and his Brothers*, a tetralogy which was published between 1933 and 1943, and *Doktor Faustus* (1948). The former is a massive retelling of the Joseph story in the Bible (Genesis 37–50), in which Mann develops his views on religion and myth; the latter makes use of the archetypal Faust theme (see Chapter 5) to develop a political allegory about Germany's selling of its soul to Nazism. It also features another of Mann's diseased artists, this time a musician. After his brief post–World War II visit to Germany in 1949, Mann settled in Switzerland near Zurich. There he wrote *The Confessions of Felix Krull, Confidence Man* (1954), a longer version of an earlier story. This novel rang down the curtain on Mann's rich literary life, for he died in 1955.

At the time when *Mario and the Magician* appeared (1929), fascism was well established in Italy under Benito Mussolini and on the rise in Germany under Adolf Hitler (he became chancellor in 1933). It is surprising, therefore, that many readers at first failed to recognize the political implications of the story. It is set in Italy and therefore directly reflects conditions under Italian fascism. But its examination of the nature of the fully developed fascist mind reveals Mann's anxieties concerning parallel trends in Germany.

The story is told by a German patrician who has brought his family to Torre di Venere, on the Tyrrhenian coast, for a vacation. It is divided into two parts, the first focusing on the events occurring at the beach, the second on the performance of the magician Cipolla. The critic Henry C. Hatfield has pointed out that it is the theme of politics that binds the two parts together, for the reader is introduced to a fascist people in a beach incident and to the fascist leader in Cipolla[7]. The beach incident partakes of the comical, though revealing the overheated patriotism of the Italian people under Mussolini. (Indeed, even before this occurrence, the Italian children manifest an aggressive chauvinism toward foreigners, the adults joining in and behaving as childishly.) The narrator relates how his eight-year-old daughter, with her parents' permission, removes her bathing suit, rinses it free of sand in the sea, and puts it on again. Immediately, he relates, the beach erupts in a united outcry against this "offense to the public morals." The narrator and his family are then accused of insulting Italy's hospitality and offending its "national dignity." In fact, they are fined by the public officials.

Shortly afterward, Cipolla makes his appearance. A traveling magician, he has come to Torre di Venere to give a performance. The narrator does not at first take him seriously, and even consents to take his children to the performance; but as the evening progresses, he is more and more convinced of the occult powers of the grotesque hunchback. At first, Cipolla ("onion," probably an allusion to the bald pate of Mussolini) merely makes some of the local youth look foolish by causing them to act contrary to their wills. More and more, however, he assumes control over the minds and wills of the audience, eventually subduing educated members of the upper class, those most resistant to him. Many of these people lapse into an "epileptic ecstasy," as Mann, in his "Appeal to Reason" speech one year later, was to describe the effect of the Nazi movement on the German people. Thus they become puppets on Cipolla's string, dancing dissolutely on the stage in a "drunken abdication of the critical spirit," as the narrator calls it.

Cipolla manifests the same irrational patriotism as the people at the beach. Much more ominous, however, is the way in which he defines his relationship to the will of the audience. He so completely identifies with their wills, he explains, that his actions are, in effect, their actions. Thus, although he may seem to be manipulating their wills by the force of his own will, in fact, he is bearing the burden of

their united wills and implementing them. "Commanding and obeying form together one single principle, one indissoluble unity; he who knew how to obey knew also how to command, and conversely; the one idea was comprehended in the other, as people and leader were comprehended in one another."[8] As Hatfield points out, this sounds like a quotation from a handbook of fascist dogma.

One young "apostle of freedom," as the narrator calls him, sets himself in opposition to Cipolla, believing that his rational decision to preserve his freedom of will and not to submit will enable him to resist the will of the magician. Cipolla, however, asserts that "freedom of the will does not exist, for a will that aims at its own freedom aims at the unknown."[9] Here Mann is following Nietzsche, a major influence on his thought, who said that freedom must be to some end. Mann seems to imply that the hypnotic powers of the dictator cannot be resisted by a merely negative will. Against such powers the will must be sustained by commitment to a higher ideal. Thus this is a story about morality as well as politics. Indeed, the two themes are intertwined.

How, then, can such negative forces be thwarted? Mann's answer is his character Mario, a rather simple young man who waits on tables in a café frequented by the narrator and his family. Cipolla calls Mario to the stage and proceeds to humiliate him about his failure to capture the love of his girlfriend, Silvestra. Gradually bringing Mario under his hypnotic powers, he suddenly presents himself to Mario as Silvestra, posturing grotesquely and inviting Mario's kiss. Overcome with bliss, Mario gladly responds. At that moment Cipolla breaks the spell, causing Mario to realize with horror what has happened. Stumbling from the stage, he suddenly wheels around and fires two shots from a small pistol, killing Cipolla. In the uproar that follows, the narrator leads his uncomprehending children from the hall, assuring them that the evening's entertainment is at an end. He concludes: "an end of horror, a fatal end. And yet a liberation—for I could not, and I cannot, but find it so!"[10]

Mann thus makes a statement about the ultimate safeguard of the human soul against political and moral tyranny. Will and reason fail to resist the power of Cipolla. But in his humiliation of Mario, who has no desire to resist him, Cipolla crosses an invisible line and encroaches upon a sacred domain, the realm of human dignity. The consequence is drastic and fatal. "This dignity," Mann seems to imply, "is in itself a force stronger than free will or the conscious mind. It brings down the tyrant after they have failed."[11]

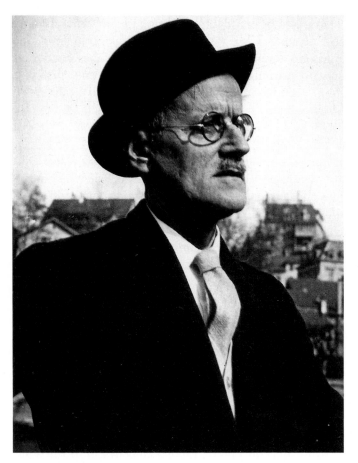

10.6 James Joyce

Joyce

Although he published only six books, James Joyce (1882–1941) is the dominant figure of Modernist literature. His works include a book of poems, a play, a collection of short stories (*Dubliners*, 1914), and three novels: *A Portrait of the Artist as a Young Man* (1916), *Ulysses* (1922), and *Finnegans Wake* (1939).

Perhaps Joyce's best known contribution to the literary techniques of Modernism is the stream-of-consciousness narrative. This device, employed originally in an obscure French novel, attempts to trace the restlessly shifting consciousness of the literary character. The result, as one might expect, is a narrative that is disconnected, lacking the plot linearity of the traditional novel.

The literary sense of *epiphany* also originated with Joyce. Originally denoting religious enlightenment resulting from a revelation of divine truth (St. Paul's encounter with the risen Christ is an example), the word was used by Joyce for the sudden insight experienced by a fictional character by which he or she glimpses some meaning in the turbulence of life.

Joyce also exerted a significant influence on modern literature through his extensive use of myth. Human beings, in Joyce's view, are surrounded by myth: the life of the ordinary person is linked with the past, his own actions and deeds recapitulating the mythical patterns traced in the great literature of the Western tradition. Thus, for example, his novel *Ulysses* (the Latin form of Odysseus) is a modern re-enactment of Homer's great epic, the *Odyssey* (see Chapter 1).

Joyce also became a seminal figure in modern literature because of his playful manipulation of words and their sounds, a passion revealed in his use of images of sound and his careful attention to the rhythms of language. It is also revealed in his coining of new terms out of combined words: for example, *bluddlefilth*, a fusion of "battlefield," "blood," and "filth." In his playful, experimental approach to language, Joyce not only influenced Modernist writers but also foreshadowed the Post-Modern writers' focus on the artful management of language as the essential element of fiction (see Chapter 12).

Born in a suburb of Dublin, Joyce was brought up with nine brothers and sisters and educated in Jesuit schools. Upon receiving his BA in 1902, he left for Paris to study medicine, only to return to Ireland in 1903 because he had received word that his mother was dying. In 1904, he left again, taking with him Nora Barnacle, a young woman from Galway. He later immortalized his first date with her (June 16, 1904) by setting the action of *Ulysses* on that same day. Their relationship did not become legal until 1932. Although Joyce was to return to Ireland only briefly on two occasions in 1909, Dublin and the Catholic faith he had rejected early in life were to be dominant influences in his writing. After a short stay in Pola, on the Adriatic, Joyce and Nora moved to Trieste, where Joyce, an excellent linguist, taught English in a Berlitz school. Two children were born to them, Georgio (1905) and Lucia Ann (1907). (In later years his daughter's gradually developing mental illness was to contribute to Joyce's own depressive mental state.) Joyce continued to support his family by teaching English during stays in Rome and Zurich, where they lived during World War I. Finally, in 1920, they settled in Paris. Through the financial aid given him by a wealthy Englishwoman, Joyce eventually gained the freedom to devote himself to his writing.

Although *Dubliners* was submitted to a publisher in 1905, this collection of short stories, which Joyce called "epiphanies," was not published until 1914. The last of these stories, *The Dead*, regarded by some critics as one of the best short stories ever written in English, has as its setting a concert in a private home. The chief characters are Gabriel Conroy, a writer, and his wife, Gretta, a quite simple woman from western Ireland. Thus Gabriel and Gretta are partially modeled on Joyce and Nora. Gretta, hearing a song about death, becomes so engrossed in her memory of a young man, Michael Furey, that, later that night, she does not respond to her husband's amorous advances. Michael, she relates, was in love with her, and died at 17 because he came through the rain to see her one more time before she left for Dublin. (Nora Joyce had had a similar experience: a certain Michael Bodkin had died after serenading her in the rain.) Thus Gabriel experiences the power of the dead over the living, a theme that appears often in Joyce's writings. The story draws to a close with Gabriel's recognition that it is better to "pass boldly into that other world, in the full glory of some passion, than fade and wither dismally with age." He himself had never experienced the love that compelled young Michael to say that he would rather die than lose Gretta. As he peers out the window at the falling snow which is gradually covering everything, falling "upon all the living and the dead," he experiences an epiphany: the recognition of the unity of the two worlds. Thus the story ends.

During his brief stay in Ireland after his mother's death, Joyce had begun an autobiographical work entitled *Stephen Hero*. In 1914 he published a revised and enlarged version of this work as *A Portrait of the Artist as a Young Man.* This book and *Dubliners* assured Joyce's literary reputation.

In *Ulysses*, published in 1922 and banned as obscene in England and the United States for more than ten years, Joyce employed the stream-of-consciousness technique consistently for the first time; he also extensively displayed his propensity for making new words. This huge novel—which grew out of a short story intended for *Dubliners*—is set in Dublin and the action takes place on one day, June 16, 1904. This in itself is an ironic contrast to the novel's inspiration, the *Odyssey*, which spans many years. Like the *Odyssey*, it is about exile, though in a more psychological sense: the sense of alienation felt by the young Stephen Dedalus (the protagonist of *A Portrait of the Artist as a Young Man*), who has just returned from Paris to be with his dying mother, but can no longer profess her Catholic faith, and that experienced by Leopold Bloom, who, as a Jew, is treated as an outsider in his own country. The various episodes that form the story line take these two characters around Dublin—their wanderings forming another parallel to the *Odyssey*—and provide a framework for the stream of consciousness revealing their thoughts and feelings. In the evening, at a brothel, they eventually meet. Bloom (who represents Ulysses) is looking for a son; Dedalus (who represents Telemachus) is looking for a father. The comparisons and contrasts between them and their mythical counterparts are worked out in great detail, as is the ironic contrast between Bloom's adulterous wife Molly (whose extended erotic soliloquy concludes the novel) and the faithful Penelope. The novel's many layers of meaning have intrigued and baffled readers for decades.

Joyce spent 17 years on his last major work, *Finnegans Wake.* Although to the uninitiated the work seems so jumbled as to be meaningless, it is the story of one family—the publican (tavernkeeper) H. C. Earwicker, his wife, and his two sons—whose relations are revealed through their dreams during one night. This narrow scope is universalized by the fact that this single family is enfolded by the garment of history and myth.

If *Ulysses* is difficult to read, *Finnegans Wake* is impossible without extensive critical assistance. The inexperienced reader, seeking an introduction to Joyce, should probably begin with *Dubliners.* In any case, Joyce must not be neglected if one is to understand the nature of literary Modernism in the twentieth century.

Eliot

Just as James Joyce is a major figure in the development of the prose of twentieth-century Modernism, so T. S. (Thomas Stearns) Eliot (1888–1965), who was deeply influenced by Joyce's *Ulysses*, is a major figure in the development of the poetry of this movement. Both Joyce and Eliot, in their attempts to trace the paths of consciousness as it seeks to unify the disparate elements of experience and observation, have had a powerful effect on the way Modernist novelists and poets conceive their task. Like Joyce, Eliot was an experimenter with language and literary forms, especially the structure of the poem. Unlike the Victorian and Romantic poets, who provided readers with a coherent development of their poetical ideas, Eliot juxtaposed images, mythical elements, and quotations from a broad range of literary traditions, leaving with the reader the responsibility of providing the connections from his or her own consciousness and experience.

Related to this is Eliot's concept of the refined sensibility and the literary tradition. By this he meant that well-read poets are constantly under the influence of the great writers whom they have read and digested. Thus a dynamic interaction takes place in their minds between literary traditions of the past and their perspectives on the complexities of the present as they seek to render their own poetic visions. Like Joyce, therefore, Eliot commingles the present and the past in order to give universal significance to both. This linking of present and past also illustrates Eliot's obsession with time. His symbolic use of time has been compared with the artist Salvador Dali's painting of limp clock faces in the midst of a wasteland, suggesting the timeless merging of past and present in a world without meaning.

Another contribution that Eliot made to the creation and criticism of poetry is the "objective correlative," a concept which he introduced in a lecture on *Ulysses* and later developed more fully in an essay on *Hamlet*. Although the term had been used earlier by an art critic, Eliot, through his special usage, gave it new meaning which has been widely employed in twentieth-century literary criticism. Eliot conceived the term in the sense of "a set of objects, a situation, a chain of events" that would serve as the "formula" of a "particular emotion." Thus when the "external facts" are presented, "the emotion is immediately evoked." Although Eliot called himself a "classicist in literature," this concept of the objective correlative accommodated both the objective (Classical) and the subjective (Romantic) approaches to the writing of poetry. That is, Eliot employed precise images, as opposed to the sometimes hazy symbols of the Romantic poets, but he did so in order to evoke emotions— "particular" emotions, however, not the emotionalism in which the Romantics at times wallowed. There is a problem with the "objective correlative," of course, in that the "formula" does not unfailingly produce the results sought by the poet: a different emotion than is intended may be evoked by the objective details.

Although Eliot spent most of his adult life in England— he moved to England in 1914 and became a citizen in 1927—he was born, of a well-to-do family, in St. Louis, Missouri. His roots were in New England, however, and his grandfather had graduated from Harvard; Eliot also studied at Harvard, as well as at the universities of Paris and Oxford. While in France he read the French Symbolist poets, and came to be heavily influenced by that movement (see page 385).

In England he first taught, then worked in a bank, and finally became associated with the publishers Faber and Faber. In 1915 he married Vivien Haigh-Wood—a relationship that proved to be an unhappy one because of her mental illness. They separated in 1932. Many years later (1957), after the death of Vivien (1947), Eliot married Valerie Fletcher; this was to be a happier relationship.

Eliot's publication of "The Love Song of J. Alfred Prufrock" in the magazine *Poetry* (1915), and later in a collection of poems (1917), was to have a profound influence on the world of poetry. Indeed, its appearance is, in the opinion of some critics, analogous to the publication of *Lyrical Ballads* (1798) by Wordsworth and Coleridge (see Chapter 5). As *Lyrical Ballads* served as a model for Romantic poetry, so did *Prufrock* for Modernist poetry.

But it was *The Waste Land*, published in 1922, that made Eliot the spokesman for the disillusioned and cynical post-World War I generation. Not a long poem (434 lines), it was accompanied by several pages of Eliot's notes explaining his numerous quotations and allusions. It has been graphically described, rather like a Cubist painting, as "a poem . . . of collapse, of fragmentation: the vase of the old order, with all its certainties, its patterns, systems and placings, has fallen upon the marble and has broken into a thousand pieces. Nine-tenths of them are missing. Yet each of the remaining pieces is exact, bright and delicately articulated, as Eliot jiggles all of them into a significant kaleidoscope."[12] The disorder of this poem, attacked by the traditionalists, is the result of Eliot's clear vision of the traditional order and of the departure of the modern world from that order. Thus *The Waste Land* is Eliot's image of twentieth-century culture and life. His original intention to use as an epigraph the last words of Conrad's Kurtz, "The horror! the horror!", suggests his agreement with Conrad's somber portrayal in *Heart of Darkness* of the failure of European humanism.

In the same year in which Eliot became a British citizen (1927), he also became a member of the Anglican Church, a religious commitment that bore fruit in such poems as *The Hollow Men* (1925), *The Journey of the Magi* (1927), *Ash Wednesday* (1930), and *Four Quartets* (1935). *The Hollow Men* revisits *The Waste Land*, but with allusions

10.7 T. S. Eliot

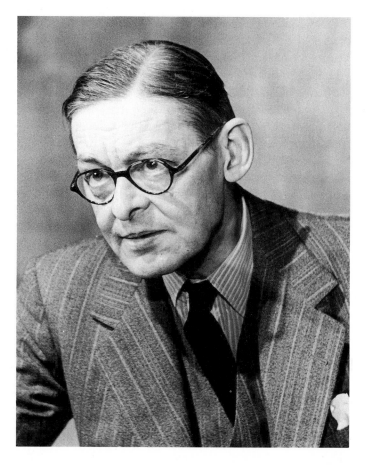

to a faith, now lost, which once gave substance and structure to life. It also reveals the influence of Conrad in its epigraph: *"Mistah Kurtz—he dead."* Like Kurtz, the modern humans that Eliot describes, whose lives have been emptied of all conviction, are hollow, inhabitants of a wasteland shrouded in twilight. The other major influence on the poem is Dante's *Divine Comedy* (see Chapter 7), which is reflected, for example, in the allusion to the "Multifoliate rose," Dante's vision of the redeemed in Paradise. *Four Quartets*, Eliot's last major poem, is a meditation on the tension between time and eternity, between the ever-changing face of history and the changeless transcendence of the Christian faith.

In the 1930s Eliot sought to revive verse drama; and here also he continued his religious pilgrimage. His *Murder in the Cathedral* (1935) is a play about Thomas à Becket in which Eliot dramatized the spiritual struggle that ended in the medieval saint's acceptance of a martyr's death. Here, too, is a "wasteland" world, but hope is offered to those who steel themselves to live—and die—by the discipline of Christian faith. *The Cocktail Party* (1949) also dramatizes the search for salvation, but in the context of the modern English drawing room instead of medieval Canterbury.

Eliot exerted his influence not only through his poetry but also through his literary and social criticism. These writings include *For Lancelot Andrewes* (1929), in the introduction of which he described himself as "an Anglo-Catholic in religion, a classicist in literature, and a royalist in politics," thus avowing his generally conservative views. Among his other critical works are *The Sacred Wood* (1920), *Homage to John Dryden* (1924), *Selected Essays* (1932), *The Use of Poetry and the Use of Criticism* (1933), *After Strange Gods* (also 1933), *The Idea of a Christian Society* (1940), and *Notes Toward the Definition of Culture* (1948).

In view of Eliot's role as the definitive Modernist poet and his authorship of such an impressive body of literary and social criticism, it is no surprise that, in 1948, he was awarded the Noble Prize for literature.

Painting

In the context of art the adjective "Modern" (or "Modernist") refers to abstract or partially abstract works made as early as the beginning of this century, while "Modern movement" refers to dramatic changes in art that began even earlier. The Modern movement ultimately reversed the direction of increasing realism that had begun with Giotto. Some say the reversal started with Impressionism (see Chapter 9). Some say it began with Courbet. Though a realist himself, Courbet (see page 370) was also the first artist to challenge the establishment. The matter will probably never be settled. Nevertheless there are good reasons for identifying Edouard Manet (see page 373) as a pivotal figure between the old and the new.

The Avant-Garde

In the 1860s Manet's ideas about art were a catalyst for the ideas of other young artists—even though most of them pursued different directions. One reason for Manet's following was the fact that he had so much difficulty with the official world of art. The more he and his work were ridiculed, the more both were respected by these artists. Indeed the latter sought Manet's opinions, meeting with him every week to share ideas. Out of these meetings grew Impressionism, a fundamentally new approach to paint-ing which also met with official disapproval. Thus Manet, through his personality and the circumstances of his career even more than through his art, helped to initiate two important aspects of Modernism: the readiness to experiment with the basic language of art, and the existence of an *avant-garde*—leaders of a movement whose work and ideas are seen as nonconformist. Developments in all of the arts from the late nineteenth century to the present have been marked by ceaseless innovation and a succession of artistic movements.

The first avant-garde was Impressionism; its development, style, and implications have been described in Chapter 9. When that movement was on the verge of gaining public acceptance in the late 1880s, another avant-garde, *Post-Impressionism*, was already underway.

Post-Impressionism

The label "Post-Impressionism" was invented by a twentieth-century art historian to identify not a cohesive movement in itself, but a group of artists active in the 1880s and '90s whose works exemplified the next phase of the modern movement. Of those, three—Cézanne, Van Gogh, and Gauguin—are considered the most important. The three had been in contact with one or more of the

Impressionists, but all broke with them to pursue different goals. Although, like their mentors, they continued to favor bright colors, thicker paint and relatively free brushwork, their subject matter was more wide-ranging, and they showed no interest in the science of color. They also took much greater liberties with realism, but not all in the same way.

Cézanne

Paul Cézanne (1839–1906), son of a wealthy family of Aix-en-Provence, was 24 before he started to paint, and in

his thirties before his style began to crystallize. In this he received help from an Impressionist, Camille Pissarro, who taught him the use of brighter color and more disciplined design. Of all the Impressionists, Pissarro was probably the most compassionate and generous. In any case he was the only one who could get along with Cézanne, a solitary man, who was seen by the others as rather boorish. Despite an ardent temperament, Cézanne was shy and ill-at-ease with people. He continued to work with Pissarro, but stayed on the fringes of Impressionism until the late 1870s, when he withdrew to southern France, far from the activities of Paris. There he methodi-

10.8 PAUL CEZANNE
Fruit Bowl, Glass, and Apples, 1879–82
Oil on canvas, $18 \times 12\frac{1}{2}$ ins (45.7×54.6 cm)
Collection Rene Lecompte, Paris

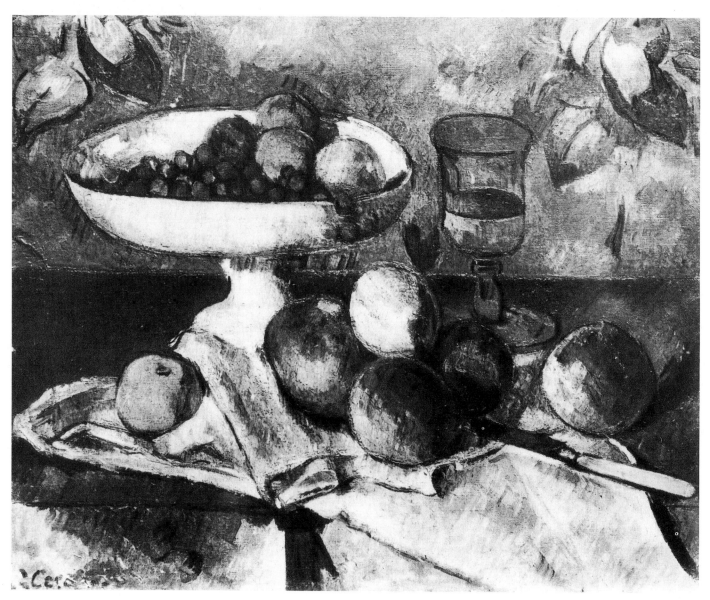

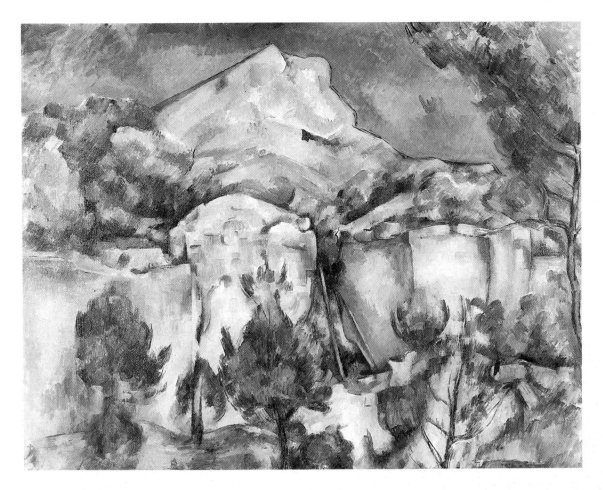

10.9 PAUL CEZANNE
Mont Sainte-Victoire seen from Bibemus Quarry, c. 1898–1900
Oil on canvas, $25\frac{1}{2} \times 32$ ins (64.8 × 81 cm)
The Cone Collection, Baltimore Museum of Art

cally developed and refined his style.

Never sharing Monet's fondness for the effects of reflected light, Cézanne strove to get to the root of things. He desired a more structured art, something "solid and durable, like the art of the museums." The realization of his aim is visible in paintings such as *Fruit Bowl, Glass, and Apples* (Fig. **10.8**), in which the sense of solidity is imparted by a system of diagonal strokes of color rather than by the usual realistic methods of shading and foreshortening. Because of the brushwork, everything—tablecloth, wallpaper, fruit, and bowl—seems to have a physical presence. Equally important are the ways in which Cézanne controlled the abstract elements of the composition. Not only are visual weights and directions kept in balance, but spatial depth is kept within bounds. No object is seen to be very near; no pocket of space is allowed to penetrate too deeply, as variations in depth are distributed rather evenly throughout the canvas. To accomplish his ends, Cézanne took liberties with the rules of perspective: different eye levels exist for the table top, and for the sides of the bowl

and glass and their rims. Needless to say, the nineteenth-century public viewed such liberties as either license or incompetence.

These liberties are even more pronounced in *Mont Sainte-Victoire Seen from Bibemus Quarry* (Fig. **10.9**) in which the space is broken up by multiple eye levels and focal points. Again, depth is evenly dispersed—the view of a distant mountain notwithstanding. The foreground has been pushed back; the mountain has been pulled forward. Hollows of depth are determined by these devices, as well as by the multiple points of view. However, the tensions created by these conflicting viewpoints are moderated by the balancing of weights and directions. Although the brushwork is as rhythmic as in the still life, it is more open, at times almost suggestive of atmosphere, as if Cézanne had responded to the subject like an orthodox Impressionist. "Look at this Sainte-Victoire! What dash, what an urgent thirst for sunlight!" he remarked to a friend. As Rouen Cathedral was to Monet, Sainte-Victoire was to Cézanne—a challenge to which he returned again and again. The pulsations of Monet's motif are on the surface; those of Cézanne's throb beneath the surface, suggesting that "... colors ... rise up from the roots of the world."[13]

Although Impressionism was in many ways a striking departure from tradition, it did not attack the fundamental premise that realism, the imitation of appearances, is a necessary condition for a picture to be a work of art. Cézanne did not disregard appearances completely, but his painting of Mont Sainte-Victoire begins to refute that premise. To understand his art, one must accept a new premise, one asserting that the demands of pictorial design take priority over realism. Cézanne's aim was not to make abstract art. He believed in representing the real world, but in painterly terms. As he expressed it: "Art is a harmony parallel to nature's."[14] While this statement respects nature, it also asserts that a work of art has a life of its own, independent of the visual world.

During the time he was involved with the Paris art world, Cézanne never had a work of his accepted by the official Salon. Moreover, the works of his that were shown in the Impressionist exhibitions of the 1870s were ridiculed. In southern France, he pursued his demanding art in isolation. As his paintings were mostly ignored, he sold few. Because of a substantial family inheritance, he did not have to sell, but he must have suffered from the indifference accorded his efforts. In the early twentieth century, however, when his work was discovered by new avant-gardes, the indifference came to a sudden end. Cézanne's paintings began to be appreciated, and his influence became considerable. The art world had at last come around to his belief that "Art is a harmony parallel to nature's."

Van Gogh

The tragic life of Vincent van Gogh (1853–1890), born in Holland of Dutch-Reformed missionaries, paralleled that of Cézanne in some respects. Both had a tendency to alienate people, particularly Van Gogh. Both started their careers late; both worked in Paris before moving to the south of France. As artists, both were outsiders as far as the official art world was concerned; both were on the edges of Impressionism. In the works of both, the abstract elements of form begin to infringe on the sovereignty of traditional realism, but in different ways: Cézanne, the classicist of the two, emphasized structure; Van Gogh, the romanticist, emphasized the expression of emotion.

After trying and failing at a number of pursuits—theology, missionary work, and selling art—Van Gogh turned to painting at the age of 27. Ever mindful of his Protestant background and former work as an evangelist, Van Gogh often looked to the paintings of Rembrandt, believing him to be the only artist to merge art and religion. Although Van Gogh had no urge to make religious art *per se*, he did want to express his feelings of compassion through paintings of downtrodden people. His first masterpiece, *The Potato Eaters* (Fig. **10.10**), reflects this desire. Van Gogh wrote, "I have tried to emphasize that those people, eating their potatoes in the lamplight, have dug the earth with those very hands they put in the dish...."[15] Courbet, also motivated by humanitarian impulses, had painted the same kind of people. But there is a fundamental difference between his approach and Van Gogh's—indeed between Rembrandt's and Van Gogh's. The emotional content in either Courbet or Rembrandt is largely built on realism, the believability of the subject as depicted. Important, but less so, are colors and elements of composition. In a Van Gogh, however, the latter is all-important. Although the artist claimed to have focused on the coarseness of the hands, he nevertheless repeated the quality of coarseness throughout: clothing, faces, background, and the entire composition have a gnarled quality. The colors are dark and earthy: browns, blacks, and bluish-blacks; as Van Gogh said, "like the color of a very dusty potato."

The first six years of Van Gogh's career were spent in the Low Countries, where he depicted peasant life in dreary, dark tones, as in *The Potato Eaters*. Although compassionate toward the people he painted, Van Gogh was so moody and unpredictable that he was unable to get along with associates. His meager income forced him to be dependent on relatives and friends for support. After several moves, quarrels, and a failed attempt at studying art in Belgium, he was physically and emotionally exhausted. In 1886 he joined his brother Theo, an art dealer, in Paris. That city was good for his health (at least at first) and for his art. Coming into contact with the Impressionists, he was encouraged to cease using muddy colors in favor of a lighter and brighter palette; the influence of Japanese art led him to simplify and strengthen his design. But the Paris interlude lasted less than two years. Tensions developed between him and Theo, and in February 1888—perhaps at the suggestion of Toulouse-Lautrec (see below)—Van Gogh moved to Arles, in Provence.

There he entered on the last two years of a short life and an even shorter career. But those years saw an outpouring of productivity and the final maturing of Van Gogh's style. The skies at Arles had the same wholesome effect on him as those at Sainte-Victoire had on Cézanne. To artists and visitors alike, the environment of southern France is especially salutary. Many of the artist's Arles paintings express euphoria through vivid colors and lively brushstrokes. Typically, like *Wheatfield and Cypress Trees* (Fig. **10.11**) they feature yellow, the color used by children to

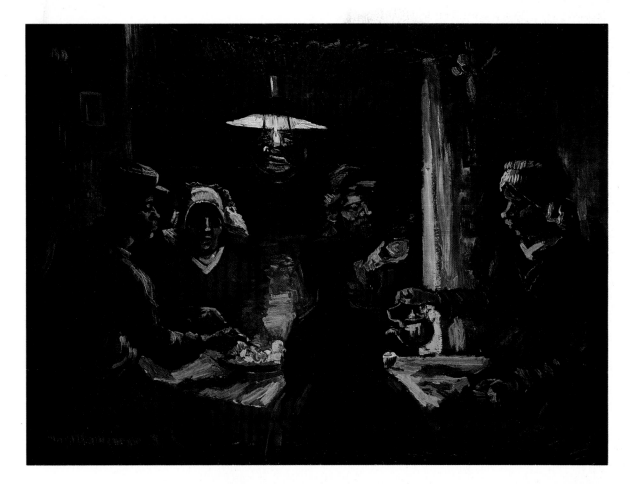

10.10 VINCENT VAN GOGH
The Potato Eaters, 1885
Oil on canvas, $32\frac{1}{4} \times 45$ ins
(82×114.3 cm)
National Museum, Amsterdam

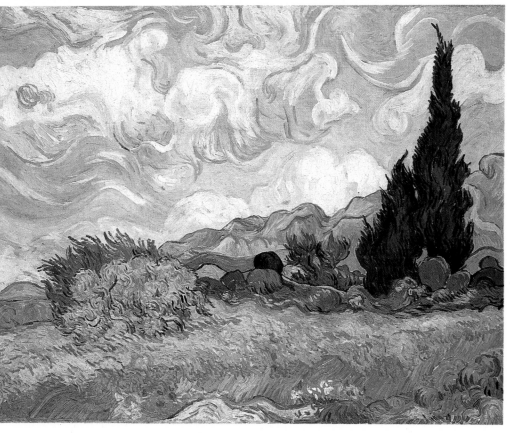

10.11 VINCENT VAN GOGH
Wheatfield and Cypress Trees,
1889
Oil on canvas, $28\frac{1}{2} \times 36$ ins
(72×91.5 cm)
National Gallery, London

symbolize joy. However, in this painting, yellow is offset by other colors and compositional factors, creating an ambivalence between joy and anxiety. It is opposed by the cool greens of the trees and the icy blue of the mountains. The open sky on one side of the design is opposed by dark cypresses, an ancient symbol of death: "a splash of *black* in a sunny landscape," as Van Gogh described it.[16] Meanwhile the surface is animated throughout by lively, ribbon-like strokes of paint. The entire landscape seems enlivened and set in motion, as it were, by some unseen force. In Cézanne's *Mont Sainte-Victoire* the energies of nature are stabilized; in this painting they threaten to erupt.

In some paintings, the energies did erupt. When he was disturbed, Van Gogh vented his feelings in harsh colors, serpentine shapes, restless brushwork, and dizzying perspectives. Thus, to some extent, his art constitutes a record of his mood swings. The Arles work represents a full range of mental states: composure, ecstasy, anxiety, and combinations of these, as in *Wheatfield and Cypress Trees*. The years in southern France were marked by many ups and downs, some more dramatic than in earlier periods of his life. One episode involved the artist Paul Gauguin (see below) who was invited by Van Gogh to join him in the fall of 1888. At first, things went well, but eventually their relationship led to a series of breakdowns and hospital stays on the part of Van Gogh. Still, he continued to produce paintings—sometimes joyful, sometimes disturbed, sometimes incorporating a mixture of emotions— until the summer of 1890, when he committed suicide.

His paintings, like those of Cézanne, were discovered by avant-garde artists of the early twentieth century who believed in the validity of expressing ideas through abstract forms. In Van Gogh's case, these artists were inspired by the intensity of his color and the emotionalism of his forms. He is the ancestor of all the *expressionistic* arts movements of the twentieth century.

Gauguin

In his forties Paul Gauguin (1848–1903) left his wife, family, and a career as a stockbroker in Paris to take up painting. In this relatively late start his career resembles those of Cézanne and Van Gogh; and Gauguin even shared some of their artistic beliefs. But he differed markedly from them in personality, being highly extrovert and a notorious adventurer—in short, the archetypal bohemian artist.

As in the case of Cézanne, it was the amiable Pissarro who, in 1879, introduced Gauguin to the techniques of the Impressionists. Gauguin emulated their style and entered works in their shows until 1886, when he began to indulge his own taste for the exotic. In terms of subject matter, this led him away from painting the countryside around Paris to exploring unfamiliar territory such as the landscape and provincial life of Brittany in northern France. In terms of style, it led him far away from the Impressionists' dependence on realism and scientific color theory.

Although his work is similar in some respects to that of Cézanne and Van Gogh, it is quite individual. His colors, like Van Gogh's, are bright, but sensuous, rather than vivid or provocative. Unlike Van Gogh's ridged brushwork, his painting surface is relatively smooth. Although he experimented with Cézanne's diagonal strokes, Gauguin avoided his multiple planes and viewpoints in favor of flattened, decorative forms. His compositions, bearing the influence of Japanese prints (which had recently seized the imagination of the French art world), are unusually ornamental. Unlike the basically traditional subject matter depicted by both Cézanne and Van Gogh, his tends toward the exotic.

Many of these traits are summarized in a painting finished in 1888, shortly before the artist visited Van Gogh in Arles: *Vision After the Sermon, Jacob Wrestling with the Angel* (Fig. 10.12). The vision is observed by Brittany women, the same kind of rural people Van Gogh painted in Holland. Gauguin's treatment of peasants, however, was motivated by a fascination for "primitive culture" rather than by compassion. To him, the only thing that mattered was the fact that they, like all simple people, were picturesque, and therefore, ideal subjects for a painting. He simplified and stylized the bonnets of the women to stress their abstract shapes and lines. The field on which Jacob and the angel struggle slopes upward to provide a backdrop for the foreground shapes, and is painted red-orange to contrast with the white of the bonnets and the greens and blues in the rest of the picture. The women are separated from the vision by a tree trunk, a bold diagonal in the center. *Vision After the Sermon* is intended to be read as a two-dimensional surface, a composition of silhouettes. The flattening of form, of course, emphasizes the aspects of pattern and color, Gauguin's specialty. But it also supports the mood of naive sincerity that the artist wanted to capture.

Gauguin's romantic quest for primitive culture eventually led him to Tahiti in the South Pacific. But he was in France long enough to become known both as an artist and as a figure in the avant-garde. Colorful, gregarious and articulate, he publicized his theories about art—in particular, the "autonomy" of color, shape, and line. Like Manet, he had a magnetic personality, and he was the inspiration for a group of young artists called "Nabis" (Hebrew, "prophets"). His influence extended even

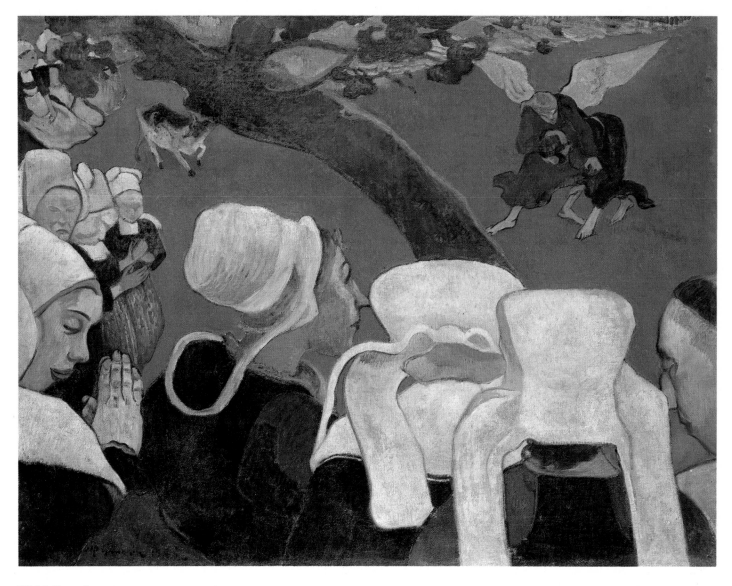

10.12 PAUL GAUGUIN
The Vision After the Sermon (Jacob Wrestling with the Angel), 1888
Oil on canvas, $28\frac{3}{4} \times 36\frac{1}{4}$ ins (73 × 92 cm)
National Gallery of Scotland, Edinburgh

beyond artists. The Symbolist writers (see above) perceived him as a kindred spirit and even reviewed his work in their literary journals. Because of such followings, Gauguin's impact on art developments occurred earlier than that of either Cézanne or Van Gogh—who were too introverted to promote their ideas in any way except through their painting. Gauguin's contributions helped prepare the way for a new art and, eventually, the acceptance of all three Post-Impressionists into the canon of art history.

Fin de Siècle Art

The decade of the 1890s, often referred to as the *fin de siècle* (French "end of the century"), saw the culmination of Post-Impressionism, the second generation avant-garde. Before reviewing further examples, we should be reminded that this decade was a pluralistic one for art. Although Impressionism had triumphed, traditional salon art had not disappeared; optically realistic styles, of all varieties, were still very popular. On the other hand, Post-Impressionism and developments related to it were gaining more and more visibility. Gauguin's influence was felt by proxy through the Nabis and the Symbolists. This influence spread to the public realm, as simplified imagery and flattened forms reminiscent of Gauguin were showing up in the popular arts—particularly posters and newspaper caricatures.

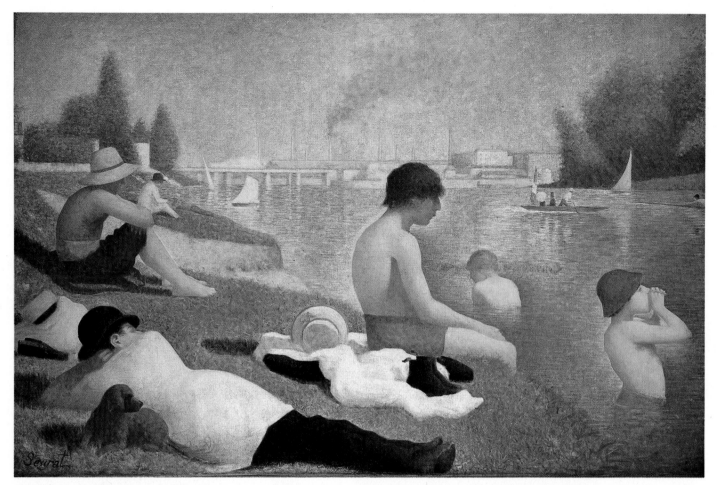

10.13 GEORGES SEURAT
Bathers, 1883–84
Oil on canvas, 6 ft 7 ins × 9 ft 11 ins (2 × 3.02 m)
Tate Gallery, London

Of all those who participated in the second generation avant-garde, the one most celebrated by his contemporaries was Georges Seurat (1859–1891). Although his life and career were even shorter than those of Van Gogh, he matured rapidly in art and, by the time of his death, was the leader of a movement called "Neo-Impressionism." Yet his works, when compared to those of Cézanne, Van Gogh, and Gauguin, are conservative—that is, much closer to Impressionism in both style and subject matter. Mainly, Seurat attempted to make Impressionism more systematic: first, by creating forms in terms of clear, geometric solids, as in the men, boys, and trees of *Bathers at Asnières* (Fig. **10.13**); second, by organizing these forms into a perfectly integrated and balanced composition; and third, by systematizing the Impressionists' method of broken color. This last technique—only partially realized in this example—evolved into a scientific system of separating colors of the spectrum into individual dots, called *pointillism*. Paintings made by this method tend to shimmer like mosaics. For his efforts Seurat was accused of turning a fresh, spontaneous style into something static. On the other hand, he was praised for introducing the classical qualities of serenity and monumentality into Impressionism. His works have been compared in this respect to those of Piero della Francesca (Fig. 3.21) and Poussin (Fig. 4.14). Still, as far as developments in the Modern movement were concerned, pointillism was his single most important contribution. Although it was not pursued in significant ways by other artists, its special luminosity did have implications for the abstract possibilities of color.

Like Seurat, Henri de Toulouse-Lautrec (1864–1901) held to the general principles of Impressionism. But his relationship to that style was the opposite of Seurat's. Instead of making it more monumental and methodical, he made it even more spontaneous and informal. His people are depicted with impetuous strokes of color rather than in terms of shaded volumes and rounded contours.

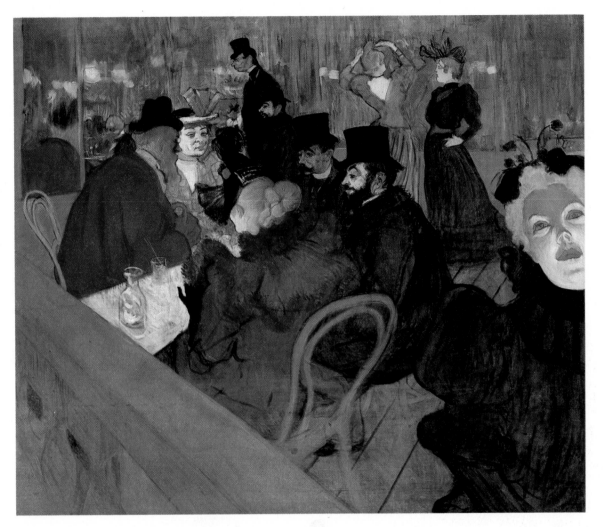

10.14 Henri De Toulouse-Lautrec
At the Moulin-Rouge, 1892
Oil on canvas, $48\frac{3}{8} \times 55\frac{1}{4}$ ins (123×140.5 cm)
Art Institute of Chicago

His compositions have the haphazard quality of snapshots, as opposed to the studied effects of Seurat's. But the aspect of his art that is the most original—distinguishing it not only from Seurat's but also from the Impressionists'—is its subject matter. It reflects the mood of decadence characteristic of the *fin de siècle*—a syndrome of boredom, cynicism, and defeatist attitudes about modern life—perhaps the final aftershock of the traumas of industrialism and urbanism. An aristocrat by birth and stunted in growth as a result of a childhood accident, Toulouse-Lautrec was a habitué of Paris nightlife: cafés, brothels, and bawdy cabarets. Indeed, he is the little man strolling beside a taller man in the background of *At the Moulin Rouge* (Fig. **10.14**). Similarities between this painting and Degas' *The Glass of Absinthe* (Fig. 9.16) are no coincidence, as Toulouse-Lautrec admired Degas enormously. In *At the*

Moulin Rouge, however, the brushwork is looser; the design, featuring a large figure cut by the right edge of the canvas, more radical; and the mood more decadent. Although his work is far from realistic in the optical sense, it is more penetrating in the existential sense than, for example, that of Courbet or Degas. Toulouse-Lautrec's account of this kind of society, recorded with the empathy of an insider and the detachment of an artist, is unique in the history of art.

Consistent with the spiritual malaise of the times, much *fin-de-siècle* art was preoccupied with mysticism and eroticism. The art of Edvard Munch (1863–1944) is permeated with despair and paranoia. A Norwegian who spent much of his creative life in Berlin and Paris, Munch was not in contact with the Impressionists, but apparently was aware of the works of the Post-Impressionists. The

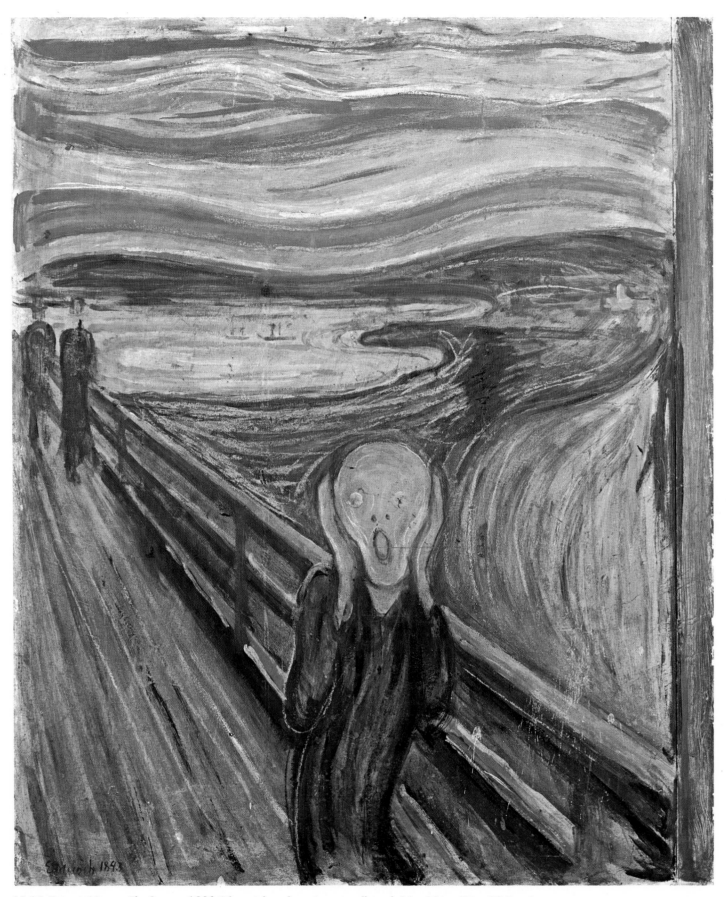

10.15 EDVARD MUNCH *The Scream*, 1893 Oil, pastel, and casein on cardboard, 36 × 29 ins (91 × 73.5 cm) National Museum, Oslo

flattened forms of *The Scream* (Fig. **10.15**) are reminiscent of the shapes in Gauguin's scene of Brittany peasants; the long, parallel lines call to mind similar lines in the cypress trees of Van Gogh's landscape. And like the latter, *The Scream* represents an intense emotional state. The agitated figure at the near end of a bridge on a boardwalk may be threatened by the two shadowy figures in the distance. But paranoia is evoked mainly by the nature of the forms: the exaggerated perspective, the wraith-like shape of the screaming figure, and especially the lines which echo the scream and imprison the rest of the forms.

The drawings of Aubrey Beardsley (1872–1898) relate to *art nouveau*, a style in decorative arts and architecture which flourished in Europe in the 1890s. Still, the striking patterns and sinuous lines in his illustration for Oscar Wilde's *Salome* (Fig. **10.16**) are almost a caricature of the forms in Gauguin's and Van Gogh's paintings, while Salome's morbid fascination with the head of John the Baptist—made all the more perverse by Beardsley's elegant style—is another reflection of the climate of decadence that pervaded the *fin de siècle*.

Early Twentieth Century

More changes and breakthroughs occurred in art in the first two decades of the twentieth century than in any other comparable period—including the first two decades of the sixteenth century (see Chapter 3). These changes may not have been greeted with the same enthusiasm that met, say, Michelangelo's *David* (Fig. 3.36) 400 years earlier. But they were not denounced so universally as those of the Impressionists; twentieth-century critics were a little more open minded than their nineteenth-century predecessors. Collectors, also mindful of the past, often bought new art for the same reasons people buy stocks in a growth industry: the new art seemed likely to increase in value. To start things off, major shows of Cézanne, Van Gogh, and Gauguin (in 1899, 1901, and 1903, respectively) greeted the new century. Post-Impressionism had not only triumphed, it was now the main inspiration for further change in the Modern movement.

Fauvism: Matisse

Henri Matisse (1869–1954) was the first artist of the new century to capitalize on this artistic ferment. His apprenticeship had started in 1891 when he switched from the study of law to art. He began by imitating the Old Masters. By mid-decade he had discovered Impressionism; by the turn of the century, Cézanne and Gauguin. Then, after experimenting with Neo-Impressionism and pointillism, he improved his understanding of color. In 1904 he

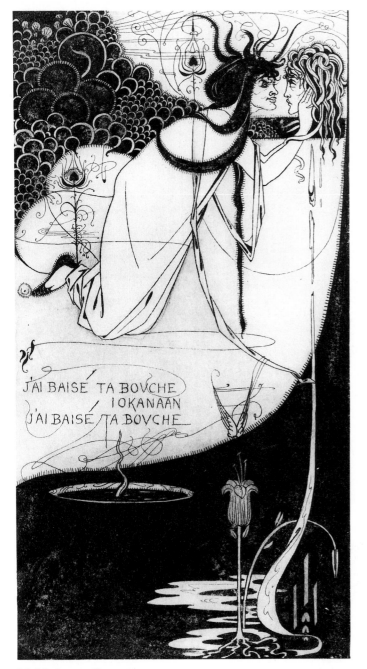

10.16 AUBREY BEARDSLEY
Salome, 1892
Pen drawing
Princeton University Library, Princeton, New Jersey

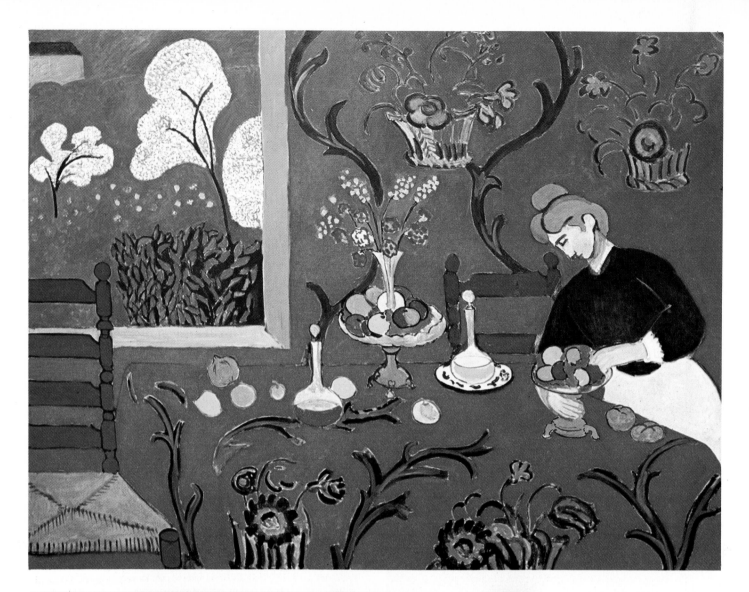

10.17 HENRI MATISSE
The Red Room, 1908–9
Oil on canvas, 71 × 97 ins
(180 × 246 cm)
Hermitage Museum, Leningrad

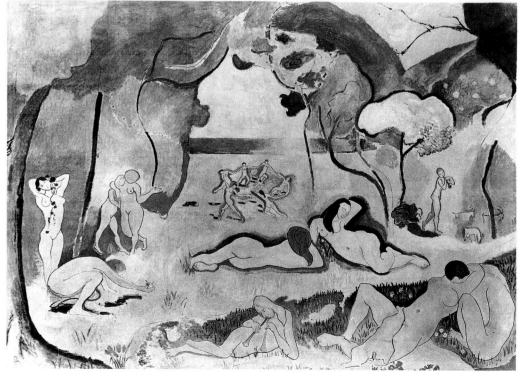

10.18 HENRI MATISSE
The Joy of Life, 1905–6
Oil on canvas, 68½ × 93¾ ins
(174.6 × 239 cm)
The Barnes Foundation,
Merian, Pennsylvania

discovered the color of Van Gogh at a retrospective show. Like Dürer, who progressed from Late Gothic to High Renaissance (see page 332), Matisse progressed from academicism to Post-Impressionism in a little more than a decade; but he was soon to go even further. After spending the summer of 1905 painting at the village of Collioure on the Mediterranean, he joined others to show paintings in a salon specializing in progressive art, which in those days meant Impressionism and Post-Impressionism. As it turned out, the work of Matisse and his friends was much more progressive than the show sponsors had expected. Taking offense at what appeared to be an orgy of color, a critic referred to the group as "fauves" (French, "wild beasts").

The critic's epithet was aimed at paintings similar to Mattisse's *The Red Room* (Fig. **10.17**), a work that employs audacious color along with the simplest of pictorial means. Its subject, a room with a window, a table setting, and a maid, together with its rectangular composition, is reminiscent of Vermeer's *Young Woman with a Water Jug* (Fig. 9.7). But beyond these similarities, the two paintings could not be more different. Vermeer's room is permeated with the glow of reflected light. Matisse's is permeated with the color red—physiologically and psychologically the most potent of all hues—tempered only by the cool colors in the rectangle of the window, the color of the woman's blouse, and the blue of the many arabesque lines. *Young Woman with a Water Jug*, through its studied and almost photographic representation of a Dutch interior, invokes the harmony of domestic tranquillity. *The Red Room*, through its balancing of the forces of brilliant color, the variable tendencies of light and dark and warm and cool to advance or recede, also evokes a harmony. But it is a kind of harmony that appeals directly to the senses rather than to the imagination. Matisse's genius lay in his use of color, which is sometimes subtle, sometimes daring, but always original. The lessons he learned from pointillism were no doubt helpful, though his intuition probably played a bigger role.

The Red Room, clearly, is a new kind of painting. It could have been made at any time in this century. The 1905 fall salon, now remembered as the Fauves show, was the first exhibit of truly twentieth-century art, that is, "modern art" as we know it even today. The Fauves, or Fauvism, as a movement did not last. Of the nine original members, only four—Matisse, Roualt, Derain, and Vlaminck—transcended the Fauves label to become well-known artists in their own right. Thus, the importance of Fauvism, apart from its being a historical event, lay in its usefulness in launching a new avant-garde, headed by Matisse.

Shortly after the Fauves show, Matisse consolidated his

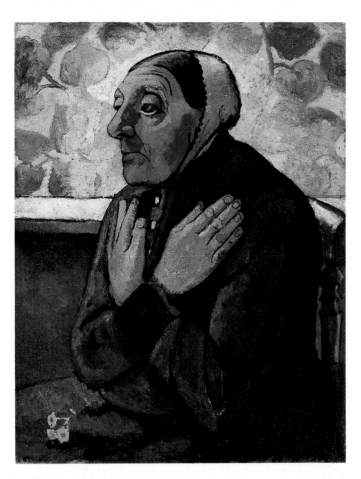

10.19 Paula Modersohn-Becker
Old Peasant Woman Praying, 1906
Oil on canvas, $29\frac{3}{4} \times 22\frac{3}{4}$ ins (75.5 × 57.8 cm)
The Detroit Institute of Arts

leadership of the avant-garde by creating *Joy of Life* (Fig. **10.18**), a pastoral scene of naked nymphs and lovers. Like *The Red Room*, this work subverts all the conventions of pictorial realism, while extolling color for color's sake. In *Joy of Life*, however, the shapes and lines are more fluid, the tonal areas more continuous. It contains most of the essentials of a style that Matisse was to continue for the rest of his long career. In the final analysis, the flattened forms and beautiful colors of both this work and *The Red Room* relate to Gauguin's style more than to Cézanne's or Van Gogh's. The joy in *Joy of Life* is proclaimed not by the dancing nymphs but by lyrical pattern and subtle color—hallmarks of a style that Matisse was to pursue. It fulfills his dream of "an art of balance, of purity and serenity devoid of troubling or depressing subject matter ..."[17]

German Expressionism

Up to now we have been talking mostly about French artists. By 1905, the year of the Fauves show, there were young artists in other parts of Europe, particularly Germany, who were just as rebellious. A group in Dresden gave form to this spirit by organizing a society called Die

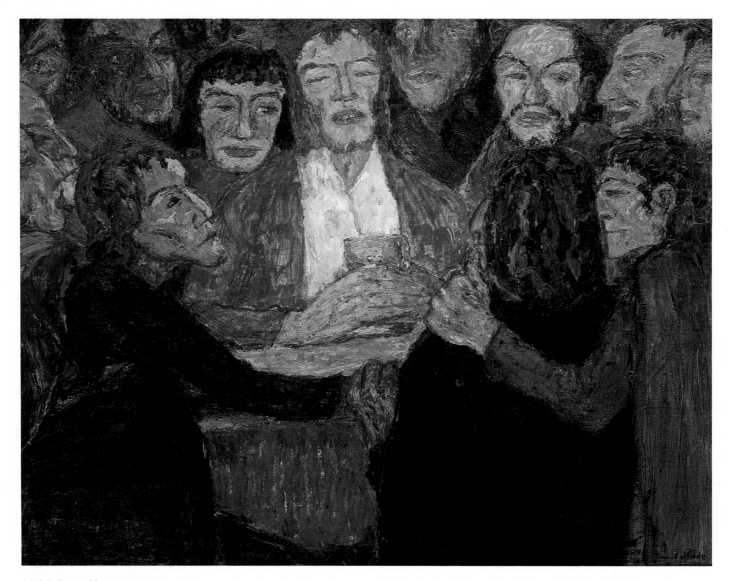

10.20 EMILE NOLDE
The Last Supper, 1909
Oil on canvas, $32\frac{1}{2} \times 42$ ins (82.5×106 cm)
Neukirchen, Schleswig, Germany

Brücke ("The Bridge"). A few years later another group, called Der Blaue Reiter ("The Blue Rider"), which included Germans and other nationalities, was formed in Munich. The work of these groups, and that of kindred artists active in central Europe up to the time of the Nazi takeover of Germany, has come to be known as *German Expressionism.*

Paula Modersohn-Becker (1876–1907), seen now as one of the earliest exponents of the movement, was the first to make use of Post-Impressionism in original ways. For example, in *Old Peasant Woman* (Fig. **10.19**), the solid construction of the head and figure reflects Cézanne, while the sympathetic approach to the subject is reminiscent of Van Gogh. Though not affiliated with the Brücke,

Modersohn-Becker's art was admired by members of the German avant-garde, and she would have been a leader in the movement had she not died of complications related to childbirth at the age of 31.

The German Expressionists immediately following Modersohn-Becker broke with the past in more radical ways than she did. Although the German avant-garde was inspired by the French avant-garde—the Fauve label described their own mood, and paintings like *The Red Room* stimulated them to be bold—their artistic goals differed from the latter in fundamental ways. The themes chosen by the French painters were essentially non-controversial: their use of distortion and bright color was intended to please, not shock, though at first it did shock the public. On the other hand, Expressionist themes were often selected for their personal, moral, social, or religious implications, while bright color and distorted forms were exploited for their power to disturb and to express the artist's feelings about life; often, these feelings were anxious ones. In other words, German Expressionist art was diametrically opposed to Matisse's serene art "devoid of troubling or depressing subject matter."

Seriousness in art had had (and perhaps still has) a long history in northern Europe. The Expressionists' immediate predecessors—indeed their heroes—were Munch and Van Gogh. Earlier predecessors, in regard to seriousness, might be said to include such people as Friedrich (see Chapter 5), Dürer, Grünewald, Rembrandt (see Chapter 8), and Sluter (see Chapter 7). However the German avant-garde also sought inspiration from such exotic sources as African sculpture—an interest shared by the Fauves, who collected African masks.

The Last Supper (Fig. **10.20**) by Emil Nolde (1867–1956) typifies these tendencies. Part of a series on the life of Christ, this one is less agitated than some of the others. The composition, which is almost banal in its simple frontality, is matched by the crude drawing and the primitive manner of the painting; the paint surface is thick and rough, and the colors are "raw" in some places, muddy in others. *The Last Supper* is an example of deliberate, even calculated, primitivism—perhaps intended to evoke primal responses in the viewer.

Though also roughly painted and simple in composition, *Self-Portrait* (Fig. **10.21**) by Oskar Kokoschka (1886–1980) is anything but primitive in style or concept. Like Van Gogh, Kokoschka constructed the figure with strokes of thick paint that endow it with intensity. The result is very personal, providing a glimpse of Kokoschka as tragic artist-hero—a somewhat self-indulgent notion which was a legacy of the Romantic period (see Chapter 5). More probing even than Rembrandt's *Self Portrait* (Fig. 8.23), Kokoschka's reveals his inner life not through natural gestures and signs of age but through exaggeration of the eyes, the length of the head, and the size of the hand, and by the way the figure is located in a field of expressionistic paint. It is one of the most compelling portraits in modern painting.

The most important artist involved in German Expressionism was neither German nor preoccupied with anxiety: Wassily Kandinsky (1866–1944). Like Matisse, Kandinsky studied the Post-Impressionists for their color, not their themes. For some years his own paintings were very Fauvist in nature. When he went to Munich he soon became the leader of the Blaue Reiter group; indeed the name was derived from one of his brightly-colored

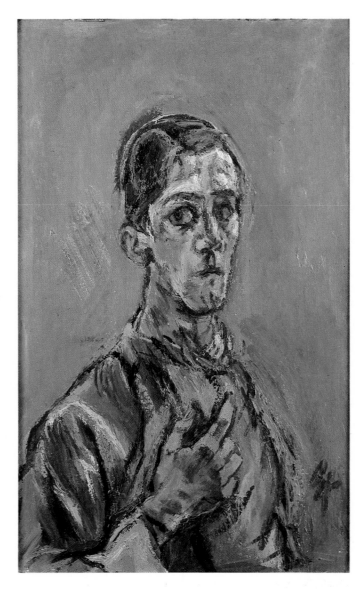

10.21 OSKAR KOKOSCHKA
Self Portrait, 1913
Oil on canvas, 32 × 19½ ins (81.2 × 49.5 cm)
Museum of Modern Art, New York

paintings. At about that time he also achieved one of the Modern movement's major breakthroughs: the first completely abstract painting. Dispensing altogether with subject matter and references to objects, Kandinsky painted his first abstraction, a watercolor, in 1910. He continued to make more after that, in both watercolors and oils. To counteract tendencies of viewers in those days to read images into his work, Kandinsky titled his paintings as if they were musical scores—a practice that also reflected his belief in the analogies between abstract art and music. His *Sketch I for "Composition VII"* (Fig. **10.22**) has neither a subject nor a title, but it has little need for such cues to convey its emotional surge. The

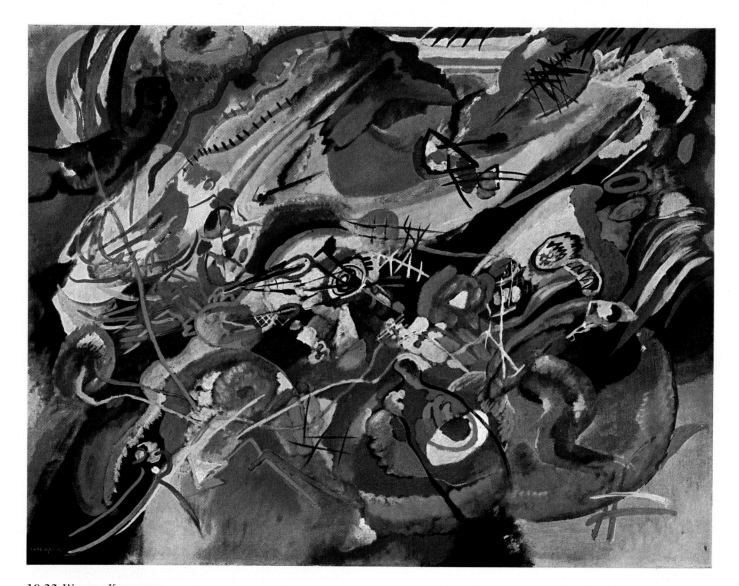

10.22 Wassily Kandinsky
Sketch I for "Composition VII", 1913
Oil on canvas $30\frac{3}{4} \times 39\frac{3}{8}$ ins (78×99.5 cm)
Städtische Galerie in Lenbachhaus, Munich

color, energy, and boiling turbulence of the forms speak for themselves. They also link this painting to the tradition of Expressionism out of which it grew. Kandinsky, a Russian Orthodox Christian, had come to believe in the need for a spiritual revival, and his experiments in abstract art were part of that quest. Because of the newness of his art and ideas, he felt compelled to defend them in a treatise, *Concerning the Spiritual in Art* written in 1910.

Cubism: Picasso

In 1905, the year of the Fauves exhibit, Pablo Picasso (1881–1973), the twentieth century's most famous artist, was a struggling young painter living in Paris. Born in

Spain, the son of an art teacher, and a child prodigy who received academic training in his home country, Picasso decided in 1901 to broaden his horizons in Paris. During his early years there, he absorbed many sources in an attempt to catch up with the Modern movement. The elongated figure in *The Old Guitarist* (Fig. **10.23**), one of his "blue-period" works, is indicative of his originality in applying the lessons of Post-Impressionism. In 1904 he studied Greek vase painting, pre-Roman Spanish sculpture, and African sculpture. By 1905 he was beginning to assimilate these sources into his work, as his experiments in style showed increasing originality.

But that year he was to encounter another, newer, source: Fauvism and the art of Matisse. There is reason to

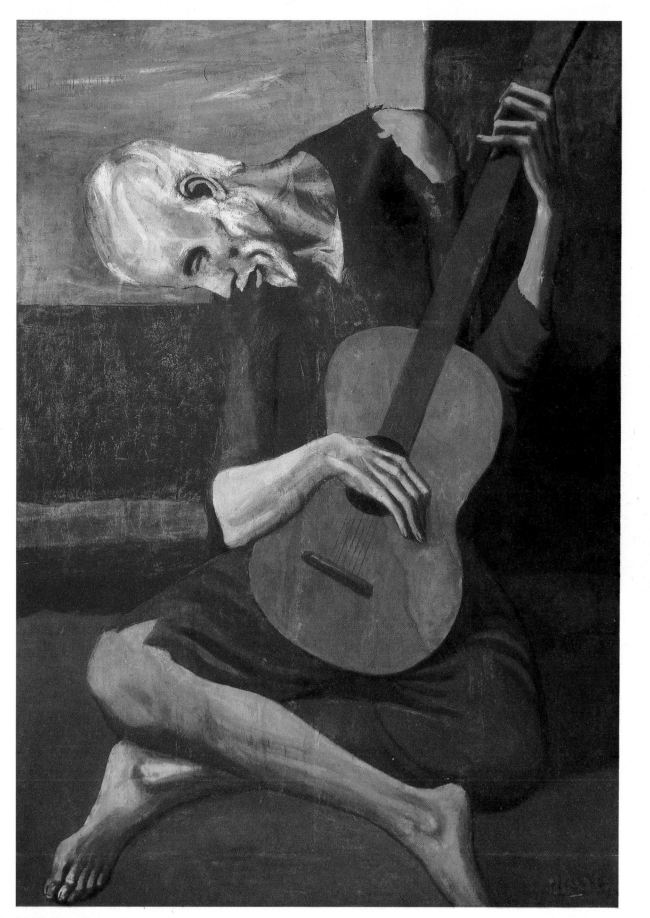

10.23 Pablo Picasso
The Old Guitarist, 1903
Oil on panel, 47¾ × 32½ ins (121 × 82.5 cm) Art Institute of Chicago

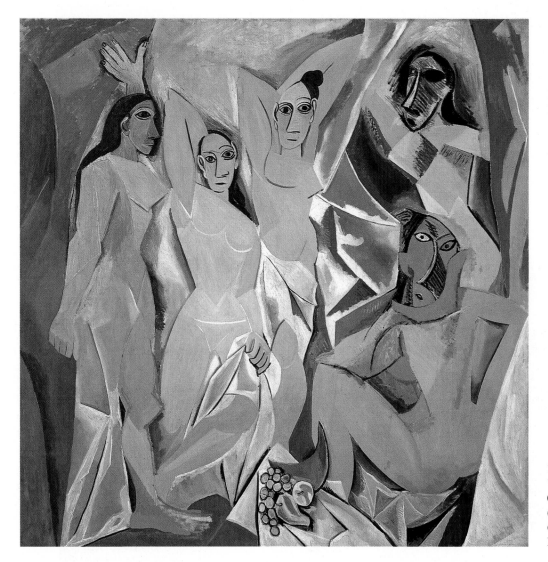

10.24 PABLO PICASSO
Les Demoiselles d'Avignon,
1906–7
Oil on canvas, 96 × 92 ins
(2.24 × 2.34 m)
Museum of Modern Art,
New York

10.25 (right) GEORGES BRAQUE
Violin and Palette, 1910
Oil on canvas, $36\frac{1}{4} \times 16\frac{7}{8}$ ins
(92 × 42 cm)
Guggenheim Museum,
New York

believe that the latter's *Joy of Life* inspired the restless Picasso to make a similarly important work of his own. If so, the result — *Les Demoiselles d'Avignon* (Fig. **10.24**) — is a reaction to Matisse's style rather than an attempt to assimilate it. Without question, this incongruous scene of five deformed bodies was radical for its time, in this respect surpassing even the Fauves. Matisse himself was shocked, calling it an outrage and a mockery of the Modern movement. In terms of subject matter, it both borrows from and devastates a tradition going back to Botticelli. In terms of form, it attacks tradition more aggressively than anything ever seen before. Even today, after nearly a century of modern art, it still looks raw. Yet, behind its seeming irrationality, there is precedent and method. The warping of the forms, together with the peaks and valleys of shallow depth, are indebted to Cézanne. The severity of some of the forms — especially those of the faces on the right — is indebted to African sculpture.

Although the art world was not at first aware of its significance, *Les Demoiselles* turned out to be not only a landmark in twentieth-century art, but the precursor of a major style called *Cubism*. In the process of bringing this style to maturity Picasso was aided by the French artist Georges Braque (1882–1963). Between 1907 and 1913 the two worked so closely that their paintings—each an individual experiment in pictorial structure—are hard to tell apart. By 1909 they arrived at a phase called Analytical Cubism, represented here by Braque's *Violin and Palette* (Fig. **10.25**).

The subject matter of a Cubist work is less important than the ways in which it has been deconstructed and reconstructed in the process of creating the work. Instead of the shocking deformities and disjunctions characteristic of *Les Demoiselles*, for example, Analytical Cubism presents a consistent system of interlocking, semi-transparent planes. The objects, like the nudes in the earlier work,

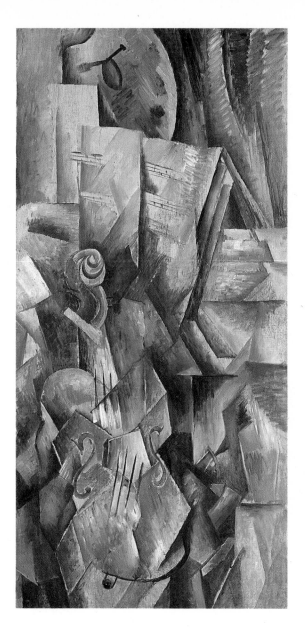

other movements. But Picasso and Braque, not content to leave it at that, continued to experiment. Because references to objects tended increasingly to be dissolved into a sea of Cubist facets, the artists had to make a choice between allowing their work to drift into complete abstraction or re-establishing the connection between it and the world of objects. Choosing the latter course, they began adding letters, scraps of paper, and other extraneous materials to their paintings—at first, tentatively, but by 1912, more confidently, using a technique known as *collage* (French, "pasting"). Braque's *Le Courrier* (Fig. **10.26**) consists mostly of cut and pasted scraps of material—imitation wood, a tobacco wrapper, a playing card, newspaper, and so forth—with just a few painted lines. In less than two years Picasso and Braque had moved from the rationality of Analytical Cubism to the caprice of pasting up random scraps. Purists who saw this as paradoxical, if not an insult to the dignity of painting, found little comfort in Picasso's jest: "Look, we can make works of art out of the contents of waste baskets."[18]

Collages soon led to *Synthetic Cubism*, which in some respects is the antithesis of Analytical Cubism. Instead of a system of shaded planes and spatial depth, Synthetic Cubism consists of flat, overlapping shapes; instead of monochromatic tones, it features color and textural variety. About the only things the two styles share are angular shapes and interlocking design. Picasso's *Three Musicians* (Fig. **10.27**) is a painting in the Synthetic Cubist

10.26 GEORGES BRAQUE
Le Courrier, 1913
Pasted paper and charcoal, $20 \times 22\frac{1}{2}$ ins (51×57 cm)
Philadelphia Museum of Art: A. E. Gallatin Collection

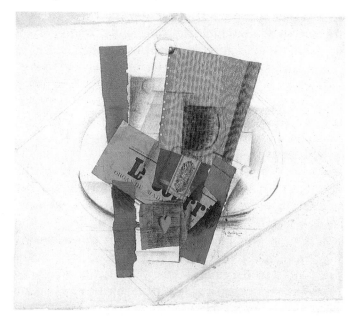

have been broken up, but, in this case, reassembled into rather appealing prismatic forms. Note that the front, bottom, and sides of the violin are visible at once, demonstrating a principle in Analytical Cubism called "simultaneity." The background, like the objects, has been broken up and reassembled, so that the whole becomes an integrated, multi-faceted composition. Unlike Fauvist and German Expressionist painting, Analytical Cubism uses mainly monochromatic colors (various tones of one color), and the forms have a degree of depth. Indeed, to create a Cubist work, a painter must employ the time-tested methods of shading and foreshortening. Meanwhile the spirit of Cézanne lives in Analytical Cubism's shaded planes, its controlled, evenly distributed depth, and its multiple viewpoints.

By 1910 Picasso rivaled Matisse as leader of the avant-garde. Now, he was his own best source. Analytical Cubism began to influence other artists, even to spawn

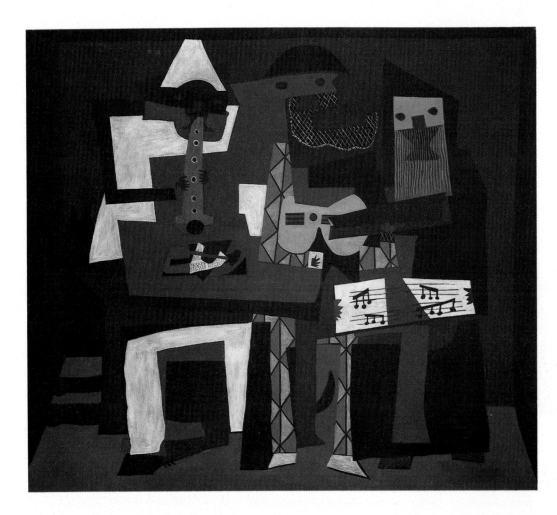

10.27 PABLO PICASSO
Three Musicians, 1921
Oil on canvas, $79 \times 87\frac{3}{4}$ ins
$(2 \times 2.23\,\text{m})$
Museum of Modern Art,
New York

style which reveals its collage heritage in the heterogeneity of its shapes and patterns, and in the whimsy of the idea. Its playfulness, however, belies a sophisticated, powerful design. Synthetic Cubism's livelier aesthetic surface compensates for the loss of Analytical Cubism's transparency and multiple viewpoints. Many artists, including Braque, who remained wedded to Cubism for the rest of his career, combined elements of both styles.

Variations of Cubism

So far, we have studied Cubism in its original "orthodox" forms. Because of its popularity—almost from the moment it was invented—it appeared in sundry, less orthodox forms. Artists such as Marc Chagall (1887–1985) whose artistic goals were different from Braque's and Picasso's, found it to be adaptable to their own. A Jew from rural Russia, who could not endure the art academies of his homeland, Chagall traveled to Paris, where he came into contact with members of the avant-garde. In this new environment Chagall's naive artistic ideas were admired rather than disparaged. Chagall, meanwhile, was very

attracted to the ideas of the avant-garde. The use of bright color and abstract forms came easy to one who had not liked academic art in the first place. Furthermore, these tendencies were appropriate for describing childhood memories, as in *I and the Village* (Fig. **10.1**). The Cubist system of faceted planes enabled Chagall to express his fantasies on different spatial, temporal, and symbolic levels, while uniting them into a consistent nostalgic theme.

Chagall's contemporary, Marcel Duchamp (1887–1968), was his opposite in many ways. Sophisticated and urbane, Duchamp moved rapidly through the various stages of the Modern movement before arriving at Cubism. He and his brothers, Jacques Villon and Duchamp-Villon, formed the nucleus of a splinter movement which combined Analytical methods with the science of color (a pursuit considered heretical in the eyes of Braque and Picasso). Marcel himself was influenced by *Italian Futurism*, a quasi-political movement committed to celebrating the dynamism of modern technology. To carry out their programs Futurists adopted Analytical Cubism's principle of simultaneity as their own, using it to express the

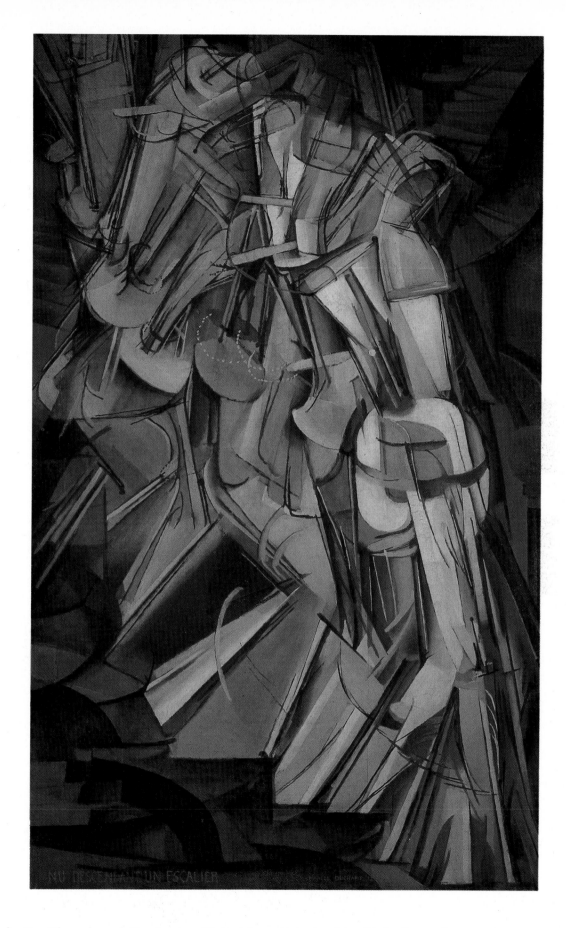

10.28 MARCEL DUCHAMP
*Nude Descending a Staircase
No. 2*, 1912
Oil on canvas, 58 × 35 ins
(147 × 89 cm)
Philadephia Museum of Art

qualities of power and velocity. Though not the least interested in either their politics or their philosophy, Duchamp did employ overlapping planes to suggest Futurist motion in his *Nude Descending a Staircase* (Fig. **10.28**)—a painting that scandalized American audiences at a show in New York (see below).

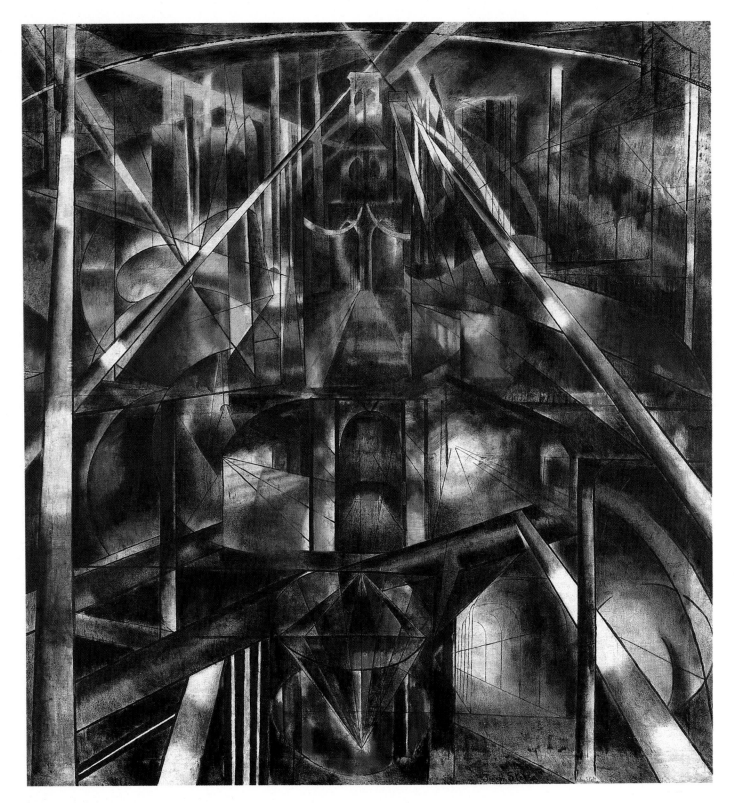

10.29 JOSEPH STELLA
Brooklyn Bridge, 1917
Oil on canvas, 84 × 76 ins (2.13 × 1.93 m)
Yale University Art Gallery, Gift of Collection Société Anonyme

10.30 PIET MONDRIAN
*Composition with Red, Blue and
Yellow*, 1930
Oil on canvas, 20 × 20 ins
(51 × 51 cm)
Photo Christie's, London

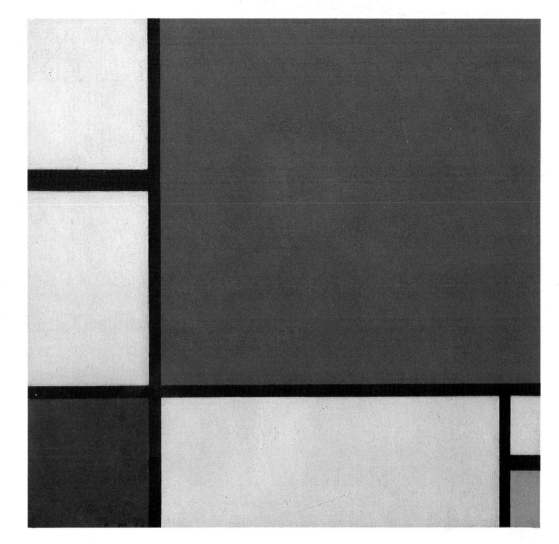

The Italian-American painter Joseph Stella (1880–1946) also brought Futurism to New York, but in a different way. He used the city itself—which even then pulsated with speed and aggression—as his subject matter. His *Brooklyn Bridge* (Fig. **10.29**), a kaleidoscopic impression of a modern city, probably embodies the spirit of Italian Futurism as well as any of the works of its original founders in Italy. Cubism's multiple planes were thus found to be as adaptable to the poetry of the city as they were to the poetry of rural Russia.

Piet Mondrian (1872–1944) was responsible for the most radical transformation of all. He found in Analytical Cubism's faceted planes the road to total abstraction—as Kandinsky had in the bold colors and impetuous brushwork of German Expressionism. There are other parallels between the two artists, for both were mystics and theorists, leaders of movements (Mondrian founded *De Stijl* ["The Style"], a Dutch movement in the fine and decorative arts), and authors of books on their ideas. But

Mondrian spent more years than Kandinsky in refining his style. Starting with a Cubist version of trees, he simplified his motif until the trees disappeared, leaving only Cubist planes; then he simplified the planes until they disappeared, leaving only an austere display of rectangles, primary colors, and thin black bars. His style, referred to by him as *Neoplasticism*, did not reach maturity until the 1920s. The simplicity of *Composition with Red, Blue, and Yellow* (Fig. **10.30**), an example of this style, is deceptive. No two rectangles are the same size and shape; none of the colors are repeated; the composition is off-center, with the large red rectangle, occupying two-thirds of the canvas, being offset by the small blue rectangle on the left and the small yellow one in the bottom right. Yet the visual tensions of this variety are resolved, so that the painting is a display of serene balance. According to Mondrian, the simplicity of Neoplasticism lays bare the basic principles not only of art but even of the universe. He raised the issue of balance to the level of religion, and, like Kandinsky,

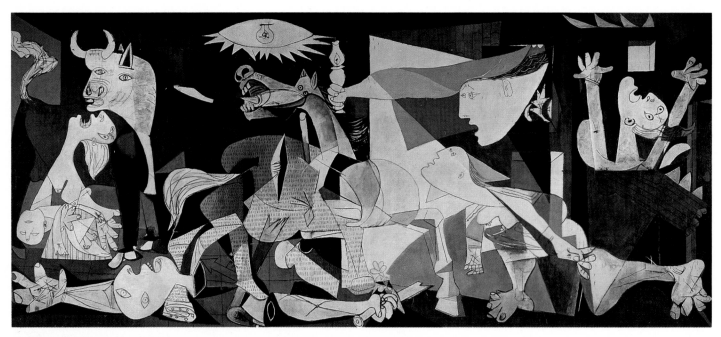

10.31 PABLO PICASSO
Guernica, 1937
Oil on canvas, 11 ft 6 ins × 25 ft 6 ins (3.5 × 7.8 m)
Museum of Modern Art, New York

hoped that his art would play a part in satisfying people's spiritual needs.

Although Picasso, the co-inventor of Cubism, experimented with other styles, he often returned to this style. Whatever his style at any given moment, however, Picasso tended to shun the use of serious themes. Cubism itself had a reputation for being the style of still lifes and innocuous subjects, and of being inadequate for expressing anything more provocative than Futurist motion. So the art world was unprepared for *Guernica* (Fig. 10.31), a large, angry mural executed in the style of Synthetic Cubism on the theme of death and destruction. Outraged at the senseless bombing, during the Spanish Civil War, of Guernica, a city in northern Spain, Picasso painted the mural as a reaction to the horrors of war and as a memorial to the victims. Containing not a single airplane or bomb, it is filled instead with women, a fallen statue, a speared horse, and a bull—direct or indirect references to the victims. Whether taken as images or symbols, these references in themselves are indirect. The message of *Guernica* is contained mostly in the anguish of its forms: the tortured proportions of the running, stretching figures, the grotesque mouth of the screaming horse, the paroxysms of the mother and child, and the convulsions of the shapes in the center. Presiding over the carnage is the placid bull, who is all the more terrifying because of his vacant expression. *Guernica*, a monument to darkness,

proclaims its message in a new language, that of Cubism. The fractured images, the dislocated forms, and the sharp contrasts of light and dark (like those of photojournalism) symbolize a broken world. Picasso showed that Cubism can express brutality as well as playfulness. Even more than Grünewald's *Crucifixion* (Fig. 8.12), *Guernica* is a portrait of suffering.

Duchamp, Dada, and Surrealism

So far, this survey has chronicled developments on the European side of the Atlantic. Except for a handful of American expatriates in France, American art was relatively unaffected by the many new trends in European art, and the American public was ignorant of them. In short, so far as international art was concerned, America was provincial.

In 1913 America lost her innocence. The cause of this loss was the *Armory Show* (officially, the *International Exhibition of Modern Art* held in New York's 69th Regiment Armory). Two-thirds of the works in the show were American (the most advanced in style being watered-down versions of Impressionism), while only one-third were European—including everything from Impressionism to Futurism. But the European third received the most attention, turning the Armory Show into a major "media" event. Banner headlines and political cartoons gleefully satirized styles such as Cubism. The European section also accounted for 80 percent of the sales. Thus it stole the show, while at the same time bringing the Modern movement to American soil. American art was never to be quite the same again.

Another story involves one of the works in the show, Duchamp's *Nude Descending a Staircase*. Like Manet's *Déjeuner sur l'Herbe* (Fig. 9.10) 50 years earlier, this one became a target of ridicule: "an explosion in a shingle factory" and "a staircase descending a nude" were among the one-liners used to mock it. In view of the status of the European avant-garde in 1913, this work was not as extreme as, say, Kandinsky's abstractions or Picasso's collages. But, in view of some of Duchamp's other works, the American public had unwittingly identified the *enfant terrible* of the day.

As early as 1912 Duchamp embarked on projects that have become the source of endless philosophical discourse. The most controversial of these involved his collection of *ready-mades*—ordinary objects which he transformed into art objects by simply placing them in art galleries or giving them titles. His most legendary ready-made, a urinal turned upside down and titled *Fountain* (Fig. **10.32**), was submitted to a show in 1917, but

10.32 Marcel Duchamp
Fountain, 1917
Porcelain, 24.5 ins (62.5 cm) high
Arturo Schwarz Collection, Milan

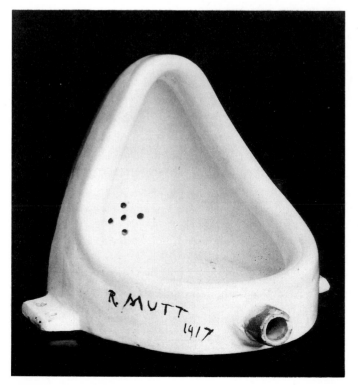

rejected. Duchamp defended it as a work of art in *Wrong-Wrong*, his own art magazine. Today, *Fountain* is on view in a Milan art collection. Thus it could be said that the artist was, in the end, "right-right." Duchamp also made art out of panes of plate glass painted with whimsical abstract shapes. When one of his glass projects was accidently cracked, Duchamp declared the unexpected fissures to be part of the design. That project, cracks and all, is part of the permanent collection of the Museum of Modern Art in New York. In the final analysis, it is not the objects themselves but the decisions and gestures made on their behalf that were (and still are) so radical, further confounding an already bewildering art scene. Duchamp's activities raised questions that are still asked to this day: What are the necessary and sufficient conditions for an object to be called a work of art? Is the term honorific or not? What is the role of intention? Should the results of chance or accident be considered legitimate elements in art?

Duchamp's activities were associated with *Dada*, a movement noted for cynicism, buffoonery, and nihilism. Born in neutral Zurich in 1916, during World War I, the movement was made up of a mixture of deserters, writers, artists, and refugees from European civilization. They met in a Zurich cabaret, initially to protest the insane war, but eventually their meetings spawned an arts movement involving preposterous activities. Among other things, they wrote poetry by cutting words out of seed catalogs, wore silly costumes, danced to the sound of barking dogs, and created pictures out of random arrangements of cut-out shapes. The name Dada (French, "hobbyhorse") was allegedly selected by opening a German-French dictionary and taking the first word that appeared. These actions, by implication, attacked all cultural endeavors, including art. Although Dadaist artists used collage and other avant-garde methods, they did not spare the heroes of the Modern movement. One mounted a toy monkey inside a frame and called it "Portrait of Cézanne."

Dada spread to other cities: Paris, Cologne, and New York (where Duchamp was active). But by 1922 it had faded away, leaving few lasting works of art. Despite its small output and its alleged nihilism, it left a legacy. "Automatic drawing," a sort of spontaneous doodling, anticipated an American style of abstraction that appeared in the 1940s. Duchamp's ideas also had an impact on avant-garde music of the 1950s. Dada's nonsense performances were revived in "happenings" and the performance art of the 1960s and '70s. Even its graphics, which seemed reckless at the time, foreshadowed modern advertising design. More importantly, the examples of Duchamp and Dada gave rise to a reassessment of aesthetic values, a questioning that goes on to this day.

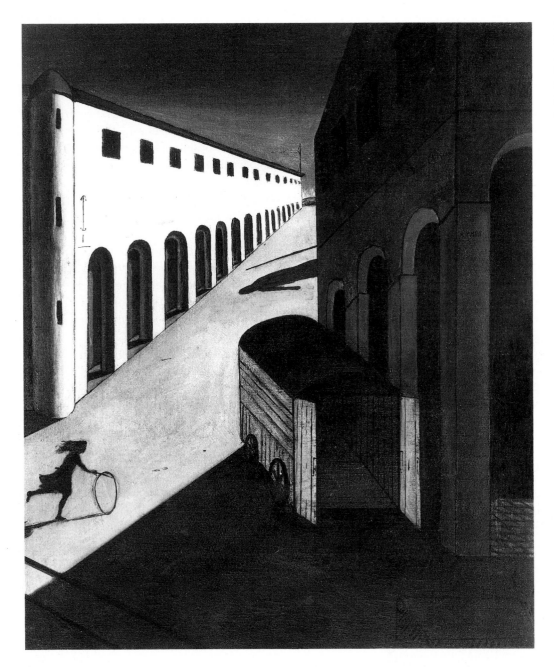

10.33 GIORGIO DE CHIRICO
The Mystery and Melancholy of a Street, 1914
Oil on canvas, $33\frac{1}{2} \times 27$ ins
(85×69 cm)
Resor Collection, New Canaan, Connecticut

They also played a role in fostering three major preoccupations of twentieth-century high culture: irony, absurdity, and the unconscious. Some Dadaist leaders brought these preoccupations with them to the next and last movement in European twentieth-century art, *Surrealism.*

Surrealism began in 1924 as a mainly literary movement. Unlike most movements, which occur more or less spontaneously, this one was formally founded and christened by the Dadaist poet André Breton and his associates. Breton even wrote a manifesto outlining the purpose of Surrealism: to merge dream and reality into an "absolute reality, a super-reality." In Breton's conception of the movement, the unconscious—whether in dreams or in the undirected play of thought that occurs when one is awake—was to be given the highest priority. The enemy of Surrealism was reason and logic. Among the Surrealists' favorite sources were the writings of Sigmund Freud, especially his *Interpretation of Dreams* (1900). They also looked to the poetry of the Symbolists and Dadaists, and to Picasso's early Cubist paintings (which Surrealists attributed to the workings of the unconscious), and the paintings of Duchamp, Chagall, and Giorgio de Chirico (1888–1978).

There are, basically, two kinds of Surrealist painting: realistic (sometimes called *veristic*) and abstract. In terms of style, the realistic variety is quite traditional; to a greater or lesser degree it indulges in all the devices of optical realism: shading, perspective, even cast shadows. In terms of subject matter, however, it is quite original. Essentially, it seeks to illustrate dreams. Like real dreams, Surrealist images range from the mildly puzzling to the bizarre. (One is reminded of Kafka's fusion of clarity of style with obscurity of meaning.)

It has already been noted that the work of De Chirico was a source of inspiration for the movement. Between 1913 and 1919 he created paintings that he called "metaphysical pictures." Because this body of work captures the spirit of realistic Surrealism as well as, if not better than, any other, we shall use it as the main example of the style—though it was created long before the Surrealist movement was born. Typical of them is *The Mystery and Melancholy of a Street* (Fig. **10.33**). Its somber colors, dry paint surface, harsh lighting and cast shadows do not partake of any of the twentieth-century "isms," or even of Post-Impressionism. Yet its mood is distinctly and uniquely twentieth-century. One of De Chirico's

strategies, typical of Surrealism proper, involves the use of irrational combinations: the lone girl sharing a deserted square with a gypsy wagon and a mysterious figure which casts a long shadow. The perspective is also irrational; note the contradictory vanishing points as well as the "yearning" length of the building on the left. Whether *The Mystery and Melancholy of a Street* is seen as a haunted post-Christian environment or as someone's private hallucination, it is certainly disturbing. From 1919 onward, De Chirico abandoned his metaphysical style for a romantic neoclassicism, an act for which the Surrealists never forgave him.

The Surrealism of Salvador Dali (born 1904), who joined the movement in 1929, is not as subtle as De Chirico's. Dali's style is supremely realistic; his subjects tend to be nightmarish. His goal was to represent the world of dreams as vividly as possible, or, as he explained, to employ the "paranoiac-critical" method to make "portraits of hallucinations." By means of optical realism, along with a vivid imagination, hallucinations like the

10.34 SALVADOR DALI
Soft Construction with Boiled Beans: Premonition of Civil War,
1936
Oil on canvas, 39 × 39 ins
(99 × 99 cm)
Philadelphia Museum of Art

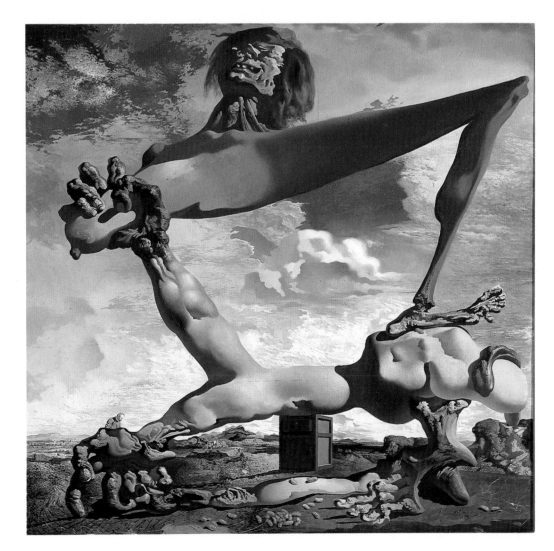

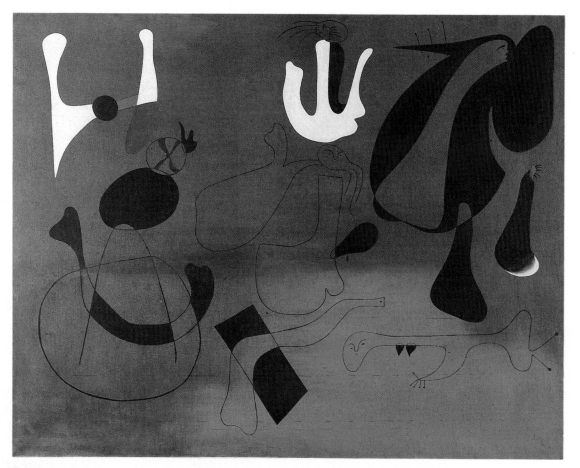

10.35 JOAN MIRO
Painting, 1933
Oil on canvas, $51\frac{3}{8} \times 64$ ins (130.5×163 cm)
Wadsworth Atheneum, Hartford, Connecticut

one in *Soft Construction with Boiled Beans: Premonition of Civil War* (Fig. **10.34**) are given the credibility of photographs. Dali's Surrealism tends to provoke, even to shock, rather than to disturb. Compare this as a statement on the horrors of war to *Guernica*, made just one year later.

The abstract branch of Surrealist painting took two directions. Some artists employed "automatic" methods—doodling, capitalizing on accidental effects, and so forth—to allow the unconscious to dominate in the creation of their works. Others, using more conventional painting methods, managed nevertheless to suggest that the unconscious was dominant and that their imagery was the result of automatic thought processes and free associations. The drifting free forms and inchoate images in *Composition* (Fig. **10.35**) by Joan Miró (born 1893) give this impression. How much of this is free association, how much is calculation, we will never know. Although his images are often vaguely demonic, Miró's paintings emphasize the playful, rather than the dark side of the unconscious. Instead of attempting to illustrate a child's

nightmare, as De Chirico or Dali might, Miró represents it as a child might. But this childlike element was employed with great sophistication. Miró invented a unique kind of abstraction which not only evoked a mixture of mystery and humor, but came to be one of the more important influences on American abstract art of the 1940s.

Although some of the paintings we have examined were produced in the 1930s, it is important to emphasize that the breakthroughs themselves occurred between 1905 and 1914, perhaps the most fertile nine years in the whole history of art. Fauvism, the Brücke, the Blaue Reiter, Cubism, and Futurism all emerged within those years. Mondrian's style, though not fully developed until the 1920s, had arrived at a stage of grid-like flatness as early as 1914; Dada did not officially begin until 1916, but its madcap innovations were anticipated by Duchamp's ready-mades of 1913; and Surrealist painting was precisely foreshadowed by De Chirico's metaphysical pictures, begun in 1913. The next series of breakthroughs would not occur until the 1940s.

Sculpture

Because Rodin's *The Kiss* (Fig. 5.19) epitomizes the Romantic preoccupation with love and yearning, this nineteenth-century sculptor was treated in Chapter 5 as the last of the Romantics (in the visual arts). He certainly was that; other works of his are even more Romantic than *The Kiss*. But he was also an Impressionist, a Symbolist, and a one-man avant-garde. Because many of his sculptures possess vibrant light-reflecting surfaces, he was the leading exponent of Impressionism in sculpture. Because some of his later sculptures are unorthodox in form and allegorical in content, he was considered a Symbolist. And, because of his nonconformist solutions, he was in continual conflict with both critics and public. When he finished the monument to Balzac (Fig. 10.36), it was refused by the people who commissioned it. They were disappointed by what looked like a mountain covered with a cloak and topped by an unfinished head. They were also offended by its haughty aloofness—actually just the effect Rodin was striving for. *Balzac* was intended not to portray the author but to symbolize godlike genius and creativity. However, Rodin's reputation, like that of other progressive artists, improved with time. He is given credit for reviving a "lost art"—so low was the state of academic sculpture when he started his career.

Although sculpture experienced rapid and fundamental changes in the early decades of the twentieth century, it tended to lag behind painting in this respect. Indeed, some of the most interesting three-dimensional works were made by painters such as Matisse, Picasso, and Umberto Boccioni (1882–1916), who essayed in sculpture some of the ideas they had originally expressed in painting, and vice versa. For their part, sculptors often were associated with, or responded to, avant-garde developments in painting. German Expressionism is reflected in the works of such artists as Ernst Barlach (1870–1938) and Wilhelm Lehmbruck (1881–1919), whose treatment of the human figure can be traced to Rodin's style. Cubism/Futurism is best represented by the experimental bronzes of Boccioni, an Italian Futurist who took leave of painting for a year just to do sculptures. Concepts like *Development of a Bottle in Space* (Fig. 10.37), when projected in the third dimension, assume a new character: their fractured planes and varied perspectives are no longer illusions, while the principle of simultaneity turns the forms inside-out.

The Rumanian-born sculptor Constantin Brancusi (1876–1957), who looked upon Rodin's *Balzac* as a "starting point," emulated not the nineteenth-century

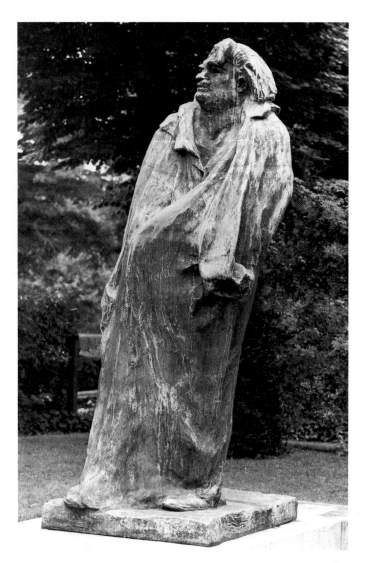

10.36 AUGUSTE RODIN
Balzac, 1892–97
Plaster, 9 ft 10 ins (3 m) high
Rodin Museum, Paris

10.37 Umberto Boccioni
Development of a Bottle in Space, 1912
Silvered bronze, $15 \times 12\frac{7}{8} \times 23\frac{3}{4}$ ins ($38 \times 32.7 \times 60$ cm)
Museum of Modern Art, New York, Aristide Maillol Fund

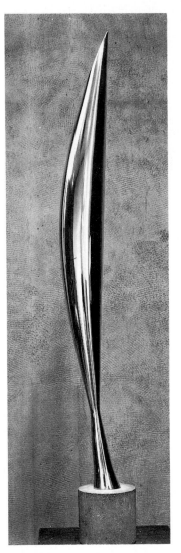

10.38 (left)
Constantin Brancusi
Bird in Space, 1919
Bronze, 54 ins (137 cm) high
Museum of Modern Art,
New York

10.39 Julio Gonzalez
Head, c. 1935
Wrought iron, 18 ins
(45 cm) high
Museum of Modern Art,
New York

10.40 ALEXANDER CALDER
Lobster Trap and Fish Tail, 1939
Mobile (steel wire and sheet
aluminium), c. 8 ft 6 ins ×
9 ft 6 ins (2.59 × 2.9 m)
Museum of Modern Art,
New York

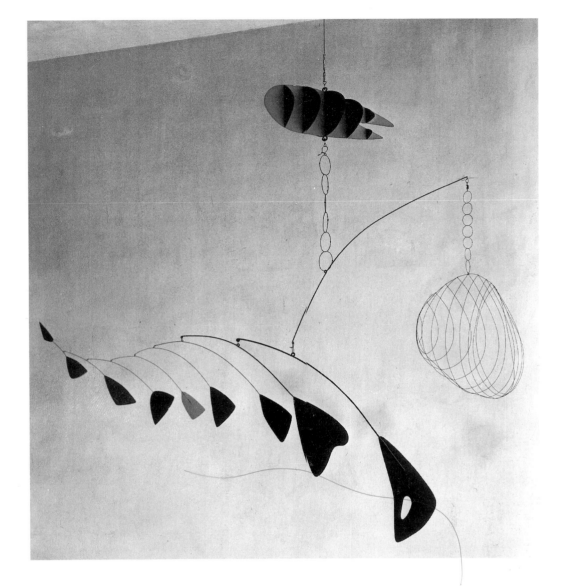

master's style, but his tendency to symbolize ideas. In an attempt to embody an essence, Brancusi would start with an animal motif and reduce it to a simplified abstract form—as Mondrian had used a tree motif to arrive at his grids. Indeed, the form of *Bird in Space* (Fig. **10.38**) shares with Mondrian's paintings a similar purity and elegance. Both artists were mystics, sharing an interest in Eastern religions, and both were Platonic in their art. But Brancusi aimed at single essences; Mondrian, at principles of organization.

Julio González (1876–1942), whose work is as abstract as Brancusi's but much less pure, joined with Picasso to pioneer a new medium: welded metal. Prior to this, Picasso and Braque had invented the *assemblage*—nailing or gluing together three-dimensional scraps—in essence, an extension of the two-dimensional collage. Aesthetically it was an easy step to move from assemblage to welded sculpture, provided one could weld. As a former wrought-iron craftsman, González could weld. Out of the fusion of rods, nails, and pieces of scrap iron, as seen in *Head* (Fig. **10.39**), González arrived at a new concept of three-dimensional art: open sculpture. Unlike traditional sculpture, which is built up from a lump of clay or cut down from a mass of stone, *Head* was constructed around empty space. The American sculptor Alexander Calder (1898–1976) carried open sculpture even further. A Yankee tinkerer as well as a sculptor, Calder was also adept at working with metal, but his main interest was sculpture that moved. This entailed linking pieces, rather than welding them together. Eventually he invented the *mobile*, an open sculpture with movable parts—rods and thin forms connected by swivels and suspended on wires—set in motion by air currents. Usually, the movement is too slow to be perceptible; but over time, a mobile such as *Lobster Trap and Fish Tail* (Fig. **10.40**) changes its composition.

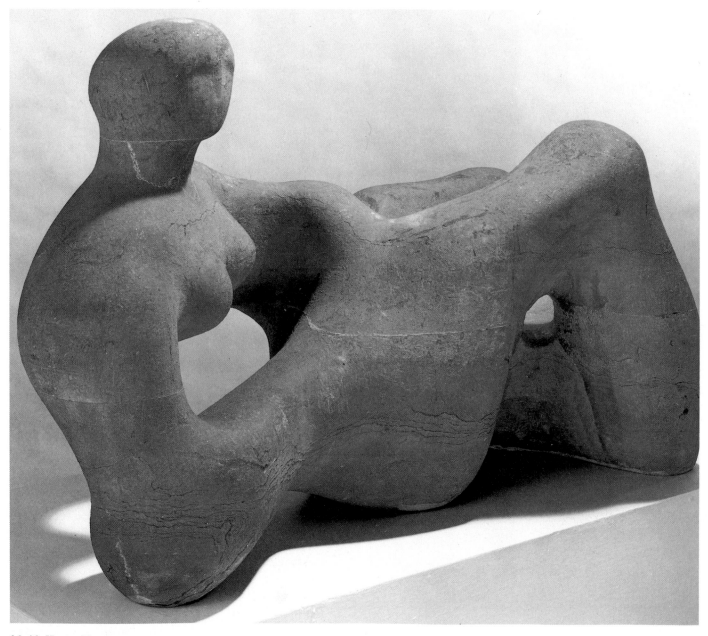

10.41 HENRY MOORE
Recumbent Figure, 1938
Green Hornton stone, c. 54 ins (137 cm) long
Tate Gallery, London

Although *Recumbent Figure* (Fig. **10.41**) by Henry Moore (born 1898) is penetrated with openings, it is derived from a solid mass—in the tradition of monumental sculpture going back to the Egyptians. Abstract in character, it is, however, clearly related to the human figure. Like Brancusi, Moore aims at embodying timeless concepts—in this case, woman as earth mother. But Moore's art contains a richer mixture of forms—both anatomical and abstract—for the mind and senses to respond to. The figure's overall aspect—the reclining position, the roundness of the shapes, the breasts—leads immediately to the theme of woman. The holes, which refer metaphorically to the vagina, amplify the theme. Associations stemming from the landscape-like forms and surface qualities of the stone suggest permanence and link the theme of femaleness to the theme of earth. In this and other works, Moore has managed to preserve and express the humanistic concerns of traditional sculpture by means of a modern sculptural language.

Architecture

Architecture in the late nineteenth century was even less related to avant-garde painting than was sculpture. Unlike many past styles—Renaissance, Baroque, Rococo, and so forth—Impressionism and Post-Impressionism did not have equivalents in architecture. If the Chicago School (see page 381), the only true architectural avant-garde of the time, were to be related to any style, it would be Realism. Sullivan's first skyscraper (Fig. 9.18) stands as an early embodiment of the concept of functionalism. Like Realism, functionalism tends to be practical, democratic, and non-idealistic.

But at least one *fin-de-siècle* style was emulated in architecture: Art Nouveau. The staircase of the Tassel House (Fig. **10.42**) by Victor Horta (1861–1947) brandishes lines in metal that rival Beardsley's lines in ink (Fig. 10.16). Curves of all kinds—arching, sinuous, thin, curling, "whiplash"—are expressed in iron bars, some

serving as decoration and support, some just as decoration. Based on abstract plant forms and Japanese designs, rather than the usual classical or Gothic motifs, Art Nouveau was perceived as simple and modern in its day, though, from our perspective, it looks as ornate as any of the others.

Curiously, Sullivan, the prophet of functionalism, was also the leading American advocate of Art Nouveau. In his Carson Pirie and Scott department store (Fig. **10.43**) one can see both of these tendencies in marvelous combination. The interstices between the windows, covered with plain sheets of white-glazed terra cotta, express the grid of the metal frame in a way that was unusually austere for 1904. Opposing this is the orgy of Art Nouveau richness decorating the first and second floors. This decoration has been criticized as too ornate for a commercial building. But Sullivan held that street-level windows

10.42 VICTOR HORTA
Staircase of Tassel House, 1892–93

10.43 LOUIS SULLIVAN
Carson Pirie and Scott department store, Chicago, 1899–1904

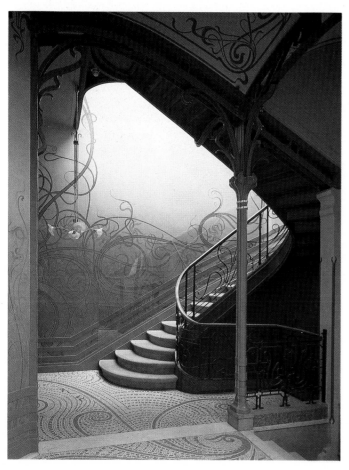

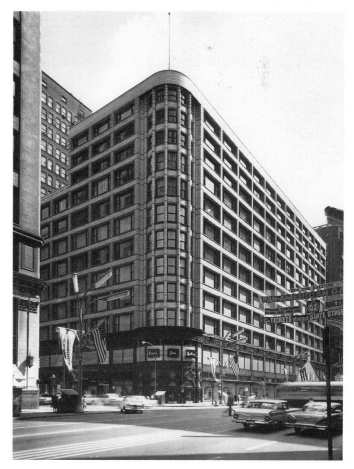

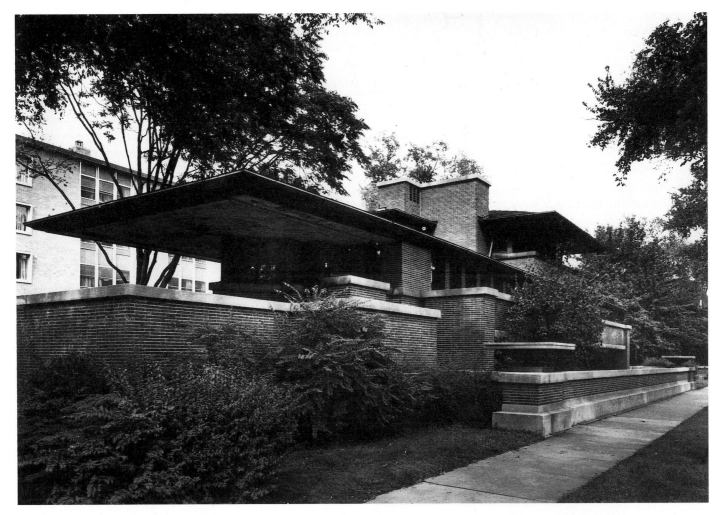

10.44 FRANK LLOYD WRIGHT
Robie House, Chicago, exterior view 1909

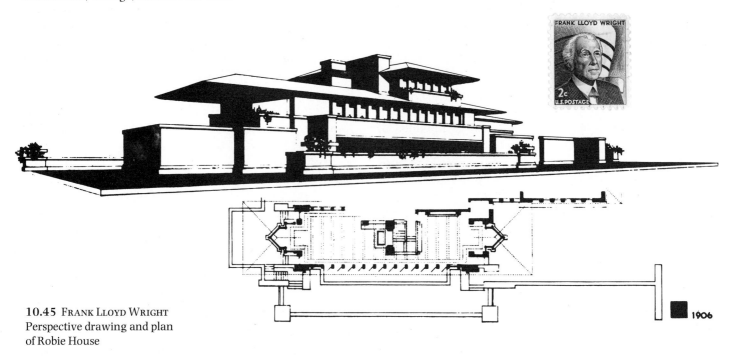

10.45 FRANK LLOYD WRIGHT
Perspective drawing and plan
of Robie House

should have richly ornamented frames. Indeed, the flourish of this level is a dramatic foil to the rest, making Carson's one of the most exciting of early commercial buildings. But in 1904, even as it was being completed, it was already considered out of fashion. New York architects, who were designing skyscrapers in various eclectic styles (though employing steel-frame technology), had captured the imagination of the commercial world. Meanwhile, Sullivan was forced to be content with minor commissions such as designing small-town banks. Functionalism, or more precisely, honestly-stated functionalism, was put on hold in downtown American architecture for some time.

Wright

One of Sullivan's apprentices, Frank Lloyd Wright (1867–1959) went on to become one of the most original and visionary architects of the twentieth century. Wright was the first designer, European or American, to create a distinctive style out of the new technologies. Many of his early projects, (like the paintings of Matisse and Picasso) have retained their modernity for nearly a century. Although he designed all kinds of buildings—skyscrapers, factories, hotels, churches, art museums—he is best known for his houses. His cardinal principle—whether designing houses or public buildings—involved what he called "organic" design: developing a structure from the inside out to suit the occupants and the site. Though considering himself Sullivan's heir, he did not share the older architect's interest in designing downtown buildings; Wright's commitment to the countryside bordered on nature-worship. His most original concepts involved the ways in which a particular building was adapted to its natural surroundings.

The topography of residential Chicago, the vicinity of Wright's early practice, is undramatically flat. Flatness notwithstanding, Wright came up with a dramatic style: the "prairie house," a low-profile building intended to harmonize with the windswept plains of northern Illinois. The perfect example of the style is a twentieth-century landmark, the Robie House (Fig. 10.44). The house is organized around a large central hearth, with the rooms extending outward from the hearth on three separate levels under long sweeping roofs. Though three-storied, the height of the Robie House is opposed by the strong horizontal effect of deep eaves, continous ribbons of windows, and long balconies (Fig. 10.45). By breaking up the wall plane, the balconies also tend to erase the distinction between indoors and outdoors. The lack of a simple plane and the resulting interpretation of spaces bring to mind the facets of Analytical Cubism—though

there is little evidence to suggest that Wright was aware of Picasso's and Braque's experiments. Finally, the Robie exterior has no ornament of any kind to detract from the impact of its sculptural forms (though, at close range, Art Nouveau designs can be seen in the windows).

The Bauhaus and the International Style

In 1910 European architects, who were as unaware of the Chicago School as the American art public was of Fauvism and Cubism before 1913, received an unexpected surprise: a portfolio of Wright's designs, including the Robie House, was published in Berlin in 1910 and 1911. Wright's work, as new to the Germans as it had been to the Americans, left a lasting impression. Thus, through Wright, the Chicago School played a seminal role in the development of twentieth-century European architecture.

Another important influence was Peter Behrens (1868–1940), whose apprentices included three of Europe's most important architects: Walter Gropius (1883–1969), Ludwig Mies van der Rohe (1886–1969), and Charles Eduoard Jeanneret (1887–1965), a Swiss who called himself Le Corbusier. Commissioned by a turbine manufacturer, Behrens designed not only the factory, but the factory products, advertising displays, and even the workers' houses; he may have been the first of a new breed: the industrial designer. More important as an inspiring employer than as an architectural innovator, Behrens instilled in his students an appreciation for the aesthetics of machine technology.

In 1919 Gropius combined two art academies in Weimar to create the *Bauhaus* (German, "house of building"), a school that came to be legendary in the field of design. Basic courses included direct experience with materials and the study of form, after which students could specialize in graphic design, one of the crafts, furniture design, or architecture—but not painting and sculpture. This, despite the fact that painters such as Kandinsky and Paul Klee (1879–1940) were on the staff, and Mondrian, who often lectured there, influenced the aesthetic direction of the school as much as any single figure. Under Mondrian's influence, and that of the Dutch De Stijl architects, the design philosophy came to resemble more and more the puritanical simplicity of Mondrian's art. Out of this grew a new architecture known as the "International Style."

The Bauhaus's own complex of buildings, designed by Gropius in 1925–26, after the school moved to Dessau, is an early example of the style (Fig. 10.46). Because the floors of the Shop Block, the main building of the complex, are supported on pillars set back from the façade, Gropius was able to face the building with continuous walls of

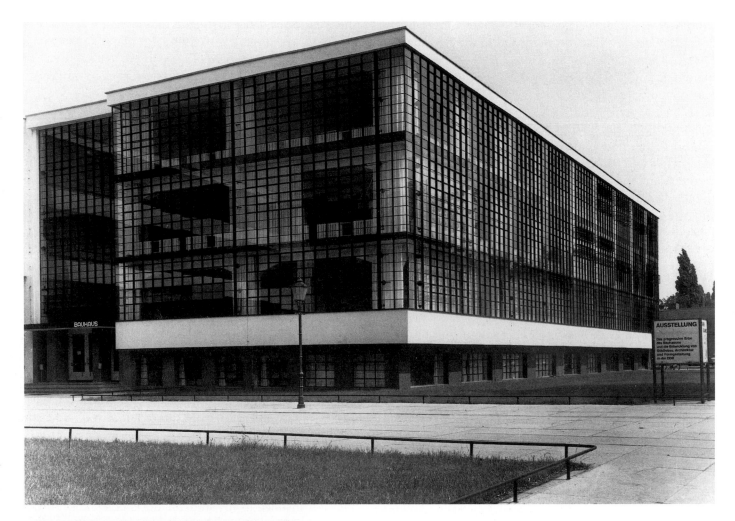

10.46 Walter Gropius
Shop block, The Bauhaus,
Dessau, Germany, 1925–26

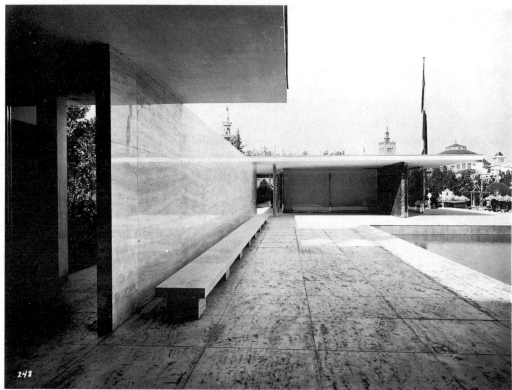

10.47 Ludwig Mies van der Rohe
German Pavilion at the
International Exhibition,
Barcelona, 1929

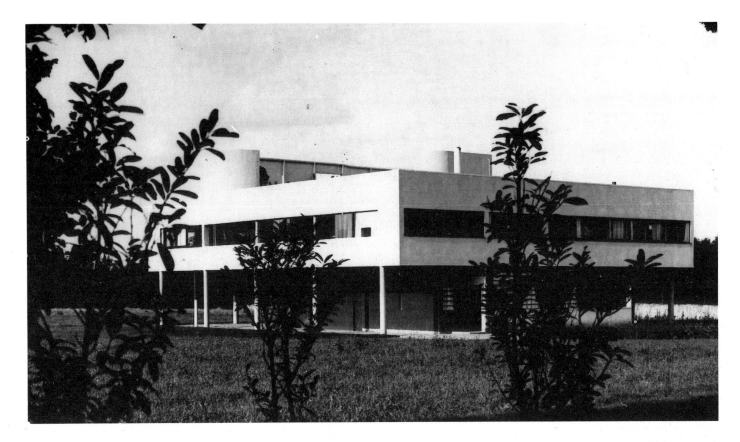

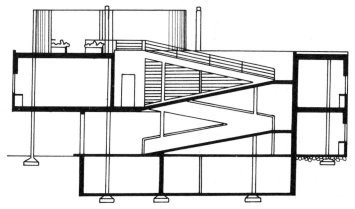

10.48 (top) LE CORBUSIER
Villa Savoye, Poissy-sur-Seine, France, 1929–30

glass. Such a step was anticipated by the Crystal Palace; but the Bauhaus is the first multi-storied, permanent building to boast such an exterior, making the statement that in modern architecture the wall is no more than a shield against the weather.

Quite a different expression of the International Style is seen in the German Pavilion at the Barcelona International Exhibition (Fig. **10.47**), an elegant assembly of reinforced concrete, glass, and travertine marble by Mies van der Rohe (who inherited the directorship of the Bauhaus from Gropius in 1930). Echoes of the Robie House can be seen in its horizontal emphasis, overhanging slab roof and abstract divisions of space. Otherwise its carefully studied proportions and rectilinear composition are indebted to Mondrian.

Similar in spirit to the German Pavilion is Le Corbusier's Villa Savoye near Paris (Fig. **10.48**). The shapes are ultrasimple; the surfaces and lines are uncluttered; the proportions reflect the passionate discipline of Mondrian. The fact that the material is reinforced concrete is belied by the Villa Savoye's lightweight appearance. This is achieved by the flat roof, ribbon windows, and delicate columns—pilotis—which open the space under the living area for circulation. To Le Corbusier, a house was a *machine à habiter* ("machine to be lived in"), an expression that succinctly reflects the International Style and the ideals of the Bauhaus.

Music

The Late Nineteenth Century

When the Impressionists had won the day in art and the young Matisse was already beginning a series of experiments that would lead to Fauvism, European composers were still writing music in a Romantic vein. This period, called Late Romanticism (or "Post-Romanticism"), continued into the early twentieth century and served as the transition between Romanticism proper and the new musical languages of the twentieth century. As we noted in Chapter 5, most European mus.c was under the spell of Wagner. Some of the most brilliant and expansive works ever written were produced at this time. Gustav Mahler, for example, wrote long, complex symphonies for enormous orchestras. Though much of Mahler's symphonic music is overwhelming, some of it is as intimate and probing as chamber music. Indeed, because of its subjective intensity, it is often associated with Vienna, the city of both Mahler and Freud.

A new musical nationalism came into being at this time, as composers of different nationalities began to assert their independence and to liberate their music from the influence of Wagner. To do so, they attempted to base their music on patriotic themes and their styles on the folk music traditions of their own lands. Among those who emphasized such themes and styles, yet also contributed significantly to the repertoire of serious, or "art," music, were Modest Mussorgsky (1839–1881) and Nikolai Rimsky-Korsakov (1844–1908) of Russia, Antonín Dvořák (1841–1904) of Czechoslovakia, Edvard Grieg (1843–1907) of Norway, Jean Sibelius (1865–1957) of Finland, Edward Elgar (1857–1934) of England, Manuel de Falla (1876–1946) of Spain, and Charles Ives (1874–1954) of the United States.

The situation in France was somewhat different. Instead of looking to their folk music for inspiration, French composers turned to their tradition of aristocratic music—specifically to the early eighteenth century, the period of such composers as François Couperin (see Chapter 4). French music of this period is distinguished by its restraint, serenity, and clarity. Elegant and charming, it evokes the world represented in the paintings of Watteau (see Chapter 5). It was these qualities that the founders of the new National Society for French Music (established in 1871) sought to encourage. The new generation of French composers, such as Camille Saint-Saëns (1835–1921) employed Romantic methods to create beautiful harmonies and smooth melodies, and Gabriel Fauré (1845–1924), one of the founders of the Society, who composed, among other works, superbly crafted songs. But it was Claude Debussy, a student of another French composer of the era, Cesar Franck (1822–1890), who steered the course of music away from the spell of Wagner.

Debussy

Though reflective of the French tradition, the music of Claude Debussy (1862–1918) transcends national boundaries. Often called "Impressionistic" (a term that Debussy himself disliked), his music is especially capable of describing atmosphere, whether of an imaginary place or a pervasive mood. Above all, it is music of understatement, nuance, and suggestion, as opposed to the heavy rhetoric of, say, Wagner or Mahler.

Although, like German composers, Debussy wrote for large orchestras, his aim was to exploit a large array of instruments for new and different sounds rather than overwhelming effects. Often using unusual instruments—harps, glockenspiels, xylophones, and so forth—or unusual combinations thereof, he added new tone colors (the qualities that distinguish one instrument from another) to the orchestral mix. His melodies tend to be short and to fall within a narrow range, whereas his harmonies, even richer and more varied than those of the German repertoire, tend to be as exotic as the colors. As painters in his generation borrowed from Japanese art, Debussy looked to the medieval church modes (see page 263) and Chinese music. Typical of his music is the use of the whole-tone scale (Fig. 10.49)—an octave divided into six whole-step intervals, rather than the traditional seven whole- and half-step intervals. Another distinguishing feature is his unique way with chords. Western ears had become accustomed to harmonies that always returned to the tonic (home key); in this system, chords are seen as functional elements within a progression. By contrast, Debussy's chords are often "non-functional"—that is, individual units designed not to direct the progression of the harmony, but to relate to the drift of a melody or the particular color of the moment.

10.49 Whole-tone scale

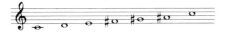

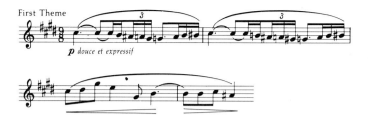

First Theme

p douce et expressif

10.50 Opening theme of *Prélude à l'après-midi d'un faune,*
Debussy

The *Prélude à "L'après-midi d'un faune"* ("The Afternoon of a Faun"; 1894), one of Debussy's best-known orchestral works, was inspired by a poem about a faun (half-man, half-beast creature of myth) and wood nymphs, written by the Symbolist poet Stéphane Mallarmé. The opening theme (Fig. 10.50), an airy, gliding melody, is introduced by the soft sounds of a flute in the low register. The sounds of harp and muted horns soon join that of the flute to echo the first theme and to accompany it in an ornamented repetition of the theme. At one point, an almost imperceptible transition from flute to oboe occurs, providing a subtle change of color. The harmonic strands thicken as muted strings and more winds are added to the mix and the music swells, only to return to solo flute. Unlike most traditional orchestral works, in which a definite musical structure can be sensed, *Prélude* seems unfocused and lacking a clear sense of direction: rhythm is irregular, changing from one meter to another; harmony is basically chromatic; the sense of a home key is quite tenuous (though never completely lost). *Prélude* inspires a sense of infinity, a sort of seamless reverie. It also evokes images, but in vague, allusive ways. One is prompted to imagine a dreamy, sylvan setting, perhaps like the one depicted in Watteau's *A Pilgrimage to Cythera* (Fig. 5.7).

With its Symbolist subject matter, along with its pervasive quality of fantasy, *Prélude* is closer in spirit to the work of Gauguin, the Post-Impressionist, than to that of the Impressionists. Even so, many of its other qualities—richness of color, diffusion of form, sense of flux, and serenity—do evoke Impressionist painting, especially the late work of Monet, whose many interpretations of his water garden at Giverny, could easily serve as settings for a mythical faun and nymphs. Just as Monet and other Impressionists and Post-Impressionists led the way to a new conception of painting, while remaining within the limits of Western realism, Debussy introduced new harmonies and colors, which were to have an enormous influence on modern Western music, yet never completely abandoned tonality.

Next to Debussy, the most famous French composer in the Impressionist idiom is Maurice Ravel (1875–1937).

The colors and textures of his ballet *Daphnis and Chloe* (1912), a mythical pastorale like Debussy's *Prélude*, are at least as rich. But its melodies, phrasing, rhythms, and tonality are easier to grasp, for even Ravel's most Impressionistic works retain some ties to the classical tradition. A musical eclectic, the composer wrote pieces in other styles, in which the use of Impressionistic devices is only marginal. As a sort of "nationalist-in-reverse," he liked to parody the music of other cultures and times: waltz music of Vienna in *La Valse* (1920), Spanish folk music in the popular *Boléro* (1928), and American jazz in *Concerto for Left Hand* (1930).

Eric Satie (1866–1925), a rather eccentric composer, has been called an "anti-Impressionist"; at the very least, he was anti-Romantic. His early compositions anticipated the cool melodies and unorthodox harmonies of Debussy, but with very lean textures in an overall dry style. His later compositions, written in the early twentieth century, were well suited to the iconoclasm of that era. Mostly satirical with incongruous titles such as *Three Pieces in the Form of a Pear* and *Dehydrated Embryos*, which mock the titles of Impressionist paintings, they have irony and humor, tendencies also found in collage, Synthetic Cubism, Dada, and Surrealism.

From 1900 to 1950

The new century was to have the same intoxicating effect on music as it did on art, although the spell of Romanticism lingered on for a few years before revolutionary trends got under way. The years 1910–1930 in music correspond to the years 1905–1914 in art, as more new things happened in music in those two decades than in any similar period in its previous history. And, as artists systematically razed the edifice of Western realism, composers dismantled the pillars of tonality and metered rhythm which had supported Western music since the sixteenth century.

Between 1930 and 1950 the experimentation slowed down, though it did not stop completely. Many composers went back to older styles or attempted syntheses between old and new. In Soviet Russia and Nazi Germany this tendency was encouraged, if not enforced, by the government; in democracies it happened spontaneously, as composers such as Stravinsky (see below) combined older forms with newer ones. Similarly in art, painters under totalitarian regimes were forced to work in realistic styles, while artists in other parts of the world tended to retreat to these styles on their own. Even the venerable radical Picasso dabbled in realism between the wars.

One aspect of music not paralleled in art was the continuing importance of nationalism as a source of creative energy in the first half of the century. (With the possible exceptions of Chagall and Kandinsky, no early twentieth-century artist of stature made a particular point of stressing the themes and styles of his/her native country.) Any discussion of nationalism would be incomplete without including Béla Bartók (1881–1945), the most prominent twentieth-century musician identified with folk idioms. Involved in folk music as both a scholar and a composer, Bartók collected nearly 6,000 folk tunes from different countries (mostly Hungary and Rumania), while incorporating folk elements into his own music throughout his career. But these elements are integrated so thoroughly that Bartók's work never sounds parochial or narrowly national. It stands on its own as sophisticated, often powerful, modern music—though much of its originality is due both to Bartók's direct use of folk music and to his many experiments in harmony and rhythm based on folk-music research. As a leader in developing new musical languages Bartók is exceeded by perhaps two composers in his generation, one of whom also made great use of folk music.

Stravinsky

Igor Stravinsky (1882–1971) utilized Russian folk styles in his early compositions, but this fact is overshadowed by his reputation as the twentieth century's most celebrated composer. In many ways he is to modern music what his contemporary Picasso is to modern art. Both Stravinsky and Picasso had long, active careers which extended well beyond World War II; yet both are remembered more for their contribution to world culture in the years before World War I when both worked in Paris. We saw in the previous section how restlessly experimental Picasso was: moving rapidly from Analytical Cubism to collage to Synthetic Cubism, and so on. We shall see in this section that Stravinsky, too, was very protean in his creativity.

Stravinsky's most famous works are three ballets that were first performed at the same time that Picasso and Braque were pioneering Cubism. Commissioned by Sergei Diaghilev, a Russian ballet producer whose company, the Ballets Russes, attracted the best dancers and was the sensation of Paris, these works thrust Stravinsky into the forefront, but each in different ways. The *Firebird* (1910), based on a Russian fairy tale and suffused with the exotic colors of Russian nationalism, was an immediate success with the public and the music world. *Petrushka* (1911), a ballet about puppets and a Russian street fair, though less traditional and much more piquant, was also a popular success. But *The Rite of Spring* (*Le Sacré du printemps*) was another story. Its first performance in 1913 caused a riot. Like the Fauves show and Picasso's *Les Demoiselles d'Avignon*, *The Rite* was a scandal that has since come to be seen as a landmark.

In the tradition of Debussy's *Prélude* and Ravel's *Daphnis and Chloe*, *The Rite of Spring* is a pastorale; but there the similarity ends. Rather than a lovely forest filled with mythical creatures, it offers a glimpse of pagan Russia, with primitive people enacting a rite of human sacrifice. The introduction opens with a solo bassoon intoning a somber, plaintive Russian folk tune (Fig. **10.51**). Other winds join the bassoon and the music becomes more animated as it describes the stirring of a dark forest in the early hours before the annual springtime sacrifice. The "Dance of the Youth and Maidens," the first episode of the rite, has a robust rhythm of repeated chords pounded out by the strings. The monotony of the relentless four-beat rhythm is relieved by the irregular placement of strong accents: sometimes on the second and fourth beats of the bar, sometimes on just the first, sometimes on none (Fig. **10.52**). Among other things, such a pattern defies the traditional practice of a consistent pattern of accents between measures and/or strong accents coinciding with changes of harmony. At times the rhythm is interrupted altogether, an action as jolting as the rhythm itself. Interwoven with the rhythm are groans and screams of winds and horns. The following movements (there are 14 in all) are typically introduced by, and interspersed with, modal-sounding folk tunes. Transitions between the movements, as well as the integrity of each movement, are difficult to determine, for one segment tends to merge and mingle with the next. Not all the movements are wild, but even the quiet ones are filled with restless rhythms, ominous sounds, and other evocations of a pagan rite. The

10.51 Introduction from Stravinsky's
Le Sacré du printemps

10.52 Stravinsky's rhythms from
Le Sacré du printemps

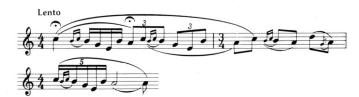

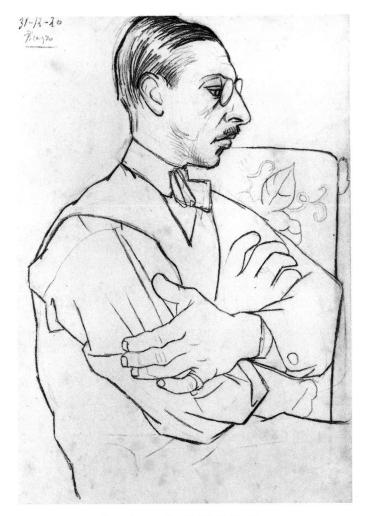

10.53 *Portrait of Igor Stravinsky*, 1920, Pablo Picasso
Private collection, Geneva

music of the final movement, "Sacrificial Dance," has been reduced to little more than savage, convulsive rhythms which build powerfully to a crashing conclusion as the chosen one dances to her death.

Stravinsky's approach in *Rite* was to invoke new and powerful musical forces through the use of "primitive" melodies and rhythms. The result was "a pastorale of the pre-historic world," according to the French poet and playwright Jean Cocteau (1891–1963). This fascination with primitivism, as we have seen, was shared by artists such as Matisse, Nolde, and Picasso. The dissonances are bolder than those even of *Petrushka.* But the most radical aspect of *Rite* is its unpredictable, furious rhythms. To the 1913 public they were as senseless and repugnant as the forms in Picasso's *Les Demoiselles.* Nevertheless, Stravinsky's ballet, like *Les Demoiselles*, was to have a lasting impact on its field. Its effect, according to the musical scholar Donald Grout, was "an explosion that so scattered the elements of musical language that they

could never again be put together as before."[19]

After gaining such spectacular recognition (or notoriety), Stravinsky felt the need to experiment with scores written for small ensembles. *The Soldier's Tale* (*L'Histoire du Soldat*; 1918) an "entertainment" with dancing and narration, written during the war for seven instrumentalists, also marked the composer's turning away from Russian styles. This work, like *The Rite of Spring*, stresses rhythm, but its style is witty and satirical rather than exotic, and its rhythms tend to be more percussive and perhaps even more inventive. In the final section they call to mind virtuoso drum performances heard in American jazz—an interest of Stravinsky's which he pursued in such pieces as *Ragtime* (1918) and *Piano Rag Music. Pulcinella* (1919), a ballet scored for small orchestra, was the only Stravinsky project to benefit from the hand of Picasso, who designed its sets and costumes. Nine days after the première, composer sat for artist, who sketched what has now come to be a famous portrait (Fig. **10.53**). Derived from the music of the eighteenth-century Italian composer Giovanni Battista Pergolesi, *Pulcinella* signals the beginning of Stravinsky's "neo-classical" period, which continued for the next few years. The works in this style, far from being regressions to an earlier era, have their moments of dissonance, odd rhythms, and above all, the inimitable Stravinsky quality of surprise.

A good example of Stravinsky's neo-classicism, and a work acclaimed by many as a twentieth-century masterpiece, is the *Symphony of Psalms* (1930). The composer set three psalms of David (from the Latin Vulgate) to music which he scored for both chorus and orchestra; thus, *Symphony of Psalms* is, in effect, a modern cantata. For this work Stravinsky decided to eliminate from his orchestration the warm colors of violins, violas, and clarinets. The brief first movement (Psalm 39 in the King James version) features a spare theme (Fig. **10.54**) sung initially by altos and later by the whole chorus, is as stark and austere as Gregorian chant. The second movement (Psalm 40), featuring themes sung contrapuntally and homophonically, begins to remind us a little of the eighteenth century. It is the third movement (Psalm 150) that is the most intriguing. The opening orchestral chords are sounded quietly, followed by the chorus, which softly

10.54 Theme from first movement of
Symphony of Psalms, Stravinsky

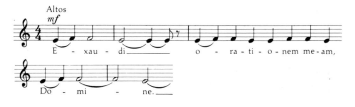

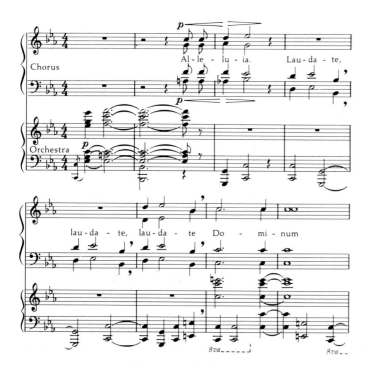

10.55 *Symphony of Psalms*, Stravinsky
Chorus and orchestra parts

intones the lines "Alleluia, Laudate, laudate, laudate Dominum" (Hallelujah, praise the Lord). The chords sung by the chorus modulate to E-flat major on the last syllable of "Alleluia," ending on a C-major chord in "Dominum" (Fig. **10.55**). Musically, the resolution from E-flat to C is odd, but religiously, the soft, prayer-like accent on words usually sung loudly—as in Handel's *Hallelujah Chorus*—is even stranger. It is a moment of tenderness which is very moving. This moment returns twice—between loud interludes by both orchestra and chorus—in the middle and at the end of the movement, as the piece ends, almost on a sigh.

In the latter part of his career, while living in the United States, Stravinsky adapted to his own needs the techniques of 12-tone music which had been pioneered by Schoenberg and his followers (see below). Though not the inventor of this system, Stravinsky used it in very individual and original ways. Thus before the end of his remarkable career, the composer had written in the manner of Russian nationalism (with influences stemming from Strauss and Debussy as well as folk idioms), shocked the musical world with his adventure in primitivism, experimented with American jazz, revived earlier traditions in neo-classicism, and expanded upon the 12-tone system. He wrote ballets, choral music, two operas, symphonies, and compositions for both very large and very small ensembles. Throughout the diversity of this output there remains a pervasive Stravinsky style: clear

and dry tone colors, stark contrasts, unpredictable rhythms, and, above all, musical excitement.

Schoenberg

Born in Vienna, the city of Mozart, Beethoven, and Mahler, Arnold Schoenberg (1874–1951) came under the spell of that city's lively culture at a young age. However, because of the early death of his father, he was unable to afford the study of music until he was 21. Much of his musical career was spent as a teacher in a variety of settings: Vienna, the Prussian Academy in Berlin, and the University of California at Los Angeles. Unlike Stravinsky, Schoenberg was never a celebrity, or even particularly well known during his life. But he had the respect of progressive composers as the most original and important thinker in modern music. He also had a loyal following of students, including Berg and Webern (see below) who became famous in their own right.

His early music was clearly in the tradition of the Late Romantic style, reflecting in particular Wagner's legacy of chromaticism and expansive orchestrations. In 1900, not to be outdone in large-scale music by contemporaries such as Strauss and Mahler, Schoenberg began writing a cantata that featured a narrator, five vocal soloists, four choruses, and an immense orchestra. (This work, the *Gurrelieder* was finally performed in 1913, to great acclaim.) However, around 1908, his interest in giant compositions faded, and his chromatic harmony became increasingly atonal. Thoroughly atonal music is characterized by its complete avoidance of a home key, as well as the avoidance of the familiar musical progressions that had become (and still are) so deeply rooted in our musical thinking that they seem almost a part of nature. Therefore, it is very difficult for unfamiliar (or intolerant) ears to listen to purely atonal music. As its chords are committed neither to a basic key nor to the familiar scales, the dissonance seems unrelieved. The melodies, having no basis in a particular key, seem to go nowhere and end nowhere.

But to Schoenberg and his followers atonal music was simply the logical next stage of a musical evolution that had started with Gregorian chant (see page 263). Dissonance, they would say, is relative: medieval polyphony sung in one of the old church modes would sound dissonant to us; but then, our four-part harmony using a major or minor key would sound just as dissonant to them. Indeed, by dispensing with keys altogether, atonal music solves the issue of dissonance; as Schoenberg said, it "emancipates dissonance." Still, neither Schoenberg nor his followers would try to persuade anyone that his music is easy or pleasant to listen to. Like German Expressionist

10.56 Arnold Schoenberg, *Self-Portrait*, 1910 Arnold Schoenberg Institute, Los Angeles

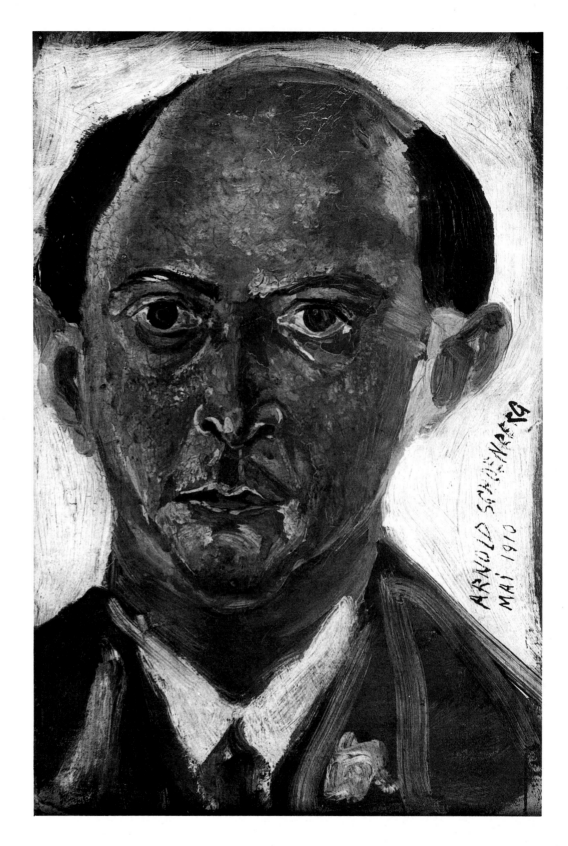

10.56 Arnold Schoenberg, *Self-Portrait*, 1910 Arnold Schoenberg Institute, Los Angeles

art and Kafka's stories, it is meant to disturb, to communicate ideas and feelings intensely. For this reason and others, the music of Schoenberg and Alban Berg (1885–1935) is often called expressionistic. It originated at about the same time and under the same cultural conditions as German Expressionist painting; Schoenberg himself knew Nolde and Kandinsky, sat for Kokoschka, and even exhibited his own paintings (Fig. 10.56) in their shows. Schoenberg's explorations of atonality are analogous to Kandinsky's experiments in total abstraction. Each took the radical step of dispensing with the fundamental components of a formal system which had been in use for centuries. Each, therefore, was compelled to solve creative problems without the reference points of well-established conventions.

In lieu of these reference points Schoenberg often relied on texts to provide meaning and continuity. His *Pierrot Lunaire* (Moonstruck Pierrot), written in 1912, not long after Kandinsky produced his first abstract painting, is a good example. Essentially it is a song cycle—in this case, the setting of a German translation of a somewhat exotic poem. Consisting of 21 movements, *Pierrot* is scored for female voice and five players, using the following instruments: flute and piccolo, clarinet and bass clarinet, violin and viola, cello, and piano. The lines of the poem are vocalized in a singing style called *Sprechstimme* (German: speaking voice), actually a highly stylized, freely inflected form of recitation in which the pitches are not always definite. (The examples below are in English; the syllables that are lengthened and/or stressed in the music are so indicated.) After a sprightly instrumental motif (Fig. **10.57**), the opening lines of the poem are sung/recited while the instruments continue contrapuntally in the background:

> *The wine which toward the eyes we drink*
> *Flows nightly from the M-O-O-N in t-o-r-rents.*

Between stanzas the orchestra sometimes echoes the vocalist, especially in the violin. Changes in dynamics are sometimes pronounced. The opening lines of the third stanza are quite loud:

> *The POET in an E-C-STASY*
> *DRINKS D-E-E-PLY from the HOLY C-H-A-LICE*

On the other hand, some lines in the second movement are recited almost in a whisper:

> *With gentle care* [pause] *this sprinkle*
> *Upon your dark-brown hair,*
> *The m-o-o-nlight p-a-l-lid b-l-o-s-soms*

Throughout, the capricious mood swings suggested by the poem are closely reflected in changes of pitch, loudness, tempo, and color in the instruments, as well as changes of pitch, accent, and cadence in the voice. Because the vocal part is recited in a variety of tones, from high-pitched ones to low, "throaty" ones, it is reminiscent somewhat of the style of a blues singer. Far from being an incoherent medium, atonal music can describe certain kinds of

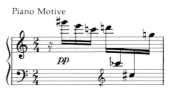

Piano Motive

10.57 Opening motive of *Pierrot lunaire*, Schoenberg

emotions and mental states as well as, if not better than, traditional music. Since it is not committed to particular keys, scales, and progressions, it is freer to pursue the meaning of a text, especially one that emphasizes, as *Pierrot Lunaire* does, intensely subjective experiences.

During World War I and the immediate postwar period, while Stravinsky was specializing in music for small ensembles, Schoenberg published no music at all. Instead he was occupied with inventing a new idiom: the 12-tone system. By the early 1920s Schoenberg had more or less completed the task, and was beginning to compose music in the new idiom. Basically, the 12-tone system (also known as *serialism*) provides a structure for atonal music. As opposed to the tonal system, which tends to emphasize tones harmonically related to a particular home key (as in C, E, and G for the key of C), the new system gave equal importance to each of the 12 tones in the octave. To write a piece of music in this system, the composer establishes a *tone row*, simply an arrangement—any arrangement—of the 12 tones; however, each of the 12 tones must be deployed in order, and none is to be deployed more than once in a group of 12 (almost 500,000,000 patterns are possible). The original 12-note row is then manipulated in three additional ways—retrograde (backwards), inverted (upside down), and retrograde inverted—to create a total of four rows (Fig. **10.58**). Now the composer is ready to write a score, normally following certain procedures: to create melodies, notes are used successively according to the pattern of one or the other of the four rows. To create chords, notes are used simultaneously in accordance with the same patterns. Notes may be shifted to any pitch level, so long as the pattern is maintained. Notes may appear in any register (g or G). The system applies to the melodic and harmonic elements of a composition, not to the choices of rhythm, tempo, and orchestration.

In essence, a composer pre-selects his/her row and follows the rules of the 12-tone system, much as a composer would do using a major or minor in a tonal system. A 12-tone composition derives from several types of manipulations of a basic row in much the same way that a tonal composition derives from several types of manipulations of the tones contained in the major-minor

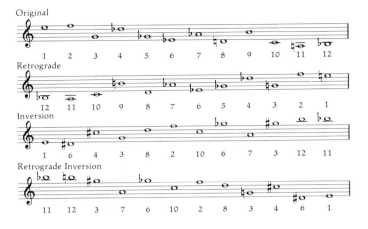

Original

Retrograde

Inversion

Retrograde Inversion

10.58 12-note row and variations

scale system. Schoenberg, in effect, provided a framework for unifying atonal compositions, so that each can be organized around a given pattern of tones.

Atonal music seems especially well suited for expressing negative emotional states. *Pierrot Lunaire*, for example, demonstrates its effectiveness in expressing neurosis and decadence. One of Schoenberg's works, *A Survivor from Warsaw*, a cantata based on a single incident related to the Holocaust of World War II, demonstrates its capacity for conveying tension, despair, fear, and even pain. Scored for male chorus, narrator, and orchestra, the music is clearly atonal, in this case using the 12-tone technique. Like Picasso's *Guernica*, it evokes the horror of its subject in a twentieth-century idiom. Schoenberg represents his subject—Polish Jews being herded by Nazi soldiers for shipment to a death camp—in an explicit way through the use of a narrator. Except for the shouts of German soldiers, English is used to relate the incident, which culminates in the victims' singing of a Hebrew prayer *Shema Yisroel* ("Hear, O Israel"). Meanwhile, the atonal music establishes the emotional atmosphere and reinforces the action. The two modes of expression, narration and music, combine to create an experience so vivid that is almost felt by the listener in a personal way. In

addition, the cantata demonstrates that atonal music can express positive as well as negative emotions. The concluding prayer sung by the chorus is as overwhelming in its sense of triumph as the previous moments are in their sense of fear and despair.

Schoenberg's influence on twentieth-century music may have been even greater than Stravinsky's. But it has also been controversial. Critics of his music not only complain about the dissonance and lack of tonal centers, they also accuse it of being too intellectual—lacking in emotional content. Yet the example of *A Survivor from Warsaw* tends to refute that charge.

The charge is also refuted by the music of Alban Berg (1885–1935). Although Berg's music is mainly atonal, it does not lack emotional content. A student of Schoenberg's in Vienna, Berg is the "romantic" among this group of composers. In his 12-tone music he created tone rows that allow for more tonal-sounding harmonies and lyrical melodies. His music has a reputation for warmth, drama, and vivid colors; as a result, it has some popular appeal. Among his better known works is *Wozzeck* (1925), a theatrical opera about a soldier who is driven to murder and suicide by a hostile society.

Schoenberg's other famous student, Anton Webern (1883–1945), was the "classicist" of the 12-tone school. Killed just outside his home in a war-related accident in 1945, Webern did not live to see his music gain considerable recognition in the 1950s. In contrast to Berg's exuberant compositions, Webern's are brief and spare; whereas the former stress warmth and lyricism, the latter stress discipline and clarity. Because of the extreme brevity of many of his works—a symphony that runs for nine minutes, movements averaging 30 seconds, and so forth—Webern's music is extremely concentrated. And, because of his novel use of instruments and skillful use of contrasting colors, as in his Symphony Opus 21 (1928), it is also fresh and original-sounding.

Thus, by the middle of the twentieth century, music, like art and literature, could look back on a chronology of radical change.

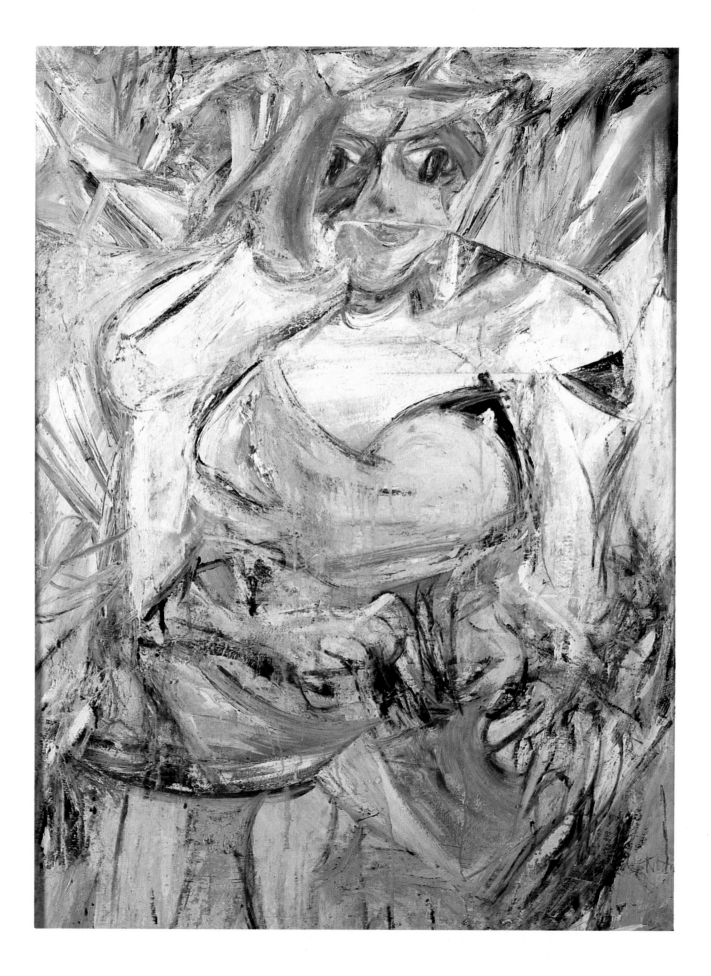

CHAPTER ELEVEN

Modernism II

They have had to forge for themselves an art of living through times of catastrophe, in order to be reborn, and then to fight openly against the death-instinct which is at work in our time.

CAMUS

11.1 WILLEM DE KOONING
Woman II, 1952
Oil on canvas, 59 × 43 ins (149 × 109 cm)
Museum of Modern Art, New York

Modernism and the Transcendent

Speaking for his own generation at the time he received the Nobel Prize for literature (1957), Albert Camus said,

> Those men who were born at the beginning of the first world war and were twenty at the time of Hitler's coming to power and the first revolutionary trials, who were then confronted, to complete their education, with the Spanish war, the second world war, the universal concentration camp, Europe ruled by the gaoler and the torturer, have now to bring up their sons and produce their works in a world threatened by nuclear destruction. Nobody, surely, can expect them to be optimists. And I believe, indeed, that we should understand, while continuing to oppose it, the mistaken attitude of those who, through excess of despair, have asserted the right to dishonour, and have rushed headlong into the nihilism of our day. None the less, the greater number of us, in my own country and throughout Europe, have rejected such nihilism and have tried to find some law to live by. They have had to forge for themselves an art of living through times of catastrophe, in order to be reborn, and then to fight openly against the death-instinct which is at work in our time.[1]

Camus' litany of twentieth-century horrors and his analysis of their effects on human thought and behavior provide an appropriate introduction to the literature and art of this period. The events Camus cites, the pessimism and nihilism resulting from them, and the existential attempt to create meaning where there seems to be none are mirrored in the significant art and literature of our century. Camus' symbolic portrayal of the Nazi occupation of France in *The Plague*, Elie Wiesel's harrowing autobiographical rendering of the Nazi Holocaust in *Night*, Solzhenitsyn's realistic portrayal of the cruelty of a Russian concentration camp in *One Day in the Life of Ivan Denisovich*, Picasso's *Guernica* (see page 420), Schoenberg's *Survivor from Warsaw* (see page 441)—all bear witness to the terrible events of our century and in their very existence as works of art give a kind of meaning to what otherwise seems absurd. The lure of nihilism of which Camus speaks—the view that nothing has meaning—is also reflected, for example, in the attenuated and forlorn protagonists of Kafka (see Chapter 10) and Beckett (see below), the fractured images of human beings in Cubism (see Chapter 10), the diminution and disappearance of human themes in Hard-Edge abstraction and Op Art, and the reduction of music to silence in John

11.2 The Modern World

DATES	SOCIAL AND POLITICAL DEVELOPMENTS	LITERATURE AND PHILOSOPHY	VISUAL ARTS	ARCHITECTURE	MUSIC
1940	Second World War Holocaust First atomic bomb United Nations The Cold War	Sartre Camus (11.4) Existentialism	O'Keeffe (11.7) Benton (11.8) Hopper (11.9) Gorky (11.10) Smith (11.23, 11.25)	Le Corbusier: Unité d'Habitation Apartment House (11.33)	Messiæn Ives Cowell Sessions Varèse Thompson Harris Copland Babbit Carter Partch Hindemith
1950	Korean conflict	Beckett Wiesel (11.5)	Pollock (11.11, 11.12) De Kooning (11.1) Kline (11.13) Rothko (11.14) Frankenthaler (11.15) Rivers (11.16) Johns (11.17) Nevelson (11.25)	Mies van der Rohe: Lake Shore Drive Apartment Houses (11.31) Seagram Building (11.32)	Boulez Stockhausen Penderecki Electronic music Cage (11.38) Brown (11.40) Feldman (11.39) Wolff
1960	Vietnam War Civil Rights Movement First man on moon Student unrest Women's Movement	Solzhenitsyn (11.6)	Kaprow's *Happening* (11.29) Lichtenstein (11.18) Riley (11.20) Stella Anuszkiewicz (11.21) Judd (11.26) Oldenburg (11.28) Heizer (11.30) Baldessari Goings (11.22)	Utzon: Sydney Opera House (11.34) Buckminster-Fuller: United States Pavilion (11.35)	
1970					

Cage's experiment *4′33″* (see *Visual Arts* and *Music*, below). Belief in a transcendent reality that guarantees cosmic meaning and order has become a rare commodity; in a world without such a belief, human beings must try to create meaning and order for themselves. In the words of Camus, they must "find some law to live by." This is precisely what the Existentialists, including Camus, Sartre, and some Modern artists, attempted to do. Indeed, this search for meaning typifies much of Modernist culture, especially in the years following World War II when Existentialist philosophy had its greatest influence.

But twentieth-century culture is not monolithic. In the first place, it should be emphasized that there are many people, including intellectuals and artists, who have not suffered a loss of faith in transcendent meaning; also, that such loss is articulated mainly by "high" culture (though no doubt intuited by "ordinary" people who are incapable of giving precise definition to their sense of malaise). Moreover, not all Modernists reflect the prevailing pessimism. Kandinsky (see page 412) believed that modern art would play a role in a spiritual revival. Mondrian (see page 419) intended his art to "express the universal within us"; in his view, such things as balance and harmony were divine principles. Between the wars, a spirit of optimism animated the work of some American painters and composers, such as Thomas Hart Benton and Aaron Copland, who idealized rural America and the laboring-class American. Even Camus, in *The Plague*, affirmed his faith in the capacity of human beings to act heroically when confronted by crisis. The Rumanian-born writer Elie Wiesel, though painfully aware of the abyss of meaninglessness because of his personal experience of the Holocaust, does not reject God; but, like Job, carries on an argumentative dialogue with him in his writings. And Alexander Solzhenitsyn is a friend of Christianity, who advocates the return of his people to the Russian Orthodox faith.

Much of the visual art produced since 1960 is neither pessimistic nor optimistic in its world-view. It is mainly indifferent; indeed, it sometimes seems almost embarrassed by the existential preoccupations of the 1950s generation of artists. Still, its disparagement of artists who affirm meaning—and even of the traditional concept of art itself, as a process of imposing order on raw materials—has nihilistic implications. The work of John Cage (see below), which negates all traditional values in music, also seems to betray a nihilistic drift, notwithstanding his personal acceptance of a kind of Zen mysticism.

In the overall picture of Modernism, despite the exceptions cited above, there can be no question but that there is a major trend toward the loss of meaning. According to the literary critic Irving Howe, nihilism is "the central preoccupation of Modernist literature." Prophesied by Dostoyevsky in his dictum that meaning is impossible without belief in a transcendent God, this state of mind is dramatized by Kafka's endless struggle, as Howe puts it, with the "angel of nothingness." Art itself had a nihilistic dimension for Thomas Mann because of his belief that there is something essentially diseased about art and the artist.[2] Indeed, Camus' melancholy assessment at mid-century continues to be relevant for much of Western culture as the century draws toward a close, although there is now perhaps even less confidence in the human capacity to forge meaning out of meaninglessness.

Literature

Camus

Albert Camus (1913–1960) and Jean-Paul Sartre (1905–1980), comrades in the French Resistance during the Nazi occupation of France in World War II, exerted a powerful influence on young intellectuals in the years following the War. Although Camus rejected labels, both he and Sartre are generally regarded as Existential writers.

Traditional philosophical thought attempted to define human nature through abstract concepts that would capture the *essence* of humanness. Existential philosophers stress instead that human essence is determined only by the concrete *existence* of the individual human being in the physical world. Thus the human being, according to Sartre, begins at ground zero and is at every point in life merely the sum total of the choices that he or she has previously made. Although there are theistic Existentialists—indeed, Kierkegaard, a seminal influence on Existentialism, was a Christian—Camus, Sartre, and other atheistic Existentialists rejected all moral and philosophical absolutes, including belief in a God who gives meaning to human existence. Thus they sought to forge values that are completely human-centered in an indifferent world.

Camus was born in Mondovi, French Algeria. Soon after his birth his Alsatian father, a farm laborer, was

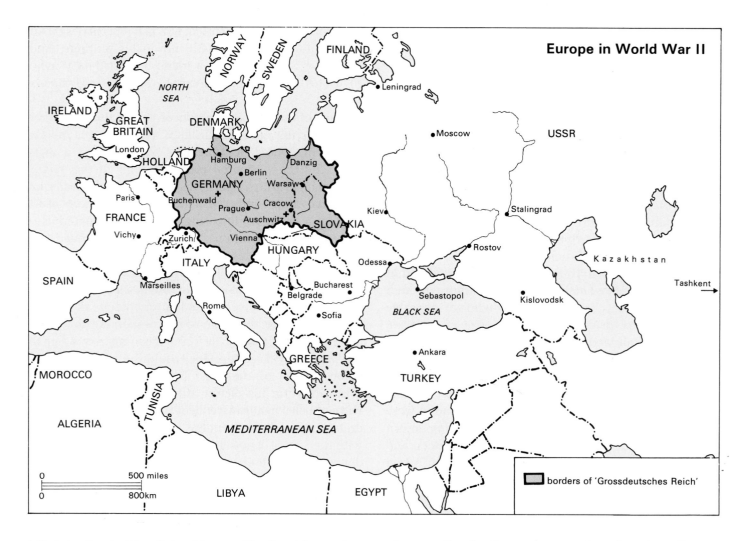

killed in the battle of the Marne. His Spanish mother moved her family—including Albert, an older brother, his grandmother, and a sickly uncle—to Algiers, where she supported them by working as a cleaning woman. Camus' abilities were recognized early by one of his primary teachers, Louis Germain—to whom Camus would dedicate his Nobel Prize speech—who assisted his young pupil in obtaining a scholarship to the *lycée* (secondary school). Later Camus studied philosophy at the University of Algiers, writing a dissertation that compared Greek and Christian thought in Plotinus and St. Augustine. During this period he manifested a passionate interest in sports (especially soccer) and the theater, enthusiasms that he retained throughout his life. For a short time during his student days, he was a member of the Communist party. He also experienced his first serious bout of tuberculosis, which interrupted his university studies; the disease recurred periodically throughout his life.

At the outbreak of World War II in 1939, Camus attempted to enlist but was rejected because of his health. Traveling to Paris in March of 1940, he became a reporter for *Paris-Soir*; but he returned to North Africa in January

of 1941, after the German occupation of northern France. There he completed his essay *The Myth of Sisyphus* and began writing *The Plague*, which was not completed until 1947. He had previously written *The Stranger*, which, along with *The Myth of Sisyphus*, was published in 1942. These two works made him famous. In this same year Camus returned to France and joined the Resistance group called "Combat," working on the newspaper of the same name. After the liberation of Paris in 1944, he became the editor of *Combat*. His editorials and articles for this paper, as well as his plays—*Caligula* (1945), for example—also contributed to his postwar reputation.

In 1951 Camus published *The Rebel*, a book stating his philosophy, and came under attack from the French Marxists, who were upset by his rejection of revolutionary violence. His controversy with Sartre over this work—though Sartre, like Camus, was not a member of the Communist party—led to the rupture of a friendship that for some time had been shaky. Camus' novel *The Fall* was published in 1956, and a volume of short stories, *The Exile and the Kingdom*, in 1957. In that same year, at the age of 44, he was awarded the Nobel Prize for literature, a remarkable achievement for one so young. In 1959, André Malraux, himself a famous French author and minister of cultural affairs, appointed Camus as the director of the new state-supported experimental theater. He was never to fulfill the promise of this position, however; for on January 4, 1960, he was killed in an automobile accident while traveling from Loumarin to Paris. An unused railroad ticket for this journey was found in his pocket. Apparently, after purchasing it, he had changed his mind about his mode of transportation.

Because his writings are informed by metaphysical views, Camus is regarded as a philosophical writer. Basic to all his thinking is the idea of *the absurd*. This absurdity results from un-met human demands upon an enigmatic universe which is indifferent to our strivings after meaning and coherence. Above all, however, the absurd is evident in the fact that, however we have lived or however passionately we desire to live on, we must die. Death thus writes an eternal *finis* to all our human possibilities. Camus' lifetime task as a writer, therefore, was to forge an answer to the question of how one must live in a world without meaning. Although he did not always arrive at the same answer, the absurd was always his starting point. Thus the absurd was his absolute—paradoxical, since he claimed to reject all absolutes. Contradiction is also implicit in Camus' efforts to define the absurd, for any attempt to put a philosophy of the absurd into words implies a measure of coherence and therefore contradicts itself.

Camus was keenly aware of the danger of nihilism in the idea of the absurd, for he recognized that it was but a short step to the denial of all values. His awareness of this danger is evident in his *Letters to a German Friend* (1945), in which he identifies, and rejects, the absurdist-nihilist impulse in the nationalistic aggression and violence of Nazism.

The concept of the absurd is especially clear in *The Myth of Sisyphus* and *The Stranger*. The former refers to the Greek myth of Sisyphus, who was eternally condemned by the gods to push a rock to the top of a hill, only to see it tumble to the bottom each time. Sisyphus, who refuses to capitulate to the inevitable and whose recognition of his absurd destiny makes him superior to it, is Camus' image of the absurd hero. He begins this essay with what to him is the most important philosophical question: Should one commit suicide? Obviously, one possible response to the absurd is to exit the stage on which the drama of the absurd is enacted. This is the ultimate issue, in Camus' view, because it deals with the question of whether life is worth living. Camus rejects suicide on the basis that since it implies an appeal to a value that is denied the victim by an absurd universe, it is collusion with the absurd because it prevents any further appeal in the name of that value.

Meursault, the narrator and protagonist of *The Stranger*, is, like Sisyphus, a victim of the absurd. In this case, the aspect of absurdity focused on is death. At the beginning of the novel Meursault's mother dies, at mid-point he kills an Arab, and at the end he awaits his own death by execution. Meursault lives an apparently meaningless life which reflects the absurd perspective; he is without commitments or values except those that give him pleasure, such as sun, sea, food and drink, and sex. However, he is not cognizant of the cause of this behavior until, near the end of the novel, he articulates his justification in response to a priest who has come to prepare him for death by turning him to God. Although Meursault tells him that he does not believe in God or the afterlife, the priest persists. Meursault finally becomes angry, seizes the priest and begins to shout that it makes no difference how he has lived his life. Indeed, he claims, "I'd been right, I was still right, I was always right."[3] He might have lived his life another way, but what difference would it have made? Death is the great leveler, he contends, wiping out all the distinctions that society

11.4 Albert Camus

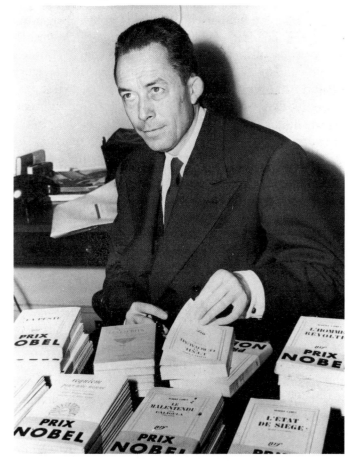

makes as to how life should be lived, justifying the rejection of all moral imperatives. It is the ultimate triumph of the absurd. Meursault thus discovers the hidden perspective that justifies his indifferently lived life, an indifference that matches the "benign indifference of the universe."[4]

Thus Camus, in *The Myth of Sisyphus* and *The Stranger*, argued that because of the absurd there are no moral absolutes. ("There are some words I do not understand," he once wrote; "one of them is sin.") How, then, is life to be made worthwhile? His answer: live it intensely; fill each moment to the full. This is, of course, an ethic of quantity, not quality. But Camus did not sustain this position, for after 1942 he began to press toward a qualitative ethic in an attempt to justify moral imperatives in a meaningless world. Unlike Dostoyevsky, who argued that the only basis for ethical values is God, Camus rejected God, yet also sought to establish ethical imperatives. It has been suggested that Camus' shift in his response to the absurd was brought about by the circumstances of the Nazi occupation of France and the Resistance movement—a situation that starkly revealed the inadequacy of an ethic that focused on pleasure as the appropriate response to the absurd, to the neglect of sacrificial public duty. Thus Camus' next major novel, *The Plague* (1947), dramatized the necessity of revolt against the absurd.

The Plague is a symbolic novel; that is, its literal meaning points beyond itself to additional meanings. Such symbolism is distinguished from allegory, like that of Dante's *Divine Comedy* (see Chapter 7), by the fact that allegory sustains its symbolism more consistently, while the figurative dimension of the symbolic novel is intermittent. On the literal level, *The Plague* is the fictional story of the ravaging of Oran, in 1940, by the bubonic plague, the efforts to resist it, and its eventual disappearance. Symbolically, at the historical level, *The Plague* represents the Nazi occupation of France, the resistance to it, and the deliverance from that "plague." At the metaphysical level, however, *The Plague* symbolizes the problem of evil and suffering (in Camusian terms, the absurd) and the necessity of revolt against the absurd, a revolt that is represented in the novel by the cooperative efforts to reduce the ravages of the plague.

The symbolism works very well at this level. The plague appears arbitrarily and mysteriously; human effort does not diminish its dreadful force; and it disappears as mysteriously as it appeared. It is truly a manifestation of the absurd. The validity of the ethic of revolt against such destructiveness is obvious. Not everyone fights against the plague, but it is apparent that those who do are acting as they must. Also, it is clear that human beings are not responsible for the plague—they are simply its victims,

although the priest, Father Paneloux, preaches a sermon in which he contends that the plague is God's judgment upon a sinful city. However, Camus' protagonist and narrator, Dr. Rieux, takes issue with the priest, arguing for the essential innocence of human beings. Thus they are the guiltless victims of absurd suffering in a meaningless universe and must band together to revolt against such irrational evil.

But it is much more difficult to make Camus' symbolism work at the historical level, for the Nazi occupation and the suffering it inflicted upon the French people was humanly instigated and implemented. Also, the question of whether this manifestation of absurd evil should be resisted, and if so, how, is much more complex than that of resistance to the plague. Thus the vast and complicated questions of human responsibility for the absurd and the nature of the duty to oppose such evil must be dealt with— questions that Camus (though acknowledging that human beings can be plague carriers) plays down in his novel. In his next book, however, his positioning of the locus of evil underwent a drastic shift.

In *The Fall* (1956), instead of emphasizing the innocence of human beings ravaged by the absurd, Camus presents a protagonist, a representative European, who is both responsible and guilty. As the title indicates, his exploration of the human heart is developed through biblical and Christian symbols. Thus his protagonist, the sole speaker in the novel, is named Jean-Baptiste Clamence, an allusion to John the Baptist, harbinger of the Messiah, as a *vox clamantis in deserto* ("a voice crying out in the wilderness"; Mark 1:3). Camus, however, far from using these symbols in a traditional manner, employs them ironically—an irony resulting from the juxtaposition of the negative but hopeful biblical view of the human condition with the wholly negative and hopeless view of humans in the novel. Biblical humans are fallen but redeemable by God's grace; in *The Fall* they are also fallen but unredeemable because there is no divine grace. Clamence, like his biblical prototype, denounces his contemporaries for their sins; but, unlike John the Baptist, he himself is a rank hypocrite and he announces no Messiah to come who will bring divine forgiveness and reconciliation. Moreover, he has adopted the role of "judge-penitent," that is, he "penitently" confesses his duplicity and misdeeds to his auditor so that, by duping him into confessing his own sins, he can judge his silent listener and therefore maintain his own egoistic sense of superiority. Thus Camus parodies the biblical story so that it no longer offers assurance of divine grace to fallen humans but rather mocks them. *The Fall* indicates that Camus' thinking on guilt had done an about-face. No longer are human beings seen as essentially innocent victims of the absurd; rather they are in complicity with and responsible for evil in the world. Where such thinking would have ultimately taken Camus, we cannot say. His absurd death precludes an answer.

Beckett and the Theater of the Absurd

Although Camus' works communicate the image of the world from the perspective of the absurd, they are written in a clear and coherent style, thus imposing order and meaning on an absurd world. A tension is therefore created between the coherent form of the work and its absurd theme. The theater of the absurd seeks to resolve this tension by making the literary work itself a metaphor for the absurd. The work becomes, not merely a means of communicating the idea of the absurd, but an embodiment of it. Samuel Beckett (born 1906), in what may be taken as a programmatic statement for the theater of the absurd, has said that the "task" of the artist is "to find a form that accommodates the mess," referring to the chaos of the world.

Influenced by Camus, the theater of the absurd emerged in Paris in the 1950s. It caught on quickly and soon spread to the rest of Europe, to England, and America. But the experience of the absurd, as contrasted with Camus' philosophical principle, had already been given literary expression in the works of Kafka (see Chapter 10). Indeed, a dramatized version of Kafka's novel *The Trial* was presented in Paris as early as 1947. Thus Kafka's Joseph K., with his sense of undefined guilt and his inability to justify his existence before the amorphous and arbitrary court that condemns him to death, is the first protagonist of absurdist drama.

The anti-literary nature of absurdist drama is demonstrated by its attempt to reduce radically the elements of traditional drama: plot, characterization, dialogue, exposition, conflict and resolution. Thus it seeks to make the play itself an expression of the idea of meaninglessness, even nothingness. Beckett often quotes the dictum of Democritus (c. 460–c. 370 BC): "Nothing is more real than nothing." The absurdist playwright seeks to give existential reality, *on stage*, to this concept of nothingness, the essence of the absurd. Thus the play *itself*—through its lack of coherence and logical development, and through its truncated characters with their empty words and gestures—becomes a metaphor for the absurd.

Largely because of his work *Waiting for Godot* (1952), the best-known playwright of the theater of the absurd—indeed, regarded by some as the most influential writer of the latter half of the twentieth century—is Samuel Beckett. Beckett, like James Joyce (see Chapter 10), was born in Ireland but has chosen to live in France through-

out most of his life. Unlike Joyce, whose parents were Catholic, he was brought up as a Protestant. After earning a BA degree in Romance languages at Trinity College, Dublin (1927), he taught English in Paris (1928–1930). During this period he met Joyce and was strongly attracted to his literary style, serving for a while as his secretary. He helped translate *Finnegans Wake* into French and wrote an interpretive essay on it. In this same period he won a prize for a poem *Whoroscope* (1930), which marked the beginning of his career as a creative writer. Returning to Dublin in 1931, he taught French and took an MA degree at Trinity. Concluding that he was not suited to the academic life, he left Ireland to wander on the Continent for five years, settling permanently in Paris in 1937. Although he published a volume of short stories in English (1934) and a novel, *Murphy* (1938), also in English, these works attracted little recognition. Like Camus, he joined the French Resistance when World War II broke out; but, fearful of arrest when members of his group were rounded up by the Nazis, he fled to the unoccupied zone of southern France, remaining there until the war ended. In this period he wrote his second novel, *Watt* (published in 1953).

After the war, in a flurry of creative activity between 1946 and 1950, he published three novels which form a trilogy and which were included in the category of the *nouveau roman* ("new novel"), a term used to designate the work of a group of French experimental writers. These three novels, written in French and later translated into English by Beckett himself, were *Molloy* (1951), *Malone Dies* (1952), and *The Unnameable* (1953). As one critic has stated, "Stripped of narrative and extensive dialogue and reduced to laconic commentary," these novels are characterized "by a sobriety and irony recalling Swift [see Chapter 4], with a Swiftian delight in the cool everyday tone for conveying the unspeakable and the indescribable."[5]

But it was *Waiting for Godot*, first published in French in 1952 as *En attendant Godot*, and produced in Paris in 1953, that gave Beckett an international reputation. *Godot* appeared in English, translated by Beckett, in 1954 and was produced on Broadway in 1956, with Bert Lahr as Gogo and E. G. Marshall as Didi. Wherever the play appeared it was highly controversial. On the one hand, it was criticized because of its lack of significant action and condemned as nihilistic. On the other, it was praised for its sensitivity to the human condition and even described as having profound religious meaning.

The action of Godot, which is subtitled a "tragicomedy in two acts," can be described briefly. Two tramps, Vladimir (Didi) and Estragon (Gogo) while away their time in empty conversation and empty actions as they wait for a Mr. Godot. Two times, once in each act, Pozzo, the master, and Lucky, his slave, pass through, with the difference that in the second act Pozzo is blind and Lucky is mute. Each act ends with the appearance of the goat-boy, who announces that Godot will come tomorrow. Each act also ends with one tramp suggesting to the other that they leave, but the stage direction in both instances is "they do not move," echoing the opening line of the play spoken by Gogo, "nothing to be done." One waggish critic described the two acts with the remark, "nothing happens twice." But the "nothingness" of *Godot* is in itself a significant commentary on the emptiness of human existence. Related to this is the major image of waiting. Human beings, deprived of any transcendent significance, seek to give meaning to their lives by convincing themselves that salvation will come from some external source, perhaps a supernatural being, at some point in the future. Thus, they "wait."

"Godot" is the symbol of their empty hope. But who is he? Or does he even exist? We do not know because he never appears. Is he God, as the name suggests? Although the French word for God is *Dieu*, this is not a decisive argument against identifying Godot as God. Beckett, after all, is multilingual, and he may have intended "Godot" in his orginal French version to have its English connotation. In support of this view, Lucky is called by his English name in both the French and English versions. But whether or not we identify Godot as God, it is clear that he is the antithesis of the void, the possibility of meaning in the empty lives of Didi and Gogo, an external possibility that never becomes a reality.

Critics have often remarked on the religious significance of *Godot*. Thus, in Christian terms, Godot might represent the hope of the Second Coming of Christ, or in the Jewish faith, the long-awaited Messiah. Moreover, the lone tree on stage is reminiscent of the cross of Christ. At one point Didi says that Godot told them that they were to wait by the tree and that he would come on Saturday. The cross of Christ was, of course, empty on Saturday, for Christ was in the tomb. In Christian faith, however, he was resurrected early on the first day of the week (Sunday). In the world of *Godot*, that Saturday never ends. There is no glorious resurrection and therefore no hope of salvation. Thus the tramps wait futilely by the tree for the appearance of Godot. Like other modern humans, they know the crucifixion story and refer to "our Savior," but this signifies nothing for their lives.

At one point, when Pozzo has fallen and is crying out for help, Didi and Gogo discuss what they should do. Didi makes a magnificent speech, an existential call to significant action on behalf of a fellow human being in distress; one is reminded of Camus' concept of revolt against the absurd, as dramatized in *The Plague*. But the rhetoric of meaningful action fades as Didi offers an apologetic for inaction and finally concludes: "What are we doing here, *that* is the question. And we are blessed in this, that we happen to know the answer. Yes, in the immense confusion one thing alone is clear, we are waiting for Godot to come—"[6] Thus their empty hope for the coming of Godot is offered as a substitute for existential commitment to compassionate action.

Is there any hope for mankind in *Godot*? The play offers little basis for optimism. The tree apparently sprouts "four or five leaves" between the two acts, but this meager sign of spring—the leaves are barely noticeable to the audience—merely points up the fact that there is little difference between winter and spring in the world of the play. A Christian interpretation of the play might argue that it indeed demonstrates the hopeless plight of modern human beings without God. One Christian critic, affirming that Godot *has* come, states that "Godot appeared 20 centuries ago in the form of a child."[7] Though this is one way of understanding what the play implies, it cannot be Beckett's meaning; Godot does not come and there is no basis for hoping that he will. The existential interpreter might contend that *Godot* dramatizes the need of humans to create meaning for their lives through significant action instead of depending on some external source, such as a supernatural being. There is no *deus ex machina* to tidy up the stage of life before the curtain falls. We are merely the sum total of our choices, and no God can change that fact. But *Godot*, unlike *The Plague*, does not dramatize this alternative, except through the fruitless rhetoric of Didi. This interpretation, like the Christian view, must extrapolate on the evidence of the play to build its case. We are thus left with what would appear to be Beckett's meaning: there is no hope. Perhaps, however, Beckett's sensitive portrayal of the tragic plight of modern human beings without God in itself is a reason for a modest hope. For the greater tragedy would be a world in which humans, infected with the fatal sickness of emptiness, were deprived of sensitive artists who, with their fingers on the pulse of the human condition, could correctly diagnose the disease—even though, as in the case of Beckett, they prescribe no remedy. Painful as it may be, the awareness of who and what we are is essential to our humanness.

But Beckett's somber presentation is not the only, let alone the final, word on the human condition as portrayed by modern writers. The writings of Elie Wiesel and Alexander Solzhenitsyn demonstrate that the problem of God has not been relegated to the trash can of history, and that human beings continue to struggle against the demon of meaninglessness rampant in the modern world.

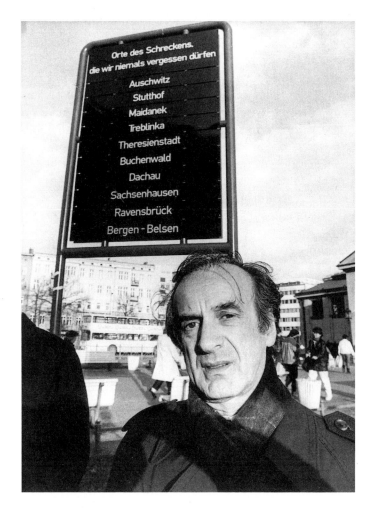

11.5 Elie Wiesel

Wiesel

Camus' concept of the *absurd* takes on a precise historical meaning in the Holocaust, the attempt by the Nazis in World War II to wipe out European Jewry, resulting in the systematic destruction of 6,000,000 Jews. (The Nazis were also responsible for the murder of millions of persons belonging to other minority groups, as well as persons they considered expendable for their purposes.) The term Holocaust refers to a whole burnt sacrifice; but the Hebrew word for the Holocaust, *Shoah* ("annihilation"), the title of a recent major film on the Holocaust, does not connote sacrifice.

Professor Terrence des Pres has written, "Every age produces the event which defines it, and in our time the Holocaust is *ours*. It demands that one face the kind of limitless horror our technological and bureaucratic civilization makes possible."[8] He also raises the question of where human beings will find the resources to deal with the implications of this horror. This is, of course, the crucial question, for it was not demons but human beings

who perpetrated the Holocaust; and it is human beings who will determine whether the threat of nuclear conflict—of which we have had a foretaste in the bombing of Hiroshima and Nagasaki—will become reality in a universal holocaust. The Holocaust is a defining event for our age because it dramatically points to the question of whether human beings have the spiritual resources to overcome the death instinct within them and to avert ultimate disaster. Indeed, the Holocaust has dramatized, on a stupendous scale, a disturbing dimension of human nature which has manifested itself repeatedly through the ages: that of cruelty. But besides raising questions about human nature, it also points to ultimate theological questions with which both Jewish and Christian theologians continue to struggle. How could God permit such horror? Indeed, can one believe in an all-powerful and all-good God after the Holocaust? Is traditional Christian theology, with its censure of the Jews for rejecting Christ, somehow responsible for the Holocaust? After all, it was a "Christian" civilization that perpetrated it.

These are but a few of the painful questions posed for all thoughtful Jews and Christians by the Holocaust. But for the survivors of the death camps, the heavy burden of these profound questions is truly crushing. For in addition to these questions, they must also grapple with the questions of why they survived when their friends and loved ones perished, and what their responsibility is to the dead—and to the living—as surviving victims and witnesses of the Holocaust obscenities, a responsibility that becomes increasingly crucial as their generation gradually dies out.

Although the volume of Holocaust literature is immense, the foremost spokesman for the survivors to date is Elie Wiesel (born 1928), who in 1985 received a Congressional Medal of Honor "in recognition of his humanitarian efforts and outstanding contributions to world literature and human rights."[9] In 1986 he received the Nobel Peace Prize.

Wiesel was a 15-year-old Jewish boy living in Sighet, Transylvania—which had been annexed by Hungary from Rumania in 1940—when the Germans entered Hungary in 1944 and began their mass deportation of the Jews. Devoutly committed to the study of the writings of his people, including the Talmud, the Kabbala, and the teachings of the Hassidic rabbis, he probably would have become a rabbinical scholar had it not been for the Holocaust. He and his family—including his father, mother, and three sisters—were deported to Auschwitz in the spring of 1944. There, his mother and youngest sister quickly perished in the gas chambers. His two older sisters somehow survived. He and his father remained together until his father's death at Buchenwald shortly before the liberation of that camp in the spring of 1945 by American troops.

After his liberation, Wiesel was taken to France along with 400 other Jewish children. There he resumed his study of the Talmud and taught Hebrew, Yiddish, and the Bible. He also learned French and studied philosophy and literature at the Sorbonne. In this period, he encountered the Existentialist thinking of writers such as Camus and Sartre, whose grappling with moral issues was to influence his own writings. In 1948 Wiesel became a foreign correspondent, reporting at times for Israeli, French, and American newspapers.

In 1954 he had what was to become a crucial interview with François Mauriac, the noted French Catholic novelist.[10] Mauriac, drawn to the young Jewish correspondent, told him how deeply moved he had been by Madame Mauriac's story of the trainloads of Jewish children she had seen waiting at Austerlitz station for deportation. He saw this event, he said, as the shattering of the optimistic hope of the Enlightenment for steady human progress based on scientific discoveries and education. Even so, he pointed out, he was unaware at the time that these children were destined for the gas chambers and crematoria. Wiesel responded, "I was one of those children."

Mauriac urged Wiesel to tell his story publicly. After his release from Buchenwald, Wiesel had vowed to remain silent about his experiences for ten years—aware that putting them into words might distort them. These years of reflection and study had prepared him for his encounter with Mauriac and the undertaking of his task.

Two years after his interview, he published a lengthy version in Yiddish of his Auschwitz experience. The condensed French version (*La Nuit*) appeared in 1958. "The text became a personal Bible for Wiesel," states the critic Ellen S. Fine, "forming the nucleus of his subsequent volumes, the center around which all of his tales revolved."[11] Thus began the literary career of Wiesel and also his mission of bearing witness to the evil of the Holocaust and the suffering of its victims. In 1960, *La Nuit* was published in the United States as *Night*. To date Wiesel has written some 20 books, including such novels as *Dawn* (1960), *The Accident* (1961), *The Town Behind the Wall* (1962), *The Gates of the Forest* (1964), *A Beggar in Jerusalem* (1968), *The Oath* (1973), *The Testament* (1980), and *The Fifth Son* (1984). He has also written books on biblical characters, the plight of the Russian Jews, and the Hassidic masters, among others. (In 1981 he was appointed honorary chairman of the World Gathering of Jewish Holocaust Survivors, in Jerusalem.)

Although Auschwitz is a somber presence in all of Wiesel's writings, he generally approaches it obliquely rather than directly. *Night*, the story of his own journey into the darkness of Auschwitz, is an exception. Wiesel sees himself as responsible for giving a voice to those whose voices were stilled by the gas chambers. Only so long as these people are remembered will the death factories be cheated of their final victory. Wiesel also struggles in his writings with the question of belief in God—an ongoing struggle that suggests his unwillingness to settle the question definitively by embracing atheism. Indeed, he writes, "there comes a time when only those who do not believe in God will not cry out to him in wrath and anguish."[12] *Night* is such an outcry.

Wiesel begins his narrative at Sighet, where, in 1942, he heard a horror story of mass execution of Jews by German soldiers from a friend and mentor who, deported in 1942, escaped and returned to warn the Jews. Everyone, including Wiesel, thought the man was mad. Not much later, German troops entered Hungary; soon afterward they began deporting Jews to the camps. Wiesel's narrative describes the subsequent events in harrowing detail: the long journey in a sealed railroad car; the arrival at Auschwitz, where they could see the flames of the crematoria; being separated, along with his father, from his mother and little sister, never to see them again; and the massacre and burning of infants:

> *Never shall I forget that night, the first night in camp, which has turned my life into one long night, seven times cursed and seven times sealed.*
> *Never shall I forget that smoke. Never shall I forget the little faces of the children, whose bodies I saw turned into wreaths of smoke beneath a silent blue sky.*
> *Never shall I forget those flames which consumed my faith forever.*
> *Never shall I forget that nocturnal silence which deprived me, for all eternity, of the desire to live.*
> *Never shall I forget those moments which murdered my God and my soul and turned my dreams to dust.*
> *Never shall I forget these things, even if I am condemned to live as long as God Himself. Never.*[13]

This passage, as Fine has written, "summarizes the principal themes of Wiesel's first book, joining the theme of night, to those of fire, silence, and the death of children, of God, and of the self."[14] But the paradox of Wiesel's relationship with God is suggested by the last line of the quoted passage. Although the God of his childhood faith was "murdered," his protest is not an absolute denial, for he can also speak of God as living. Later, he writes, "How I sympathized with Job! I did not deny God's existence, but I doubted his absolute justice."[15] Indeed, Wiesel's protest to God against God, the arraignment of God on the grounds of apparent failure to be, as promised, a God of justice and mercy, is an honored Jewish tradition, rooted in the Bible itself, as shown in our discussion of Job (see Chapter 1).

His alienation from God and from his childhood self also alienated him from the worshiping Jewish community. On the eve of Rosh Hashanah, the beginning of the Jewish New Year, thousands of Jewish prisoners gathered in the camp to bless God and to plead for forgiveness. Wiesel could no longer do this, for God had "allowed" Jews "to be tortured, butchered, gassed, burned." Thus, Wiesel tells us, he "had ceased to plead. I was no longer capable of lamentation ... I was the accuser, God the accused.... I was alone—terribly alone in a world without God and without man.... I stood amid that praying congregation, observing it like a stranger."[16]

But Wiesel never became alienated from his father. Their relationship is a humanizing factor in the midst of his account of the calculated dehumanizing process of the death camps. After their arrival in Buchenwald, however, his father, who was suffering from dysentery and a blow on the head, was taken away one night, not to return. To his distress, Wiesel could not weep for his father—and even experienced a tinge of relief. He relates that the night before the deportation of the Jews to Auschwitz began, his father was telling a good story to a group of people in his family's backyard. The story was never finished, because his father was called away to a meeting where he received the news of the deportation. Wiesel's Holocaust writings, as Fine has pointed out, are an attempt to finish, in a sense, his father's truncated story and the story of every Jew whose voice was silenced by the Nazi death camps.[17]

But Wiesel speaks not only for his own people destroyed by the Nazis, but for all peoples who have been or are the victim of oppression. "The Jewish and human conditions become one," he affirms, "a concentric circle, one within the other, not one against the other or one replacing the other."

In *Night* we can see a parallel with the world described in *The Plague*, in which people are trapped within a closed environment, at the mercy of an absurd evil. Auschwitz and the other camps are a real-life, magnified version of the closed world of meaningless suffering depicted by Camus. But unlike the plague bacillus which inflicts suffering and death upon the inhabitants of Oran, the evil and horror of the death camps was inflicted on humans by humans.

Solzhenitsyn

The twentieth century has provided three major symbols of the pain and destruction human beings inflict on one another: the mushroom-shaped cloud of a nuclear attack, the Nazi death camp, and the *Gulag*. The first two of these horrors are now indelibly etched on the mental landscape of most Western peoples. But the Gulag has more recently

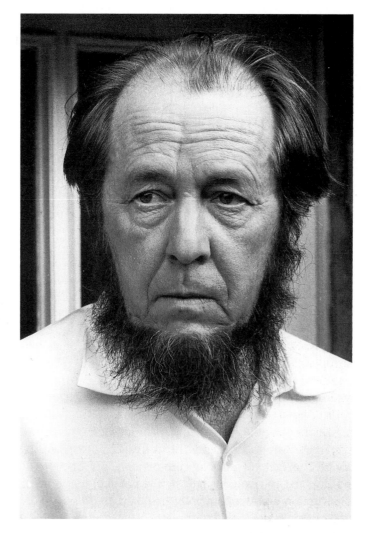

11.6 Alexander Solzhenitsyn

become familiar to us, thanks to the writings of Alexander Solzhenitsyn, and, in particular, to his three-volume work *The Gulag Archipelago*, in which he reveals in detail the brutality of the Russian labor camps. Indeed, according to Solzhenitsyn, Russian totalitarian cruelty provided the model for Hitler's own techniques.

Born in 1918 in Kislovodsk in the Caucasus, Solzhenitsyn was brought up by his mother—his father having been killed in a hunting accident before he was born. Although he preferred the study of literature, he obtained a degree in mathematics and physics from the University of Rostov. He began his formal study of literature at the age of 21, when he took a correspondence course from Moscow University. After the Germans invaded Russia, Solzhenitsyn joined the Red Army, where he became an artillery officer. Twice decorated for bravery, he was nonetheless arrested by Soviet counter-intelligence agents in 1945 on the charge that he had slandered the Russian dictator, Stalin, in letters written to a friend. He was sentenced to eight years imprisonment. Because of his education, he was first sent to Mavrino, a prison research institute. His experiences there eventually provided him with material for his novel *The First Circle* (1968). But his first and most famous book, the novella *One Day in the Life of Ivan Denisovich* (1962), grew out of the last two years of his sentence, which he served in a forced labor camp in Kazakhstan. While there, he underwent surgery for cancer.

Released in 1953, shortly before the death of Stalin, Solzhenitsyn was sentenced to "perpetual" exile in Kazakhstan. He began to write, but the cancer recurred, necessitating his treatment at the hospital in Tashkent. This experience later became the basis for his novel *Cancer Ward* (1968). After his release from the hospital, Solzhenitsyn taught high school mathematics in the village of Kok-Terek. His story *Matryona's House* (1963) reflects this period. Rehabilitated by the Twentieth Party Congress in the post-Stalin era, he was able to move to Ryazan in European Russia. There he obtained a job teaching mathematics in a school and was able to continue his writing.

Until 1961, however, Solzhenitsyn was convinced that his writings would never see print. Indeed, he dared not even read them to his friends. He was especially concerned about the lack of critical commentary on his works. Finally, in 1961, encouraged by the political thaw under the Russian premier Nikita Khrushchev and a speech by Alexander Tvardovsky, the editor of *Novy Mir* ("New World"), he submitted his manuscript of *One Day in the Life of Ivan Denisovich* to this journal. Tvardovsky, deeply impressed by the story, obtained the support of Khrushchev for its publication. In November, 1962, the story was published in *Novy Mir* with Khrushchev's approval. *One Day*, an account of conditions in a Stalinist labor camp, served Khrushchev's purpose to downgrade the image of Stalin in the interest of consolidating his own position. In his introduction to the English edition of this novella, which appeared in 1963, Marvin Kalb wrote, "within a day all of the 95,000 copies of the November issue of the magazine were snapped up by eager Russians. Within a week Solzhenitsyn skyrocketed to international fame."[18]

But official approval was ephemeral. Although *Novy Mir*, in 1963, published three of Solzhenitsyn's short stories—*Matryona's House, The Incident at Krechetovka Station* and *For the Good of the Cause*—in 1964 he was officially rejected as a potential recipient of the prestigious Lenin Prize for *One Day*. Moreover, when he completed *The First Circle*, also in 1964, the manuscript, along with other private papers, was confiscated. Solzhenitsyn then began a series of unsuccessful appeals to the Soviet Writers' Union in the hope of gaining their support. He was in fact expelled from the Ryazan branch of the union in 1969. Both Western writers and Soviet dissidents protested his expulsion. In the meantime, both *The First Circle* and *Cancer Ward* had appeared in English.

In 1970 Solzhenitsyn was awarded the Nobel Prize for literature. Fearing that if he went to Stockholm to receive the award he would not be readmitted to Russia, he accepted it *in absentia*. In 1971 he permitted his novel on World War I, *August, 1914*, to be published in Russian by a Paris press. But when the first volume of *The Gulag Archipelago* was published by a foreign press, he was arrested and expelled from Russia. From 1974 to 1976 he lived in Zurich, afterward moving to the United States, where, on a farm in Vermont, he has continued to live and write.

One Day in the Life of Ivan Denisovich is undoubtedly Solzhenitsyn's best-known work. The publication of this novella marked the first exposé of the Stalinist labor camps; thus its political significance has tended to overshadow its literary value. This imbalance, however, has been righted by those critics who have called attention to Solzhenitsyn's unsentimental and skillfully understated tracing of the ordinary activities of a prisoner from the clanging of the iron rail at 5 a.m. until he returns to camp that night. Solzhenitsyn does not play upon our sympathy in his presentation of the suffering of the protagonist, Ivan Denisovich Shukhov, an uneducated peasant and the least autobiographical of the characters in his novels. Yet the circumstances of his day are so rigorous and painful that one wonders how men can survive the sentence of a year, much less ten years (Shukhov's sentence) or twenty-five years (the sentence given Alyosha the Baptist because of his religious beliefs).

Remarkably, although this novella is a searing witness to man's inhumanity to man, it is, above all, an affirmation of the indomitability of the human spirit and the ineradicability of human dignity. As in the work of Dostoyevsky (see Chapter 9), Solzhenitsyn's persistent theme is the purification of the human spirit through suffering, evident in the character of Shukhov, as well as others in the book. Shukhov's concern for others is especially evident in his relationship with Alyosha, the Christian. He feels that Alyosha neglects his own interests. "Makes himself nice to everyone but doesn't know how to do favors that get paid back." Although Shukhov is adept at doing such favors, it is apparent that he is not motivated merely by self-interest; for he gives Alyosha one of the precious biscuits that he had received for doing a favor. "Alyosha smiled. 'Thank you, but you've got nothing yourself.'" Urging Alyosha to eat the biscuit, Shukhov reflects, "We've got nothing but we always find a way to make something extra."[19] It is that "something extra" emerging from "nothing," that manifestation of sensitivity and compassion revealed in the wretched and brutal circumstances of a Stalinist labor camp, that lights up this story like a candle in a darkened room.

Just as *One Day* reflects Solzhenitsyn's experiences in the labor camp at Kazakhstan, so *The First Circle* portrays his experiences in the Mavrino Institute in Moscow, where he worked as a mathematician before being sent to the labor camp. The title of the novel is of course derived from the 'first circle' of Dante's Hell, which is reserved for unbaptized pagans of superior enlightenment and moral stature (see Chapter 7). Their punishment is the least severe, and so is that of the prisoners who work in the Mavrino Institute, as compared with those who work in the labor camps. But in both cases it is still Hell! And the better care of the prisoners does not result from humanitarian concerns but has the practical purpose of making them more productive at their task: the discovery of a method of identifying telephone voices, a valuable tool in a totalitarian society.

Cancer Ward had its origins in Solzhenitsyn's treatment for cancer at the hospital in Tashkent. Thirteen people from various walks of life inhabit the ward, Solzhenitsyn's image for Russian society. All however, share in the suffering caused by cancer, the treatment given without explanation of possible side effects, and the threat of death. Most important, because they read a story by Leo Tolstoy, they are confronted by the question posed by its title: *What Do Men Live By?* The futility of relying on collectivist ideology to answer such a question is pointed up by Oleg Kostoglotov, the most autobiographical character, when he states that one must die, not as a member of a collective, but as an individual. It is the individual human being who must learn how to die, by learning how to live.

In *The Gulag Archipelago*, Solzhenitsyn continued to write about the Stalinist labor camps. Here, however, the vista is much more panoramic, as indicated by the term "archipelago," for the labor camps stretch across Russia like the islands of an archipelago. Gulag is an acronym for the Russian equivalent of "Chief Administration of Corrective Labor Camps." In this massive non-fiction work, which Solzhenitsyn regards as both history and literature, he draws not only upon personal experience but also upon historical sources, such as eye witness testimony. Like Elie Wiesel, he seeks to give voice to those whose voices have been stilled by oppression. The power and pathos of this vast document are epitomized by the story of how it came to be printed. Solzhenitsyn had left a copy of the work with Elizaveta Voronyanskaya, who had typed the manuscript. Subsequently (September, 1973), the KGB arrested her. For five days and nights, they relentlessly questioned her until her resistance broke and she revealed where she had placed the manuscript. She then went home and killed herself. When Solzhenitsyn realized what had happened, knowing that the KGB might publish misleading out-of-context portions of the confiscated manuscript, he decided to publish the work in the West. Two of the seven parts appeared in Russian in December, 1973, and in various translations soon after. This led to Solzhenitsyn's arrest on February 12, 1974, and his exile.

Nihilism in twentieth-century thought, identified by Camus in his Nobel Prize speech as the logical consequence of the absurd and dramatized in the writings of Beckett and the theater of the absurd, has created a moral and spiritual vacuum that totalitarian regimes, with their *realpolitik* and their concept of the supremacy of the state, have not hesitated to fill, a phenomenon writ large in the fascist and communist political systems in the twentieth century. Thus the all-powerful state, stepping into the shoes left empty by the loss of transcendent meaning, has sought to provide the structure and stability forfeited in this loss. But the writings of Camus, Wiesel, and Solzhenitsyn demonstrate that human beings cannot accept the price paid for such state-controlled purpose and meaning and urge that they must not only oppose such regimes but also seek the personal sense of meaning without which the human spirit withers.

Visual Arts

From the Armory Show to World War II

Although the Armory Show (see page 420) stimulated the development of a small avant-garde in America, it did not lead to a radical redirection of American art. Modernism never achieved a significant niche in American culture before World War II. Constantly assailed by a philistine press and unable to establish a market for abstract works, the American avant-garde ceased to function as a viable movement after 1917. Wealthy Americans interested in contemporary art bought works by Matisse and Picasso. Adding insult to injury, European artists and writers

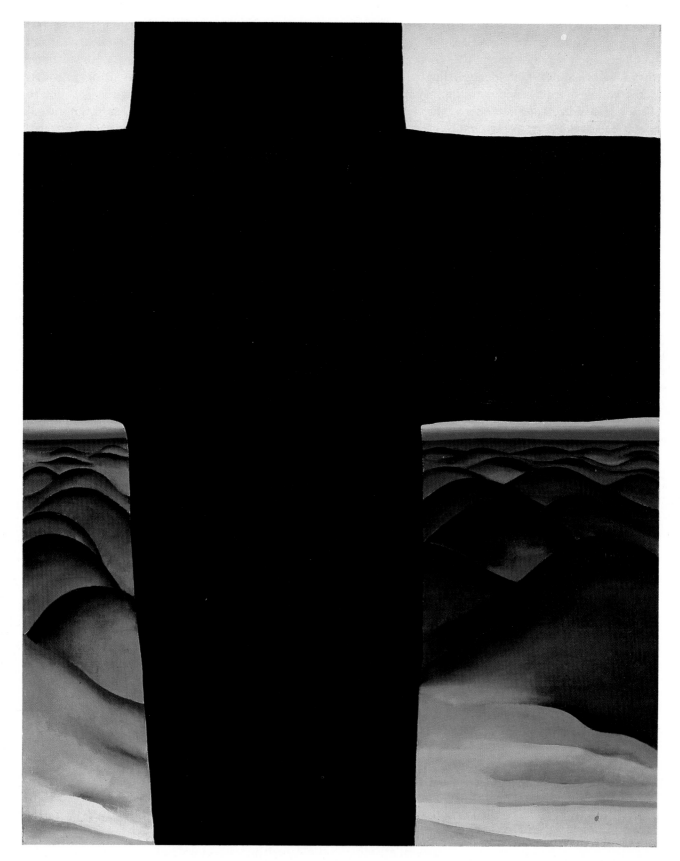

11.7 GEORGIA O'KEEFFE
Black Cross, New Mexico, 1929
Oil on canvas, 36 × 30 ins (91.5 × 76 cm)
Art Institute of Chicago

disparaged American art as derivative and weak—despite the fact that works such as *Black Cross, New Mexico* (Fig. 11.7) by Georgia O'Keeffe (1887–1986), were quite original. Like Mondrian and Brancusi, O'Keeffe often used natural motifs as points of departure for simplification and reduction. But in her hands, the process did not lead to total abstraction, nor to the revelation of some abstract principle or essence, but to a clearer revelation of the form itself.

The little momentum that did exist for a modern movement was overwhelmed by Regionalism, a conservative style emphasizing American subject matter. Its appearance coincided with that of a similar focus in literature on the American way of life. But whereas authors such as Sinclair Lewis (1885–1951) criticized the narrowness and provincialism of small-town life, artists such as Thomas Hart Benton (1889–1975) tended to celebrate it. Involved in Cubism before the war, Benton turned against what he called the "cockeyed isms" of Modern art and took up Regionalism. Still, the elongations of the figures in his *Arts of the West* (Fig. 11.8) recall similar tendencies not only in El Greco (Fig. 8.16) but also

in the early Picasso (Fig. 10.23), while the geometry of the figures, and the dynamic, interlocking composition are based on the artist's early experience with Cubism. If Benton's artistic sources were not as local as he claimed, his thematic sources were. Suggesting that America's frontier-cowboy culture was still alive, Benton's subject matter was, to say the least, nationalistic.

At the other end of the Regionalist spectrum stand the works of Edward Hopper (1882–1967), who is also considered a Realist in the tradition of Winslow Homer (Fig. 9.9). Unlike Benton's lively people and compositions, Hopper's figures are motionless, almost frozen, while his view of America is anything but sanguine. In his paintings Hopper observed and depicted the spiritually empty side of American life. In some respects, his *Nighthawks* (Fig. 11.9) can be likened to Degas' *Glass of Absinthe* (Fig. 9.16). Both have off-center compositions, both express the modern condition of anomie in a social setting (a café and a diner, respectively). But, whereas Degas' Japanese-inspired open spaces are imbued with Impressionistic tension, Hopper's are just plain empty; and, whereas Degas treats his subject with clinical detachment, Hopper gives his overtones of

11.8 THOMAS HART BENTON
Arts of the West, 1932
Tempera, 8 ft × 13 ft (2.43 × 4 m)
New Britain Museum of American Art, New Britain, Connecticut

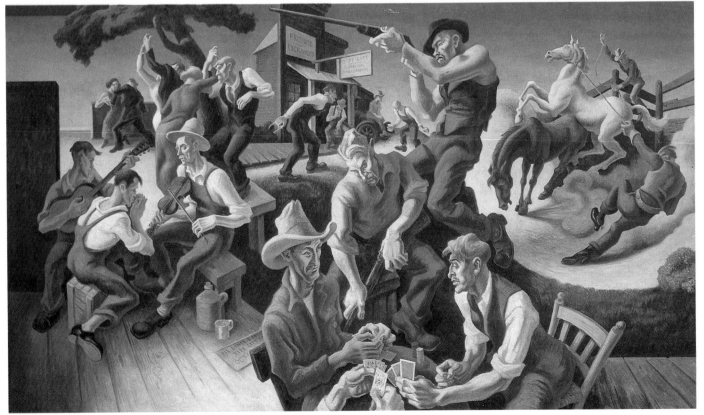

pathos. *Nighthawks* can also be likened to De Chirico's *Mystery and Melancholy of a Street* (Fig. 10.33), for both describe anomie in terms of an oppressively still environment. But Hopper's world is reality, not a fantasy or hallucination.

Hopper has stood the test of time better than any other Regionalist. Although, as a school of art, Regionalism was popular with the American public and press, it was obviously too nationalistic and provincial to enjoy international status. Thus, by World War II, when America had become a principal power in a world-wide struggle, young American artists seemed to be offered a choice between one of two traditions: a weak, discredited Modernism or a popular but provincial Realism.

The Crisis of Transition

In fact, young American artists chose a third option: creating their own tradition. But doing so was not easy, nor was anyone aware of what was happening until after the fact. Aside from Pearl Harbor, the leading factors contributing to dramatic changes in American art in the 1940s were the influx of European art and artists, the philosophy called Existentialism, and the restlessness of young American artists. All of these factors converged on the art world of New York, the crucible of these changes.

New York art galleries, particularly the Museum of Modern Art, became more aggressive in collecting and exhibiting works of European masters. By the early 1940s young American artists had become exposed to such influences as Synthetic Cubism, abstract Surrealism, and the works of Kandinsky. Meanwhile, New York itself had become a haven for European intellectuals fleeing from the political crises on their own continent. Among the emigré artists were Chagall, Dali, Duchamp, and Mondrian; among the writers, Breton; among the composers, Bartók, Schoenberg, and Stravinsky. Of all the various groups, it was the Surrealists who made the biggest impression on American artists.

In the immediate postwar period the influence of Existentialism, especially as articulated in the writings of Albert Camus and Jean-Paul Sartre (see above), was particularly strong among young American intellectuals. Central to Existentialism was the belief that people are free to shape their own destinies, but, at the same time, they are physically and spiritually abandoned in the world. Sartrean Existentialists also placed a great deal of emphasis on the individual personality and inter-personal

11.9 EDWARD HOPPER
Nighthawks, 1942
Oil on canvas, 33 × 60 ins (84 × 152 cm)
Art Institute of Chicago

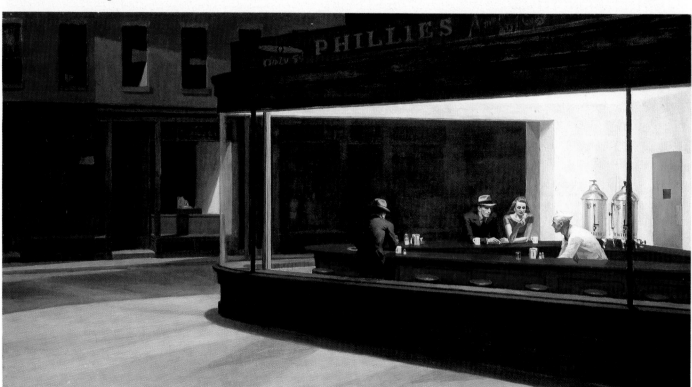

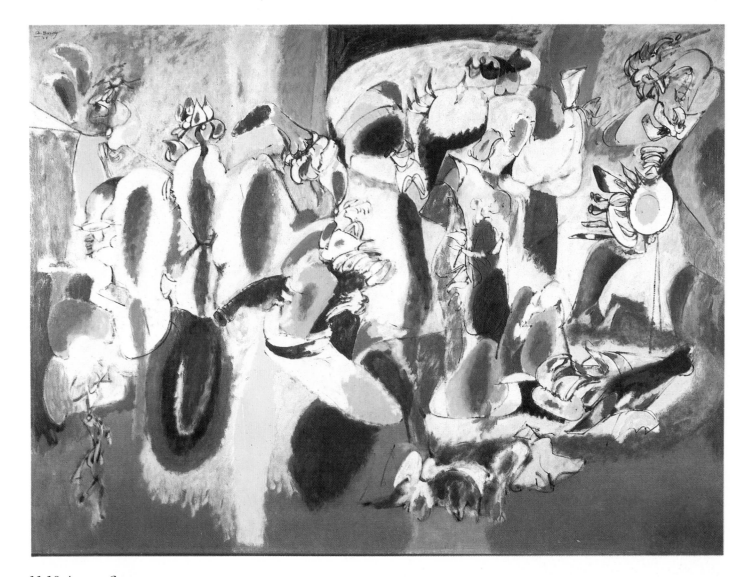

11.10 ARSHILE GORKY
The Liver Is the Cock's Comb, 1944
Oil on canvas, 6 ft × 8 ft 2 ins (1.83 × 2.49 m)
Albright-Knox Art Gallery, Buffalo, New York

relationships. Whether young American painters read Sartre or not, they had reached similar conclusions on their own. According to Willem de Kooning: "We weren't influenced directly by Existentialism, but it was in the air, and we felt it without knowing too much about it. We were in touch with the mood."[20]

In this unstable period, young painters such as Jackson Pollock, Arshile Gorky, and De Kooning were living out the themes of Existentialism more literally than they probably intended. Among other things, they were trying to find their artistic identities in a cultural vacuum. Without an acceptable local tradition (either to work within or react against), a sympathetic cultural infrastructure, or even a mythology of American artists, they often experienced the deep despair that Existentialists

speak of. Of the group, Gorky (1905–1948) showed the earliest promise. His painting *The Liver is the Cock's Comb* (Fig. 11.10) is a competent synthesis of influences from Picasso, Miró, and Kandinsky. The title, along with the many squiggly lines, prompts one to look for images and symbols, no matter how vague. The use of free-form imagery can be related to Synthetic Cubism and abstract Surrealism, while the strong colors and undulating composition bring to mind Kandinsky's abstractions. Despite the borrowing from European sources, Gorky's painting manifests the nucleus of an original style. Had he not committed suicide in 1948, he might have gone on to become one of the leading American artists of the 1950s.

Of this group, Pollock (1912–1956) was the most restless. His works, more than those of the others, have

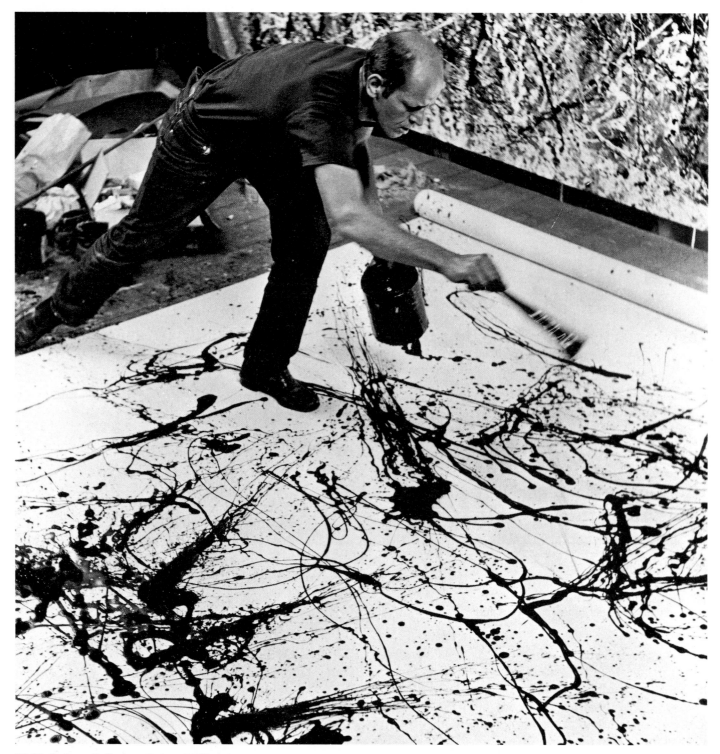

11.11 Jackson Pollock, painting, 1950
Photo Hans Namuth

come to symbolize the heroic experimentation of the period. Born in Wyoming, a student of Benton's, and an alcoholic with a record of aggressive behavior, Pollock himself has come to symbolize the American artist as romantic rebel. His fiery temperament, together with his brooding art, established a myth of American creativity—a myth that sprang from the narrative that he acted out in real life. Like Gorky, Pollock borrowed bits and pieces from Picasso and Miró in the early 1940s, but his assimilation of these sources was, compared to Gorky's, undigested. His own instability and anger were poured into paintings distinguished by their turgid textures, heavy forms, and baroque composition (influenced by Benton). But, whatever they may have lacked in sophistication, they made up for in excitement; Pollock's work began to attract the attention of critics and the patronage of Peggy Guggenheim, a wealthy heiress. This piece of success, however, was just a prelude to his breakthroughs in the late 1940s.

Ever restless, he continued to experiment. In 1946, the vague images and symbols of his earlier paintings disappeared, becoming subsumed into an all-over pattern of abstract, circular strokes. Although this discovery of total abstraction had been anticipated by European artists, notably Kandinsky (see page 412), Pollock's particular brand of abstraction was original. But the real breakthrough came in 1947 when he began his famous "drip" paintings. Having spread a large canvas on the floor, Pollock would spill, splash, fling, and drag paint across its surface while walking on it (Fig. 11.11). The result of this method can be seen in the teeming webs of lines in *One* (*#31, 1950*) (Fig. 11.12). Varying in color, length, width, and viscosity, the lines reflect the patterns and rhythms of the process in which they were made.

Pollock's drip style was not only an original form of abstraction, it was a new kind of art. Although it related to Surrealists' experiments in "automatic" methods, the world had never seen anything like this done on so large a scale and with so much passion. In many respects Pollock's style of working was more important than the style of his paintings. In addition to eliminating the easel and traditional methods of applying paint, he also speeded up the process. A painting like *One* supposedly had to be made in a single period of time. To take leave of it before finishing would break the "spell." According to Pollock:

> When I am in my painting, I'm not aware of what I'm doing. It is only after a sort of "get acquainted" period that I see what I have been about. I have no fears about making changes, destroying the image, etc., because the painting has a life of its own. I try to let it come through. It is only when I lose contact with the painting that the result is a mess. Otherwise there is pure harmony, an easy give and take, and the painting comes out well.[21]

The process was more important than the product. The act of painting became a psychological event, the product being a record of that event. All images, symbols, and thoughtful composition were eliminated, so that nothing would intervene between the subjective world of the artist's feeling and the objective world of paint and canvas. Pollock had created an ethos as well as a style.

11.12 JACKSON POLLOCK
One (No. 31, 1950), 1950
Oil and duco enamel on canvas, 8 ft 10 ins × 17 ft 5⅝ ins (2.69 × 5.32 m)
Museum of Modern Art, New York

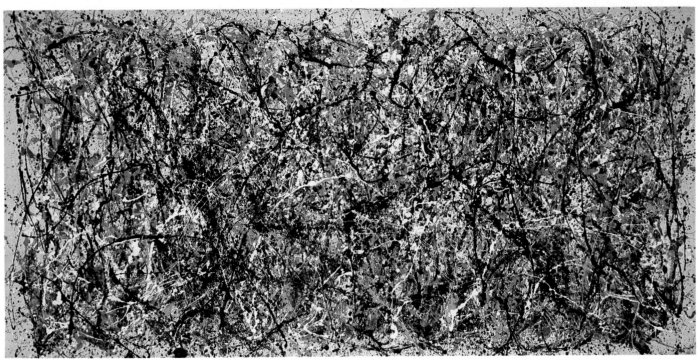

Abstract Expressionism

Pollock's hard-won discoveries led to the first home-grown American style: Abstract Expressionism. What had been a struggling avant-garde in the 1940s blossomed in the 1950s to become an established school (sometimes called the "New York School"). Pollock, of course, was not the only one to share in this triumph; indeed, he and a number of others with common aims were identified with a group known as "Action" painters. The label, coined by an art critic in 1951, aptly describes their athletic methods of painting—though not necessarily involving Pollock's particular techniques. They produced "action paintings," large "heroic " canvases filled with fluid shapes, color variety, and agitated surfaces ("energized marks of paint" as Pollock called them). But within this family of traits there are many varieties and some exceptions. For example, Franz Kline (1910–1962) limited his palette to black and white, a fact that did not detract from his work's sense of vitality. Indeed, in *Mahoning* (Fig. 11.13) the broad, athletic strokes are more stark than if additional colors had been used, while the polar contrast of black and white evokes such fundamental dualisms as male/female or life/death. The works of De Kooning (born 1904) best epitomize the style; paintings like *Woman II* (Fig. 11.1) possess all of its typical traits. The aggressive brushwork which slashes in all

directions is at least as violent as Kline's. But instead of stark or somber colors, De Kooning often used flesh tones and pastel hues, an incongruity that is especially unsettling when used in conjunction with a human image, as in *Woman II*, in which the vague presence of a seated woman has disturbing connotations of eroticism mingled with violence.

"Chromatic Abstraction," the other branch of Abstract Expressionism was less dramatic, but just as original. Like action painters, exponents of this style went in for heroic scale, though without the "energized marks of paint." Paring their designs down to one or two shapes, and eliminating all distracting details, they aimed at engulfing viewers with visions of boundless color. Their canvases are passive rather than active, intended not to assault the senses but to soothe them, and perhaps to evoke meditative responses. Typical is *Green on Blue* (Fig. 11.14) by Mark Rothko (1903–1973), in which two blurred rectangles, one green, one white, seem to float in bluish space. By dulling the white, green, and blue, and making their values (lightness-darkness) relatively equal, Rothko minimized their contrasts. Unlike the action painters, Rothko minimized effects rather than intensifying them. Although in the early 1950s Chromatic Abstraction received less attention than Action painting, by the end of the decade it had grown to be an important influence on the next generation of abstract artists (see below).

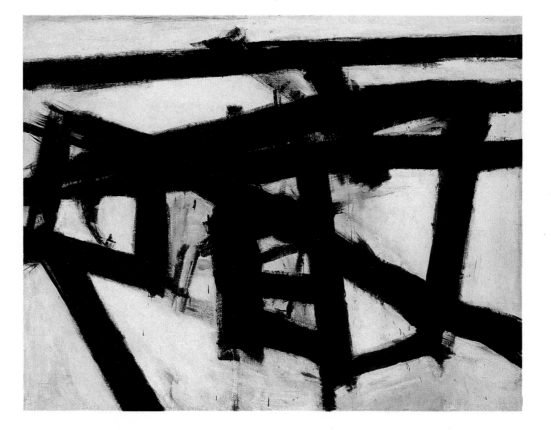

11.13 FRANZ KLINE
Mahoning, 1956
Oil on canvas, 80 × 100 ins
(2.03 × 2.54 m)
Whitney Museum of
American Art, New York

11.14 MARK ROTHKO
Green on Blue, 1956
Oil on canvas, $89\frac{3}{4} \times 63\frac{1}{4}$ ins (228×161 cm)
University of Arizona Museum of Art, Gift of Edward J. Gallagher, Jr.

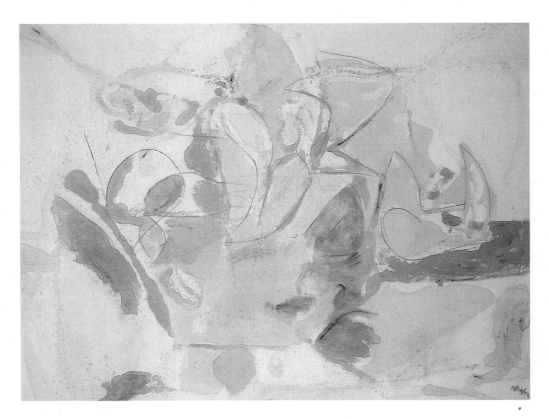

11.15 HELEN FRANKENTHALER
Mountains and Sea, 1952
Oil on canvas,
7 ft 2⅝ ins × 9 ft 9¼ ins
(2.1 × 2.9 m)
Collection the artist,
on extended loan to the
National Gallery of Art,
Washington, D.C.

11.16 (right) LARRY RIVERS
Europe II, 1956
Oil on canvas, 58 × 48 ins
(147 × 122 cm)
Collection Mrs Donald M.
Weisberger, New York

Meanwhile, a species of painting that flaunted loosely painted abstract forms had emerged in Europe. Under a number of different labels—*Art Informel, Abstraction Lyrique* and *Tachisme* (from the French *tache*, "stain" or "mark")—this painting developed independently of its American counterpart until 1950, when the two were brought together in a major Paris exhibition. By comparison, the European version was less impressive; the American appeared bolder and more original. This moment marked a historic turning point in the relationship between European and American art. Since then, American art has continued to rival, if not dominate, European art as a force in international culture. Thus, one of the most important achievements of Abstract Expressionism was that of bringing American art out of its cultural isolation and into a position of world leadership. In this respect De Kooning said that Pollock had "broken the ice."

The effect of Abstract Expressionism on American culture is harder to determine. There is reason to believe, however, that its success may have been an inspiration for the poetry of the Beat Generation and for cool jazz—forms of culture in the 1950s that also emphasized artistic freedom and improvisation. To the extent that it planted the seeds of rebellion in the American psyche, Abstract Expression may have fostered attitudes that led to the counter-culture manifestations of the 1960s. Its stress on the inner life as source material for art anticipated the

modern obsession with self-discovery. Jackson Pollock broke the ice in more ways than one.

Alternatives to Abstract Expressionism

As we have seen, Abstract Expressionism dominated art and thinking about art during the 1950s. Reviewers and critics writing for art magazines—which were growing in number and slickness, partly because of the ascendancy of American art—made common cause with all forms of abstract art. Those writing for major newspapers and news magazines generally also supported it. Regionalism was discredited, and most realistic styles were disparaged as retrograde. As a style and mode of belief, Abstract Expressionism tends to be serious and high-minded. It makes no comment, good or bad, on everyday American culture. This is so partly because it is abstract, but also because its adherents saw American culture as so corrupt and debased that it was not worth commenting on. Yet these same adherents maintained that the new style had content, that it referred in mysterious, but significant ways, to the human condition. Thus, Abstract Expressionism was in the curious position of turning its back on life while claiming the right to pontificate about it. Even during its heyday some artists took issue with that position by bringing forth alternatives that challenged Abstract Expressionism on its own terms.

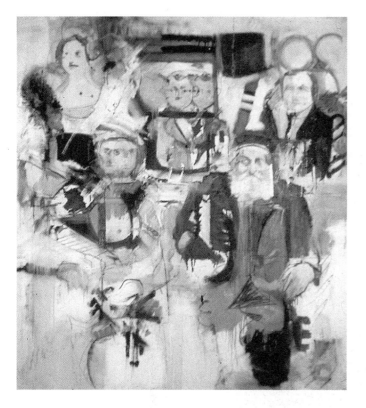

One alternative involved a type of abstract painting that stresses formal effects rather than self-discovery. Its exponents, even more indifferent to the external world than Abstract Expressionists, were also indifferent to the human condition, feeling that the proper role of abstract art was to investigate problems of color and space. As early as 1952, Helen Frankenthaler (born 1928) experimented with staining raw canvas with thin washes of paint. Although her methods bore some resemblance to Pollock's, Frankenthaler allowed the paint to run, spread, and sink into the fabric of the canvas, rather than resting on top of it. *Mountains and Sea* (Fig. 11.15), her first experiment in this idiom, is somewhat tentative. Since then she has developed the method into a major style. Expanding her range of techniques to include practically every way that paint can be spread—pouring, flooding, sponging, even warping the canvas—Frankenthaler creates huge, luminous fields of color. Indeed, when others followed her lead and took up the practice of staining, someone invented the label "Color-Field" to describe what they were doing. Attuned more to Rothko's Chromatic Abstraction than to Action painting, Color-Field painters achieved their effects not from unconscious bodily gestures but from conscious manipulations of canvas and paint.

Another alternative involved the introduction of subject matter to abstract painting—that is, making refer-

ences to the external world. The brushwork in *Europe II* (Fig. 11.16) by Larry Rivers (born 1923) is as smeary and vibrant as that in a De Kooning. But woven into the smears are indications of people—not the wild kind found in *Woman II*, but the ordinary kind. As images they are quite sketchy, some only marginal; all seem on the brink of merging with their painterly environment. Yet the few that are recognizable are quite realistic, suggesting that they are derived from photos—an alien element when considered from the standpoint of traditional Abstract Expressionism. Though vague, these images, rather than the brushwork, are the emotional focus in *Europe II*. Meanwhile, the challenge of *Three Flags* (Fig. 11.17) by Jasper Johns (born 1930) was much more unsettling to the principles of the Abstract Expressionist generation. Such an overt use of a national symbol was considered unorthodox, if not heretical. From a patriotic standpoint this needs no explaining. From an artistic standpoint the explanation is quite different. To Abstract Expressionists, popular emblems—especially national flags—were visual clichés, and thus inappropriate, if not absurd, to use as subject matter. Therefore, paintings like this one were regarded as jokes and affronts to the dignity of art. But *Three Flags* was not to be taken lightly. Its novel mix of art and symbol explores the relationship between sign and art, and between popular culture and high culture. Like a Duchamp ready-made (see page 421), it is a form of investigation that raises more questions than it answers. Is Johns' painting an abstract display of color or an imitation of an American flag? If the latter, does it refer to the flag itself or to what it stands for?

Pop Art

An art movement of the 1960s that parodies popular culture, Pop Art made its debut in 1962 with several shows featuring enlarged images of billboard advertisements, commercial logos, lettered signs, and comic strips. These shows were met with the same kind of shock that accompanied the Salon des Refusés a century earlier. If Johns' *Three Flags* astonished critics, *Whaam!* (Fig. 11.18) an enlarged comic-strip illustration by Roy Lichtenstein (born 1923), must have amazed them even more. It seems to scoff at the notion of art being a one-of-a-kind, personal creation. Worse, it seems passively to accept comic-strip art and therefore to confirm American popular culture, with all its dehumanizing tendencies. These concerns, of course, reflect the prejudices of the Abstract Expressionist generation. In fact, however, Lichtenstein's work is not a servile imitation of popular culture. By subtle adjustments of the comic-strip idiom the artist created a satisfying formal arrangement of black and white spaces in terms of

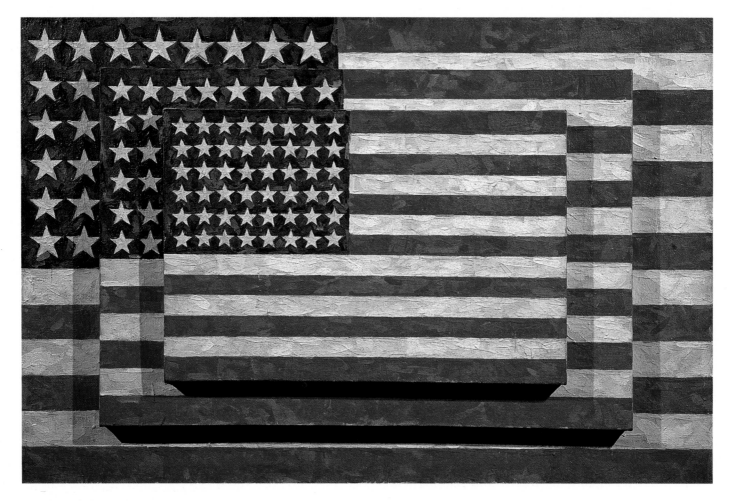

11.17 JASPER JOHNS *Three Flags*, 1958
Encaustic on canvas, 31 × 45 ins (78 × 115 cm) Whitney Museum of American Art, New York

11.18 ROY LICHTENSTEIN *Whaam!* 1963
Acrylic on canvas, 68 × 160 ins (172.7 × 406.4 cm) Tate Gallery, London

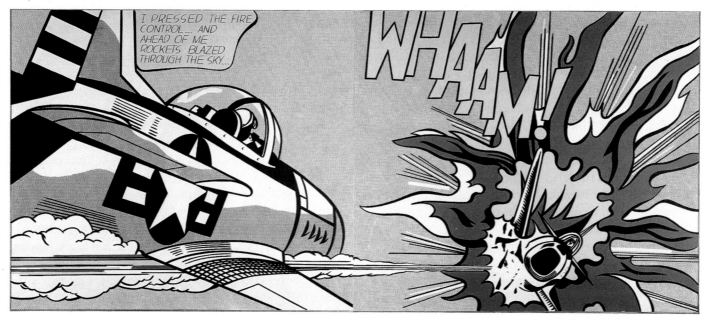

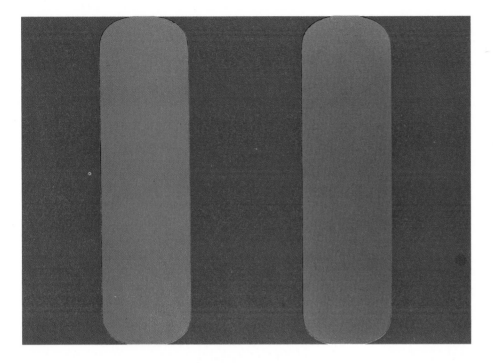

11.19 ELLSWORTH KELLY
Green, Blue, Red, 1964
Oil on canvas, 6 ft 1 in × 8 ft 4 ins
(1.8 × 2.5 m)
Whitney Museum of American Art

abstract principles. A more significant transformation is his radical enlargement of a single comic-strip frame. By so doing, he brings to the viewer's attention not only the fact that comics are extremely stylized (including even the relatively realistic adventure variety), but also the ways in which their forms function as visual codes. Lichtenstein, therefore, induces people to confront aspects of their culture that, because of habit and apathy, generally go unnoticed. In an interview entitled "What is Pop Art?" he stated:

> *Well, it is an involvement with what I think to be the most brazen and threatening characteristics of our culture, things we hate, but which are also powerful in their impingement on us. I think art since Cézanne has become extremely romantic and unrealistic, feeding on art; it is utopian. It has had less and less to do with the world, it looks inward....*

Pop Art, by looking outward into the world, may have done more to dissent against that world and to redeem popular culture than all the posturings of the Action painters.

Hard-Edge Abstraction

The major kind of abstract painting of the 1960s turned out to be a new species of geometric abstraction. Although appearing in different varieties and under different headings—"Minimal," "Shaped Canvas," "Systemic"—this painting features geometric shapes with clearly contoured forms; therefore, the generic label "Hard-Edge

Abstraction" seems appropriate. (Some call it "ABC" art, because it is so basic and simple.) Growing out of Color-Field, Hard-Edge painting is a reflection of the desire on the part of many artists to put even greater distance between their work and the energetic gestures of the Abstract Expressionists. So, by hardening the forms as well as flattening the textures, they "dried out" the emotions of abstract art even more than had the Color-Field artists. About the only thing Hard-Edge painting shares with Abstract Expressionism is a firm commitment to abstraction. Superficially, this style would seem to have a lot in common with the paintings of Mondrian and the art of De Stijl (see page 419), but, in fact, it does not. Although both kinds of abstraction are geometric, the Hard-Edge variety differs significantly from Mondrian's in its basic approach. The 1960s artists did not share Mondrian's mystical ideas about order and harmony, and defied his principle of creating balance out of variety. Artists such as Ellsworth Kelly (born 1923) were not at all opposed to making symmetrical paintings with uniform, repeatable shapes as in his *Green, Blue, Red* (Fig. 11.19). In the final analysis, the dry and simple patterns of Hard-Edge painting have much in common with the cool, deadpan images of its 1960s sibling, Pop Art.

Just as Pollock and his generation had been influenced by the emphasis on subjectivity in Existentialism, Kelly and his generation have been influenced by the objectivity of analytical philosophy. This is reflected in the disciplined and matter-of-fact character of Kelly's art. In Kelly's *Green, Blue, Red* he consolidated a painting into a single, indivisible image by means of symmetry, limited colors,

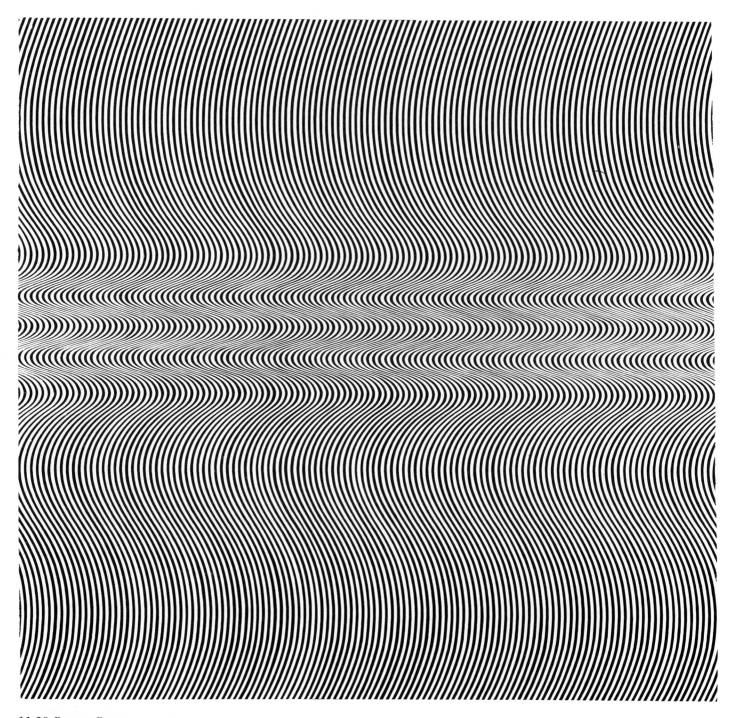

11.20 BRIDGET RILEY
Current, 1964
Synthetic polymer paint on composition board, $58\frac{3}{4} \times 58\frac{7}{8}$ (149×149.5 cm)
Museum of Modern Art, New York, Phillip Johnson Fund

repeatability, and redundancy. His desire was to make his art refer to nothing besides itself; in effect, to eliminate content. This approach is neatly reflected in a remark of another Hard-Edge painter, Frank Stella, who said, "My painting is based on the fact that only what can be seen there *is* there. It really is an object."

Op Art

Op Art (derived from the word "optical") shares with Pop Art an easy-to-remember, similar-sounding name. Like Hard-Edge painting, it is abstract, precise, and geometric. Like both Pop and Hard-Edge, it flourished in the 1960s. But it differs markedly in its origins and agenda. Growing out of the investigations of Bauhaus artists and Gestalt psychologists in the 1920s and, later, the researches of Victor Vasarély (born 1908) in Paris in the 1940s and 1950s, optical painting has a scientific theoretical base and a European geographical base. Most optical painters aimed at creating works with very active visual fields, which would impinge directly, almost physically, on the eyes. Through scientific (and clever) manipulations of pattern and color, they made flat surfaces appear to advance, recede, and bend in ways that deceive, disorient, and tantalize all at the same time. The paintings of the British artist, Bridget Riley (born 1931) were among the most popular of the 1960s. By means of closely spaced patterns of line, as in *Current* (Fig. 11.20), Riley created the artistic version of motion sickness. As a visual field the lines are relentlessly monotonous, forbidding the eye to rest—an effect that is both exciting and annoying. The American artist Richard Anuszkiewicz (born 1930) experimented extensively with the potentials of color, together with particular geometric patterns, to impart the illusion of depth. The illusionistic effect of his *Entrance to Green* (Fig. 11.21) is ambiguous. Does it recede toward infinity in the center, or advance to form the razor's edge of an oblong pyramid? Further compounding this effect is the tendency of small units of color to shift their tones when juxtaposed with one another. The green, for example, seems to change its hue and value depending on changes in its neighboring colors.

Op Art eliminates almost all factors of meaning except visual effects. Unlike all other kinds of visual art, it depends not on cultural norms, symbolism, or the observer's past experiences but on the physiology of the human eye and on the brain's ability to respond to pure color and pattern.

Photo-Realism

Following in the wake of Pop Art and the tendency of 1960s artists to break rules—even those established by the avant-garde—a new kind of realistic painting evolved. Called Photo-Realism, it entails copying photographs, often in very literal ways. After all, reasoned the Photo-Realists, if Lichtenstein could get away with imitating comics, they might as well imitate photographs. And, like Pop artists, they made rather obvious references to the popular culture, for their subjects (or, rather, the subjects of their photographs) tend to be banal scenes of American life. At first wary, the art world condoned Photo-Realism when it learned that the trend was not just another revival of traditional realism but an attempt to make use of the unique characteristics of camera images. By meticulously copying photographs, these artists call attention to the abstract effects of the camera's special way of seeing.

Supposedly, when he painted *Windows* (Fig. 11.22) Ralph Goings (born 1928) was concerned entirely with painting problems. Theoretically, no meaning—no interpretation of modern life—is to be attributed to the restaurant and cars seen in the picture. Only the surface effects of pattern and color peculiar to photography are at issue. Even so, it is difficult not to see the subject itself, and compare it to similar subjects in paintings by Degas (Fig. 9.16) and Hopper (Fig. 11.9). Common to all three is an eating establishment where ordinary people gather— respectively, an 1870s tawdry café, a 1940s lonely diner, and a 1970s antiseptic fast-food restaurant. Each is representative of an era. Viewers may draw their own conclusions.

Three-Dimensional Postwar Art

Dramatic changes had occurred in modern sculpture even before World War II. Welded metal and assemblages (collections of disparate materials) joined carved stone and cast bronze as acceptable media; open forms became as common as the traditional solid forms (see Chapter 10). But compared to postwar sculpture, prewar sculpture seems conservative. Indeed, the incredible variety of forms and materials used in recent sculpture brings us to use the general term *three-dimensional art*, rather than sculpture.

David Smith (1906–1965), perhaps America's greatest modern sculptor, was the first American to work in welded metal. His introduction to Modern art came in the 1930s, when he was studying painting—a fact that may explain why he was so attuned to the changing developments in both Europe and New York. After discovering the art of González (see page 427) and learning how to weld in a factory, he switched to sculpture. From the start he preferred working directly in iron and steel rather than alloys. As he often used unmodified pieces of scrap iron, his work was rugged, unfinished, energetic, a sort of sculptural counterpart to Pollock's early paintings. In-

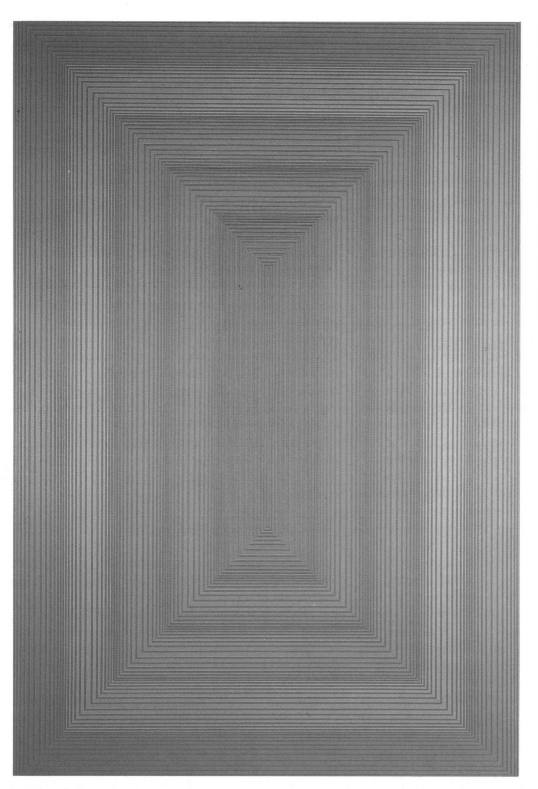

11.21 RICHARD ANUSKIEWICZ
Entrance to Green, 1970
Acrylic on canvas, 108 × 72 ins
(2.74 × 1.83 m)
Collection Sidney Janis Gallery,
New York

11.22 (top right)
RALPH GOINGS
Windows, 1984
Oil on canvas, 44 × 66 ins
(112 × 168 cm)
Private Collection

11.23 (bottom right)
DAVID SMITH
Hudson River Landscape, 1951
Welded steel,
75 × 49½ × 16¾ ins
(190.5 × 125.7 × 42.5 cm)
Whitney Museum of American
Art, New York

deed, like both Gorky and Pollock, Smith loaded his pieces with symbolism in the 1940s, and was considered a Surrealist. Again, like Pollock, he dropped symbolism in the late 1940s and began making lyrical works such as *Hudson River Landscape* (Fig. **11.23**). This work's curvilinear rhythms and all-over composition are somewhat reminiscent of Pollock's *One* (see Fig. **11.12**), made about the same time. In fact, there are many similarities of form and aesthetic sensibility between Action painting and the sculpture of the 1950s.

The transition from Abstract Expressionism to Pop Art is best reflected in the works of Robert Rauschenberg

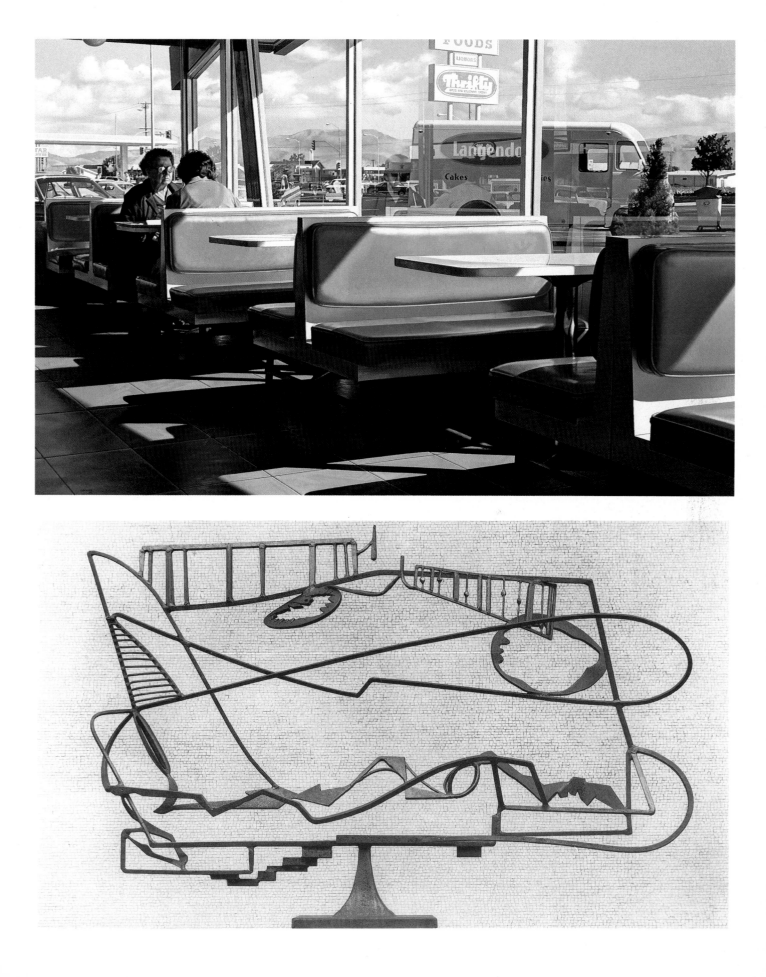

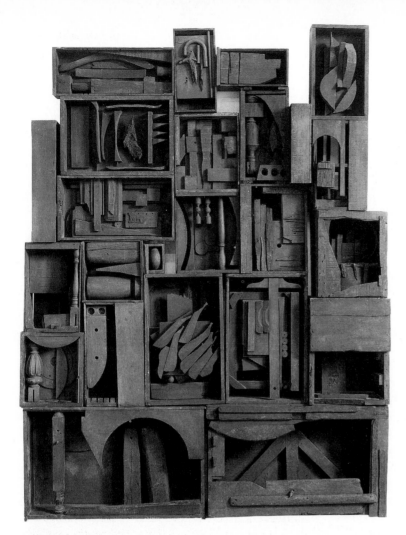

11.24 LOUISE NEVELSON
Black Wall, 1959
Gilded wood, $112 \times 85\frac{1}{4} \times 25\frac{1}{2}$ ins
Tate Gallery, London ($264.2 \times 216.5 \times 64.8$ cm)

11.25 DAVID SMITH
Cubi series, 1963/4
Stainless steel
Tate Gallery, London

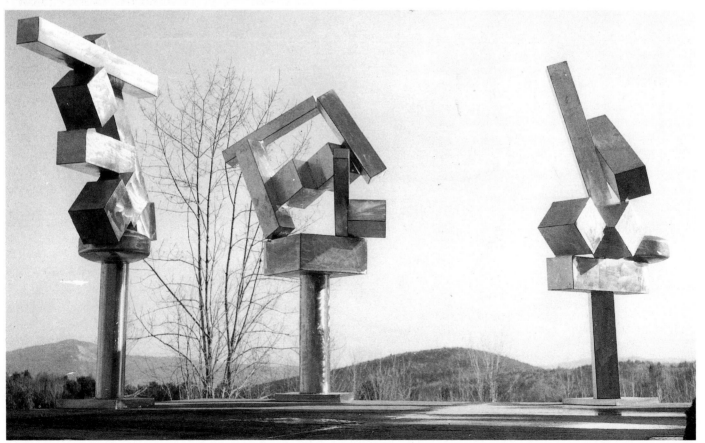

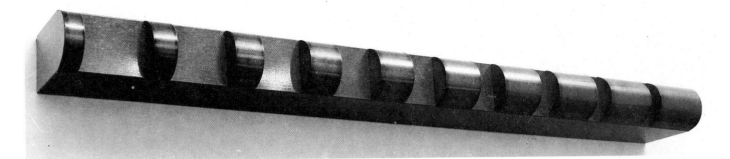

11.26 DONALD JUDD
Untitled. 1965
Galvanized iron
$5 \times 69 \times 8\frac{3}{4}$ ins ($12.7 \times 175 \times 22$ cm)
Leo Castelli Gallery, New York

(born 1925), an artist of the same generation as Rivers and Johns. Though primarily a painter, Rauschenberg expanded his media to include assemblages of what he called "combine-painting." Like Rivers' *Europe II* (Fig. 11.16), this style of work combines De Kooning-style brushwork with pictures, but goes much further by including such alien materials as stuffed animals and pillows. Rauschenberg tried to bring art and life closer together by mixing the strokes of Action painters with random pieces of junk. Of course this was seen as an outrageous mockery of Action painting, and it may have been. Rauschenberg's art, like that of Rivers and Johns, fostered a climate of irreverence toward art and society that eventually produced Pop Art.

The assemblages of Louise Nevelson (1900–1988) also incorporate discarded objects, in this case chair legs, newel posts, knobs, and sundry other bits of carpentry. But Nevelson toned down the variety by "abstracting" it—specifically, restricting the material to wood, organizing the little components into shallow boxes, and spraying them one color. As a result of the artist's tasteful manipulations, assemblages like *Black Wall* (Fig. 11.24) consist of organized miscellany, as opposed to the hectic miscellany of a Rauschenberg combine. In the light of what her colleagues were doing in painting, Nevelson capitalized on both trends of the late 1950s: making references to the external world, as in the works of Rivers and Johns, and creating elegant abstractions, as in the works of the Color-Field painters. Although their original identities have been muted by her transformations, Nevelson's little objects are still recognizable, still show the signs of wear and aging, and thus convey an aura of their former human use.

Of the Abstract Expressionist generation—both sculptors and painters—David Smith was the most adaptable to change. Earlier, as we saw, he made the transition from

symbolism in the 1940s to all-over abstraction in the 1950s. Picking up on the reaction against Action painting in the early 1960s, Smith embarked on his *Cubi* series, three of which are shown here as they appeared on his farm (Fig. 11.25). As the name suggests, Smith had Cubism in mind, and although the series does serve as a link between the old idiom and 1960s art, the rugged scale and the starkly simple cubes and cylinders stand in marked contrast to the intimate and refined paintings of Picasso and Braque. Ironically, the highly structured forms are organized in very unstructured ways—almost as if Smith had tossed them in the air and fused them on the way down. This, together with the randomly buffed surfaces, makes the *Cubi* series among the most interesting sculptures produced in recent years. Despite these touches of novelty, the series prophesied the coldly impersonal geometry of *Minimal* sculpture (see below) and Hard-Edge painting.

Donald Judd (born 1928) was the leading exponent of Minimal sculpture (sometimes called *Primary structures*) in the 1960s. The only concession to variety in his *Untitled* (Fig. 11.26) consists of the fact that the projections progress from small to large (at the same rate that the intervals between them progress from large to small). To ensure the impersonality of his work—literally as well as expressively—Judd had most of his sculptures produced in factories. He also took pains to ensure that the finish was as unadorned, polished, and impersonal-looking as that, say, on an air-conditioner. The simplicity, redundancy, and calculated monotony of Judd's sculpture are reminiscent of Kelly's paintings. Minimal sculpture's moment in art history probably marked the greatest distance in philosophy between two generations of American art: its deliberate suppressions of both content and the artist's ego implied a total renunciation of what the Abstract Expressionists stood for.

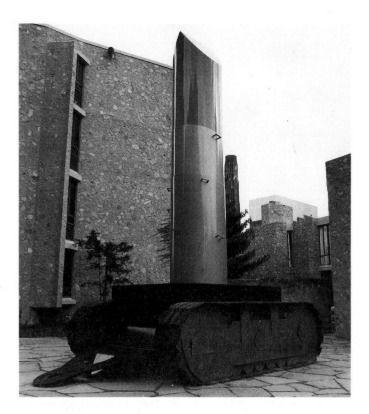

As abstract shapes, the simple forms of *Yale Lipstick* (Fig. 11.27), a Pop-Art sculpture by Claes Oldenburg (born 1929), resemble those of a Minimal sculpture—a fact that was probably more than coincidental, as Oldenburg and Judd were operating within the same aesthetic climate. But beyond that the similarity ends, for *Yale Lipstick* does relate, or at least it *did* relate, to contemporary life in rather tangible ways. In the early 1960s Oldenburg stuffed pieces of canvas with foam rubber to create monster imitations of junk food. From there he graduated to making household appliances out of pieces of vinyl stuffed with kapok. By the late 1960s he was designing monumental imitations of banal objects for major cities: among others, a floating toilet ball for the Thames River at London, a handsaw for Oslo, a Good-Humor bar for New York, and a giant clothespin for Chicago (Fig. 11.28). Needless to say, most of these projects never got beyond the proposal stage. But a few of the less ambitious conceptions, like the *Yale Lipstick*, have actually been built. Like those that remained proposals, this one is a mockery of public art: a commonplace object mounted on treads. But that is only the beginning of its contradictions.

11.27 CLAES OLDENBERG *Yale Lipstick*, 1969, reworked 1974. Steel, aluminium, fiberglass, and paint, 24 ft (7.3 m) high. Yale University Art Gallery

11.28 CLAES OLDENBERG *Late Submission to the Chicago Tribune Architectural Competition of 1922: Clothespin (Version Two)*, 1967. Pencil and colored crayon on paper, 22 × 23¼ ins (55.8 × 59 cm) Des Moines Art Center

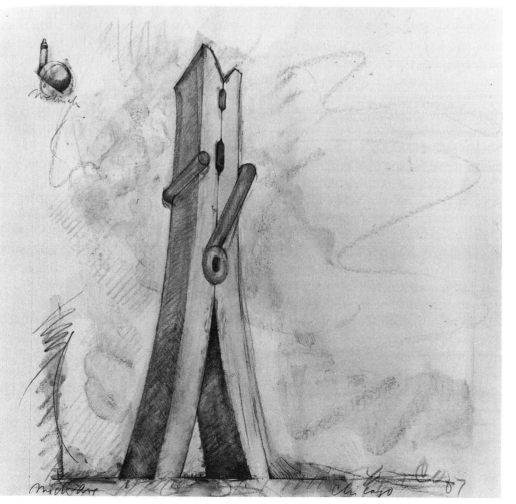

Ordinarily we do not associate treads, which make us think of military vehicles, with a lipstick, which makes us think of kissing. Thus, as symbols, the treads suggest aggression, the lipstick eroticism. But, as abstract shapes, the relationship is reversed. The oval shape of the treads is relatively passive, and far less aggressive than the vertical shape of the lipstick, with its phallic/militaristic overtones. The lipstick monument is an incongruous blend of male-female symbolism. Finally, because *Yale Lipstick* was built for a college campus in 1969, at the peak of the Vietnam war, its provocative qualities were compounded by the political climate of the time. It was such a focal point of controversy that it became the target of graffiti and radical posters, and had to be removed. At any rate, no one could say that Oldenburg's art did not relate to life. The lipstick monument was not returned to Yale until 1974.

Temporary Art

With the possible exception of Dadaist art, all the art examined in this book so far has consisted of relatively stable objects—whether paintings, sculptures, murals, mosaics, or prints. Virtually all may be seen somewhere in the world, in public collections, private collections, or attached to buildings. But recently some kinds of art have been made that are not on view, or at least not on view in their original states. For convenience, we are calling all of these *temporary* art, though this is not an official title. Due to space limitations, only three types of temporary art—Happenings, Earth Art, and Conceptual Art—will be discussed, but it should be remembered that there are many others bearing such labels as "performances," "body art," "process art," "environments," and so forth.

This kind of art did not occur to any great extent until the late 1960s, when it became quite popular for a while. But one artist, Allan Kaprow (born 1927), must have been prescient, for he invented the Happening as early as 1959. A kind of improvisational play in which the viewer participates, a Happening can take many forms and be enacted anywhere, indoors or out. The first one, called *18 Happenings in 6 Parts* (Fig. 11.29) was produced in a New York gallery which Kaprow had outfitted with plastic partitions, slide projectors, tape recorders, and assemblages of junk, as well as "performers" who played musical instruments, spoke double talk, and painted on the walls, among other activities. Gallery-goers, who were given instructions on how to move through this miscellany, themselves became part of the work. Happenings differ from conventional theater in many ways: the viewer-participant is *in* the work, rather than being separated from it by a proscenium; the performers, if any, do not play fictitious roles; and usually there is no script,

plot, or even a focused structure of events that can be replicated. Like Rauschenberg, Kaprow was an advocate of breaking down the barrier between art and life; and like Rauschenberg, he specialized in the inspired use of junk, or perishable material. In the Happening, however, Kaprow succeeded in literally bringing life and art together and extending the concept of perishable material into action, which by its very nature is perishable.

Kaprow's invention suggested at least two directions: performance art—works involving actions of some sort; and environments—works that surround the viewer on all, or nearly all, sides. In the late 1960s some artists expanded the concept of the environment by moving it outdoors. Thus, *Earth Art* was brought into being. Earth Art may be as simple as etching designs in snow or as ambitious as wrapping one million square feet (93,000 square meters) of coastline in plastic sheets using hundreds of volunteers. In order to execute his works in the desert Michael Heizer (born 1944), had to use heavy equipment rather than volunteers. Some 200,000 tons (181,000 metric tons) of dirt and rock were excavated to create his *Double Negative* (Fig. 11.30), an Earth work involving an enormous trench at the edge of a canyon. The name refers to the two negative spaces—that of the trench and that of the canyon—which overlap in the center. Wide enough to accommodate a two-lane high-

11.29 ALLAN KAPROW
18 Happenings in 6 Parts 1959
Photo by Fred W. McDarrah

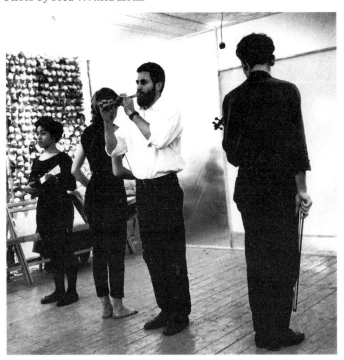

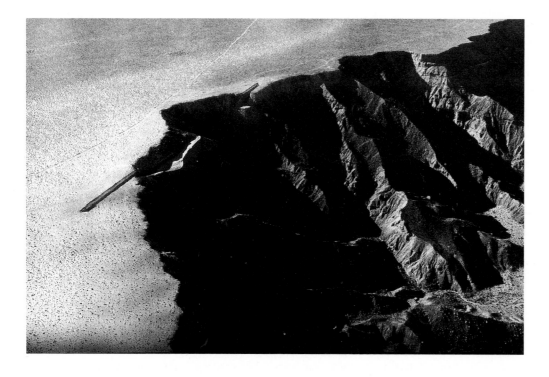

11.30 MICHAEL HEIZER
Double Negative, 1969–70
Two-hundred-thousand-ton
displacement in rhyolite and
sandstone, 50 × 1500 × 30 ft
(15.25 × 457.2 × 9.1 m)
Collection Virginia Duran

way, the trench's human scale is belied by its appearance in the aerial photograph. Because *Double Negative* is located in a very remote area, its full impact may have been restricted to those involved in making it and the intrepid few who bothered to visit it. "The sense of its grandeur," as the art historian Sam Hunter explains, "thus becomes as inaccessible and abstract as the feat of conquering some particularly remote and dangerous mountain peak...."[22] So, although *Double Negative* is not as temporary as a Kaprow Happening, the possibility of experiencing it first hand is nevertheless very limited. Also, being vulnerable to the erosions of time and weather, it is not as permanent as, say, a typical outdoor sculpture. A hundred years from now the trench will be all but completely filled with drifting sand; all that will remain of *Double Negative* are the photographs that document it.

Not all examples of Earth Art involved moving tons of dirt. Some have been insignificant physically, but very ambitious geographically, for example: extending a chalk-line across miles of desert, dropping leaflets at designated places over a state-wide area, traveling the length of the United States on the 42nd parallel, and so forth. In such cases the art "object," if any, was overshadowed by the activities of the artist(s). In its place were various records—photographs, maps, letters, receipts, written reports, and so forth—of the undertaking. Some projects were never carried out, remaining embodied in plans or written proposals. Still others were invisible. Oldenburg, for example, commissioned a 108 cubic foot (3 cubic

meter) hole to be dug in Central Park in New York, after which he had it filled in and entitled *Placid City Monument*. Another artist buried a 60-inch (1.5-meter) aluminum cube in Holland. Called simply *Box in the Hole*, the entire operation was thoroughly documented with photographs. Out of these kinds of activities came *Conceptual Art*, a type of art in which the idea or "concept" takes priority over everything else. In the late 1960s Conceptual artists argued that the creation of art is possible without the use of objects. By collapsing art and idea, they echoed—knowingly or not—the idealism of Plato (see page 60). Yet despite their arguments, these artists made concessions to the objective world—since it is impossible to communicate a "disembodied" idea. Visible or verbal evidence of some kind was required to verify their actions.

Summary of Postwar Art

In retrospect the hectic developments of the 1960s were anticipated in the paintings of Rivers and Johns, the Color-Field experiments of Frankenthaler, the "combines" of Rauschenberg, and the Happenings of Kaprow. The real breakthrough, however, did not occur until the debut of Pop Art in 1962. From that moment the mainstream of art has been flooded with avant-garde movements: Op, Hard-Edge abstraction, Photo-Realism, Minimal sculpture, Earth Art, and Conceptual Art, to name just a few. In less than a decade, a relatively unitary art world had become very pluralistic. But in this pluralism there is a common thread of Neo-Dada or self-ridicule which mocks the high seriousness of Abstract Expressionism. This thread, of course, is obvious in the irreverent creations of Pop and Conceptual Art. It is less so in some of the more puritanical creations of Hard-Edge, Minimal, and Earth

Art. Yet because so many of these have been carried to absurd extremes of reduction, the thread of self-ridicule continues in them as well.

Architecture

During the political crisis in Europe in the 1930s and '40s, America had become a haven for that continent's designers and architects, as well as its artists. Because of the closing of the Bauhaus, many came in the 1930s: notably, the architects Walter Gropius (1883–1969) and Marcel Breur (born 1902) to Harvard; the designer Laszlo Moholy-Nagy (1895–1946) and the architect Ludwig Mies van der Rohe (1886–1969) to Chicago. In 1938 the latter took over the architectural department of the Illinois Institute of Technology, where he soon became known as

the leading exponent of the International Style (see page 431) in the United States. Others have pointed out that his presence in Chicago returned to that city the tradition "form follows function," which had originated with Sullivan at the turn of the century (see page 381).

In the immediate postwar period Mies helped to stimulate a renaissance—a sort of "Chicago School II"—in urban commercial architecture. The glass-enclosed metal towers of the Lake Shore Apartments (Fig. 11.31) are early examples of this renaissance, and among the earliest

11.31 Ludwig Mies Van Der Rohe
Lake Shore Drive Apartment Houses,
Chicago, 1950–52

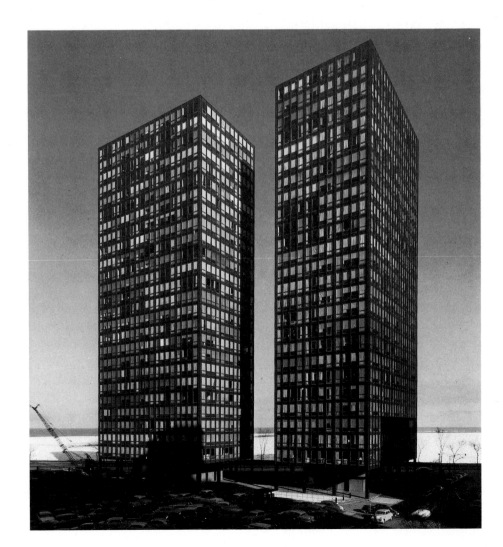

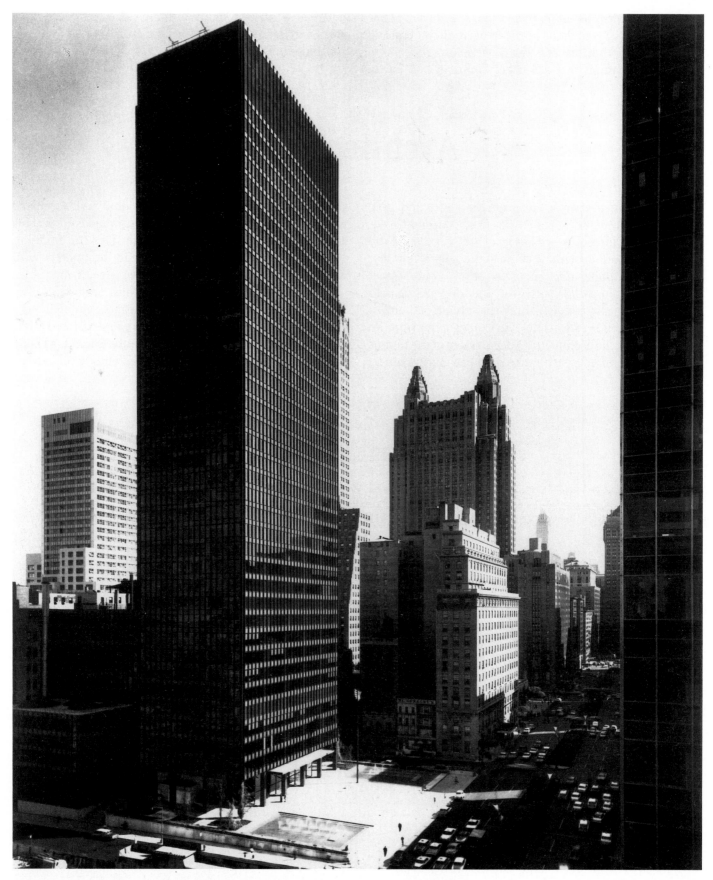

11.32 LUDWIG MIES VAN DER ROHE and PHILP JOHNSTON
Seagram Building, New York, 1956–58

structures in America to flaunt their metal skeletons openly. Completely free of ornament and projections, the towers reflect the severity of Judd's Minimalist boxes (or, to put it more accurately, Judd's boxes reflect Miesian architecture). Paradoxically, these Modernist buildings also have something in common with the Parthenon (Fig. 2.27): both are products of exacting attention to detail and proportion. One has to look closely at the apartments to perceive that the supporting verticals (which, at ground level, serve as pillars) are slightly wider than the verticals in between; the windows next to them are slightly narrower than those in the middle, which are also distinguished by I-beams; and so forth—all of these adjustments provide variety and "optical" perfection within severely limited means.

The classic of this style is New York's glass- and bronze-clad Seagram Building (1958), which Mies designed in collaboration with Philip Johnson (Fig. 11.32). The proportions of the Seagram Building are as impeccable as those of a Doric column. The raised level at the bottom is balanced at the top by a four-story "cap," distinguishable

in the daylight by a subtle shift in tone. Mies's style, sometimes symbolized by the phrase "less is more," embodies a philosophy of architectural design that has enjoyed a large following (notably in the firm of Skidmore, Owings, and Merrill), and has changed the face not only of corporate America but of cities all over the world. The most successful solutions of this philosophy are found in downtown Chicago—and not just in the buildings designed by Mies—where "less is more" has been employed most imaginatively, and where recent metal-frame examples reflect the zest of the Sullivan era. But in many cities it has led to glass-coated monotony and architectural boredom.

Like Mies, Le Corbusier began his career under the spell of Mondrian and the International School (Fig. 10.30). But instead of extending and refining that influence, he turned his back on much of it. Preferring the medium of ferroconcrete (concrete reinforced with steel rods) over that of the metal frame, Le Corbusier devised a postwar alternative to the glass block. His Unité d'Habitation (1952) apartments in Marseilles (Fig. 11.33), like the Lake

11.33 Le Corbusier
Unité d'Habitation Apartment House, Marseilles, 1947–52

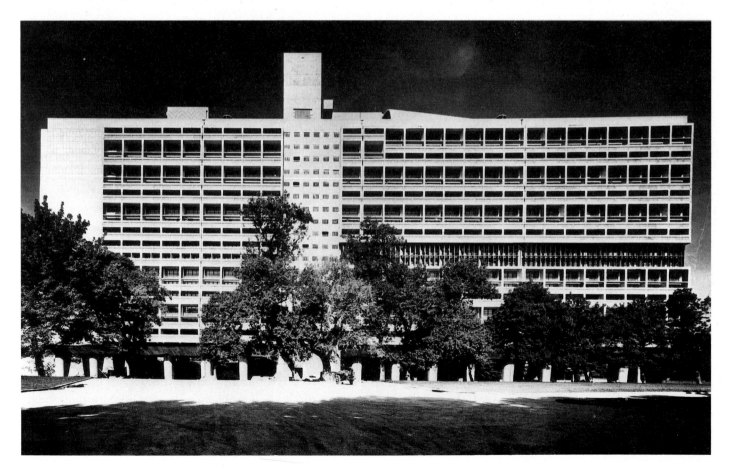

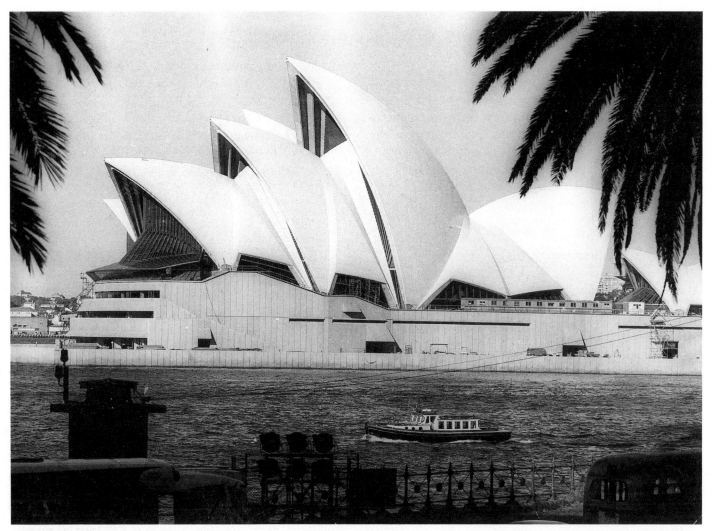

11.34 JÖRN UTZON
Sydney Opera House, Australia, 1959–72

Shore Apartments finished the previous year, are based on a rectangular module and raised on supports. But how different they are in spirit! The concrete supports, like archaic columns, are tapered and massive; the windows are not on the same plane as the wall but deeply recessed; the wall is not a smooth envelope of metal and glass but unadorned concrete which still bears the impressions of the casting forms. The word "sculptural," often used to describe the qualities of Le Corbusier's style and of latter-day concrete construction in general, is certainly not intended to mean Minimalist sculpture, but sculpture on the order of Henry Moore's (Fig. 10.41). Like Moore's works, Le Corbusier's buildings are tactile, earthy, and penetrated with openings; both resonate with similar allusions to the womb, the cave, and the earth. Le Corbusier designed projects in France and other parts of the world that are much more sculptural even than Unité d'Habitation. More importantly, he and his imaginative

use of ferroconcrete inspired other architects, for example Jørn Utzon (born 1918), who designed for Sydney Opera House (Fig. **11.34**). Situated in Sydney Harbor, Utzon's project resonates with allusions to the sea rather than the earth, as its dramatic concrete vaults bring to mind swelling sails, gull wings, or breaking waves. Thus in postwar architecture there exists a striking dualism: the rational, Euclidian classicism of Mies's following versus the sculptural freedom of Le Corbusier's following.

The geodesic dome could be seen as a third alternative, though it has not generated a significant following. Invented by Buckminster Fuller (1895–1983), a man who combined the attributes of Yankee tinkerer and visionary, it is a frame type of construction. But instead of square modules, it employs a hexagonal pyramid which, when repeated, forms a shell, as opposed to a plane. The dome of the United States Pavilion at Expo 67 in Montreal (Fig. **11.35**) employs an additional system of metal rods to bridge the apexes of the pyramids. The usefulness of the geodesic dome is problematical. Its potential is great, as it is probably the most rapid and efficient construction method to date. In terms of space per pound of material it is unexcelled. The Pavilion at Montreal, for example, is higher than the tallest vault at the Sydney Opera House, but its weight is only a fraction of the weight of that building. Yet, because the geodesic dome seems to be limited to a shell configuration, it is also limited as a style.

Ever the visionary, Fuller proposed a two-mile- (3.2-km-) diameter shell to cover part of Manhattan. Unlike Oldenburg, he was serious; but this project also died in the proposal stage. Besides world's fair pavilions the dome has been used effectively for covering botanical gardens, military radar installations, and swimming pools. It remains to be seen whether it will ever play as significant a role in architecture as rectangular steel-frame construction does today.

11.35 BUCKMINSTER FULLER
United States Pavilion, EXPO 67, Montreal, 1967

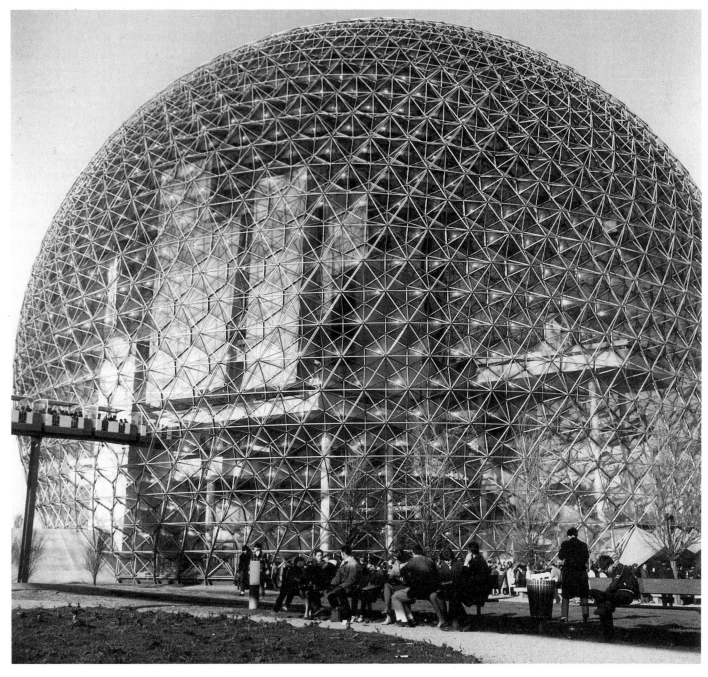

The New Music

Developments in Postwar Europe

In a tragic case of mistaken identity, the Austrian serialist composer Anton Webern (see Chapter 10) was shot near his home at the end of World War II by American soldiers pursuing a black-marketeer. Had the composer lived, he would have seen his highly disciplined brand of music become the basis of a new movement. In the late 1940s his music was "in the air." A Webern cult had grown up in Darmstadt, West Germany, where his admirers—principally Pierre Boulez (born 1925) of Paris and Karlheinz Stockhausen (born 1928) of Cologne—enlarged upon his ideas. Even Stravinsky, in far-away Los Angeles, hailed him as a hero on the tenth anniversary of his death in 1955.

Webern's spare, abstract music, a direct product of the 12-tone method, was seen as the most advanced form of music to date, and therefore more capable of extension into a new idiom than Schoenberg's. The new idiom, called *total serialism*, was an attempt to extend the serial principle beyond pitch into other elements: note duration (including rests), dynamics, and even tone color. In many ways it was also an attempt to disengage from the old heritage, to set music on a completely new path. The term "avant-garde," familiar in the visual arts for almost a century, was embraced by serialist composers to signify their break with the past. In *Structures I* (1951), a work for two pianos, Boulez applied the tone-row method (see page 440) to durations, dynamics, and *attacks* (ways in which a

note may be struck), as well as to pitches. Note durations, for example, ranged from that of a thirty-second note to that of a thirty-second note times 12 ("dotted quarter note"); the 12 values of loudness ranged from *pppp* (extremely soft) to *ffff* (extremely loud). As we noted in Chapter 10, a tone row can be manipulated in four ways: original, retrograde, inverted, and retrograde-inverted. In order to manage such complexity, to submit all the variables to the serial method, Boulez had to resort to the use of elaborate number matrices (Fig. 11.36). Total serialism may have been on the cutting edge of musical developments in the late twentieth century, but its principles are as old as antiquity, when music was conceived of in terms of ideal numbers (see page 74). Still, although the genesis of musical ideas in total serialism tends to be numerical rather than musical, it is possible to produce sensitive music with this method, as is demonstrated by Stockhausen's *Kontra-Punkte* (1953). Scored for ten instruments, *Kontra-Punkte* begins with relatively long phrases and a polyphonic texture of widely-spaced orchestral sounds, and ends with notes of shorter duration using only a few of the original ten instruments—a progression from loud to soft, and from complex to simple. The title ("Counter-Point") has a double meaning in this case: the contrapuntal structure of the music itself and the fact that it is "counter" to an earlier work written in a classical 12-tone idiom entitled "Punkte" (1952).

Commitment to total serialism soon ended, at least in Europe. Despite heroic efforts to manipulate numbers and

11.36 Number matrices used by Boulez

'O' matrix

1	2	3	4	5	6	7	8	9	10	11	12
2	8	4	5	6	11	1	9	12	3	7	10
3	4	1	2	8	9	10	5	6	7	12	11
4	5	2	8	9	12	3	6	11	1	10	7
5	6	8	9	12	10	4	11	7	2	3	1
6	11	9	12	10	3	5	7	1	8	4	2
7	1	10	3	4	5	11	2	8	12	6	9
8	9	5	6	11	7	2	12	10	4	1	3
9	12	6	11	7	1	8	10	3	5	2	4
10	3	7	1	2	8	12	4	5	11	9	6
11	7	12	10	3	4	6	1	2	9	5	8
12	10	11	7	1	2	9	3	4	6	8	5

'I' matrix

1	7	3	10	12	9	2	11	6	4	8	5
7	11	10	12	9	8	1	6	5	3	2	4
3	10	1	7	11	6	4	12	9	2	5	8
10	12	7	11	6	5	3	9	8	1	4	2
12	9	11	6	5	4	10	8	2	7	3	1
9	8	6	5	4	3	12	2	1	11	10	7
2	1	4	3	10	12	8	7	11	5	9	6
11	6	12	9	8	2	7	5	4	10	1	3
6	5	9	8	2	1	11	4	3	12	7	10
4	3	2	1	7	11	5	10	12	8	6	9
8	2	5	4	3	10	9	1	7	6	12	11
5	4	8	2	1	7	6	3	10	9	11	12

generate permutations, composers could not seem to come up with very original results beyond a certain point. Furthermore, the complexities of the system were too demanding for most performers. By the mid 1950s it was supplanted by less rigid forms of atonality. Boulez's *Le Marteau sans maître* ("The Masterless Hammer"), written in 1954 and revised in 1957, exemplifies this freer approach and has been praised as one of the finest works of late atonalism. Intended as a setting for three poems by the Surrealist poet René Char, it is divided into nine movements, and is scored for alto voice, flute, xylorimba (an instrument that combines the qualities of xylophone and marimba), vibraphone, guitar, viola, and light percussion instruments. The sequence and the use of solo voice are reminiscent of Schoenberg's *Pierrot Lunaire* (see page 440), but in the Boulez piece the percussive sounds of the instruments contrast with the flowing lines of the vocalist, rather than echoing them. And Boulez's colors, the product of unconventional instruments and unusual combinations of these instruments, are both more exotic and more resonant, suggestive of Balinese music. Because of this and the relative isolation of the individual notes, *Le Marteau* has been associated with the "pointillist" style—named after the style of painting invented by Seurat (see Chapter 10).

Besides a commitment to restructuring composition, whether by the 12-tone system or by some other means, many new composers are especially known for experimenting with new sounds and tone colors. Some of these involve novel ways of playing conventional instruments: "flutter-tongueing," special lip methods, or unorthodox fingering, in the case of wind instruments; unusual bowing techniques with stringed instruments; special ways of blowing and/or muting horns; and many others. Some involve careful clusterings of instruments to create delicate shadings. *Threnody to the Victims of Hiroshima* (1961) by Krzystof Penderecki (born 1933) calls for the violin to be bowed between the bridge and the tailpiece. When a number of violins are played this way—all sounding the same or closely-spaced tones—this method produces an ethereal, haunting sound, reminiscent of electronic music. Some involve conventional instruments enhanced by electronic means as in placing a microphone inside the sound tube of a woodwind. Still others involve the use of non-Western instruments, especially percussive varieties. The teacher of Boulez and Stockhausen, Olivier Messiaen (born 1908), is fascinated with Oriental versions: gongs, temple blocks, wood and glass chimes, and Chinese cymbals, among others. Latin-American bongos, congas, maracas, marimbas, timbales, and so forth, in addition to African drums, have added enormously to the rhythmic, as well as coloristic possibilities of new music.

Finally, some musicians—in particular, Harry Partch (1901–1976)—have invented new instruments of their own.

But the sounds with the most far-reaching implications are those produced synthetically, that is, on tape recorders, as opposed to instruments. Though often lumped together under the heading "electronic," only some of this music is produced initially by electronic means. *Musique concrète* ("concrete music"), considered to be the earliest form of synthetic music, uses existing sounds, but manipulates them in special ways before playing them back on tape. Some of these manipulations simply capitalize on the tape recorder's mechanical capabilities—changing speeds, reversing tape direction, cutting and editing, superimposing sounds, and so forth—while others involve modifications of the sound by actual electronic means: mainly, filtering (similar to the tone controls on a radio) and creating reverberations or echoes. The concept was born in Paris in the late 1940s out of the efforts of a musical research group and the French radio. Over the years the group has invited numerous new musicians, including Messiaen, Boulez, Stockhausen, and Edgard Varèse (1883–1965), to work in its studios, and has exerted a wide influence on new music. Varèse's *Poème électronique*, perhaps the best-known masterpiece of musique concrète, was embodied in the most ambitious performance of the idiom so far. In some respects a matter of "musique concrète meets ferroconcrete," the performance was the product of collaboration between Varèse and Le Corbusier, in which the composer furnished sounds to permeate the spaces of the Corbusier-designed *Philips Pavilion* (Fig. 11.37) at the 1958 Brussels World's Fair. Varèse created an eight-minute, three-track tape of electronically-processed sounds from a variety of sources: piano chords, bells, organs, kettledrums, sirens, human voices, and machines, together with some electronically generated sounds. With the aid of 425 loudspeakers placed along sound paths designed into its walls, the whole pavilion was awash with the sounds of *Poème électronique*. "I heard my music," said Varèse, "literally in space, for the first time." During the performance, slides of girls both naked and dressed, birds and beasts, fish and reptiles, cities, and a mushroom cloud were projected on the walls; Le Corbusier selected the slides in collaboration with the composer, but no attempt was made to synchronize image and sound.

Through trial and error, a composer of musique concrète discovers possibilities in existing sounds, and molds them into a piece of music, much as Rauschenberg discovers found images and makes them into a combine painting. "Pure" electronic music, on the other hand, consists of electronically generated tones which often

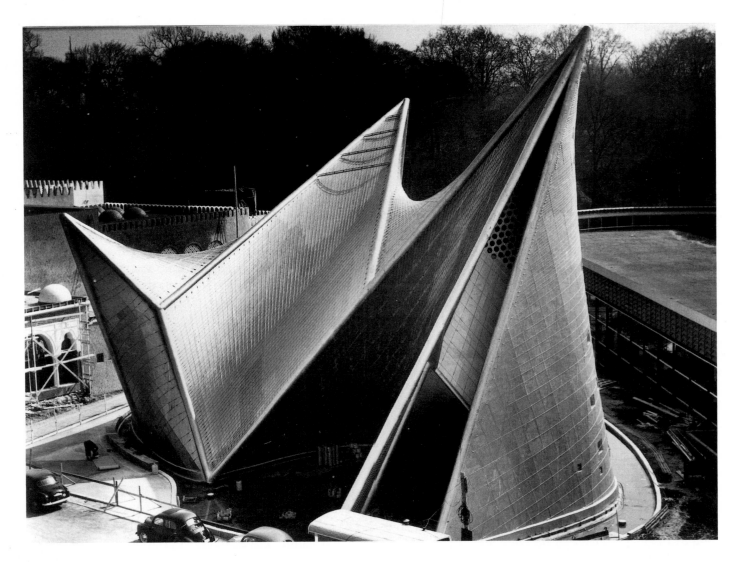

11.37 LE CORBUSIER
The Philips Pavilion at the Brussels Exposition (World's Fair)

have to be composed like traditional music—that is, conceived in the composer's mind, and then realized in sound. But the analogy to traditional music goes only so far. Early composers of electronic music, unlike their traditional counterparts, did not have a "language," a notational system to indicate pitches, durations, and other musical variables; nor did they have at their command an array of musical instruments, all calibrated to play Western scales. Lacking these means, they were forced to use the language of audio-technicians, that is to indicate on graph paper the values for pitch in terms of frequencies, duration in terms of tape length, and so on for each of the musical variables; then build each sound according to these variables with the help of sine-tone generators, white-sound generators, filters, ring modulators, variable-speed tape recorders, and dynamic suppressors, to mention just some of the equipment. To prepare even a short

piece of music was a tedious, time-consuming process. Such was the situation when the first electronic music studio was established in Cologne in 1951, and it is little wonder that the first concert of its compositions was not broadcast until late 1954. The situation changed dramatically in 1965, when the inventor Robert Moog developed a practical and relatively portable version of the *synthesizer*, a device that produces original electronic sounds almost at the will of the user. Capable of varying pitches, durations, loudness, tone colors, and attacks, and, when connected to a digital computer, of "remembering" sequences and creating polyphonically, the Moog synthesizer has come to be more than a time-saving device; it is a new and liberating musical medium. Composers of electronic music can discard not only generators, filters, and ring modulators, but also (by storing sounds on tape for playback) notation and instruments. Like painters, they can express ideas directly in their medium, realizing their inspirations without the intervention of such agencies as sheet music and performers.

But computer music seems to have made more of an impression on the popular culture than on the world of art music. It has spread from the studios of experimental musicians to those of rock musicians, and from sound laboratories to universities and even homes. Its tunes are commonly used on radio and television for commercials and station breaks. Yet despite, or maybe because of, the public acceptance of electronic music, serious musicians have not shown much enthusiasm for it in the decades since the synthesizer came into use. This is due, at least in part, to a major drawback: performances of electronic music by serious (as opposed to pop music) composers are not very interesting to watch.

Developments in pre-war America

Between the wars, American music, like American art, was largely dependent on European developments. But there were exceptions: Charles Ives (1874–1954), a composer who made his living by selling insurance, could afford to experiment. Ignoring convention, he wrote pieces in which, for example, singers sang different versions of the same melody while the orchestra played four different themes simultaneously. Obviously, American culture was not ready for music like this in the early 1900s. It went unpublished until the composer began publishing it himself in 1918. And then it went unperformed until the 1930s. Schoenberg, upon first hearing it, called Ives a great composer who "responds to negligence by contempt."[23] The French emigré Varèse, a very independent spirit, did something about the neglect of his music and that of other American moderns by forming the International Composers' Guild (ICG), an organization for performing new scores. Henry Cowell (1897–1965), a follower of both Ives and Varèse, receives credit for being the first to invent "tone clusters," the massing of adjacent pitches (as used so effectively by Penderecki in *Threnody*). But on the whole, America's modern composers—among them: Roger Sessions (1896–1985), Virgil Thomson (born 1896), Roy Harris (1898–1979), Aaron Copland (born 1900), and Elliot Carter (born 1908)—were indebted to European Modernism. The major initiative in musical innovation still lay with such composers as Stravinsky, Schoenberg, Berg, and Webern.

Meanwhile Varèse's ICG inspired the formation of other societies dedicated to Modern music; by the early 1930s, famous conductors such as Serge Koussevitzky (1874–1951) and Leopold Stokowski (1882–1977) were performing and championing new scores. The possibility

for the growth of an indigenous Modern music was not an empty hope. But by the middle of the decade, the Modern momentum ended. A retrenchment to conservative styles, as we have already seen in Chapter 10, occurred in European music and art and in American art. American music was equally responsive to the Depression and the need to seek a wider public. American composers, therefore, were inspired to write in more popular idioms and to celebrate national themes. Copland, reversing direction to become a sort of musical "Regionalist," merged symphonic music with various New World folk styles: Mexican songs in *El Salón México* (1936), Cuban dance rhythms in *Danzón Cubano* (1942), and cowboy songs in *Billy the Kid*. His crowning achievement is the ballet *Appalachian Spring*, commissioned by Martha Graham, an American masterpiece which incorporates a Shaker hymn, *The Gift to Be Simple*. Written in 1944, it exemplifies the style of pre-war American music. But, like American art, American music was soon to submit to the forces of change: the disruption of the war itself, the discrediting of nationalistic music, the need for artistic renewal, and even the atomic bomb. Add to these the considerable influence of European emigrés in America—in addition to Varèse, who came in 1915, Bartók, Schoenberg, Stravinsky, and Paul Hindemith (1895–1963).

Developments in postwar America

Two opposing approaches emerged in American music in the immediate postwar period: One, which followed the lead of European music, emphasized structure and control; the other, which ultimately influenced Europe's composers, emphasized the absence of control. The first could be likened to the disciplined art of Mondrian (see page 419); the second to the unrestrained art of the Abstract Expressionists.

After graduation from New York University, Milton Babbitt (born 1916) decided to adopt the 12-tone method. This was in 1939, when Schoenberg's music was out of favor; even Roger Sessions, Babbitt's teacher, opposed it. But the young composer persisted, and some years later began to expand the method into other musical elements around the time that Boulez and Stockhausen were doing the same. This development was rather ironic, as neither side was aware of the other's efforts (a situation not unlike that of painting in the early postwar years). In effect, Babbitt created the American version of total serialism. Today, he and his followers remain committed to the concept, while their counterparts in Europe have long since abandoned it. American serialists seek, even more than the Europeans did, to control every aspect of the musical material so that all elements are interrelated in a

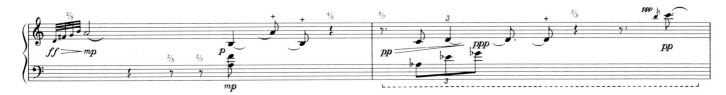

11.38 Extract from John Cage's *Music of Changes*, showing his use of traditional notation

complex syntax. Because orchestras then (and even now) could not easily handle this syntax, Babbitt was one of the first Americans to turn to technology and electronic sound: "I love going to the studio with my work in my head, realizing it while I am there,... knowing exactly how it will sound."[24] Babbitt sees an analogy between his kind of music and modern physics. Both are intellectual, esoteric, and, one might add, intelligible only to a professional elite. Like mathematicians and physics professors, serial composers study their profession in American universities, where Babbit has been successful in winning for music the intellectual status of academic subjects.

Another group of American composers—John Cage (born 1912), Earle Brown (born 1926), Morton Feldman (born 1926), and Christian Wolff (born 1934), among others—have followed a very different path. Centered around Cage, they share an interest in the paintings of Pollock, De Kooning, and Rothko, and, like these artists, are bold and iconoclastic. Neither the past nor the heritage of Europe—least of all, the 12-tone system—hold them in thrall. Unlike Babbitt and his followers, whose goal was to control all musical elements, these people have championed "indeterminacy"—the philosophy and practice of leaving such things as pitch and note duration to chance. Theoretically, indeterminacy means total unpredictability about outcomes, but, in practice, it is much less than total. Basically, indeterminacy may take one of two forms: composer indeterminacy and performer indeterminacy. In the first, a score is written with the use of some type of chance method, as in throwing dice or referring to a table of random numbers. But once the music is down on paper,

performances of it are rather predictable. To select the compositional elements of his *Music of Changes* (1951), Cage used *I Ching*—an ancient Chinese technique in which all values are based on tossing coins or numbered sticks. Although control over Cage's score was surrendered to chance, control over performances of his piece was guaranteed by his use of traditional notation (Fig. 11.38). In performer indeterminacy, the composer allows performers such a wide latitude of interpretation that no two performances of a single piece could ever sound the same. To yield control to performers, a composer usually has to abandon traditional notation. Feldman's score for *Intersection I* (Fig. 11.39) is an example of an improvised system of notation in which the elements of pitch, dynamics, and times of entry are deliberately undefined, leaving these matters to the discretion of the performers. Brown's score for *Available Forms I* (Fig. 11.40) contains traditional staffs and symbols for treble and bass, but leaves undefined the order in which the five numbered "events" are to be played. Brown's inspiration came from the ever-changing, "indeterminate," forms of Calder's mobiles (see page 427).

European composers, particularly Stockhausen and Boulez, have become involved with indeterminacy, though not until a decade or so after the Americans began to experiment with it. Their conversion was due to the confluence of at least three factors: disenchantment with serialism, experiments with musique concrète, and a visit by Cage in 1958. Stockhausen's *Hymnen* (1967), for example, incorporates fragments of words and melodies from numerous national anthems, all arranged haphazardly and overlaid with apparently random noises resem-

11.39 Morton Feldman's score for *Intersection I*

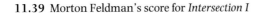
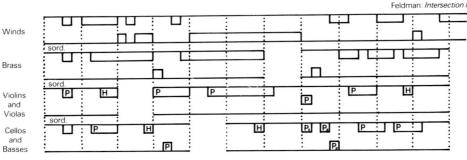

11.40 Earl Brown's score for *Available forms I*

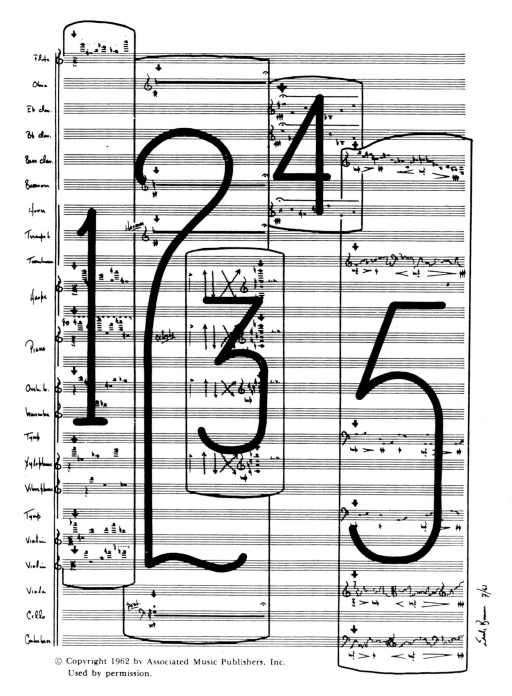

bling static and radio interference. Boulez coined the term "aleatory" (*alea*, Latin for "dice") to describe chance techniques within a controlled framework. Generally, the Europeans' approach to chance has been less extreme than the Americans'; Feldman has accused them of compromising in order to preserve "their precious integrity." Boulez, on the other hand, felt that the use of chance "can bring something interesting only one time in a million . . . . and, if you do get it, you get it in the midst of a hundred thousand possibilities which are not interesting."[25] Furthermore, according to Boulez, indeterminacy as practiced by American composers is a refusal of choice. Over the years the division between American and European concepts of chance has grown wider. On the American side of this divide is an underlying philosophy which is summarized by the music scholar David Cope:

Indeterminacy, as a step-by-step (even pedagogical) approach to erase control over compositional elements which so many have fought to retain, must first transcend man's loss of individual and "racial" ego. As such, it is merely the first step to a far-reaching eventuality: rejection of all homocentered creativity, and acceptance of all of the life around us, with man no longer in control, no longer the creator or destroyer of images or ideals, real or imagined.[26]

Cage

"Transcending loss of ego," "rejection of homocentered creativity," and "acceptance of life around us" are concepts articulated by John Cage, whose impact on the field of new music may be greater than that of any other single person. Openness—to nature, to new ideas, to new musical elements—has been a fundamental principle of Cage's. The music critic William Brooks believes that his entire career has been motivated by a desire to accept into the musical context those things that heretofore had been rejected: when young, Cage was committed to the acceptance of atonality (which put him in league with Schoenberg); after that he championed noise, then silence, then the operation of chance and so on, each time moving on to a new element as soon as the one previously rejected became acceptable.

Although Cage's peak influence occurred during the 1950s and 1960s, his total productivity covers more than five decades—going back to 1932. In the 1940s, motivated by a belief that duration was the most fundamental principle of music, he began to structure his music by lengths of time rather than by some harmonic system, thus tending to emphasize meter and percussion over other musical variables. The influence of the Dadaist artist Duchamp (see page 421) led him to use found and invented objects in *Living Room Music* (1940) and *Third Construction* (1941). As early as 1942 he anticipated musique concrète by employing radio noises in *Credo in Us*. About that time he invented the "prepared piano" by inserting miscellaneous materials—wood, cardboard, weather stripping, nuts, bolts, and so forth—between the strings of a piano, literally placing at one's fingertips a variety of percussion sounds.

By most accounts, 1951 is seen as a breakthrough in both Cage's career and new music. In that year his *Music of Changes*, the first major work composed by chance operations, was completed. Although Cage yielded control over these elements to chance, the overall project was highly structured. As Cage explains: "You have to envisage exactly what are the questions you ask when you write music, and then toss coins to help you answer each question."[27] Thus, the resulting score, written for prepared piano, leaves nothing to chance in the perfor-

mance. But, in the final analysis, one must ask: what effect does all this have on the music itself? Surprisingly, *Music of Changes* expresses Cage's intentions and personality, notwithstanding the fact that he surrendered many of his prerogatives as a composer to *I Ching*. Unlike 12-tone music, which is quite demanding on the listener, intellectually and emotionally, the Cage work is relaxed and undemanding. It is simply a non-melodic sequence of relatively short-duration piano sounds alternating with silences of varying length (some as long as 15 seconds); some sounds have relatively ordinary pitch and timbre, others are very percussive. Although most of the notes are unconnected, some are joined to form short trills or arpeggios. On the whole, *Music of Changes* is unfocused, with no emotional surge and no particular destination.

As time went on, Cage increasingly wrote scores that left decisions to performers; by 1957, he began devising pieces in which virtually all aspects were performer-indeterminate. But his most controversial work, *4'33"*, involves neither composer nor performer indeterminacy, but *listener* indeterminacy. In its first performance in 1952 a piano was used; the pianist, at the beginning of each "movement," closed the keyboard with the cover and played nothing while timing the silence of each "movement" with a stopwatch; the entire silence lasted four minutes and thirty three seconds. To the extent that the score of *4'33"* mentions no instrumentation—a performance could utilize any instrument, including a symphony orchestra—it is performer-indeterminate. But mainly, it requires the listener to fill the void. Behind what may seem to be little more than a stunt (or, in the opinion of some people, the ultimate gesture of twentieth-century nihilism) is a seriousness of purpose, along with a concept related to Cage's world-view. During the silence, the incidental sounds of the environment—whether it be a room or concert hall—take on added importance, so much so that members of the audience turn to these sounds. As Cage further explains:

The turning is psychological and seems at first to be a giving up of everything that belongs to humanity—for a musician, the giving up of music. This psychological turning leads to the world of nature, where, gradually or suddenly, one sees that humanity and nature, not separate, are in this world together; that nothing was lost when everything was given away.[28]

Cage's influences are diverse. In music his teachers included Cowell and Schoenberg (who accused him of having no feeling for harmony). Cage is also a great admirer of Satie (see page 435). His philosophy is drawn from Meister Eckart, a fourteenth-century German mystic, and Zen Buddhism, a Japanese sect noted for austerity and the use of paradoxical ideas to achieve personal tranquillity. Perhaps the most important influences on his work stem from his collaborations with artists—who, in turn, have been influenced by him. We have already mentioned Duchamp (with whom he played chess). The West Coast artist Morris Graves is an old friend. In 1941 the famous designer Laszlo Moholy-Nagy invited him to teach at the Chicago Institute of Design. The Museum of Modern Art was the site of his first concerts in New York. The Abstract Expressionist Robert Motherwell (born 1915) invited him to participate in the Artists' Club, where he came into contact with other artists of that generation. In 1952 Johns and Rauschenberg worked with him at Black Mountain College in North Carolina; while there, they collaborated on prototypes for the art of Happenings. The following year Rauschenberg's New York exhibition of all-white paintings made a big impression on the composer. In 1958 Kaprow was one of his students at the New School for Social Research in New York.

Cage and Jackson Pollock (see page 459) had much in common: both were born in 1912, grew up in the West, went to high school in Los Angeles, eventually moved to New York, and created important works which made them the leaders of their respective arts. Parallels also exist in their creative approaches, for both were fearless experimenters, renounced premeditation in the creative act, were open to accident, and claimed to value the process of creativity over the final product. But the fundamental differences between the two almost overshadow the similarities. Pollock, influenced by Existentialism, made paintings that enshrined his struggles as a person and artist in frenetic, energized marks of paint. His canvases have been called "heroic"—a reference not only to their scale but to the epic creative endeavor that brought them into being. In many ways, Cage's work calls into question all of these things—the very premises that underlie the work of Pollock and the other Abstract Expressionists. His music stands for the abnegation of the ego, not its glorification. In place of high seriousness, it extols quiet mysticism, simplicity, humor, and irony. It is Zen rather than Existential. Indeed, Cage has described the difference between the two philosophies as optimism versus pessimism. Cage found inspiration in Eastern cultures; the Abstract Expressionists were still tied to European culture.

Finally, it should be emphasized that the relationship between Cage and art in the 1950s was not a one-way street. Just as the composer gained much from art and his artist friends, they gained much from him. The assemblages of Johns and Rauschenberg owe much to Cage's own inventive use of disparate sources; Kaprow's Happenings and, later, Environmental art grew directly out of Cage's experiments at Black Mountain College; the Pop Art movement of the 1960s was anticipated by his use of banal sounds along with the impersonality and implied irony of his work; Systemic painting, Minimal Sculpture, and Conceptual Art were anticipated by more than a decade by the revolutionary gesture of 4'33". Echoes of its tendencies—radical reduction, using a concept as the very structure of a work, and even the silence—could be heard in the artistic avant-garde throughout the late 1960s and early '70s.

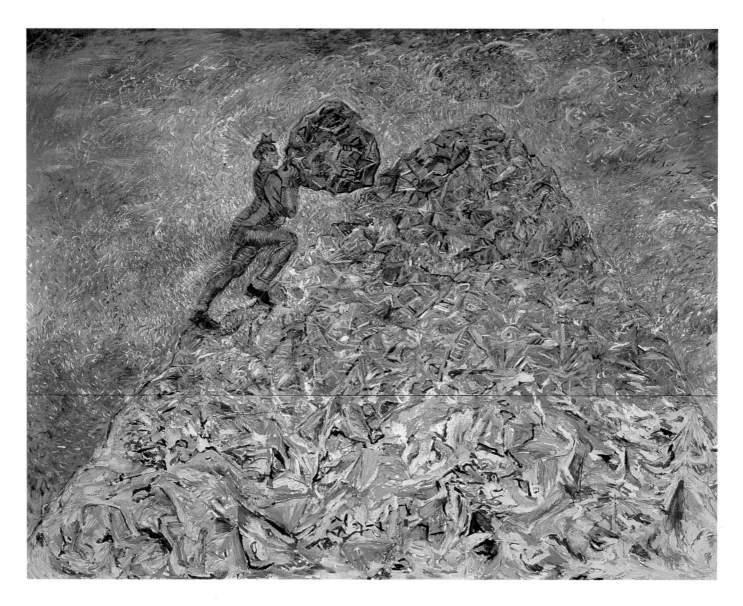

12.1 SANDRO CHIA
The Idleness of Sisyphus, 1981
Oil on canvas, 10 ft 2 ins × 12 ft 8 ins (3.1 × 3.86 m)
Museum of Modern Art, New York

CHAPTER TWELVE

Post-Modernism

Thus, against the aesthetic justification for life, post-modernism has completely substituted the instinctual. Impulse and pleasure alone are real and life-affirming; all else is neurosis and death.

DANIEL BELL

Introduction

The previous two chapters surveyed the developments of Modernism from approximately the mid-1880s to the mid-1970s—a 90-year period that, taken as a whole, witnessed more changes, movements, and "isms" in the arts than any other comparable period in Western history. But since the mid-1970s, few, if any, significant new developments in the arts have occurred, a fact that has led some to wonder whether or not Modernism—that many-colored, but coherent chain of developments—has come to an end. Increasingly the protean term "Post-Modernism" is being invoked to describe current trends in the arts. This final chapter, therefore, will attempt to shed some light on the present time and the meaning(s) of Post-Modernism.

As a term, Post-Modernism is not new. Before World War II literary scholars had used it as a reaction to aspects of Modernism; in 1947 Arnold Toynbee used it in *A Study of History* to identify a new cycle in Western civilization starting in the late nineteenth century; in the 1960s the term was broached in the theoretical writings of sociologists and cultural historians. Recently, however, the concept of Post-Modernism has become pervasive, especially with reference to the current status of Western culture. Its use is no longer confined to isolated contexts, and it appears in the literature of several fields besides the arts: theology, philosophy, and politics, among others. But its meaning across these fields and among different writers varies greatly.

As a socio-cultural phenomenon Post-Modernism is perhaps best articulated by Daniel Bell in *The Cultural Contradictions of Capitalism* (1976). He defines Modernism—"the self-willed effort of a style and sensibility to remain in the forefront of 'advancing consciousness'"[1]—much as we have in this book defined "avant-garde." What is striking about Bell's argument is his claim that Modernism replaced religion as the dominant cultural mode, not just of the arts but of the whole of Western society, around a hundred years ago. It entered America as a significant force around the time of the Armory Show (see page 420), when the puritan temper and Protestant ethic were being challenged by young intellectuals. Evidence of Modernism's dominance in recent times lies in the fact that its point of view pervades all major cultural establishments: theaters, music societies, publishing houses, urban news media, cultural weeklies, universities, and so forth, in addition to museums and galleries. Its potency has stemmed from its role as adversary—by definition constantly in the fore-front, sitting in judgment not only over traditional culture but also over its own contemporary culture. Its overriding values, whether implied or expressed, have centered around the immediacy of experience and the primacy of the "self." Rising out of these, of course, is the implied promise of a "liberated future," but beyond these values and its future-orientation, Modernism has failed to provide a comprehensive set of ultimate meanings to replace those of Christianity. According to Bell, the ethos of Modernism, formerly the possession only of a cultural elite, has by now trickled down to the masses. Since the 1960s, Western mass culture—particularly as seen in the consumer-oriented, credit-card life-styles of Americans—has emphasized the pursuit of pleasure and narcissistic self-fulfillment, including sexual promiscuity and drug abuse. When reality has more shock-value than Modernism itself, there is no longer a raison d'être for an artistic avant-garde, and Modernism dies of its own success; the future is here. In the present Post-Modern period, according to Bell, "Impulse and pleasure alone are real and life-affirming; all else is neurosis and death."[2] This contrasts with the Modern period to the extent that, according to its ethos, such impulses were played out "in the imagination, within the constraints of art."[3] Although Bell does not explain what Post-Modern art and literature are, or what they should be, he does refer to the art of the 1960s, particularly the Happening, as a model for satisfying immediate experience, and to Pop Art as a sardonic, though accurate, reflection of a consumer-oriented, narcissistic culture.

The interpretation of Post-Modernism among scholars in the arts and humanities and cultural historians focuses more on its manifestations in the high culture than in the society as a whole. Often writing from perspectives grounded in Existentialism, psychoanalysis, and/or Marxist aesthetics, these writers agree with Bell's view that twentieth-century high culture is in an adversarial position, a continual struggle of the free creative self at war with the majority culture. But whereas Bell approaches the subject with a certain amount of scientific detachment, these writers seem to perceive themselves as part of the adversarial culture itself. Frequently referring to works that by their nature protest the status quo—as in the poetry of the Dadaists and Surrealists, the art of Duchamp, and the music of Cage—they promote irrationality and anti-form as either superior forms of truth, or at least as antidotes to the rationalistic and technocratic tendencies of modern capitalism. They admit that Post-

Modernism as a concept is vague and semantically unstable. To separate their notion of it from that of Modernism proper is difficult, for some seem to see Post-Modernism as a playing out of the agenda of late Modernism, continuing, among other things, Modernism's traditional adversarial role. Others see it not as just another avant-garde, but more of a "neo-avant-garde," a departure from the continuum of previous avant-gardes. If so, it is a flabby movement which lacks the Dionysian energy of earlier avant-gardes. In the final analysis, Post-Modernism probably is an adversary culture, but one that has lost faith in the corrective possibilities of protest and change. The whole point about this loss, according to Frederic Jameson, "is that it also involves a sense that nothing will change and there is no hope. I think one must start with that."[4]

Literature

The conceptual vagueness of "Post-Modernism" is illustrated by the fact that both the chronology and the meaning of literary Post-Modernism are in dispute. Some critics date it from the 1930s, some from the end of World War II, and others from the 1960s. Chronology does not necessarily determine who is identified with it. For example, Kafka (see Chapter 10), who died in 1924, is often claimed by the Post-Modernists. Moreover, the advent of Post-Modernism (whenever that was) does not mark the end of Modernist writing. Modernist and Post-Modernist writers coexist in the period of Post-Modernism.

"Post-Modernism" implies a connection of some kind with Modernism. But is "post" to be understood merely in the literal sense of coming after Modernism? Or does it imply some kind of contrast? And if so, what kind? Is it a further development, a pushing to logical conclusion of the tendencies always present in Modernism? Or does it imply a radical rejection of something essential to Modernism? There is no critical consensus on these questions. Indeed, as yet, Post-Modernism cannot be defined as a well-formed literary movement with universally recognized representatives. The critic Ihab Hassan fills almost a full page with the names of artists, writers, and other intellectuals whom he regards as "adumbrating" Post-Modernism, and then concludes: "Indubitably, these names are far too heterogeneous to form a movement, paradigm, or school. Still, they may evoke a number of related cultural tendencies, a constellation of values, a repertoire of procedures and attitudes. These we call postmodern."[5] Among the artists, Hassan lists such people as Duchamp, Rauschenberg, and Kaprow, who are involved in creating experimental forms that call into question the nature of art. Among the writers, he includes Samuel Beckett, Eugène Ionesco, Jorge Luis Borges, Vladimir Nabokov, Harold Pinter, Peter Handke, Gabriel García Márquez, Alain Robbe-Grillet, John Barth, Thomas Pynchon, William Burroughs, and Sam Shepard. Thus Post-Modernism, unlike Modernism, has yet to acquire a clearly defined identity.

Still, it can be said that there are certain methods and styles that "adumbrate" literary Post-Modernism. For example, literary character and structure, as well as the relationship of the literary work to the world, have all been affected profoundly by Post-Modernist theory. Traditionally, it has been assumed that a writer can convincingly render a human character—with all of his or her attendant feelings, thoughts, and actions—and position that character in an imaginary world not unlike our own, thus symbolizing the actual human condition. Post-Modernist literary theory denies that this is possible. In his essay, "The Death of the Novel," Ronald Sukenick puts it well:

> Realistic fiction presupposed chronological time as the medium of a plotted narrative, an irreducible individual psyche as the subject of its characterization, and, above all, the ultimate concrete reality of things as the object and rationale of its description. In the world of postrealism, however, all these absolutes have become absolutely problematical.[6]

Post-Modernists contend that a writer cannot create an authentic character, with the full range of his or her psychological subtleties and gradations of motivations. Rejecting this possibility, therefore, they resort to two-dimensional characterization, analogous to the approach of those artists who have replaced Renaissance three-dimensional space with the flatness of the picture plane itself. Such characters lack any consistent identity and often perform meaningless actions in a void. They experience no moment of insight or understanding, termed "epiphany" (see page 394)—an essential element in Modernist writing—in which they might discover the truth about themselves and thus lend significance to the world created by the writer. Samuel Beckett's often-produced play *Waiting for Godot* (see Chapter 11) illus-

DATES	SOCIAL AND POLITICAL DEVELOPMENTS	LITERATURE AND PHILOSOPHY	VISUAL ARTS	ARCHITECTURE	MUSIC
1950	The Cold War Korean conflict	Beckett Ionesco Borges Nabokov Pinter Handke Marquez Robbe-Grillet			
1960	Vietnam War Civil Rights Movement First man on moon Student unrest Women's Movement	Barth Pynchon Burroughs Shepard Doctorow Coover	Chia (12.1) Kiefer (12.7) Attie (12.5) Salle (12.6) Sherman (12.8)	Boston City Hall (12.4) Venturi: Guild House (12.9)	Cage Del Tredici Minimalism Riley Reich Glass (12.12)
1970				Johnson: AT & T Building (12.11)	
	Iranian Revolution – Khomeini				
1980	Reagan presidency				

12.2 Post-Modernism

trates this lack. Post-Modernist writers also reject the traditional linear development of character, which, in their view, suggests a continuity of development that is not credible. Thus their characters are given to improvisation which adds up to nothing in the way of identity or significance. For Post-Modernist writers, therefore, literary characters do not imitate "reality" but are "made of words," as Philip Stevick states, summarizing the view of William Gass, "and the medium within which they exist is a linguistic construct."[7]

Indeed, these writers reject any attempt to imitate "reality," calling attention to the fact that what they create is merely a linguistic artifice. For example, the protagonist of *Giles Goat-Boy* (1966), by John Barth (born 1930), encounters a girl who is reading *Giles Goat-Boy* and has just arrived at the point where she is described as reading. In his *Lost in the Funhouse* (1968) he calls attention to the artifice of his craft by commenting on his narrative method as he tells his story.[8] "At no previous time," Stevick writes, "have so many writers of consequence entertained the idea, at least provisionally and intermittently, that fiction does not exist to imitate the 'real world,' does not even exist to abstract from or superimpose upon the world a thematic organization, but that fiction exists as a nonmimetic [non-imitative] object, made of words, for its own sake."[9] In this respect, Post-Modern literary method resembles the approach of artists such as Johns and Lichtenstein and composers such as Cage (see Chapter 11), who focus on the conventions and premises of the medium itself, rather than on what it expresses.

The classic (and classical) definition of literary structure for Western culture, set forth by Aristotle in his *Poetics*, states that a play (and we may include other literature) must have a beginning, middle, and end. The action begins at a certain point, unfolds so as to rise to a climax, and then falls off in a resolution or dénouement. The climax grows logically out of what precedes it and leads logically to what follows. Indeed, each segment of the drama emerges logically from what has gone before. Thus plot is conceived as linear. Another factor that has contributed to the dominance of plot linearity in the West, according to Stevick, is the dominance of print since the Renaissance invention of printing from moveable type. By its very nature, print is linear and causal and thus influences those who are oriented to it to think in the same terms. But the modern electronic media, with their orally and visually transmitted messages, have profoundly altered this print orientation. Thus, Stevick states, "that narration which is closely in touch with the general culture will show the erosion of that linear, causal arrangement of words, presumably as a form more fragmented, less end-directed, more playfully aware of itself," and thus also close to the non-linear and improvisational oral culture that was largely replaced, four centuries ago, by print culture.[10]

The lack of logical structure in Post-Modernist writing, of course, reflects a world view. Lacking logic, coherence, linearity, climax, and thus probability, Post-Modernist literature makes a statement about the disorder and irrationality of the world as experienced. But so does Modernism. So what is the difference? T. S. Eliot (see

Chapter 10), commenting on the apparent chaos of James Joyce's *Ulysses* (see page 395), observed that the author's method was "simply a way of controlling, of ordering, of giving a shape and significance to the immense panorama of futility and anarchy which is contemporary history."[11] Thus Modernist writers "control" and "shape" their material in imitation of chaotic "reality." Post-Modernist writers, however, do not attempt to represent any kind of reality but rather to create an alternate reality for the purpose of showing that all fictional realities are artificial constructs. Post-Modernism thus seeks to divorce literature altogether from the mimetic tradition that has dominated Western culture. "Fiction will no longer be regarded as a mirror of life, as a pseudo-realistic document that informs us about life," writes Raymond Federman.[12]

But Post-Modernism goes beyond arguing that fiction is an artificial linguistic construct. It asserts much the same about history; indeed, it contends that all meaning systems are human constructs. Challenging the objectivity of history, some Post-Modernists write "historical" novels that combine historical figures and events with imaginary ones. E. L. Doctorow's *Ragtime* (1975), for example, includes historical personages—Harry Houdini, Emma Goldman, Henry Ford—but its events are largely fictional. In *The Public Burning* (1977), Robert Coover writes about the Rosenberg trial and makes Richard Nixon his main character; but he interweaves facts based on assiduous historical research with his imagined alternative facts. (One is also reminded of Woody Allen's film *Zelig*, in which Woody's character appears in documentary films featuring historical figures such as Adolf Hitler and Lou Gehrig.) Thus Post-Modern writers seek to break down the distinction between the "facts" of history and the imaginary world of fiction. Both, they are saying, are basically linguistic meaning systems imposed on the "real" world.

Our task here has been that of explicating Post-Modernism in literature, but the attention given it should not suggest to the reader that it is the only approach to literature in our time. It is given special attention because, in the minds of some critics and writers, it has succeeded Modernism and is thus an avant-garde, or neo-avant-garde literary "movement." There are fine writers in our time—Solzhenitsyn and Wiesel, for example (see Chapter 11)—who conceive literature in the traditional manner: as a means of exploring the profound moral questions of our day and therefore of supreme relevance to the "real" world. Some are explicitly critical of the lack of moral concern in Post-Modernism. The late John Gardner, an American novelist of some stature, complained, "The term 'post-modernism' not only isolates a few writers and praises them beyond their due, depressing the stock of others or willfully misreading them; it judges cynical or nihilist writers as characteristic of the age and therefore significant, and thus supports, even celebrates ideas no father would wittingly teach his children."[13]

How important Post-Modernism will be for the critics of the twenty-first century who will evaluate and label the literature of the late twentieth century, we cannot say. But, at the least, if Post-Modernism compels us to study the relationship of language to reality more closely and thereby to become more sophisticated readers, it has made a significant contribution to literature.

Visual Arts

In the previous chapter we discussed developments in art up to the decade of the 1970s. By that time Performance pieces, Earth Art, and Conceptual Art were the most fashionable, while Photo-Realistic painting, at the opposite end of the avant-garde spectrum, was just getting started. Minimal sculptures and Hard-Edge paintings were still fashionable, but past their peak. Op and Pop were passé, but had not disappeared from the scene. Architecture was still under the influence of the two giants: Mies van der Rohe and Le Corbusier. Although their main innovations occurred in the 1950s, the styles they inspired were being reflected in such megastructures as Chicago's John Hancock Center (Fig. 12.3) and Boston's City Hall (Fig. 12.4).

Of all the visual arts, architecture was the least pluralistic, but even it was divided between Mies van der Rohe's classical approach and Le Corbusier's organic approach. Avant-garde painting and sculpture, meanwhile, were in such a state of pluralism that the many competing styles tended to contradict one another and thus strain the credibility of the very concept of an avant-garde. This credibility became very thin during the 1980s, when the pluralism continued, yet few new ideas, and no major movements, emerged. Apparently the developments of the 1950s, and '60s had left artists with enough ideas to explore for the rest of the century. Either that, or

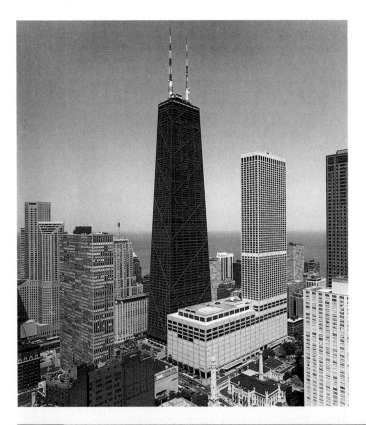

Modernism had had its day. As noted above, people began to invoke the term Post-Modernism. But what does the term signify in art and architecture?

Although the pluralism of the period makes it difficult to identify a Post-Modern style (especially in the fields of painting and sculpture), it is possible to describe a Post-Modern *sensibility*, that is, a body of shared tastes and attitudes on the part of both artists and viewers. In many respects, this sensibility is a reaction to Modernism. The latter, ironically, is now attacked for its inherent conservatism—especially the tendency of avant-gardes to be dogmatic, to traffic in inflated rhetoric, and to reject not only the past but revisionist tendencies within their own movements. Thus, the only rules left to break are those that Modernism itself established. This has led to pursuits that in the 1950s and '60s would have been branded as Modernist heresies: art historians researching and reviv-

12.3 Skidmore, Owings, and Merrill
John Hancock Center, Chicago, 1965

12.4 Kallman, McKinnell, and Knowles
City Hall, Boston, 1963

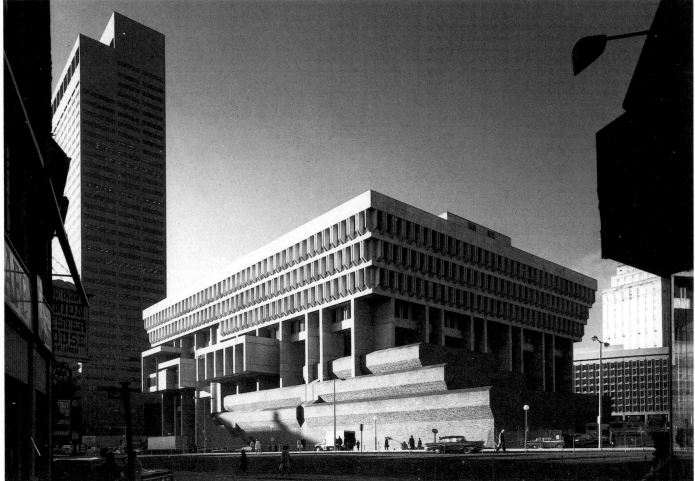

ing interest in such formerly despised styles as Victorian-era Realism; painters returning to subject matter and reviving the tools of optical realism; and architects reconsidering eclecticism as a viable mode of design. The art scholar Peter Fuller contrasts attitudes in the late 1960s, when art critics talked glibly of the "death" of painting, and art students made mixed-media "events," with those of the 1980s, when interest in painting had become as strong as ever, and students had taken up the challenges of life drawing and painting still lifes. Robert Venturi, an architect and critic, has had the temerity to condemn the sacred cows of Modernist architecture in his writings, and to manifest his own beliefs in conservative "dumb" designs (see below) which make a mockery of Modernism's principles. Still, the Post-Modern sensibility is more than just a regression to the past. In painting and sculpture it is manifested in subtle ways that take into account a range of art-related issues—current and past. Knowledge of these issues is often more important in an encounter with a work than the visible qualities of the work itself. In the fields of painting and sculpture the Post-Modern sensibility is characterized by four interrelated characteristics—*pluralism, eclecticism, self-consciousness,* and *contextualism.*

Pluralism, the profusion of styles and modes of today's art, has already been discussed. But this condition can also be found in single works. David Salle's *Poverty is No Disgrace* (Fig. **12.6**) is reminiscent of the mixed-media art of Rauschenberg (see page 470). But whereas the latter tends to combine incongruous materials in a single work, Salle (born 1952) mixes different modes of art—abstractionism, expressionism, academic painting, and even assemblage (the chair attached to the lower part of the canvas)—in a single work. Because each of these modes requires not only particular "codes" of viewing but also a particular way of thinking about art, each tends to be alien to the other. Yet Salle seems to have fused them successfully. If so, he has also denatured their content, as well as mocked all the critical rationales used to explain and defend each of these modes.

What Salle does is closely related to eclecticism, a practice that was considered almost immoral by Moder-

12.5 DOTTIE ATTIE
Carolina and her Father, 1978
Pencil on paper, each drawing
2 ins (5 cm) square
AIR Gallery, New York.

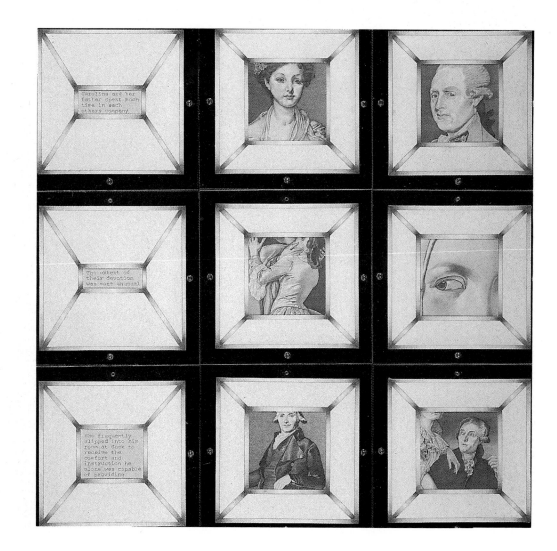

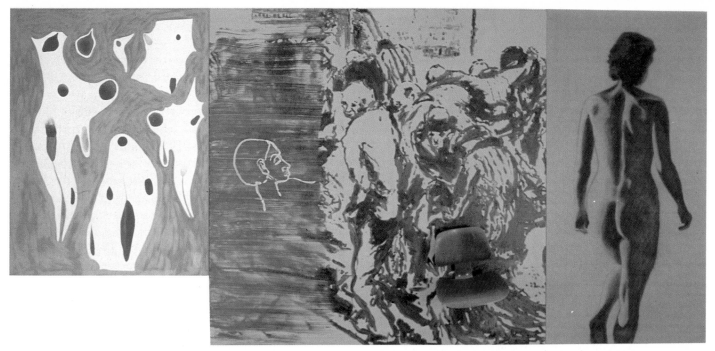

12.6 DAVID SALLE *Poverty is No Disgrace*, 1982
Oil, acrylic, chair, and canvas, 12.8 × 11.2 ft (3.9 × 3.4 m) Courtesy of Mary Boone Gallery, New York

12.7 ANSELM KIEFER *The Meistersinger*, 1982
Oil and straw on canvas, 111 × 150 ins (280 × 380 cm) Doris and Charles Saatchi, London

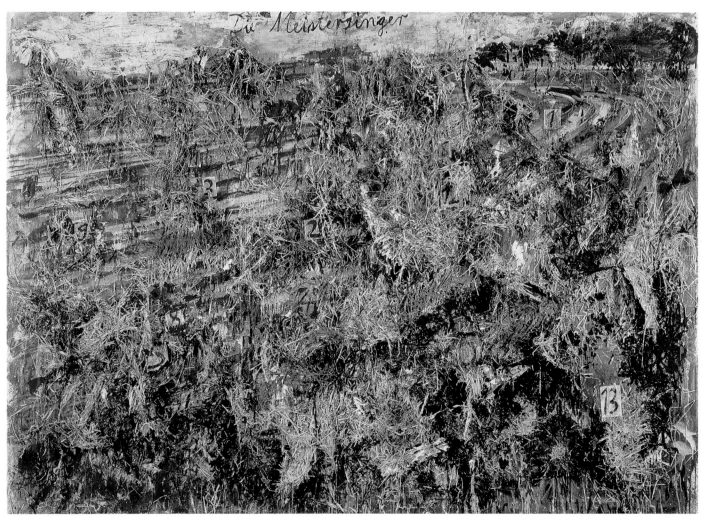

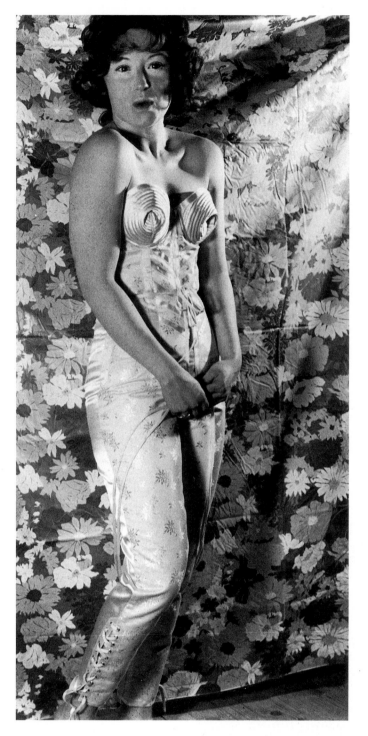

12.8 CINDY SHERMAN
Untitled, 1983
Photograph

nists. If any single thing divides Modernists from Post-Modernists it is the fact that the latter not only accept, but wholeheartedly embrace, eclecticism. Dottie Attie (born 1938) meticulously copies details from Old-Master paintings (c. 1600–1800). These details are alternated with

printed words to create a witty narrative which stretches for several feet on a gallery wall (Fig. **12.5**). Although Attie transforms the content of her Old-Master fragments, she nevertheless boldly appropriates their styles and subjects.

Often accused of being "art about art," Post-Modernism is self-conscious not only about its role in high culture but about the role of images in general. Along with semiologists (specialists in the science of signs and symbols), artists have come to the recognition that the world is given to us through language, including the language of art. This has led them to investigate the conventions of that language, sometimes placing more emphasis on the codes used to transmit content than on the content itself. The work of Cindy Sherman (born 1954) is about feminism, but it is also about the possibilities and limitations of photography to represent the world. Consisting of the artist herself as the model, in addition to costumes, props, and special lighting, a Sherman photograph (Fig. **12.8**) calls as much attention to the artistic strategies of its own making as to the issues of women in popular culture.

Sherman's work, like many other examples of Post-Modernism, evokes the sense of its own context—that is, an awareness of its socio- and art-historical roots. This is in opposition to most Modernist art, which was intended to be isolated from the concerns of society and the forces of history. Post-Modernism not only rejects Modernism's elevated stance, but seems to go to special lengths to raise the subject of its own problematical place in culture. *The Idleness of Sisyphus* (Fig. **12.1**), a "Neo-Expressionist" work by the Italian artist Sandro Chia (born 1946), refers to the myth of a king who was condemned eternally to push a huge stone up a mountain, only for it to roll down every time it neared the top; but it could just as easily be an allegory on the dilemmas of Post-Modern art. The paintings of Anselm Kiefer (born 1945) relate to the anxieties of both modern culture and the history of his native Germany. He and other contemporary German artists are concerned with their country's past, seeking to exorcise it in some cases and redeem it in others. All of Kiefer's paintings, even those which are somewhat abstract, contain specific subject matter. Through the use of visual and verbal clues, they relate directly or indirectly to various "stress moments" in German history, especially World War II and the Nazis' destruction of Jewish culture. Thickly painted, somber-colored, and embedded with additional material (such as straw), *The Meistersinger* (Fig. **12.7**) is typical of Keifer's work. Also typical is its ambiguous reference to German roots, in this case, to Wagner and the medieval tradition of Meistersingers (see Chapter 5).

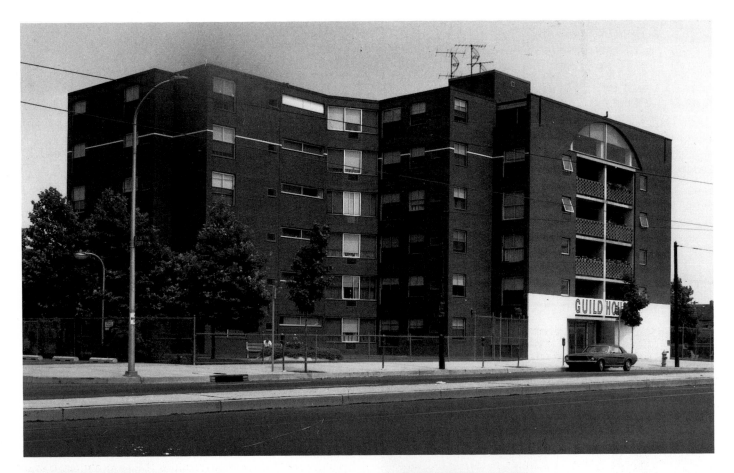

12.9 VENTURI and RAUCH, COPE and LIPPENCOTT
Guild House; Friends' Housing for the Elderly, Philadelphia, 1960–63

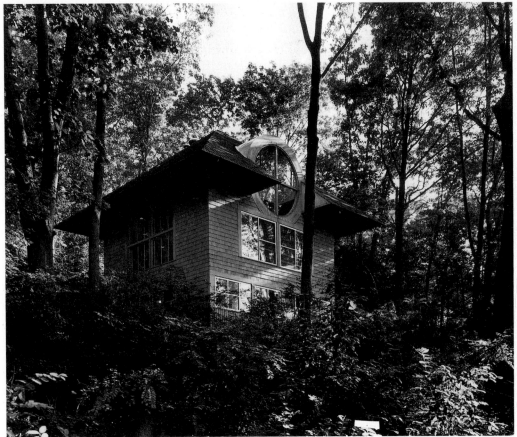

12.10 VENTURI and RAUCH
Tucker House, Katonah, New York, 1975
Photo Tom Crane

Architecture

Of all the arts, architecture presents the most coherent form of Post-Modernism. Indeed, members of the architectural profession use the term itself with much more boldness and conviction than do painters or sculptors. Many architects and architectural writers are clearly opposed to the Modernist dogmas of rationalism, functionalism, and faith in the new, and publicly acknowledge their interest in pluralism, history, semiology, and contextualism. The targets of their disapproval are, not surprisingly, the designs of Mies van der Rohe and Le Corbusier,

as well as those of their followers. (Because of its monumentality, complexity, and sheer expense, architecture had not been challenged by a significant movement of anti-art, such as that produced by artists like Duchamp, Johns, Rauschenberg, and the Pop artists.)

Inasmuch as recent architecture is less pluralistic than recent sculpture and painting, it is possible to recognize a Post-Modern style—a style that is distinguishable to some extent from late Modernist styles (see Chapter 11). What is striking is that this style seems rather traditional in both form and spirit. It replaces the continuous lines, open plan, and curtain walls of Modernist buildings with recognizable walls, mass, and self-contained rooms. It returns to a stance that the architectural writer Mary McLeod describes as "premodernist humanism." McLeod goes on to say that "postmodernism in architecture is not, as it is in some fields, a more sophisticated and comprehensive exploration of the formal discoveries of modernism.... Rather, it is a reaction against those very discoveries and their resultant destruction of accepted styles and compositional modes."[14] The "dumb design" of Venturi's project for housing for the elderly (Fig. **12.9**) employs a style and composition that are almost banal, though some features—the split façade, the sign, and the irregular scales of some of the windows—are subtly original. In his Tucker House (Fig. **12.10**), the architect has exaggerated the popular "codes" of hip roof, eaves, and picture window (the huge "oculus" at the top). Venturi's works reflect all the categories of the "Postmodern sensibility" described earlier, as well as the qualities of Post-Modern architecture outlined by the architectural writer Charles A. Jencks: "... an interest in popular and local codes of communication ..., in historical memory, urban context, ornament, representation, metaphor, participation, the public realm, pluralism and eclecticism...."[15] Jencks has referred to Venturi's projects as "ironic vernacular."

If so, New York's AT&T Building (Fig. **12.11**) is an example of "ironic monumentality." Designed by Philip Johnson (the architect who collaborated with Mies van der Rohe on the Seagram Building; Fig. **11.32**), this skyscraper embodies a memory of both historical styles and specific monuments: its arched entrance alludes to Roman architecture or to the entrance of Brunelleschi's Pazzi Chapel (Fig. **3.7**); its three-part division calls to mind the pre-modern skyscrapers of Sullivan (see page 381), and the controversial split gable echoes both classical pediments and Chippendale furniture.

12.11 JOHNSON and BURGEE
AT&T Building, New York

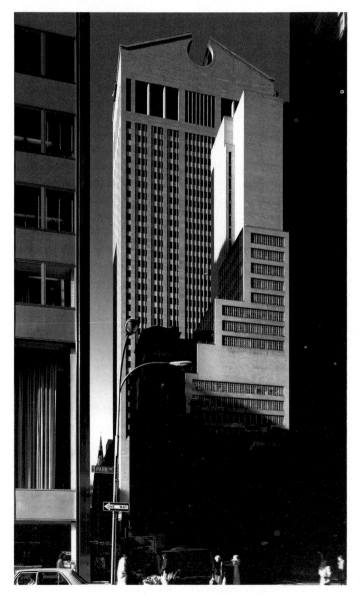

The New Music

By about 1970 serialism, post-serialism, tone clusters, musique concrète, computer-music, indeterminacy (both the composer and performer varieties), and even silence formed the landscape of what has been called "new music." Among the experimental composers, John Cage was by far the most seminal. Though his major works were produced in the 1950s, his influence in the 1960s and early '70s—not only on new music, but on experimental theater and even some forms of visual art—was at its peak.

The term Post-Modernism sometimes arises in music criticism, though less frequently than it does in art and literature. The composer and scholar Eric Salzman feels that "post-modern" music grew out of the Cage-inspired activities of the 1960s, including styles that parallel the visual arts, as in "minimal music," "conceptual music," and musical "imagery," as well as experiments in music-theater—often elaborations on the merger of musique concrète and Happenings. Meanwhile David Cope, sounding a theme similar to that of the architects Fuller and Venturi, takes issue with these models. Branding many experiments as dead ends and the avant-garde as a tyranny of the new, Cope sees a "return to faith in honest technique and musicality." He envisions a "post avant-garde" period in which composers will be free to work in any style, new or old. As models for this period he cites works by György Ligeti (born 1923), Luciano Berio (born 1925), and George Crumb (born 1929) that combine traditional and avant-garde techniques. Crumb's *Ancient Voices of Children* (1970), for example, employs experimental sounds: *Sprechstimme*,, non-Western tone colors and scales, along with classical sounds, including even some triadic (three-note) harmonies. But each of these elements is employed for an expressive purpose, and all are successfully molded into a unity of form and content. *Final Alice* (1976), a vivid concert piece for voice based on *Alice's Adventures in Wonderland*, by David Del Tredici (born 1937), is built almost entirely on traditional harmony—both chromatic and diatonic. Through the use of out-of-sync tempos and selective dissonance, the songs are surreal enough to capture the spirit of the Wonderland itself, but at the same time voluptuous enough—as much as the music of Wagner or Strauss—to suggest the affectionate relationship between Lewis Carroll and Alice Liddell, the real-life Alice. The music critic Garry E. Clarke suggests that aspects of Del Tredici's music "speak to a revival of a certain romantic sensibility, if not to a new romanticism itself."[16]

Minimalism

According to Clarke, the term Post-Modern, if it is to be used, must be applied to music that goes beyond Modern music—beyond, say, the over-organized atonality of Babbitt (see page 485) or the unpredictable anti-music of Cage. Minimalism, a variety of music that has become quite fashionable, may satisfy that criterion. Although the minimalism label itself is problematic, it continues to be used to identify a number of styles that are partial to a basic, stripped-down type of music. This music, unlike the vast majority of Modernist music, employs tonality and consonant chords. And its melodies, like the uniform, repeatable shapes of a Hard-Edge painting by Kelly (see page 467), are not only simple, but often deployed in cyclical patterns (not unlike those heard on a cracked record). But, though simple in tonality and melody, minimalism is complex in meter, creating fascinating, sometimes disconcerting, pulsating effects.

The beginnings of minimalism can be attributed either to the repetitive "trance music" of La Monte Young (born 1935), or to *In C*, a piece consisting of 53 short musical fragments repeatable according to the discretion of the performers, by Terry Riley (born 1935) and first performed in 1965. But Steve Reich (born 1936) and Philip Glass (born 1937) are the best-known exponents of the style. Though often linked, because of similarities in both their music and careers, the two insist that their music is different. Reich's emphasizes meter and is richly pulsating; Glass's is known for its novel harmonies and subtle shifts in texture. These differences are reflected in their respective ensembles: Reich's has more percussion, Glass's is more electronic. Meanwhile, the music of both has become less minimal in at least one respect: the scale and grandeur of their recent works.

Reich sees an analogy between the music of Wagner, which was dominated by an obsession with chromaticism, and his own, with its equally obsessive repetition. Reich's *The Desert Music* (1984), an ambitious setting of poems by William Carlos Williams, featuring a chorus of 27 voices and 89 musicians (strings, synthesizers, amplified woodwinds, muted brass, two pianos, and a variety of percussion), is typical. Like all his pieces, it specializes in complex poly-rhythms and interlocked patterns, but on a grander scale. The pace is established in the opening movement by rapid, almost hypnotic, pulsations. As Reich himself describes it: "The opening of the piece is a kind of chorale, only instead of individual chords sounding for a

12.12 Philip Glass

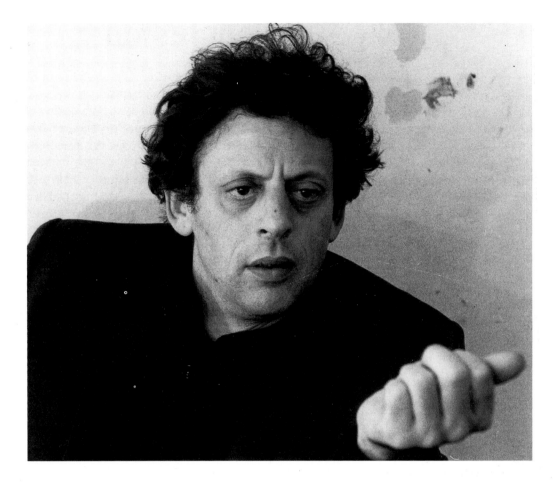

given length of held notes, they're pulsed; instead of a steady tone you get rapid eighth notes repeating over and over again, which sets up a kind of rhythmic energy...."[17]

Glass, who claims that minimalism has been dead since 1975, has completed three operas since then: *Einstein on the Beach* (1976), a large-scale music/theater piece, *Satyagraha* (1980), a Sanskrit text based on the life of Mohandas Gandhi, and *Akhnaton* (1984), a text loosely based on the life of the heretic pharaoh (see page 39). Yet despite Glass's preference for theatrical productions and his alleged renunciation of minimalism, his music nevertheless features highly economical structures. For example, the violin solo of *Einstein on the Beach* consists of spare phrases that seem relentlessly to examine and re-examine a simple four-note, ascending motive (B, C, C♯, and D♯) from slightly different angles. At times sounding like the bass part of a Baroque *basso continuo* (see page 181), and at other times like a musician practicing scales, the solo violin is almost as compelling in its permutations of a basic module as is Bach's *Goldberg Variations* (see page 185).

In addition to producing operas, Glass has been involved with rock musicians and, recently, writers of popular songs. To make an album of songs (*Songs from Liquid Days*), he enlisted the help of people such as David Byrne, Linda Ronstadt, Paul Simon, Suzanne Vega, and the performance-artist/song-writer Laurie Anderson. Such collaborations and excursions into the field of popular music have given Glass the kind of visibility and following that few other serious composers enjoy.

Thus, late twentieth-century music betrays many of the same symptoms of late twentieth-century art: pluralism (in addition to the varieties mentioned in Chapter 11, the neo-romanticism of Del Tredici and the minimalism of Reich), eclecticism (Crumb's potpourri of styles, other composers' use of non-Western forms), renunciation of the dogmas of Modernism (particularly the taboo against tonality), and even the interest in vernacular styles (Glass's collaboration with popular song-writers). However, there seem to be few, if any, examples of music designed specifically to evoke a Post-Modern sensibility, at least not in the same way that several examples of late twentieth-century art do.

Conclusion

So, again, what is Post-Modernism: a *neo* avant-garde that finds its models in the experiments of late Modernism, or a *post* avant-garde that leap-frogs Modernism to find inspiration in literary, art, or music history? Is it the final phase before the death of Western culture, or the transitional phase of a new culture? These questions cannot be answered with any finality. Nevertheless, there is a consensus on some issues. All Post-Modernists agree that Western culture has indeed entered a different phase, that Modernism has exhausted itself. Although offering conflicting interpretations, they accept the term "Post-Modernism," and agree that—whatever its true configuration may be—Post-Modernism is pluralistic, like late Modernism (that is, the era of Happenings, Pop Art, and Cage's music). But unlike its predecessor, Post-Modernism dares to be eclectic. Recent critics have grown weary of "the tradition of the new." The new and the future are no longer as venerated as they once were, while the old and the past have become legitimate concerns. Post-Modernism actually encourages the practice of appropriating elements from older styles, as in the parodying of eighteenth-century writing by Barth, the imitation of Old-Master styles by Attie, the use of arch and pediment in a skyscraper, and the aping of grand opera in *Final Alice*. But it should be pointed out that these are appropriations, not revivals. They are pastiches—writers, artists, architects, and composers making use of the codes of past styles without taking the codes themselves seriously, like Machaut composing a parody Mass (see page 318). Intended for an educated audience, they are self-conscious references to styles or motifs removed from their original contexts for their connotative, metaphoric, or even satirical potential.

Because the present is always too close to us, it can never be described fully. But, assuming that the above discussion provides a usable sketch of Post-Modernism, then we can compare this trend's features with those of other cultural periods, such as those surveyed in earlier chapters of this book.

The tendency of Post-Modern literature, art, and music to use the past as a resource is, as we have seen again and again, not unique in history. The Hellenistic Greeks, who invented eclecticism, may have been the first to borrow from the Classical Greeks. But they had many successors: the first-century Romans who made an industry out of mining Greek culture, both Classical and Hellenistic (see Chapter 2); the fourteenth-century Florentines whose "Renaissance" meant the rebirth of classical civilization

(see Chapter 3); the seventeenth-century writers and architects at Versailles who tried to make all the arts conform to classical standards; and the painters and architects of the French Revolution who literally modeled their work on classical styles (see Chapter 4). Charlemagne's artists openly copied the works of Byzantine and Early Christian artists, while his scholars transcribed their manuscripts (see Chapter 7). Bach based his Cantata No. 80 on *Ein Feste Burg*, a chorale by Luther based on a plainsong (see Chapter 8). The Romantic architects, who unashamedly appropriated from Egyptian, classical, medieval, Renaissance, Baroque, and Neoclassical sources, were the ones who finally gave eclecticism a bad reputation (see Chapter 5).

Foreshadowings of Post-Modern complexity and overrefinement can be seen in the thin piers and tracery of Late Gothic architecture, the attention to detail in fifteenth-century Flemish painting, the rhythms and melismas of *ars nova*, Mannerist painting, Baroque and Rococo architecture, almost all Romantic works, and French Symbolist poetry. Pluralism, as a cultural phenomenon, was true of the Hellenistic, late Roman, and *fin-de-siècle* periods. Note that most of the examples are from periods representing the end of an era: the Hellenistic style as the final stage of Greek culture, late Roman at the end of the Empire, Late Gothic and *ars nova* at the close of the Middle Ages, Mannerism at the end of the High Renaissance, and Richard Strauss's music and symbolist poetry as the last gasp of Romanticism. These periods were, and perhaps still are, seen as declines. Sometimes the terms used to describe them are even more negative: "weary," "jaded," "decadent," and so forth. But this depends somewhat on one's point of view. Still, history has tended to agree with the assessments of those who took up the mantle of culture after the periods under question. The successes of the Romans who assumed leadership during the Hellenistic period, of the Christians who triumphed over the late Romans, of the Renaissance humanists who denounced the Late Gothic, and of the Modernists who came after the *fin-de-siècle*, have assured these groups their deserved place in the history books (and humanities texts). Now, there is some evidence that the Post-Modernists may be supplanting the Modernists. The question of who follows the Post-Modernists, and how history judges late twentieth-century culture—our own *fin-de-siècle*—will be answered by a Humanities text written in the twenty-first century.

GLOSSARY

When a definition includes a term that is itself defined elsewhere in the Glossary, that word is printed in italics.

abbey A church or building belonging to a monastery.

absurd In atheistic existentialist philosophies, the sense that human life is meaningless in a universe indifferent to human longing. The Theater of the Absurd, which appeared in the 1950s, was an attempt to dramatize and stage this concept.

academic A disparaging term used in reference to works of art that are accomplished but unoriginal or overly conventional.

acrylic A synthetic paint medium, usually water-soluble, that has many of the qualities of oil on canvas. A painting made with acrylic.

aerial perspective The use of different shades of color to produce the illusion of atmosphere in a picture, particularly through the progressive blurring of outlines, increased use of blue, and decreased contrasts of light and dark in the distance. See *sfumato*.

aleatory music A music that is uncontrolled or left to chance. See *indeterminacy*.

allegory An extended *metaphor* whose images convey a symbolic meaning external to the narrative.

altarpiece A painting or carving of a Christian subject that rests on, or hangs above, an altar.

ambulatory An aisle of a church or cathedral that extends around the sanctuary and, if present, around the *transept*. See *basilican plan*.

amphitheater An oval or circular structure with tiers of seats sloping upward from a central stage area.

antiphon Church music performed by two or more choruses in which the verses of a psalm or hymn are sung alternately or responsively.

apocalyptic Used to describe literature or art which, like the Book of Revelation, features bizarre and cryptic symbolism and proclaims the end of the world.

apse A semicircular projection at the east end of a church or cathedral. See *basilican plan*.

arcade A series of *arches* supported by *columns*.

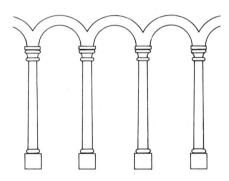

arch A curved masonry structure that spans an opening such as a doorway, window, gateway, etc., or provides support for a bridge or aqueduct.

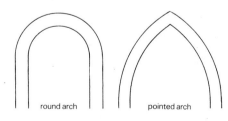

round arch   pointed arch

archetype In literary criticism, a character, plot, or image that occurs frequently in literature. In Jungian criticism, the "primordial images" in our racial memory that are expressed through religious myths and dreams. See *Jungian myth*.

architectural order A style of Classical architecture defined by the styles of the *column*, particularly the *capital*, and the *entablature*. See *Corinthian order*, *Doric order*, *Ionic order*, and *Tuscan order*.

architrave A horizontal beam resting on *columns*. The bottom part of a classical *entablature*.

aria A solo song, usually in an opera, oratorio, or cantata.

art for art's sake A slogan coined by Walter Pater to express the philosophy that art has a value all its own, with its sole purpose being to give pleasure.

assemblage An artwork created by assembling an assortment of three-dimensional scraps or objects.

atonality Music without a tonal center. See *tonality*.

avant-garde Used to describe leaders of an arts or literary movement whose work and ideas are seen as non-conformist or unconventional.

Babylonian Captivity (Exile) The exile in the sixth century BC of the leading Jews of Jerusalem and Judah resulting from their deportation by King Nebuchadnezzar of Babylon. Also used for the fourteenth-century transfer of the papacy from Rome to Avignon.

ballet A dramatic art in which dancing, mime, and music combine to tell a story or evoke a mood.

baptistery A part of a church used for baptism. A separate building designed for baptism during the Early Christian, Romanesque, and

Gothic periods, particularly in Italy.

bar lines Vertical lines on a musical score that divide the music into rhythmic units.

barrel vault A semicircular masonry *vault*.

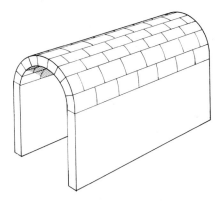

basilica In Roman times, a long building with *colonnaded aisles and apses* at both ends used as a public hall or legal center. During the Early Christian period, a style of church based on the Roman basilica with an apse at one end. See *basilican plan*.

basilican plan A rectangular style of church consisting of *narthex*, *nave*, *side aisles*, and *apse*. More complex churches also have some or all of the following: *transept*, *crossing*, *choir*, *ambulatory*, and *radiating chapels*.

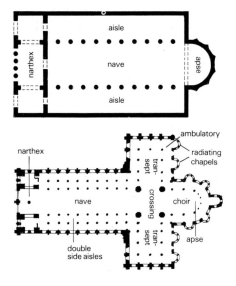

bass 1. The lowest voice of a composition; 2. The lowest male voice; 3. A string instrument with the lowest range.

basso continuo In seventeenth- and eighteenth-century music, the combination of a bass-line instrument (cello or bassoon) and a keyboard instrument that doubles the bass line and adds harmony above it.

bay In architecture, usually a single opening framed by vertical supports, as in the space between two *columns* of a Greek temple, or the *clerestory*, *gallery* and *arcade* between two *piers* of a Romanesque or Gothic cathedral.

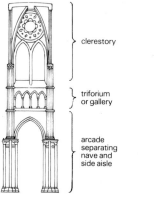

clerestory

triforium or gallery

arcade separating nave and side aisle

Bildungsroman German term for a novel about a person's gradual development to maturity.

book of hours A devotional book containing the service of the *Divine Office* and a calendar of the church seasons.

broken color Short strokes of paint that, if used with a variety of colors, produce a vibrant effect. See *pointillism*.

bronze casting A bronze sculpture cast from a mold. See *casting*.

canon A *contrapuntal* musical work in which one or more voices imitate the original subject, each beginning at different intervals of time and/or pitch. See *fugue*, *subject*.

cantata A vocal composition for chorus, solo voices, and orchestra, usually based on a religious text.

canzoniere Lyrical poems (*canzoni*) composed by Petrarch that take a variety of forms, usually that of the *sonnet*.

capital The top part of a *column*.

Cartesianism A philosophy based on the thought of René Descartes (1596–1650), who emphasized the mathematical approach to knowledge of a universe conceived as mechanical. In this view, God may be known through human reason and logic.

casting A sculpture formed by pouring liquid material (such as plaster or molten metal) into a mold which is removed when the material hardens.

catacombs A vast network of underground cemeteries used by the early Christians.

cella In a Greek temple, a walled enclosure intended to house a cult statue.

centering A temporary wooden framework used to support an *arch* during construction.

ceramic Clay that has been changed into a hard substance through baking at a high temperature. Of any material made by this process.

chain of being The concept of the universe as an hierarchical chain extending downwards from God through angels, humans, and animals, finally to nothing, with every element in its proper place.

chancel The part of a church around the altar where the sacrament of the Lord's Supper (Mass) is performed by the clergy.

chanson (French: song) A secular song, particularly popular from the fourteenth to the sixteenth century.

chanson de geste (French: song of (heroic) deeds) A French *epic* poem celebrating heroic deeds, especially those of Charlemagne and the Twelve Peers of his court.

chant *Monophonic* vocal music lacking strict meter. See *Gregorian chant.*

chiaroscuro (Italian: light-dark) In a picture, the use of varying degrees of shading to suggest the play of reflected light on a curved or uneven surface.

chivalric romance Medieval tales of adventure, often featuring ladies in distress and heroic knights motivated by love, faith, or desire for adventure.

choir Part of a Romanesque or Gothic *nave* where the singing choir performs. See *basilican plan.*

chorale A type of hymn introduced by Martin Luther during the Reformation.

chord Three or more *tones* of different *pitch* played simultaneously.

chorus In Greek drama, the group of singers and dancers who appear at frequent intervals in the play to comment perceptively on the deeper significance of the events.

chromatic Of music using half-tones and *tones* not related to the main key. See *diatonic.*

church modes The scale patterns of medieval church music. See *Gregorian chant.*

City Dionysia A festival in honor of Dionysus, god of plant and animal life, instituted in Athens in the seventh century BC and an occasion for the presenting of dramatic tragedies.

clerestory In an Early Christian, Romanesque, or Gothic church, that part of the *nave* wall which rises above the *side aisles* and is pierced by windows.

coda See *sonata form.*

collage An artwork created by applying an assortment of flat materials—paper scraps, cloth, photos, news clippings, etc.—to a flat surface.

colonnade A row of *columns*, usually supporting a roof or *arcade.*

colonnette A small *column.* In Romanesque and Gothic architecture, colonnettes are typically attached to *piers.*

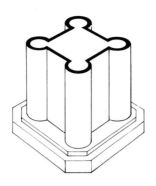

color (in music) The qualities of sound that distinguish one musical instrument from another. See *timbre.*

column An upright structural support, usually consisting of a base, cylindrical shaft, and *capital.*

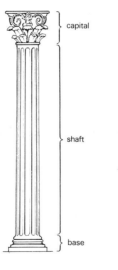

comedy A form of drama that employs wit and humor to amuse and that ends happily. More broadly, a literary work that has a positive ending.

concerto A multi-movement composition in which a solo instrument is accompanied by an orchestra.

concerto grosso A Baroque concerto in which two or more solo instruments (concertino) play with a small orchestra (ripieno).

consonance In music, harmonious sound. See *dissonance.*

contrapuntal (Latin: point against point) Pertaining to two or more melodies played simultaneously in different voices.

Corinthian order. The most elaborate of the Classical orders, employing a leaf motif in the *capital.*

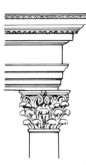

cornice In classical architecture, the horizontal molding at the top of the *entablature* and below the roof or *pediment.* Also the molding, called a *raking* cornice, that frames the sloping sides of the pediment itself. Any horizontal projection at the top of a building.

crescendo In music, gradual increase in loudness. See *decrescendo.*

crossing Where the *nave* and *transept* wings of a Gothic or Romanesque church intersect. See *basilican plan.*

cross vault A structure consisting of two *vaults* intersecting at right angles, creating four *bays.* Because the lines of intersection form v-shapes, or "groins," on the underside, the structure may be referred to as a "groin vault."

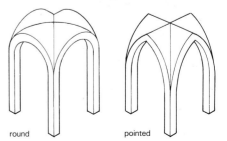

round   pointed

cruciform Cross-shaped. Of the shape of any *basilican-plan* church with a *transept*.

cuneiform Wedge-shaped writing on clay tablets, invented by the ancient Sumerians of the Tigris-Euphrates valley (Mesopotamia).

Cupid The god of love, usually represented as a young boy with wings and arrow.

decrescendo In music, gradual decrease in loudness. See *crescendo*.

deism The belief, especially popular in the eighteenth century, that conceived of God as a master watchmaker who, having created the universe, withdrew and left it to operate without his intervention, according to laws discoverable by human reason.

Delphic oracle The priestess of Apollo (god of prophecy) in the shrine at Delphi (Greece) who, when so requested, gave advice and predicted the future.

dénouement (French: unravelling) In literature, a term for the unravelling or resolution of the plot.

deus ex machina Literally, "god out of the machine." Derived from a device on the roof of the Greek stage building used to lower deities onto the stage, who would then provide resolutions to otherwise impossible conflicts. Now used for any arbitrary solution imposed upon a play or story by the writer.

development The second section of a *sonata form*.

Diaspora A technical term for the Jews living outside Palestine after the *Babylonian Captivity*.

diatonic Of music using only the *pitches* of a *major* or *minor* scale, as contrasted with *chromatic*.

dissonance In music, inharmonious sound. See *consonance*.

dithyramb A choral hymn sung and danced in honor of the dying Dionysus, god of plant and animal life. Thought to be the origin of Greek tragedy.

Divine Office Religious services celebrated in monasteries and convents throughout the day and night: Matins (6 a.m.), Lauds (9 a.m.), Prime (noon), Terce (3 p.m.), Sext (6 p.m.), Nones (9 p.m.), Vespers (midnight), and Compline (3 a.m.).

dome A *vaulted* ceiling/roof in the form of a shell—either hemispherical or ovoidal. A radial form of the *arch*.

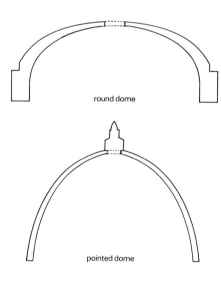

round dome

pointed dome

Doric order The simplest of the Greek orders, with each *column* having no base and a simple block as a *capital*.

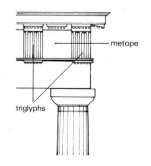

metope

triglyphs

duplum In medieval *polyphony*, the voice directly above the tenor.

dynamics The degree of loudness or softness in a musical passage.

elevation A scale drawing of any side of a building—interior or exterior. An architectural diagram of a vertical plane, as distinguished from a plan.

engraving A print made from an image cut into a copper plate by a pointed tool.

ensemble Two or more musicians performing individual parts of a composition.

entablature The horizontal part of a classical building that lies between the *pediment* and the *columns* and consists of *architrave*, *frieze*, and *cornice*.

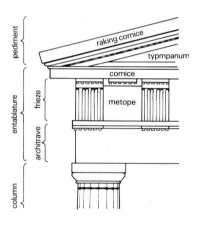

pediment
raking cornice
typmpanum
cornice
entablature
frieze
metope
architrave
column

entasis The slight outward swelling of the shaft of a Greek *column*.

epic A long narrative poem in elevated style, focusing on the deeds and adventures of a hero.

epiphany In general, a manifestation, often of a divine being. In literary criticism, a term introduced by James Joyce to denote the experience in which the essence of something is revealed. His stories are sometimes called epiphanies.

epistolary novel A novel written in the form of a series of letters.

etching A print made from an image cut into a copper plate by means of acid.

Eucharist Greek term for the sacrament of the Church in which Christians commemorate the death of Christ through partaking of the bread and wine in Holy Communion. See *transubstantiation*.

Everyman The title of a medieval morality play dramatizing the search for salvation. A term for any fictional or dramatic character who represents the universal experience of humans.

expressionism An early-twentieth-century movement in art and literature in which the artist or writer attempted to express inner, often dream-like images. *Stream of consciousness* is sometimes regarded as a type of expressionism.

façade The front of a building.

ferroconcrete Concrete reinforced with steel rods or mesh.

feudalism A political and economical system in Europe between the ninth and fifteenth centuries, whereby land was granted by a lord to his vassal in exchange for homage and service.

fluting In architecture, the vertical channels carved into the shaft of a *column*.

flying buttress An external support for a Gothic building; specifically, a half *arch* extending from a narrow masonry *pier* to the upper part of the *nave*.

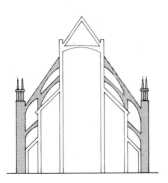

foreshorten In drawing or painting, to shorten the length of some of the contours of an object, animal, or person, to give the illusion of depth.

form The shape and structure given the elements of a literary, artistic, or musical composition.

fortissimo Loud (music)

forum In a Roman city, a center of civic, legal, and commercial activity.

frame construction A *nonload-carrying* type of construction in which thin wooden boards or metal beams are joined to form a rigid framework for supporting the walls and roof.

frame story A story that provides the vehicle for the telling of one or more separate stories, as in Boccaccio's *Decameron*.

fresco A method of painting on wet plaster with pigments mixed with water.

frieze A horizontal decoration, typically consisting of *relief* sculptures, that forms an ornamental band on the outside or inside of a building. Part of the *entablature* of a classical building.

fugue A *polyphonic* composition based on a single melody that is imitated and varied in one or more voices beginning at different intervals of time and/or *pitch*. See *contrapuntal*.

gallery In architecture, the walkway or balcony directly above the *side aisle* in a Byzantine, Romanesque, or Gothic church. See *triforium*.

general will Rousseau's term for the expression of the collective will of individuals within an organized society.

genre Type, kind, or category of literature. In art, a realistic depiction of everyday life.

geodesic dome A type of frame construction whereby lightweight metal rods are joined to create hexagons which, in turn, form a hemispherical shell.

glaze A thin, semi-transparent layer of oil or varnish mixed with pigment and applied to the surface of a painting to modify the effect of the colors. A glass-like coating for *ceramic* objects.

Golden Age In Greece, the period of the Athenian artistic and intellectual achievements of the fifth and fourth centuries BC. For the Romans, the literary achievement between 80 BC and AD 14, which included the works of such luminaries as Cicero, Lucretius, Virgil, and Ovid.

gospel (Greek: good news) A message of salvation through the death, burial and resurrection of Christ, proclaimed by the early Christians.

Gospels First four books of the New Testament—traditionally attributed to Matthew, Mark, Luke and John—which focus on highly-selective aspects of Jesus' life and teaching, especially his arrest, crucifixion, and resurrection.

Gregorian chant Monophonic melodies that formed the basis of Roman Catholic church music during the Middle Ages; sometimes called *plainsong*.

groin vault See *cross vault*.

gulag An acronym for Chief Administration of Corrective Labor Camps, referring to the Russian labor camps.

harmony A blend of simultaneously sounding *tones*.

Hasidism A Jewish religious and social movement founded in the eighteenth century in revolt against cold formalism and intellectualism in Judaism. It stresses intense personal piety and humility.

Hebrews A term for ancient biblical Israelites. Sometimes used interchangeably with "Jews," though the latter often designates the Israelites after the *Babylonian Captivity*.

hieroglyphics Ancient Egyptian writing which employed pictures of figures and objects to represent words and sounds.

holocaust Literally, a whole burnt offering. Now, when capitalized, it refers to the "final solution" of Adolf Hitler and the Nazis (World War II) in which they sought to destroy all European Jews by means of extermination camps and mass executions. Also termed "Shoah" (Hebrew: annihilation).

Holy Roman Empire A political entity in Europe which, in theory, revived the Roman empire, first under Charlemagne (crowned Holy Roman Emperor in AD 800), and later under Otto the Great (AD 962). Dissolved by Napoleon in 1806.

homophony Two or more musical parts played together at the same rhythm and *tempo*, but at different *pitch* levels.

humanism During the Renaissance, a philosophical and literary outlook largely characterized by a passion for the recovery and study of Greek and Roman literature, in which was found inspiration for an exaltation of human nature and interests. Christian humanists used their knowledge of the classical languages as a means of developing more accurate texts and interpretations of the Bible.

hunter-gatherer culture A nomadic way of life based on hunting animals and gathering edible plants, characteristic of the Paleolithic (Old Stone) Age.

hymn A religious song of praise, usually in *strophic* form.

hypocrite A Greek word meaning "answerer," the term for the actor in a play. First used for the respondent to the choral *dithyrambs*.

idée fixe (French: fixed idea) A short musical phrase that recurs throughout a multi-movement composition. See *leitmotiv*.

imitation Repetition of a musical theme by different voices or instruments.

indeterminancy A condition of unpredictable music, where such things as *pitch* and note duration are left to "chance".

indulgence A papal certificate that reduces the temporal punishment for sin, on earth and in *purgatory*, after the sin has been forgiven.

in medias res (Latin: in the midst of things) A traditional Homeric technique employed in *epic* poetry whereby the story opens in the midst of the action with information about the beginning of the action supplied through flashbacks.

instrumentation The arranging, composing, and writing of instrumental music.

interval The musical space between *pitches*.

Ionic order One of the Greek orders, employing a scroll-like *capital* with a circular base.

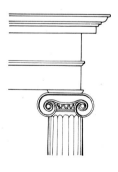

irony 1. Verbal irony: a form of speech in which what is said is the opposite of what is meant.

2. Dramatic irony: actions or words in a play that are contrary to the actual truth, as known to the audience but unknown to the dramatic characters.
3. Situational irony: when circumstances turn out the opposite of what is expected.

Jansenism An ideology named for a Catholic bishop (Jansen) who emphasized the Augustinian doctrine of predestinative grace in his theology. His teaching was the reigning theology in the nunnery at Port Royal (France). See *predestination*.

Jungian myth According to Karl Jung's psychological theory, myth is the repository of the *archetypes*, which are a part of what he termed the "collective unconscious" of the human race.

Kabbalah (also Cabala) Mystical teachings of Judaism based on a secret system of interpreting the Jewish Scriptures (Old Testament).

kerygma (Greek: proclamation) A New Testament term for the message of salvation through Christ preached by the early Christians.

key The basic scale of a musical composition as evidenced by its *tonic* note, and as indicated on the score by a symbol called a key signature.

keystone The central, crowning stone of an *arch*. The last stone to be set when constructing an arch.

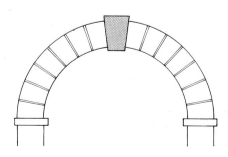

ladder of love A theory of love developed by Marsilio Ficino which combined Neoplatonic and Christian thought. According to this theory, the lover of beauty and goodness, in his meditations, moves up a hierarchy of loves attracted by created beauty until he contemplates uncreated beauty and the source of all goodness—God himself.

lantern A small structure crowning a *dome*.

leitmotiv (German: leading idea) In music, a recurring subject, often used to represent a character or mood in a multi-movement composition.

libretto The text of an opera or *oratorio*.

Lied (plural: Lieder) A German song.

linear perspective In a picture, a system for creating the illusion of depth through the convergence of lines and foreshortening. In one-point perspective, the sizes and shapes of objects and their interrelationships are determined by the locations of the *vanishing point* and the eye-level (horizon).

load-carrying Of constructions in which walls, posts, columns, or arcades support the weight of the ceiling. Distinguished from nonload-carrying constructions.

lunette A triangular or semicircular area of wall over a window or door.

lyric poem A brief poem that features imagery and sound rather than telling a story. See *narrative poem*.

madrigal A secular music composition for unaccompanied voices in Renaissance Italy and sixteenth- and early-seventeenth-century England.

major and minor scales Progressions of *tones* in steps, where the major or minor quality is determined by the placement of half and whole steps.

mal du siècle (French: sickness of the age) The melancholy associated especially with the Romantic personality. See *Weltschmerz*.

Manichaeism A religion named for Mani (died AD 277) which explained evil by positing two realms—light and darkness—originally independent but now intermingled in the world.

masonry Brickwork, stonework, or concrete.

Mass 1. Celebration of the Holy *Eucharist* consisting of a series of prayers and chants; 2. A *polyphonic* composition written to accompany the Mass, or Catholic worship service.

mastaba An ancient Egyptian tomb with a flat top and sloping sides.

measure In music, a group of beats, usually with an accent on the first beat, set off in written music by *bar lines*.

medium (pl. media) The methods and materials used to produce an artwork.

melismatic Having several notes on one syllable of text. See *neumatic*, *syllabic*.

Messiah (Hebrew: anointed one) An Old Testament term for the king promised by God who would save his people. The New Testament presents Jesus as the fulfillment of this promise. Thus he is entitled the Christ (Greek: anointed one).

metaphor A figure of speech involving an implied comparison between one thing and another in which one or more of the attributes of the one are transferred to the other—for example, "the lamp of experience" (Patrick Henry).

meter In music, an organization of beats into equal units of time. See *measure*.

metope A rectangular panel (sometimes containing *relief* sculptures) framed by *triglyphs* on the *frieze* of a Doric *entablature*.

mimetic Adjective from *mimesis* (Greek: imitation). In literary criticism, a concept derived from Aristotle's definition of dramatic plot as the imitation of an action. Later, extended to include all things that literature may imitate.

miniature A very small painting. An illustration for a devotional book such as a *book of hours*.

minor scales See *major and minor scales*.

mobile An abstract sculpture suspended from a ceiling and consisting of thin rods and metal plates that move—though almost imperceptibly—with currents of air.

mode Used to describe the patterns of notes within an *octave*. See *church modes*.

monochromatic Of an artwork in one color, or in various shades of one color. Distinguished from *polychromatic*.

monody 1. Music with a single melodic line; 2. Italian music of the seventeenth century which consists of a single solo line accompanied by instruments.

monophony Music consisting of a single melody without support of *harmony*.

mosaic Wall or floor decorations made by inlaying small pieces of stone, ceramic, or glass in plaster or cement.

motet From the late Middle Ages to the eighteenth century, a *polyphonic* composition that was usually sacred, often sung with two or more texts simultaneously, and written for unaccompanied voice.

motif A recurring thematic element in a literary, artistic, or musical work. See *motive*.

motive A short melodic and/or rhythmic musical idea which is emphasized throughout a section or movement of a composition. See *idée fixe, leitmotiv, subject.*

mot juste (French: the right word) Flaubert's theory that in each instance there is but one correct word for the writer's meaning.

movement A major part of a composition with a clear beginning and ending.

mural A picture painted directly on a wall. See *fresco.*

musicology The scholarly study of music through historical, theoretical, acoustical, psychological, sociological, or physiological analyses.

musique concrète A twentieth-century musical style in which sounds from the environment are recorded on magnetic tape and then manipulated electronically to produce new effects.

narrative poem A poem that tells a story.

narthex The entrance hall at the west end of a church. See *basilican plan.*

naturalism In literary criticism, an extension of *realism* to even the sordid, ugly, animalistic aspects of human life.

nave The central and main aisle of a church extending from the *narthex* to the *apse* or *transept.* See *basilican plan.*

Neoplatonism 1. A revival of Platonism in the third century, initiated by Plotinus and his disciples, which stressed union with the One. 2. Another such revival which began in the fifteenth century with Marsilio Ficino, head of the Platonic Academy in Florence.

neumatic Having two or three notes sung on a single syllable, falling stylistically between *syllabic* and *melismatic.*

neume Symbol for note or group of notes used in the musical notation system of the Middle Ages.

nihilism (from Latin, *nihil*: nothing) The rejection of all distinctions in moral values; often the denial of meaning and significance in human life and endeavour.

nonload-carrying Of construction in which the walls do not support the weight of a ceiling or roof but are attached to a frame.

notation The use of a system of signs and symbols to represent *pitch,* duration, and rhythm in musical compositions.

nouveau roman (French: new novel) A French experimental novel of the 1950s and 1960s characterized by the rejection of elements such as characterization and plot in favor of emphasis on an uninterpreted and unstructured portrayal of facts and images.

novella A short tale, such as those in Boccaccio's *Decameron.* Also, sometimes used to designate the short novel.

objective correlative A term used by T. S. Eliot which refers to objective elements (objects, situation, events) in a poem that communicate to the reader the emotional experience of the author or fictional character.

octave An interval of eight notes in a *diatonic* scale in which the highest tone has twice as many vibrations per second as the lowest tone. In literature, eight lines of a *sonnet.* See *canzoniere.*

Oedipus complex A component of Freudian psychoanalytic theory signifying a son's hatred of his father and erotic attachment to his mother. Derived from Oedipus' killing of his father and marriage to his mother (in Greek legend and in Sophocles' play, *Oedipus the King.*

oil-on-canvas A painting *medium* in which pigments are mixed with linseed oil and applied to canvas.

opera A drama which is set to music, including *arias,* duets, *choruses,* etc., sung to orchestral accompaniment.

oratorio Like an *opera,* a drama set to music, usually having a sacred text and rarely performed with staging or actors.

orchestra in Greek theater, the semicircular area of the focal point of the *amphitheater* in which the *chorus* danced and sang.

Ordinary In the *Mass,* texts which do not vary: Kyrie, Gloria, Credo, Sanctus, Benedictus, and Agnus Dei.

organum The earliest kind of *polyphonic* chant, which took the following forms: 1. parallel organum—two or more voices proceeding in the same direction with consistent *pitch* intervals; 2. free organum—two or more voices proceeding in different directions; 3. *melismatic* organum—two or more voices, with at least one singing syllabically; 4. discant style—two or more voices singing *syllabically* or *neumatically.*

overture A short orchestral composition used to introduce an *opera, oratorio,* or orchestral suite.

papyrus An Egyptian writing scroll prepared from the papyrus plant.

peasant-village culture A way of life in settled communities, based on domestication of plants and animals, typical of the Neolithic (New Stone) Age (c. 7000 BC).

pediment In classical architecture, a low-pitched gable above the *entablature* framed by raking *cornices* at the top and the horizontal cornice of the *entablature* at the bottom.

persona (Latin: mask) A character in a literary work who speaks for the author.

philosophes French intellectuals of the eighteenth century who sought to evaluate all things in the light of reason.

philosophical tale (novel) An episodic narrative that employs *satire* and *comedy* to defend or attack an idea, as in Voltaire's *Candide*.

phrase A short passage of music, usually from two to eight *measures*, with a clear beginning and ending.

pianissimo Soft (music).

pier A heavy masonry support, usually square.

pieta (Italian: pity) An image of Mary grieving over the dead body of Christ.

pigment Coloring matter. When mixed with such materials as oil, water, ink, or glaze, pigments furnish colors for paintings, prints, *mosaics*, etc.

pinnacle A small spire crowning the *pier* of a *flying buttress*.

pitch 1. The relative level—high or low—of a single tone; 2. The rise or fall of a melody.

pizzicato The playing of string instruments—usually those of the violin family—by plucking rather than bowing.

plainsong See *Gregorian chant*.

pointillism A painting method pioneered by the artist Georges Seurat involving the application of small dots of different colors. When seen from a distance the small dots mix optically to create new colors. See *broken color*.

polychromatic Of an artwork in two or more colors. Distinguished from *monochromatic*.

polyphony Two or more independent melody lines played or sung simultaneously.

Positivism The philosophy of Auguste Comte according to which human thinking has evolved through three stages: theological, metaphysical, and positivistic, the last characterized by scientific demonstration as opposed to dependence on authority (theological stage) or speculation (metaphysical stage).

post and lintel The most basic and ancient method of construction in which vertical members (*columns*, posts, *piers*, or solid walls) support horizontal members (beams or lintels).

predestination The doctrine, developed by Augustine and advocated by John Calvin, that God has foreordained by his grace the salvation of certain people (the elect); the rest of mankind being left to suffer eternal damnation for their sins.

program music Instrumental music that tells a story or describes a non-musical idea.

Proper In the *Mass*, texts that vary according to the religious calendar: Introit, Gradual, Alleluia, Tract, Offertory, Communion, and Ite, Missa Est.

Psalter The Book of Psalms of the Old Testament. A book containing the psalms arranged for devotional use.

purgatory In Roman Catholic theology, the state endured for a prescribed period by souls who have died in a state of grace, to atone for those sins for which they have not already paid their punishment on earth.

putto (pl putti) A plump young child, usually nude and winged, frequently represented in classical, Renaissance, and Baroque art.

radiating chapels Small chapels projecting from the *ambulatory*. See *basilican plan*.

realism In literature and art, the attempt to represent human life, especially that of the middle and lower classes, in a truthful and realistic manner. See *naturalism*.

recapitulation See *sonata form*.

recitative A declamatory type of singing used in *opera* and oratorio.

relief/in relief Raised. Of sculpture whose images or forms protrude from a flat background, varying from "high relief" to "low relief."

resolution A musical progression from a *dissonant* to a *consonant* sound.

responsorial singing A vocal practice in medieval churches in which priest and choir sang lines of a psalm or *antiphon* alternatively.

rhythm In music, an arrangement of beat patterns and their divisions, usually in *measures*.

rib In Romanesque or Gothic architecture, a slender, slightly projecting, reinforcement of a vault, typically at the groins of a *cross vault*. See *transverse arch*.

ribbed vault A *cross vault* reinforced with *ribs*.

ricercar A *contrapuntal* instrumental piece of the sixteenth and seventeenth centuries.

sarcophagus Among the Greeks, Romans, and Early Christians, a large stone coffin, usually decorated with *relief* sculptures.

satire Literature that ridicules evil and folly through the use of wit and humor.

satyr play A bawdy comedy written by the Greek playwright to accompany his *tragic trilogy*.

scale A step-wise progression of musical tones.

scholasticism A system of thought developed by medieval philosophers in which they attempted, through logic, to reconcile Christian theology and rational thought. It originated in the ninth and tenth centuries and culminated in the thirteenth with the philosophy of Thomas Aquinas.

Septuagint A Greek translation of the Hebrew Bible (Old Testament) that originated perhaps between 250 and 100 BC.

serialism A system developed in the twentieth century for ordering the twelve tones of a *chromatic* scale to create a musical composition. See *tone row*.

Servant Songs Four passages in the Book of Isaiah (42:1–4; 49:1–6; 50:4–11; 52:13–53:12) which speak of a servant of the Lord whose vicarious sufferings will be the means of redeeming mankind. See *Suffering Servant*.

sestet see *canzoniere*.

sfumato (Italian: smoke) A painting effect attributed to Leonardo and his followers in which atmospheric haze or mist is suggested by softening or blurring the outlines of the subjects. See *aerial perspective*.

side aisle A walkway on either side of, and running parallel to, the nave. In a Roman or Early Christian basilica it is separated from the *nave* by a *colonnade*; in a Romanesque or Gothic church it is separated by a heavy *arcade*. See *basilican plan*.

simoniac A person who practices simony, the buying and selling of church offices, pardons, and emoluments.

social contract Rousseau's theory that government exists because sovereign people enter into a mutual contract with their rulers by which they surrender a measure of their natural freedom but not their sovereignty. Also, the title of his landmark book on this topic.

sola Scriptura The Reformation principle that the Bible alone is the basis for authority in religion.

soliloquy A speech made by a dramatic character in isolation and intended to convey his or her inner reflections.

solmization The use of generic syllables for singing the *tones* of a *scale* as in *do, re, mi,* etc.

sonata A multi-movement composition for solo instrument with or without accompaniment.

sonata form A form of composition associated with the first movement of a Classical *symphony*, string quartet, or *sonata*, usually divided into three or four main sections: exposition: the introduction of the principal themes; development: the elaboration of the themes; recapitulation: the re-introduction of the themes; and coda: the concluding section.

sonnet A poem of fourteen lines with a fixed rhyme scheme of abba, abba, cde, cde, where the octave (first eight lines) states the problem, and the sestet (last six lines) provides the solution. An alternative (English) form divides the verse into three quatrains (four lines) and a couplet (two lines). See *canzoniere*.

sprechstimme (German: speaking voice) A twentieth-century vocal technique pioneered by Arnold Schoenberg that falls somewhere between speaking and singing.

sprezzatura An Italian Renaissance term for the ability of the *universal man* to display his manifold accomplishments with nonchalance.

staff A framework of horizontal lines used in notation to locate the *pitch* levels of notes.

stele A vertical stone slab, usually with carved decorations and inscriptions, used as a memorial or grave marker.

stream of consciousness A twentieth-century literary technique, typical of Modernism, in which the author traces the uneven flow of consciousness in a character.

strophic Of vocal music in which each stanza of a poem is sung to the same music.

Sturm und Drang (German: storm and stress) A term for the Romantic movement that occurred in Germany in the late eighteenth century.

stylobate The platform or floor of a Classical temple. A masonry base for the columns.

subject A musical theme or melody. The primary theme of a *fugue*.

Suffering Servant Servant of the Lord in the *Servant Songs* of Isaiah whose vicarious suffering will be the means of redeeming mankind. Often identified as either the nation of Israel or Jesus Christ.

suite A composition of several dance movements.

syllabic Having one note sung on each syllable; of word-related melodies.

symbol In broad terms, a form, image, or object used by artists or writers to represent another object or idea.

symbolism The self-conscious and heightened use of *symbols* in literature. French Symbolism: a nineteenth-century literary movement that sought to represent through a complex system of symbols the fleeting emotional experience of the poet in a given moment.

symphony A multi-movement orchestral composition.

syncopation In music, the alteration of rhythmic accents in order to strengthen usually weak beats or to weaken usually strong beats.

Synoptic Gospels The first three

Gospels of the New Testament (Matthew, Mark, Luke), designated synoptic (from Greek *synopsis* "a seeing together") because they present many of the same events in the life of Jesus and in much the same order.

synthesizer An instrument that produces electronic sounds. When connected with a digital computer, it can "remember" sequences of sounds.

Talmud An encyclopedic compilation of traditional rabbinical interpretations of the Jewish Scriptures (Old Testament). It is the foundation and source of authority for Judaism.

tempera A painting medium in which pigments are mixed with water and egg yolk.

tempo The rate of speed at which a musical composition is performed.

terraced dynamics Abrupt changes in dynamic level, as opposed to the use of *crescendos* and *decrescendos*. A characteristic of Baroque music.

text painting Music in which a close relationship exists between the sound of a musical passage and the meaning of a text.

texture In music, the number and interrelationship of individual voices or parts in a composition.

theme The major idea or perception developed in a literary, artistic, or musical work.

theodicy An attempt to justify God's ways as they relate to human beings, as in Leibnitz's *Theodicy*.

timbre The individual quality of a tone that distinguishes one particular sound from another.

tonality Music organized harmonically around a particular musical *key*.

tone A musical sound of constant *pitch*. A note.

tone cluster The simultaneous sounding of adjacent musical *pitches*.

tone row A melody based on a predetermined arrangement of the twelve tones of a *chromatic* scale. See *serialism*.

tonic The main note of a *key* or *scale*.

tragedy A drama that focuses on a series of causally connected incidents in the life of a protagonist, which leads to his or her catastrophic downfall. See *dithyramb*.

tragic trilogy In Greek tragedy, a set of three plays presented by the playwright to the Athenian audience at the *City Dionysia*.

transcendance (Latin: to go beyond) Belief in a realm of existence beyond the world that is perceptible to the physical senses.

transept The wing of a *basilican-plan* church that runs perpendicular to the *nave*.

transubstantiation The Catholic doctrine stating that in the celebration of the *Mass* the bread and wine are in substance actually transformed into the body and blood of Christ.

transverse arch In Romanesque architecture, a *rib* attached to a *barrel-vaulted* ceiling. Often, an extension of an attached *colonnette*.

triad A three-note chord based on intervals of a third and a fifth above the lowest note.

triforium In a Gothic cathedral, the small *gallery* between the *arcade* and the *clerestory*. A low passageway occupying the narrow space between the *vaults* of the *side aisle* and the roof.

triglyph Rectangular panels that alternate with *metopes* on a *Doric order frieze*.

Tuscan order A classical order attributed to the Romans.

twelve-tone music Music using all twelve tones of the *chromatic* scale. See *serialism, tone row*.

tympanum In classical architecture, the recessed face of a *pediment*, often decorated with sculpture. In Romanesque or Gothic architecture, the arch-shaped space over a doorway, often filled with *relief* sculptures.

tyrants (Greek: *tyrannoi*) Greek rulers of the seventh and sixth centuries BC who came to power by unconstitutional means and ruled without legal controls.

unities Three principles of dramatic structure, derived from Aristotle's *Poetics*, which stipulate that a drama should have a single plot (unity of action), a single location (unity of place), and a timespan of a single day (unity of time).

universal man An Italian Renaissance term for a person who is highly skilled in all the arts and sciences; the ideal courtier of Castiglione's *The Courtier*. See *sprezzatura*.

Utilitarianism The philosophy of John Stuart Mill, which proclaimed the ethical theory that one should always act so as to promote "the greatest good (happiness) for the greatest number."

vanishing point In *linear perspective* the point on the horizon where parallel lines appear to meet and vanish from sight.

variation A restatement of a musical theme with changes.

vault A masonry ceiling or roof in the shape of an arch, of stone, brick, or concrete. The shape of a vault could be semicircular or pointed. The plan of the vault could be oblong, square, or round. See *arch, barrel vault, cross vault, dome, ribbed vault*.

vernacular languages Regional dialects that supplanted Latin as the spoken language of the Middle Ages and eventually developed into the modern European languages.

voice A melodic line. A part in a vocal or instrumental composition.

volute A spiral, scroll-shaped decoration, found paired on an *Ionic capital.*

Vulgate Latin translation of the Bible by Jerome (AD 370–420); the official Roman Catholic Bible.

watercolor A painting medium in which pigments are mixed with water and applied to white paper.

Weltschmerz (German: world-sickness) The melancholy associated especially with the Romantic personality. See *mal du siècle.*

Weltseele Schelling's universal world soul shared by human beings and nature, a concept typical of the Romantic view of nature.

whole-tone scale A musical *scale* consisting of six whole-step intervals.

woodcut A print made from a image carved into the side of a wood block cut along the grain.

ziggurat In Mesopotamia, a large terraced pyramid, often capped with a temple.

NOTES

Chapter 1

1 Revised Standard Version. All biblical quotations in this book are from this translation.
2 James C. F. Hastings, ed. *A Dictionary of the Bible.* New York: Charles Scribner & Sons, 1906, Vol. II, pp. 668–69.

Chapter 2

1 Alfred Sendry, *Music in the Social and Religious Life of Antiquity.* Rutherford, Madison and Teaneck: Fairleigh Dickinson University Press, 1974, p. 292.
2 *Aeschylus I: Oresteia.* trans. by Richmond Lattimore. Chicago: The University of Chicago Press, 1953, p. 40, ll. 176–78.
3 Aeschylus, *op. cit.,* ll. 1485–88.
4. H. D. F. Kitto, *Greek Tragedy.* Third edition. London: Methuen & Co. Ltd, 1970, p. 138. This interpretation of Oedipus is derived from Kitto.
5 Donald J. Grout, *A History of Western Music.* Third edition. New York: W. W. Norton & Co., Inc., 1980, p. 30.
6 Oliver Strunk, *Source Readings in Music History.* New York: W. W. Norton & Co., Inc., 1950, pp. 5ff.
7 Isobel Henderson, "Ancient Greek Music," in Wellesz, Egon, ed., *The New Oxford History of Music,* Vol. I. London: Oxford University Press, 1957, p. 395.

Chapter 3

1 Vasari, quoted in Leonardo Benevolo, *The Architecture of the Renaissance,* Vol. II. Boulder, Colorado: Westview Press, 1978, p. 41.
2 Donald M. Frame, trans. and ed. *Montaigne: Selections from the Essays.* Northbrook, Illinois: AHM Publishing Corporation, 1973, p. 3.
3 Arnold, quoted in A. M. Eastmen, and G. B. Harrison, eds. *Shakespeare's Critics: From Jonson to Auden: A Medley of Judgments* Ann Arbor: The University of Michigan Press, 1964, pp. 175–76.
4 Donald J. Grout, *A History of Western Music.* Third edition. New York: W. W. Norton & Co., Inc., 1980, p. 247.

Chapter 4

1 Alexander Pope, *Essay on Man, Epistle II,* ll. 3–18, taken from John L. Mahoney, ed. *The Enlightenment and English Literature: Prose and Poetry of the Eighteenth Century,* DC Heath and Company, Lexington, Massachusetts, 1980, p. 64.
2 Pope, *op. cit., Epistle II,* ll. 289–294.
3 *St. Augustine: Confessions,* trans. by R. S. Pine-Coffin. Baltimore: Penguin Books, 1961, p. 21.
4 Edward J. Dent, *Mozart's Operas: A Critical Study.* Second edition. London: Open University Press, 1947, p. 186.

Chapter 5

1 Jean-Jacques Rousseau, *The Confessions,* trans. by J. M. Cohen. Baltimore: Penguin Books, 1967, p. 17.
2 Johann Wolfgang von Goethe, *Faust, Part I with Part II, Act V,* trans. by Bayard Quincy Morgan. Indianapolis and New York: The Bobbs-Merrill Company, Inc., 1957, p. 10. Subsequent quotations from the prologue of *Faust* are from this edition (pp. 9–11).
3 Goethe, *op. cit.,* p. 40.
4 Goethe, *op. cit.,* p. 13.
5 Goethe, *op. cit.,* pp. 131, 139.
6 Michael Levey, *Rococo to Revolution: Major Trends in Eighteenth-Century Painting.* New York: Frederick Praeger, 1966, p. 63.
7 Quoted in Hugh Honour, *Romanticism,* London: Penguin Books Ltd, 1979, p. 46.
8 Honour, *op. cit.,* p. 31.
9 Philip Wayne, ed. *Wordsworth's Poems,* Volume 1. London: J. M. Dent & Sons, Ltd., 1907, p. 133.
10 Alfred Einstein. *Mozart: His Character, His Work.* London: Oxford University Press, 1945, p. 50.
11 Quoted in Will and Ariel Durant, "The Age of Napoleon," from *The Story of Civilization, Part XI.* New York: Simon and Schuster, 1975, p. 573.
12 Quoted in Denis Arnold and Nigel Fortune, *The Beethoven Reader.* New York: W. W. Norton and Co., Inc., 1971, p. 300.
13 Gerald Abraham, ed. *Schumann: A Symposium.* Westport,

Connecticut: Greenwood Press, 1977, p. 106.

14 Quoted in Ronald Taylor, *Richard Wagner: His Life, Art, and Thought*. London: Paul Elek, 1979, p. 265.

Chapter 6

1 *St. Augustine: Confessions*, trans. by R. S. Pine-Coffin. Baltimore: Penguin Books, 1961, p. 178.

2 Calvin S. Brown, ed. *The Reader's Companion to World Literature*. Holt, Rinehart & Winston, Inc., 1956, p. 106.

3 F. L. Cross, ed. *The Oxford Dictionary of the Christian Church*. London: Oxford University Press, 1957, p. 107.

4 John Beckwith, *Early Christian and Byzantine Art*. Harmondsworth, Middlesex: Penguin Books Ltd, 1970, p. 46.

5 Erik Routley, *The Church and Music*. London: Gerald Duckworth & Co., 1950, p. 234.

6 Alfred Sendrey, *Music in Ancient Israel*. New York: Philosophical Library, 1969, p. 196.

7 Donald J. Grout, *A History of Ancient Music*. Third edition. New York: W. W. Norton & Co., Inc., 1980, p. 36.

Chapter 7

1 Frederick Goldin, trans. *The Song of Roland*. New York: W. W. Norton & Co., Inc., 1978, p. 7 (pp. 3–28 for complete discussion).

2 Charles T. Wood, *The Quest for Eternity: Medieval Manners and Morals*. Garden City, New York: Anchor Books, Doubleday & Co., Inc., 1971, p. 141.

3 Robert Steele, trans., *The Little Flowers of St. Francis*. New York: E. P. Dutton & Co., Inc., 1951, pp. 387–89.

4 Henri Focillon, *The Art of the West: Vol II: Gothic Art*, trans. by Donald King. London: Phaidon Press Ltd, 1963.

5 Giorgio Vasari, *Lives of the Artists*, trans. by Betty Burroughs. New York: Simon and Schuster, 1946.

6 Dante quoted in Millard, Meiss, *Painting in Florence and Siena after the Black Death*. New York: Harper & Row, Inc., 1951.

7 Richard H. Hoppin, *Medieval Music*, New York: W. W. Norton & Co., Inc., 1978, p. 60.

8 Jacob of Liege quoted in D. Hughes and G. Abraham, (eds). *Oxford History of Music*: Volume III, *Ars Nova and the Renaissance 1300–1540*, London: Oxford University Press.

Chapter 8

1 Harold J. Grimm, *The Reformation Era: 1500–1650*. Second edition. New York: Macmillan Co., 1973, p. 75.

2 From a lecture by Professor Rudolf Gottfried, Indiana University, March 6, 1961.

3 Desiderius Erasmus, *The Praise of Folly*, trans. by Leonard F. Dean. New York: Hendricks House, 1959, p. 71.

4 Erasmus, *op. cit.*, pp. 111–13.

5 Erasmus, *op. cit.*, p. 125.

6 Quoted in Roland H. Bainton, *Here I Stand: A Life of Martin Luther*, New York: Abingdon Press, 1950, p. 230–1.

7 Bainton, *op. cit.*, p. 326.

8 John T. McNeill, ed. *On the Christian Faith: Selections from the Institutes, Commentaries, and Tracts: John Calvin*. Indianapolis: Bobbs-Merrill Co., Inc., 1957, p. vii.

9 McNeill, *op. cit.*, p. xii.

10 McNeill, *op. cit.*, p. xxvi.

11 Grimm, *op. cit.*, p. 310.

12 Otto Benesch, *The Art of the Renaissance in Northern Europe: Its Relation to the Contemporary Spiritual and Intellectual Movements*. Greenwich, Conn.: Phaidon Publishers Inc., 1965, p. 75.

13 Quoted in Will Durant, "The Reformation," from *The Story of Civilization, Part VI*, New York, Simon & Schuster, 1957, p. 902.

14 Friedrich Blume, *Protestant Church Music: A History*. New York: W. W. Norton and Co., Inc., 1974, p. 10.

15 Jaroslav Pelikan, *Jesus Through the Centuries: His Place in the History of Culture*. New Haven, Conn.: Yale University Press, 1985, pp. 7–8.

Chapter 9

1 Martin Turnell, "Madame Bovary," in *Flaubert: A Collection of Critical Essays*, ed. Raymond Giraud. Englewood Cliffs, New Jersey: Prentice-Hall, Inc., p. 98.

2 Fyodor Dostoyevsky, *Crime and Punishment*, trans. by David Magarshack. Baltimore: Penguin Books Inc., 1967, p. 84.

3 Dostoyevsky, *op. cit.*, pp. 558–59.

4 Dostoyevsky, *op. cit.*, pp. 433–34.

5 Leo Tolstoy, *Great Short Works*, trans. by Louise and Aylmer Maude. New York: Harper & Row, Inc., 167, p. 255. Hereafter page numbers from Tolstoy's story will be cited from this edition parenthetically within the text. Substantially, this discussion of *Ivan Ilych* appeared originally in *The University of Dayton Review*, Spring 1981, Vol. 15, No. 1, pp. 99–106.

6 Arnold Hauser, *The Social History of Art. Vol. II*. New York: Alfred A. Knopf, 1961, p. 775.

Chapter 10

1 Irvin Howe, ed. *Literary Modernism*. Greenwich, Conn.: Fawcett Publications, Inc., 1967, pp. 21–22.

2 Howe, *op. cit.*, p. 36.

3 Leo Hamalian and Edmund L. Volpe, eds. *Eleven Modern Short Novels*. Second edition. New York: G. P. Putnam & Sons, 1970, p. 69.

4 Hamalian and Volpe, *op. cit.*, p. 97.

5 Hamalian and Volpe, *op. cit.*, p. 220.

6 Hamalian and Volpe, *op. cit.*, p. 243.

7 Henry C. Hatfield, "Thomas Mann's *Mario und der Zauberer*: An Interpretation," *Germanic Review*, 21, 1946, p. 306. This discussion is indebted to Hatfield at several points.

8 Hamalian and Volpe, *op. cit.*, p. 433–34.

9 Hamalian and Volpe, *op. cit.*, p. 432.

10 Hamalian and Volpe, *op. cit.*, p. 448.

11 Hatfield, *op. cit.*, p. 312.

12 Geoffrey Grigson, ed. *The Concise Encyclopedia of Modern World Literature*. New York: Hawthorn Books, Inc., 1963, p. 131.

13 Werner Haftmann, *Painting in the Twentieth Century*. Vol. I, *An Analysis of the Artists and Their Work*. New York: Praeger Publishers, 1965, p. 34.

14 Haftmann, *op. cit.*, p. 32.

15 Bruce Bernard, ed. *Vincent by Himself: A Selection of Van Gogh's Paintings and Drawings together with Extracts from his Letters*. New York: Little, Brown and Co., Inc., 1985, p. 65.

16 Bernard, *op. cit.*, p. 203.

17 John Canaday, *Mainstreams of Modern Art*. Second edition. New York: Holt, Rinehart and Winston, 1981, p. 387.

18 Alfred Barr, *Picasso: Fifty Years of His Art*. New York: The Museum of Modern Art, 1946, p. 80.

19 Donald J. Grout, *A History of Western Music*. Third edition. New York: W. W. Norton & Co., Inc., 1980, p. 691.

Chapter 11

1 John Cruickshank, *Albert Camus and the Literature of Revolt*. New York: Oxford University Press, 1960, p. x.

2 Irving Howe, ed., *Literary Modernism*, Greenwich, Connecticut: Fawcett Publications, Inc., 1967, p. 36–39.

3 Albert Camus, *The Stranger*, trans. by Stuart Gilbert. New York: Random House, Vintage Books, 1946, pp. 151–52.

4 Camus, *op. cit.*, p. 154.

5 Geoffrey Grigson, ed., *The Concise Encyclopedia of Modern World Literature*. New York: Hawthorn Books, Inc., 1963, p. 47.

6 Samuel Beckett, *Waiting for Godot: Tragicomedy in 2 Acts, New York: Grove Press, Inc., 1954, p. 51.*

7 Fred E. Luchs, "Waiting for Godot," *Christianity Today*, June 6, 1960, p. 8.

8 Foreword to Fine, S. Ellen, *Legacy of Night: The Literary Universe of Elie Wiesel*. Albany: State University of New York Press, 1982, p. xi.

9 Quoted in *Time*, March 18, 1985, p. 79.

10 See Mauriac's account of this interview in his Foreword to Elie Wiesel's autobiographical novel *Night*, trans. by Stella Rodway. New York: Bantam Books, 1982.

11 Fine, *op. cit.*, p. 7.

12 Alvin H. Rosenfeld, and Irving Greenberg, eds. "Why I Write" in *Confronting the Holocaust*. Bloomington: Indiana University Press, 1978, p. 205.

13 Wiesel, *op. cit.*, p. 32.

14 Fine, *op. cit.*, pp. 13–14, 8–9.

15 Wiesel, *op. cit.*, p. 55–56.

16 Wiesel, *op. cit.*, p. 79.

17 Fine, *op. cit.*, p. 15.

18 Alexander Solzhenitsyn, *One Day in the Life of Ivan Denisovich*, trans. by Ralph Parker, New York: E. P. Dutton & Co., Inc. 1963, p. 5.

19 Solzhenitsyn, *op. cit.*, p. 159.

20 Quoted in Irving Sandler, *The Triumph of America: A History of Abstract Expressionism*. New York: Praeger Publishers, 1970, p. 98.

21 Quoted in Jack Hobbs, *Art in Context*, Third edition. San Diego: Harcourt Brace Jovanovich, 1986, p. 201.

22 Sam Hunter and John Jacobus, *American Art of the Twentieth Century*. New York: Harry N. Abrams, Inc., 1973, p. 454.

23 Joan Peyser, *The New Music: The Sense Behind the Sound*. New York: Dell Publishing Co., Inc., 1972, p. 150.

24 Peyser, *op. cit.*, p. 176.

25 David H. Cope, *New Directions in Music*. Fourth edition. Dubuque, Iowa, Wm. C. Brown Publishers, 1984, p. 268.

26 Cope, *op. cit.*, p. 269.

27 Richard Kostelanetz, *John Cage*. New York: Praeger Publishers, 1970, p. 19.

28 John Cage, *Silence*. Cambridge, Mass.: The M.I.T. Press, 1961, p. 8.

Chapter 12

1 Daniel Bell, *The Cultural Contradictions of Capitalism*. New York: Basic Books, Inc., 1976.

2 Bell, *op. cit.*, p. 51.

3 Bell, *op. cit.*, p. 51.

4 Anders Stephenson, "Interview with Frederic Jameson" in *Flash Art* No. 131, December 1986/January 1987, pp. 69–73.

5 Ihab Hassan, *The Dismemberment of Orpheus: Toward a Postmodern Literature*. Second edition. Madison, Wisc.: The University of Wisconsin Press, 1982, p. 260.

6 Quoted by Philip Stevick, in "Literature," in Stanley Trachtenberg, ed. *The Postmodern Moment: A Handbook of Contemporary Innovation in the Arts*. Westport Connecticut: Greenwood Press, 1985, p. 141. This discussion of Postmodernism in literature is greatly indebted to Stevick's chapter.

7 *Trachtenberg*, p. 141.

8 John O. Stark, *The Literature of Exhaustion: Borges, Nabokov, and Barth*. N. C. Durham: Duke University Press, 1974, p. 133.

9 Trachtenberg, *op. cit.*, p. 142.

10 Trachtenberg, *op. cit.*, p. 143.

11 Trachtenberg, *op. cit.*, p. 146.

12 Trachtenberg, *op. cit.*, p. 147.

13 John Gardner, *On Moral Fiction*. New York: Basic Books, Inc., 1978, pp. 55–56.

14 Mary McLeod, "Architecture," in Trachtenberg, *op. cit.*, p. 24.

15 Charles A. Jencks, *The Language of Post-Modern Architecture*. New York: Rizzoli International Publications, 1977, p. 60.

16 Garry E. Clarke, "Music" in Trachtenberg, *op. cit.*, p. 157–76.

17 Jonathan Cott, "Steven Reich in Conversation with Jonathan Cott," (New York, 1985) from album cover of *The Desert Music* by Reich. Nonesuch Digital Recordings E1–79101.

FURTHER READING

Chapter 1

LITERATURE

Old Testament

Ackroyd, P. R. and C. F. Evans, eds. *The Cambridge History of the Bible. Volume I: From the Beginnings to Jerome*. Cambridge: Cambridge University Press, 1975.

Barker, Kenneth, ed. *The NIV Study Bible: New International Version*. Grand Rapids, Michigan: Zondervan, 1985.

Black, Matthew and Harold H. Rowley, eds. *Peake's Commentary on the Bible*. London: Thomas Nelson and Sons, Ltd, 1962.

Bright, John, *A History of Israel*. Third edition. Philadelphia: The Westminster Press, 1981.

Brown, Raymond, Joseph A. Fitzmyer and Roland E. Murphy, *The Jerome Biblical Commentary*. Englewood Cliffs, New Jersey: Prentice-Hall, Inc., 1968.

Buttrick, George A., ed. *The Interpreter's Bible*, 12 vols. New York and Nashville: Abingdon Cokesbury Press, 1952.

Buttrick, George A., ed. *The Interpreter's Dictionary of the Bible: An Illustrated Encyclopedia* 4 vols. New York and Nashville: Abingdon Press, 1962. *Supplementary Volume*, ed. Keith Crim. Nashville: Abingdon Press, 1976.

Eissfeldt, Otto, *The Old Testament: An Introduction*, 1934, trans. by Peter R. Ackroyd. Oxford: Basil Blackwell, 1965.

Guthrie, D. and J. A. Motyer, eds. *The New Bible Commentary: Revised*. Third edition. Grand Rapids, Michigan: Wm. B. Eerdmans Publishing Company, 1970.

LaSor, William Sanford, David Allen Hubbard and William Frederic Bush, *Old Testament Survey: The Message, Form, and Background of the Old Testament*. Grand Rapids, Michigan: William B. Eerdmans Publishing Company, 1982.

May, Herbert G., and Bruce M. Metzger, *The New Oxford Annotated Bible*. New York: Oxford University Press, 1977.

ART

Groenewegen, Frankfort, and Bernard Ashmole, *Art of the Ancient World.* New York: Abrams, 1971.

Harris, James Renel, *Egyptian Art.* London: Spring Books, 1966.

Maringer, Johannes, and Hans Bandi, *Ice Age Art, Spanish Levant Art. Arctic Art.* New York: Praeger, 1953.

Michalowski, Kazimlerz, *The Art of Ancient Egypt.* New York: Harry N. Abrams, 1969.

Woldering, Irmgard, *The Art of Egypt: The Time of the Pharaohs*, trans. by Ann E. Keep. New York: Crown Publishers, Inc., 1963.

MUSIC

Goldron, Romain, *Ancient and Oriental Music.* New York: H. S. Stuttman and Co. Inc., 1968.

Sachs, Curt, *The Rise of Music in the Ancient World: East and West.* New York: W. W. Norton and Co., Inc., 1943.

Chapter 2

LITERATURE

Baldry, H. C., *Ancient Greek Literature in Its Living Context.* New York: McGraw-Hill Book Company, 1968.

Ferguson, John, *A Companion to Greek Tragedy.* Austin and London: University of Texas Press, 1972.

Kitto, H. D. F., *Greek Tragedy.* Third edition. London: Methuen and Co., Ltd., 1970.

Kitto, H. D. F., *The Greeks.* Harmondsworth, Middlesex: Penguin Books Ltd., 1951.

Homer

Camps, W. A., *An Introduction to Homer.* Oxford: Clarendon Press, 1980.

Clark, Howard, *Homer's Readers.* Newark: University of Delaware Press, 1981.

Finley, M. I., *The World Of Odysseus.* Revised edition. New York: Viking Press, 1978.

Griffin, J., *Homer.* Oxford: Oxford University Press, 1980.

Steiner, George, and Robert Fagles, eds. *Homer: A Collection of Critical Essays.* Englewood Cliffs, New Jersey: Prentice-Hall, Inc., 1962.

Aeschylus

Kitto, H. D. F., *Form and Meaning in Drama.* New York: Barnes & Noble, 1960 (1956).

Hogan, James C., *A Commentary on the Complete Greek Tragedies: Aeschylus.* Chicago: University of Chicago Press, 1984.

McCall, Marsh H., ed. *Aeschylus: A Collection of Critical Essays.* Englewood Cliffs, New Jersey. Prentice-Hall, Inc., 1972.

Murray, Gilbert, *Aeschylus: The Creator of Tragedy.* Oxford: The Clarendon Press, 1940.

Sophocles

Kitto, H. D. F., *Sophocles: Dramatist and Philosopher.* London: Oxford University Press, 1958, 1981.

Knox, Bernard M. W., *The Heroic Temper: Studies in Sophoclean Tragedy.* Berkeley: University of California Press, 1964.

Whitman, C. H., *Sophocles: A Study of Heroic Humanism.* Cambridge: Harvard University Press, 1951.

Woodward, Thomas Marion, *Sophocles: A Collection of Critical Essays.* Englewood Cliffs, New Jersey: Prentice-Hall, Inc., 1966.

Euripides

Murray, Gilbert, *Euripides and His Age.* London & New York: Oxford University Press, 1965.

Segal, Erich, ed. *Euripides: A Collection of Critical Essays.* Englewood Cliffs, New Jersey. Prentice-Hall, Inc., 1968.

Webster, T. B. L., *The Tragedies of Euripides.* New York: Barnes & Noble, 1968.

Virgil

Commager, Steele, ed. *Virgil: A Collection of Critical Essays.* Englewood Cliffs, New Jersey: Prentice-Hall, Inc., 1966.

Jackson Knight, W. F., *Roman Vergil.* London: Faber and Faber, 1966 (1944).

Rand, E. K., *The Magical Art of Virgil.* Cambridge, Mass.: Harvard University Press, 1931.

ART

Ashmole, Bernard, *Architect and Sculptor in Classical Greece.* London & New York: Phaidon Press Ltd, 1972.

Bruno, Vincent J., ed. *The Parthenon.* New York: W. W. Norton & Co., Inc., 1974.

Carpenter, Rhys, *The Esthetic Basis of Greek Art.* Bloomington, Indiana: Indiana University Press, 1959.

Cook, Robert, *Greek Art: Its Development, Character and Influence.* Harmondsworth: Penguin Books Ltd, 1976.

Lullies, Reinhard, *Greek Sculpture.* New York: Harry N. Abrams, Inc., 1960.

Richter, Gisela M. A., *Ancient Italy: A Study of the Interrelations of Its Peoples as Shown in Their Arts.* Ann Arbor, Michigan: University of Michigan Press, 1955.

Richter, Gisela M. A., *A Handbook of Greek Art.* Seventh edition. London & New York: Phaidon Press Ltd, 1974.

Sear, Frank, *Roman Architecture.* London: B. T. Batsford Ltd, 1982.

MUSIC

Crossley-Holland, Peter, "Non-western Music" in Robertson and Stevens, ed., *The Pelican History of Music*, Vol. I. Baltimore: Penguin Books Ltd, 1960.

Grout, Donald J., *A History of Western Music.* Third edition. New York: W. W. Norton & Co., Inc., 1980.

Henderson, Isobel, "Ancient Greek Music" in Wellesz, Egon, ed., *The New Oxford History of Music*, Vol. I. London: Oxford University Press, 1957.

Sachs, Curt, *The Rise of Music in the Ancient World: East and West.* New York: W. W. Norton & Co., Inc., 1943.

Scott, The Reverend J. E., "Roman Music" in Wellesz, Egon, ed., *The New Oxford History of Music*, Vol. I. London: Oxford University Press, 1957.

Sendry, Alfred, *Music in the Social and Religious Life of Antiquity.* Rutherford, Madison, and Teaneck: Fairleigh Dickinson University Press, 1974.

Strunk, Oliver, *Source Readings in Music History.* New York: W. W. Norton & Co., Inc., 1950.

Chapter 3

LITERATURE

Kristeller, Peter Oskar, *Renaissance Thought: The Classic, Scholastic, and Humanist Strains.* New York: Harper & Row, Inc., 1961.

Petrarch

Bergin, Thomas G., *Petrarch.* New York: Twayne Publishers, 1970.

Bishop, Morris, *Petrarch and His World.* Bloomington: Indiana University Press, 1963.

Wilkins, Ernest Hatch, *The Life of Petrarch.* Chicago: University of Chicago Press, 1961.

Boccaccio

Bergin, Thomas G., *Boccaccio.* New York: Viking Press, 1981.

Osgood, Charles G., *Boccaccio on Poetry.* Princeton: Princeton University Press, 1930.

Scaglione, A. D., *Nature and Love in the Middle Ages*. Berkeley: University of California Press, 1963.

Machiavelli

Gilbert, Allen H., *Machiavelli's "Prince" and Its Forerunners*. New York: Barnes & Noble, 1968 (1938).

Hale, J. R., *Machiavelli and Renaissance Italy*. New York: Macmillan, Inc., 1960.

Skinner, Quentin, *Machiavelli*. New York: Hill and Wang, 1981.

Castiglione

Hanning, Robert W. and David Rosand, eds. *Castiglione: The Ideal and the Real in Renaissance Culture*. New Haven: Yale University Press, 1983.

Montaigne

Frame, Donald M., *Montaigne: A Biography*. New York: Harcourt, Brace & World, Inc., 1965.

Frame, Donald M., *Montaigne's Essais: A Study*. Englewood Cliffs, New Jersey: Prentice-Hall, Inc., 1969.

McGowan, Margaret M., *Montaigne's Deceits: The Art of Persuasion in the "Essais."* London: University of London Press, 1974.

Shakespeare

Bradley, A. C., *Shakespearean Tragedy*. Second edition. New York: St. Martin's Press, 1956, reprint of 1905 edition.

Burgess, Anthony, *Shakespeare*. Baltimore: Penguin Books Ltd, 1972 (1970).

Dean, Leonard F., ed. *Shakespeare: Modern Essays in Criticism*. Revised edition. New York: Oxford University Press, 1967.

ART

Benevolo, Leonardo, *The Architecture of the Renaissance* Vol. I. Boulder, Colorado: Westview Press, 1978.

Berenson, Bernard, *The Italian Painters of the Renaissance*. London: Phaidon Press Ltd, 1952.

Da Vinci, Leonardo, *The Art of Painting*. New York: Philosophical Library Incorporation, 1957.

DeWald, Ernest, *Italian Painting*. New York: Holt Rinehart & Winston, Inc., 1961.

Gombrich, E. H., *Norm and Form: Studies in the Art of the Renaissance*. London: Phaidon Press Ltd, 1966.

Gombrich, E. H., *Symbolic Images: Studies in the Art of the Renaissance*. London: Phaidon Press Ltd, 1972.

Hartt, Frederick, *History of Italian Renaissance Art: Painting, Sculpture and Architecture*. New York: Harry N. Abrams, Inc., 1970.

Pater, Walter, *The Renaissance: Studies in Art and Poetry*. London: Macmillan and Co., 1912.

Pope-Hennessy, John, *Italian Renaissance Sculpture*. London: Phaidon Press Ltd, 1971.

Seymour, Charles, Jr., *Sculpture in Italy: 1400 to 1500*. Baltimore: Penguin Books Ltd, 1968.

Valentiner, W. R., *Studies of Italian Renaissance Sculpture*. London: Phaidon Press Ltd, 1950.

Vasari, Giorgio, *Lives of the Artists*, trans. by Betty Burroughs. New York: Simon and Schuster, 1946.

Wittkower, Rudolph, *Architectural Principles in the Age of Humanism*. New York: Random House, 1962.

Wolfflin, Heinrich, *Classic Art: An Introduction to the Italian Renaissance*. Second edition. London: Phaidon Press, 1953.

MUSIC

Blume, Friedrich, *Renaissance and Baroque Music: A Comprehensive Survey*, trans. by M. D. H. Norton. New York: W. W. Norton and Co., Inc.

Bridgman, Nanie, "The Age of Ockeghem and Josquin" in *Ars Nova and the Renaissance: 1300–1540*. London: OUP, 1960.

Grout, Donald J., *A History of Western Music*. Third edition. New York: W. W. Norton and Co., Inc., 1980.

Hayes, Gerald, "Musical Instruments" in *Ars Nova* (see Bridgman above).

Helm, Everett, "Secular Vocal Music in Italy (1400–1530)" in *Ars Nova* (see Bridgman above).

Pattison, Bruce, *Music and Poetry of the English Renaissance*. New York: Da Capo Press, 1971.

Rokseth, Yvonne, "The Instrumental Music of the Middle Ages and Early Sixteenth Century" in *Ars Nova* (see Bridgman above).

Vandenborren, Charles, "Dufay and his School" in *Ars Nova and the Renaissance: 1300–1540*. London: OUP, 1960.

Chapter 4

LITERATURE

Turnell, Martin, *The Classical Movement*. Norfolk, Conn.: J. Laughlin, 1963 (1948).

Moliere

Gossman, Lionel, *Men and Masks: A Study of Moliere*. Baltimore: Johns Hopkins University Press, 1963.

Hubert, J. D., *Moliere and the Comedy of Intellect*. Berkeley: University of California Press, 1962.

Lewis, D. B. Wyndham, *Moliere: The Comic Mask*. London: Eyre & Spottiswoode Ltd, 1959.

Mander, Gertrud, *Moliere*, trans. by Diana Stone Peters. New York: Ungar Publishing Co., 1973.

Racine

Breton, Geoffrey, *Jean Racine: A Critical Biography*. New York: Barnes & Noble, 1973.

Weinberg, Bernard, *The Art of Jean Racine*. Chicago: University of Chicago Press, 1963.

Swift

Eddy, William A., *"Gulliver's Travels": A Critical Study*. New York: Russell & Russell, 1923, rpt. 1963.

Ehrenpreis, I., *The Personality of Jonathan Swift*. London: Methuen & Co. Ltd, 1958.

Monk, Samuel, "The Pride of Lemuel Gulliver," *The Sewanee Review*, 63 (1955), 48–71.

Rowse, A. L., *Jonathan Swift: Major Prophet*. London: Thames and Hudson Ltd, 1975.

Voltaire

Aldridge, Owen, *Voltaire and the Century of Light*. Princeton, New Jersey: Princeton University Press, 1975.

Besterman, T., *Voltaire*. Third edition. Oxford: Blackwell, 1976.

Foster, Milton P., *Voltaire's "Candide" and the Critics*. Bellmont, California: Wadsworth Publishing Company, Inc., 1962.

Mason, Haydn, *Voltaire: A Biography*. Baltimore, Md.: Johns Hopkins University Press, 1981.

Wade, Ira O., *Voltaire and "Candide"; A Study in the Fusion of History, Art, and Philosophy*. Princeton: Princeton University Press, 1959.

ART

Honour, Hugh, *Neo-Classicism*. Harmondsworth, England: Penguin Books Ltd, 1968.

Levey, Michael, *Rococo to Revolution: Major Trends in Eighteenth-Century Painting*. New York: Frederick Praeger, 1966.

MUSIC

Davison, Archibald, T., *Bach and Handel: The Consummation of the Baroque in Music*. Harvard University Press, 1951.

Dent, Edward J., *Mozart's Operas: A Critical Study*. Second edition. London: Oxford University Press, 1947.

Einstein, Alfred, *Mozart: His Character, His Work.* London: Oxford University Press, 1945.

Kamien, Roger, *Music: An Appreciation.* New York: McGraw-Hill, Inc., 1976.

Landon, H. C. Robbins, *Haydn: A Documentary Study.* London: Thames and Hudson, 1981.

Landon, H. C. Robbins, *Handel and His World.* Boston: Little, Brown and Co., 1984.

Lang, Paul Henry, *George Frederic Handel.* New York: W. W. Norton and Co., Inc., 1966.

Mellers, Wilfrid, *Bach and the Dance of God.* London: Faber and Faber, 1980.

Pauley, Reinhard G., *Music in the Classic Period.* Englewood Cliffs, New Jersey: Prentice-Hall, Inc., 1965.

Politoske, Daniel T., *Music.* Fourth edition. Englewood Cliffs, New Jersey: Prentice-Hall, Inc., 1987.

Sadie, Stanley, *Handel.* London: Faber and Faber, 1968.

Young, Percy M., *The Bachs 1500–1850.* Thomas Y. Cromwell, 1970.

Chapter 5

LITERATURE

Rousseau

Dobinson C. H., *Jean-Jacques Rousseau: His Thought and Its Relevance Today.* London: Methuen & Co. Ltd., 1969.

Green, F. C., *Jean-Jacques Rousseau: A Critical Study of His Life and Writings.* Cambridge, England: Cambridge University Press, 1955.

Winwar, Frances, *Jean-Jacques Rousseau: Conscience of an Era.* New York: Random House, Inc., 1961.

Goethe

Dieckmann, Liselotte, *Goethe's Faust: A Critical Reading.* Englewood Cliffs, New Jersey: Prentice-Hall, Inc. 1972.

Gray, Ronald, *Goethe: A Critical Introduction.* London: Cambridge University Press, 1967.

Haile, H. G., *Invitation to Goethe's "Faust."* University of Alabama Press, 1978.

Hatfield, H., *Goethe: A Critical Introduction.* Cambridge, Mass.: Harvard University Press, 1964.

Lange, V., ed., *Goethe: A Colllection of Critical Essays.* Englewood Cliffs, New Jersey: Prentice-Hall, Inc., 1960.

Wordsworth

Darbishire, Helen, *The Poet Wordsworth.* Oxford: Clarendon Press, 1950.

Harper, G. M., *William Wordsworth: His Life, Works, and Influence.* London: John Murray Ltd, 1916.

Hartman, Geoffrey H., *Wordsworth's Poetry.* New Haven: Yale University Press, 1964.

Woodring, Carl, *Wordsworth.* Boston: Houghton Mifflin Company, 1965.

ART

Clark, Kenneth, *The Romantic Rebellion.* New York: Harper and Row, 1973.

De La Croix, Horst, and Tansey, Richard G., *Gardner's Art Through the Ages*, Seventh edition. New York: Harcourt Brace Jovanovich, 1980.

Honour, Hugh, *Romanticism.* London: Penguin Books Ltd, 1979.

MUSIC

Abraham, Gerald, *A Hundred Years of Music.* Third edition. Chicago: Aldine Publishing Company, 1964.

Abraham, Gerald, ed. *The New Oxford History of Music* Vol. VIII: *The Age of Beethoven 1790–1830.* London: Oxford University Press, 1982.

Adorno, Theodor, *In Search of Wagner*, trans. by Livingston. London: NLB, 1981.

Arnold, Denis and Fortune, Nigel, *The Beethoven Reader.* New York: W. W. Norton and Co., Inc., 1971.

Barzun, Jacques, *Berlioz and the Romantic Century* Vol. I. Boston: Little, Brown and Co., 1950.

Blume, Friedrich, *Classic and Romantic Music.* New York: W. W. Norton and Co., Inc., 1970.

Clarson-Leach, Robert, *Berlioz: His Life and Times.* New York: Midas Books, 1983.

Cooper, Martin, "The Songs" in Abraham, Gerald, ed., *Schumann: A Symposium.* Westport, Connecticut: Greenwood Press, 1977.

Dahlhaus, Carl (Whittall, trans.). *Richard Wagner's Music Dramas*, Cambridge: Cambridge University Press, 1971.

Dickinson, A. E. F., *Music of Berlioz.* London: Faber and Faber, 1972.

Einstein, Alfred, *Music in the Romantic Era.* New York: W. W. Norton and Co., Inc., 1947.

Finck, Henry, *Wagner and his Works.* London: Grevel and Co., 1893.

Grout, Donald J., *A History of Western Music.* Third edition. New York: W. W. Norton and Co., Inc., 1980.

Gutman, Robert W., *Richard Wagner: The Man, His Mind and His Music.* New York: Harcourt, Brace and World, Inc., 1968.

James, Burnett, *Wagner and the Romantic Disaster.* New York: Midas Books, 1983.

Kirby, F. E., "Beethoven's Pastoral Symphony as a Synfonia Caracteristica" in Lang, Paul Henry, ed. *The Creative World of Beethoven.* New York: W. W. Norton and Co., Inc., 1970.

Longyear, Rey M., *Nineteenth-Century Romanticism in Music.* Englewood Cliffs, New Jersey: Prentice-Hall, Inc., 1969.

Mander, Raymond and Mitchenson, Joe, *The Wagner Companion.* London: W. H. Allen & Co., plc, 1977.

Taylor, Ronald, *Richard Wagner: His Life, Art, and Thought.* London: Paul Elek, 1979.

Taylor, Ronald, *Robert Schumann: His Life and Work.* New York: Universe Books, 1982.

Chapter 6

LITERATURE

Latourette, Kenneth Scott, *A History of Christianity.* New York: Harper & Row, Inc., 1953.

Cross, F. L., and E. A. Livingstone, eds. *The Oxford Dictionary of the Christian Church.* Second edition. London and New York: Oxford University Press, 1974.

New Testament

See bibliography of Chapter 1 for additional bibilical reference works and commentaries.

Guthrie, Donald, *New Testament Introduction.* London: Tyndale, 1970.

Metzger, Bruce M., *The New Testament: its background, growth, and content.* Nashville: Abingdon Press, 1965.

Augustine

Battenhouse, Roy W., ed. *A Companion to the Study of Saint Augustine.* New York: Oxford University Press, 1955.

Brown, Peter, *Augustine of Hippo.* Berkeley: University of California Press, 1967.

Guitton, Jean, *The Modernity of Saint Augustine.* Baltimore: Helicon Press, 1959.

O'Meara, John J., *The Young Augustine: An Introduction to the Confessions of Augustine.* London and New York: Longman, Inc., 1980 (1954).

ART

Beckwith, John, *Early Christian and Byzantine Art.* Harmondsworth, Middlesex: Penguin Books Ltd, 1970.

Hauser, Arnold, *The Social History of Art*, Vol. I. New York: Vintage Books (originally Knopff, Inc.), 1951.

Hutter, Imgard, *Early Christian and Byzantine Art.* New York: Universe Books, 1971.

Lowrie, Walter, *Art in the Early Church.* New York: Pantheon Books, Inc., 1947.

MacDonald, William L., *Early Christian and Byzantine Architecture.* London: Prentice-Hall, Inc., 1962.

Rice, David T., Inc., *Art of the Byzantine Era.* New York: Frederick Praeger, 1963.

Van der Meer, F., and P. Brown, *Early Christian Art.* London: Faber and Faber Ltd., 1967.

MUSIC

Fellerer, Karl, *The History of Catholic Church Music*, trans. by Bruner. Baltimore: Helicon Press, 1961.

Grout, Donald J., *A History of Western Music.* Third edition. New York: W. W. Norton & Co., Inc., 1980.

Hoppin, Richard H., *Medieval Music.* New York: W. W. Norton and Co., Inc., 1978.

Palisca, Claude, ed. *Norton Anthology of Western Music*: Vol. I. New York: W. W. Norton and Co., Inc., 1980.

Routley, Erik, *The Church and Music.* London: Gerald Duckworth and Co., 1950.

Sendrey, Alfred, *Music in Ancient Israel.* New York: Philosophical Library, 1969.

Squire, Russel N., *Church Music.* St. Louis: Bethany Press, 1962.

Strunk, Oliver, *Essays on Music in the Byzantine World*, New York: W. W. Norton and Co., Inc., 1977.

Strunk, Oliver, *Source Readings in Music History: From Classical Antiquity Through the Romantic Era.* New York: W. W. Norton and Co., Inc., 1950.

Chapter 7

LITERATURE

Artz, Frederick B., *The Mind of the Middle Ages: A.D. 200–1500: An Historical Survey.* Third edition. Chicago: University of Chicago Press, 1980.

Ker, W. P., *Epic and Romance.* Second edition. London: Macmillan and Co., Ltd., 1926 (1896).

Lewis, C. S., *The Discarded Image.* Cambridge, England: Cambridge University Press, 1964.

Song of Roland

Brault, Gerard S., *The Song of Roland: An Analytical Edition.* University Park: Pennsylvania State University Press, 1984.

Fox, John, *A Literary History of France: The Middle Ages*, Vol. I, Pt. I. New York: Barnes & Noble, 1974.

Saint Francis of Assisi

Bishop, M., *St. Francis of Assisi.* Boston: Little, Brown, and Co., 1974.

Cunningham, L., *St. Francis of Assisi.* Boston: Twayne Publishers, 1976.

Green, Julien, *God's Fool: The Life and Times of Francis of Assisi.* trans. by Peter Heinegg. San Francisco: Harper & Row, Inc., 1985.

Dante

Auerbach, Erich, *Dante, Poet of the Secular World*, trans. by Ralph Manheim. Chicago: University of Chicago Press, 1961. (1929).

Eliot, T. S., "Dante," in *Selected Essays.* New York: Harcourt, Brace, & World, Inc., 1932.

Holmes, George, *Dante.* Oxford and New York: Oxford University Press, 1980.

Sayers, Dorothy, *Introductory papers on Dante.* New York: Barnes & Noble, 1969. (1954).

Sayers, Dorothy, *Further Papers on Dante.* New York: Harper & Row, Inc., 1957.

Art

Benesch, Otto, *The Art of the Renaissance in Northern Europe.* London: Phaidon Press Ltd, 1965.

Branner, Robert, *Gothic Architecture.* New York: George Braziller, 1967.

Cole, Bruce, *Giotto and Florentine Painting 1280 to 1375.* New York: Harper and Row, Inc., 1976.

Cole, Bruce, *Sienese Painting.* New York: Harper and Row, Inc., 1980.

Conant, Kenneth J., *Carolingian and Romanesque Architecture 800 to 1200.* Baltimore: Penguin Books Ltd, 1973.

Focillon, Henri, *The Art of the West*: Vol. I *Romanesque Art* trans. by Donald King. London: Phaidon Press Ltd, 1963.

Focillon, Henri, *The Art of the West*: Vol. II *Gothic Art*, London: Phaidon Press Ltd, 1963.

Frey, Roger, *Flemish Art.* New York: Brentano's, 1927.

Genaille, Robert, *From Van Eyck to Brueghel*, trans. by Leslie Schenk. London: A. Zwemmer Ltd., 1954.

Hauser, Arnold, *The Social History of Art.* Vol. I, New York: Vintage Books (originally Knopf, Inc.) 1951.

Henderson, George, *Gothic.* Baltimore: Penguin Books Ltd., 1967.

Lassaigne, Jacques, *Flemish Painting: The Century of Van Eyck*, trans. by Stuart Gilbert. Paris: Abert Skira.

Meiss, Millard, *Painting in Florence and Siena After the Black Death.* New York: Harper & Row, Inc., 1951.

Panofsky, Erwin, *Gothic Architecture and Scholasticism.* Cleveland and New York: World Publishing, 1957.

Panofsky, Erwin, *Renaissance and Renascences in Western Art.* Second edition. Stockholm: Almqvist and Wiksell, 1965.

Panofsky, Erwin, *Studies in Iconology*, New York: Harper and Row, Inc., 1962.

Schneider, Laurie, ed. *Giotto in Perspective*, Engelwood Cliffs, New Jersey: Prentice Hall Inc., 1974.

MUSIC

Fellerer, Karl, *The History of Catholic Church Music*, trans. by Brunner. Baltimore: Helicon Press, 1961.

Grout, Donald, J., *A History of Western Music* Third edition. New York: W. W. Norton & Co., Inc., 1980.

Hoppin, Richard H., *Medieval Music*, New York: W. W. Norton and Co., Inc., 1978.

Hughes, D., and G. Abraham, eds. *Oxford History of Music, III: Ars Nova and the Renaissance 1300 to 1540*, London: Oxford University Press.

Palisca, Claude, ed., *Norton Anthology of Western Music*: Vol. I, New York: W. W. Norton and Co., Inc., 1980.

Routley, Erik, *The Church and Music.* London: Gerald Duckworth and Co., 1950.

Squire, Russel N., *Church Music.* St. Louis: Bethany Press, 1962.

Strunk, Oliver, *Source Readings in Music History: From Classical Antiquity Through the Romantic Era*, New York: W. W. Norton and Co., Inc., 1950.

Chapter 8

LITERATURE

Bainton, Roland H., *The Reformation of the Sixteenth Century.* Boston:

The Beacon Press, 1952.

Grimm, Harold J., *The Reformation Era: 1500–1650.* Second edition. New York: Macmillan Co., 1973.

Erasmus

Bainton, Roland H., *Erasmus of Christendom.* New York: Scribner, 1969.

Phillips, M. M., *Erasmus and the Northern Renaissance.* New York: Macmillan Co., 1950.

Williams, Kathleen, ed. *Twentieth Century Interpretations of "The Praise of Folly": A Collection of Critical Essays.* Englewood Cliffs, New Jersey: Prentice-Hall, Inc., 1969.

Luther

Bainton, Roland H., *Here I Stand, A Life of Martin Luther.* New York: Abingdon Press, 1950.

Boehmer, H., *Martin Luther: Road to Reformation.* Philadelphia, Pa: Muhlenberg Press, 1946.

Fife, R. H. *The Revolt of Martin Luther.* New York: Columbia University Press, 1957.

Luther, Martin, *Three Treatises,* trans. by C. M. Jacobs, A. T. W. Steinhaueser, and W. A. Lambert. Philadelphia: The Muhlenberg Press, 1943.

Schweibert, E. G., *Luther and His Times.* St Louis: Concordia Publishing House, 1950.

Calvin

Calvin, John, *On the Christian Faith,* ed. John E. McNeill. New York: Liberal Arts Press, 1957.

Mackinnon, James, *Calvin and the Reformation.* New York: Russell & Russell, 1962 (1936).

Parker, T. H. L., *John Calvin.* London: Dent, 1975.

Walker, Williston, *John Calvin: The Organizer of Reformed Protestantism.* New York: Schocken Books, 1969. (1906).

Loyola

Foss, M., *The Founding of the Jesuits: 1540.* New York: Weybright and Talley, 1969.

Van Dyke, Paul, *Ignatius Loyola, the Founder of the Jesuits.* Port Washington, New York: Kennikat Press, 1968 (1926).

ART

Benesch, Otto, *The Art of the Renaissance in Northern Europe: Its Relation to the Contemporary Spiritual and Intellectual Movements,* (trans?). Greenwich, Conn.: Phaidon Publishers Inc., 1965.

Benesch, Otto, *German painting, from Dürer to Holbein,* trans. by H. S. B. Harrison. Geneva: Skira, 1966.

Davies, David, *El Greco.* New York: Dutton, 1976.

Deusch, Werner, *German Painting of the Sixteenth Century.* New York: Hacker Art Books, 1973.

Held, Julius S. and Posner, Donald, *17th and 18th Century Art.* New York: Harry N. Abrams, Inc., 1971.

MUSIC

Blume, Friedrich, *Protestant Church Music: A History.* New York: W. W. Norton and Co., Inc., 1974.

Grout, Donald J. *A History of Western Music.* Third edition. New York: W. W. Norton and Co., Inc., 1980.

Politoske, Daniel T., *Music.* Fourth edition. Englewood Cliffs, New Jersey: Prentice-Hall, Inc., 1987.

Poultney, David, *Studying Music History.* Englewood Cliffs, New Jersey: Prentice-Hall, Inc., 1983.

Routley, Eric, *Words, Music, and the Church.* New York: Abingdon Press, 1968.

RELIGION

Pelikan, Jaroslav, *Jesus Through the Centuries: His Place in the History of Culture.* New Haven, Conn.: Yale University Press, 1985.

Chapter 9

LITERATURE

Auerbach, Erich, *Mimesis: The Representation of Reality in Western Literature,* trans. by Willard R. Trask. Princeton: Princeton University Press, 1953.

Levin, H., *The Gates of Horn: A Study of Five French Realists.* New York: Oxford University Press, 1963.

Flaubert

Brombert, Victor, *The Novels of Flaubert.* Princeton, New Jersey: Princeton University Press, 1966.

Cortland, Peter, *A Reader's Guide to Flaubert.* New York: Helios Books, 1968.

Steegmuller, Francis, *Flaubert and Madame Bovary.* New York: Noonday Press, 1968.

Turnbell, Martin, "*Madame Bovary,*" in *Flaubert: A Collection of Critical Essays,* ed. Raymond Giraud. Englewood Cliffs, New Jersey: Prentice-Hall, Inc., 1964.

Dostoyevsky

Hingley, Ronald, *Dostoyevsky: His Life and Work.* London: Paul Elek, 1978.

Mochulsky, Konstantin, *Dostoyevsky: Life and Work,* trans. by Michael Minihan. Princeton, New Jersey: Princeton University Press, 1967.

Peace, Richard, *Dostoyevsky: An Examination of the Major Novels.* Cambridge, England: Cambridge University Press, 1971.

Wasiolek, Edward, *Dostoevsky: The Major Fiction.* Cambridge, Mass.: M.I.T. Press, 1964.

Wellek, Rene, ed. *Dostoevsky: A Collection of Critical Essays.* Englewood Cliffs, New Jersey: Prentice-Hall, Inc., 1962.

Tolstoy

Bayley, John, *Tolstoy and the Novel.* New York: Viking Press, 1967.

Berlin, Isaiah, *The Hedgehog and the Fox.* New York: Simon and Schuster, 1953.

Christian, R. F., *Tolstoy: A Critical Introduction.* London: Cambridge University Press, 1969.

Matlaw, Ralph E., ed. *Tolstoy: A Collection of Critical Essays.* Englewood Cliffs, New Jersey: Prentice-Hall, Inc., 1967.

Simmons, Ernest J., *Leo Tolstoy.* London and Boston: Routledge and Kegan Paul, 1973.

ART

A Day in the Country: Impressionism and the French Landscape. Los Angeles: Los Angeles County Museum of Art, 1984.

Clark, T. J., *The Painting of Modern Life: Paris in the Art of Manet and His Followers.* New York: Alfred A. Knopf, 1985.

Condit, Carl W., *The Chicago School of Architecture: A History of Commercial and Public Building in the Chicago Area 1875–1925.* Chicago: The University of Chicago Press, 1964.

De La Croix, Horst, and Tansey, Richard G., *Gardner's Art Through the Ages.* Eighth edition. New York: Harcourt Brace Jovanovich, Inc., 1986.

Giedion, Sigfried, *Space, Time and Architecture: The Growth of a New Tradition.* Fifth edition. Cambridge, Mass.: Harvard University Press, 1967.

Hauser, Arnold, *The Social History of Art.* Vol. II. New York: Alfred A. Knopf, 1961.

Hibbert, Christopher, *Rome: The Biography of a City.* New York: W. W. Norton and Co., Inc., 1985.

Rewald, John, *The History of Impressionism.* Fourth edition. New York: N.Y. Graphic Society for the Museum of Modern Art, 1973.

Siegel, Arthur, *Chicago's Famous Buildings.* Second edition. Chicago: Chicago University Press, 1969.

Chapter 10

LITERATURE

Howe, Irving, ed. *Literary Modernism*. Greenwich, Conn.: Fawcett Publications, Inc., 1967.

Conrad

Baines, Jocelyn, *Joseph Conrad: A Critical Biography*. McGraw-Hill: New York, 1960.

Guerard, Albert, *Conrad the Novelist*. Cambridge: Howard University Press, 1958.

Karl, Frederick R., *A Reader's Guide to Joseph Conrad*. New York: Farrar, Straus & Giroux, 1960 (Rev. ed. 1969).

Kafka

Gray, Ronald, ed. *Kafka: A Collection of Critical Essays*. Englewood Cliffs, New Jersey: Prentice-Hall, Inc., 1962.

Greenberg, Martin, *The Terror of Art: Kafka and Modern Literature*. New York: Basic Books, 1968.

Heller, Erich, *Franz Kafka*. New York: Viking Press, 1975.

Politzer, Heinz, *Franz Kafka: Parable and Paradox*. Ithaca: Cornell University Press, 1966.

Sokel, Walter Herbert, *Franz Kafka*. New York: Columbia University Press, 1966.

Mann

Feuerlicht, Ignace, *Thomas Mann*. New York: Twayne Publishers, 1968.

Hatfield, Henry C., ed. *Thomas Mann: A Collection of Critical Essays*. Englewood Cliffs, New Jersey: Prentice-Hall, Inc., 1964.

Hatfield, Henry C., *Thomas Mann*. Norfolk: New Directions, 1951.

Heller, Erich, *Thomas Mann: The Ironic German*. Boston: Little, Brown and Co., 1958, rev. 1961.

Reed, Terence, J., *Thomas Mann: The Uses of Tradition*. Oxford: Clarendon Press, 1974.

Joyce

Bloom, Harold, ed. *James Joyce*. New York: Chelsea House, 1986.

Chace, William M. ed. *Joyce: A Collection of Critical Essays*. Englewood Cliffs, N.J.: Prentice-Hall, 1974.

Ellmann, Richard, *James Joyce*. rev. ed. New York: Oxford University Press, 1982.

Kenner, Hugh, *Dublin's Joyce*. Gloucester, Mass.: P. Smith, 1969.

Levin, Harry, *James Joyce: A Critical Introduction*. Norfolk, Conn.: New Directions Books, 1941.

Tindall, William York, *A Reader's Guide to James Joyce*. New York: Noonday Press, 1959.

Eliot

Bergonzi, Bernard, *T. S. Eliot*. Second edition, London: Macmillan, 1978.

Drew, Elizabeth, *T. S. Eliot, The Design of his Poetry*. New York: C. Scribner & Sons, 1949.

Kenner, Hugh, ed. *T. S. Eliot: A Collection Of Critical Essays*. Englewood Cliffs, New Jersey: Prentice-Hall, Inc., 1962.

Williamson, George, *A Reader's Guide to T. S. Eliot: A Poem by Poem Analaysis*. Second edition, New York: Octagon Books, 1974.

ART

Barr, Alfred, *Picasso: Fifty Years of His Art*. New York: The Museum of Modern Art, 1946.

Bernard, Bruce, ed. *Vincent by Himself: A Selection of Van Gogh's Paintings and Drawings together with Extracts from his Letters*. New York: Little, Brown and Co., Inc., 1985.

Bowness, Alan, *Modern European Art*. New York: Harcourt Brace Jovanovich, Inc., 1972.

Canaday, John, *Mainstreams of Modern Art*, Second edition. New York: Holt, Rinehart and Winston, Inc., 1981.

Condit, Carl W., *The Chicago School of Architecture: A History of Commercial and Public Building in the Chicago Area 1875–1925*. Chicago: University of Chicago Press, 1964.

Giedion, Sigfried, *Space, Time and Architecture: The Growth of a New Tradition*. Fifth edition. Cambridge, Mass.: Harvard University Press, 1967.

Haftmann, Werner, *Painting in the Twentieth Century*. Vol. I, *An Analysis of the Artists and Their Work*. New York: Praeger Publishers, 1965.

Rewald, John, *Post Impressionism: From Van Gogh to Gauguin*. New York: Museum of Modern Art, 1962.

Schapiro, Meyer, *Modern Art: 19th and 20th Centuries*. New York: George Braziller, 1978.

Siegel, Arthur, *Chicago's Famous Buildings*. Second edition. Chicago: University of Chicago Press, 1969.

Stern, Robert A. M., *Pride of Place: Building the American Dream*. Boston: Houghton Mifflin Company, 1986.

MUSIC

Adorno, Theodor W., *Philosophy of Modern Music*, trans. by A. G. Mitchell and W. V. Blomster. New York: The Seabury Press, 1973.

Austin, William, *Music in the Twentieth Century*. New York: W. W. Norton and Co., Inc., 1966.

Machlis, Joseph, *Introduction to Contemporary Music*. Second edition. New York: W. W. Norton and Co., Inc., 1979.

Politoske, Daniel T., *Music*. Fourth edition. Englewood Cliffs, New Jersey: Prentice-Hall, 1987.

Salzman, Eric, *Twentieth-Century Music: An Introduction*. Second edition. Englewood Cliffs, New Jersey: Prentice-Hall, Inc., 1974.

Chapter 11

LITERATURE

Camus

Brée, Germaine, *Albert Camus*. New Brunswick: Rutgers University Press, 1964.

Brée, Germaine, ed. *Camus: A Collection of Critical Essays*. Englewood Cliffs, New Jersey: Prentice-Hall, Inc., 1961.

Cruickshank, John, *Albert Camus and the Literature of Revolt*. New York: Oxford University Press, 1960 (1959).

Lottman, Herbert, *Albert Camus: A Biography*. New York: George Braziller, 1980.

O'Brien, Conor Cruise, *Albert Camus of Europe and Africa*. New York: The Viking Press, 1970.

Thody, Philip, *Albert Camus, 1933–1960*. New York: Macmillan & Co., 1962.

Beckett

Cohn, Ruby, ed. *Samuel Beckett: A Collection of Criticism*. New York: McGraw-Hill, 1975.

Esslin, Martin, ed. *Samuel Beckett: A Collection of Critical Essays*. Englewood Cliffs, New Jersey: Prentice-Hall, Inc., 1965

Hayman, Ronald, *Samuel Beckett*. Third edition, London: Heinemann, 1980.

Kenner, Hugh, *A Reader's Guide to Samuel Beckett*. New York: Farrar, Straus and Giroux, 1973.

Wiesel

Cargas, Harry James, ed. *Responses to Elie Wiesel, Critical Essays by Major Jewish and Christian Scholars*. New York: Persea Books, 1978.

Estess, Ted L., *Elie Wiesel*. New York: Frederick Ungar Pub. Co., 1980.

Fine, Ellen S., *Legacy of Night: The Literary Universe of Elie Wiesel*.

Albany: State University of New York Press, 1982.

Halperin, Irving, *Messengers from the Dead*. Philadelphia: The Westminster Press, 1970.

Langer, Lawrence, *The Holocaust and the Literary Imagination*. New Haven: Yale University Press, 1976.

Rosenfeld, Alvin H. and Irving Greenberg, eds. *Confronting the Holocaust: The Literary Impact of Elie Wiesel*. Bloomington and London: Indiana University Press, 1978.

Roth, John K., *A Consuming Fire: Encounters with Elie Wiesel and the Holocaust*. Prologue by Elie Wisel. Atlanta, Ga.: John Knox Press, 1979.

Solzhenitsyn

Ericson, Edward E., Jr., *Solzhenitsyn: The Moral Vision*. Grand Rapids, Mich.: William B. Eerdmans Publishing Company, 1980.

Feuer, Kathryn B., ed. *Solzhenitsyn: A Collection of Critical Essays*. Englewood Cliffs, New Jersey: Prentice Hall, Inc., 1976.

Kodjak, Andrej, *Alexander Solzhenitsyn*. Boston: G. K. Hall & Co., 1978.

Rothberg, Abraham, *Aleksandr Solzhenitsyn: The Major Novels*. Ithaca and London: Cornell University Press, 1971.

ART

Giedion, Sigfried, *Space, Time and Architecture: The Growth of a New Tradition*. Fifth edition. Cambridge, Mass.: Harvard University Press, 1967.

Hobbs, Jack, *Art in Context*, Third edition. San Diego: Harcourt Brace Jovanovich, 1986.

Hughes, Robert, *The Shock of the New*. New York: Alfred A. Knopf, 1981.

Hunter, Sam, and Jacobus, John, *American Art of the Twentieth Century*. New York: Harry N. Abrams, Inc., 1973.

Siegel, Arthur, ed. *Chicago's Famous Buildings*. Second edition. Chicago: University of Chicago Press, 1969.

Stern, Robert A. M., *Pride of Place: Building the American Dream*. Boston: Houghton Mifflin Company, 1986.

MUSIC

Brindle, Reginald Smith, *The New Music*. London: Oxford University Press, 1975.

Brooks, William, "Choice and Change in Cage's Recent Music," in *A John Cage Reader*. New York: C. F. Peters Corporation, 1982.

Cage, John, *Silence*. Cambridge, Mass.: The M.I.T. Press, 1961.

Cope, David H., *New Directions in Music*. Fourth edition. Dubuque, Iowa: Wm. C. Brown Publishers, 1984.

Gena, P., Brent, J. and D. Gillespie, eds. *A John Cage Reader*. New York: C. F. Peters Corporation, 1982.

Griffiths, Paul, *Cage*. London: Oxford University Press, 1981.

Kostelanetz, Richard, *John Cage*. New York: Praeger Publishers, 1970.

Machlis, Joseph, *Introduction to Contemporary Music*. Second edition. New York: W. W. Norton and Co., Inc., 1979.

Peyser, Joan, *The New Music: The Sense Behind the Sound*. New York: Dell Publishing Co., Inc., 1972.

Salzman, Eric, *Twentieth-Century Music: An Introduction*. Second edition. Englewood Cliffs, New Jersey: Prentice-Hall, Inc., 1974.

Sandler, Irving, *The Triumph of America. A History of Abstract Expressionism*. New York: Praeger Publishers, 1970.

Lewisburg, Penn.: Bucknell University Press, 1977.

Hassan, Ihab, *The Dismemberment of Orpheus: Toward a Postmodern Literature*. Second edition. Madison: The University of Wisconsin Press, 1982 (1971).

Stark, John O., *The Literature of Exhaustion: Borges, Nabokov, and Barth*. Durham, N. C.: Duke University Press, 1974.

GENERAL

Bell, Daniel, *The Cultural Contradictions of Capitalism*. New York: Basic Books, Inc., 1976.

Bloom, Allan, *The Closing of the American Mind*. New York: Simon and Schuster, 1987.

Francklin, Catherine, "Interview with Julia Kristeva," trans. by Nancy Blake in *Flash Art*, No. 126, February/March 1986, 44–46.

Francklin, Catherine, "Interview with Jean Baudrillard," trans. by Nancy Blake in *Flash Art*, No. 130, October/November 1986, 54–55.

Guattari, Felix, "The Postmodern Dead End," trans. by Nancy Blake in *Flash Art*, No. 128, May/June 1986, 40–41.

Stephanson, Anders, "Interview with Frederic Jameson" in *Flash Art*, No. 131, December 1986/January 1987, 69/73.

"Supplement on Postmodernism" in *Art and Artists* 15 (3), May/June 1986, 3–13.

Toynbee, Arnold Joseph, *A Study of History* (abridgement of volumes I–X by D. C. Somervell). London: Oxford University Press, 1947.

Trachtenberg, Stanley, ed. *The Postmodern Moment: A Handbook of Contemporary Innovation in the Arts*. Westport, Conn. Greenwood Press, 1985.

ARTS and MUSIC

Clarke, Garry E., "Music" in Trachtenberg (*see* General, above).

Cope, David H., *New Directions in Music*, Fourth edition. Dubuque, Iowa: Wm. C. Brown Publishers, 1984.

Filler, Martin, "High Ruse, Part I" in *Art in America* 72 (8), September, 1984, 156–60.

Foucault, M., and P. Boulez, "Contemporary Music and the Public" in *Perspectives of new Music* 24 (1), Fall-Winter 1985, 6–12.

Fuller, Peter, *Aesthetics after Modernism*. London: Writers and Readers Publishing Cooperative Society Ltd, 1983.

Hughes, Robert, *The Shock of the New*. New York: Alfred Knopf, 1981.

Jencks, Charles A., *The Language of Post-Modern Architecture*. New York: Rizzoli International Publications, 1977.

Machlis, Joseph, *Introduction to Contemporary Music*. Second edition. New York: W. W. Norton and Co., Inc., 1979.

Paoletti, John T., "Art" in Trachtenberg (*see* General, above).

Salzman, Eric, *Twentieth-Century Music: An Introduction*. Second edition. Englewood Cliffs, New Jersey: Prentice-Hall, Inc., 1974.

Tafuri, Manfredo. *Theories and History of Architecture*, trans. by Giorgio Verrecchia. New York: Harper and Row, Inc., 1976.

Venturi, R., Brown, D. A., and Izenour, S., *Learning from Las Vegas: The Forgotten Symbolism of Architectural Form*. Cambridge, Mass.: The MIT Press, 1977.

Venturi, Robert, *Complexity and Contradiction in Architecture*. Second edition. New York: The Museum of Modern Art, 1977.

Chapter 12

LITERATURE

Garvin, Harry R., ed., *Romanticism, Modernism, Postmodernism*.

Index

Numbers in bold type refer to illustrations.

Aachen, Germany: Palace Chapel of Charlemagne 279, **7.8, 7.9**
Abstract Expressionism 462, 464–5
"Action" painters 462
Aeschylus 55–6, 60, 73, **2.13**; *Oresteia* 56–7
Akhnaton 39–40, **1.25**
Alcuin 269, 281, 314
Altamira, Spain: cave paintings 25, 26, **1.1, 1.7**
Ambrose, St. 235, 241, 263
Amenhotep IV 39
Amiens, France: Cathedral 297–8, **7.31–33**
Anuskiewicz, Richard: *Entrance to Green* 469, **11.21**
Aqueducts, Roman 82, **2.44**
Aquinas, St. Thomas 274; *Summa Theologica* 271, 274–5
Archaic period 50–1, 52–3
Aristophanes 60, 73, 74
Aristotle 60, 74, 153, 358, **2.18**
Armory Show (1913) 420–1, 455
Arnold, Matthew 123, 359
Ars nova 316, 317
Art Nouveau 429
Ashurnasirpal II 32, **1.14**
Assyrian Empire 18; architecture 32; relief carvings 32
Athens 46–7, 61, 62; Acropolis 44, 62, **2.1, 2.19, 2.20**; Parthenon 65–6, 68–9, **2.24–28**
Attie, Dottie 499; *Carolina and her Father* 499, **12.5**
Augustine, St. 61, 160, 235, 239–42, **6.6**
Augustus, Emperor 48, 75, 82, 85, *Augustus of Primaporta* 80, **2.42**

Babbitt, Milton 485–6
Babylon 9, **1.11**
Babylonian Empire 18–19, 29
Bach, Carl Philipp Emanuel 185, 187, 223
Bach, Johann Sebastian 184–5, 323, 353, **4.38**; *Ein feste Burg* (Cantata No. 80) 352, 353–4, **8.27**; *Goldberg Variations* 185–6, 187, **4.40–43**; *Passion According to St. Matthew* 186, 223
Barlach, Ernst 425
Baroque style: art and architecture 150, 151, 161, 163–4, 166, 344–6; music 151, 181–4, 187, 353–4
Barry, Charles: Houses of Parliament, London 220, **5.21**
Barth, John 493, 494
Bartók, Béla 436, 485
Baudelaire, Charles 386
Bauhaus 431, 433, 477, **10.46**
Beardsley, Aubrey 407; *Salome* 407, **10.16**
Beckett, Samuel 444, 449, 493; *Waiting for Godot* 449–50, 493–4
Beethoven, Ludwig van 196, 223–5, **5.23**; 5th Symphony 225, **5.24–28**; 6th Symphony 225–6
Behrens, Peter 431
Benedict, St. 263, 269
Benton, Thomas Hart 445, 457, 460, 461; *Arts of the West* 457, **11.8**
Berg, Alban 439, 441
Berio, Luciano 502
Berlinghieri, Bonaventura: *St Francis of Assisi* **7.5**
Berlioz, Hector 226, 231; *Symphonie fantastique* 226–7, **5.29–30**
Bernini, Gianlorenzo 323, 345; *Baldacchino*, St. Peter's, Rome 163,

4.10; Colonnade, St. Peter's, Rome 163, **4.9**; *Ecstasy of St. Theresa* 345–6, **8.19, 8.20**
Bible, The: New Testament 234, 235, 237–9, 244, 262; Old Testament 18–19, 20–24, 41, 42, 244, 264
Blaue Reiter, Der 411
Boccaccio, Giovanni 98, 99, **3.5**; *Decameron* 98–9
Boccioni, Umberto 425; *Development of a Bottle in Space* 425, **10.37**
Boethius 263
Borges, Jorge Luis 493
Borromini, Francesco: San Carlo alle Quattro Fontane, Rome 163–4, **4.11**
Boston, Mass.: City Hall 495, **12.4**
Botticelli, Sandro 113; *Birth of Venus* 113, **3.20**
Boffrand, Germain: Salon de la Princesse, Palais Soubise, Paris 172, **4.21**
Bouguereau, Guillaume Adolphe: *Nymphs and Satyr* **9.13**
Boulez, Pierre 229, 482, 485, 486, 487; *Le Marteau sans maître* 483; number matrices **11.36**; *Structures I* 482
Brahms, Johannes 231
Bramante, Donato: St. Peter's, Rome 138, **3.45**; Tempietto 138, **3.44**
Brancusi, Constantin 425, 427; *Bird in Space* 427, **10.38**
Braque, Georges 414, 415, 427; *Le Courrier* 415, **10.26**; *Violin and Palette* 414, **10.25**
Breton, André 422
Breuer, Marcel 477
Brighton, England: Royal Pavilion 220, **5.22**
Brown, Earle 486; *Available Forms I* 486, **11.40**
Brücke, Die 409–10
Bruckner, Anton 231
Brunelleschi, Filippo 103; Dome of Florence Cathedral 103, 118, **3.8**; Ospedale degli Innocenti, Florence 103, **3.10**; Pazzi Chapel, Florence 99, 100, 103, **3.7**
Brussels, Belgium: Philips Pavilion, World Fair (1958) 483, **11.37**; Tassel House 429, **10.42**
Burroughs, William 493
Byzantine Empire 235, 249, 254–5, 268–9; art and architecture 255, 257, 259–61

Cage, John 486, 488–9, 494; *4′33″* 44–5, 488, 489; *Music of Changes* 486, 488, **11.38**
Calder, Alexander 427; *Lobster Trap and Fish Tail* 427, **10.40**
Calf-bearer (marble statue) **6.9**
Calvin, John 323, 329–31, 341, 352, **8.6**
Camus, Albert 444, 445–8, 455, **11.4**; *The Exile and the Kingdom* 446; *The Fall* 446, 448–9; *The Myth of Sisyphus* 386, 446, 447, 448; *The Plague* 444, 445, 446, 448; *The Rebel* 446; *The Stranger* 446, 447–8
Canova, Antonio 179; *Napoleon* 179, **4.29**
Cantata 183–4, 353, 506
Caravaggio, Michelangelo da 344–5; *Conversion of St. Paul* 345, **8.18**
Carolingian Renaissance 269, 279, 281
Carter, Elliot 485
Castiglione, Baldassare 94, 120, 137–8, **3.43**; *Book of the Courtier* 120–1

Catacombs 243–5, **6.7, 6.8**
Cézanne, Paul 397, 398–9, 400, 402; *Fruit Bowl, Glass, and Apples* 399, **10.8**; *Mont Sainte-Victoire seen from Bibémus Quarry* 399–400, 402, **10.9**
Chagall, Marc 416, 436; *I and the Village* 416, **10.1**
Chanson de Roland see Roland, Song of
Chardin, Jean-Baptiste 175, 177; *Grace at Table* 175, **4.24**
Charlemagne 269, 271, 272, 279, 281, 314
Chartres, France: Cathedral 293–4, 296–7, 300–2, **7.27–30, 7.38–40**
Chia, Sandro: *The Idleness of Sisyphus* 499, **12.1**
Chicago, Illinois: Carson, Pirie and Scott Dept. Store 429, 431, **10.43**; Hancock Center 495, **12.3**; Lake Shore Drive apartment houses 477, 479, **11.31**; Robie House 431, **10.44, 10.45**
Chicago School 381, 429, 431
Chirico, Giorgio de 422, 423; *The Mystery and Melancholy of a Street* 423, 458, **10.33**
Chromatic Abstraction 462
Cimabue, Giovanni 307; *Madonna Enthroned* 307, **7.44**
Claude Gellée (Claude Lorraine) 167; *The Marriage of Isaac and Rebekah* 167, **4.15**
Cleisthenes 46
Cluny Abbey, France 269, 282–3, **7.13**
Cologne, Germany: Cathedral 300, **7.36**
Color-Field artists 465, 467
Comte, Auguste 359, 360
Conceptual art 475, 476
Conrad, Joseph 385, 387–8, **10.3**; *Heart of Darkness* 385, 386, 387, 388–9, 396, 397
Constable, John 217–18; *The Hay Wain* 208, 218, **5.18**
Constantine, Emperor 245, 247, 257
Constantinople 235, 254, 255, 268
Coover, Robert: *The Public Burning* 495
Copland, Aaron 445, 485; *Appalachian Spring* 485
Corelli, Arcangelo 184
Corinth, Greece **6.3**
Counter Reformation 323, 331–2; art 341; music 352–3
Couperin, François 187
Courbet, Gustave 359, 371, 373, 397; *Burial at Ornans* 370–1, **9.1, 9.8**
Cowell, Henry 485, 488
Cranach, Lucas, the Elder 332
Crumb, George 502, 503
Cubism 412, 414–16

Dadaism 421–2, 424
Dali, Salvador 423; *Soft Construction with Boiled Beans: Premonition of Civil War* 424, **10.34**
Dante 98, 275, **7.6**; *Divine Comedy* 79, 271, 275–8, 397
Darwin, Charles 359, 360, 385
David, Jacques-Louis 178, 179, 180; *Oath of the Horatii* 177–8, 208, **4.26**
Debussy, Claude 434; *L'Après-midi d'un faune* 435, **10.50**
Degas, Edgar 379; *The Glass of Absinthe* 379, 405, 457, 469, **9.16**
Delacroix, Eugène 208, 212, 213, 220; *The Death of Sardanapalus* 212, **5.12**
Delian League, the 46

Dessau, Germany: Bauhaus shop block 431, 433, **10.46**
Diaghilev, Sergei 436
Diderot, Denis 200; *Encyclopedia* 153
Didyma, Turkey: Temple of Apollo 72, **2.34, 2.35**
Doctorow, E. L.: *Ragtime* 495
Doidalsas: *Aphrodite* 70, **2.31**
Donatello 105, 113; *David* 105–6, **3.12**; *Equestrian statue of Gattamelata* 106, **3.13**; *St. Mark* 105, 106, 113, **3.11**
Dostoyevsky, Fyodor 362–3, 364–5, 385, 386, 445, 448, **9.4**; *Brothers Karamazov* 362, 363; *Crime and Punishment* 360, 363–4; *Notes from Underground* 359, 363, 364, 387
Draco 46
Duchamp, Marcel 416, 417, 421, 488, 489, 493; *Fountain* 421, **10.32**; *Nude Descending a Staircase No. 2* 417, 421, **10.28**
Dufay, Guillaume 118, **3.27**
Dunstable, John 116, **3.23**
Dürer, Albrecht 322, 332, 335, 336; *Adam and Eve* 335, **8.10**; *Four Apostles* 336, **8.1, 8.11**; *Four Horsemen of the Apocalypse* 332, **8.9**; *Self-Portrait in a Fur Coat* 332, **8.8**
Durham, England: Cathedral 289, **7.20, 7.21**
Dur Sharrukin: Citadel of Sargon II 32, **1.15, 1.16**
Dvořák, Antonín 434

Earth Art 475–6
Egypt, ancient 19–20; art and architecture 34–6, 38–9; map 19, **1.4**; music 42, 43
Electronic music 483–5
Elgar, Edward 231, 434
Eliot, T. S. 275, 395–7, 494–5, **10.7**; *Murder in the Cathedral* 397; *The Waste Land* 396
Enlightenment, The 151, 153, 160
Epidaurus, Greece: theatre **2.12**; tholos **2.30**
Erasmus, Desiderius 323, 325–6, 341, **8.4**; *Praise of Folly* 323, 326–7
Euripides 55–6, 59–60, 73, 196, **2.15**
Existentialism 458–9
Expressionism 409–10, 411, 425
Eyck, Hubert and Jan van: *Ghent Altarpiece* 311, 312–13, 332, **7.48–50**

Falla, Manuel de 434
Fauré, Gabriel 434
Fauvel, Roman de 317
Fauvism 407, 409, 410, 411, 414
Feldman, Morton 486, 487; *Intersection I* 486, **11.39**
Ficino, Marsilio 99, 113, 510
Fin de siècle art 403–5, 407, 429
Flaubert, Gustave 360–1, 9.2; *Madame Bovary* 358, 360, 361–2
Florence, Italy 100; Baptistery 110, 113, **3.17, 3.18**; Cathedral 103, **3.1, 3.8, 3.9**; Ospedale degli Innocenti 103, 138, 140, **3.10**; Pazzi Chapel 99, 100, 103, **3.7**
Fragonard, Jean-Honoré: *The Swing* 172, 174, **4.22**
Frame construction 379–80, 381, 509
Francis of Assisi, St. 196, 269, 272, 274, 291, **7.5**
Franck, César 434
Frankenthaler, Helen 465; *Mountains and Sea* 465, **11.15**
Freud, Sigmund 422

Friedrich, Casper David 214; *Cross in the Mountains* 214–15, **5.14**; *The Polar Sea* 215–16, **5.15**; *Winter* 220, **5.20**
Fuller, Buckminster: US Pavilion, EXPO 67, Montreal 480–1, **11.35**
Futurism, Italian 416–17

Gardner, John 495
Gauguin, Paul 384, 386, 397–8, 402–3; *The Vision After the Sermon (Jacob Wrestling with the Angel)* 402, **10.12**
Gentile da Fabriano: *Adoration of the Magi* 107, 310, 311, **3.14**
Géricault, Théodore 211; *Portrait of a Young Man in an Artist's Studio* 210, **5.10**; *Raft of the Medusa* 211–12, **5.11**
Ghent Altarpiece 311, 312–13, 332, **7.48–50**
Ghiberti, Lorenzo: *Gates of Paradise* 110, 113, **3.17**, **3.18**
Gilgamesh epics 17
Giotto di Bondone 304, 307, 308; *The Kiss of Judas* 308, **7.45**; *Madonna Enthroned* 308, **7.32**; (?) *Portrait of Dante* **7.6**; (?) *St. Francis' Sermon to the Birds* 272, **7.1**
Giza, Egypt: Pyramids 35, 38, **1.17–20**
Glass, Philip 502, 503, **12.12**
Goethe, Johann Wolfgang von 196, 201–3, **5.5**; *Faust* 202–3
Gogh, Vincent van 397–8, 400, 402; *The Potato Eaters* 400, **10.10**; *Wheatfield and Cypress Trees* 400, 402, **10.11**
Goings, Ralph: *Windows* 469, **11.22**
González, Julio 427; *Head* 427, **10.39**
Gorky, Arshile 459, 460; *The Liver Is the Cock's Comb* 459, **11.10**
Gospel Book of Archbishop Ebbo of Reims 281, **7.11**
Gospel Book of Charlemagne 281, **7.10**
Gothic style: architecture 220, 291, 293–4, 296–9; sculpture 300–2, 304
Goya, Francesco 207–8; *Los Caprichos* 208, **5.8, 5.9**; *The Third of May* 198, 208, **5.4**
Greco, El (Kyriakos Theotokopoulos) 323, 342; *The Burial of Count Orgaz* 342–3, 346, **8.16**
Greece, ancient 46–7; architecture 52–3, 66, 68–70, 72; literature 49–50, 55–61, map 47, **2.2**; music 54, 73–5; sculpture 50–1, 62–3, 65–6, 70, 72
Gregorian chant 263–5, 509
Gregory I, Pope 263–4, **6.31**
Gregory VII, Pope 269
Grieg, Edvard 434
Gropius, Walter 431, 477; Bauhaus shop block 431, 433, **10.46**
Grünewald, Matthias 332, 337, 339–40; *Isenheim Altarpiece* 337–9, 343, **8.12, 8.13**
Guido d'Arezzo 313, 314

Hammurabi 18, 31, **1.13**
Handel, George Frideric 151, 184; *Messiah* 354–5, **8.28, 8.29**; *Water Music* 184, 185, 187, **4.39**
Handke, Peter 493
Happenings 475
Hard-Edge Abstraction 467
Harris, Roy 485
Hatshepsut, Queen: Temple 39, **1.24**
Haydn, Joseph 189, 191, 192, 223, 224; *Symphony No. 94* 188–9, **4.45–47**
Hegel, Georg Wilhelm Friedrich 198–9
Heine, Heinrich 228, 229
Heizer, Michael: *Double Negative* 475–6, **11.30**
Hellenistic art *see* Greece, ancient
Helmet-maker (bronze statue) 50, **2.5**
Herder, Johann Gottfried 202

Hindemith, Paul 485
Hogarth, William 151, 174–5; *The Marriage Contract* 175, **4.23**
Holbein, Hans, the Younger: *Erasmus of Rotterdam* **8.4**
Homer 2.4; *Iliad* 46, 49, 55; *Odyssey* 46, 49–50, 55
Homer, Winslow 371, 372–3; *The Country School* 371–2, **9.9**
Hooch, Pieter de: *Interior of a courtyard, Delft* 164, **4.13**
Hopper, Edward 457; *Nighthawks* 457–8, 469, **11.9**
Horta, Victor: staircase of Tassel House 429, **10.42**
Houdon, Jean-Antoine: *Voltaire* 179, **4.28**
Hus, Jan 322

Ice Age 16; art 25–8
Impressionism 376–7, 378
Indeterminacy (music) 486, 488, 510
Ingres, Jean-Auguste-Dominique 178; *La Grande Odalisque* 178–9, **4.27**
Innocent III, Pope: *De contemptu mundi* 272
International Style: 15th c. 310–11; 1930s 431
Ionesco, Eugène 493
Isenheim Altarpiece 337–9, 343, **8.12, 8.13**
Islamic religion 269
Istanbul, Turkey: Hagia Sophia 255, 257, 6.20–24
Ives, Charles 434, 485

James, Henry 372
Jefferson, Thomas 180; State Capitol, Richmond, Va 180, **4.30**
Jesuits (Society of Jesus) 331–2
Johns, Jasper 473, 489, 494; *Three Flags* 465, **11.17**
Johnson, Philip: AT&T Building, New York 501, **12.11**; Seagram Building, New York 479, **11.32**
Josquin des Prez 146, **3.52, 3.53**
Joyce, James 394, 449, **10.6**; *Dubliners* 394–5; *Finnegans Wake* 394, 395, 449; *Ulysses* 395, 495
Judd, Donald 473, 479; *Untitled* (1965) 473, **11.26**
Justinian, Emperor 235, 255, 259, 268–9
Justinian and Attendants (mosaic) 259, 261, **6.1, 6.28, 6.30**

Kafka, Franz 386, 389–92, 444, 445, 449, 493, **10.4**
Kallman, McKinnell and Knowles: City Hall, Boston 495, **12.4**
Kandinsky, Wassily 411, 412, 419, 431, 436, 439, 440, 445, 459, 461; *Sketch I for "Composition VII"* 411–12, **10.22**
Kant, Immanuel 198
Kaprow, Allan 475, 489, 493; *18 Happenings in 6 Parts* 475, **11.29**
Kelly, Ellsworth 467, 469; *Green, Blue, Red* 467, **11.19**
Kiefer, Anselm 499; *The Meistersinger* 499, **12.7**
Klee, Paul 431
Kline, Franz 462; *Mahoning* 462, **11.13**
Kokoschka, Oskar 439; *Self Portrait* 411, **10.21**
Kooning, Willem de 459, 462, 464; *Woman II* 462, 465, **11.1**
Koussevitzky, Serge 485
Kritios Boy 63, **2.21**

La Madeleine, Dordogne: *Bison* **1.6**
Laocoon and his Two Sons 70, **2.32**
Lascaux Caves, Dordogne 25, **1.5**
Le Brun, Charles 169; Hall of Mirrors, Versailles 169, **4.16**
Le Corbusier (Charles-Édouard Jeanneret) 431, 479, 480, 495, 501; Philips Pavilion 483, **11.37**;

Unité d'Habitation Apartment House, Marseilles 479–80, **11.33**; Villa Savoye 433, **10.48**
Lehmbruck, Wilhelm 425
Leonardo da Vinci 125–6, 332; *Adoration of the Magi* 126, 128, **3.33**; *Embryo in the Womb* **3.31**; *The Last Supper* 126, 128, **3.34**; *Mona Lisa* 128, 130, 138, **3.35**; *Project for a Church* **3.32**
Lewis, Sinclair 457
Lichtenstein, Roy 467, 494; *Whaam!* 465, **11.18**
Ligeti, György 502
Limbourg Brothers: *May* from *Les Très Riches Heures du Duc de Berry* 310–11, **7.47**
Locke, John 159, 200
London: Crystal Palace 380–1, **9.17**; Houses of Parliament 220, **5.21**; St. Paul's Cathedral 170, **4.19, 4.20**
Louis XIV, King of France 150–1
Loyola, St. Ignatius 331, **8.7**
Lully, Jean-Baptiste 183; *Les Fêtes de l'amour et de Bacchus* **4.37**; *Phaëton* **4.36**
Luther, Martin 322–3, 324, 325, 326, 327–9, 341, 351–2, **8.5**

Machaut, Guillaume de 317–19
Machiavelli, Niccolò 119, **3.28**; *The Prince* 119–20, 326
Maderno, Carlo: façade of St. Peter's, Rome 140, **3.47**
Madrigals 147
Mahler, Gustav 231, 434
Mallarmé, Stéphane 385, 386
Malraux, André 447
Manet, Édouard 373, 378, 386, 397; *Le Déjeuner sur l'herbe* 373, 374, **9.10**
Mann, Thomas 385, 391–3, 445, **10.5**
Mannerism 145
Mansart, Jules Hardouin: Hall of Mirrors, Versailles 169, **4.16**
Mantegna, Andrea 113; *St. James Led to his Execution* 113, 115, **3.22**
Marco Antonio: *Ricercar for organ* 147, **3.54**
Márquez, Gabriel Garcia 493
Marseilles, France: Unité d'Habitation Apartment House 479–80, **11.33**
Marx, Karl: *Das Kapital* 360
Masaccio (Tommaso Guidi) 107; *The Holy Trinity with the Virgin and St John* 109, **3.15**; *The Tribute Money* 109–10, **3.16**
Mastabas 36, 38, **1.21**
Matisse, Henri 407, 409, 414, 415; *The Joy of Life* 409, 414, **10.18**; *The Red Room* 409, **10.17**
Mauriac, François 452
Mendelssohn, Felix 186, 223, 231
Mesolithic era 16
Mesopotamia 17–19, 20, **1.4**; art and architecture 29, 31–2
Messiaen, Oliver 483
Michelangelo Buonarroti 130–1, 196, 224; *David* 130, **3.36**; *The Last Judgment* (Sistine Chapel) 341, **8.14**; St Peter's, Rome 138, 140, **3.46**; Sistine Chapel ceiling frescoes 131, 135–6, **3.37–41**; Tomb of Lorenzo 145, **3.51**
Mies van der Rohe, Ludwig 431, 433, 477, 479, 495, 501; German Pavilion 433, **10.47**; Lake Shore Drive apartment houses, Chicago 477, **11.31**; Seagram Building, New York 479, **11.32**
Mill, John Stuart 355, 359
Minimalism 473–4, 502–3
Miró, Joan 424; *Composition* 424, **10.35**
Modersohn-Becker, Paula 410; *Old Peasant Woman Praying* 410, **10.19**
Moholy-Nagy, Laszlo 477, 489

Moissac, France: St Pierre 289, 290, 300–1, 302, **7.22, 7.23**
Molière 153–4, **4.5**; *Imaginary Invalid* 153, 154; *Misanthrope* 153, 154–5; *Tartuffe* 153, 154
Mondrian, Piet 419, 431, 445, 467; *Composition with Red, Blue and Yellow* 419, **10.30**
Monet, Claude 375–6, 377; *La Grenouillère* 375, 378, **9.13**; *Rouen Cathedral in Full Sunlight* 376, 378, **9.15**
Montaigne, Michel de 121–2, 123, 124, **3.29**
Monteverdi, Claudio 182
Moog, Robert 484
Moore, Henry 428; *Recumbent Figure* 428, **10.41**
Mosaics: Byzantine 255, 259–61; Christian 251
Motherwell, Robert 489
Mozart, Wolfgang Amadeus 191–2; *Don Giovanni* 192, **4.50**
Munch, Edvard 405, 407; *The Scream* 407, **10.15**
Music 41–3; ancient Greek 54, 73–5; ancient Roman 91; Baroque 181–2, 184, 187; early Christian 261–5; Classical 187–8, 223; Counter Reformation 352–3; Medieval 313–17; 19th c. 434; Reformation 351–2; Renaissance 95–6, 116–19, 147; Romantic 222–3; 16th c. 145–7; 20th c. 435–6, 482–8, 502–3
Mussorgsky, Modest 434

"Nabis" painters 402, 403
Nabokov, Vladimir 493
Nakht, tomb of: mural 41, **1.27**
Napoleon Bonaparte 179, 197, 224, **4.29**
Nash, John: Royal Pavilion, Brighton 220, **5.22**
Naturalism 358, 360
Neoclassicism: architecture 151, 166, 180; art 151, 166, 177–8, 196, 208, 210; literature 150, 151, 153; sculpture 179
Neolithic era 16
Nero, Emperor 91
Nevelson, Louise 473; *Black Wall* 473, **11.24**
Newton, Isaac: *Principia* 151
New York: AT&T Building 501, **12.11**; Seagram Building 479, 501, **11.32**
Nietzsche, Friedrich 386
Nolde, Emil: *The Last Supper* 411, **10.20**
Notre Dame, School of 315–16

Ockeghem, Johannes 118
O'Keeffe, Georgia 457; *Black Cross, New Mexico* **11.7**
Oldenberg, Claes 474, 476; *Clothespin (Version Two)* 474, **11.28**; *Yale Lipstick* 474–5, **11.27**
Op Art 469
Opera 182–3, 191–2, 512
Opera buffa 187
Oratorio 183, 354, 512

Padua, Italy: Arena Chapel 308, **7.46**
Paestum, Italy: Basilica 53, **2.11**
Paleolithic era 16
Palestrina, Giovanni Pierluigi da 353; *Missa Brevis* 353, **8.26**
Palladio, Andrea 140
Palma de Majorca, Spain: Cathedral 300, **7.37**
Paris, France: Notre Dame Cathedral 293; Palais Soubise 172, **4.21**; St-Denis abbey church 293, **7.24**; Sainte-Chapelle 99–100, 298, **3.6**
Parmigianino: *Madonna with the Long Neck* 145, **3.50**
Partch, Harry 483
Parting of Lot and Abraham (mosaic) 251, **6.17**

Pascal, Blaise 160
Paul, St. 234, 235, 238, 243
Paxton, Joseph: Crystal Palace, London 380–1, **9.17**
Peisistratus 46
Penderecki, Krzystof: *Threnody to the Victims of Hiroshima* 483, 485
Peplos Maiden 51, **2.7**
Pericles 46, 62
Perugino 136–7
Petrarch 94, 97–8, **3.4**
Phidias: Parthenon 65–6, 68–9, **2.24–28**
Philadelphia, Pa: Guild House 501, **12.9**
Philosophes 153, 160, 177, 187
Photo-realism 469
Picasso, Pablo 412, 415, 420, 427, 435, 436; *Demoiselles d'Avignon* 414, **10.24**; *Guernica* 420, **10.31**; *The Old Guitarist* 412, **10.23**; *Portrait of Stravinsky* **10.53**; *Three Musicians* 415–16, **10.27**
Pico della Mirandola 99
Piero della Francesca 113; *St. Augustine* **6.6**; *Resurrection* 113, 339, **3.21**
Pinter, Harold 493
Piranesi, Giovanni Battista: *The Temple of Saturn* 177, **4.25**
Pisa, Italy: Cathedral 286–7, **7.18**, **7.19**
Pissarro, Camille 398
Plato 60–1, 63, 74, **2.17**; *The Republic* 367–8
Pointillism 404
Poissy-sur-Seine, France: Villa Savoye 433, **10.48**
Pollock, Jackson 459–61, 462, 464, 489, **11.11**; *One (No. 31, 1950)* 461, 470, **11.12**
Polyeuktos: *Demosthenes* 72, **2.33**
Polykleitos: *Spear Carrier* 63, 80, 290, **2.22**
Polyphonic music 314–15, 513
Pont du Gard, France: Aqueduct **2.44**
Pop Art 465, 467, 476, 492
Pope, Alexander 151; *Essay on Man* 157, 159
Post-Impressionism 397–8, 403, 407
Post-Modernism 492–4; architecture 495–6, 501; art 496–7, 499; literature 493–5
Poussin, Nicolas 166–7, 169; *Landscape with the Burial of Phocion* 167, 213, **4.14**
Praetorius, Michael: *Syntagma musicum* **3.26**
Praxiteles 63; *Hermes and Dionysus* 65, **2.23**
Puccini, Giacomo 231
Pugin, A. W. N.: Houses of Parliament, London 220, **5.21**
Purcell, Henry 151, 183
Pynchon, Thomas 493
Pythagoras 68, 73–4

Racine, Jean 153, 155, **4.6**; *Phaedra* 153, 155–6
Raimondi, Marcantonio: *The Judgement of Paris* 373, **9.12**
Raphael (Raffaello Sanzio) 136; *Castiglione* 137–8, **3.43**; *School of Athens* 137, **3.42, cover**
Rationalism 153
Rauschenberg, Robert 470, 473, 475, 489, 493, 497
Ravel, Maurice 435

Ravenna, Italy: S. Vitale 259–61, **6.25–30**
Realism: art 367–8, 370, 373, 379; literature 358–9, 360
Reformation, The 322–4, 327; art 332; music 351–2
Regionalism 457, 458
Reich, Steve 502–3
Rembrandt van Rijn 323, 347–9, 351, 400; *Blinding of Samson* 349, **8.21**; *Descent from the Cross* (1633) 349, **8.22**; *Descent from the Cross* (1651) 350–1, **8.24**; *Return of the Prodigal Son* 351, **8.25**; *Self-Portrait* 349, **8.23**
Renaissance, the 94–6; architecture 99, 138; art 124–5; music 95–6, 116–19, 147
Renoir, Auguste: *Le Moulin de la Galette* 376, **9.14**
Richmond, Va: State Capitol 180, **4.30**
Riley, Bridget: *Current* 469, **11.20**
Riley, Terry: *In C* 502
Rimsky-Korsakov, Nikolai 434
Rivers, Larry: *Europe II* 465, 473, **11.16**
Robbe-Grillet, Alain 493
Rococo style 151, 172, 174, 177
Rodin, Auguste 218, 425; *Balzac* 425, **10.36**; *The Kiss* 218–19, 425, **5.19**
Roland, Song of 269, 270, 271–2, **7.4**
Roman Empire 47–8; architecture 82, 85–7, 89–90, *see also* Rome; art 79–80; literature 75–9; map 77, **2.37**; music 91; sculpture 80
Romanesque style 281–3, 285–7, 289–91
Romanticism 196–9; architecture 220; art 208, 212, 213; music 222–3
Rome, ancient **2.36**, *see also* Roman Empire; Arch of Constantine 245, **6.10, 6.11**; Colosseum 87, 89, **2.50–52**; Forums 82, **2.45, 2.47**; Medici Chapel, Tomb of Lorenzo 145, **3.51**; Pantheon 89–90, **2.53–55**; S. Carlo alle Quattro Fontane 163–4, **4.11**; S. Costanza 249, 251, **6.15, 6.16**; S. Maria Maggiore 247, 249, 251, **6.12–14, 6.17**; St. Peter's 138, 140, 163, **3.45–47, 4.9, 4.10**; Sistine Chapel 131, 135–6, 341, **3.37–41, 8.14**; Tempietto, S. Pietro in Montorio 138, **3.44**; Temple of Fortuna **2.43**; Temple of Mars Ultor 85, **2.46**
Rothko, Mark: *Green on Blue* 462, **11.14**
Rousseau, Jean-Jacques 160, 197, 200, 201, **5.2**; *Confessions* 196, 200; *Émile* 201; *Social Contract* 197, 200–1
Rubens, Peter Paul 323, 346; *The Raising of the Cross* 344, 345, 349, **8.17**; *Rape of the Daughters of Leucippus* 164, 166, **4.12**
Ruisdael, Jacob van: *View of Haarlem from the Dunes at Overveen* 213, **5.13**

St. Louis, Missouri: Wainwright Building 381, 429, **9.18**
Saint-Saëns, Camille 231, 434
Salisbury, England: Cathedral 299, **7.34, 7.35**
Salle, David 497: *Poverty is No Disgrace* 497, **12.6**
Salzman, Eric 502

Sarcophagus of Junius Bassus 252, **6.18, 6.19**
Sartre, Jean-Paul 445, 446, 458–9
Satie, Eric 435
Scarlatti, Domenico 184
Schelling, Friedrich W. J. 198
Schoenberg, Arnold 231, 438–41, 485, 488; *Pierrot Lunaire* 440, 441, **10.57**; *Self-Portrait* **10.56**
Schopenhauer, Arthur 386
Schubert, Franz: *Lieder* 228
Schumann, Robert 227–8; *Lieder* 228–9, **5.31, 5.32**
Serialism 440, 482–3, 485
Sessions, Roger 485
Seurat, Georges 404; *Bathers at Asnières* 404, **10.13**
Shakespeare, William 122–3, **3.30**; *Hamlet* 123–4
Shephard, Sam 493
Sherman, Cindy 499; *Untitled* (photograph) 499, **12.8**
Sibelius, Jean 434
Skidmore, Owings, and Merrill: Hancock Center, Chicago 495, **12.3**
Sluter, Claus 304; *Well of Moses* 304, **7.42**
Smith, David 469–70, 473; *Cubi* series 473, **11.25**; *Hudson River Landscape* 470, **11.23**
Socrates 60, **2.16**
Solon 46
Solzhenitsyn, Alexander 444, 445, 450, 453–5, 495, **11.6**
Sophocles 55–6, 57–9, **2.14**
Stein, Johann Andreas: piano **4.44**
Stella, Frank 467, 469
Stella, Joseph: *Brooklyn Bridge* 419, **10.29**
Stevick, Philip 494
Stockhausen, Karlheinz 482, 485, 486; *Hymnen* 486–7; *Kontra-Punkte* 482
Stokowski, Leopold 485
Strauss, Richard 231
Stravinsky, Igor 436, 438, 482, 485, **10.53**; *Pulcinella* 437; *Rite of Spring* (*Sacré du printemps*) 385, 436–7, **10.51, 10.52**; *The Soldier's Tale* 437; *Symphony of Psalms* 437–8, **10.54, 10.55**
Sturm und Drang 196, 202
Sukenick, Ronald 493
Sullivan, Louis 381, 429, 431; Carson, Pirie and Scott Dept. Store, Chicago 429, 431, **10.43**; Wainwright Building, St. Louis 381, 429, **9.18**
Sumerians 17–18; architecture 18, 29, **1.9, 1.10**; art 29, 31; literature 17
Surrealism 422–3
Susa, Iran: painted beaker 29, **1.8**
Sutton Hoo Ship Burial: purse cover **7.7**
Swift, Jonathan 151, 153, 156, **4.7**; *Gulliver's Travels* 156, 157–8
Sydney, Australia: Opera House 480, **11.34**
Symbolism 385, 403

Tachisme 464
Telemann, Philipp 353
Theodora, Empress 255
Theodora and Attendants (mosaic) 259–60, **6.29**
Thomson, Virgil 485
Tintoretto, Jacopo: *Last Supper* 342, **8.15**

Titian (Tiziano Vecillio) 141; *Christ Crowned with Thorns* 142, 145, **3.49**; *Venus of Urbino* 141–2, **3.48**
Tolstoy, Leo 358, 364–5, **9.5**; *Anna Karenina* 365, 366; *Death of Ivan Ilych* 366–7; *Resurrection* 366; *War and Peace* 365–6
Toulouse, France: St. Sernin 283, 285–6, **7.14–17**
Toulouse-Lautrec, Henri de 404–5; *At the Moulin Rouge* 405, **10.14**
Toynbee, Arnold 492
Tredici, David Del: *Final Alice* 502
Troubadours 316
Turner, Joseph M. W. 216, 222; *The Fighting Temeraire* 216, **5.1, 5.17**; *The Shipwreck* 215–16, **5.16**

Ur 17; Ziggurat of King Urnammu 29, **1.9, 1.10**
Utilitarianism 359
Utzon, Jørn: Sydney Opera House 480, **11.34**

Varèse, Edgard 485; *Poème électronique* 483
Vasarély, Victor 469
Velázquez, Diego 368, 373; *Water Carrier of Seville* 368–9, **9.6**
Venturi, Robert 497
Venturi and Rauch: Tucker House, Katonah, NY 501, **12.10**
Venturi and Rauch, Cope and Lippencott: Guild House, Philadelphia 501, **12.9**
Verdi, Giuseppe 231
Vermeer, Jan 368, 369–70; *Young Woman with a Water Jug* 369, 409, **9.7**
Verrocchio, Andrea del 125; *Doubting of Thomas* 113, **3.19**
Versailles, Palace of 150, 169, **4.1, 4.16–18**
Vienna: St. Peter's church and square **4.49**
Virgil 75, 79, **2.38**; *Aeneid* 76–9, **2.39**; *Eclogues* 75; *Georgics* 75–6
Virgin of Paris, The (sculpture) 304, **7.41**
Vitry, Philippe de 317; *Fauvel* motet 317, **7.55**
Vivaldi, Antonio 184
Voltaire (François-Marie Arouet) 153, 158–9, **4.8, 4.28**; *Candide* 159–60

Wagner, Richard 229–31; *Die Meistersinger* 230, **5.34**; *Tristan und Isolde* 230, **5.34**
Watteau, Jean-Antoine 207; *A Pilgrimage to Cythera* 207, **5.7**
Webern, Anton 441, 482
Wiesel, Elie 445, 450, 451–2, 455, 495, **11.5**; *Night* 444, 452–3
Winckelmann, Johann Joachim 177
Wolff, Christian 486
Wordsworth, William 203–4, 217, **5.6**; *Lyrical Ballads* 204–6
Wright, Frank Lloyd 431; Robie House 431, **10.44, 10.45**
Wren, Christopher 151; St. Paul's Cathedral, London 170, **4.19**
Wycliffe, John 322

Young, La Monte 502
Youth from Tenea 50–1, **2.6**

Ziggurats 29, **1.9, 1.10**
Zola, Émile 374
Zwingli, Ulrich 352